Perrine's

Literature
Structure, Sound, and Sense

Perrine's

Literature
Structure, Sound, and Sense
Ninth Edition

Thomas R. Arp
Southern Methodist University

Greg Johnson
Kennesaw State University

THOMSON
WADSWORTH

Australia • Canada • Mexico • Singapore • Spain • United Kingdom • United States

Perrine's Literature: Structure, Sound, and Sense, Ninth Edition
Thomas R. Arp / Greg Johnson

Publisher: Michael Rosenberg
Acquisitions Editor: Aron Keesbury
Development Editor: Helen Triller-Yambert
Editorial Assistant: Cheryl Forman
Technology Project Manager: Cara Douglass-Graff
Senior Marketing Manager: Mary Jo Southern
Marketing Assistant: Dawn Giovanniello
Associate Marketing Communications Manager:
    Patrick Rooney

Senior Project Manager, Editorial Production:
    Samantha Ross
Manufacturing Manager: Marcia Locke
Permissions Editor: Roberta Broyer
Production Service/Compositor: Graphic
    World, Inc.
Cover Designer: Bill Reuter
Cover Printer: Phoenix Color Corporation
Printer: West Group

For more information about
our products, contact us at:
Thomson Learning Academic Resource Center
1-800-423-0563
For permission to use material from this text
or product, submit a request online at
http://www.thomsonrights.com.
Any additional questions about
permissions can be submitted by email to
thomsonrights@thomson.com.

Thomson Higher Education
25 Thomson Place
Boston, MA 02210-1202
USA

Asia (including India)
Thomson Learning
5 Shenton Way
#01-01 UIC Building
Singapore 068808

Australia/New Zealand
Thomson Learning Australia
102 Dodds Street
Southbank, Victoria 3006
Australia

Canada
Thomson Nelson
1120 Birchmount Road
Toronto, Ontario M1K 5G4
Canada

UK/Europe/Middle East/Africa
Thomson Learning
High Holborn House
50–51 Bedford Road
London WC1R 4LR
United Kingdom

Library of Congress Control Number: 2005923051

Student Edition ISBN 1-4130-0654-X
Instructor's Edition ISBN 1-4130-2274-X

Credits appear on pages 1673-1684, which
constitute a continuation of the copyright page.

Brief Contents

Contents

Fiction   The Elements of Fiction   59

Chapter One   Reading the Story   61

Chapter Two   Plot and Structure   103

Chapter Three   Characterization   161

Chapter Four   Theme   188

Stories for Further Reading   509

Poetry Elements of Poetry   645

Chapter One What Is Poetry?   647

Chapter Four   Imagery   700

Chapter Five   Figurative Language I: Simile, Metaphor, Personification, Apostrophe, Metonymy   714

Chapter Twelve   Rhythm and Meter   838

Chapter Thirteen   Sound and Meaning   864

Featured Poets

The following poems appear as illustrations in various chapters of the poetry section, but these four poets are represented by a sufficient number of poems to warrant studying them as individual artists.

Drama The Elements of Drama   1025

Chapter One The Nature of Drama   1027

Chapter Two Realistic and Nonrealistic Drama   1074

Chapter Three Tragedy and Comedy   1209

Plays For Further Reading   1429

Preface

In preparing this ninth edition of *Perrine's Literature: Structure, Sound, and Sense*, we have striven to be true to the principles established by Laurence Perrine almost fifty years ago, while at the same time acknowledging the developing nature of literature. The book as always works to balance the classic with the contemporary, to represent a wide diversity of writers, and to emphasize the importance of the close reading of literature as the avenue to enjoying and appreciating it. While there are many flourishing approaches to literature and its effects, we believe that the initial step must be to understand the elements of fiction, poetry, and drama through which they present themselves.

This book is addressed to the student who is beginning a serious study of imaginative literature. It seeks to give that student a sufficient grasp of the nature and variety of fiction, poetry, and drama; some reasonable means for reading with appreciative understanding; and a few primary ideas of how to evaluate literature. One important principle established in the earliest editions is the need for conciseness and compactness, so that the book will have a friendly, welcoming appeal and will not seem daunting in its comprehensiveness. In matters of theory, in an introductory textbook some issues are undoubtedly simplified, but none we hope seriously so, and some more sophisticated theoretical approaches have had to be excluded in the interests of space. Another principle is that the elements of literature are presented in a progression in which each new topic builds on what preceded it. The separate chapters gradually introduce the student to the elements of the three genres, putting the emphasis always on *how* and *why: How* can the reader use these elements to get at the meaning of the work, to interpret it sensibly, and to respond to it adequately? *Why* does the writer use these elements? What values have they for the writer and reader?

The ninth edition of *Literature* maintains the balance between classic and modern writers and continues to offer a wide sampling of vicarious experiences through the works of women as well as men, ethnic minorities as well as authors representing the varieties of American and world literatures. The structure of the book reflects the step-by-step approach to understanding literature. Each chapter contains two parts: (1) a discussion of the topic indicated by the chapter title, with illustrative works, and (2) a relevant selection of works with study questions for further illustration of the topic.

Although the book emphasizes the study of literature, not writers, we have continued the practice of representing some authors with a sufficient number of works to support the study of them as individual artists. In the fiction section we include three stories each by a great twentieth-century writer (Flannery O'Connor) and one of the classic pioneers in the short story form (James Joyce). In this edition, there are also four poets amply represented: Emily Dickinson, John Donne, Robert Frost, and the contemporary poet Adrienne Rich (a large assortment of whose poems we are pleased to include, but at the instruction of her publisher we have not been permitted to supply study questions for them). The Instructor's Manual available to teachers using this book will supply some questions as well as the usual explanatory discussions of the poems.

This ninth edition differs from the eighth chiefly in the inclusion of Adrienne Rich as a featured poet and the introduction of several contemporary fiction writers and playwrights in the fiction and drama sections. It has again increased the number of works by women and by members of ethnic minorities. Part One, "Writing about Literature," has been augmented and continues to hold a prominent place in the book, as have the "Suggestions for Writing" at the ends of the chapters. A new feature of the book is the inclusion of review topics within each chapter for the student's more efficient studying. The advice of many users has led us to revise the chapter on "Pattern" in the poetry section, dropping the subliterary verse form the limerick and increasing the number of sonnets represented there. Molière's *Tartuffe, or The Impostor* replaces his *The Misanthrope* as an example of satiric comedy.

Through the nine editions of a book that originated in the middle of the twentieth century, *Perrine's Literature: Structure, Sound, and Sense* has evolved in many ways, responding to shifts in interest, concern, and taste expressed by its users. But certain abiding principles remain as relevant to this new century as they were in the last. Among these are the conviction that the close reading of a text is basic to the understanding and appreciation of literature; that to understand the means by which a work achieves its ends is an essential part of experiencing it fully; and that reading literature is important to the development of the whole person. The first assumptions of this book are that literature needs to be read carefully and thought about considerably and that, when so read, it gives its readers continuing rewards in experience and understanding.

T. R. A. and G. J.

Professional Acknowledgments

The following instructors have offered helpful reactions and suggestions for this ninth edition of *Perrine's Literature: Structure, Sound, and Sense:*

Frank J. Albert
Community College of Beaver County

Denise T. Askin
Saint Anselmo College

Dorothy Z. Baker
University of Houston

Susan M. Bamberg
Shelton State Community College

Charles L. Batten
University of California, Los Angeles

Donna Bauerly
Loras College

William R. Bell
Liberty University

John Bellue
West Virginia University Institute of Technology

Paul Benson
Mountain View College

Mark Bernheim
Miami University of Ohio

Steve Bidlake
Central Oregon Community College

John D. Boyd
University of Georgia

Renie Stewart Braswell
Mayland Community College

Robert A. Brown
Champlain College

Douglas Burger
University of Colorado, Boulder

Merlin G. Chaney
Weber State University

Greg Chapman
Snead State Community College

Johnson Cheu
Ohio State University

William Clarkson
Sewanee: The University of the South

John R. Combs
Kentucky Wesleyan College

John J. Covolo
Lakeland Community College

Jack Culross
Eastern Kentucky University

Sharon Cumberland
Seattle University

Patricia Curran
Northern Kentucky University

Jerome Curry
Pennsylvania State University

Carl C. Curtis
Liberty University

Richard Daniels
Oregon State University

Sherry B. Darnell
University of Southern Indiana

Pam Davis
Shelton State Community College

Annie Dawid
Lewis and Clark College

Beth DeMeo
Alvernia College

Linda Desjardins
Northern Essex Community College

Cecilia Donohue
Madonna University

Richard Downing
Pasco-Hernando Community College

Janet Eber
County College of Morris

T. T. Eiland
Citrus College

Roberta Eisel
Citrus College

Bonnie W. Epstein
Plymouth State University

Roger Ernest
Cerritos College

Kevin Eyster
Madonna University

Denise A. Ezell
Colorado Mountain College

Laura Fasick
*Minnesota State University,
    Moorhead*

Maryanne Felter
Cayuga Community College

Paul J. Ferlazzo
Northern Arizona University

Dennis Flynn
Bentley College

Grable M. Ford
Miami University of Ohio

Meredith Fosque
Northern Carolina State University

Margaret H. Freeman
Los Angeles Valley College

Dan Giancola
Suffolk County Community College

C. Herbert Gilliland
U.S. Naval Academy, Annapolis

Gary Grassinger
*Community College of Allegheny
    County*

Mitchell Hagler
*Central Piedmont Community
    College*

Kent Harrison
Dalton State College

Adam Hartman
*California State University, San
    Bernardino*

Herbert Jack Heller
Huntington College

Allen Helmstetter
University of North Dakota

Darci Hill
Sam Houston State University

Marion C. Hodge, Jr.
High Point University

James Hoggard
Midwestern State University

John B. Humma
Georgia Southern University

Joan M. Irons
North Shore Community College

Maude M. Jennings
Ball State University

Kitty Johnson
Shelton State Community College

Mary Susan Johnston
Minnesota State University, Mankato

Cris Karmas
Graceland University

Richard Keenan
*University of Maryland, Eastern
    Shore*

Julie King
University of Wisconsin, Parkside

Robert Kinpoitner
Molloy College

Mary Kramer
University of Massachusetts, Lowell

Dallas Liddle
Augsburg College

Judy Logan
Eastern Washington University

Kelley K. Mahoney
Dalton State College

John A. Matthew
Ball State University

Michael P. McClung
Northwest-Shoals Community College

James McCurry
Carl Sandberg College

Mark Medvetz
University of Montana

John Mintioer
Wilbur Wright College

Anna Moore
Citrus College

Harry Moore
Calhoun Community College

Robert Mugford
Scottsdale Community College

Barbara Murray
Dalton State College

Kimberly Myers
Montana State University

Kevin Nebergall
Kirkwood Community College

Channa Newman
Point Park College

Nicholas Nownes
Yavapai College

Lawrence O'Brien
Western New England College

Jaime O'Neill
Butte College

Britt Osgood-Treston
Riverside Community College

John Panza
Cuyahoga Community College–East

James Persoon
Grand Valley State University

Bonnie Pickett
Viterbo University

Kenn Pierson
Rio Hondo College

Mary Pollock
Stetson University

Suzanne Radigan
University of South Dakota

Barbara Ragan
Mount Vernon Nazarene College

Scott Redmond
Cleveland State Community College

Lisa Sandlin
Wayne State College

Richard B. Schrader
Boston College

Barbara Scrafford
City College of San Francisco

Stephen Shepherd
Southern Methodist University

Lyle E. Smith
California State University, Dominguez Hills

Roxanne Solomon
Palm Beach Community College

David Starnes
Georgia Southern University

David E. Stooke
Marshall University

Paul Strong
Alfred University

Margaret Judith Sullivan
Western Connecticut State University

Mitchell E. Summerlin
John C. Calhoun State Community College

Kathryn Swanson
Augsburg College

Karl Terryberry
Daemen College

Charles J. Thomas
Bergen Community College

Frieda E. Thompson
University of Texas Pan American

Burt Thorp
University of North Dakota

Jim Toner
Columbia College

Linda Urschel
Huntington College

Mark Vinz
Minnesota State University, Moorhead

Linda S. VonBergen
Georgia Southern University

Margaret Whitt
University of Denver

Sheila D. Willard
Middlesex Community College

Jack Wood
Citrus College

John T. Young
Gannon University

Dede Yow
Kennesaw State University

Rosemary Ziegler
Mount Vernon Nazarene University

David H. Zucker
Quinnipiac University

Foreword to Students

You've been reading stories ever since you learned to read; your first expo-sure to verse came with "Pat-a-cake, pat-a-cake, baker's man"; you've been watching dramatized life since your family planted you in front of the TV. You've developed your own tastes and your own attitudes toward what these varieties of "literature" can give you. In a sense, there's no need to take an introductory course in reading literature, because you've moved beyond the "introductory" phase. Let's say, then, that it's time to become familiar and friendly with the literary arts.

But let's take stock of where you stand. What have you been getting out of the things that you enjoy reading and watching? For most people, the first answer is "vicarious experience," the impression that you are tem-porarily able to live in some other world than your own private one—a world that may be as familiar as your own neighborhood or as alien to your experience as space travel in some future time or the adventures of ex-plorers of the past. What you want is for the author to take you to where you have never been, so that you can imagine yourself as a person in a world other than your own.

You probably also want to be able to "relate" to the characters in the things you read or watch, discovering in them some features of yourself or some qualities that you would like to have. Or you like to share vicariously the excitements, joys, and sorrows of people who are not very much like you, but whose lives seem rich and interesting. Or you get a lift from watching some characters making major mistakes with their lives, and turning themselves around just in time—or maybe you are thrilled to see such people brought to justice and punished for misdeeds.

Whatever the sources of your pleasure and enjoyment from reading, you may now be ready to find both broader and deeper reasons for continuing that pastime. No matter how much experience you bring to the study of these works, you're in for a few surprises. Some of them will be the surprises that come from broadening your vicarious experience, from "traveling" with us to India and Russia and Nigeria, to Harlem and Pittsburgh and Dublin, to sixteenth-century London and seventeenth-century Massachu-setts and nineteenth-century Wall Street. Some will be the surprises that come from penetrating to the secret recesses of the human mind and soul in joys and agonies, from observing people whom you have never met or imagined and with whom you have nothing in common but your humanness.

And, we hope, there will be the surprises and pleasures that come from feeling yourself growing in control or even mastery of your responses and reactions as you learn *how* literature does what it does. This, of course, is what the formal study of literature can bring you. We all know how we *feel* when we first read through a work. We probably start by thinking "I like this" or "it doesn't say much to me" or "what in the world is that supposed to mean?" If you could, you'd act on your first reaction and read the work again, or try to see what it's trying to say, or drop it and go on to do something more pleasurable.

But you're in a special situation. You're taking a course (either by your own choice or because you're required to), and one of the rules of the game is that you're supposed to move from your initial reaction to some sort of "serious" response that will satisfy your teacher. If you like something and want to reread it, your teacher will pester you with wanting to know *why* you liked it, and might even insist that you offer reasons why other people should like it too. If you are only a little bit curious about it, or think that it is a waste of time, your teacher will lead (or nudge, or bash) you into finding things in it that might change your first opinion. In any case, the terms of your special situation, as a student in a course with a grade on the horizon, make it necessary for you to have more than an initial reaction. You'll need to have a developing understanding of the work, and you'll need to show in discussion or writing both what you understand and how the work itself led to that understanding.

That's where this book will help. In addition to a systematic guide for discovering how and what a literary work means, we've provided you with suggestions for writing at the ends of the chapters and standards for your written work in the first section of the book.

Why is writing so important? It's the most straightforward way of sorting out your feelings and ideas, putting them into shape, nailing down your own experience. All writing about literature has a double motive—it sharpens your grasp of the work, and it helps you to lead other people to share your experience. Writing about literature is writing persuasively, and persuading others to see what you see helps you to see it more clearly.

So in the barest sense, this book (and your course) want to help you with reading and writing. But you have every right to ask, "Why literature?" That's a good question, because in our world there are so many ways of gaining experience and insight into our lives and the lives of others that focusing on one resource based on the spoken and written word may seem narrow and old-fashioned. We're willing to grant that, and we'll go even further: in a sense, it is also elitist, and turning to literature as a source of experience will set you apart from the majority of people. Thus, literature provides not only vicarious experience and opportunities to relate to others' lives, but it also permits you to join a special group of scholars, instructors, critics, and other students who share in the wealth of enjoyment and intellectual challenge that it has to offer.

Perrine's

Literature
Structure, Sound, and Sense

Writing
about
Literature

I. Why Write about Literature?

Written assignments in a literature class have two purposes: (1) to give you additional practice in writing clearly and persuasively, and (2) to deepen your understanding of literary works by leading you to read and think about a few works more searchingly than you might otherwise do. But these two purposes are private. To be successful, your paper must have a public purpose as well: it should be written to enlighten others besides yourself. Even if no one else ever reads your paper, you should never treat it as a private note to your instructor. You should write every paper as if it were intended for publication.

II. For Whom Do You Write?

The audience for whom you write will govern both the content and the expression of your paper. You need to know something about your readers' backgrounds—national, racial, social, religious—and be able to make intelligent guesses about their knowledge, interests, and previous reading. In writing about George Herbert's "Peace" (page 743) for a Hindu audience, you would need to include explanations of Christian belief and biblical stories that would be unnecessary for a western European or American audience. In presenting Graham Greene's "The Destructors" (page 111), your editors have felt it necessary to provide information (in footnotes) that would not be needed by a British audience; for "Los Vendidos" by Luis Valdez (page 1195), footnotes provide translations and explanations that would not be necessary for an audience familiar with the Spanish-language slang of contemporary America. But the most crucial question about an audience is: *Has it read the work you are writing about?* The book reviewer in your Sunday paper generally writes about a newly published book that the audience has not read. A reviewer's purpose is to let readers know something of what the book is about and to give them some notion of whether they will enjoy or profit from reading it. At an opposite extreme, the scholar writing in a specialized scholarly journal can generally assume an audience that *has* read the work, that has a knowledge of previous interpretations of the work, and that is familiar with other works in its period or genre. The scholar's purpose, not infrequently, is to persuade this audience that some new information or some new way of looking at the work appreciably deepens or alters its meaning or significance.

Clearly, essays written for such different audiences and with such different purposes differ considerably in content, organization, and style. Book reviewers reviewing a new novel will include a general idea of its plot while being careful not to reveal the outcome. Scholars will assume that readers already know the plot, and will have no compunction about discussing its outcome. Reviewers will try to write interestingly and engagingly about the novel and to persuade readers that they have valid grounds for their opinions of its worth, but their manner will generally be informal. Scholars are more interested in presenting a cogent argument, logically arranged and solidly based on evidence. They will be more formal, and may use critical terms and refer to related works that would be unfamiliar to nonspecialized readers. In documentation the two types of essays will be quite different. Reviewers' only documentation is normally the identification of the novel's title, author, publisher, and price, at the top of the review. For other information and opinions, they hope that a reader will rely on their intelligence, knowledge, and judgment. Scholars, on the other hand, may furnish an elaborate array of citations of other sources of information, allowing the reader to verify the accuracy or basis of any important part of their argument. Scholars expect to be challenged, and they see to it that all parts of their arguments are buttressed.

For whom, then, should *you* write? Unless your instructor stipulates (or you request) a different audience, the best plan is to assume that you are writing for the other members of your class. Pretend that your class publishes a journal of which it also constitutes the readership. Your instructor is the editor and determines editorial policy. If you write on a work that has been assigned for class reading, you assume that your audience is familiar with it. (This kind of paper is generally of the greatest educational value, for it is most open to challenge and class discussion and places on you a heavier burden of proof.) If you compare an assigned work with one that has not been assigned, you must gauge what portion of your audience is familiar with the unassigned work and proceed accordingly. If the unassigned story were A. Conan Doyle's "The Adventure of the Speckled Band," you would probably not need to explain that "Sherlock Holmes is a detective" and that "Dr. Watson is his friend," for you can assume that *this* audience, through movies, TV, or reading, is familiar with these characters; but you could not assume familiarity with this particular story. You know that, as members of the same class, your readers have certain backgrounds and interests in common and are at comparable levels of education. Anything you know about your audience may be important for how you write your paper and what you put in it.

Assuming members of your class as your audience carries another advantage: you can also assume that they are familiar with the definitions and examples given in this book, and therefore you can avoid wasting space by quoting or paraphrasing the book. There will be no need to tell them that an indeterminate ending is one in which the central conflict is left unresolved, or that Emily Dickinson's poems are untitled, or that Miss Brill is an unmarried Englishwoman living in France.

III. Two Basic Approaches

In a beginning study of literature, most writing will focus on a careful reading of details of the assigned work as the basis for any further exploration. Traditionally, the approach will be structured as an *explication* or an *analysis*.

1. Explication

An *explication* (literally, an "unfolding") is a detailed elucidation of a work, sometimes line by line or word by word, which is interested not only in *what* that work means but in *how* it means what it means. It thus considers all relevant aspects of a work—speaker or point of view, connotative words and double meanings, images, figurative language, allusions, form, structure, sound, rhythm—and discusses, if not all of these, at least the most important. (There is no such thing as exhausting the meanings and the ways to those meanings in a complex piece of literature, and the explicator must settle for something less than completeness.) Explication follows from what we sometimes call "close reading"—looking at a piece of writing, as it were, through a magnifying glass.

Clearly, the kinds of literature for which an explication is appropriate are limited. First, the work must be rich enough to repay the kind of close attention demanded. One would not think of explicating "Little Jack Horner" (page 791) unless for purposes of parody, for it has no meanings that need elucidation and no "art" worthy of comment. Second, the work must be short enough to be encompassed in a relatively brief discussion. A thorough explication of *Othello* would be much longer than the play itself and would tire the patience of the most dogged reader. Explications work best with short poems. (Sonnets like Shakespeare's "That time of year" [page 887] and Frost's "Design" [page 796] almost beg for explication.) Explication sometimes may also be appropriate for passages in long poems, as, for example, the lines spoken by Macbeth after the death of his wife (page 780) or the "sonnet" from *Romeo and Juliet* (page 891), and occasionally for exceptionally rich or crucial passages of prose, perhaps the final paragraphs of stories like "Paul's Case" (page 234) or "Miss Brill" (page 175). But explication as a critical form should perhaps be separated from explication as a method. Whenever you elucidate even a small part of a literary work by a close examination that relates it to the whole, you are essentially explicating (unfolding). For example, if you point out the multiple meanings in the title of "Time Flies" (page 1061) as they relate to that play's themes, you are explicating the title.

For examples of explication, see the three sample essays in Part XII of this section (pages 40–58). The discussions in this book display the explicative method frequently, but except for the sample essays, there are no pure examples of explication. The discussions of "A Noiseless Patient Spider" (pages 737–739) and "Digging" (pages 740–742) come close to being explications and might have been so had they included answers to the study questions and one or two other matters. The exercises provided in "Understanding and Evaluating Poetry" on page 655 should be helpful to you in writing an explication of a poem. Not all the questions will be applicable to every poem, and you need not answer all those that are applicable, but you should start by considering all that apply and then work with those that are central and important for your explication.

2. Analysis

An *analysis* (literally a "breaking up" or separation of something into its constituent parts), instead of trying to examine all parts of a work in relation to the whole, selects for examination *one* aspect or element or part that relates to the whole. Clearly, an analysis is a better approach to longer works and to prose works than is an explication. A literary work may be usefully approached through almost any of its elements—point of view, characterization, plot, setting, symbolism, structure, and the like— so long as you relate this element to the central meaning or the whole. (An analysis of meter is meaningless unless it shows how meter serves the meaning; an analysis of the vocabulary and grammar of "The Lesson" [page 195] or "The Sandbox" [page 1054] would be pointless unless related to the characterization of the speakers.) The list of exercises on pages 100–102 may suggest approaches to stories, plays, and narrative poems; the list on page 655 to anything written in verse; and that on pages 1030–1031 to dramas. As always, it is important to choose a topic appropriate to the space available. "Characterization in Flannery O'Connor's 'Greenleaf'" is too large a topic to be usefully treated in a few pages, but a character analysis of Mrs. May or of her two sons might fit the space neatly. For examples of analyses of three literary forms, see the sample essays in Part XII of this section (pages 40–58).

IV. Choosing a Topic

As editor of this imaginary publication, your instructor is responsible for the nature of its contents. Instructors may be very specific in their assignments, or they may be very general, inviting you to submit a paper on any subject within a broadly defined area of interest. They will also have editorial policies concerning length of papers, preparation of manuscripts, and deadlines for submission (all of which should be meticulously heeded). Instructors may further specify whether the paper should be entirely the work of your own critical thinking, or whether it is to be an investigative assignment—that is, one involving research into what other writers have written concerning your subject and the use of their findings, where relevant, to help you support your own conclusions.

Let us consider four kinds of papers you might write: (1) papers that focus on a single literary work, (2) papers of comparison and contrast, (3) papers on a number of works by a single author, and (4) papers on a number of works having some feature other than authorship in common.

1. Papers That Focus on a Single Literary Work

If your assignment is a specific one (How is the landscape symbolic in "The Guest"? [page 358] What emotions are evoked by the imagery in "The Widow's Lament in Springtime"? [page 704] How does music contribute to the effect of *Death of a Salesman?* [page 1445]), your task is clear-cut. You have only to read the selection carefully (obviously more than once), formulate your answer, and support it with corroborating evidence from within the text as cogently and convincingly as possible. In order to convince your readers that your answer is the best one, you will need to examine and account for apparently contrary evidence as well as clearly supportive evidence; otherwise, skeptical readers, reluctant to change their minds, might simply refer to "important points" that you have "overlooked."

Specific questions like these, when they are central to the work and may be a matter of dispute, make excellent topics for papers. You may discover them for yourself when you disagree with a classmate about the interpretation of a story or poem or play. The study questions following many of the selections in this anthology frequently suggest topics of this kind.

If your assignment is more general, and if you are given some choice as to what selection you wish to write on, it is usually best to choose one you enjoyed, whether or not you entirely understood it. (You are more likely to write a good paper on a selection you liked than on one you disliked, and you should arrive at a fuller understanding of it while thinking through your paper.) You must then decide what kind of paper you will write, taking into account the length and kind of selection you have chosen and the amount of space at your disposal.

2. Papers of Comparison and Contrast

The comparison and contrast of two stories, poems, or plays having one or more features in common may be an illuminating exercise because the similarities highlight the differences, or vice versa, and thus lead to a better understanding not only of both pieces but of literary processes in general. The works selected may be similar in plot but different in theme, similar in subject but different in tone, similar in theme but different in literary value, or, conversely, different in plot but similar in theme, different in subject but similar in tone, and so on. In writing such a paper, it is usually best to decide first whether the similarities or the differences are more significant, begin with a brief summary of the less significant, and then concentrate on the more significant.

A number of selections in this collection have been included to encourage just this kind of study: "The Most Dangerous Game" and "Hunters in the Snow" in chapter 1 of the Fiction section; "A Municipal Report" and "A Jury of Her Peers," and "Roman Fever" and "A New Leaf" in chapter 8; in the Poetry section, "Terence, this is stupid stuff" and "Ars Poetica" in chapter 1; "Spring" and "The Widow's Lament in Springtime" in chapter 4; "Ulysses" and "Curiosity" in chapter 6; "The Unknown Citizen" and "Mr. Z" in chapter 7; except for "Little Jack Horner," all six pairs of poems in chapter 9; "For a Lamb" and "Apparently with no surprise," "Crossing the Bar" and "The Oxen," "One dignity delays for all" and "'Twas warm—at first—like Us," "The Apparition" and "The Flea," and "Dover Beach" and "Church Going" in chapter 10; "Had I the Choice" and "The Aim Was Song" in chapter 12; and all seven pairs of poems in chapter 15; in the Drama section, *Oedipus Rex* and "Oedi," and *The Glass Menagerie* and "For Whom the Southern Belle Tolls." In addition, many of the Suggestions for Writing at the ends of chapters group together comparable works.

3. Papers on a Number of Works by a Single Author

Most readers, when they discover a work they particularly like, look for other works by the same author. The paper that focuses on a single author rather than a single work is the natural corollary of such an interest. The most common concern in a paper of this type is to identify the characteristics that make this author different from other authors and therefore of particular interest to the writer. What are the author's characteristic subjects, settings, attitudes, or themes? With what kinds of life does the author characteristically deal? What are the author's preferred literary forms? Is the author's approach ironic, witty, serious, comic, tragic? Is the author's vision directed principally inward or outward? In short, what configuration of patterns makes the author's fingerprints unique? Your paper may consider one or more of these questions.

Several writers are represented in this book by a sufficient number of works to support such a paper without turning to outside sources. In the Fiction section, three stories each by James Joyce and Flannery O'Connor are grouped together for comparative study. In the Poetry section, there are numerous poems by John Donne, Emily Dickinson, Robert Frost, and Adrienne Rich, as well as three or more poems by W. H. Auden, William Blake, Gwendolyn Brooks, Robert Browning, Billy Collins, Countee Cullen, Thomas Hardy, George Herbert, A. E. Housman, Langston Hughes, John Keats, Phillip Larkin, Sharon Olds, Sylvia Plath, Edwin Arlington Robinson, Theodore Roethke, William Shakespeare, Wallace Stevens, Alfred, Lord Tennyson, Walt Whitman, Richard Wilbur, William Carlos Williams, William Wordsworth, and William Butler Yeats. The author listings in the index will help you locate the multiple poems by a single author.

A more ambitious type of paper on a single author examines the works for signs of development. The attitudes that any person, especially an author, takes toward the world may change with the passing from adolescence to adulthood to old age. So also may the author's means of expressing attitudes and judgments. Though some writers are remarkably consistent in outlook and expression throughout their careers, others manifest surprising changes. To write a paper on the development of an author's work, you must have accurate information about the dates when works were written, and the works must be read in chronological order. When you have mastered the differences, you may be able to illustrate them through close examination of two or three works, one for each stage.

When readers become especially interested in the works of a particular author, they may develop a curiosity about that author's life as well. This is a legitimate interest, and, if there is sufficient space and your editor/instructor permits it, you may want to incorporate biographical information into your paper. If so, however, you should heed three caveats. First, your main interest should be in the literature itself: the biographical material should be subordinated to and used in service of your examination of the work. In general, discuss only those aspects of the author's life that bear directly on the work: biography should not be used as "filler." Second, you should be extremely cautious about identifying an event in a work with an event in the life of the author. Almost never is a story, poem, or play an exact transcription of its author's personal experience. Authors fictionalize themselves when they put themselves into imaginative works. If you consider that even in autobiographies (where they intend to give accurate accounts of their lives) writers must select incidents from the vast complexity of their experiences, that the memory of past events may be defective, and that at best writers work from their own points of view—in short, when you realize that even autobiography cannot be an absolutely reliable transcription of historical fact—you should be more fully prepared not to expect such an equation in works whose object is imaginative truth. Third, you must document the sources of your information about the author's life (see pages 23–31).

4. Papers on a Number of Works with Some Feature Other Than Authorship in Common

You might also write a successful paper on works by various authors that have some features in common, such as subject matter, form, setting, point of view, literary devices, and the like; discovering the ways in which different works employ a particular feature can be illuminating. Probably the most familiar paper of this type is the one that treats works having a similar thematic concern (love, war, religious belief or doubt, art, adolescence, initiation, maturity, old age, death, parents and children, racial conflict, social injustice). But a paper may also examine particular forms of literature, for example, the Italian sonnet, the dramatic monologue, the short story with an unreliable narrator. Topics of this kind may be further limited by time or place or number—four attitudes toward death; Elizabethan love lyrics; poetry of the Vietnam War; satires of bureaucracy.

V. Proving Your Point

In writing about literature, your object generally is to convince your readers that your understanding of a work is valid and important and to lead them to share that understanding. When writing about other subjects, it may be appropriate to persuade your readers through various rhetorical means—through eloquent diction, structural devices that create suspense, analogies, personal anecdotes, and the like. But readers of essays about literature usually look for "proof." They want you to show them *how* the work, or the element you are discussing, does what you claim it does. Like scientists who require proof of the sort that they can duplicate in their own laboratories, readers of criticism want access to the process of inference, analysis, and deduction that has led to your conclusions, so that they may respond as you have done.

To provide this proof is no easy task, for it requires the development of your own reading and writing skills. In addition, you must have developed a responsible interpretation of the work and of the way it achieves its effect; you should be able to point out precisely how it communicates its meanings; and you should be able to present your experiences of it clearly and directly. When you have spent considerable time in coming to understand and respond to a work of literature, it may become so familiar that it seems self-evident to you, and you will need to "back off" sufficiently to be able to put yourself in your readers' position—they may have vague feelings about the work ("I like it" or "It moves me deeply"), without knowing what it is that produced those feelings. It is your job to refine the feelings and define away the vagueness.

Some forms of "proof" rarely do the job. Precision does not result from explaining a metaphor metaphorically ("When Shakespeare's Juliet calls parting from Romeo a 'sweet sorrow,' the reader is reminded of taking bitter-tasting medicine"). Nor can you prove anything about a work by hypothesizing about what it might have been if it did not contain what it does ("If Desdemona had not lost her handkerchief, Othello would never have murdered her" —this is equivalent to saying, "If the play were not what it is, it would not be what it is"). Your own personal experiences will rarely help your readers ("My anxiety, excitement, and awkwardness at my first skiing lesson were like the mixed feelings Prufrock imagines for himself at the tea party"—*your* reader hasn't shared your experience of that lesson). Even your personal history of coming to understand a literary work will seldom help, though you present it in more general terms ("At a first reading, the opening paragraphs of 'Eveline' are confusing because they do not explain Eveline's reason for reminiscing about her childhood"—most literature does not yield up its richness on a first reading, so this approach has nothing to add to your reader's understanding). Just as argument by analogy is not regarded as valid in formal logic, so in critical discourse analogies are usually unconvincing ("Desdemona's ignorance about adultery is like a child's inability to balance a checkbook"). These strategies all have in common the looseness and vagueness of trying to define something by saying what it is not, or what it is like, rather than dealing with what it *is*.

"Proof" in writing about literature is primarily an exercise in strict definition. Juliet's phrase "sweet sorrow" (quoted in the preceding paragraph) derives its feeling from the paradoxical linking of sweetness and grief as a representation of the conflicting emotions of love. To provide an appropriate definition of the effect of the phrase, you would need to identify the figure of speech as paradox and to investigate the way in which love can simultaneously inflict pain and give pleasure, and you might find it useful to point to the alliteration that ties these opposites together. Obviously, comparing this kind of proof to that required by science is inexact, since what you are doing is reminding your readers, or perhaps informing them, of feelings that are associated with language, not of the properties of chemical compounds. Furthermore, a scientific proof is incomplete if it does not present every step in a process. If that requirement were placed on literary analysis, a critical essay would be interminable, since more can always be said about any interpretive point. So, rather than attempting to prove every point that you make, you should aim to demonstrate that your *method* of analysis is valid by providing persuasive proof of your major point or points. If you have shown that your handling of a major point is sound, your readers will tend to trust your judgment on lesser matters.

VI. Writing the Paper

The general procedures for writing a good paper on literature are much the same as the procedures for writing a good paper on any subject.

1.   As soon as possible after receiving the assignment, read carefully and thoughtfully the literary materials on which it is based, mulling over the problem to be solved or—if the assignment is general—a good choice of subject, jotting down notes, and sidelining or underlining important passages if the book is your own. (If you use a library book, note the page or line numbers of such passages so that you can readily find them again.) Be sure to read the assigned material more than once.

2.   Then, rather than proceeding directly to the writing of the paper, put the materials aside for several days and let them steep in your

mind. The advantage of this is that your subconscious mind, if you have truly placed the problem in it, will continue to work on the problem while you are engaged in other activities, indeed even while you are asleep. Repeated investigations into the psychology of creativity have shown that great solutions to scientific and artistic problems frequently occur while the scientist or artist is thinking of something else; the answer pops into consciousness as if out of nowhere but really out of the hidden recesses of the mind, where it has been quietly incubating. Whether this apparent "miracle" happens to you or not, it is probable that you will have more ideas when you sit down to write after a period of incubation than you will if you try to write your paper immediately after reading the materials.

3. When you are ready to write (allow yourself as long an incubation period as possible, but also allow ample time for writing, looking things up, revising, copying your revision, and correcting your final copy), jot down a list of the ideas you have, select connecting ideas relevant to your problem or to a single acceptable subject, and formulate a thesis statement that will clearly express in one sentence what you wish to say about that subject. Make a rough outline, rearranging your ideas in the order that will best support your thesis. Do they make a coherent case? Have you left out anything necessary to demonstrate your thesis? If so, add it in the proper place. Then begin to write, using your rough outline as a guide. Write this first draft as swiftly as possible, not bothering about sentence structure, grammar, diction, spelling, or verification of sources. Concentrate on putting on paper what is in your head and on your outline without interrupting the flow of thought for any other purpose. If alternative ways of expressing a thought occur to you, put them all down for a later decision. Nothing is more unprofitable than staring at a blank sheet of paper, chewing on a pencil—or staring at a blank monitor, hearing the computer's hum—wondering, "How shall I begin?" Just begin. Get something down on paper. It may look awful, but you can shape and polish it later.

4. Once you have something on paper, it is much easier to see what should be done with it. The next step is to revise. Does your paper proceed from an introductory paragraph that either defines the problem to be solved or states your thesis, through a series of logically arranged paragraphs that advance toward a solution of the problem or demonstrate your thesis, to a final paragraph that either solves the problem or sums up and restates your thesis but in somewhat different words? If not, analyze the difficulty. Do the paragraphs need reorganization or amplification? Are more examples needed? Does the thesis itself need modification? Make whatever adjustments are necessary for a logical and convincing demonstration. This may require a rewriting of the paper, or it may call

only for deletions, insertions, and circlings with arrows showing that a sentence or paragraph should be shifted from one place to another.

Notice that you are expected to organize your paper according to *your* purpose or thesis. This frequently will mean that you will not be moving paragraph-by-paragraph through a story, line-by-line through a poem, or speech-by-speech through a play, following the structure that the author created, but rather ordering your paper in the most effective way to make your point. If you do discuss a work following the order in which its materials are presented, your reader will naturally expect your thesis to include some comment on the structure of the work. The exception to this is a paper devoted entirely to explication, since in that case you will be expected to follow the structure of the poem or the passage you are explicating.

5.   In your revision (if not earlier), make sure that the stance expressed in your statements and judgments is firm and forthright, not weak and wishy-washy. Don't allow your paper to become a sump of phrases like "it seems to me that," "I think [or feel] that," "this word might connote," "this line could mean," and "in my opinion." Your readers know that the content of your paper expresses your thoughts; you need to warn them only when it expresses someone else's. And don't be weak-kneed in expressing your opinion. Even though you are not 100 percent sure of your rightness, write as if you are presenting a truth. Realizing beforehand that you will need to state your interpretations and conclusions confidently should also help you to strive for a greater degree of certainty as you read and interpret.

6.   Having revised your paper for the logic, coherence, confidence, and completeness of its argument, your next step is to revise it for effectiveness of expression. Do this slowly and carefully. How many words can you cut out without loss of meaning? Are your sentences constructed for maximum force and economy? Are they correctly punctuated? Do the pronouns have clear antecedents? Do the verbs agree with their subjects? Are the tenses consistent? Have you chosen the most exact words and spelled them correctly? Now is the time to use the dictionary, to verify quotations and other references, and to supply whatever documentation is needed. A conscientious writer may put a paper through several revisions.

7.   After all is in order, write or type your final copy, being sure to follow the editorial policies of your instructor for the submission of manuscripts.

8.   Read over your final copy slowly and carefully, and correct any mistakes (omissions, repetitions, typographical errors) you may have made in copying from your draft. This final step—too often omitted due

to haste or fatigue—is extremely important and may make the difference between an A or a C paper, or between a C paper and an F. It is easy to make careless mistakes in copying, but your reader should not be counted on to recognize the difference between a copying error and one of ignorance. Moreover, the smallest error may utterly destroy the sense of what you have written: omission of a "not" may make your paper say exactly the opposite of what you meant it to say. Few instructors require or want you to recopy or retype a whole page of your paper at this stage. It is enough to make neat corrections in ink on the paper itself.

VII. Writing In-Class Essays or Essay Tests

You will often be asked in your literature courses to write essays in class or to write essay tests. The topic or assignment may be given to you in advance so that you can prepare for writing in the classroom, or you may be given the topic in the class when you will do the writing. If you have the topic early enough to prepare, you will want to follow the preparatory suggestions offered for writing a formal out-of-class essay. If the topic for your essay or tests is not given out in advance, the following general approaches may be useful.

1. Analyze the topic. If you are asked to compare characters, or to discuss the implications of an event, or to define a concept and exemplify it, be sure that you do so. Pay attention to key words and such instructions as *compare, show how,* and especially *define.* If asked to compare, be sure you are drawing the comparison and not just giving two summaries; if asked to define, be sure your statement is in the form of a definition and does not just give examples. And be sure that you answer all parts of a question: consider whether it contains two or even three tasks within a single instruction.

2. For each question, take a little time to jot down a few key words or ideas that seem to be essential in answering the question, to keep yourself from spending all your time on one of the points but leaving out others of equal importance. If you can, decide which points are the *most* important, to be sure to include them.

3. Try to begin your answer with a topic sentence that includes all the major points you intend to use in your essay. You can often get a good topic sentence out of the question itself: if it says "Show how the frame story of Gordimer's 'Once upon a Time' is related to the main story," you might begin your essay, "The frame story involving a writer awakened by a frightening noise in the night introduces fear, the central topic of the main story, but the kinds of fear are distinctly different."

4. Don't give summaries of actions and plots unless you need to do so. You may need to give a brief summary, for example, in order to support a point; but be sure you are doing that rather than assuming that a summary will *make* a point. An essay test is not usually the place to prove that you have read the assigned material, but that you can use your reading.

5. Be specific and concrete. Prove your points with facts—named characters, specific actions, concrete details of plot, and even paraphrases or quotations from speeches if you can recall them (but don't quote unless you have indeed memorized them, and do not place quotation marks around paraphrases).

6. Keep an eye on the clock and budget your time. If you are asked to write two essays with equal time allotments, and you answer only one, then your maximum score can be no more than 50%—no matter how well you answer the one. If you have time, review and revise your writing, making corrections as neatly as you can. When moving whole paragraphs or blocks of writing, be sure your final intention is clear. And take all the time that is allotted to you—if you think you have said everything you can, then spend the time in revision.

VIII. Introducing Quotations

In writing about literature it is often desirable, sometimes imperative, to quote from the work under discussion. Quoted material is needed (1) to provide essential evidence in support of your argument, and (2) to set before your reader any passage that you are going to examine in detail. It will also keep your reader in contact with the text and allow you to use felicitous phrasing from the text to enhance your own presentation. You must, however, be careful not to overquote. If a paper consists of more than 20 percent quotation, it loses the appearance of closely knit argument and seems instead merely a collection of quotations strung together like clothes hung out on a line to dry. Avoid, especially, unnecessary use of long quotations. Readers tend to skip them. Consider carefully whether the quoted material may not be more economically presented by paraphrase, or whether the quotation, if judged necessary, may not be effectively shortened by ellipsis (see Q9 below). Readers faced with a long quotation may reasonably expect you to examine it in some detail; that is, the longer your quotation, the more you should do with it.

As a general rule in analytical writing, quotation should be included for the purpose of supporting or proving a point, not for the purpose of re-creating the experience of a work for your reader. You may assume that your reader has already read the work and does not need to have it summarized—but on the other hand, you should not send your reader back to the book to reread in order to understand what you are referring to. Analysis is the process of demonstrating how the parts work together to create the whole; it must examine these parts in detail and show how they work together. Quoting presents details, and analysis shows how the details do what you say they do. If a quotation seems entirely self-evident to you, so that you have nothing to explain about it, then it is not really worth quoting. If it is self-evident, your reader has already understood all there is to know about it.

As with every other aspect of good writing, the use of quotation is a matter of intelligence and tact. There are no hard-and-fast rules, since the amount of material you quote and the way you explain the significance of your quotations will vary, depending on the work you are writing about and the kind of paper you are writing. In general, however, you should limit direct quotation to words, phrases, or short passages that are so well written and illuminating that to paraphrase them would dilute the force of your argument. Such quotation strengthens your own writing by showing that you have mastered the material and can offer the crucial evidence directly from the text. On the other hand, if the *content* of a passage (especially a long passage) is more significant than the specific language the author uses, then a paraphrase is probably adequate. Either way, be sure that you quote or paraphrase selectively, keeping your own ideas about the work in the foreground; and also be sure that your quotation or paraphrase directly supports your argument.

Principles and Guidelines

There is no legislative body that establishes laws governing the formal aspects of quoting, documenting, or any other aspect of writing. The only "rules" are the editorial policies of the publisher to whom you submit your work. (In the case of papers being written as class assignments, your "publisher" is your instructor.) There is, however, a national organization—the Modern Language Association of America—that is so influential that its policies for its own publications and its recommendations for others are adopted by most journals of literary criticism and scholarship. The instructions below are in general accord with those stated in the *MLA Handbook for Writers of Research Papers*, 6th edition, by Joseph Gibaldi (New York: MLA, 2003). In your course, your instructor will inform you of any editorial policies in effect that differ from those given here or in the *MLA Handbook*. The examples we use here are all drawn from act 5, scene 2 of *Othello*.

Q1. If the quotation is short (normally not more than four typed lines of prose or not more than two or three lines of verse), put it in quotation marks and introduce it directly into the text of your essay.

> a Othello, before stabbing himself, reminds his listeners,
>   "I have done the state some service and they know 't."
> b He speaks of himself as "one that loved not wisely but
>   too well" and compares himself to "the base Indian"
> c who "threw a pearl away / Richer than all his tribe"
>   (5.2.338–47).

Q2. If the quotation is long (normally more than four typed lines of prose or more than three lines of verse), begin it on a new line (and resume the text of your essay on a new line also); double-space it (like the rest of your paper); and indent it twice as far from the left margin (ten spaces or one inch) as you do for a new paragraph indentation (five spaces or one-half inch). If it is verse and has lines either too long or too short to look good with a ten-space indentation, center the quotation between the margins. Whether verse or prose, *do not enclose it in quotation marks*. Since the indentation and the line arrangement both signal a quotation, the use of quotation marks would be redundant.

> In the final scene, convinced that Desdemona is en-
> tirely innocent and having decided to kill himself,
> Othello says to his auditors:
>
> > I pray you, in your letters,
> > When you shall these unlucky deeds relate,
> > Speak of me as I am, nothing extenuate,
> > Nor set down aught in malice. (5.2.339–42)

The two boxed examples illustrate the "run-in" quotation (Q1), where the quotation is "run in" with the writer's own text, and the "set-off" or "block" quotation (Q2), which is separated from the writer's text.

Q3. In quoting verse, it is extremely important to preserve the line arrangement of the original because the verse line is a rhythmical unit and thus affects meaning. When more than one line of verse is run in, the lines are separated by a virgule (or diagonal slash) with one letter-space on each side, and capitalization after the first line follows that of the original. (See Q1.c. above.)

Q4. In general, sentences containing a quotation are punctuated as they would be if there were no quotation. In Q1.a. above, a comma precedes the quoted statement as it would if there were no quotation marks. In Q2, a colon precedes the quoted sentence because it is long and complex. In Q1.b. and Q1.c., there is no punctuation at all before the quotation. Do not put punctuation before a quotation unless it is otherwise called for.

Q5. Your quotation must combine with its introduction to make a grammatically correct sentence. The normal processes of grammar and syntax, like the normal processes of punctuation, are unaffected by quoting. Subjects must agree with their verbs, verbs must be consistent in tense, pronouns must have their normal relation with antecedents.

WRONG	Othello says, "One that loved not wisely but too well" (5.2.343).
	(Incomplete sentence)
RIGHT	Othello speaks of himself as "one that loved not wisely but too well" (5.2.343).

WRONG	Othello asks his auditors to "speak of me as I am" (5.2.341).
	(The pronouns "me" and "I" do not agree in person with their antecedent.)
RIGHT	Othello bids his auditors,
	Speak of me as I am, nothing extenuate, Nor set down aught in malice. Then must you speak Of one that loved not wisely but too well. (5.2.341–43)

| WRONG | Othello says that "I have done the state some service" (5.2.338).
(Incorrect mixture of direct and indirect quotation) |
| RIGHT | Othello says, "I have done the state some service" (5.2.338). |

| WRONG | Othello says that he "have done the state some service" (5.2.338).
(Subject and verb of subordinate clause lack agreement.) |
| RIGHT | Othello says that he has "done the state some service" (5.2.338). |

Q6. Your introduction must supply enough context to make the quotation meaningful. Be careful that all pronouns in the quotation have clearly identifiable antecedents.

| WRONG | In the final speech of the play, Lodovico says, "Look on the tragic loading of this bed: / This is thy work" (5.2.362–63).
(Whose work?) |
| RIGHT | In the final speech of the play, Lodovico says to Iago, "Look on the tragic loading of this bed: / This is thy work" (5.2.362–63). |

Q7. The words within your quotation marks must be quoted *exactly* from the original.

| WRONG | Though Iago bids his wife to "hold her peace," Emilia declares, "I will speak as liberally as the north wind" (5.2.218–19). |

Q8. It is permissible to insert or supply words in a quotation *if* you enclose them within brackets. Brackets (parentheses with square corners) indicate *your* changes or additions. If parentheses were used, the reader might interpret the enclosed material as the *author's* (as part of what you are quoting). Avoid excessive use of brackets: they make quotations more difficult to read and comprehend. Often paraphrase will serve as well as quotation, particularly if you are not explicitly analyzing the language of a passage.

| CORRECT | Though Iago bids his wife to "hold [her] peace," Emilia declares, "I will speak as liberal[ly] as the north [wind]" (5.2.218–19). |
| BETTER | Though Iago bids his wife to hold her peace, Emilia declares that she will speak as liberally as the north wind. |

Notice that a word within brackets can either replace a word in the original (as in the substitution of *her* for "your" above) or be added to explain or complete the original (as with *-ly* and *wind* above). Since a reader understands that brackets signal either substitutions or additions, it is superfluous to include the words for which substitutions have been made.

| WRONG | Iago bids his wife to "hold your [her] peace" (5.2.218). |

Your sentences, including bracketed words, must read as if there were no brackets:

RIGHT

After Iago's treachery has been completely exposed, Lodovico tells Othello:

> You must forsake this room, and go with us.
> Your power and your command is taken off.
> And Cassio rules in Cyprus. For this slave [Iago],
> If there can be any cunning cruelty
> That can torment him much and hold him long,
> It shall be his. (5.2.329–34)

Q9. It is permissible to omit words from quoted material, but *only* if the omission is indicated. Three *spaced* periods are used to indicate the omission (technically they are called "ellipsis points"). If there are four periods, the first is the normal period at the end of a sentence; the other three indicate the ellipsis.

The statement just concluded, if quoted, might be shortened in the following way: "It is permissible to omit words . . . *if* the omission is indicated. Three *spaced* periods are used to indicate the omission. . . . If there are four periods, the first is the normal period at the end of a sentence."

It is usually not necessary to indicate ellipsis at the beginning or ending of a quotation (the very act of quoting implies that something precedes and follows)—unless what you quote is in some way contradicted by its context, as for example by a "not" preceding the material you quote.

Q10. Single quotation marks are used for quotations within quotations. Thus, if the material you are quoting in a run-in quotation includes a quotation, you should reduce the original double quote marks to single quote marks. (In a block quotation, the quotation marks would remain unchanged.)

In her dying speech, Emilia asks her dead mistress, "Hark, canst thou hear me? I will play the swan, / And die in music. 'Willow, willow, willow'" (5.2.246–47)

Single quotation marks are not used for any other purposes and should not be substituted for double quotes.

Q11. At the conclusion of a run-in quotation, commas and periods are conventionally placed *within* quotation marks; semicolons and colons are placed outside. (The convention is based on appearance, not on logic.) Question marks and exclamation marks are placed inside if they belong to the quoted sentence, outside if they belong to your sentence. (This *is* based on logic.) Special rules apply when the quotation is followed by parenthetical documentation (see PD3 and PD4, page 36). The following examples are all correct:

> "I am not valiant neither," says Othello (5.2.242).
>
> Othello says, "I am not valiant neither" (5.2.242).
>
> "Who can control his fate?" cries Othello (5.2.264).
>
> Does Shakespeare endorse Othello's implication that no one "can control his fate"? (5.2.264).

IX. Documentation

Documentation is the process of identifying the sources of materials used in your paper. The sources are of two kinds: primary and secondary. *Primary* sources are materials written *by* the author being studied, and may be confined to the single work being discussed. *Secondary* sources are materials by other writers *about* the author or work being discussed, or materials having some bearing on that work. Documentation serves two purposes: (1) it enables your readers to check any material they may think you have misinterpreted; (2) it enables you to make proper acknowledgment of information, ideas, opinions, or phraseology that are not your own.

It is difficult to overemphasize the second of these purposes. The use of someone else's ideas or insights in your own words, since it does not require quotation marks, makes an even heavier demand for acknowledgment than does quoted material. Although you need not document matters of common knowledge, your use without acknowledgment of material that is uniquely someone else's is not only dishonest but also illegal (plagiarism), and could result in penalties ranging from an F on the paper through expulsion from school to a term in jail, depending on the magnitude of the offense.

Documentation may be given in (1) the text of your essay; (2) parentheses placed within the text of your essay; or (3) a list of Works Cited placed at the end of your essay but keyed to parenthetical references within the essay. The three methods are progressively more formal.

In any case, the type of documentation required in your class will be chosen by your instructor, who may wish to have you practice several methods so that you will learn their use.

1. Textual Documentation

Every literary essay contains textual documentation. A title like "Dramatic Irony in *Oedipus Rex*" identifies the play that will furnish the main materials in the paper. A paragraph beginning "In scene 2 . . ." locates more specifically the source of what follows. An informally documented essay is one that relies on textual documentation exclusively. Perhaps the majority of articles published in newspapers and periodicals with wide circulation are of this kind. Informal documentation works best for essays written on a single short work, without use of secondary sources, for readers without great scholarly expectations. A first-rate paper might be written on Herman Melville's "Bartleby the Scrivener" using only textual documentation. The author's name and the title of the story mentioned somewhere near the beginning of the essay, plus a few phrases like "In the opening paragraph" or "When Bartleby answers the lawyer's advertisement for additional scriveners" or "At the story's conclusion" might provide all the documentation needed for this audience. The action of the story is straightforward enough that the reader can easily locate any detail within it. If the essay is intended for our hypothetical journal published by your literature class (all of whose members are using the same anthology and have presumably read the story), its readers can readily locate the story and its events. But textual documentation, although less appropriate, can also be used for more complex subjects, and can even accommodate secondary sources with phrases like "As Yvor Winters points out in his essay on Melville in *In Defense of Reason* . . . ."

Principles and Guidelines

TD1. Enclose titles of short stories, articles, one-act plays, and poems (unless they are book-length) in quotation marks; underline titles of full-length plays, magazines, newspapers, and books. Do not underline or put the title of your own paper in quotation marks. The general principle is that titles of separate publications are underlined; titles of selections or parts of books are put within quotation marks. Full-length plays, like *Othello* and *Oedipus Rex,* though often reprinted as part of an anthology, are elsewhere published as separate books and should be underlined. Underlining, in manuscripts, is equivalent to italics in printed matter. Many word-processing programs include italic fonts, so you should check with your instructor for the preferred style.

TD2.   Capitalize the first word and all important words in titles. Do not capitalize articles, prepositions, and conjunctions except when they begin the title ("The Interview," "For Whom the Southern Belle Tolls," "To the Virgins, to Make Much of Time").

TD3.   When the title above a poem is identical with its first line or a major part of its first line, there is a strong presumption that the poet left the poem untitled and the editor or anthologist has used the first line or part of it to serve as a title. In such a case you may *use* the first line as a title, but should not *refer* to it as a title. For example, you might write that "Dickinson's 'There's a certain slant of Light' is a powerful poem about a depressed psychological state." But you should not write, "Dickinson repeats her title in the first line of 'There's a certain slant of Light' because she wants to emphasize her main point." In using it as a title, capitalize only those words that are capitalized in the first line.

TD4.   Never use page numbers in the body of your discussion because a page is not a structural part of a story, poem, or play. You may refer in your discussions to paragraphs, sections, stanzas, lines, acts, or scenes, as appropriate, but use page numbers *only* in parenthetical documentation where a specific edition of the work has been named.

TD5.   Spell out numerical references when they precede the unit they refer to; use numbers when they follow the unit (the fifth act, or act 5; the second paragraph, or paragraph 2; the fourth line, or line 4; the tenth stanza, or stanza 10). Use the first of these alternative forms sparingly, and only with small numbers. Never write "In the thirty-fourth and thirty-fifth lines . . . ," for to do so is to waste good space and irritate your reader; write "In lines 34–35. . . ."

2. Parenthetical Documentation

Parenthetical documentation makes possible fuller and more precise accrediting without a forbidding apparatus of footnotes or an extensive list of Works Cited. With a full-length play like Tennessee Williams's *The Glass Menagerie*, a phrase like "midway through scene 4" is insufficient to allow the reader to locate the passage readily. This can be done by giving a page number, within parentheses, after the passage cited. But the reader needs to know also what book or edition the page number refers to, so this information must be supplied the first time such a citation is made.

Parenthetical documentation is the method most often required for a paper using only the primary source, or, at most, two or three sources—as, for example, most of the writing assigned in an introductory literature course. The information given in parenthetical documentation should enable your reader to turn easily to the exact source of a quotation or a reference. At the first mention of a work (which may well precede the first quotation from it), full publishing details should be given, but parenthetical documentation should supplement textual documentation; that is, information provided in the text of your essay should not be repeated within the parentheses. For the readers of our hypothetical class journal, the first reference in a paper on Williams's play might look like this:

> In Tennessee Williams's *The Glass Menagerie* (reprinted in Thomas R. Arp and Greg Johnson, *Perrine's Literature: Structure, Sound, and Sense*, 9th ed. [Boston: Wadsworth, 2006] 1141), Tom occasionally addresses the audience directly.

Notice in this entry that brackets are used for parentheses within parentheses. In subsequent references, provided no other source intervenes, only the page number need be given:

> Amanda defines her fear that she and Laura will be deserted when she compares Tom to his father: "He was out all hours without explanation!—Then *left! Good-bye!* And me with the bag to hold" (1161).

If you use more than one source, each must be identified—if referred to a second time, by an abbreviated version of the first citation; normally this will be the author's last name or, if you cite several works by a single author, the work's title or a shortened version of it; in any case, use the shortest identification that will differentiate the source from all others.

Principles and Guidelines

PD1. For the first citation from a book, give the author's name; the title of the selection; the name of the book from which it is taken; the editor (preceded by the abbreviation *ed.* for "edited by") or the trans-lator (preceded by the abbreviation *trans.* for "translated by"); the edi-tion (designated by a number) if there has been more than one; the city of publication (the first one will suffice if there is more than one); the publisher (this may be given in shortened form, dropping all but the first name); the year of publication or of most recent copyright; and the page number. The following example correctly combines textual with parenthetical documentation:

> In "Home Burial," Frost has a husband complain, "'A man must partly give up being a man / With womenfolk'" (*The Poetry of Robert Frost,* ed. Edward Connery Lathem [New York: Holt, 1969] 52).

PD2.   For your principal primary source, after the first reference, only a page number is required. Since the paragraphs of the stories in this book are numbered, your instructor may prefer you to supply the para-graph number rather than the page number. For long poems, it may be useful to give line numbers or stanza numbers rather than page num-bers. If a poem is short, line numbers are unnecessary and should be omitted. For plays in verse, citation by line number (preceded by act and scene number) will usually be more useful than citation by page number—for example, *Othello* (5.2.133).

PD3.   Documentation for run-in quotations always follows the quota-tion marks. If the quotation ends with a period, remove it to the end of the documentation. If it ends with an exclamation point or question mark, leave it, but put a period after the documentation as well. The following examples are from *Othello:*

"She was false as water" (5.2.133).

"Alas, what cry is that?" (5.2.116).

PD4.   With block quotations, parenthetical documentation follows the last mark of punctuation without further punctuation after the parentheses:

> Out and alas! That was my lady's voice.
> Help! Help, ho! Help! O lady, speak again!
> Sweet Desdemona! O sweet mistress, speak!
>   (5.2.118–20)

PD5.   Avoid cluttering your paper with excessive documentation. When possible, use one note to cover a series of short quotations. (See example, Q1.) Remember that short poems need no parenthetical documentation at all after the first reference. Do not document well-known sayings or proverbs that you use for stylistic purposes and that form no part of the substance of your investigation (and of course be wary of including hackneyed commonplaces in your formal writing).

PD6.   It is customary in a formal paper to document all quoted materials. Do not, however, assume that *only* quotations need documentation. The first purpose of documentation (see page 23) is to allow the reader to check the primary text concerning any major or possibly controversial interpretation. If you declare that the turning point in a long story occurs with an apparently minor event, it may be more important for the reader to have a page number for that event than for any quotation from the story. Judgment must be exercised. You cannot and should not provide page numbers for every detail of a story; but neither should you think that you have necessarily done your duty if you only document all quotations.

3. Documentation by Works Cited

When your assignment involves the use of secondary sources, your instructor may require you to create a list of "Works Cited," to be located at the end of your paper. Any book, article, website, or other source you use or quote from must be referenced parenthetically in the body of your paper so that the reader can easily locate the source in your Works Cited list.

Your first step should be to create the Works Cited list (no longer called a "bibliography") in the format detailed in the *MLA Handbook for Writers of Research Papers* mentioned earlier. Then you should locate each instance in your paper where you have quoted from or paraphrased a source or where your ideas have been formed by reading a source. In order to identify the source, you should normally give the author's last name and the page number to which you are indebted.

For example, let's say you are writing a research paper on Emily Dickinson and one of your sources is David Porter's book *The Art of Emily Dickinson's Early Poetry*. Typically you would cite a reference to the book in this manner: (Porter 141). There are some instances, however, where more information might be needed. David Porter wrote a second book on Dickinson called *Dickinson: The Modern Idiom*. If both of Porter's titles are in your Works Cited list, you need to identify the source parenthetically with an abbreviation of the particular book you are citing. These might read as follows: (Porter, *Early Poetry* 141) or (Porter, *Modern Idiom*

252). The key principle is that you should keep the parenthetical citations both as brief and as clear as possible, so that the reader will have no trouble finding the particular source you are citing.

Here is another example of when you must provide some information in addition to the last name and page number: you might have two authors on your Works Cited list with the last name of Smith. In this case, you need to be specific about which of the two authors you are quoting. Thus the parenthetical citations might read (Mary Smith 88) or (John Smith 138). Note that the first name is required only when there are two sources on the Works Cited list whose authors have the same last name.

Always keep nearby the *MLA Handbook* when preparing the parenthetical documentation and the Works Cited list. Different types of sources—for instance, a newspaper story or an article from an anthology with multiple editors—require different formats, and examples of all these are located in the *Handbook.*

Here is a sample Works Cited page from a paper on Emily Dickinson. Note that the list should start on a new page and be double-spaced. Also note the proper method of abbreviation for publishers' names—for example, "Harvard UP" rather than "Harvard University Press." Also remember to indent after the first line of an entry. When two titles are by the same author, like the entries for David Porter here, the second and any subsequent listings of the author's name should be replaced by a straight line.

Works Cited

Buckingham, Willis J. Emily Dickinson: An Annotated Bibliography. Bloomington: Indiana UP, 1970.

Cameron, Sharon. Lyric Time: Dickinson and the Limits of Genre. Baltimore: Johns Hopkins UP, 1979.

Diehl, Joanne Feit. "Dickinson and Bloom: An Antithetical Reading of Romanticism." Texas Studies in Literature and Language 23 (1981): 414–41.

Porter, David. The Art of Dickinson's Early Poetry. Cambridge: Harvard UP, 1966.

——————. Dickinson: The Modern Idiom. Cambridge: Harvard UP, 1981.

Wilson, Suzanne M. "Structural Patterns in the Poetry of Emily Dickinson." American Literature 35 (1963): 53–59.

4. Documentation of Electronic Sources

If your instructor encourages or permits you to do research on the Internet or other electronic sources, you need to be sure that the information is reliable, since much of what is available is uncredited or incorrect. As with all research, the quality of your paper will be directly affected by the quality of its sources.

Electronic sources are cited in your paper as parenthetical references and then included in your list of Works Cited. Examples include personal websites; online books, magazines, and newspapers; and materials obtained from a library subscription service such as Lexis-Nexis or Expanded Academic ASAP. Unlike textual sources, which usually clearly state author, title, date of publication, and publisher, electronic sources may or may not provide such information. Whatever the format, you will need to provide information that enables your reader to access the exact source of your materials.

Your parenthetical citations normally will include the name of the author and a page number. If the source is not paginated, the name of the author may suffice; if it is divided by paragraphs, sections, or screen numbers, after the author's name use the abbreviations "par.," "sec.," or the word "screen" followed by the appropriate number. Here are some examples from a paper on James Joyce's "Araby":

A scholarly project or information database:
According to many scholars, James Joyce's "Araby" is best understood if studied at both a realistic and a symbolic level (Gray 1).

A document within a scholarly project or information database:
"Araby" was first published in *Irish Homestead* in 1904 ("James Joyce").

An article in a scholarly journal:
Most scholars contend that "Araby" is an initiation story recounting a young man's first bitter taste of reality (Coulthard).

An article in an encyclopedia:
Joyce often used stream of consciousness, a technique that allows authors to capture their character's complete flow of interior thoughts and feelings ("Stream of Consciousness" par. 2).

Works from online services:
Often lacking courage and honesty, the anti-hero reflects modern man's ambivalence towards traditional social mores ("Anti-hero" sec. 2).

Dublin, and its long history of legal and cultural repression, heavily influenced Joyce's writing ("Dublin" par. 2).

A CD-ROM nonperiodical publication:
According to the *Oxford English Dictionary*, the word "araby" is a romantic word for the Middle East ("Araby").

In your list of Works Cited, Internet sources should include both the date of the electronic publication (if available) and the date you accessed the source, and should also include the URL. These are the Works Cited for the examples above:

Gray, Wallace. "James Joyce's Dubliners: An Introduction by Wallace Gray." World Wide Dubliners by James Joyce. Ed. Roger B. Blumberg and Wallace Gray. 1997. Brown U. 5 Sep. 2004 <http://www.mendele.com/WWD/home.html>.

"James Joyce." Contemporary Authors. 2003. Gale Group. 3 Sep. 2004. <http://www.galenet.com/servlet/ LitIndex/form?1=1&u=LitIndex&o=DocTitle>.

Coulthard, A.R. "Joyce's 'Araby'." Explicator 52 (1994): 97-100. Academic Search Premier. EBSCOhost. University of Texas Lib. Austin, TX. 6 Sep. 2004 <http://www.lib.utexas.edu/ indexes/s-literaturesinenglish.html>.

"Stream of Consciousness." Britannica Online. 2004. Encyclopedia Britannica. 2 Sep. 2004 <http://www.britannica.com>.

"Anti-hero." Encyclopedia. 2004. Infoplease.com. 1 Sep. 2004. Keyword: James Joyce.

"Dublin." Encyclopedia. 2004. Infoplease.com. 6 Sep. 2004. Path: James Joyce; Irish Literary Renaissance; History; Republic of Ireland.

"Araby." The Oxford English Dictionary. 2nd ed. CD-ROM. Oxford: Oxford UP, 2001.

The Internet and other electronic sources provide a great variety of materials, and there are many complex variations on the examples we have given you. For the fullest possible range of correct references, consult the *MLA Handbook*.

X. Stance and Style

In section II, "For Whom Do You Write?" we discussed the assumed audience for your critical writing. Now we must consider the
other half of the reader/writer equation. We might ask the parallel
question "Who Are You?" except that that would imply that we are
asking about your own personal identity. Rather, since we defined
your audience hypothetically as members of your class, we need to
define "you" in terms of the voice that your audience will expect and
appreciate. There are certain conventional expectations that are
aroused when we read critical analyses of literature, and the following suggestions may lead you to adopt the stance that your readers
will expect. If these sound prescriptive (or if your instructor suggests
others), remember that writing about literature is essentially persuasive writing, its purpose being to persuade your readers to agree with
your interpretation; the means of persuasion are many, and the
writer's stance is only one of them. What we advise here are a few
"hints" that have been valuable to students in the past, and may be
helpful to you.

S1. *Avoid first-person pronouns.* This injunction warns you away from
unnecessarily intruding yourself into your critical statements, with a
consequent loss of power and precision. Consider the relative force of
these approaches:

POOR	It seems to me that Welty uses the name Phoenix to symbolize endurance and persistence.
GOOD	Welty uses the name Phoenix to symbolize endurance and persistance.
BETTER	The name Phoenix symbolizes endurance and persis-tence.

The first example dilutes the statement by making it sound tentative
and opinionated. It allows your reader to respond, "Why should I consider that seriously, since the writer confesses that it's only a private
opinion rather than a fact?" As a critic, you should adopt the stance of
the sensitive person who is confident of the accuracy of her or his insights—even when in your heart you may *feel* tentative or unsure. Say
it with an air of confidence.

The third example is "better" because it observes the following suggestion:

S2. *Write about the work.* When analyzing a work of literature or some aspect of it, you should be sure that the thesis or topic of a paragraph or essay (and its thesis sentence) focuses on your topic. You will usually not be writing about an *author* but about a *work*, so try to avoid using the author's name as the subject:

POOR	Welty uses the name to symbolize endurance. *(This focuses on Welty [subject] and uses [verb].)*
GOOD	The name symbolizes endurance. (*Subject,* name; *verb,* symbolizes.)

Try also to avoid the verb *uses*, since your focus is not on a writer using a technical device but on the result of that use; not on an author selecting a device to achieve a purpose but on the result of that selection. The easiest way to get rid of the word *use* or the idea of *using* is simply to delete them:

POOR	Welty uses the name to symbolize . . .
GOOD	The name symbolizes . . .

The revised version cuts the wordiness and is more direct.

S3. *Be cautious about passive constructions.* In analyzing literature, the passive voice presents three potential problems: (1) it may fail to identify its subject and thus (2) may introduce vagueness, and (3) it is often a weak and wordy way to say something that you can say directly and forcefully. It may also be a roundabout way to write about an author rather than a work:

POOR	The plot is structured on Phoenix's journey.
GOOD	Phoenix's journey gives structure to the plot.

S4. *Be cautious about praise.* Praising a work or writer with such adverbs as *cleverly, remarkably, beautifully,* and so forth, is much less effective than presenting and analyzing the details that you find praiseworthy. Your opinion is important, but your reader wants the opportunity to share it—and such labeling doesn't really afford that opportunity.

S5. *Avoid preparatory circumlocution.* Don't write a "table of contents" as an introductory paragraph, and eliminate such phrases as "in order to understand X we must examine Y." Just go ahead and examine Y, and trust your reader to recognize its relevance. Another example: "Z is a significant aspect of the poem" (or, a little worse, "It is interesting to note that Z is a significant aspect"). If Z is significant, just go ahead and say what it signifies; if it is interesting, let what is interesting about it be your topic.

Such circumlocution is sometimes called "treading water," since it is generally only a way of keeping afloat on the page until you get a good idea of the direction you really want to swim. You wouldn't walk into a room and announce, "I am now going to tell you that I'm here," or "I will tell you how interested you'll be to notice that I'm here." You'd say, "Here I am!"

It is perfectly all right to use such space-wasters in preliminary drafts—as ways of keeping your pen or keyboard in action while you are figuring out which way you are going to swim. Just be sure to edit them from your finished text.

S6. *Avoid negative hypotheses.* Negative hypothesis is introduced with an example on page 11, "Proving Your Point." Here's another: "If Phoenix Jackson's grandson had not swallowed lye, she would not have made her trip to the city." But he did, so a critical analysis can neither speculate about what might have happened under other circumstances, nor prove by comparison that what happens is better or worse—there is nothing to compare.

On the other hand, in the process of coming to understand a work (as distinct from presenting the results of that process in your writing), it can be valuable to entertain such hypotheses. For example, in discussing connotation, we suggest that imagining possible alternative words can sharpen your appreciation of the poet's actual choice (see study questions for Dickinson, "There is no Frigate like a Book" [page 687] or Kay, "Pathedy of Manners" [page 690]).

XI. Grammar, Punctuation, and Usage: Common Problems

1. Grammar

G1. In discussing the action of a literary work, rely primarily on the present tense (even when the work itself uses the past), keeping the past, future, and perfect tenses available for prior or subsequent actions; for example,

> When Mrs. May imagines that the bull may have gored Greenleaf and killed him, and thinks of this as the "perfect ending" for a story she has been telling her friends, the situation is highly ironic, for she does not guess that the bull will cause her own death.

G2.   Do not let pronouns refer to nouns in the possessive case. Antecedents of pronouns should always hold a strong grammatical position: a possessive is a mere modifier, like an adjective:

WRONG	In Shakespeare's play *Othello,* he writes . . .
	(Antecedent of "he" is in possessive case.)
RIGHT	In his play *Othello,* Shakespeare writes . . .
	(Antecedent of "his" is the subject of the sentence.)

2. Punctuation

P1.   The insertion of a parenthetical phrase in your sentence structure (as, for example, in parenthetical documentation) does not alter the normal punctuation of the rest of the sentence. Do not, as the preceding sentence doesn't, place a comma after a parenthetical phrase unless it belonged there before the parenthesis was inserted. You wouldn't write, "Welty's story, touches upon racial issues," so don't include that comma when you insert a parenthesis.

WRONG	Welty's "A Worn Path" (rpt. in Thomas R. Arp and Greg Johnson, *Perrine's Literature: Structure, Sound and Sense, 9th ed* [Boston: Wadsworth, 2006] 212), touches upon racial issues in the early twentieth century.
	(Delete the comma after the parenthesis.)

And it is an inflexible rule of punctuation: never place a comma immediately before a parenthesis.

P2.   Do not set off restrictive appositives with commas. A restrictive appositive is one necessary to the meaning of the sentence; a nonrestrictive appositive could be left out without changing the meaning.

WRONG	In her story, "A Worn Path," Welty . . .
	(The title of the story is necessary to the meaning of the statement. As punctuated, the sentence falsely implies that Welty wrote only one story.)
RIGHT	In her story "A Worn Path," Welty . . .
RIGHT	In her story in chapter 4 of *Perrine's Literature,* "A Worn Path," Welty . . .
	(The chapter number identifies the story. The title simply supplies additional information and could be omitted without changing the meaning.)

P3.   Words used simply as words should be either underlined or italicized or put in quotation marks.

WRONG	The word describing the seal and frame is gold.
	(This statement is false; all the words in the story are black.)
RIGHT	The word describing the seal and frame is "gold."

Since the word "gold" is quoted from the story, it has here been put in quotation marks. However, if you list a series of words from various parts of the story, you may prefer underlining for the sake of appearance. Whichever system you choose, be consistent throughout your paper.

P4.   Observe the conventions of typed manuscripts: (1) put a space after an abbreviating period (p. 7, not p.7; pp. 10–13, not pp.10–13);

(2) use two hyphens to represent a dash--and do not put spaces before and after them.

P5. Observe the standard for forming possessives. For a singular noun, add an apostrophe and an *s* (a student's duty, yesterday's mail, the dress's hemline). For a plural noun, add only an apostrophe (the students' duties, seven days' mail). For proper nouns, the same rules apply (Camus's "The Guest," Chekhov's "Gooseberries," Oates's play).

Do not confuse the contraction *it's* (it is) with the possessive *its* (belonging to it). *Its* is an exception to the general rule requiring apostrophes for possessives.

3. Usage

U1. Though accepted usage changes with time, and the distinctions between the following pairs of words are fading, many instructors will bless you if you try to preserve them.

convince, persuade   *Convince* pertains to belief (conviction); *persuade* pertains to either action or belief. The following sentences observe the distinction. "In 'Eveline,' Frank persuades Evvie to sail away with him." "In 'Eveline,' Frank seems to have convinced Evvie that she will be happy in Argentina." "Although Eveline has been persuaded to leave, finally she is not convinced that she should go."

describe, define   *Describe* means to delineate the visual appearance of something; *define* means to state the meaning of a word or phrase, or to explain the essential quality of something. Reserve *describe* and *description* for talking about how things look.

disinterested, uninterested   A disinterested judge is one who has no stake or personal interest in the outcome of a case and can therefore judge fairly; an uninterested judge goes to sleep on the bench. A good judge is interested in the case but disinterested in its outcome. An uninterested reader finds reading boring. A disinterested reader? Perhaps one who can enjoy a good book whatever its subject matter.

imply, infer   A writer or speaker implies; a reader or listener infers. An implication is a meaning hinted at but not stated outright. An inference is a conclusion drawn from evidence not complete enough for proof. If you imply that I am a snob, I may infer that you do not like me.

lover, beloved   In older literature, the word *lover* usually meant one of two things—a man who is sexually involved, or any person who feels affection or esteem for another person or persons. In the case of the former, *lover* generally designated the male partner and *beloved* his female partner. In the case of the latter usage, no sexual implications are involved.

quote, quotation   The word *quote* was originally only a verb. Today the use of the terms "single quotes" and "double quotes" in reference to quotation marks is almost universally accepted; but, although the use of "quote" for the noun "quotation" is common in informal speech, it is still unacceptable in formal writing.

Note also that quoting is an act performed by the writer *about* literature, not by the writer *of* literature:

WRONG	Shakespeare's famous quotation "To be or not to be" . . .
RIGHT	The famous quotation from Shakespeare, "To be or not to be" . . .

sensuous, sensual   *Sensuous* normally pertains to the finer senses, *sensual* to the appetites. Good poetry is sensuous: it appeals through the imagination to the senses. A voluptuous woman, an attractive man, or a rich dessert may have a sensual appeal that stirs a desire for possession.

U2.   Some words and phrases to avoid are the following.

center around   A geometrical impossibility. A story may perhaps center *on* a certain feature, but to make it center *around* that feature is to make the hub surround the wheel.

just as   This phrase as a term of comparison is too precise for literary analysis because the adjective *just* means *exactly* or *identical in every possible way*, almost an impossibility when discussing literature. You should take the trouble to establish the points of similarity and dissimilarity between things that you are comparing.

lifestyle   An overused neologism, especially inappropriate for use with older literature, that is too general to mean much. One dictionary defines it as "a person's typical approach to living, including his moral attitudes, preferred entertainment, fads, fashions, etc." If you wish to define someone's moral attitudes, do so; if you try to define a person's "lifestyle," you have a monumental task of all-inclusive definition. It's easier just to avoid it.

society   The problem with this word is that it is too often used only vaguely as a substitute for some more precise idea. Any story, poem, or play that does deal with "society" will clearly indicate a *particular* society—the world of segregated white middle-class people in South Africa's apartheid system in "Once upon a Time," or the paternalistic society of Norway in the late nineteenth century in *A Doll House*. In those cases, once one has defined the particular society and its characteristics, the term might legitimately be used. But don't use it simply to mean "people in general at that time in that place." And it is important to avoid the glib assumption that *society* makes a person do something. A person's desire to be a member of a social group may lead to actions that appear to be imposed or forced, but what makes a person conform is the desire to be or remain a member, not the fact that there are codes of behavior. See Ellen Kay's "Pathedy of Manners" (page 689).

somewhat (also *rather, more or less, as it were, in a manner*)   All of these terms are specifically designed to avoid or evade precision—to create a sense of vagueness. Since clarity and precision are the goals of critical analysis, these terms should be avoided. They also sound wishy-washy, while you should strive to sound firm and convinced.

upset   As an adjective to define an emotional condition, the word is just too vague. Your dictionary will tell you that its synonyms are "distressed, disturbed, agitated, perturbed, irritated," and so forth. All of those terms are more precise than *upset,* and the one that most nearly indicates your meaning should be chosen.

what the author is trying to say is   The implication of this expression is that the author *failed* to say it. You don't say "I'm trying to get to Boston" if you are already there; give the author credit for having got where he or she was going.

Others suggested by your instructor:

_____   _____

_____   _____

_____   _____

_____   _____

_____   _____

_____   _____

_____   _____

_____   _____

XII. Writing Samples

1. Fiction Explication

"Darkness" in the Conclusion of "The Child by Tiger"

The concluding paragraph of Thomas Wolfe's "The Child by Tiger" (rpt. in Thomas R. Arp and Greg Johnson, *Perrine's Literature: Structure, Sound, and Sense,* 9th ed. [Boston: Wadsworth, 2006] 625) resonates with the words "darkness," "dark," and "night." This conclusion presents the final discoveries of the narrator Spangler, twenty-five years after the horrific events that he witnessed or heard about when a child; it is the result of his having been haunted by the mystery of those events. The story was published in 1937, and we may safely infer that Dick Prosser's murderous rampage occurred in 1912, the year in which Wolfe himself would have been twelve years old—that is, for purposes of dating the events, it is not unreasonable to identify the narrator with the author, and Wolfe's writing has been called "patently autobiographical" (*Cambridge Biographical Dictionary,* ed. Magnus Magnusson [Cambridge: Cambridge UP, 1990] 1576). The potential identification of Spangler with Wolfe will be a component part of our understanding of the story.

The events of the story center upon Dick Prosser, an African American general handyman working for a middle-class family in a southern town at the foot of the Great Smoky Mountains. Dick is remarkable in every way, a superior worker of many skills who adapts his social behavior to the racist norms of a society that oppresses and denigrates his race. He is deeply religious and a model of "proper" behavior. For example, he not only abases himself before the white adults but even treats the children as if they were his superiors, calling the boys "Cap'n" or "Mister" (Wolfe 626). Despite their extravagant admiration for Dick's skills, the boys feel some unnamed uneasiness about him, and this feeling foreshadows Dick's climactic actions. Perhaps out of jealousy (and perhaps not), Dick begins a shooting rampage by killing the husband of a woman, and then goes on to kill indiscriminately white policemen, black by-standers, and members of the white lynch mob who track him down and finally destroy him.

The conclusion that Spangler reaches is phrased in terms of Dick's origins rather than his motives. Although the essential question would seem to be why such a good man would commit so many murders, the narrator finds his explanation not in terms of Dick's uniqueness but in the origins of evil in all men. Here is his answer:

> He came from darkness. He came out of the heart of darkness, from the dark heart of the secret and undiscovered South. He came by night, just as he passed by night. He was night's child and partner, a token of the other side of man's dark soul, a symbol of those things that pass by darkness and that still remain, a symbol of man's evil innocence, and the token of his mystery, a projection of his own unfathomed quality, a friend, a brother and a mortal enemy, an unknown demon, two worlds together—a tiger and a child. (643)

This rhapsodic (even bombastic) paragraph shifts the mystery of Dick's motivation from the individual man to what he represents in all of us, the potential for unspeakable evil that is the heritage of the *human* race, not the *black* race. The darkness and night in this passage are not physical but metaphysical, as Wolfe says, a "symbol" and "token" of the evil shared by all. The point is shifted from solving the mystery of Dick's motives to trying to account for the "darkness" in humanity. Wolfe's explanation is put in Manichean terms—dark evil vs. (presumably) bright goodness. Like the story of Adam's fall, this is one way of explaining the fact that people do do evil things even when they are conscious of the wrongness of the action and aware of its self-destructive consequences. Wolfe frames a paradoxical phrase to encompass this, "man's evil innocence," and embodies it in the title and the references to Blake's poem—man is a tiger, and also a child. Dick was fierce, and Dick was pure of heart.

But in a story in which race relations are an inescapable center of attention, there are still lingering problems. The imagery of darkness and night must inevitably reverberate with the racist implications of dark skin. Has Wolfe actually managed to separate Dick's "dark soul" from his skin color, or do the evils of racism continue to be relevant to this story? While it is true that Wolfe is evenhanded in showing that Dick's murders are not essentially race-based, and suggests thereby that Dick's revolt is not a blow against the racism of his society, we cannot escape seeing the other kind of "darkness" in the story. The members of the racist lynch mob also display the darkness of the soul, but they are focused on the dark skin as the badge of evil, and they certainly congratulate themselves for destroying Dick in the most savage way (their savagery is in contrast to Dick's sharpshooter skill, one bullet precisely placed in each victim versus the "three hundred holes" in his "riddled carcass"). In terms of the story, their viciousness is more disgusting than the surgical kills of Dick Prosser.

Wolfe says that the origin of Dick was "the dark heart of the secret and undiscovered South," that is, his evil actions were molded in the cruelty and inequality of a social system itself mysterious and dark in its origins. However, in universalizing Dick's evil he replaces that social evil with intrinsic evil. In converting Dick into a symbol, he moves the focus away from the evil system. Nowadays, we might have preferred that the story find a resolution in *both* the intrinsic nature of mankind and its manifestation in social evils. Equally, we might have preferred that Wolfe not use the kind of language that we find so offensive, the "nigger" from "Niggertown," "the comely Negro wench, young, plump, black as the ace of spades," and the rest (Wolfe 634, 629). But we must remember that in 1937 (publication date) and certainly in 1912 (year of the actions) such language was commonplace, a straightforward symbol of the embedded racism of the times, and not limited to the "South." It would probably be asking for more than could be expected for Wolfe to employ inoffensive language in representing that world.

Perhaps one signal that he was fully aware of the distorting nature of such language is his allusion to another story of racism and its debasing effects on a man's "innocence" : "he came out of the heart of darkness," the narrator reports. Joseph Conrad's tale of unspeakable viciousness and the fall from the highest human potentiality to its most degraded evil, "Heart of Darkness," was published in 1902, and deals directly with the maltreatment of the black race as a cause for the degeneration of the white man. Trapped in the language and assumptions of his time and place, Spangler does not overtly reach that conclusion. But the allusion to Conrad's story may be seen as the ironic wedge that separates Spangler from Wolfe and points to a symbolic meaning that eludes the narrator. The racism that shaped Prosser's humiliating self-abasement also fed the evil side of his "evil innocence," and even more overtly it also shaped the viciousness of his destroyers.

Comments

While this essay does not provide a line-by-line explication of the passage, its handling of key words and phrases and its limitation to one paragraph for its evidence qualify it as explicative. It summarizes the major event in the story not for purposes of narration but in order to provide necessary background material for explicating the mystery that it presents. Biographical information is relevant to the conclusion that there may be an ironic distance between narrator and author, and is documented properly. The essay introduces the question of the identification of author and narrator in the opening paragraph, and completes the thought in the conclusion after presenting its explication of the language. Because there are two documented sources, the citations from the story must use the author's name. The date of publication of the story is not documented since it is known to the hypothetical readers of the essay who have read the introductory footnote in the text.

2. Fiction Analysis

The Function of the Frame Story in "Once upon a Time"

Nadine Gordimer's "Once upon a Time" (rpt. in Thomas R. Arp and Greg Johnson, *Perrine's Literature: Structure, Sound, and Sense,* 9th ed. [Boston: Wadsworth, 2006] 220) is a complex, ironic presentation of the results of fear and hatred. This "children's story," so flat in its tone, characterization, and reporting of events, proceeds by gradual steps to show a family systematically barricading itself behind various security devices, the last of which has an effect opposite of what was intended in destroying the child that the parents are trying to protect.

The tale is especially harrowing because of the tone hinted at in the title. This is an easy, casual narration that repeats such standard storybook phrases as "living happily ever after" (221) and identifies its characters only by their functions and relationships, never exploring motivations or revealing the steps of their decision making. The deeper causes for fear are not defined in the tale. All these qualities, and others, establish the tone of fairy tales and other stories for children. In this story, however, no one lives "happily ever after," for in attempting to safeguard themselves, the parents destroy their lives.

But that tale doesn't begin until the ninth paragraph of Gordimer's story. What precedes it is the frame story of a writer who has been asked to write a story for a children's collection, who refuses to contribute, and then is awakened in the night by some noise that frightens her. Her fear first chillingly conjures up a burglar or murderer "moving from room to room, coming up the passage—to [her] door" (220). Then the actual cause of her waking comes to her: deep down, "three thousand feet below" her house, some rock face has fallen in the gold mine beneath (221). She is not in personal danger, then. Yet she cannot return to sleep, so she tells herself "a bedtime story" to relax her mind—and the story is of the family that grows obsessed with security and protection, the awful story of the mutilation of the little boy.

The frame story initially seems little more than an introductory explanation of how the tale came to be written, against the writer's will and purpose. Its details are unrelated to the children's tale—explicitly so, as the writer, despite her knowledge of two recent murders in her neighborhood, and the rational fears that such events arouse, has "no burglar bars, no gun under the pillow" (220), in contrast to the precautions taken in the tale. There is no fairy-tale gold mine in her life, only the knowledge of the mining of gold a half-mile beneath her. So what does this frame have to do with the tale, other than to place the reader within the literal reality of a writer's time and place, from which the imagination journeys to "once upon a time"? Is it more than an ironic contrast in subject and tone?

For answers, we need to consider the writer's time and place as parallels to those of the tale. Both are located in South Africa, both are in the present (even though the phrase "once upon a time" normally signals a long time ago, in a far-off place). The family in the tale, with their burglar bars, walls, alarms, and finally "the razor-bladed coils all round the walls of the house," are like those people in the writer's world who *do* keep guns under their pillows. Like the real people of the writer's neighborhood, the family focuses its fears on the black African populace who surround and outnumber them. On the one hand, in the writer's world, the fears focus on "a casual laborer . . . dismissed without pay" who returns to strangle the watchdogs and knife the man who treated him unfairly (221); on the other hand, in the children's story, the fears focus on the hungry, out-of-work, and begging multitudes who fill and spoil the suburban streets of the fictitious family's neighborhood. In both worlds, unfairness, want, and deprivation mark the blacks, while the whites feel surrounded and threatened by them.

Why cannot the writer return to sleep after she has discovered the innocent cause of her awakening? Because the comforting natural explanation, which removes her from personal danger, is in fact more horrifying than a murderous prowler. She thinks of

> the Chopi and Tsonga migrant miners who might [be] down there, under [her] in the earth at that moment. The stope where the [rock] fall was could have been disused, dripping water from its ruptured veins; or men might now be interred there in the most profound of tombs. (221)

Two possibilities occur to her—one of no harm to men, the other of burial alive—both a consequence of the wage-slavery of "migrant miners" over whose heads (literally and figuratively) the white society lives in "uneasy strain . . . of brick, cement, wood and glass" (221). If no miner has been harmed by *this* rock fall, others have been and will be; and moreover, being killed in that subterranean world of "ruptured veins" is not the only harm that the whites have inflicted on the original inhabitants of the country they control, nor on their own sensitivities and consciences.

The frame story of "Once upon a Time," then, foreshadows the fear, the violence, and the pain of the children's tale, and points to the ultimate cause of its terrible sacrifice of a child—the systematic maltreatment of one race by another and the brutality and self-destruction that are its result.

Comments

This analysis has as its subject an aspect of the story that the writer can fully develop in the limited space. It is written for our hypothetical class journal, as indicated by the way in which the writer refrains from giving a detailed summary of the tale enclosed in the frame (since the audience is known to be familiar with the story), and presents details from the frame narration as they support the writer's argument. It employs some information about the author that is common knowledge to the class (her nationality and her contemporaneity are in the introductory footnote to the story). Quotations are integrated into the writer's sentence structures, and the writer interpolates words within the extended quotation.

3. Poetry Explication

"A Study of Reading Habits"

The first noteworthy feature of Philip Larkin's "A Study of Reading Habits" (rpt. in Thomas R. Arp and Greg Johnson, *Perrine's Literature: Structure, Sound, and Sense,* 9th ed. [Boston: Wadsworth, 2006] 671) is the ironic discrepancy between the formal language of its title and the colloquial, slangy, even vulgar language of the poem itself. The title by its tone implies a formal sociological research paper, possibly one that samples a cross section of a population and draws conclusions about people's reading. The poem presents, instead, the confessions of one man whose attitudes toward reading have progressively deterio-rated to the point where books seem to him "a load of crap." The poem's real subject, moreover, is not the man's reading habits but the revelation of life and character they provide.

The poem is patterned in three stanzas having an identical rhyme scheme (*abcbac*) and the same basic meter (iambic trimeter). The stanzaic division of the poem corresponds to the internal structure of meaning, for the three stanzas present the speaker at three stages of his life: as schoolboy, adolescent, and adult. Larkin signals the chrono-logical progression in the first lines of the stanzas by the words "When," "Later," and "now." The "now" is the present out of which the adult speaks, recalling the two earlier periods.

The boy he remembers in stanza 1 was unhappy, both in his home and, even more so, at school. Perhaps small and bullied by big-ger boys, probably an indifferent student, making poor grades, and scolded by teachers, he found a partial escape from his miseries through reading. The books he read—tales of action and adventure, pitting good guys against bad guys, full of physical conflict, and ending with victory for the good guy—enabled him to construct a fan-tasy life in which he identified with the virtuous hero and in his imagi-nation beat up villains twice his size, thus reversing the situations of his real life.

In stanza 2 the speaker recalls his adolescence when his dreams were of sexual rather than muscular prowess. True to the prediction of "ruining [his] eyes" in stanza 1, he had to wear spectacles, which he describes hyperbolically as "inch-thick"—a further detriment to his so-cial life. To compensate for his lack of success with girls, he envi-sioned himself as a Dracula figure with cloak and fangs, enjoying a se-ries of sexual triumphs. His reading continued to feed his fantasy life, but, instead of identifying with the virtuous hero, he identified with the glamorous, sexually ruthless villain. The poet puns on the word "rip-ping" (the speaker "had ripping times in the dark"), implying both the British slang meaning of "splendid" and the violence of the rapist who rips the clothes off his victim.

In stanza 3 the speaker, now a young adult, confesses that he no longer reads much. His accumulated experience of personal failure and his long familiarity with his shortcomings have made it impossible for him to identify, even in fantasy, with the strong virtuous hero or the viciously potent villain. He can no longer hide from himself the truth that he resembles more closely the weak secondary characters of the escapist tales he picks up. He recognizes himself in the undependable dude who fails the heroine, or the cowardly storekeeper who knuckles under to the bad guys. He therefore has turned to a more powerful means of escape, one that protects him from dwelling on what he knows about himself: drunkenness. His final words are memorable—so "unpoetical" in a traditional sense, so poetically effective in characterizing this speaker. "Get stewed," he tells himself. "Books are a load of crap."

It would be a serious mistake to identify the speaker of the poem, or his attitudes or his language, with the poet. Poets, unless they are in a cynical or depressed mood, do not think that "books are a load of crap." Philip Larkin, moreover, an English poet and a graduate of Oxford, was for many years until his death a university librarian (Ian Hamilton, ed., *Oxford Companion to Twentieth-Century Poetry* [Oxford: Oxford UP, 1994] 288). "A Study of Reading Habits" is both dramatic and ironic. It presents a first-person speaker who has been unable to cope with the reality of his life in any of its stages and has therefore turned toward various means of escaping it. His confessions reveal a progressive deterioration of values (from good to evil to sodden indifference) and a decline in reading tastes (from adventure stories to prurient sexual novels to none) that reflect his downward slide.

Comments

The title of this paper is enclosed in quotation marks because the writer has used the title of the poem for the title of the paper. The paper uses textual and parenthetical documentation. Line numbers for quotations from the poem are not supplied because the poem is too short to require them: they would serve no useful purpose. Notice that in quoting from stanza 1, the writer has changed the phrase "ruining my eyes" to fit the essay's syntax, but has indicated the alteration by putting the changed word within brackets. The paper is written for an American audience; if it had been written for an English audience, the writer would not have needed to explain that "ripping" is British slang or to have made it a point that the poet is English. The paper is documented for an audience using this textbook. If it were directed toward a wider audience, the writer would want to refer for his text of the poem not to a textbook or anthology but to the volume of Larkin's poetry containing this poem (*Collected Poems*, ed. Anthony Thwaite [London: Faber, 1988] 31). Also, the writer would probably wish to include the poet's name in the title: Philip Larkin's "A Study of Reading Habits" (or) An Examination of Larkin's "A Study of Reading Habits." Since Larkin's nationality and his profession as a librarian are not common knowledge, the paper documents a biographical source where that information is found.

4. Poetry Analysis

Diction in "Pathedy of Manners"

Ellen Kay's "Pathedy of Manners" (rpt. in Thomas R. Arp and Greg Johnson, *Perrine's Literature: Structure, Sound, and Sense,* 9th ed. [Boston: Wadsworth, 2006] 689) surprisingly shifts its time focus after the first four stanzas. Until the beginning of the fifth stanza, the poem reads as a biographical narrative summarizing the development of a young woman; stanzas 5–8 shift to the present and future for a summary evaluation of the consequences of the woman's choices and a definition of her life as a "pathedy"—a pathetic drama, in the poet's coined term.

From the fifth stanza to the end, the poem straightforwardly defines the emotional condition of a woman who chooses a course of life that ultimately brings neither contentment nor happiness. She is alone, widowed, and separated from her children, and has begun entertaining the idea of recapturing her missed opportunities. However, as the speaker explains it, she is

> Toying with plots to kill time and re-wed
> Illusions of lost opportunity.

The diction in these lines, along with the structural placement of the word "re-wed" at the end of a line, creates a complexity of feeling that goes beyond what the woman herself is willing to confront. The phrase "Toying with plots"—particularly when it goes on "to kill"—combines the superficiality of idle conjecture with the melodramatic action suggested by "plots to kill." The phrase continues: it's only "time" that she is plotting to kill, and the whole project seems to collapse with the cliché "to kill time." Thus in her daydreaming the woman spans the contrasts contained in the superficiality of "Toying," the violence of "plots to kill," and the blandness of the cliché for escaping boredom—killing time.

The concluding phrase contains the misleading implication that she might escape her boredom by remarrying—misleading, because the object of the verb "re-wed" is not a second husband, but rather her youthful "illusions." One way to "kill [the passage of] time" is to return to one's past, and this seems to be her desire. But the phrase "Illusions of lost opportunity" presents further complications of feeling. One might easily sympathize with a person who thinks her life has gone sour because she was denied the opportunity to achieve "all that wealth and mind had offered her" (as the next stanza says). However, that is not the issue here. The woman wants to recapture "illusions" that she has missed her opportunities. It's an odd idea—the desire to get back to the point where she might pretend that her failures in life amounted to missing out on what was offered to her. She wants to comfort herself with the thought that she was not responsible for her choices.

In order to test this interpretation, we may turn to the kind of language that showed the woman moving from her early brilliance to the emptiness of the present. What we find is a purposeful progression from opportunities to the fulfillment of them—a woman who made her choices based on her desire to seem a part of the well-bred social elite. As the first stanza implies, she was "brilliant" in two ways: she was extraordinarily intelligent and spectacularly resplendent in appearance. She was elected (as a junior) to the honor society for liberal arts graduates, and she was enormously popular on the social scene. All her opportunities seemed to point to a doubly successful life growing out of the doubleness of her brilliance.

But she made a choice: "when she might have thought, [she] conversed instead." She chose the path of social brilliance over the development of her mind. Knowing that she was not "bred to" the appreciation of beautiful, expensive objects, she set out to learn the tastes of those who had been raised among them. The diction again provides a double-edged valuation. As line 5 puts it, "She learned the *cultured jargon*" of the class to which she aspired. "Cultured" denotes both the taste and intellect of the elite and the artificiality of imitations (as in *cultured pearls,* a second meaning later reinforced when she marries a man for his "real . . . pearl cufflinks"). "Jargon" denotes both the specialized language of a particular group and the meaningless gibberish of empty repetition. In their opposed denotations, the two words also bear contrasted connotations, each of them both positive and negative. What was it, then, that the young woman set out to learn—a language that would offer her entry into a higher social class, or empty artificialities? Pathetically, what she attained was both, a dulling of her brilliant mind in order to reach social brilliance.

Such ambivalent and ambiguous diction pervades the first five stanzas, which ironically show the woman deteriorating intellectually while she climbs the social ladder. Lines 5–6 focus this irony by calling her children both "ideal" (by what standards?) and "lonely." In light of her accumulation of the trappings of class, one of her lessons has an even sharper point: she who has become a fraud "learned to tell real Wedgwood [china] from a fraud."

In effect, then, there were no "lost" opportunities, for she seems to have seized every one that she desired. For this unhappy woman, it would be most comforting to suppose that there were some that she missed—but that would be an "illusion." She began in possibilities, "brilliant and adored," but she will end "alone in brilliant circles." She will be surrounded by the glitterati, going round and round with them in meaningless circling. By her own actions, she limited her brilliance to a single denotative meaning—a shiny surface—without the intellectual keenness that she discarded.

Comments

The title of this paper is not enclosed in quotation marks—the writer uses them only to set off the title of the poem. The paper uses textual and parenthetical documentation, but line numbers are not included for each quoted word or phrase because the poem is too short to require them. When the paper does focus on a pair of lines, numbers in the text locate them. Because this is an analysis, the writer does not feel constrained to follow the order of presentation of materials in the poem, but rather organizes the paper according to the progression of its topics. Also as an analysis, the paper does not attempt commentary on every detail, but selects a few from various places in the poem to support the thesis, and analyzes them from the perspective of their denotative and connotative meanings. The paper includes the general meaning of the poem as an orientation for the meaningful presentation of the details, but its main focus is on the quality of language as that contributes to the general meaning.

5. Drama Explication

Iago's First Soliloquy

At the end of the first act of *Othello, the Moor of Venice* (rpt. in Thomas R. Arp and Greg Johnson, *Perrine's Literature: Structure, Sound, and Sense,* 9th ed. [Boston: Wadsworth, 2006], 1261), Iago delivers the first of his several soliloquies (1.3.363–84). In this act Iago has initiated the action by leading Roderigo to announce to her father Desdemona's elopement with Othello. The result is Brabantio's violent accusation of Othello and his estrangement from his daughter. Most of Iago's time on the stage has been with Roderigo, whom he manipulates first in inducing him to cause trouble for Othello and dismay to Brabantio, and then at length in persuading him to pursue Desdemona to Cyprus (having first gathered up as much money as he can).

Iago begins the soliloquy justifying to himself spending time with such a fool as Roderigo:

> Thus do I ever make my fool my purse,
> For I mine own gained knowledge should profane
> If I would time expend with such a snipe   365
> But for my sport and profit.

That he feels the need to justify such an association is implied by the terms he uses to describe him—"fool," "snipe," and, at the end of the soliloquy, "ass." Roderigo is no fit companion for a man of such "gained knowledge"—that is, a man of Iago's accomplishments and wisdom. We may sense in this not only his contempt for Roderigo, but pride in his own superiority, a pride that is evidenced elsewhere in this soliloquy as well. For example, he alludes to Roderigo at the end when he says that Othello "will be as tenderly led by the nose / As asses are." What he gains from associating with this "snipe" is "sport and profit"—the pleasure of manipulating and controlling someone, and the monetary gain that he plans to receive. How Roderigo's money becomes Iago's we learn much later: he persuades Roderigo to give him cash to purchase jewels to bribe Desdemona into sleeping with the young man, but of course he pockets the money rather than buying her presents (see 4.2.184–88 and 5.1.15–17).

After these four lines of self-justification, Iago turns to Othello. He has already at length told Roderigo of his duplicity in serving the general, and has given a reason for hating him: Othello has promoted Cassio ahead of Iago, thus thwarting his ambitions (1.1.8-65). In the soliloquy, ambition takes a back seat to other motives:

> I hate the Moor,
> And it is thought abroad that 'twixt my sheets
> He's done my office. I know not if 't be true,
> But I for mere suspicion in that kind
> Will do as if for surety.   370

We must not read this too quickly, or we might miss the disconnect between the first line and what follows. He does not say "I hate the Moor" *because* I suspect him of sleeping with my wife; rather, those appear as two distinct motives, one explicit, the other general and vague. His hatred is almost abstract, a flat statement of loathing without a supporting cause. His jealousy, on the other hand, though based merely on rumors (and vigorously refuted by Emilia later in the play), is at least a humanly comprehensible motivation. And he does not repeat what he has told Roderigo, that he hates Othello because he by-passed him for promotion. Rather, that comes in as he begins to plot his revenge for having been cuckolded:

> [Othello] holds me well,   370
> The better shall my purpose work on him.
> Cassio's a proper man. Let me see now,
> To get his place, and to plume up my will
> In double knavery.—How, how?—Let's see.—

He enjoys the irony that Othello's admiration for him will make the general more vulnerable to his plotting. But even more delightful to him is the proud prospect of "double knavery," taking revenge on Othello and supplanting Cassio as lieutenant, and thus "plum[ing] up [his] will" by creating a two-part plot that will bring down Cassio as well as Othello. What he has against Cassio personally (as opposed to his professional jealousy) is implied in the brief sentence referring to Cassio's handsomeness. As he explains much later, Cassio "hath a daily beauty in his life / That makes me ugly" (5.1.19–20). He is jealous of Cassio's social and physical superiority; Cassio is as far above him in grace as he himself is superior to Roderigo in craft and intelligence. And as he goes on to say, Cassio

> hath a person and a smooth dispose
> To be suspected, framed to make women false.

It is characteristic of Iago that he perceives the virtues in others, and in his thinking twists them into weaknesses or vices. Othello esteems him, which will make him less suspicious; Cassio is handsome, which makes him a threat to women. He goes on in this vein:

> The Moor is of a free and open nature
> That thinks men honest that but seem so . . .

Othello's lack of guile, his own honesty, make him the more vulnerable to a guileful, dishonest schemer like Iago.

He concludes the soliloquy with an echo of an earlier remark of his:

> I have 't. It is engendered. Hell and night
> Must bring this monstrous birth to the world's light.

In advising Roderigo to prepare for his trip to Cyprus, Iago tells him, "There are many events in the womb of time which will be delivered" (1.3.353–54). He ends the soliloquy proudly announcing that he himself has impregnated that "womb of time," and the offspring will be "monstrous."

The essence of the plot is expressed with great simplicity:

> After some time, to abuse Othello's ear   375
> That [Cassio] is too familiar with [Othello's] wife.

This monstrous lie seems to Iago a perfect revenge—and one that inadvertently suggests Iago is not in fact jealous of Othello's sleeping with Emilia, for this perfect circle of wife-for-wife will culminate not in Desdemona's infidelity but in the illusion of it. We may well wonder if Iago does in fact believe in his own wife's disloyalty, since he is plotting a lie about Desdemona's.

There is one more example of Iago's proud self-estimation in the soliloquy, his assertion of his strong will. Of Othello's supposed sexual relations with Emilia, he says,

> I know not if 't be true,
> But I for mere suspicion in that kind
> Will do as if for surety.   370

His boast is that he is not the sort of man who waits and investigates (a man of "gained knowledge"), but one who will take drastic action even on "mere suspicion." It is a curious assertion, since the subsequent events seem to show the opposite—and may even be contradicted here by his plan to induce Othello's jealousy only "After some time."

What this soliloquy reveals is that Iago takes great pride in his manipulative abilities, that he has a mixture of motives, and that he is not entirely consistent. These are traits that we can follow throughout the play.

Comments

The essay restricts its references to the text of the play, so parenthetical documentation is appropriate. While it explicates the whole soliloquy, it does not simply "read" the speech from beginning to end, but rather structures its argument according to the writer's several points that characterize Iago. Its conclusion draws attention to the importance of the speech in establishing character traits that can be observed in the rest of the play.

6. Drama Analysis

Othello's Race

The subtitle of *Othello* is *The Moor of Venice,* a term that can be misleading if we rely on a standard desk dictionary for a definition of "moor." For example, the *Random House College Dictionary* defines it thus: "Moor . . . a Muslim of mixed Berber and Arab people inhabiting NW Africa." *The American Heritage Dictionary* agrees with that definition and adds an alternative: "one of the Saracens who invaded Spain in the eighth century A.D." But these definitions do not match the facts in the play.

Othello is presented as a Christian, not a Muslim. Iago refers to his "baptism" (2.3.308), and in his first meeting with Desdemona on Cyprus he clearly alludes to their shared belief in Christian salvation (2.1.184–90).

But more importantly, he is throughout the play characterized as a black African. A fuller definition of the word "moor" can be found in the *Oxford English Dictionary:* "in the Middle Ages, and as late as the 17 c., Moors were commonly supposed to be mostly black, . . . and hence the word was often used for 'negro.'"

In the opening scene Roderigo refers to Othello's negroid features by calling him "the thick-lips" (1.1.66), and Iago insultingly refers to his race ("an old black ram," "a Barbary horse" [1.1.88, 110–11]). Brabantio's public denunciation of him in 1.3 is clearly calling him black. He himself in his soliloquy trying to cope with Desdemona's supposed rejection of him in favor of Cassio explicitly calls himself "black" (3.3.264), and later in that scene in referring to Desdemona's supposed sinful lust says:

> Her name, that was as fresh
> As Dian's visage, is now begrimed and black
> As mine own face. (3.3.387–89)

The play also establishes a racist bigotry about Othello's color, chiefly in the assumptions revealed by Brabantio in his distress over Desdemona's marriage to the Moor. When he learns of it from Iago and Roderigo in 1.1, he declares to Roderigo "would you had had her" (1.1.173), though he has already reminded Roderigo that he had rejected him as a suitor for his daughter—that is, *any* white man would be preferable to a black. This attitude is supported by his assumption that a mixed marriage is "in spite of nature" and "against all rules of nature" (1.3.96, 101). That she is aware of her father's prejudices is implied in Desdemona's defense of her choice: "I saw Othello's visage in his mind" (1.3.249), not in the superficial coloring of his skin. That the racism is not limited to Brabantio is indicated by the nature of the insults mouthed to him by Iago and Roderigo, and even by the good-hearted Duke who tries to patch up the quarrel between Brabantio and Othello. He says to Brabantio, "If virtue no delighted beauty lack / Your son-in-law is far more fair than black" (1.3.286–87), by which he means that Othello's virtues outweigh his unfortunate blackness.

Surprisingly, Othello himself seems partially to subscribe to the racist argument that it is unnatural for whites and blacks to marry. Having been reminded by Iago of Brabantio's warning that Desdemona had deceived her father and therefore could deceive her husband, Othello echoes Brabantio: "nature erring from itself" (3.3.228) he says of his wife's accepting him as a husband.

The importance of correctly identifying Othello's race and recognizing the social attitude toward it is that we can more clearly see the deeply ironic reversal of expectations enacted in this tragedy. By tradition, black was the color ascribed to the devil (hence Emilia's charge that by murdering Desdemona Othello has shown himself to be "a blacker devil" [5.2.130]). Evil itself was popularly referred to as a black deed. Again, the *OED* provides full and useful definitions of two figurative meanings of the word "black":

> Having dark or deadly purposes, malignant; pertaining to or involving death, deadly; baneful, disastrous, sinister . . . Foul, iniquitous, atrocious, horribly wicked.

But in the play, the "horribly wicked" character is Iago, the white Venetian, and Othello is a great, virtuous man who makes the terrible mistake of supposing his wife to be a criminal deserving execution at the hands of "justice." The dramatic effect is overwhelming, as we see the viciousness of white Iago overcoming the virtue of black Othello.

Works Cited

"Black," "Moor." The Compact Edition of the Oxford English Dictionary.
     1971.
"Moor." The American Heritage Dictionary of the English Language.
     1981.
"Moor." The Random House College Dictionary. Rev. ed. 1980.
Shakespeare, William. Othello, the Moor of Venice. Rpt. in Thomas R.
     Arp and Greg Johnson, Perrine's Literature: Structure, Sound, and
     Sense. 9th ed. Boston: Wadsworth, 2006.

Comments

This analysis makes use of references from four sources, three dictionaries and the text of the play, so a Works Cited list is appropriate. The textual material is not presented in the order of its appearance in the play but is instead arranged according to the writer's thesis. The essay proceeds by defining Othello's race, then establishing the prevailing attitudes toward it, and finally reaching a conclusion about the effect of reversing racial expectations.

Fiction

The Elements
of Fiction

Chapter One

Reading the Story

Before embarking on a study of fiction, we might ask a basic question: Why bother to read it? With so many pressing demands on our time, and with so many nonfiction books of history, memoir, politics, and cultural discussion competing for our attention, why should we spend our scarce free time on works of imagination?

The eternal answers to this question are two: enjoyment and understanding.

Since the invention of language, human beings have enjoyed hearing and reading stories, participating in the fictional experiences and adventures of imaginary people. The bedtime stories read to children, the thrillers and romances many adults take to the beach, the historical novels and inspirational fiction elderly people often enjoy—any such harmless activity that helps make life less tedious or stressful surely needs nothing else to recommend it. Simple enjoyment has always been a primary aim and justification for reading fiction.

Fiction whose sole purpose is to entertain, however, requires no serious or intensive study. Unless a story expands or refines our thinking on a significant topic or quickens our sense of life, its value is not appreciably greater than that of video games or crossword puzzles. A story written with serious artistic intentions, on the other hand, must yield not only enjoyment but also understanding.

Like all serious art, fiction of this latter kind provides an imagined experience that yields authentic insights into some significant aspect of life. "Art is a lie," Picasso said, "that leads to the truth," and since a short story is a fiction, and thus a kind of "lie," this statement perfectly sums up the kind of story that provides entertainment but also may become part of an enduring literature. Most fiction, of course, is of the other sort: it has no aspirations beyond merely entertaining the reader. In order to distinguish these types of fiction, therefore, we should begin by defining two broad classifications, employing the terms most often used today: **commercial fiction**, the kind intended solely to entertain; and **literary fiction**, which is the primary subject of this book.

Commercial fiction, such as the legal thrillers and romance novels that make up best-seller lists and the easy-to-read short stories that appear in mass-market magazines, is written and published primarily to make money, and it makes money because it helps large numbers of people escape the tedium and stress of their lives. Literary fiction, however, is written by someone with serious artistic intentions who hopes to broaden, deepen, and sharpen the reader's awareness of life. Commercial fiction takes us *away* from the real world: it helps us temporarily to forget our troubles. Literary fiction plunges us, through the author's imaginative vision and artistic ability, more deeply *into* the real world, enabling us to understand life's difficulties and to empathize with others. While commercial fiction has the reader's immediate pleasure as its object, literary fiction hopes to provide a complex, lasting aesthetic and intellectual pleasure rather than a simple, escapist diversion; its object is to offer pleasure *plus* understanding.

We should immediately make the point that these two categories of fiction are not clear-cut. Not every given story can simply be tossed into one of two bins marked "commercial" or "literary." Rather the two categories suggest opposite ends of a spectrum; some works may fall close to the middle rather than to one end, and genres normally associated with commercial purposes and categories are sometimes used successfully by authors with literary intentions. A famous work such as Harriet Beecher Stowe's *Uncle Tom's Cabin* (1852), for instance, seems to straddle the line between commercial and literary fiction; immensely popular in its own time, it was written with serious intentions but is marred by significant aesthetic flaws. Because it does have some literary quality, however, and because it is an historically important work of its century, it is still read today by general readers and scholars alike. Another example of the occasional blending of our two broad categories is Charlotte Brontë's novel *Jane Eyre* (1847), which adheres to certain conventions of the romance novel and has been commercially successful since it was first published; but it also remains one of the finest literary novels ever written. Similarly, writers such as Charles Dickens, Edith Wharton, and John Updike have published novels that were simultaneously best-sellers and highly praised by literary critics.

The terms "commercial" and "literary" should be applied to novels or stories themselves, not necessarily to their authors. Dickens, in fact, is a good example of a single author capable of writing different works that fall into one category or the other. His novel *Martin Chuzzlewit* (1844), for instance, had disappointing sales when first published but today is greatly admired and discussed by literary scholars; on the other hand, his sentimental but hugely popular *A Christmas Carol* (1843) is essentially a commercial work. More recently, Graham Greene wrote some novels he subtitled "entertainments" as a way of setting them apart from his more serious, literary novels.

It should likewise be stressed that the difference between commercial and literary fiction does not necessarily relate to the absence or presence of a "moral." A story whose incidents and characters are notably shallow may have an unimpeachable moral, while a literary story or novel may have no "moral" at all in the conventional sense; it may choose to dramatize human experience rather than to moralize about it. Similarly, the difference between commercial and literary fiction does not lie in the absence or presence of "facts." An historical romance may be packed with reliable information and yet be pure escape in its depiction of human behavior. Nor does the difference lie in the presence or absence of an element of fantasy. Commercial fiction may have the surface appearance of everyday reality—a police detective novel is a good example—but have little significance beyond the reality depicted; on the other hand, a wildly fanciful tale may impress the reader with a profound and surprising truth. The differences between the two kinds of fiction are deeper and more subtle than any of these distinctions.

Perhaps we can clarify the difference by analogy. Commercial writers are like inventors who devise a contrivance for our diversion. When we push a button, lights flash, bells ring, and cardboard figures move jerkily across a painted horizon. Such writers are full of tricks and surprises: they pull rabbits out of hats, saw beautiful women in two, and juggle brightly colored balls in the air. By contrast, literary writers are more like explorers: they take us out into the midst of life and say, "Look, here is the world in all its complexity." They also take us behind the scenes, where they show us the props and mirrors and seek to dispel the illusions. This is not to say that literary writers are merely reporters. More surely than commercial writers, they carefully shape their materials. But they shape them always with the intent that we may see, feel, and understand them better, not for the primary purpose of furnishing entertainment. In short, any fiction that illuminates some aspect of human life or behavior with genuine originality and power may be called "literary." Such a story presents an insight—whether large or small—into the nature and condition of our existence. It gives us a keener awareness of our humanity within a universe that is sometimes friendly, sometimes hostile. It helps us to understand our world, our neighbors, and ourselves.

The distinctions we have drawn between the two types of fiction are true of both the full-length novel and the short story. Since the latter form is the focus of this text, however, we should stress that the short story, by its very nature, is a more literary genre. Writers hoping to succeed as commercial authors usually work in the novel form, which has proved more popular with large masses of people than has the more refined and subtle art of the story. (A collection of short stories appearing on any best-seller list is an extremely rare event.) Although there are types of commercial short stories that appear in men's adventure magazines, mystery and horror anthologies, and women's publications, the majority of short fiction published today appears in journals that are called, in fact, "literary magazines." Because of their serious intentions and their brevity, short stories provide the ideal vehicle for studying those elements of storytelling common to all literary fiction.

As you read and reread the stories in this book, you will become aware that the term "short story" is a highly elastic one. While brevity is an obvious characteristic of the genre, short narratives have always been part of the human storytelling impulse and have shown an impressive diversity throughout history. Ancient fairy tales and fables were the precursors of the modern short story, but only in the last two centuries has the short story assumed the generally accepted characteristics, outlined in the following chapters, which constitute its uniqueness as a literary genre. Authors of short stories continually seek new ways to exploit the genre, however, using fresh techniques and storytelling approaches in order to advance and refine this sophisticated form. A seemingly conventional tale may veer in an unexpected direction; a fragmented structure may help to mirror the world of one story, while an experimental approach to language or style may distinguish another from anything you have read before. The short story's lack of commercial appeal has, in a way, helped its development as an art form, for writers of short fiction, unconstrained by the demands of the marketplace and a mass audience, are able to give free rein to their creativity and imagination. Noting the "freedom and promise of the form," author Joyce Carol Oates has observed that "radical experimentation, which might be ill-advised in the novel, is well suited for the short story." This outlook, shared by most literary writers, has helped to maintain the status of the short story as a genre capable of ongoing diversity, richness, and self-renewal.

Before beginning a serious study of fiction, you should be aware that literary fiction requires a different way of reading than commercial fiction does. When we take a novel by Stephen King or Danielle Steel to the beach, we do not want to have to think much, if at all, about what we are reading; we simply want a diverting way of passing the time.

When we read a literary novel or story, however, we are seeking something different. We expect a serious work to offer some of the immediate pleasures of a well-told story—an original premise and intriguing characters, for instance; but we also know that a literary work may be more demanding of the reader in terms of its language, structure, and complexity. Ultimately we expect to come away from a literary work with an enhanced understanding of life.

In order to appreciate how it operates as a work of narrative art, we should read any piece of literary fiction *at least twice* before we can fully grasp what it has to offer. This is another reason the short story represents an ideal medium for the intensive study of fiction, since its length enables us to reread a story without making unreasonable demands on our time. As you read the stories included in this book, try following this general procedure: (1) read the story the first time simply to enjoy and familiarize yourself with it; (2) read the story a second time, more slowly and deliberately, in the attempt to understand its full artistic significance and achievement. As you proceed through the chapters, learning about plot, characterization, theme, and so forth, you will gradually develop the instincts of a serious reader: it is important to ask, for instance, why a story is constructed in a certain way, or why an author explores a specific character's inner life. With commercial fiction, such questions are irrelevant: there the focus is usually on what happens next, not on the techniques the author uses to tell the story. But with literary fiction, we are willing to invest more time and energy into reading more deliberately, and into careful rereading, because we know the personal rewards will be greater.

When we speak of different kinds of reading, of course, we aren't necessarily talking about different kinds of people. Avid readers may read both commercial and literary fiction at different times, just as an individual may sometimes want fast food, or "junk food," and at other times be willing to invest considerable time and money in savoring a gourmet meal. An English professor may buy a paperback thriller to enjoy during a vacation, while a factory worker might read *Jane Eyre* during her work breaks. So the primary distinction is between kinds of reading, not kinds of readers.

We also bring different expectations to our reading of these two different types of fiction. When we pick up a commercial novel, we come to the book with specific, fixed expectations and will feel frustrated and disappointed unless those expectations are met. Depending on the genre, some of these expectations may include (1) a sympathetic hero or heroine—someone with whom the reader can identify and whose adventures and triumphs the reader can share; (2) a defined plot in which something exciting is always happening and in which there is a strong element of suspense (thus the term "page-turner," often applied to a successful commercial novel); (3) a happy ending that sends the reader away undisturbed and optimistic about life; (4) a general theme, or "message," that affirms widely held, conventional views of the world.

By contrast, when we come to a novel or story with literary intentions, we approach the work with a different set of expectations. For one thing, we are willing to expect the unexpected: instead of adopting a conventional way of storytelling, a literary author may create a unique style or angle of vision in order to express his or her artistic truth; and instead of a happy or conventional ending in which everything is tied together in a neat package, a literary work may end in an unsettling or even unresolved way, forcing us to examine our own expectations about the story itself, about the way the story is told, and about our ingrained, perhaps unconscious way of viewing a certain topic or idea that may have been challenged or changed by what we have read. In short, when reading literary fiction we must keep an open mind and stay receptive to the author's imaginative vision, however different it may be from our own habits of perceiving and "reading" the world.

Reading effectively, it should be stressed, involves evaluating what we read. A typical library contains thousands of books, and any individual has time to read only a fraction of them. To choose our reading wisely, we need to know two things: (1) how to get the most out of any book we read and (2) how to choose the books that will best repay the time and attention we devote to them. The assumption of this book is that a proper selection will include both fiction and nonfiction—nonfiction as an indispensable fund of information and ideas that constitute one kind of knowledge of the world; literary fiction as an equally indispensable source of a different kind of knowledge, a knowledge of experience, felt in the emotions as well as apprehended by the mind. One aim of this book is to help you develop your understanding and judgment in evaluating what you read.

If we approach a literary story in a serious, committed way, after all, we will probably have a more memorable and satisfying reading experience than the kind we derive from commercial fiction, which we tend to forget as soon as we have consumed it. Especially if you are accustomed to reading fiction quickly and without much thought about its possible complex meanings, try to adopt a slower, more thoughtful approach as you read the stories in this and later chapters. Inevitably, as with different commercial works, you will find some of the stories in

this book more appealing than others. They have been chosen carefully, however, to help you explore the elements of fiction and to illustrate the diversity of the short-story form as practiced by a broad range
of writers. Ideally, a careful reading of these stories will convince you
that while nonfiction may be an indispensable fund of information and
ideas, and one way of knowing about the world, fiction is an equally indispensable source of knowledge, and a knowledge apprehended not
only by your intellect but by your emotions and imagination as well.
Through the act of reading a story and sharing an author's imaginative
vision, you will gain not only a pleasurable experience but growth in
your understanding of the world and of the human condition.

REVIEWING CHAPTER ONE

1. Differentiate between commercial fiction and literary fiction.
2. Explain the purposes of literary fiction.
3. Review the different types of short stories.
4. Describe the best way to read a short story for the purpose of
   serious study.
5. List the differing expectations we bring to the reading of commercial and literary fiction.

Richard Connell

The Most Dangerous Game

"Off there to the right—somewhere—is a large island," said
Whitney. "It's rather a mystery—"

"What island is it?" Rainsford asked.

"The old charts call it 'Ship-Trap Island,'" Whitney replied. "A
suggestive name, isn't it? Sailors have a curious dread of the place. I
don't know why. Some superstition—"

"Can't see it," remarked Rainsford, trying to peer through the dank
tropical night that was palpable as it pressed its thick warm blackness
in upon the yacht.

THE MOST DANGEROUS GAME   First published in 1924. Richard Connell (1893–
1949) was a native of New York State, graduated from Harvard, and served a year
in France with the United States Army during World War I.

5   "You've good eyes," said Whitney, with a laugh, "and I've seen you pick off a moose moving in the brown fall bush at four hundred yards, but even you can't see four miles or so through a moonless Caribbean night."

"Nor four yards," admitted Rainsford. "Ugh! It's like moist black velvet."

"It will be light in Rio," promised Whitney. "We should make it in a few days. I hope the jaguar guns have come from Purdey's. We should have some good hunting up the Amazon. Great sport, hunting."

"The best sport in the world," agreed Rainsford.

"For the hunter," amended Whitney. "Not for the jaguar."

10   "Don't talk rot, Whitney," said Rainsford. "You're a big-game hunter, not a philosopher. Who cares how a jaguar feels?"

"Perhaps the jaguar does," observed Whitney.

"Bah! They've no understanding."

"Even so, I rather think they understand one thing—fear. The fear of pain and the fear of death."

"Nonsense," laughed Rainsford. "This hot weather is making you soft, Whitney. Be a realist. The world is made up of two classes—the hunters and the huntees. Luckily, you and I are the hunters. Do you think we've passed that island yet?"

15   "I can't tell in the dark. I hope so."

"Why?" asked Rainsford.

"The place has a reputation—a bad one."

"Cannibals?" suggested Rainsford.

"Hardly. Even cannibals wouldn't live in such a God-forsaken place. But it's gotten into sailor lore, somehow. Didn't you notice that the crew's nerves seemed a bit jumpy today?"

20   "They were a bit strange, now you mention it. Even Captain Nielsen—"

"Yes, even that tough-minded old Swede, who'd go up to the devil himself and ask him for a light. Those fishy blue eyes held a look I never saw there before. All I could get out of him was: 'This place has an evil name among seafaring men, sir.' Then he said to me, very gravely: 'Don't you feel anything?'—as if the air about us was actually poisonous. Now, you mustn't laugh when I tell you this—I did feel something like a sudden chill.

"There was no breeze. The sea was as flat as a plate-glass window. We were drawing near the island then. What I felt was a—a mental chill; a sort of sudden dread."

"Pure imagination," said Rainsford. "One superstitious sailor can taint the whole ship's company with his fear."

"Maybe. But sometimes I think sailors have an extra sense that tells them when they are in danger. Sometimes I think evil is a tangible thing—with wave lengths, just as sound and light have. An evil place can, so to speak, broadcast vibrations of evil. Anyhow, I'm glad we're getting out of this zone. Well, I think I'll turn in now, Rainsford."

"I'm not sleepy," said Rainsford. "I'm going to smoke another pipe   25
on the after deck."

"Good night, then, Rainsford. See you at breakfast."

"Right. Good night, Whitney."

There was no sound in the night as Rainsford sat there, but the muffled throb of the engine that drove the yacht swiftly through the darkness, and the swish and ripple of the wash of the propeller.

Rainsford, reclining in a steamer chair, indolently puffed on his favorite brier. The sensuous drowsiness of the night was on him. "It's so dark," he thought, "that I could sleep without closing my eyes; the night would be my eyelids—"

An abrupt sound startled him. Off to the right he heard it, and his   30
ears, expert in such matters, could not be mistaken. Again he heard the sound, and again. Somewhere, off in the blackness, some one had fired a gun three times.

Rainsford sprang up and moved quickly to the rail, mystified. He strained his eyes in the direction from which the reports had come, but it was like trying to see through a blanket. He leaped upon the rail and balanced himself there, to get greater elevation; his pipe, striking a rope, was knocked from his mouth. He lunged for it; a short, hoarse cry came from his lips as he realized he had reached too far and had lost his balance. The cry was pinched off short as the blood-warm waters of the Caribbean Sea closed over his head.

He struggled up to the surface and tried to cry out, but the wash from the speeding yacht slapped him in the face and the salt water in his open mouth made him gag and strangle. Desperately he struck out with strong strokes after the receding lights of the yacht, but he stopped before he had swum fifty feet. A certain cool-headedness had come to him; it was not the first time he had been in a tight place. There was a chance that his cries could be heard by some one aboard the yacht, but that chance was slender, and grew more slender as the yacht raced on. He wrestled himself out of his clothes, and shouted with all his power. The lights of the yacht became faint and ever-vanishing fireflies; then they were blotted out entirely by the night.

Rainsford remembered the shots. They had come from the right, and doggedly he swam in that direction, swimming with slow, deliberate strokes, conserving his strength. For a seemingly endless time he fought the sea. He began to count his strokes; he could do possibly a hundred more and then—

Rainsford heard a sound. It came out of the darkness, a high screaming sound, the sound of an animal in an extremity of anguish and terror.

35   He did not recognize the animal that made the sound; he did not try to; with fresh vitality he swam toward the sound. He heard it again; then it was cut short by another noise, crisp, staccato.

"Pistol shot," muttered Rainsford, swimming on.

Ten minutes of determined effort brought another sound to his ears—the most welcome he had ever heard—the muttering and growling of the sea breaking on a rocky shore. He was almost on the rocks before he saw them; on a night less calm he would have been shattered against them. With his remaining strength he dragged himself from the swirling waters. Jagged crags appeared to jut into the opaqueness; he forced himself upward, hand over hand. Gasping, his hands raw, he reached a flat place at the top. Dense jungle came down to the very edge of the cliffs. What perils that tangle of trees and underbrush might hold for him did not concern Rainsford just then. All he knew was that he was safe from his enemy, the sea, and that utter weariness was on him. He flung himself down at the jungle edge and tumbled headlong into the deepest sleep of his life.

When he opened his eyes he knew from the position of the sun that it was late in the afternoon. Sleep had given him new vigor; a sharp hunger was picking at him. He looked about him, almost cheerfully.

"Where there are pistol shots, there are men. Where there are men, there is food," he thought. But what kind of men, he wondered, in so forbidding a place? An unbroken front of snarled and ragged jungle fringed the shore.

40   He saw no sign of a trail through the closely knit web of weeds and trees; it was easier to go along the shore, and Rainsford floundered along by the water. Not far from where he had landed, he stopped.

Some wounded thing, by the evidence a large animal, had thrashed about in the underbrush; the jungle weeds were crushed down and the moss was lacerated; one patch of weeds was stained crimson. A small, glittering object not far away caught Rainsford's eye and he picked it up. It was an empty cartridge.

"A twenty-two," he remarked. "That's odd. It must have been a fairly large animal too. The hunter had his nerve with him to tackle it with a light gun. It's clear that the brute put up a fight. I suppose the first three shots I heard was when the hunter flushed his quarry and wounded it. The last shot was when he trailed it here and finished it."

He examined the ground closely and found what he had hoped to find—the print of hunting boots. They pointed along the cliff in the direction he had been going. Eagerly he hurried along, now slipping on a rotten log or a loose stone, but making headway; night was beginning to settle down on the island.

Bleak darkness was blacking out the sea and jungle when Rainsford sighted the lights. He came upon them as he turned a crook in the coast line, and his first thought was that he had come upon a village, for there were many lights. But as he forged along he saw to his great astonishment that all the lights were in one enormous building—a lofty structure with pointed towers plunging upward into the gloom. His eyes made out the shadowy outlines of a palatial château; it was set on a high bluff, and on three sides of it cliffs dived down to where the sea licked greedy lips in the shadows.

"Mirage," thought Rainsford. But it was no mirage, he found, when   45
he opened the tall spiked iron gate. The stone steps were real enough; the massive door with a leering gargoyle for a knocker was real enough; yet about it all hung an air of unreality.

He lifted the knocker, and it creaked up stiffly, as if it had never before been used. He let it fall, and it startled him with its booming loudness. He thought he heard steps within; the door remained closed. Again Rainsford lifted the heavy knocker, and let it fall. The door opened then, opened as suddenly as if it were on a spring, and Rainsford stood blinking in the river of glaring gold light that poured out. The first thing Rainsford's eyes discerned was the largest man Rainsford had ever seen—a gigantic creature, solidly made and black-bearded to the waist. In his hand the man held a long-barreled revolver, and he was pointing it straight at Rainsford's heart.

Out of the snarl of beard two small eyes regarded Rainsford.

"Don't be alarmed," said Rainsford, with a smile which he hoped was disarming. "I'm no robber. I fell off a yacht. My name is Sanger Rainsford of New York City."

The menacing look in the eyes did not change. The revolver pointed as rigidly as if the giant were a statue. He gave no sign that he understood Rainsford's words, or that he had even heard them. He was dressed in uniform, a black uniform trimmed with gray astrakhan.

"I'm Sanger Rainsford of New York," Rainsford began again. "I fell   50
off a yacht. I am hungry."

The man's only answer was to raise with his thumb the hammer of his revolver. Then Rainsford saw the man's free hand go to his forehead in a military salute, and he saw him click his heels together and stand at attention. Another man was coming down the broad marble steps, an erect, slender man in evening clothes. He advanced to Rainsford and held out his hand.

In a cultivated voice marked by a slight accent that gave it added precision and deliberateness, he said: "It is a very great pleasure and honor to welcome Mr. Sanger Rainsford, the celebrated hunter, to my home."

Automatically Rainsford shook the man's hand.

"I've read your book about hunting snow leopards in Tibet, you see," explained the man. "I am General Zaroff."

55   Rainsford's first impression was that the man was singularly handsome; his second was that there was an original, almost bizarre quality about the general's face. He was a tall man past middle age, for his hair was a vivid white; but his thick eyebrows and pointed military mustache were as black as the night from which Rainsford had come. His eyes, too, were black and very bright. He had high cheek bones, a sharp-cut nose, a spare, dark face, the face of a man used to giving orders, the face of an aristocrat. Turning to the giant in uniform, the general made a sign. The giant put away his pistol, saluted, withdrew.

"Ivan is an incredibly strong fellow," remarked the general, "but he has the misfortune to be deaf and dumb. A simple fellow, but, I'm afraid, like all his race, a bit of a savage."

"Is he Russian?"

"He is a Cossack," said the general, and his smile showed red lips and pointed teeth. "So am I.

"Come," he said, "we shouldn't be chatting here. We can talk later. Now you want clothes, food, rest. You shall have them. This is a most restful spot."

60   Ivan had reappeared, and the general spoke to him with lips that moved but gave forth no sound.

"Follow Ivan, if you please, Mr. Rainsford," said the general. "I was about to have my dinner when you came. I'll wait for you. You'll find that my clothes will fit you, I think."

It was to a huge, beam-ceilinged bedroom with a canopied bed big enough for six men that Rainsford followed the silent giant. Ivan laid out an evening suit, and Rainsford, as he put it on, noticed that it came from a London tailor who ordinarily cut and sewed for none below the rank of duke.

The dining room to which Ivan conducted him was in many ways remarkable. There was a medieval magnificence about it; it suggested a baronial hall of feudal times with its oaken panels, its high ceiling, its vast refectory table where twoscore men could sit down to eat. About

the hall were the mounted heads of many animals—lions, tigers, elephants, moose, bears; larger or more perfect specimens Rainsford had
never seen. At the great table the general was sitting, alone.

"You'll have a cocktail, Mr. Rainsford," he suggested. The cocktail
was surpassingly good; and, Rainsford noted, the table appointments
were of the finest—the linen, the crystal, the silver, the china.

They were eating *borsch*, the rich, red soup with whipped cream so   65
dear to Russian palates. Half apologetically General Zaroff said: "We do
our best to preserve the amenities of civilization here. Please forgive
any lapses. We are well off the beaten track, you know. Do you think
the champagne has suffered from its long ocean trip?"

"Not in the least," declared Rainsford. He was finding the general
a most thoughtful and affable host, a true cosmopolite. But there was
one small trait of the general's that made Rainsford uncomfortable.
Whenever he looked up from his plate he found the general studying
him, appraising him narrowly.

"Perhaps," said General Zaroff, "you were surprised that I recog-
nized your name. You see, I read all books on hunting published in
English, French, and Russian. I have but one passion in my life,
Mr. Rainsford, and it is the hunt."

"You have some wonderful heads here," said Rainsford as he ate a
particularly well cooked filet mignon. "That Cape buffalo is the largest
I ever saw."

"Oh, that fellow. Yes, he was a monster."

"Did he charge you?"   70

"Hurled me against a tree," said the general. "Fractured my skull.
But I got the brute."

"I've always thought," said Rainsford, "that the Cape buffalo is the
most dangerous of all big game."

For a moment the general did not reply; he was smiling his curious
red-lipped smile. Then he said slowly: "No. You are wrong, sir. The
Cape buffalo is not the most dangerous big game." He sipped his wine.
"Here in my preserve on this island," he said in the same slow tone, "I
hunt more dangerous game."

Rainsford expressed his surprise. "Is there big game on this island?"

The general nodded. "The biggest."   75

"Really?"

"Oh, it isn't here naturally, of course. I have to stock the island."

"What have you imported, general?" Rainsford asked. "Tigers?"

The general smiled. "No," he said. "Hunting tigers ceased to interest me some years ago. I exhausted their possibilities, you see. No thrill
left in tigers, no real danger. I live for danger, Mr. Rainsford."

80   The general took from his pocket a gold cigaret case and offered his
guest a long black cigaret with a silver tip; it was perfumed and gave off
a smell like incense.

"We will have some capital hunting, you and I," said the general.
"I shall be most glad to have your society."

"But what game—" began Rainsford.

"I'll tell you," said the general. "You will be amused, I know. I think
I may say, in all modesty, that I have done a rare thing. I have invented
a new sensation. May I pour you another glass of port, Mr. Rainsford?"

"Thank you, general."

85   The general filled both glasses, and said: "God makes some men
poets. Some He makes kings, some beggars. Me He made a hunter. My
hand was made for the trigger, my father said. He was a very rich man
with a quarter of a million acres in the Crimea, and he was an ardent
sportsman. When I was only five years old he gave me a little gun,
specially made in Moscow for me, to shoot sparrows with. When I
shot some of his prize turkeys with it, he did not punish me; he com-
plimented me on my marksmanship. I killed my first bear in the Cau-
casus when I was ten. My whole life has been one prolonged hunt. I
went into the army—it was expected of noblemen's sons—and for a
time commanded a division of Cossack cavalry, but my real interest
was always the hunt. I have hunted every kind of game in every land.
It would be impossible for me to tell you how many animals I have
killed."

The general puffed at his cigaret.

"After the debacle in Russia I left the country, for it was imprudent for an officer of the Czar to stay there. Many noble Russians lost
everything. I, luckily, had invested heavily in American securities, so
I shall never have to open a tea room in Monte Carlo or drive a taxi
in Paris. Naturally, I continued to hunt—grizzlies in your Rockies,
crocodiles in the Ganges, rhinoceroses in East Africa. It was in Africa
that the Cape buffalo hit me and laid me up for six months. As soon
as I recovered I started for the Amazon to hunt jaguars, for I had
heard they were unusually cunning. They weren't." The Cossack
sighed. "They were no match at all for a hunter with his wits about
him, and a high-powered rifle. I was bitterly disappointed. I was lying
in my tent with a splitting headache one night when a terrible
thought pushed its way into my mind. Hunting was beginning to bore
me! And hunting, remember, had been my life. I have heard that in
America businessmen often go to pieces when they give up the business that has been their life."

"Yes, that's so," said Rainsford.

The general smiled. "I had no wish to go to pieces," he said. "I must do something. Now, mine is an analytical mind, Mr. Rainsford. Doubtless that is why I enjoy the problems of the chase."

"No doubt, General Zaroff."   90

"So," continued the general, "I asked myself why the hunt no longer fascinated me. You are much younger than I am, Mr. Rainsford, and have not hunted as much, but you perhaps can guess the answer."

"What was it?"

"Simply this: hunting had ceased to be what you call 'a sporting proposition.' It had become too easy. I always got my quarry. Always. There is no greater bore than perfection."

The general lit a fresh cigaret.

"No animal had a chance with me any more. That is no boast; it is   95
a mathematical certainty. The animal had nothing but his legs and his instinct. Instinct is no match for reason. When I thought of this it was a tragic moment for me, I can tell you."

Rainsford leaned across the table, absorbed in what his host was saying.

"It came to me as an inspiration what I must do," the general went on.

"And that was?"

The general smiled the quiet smile of one who has faced an obstacle and surmounted it with success. "I had to invent a new animal to hunt," he said.

"A new animal? You're joking."   100

"Not at all," said the general. "I never joke about hunting. I needed a new animal. I found one. So I bought this island, built this house, and here I do my hunting. The island is perfect for my purposes—there are jungles with a maze of trails in them, hills, swamps—"

"But the animal, General Zaroff?"

"Oh," said the general, "it supplies me with the most exciting hunting in the world. No other hunting compares with it for an instant. Every day I hunt, and I never grow bored now, for I have a quarry with which I can match my wits."

Rainsford's bewilderment showed in his face.

"I wanted the ideal animal to hunt," explained the general. "So I   105
said: 'What are the attributes of an ideal quarry?' And the answer was, of course: 'it must have courage, cunning, and, above all, it must be able to reason.'"

"But no animal can reason," objected Rainsford.

"My dear fellow," said the general, "there is one that can."

"But you can't mean—" gasped Rainsford.

"And why not?"

110   "I can't believe you are serious, General Zaroff. This is a grisly joke."

"Why should I not be serious? I am speaking of hunting."

"Hunting? Good God, General Zaroff, what you speak of is murder."

The general laughed with entire good nature. He regarded Rainsford quizzically. "I refuse to believe that so modern and civilized a young man as you seem to be harbors romantic ideas about the value of human life. Surely your experiences in the war—"

"Did not make me condone cold-blooded murder," finished Rainsford stiffly.

115   Laughter shook the general. "How extraordinarily droll you are!" he said. "One does not expect nowadays to find a young man of the educated class, even in America, with such a naive, and, if I may say so, mid-Victorian point of view. It's like finding a snuff-box in a limousine. Ah, well, doubtless you had Puritan ancestors. So many Americans appear to have had. I'll wager you'll forget your notions when you go hunting with me. You've a genuine new thrill in store for you, Mr. Rainsford."

"Thank you, I'm a hunter, not a murderer."

"Dear me," said the general, quite unruffled, "again that unpleasant word. But I think I can show you that your scruples are quite ill founded."

"Yes?"

"Life is for the strong, to be lived by the strong, and, if need be, taken by the strong. The weak of the world were put here to give the strong pleasure. I am strong. Why should I not use my gift? If I wish to hunt, why should I not? I hunt the scum of the earth—sailors from tramp ships—lascars, blacks, Chinese, whites, mongrels—a thoroughbred horse or hound is worth more than a score of them."

120   "But they are men," said Rainsford hotly.

"Precisely," said the general. "That is why I use them. It gives me pleasure. They can reason, after a fashion. So they are dangerous."

"But where do you get them?"

The general's left eyelid fluttered down in a wink. "This island is called Ship-Trap," he answered. "Sometimes an angry god of the high seas sends them to me. Sometimes, when Providence is not so kind, I help Providence a bit. Come to the window with me."

Rainsford went to the window and looked out toward the sea.

"Watch! Out there!" exclaimed the general, pointing into the   125
night. Rainsford's eyes saw only blackness, and then, as the general
pressed a button, far out to sea Rainsford saw the flash of lights.

The general chuckled. "They indicate a channel," he said, "where
there's none: giant rocks with razor edges crouch like a sea monster
with wide-open jaws. They can crush a ship as easily as I crush this
nut." He dropped a walnut on the hardwood floor and brought his heel
grinding down on it. "Oh, yes," he said, casually, as if in answer to a
question, "I have electricity. We try to be civilized here."

"Civilized? And you shoot down men?"

A trace of anger was in the general's black eyes, but it was there for
but a second, and he said, in his most pleasant manner: "Dear me, what
a righteous young man you are! I assure you I do not do the thing you
suggest. That would be barbarous. I treat these visitors with every consideration. They get plenty of good food and exercise. They get into
splendid physical condition. You shall see for yourself tomorrow."

"What do you mean?"

"We'll visit my training school," smiled the general. "It's in the cel-   130
lar. I have about a dozen pupils down there now. They're from the
Spanish bark *San Lucar* that had the bad luck to go on the rocks out
there. A very inferior lot, I regret to say. Poor specimens and more accustomed to the deck than to the jungle."

He raised his hand, and Ivan, who served as waiter, brought thick
Turkish coffee. Rainsford, with an effort, held his tongue in check.

"It's a game, you see," pursued the general blandly. "I suggest to one
of them that we go hunting. I give him a supply of food and an excellent hunting knife. I give him three hours' start. I am to follow, armed
only with a pistol of the smallest caliber and range. If my quarry eludes
me for three whole days, he wins the game. If I find him"—the general
smiled—"he loses."

"Suppose he refuses to be hunted?"

"Oh," said the general, "I give him his option, of course. He need
not play that game if he doesn't wish to. If he does not wish to hunt, I
turn him over to Ivan. Ivan once had the honor of serving as official
knouter to the Great White Czar, and he has his own ideas of sport. Invariably, Mr. Rainsford, invariably they choose the hunt."

"And if they win?"   135

The smile on the general's face widened. "To date I have not lost,"
he said.

Then he added, hastily: "I don't wish you to think me a braggart,
Mr. Rainsford. Many of them afford only the most elementary sort of

problem. Occasionally I strike a tartar. One almost did win. I eventually had to use the dogs."

"The dogs?"

"This way, please. I'll show you."

140   The general steered Rainsford to a window. The lights from the
windows sent a flickering illumination that made grotesque patterns on
the courtyard below, and Rainsford could see moving about there a
dozen or so huge black shapes; as they turned toward him, their eyes
glittered greenly.

"A rather good lot, I think," observed the general. "They are let out
at seven every night. If anyone should try to get into my house—or
out of it—something extremely regrettable would occur to him." He
hummed a snatch of song from the Folies Bergère.

"And now," said the general, "I want to show you my new collection of heads. Will you come with me to the library?"

"I hope," said Rainsford, "that you will excuse me tonight, General
Zaroff. I'm really not feeling at all well."

"Ah, indeed?" the general inquired solicitously. "Well, I suppose
that's only natural, after your long swim. You need a good, restful night's
sleep. Tomorrow you'll feel like a new man, I'll wager. Then we'll hunt,
eh? I've one rather promising prospect—"

145   Rainsford was hurrying from the room.

"Sorry you can't go with me tonight," called the general. "I expect
rather fair sport—a big, strong black. He looks resourceful— Well,
good night, Mr. Rainsford; I hope you have a good night's rest."

The bed was good, and the pajamas of the softest silk, and he was
tired in every fiber of his being, but nevertheless Rainsford could not
quiet his brain with the opiate of sleep. He lay, eyes wide open. Once
he thought he heard stealthy steps in the corridor outside his room. He
sought to throw open the door; it would not open. He went to the window and looked out. His room was high up in one of the towers. The
lights of the château were out now, and it was dark and silent, but there
was a fragment of sallow moon, and by its wan light he could see, dimly,
the courtyard; there, weaving in and out in the pattern of shadow, were
black, noiseless forms; the hounds heard him at the window and looked
up, expectantly, with their green eyes. Rainsford went back to the bed
and lay down. By many methods he tried to put himself to sleep. He
had achieved a doze when, just as morning began to come, he heard, far
off in the jungle, the faint report of a pistol.

General Zaroff did not appear until luncheon. He was dressed
faultlessly in the tweeds of a country squire. He was solicitous about the
state of Rainsford's health.

"As for me," sighed the general, "I do not feel so well. I am worried, Mr. Rainsford. Last night I detected traces of my old complaint."

To Rainsford's questioning glance the general said: "Ennui. Boredom."   150

Then, taking a second helping of Crêpes Suzette, the general explained: "The hunting was not good last night. The fellow lost his head. He made a straight trail that offered no problems at all. That's the trouble with these sailors; they have dull brains to begin with, and they do not know how to get about in the woods. They do excessively stupid and obvious things. It's most annoying. Will you have another glass of Chablis, Mr. Rainsford?"

"General," said Rainsford firmly, "I wish to leave this island at once."

The general raised his thickets of eyebrows; he seemed hurt. "But, my dear fellow," the general protested, "you've only just come. You've had no hunting—"

"I wish to go today," said Rainsford. He saw the dead black eyes of the general on him, studying him. General Zaroff's face suddenly brightened.

He filled Rainsford's glass with venerable Chablis from a dusty   155
bottle.

"Tonight," said the general, "we will hunt—you and I."

Rainsford shook his head. "No, general," he said. "I will not hunt."

The general shrugged his shoulders and delicately ate a hothouse grape. "As you wish, my friend," he said. "The choice rests entirely with you. But may I not venture to suggest that you will find my idea of sport more diverting than Ivan's?"

He nodded toward the corner to where the giant stood, scowling, his thick arms crossed on his hogshead of chest.

"You don't mean—" cried Rainsford.   160

"My dear fellow," said the general, "have I not told you I always mean what I say about hunting? This is really an inspiration. I drink to a foeman worthy of my steel—at last."

The general raised his glass, but Rainsford sat staring at him.

"You'll find this game worth playing," the general said enthusiastically. "Your brain against mine. Your woodcraft against mine. Your strength and stamina against mine. Outdoor chess! And the stake is not without value, eh?"

"And if I win—" began Rainsford huskily.

"I'll cheerfully acknowledge myself defeated if I do not find you by   165
midnight of the third day," said General Zaroff. "My sloop will place you on the mainland near a town."

The general read what Rainsford was thinking.

"Oh, you can trust me," said the Cossack. "I will give you my word as a gentleman and a sportsman. Of course you, in turn, must agree to say nothing of your visit here."

"I'll agree to nothing of the kind," said Rainsford.

"Oh," said the general, "in that case— But why discuss that now? Three days hence we can discuss it over a bottle of Veuve Cliquot, unless—"

170   The general sipped his wine.

Then a businesslike air animated him. "Ivan," he said to Rainsford, "will supply you with hunting clothes, food, a knife. I suggest you wear moccasins; they leave a poorer trail. I suggest too that you avoid the big swamp in the southeast corner of the island. We call it Death Swamp. There's quicksand there. One foolish fellow tried it. The deplorable part of it was that Lazarus followed him. You can imagine my feelings, Mr. Rainsford. I loved Lazarus; he was the finest hound in my pack. Well, I must beg you to excuse me now. I always take a siesta after lunch. You'll hardly have time for a nap, I fear. You'll want to start, no doubt. I shall not follow till dusk. Hunting at night is so much more exciting than by day, don't you think? Au revoir, Mr. Rainsford, au revoir."

General Zaroff, with a deep, courtly bow, strolled from the room.

From another door came Ivan. Under one arm he carried khaki hunting clothes, a haversack of food, a leather sheath containing a long-bladed hunting knife; his right hand rested on a cocked revolver thrust in the crimson sash about his waist. . . .

Rainsford had fought his way through the bush for two hours. "I must keep my nerve. I must keep my nerve," he said through tight teeth.

175   He had not been entirely clear-headed when the château gates snapped shut behind him. His whole idea at first was to put distance between himself and General Zaroff, and, to this end, he had plunged along, spurred on by the sharp rowels of something very like panic. Now he had got a grip on himself, had stopped, and was taking stock of himself and the situation.

He saw that straight flight was futile; inevitably it would bring him face to face with the sea. He was in a picture with a frame of water, and his operations, clearly, must take place within that frame.

"I'll give him a trail to follow," muttered Rainsford, and he struck off from the rude paths he had been following into the trackless wilderness. He executed a series of intricate loops; he doubled on his trail again and again, recalling all the lore of the fox hunt, and all the dodges of the fox. Night found him leg-weary, with hands and face lashed by the branches, on a thickly wooded ridge. He knew it would be insane to blunder on through the dark, even if he had the strength. His need for rest was imperative and he thought: "I have played the fox, now I must play the cat of the fable." A big tree with a thick trunk and outspread branches was nearby, and, taking care to leave not the slightest mark, he climbed up into the crotch, and stretching out on one of the broad limbs, after a fashion, rested. Rest brought him new confidence and almost a feeling of security. Even so zealous a hunter as General Zaroff could not trace him there, he told himself; only the devil himself could follow that complicated trail through the jungle after dark. But, perhaps, the general was a devil—

An apprehensive night crawled slowly by like a wounded snake, and sleep did not visit Rainsford, although the silence of a dead world was on the jungle. Toward morning when a dingy gray was varnishing the sky, the cry of some startled bird focused Rainsford's attention in that direction. Something was coming through the bush, coming slowly, carefully, coming by the same winding way Rainsford had come. He flattened himself down on the limb, and through a screen of leaves almost as thick as tapestry, he watched. The thing that was approaching was a man.

It was General Zaroff. He made his way along with his eyes fixed in utmost concentration on the ground before him. He paused, almost beneath the tree, dropped to his knees and studied the ground. Rainsford's impulse was to hurl himself down like a panther, but he saw the general's right hand held something metallic—a small automatic pistol.

The hunter shook his head several times, as if he were puzzled.   180 Then he straightened up and took from his case one of his black cigarets; its pungent incense-like smoke floated up to Rainsford's nostrils.

Rainsford held his breath. The general's eyes had left the ground and were traveling inch by inch up the tree. Rainsford froze there, every muscle tensed for a spring. But the sharp eyes of the hunter stopped before they reached the limb where Rainsford lay; a smile spread over his brown face. Very deliberately he blew a smoke ring into the air; then he turned his back on the tree and walked carelessly away, back along the trail he had come. The swish of the underbrush against his hunting boots grew fainter and fainter.

The pent-up air burst hotly from Rainsford's lungs. His first thought made him feel sick and numb. The general could follow a trail through the woods at night; he could follow an extremely difficult trail; he must have uncanny powers; only by the merest chance had the Cossack failed to see his quarry.

Rainsford's second thought was even more terrible. It sent a shudder of cold horror through his whole being. Why had the general smiled? Why had he turned back?

Rainsford did not want to believe what his reason told him was true, but the truth was as evident as the sun that had by now pushed through the morning mists. The general was playing with him! The general was saving him for another day's sport! The Cossack was the cat; he was the mouse. Then it was that Rainsford knew the full meaning of terror.

185   "I will not lose my nerve. I will not."

He slid down from the tree, and struck off again into the woods. His face was set and he forced the machinery of his mind to function. Three hundred yards from his hiding place he stopped where a huge dead tree leaned precariously on a smaller, living one. Throwing off his sack of food, Rainsford took his knife from its sheath and began to work with all his energy.

The job was finished at last, and he threw himself down behind a fallen log a hundred feet away. He did not have to wait long. The cat was coming again to play with the mouse.

Following the trail with the sureness of a bloodhound, came General Zaroff. Nothing escaped those searching black eyes, no crushed blade of grass, no bent twig, no mark, no matter how faint, in the moss. So intent was the Cossack on his stalking that he was upon the thing Rainsford had made before he saw it. His foot touched the protruding bough that was the trigger. Even as he touched it, the general sensed his danger and leaped back with the agility of an ape. But he was not quick enough; the dead tree, delicately adjusted to rest on the cut living one, crashed down and struck the general a glancing blow on the shoulder as it fell; but for his alertness, he must have been smashed beneath it. He staggered, but he did not fall; nor did he drop his revolver. He stood there, rubbing his injured shoulder, and Rainsford, with fear again gripping his heart, heard the general's mocking laugh ring through the jungle.

"Rainsford," called the general, "if you are within the sound of my voice, as I suppose you are, let me congratulate you. Not many men know how to make a Malay man-catcher. Luckily, for me, I too have hunted in Malacca. You are proving interesting, Mr. Rainsford. I am going now to have my wound dressed; it's only a slight one. But I shall be back. I shall be back."

190   When the general, nursing his bruised shoulder, had gone, Rainsford took up his flight again. It was flight now, a desperate, hope-

less flight, that carried him on for some hours. Dusk came, then darkness, and still he pressed on. The ground grew softer under his moccasins; the vegetation grew ranker, denser; insects bit him savagely. Then, as he stepped forward, his foot sank in the ooze. He tried to wrench it back, but the muck sucked viciously at his foot as if it were a giant leech. With a violent effort, he tore loose. He knew where he was now. Death Swamp and its quicksand.

His hands were tight closed as if his nerve were something tangible that some one in the darkness was trying to tear from his grip. The softness of the earth had given him an idea. He stepped back from the quicksand a dozen feet or so, and, like some huge prehistoric beaver, he began to dig.

Rainsford had dug himself in in France when a second's delay meant death. That had been a placid pastime compared to his digging now. The pit grew deeper; when it was above his shoulders, he climbed out and from some hard saplings cut stakes and sharpened them to a fine point. These stakes he planted at the bottom of the pit with the points sticking up. With flying fingers he wove a rough carpet of weeds and branches and with it he covered the mouth of the pit. Then, wet with sweat and aching with tiredness, he crouched behind the stump of a lightning-charred tree.

He knew his pursuer was coming; he heard the padding sound of feet on the soft earth, and the night breeze brought him the perfume of the general's cigaret. It seemed to Rainsford that the general was coming with unusual swiftness; he was not feeling his way along, foot by foot. Rainsford, crouching there, could not see the general, nor could he see the pit. He lived a year in a minute. Then he felt an impulse to cry aloud with joy, for he heard the sharp crackle of the breaking branches as the cover of the pit gave way; he heard the sharp scream of pain as the pointed stakes found their mark. He leaped up from his place of concealment. Then he cowered back. Three feet from the pit a man was standing, with an electric torch in his hand.

"You've done well, Rainsford," the voice of the general called. "Your Burmese tiger pit has claimed one of my best dogs. Again you score. I think, Mr. Rainsford, I'll see what you can do against my whole pack. I'm going home for a rest now. Thank you for a most amusing evening."

At daybreak Rainsford, lying near the swamp, was awakened by the sound that made him know that he had new things to learn about fear. It was a distant sound, faint and wavering, but he knew it. It was the baying of a pack of hounds.

195

Rainsford knew he could do one of two things. He could stay where he was and wait. That was suicide. He could flee. That was postponing the inevitable. For a moment he stood there, thinking. An idea that held a wild chance came to him, and, tightening his belt, he headed away from the swamp.

The baying of the hounds drew nearer, then still nearer, nearer, ever nearer. On a ridge Rainsford climbed a tree. Down a watercourse, not a quarter of a mile away, he could see the bush moving. Straining his eyes, he saw the lean figure of General Zaroff; just ahead of him Rainsford made out another figure whose wide shoulders surged through the tall jungle weeds; it was the giant Ivan, and he seemed pulled forward by some unseen force; Rainsford knew that Ivan must be holding the pack in leash.

They would be on him any minute now. His mind worked frantically. He thought of a native trick he had learned in Uganda. He slid down the tree. He caught hold of a springy young sapling and to it he fastened his hunting knife, with the blade pointing down the trail; with a bit of wild grapevine he tied back the sapling. Then he ran for his life. The hounds raised their voices as they hit the fresh scent. Rainsford knew now how an animal at bay feels.

He had to stop to get his breath. The baying of the hounds stopped abruptly, and Rainsford's heart stopped too. They must have reached the knife.

200   He shinnied excitedly up a tree and looked back. His pursuers had stopped. But the hope that was in Rainsford's brain when he climbed died, for he saw in the shallow valley that General Zaroff was still on his feet. But Ivan was not. The knife, driven by the recoil of the springing tree, had not wholly failed.

"Nerve, nerve, nerve!" he panted, as he dashed along. A blue gap showed between the trees dead ahead. Ever nearer drew the hounds. Rainsford forced himself on toward that gap. He reached it. It was the shore of the sea. Across a cove he could see the gloomy gray stone of the château. Twenty feet below him the sea rumbled and hissed. Rainsford hesitated. He heard the hounds. Then he leaped far out into the sea. . . .

When the general and his pack reached the place by the sea, the Cossack stopped. For some minutes he stood regarding the blue-green expanse of water. He shrugged his shoulders. Then he sat down, took a drink of brandy from a silver flask, lit a perfumed cigaret, and hummed a bit from *Madame Butterfly*.

General Zaroff had an exceedingly good dinner in his great paneled dining hall that evening. With it he had a bottle of Pol Roger and half a bottle of Chambertin. Two slight annoyances kept him from perfect enjoyment. One was the thought that it would be difficult to replace Ivan; the other was that his quarry had escaped him; of course the American hadn't played the game—so thought the general as he tasted his after-dinner liqueur. In his library he read, to soothe himself, from the works of Marcus Aurelius. At ten he went up to his bedroom. He was deliciously tired, he said to himself, as he locked himself in. There was a little moonlight, so, before turning on his light, he went to the window and looked down at the courtyard. He could see the great hounds, and he called: "Better luck another time," to them. Then he switched on the light.

A man, who had been hiding in the curtains of the bed, was standing there.

"Rainsford!" screamed the general. "How in God's name did you   205
get here?"

"Swam," said Rainsford. "I found it quicker than walking through the jungle."

The general sucked in his breath and smiled. "I congratulate you," he said. "You have won the game."

Rainsford did not smile. "I am still a beast at bay," he said, in a low, hoarse voice. "Get ready, General Zaroff."

The general made one of his deepest bows. "I see," he said. "Splendid! One of us is to furnish a repast for the hounds. The other will sleep in this very excellent bed. On guard, Rainsford. . . ."

He had never slept in a better bed, Rainsford decided.   210

QUESTIONS

1. Discuss the two meanings of the title.
2. How important is suspense in the story? How is it developed and sustained? What roles do chance and coincidence play in the story?
3. Discuss the characterizations of Rainsford and General Zaroff. Which one is more fully characterized? Are both characters plausible?
4. Why does Connell include the "philosophical" discussion between Whitney and Rainsford at the beginning of the story (paragraphs 7–24)? Does it reveal a personal limitation on Rainsford's part? Does Rainsford undergo any significant changes in the course of the story? Do we come to know him better as the story proceeds?
5. Compare the discussion between Whitney and Rainsford and the after-dinner conversation between Rainsford and Zaroff (paragraphs 68–145). In these discussions, is Rainsford more like Whitney or Zaroff? How does he differ from Zaroff? Does the end of the story resolve that difference?

6. As you read the story, do you develop any expectations of how it might be resolved? Are these expectations met or overturned?
7. As you go through the story a second time, do you find more significance in any of the action or description than you noticed during the first reading?
8. Would you describe this story as commercial fiction or literary fiction? Support your answer.

Tobias Wolff

Hunters in the Snow

Tub had been waiting for an hour in the falling snow. He paced the sidewalk to keep warm and stuck his head out over the curb whenever he saw lights approaching. One driver stopped for him but before Tub could wave the man on he saw the rifle on Tub's back and hit the gas. The tires spun on the ice.

The fall of snow thickened. Tub stood below the overhang of a building. Across the road the clouds whitened just above the rooftops, and the street lights went out. He shifted the rifle strap to his other shoulder. The whiteness seeped up the sky.

A truck slid around the corner, horn blaring, rear end sashaying. Tub moved to the sidewalk and held up his hand. The truck jumped the curb and kept coming, half on the street and half on the sidewalk. It wasn't slowing down at all. Tub stood for a moment, still holding up his hand, then jumped back. His rifle slipped off his shoulder and clattered on the ice, a sandwich fell out of his pocket. He ran for the steps of the building. Another sandwich and a package of cookies tumbled onto the new snow. He made the steps and looked back.

The truck had stopped several feet beyond where Tub had been standing. He picked up his sandwiches and his cookies and slung the rifle and went up to the driver's window. The driver was bent against the steering wheel, slapping his knees and drumming his feet on the floorboards. He looked like a cartoon of a person laughing, except that

HUNTERS IN THE SNOW   First published in 1981. Tobias Wolff (b. 1945), a winner of the PEN/Faulkner award, has also won many awards for his short fiction, including places in the annual *Prize Stories: The O. Henry Awards* and *The Best American Short Stories* volumes. Raised in the state of Washington, he dropped out of high school and worked as an apprentice seaman, then later served as a paratrooper in Vietnam. He then earned degrees at Oxford University and Stanford, where he now teaches.

his eyes watched the man on the seat beside him. "You ought to see yourself," the driver said. "He looks just like a beach ball with a hat on, doesn't he? Doesn't he, Frank?"

The man beside him smiled and looked off.   5

"You almost ran me down," Tub said. "You could've killed me."

"Come on, Tub," said the man beside the driver. "Be mellow. Kenny was just messing around." He opened the door and slid over to the middle of the seat.

Tub took the bolt out of his rifle and climbed in beside him. "I waited an hour," he said. "If you meant ten o'clock why didn't you say ten o'clock?"

"Tub, you haven't done anything but complain since we got here," said the man in the middle. "If you want to piss and moan all day you might as well go home and bitch at your kids. Take your pick." When Tub didn't say anything he turned to the driver. "Okay, Kenny, let's hit the road."

Some juvenile delinquents had heaved a brick through the wind-   10 shield on the driver's side, so the cold and snow tunneled right into the cab. The heater didn't work. They covered themselves with a couple of blankets Kenny had brought along and pulled down the muffs on their caps. Tub tried to keep his hands warm by rubbing them under the blanket but Frank made him stop.

They left Spokane and drove deep into the country, running along black lines of fences. The snow let up, but still there was no edge to the land where it met the sky. Nothing moved in the chalky fields. The cold bleached their faces and made the stubble stand out on their cheeks and along their upper lips. They stopped twice for coffee before they got to the woods where Kenny wanted to hunt.

Tub was for trying someplace different; two years in a row they'd been up and down this land and hadn't seen a thing. Frank didn't care one way or the other, he just wanted to get out of the goddamned truck. "Feel that," Frank said, slamming the door. He spread his feet and closed his eyes and leaned his head way back and breathed deeply. "Tune in on that energy."

"Another thing," Kenny said. "This is open land. Most of the land around here is posted."

"I'm cold," Tub said.

Frank breathed out. "Stop bitching, Tub. Get centered."   15

"I wasn't bitching."

"Centered," Kenny said. "Next thing you'll be wearing a night-gown, Frank. Selling flowers out at the airport."

"Kenny," Frank said, "you talk too much."

"Okay," Kenny said. "I won't say a word. Like I won't say anything about a certain babysitter."

20   "What babysitter?" Tub asked.

"That's between us," Frank said, looking at Kenny. "That's confidential. You keep your mouth shut."

Kenny laughed.

"You're asking for it," Frank said.

"Asking for what?"

25   "You'll see."

"Hey," Tub said, "are we hunting or what?"

They started off across the field. Tub had trouble getting through the fences. Frank and Kenny could have helped him; they could have lifted up on the top wire and stepped on the bottom wire, but they didn't. They stood and watched him. There were a lot of fences and Tub was puffing when they reached the woods.

They hunted for over two hours and saw no deer, no tracks, no sign. Finally they stopped by the creek to eat. Kenny had several slices of pizza and a couple of candy bars; Frank had a sandwich, an apple, two carrots, and a square of chocolate; Tub ate one hard-boiled egg and a stick of celery.

"You ask me how I want to die today," Kenny said, "I'll tell you burn me at the stake." He turned to Tub. "You still on that diet?" He winked at Frank.

30   "What do you think? You think I like hard-boiled eggs?"

"All I can say is, it's the first diet I ever heard of where you gained weight from it."

"Who said I gained weight?"

"Oh, pardon me. I take it back. You're just wasting away before my very eyes. Isn't he, Frank?"

Frank had his fingers fanned out, tips against the bark of the stump where he'd laid his food. His knuckles were hairy. He wore a heavy wedding band and on his right pinky another gold ring with a flat face and an "F" in what looked like diamonds. He turned the ring this way and that. "Tub," he said, "you haven't seen your own balls in ten years."

35   Kenny doubled over laughing. He took off his hat and slapped his leg with it.

"What am I supposed to do?" Tub said. "It's my glands."

They left the woods and hunted along the creek. Frank and Kenny worked one bank and Tub worked the other, moving upstream. The snow was light but the drifts were deep and hard to move through. Wherever Tub looked the surface was smooth, undisturbed, and after a time he lost interest. He stopped looking for tracks and just tried to keep up with Frank and Kenny on the other side. A moment came when he realized he hadn't seen them in a long time. The breeze was moving from him to them; when it stilled he could sometimes hear Kenny laughing but that was all. He quickened his pace, breasting hard into the drifts, fighting away the snow with his knees and elbows. He heard his heart and felt the flush on his face but he never once stopped.

Tub caught up with Frank and Kenny at a bend of the creek. They were standing on a log that stretched from their bank to his. Ice had backed up behind the log. Frozen reeds stuck out, barely nodding when the air moved.

"See anything?" Frank asked.

Tub shook his head.   40

There wasn't much daylight left and they decided to head back toward the road. Frank and Kenny crossed the log and they started downstream, using the trail Tub had broken. Before they had gone very far Kenny stopped. "Look at that," he said, and pointed to some tracks going from the creek back into the woods. Tub's footprints crossed right over them. There on the bank, plain as day, were several mounds of deer sign. "What do you think that is, Tub?" Kenny kicked at it. "Walnuts on vanilla icing?"

"I guess I didn't notice."

Kenny looked at Frank.

"I was lost."

"You were lost. Big deal."   45

They followed the tracks into the woods. The deer had gone over a fence half buried in drifting snow. A no hunting sign was nailed to the top of one of the posts. Frank laughed and said the son of a bitch could read. Kenny wanted to go after him but Frank said no way, the people out here didn't mess around. He thought maybe the farmer who owned the land would let them use it if they asked. Kenny wasn't so sure. Anyway, he figured that by the time they walked to the truck and drove up the road and doubled back it would be almost dark.

"Relax," Frank said. "You can't hurry nature. If we're meant to get that deer, we'll get it. If we're not, we won't."

They started back toward the truck. This part of the woods was mainly pine. The snow was shaded and had a glaze on it. It held up Kenny and Frank but Tub kept falling through. As he kicked forward, the edge of the crust bruised his shins. Kenny and Frank pulled ahead of him, to where he couldn't even hear their voices any more. He sat down on a stump and wiped his face. He ate both the sandwiches and half the cookies, taking his own sweet time. It was dead quiet.

When Tub crossed the last fence into the road the truck started moving. Tub had to run for it and just managed to grab hold of the tailgate and hoist himself into the bed. He lay there, panting. Kenny looked out the rear window and grinned. Tub crawled into the lee of the cab to get out of the freezing wind. He pulled his earflaps low and pushed his chin into the collar of his coat. Someone rapped on the window but Tub would not turn around.

50   He and Frank waited outside while Kenny went into the farmhouse to ask permission. The house was old and paint was curling off the sides. The smoke streamed westward off the top of the chimney, fanning away into a thin gray plume. Above the ridge of the hills another ridge of blue clouds was rising.

"You've got a short memory," Tub said.

"What?" Frank said. He had been staring off.

"I used to stick up for you."

"Okay, so you used to stick up for me. What's eating you?"

55   "You shouldn't have just left me back there like that."

"You're a grown-up, Tub. You can take care of yourself. Anyway, if you think you're the only person with problems I can tell you that you're not."

"Is something bothering you, Frank?"

Frank kicked at a branch poking out of the snow. "Never mind," he said.

"What did Kenny mean about the babysitter?"

60   "Kenny talks too much," Frank said. "You just mind your own business."

Kenny came out of the farmhouse and gave the thumbs-up and they began walking back toward the woods. As they passed the barn a large black hound with a grizzled snout ran out and barked at them. Every time he barked he slid backwards a bit, like a cannon recoiling. Kenny got down on all fours and snarled and barked back at him, and the dog slunk away into the barn, looking over his shoulder and peeing a little as he went.

"That's an old-timer," Frank said. "A real graybeard. Fifteen years if he's a day."

"Too old," Kenny said.

Past the barn they cut off through the fields. The land was unfenced and the crust was freezing up thick and they made good time. They kept to the edge of the field until they picked up the tracks again and followed them into the woods, farther and farther back toward the hills. The trees started to blur with the shadows and the wind rose and needled their faces with the crystals it swept off the glaze. Finally they lost the tracks.

Kenny swore and threw down his hat. "This is the worst day of hunt-   65
ing I ever had, bar none." He picked up his hat and brushed off the
snow. "This will be the first season since I was fifteen I haven't got my
deer."

"It isn't the deer," Frank said. "It's the hunting. There are all these
forces out here and you just have to go with them."

"You go with them," Kenny said. "I came out here to get me a deer,
not listen to a bunch of hippie bullshit. And if it hadn't been for dimples here I would have, too."

"That's enough," Frank said.

"And you—you're so busy thinking about that little jailbait of
yours you wouldn't know a deer if you saw one."

"Drop dead," Frank said, and turned away.   70

Kenny and Tub followed him back across the fields. When they
were coming up to the barn Kenny stopped and pointed. "I hate that
post," he said. He raised his rifle and fired. It sounded like a dry branch
cracking. The post splintered along its right side, up towards the top.
"There," Kenny said. "It's dead."

"Knock it off," Frank said, walking ahead.

Kenny looked at Tub. He smiled. "I hate that tree," he said, and
fired again. Tub hurried to catch up with Frank. He started to speak but
just then the dog ran out of the barn and barked at them. "Easy, boy,"
Frank said.

"I hate that dog." Kenny was behind them.

"That's enough," Frank said. "You put that gun down."   75

Kenny fired. The bullet went in between the dog's eyes. He sank
right down into the snow, his legs splayed out on each side, his yellow
eyes open and staring. Except for the blood he looked like a small
bearskin rug. The blood ran down the dog's muzzle into the snow.

They all looked at the dog lying there.

"What did he ever do to you?" Tub asked. "He was just barking."

Kenny turned to Tub. "I hate you."

Tub shot from the waist. Kenny jerked backward against the fence   80
and buckled to his knees. He folded his hands across his stomach.
"Look," he said. His hands were covered with blood. In the dusk his
blood was more blue than red. It seemed to belong to the shadows. It
didn't seem out of place. Kenny eased himself onto his back. He sighed
several times, deeply. "You shot me," he said.

"I had to," Tub said. He knelt beside Kenny. "Oh God," he said.
"Frank. Frank."

Frank hadn't moved since Kenny killed the dog.

"Frank!" Tub shouted.

"I was just kidding around," Kenny said. "It was a joke. Oh!" he said, and arched his back suddenly. "Oh!" he said again, and dug his heels into the snow and pushed himself along on his head for several feet. Then he stopped and lay there, rocking back and forth on his heels and head like a wrestler doing warm-up exercises.

85   Frank roused himself. "Kenny," he said. He bent down and put his gloved hand on Kenny's brow. "You shot him," he said to Tub.

"He made me," Tub said.

"No no no," Kenny said.

Tub was weeping from the eyes and nostrils. His whole face was wet. Frank closed his eyes, then looked down at Kenny again. "Where does it hurt?"

"Everywhere," Kenny said, "just everywhere."

90   "Oh God," Tub said.

"I mean where did it go in?" Frank said.

"Here." Kenny pointed at the wound in his stomach. It was welling slowly with blood.

"You're lucky," Frank said. "It's on the left side. It missed your appendix. If it had hit your appendix you'd really be in the soup." He turned and threw up onto the snow, holding his sides as if to keep warm.

"Are you all right?" Tub said.

95   "There's some aspirin in the truck," Kenny said.

"I'm all right," Frank said.

"We'd better call an ambulance," Tub said.

"Jesus," Frank said. "What are we going to say?"

"Exactly what happened," Tub said. "He was going to shoot me but I shot him first."

100   "No sir!" Kenny said. "I wasn't either!"

Frank patted Kenny on the arm. "Easy does it, partner." He stood. "Let's go."

Tub picked up Kenny's rifle as they walked down toward the farmhouse. "No sense leaving this around," he said. "Kenny might get ideas."

"I can tell you one thing," Frank said. "You've really done it this time. This definitely takes the cake."

They had to knock on the door twice before it was opened by a thin man with lank hair. The room behind him was filled with smoke. He squinted at them. "You get anything?" he asked.

105   "No," Frank said.

"I knew you wouldn't. That's what I told the other fellow."

"We've had an accident."

The man looked past Frank and Tub into the gloom. "Shoot your friend, did you?"

Frank nodded.

"I did," Tub said.

"I suppose you want to use the phone."

"If it's okay."

The man in the door looked behind him, then stepped back. Frank and Tub followed him into the house. There was a woman sitting by the stove in the middle of the room. The stove was smoking badly. She looked up and then down again at the child asleep in her lap. Her face was white and damp; strands of hair were pasted across her forehead. Tub warmed his hands over the stove while Frank went into the kitchen to call. The man who had let them in stood at the window, his hands in his pockets.

"My friend shot your dog," Tub said.

The man nodded without turning around. "I should have done it myself. I just couldn't."

"He loved that dog so much," the woman said. The child squirmed and she rocked it.

"You asked him to?" Tub said. "You asked him to shoot your dog?"

"He was old and sick. Couldn't chew his food any more. I would have done it myself but I don't have a gun."

"You couldn't have anyway," the woman said. "Never in a million years."

The man shrugged.

Frank came out of the kitchen. "We'll have to take him ourselves. The nearest hospital is fifty miles from here and all their ambulances are out anyway."

The woman knew a shortcut but the directions were complicated and Tub had to write them down. The man told them where they could find some boards to carry Kenny on. He didn't have a flashlight but he said he would leave the porch light on.

It was dark outside. The clouds were low and heavy-looking and the wind blew in shrill gusts. There was a screen loose on the house and it banged slowly and then quickly as the wind rose again. They could hear it all the way to the barn. Frank went for the boards while Tub looked for Kenny, who was not where they had left him. Tub found him farther up the drive, lying on his stomach. "You okay?" Tub said.

"It hurts."

"Frank says it missed your appendix."

"I already had my appendix out."

"All right," Frank said, coming up to them. "We'll have you in a nice warm bed before you can say Jack Robinson." He put the two boards on Kenny's right side.

"Just as long as I don't have one of those male nurses," Kenny said.

"Ha ha," Frank said. "That's the spirit. Get ready, set, *over you go,*" and he rolled Kenny onto the boards. Kenny screamed and kicked his legs in the air. When he quieted down Frank and Tub lifted the boards and carried him down the drive. Tub had the back end, and with the snow blowing into his face he had trouble with his footing. Also he was tired and the man inside had forgotten to turn the porch light on. Just past the house Tub slipped and threw out his hands to catch himself. The boards fell and Kenny tumbled out and rolled to the bottom of the drive, yelling all the way. He came to rest against the right front wheel of the truck.

130   "You fat moron," Frank said. "You aren't good for diddly."

Tub grabbed Frank by the collar and backed him hard up against the fence. Frank tried to pull his hands away but Tub shook him and snapped his head back and forth and finally Frank gave up.

"What do you know about fat," Tub said. "What do you know about glands." As he spoke he kept shaking Frank. "What do you know about me."

"All right," Frank said.

"No more," Tub said.

135   "All right."

"No more talking to me like that. No more watching. No more laughing."

"Okay, Tub. I promise."

Tub let go of Frank and leaned his forehead against the fence. His arms hung straight at his sides.

"I'm sorry, Tub." Frank touched him on the shoulder. "I'll be down at the truck."

140   Tub stood by the fence for a while and then got the rifles off the porch. Frank had rolled Kenny back onto the boards and they lifted him into the bed of the truck. Frank spread the seat blankets over him. "Warm enough?" he asked.

Kenny nodded.

"Okay. Now how does reverse work on this thing?"

"All the way to the left and up." Kenny sat up as Frank started forward to the cab. "Frank!"

"What?"

145   "If it sticks don't force it."

The truck started right away. "One thing," Frank said, "you've got to hand it to the Japanese. A very ancient, very spiritual culture and they can still make a hell of a truck." He glanced over at Tub. "Look, I'm sorry. I didn't know you felt that way, honest to God I didn't. You should have said something."

"I did."

"When? Name one time."

"A couple of hours ago."

"I guess I wasn't paying attention."   150

"That's true, Frank," Tub said. "You don't pay attention very much."

"Tub," Frank said, "what happened back there, I should have been more sympathetic. I realize that. You were going through a lot. I just want you to know it wasn't your fault. He was asking for it."

"You think so?"

"Absolutely. It was him or you. I would have done the same thing in your shoes, no question."

The wind was blowing into their faces. The snow was a moving   155
white wall in front of their lights; it swirled into the cab through the hole in the windshield and settled on them. Tub clapped his hands and shifted around to stay warm, but it didn't work.

"I'm going to have to stop," Frank said. "I can't feel my fingers."

Up ahead they saw some lights off the road. It was a tavern. Outside in the parking lot there were several jeeps and trucks. A couple of them had deer strapped across their hoods. Frank parked and they went back to Kenny. "How you doing, partner," Frank said.

"I'm cold."

"Well, don't feel like the Lone Ranger. It's worse inside, take my word for it. You should get that windshield fixed."

"Look," Tub said, "he threw the blankets off." They were lying in a   160
heap against the tailgate.

"Now look, Kenny," Frank said, "it's no use whining about being cold if you're not going to try and keep warm. You've got to do your share." He spread the blankets over Kenny and tucked them in at the corners.

"They blew off."

"Hold on to them then."

"Why are we stopping, Frank?"

"Because if me and Tub don't get warmed up we're going to freeze   165
solid and then where will you be?" He punched Kenny lightly in the arm. "So just hold your horses."

The bar was full of men in colored jackets, mostly orange. The waitress brought coffee. "Just what the doctor ordered," Frank said, cradling the steaming cup in his hand. His skin was bone white. "Tub,

I've been thinking. What you said about me not paying attention, that's true."

"It's okay."

"No. I really had that coming. I guess I've just been a little too interested in old number one. I've had a lot on my mind. Not that that's any excuse."

"Forget it, Frank. I sort of lost my temper back there. I guess we're all a little on edge."

170 Frank shook his head. "It isn't just that."

"You want to talk about it?"

"Just between us, Tub?"

"Sure, Frank. Just between us."

"Tub, I think I'm going to be leaving Nancy."

175 "Oh, Frank. Oh, Frank." Tub sat back and shook his head.

Frank reached out and laid his hand on Tub's arm. "Tub, have you ever been really in love?"

"Well—"

"I mean *really* in love." He squeezed Tub's wrist. "With your whole being."

"I don't know. When you put it like that, I don't know."

180 "You haven't then. Nothing against you, but you'd know it if you had." Frank let go of Tub's arm. "This isn't just some bit of fluff I'm talking about."

"Who is she, Frank?"

Frank paused. He looked into his empty cup. "Roxanne Brewer."

"Cliff Brewer's kid? The babysitter?"

"You can't just put people into categories like that, Tub. That's why the whole system is wrong. And that's why this country is going to hell in a rowboat."

185 "But she can't be more than—" Tub shook his head.

"Fifteen. She'll be sixteen in May." Frank smiled. "May fourth, three twenty-seven p.m. Hell, Tub, a hundred years ago she'd have been an old maid by that age. Juliet was only thirteen."

"Juliet? Juliet Miller? Jesus, Frank, she doesn't even have breasts. She doesn't even wear a top to her bathing suit. She's still collecting frogs."

"Not Juliet Miller. The real Juliet. Tub, don't you see how you're dividing people up into categories? He's an executive, she's a secretary, he's a truck driver, she's fifteen years old. Tub, this so-called babysitter, this so-called fifteen-year-old has more in her little finger than most of us have in our entire bodies. I can tell you this little lady is something special."

Tub nodded. "I know the kids like her."

"She's opened up whole worlds to me that I never knew were   190
there."

"What does Nancy think about all of this?"

"She doesn't know."

"You haven't told her?"

"Not yet. It's not so easy. She's been damned good to me all these
years. Then there's the kids to consider." The brightness in Frank's eyes
trembled and he wiped quickly at them with the back of his hand. "I
guess you think I'm a complete bastard."

"No, Frank. I don't think that."   195

"Well, you *ought* to."

"Frank, when you've got a friend it means you've always got someone on your side, no matter what. That's the way I feel about it, anyway."

"You mean that, Tub?"

"Sure I do."

Frank smiled. "You don't know how good it feels to hear you say that."   200

Kenny had tried to get out of the truck but he hadn't made it. He
was jackknifed over the tailgate, his head hanging above the bumper.
They lifted him back into the bed and covered him again. He was
sweating and his teeth chattered. "It hurts, Frank."

"It wouldn't hurt so much if you just stayed put. Now we're going
to the hospital. Got that? Say it—I'm going to the hospital."

"I'm going to the hospital."

"Again."

"I'm going to the hospital."   205

"Now just keep saying that to yourself and before you know it we'll
be there."

After they had gone a few miles Tub turned to Frank. "I just pulled
a real boner," he said.

"What's that?"

"I left the directions on the table back there."

"That's okay. I remember them pretty well."   210

The snowfall lightened and the clouds began to roll back off the
fields, but it was no warmer and after a time both Frank and Tub were
bitten through and shaking. Frank almost didn't make it around a
curve, and they decided to stop at the next roadhouse.

There was an automatic hand-dryer in the bathroom and they took
turns standing in front of it, opening their jackets and shirts and letting
the jet of hot air breathe across their faces and chests.

"You know," Tub said, "what you told me back there, I appreciate it. Trusting me."

Frank opened and closed his fingers in front of the nozzle. "The way I look at it, Tub, no man is an island. You've got to trust someone."

215   "Frank—"

Frank waited.

"When I said that about my glands, that wasn't true. The truth is I just shovel it in."

"Well, Tub—"

"Day and night, Frank. In the shower. On the freeway." He turned and let the air play over his back. "I've even got stuff in the paper towel machine at work."

220   "There's nothing wrong with your glands at all?" Frank had taken his boots and socks off. He held first his right, then his left foot up to the nozzle.

"No. There never was."

"Does Alice know?" The machine went off and Frank started lacing up his boots.

"Nobody knows. That's the worst of it, Frank. Not the being fat, I never got any big kick out of being thin, but the lying. Having to lead a double life like a spy or a hit man. This sounds strange but I feel sorry for those guys, I really do. I know what they go through. Always having to think about what you say and do. Always feeling like people are watching you, trying to catch you at something. Never able to just be yourself. Like when I make a big deal about only having an orange for breakfast and then scarf all the way to work. Oreos, Mars Bars, Twinkies. Sugar Babies. Snickers." Tub glanced at Frank and looked quickly away. "Pretty disgusting, isn't it?"

"Tub. Tub." Frank shook his head. "Come on." He took Tub's arm and led him into the restaurant half of the bar. "My friend is hungry," he told the waitress. "Bring four orders of pancakes, plenty of butter and syrup."

225   "Frank—"

"Sit down."

When the dishes came Frank carved out slabs of butter and just laid them on the pancakes. Then he emptied the bottle of syrup, moving it back and forth over the plates. He leaned forward on his elbows and rested his chin in one hand. "Go on, Tub."

Tub ate several mouthfuls, then started to wipe his lips. Frank took the napkin away from him. "No wiping," he said. Tub kept at it. The syrup covered his chin; it dripped to a point like a goatee. "Weigh in, Tub," Frank said, pushing another fork across the table.

"Get down to business." Tub took the fork in his left hand and lowered his head and started really chowing down. "Clean your plate," Frank said when the pancakes were gone, and Tub lifted each of the four plates and licked it clean. He sat back, trying to catch his breath.

"Beautiful," Frank said. "Are you full?"

"I'm full," Tub said. "I've never been so full."   230

Kenny's blankets were bunched up against the tailgate again.

"They must have blown off," Tub said.

"They're not doing him any good," Frank said. "We might as well get some use out of them."

Kenny mumbled. Tub bent over him. "What? Speak up."

"I'm going to the hospital," Kenny said.   235

"Attaboy," Frank said.

The blankets helped. The wind still got their faces and Frank's hands but it was much better. The fresh snow on the road and the trees sparkled under the beam of the headlight. Squares of light from farmhouse windows fell onto the blue snow in the fields.

"Frank," Tub said after a time, "you know that farmer? He told Kenny to kill the dog."

"You're kidding!" Frank leaned forward, considering. "That Kenny. What a card." He laughed and so did Tub. Tub smiled out the back window. Kenny lay with his arms folded over his stomach, moving his lips at the stars. Right overhead was the Big Dipper, and behind, hanging between Kenny's toes in the direction of the hospital, was the North Star, Pole Star, Help to Sailors. As the truck twisted through the gentle hills the star went back and forth between Kenny's boots, staying always in his sight. "I'm going to the hospital," Kenny said. But he was wrong. They had taken a different turn a long way back.

QUESTIONS

1. Discuss the way Tub is presented in the opening scene. Does your assessment of his character change in the later scenes?
2. How does the cold, hostile environment in the story relate to its meaning?
3. Which is the most sympathetic of the three characters? The story deals, in part, with the power struggle among the characters. Which character is the most powerful? Do the balance of power and alliances between the characters shift as the story proceeds?
4. How do the physical descriptions of the characters help us to understand them? For example, how is Tub's obesity relevant to his character?

5. The second half of the story includes some surprising twists and turns. How are these more meaningful and substantial than the random plot twists one might find in a purely commercial work of fiction?

6. What other elements of the story suggest that this is a serious, literary work rather than merely an entertaining yarn about three hapless hunters?

7. What is the purpose of the scene in which Frank and Tub stop at the tavern for food and coffee, leaving the wounded Kenny in the back of the truck? During their conversation, Frank analyzes his own character and expresses remorse. Are his insights and remorse genuine? Why or why not?

8. The final plot twist comes in the last two sentences of the story. Here the narrator speaks directly to the reader, giving us information the characters don't know. How is this an appropriate conclusion to the story? What final statement is being made about the characters?

Understanding and Evaluating Fiction

Most of the stories in this book are accompanied by study questions that are by no means exhaustive. The following is a list of questions that you may apply to any story. You may be unable to answer many of them until you have read further in the book.

Plot and Structure

1. Who is the protagonist of the story? What are the conflicts? Are they physical, intellectual, moral, or emotional? Is the main conflict between sharply differentiated good and evil, or is it more subtle and complex?

2. Does the plot have unity? Are all the episodes relevant to the total meaning or effect of the story? Does each incident grow logically out of the preceding incident and lead naturally to the next? Is the ending happy, unhappy, or indeterminate? Is it fairly achieved?

3. What use does the story make of chance and coincidence? Are these occurrences used to initiate, to complicate, or to resolve the story? How improbable are they?

4. How is suspense created in the story? Is the interest confined to "What happens next?" or are larger concerns involved? Can you find examples of mystery? Of dilemma?

5. What use does the story make of surprise? Are the surprises achieved fairly? Do they serve a significant purpose? Do they divert the reader's attention from weaknesses in the story?

6. To what extent is this a "formula" story?

Characterization

7. What means does the author use to reveal character? Are the characters sufficiently dramatized? What use is made of character contrasts?
8. Are the characters consistent in their actions? Adequately motivated? Plausible? Does the author successfully avoid stock characters?
9. Is each character fully enough developed to justify its role in the story? Are the main characters round or flat?
10. Is any of the characters a developing character? If so, is the change a large or a small one? Is it a plausible change for such a person? Is it sufficiently motivated? Is it given sufficient time?

Theme

11. Does the story have a theme? What is it? Is it implicit or explicit?
12. Does the theme reinforce or oppose popular notions of life? Does it furnish a new insight or refresh or deepen an old one?

Point of View

13. What point of view does the story use? Is it consistent in its use of this point of view? If shifts are made, are they justified?
14. What advantages has the chosen point of view? Does it furnish any clues as to the purpose of the story?
15. If the point of view is that of one of the characters, does this character have any limitations that affect her or his interpretation of events or persons?
16. Does the author use point of view primarily to reveal or conceal? Is important information known to the focal character ever unfairly withheld?

Symbol, Allegory, and Fantasy

17. Does the story make use of symbols? If so, do the symbols carry or merely reinforce the meaning of the story?
18. Does the story make use of symbolic settings?
19. Does the story employ allegory? Is the use of allegory clear-cut or ambiguous?
20. Does the story contain any elements of fantasy? If so, what is the initial assumption? Does the story operate logically from this assumption?
21. Is the fantasy employed for its own sake or to express some human truth? If the latter, what truth?

Humor and Irony

22. If the story employs humor, is the humor present merely for its own sake or does it contribute to the meaning?
23. Does the story anywhere use irony of situation? Dramatic irony? Verbal irony? What functions do the ironies serve?

General

24. Is the primary interest of the story in plot, character, theme, or some other element?
25. What contribution to the story is made by its setting? Is the particular setting essential, or could the story have happened anywhere?
26. What are the characteristics of the author's style? Are they appropriate to the nature of the story?
27. What light is thrown on the story by its title?
28. Do all the elements of the story work together to support a central purpose? Is any part irrelevant or inappropriate?
29. What do you conceive to be the story's central purpose? How fully has it achieved that purpose?
30. Is the story commercial or literary? How significant is the story's purpose?
31. Is the story more or less impressive on a second reading?

SUGGESTIONS FOR WRITING

1. After reviewing the distinguishing characteristics of literary and commercial fiction, and bearing in mind that the two types of fiction represent a spectrum of qualities rather than hard-and-fast opposites, examine one of the following stories for its mix of literary and commercial characteristics:
   a. O. Henry, "A Municipal Report" (page 375).
   b. Hurston, "The Gilded Six-Bits" (page 567).
   c. Poe, "The Cask of Amontillado" (page 611).
   d. Wharton, "Roman Fever" (page 409).
   On balance, determine whether your choice is predominantly commercial or literary.
2. Connell's "The Most Dangerous Game" (page 67) and Wolfe's "The Child by Tiger" (page 625) have in common the same central action, a manhunt, complete with the use of hounds. In a comparative essay, determine which is the literary and which is the commercial story.

Chapter Two

Plot and Structure

Plot is the sequence of incidents or events through which an author constructs a story; skilled authors are careful to present the sequence in a significant order. When described in isolation, the plot bears about the same relationship to a story that a map does to a journey. Just as a map may be drawn on a finer or grosser scale, so may a plot be recounted with lesser or greater detail. A plot summary may include what characters say or think, as well as what they do, but it leaves out description and analysis and concentrates primarily on major events.

Plot should not be confused with the content of the work. The plot is not the action itself, but the way the author *arranges* the action toward a specific end. In commercial fiction, the plot may include many surprising twists and turns and a culminating, climactic incident; because the main goal is to keep the reader turning the pages, a commercial author is likely to use a tried-and-true, fairly conventional **structure** in arranging the plot elements. The story may follow a standard chronology, for instance, and may employ familiar structural patterns. Connell's "The Most Dangerous Game" has a chronological structure and includes the familiar structural tactic (one as old as the story of Goldilocks and the Three Bears) of using a three-part sequence in narrating Rainsford's attempts to entrap General Zaroff: first he tries the Malay man-catcher, and fails; then he tries the Burmese tiger pit, and fails; but on the third try, with the "native trick" learned in Uganda, he manages to kill Ivan and ultimately outwit Zaroff. Although Wolff's "Hunters in the Snow" also employs a chronological structure, the plot elements are arranged in a complex way in order to explore the relationships among the three principal characters. Compared with "The Most Dangerous Game," the plot structure in "Hunters in the Snow" is more experimental and unpredictable, taking unexpected excursions into the thought processes of all three characters. For a literary writer, a complex structure is often required to convey complex meanings. In

Wolff's story, the *significance* of the action is more important than the action itself, and subtle exchanges of words among characters may be just as significant as the more action-oriented sequences of the hunting expeditions.

Ordinarily, however, both the surface excitement required in commercial fiction and the significant meaning found in literary fiction arise out of some sort of **conflict**—a clash of actions, ideas, desires, or wills. Characters may be pitted against some other person or group of persons (conflict of person against person); they may be in conflict with some external force—physical nature, society, or "fate" (conflict of person against environment); or they may be in conflict with some elements in their own natures (conflict of person against himself or herself). The conflict may be physical, mental, emotional, or moral. There is conflict in a chess game—during which the competitors sit quite still for hours—as surely as in a wrestling match; emotional conflict may be raging within a person sitting alone in a silent room.

The central character in a conflict, whether sympathetic or unsympathetic as a person, is called the **protagonist;** occasionally there may be more than one protagonist in a story. (The technical term "protagonist" is preferable to the popular term "hero" or "heroine" because it is less ambiguous. The protagonist is simply the central character; the term "hero" or "heroine" implies that the central character has heroic qualities, which is often not the case.) Any force arranged against the protagonist—whether persons, things, conventions of society, or the protagonist's own character traits—is the **antagonist.** In some stories the conflict is single, clear-cut, and easily identifiable. In others it is multiple, various, and subtle. A person may be in conflict with other individuals, with social norms or nature, and with herself or himself all at the same time, and sometimes may be involved in conflict without being aware of it.

"The Most Dangerous Game" illustrates most of these kinds of conflict. Rainsford, the protagonist, is pitted first against other men—against Whitney and General Zaroff in the discussions preceding the manhunt, against Zaroff and Ivan during the manhunt. Early in the story he is pitted against nature when he falls into the sea and cannot get back to the yacht. At the beginning of the manhunt, he is in conflict with himself when he tries to fight off panic by repeating to himself, "I must keep my nerve. I must keep my nerve." The various conflicts illuminated in this story are physical (Rainsford against the sea and Zaroff), mental (Rainsford's initial conflict of ideas with Whitney and his battle of wits with Zaroff during the manhunt, which Zaroff refers to as "outdoor chess"), emotional (Rainsford's efforts to control his terror), and moral (Rainsford's refusal to "condone cold-blooded murder," in contrast to Zaroff's contempt for "romantic ideas about the value of human life").

Excellent literary fiction has been written utilizing all four of these major kinds of conflict. Much commercial fiction, however, emphasizes only the confrontation between man and man, depending on the element of physical conflict to supply the primary excitement. For instance, it is hard to conceive of a western story without a fistfight or a gunfight. Even in the most formulaic kinds of fiction, however, something more will be found than mere physical action. Good people will be arrayed against bad ones, and thus the conflict will also be between moral values. In commercial fiction this conflict often is clearly defined in terms of moral absolutes: the "good guy" versus the "bad guy." In literary fiction, the contrasts are usually less distinct. Good may be opposed to good, or half-truth to half-truth. There may be difficulty in determining what *is* good or bad, causing internal conflict rather than physical confrontation. In the real world, of course, significant moral issues are seldom sharply defined—judgments are difficult, and choices are complex rather than simple. Literary writers are aware of this complexity and are more concerned with displaying its various shadings of moral values than with presenting glaring, simplistic contrasts of good and evil, right and wrong.

Suspense is the quality in a story that makes readers ask "What's going to happen next?" or "How will this turn out?" Such questions compel them to keep reading. Suspense increases when a reader's curiosity is combined with anxiety about the fate of a likable, sympathetic character. Thus, in old serial movies—often appropriately called "cliffhangers"—a strong element of suspense was created at the end of each episode by leaving the hero hanging from the edge of a cliff or the heroine tied to railroad tracks with an express train rapidly approaching. In murder mysteries—often called "whodunits"—the main element of suspense is the reader's desire to know who committed the murder. In love stories the reader wants to know if the boy will win the girl, or if the lovers will be reunited.

In more literary forms of fiction the suspense often involves not so much the question *what* as the question *why*—not "What will happen next?" but "Why is the protagonist behaving this way? How is the protagonist's behavior to be explained in terms of human personality and character?" The forms of suspense range from crude to subtle and may involve not only actions but psychological considerations and moral issues as well. There are two common devices writers use to create suspense: they introduce an element of **mystery** (an unusual set of circumstances for which the reader craves an explanation) or they place the protagonist in a **dilemma** (a position in which he or she must choose between two courses of action, both undesirable). But suspense can readily be created for most readers by placing *anybody* on a seventeenth-story window ledge or simply by bringing together two attractive, sexy young people.

In "The Most Dangerous Game," the author initiates suspense in the opening sentences with Whitney's account of the mystery of "Ship-Trap Island," of which sailors "have a curious dread"—a place that seems to emanate evil. The mystery grows when, in this out-of-the-way spot, Rainsford discovers an enormous château with a leering gargoyle knocker on its massive door and confronts a bearded giant pointing a long-barreled revolver straight at his heart. Connell introduces a second mystery when General Zaroff tells Rainsford that he hunts "more dangerous game" on this island than the Cape buffalo. He then frustrates Rainsford's (and the reader's) curiosity for some thirty-six paragraphs before revealing what the game is. Meanwhile, by placing the protagonist in physical danger, Connell introduces a second kind of suspense. Initiated by Rainsford's fall into the sea and his confrontation with Ivan, this second kind becomes the principal source of suspense in the second half of the story. Simply put, the issues of whether Rainsford will escape and how he will escape are what keep the reader absorbed in the story. The manhunt itself begins with a dilemma. Rainsford must choose among three undesirable courses of action: he can hunt men with Zaroff; he can let himself be hunted; or he can submit to a presumably torturous death at the hands of Ivan. During the hunt, he is faced with other dilemmas. For instance, on the third day, pursued by Zaroff's hounds, "Rainsford knew he could do one of two things. He could stay where he was and wait. That was suicide. He could flee. That was postponing the inevitable."

Suspense is usually the most important criterion for good commercial fiction; unless a story makes us want to keep reading it, it can have little merit. In literary fiction, however, suspense is less important than other elements the author uses to engage the reader's interest: such a story may be amusing, well written, morally penetrating, peopled by intriguing characters; or it may feature some combination of all these elements. One test of a literary story is to determine whether it creates a desire to read it again. Like a play by Shakespeare, a successful literary story should create an even richer reading experience on the second or third encounter—even though we already know what is going to happen—than on a first reading. By contrast, when an author creates suspense artificially—by the simple withholding of vital information, for instance—readers will feel that the author's purpose is simply to keep them guessing what will happen next, not to reveal some insight into human experience. Either a commercial or a literary story could be written, for example, about the man on the seventeenth-story window ledge; but the literary story would focus less upon whether the man will jump than upon the psychological factors and life experiences that brought him to the ledge in the first place. The commercial story would keep us asking, "What happens next?" The literary story will make us wonder, "*Why* do things happen as they do?" or "What is the significance of this event?"

Closely connected with the element of suspense in fiction is the element of **surprise.** If we know ahead of time exactly what is going to happen in a story and why, there can be no suspense; as long as we do not know, whatever happens comes with an element of surprise. The surprise is proportional to the unexpectedness of what happens; it becomes pronounced when the story departs radically from our expectation. In the short story such radical departure is most often found in a **surprise ending:** one that features a sudden, unexpected turn or twist.

As with physical action and suspense, commercial fiction tends to feature a surprise ending more frequently than literary fiction. But in either type of story, there are two ways by which the legitimacy and value of a surprise ending may be judged: (1) by the fairness with which the surprise is achieved and (2) by the purpose that it serves. If the surprise is contrived through an improbable coincidence or series of coincidences, or by the planting of false clues (details whose only purpose is to mislead the reader), or through the arbitrary withholding of information, then we may well dismiss it as a cheap trick. If, on the other hand, the ending that at first is such a surprise comes to seem, the more we think about it and look back over the story, perfectly logical and natural, we will feel the surprise was achieved fairly. Again, a surprise ending may be judged as trivial if it exists simply for its own sake—to shock or to titillate the reader. We may judge it as a fraud if it serves, as it does in more formulaic commercial fiction, to conceal earlier weaknesses in the story by giving us a shiny bauble at the end to absorb and concentrate our attention. We will consider a surprise ending justified, however, when it serves to broaden or to reinforce the meaning of the story. In literary fiction, the surprise is one that furnishes meaningful illumination, not just a reversal of expectation.

Whether or not a commercial story has a surprise ending, it almost always has a **happy ending:** the protagonist must solve her problems, defeat an adversary, win her man, "live happily ever after." A common obstacle confronting readers who are making their first attempt to enjoy literary fiction is that such fiction often (though certainly not always) ends unhappily. They are likely to label such stories as "depressing" and to complain that "real life has enough troubles of its own" or, conversely, that "real life is seldom as unhappy as all that."

Two justifications may be made for the **unhappy ending.** First, many situations in real life do have unpleasant outcomes; therefore, if fiction is to reflect and illuminate life, it must acknowledge human defeats as well as triumphs. Commercial writers of sports fiction usually write of how an individual or a team achieves victory against formidable odds. Yet if one team wins the pennant, thirteen others must lose it; if a golfer wins a tournament, fifty or a hundred others must fail to win. In situations like these, at least, success is much less frequent than failure. Varying the formula, a sports writer might tell how an individual lost the game but learned some important moral lesson—for instance, the importance of fair play. But here again, in real life, people achieve such compensations only occasionally. Defeat, in fact, sometimes embitters people and makes them less able to cope with life than before. Thus we need to understand and perhaps expect defeat as well as victory.

The second justification for an unhappy ending is its value in forcing us to ponder the complexities of life. The story with a happy ending has been "wrapped up" for us: it sends the reader away feeling pleasantly and vaguely satisfied with the world, and it requires no further thought. The unhappy ending, on the other hand, may cause readers to brood over the outcome, to relive the story in their minds, and by searching out its implications to get much more meaning and significance from it. Just as we can judge individuals better when we see how they behave in times of trouble, so we can see deeper into life when it is pried open for inspection. The unhappy ending is also more likely to raise significant issues. Shakespeare's tragedies reverberate in our minds much longer and more resonantly than his comedies. The ending of "The Most Dangerous Game" resolves all our anxieties, but the ending of "Hunters in the Snow" forces us to think about the mysteries and contradictions of human nature.

Readers of literary fiction evaluate an ending not by whether it is happy or unhappy but by whether it is logical within the story's own terms and whether it affords a full, believable revelation. An ending that meets these tests can be profoundly satisfying, whether happy or unhappy. In fact, some artistically satisfying stories have no ending at all in the sense that the central conflict is resolved in favor of protagonist or antagonist. In real life some problems are never solved and some battles never permanently won. A story, therefore, may have an **indeterminate ending,** one in which no definitive conclusion is reached. There must be some kind of conclusion, of course; a story, which must have artistic unity, cannot simply stop. But the conclusion need not be in terms of a resolved conflict. We cannot be sure whether Tub and Frank in "Hunters in the Snow" will maintain their alliance, or what the ultimate fate of their "friendship" might be. But the story is more effective without a definite resolution, for it leaves us to ponder the complex psychological dynamics that operate within human relationships.

Artistic unity is essential to a good plot. There must be nothing in the story that is irrelevant, that does not contribute to the meaning; there should be nothing there for its own sake or its own excitement. Good writers exercise rigorous selection: they include nothing that does not advance the central intention of the story. But they not only select; they also arrange. Authors place the story's incidents and scenes in the most effective order, which is not necessarily the chronological order (although, when we place them in chronological order, they must form a logical progression). In a carefully unified story each event grows out of the preceding one and leads logically to the next. The author links scenes together in a chain of cause and effect. With such a story the reader should not feel that events might as easily have taken one turn as another; at the same time, the author's handling of plot should not be heavy-handed but should have a quality of natural inevitability, given the specific set of characters and the initial situation.

An author who includes a turn in the plot that is unjustified by the situation or the characters is indulging in **plot manipulation.** An unmotivated action is one instance of such manipulation. Similarly, the reader feels manipulated if the plot relies too heavily on chance or on coincidence to provide a resolution to a story. This kind of resolution is sometimes called a **deus ex machina** (Latin for "god from a machine") after the practice of some ancient Greek dramatists in having a god descend from heaven at the last minute (presented in the theater by means of a mechanical stage device) to rescue the protagonist from some impossible situation. But while this was an accepted convention in Greek drama, such a resolution is seldom convincing in fiction. The action should grow organically out of the plot rather than end with an arbitrary, chance resolution for which the author has laid no groundwork earlier in the story.

Chance cannot be barred from fiction, of course, any more than it can be barred from life; the same is true of **coincidence.** Chance is the occurrence of an event that has no apparent cause in previous events or in predisposition of character, while coincidence is the chance occurrence of *two* events that may have a peculiar correspondence. But if an author uses an improbable chance event to resolve a story, the story loses its sense of conviction and thus its power to move the reader. The use of coincidence in fiction is even more problematic, since coincidence is chance compounded. Coincidence may justifiably be used to initiate a story, and occasionally to complicate it, but not to resolve it. Its use is objectionable in proportion to its improbability, its importance to the story, and its nearness to the ending. If two characters in a story both start talking of the same topic at once, it may be a coincidence but not necessarily an objectionable one. But if both decide suddenly and at the same time to kill their mothers, the coincidence would be less believable. The use of even a highly improbable coincidence may be perfectly appropriate at the start of a story. Just as a chemist may wonder what will happen if he places certain chemical elements together in a test tube, an author may wonder what will happen if two former lovers accidentally meet in Majorca, where they longed as young lovers to go, many years after they have each married someone else. The improbable initial situation is justified because it offers a chance to observe human nature in conditions that may be particularly revealing, and readers of literary fiction should demand only that the author develop a story logically from that initial situation. But the writer who uses a similar coincidence to resolve a story is imposing an unlikely pattern on human experience rather than revealing any human truth. It is often said that fact is stranger than fiction: in fact, convincing fiction often cannot include some of the more bizarre occurrences (including chance and coincidence) that sometimes happen in life. In life, almost any sequence of events is possible; but in a story the sequence must be plausible in order to convince and hold the reader.

There are various approaches to the analysis of plot. We may, if we wish, draw diagrams of different kinds of plots or trace the development of **rising action, climax,** and **falling action.** Tracing such structural patterns, however, if they are concerned only with examining the plot in isolation, will not take us very far into the story. A more profitable approach is to consider the *function* of plot in trying to understand the relationship of each incident to the larger meaning of the story. In literary fiction, plot is important for what it reveals. Analyzing a story by focusing on its central conflict may be especially fruitful, for this quickly takes the reader to the primary issue in the story. In evaluating fiction for its quality, it is useful to examine the way incidents and scenes are connected as a way of testing the story's plausibility and unity. In any good story, plot is inextricable from other elements of fiction to be considered in later chapters: characterization, point of view, and so forth. It provides a kind of map, or guide, but it cannot serve as a substitute for the reader's journey into the author's fictional landscape.

> **REVIEWING CHAPTER TWO**
> 1. Define the term "plot."
> 2. Describe the importance of conflict in fiction.
> 3. Differentiate between the protagonist and the antagonist in a story.
> 4. Explore the importance of the element of surprise in fiction.
> 5. Consider the differences between a happy, an unhappy, and an indeterminate ending.
> 6. Review the importance of artistic unity in literary fiction.

Graham Greene

The Destructors

1

It was the eve of August Bank Holiday° that the latest recruit became the leader of the Wormsley Common Gang. No one was surprised except Mike, but Mike at the age of nine was surprised by everything. "If you don't shut your mouth," somebody once said to him, "you'll get a frog down it." After that Mike had kept his teeth tightly clamped except when the surprise was too great.

The new recruit had been with the gang since the beginning of the summer holidays, and there were possibilities about his brooding silence that all recognized. He never wasted a word even to tell his name until that was required of him by the rules. When he said "Trevor" it was a statement of fact, not as it would have been with the others a statement of shame or defiance. Nor did anyone laugh except Mike,

---

THE DESTRUCTORS   First published in 1954. The setting is London nine years after the conclusion of World War II (1939–1945). During the first sustained bombing attacks on London ("the first blitz") from September 1940 to May 1941, many families slept in the Underground (i.e., subway) stations, which were used as bomb shelters. "Trevor" was typically an upper-class English name. Sir Christopher Wren (1632–1723), England's most famous architect, designed St. Paul's Cathedral and many other late seventeenth- and early eighteenth-century buildings. Graham Greene (1904–1991), who was born just outside London, lived in that city at various stages of his life.

Bank Holiday: three-day weekend in Britain, one of several during the year

who finding himself without support and meeting the dark gaze of the newcomer opened his mouth and was quiet again. There was every reason why T., as he was afterwards referred to, should have been an object of mockery—there was his name (and they substituted the initial because otherwise they had no excuse not to laugh at it), the fact that his father, a former architect and present clerk, had "come down in the world" and that his mother considered herself better than the neighbors. What but an odd quality of danger, of the unpredictable, established him in the gang without any ignoble ceremony of initiation?

The gang met every morning in an impromptu car-park, the site of the last bomb of the first blitz. The leader, who was known as Blackie, claimed to have heard it fall, and no one was precise enough in his dates to point out that he would have been one year old and fast asleep on the down platform of Wormsley Common Underground Station. On one side of the car-park leant the first occupied house, No. 3, of the shattered Northwood Terrace—literally leant, for it had suffered from the blast of the bomb and the side walls were supported on wooden struts. A smaller bomb and some incendiaries had fallen beyond, so that the house stuck up like a jagged tooth and carried on the further wall relics of its neighbor, a dado, the remains of a fireplace. T., whose words were almost confined to voting "Yes" or "No" to the plan of operations proposed each day by Blackie, once startled the whole gang by saying broodingly, "Wren built that house, father says."

"Who's Wren?"

5   "The man who built St. Paul's."

"Who cares?" Blackie said. "It's only Old Misery's."

Old Misery—whose real name was Thomas—had once been a builder and decorator. He lived alone in the crippled house, doing for himself: once a week you could see him coming back across the common with bread and vegetables, and once as the boys played in the car-park he put his head over the smashed wall of his garden and looked at them.

"Been to the lav," one of the boys said, for it was common knowledge that since the bombs fell something had gone wrong with the pipes of the house and Old Misery was too mean to spend money on the property. He could do the redecorating himself at cost price, but he had never learnt plumbing. The lav was a wooden shed at the bottom of the narrow garden with a star-shaped hole in the door: it had escaped the blast which had smashed the house next door and sucked out the window-frames of No. 3.

The next time the gang became aware of Mr. Thomas was more surprising. Blackie, Mike and a thin yellow boy, who for some reason was called by his surname Summers, met him on the common coming back from the market. Mr. Thomas stopped them. He said glumly, "You belong to the lot that play in the car-park?"

Mike was about to answer when Blackie stopped him. As the leader 10 he had responsibilities. "Suppose we are?" he said ambiguously.

"I got some chocolates," Mr. Thomas said. "Don't like 'em myself. Here you are. Not enough to go round, I don't suppose. There never is," he added with somber conviction. He handed over three packets of Smarties.

The gang were puzzled and perturbed by this action and tried to explain it away. "Bet someone dropped them and he picked 'em up," somebody suggested.

"Pinched 'em and then got in a bleeding funk," another thought aloud.

"It's a bribe," Summers said. "He wants us to stop bouncing balls on his wall."

"We'll show him we don't take bribes," Blackie said, and they sacri- 15 ficed the whole morning to the game of bouncing that only Mike was young enough to enjoy. There was no sign from Mr. Thomas.

Next day T. astonished them all. He was late at the rendezvous, and the voting for the day's exploit took place without him. At Blackie's suggestion the gang was to disperse in pairs, take buses at random and see how many free rides could be snatched from unwary conductors (the operation was to be carried out in pairs to avoid cheating). They were drawing lots for their companions when T. arrived.

"Where you been, T.?" Blackie asked. "You can't vote now. You know the rules."

"I've been *there*," T. said. He looked at the ground, as though he had thoughts to hide.

"Where?"

"At Old Misery's." Mike's mouth opened and then hurriedly closed 20 again with a click. He had remembered the frog.

"At Old Misery's?" Blackie said. There was nothing in the rules against it, but he had a sensation that T. was treading on dangerous ground. He asked hopefully, "Did you break in?"

"No. I rang the bell."

"And what did you say?"

"I said I wanted to see his house."

"What did he do?" 25

"He showed it to me."

"Pinch anything?"

"No."

"What did you do it for then?"

30   The gang had gathered round: it was as though an impromptu court were about to form and to try some case of deviation. T. said, "It's a beautiful house," and still watching the ground, meeting no one's eyes, he licked his lips first one way, then the other.

"What do you mean, a beautiful house?" Blackie asked with scorn.

"It's got a staircase two hundred years old like a corkscrew. Nothing holds it up."

"What do you mean, nothing holds it up. Does it float?"

"It's to do with opposite forces, Old Misery said."

35   "What else?"

"There's paneling."

"Like in the Blue Boar?"

"Two hundred years old."

"Is Old Misery two hundred years old?"

40   Mike laughed suddenly and then was quiet again. The meeting was in a serious mood. For the first time since T. had strolled into the car-park on the first day of the holidays his position was in danger. It only needed a single use of his real name and the gang would be at his heels.

"What did you do it for?" Blackie asked. He was just, he had no jealousy, he was anxious to retain T. in the gang if he could. It was the word "beautiful" that worried him—that belonged to a class world that you could still see parodied at the Wormsley Common Empire° by a man wearing a top hat and a monocle, with a haw-haw accent. He was tempted to say, "My dear Trevor, old chap," and unleash his hell hounds. "If you'd broken in," he said sadly—that indeed would have been an exploit worthy of the gang.

"This was better," T. said. "I found out things." He continued to stare at his feet, not meeting anybody's eye, as though he were absorbed in some dream he was unwilling—or ashamed—to share.

"What things?"

"Old Misery's going to be away all tomorrow and Bank Holiday."

45   Blackie said with relief, "You mean we could break in?"

"And pinch things?" somebody asked.

Blackie said, "Nobody's going to pinch things. Breaking in—that's good enough, isn't it? We don't want any court stuff."

"I don't want to pinch anything," T. said. "I've got a better idea."

"What is it?"

50   T. raised his eyes, as grey and disturbed as the drab August day. "We'll pull it down," he said. "We'll destroy it."

Wormsley Common Empire: a music hall for revues and popular entertainments

Blackie gave a single hoot of laughter and then, like Mike, fell quiet, daunted by the serious implacable gaze. "What'd the police be doing all the time?" he asked.

"They'd never know. We'd do it from inside. I've found a way in." He said with a sort of intensity, "We'd be like worms, don't you see, in an apple. When we came out again there'd be nothing there, no staircase, no panels, nothing but just walls, and then we'd make the walls fall down—somehow."

"We'd go to jug," Blackie said.

"Who's to prove? And anyway we wouldn't have pinched anything." He added without the smallest flicker of glee, "There wouldn't be anything to pinch after we'd finished."

"I've never heard of going to prison for breaking things," Summers said.   55

"There wouldn't be time," Blackie said. "I've seen housebreakers at work."

"There are twelve of us," T. said. "We'd organize."

"None of us know how . . ."

"I know," T. said. He looked across at Blackie. "Have you got a better plan?"

"Today," Mike said tactlessly, "we're pinching free rides . . ."   60

"Free rides," T. said. "You can stand down, Blackie, if you'd rather . . ."

"The gang's got to vote."

"Put it up then."

Blackie said uneasily, "It's proposed that tomorrow and Monday we destroy Old Misery's house."

"Here, here," said a fat boy called Joe.   65

"Who's in favor?"

T. said, "It's carried."

"How do we start?" Summers asked.

"He'll tell you," Blackie said. It was the end of his leadership. He went away to the back of the car-park and began to kick a stone, dribbling it this way and that. There was only one old Morris in the park, for few cars were left there except lorries: without an attendant there was no safety. He took a flying kick at the car and scraped a little paint off the rear mudguard. Beyond, paying no more attention to him than to a stranger, the gang had gathered round T.; Blackie was dimly aware of the fickleness of favor. He thought of going home, of never returning, of letting them all discover the hollowness of T.'s leadership, but suppose after all what T. proposed was possible—nothing like it had ever been done before. The fame of the Wormsley Common car-park gang would surely reach around London. There would be headlines in the papers. Even the grown-up gangs who ran the betting at the all-in wrestling and the barrow-boys would hear with respect of how Old Misery's house had been destroyed. Driven by the pure, simple and altruistic ambition of fame for the gang, Blackie came back to where T. stood in the shadow of Misery's wall.

70 T. was giving his orders with decision: it was as though this plan had been with him all his life, pondered through the seasons, now in his fifteenth year crystallized with the pain of puberty. "You," he said to Mike, "bring some big nails, the biggest you can find, and a hammer. Anyone else who can better bring a hammer and a screwdriver. We'll need plenty of them. Chisels too. We can't have too many chisels. Can anybody bring a saw?"

"I can," Mike said.

"Not a child's saw," T. said. "A real saw."

Blackie realized he had raised his hand like any ordinary member of the gang.

"Right, you bring one, Blackie. But now there's a difficulty. We want a hacksaw."

75 "What's a hacksaw?" someone asked.

"You can get 'em at Woolworth's," Summers said.

The fat boy called Joe said gloomily, "I knew it would end in a collection."

"I'll get one myself," T. said. "I don't want your money. But I can't buy a sledge-hammer."

Blackie said, "They are working on No. 15. I know where they'll leave their stuff for Bank Holiday."

80 "Then that's all," T. said. "We meet here at nine sharp."

"I've got to go to church," Mike said.

"Come over the wall and whistle. We'll let you in."

2

On Sunday morning all were punctual except Blackie, even Mike. Mike had had a stroke of luck. His mother felt ill, his father was tired after Saturday night, and he was told to go to church alone with many warnings of what would happen if he strayed. Blackie had had difficulty in smuggling out the saw, and then in finding the sledge-hammer at the back of No. 15. He approached the house from a lane at the rear of the garden, for fear of the policeman's beat along the main road. The tired evergreens kept off a stormy sun: another wet Bank Holiday was being prepared over the Atlantic, beginning in swirls of dust under the trees. Blackie climbed the wall into Misery's garden.

There was no sign of anybody anywhere. The lav stood like a tomb in a neglected graveyard. The curtains were drawn. The house slept. Blackie lumbered nearer with the saw and the sledge-hammer. Perhaps after all nobody had turned up: the plan had been a wild invention: they had woken wiser. But when he came close to the back door he could hear a confusion of sound hardly louder than a hive in swarm: a clickety-clack, a bang bang, a scraping, a creaking, a sudden painful crack. He thought: it's true, and whistled.

They opened the back door to him and he came in. He had at once   85 the impression of organization, very different from the old happy-go-lucky ways under his leadership. For a while he wandered up and down stairs looking for T. Nobody addressed him: he had a sense of great urgency, and already he could begin to see the plan. The interior of the house was being carefully demolished without touching the outer walls. Summers with hammer and chisel was ripping out the skirting-boards in the ground floor dining-room: he had already smashed the panels of the door. In the same room Joe was heaving up the parquet blocks, exposing the soft wood floor-boards over the cellar. Coils of wire came out of the damaged skirting and Mike sat happily on the floor clipping the wires.

On the curved stairs two of the gang were working hard with an inadequate child's saw on the banisters—when they saw Blackie's big saw they signaled for it wordlessly. When he next saw them a quarter of the banisters had been dropped into the hall. He found T. at last in the bathroom—he sat moodily in the least cared-for room in the house, listening to the sounds coming up from below.

"You've really done it," Blackie said with awe. "What's going to happen?"

"We've only just begun," T. said. He looked at the sledge-hammer and gave his instructions. "You stay here and break the bath and the wash-basin. Don't bother about the pipes. They come later."

Mike appeared at the door. "I've finished the wires, T.," he said.

"Good. You've just got to go wandering round now. The kitchen's   90 in the basement. Smash all the china and glass and bottles you can lay hold of. Don't turn on the taps—we don't want a flood—yet. Then go into all the rooms and turn out drawers. If they are locked get one of the others to break them open. Tear up any papers you find and smash all the ornaments. Better take a carving-knife with you from the kitchen. The bedroom's opposite here. Open the pillows and tear up the sheets. That's enough for the moment. And you, Blackie, when you've finished in here crack the plaster in the passage up with your sledge-hammer."

"What are you going to do?" Blackie asked.

"I'm looking for something special," T. said.

It was nearly lunch-time before Blackie had finished and went in search of T. Chaos had advanced. The kitchen was a shambles of broken glass and china. The dining-room was stripped of parquet, the skirting was up, the door had been taken off its hinges, and the destroyers had moved up a floor. Streaks of light came in through the closed shutters where they worked with the seriousness of creators—and destruction after all is a form of creation. A kind of imagination had seen this house as it had now become.

Mike said, "I've got to go home for dinner."

95   "Who else?" T. asked, but all the others on one excuse or another had brought provisions with them.

They squatted in the ruins of the room and swapped unwanted sandwiches. Half an hour for lunch and they were at work again. By the time Mike returned, they were on the top floor, and by six the superficial damage was completed. The doors were all off, all the skirtings raised, the furniture pillaged and ripped and smashed—no one could have slept in the house except on a bed of broken plaster. T. gave his orders—eight o'clock next morning, and to escape notice they climbed singly over the garden wall, into the car-park. Only Blackie and T. were left: the light had nearly gone, and when they touched a switch, nothing worked—Mike had done his job thoroughly.

"Did you find anything special?" Blackie asked.

T. nodded. "Come over here," he said, "and look." Out of both pockets he drew bundles of pound notes. "Old Misery's savings," he said. "Mike ripped out the mattress, but he missed them."

"What are you going to do? Share them?"

100   "We aren't thieves," T. said. "Nobody's going to steal anything from this house. I kept these for you and me—a celebration." He knelt down on the floor and counted them out—there were seventy in all. "We'll burn them," he said, "one by one," and taking it in turns they held a note upwards and lit the top corner, so that the flame burnt slowly towards their fingers. The grey ash floated above them and fell on their heads like age. "I'd like to see Old Misery's face when we are through," T. said.

"You hate him a lot?" Blackie asked.

"Of course I don't hate him," T. said. "There'd be no fun if I hated him." The last burning note illuminated his brooding face. "All this hate and love," he said, "it's soft, it's hooey. There's only things, Blackie," and he looked round the room crowded with the unfamiliar shadows of half things, broken things, former things. "I'll race you home, Blackie," he said.

3

Next morning the serious destruction started. Two were missing—Mike and another boy whose parents were off to Southend and Brighton in spite of the slow warm drops that had begun to fall and the rumble of thunder in the estuary like the first guns of the old blitz. "We've got to hurry," T. said.

Summers was restive. "Haven't we done enough?" he said. "I've been given a bob for slot machines. This is like work."

"We've hardly started," T. said. "Why, there's all the floor left, and   105
the stairs. We haven't taken out a single window. You voted like the others. We are going to *destroy* this house. There won't be anything left when we've finished."

They began again on the first floor picking up the top floorboards next to the outer wall, leaving the joists exposed. Then they sawed through the joists and retreated into the hall, as what was left of the floor heeled and sank. They had learnt with practice, and the second floor collapsed more easily. By the evening an odd exhilaration seized them as they looked down the great hollow of the house. They ran risks and made mistakes: when they thought of the windows it was too late to reach them. "Cor," Joe said, and dropped a penny down in the dry rubble-filled well. It cracked and span among the broken glass.

"Why did we start this?" Summers asked with astonishment; T. was already on the ground, digging at the rubble, clearing a space along the outer wall. "Turn on the taps," he said. "It's too dark for anyone to see now, and in the morning it won't matter." The water overtook them on the stairs and fell through the floorless rooms.

It was then they heard Mike's whistle at the back. "Something's wrong," Blackie said. They could hear his urgent breathing as they unlocked the door.

"The bogies?"° Summers asked.

"Old Misery," Mike said. "He's on his way." He put his head be-   110
tween his knees and retched. "Ran all the way," he said with pride.

"But why?" T. said. "He told me . . ." He protested with the fury of the child he had never been, "It isn't fair."

"He was down at Southend," Mike said, "and he was on the train coming back. Said it was too cold and wet." He paused and gazed at the water. "My, you've had a storm here. Is the roof leaking?"

"How long will he be?"

bogies: police

"Five minutes. I gave Ma the slip and ran."

115   "We better clear," Summers said. "We've done enough, anyway."

"Oh, no, we haven't. Anybody could do this—" "This" was the shattered hollowed house with nothing left but the walls. Yet the walls could be preserved. Façades were valuable. They could build inside again more beautifully than before. This could again be a home. He said angrily, "We've got to finish. Don't move. Let me think."

"There's no time," a boy said.

"There's got to be a way," T. said. "We couldn't have got this far . . ."

"We've done a lot," Blackie said.

120   "No. No, we haven't. Somebody watch the front."

"We can't do any more."

"He may come in at the back."

"Watch the back too." T. began to plead. "Just give me a minute and I'll fix it. I swear I'll fix it." But his authority had gone with his ambiguity. He was only one of the gang. "Please," he said.

"Please," Summers mimicked him, and then suddenly struck home with the fatal name. "Run along home, Trevor."

125   T. stood with his back to the rubble like a boxer knocked groggy against the ropes. He had no words as his dreams shook and slid. Then Blackie acted before the gang had time to laugh, pushing Summers backward. "I'll watch the front, T.," he said, and cautiously he opened the shutters of the hall. The grey wet common stretched ahead, and the lamps gleamed in the puddles. "Someone's coming, T. No, it's not him. What's your plan, T.?"

"Tell Mike to go out to the lav and hide close beside it. When he hears me whistle he's got to count ten and start to shout."

"Shout what?"

"Oh, 'Help,' anything."

"You hear, Mike," Blackie said. He was the leader again. He took a quick look between the shutters. "He's coming, T."

130   "Quick, Mike. The lav. Stay here, Blackie, all of you till I yell."

"Where are you going, T.?"

"Don't worry. I'll see to this. I said I would, didn't I?"

Old Misery came limping off the common. He had mud on his shoes and he stopped to scrape them on the pavement's edge. He didn't want to soil his house, which stood jagged and dark between the bomb-sites, saved so narrowly, as he believed, from destruction. Even the fan-light had been left unbroken by the bomb's blast. Somewhere somebody whistled. Old Misery looked sharply round. He didn't trust whistles. A child was shouting: it seemed to come from his own garden.

Then a boy ran into the road from the car-park. "Mr. Thomas," he called. "Mr. Thomas."

"What is it?"

"I'm terribly sorry, Mr. Thomas. One of us got taken short, and we   135
thought you wouldn't mind, and now he can't get out."

"What do you mean, boy?"

"He's got stuck in your lav."

"He'd no business . . . Haven't I seen you before?"

"You showed me your house."

"So I did. So I did. That doesn't give you the right to . . ."   140

"Do hurry, Mr. Thomas. He'll suffocate."

"Nonsense. He can't suffocate. Wait till I put my bag in."

"I'll carry your bag."

"Oh no, you don't. I carry my own."

"This way, Mr. Thomas."   145

"I can't get in the garden that way. I've got to go through the house."

"But you *can* get in the garden this way, Mr. Thomas. We often do."

"You often do?" He followed the boy with a scandalized fascination. "When? What right? . . ."

"Do you see . . . ? The wall's low."

"I'm not going to climb walls into my own garden. It's absurd."   150

"This is how we do it. One foot here, one foot there, and over." The boy's face peered down, an arm shot out, and Mr. Thomas found his bag taken and deposited on the other side of the wall.

"Give me back my bag," Mr. Thomas said. From the loo° a boy yelled and yelled. "I'll call the police."

"Your bag's all right, Mr. Thomas. Look. One foot there. On your right. Now just above. To your left." Mr. Thomas climbed over his own garden wall. "Here's your bag, Mr. Thomas."

"I'll have the wall built up," Mr. Thomas said. "I'll not have you boys coming over here, using my loo." He stumbled on the path, but the boy caught his elbow and supported him. "Thank you, thank you, my boy," he murmured automatically. Somebody shouted again through the dark. "I'm coming, I'm coming," Mr. Thomas called. He said to the boy beside him, "I'm not unreasonable. Been a boy myself. As long as things are done regular. I don't mind you playing round the place Saturday mornings. Sometimes I like company. Only it's got to be regular. One of you asks leave and I say Yes. Sometimes I'll say No. Won't

loo: outdoor toilet (an older term for "lav")

feel like it. And you come in at the front door and out at the back. No
garden walls."

155   "Do get him out, Mr. Thomas."

"He won't come to any harm in my loo," Mr. Thomas said, stumbling slowly down the garden. "Oh, my rheumatics," he said. "Always
get 'em on Bank Holiday. I've got to go careful. There's loose stones
here. Give me your hand. Do you know what my horoscope said yesterday? 'Abstain from any dealings in first half of week. Danger of serious crash.' That might be on this path," Mr. Thomas said. "They speak
in parables and double meanings." He paused at the door of the loo.
"What's the matter in there?" he called. There was no reply.

"Perhaps he's fainted," the boy said.

"Not in my loo. Here, you come out," Mr. Thomas said, and giving
a great jerk at the door he nearly fell on his back when it swung easily
open. A hand first supported him and then pushed him hard. His head
hit the opposite wall and he sat heavily down. His bag hit his feet. A
hand whipped the key out of the lock and the door slammed. "Let me
out," he called, and heard the key turn in the lock. "A serious crash," he
thought, and felt dithery and confused and old.

A voice spoke to him softly through the star-shaped hole in the
door. "Don't worry, Mr. Thomas," it said, "we won't hurt you, not if you
stay quiet."

160   Mr. Thomas put his head between his hands and pondered. He had
noticed that there was only one lorry in the car-park, and he felt certain that the driver would not come for it before the morning. Nobody
could hear him from the road in front, and the lane at the back was seldom used. Anyone who passed there would be hurrying home and
would not pause for what they would certainly take to be drunken cries.
And if he did call "Help," who, on a lonely Bank Holiday evening,
would have the courage to investigate? Mr. Thomas sat on the loo and
pondered with the wisdom of age.

After a while it seemed to him that there were sounds in the silence—they were faint and came from the direction of his house. He
stood up and peered through the ventilation-hole—between the cracks
in one of the shutters he saw a light, not the light of a lamp, but the wavering light that a candle might give. Then he thought he heard the
sound of hammering and scraping and chipping. He thought of burglars—perhaps they had employed the boy as a scout, but why should
burglars engage in what sounded more and more like a stealthy form of
carpentry? Mr. Thomas let out an experimental yell, but nobody answered. The noise could not even have reached his enemies.

4

Mike had gone home to bed, but the rest stayed. The question of leadership no longer concerned the gang. With nails, chisels, screwdrivers, anything that was sharp and penetrating, they moved around the inner walls worrying at the mortar between the bricks. They started too high, and it was Blackie who hit on the damp course and realized the work could be halved if they weakened the joints immediately above. It was a long, tiring, unamusing job, but at last it was finished. The gutted house stood there balanced on a few inches of mortar between the damp course and the bricks.

There remained the most dangerous task of all, out in the open at the edge of the bomb-site. Summers was sent to watch the road for passers-by, and Mr. Thomas, sitting on the loo, heard clearly now the sound of sawing. It no longer came from his house, and that a little re-assured him. He felt less concerned. Perhaps the other noises too had no significance.

A voice spoke to him through the hole. "Mr. Thomas."

"Let me out," Mr. Thomas said sternly.   165

"Here's a blanket," the voice said, and a long grey sausage was worked through the hole and fell in swathes over Mr. Thomas's head.

"There's nothing personal," the voice said. "We want you to be comfortable tonight."

"Tonight," Mr. Thomas repeated incredulously.

"Catch," the voice said. "Penny buns—we've buttered them, and sausage-rolls. We don't want you to starve, Mr. Thomas."

Mr. Thomas pleaded desperately. "A joke's a joke, boy. Let me out   170
and I won't say a thing. I've got rheumatics. I got to sleep comfortable."

"You wouldn't be comfortable, not in your house, you wouldn't. Not now."

"What do you mean, boy?" but the footsteps receded. There was only the silence of night: no sound of sawing. Mr. Thomas tried one more yell, but he was daunted and rebuked by the silence—a long way off an owl hooted and made away again on its muffled flight through the soundless world.

At seven next morning the driver came to fetch his lorry. He climbed into the seat and tried to start the engine. He was vaguely aware of a voice shouting, but it didn't concern him. At last the engine responded and he backed the lorry until it touched the great wooden shore that supported Mr. Thomas's house. That way he could drive right out and down the street without reversing. The lorry moved forward, was momentarily checked as though something were pulling it from behind, and then went on to the sound of a long rumbling crash. The driver was astonished to see bricks bouncing ahead of him, while stones hit the roof of his cab. He put on his brakes. When he climbed out the whole landscape had suddenly altered. There was no house beside the car-park, only a hill of rubble. He went round and examined the back of his car for damage, and found a rope tied there that was still twisted at the other end round part of a wooden strut.

The driver again became aware of somebody shouting. It came from the wooden erection which was the nearest thing to a house in that desolation of broken brick. The driver climbed the smashed wall and unlocked the door. Mr. Thomas came out of the loo. He was wearing a grey blanket to which flakes of pastry adhered. He gave a sobbing cry. "My house," he said. "Where's my house?"

175 "Search me," the driver said. His eye lit on the remains of a bath and what had once been a dresser and he began to laugh. There wasn't anything left anywhere.

"How dare you laugh," Mr. Thomas said. "It was my house. My house."

"I'm sorry," the driver said, making heroic efforts, but when he remembered the sudden check to his lorry, the crash of bricks falling, he became convulsed again. One moment the house had stood there with such dignity between the bomb-sites like a man in a top hat, and then, bang, crash, there wasn't anything left—not anything. He said, "I'm sorry. I can't help it, Mr. Thomas. There's nothing personal, but you got to admit it's funny."

QUESTIONS

1. Who is the protagonist in this story—Trevor, Blackie, or the gang? Who or what is the antagonist? Identify the conflicts of the story.
2. How is suspense created?
3. This story uses the most common basic formula of commercial fiction: protagonist aims at a goal, is confronted with various obstacles between himself and his goal, overcomes the obstacles, and achieves his goal. How does this story differ from commercial fiction in its use of this formula? Does the story have a happy ending?
4. Discuss the gang's motivations, taking into account (a) the age and beauty of the house, (b) Blackie's reasons for not going home after losing his position of leadership, (c) the seriousness with which the boys work at their task, and their loss of concern over their leadership, (d) the burning of the pound notes, (e) their consideration for Old Misery, (f) the lorry driver's reaction. What characteristics do the gang's two named exploits—pinching free rides and destroying the house—have in common?

5. Of what significance, if any, is the setting of this story in blitzed London? Does the story have anything to say about the consequences of war? About the causes of war?

6. Explain as fully as you can the causes of the gang's delinquency, taking into account (a) their reaction to the name Trevor, (b) their reaction to Old Misery's gift of chocolates, (c) Blackie's reaction to the word "beautiful," (d) Trevor's comments on "hate and love," (e) Summers's reaction to the word "Please," (f) the setting.

7. What good qualities do the delinquents in this story have? Do they differ as a group from other youth gangs you have read or know about? If so, account for the differences.

8. On the surface this is a story of action, suspense, and adventure. At a deeper level it is about delinquency, war, and human nature. Try to sum up what the story says about human nature in general.

Alice Munro
How I Met My Husband

We heard the plane come over at noon, roaring through the radio news, and we were sure it was going to hit the house, so we all ran out into the yard. We saw it come over the treetops, all red and silver, the first close-up plane I ever saw. Mrs. Peebles screamed.

"Crash landing," their little boy said. Joey was his name.

"It's okay," said Dr. Peebles. "He knows what he's doing." Dr. Peebles was only an animal doctor, but had a calming way of talking, like any doctor.

This was my first job—working for Dr. and Mrs. Peebles, who had bought an old house out on the Fifth Line, about five miles out of town. It was just when the trend was starting of town people buying up old farms, not to work them but to live on them.

We watched the plane land across the road, where the fairgrounds used to be. It did make a good landing field, nice and level for the old race track, and the barns and display sheds torn down now for scrap   5

How I Met My Husband   First published in her collection *Something I've Been Meaning to Tell You* in 1974. Alice Munro (b. 1931) grew up in rural southwestern Ontario, where much of her fiction is set. She attended the University of Western Ontario for two years and moved to British Columbia, where she lived until 1972; she now lives in Clinton, Ontario. She is the author of nine collections of short fiction, most recently *Runaway* (2004).

lumber so there was nothing in the way. Even the old grandstand bays had burned.

"All right," said Mrs. Peebles, snappy as she always was when she got over her nerves. "Let's go back in the house. Let's not stand here gawking like a set of farmers."

She didn't say that to hurt my feelings. It never occurred to her.

I was just setting the dessert down when Loretta Bird arrived, out of breath, at the screen door.

"I thought it was going to crash into the house and kill youse all!"

10   She lived on the next place and the Peebleses thought she was a country-woman, they didn't know the difference. She and her husband didn't farm, he worked on the roads and had a bad name for drinking. They had seven children and couldn't get credit at the HiWay Grocery. The Peebleses made her welcome, not knowing any better, as I say, and offered her dessert.

Dessert was never anything to write home about, at their place. A dish of Jell-O or sliced bananas or fruit out of a tin. "Have a house without a pie, be ashamed until you die," my mother used to say, but Mrs. Peebles operated differently.

Loretta Bird saw me getting the can of peaches.

"Oh, never mind," she said. "I haven't got the right kind of a stomach to trust what comes out of those tins, I can only eat home canning."

I could have slapped her. I bet she never put down fruit in her life.

15   "I know what he's landed here for," she said. "He's got permission to use the fairgrounds and take people up for rides. It costs a dollar. It's the same fellow who was over at Palmerston last week and was up the lakeshore before that. I wouldn't go up, if you paid me."

"I'd jump at the chance," Dr. Peebles said. "I'd like to see this neighborhood from the air."

Mrs. Peebles said she would just as soon see it from the ground. Joey said he wanted to go and Heather did, too. Joey was nine and Heather was seven.

"Would you, Edie?" Heather said.

I said I didn't know. I was scared, but I never admitted that, especially in front of children I was taking care of.

20   "People are going to be coming out here in their cars raising dust and trampling your property, if I was you I would complain," Loretta said. She hooked her legs around the chair rung and I knew we were in for a lengthy visit. After Dr. Peebles went back to his office or out on his next call and Mrs. Peebles went for her nap, she would hang around me while

I was trying to do the dishes. She would pass remarks about the Peebleses in their own house.

"She wouldn't find time to lay down in the middle of the day, if she had seven kids like I got."

She asked me did they fight and did they keep things in the dresser drawer not to have babies with. She said it was a sin if they did. I pretended I didn't know what she was talking about.

I was fifteen and away from home for the first time. My parents had made the effort and sent me to high school for a year, but I didn't like it. I was shy of strangers and the work was hard, they didn't make it nice for you or explain the way they do now. At the end of the year the averages were published in the paper, and mine came out at the very bottom, 37 percent. My father said that's enough and I didn't blame him. The last thing I wanted, anyway, was to go on and end up teaching school. It happened the very day the paper came out with my disgrace in it, Dr. Peebles was staying at our place for dinner, having just helped one of our cows have twins, and he said I looked smart to him and his wife was looking for a girl to help. He said she felt tied down, with the two children, out in the country. I guess she would, my mother said, being polite, though I could tell from her face she was wondering what on earth it would be like to have only two children and no barn work, and then to be complaining.

When I went home I would describe to them the work I had to do, and it made everybody laugh. Mrs. Peebles had an automatic washer and dryer, the first I ever saw. I have had those in my own home for such a long time now it's hard to remember how much of a miracle it was to me, not having to struggle with the wringer and hang up and haul down. Let alone not having to heat water. Then there was practically no baking. Mrs. Peebles said she couldn't make pie crust, the most amazing thing I ever heard a woman admit. I could, of course, and I could make light biscuits and a white cake and dark cake, but they didn't want it, she said they watched their figures. The only thing I didn't like about working there, in fact, was feeling half hungry a lot of the time. I used to bring back a box of doughnuts made out at home, and hide them under my bed. The children found out, and I didn't mind sharing, but I thought I better bind them to secrecy.

The day after the plane landed Mrs. Peebles put both children in   25
the car and drove over to Chesley, to get their hair cut. There was a good woman then at Chesley for doing hair. She got hers done at the same place, Mrs. Peebles did, and that meant they would be gone a good while. She had to pick a day Dr. Peebles wasn't going out into the

country, she didn't have her own car. Cars were still in short supply then, after the war.

I loved being left in the house alone, to do my work at leisure. The kitchen was all white and bright yellow, with fluorescent lights. That was before they ever thought of making the appliances all different colors and doing the cupboards like dark old wood and hiding the lighting. I loved light. I loved the double sink. So would anybody new-come from washing dishes in a dishpan with a rag-plugged hole on an oilcloth-covered table by light of a coal-oil lamp. I kept everything shining.

The bathroom too. I had a bath in there once a week. They wouldn't have minded if I took one oftener, but to me it seemed like asking too much, or maybe risking making it less wonderful. The basin and the tub and the toilet were all pink, and there were glass doors with flamingos painted on them, to shut off the tub. The light had a rosy cast and the mat sank under your feet like snow, except that it was warm. The mirror was three-way. With the mirror all steamed up and the air like a perfume cloud, from things I was allowed to use, I stood up on the side of the tub and admired myself naked, from three directions. Sometimes I thought about the way we lived out at home and the way we lived here and how one way was so hard to imagine when you were living the other way. But I thought it was still a lot easier, living the way we lived at home, to picture something like this, the painted flamingos and the warmth and the soft mat, than it was anybody knowing only things like this to picture how it was the other way. And why was that?

I was through my jobs in no time, and had the vegetables peeled for supper and sitting in cold water besides. Then I went into Mrs. Peebles' bedroom. I had been in there plenty of times, cleaning, and I always took a good look in her closet, at the clothes she had hanging there. I wouldn't have looked in her drawers, but a closet is open to anybody. That's a lie. I would have looked in drawers, but I would have felt worse doing it and been more scared she could tell.

Some clothes in her closet she wore all the time, I was quite familiar with them. Others she never put on, they were pushed to the back. I was disappointed to see no wedding dress. But there was one long dress I could just see the skirt of, and I was hungering to see the rest. Now I took note of where it hung and lifted it out. It was satin, a lovely weight on my arm, light bluish-green in color, almost silvery. It had a fitted, pointed waist and a full skirt and an off-the-shoulder fold hiding the little sleeves.

30   Next thing was easy. I got out of my own things and slipped it on. I was slimmer at fifteen than anybody would believe who knows me now and the fit was beautiful. I didn't, of course, have a strapless bra on,

which was what it needed, I just had to slide my straps down my arms under the material. Then I tried pinning up my hair, to get the effect. One thing led to another. I put on rouge and lipstick and eyebrow pencil from her dresser. The heat of the day and the weight of the satin and all the excitement made me thirsty, and I went out to the kitchen, got up as I was, to get a glass of ginger ale with ice cubes from the refrigerator. The Peebleses drank ginger ale, or fruit drinks, all day, like water, and I was getting so I did too. Also there was no limit on ice cubes, which I was so fond of I would even put them in a glass of milk.

I turned from putting the ice tray back and saw a man watching me through the screen. It was the luckiest thing in the world I didn't spill the ginger ale down the front of me then and there.

"I never meant to scare you. I knocked but you were getting the ice out, you didn't hear me."

I couldn't see what he looked like, he was dark the way somebody is pressed up against a screen door with the bright daylight behind them. I only knew he wasn't from around here.

"I'm from the plane over there. My name is Chris Watters and what I was wondering was if I could use that pump."

There was a pump in the yard. That was the way the people used   35
to get their water. Now I noticed he was carrying a pail.

"You're welcome," I said. "I can get it from the tap and save you pumping." I guess I wanted him to know we had piped water, didn't pump ourselves.

"I don't mind the exercise." He didn't move, though, and finally he said, "Were you going to a dance?"

Seeing a stranger there had made me entirely forget how I was dressed.

"Or is that the way ladies around here generally get dressed up in the afternoon?"

I didn't know how to joke back then. I was too embarrassed.   40

"You live here? Are you the lady of the house?"

"I'm the hired girl."

Some people change when they find that out, their whole way of looking at you and speaking to you changes, but his didn't.

"Well, I just wanted to tell you you look very nice. I was so surprised when I looked in the door and saw you. Just because you looked so nice and beautiful."

I wasn't even old enough then to realize how out of the common   45
it is, for a man to say something like that to a woman, or somebody he is treating like a woman. For a man to say a word like *beautiful*. I wasn't old enough to realize or to say anything back, or in fact to do anything

but wish he would go away. Not that I didn't like him, but just that it upset me so, having him look at me, and me trying to think of something to say.

He must have understood. He said good-bye, and thanked me, and went and started filling his pail from the pump. I stood behind the Venetian blinds in the dining room, watching him. When he had gone, I went into the bedroom and took the dress off and put it back in the same place. I dressed in my own clothes and took my hair down and washed my face, wiping it on Kleenex, which I threw in the wastebasket.

The Peebleses asked me what kind of man he was. Young, middle-aged, short, tall? I couldn't say.

"Good-looking?" Dr. Peebles teased me.

I couldn't think a thing but that he would be coming to get his water again, he would be talking to Dr. or Mrs. Peebles, making friends with them, and he would mention seeing me that first afternoon, dressed up. Why not mention it? He would think it was funny. And no idea of the trouble it would get me into.

50   After supper the Peebleses drove into town to go to a movie. She wanted to go somewhere with her hair fresh done. I sat in my bright kitchen wondering what to do, knowing I would never sleep. Mrs. Peebles might not fire me, when she found out, but it would give her a different feeling about me altogether. This was the first place I ever worked but I really had picked up things about the way people feel when you are working for them. They like to think you aren't curious. Not just that you aren't dishonest, that isn't enough. They like to feel you don't notice things, that you don't think or wonder about anything but what they liked to eat and how they liked things ironed, and so on. I don't mean they weren't kind to me, because they were. They had me eat my meals with them (to tell the truth I expected to, I didn't know there were families who don't) and sometimes they took me along in the car. But all the same.

I went up and checked on the children being asleep and then I went out. I had to do it. I crossed the road and went in the old fairgrounds gate. The plane looked unnatural sitting there, and shining with the moon. Off at the far side of the fairgrounds, where the bush was taking over, I saw his tent.

He was sitting outside it smoking a cigarette. He saw me coming.

"Hello, were you looking for a plane ride? I don't start taking people up till tomorrow." Then he looked again and said, "Oh, it's you. I didn't know you without your long dress on."

My heart was knocking away, my tongue was dried up. I had to say something. But I couldn't. My throat was closed and I was like a deaf-and-dumb.

"Did you want to ride? Sit down. Have a cigarette."   55

I couldn't even shake my head to say no, so he gave me one.

"Put it in your mouth or I can't light it. It's a good thing I'm used to shy ladies."

I did. It wasn't the first time I had smoked a cigarette, actually. My girl friend out home, Muriel Lowe, used to steal them from her brother.

"Look at your hand shaking. Did you just want to have a chat, or what?"

In one burst I said, "I wisht you wouldn't say anything about that   60
dress."

"What dress? Oh, the long dress."

"It's Mrs. Peebles'."

"Whose? Oh, the lady you work for? Is that it? She wasn't home so you got dressed up in her dress, eh? You got dressed up and played queen. I don't blame you. You're not smoking the cigarette right. Don't just puff. Draw it in. Did anybody ever show you how to inhale? Are you scared I'll tell on you? Is that it?"

I was so ashamed at having to ask him to connive this way I couldn't nod. I just looked at him and he saw *yes*.

"Well I won't. I won't in the slightest way mention it or embarrass   65
you. I give you my word of honor."

Then he changed the subject, to help me out, seeing I couldn't even thank him.

"What do you think of this sign?"

It was a board sign lying practically at my feet.

SEE THE WORLD FROM THE SKY. ADULTS $1.00, CHILDREN 50¢. QUAL-
IFIED PILOT.

"My old sign was getting pretty beat up, I thought I'd make a new   70
one. That's what I've been doing with my time today."

The lettering wasn't all that handsome, I thought. I could have done a better one in half an hour.

"I'm not an expert at sign making."

"It's very good," I said.

"I don't need it for publicity, word of mouth is usually enough. I turned away two carloads tonight. I felt like taking it easy. I didn't tell them ladies were dropping in to visit me."

Now I remembered the children and I was scared again, in case one   75
of them had waked up and called me and I wasn't there.

"Do you have to go so soon?"

I remembered some manners. "Thank you for the cigarette."

"Don't forget. You have my word of honor."

I tore off across the fairgrounds, scared I'd see the car heading home from town. My sense of time was mixed up, I didn't know how long I'd been out of the house. But it was all right, it wasn't late, the children were asleep. I got in bed myself and lay thinking what a lucky end to the day, after all, and among things to be grateful for I could be grateful Loretta Bird hadn't been the one who caught me.

80   The yard and borders didn't get trampled, it wasn't as bad as that. All the same it seemed very public, around the house. The sign was on the fairgrounds gate. People came mostly after supper but a good many in the afternoon, too. The Bird children all came without fifty cents between them and hung on the gate. We got used to the excitement of the plane coming in and taking off, it wasn't excitement anymore. I never went over, after that one time, but would see him when he came to get his water. I would be out on the steps doing sitting-down work, like preparing vegetables, if I could.

"Why don't you come over? I'll take you up in my plane."

"I'm saving my money," I said, because I couldn't think of anything else.

"For what? For getting married?"

I shook my head.

85   "I'll take you up for free if you come sometime when it's slack. I thought you would come, and have another cigarette."

I made a face to hush him, because you never could tell when the children would be sneaking around the porch, or Mrs. Peebles herself listening in the house. Sometimes she came out and had a conversation with him. He told her things he hadn't bothered to tell me. But then I hadn't thought to ask. He told her he had been in the war, that was where he learned to fly a plane, and now he couldn't settle down to ordinary life, this was what he liked. She said she couldn't imagine anybody liking such a thing. Though sometimes, she said, she was almost bored enough to try anything herself, she wasn't brought up to living in the country. It's all my husband's idea, she said. This was news to me.

"Maybe you ought to give flying lessons," she said.

"Would you take them?"

She just laughed.

90   Sunday was a busy flying day in spite of it being preached against from two pulpits. We were all sitting out watching. Joey and Heather

were over on the fence with the Bird kids. Their father had said they could go, after their mother saying all week they couldn't.

A car came down the road past the parked cars and pulled up right in the drive. It was Loretta Bird who got out, all importance, and on the driver's side another woman got out, more sedately. She was wearing sunglasses.

"This is a lady looking for the man that flies the plane," Loretta Bird said. "I heard her inquire in the hotel coffee shop where I was having a Coke and I brought her out."

"I'm sorry to bother you," the lady said. "I'm Alice Kelling, Mr. Watters' fiancée."

This Alice Kelling had on a pair of brown and white checked slacks and a yellow top. Her bust looked to me rather low and bumpy. She had a worried face. Her hair had had a permanent, but had grown out, and she wore a yellow band to keep it off her face. Nothing in the least pretty or even young-looking about her. But you could tell from how she talked she was from the city, or educated, or both.

Dr. Peebles stood up and introduced himself and his wife and me   95
and asked her to be seated.

"He's up in the air right now, but you're welcome to sit and wait. He gets his water here and he hasn't been yet. He'll probably take his break about five."

"That is him, then?" said Alice Kelling, wrinkling and straining at the sky.

"He's not in the habit of running out on you, taking a different name?" Dr. Peebles laughed. He was the one, not his wife, to offer iced tea. Then she sent me into the kitchen to fix it. She smiled. She was wearing sunglasses too.

"He never mentioned his fiancée," she said.

I loved fixing iced tea with lots of ice and slices of lemon in tall   100
glasses. I ought to have mentioned before, Dr. Peebles was an abstainer, at least around the house, or I wouldn't have been allowed to take the place. I had to fix a glass for Loretta Bird too, though it galled me, and when I went out she had settled in my lawn chair, leaving me the steps.

"I knew you was a nurse when I first heard you in that coffee shop."

"How would you know a thing like that?"

"I get my hunches about people. Was that how you met him, nursing?"

"Chris? Well yes. Yes, it was."

"Oh, were you overseas?" said Mrs. Peebles.   105

"No, it was before he went overseas. I nursed him when he was stationed at Centralia and had a ruptured appendix. We got engaged and then he went overseas. My, this is refreshing, after a long drive."

"He'll be glad to see you," Dr. Peebles said. "It's a rackety kind of life, isn't it, not staying one place long enough to really make friends."

"Youse've had a long engagement," Loretta Bird said.

Alice Kelling passed that over. "I was going to get a room at the hotel, but when I was offered directions I came on out. Do you think I could phone them?"

110   "No need," Dr. Peebles said. "You're five miles away from him if you stay at the hotel. Here, you're right across the road. Stay with us. We've got rooms on rooms, look at this big house."

Asking people to stay, just like that, is certainly a country thing, and maybe seemed natural to him now, but not to Mrs. Peebles, from the way she said, oh yes, we have plenty of room. Or to Alice Kelling, who kept protesting, but let herself be worn down. I got the feeling it was a temptation to her, to be that close. I was trying for a look at her ring. Her nails were painted red, her fingers were freckled and wrinkled. It was a tiny stone. Muriel Lowe's cousin had one twice as big.

Chris came to get his water, late in the afternoon just as Dr. Peebles had predicted. He must have recognized the car from a way off. He came smiling.

"Here I am chasing after you to see what you're up to," called Alice Kelling. She got up and went to meet him and they kissed, just touched, in front of us.

"You're going to spend a lot on gas that way," Chris said.

115   Dr. Peebles invited Chris to stay for supper, since he had already put up the sign that said: NO MORE RIDES TILL 7 P.M. Mrs. Peebles wanted it served in the yard, in spite of the bugs. One thing strange to anybody from the country is this eating outside. I had made a potato salad earlier and she had made a jellied salad, that was one thing she could do, so it was just a matter of getting those out, and some sliced meat and cucumbers and fresh leaf lettuce. Loretta Bird hung around for some time saying, "Oh, well, I guess I better get home to those yappers," and, "It's so nice just sitting here, I sure hate to get up," but nobody invited her, I was relieved to see, and finally she had to go.

That night after rides were finished Alice Kelling and Chris went off somewhere in her car. I lay awake till they got back. When I saw the car lights sweep my ceiling I got up to look down on them through the slats of my blind. I don't know what I thought I was going to see. Muriel Lowe and I used to sleep on her front veranda and watch her sister and her sister's boy friend saying good night. Afterward we couldn't get to sleep, for longing for somebody to kiss us and rub up against us and we would talk about suppose you were out in a boat with a boy and he wouldn't bring you in to shore unless you did it, or what if somebody got you trapped in a barn, you would have to, wouldn't you, it wouldn't be your fault. Muriel said her two girl cousins used to try with a toilet paper roll that one of them was a boy. We wouldn't do anything like that; just lay and wondered.

All that happened was that Chris got out of the car on one side and she got out on the other and they walked off separately—him toward the fairgrounds and her toward the house. I got back in bed and imagined about me coming home with him, not like that.

Next morning Alice Kelling got up late and I fixed a grapefruit for her the way I had learned and Mrs. Peebles sat down with her to visit and have another cup of coffee. Mrs. Peebles seemed pleased enough now, having company. Alice Kelling said she guessed she better get used to putting in a day just watching Chris take off and come down, and Mrs. Peebles said she didn't know if she should suggest it because Alice Kelling was the one with the car, but the lake was only twenty-five miles away and what a good day for a picnic.

Alice Kelling took her up on the idea and by eleven o'clock they were in the car, with Joey and Heather and a sandwich lunch I had made. The only thing was that Chris hadn't come down, and she wanted to tell him where they were going.

"Edie'll go over and tell him," Mrs. Peebles said. "There's no   120
problem."

Alice Kelling wrinkled her face and agreed.

"Be sure and tell him we'll be back by five!"

I didn't see that he would be concerned about knowing this right away, and I thought of him eating whatever he ate over there, alone, cooking on his camp stove, so I got to work and mixed up a crumb cake and baked it, in between the other work I had to do; then, when it was a bit cooled, wrapped it in a tea towel. I didn't do anything to myself but take off my apron and comb my hair. I would like to have put some makeup on, but I was too afraid it would remind him of the way he first saw me, and that would humiliate me all over again.

He had come and put another sign on the gate: NO RIDES THIS P.M. APOLOGIES. I worried that he wasn't feeling well. No sign of him outside and the tent flap was down. I knocked on the pole.

"Come in," he said, in a voice that would just as soon have said   125
Stay out.

I lifted the flap.

"Oh, it's you. I'm sorry. I didn't know it was you."

He had been just sitting on the side of the bed, smoking. Why not at least sit and smoke in the fresh air?

"I brought a cake and hope you're not sick," I said.

130   "Why would I be sick? Oh—that sign. That's all right. I'm just tired of talking to people. I don't mean you. Have a seat." He pinned back the tent flap. "Get some fresh air in here."

I sat on the edge of the bed, there was no place else. It was one of those fold-up cots, really: I remembered and gave him his fiancée's message.

He ate some of the cake. "Good."

"Put the rest away for when you're hungry later."

"I'll tell you a secret. I won't be around here much longer."

135   "Are you getting married?"

"Ha ha. What time did you say they'd be back?"

"Five o'clock."

"Well, by that time, this place will have seen the last of me. A plane can get further than a car." He unwrapped the cake and ate another piece of it, absentmindedly.

"Now you'll be thirsty."

140   "There's some water in the pail."

"It won't be very cold. I could bring some fresh. I could bring some ice from the refrigerator."

"No," he said. "I don't want you to go. I want a nice long time of saying good-bye to you."

He put the cake away carefully and sat beside me and started those little kisses, so soft, I can't ever let myself think about them, such kindness in his face and lovely kisses, all over my eyelids and neck and ears, all over, then me kissing back as well as I could (I had only kissed a boy on a dare before, and kissed my own arms for practice) and we lay back on the cot and pressed together, just gently, and he did some other things, not bad things or not in a bad way. It was lovely in the tent, that smell of grass and hot tent cloth with the sun beating down on it, and he said, "I wouldn't do you any harm for the world." Once, when he had rolled on top of me and we were sort of rocking together on the cot, he said softly, "Oh, no," and freed himself and jumped up and got the water pail. He splashed some of it on his neck and face, and the little bit left, on me lying there.

"That's to cool us off, miss."

145   When we said good-bye I wasn't at all sad, because he held my face and said, "I'm going to write you a letter. I'll tell you where I am and maybe you can come and see me. Would you like that? Okay then. You wait." I was really glad I think to get away from him, it was like he was

piling presents on me I couldn't get the pleasure of till I considered them alone.

No consternation at first about the plane being gone. They thought he had taken somebody up, and I didn't enlighten them. Dr. Peebles had phoned he had to go to the country, so there was just us having supper, and then Loretta Bird thrusting her head in the door and saying, "I see he's took off."

"What?" said Alice Kelling, and pushed back her chair.

"The kids come and told me this afternoon he was taking down his tent. Did he think he'd run through all the business there was round here? He didn't take off without letting you know, did he?"

"He'll send me word," Alice Kelling said. "He'll probably phone tonight. He's terribly restless, since the war."

"Edie, he didn't mention to you, did he?" Mrs. Peebles said. "When   150
you took over the message?"

"Yes," I said. So far so true.

"Well why didn't you say?" All of them were looking at me. "Did he say where he was going?"

"He said he might try Bayfield," I said. What made me tell such a lie? I didn't intend it.

"Bayfield, how far is that?" said Alice Kelling.

Mrs. Peebles said, "Thirty, thirty-five miles."   155

"That's not far. Oh, well, that's really not far at all. It's on the lake, isn't it?"

You'd think I'd be ashamed of myself, setting her on the wrong track. I did it to give him more time, whatever time he needed. I lied for him, and also, I have to admit, for me. Women should stick together and not do things like that. I see that now, but didn't then. I never thought of myself as being in any way like her, or coming to the same troubles, ever.

She hadn't taken her eyes off me. I thought she suspected my lie.

"When did he mention this to you?"

"Earlier."   160

"When you were over at the plane?"

"Yes."

"You must've stayed and had a chat." She smiled at me, not a nice smile. "You must've stayed and had a little visit with him."

"I took a cake," I said, thinking that telling some truth would spare me telling the rest.

"We didn't have a cake," said Mrs. Peebles rather sharply.   165

"I baked one."

Alice Kelling said, "That was very friendly of you."

"Did you get permission," said Loretta Bird. "You never know what these girls'll do next," she said. "It's not they mean harm so much, as they're ignorant."

"The cake is neither here nor there," Mrs. Peebles broke in. "Edie, I wasn't aware you knew Chris that well."

170   I didn't know what to say.

"I'm not surprised," Alice Kelling said in a high voice. "I knew by the look of her as soon as I saw her. We get them at the hospital all the time." She looked hard at me with her stretched smile. "Having their babies. We have to put them in a special ward because of their diseases. Little country tramps. Fourteen and fifteen years old. You should see the babies they have, too."

"There was a bad woman here in town had a baby that pus was running out of its eyes," Loretta Bird put in.

"Wait a minute," said Mrs. Peebles. "What is this talk? Edie. What about you and Mr. Watters? Were you intimate with him?"

"Yes," I said. I was thinking of us lying on the cot and kissing, wasn't that intimate? And I would never deny it.

175   They were all one minute quiet, even Loretta Bird.

"Well," said Mrs. Peebles. "I am surprised. I think I need a cigarette. This is the first of any such tendencies I've seen in her," she said, speaking to Alice Kelling, but Alice Kelling was looking at me.

"Loose little bitch." Tears ran down her face. "Loose little bitch, aren't you? I knew as soon as I saw you. Men despise girls like you. He just made use of you and went off, you know that, don't you? Girls like you are just nothing, they're just public conveniences, just filthy little rags!"

"Oh, now," said Mrs. Peebles.

"Filthy," Alice Kelling sobbed. "Filthy little rags!"

180   "Don't get yourself upset," Loretta Bird said. She was swollen up with pleasure at being in on this scene. "Men are all the same."

"Edie, I'm very surprised," Mrs. Peebles said. "I thought your parents were so strict. You don't want to have a baby, do you?"

I'm still ashamed of what happened next. I lost control, just like a six-year-old, I started howling. "You don't get a baby from just doing that!"

"You see. Some of them are that ignorant," Loretta Bird said.

But Mrs. Peebles jumped up and caught my arms and shook me.

185   "Calm down. Don't get hysterical. Calm down. Stop crying. Listen to me. Listen. I'm wondering, if you know what being intimate means. Now tell me. What did you think it meant?"

"Kissing," I howled.

She let go. "Oh, Edie. Stop it. Don't be silly. It's all right. It's all a misunderstanding. Being intimate means a lot more than that. Oh, I *wondered.*"

"She's trying to cover up, now," said Alice Kelling. "Yes. She's not so stupid. She sees she got herself in trouble."

"I believe her," Mrs. Peebles said. "This is an awful scene."

"Well there is one way to find out," said Alice Kelling, getting up.   190
"After all, I am a nurse."

Mrs. Peebles drew a breath and said, "No. No. Go to your room, Edie. And stop that noise. This is too disgusting."

I heard the car start in a little while. I tried to stop crying, pulling back each wave as it started over me. Finally I succeeded, and lay heaving on the bed.

Mrs. Peebles came and stood in the doorway.

"She's gone," she said. "That Bird woman too. Of course, you know you should never have gone near that man and that is the cause of all this trouble. I have a headache. As soon as you can, go and wash your face in cold water and get at the dishes and we will not say any more about this."

Nor we didn't. I didn't figure out till years later the extent of what   195
I had been saved from. Mrs. Peebles was not very friendly to me afterward, but she was fair. Not very friendly is the wrong way of describing what she was. She had never been very friendly. It was just that now she had to see me all the time and it got on her nerves, a little.

As for me, I put it all out of my mind like a bad dream and concentrated on waiting for my letter. The mail came every day except Sunday, between one-thirty and two in the afternoon, a good time for me because Mrs. Peebles was always having her nap. I would get the kitchen all cleaned and then go up to the mailbox and sit in the grass, waiting. I was perfectly happy, waiting, I forgot all about Alice Kelling and her misery and awful talk and Mrs. Peebles and her chilliness and the embarrassment of whether she had told Dr. Peebles and the face of Loretta Bird, getting her fill of other people's troubles. I was always smiling when the mailman got there, and continued smiling even after he gave me the mail and I saw today wasn't the day. The mailman was a Carmichael. I knew by his face because there are a lot of Carmichaels living out by us and so many of them have a sort of sticking-out top lip. So I asked his name (he was a young man, shy, but good-humored, anybody could ask him anything) and then I said, "I knew by your face!" He was pleased by that and always glad to see me and got a little less shy. "You've got the smile I've been waiting on all day!" he used to holler out the car window.

It never crossed my mind for a long time a letter might not come. I believed in it coming just like I believed the sun would rise in the morning. I just put off my hope from day to day, and there was the goldenrod out around the mailbox and the children gone back to school, and the leaves turning, and I was wearing a sweater when I went to wait. One day walking back with the hydro bill stuck in my hand, that was all, looking across at the fairgrounds with the full-blown milkweed and dark teasels, so much like fall, it just struck me: *No letter was ever going to come.* It was an impossible idea to get used to. No, not impossible. If I thought about Chris's face when he said he was going to write to me, it was impossible, but if I forgot that and thought about the actual tin mailbox, empty, it was plain and true. I kept on going to meet the mail, but my heart was heavy now like a lump of lead. I only smiled because I thought of the mailman counting on it, and he didn't have an easy life, with the winter driving ahead.

Till it came to me one day there were women doing this with their lives, all over. There were women just waiting and waiting by mailboxes for one letter or another. I imagined me making this journey day after day and year after year, and my hair starting to go gray, and I thought, I was never made to go on like that. So I stopped meeting the mail. If there were women all through life waiting, and women busy and not waiting, I knew which I had to be. Even though there might be things the second kind of women have to pass up and never know about, it still is better.

I was surprised when the mailman phoned the Peebleses' place in the evening and asked for me. He said he missed me. He asked if I would like to go to Goderich, where some well-known movie was on, I forget now what. So I said yes, and I went out with him for two years and he asked me to marry him, and we were engaged a year more while I got my things together, and then we did marry. He always tells the children the story of how I went after him by sitting by the mailbox every day, and naturally I laugh and let him, because I like for people to think what pleases them and makes them happy.

QUESTIONS

1. Describe the plot structure in the story. How is the arrangement of the plot elements effective? At which points were your expectations as a reader overturned?
2. How does the story generate suspense? Which developments of the plot help to increase the suspense?
3. How do minor characters like Loretta Bird and Mrs. Peebles help advance the plot? What else do they add to the story?

4. Is Edie a sympathetic character? How does her status as "the hired girl" affect the way you respond to her as a reader?
5. Evaluate Chris Watters as a potential husband for Edie. Does her evaluation of him differ from the reader's?
6. The title "How I Met My Husband" suggests a reminiscence told from a much later, more mature vantage point. Can you detect the voice of an older, wiser Edie who is distinct from the young girl working for Dr. and Mrs. Peebles?
7. Discuss the role of Alice Kelling in advancing the plot and in the story as a whole. Could she be described as the antagonist? Why or why not?
8. Discuss the effectiveness of the surprise ending. How does Carmichael differ from Chris Watters? Can it be argued that the surprise ending is also inevitable and appropriate?

Jhumpa Lahiri
Interpreter of Maladies

At the tea stall Mr. and Mrs. Das bickered about who should take Tina to the toilet. Eventually Mrs. Das relented when Mr. Das pointed out that he had given the girl her bath the night before. In the rearview mirror Mr. Kapasi watched as Mrs. Das emerged slowly from his bulky white Ambassador, dragging her shaved, largely bare legs across the back seat. She did not hold the little girl's hand as they walked to the rest room.

They were on their way to see the Sun Temple at Konarak. It was a dry, bright Saturday, the mid-July heat tempered by a steady ocean breeze, ideal weather for sightseeing. Ordinarily Mr. Kapasi would not have stopped so soon along the way, but less than five minutes after he'd picked up the family that morning in front of Hotel Sandy Villa, the little girl had complained. The first thing Mr. Kapasi had noticed when he saw Mr. and Mrs. Das, standing with their children under the portico of the hotel, was that they were very young, perhaps not even

INTERPRETER OF MALADIES   First published in her 1999 collection *Interpreter of Maladies*, which won the 2000 Pulitzer Prize for fiction. Lahiri's book conducts an incisive exploration of Indian culture, especially as it collides with the values of western Europe and the United States. This story takes place in the state of Orissa on the eastern coast of India; the "Sun Temple at Konarak" is located on the coast near the city of Puri, where the Das family is staying. Of Indian ancestry, Jhumpa Lahiri (b. 1967) was born in London, grew up in Rhode Island, and earned an M.A. in creative writing and a Ph.D. in Renaissance Studies from Boston University. She now lives in New York City.

thirty. In addition to Tina they had two boys, Ronny and Bobby, who appeared very close in age and had teeth covered in a network of flashing silver wires. The family looked Indian but dressed as foreigners did, the children in stiff, brightly colored clothing and caps with translucent visors. Mr. Kapasi was accustomed to foreign tourists; he was assigned to them regularly because he could speak English. Yesterday he had driven an elderly couple from Scotland, both with spotted faces and fluffy white hair so thin it exposed their sunburnt scalps. In comparison, the tanned, youthful faces of Mr. and Mrs. Das were all the more striking. When he'd introduced himself, Mr. Kapasi had pressed his palms together in greeting, but Mr. Das squeezed hands like an American so that Mr. Kapasi felt it in his elbow. Mrs. Das, for her part, had flexed one side of her mouth, smiling dutifully at Mr. Kapasi, without displaying any interest in him.

As they waited at the tea stall, Ronny, who looked like the older of the two boys, clambered suddenly out of the back seat, intrigued by a goat tied to a stake in the ground.

"Don't touch it," Mr. Das said. He glanced up from his paperback tour book, which said "INDIA" in yellow letters and looked as if it had been published abroad. His voice, somehow tentative and a little shrill, sounded as though it had not yet settled into maturity.

5   "I want to give it a piece of gum," the boy called back as he trotted ahead.

Mr. Das stepped out of the car and stretched his legs by squatting briefly to the ground. A clean-shaven man, he looked exactly like a magnified version of Ronny. He had a sapphire blue visor, and was dressed in shorts, sneakers, and a T-shirt. The camera slung around his neck, with an impressive telephoto lens and numerous buttons and markings, was the only complicated thing he wore. He frowned, watching as Ronny rushed toward the goat, but appeared to have no intention of intervening. "Bobby, make sure that your brother doesn't do anything stupid."

"I don't feel like it," Bobby said, not moving. He was sitting in the front seat beside Mr. Kapasi, studying a picture of the elephant god taped to the glove compartment.

"No need to worry," Mr. Kapasi said. "They are quite tame." Mr. Kapasi was forty-six years old, with receding hair that had gone completely silver, but his butterscotch complexion and his unlined brow, which he treated in spare moments to dabs of lotus-oil balm, made it easy to imagine what he must have looked like at an earlier age. He wore gray trousers and a matching jacket-style shirt, tapered at the waist, with short sleeves and a large pointed collar, made of a thin but durable synthetic material. He had specified both the cut and the fabric to his tailor—it was his preferred uniform for giving tours because it did not get crushed during his long hours behind the wheel. Through the windshield he watched as Ronny circled around the goat, touched it quickly on its side, then trotted back to the car.

"You left India as a child?" Mr. Kapasi asked when Mr. Das had settled once again into the passenger seat.

"Oh, Mina and I were both born in America," Mr. Das announced   10
with an air of sudden confidence. "Born and raised. Our parents live here now, in Assansol. They retired. We visit them every couple years." He turned to watch as the little girl ran toward the car, the wide purple bows of her sundress flopping on her narrow brown shoulders. She was holding to her chest a doll with yellow hair that looked as if it had been chopped, as a punitive measure, with a pair of dull scissors. "This is Tina's first trip to India, isn't it, Tina?"

"I don't have to go to the bathroom anymore," Tina announced.

"Where's Mina?" Mr. Das asked.

Mr. Kapasi found it strange that Mr. Das should refer to his wife by her first name when speaking to the little girl. Tina pointed to where Mrs. Das was purchasing something from one of the shirtless men who worked at the tea stall. Mr. Kapasi heard one of the shirtless men sing a phrase from a popular Hindi love song as Mrs. Das walked back to the car, but she did not appear to understand the words of the song, for she did not express irritation, or embarrassment, or react in any other way to the man's declarations.

He observed her. She wore a red-and-white-checkered skirt that stopped above her knees, slip-on shoes with a square wooden heel, and a close-fitting blouse styled like a man's undershirt. The blouse was decorated at chest-level with a calico appliqué in the shape of a strawberry. She was a short woman, with small hands like paws, her frosty pink fingernails painted to match her lips, and was slightly plump in her figure. Her hair, shorn only a little longer than her husband's, was parted far to one side. She was wearing large dark brown sunglasses with a pinkish tint to them, and carried a big straw bag, almost as big as her torso, shaped like a bowl, with a water bottle poking out of it. She walked slowly, carrying some puffed rice tossed with peanuts and chili peppers in a large packet made from newspapers. Mr. Kapasi turned to Mr. Das.

"Where in America do you live?"   15

"New Brunswick, New Jersey."

"Next to New York?"

"Exactly. I teach middle school there."

"What subject?"

20   "Science. In fact, every year I take my students on a trip to the Museum of Natural History in New York City. In a way we have a lot in common, you could say, you and I. How long have you been a tour guide, Mr. Kapasi?"

"Five years."

Mrs. Das reached the car. "How long's the trip?" she asked, shutting the door.

"About two and a half hours," Mr. Kapasi replied.

At this Mrs. Das gave an impatient sigh, as if she had been traveling her whole life without pause. She fanned herself with a folded Bombay film magazine written in English.

25   "I thought that the Sun Temple is only eighteen miles north of Puri," Mr. Das said, tapping on the tour book.

"The roads to Konarak are poor. Actually it is a distance of fifty-two miles," Mr. Kapasi explained.

Mr. Das nodded, readjusting the camera strap where it had begun to chafe the back of his neck.

Before starting the ignition, Mr. Kapasi reached back to make sure the cranklike locks on the inside of each of the back doors were secured. As soon as the car began to move the little girl began to play with the lock on her side, clicking it with some effort forward and backward, but Mrs. Das said nothing to stop her. She sat a bit slouched at one end of the back seat, not offering her puffed rice to anyone. Ronny and Tina sat on either side of her, both snapping bright green gum.

"Look," Bobby said as the car began to gather speed. He pointed with his finger to the tall trees that lined the road. "Look."

30   "Monkeys!" Ronny shrieked. "Wow!"

They were seated in groups along the branches, with shining black faces, silver bodies, horizontal eyebrows, and crested heads. Their long gray tails dangled like a series of ropes among the leaves. A few scratched themselves with black leathery hands, or swung their feet, staring as the car passed.

"We call them the hanuman,"° Mr. Kapasi said. "They are quite common in the area."

As soon as he spoke, one of the monkeys leaped into the middle of the road, causing Mr. Kapasi to brake suddenly. Another bounced onto the hood of the car, then sprang away. Mr. Kapasi beeped his horn. The children began to get excited, sucking in their breath and covering their faces partly with their hands. They had never seen monkeys out-

hanuman: a gray monkey venerated by Hindus

side of a zoo, Mr. Das explained. He asked Mr. Kapasi to stop the car so that he could take a picture.

While Mr. Das adjusted his telephoto lens, Mrs. Das reached into her straw bag and pulled out a bottle of colorless nail polish, which she proceeded to stroke on the tip of her index finger.

The little girl stuck out a hand. "Mine too. Mommy, do mine too."   35

"Leave me alone," Mrs. Das said, blowing on her nail and turning her body slightly. "You're making me mess up."

The little girl occupied herself by buttoning and unbuttoning a pinafore on the doll's plastic body.

"All set," Mr. Das said, replacing the lens cap.

The car rattled considerably as it raced along the dusty road, causing them all to pop up from their seats every now and then, but Mrs. Das continued to polish her nails. Mr. Kapasi eased up on the accelerator, hoping to produce a smoother ride. When he reached for the gearshift the boy in front accommodated him by swinging his hairless knees out of the way. Mr. Kapasi noted that this boy was slightly paler than the other children. "Daddy, why is the driver sitting on the wrong side in this car, too?" the boy asked.

"They all do that here, dummy," Ronny said.   40

"Don't call your brother a dummy," Mr. Das said. He turned to Mr. Kapasi. "In America, you know . . . it confuses them."

"Oh yes, I am well aware," Mr. Kapasi said. As delicately as he could, he shifted gears again, accelerating as they approached a hill in the road. "I see it on *Dallas*, the steering wheels are on the left-hand side."

"What's *Dallas*?" Tina asked, banging her now naked doll on the seat behind Mr. Kapasi.

"It went off the air," Mr. Das explained. "It's a television show."

They were all like siblings, Mr. Kapasi thought as they passed a row   45
of date trees. Mr. and Mrs. Das behaved like an older brother and sister, not parents. It seemed that they were in charge of the children only for the day; it was hard to believe they were regularly responsible for anything other than themselves. Mr. Das tapped on his lens cap, and his tour book, dragging his thumbnail occasionally across the pages so that they made a scraping sound. Mrs. Das continued to polish her nails. She had still not removed her sunglasses. Every now and then Tina renewed her plea that she wanted her nails done, too, and so at one point Mrs. Das flicked a drop of polish on the little girl's finger before depositing the bottle back inside her straw bag.

"Isn't this an air-conditioned car?" she asked, still blowing on her hand. The window on Tina's side was broken and could not be rolled down.

"Quit complaining," Mr. Das said. "It isn't so hot."

"I told you to get a car with air-conditioning," Mrs. Das continued. "Why do you do this, Raj, just to save a few stupid rupees. What are you saving us, fifty cents?"

Their accents sounded just like the ones Mr. Kapasi heard on American television programs, though not like the ones on *Dallas.*

50   "Doesn't it get tiresome, Mr. Kapasi, showing people the same thing every day?" Mr. Das asked, rolling down his own window all the way. "Hey, do you mind stopping the car. I just want to get a shot of this guy."

Mr. Kapasi pulled over to the side of the road as Mr. Das took a picture of a barefoot man, his head wrapped in a dirty turban, seated on top of a cart of grain sacks pulled by a pair of bullocks. Both the man and the bullocks were emaciated. In the back seat Mrs. Das gazed out another window, at the sky, where nearly transparent clouds passed quickly in front of one another.

"I look forward to it, actually," Mr. Kapasi said as they continued on their way. "The Sun Temple is one of my favorite places. In that way it is a reward for me. I give tours on Fridays and Saturdays only. I have another job during the week."

"Oh? Where?" Mr. Das asked.

"I work in a doctor's office."

55   "You're a doctor?"

"I am not a doctor. I work with one. As an interpreter."

"What does a doctor need an interpreter for?"

"He has a number of Gujarati° patients. My father was Gujarati, but many people do not speak Gujarati in this area, including the doctor. And so the doctor asked me to work in his office, interpreting what the patients say."

"Interesting. I've never heard of anything like that," Mr. Das said.

60   Mr. Kapasi shrugged. "It is a job like any other."

"But so romantic," Mrs. Das said dreamily, breaking her extended silence. She lifted her pinkish brown sunglasses and arranged them on top of her head like a tiara. For the first time, her eyes met Mr. Kapasi's in the rearview mirror: pale, a bit small, their gaze fixed but drowsy.

Mr. Das craned to look at her. "What's so romantic about it?"

"I don't know. Something." She shrugged, knitting her brows together for an instant. "Would you like a piece of gum, Mr. Kapasi?" she asked brightly. She reached into her straw bag and handed him a small

Gujarati: from Gujarat, a state in western India

square wrapped in green-and-white-striped paper. As soon as Mr. Kapasi put the gum in his mouth a thick sweet liquid burst onto his tongue.

"Tell us more about your job, Mr. Kapasi," Mrs. Das said.

"What would you like to know, madame?"   65

"I don't know," she shrugged, munching on some puffed rice and licking the mustard oil from the corners of her mouth. "Tell us a typical situation." She settled back in her seat, her head tilted in a patch of sun, and closed her eyes. "I want to picture what happens."

"Very well. The other day a man came in with a pain in his throat."

"Did he smoke cigarettes?"

"No. It was very curious. He complained that he felt as if there were long pieces of straw stuck in his throat. When I told the doctor he was able to prescribe the proper medication."

"That's so neat."   70

"Yes," Mr. Kapasi agreed after some hesitation.

"So these patients are totally dependent on you," Mrs. Das said. She spoke slowly, as if she were thinking aloud. "In a way, more dependent on you than the doctor."

"How do you mean? How could it be?"

"Well, for example, you could tell the doctor that the pain felt like a burning, not straw. The patient would never know what you had told the doctor, and the doctor wouldn't know that you had told the wrong thing. It's a big responsibility."

"Yes, a big responsibility you have there, Mr. Kapasi," Mr. Das   75
agreed.

Mr. Kapasi had never thought of his job in such complimentary terms. To him it was a thankless occupation. He found nothing noble in interpreting people's maladies, assiduously translating the symptoms of so many swollen bones, countless cramps of bellies and bowels, spots on people's palms that changed color, shape, or size. The doctor, nearly half his age, had an affinity for bell-bottom trousers and made humorless jokes about the Congress party. Together they worked in a stale little infirmary where Mr. Kapasi's smartly tailored clothes clung to him in the heat, in spite of the blackened blades of a ceiling fan churning over their heads.

The job was a sign of his failings. In his youth he'd been a devoted scholar of foreign languages, the owner of an impressive collection of dictionaries. He had dreamed of being an interpreter for diplomats and dignitaries, resolving conflicts between people and nations, settling disputes of which he alone could understand both sides. He was a self-educated man. In a series of notebooks, in the evenings before his parents settled his marriage, he had listed the common etymologies of words, and at one point in his life he was confident that he could converse, if given the opportunity, in English, French, Russian, Portuguese, and Italian, not to mention Hindi, Bengali, Orissi, and Gujarati. Now only a handful of European phrases remained in his memory, scattered words for things like saucers and chairs. English was the only non-Indian language he spoke fluently anymore. Mr. Kapasi knew it was not a remarkable talent. Sometimes he feared that his children knew better English than he did, just from watching television. Still, it came in handy for the tours.

He had taken the job as an interpreter after his first son, at the age of seven, contracted typhoid—that was how he had first made the acquaintance of the doctor. At the time Mr. Kapasi had been teaching English in a grammar school, and he bartered his skills as an interpreter to pay the increasingly exorbitant medical bills. In the end the boy had died one evening in his mother's arms, his limbs burning with fever, but then there was the funeral to pay for, and the other children who were born soon enough, and the newer, bigger house, and the good schools and tutors, and the fine shoes and the television, and the countless other ways he tried to console his wife and to keep her from crying in her sleep, and so when the doctor offered to pay him twice as much as he earned at the grammar school, he accepted. Mr. Kapasi knew that his wife had little regard for his career as an interpreter. He knew it reminded her of the son she'd lost, and that she resented the other lives he helped, in his own small way, to save. If ever she referred to his position, she used the phrase "doctor's assistant," as if the process of interpretation were equal to taking someone's temperature, or changing a bedpan. She never asked him about the patients who came to the doctor's office, or said that his job was a big responsibility.

For this reason it flattered Mr. Kapasi that Mrs. Das was so intrigued by his job. Unlike his wife, she had reminded him of its intellectual challenges. She had also used the word "romantic." She did not behave in a romantic way toward her husband, and yet she had used the word to describe him. He wondered if Mr. and Mrs. Das were a bad match, just as he and his wife were. Perhaps they, too, had little in common apart from three children and a decade of their lives. The signs he recognized from his own marriage were there—the bickering, the indifference, the protracted silences. Her sudden interest in him, an interest she did not express in either her husband or her children, was mildly intoxicating. When Mr. Kapasi thought once again about how she had said "romantic," the feeling of intoxication grew.

80   He began to check his reflection in the rearview mirror as he drove, feeling grateful that he had chosen the gray suit that morning and not

the brown one, which tended to sag a little in the knees. From time to time he glanced through the mirror at Mrs. Das. In addition to glancing at her face he glanced at the strawberry between her breasts, and the golden brown hollow in her throat. He decided to tell Mrs. Das about another patient, and another: the young woman who had complained of a sensation of raindrops in her spine, the gentleman whose birthmark had begun to sprout hairs. Mrs. Das listened attentively, stroking her hair with a small plastic brush that resembled an oval bed of nails, asking more questions, for yet another example. The children were quiet, intent on spotting more monkeys in the trees, and Mr. Das was absorbed by his tour book, so it seemed like a private conversation between Mr. Kapasi and Mrs. Das. In this manner the next half hour passed, and when they stopped for lunch at a roadside restaurant that sold fritters and omelette sandwiches, usually something Mr. Kapasi looked forward to on his tours so that he could sit in peace and enjoy some hot tea, he was disappointed. As the Das family settled together under a magenta umbrella fringed with white and orange tassels, and placed their orders with one of the waiters who marched about in tri-cornered caps, Mr. Kapasi reluctantly headed toward a neighboring table.

"Mr. Kapasi, wait. There's room here," Mrs. Das called out. She gathered Tina onto her lap, insisting that he accompany them. And so, together, they had bottled mango juice and sandwiches and plates of onions and potatoes deep-fried in graham-flour batter. After finishing two omelette sandwiches Mr. Das took more pictures of the group as they ate.

"How much longer?" he asked Mr. Kapasi as he paused to load a new roll of film in the camera.

"About half an hour more."

By now the children had gotten up from the table to look at more monkeys perched in a nearby tree, so there was a considerable space between Mrs. Das and Mr. Kapasi. Mr. Das placed the camera to his face and squeezed one eye shut, his tongue exposed at one corner of his mouth. "This looks funny. Mina, you need to lean in closer to Mr. Kapasi."

She did. He could smell a scent on her skin, like a mixture of whiskey and rosewater. He worried suddenly that she could smell his perspiration, which he knew had collected beneath the synthetic material of his shirt. He polished off his mango juice in one gulp and smoothed his silver hair with his hands. A bit of the juice dripped onto his chin. He wondered if Mrs. Das had noticed.

She had not. "What's your address, Mr. Kapasi?" she inquired, fishing for something inside her straw bag.

85

"You would like my address?"

"So we can send you copies," she said. "Of the pictures." She handed him a scrap of paper which she had hastily ripped from a page of her film magazine. The blank portion was limited, for the narrow strip was crowded by lines of text and a tiny picture of a hero and heroine embracing under a eucalyptus tree.

The paper curled as Mr. Kapasi wrote his address in clear, careful letters. She would write to him, asking about his days interpreting at the doctor's office, and he would respond eloquently, choosing only the most entertaining anecdotes, ones that would make her laugh out loud as she read them in her house in New Jersey. In time she would reveal the disappointment of her marriage, and he his. In this way their friendship would grow, and flourish. He would possess a picture of the two of them, eating fried onions under a magenta umbrella, which he would keep, he decided, safely tucked between the pages of his Russian grammar. As his mind raced, Mr. Kapasi experienced a mild and pleasant shock. It was similar to a feeling he used to experience long ago when, after months of translating with the aid of a dictionary, he would finally read a passage from a French novel, or an Italian sonnet, and understand the words, one after another, unencumbered by his own efforts. In those moments Mr. Kapasi used to believe that all was right with the world, that all struggles were rewarded, that all of life's mistakes made sense in the end. The promise that he would hear from Mrs. Das now filled him with the same belief.

90   When he finished writing his address Mr. Kapasi handed her the paper, but as soon as he did so he worried that he had either misspelled his name, or accidentally reversed the numbers of his postal code. He dreaded the possibility of a lost letter, the photograph never reaching him, hovering somewhere in Orissa, close but ultimately unattainable. He thought of asking for the slip of paper again, just to make sure he had written his address accurately, but Mrs. Das had already dropped it into the jumble of her bag.

They reached Konarak at two-thirty. The temple, made of sandstone, was a massive pyramid-like structure in the shape of a chariot. It was dedicated to the great master of life, the sun, which struck three sides of the edifice as it made its journey each day across the sky. Twenty-four giant wheels were carved on the north and south sides of the plinth. The whole thing was drawn by a team of seven horses, speeding as if through the heavens. As they approached, Mr. Kapasi explained that the temple had been built between A.D. 1243 and 1255, with the efforts of twelve hundred artisans, by the great ruler of the

Ganga dynasty, King Narasimhadeva the First, to commemorate his victory against the Muslim army.

"It says the temple occupies about a hundred and seventy acres of land," Mr. Das said, reading from his book.

"It's like a desert," Ronny said, his eyes wandering across the sand that stretched on all sides beyond the temple.

"The Chandrabhaga River once flowed one mile north of here. It is dry now," Mr. Kapasi said, turning off the engine.

They got out and walked toward the temple, posing first for pictures by the pair of lions that flanked the steps. Mr. Kapasi led them next to one of the wheels of the chariot, higher than any human being, nine feet in diameter. 95

"'The wheels are supposed to symbolize the wheel of life,'" Mr. Das read. "'They depict the cycle of creation, preservation, and achievement of realization.' Cool." He turned the page of his book. "'Each wheel is divided into eight thick and thin spokes, dividing the day into eight equal parts. The rims are carved with designs of birds and animals, whereas the medallions in the spokes are carved with women in luxurious poses, largely erotic in nature.'"

What he referred to were the countless friezes of entwined naked bodies, making love in various positions, women clinging to the necks of men, their knees wrapped eternally around their lovers' thighs. In addition to these were assorted scenes from daily life, of hunting and trading, of deer being killed with bows and arrows and marching warriors holding swords in their hands.

It was no longer possible to enter the temple, for it had filled with rubble years ago, but they admired the exterior, as did all the tourists Mr. Kapasi brought there, slowly strolling along each of its sides. Mr. Das trailed behind, taking pictures. The children ran ahead, pointing to figures of naked people, intrigued in particular by the Nagamithunas, the half-human, half-serpentine couples who were said, Mr. Kapasi told them, to live in the deepest waters of the sea. Mr. Kapasi was pleased that they liked the temple, pleased especially that it appealed to Mrs. Das. She stopped every three or four paces, staring silently at the carved lovers, and the processions of elephants, and the topless female musicians beating on two-sided drums.

Though Mr. Kapasi had been to the temple countless times, it occurred to him, as he, too, gazed at the topless women, that he had never seen his own wife fully naked. Even when they had made love she kept the panels of her blouse hooked together, the string of her petticoat knotted around her waist. He had never admired the backs of his wife's legs the way he now admired those of Mrs. Das, walking as if for his benefit alone. He had, of course, seen plenty of bare limbs before, belonging to the American and European ladies who took his tours. But Mrs. Das was different. Unlike the other women, who had an interest only in the temple, and kept their noses buried in a guidebook, or their eyes behind the lens of a camera, Mrs. Das had taken an interest in him.

100   Mr. Kapasi was anxious to be alone with her, to continue their private conversation, yet he felt nervous to walk at her side. She was lost behind her sunglasses, ignoring her husband's requests that she pose for another picture, walking past her children as if they were strangers. Worried that he might disturb her, Mr. Kapasi walked ahead, to admire, as he always did, the three life-sized bronze avatars of Surya, the sun god, each emerging from its own niche on the temple facade to greet the sun at dawn, noon, and evening. They wore elaborate headdresses, their languid, elongated eyes closed, their bare chests draped with carved chains and amulets. Hibiscus petals, offerings from previous visitors, were strewn at their gray-green feet. The last statue, on the northern wall of the temple, was Mr. Kapasi's favorite. This Surya had a tired expression, weary after a hard day of work, sitting astride a horse with folded legs. Even his horse's eyes were drowsy. Around his body were smaller sculptures of women in pairs, their hips thrust to one side.

"Who's that?" Mrs. Das asked. He was startled to see that she was standing beside him.

"He is the Astachala-Surya," Mr. Kapasi said. "The setting sun."

"So in a couple of hours the sun will set right here?" She slipped a foot out of one of her square-heeled shoes, rubbed her toes on the back of her other leg.

"That is correct."

105   She raised her sunglasses for a moment, then put them back on again. "Neat."

Mr. Kapasi was not certain exactly what the word suggested, but he had a feeling it was a favorable response. He hoped that Mrs. Das had understood Surya's beauty, his power. Perhaps they would discuss it further in their letters. He would explain things to her, things about India, and she would explain things to him about America. In its own way this correspondence would fulfill his dream, of serving as an interpreter between nations. He looked at her straw bag, delighted that his address lay nestled among its contents. When he pictured her so many thousands of miles away he plummeted, so much so that he had an overwhelming urge to wrap his arms around her, to freeze with her, even for an instant, in an embrace witnessed by his favorite Surya. But Mrs. Das had already started walking.

"When do you return to America?" he asked, trying to sound placid.

"In ten days."

He calculated: A week to settle in, a week to develop the pictures, a few days to compose her letter, two weeks to get to India by air. According to his schedule, allowing room for delays, he would hear from Mrs. Das in approximately six weeks' time.

The family was silent as Mr. Kapasi drove them back, a little past four-thirty, to Hotel Sandy Villa. The children had bought miniature granite versions of the chariot's wheels at a souvenir stand, and they turned them round in their hands. Mr. Das continued to read his book. Mrs. Das untangled Tina's hair with her brush and divided it into two little ponytails.

Mr. Kapasi was beginning to dread the thought of dropping them off. He was not prepared to begin his six-week wait to hear from Mrs. Das. As he stole glances at her in the rearview mirror, wrapping elastic bands around Tina's hair, he wondered how he might make the tour last a little longer. Ordinarily he sped back to Puri using a shortcut, eager to return home, scrub his feet and hands with sandalwood soap, and enjoy the evening newspaper and a cup of tea that his wife would serve him in silence. The thought of that silence, something to which he'd long been resigned, now oppressed him. It was then that he suggested visiting the hills at Udayagiri and Khandagiri, where a number of monastic dwellings were hewn out of the ground, facing one another across a defile. It was some miles away, but well worth seeing, Mr. Kapasi told them.

"Oh yeah, there's something mentioned about it in this book," Mr. Das said. "Built by a Jain king or something."

"Shall we go then?" Mr. Kapasi asked. He paused at a turn in the road. "It's to the left."

Mr. Das turned to look at Mrs. Das. Both of them shrugged.

"Left, left," the children chanted.

Mr. Kapasi turned the wheel, almost delirious with relief. He did not know what he would do or say to Mrs. Das once they arrived at the hills. Perhaps he would tell her what a pleasing smile she had. Perhaps he would compliment her strawberry shirt, which he found irresistibly becoming. Perhaps, when Mr. Das was busy taking a picture, he would take her hand.

He did not have to worry. When they got to the hills, divided by a steep path thick with trees, Mrs. Das refused to get out of the car. All along the path, dozens of monkeys were seated on stones, as well as on

110

115

the branches of the trees. Their hind legs were stretched out in front and raised to shoulder level, their arms resting on their knees.

"My legs are tired," she said, sinking low in her seat. "I'll stay here."

"Why did you have to wear those stupid shoes?" Mr. Das said. "You won't be in the pictures."

120   "Pretend I'm there."

"But we could use one of these pictures for our Christmas card this year. We didn't get one of all five of us at the Sun Temple. Mr. Kapasi could take it."

"I'm not coming. Anyway, those monkeys give me the creeps."

"But they're harmless," Mr. Das said. He turned to Mr. Kapasi. "Aren't they?"

"They are more hungry than dangerous," Mr. Kapasi said. "Do not provoke them with food, and they will not bother you."

125   Mr. Das headed up the defile with the children, the boys at his side, the little girl on his shoulders. Mr. Kapasi watched as they crossed paths with a Japanese man and woman, the only other tourists there, who paused for a final photograph, then stepped into a nearby car and drove away. As the car disappeared out of view some of the monkeys called out, emitting soft whooping sounds, and then walked on their flat black hands and feet up the path. At one point a group of them formed a little ring around Mr. Das and the children. Tina screamed in delight. Ronny ran in circles around his father. Bobby bent down and picked up a fat stick on the ground. When he extended it, one of the monkeys approached him and snatched it, then briefly beat the ground.

"I'll join them," Mr. Kapasi said, unlocking the door on his side. "There is much to explain about the caves."

"No. Stay a minute," Mrs. Das said. She got out of the back seat and slipped in beside Mr. Kapasi. "Raj has his dumb book anyway." Together, through the windshield, Mrs. Das and Mr. Kapasi watched as Bobby and the monkey passed the stick back and forth between them.

"A brave little boy," Mr. Kapasi commented.

"It's not so surprising," Mrs. Das said.

130   "No?"

"He's not his."

"I beg your pardon?"

"Raj's. He's not Raj's son."

Mr. Kapasi felt a prickle on his skin. He reached into his shirt pocket for the small tin of lotus-oil balm he carried with him at all times, and applied it to three spots on his forehead. He knew that Mrs. Das was watching him, but he did not turn to face her. Instead he watched as the figures of Mr. Das and the children grew smaller, climbing up the steep path, pausing every now and then for a picture, surrounded by a growing number of monkeys.

"Are you surprised?" The way she put it made him choose his words   135
with care.

"It's not the type of thing one assumes," Mr. Kapasi replied slowly. He put the tin of lotus-oil balm back in his pocket.

"No, of course not. And no one knows, of course. No one at all. I've kept it a secret for eight whole years." She looked at Mr. Kapasi, tilting her chin as if to gain a fresh perspective. "But now I've told you."

Mr. Kapasi nodded. He felt suddenly parched, and his forehead was warm and slightly numb from the balm. He considered asking Mrs. Das for a sip of water, then decided against it.

"We met when we were very young," she said. She reached into her straw bag in search of something, then pulled out a packet of puffed rice. "Want some?"

"No, thank you."   140

She put a fistful in her mouth, sank into the seat a little, and looked away from Mr. Kapasi, out the window on her side of the car. "We married when we were still in college. We were in high school when he proposed. We went to the same college, of course. Back then we couldn't stand the thought of being separated, not for a day, not for a minute. Our parents were best friends who lived in the same town. My entire life I saw him every weekend, either at our house or theirs. We were sent upstairs to play together while our parents joked about our marriage. Imagine! They never caught us at anything, though in a way I think it was all more or less a setup. The things we did those Friday and Saturday nights, while our parents sat downstairs drinking tea . . . I could tell you stories, Mr. Kapasi."

As a result of spending all her time in college with Raj, she continued, she did not make many close friends. There was no one to confide in about him at the end of a difficult day, or to share a passing thought or a worry. Her parents now lived on the other side of the world, but she had never been very close to them, anyway. After marrying so young she was overwhelmed by it all, having a child so quickly, and nursing, and warming up bottles of milk and testing their temperature against her wrist while Raj was at work, dressed in sweaters and corduroy pants, teaching his students about rocks and dinosaurs. Raj never looked cross or harried, or plump as she had become after the first baby.

Always tired, she declined invitations from her one or two college girlfriends, to have lunch or shop in Manhattan. Eventually the friends stopped calling her, so that she was left at home all day with the baby, surrounded by toys that made her trip when she walked or wince when she sat, always cross and tired. Only occasionally did they go out after Ronny was born, and even more rarely did they entertain. Raj didn't mind; he looked forward to coming home from teaching and watching television and bouncing Ronny on his knee. She had been outraged when Raj told her that a Punjabi friend, someone whom she had once met but did not remember, would be staying with them for a week for some job interviews in the New Brunswick area.

Bobby was conceived in the afternoon, on a sofa littered with rubber teething toys, after the friend learned that a London pharmaceutical company had hired him, while Ronny cried to be freed from his playpen. She made no protest when the friend touched the small of her back as she was about to make a pot of coffee, then pulled her against his crisp navy suit. He made love to her swiftly, in silence, with an expertise she had never known, without the meaningful expressions and smiles Raj always insisted on afterward. The next day Raj drove the friend to JFK. He was married now, to a Punjabi girl, and they lived in London still, and every year they exchanged Christmas cards with Raj and Mina, each couple tucking photos of their families into the envelopes. He did not know that he was Bobby's father. He never would.

145   "I beg your pardon, Mrs. Das, but why have you told me this information?" Mr. Kapasi asked when she had finally finished speaking, and had turned to face him once again.

"For God's sake, stop calling me Mrs. Das. I'm twenty-eight. You probably have children my age."

"Not quite." It disturbed Mr. Kapasi to learn that she thought of him as a parent. The feeling he had had toward her, that had made him check his reflection in the rearview mirror as they drove, evaporated a little.

"I told you because of your talents." She put the packet of puffed rice back into her bag without folding over the top.

"I don't understand," Mr. Kapasi said.

150   "Don't you see? For eight years I haven't been able to express this to anybody, not to friends, certainly not to Raj. He doesn't even suspect it. He thinks I'm still in love with him. Well, don't you have anything to say?"

"About what?"

"About what I've just told you. About my secret, and about how terrible it makes me feel. I feel terrible looking at my children, and at Raj, always terrible. I have terrible urges, Mr. Kapasi, to throw things away. One day I had the urge to throw everything I own out the window, the television, the children, everything. Don't you think it's unhealthy?"

He was silent.

"Mr. Kapasi, don't you have anything to say? I thought that was your job."

"My job is to give tours, Mrs. Das." 155

"Not that. Your other job. As an interpreter."

"But we do not face a language barrier. What need is there for an interpreter?"

"That's not what I mean. I would never have told you otherwise. Don't you realize what it means for me to tell you?"

"What does it mean?"

"It means that I'm tired of feeling so terrible all the time. Eight years, 160 Mr. Kapasi, I've been in pain eight years. I was hoping you could help me feel better, say the right thing. Suggest some kind of remedy."

He looked at her, in her red plaid skirt and strawberry T-shirt, a woman not yet thirty, who loved neither her husband nor her children, who had already fallen out of love with life. Her confession depressed him, depressed him all the more when he thought of Mr. Das at the top of the path, Tina clinging to his shoulders, taking pictures of ancient monastic cells cut into the hills to show his students in America, unsuspecting and unaware that one of his sons was not his own. Mr. Kapasi felt insulted that Mrs. Das should ask him to interpret her common, trivial little secret. She did not resemble the patients in the doctor's office, those who came glassy-eyed and desperate, unable to sleep or breathe or urinate with ease, unable, above all, to give words to their pains. Still, Mr. Kapasi believed it was his duty to assist Mrs. Das. Perhaps he ought to tell her to confess the truth to Mr. Das. He would explain that honesty was the best policy. Honesty, surely, would help her feel better, as she'd put it. Perhaps he would offer to preside over the discussion, as a mediator. He decided to begin with the most obvious question, to get to the heart of the matter, and so he asked, "Is it really pain you feel, Mrs. Das, or is it guilt?"

She turned to him and glared, mustard oil thick on her frosty pink lips. She opened her mouth to say something, but as she glared at Mr. Kapasi some certain knowledge seemed to pass before her eyes, and she stopped. It crushed him; he knew at that moment that he was not even important enough to be properly insulted. She opened the car door and began walking up the path, wobbling a little on her square wooden heels, reaching into her straw bag to eat handfuls of puffed rice. It fell through her fingers, leaving a zigzagging trail, causing a monkey to leap down from a tree and devour the little white grains. In search of more, the monkey began to follow Mrs. Das. Others joined him, so that she was soon being followed by about half a dozen of them, their velvety tails dragging behind.

Mr. Kapasi stepped out of the car. He wanted to holler, to alert her in some way, but he worried that if she knew they were behind her, she would grow nervous. Perhaps she would lose her balance. Perhaps they would pull at her bag or her hair. He began to jog up the path, taking a fallen branch in his hand to scare away the monkeys. Mrs. Das continued walking, oblivious, trailing grains of puffed rice. Near the top of the incline, before a group of cells fronted by a row of squat stone pillars, Mr. Das was kneeling on the ground, focusing the lens of his camera. The children stood under the arcade, now hiding, now emerging from view.

"Wait for me," Mrs. Das called out. "I'm coming."

165   Tina jumped up and down. "Here comes Mommy!"

"Great," Mr. Das said without looking up. "Just in time. We'll get Mr. Kapasi to take a picture of the five of us."

Mr. Kapasi quickened his pace, waving his branch so that the monkeys scampered away, distracted, in another direction.

"Where's Bobby?" Mrs. Das asked when she stopped.

Mr. Das looked up from the camera. "I don't know. Ronny, where's Bobby?"

170   Ronny shrugged. "I thought he was right here."

"Where is he?" Mrs. Das repeated sharply. "What's wrong with all of you?"

They began calling his name, wandering up and down the path a bit. Because they were calling, they did not initially hear the boy's screams. When they found him, a little farther down the path under a tree, he was surrounded by a group of monkeys, over a dozen of them, pulling at his T-shirt with their long black fingers. The puffed rice Mrs. Das had spilled was scattered at his feet, raked over by the monkeys' hands. The boy was silent, his body frozen, swift tears running down his startled face. His bare legs were dusty and red with welts from where one of the monkeys struck him repeatedly with the stick he had given to it earlier.

"Daddy, the monkey's hurting Bobby," Tina said.

Mr. Das wiped his palms on the front of his shorts. In his nervousness he accidentally pressed the shutter on his camera; the whirring noise of the advancing film excited the monkeys, and the one with the stick began to beat Bobby more intently. "What are we supposed to do? What if they start attacking?"

175   "Mr. Kapasi," Mrs. Das shrieked, noticing him standing to one side. "Do something, for God's sake, do something!"

Mr. Kapasi took his branch and shooed them away, hissing at the ones that remained, stomping his feet to scare them. The animals retreated slowly, with a measured gait, obedient but unintimidated. Mr. Kapasi gathered Bobby in his arms and brought him back to where his parents and siblings were standing. As he carried him he was tempted to whisper a secret into the boy's ear. But Bobby was stunned, and shivering with fright, his legs bleeding slightly where the stick had broken the skin. When Mr. Kapasi delivered him to his parents, Mr. Das brushed some dirt off the boy's T-shirt and put the visor on him the right way. Mrs. Das reached into her straw bag to find a bandage which she taped over the cut on his knee. Ronny offered his brother a fresh piece of gum. "He's fine. Just a little scared, right, Bobby?" Mr. Das said, patting the top of his head.

"God, let's get out of here," Mrs. Das said. She folded her arms across the strawberry on her chest. "This place gives me the creeps."

"Yeah. Back to the hotel, definitely," Mr. Das agreed.

"Poor Bobby," Mrs. Das said. "Come here a second. Let Mommy fix your hair." Again she reached into her straw bag, this time for her hairbrush, and began to run it around the edges of the translucent visor. When she whipped out the hairbrush, the slip of paper with Mr. Kapasi's address on it fluttered away in the wind. No one but Mr. Kapasi noticed. He watched as it rose, carried higher and higher by the breeze, into the trees where the monkeys now sat, solemnly observing the scene below. Mr. Kapasi observed it too, knowing that this was the picture of the Das family he would preserve forever in his mind.

QUESTIONS

1. Define the central conflict in this story. Is the conflict resolved in the story's conclusion?
2. How does the plot help to illuminate the differing cultural viewpoints of Mr. Kapasi and of Mr. and Mrs. Das? Which cultural viewpoint is presented with greater sympathy?
3. How does Mr. Kapasi's job as an "interpreter of maladies" relate to the action in this story? Does he have the occasion to use his diagnostic ability in his interactions with the Das family?
4. Discuss the significance of Mrs. Das's requesting, and then losing, Mr. Kapasi's address. Apart from its function in the plot, how does this suggest a resolution to the story?
5. How do the characters' views of one another differ from the way the reader is encouraged to view them? How does this ironic technique help to generate suspense?
6. How do the monkeys that the group encounters in the hill country serve as a plot element, helping to advance the story?

7. Discuss the function of the "secret" Mrs. Das reveals to Mr. Kapasi. Does this scene make Mrs. Das more sympathetic?

8. What does the ending suggest about Mr. Kapasi's future? Has his encounter with the Das family created any permanent change in his outlook on life or his view of himself? Is the ending happy or unhappy?

SUGGESTIONS FOR WRITING

1. In Wolff's "Hunters in the Snow," the plot helps to illuminate the struggle for power among the three principal characters. Write an essay in which you show how this struggle for power is elucidated by some of the elements of fiction presented in Chapter Two—such as suspense, mystery, surprise, and conflict.

2. Write an essay on the ending of one of the following stories, determining whether it is happy, unhappy, or indeterminate and how the type of ending helps define the story as an example of commercial or literary fiction:
   a. Wolff, "Hunters in the Snow" (page 86).
   b. Achebe, "Civil Peace" (page 511).
   c. Cofer, "American History" (page 539).
   d. Jackson, "The Lottery" (page 251).

3. Write an essay defining the type(s) of conflict in one of these stories:
   a. Achebe, "Civil Peace" (page 511).
   b. Hurston, "The Gilded Six-Bits" (page 564).
   c. Hemingway, "Hills Like White Elephants" (page 268).
   d. Wharton, "Roman Fever" (page 409).

Chapter Three

Characterization

The preceding chapter considered plot apart from characterization, as if the two were separable. Actually, along with the other elements of fiction discussed in later chapters, plot and characterization work together in any good story. In commercial fiction, plot is usually more important than in-depth characterization, while literary writers are usually more concerned with complex characters than with the mechanics of plot. Many literary fiction writers, in fact, consider characterization to be the most important element of their art.

Analyzing **characterization** is more difficult than describing plot, for human character is infinitely complex, variable, and ambiguous. Anyone can summarize what a person in a story has done, but a writer needs considerable skill and insight into human beings to describe convincingly *who* a person is. Even the most complicated plot in a detective story puts far less strain on our understanding than does human nature. This is why commercial fiction may feature an elaborate plot but offer characters who are simple and two-dimensional, even stereotypical. In such fiction the characters must be easily identifiable and clearly labeled as good or bad; the commercial author's aim is to create characters who can carry the plot forward, not to explore human psychology and motivation.

The main character in a commercial work must also be someone attractive or sympathetic. If the protagonist is male, he need not be perfect, but usually he must be fundamentally decent—honest, goodhearted, and preferably good-looking. He may also have larger-than-life qualities, showing himself to be daring, dashing, or gallant. He may defy laws made for "ordinary" people, but this makes him even more likable because he breaks the rules for a good reason: to catch a criminal, or to prevent a disaster. In commercial fiction, the reader enjoys identifying with such a protagonist, vicariously sharing his adventures, escapes, and triumphs. If the protagonist has vices, they must be the kind a typical reader would not mind or would enjoy having. For instance, the main character in successful commercial fiction may be sexually promiscuous—James Bond is a good example—and thus allow readers to indulge imaginatively in pleasures they might not allow themselves in real life.

Literary fiction does not necessarily renounce the attractive character. Jane Eyre, Huckleberry Finn, and Holden Caulfield are literary characters beloved by millions of readers; both Mr. Kapasi in "Interpreter of Maladies" and Edie in "How I Met My Husband" are likable characters as well. But literary protagonists are less easily labeled and pigeonholed than their counterparts in commercial fiction. Sometimes they may be wholly unsympathetic, even despicable. But because human nature is not often entirely bad or perfectly good, literary fiction deals usually with characters who are composed of both good and evil impulses, three-dimensional human beings who live in our memory as "real" people long after we have stopped reading.

Such fiction offers an exciting opportunity to observe human nature in all its complexity and multiplicity. It enables us to know people, to understand them, and to develop compassion for them in a way we might not do without reading serious fiction. In some respects, we can know fictional characters even better than we know real people in our lives. For one thing, we observe fictional people in situations that are always significant and that serve to illuminate their characters in a way that our daily, routine exposure to real people seldom does. We can also view a character's inner life in a way that's impossible in ordinary life. Authors can show us, if they wish, exactly what is happening in a character's mind and emotions. In real life, of course, we can only guess at another person's thoughts and feelings from external behavior, which may be designed to conceal the person's inner life. Because of the opportunity literary fiction affords us of knowing its characters so thoroughly, it also enables us to understand the motives and behavior of people in real life.

Authors present their characters either directly or indirectly. In **direct presentation** they tell us straight out, by exposition or analysis, what the characters are like, or they have another character in the story describe them. In **indirect presentation** the author *shows* us the characters through their actions; we determine what they are like by what they say or do. Graham Greene uses direct presentation when he tells us about Blackie: "He was just, he had no jealousy." He uses indirect presentation when he shows Blackie allowing the gang to vote on Trevor's project, accepting the end of his leadership fairly calmly, taking orders from Trevor without resentment, burning banknotes with

Trevor, and racing him home. In this story, of course, the word "just" has a slight ironic twist—it applies only to behavior within the gang—and Greene presents this indirectly. Alice Munro relies on indirect presentation to show that Chris Watters is a charming but irresponsible barnstormer; Edie never directly criticizes him, but we feel her disillusionment as she waits day after day for a letter that will never come.

Sometimes the method of direct presentation has the advantages of being clear and economical, but good writers use it sparingly. In order to involve the reader in a character, the author must *show* the character in action; the axiom "show, don't tell" is therefore one of the basics of fiction writing. If characters are merely described, then the story will read more like an essay. The direct method usually has little emotional impact unless it is bolstered by the indirect. It will give us only the explanation of a character, not the impression of a living, breathing human being. In almost all good fiction, therefore, the characters are **dramatized.** They are shown speaking and behaving, as in a stage play. If we are really to believe in the selfishness of a character, we must see the character acting selfishly. Instead of telling us that Frank in "Hunters in the Snow" is a selfish, self-deluding man, Wolff gives us dramatic scenes in which Frank exhibits his selfishness and self-delusions through his dialogue and actions. Most literary writers rely on indirect presentation and may even use it exclusively.

Good fiction follows three other principles of characterization. First, the characters are consistent in their behavior: they do not behave one way on one occasion and a different way on another unless there is a clear and sufficient reason for the change. Second, the characters' words and actions spring from motivations the reader can understand and believe; if we can't understand why they behave in a certain way immediately, that understanding comes by the end of the story. Finally, the characters must be plausible or lifelike. They cannot be perfectly virtuous or monsters of evil; nor can they have some impossible combination of contradictory traits. In short, the author must convince the reader that the character might well have existed so that, at least while we're reading, we have the illusion that the person is real and forget we are reading fiction at all.

In his book *Aspects of the Novel* (1927), the British novelist E. M. Forster introduced terms that have become standard in discussing types of characters; he wrote that a literary character is either "flat" or "round." **Flat characters** usually have only one or two predominant traits; they can be summed up in a sentence or two. Richard Connell's character Ivan, for instance, is a fearsome thug, and that is all we need to know about him. By contrast, **round characters** are complex and many-sided; they have the three-dimensional quality of real people. Huck Finn, for example, because Mark Twain imagined and dramatized him so successfully as an individual, lives vigorously in the imagination of millions of readers. This is not to say that flat characters cannot be memorable. Though essentially two-dimensional, they too may be made memorable in the hands of an expert author who creates some vivid detail of their appearance, gestures, or speech. Ebenezer Scrooge, in Dickens's *A Christmas Carol*, could be defined as a stereotype of the miserly misanthrope; but his "Bah! Humbug!" has helped make him an immortal character.

Whether round or flat, all characters in good fiction are dramatized to whatever extent needed to make them convincing and to fulfill their roles in the story. Most short stories, of course, will have room for only one or two round characters. Minor characters must necessarily remain flat. There are some literary stories, of course, where the exploration of individual character is not the main focus of interest—Shirley Jackson's "The Lottery" (page 251) is an example—and in such stories none of the characters may be developed fully. Such instances, however, are relatively rare.

A special kind of flat character is the **stock character.** These are stereotyped figures who have recurred so often in fiction that we recognize them at once: the strong silent sheriff, the brilliant detective with eccentric habits, the mad scientist who performs fiendish experiments on living people, the glamorous international spy of mysterious background, the comic Englishman with a monocle, the cruel stepmother, and so forth. Commercial authors often rely on such stock characters for precisely the reason that they can be grasped quickly and easily by the reader. Such characters are like interchangeable parts that might be transferred from one story to another. When literary writers employ a conventional type, however, they usually add individualizing touches to help create a fresh and memorable character. Conan Doyle's Sherlock Holmes follows a stock pattern of the detective, but he remains more memorable than hundreds of other fictional detectives who have come and gone since he was created. Similarly, Wolff's character Tub in "Hunters in the Snow" embodies the stereotypes of the fat, comic buffoon; but certain details about him—his insecurity, his habit of hiding the food he eats so compulsively—help to make him distinctive.

Fictional characters may also be classified as either static or developing. The **static character** remains essentially the same person from the beginning of the story to the end. The **developing** (or dynamic)

character, on the other hand, undergoes some distinct change of character, personality, or outlook. The change may be a large or a small one; it may be positive or negative; but it is something significant and basic, not some minor change of habit or opinion. The Irish writer James Joyce used a term that has become widely adopted today, noting that a character in a story often experiences an **epiphany,** which he termed a moment of spiritual insight into life or into the character's own circumstances. This epiphany or insight usually defines the moment of the developing character's change.

Edie in Munro's "How I Met My Husband" is a dynamic character, for she learns a painful lesson about romance and growing up that alters the entire course of her life. Many stories show a change in the protagonist as the result of some crucial situation in his or her life. This change is usually at the heart of the story, and defining and explaining the change will be the best way to arrive at its meaning. In commercial fiction, changes in character are likely to be relatively superficial, intended mainly to effect a happy ending. Readers of literary fiction, however, usually expect that a convincing change in a character meet three conditions: (1) it must be consistent with the individual's characterization as dramatized in the story; (2) it must be sufficiently motivated by the circumstances in which the character is placed; and (3) the story must offer sufficient time for the change to take place and still be believable. Essential changes in human character, after all, do not usually occur suddenly. For this reason, good fiction will not give us a confirmed criminal who miraculously reforms at the end of a story, or a lifelong racist who wakes up one day and decides to be tolerant and open-minded. If fiction is to be convincing, it must show us believable, dynamic, but often quiet changes or turning points in a character's life. When an author has carefully laid the groundwork earlier in the story, we believe in the character's change and experience the moment of epiphany as a possibly small but significant marker in the life of an individual human being.

Ultimately it is the quality of characterization by which a literary story stands or falls. Long after we have read even the greatest novels and short stories, we tend to remember not the incidents of plot but the unforgettable characters who made our reading such a rich, vibrant experience. Through the creation of character, an author can summon up a new personality, a new voice, and an entirely new and original way of seeing the world. Such characters come alive each time a reader takes up the story, renewing the miracle of the human imagination.

REVIEWING CHAPTER THREE

1. Describe the significance of characterization in literary fiction vs. commercial fiction.
2. Distinguish between direct and indirect presentation of character in fiction.
3. Review the terms "flat character," "round character," and "stock character."
4. Consider the difference between a static character and a dynamic character.
5. Explore the authors' use of characterization in the following stories.

Alice Walker
Everyday Use

for your grandmama

I will wait for her in the yard that Maggie and I made so clean and wavy yesterday afternoon. A yard like this is more comfortable than most people know. It is not just a yard. It is like an extended living room. When the hard clay is swept clean as a floor and the fine sand around the edges lined with tiny, irregular grooves, anyone can come and sit and look up into the elm tree and wait for the breezes that never come inside the house.

Maggie will be nervous until after her sister goes: she will stand hopelessly in corners, homely and ashamed of the burn scars down her arms and legs, eying her sister with a mixture of envy and awe. She

EVERYDAY USE   First published in 1973. Alice Walker was born in Georgia in 1944, attended Spelman College for two years, earned her B.A. from Sarah Lawrence, and was active in the civil rights movement. She has taught and been writer-in-residence at various colleges including Jackson State, Tougaloo, Wellesley, the University of California at Berkeley, and Brandeis. The names adopted by two of the characters in the story reflect the practice among some members of the black community of rejecting names inherited from the period of slavery and selecting others more in keeping with their African heritage. The greetings used by Hakim and Wangero ("Asalamalakim" and "Wa-su-zo-Tean-o") are apparently adaptations of Arabic and African languages.

thinks her sister has held life always in the palm of one hand, that "no" is a word the world never learned to say to her.

You've no doubt seen those TV shows where the child who has "made it" is confronted, as a surprise, by her own mother and father, tottering in weakly from backstage. (A pleasant surprise, of course: What would they do if parent and child came on the show only to curse out and insult each other?) On TV mother and child embrace and smile into each other's faces. Sometimes the mother and father weep, the child wraps them in her arms and leans across the table to tell how she would not have made it without their help. I have seen these programs.

Sometimes I dream a dream in which Dee and I are suddenly brought together on a TV program of this sort. Out of a dark and soft-seated limousine I am ushered into a bright room filled with many people. There I meet a smiling, gray, sporty man like Johnny Carson° who shakes my hand and tells me what a fine girl I have. Then we are on the stage and Dee is embracing me with tears in her eyes. She pins on my dress a large orchid, even though she had told me once that she thinks orchids are tacky flowers.

In real life I am a large, big-boned woman with rough, man-working hands. In the winter I wear flannel nightgowns to bed and overalls during the day. I can kill and clean a hog as mercilessly as a man. My fat keeps me hot in zero weather. I can work outside all day, breaking ice to get water for washing; I can eat pork liver cooked over the open fire minutes after it comes steaming from the hog. One winter I knocked a bull calf straight in the brain between the eyes with a sledge hammer and had the meat hung up to chill before nightfall. But of course all this does not show on television. I am the way my daughter would want me to be: a hundred pounds lighter, my skin like an uncooked barley pancake. My hair glistens in the hot bright lights. Johnny Carson has much to do to keep up with my quick and witty tongue. 5

But that is a mistake. I know even before I wake up. Who ever knew a Johnson with a quick tongue? Who can even imagine me looking a strange white man in the eye? It seems to me I have talked to them always with one foot raised in flight, with my head turned in whichever way is farthest from them. Dee, though. She would always look anyone in the eye. Hesitation was no part of her nature.

Johnny Carson: former host of *The Tonight Show* on NBC

"How do I look, Mama?" Maggie says, showing just enough of her thin body enveloped in pink skirt and red blouse for me to know she's there, almost hidden by the door.

"Come out into the yard," I say.

Have you ever seen a lame animal, perhaps a dog run over by some careless person rich enough to own a car, sidle up to someone who is ignorant enough to be kind to him? That is the way my Maggie walks. She has been like this, chin on chest, eyes on ground, feet in shuffle, ever since the fire that burned the other house to the ground.

10   Dee is lighter than Maggie, with nicer hair and a fuller figure. She's a woman now, though sometimes I forget. How long ago was it that the other house burned? Ten, twelve years? Sometimes I can still hear the flames and feel Maggie's arms sticking to me, her hair smoking and her dress falling off her in little black papery flakes. Her eyes seemed stretched open, blazed open by the flames reflected in them. And Dee. I see her standing off under the sweet gum tree she used to dig gum out of; a look of concentration on her face as she watched the last dingy gray board of the house fall in toward the red-hot brick chimney. Why don't you do a dance around the ashes? I'd wanted to ask her. She had hated the house that much.

I used to think she hated Maggie, too. But that was before we raised the money, the church and me, to send her to Augusta to school. She used to read to us without pity; forcing words, lies, other folks' habits, whole lives upon us two, sitting trapped and ignorant underneath her voice. She washed us in a river of make-believe, burned us with a lot of knowledge we didn't necessarily need to know. Pressed us to her with the serious way she read, to shove us away at just the moment, like dimwits, we seemed about to understand.

Dee wanted nice things. A yellow organdy dress to wear to her graduation from high school; black pumps to match a green suit she'd made from an old suit somebody gave me. She was determined to stare down any disaster in her efforts. Her eyelids would not flicker for minutes at a time. Often I fought off the temptation to shake her. At sixteen she had a style of her own: and knew what style was.

I never had an education myself. After second grade the school was closed down. Don't ask me why: in 1927 colored asked fewer questions than they do now. Sometimes Maggie reads to me. She stumbles along good-naturedly but can't see well. She knows she is not bright. Like good looks and money, quickness passed her by. She will marry John Thomas (who has mossy teeth in an earnest face) and then I'll be free to sit here and I guess just sing church songs to myself. Although I never was a good singer. Never could carry a tune. I was always better at a man's job. I used to love to milk till I was hooked in the side in '49. Cows are soothing and slow and don't bother you, unless you try to milk them the wrong way.

I have deliberately turned my back on the house. It is three rooms, just like the one that burned, except the roof is tin; they don't make shingle roofs any more. There are no real windows, just some holes cut in the sides, like the portholes in a ship, but not round and not square, with rawhide holding the shutters up on the outside. This house is in a pasture, too, like the other one. No doubt when Dee sees it she will want to tear it down. She wrote me once that no matter where we "choose" to live, she will manage to come see us. But she will never bring her friends. Maggie and I thought about this and Maggie asked me, "Mama, when did Dee ever *have* any friends?"

She had a few. Furtive boys in pink shirts hanging about on wash- 15 day after school. Nervous girls who never laughed. Impressed with her, they worshipped the well-turned phrase, the cute shape, the scalding humor that erupted like bubbles in lye. She read to them.

When she was courting Jimmy T she didn't have much time to pay to us, but turned all her faultfinding power on him. He *flew* to marry a cheap city girl from a family of ignorant flashy people. She hardly had time to recompose herself.

When she comes I will meet—but there they are!

Maggie attempts to make a dash for the house, in her shuffling way, but I stay her with my hand. "Come back here," I say. And she stops and tries to dig a well in the sand with her toe.

It is hard to see them clearly through the strong sun. But even the first glimpse of leg out of the car tells me it is Dee. Her feet were always neat-looking, as if God himself had shaped them with a certain style. From the other side of the car comes a short, stocky man. Hair is all over his head a foot long and hanging from his chin like a kinky mule tail. I hear Maggie suck in her breath. "Uhnnnh," is what it sounds like. Like when you see the wriggling end of a snake just in front of your foot on the road. "Uhnnnh."

Dee next. A dress down to the ground, in this hot weather. A dress 20 so loud it hurts my eyes. There are yellows and oranges enough to throw back the light of the sun. I feel my whole face warming from the heat waves it throws out. Earrings gold, too, and hanging down to her shoulders. Bracelets dangling and making noises when she moves her arm up to shake the folds of the dress out of her armpits. The dress is loose and flows, and as she walks closer, I like it. I hear Maggie go "Uhnnnh" again. It is her sister's hair. It stands straight up like the wool on a sheep. It is black as night and around the edges are two long pigtails that rope about like small lizards disappearing behind her ears.

"Wa-su-zo-Tean-o!" she says, coming on in that gliding way the dress makes her move. The short stocky fellow with the hair to his navel is all grinning and he follows up with "Asalamalakim, my mother and sister!" He moves to hug Maggie but she falls back, right up against the back of my chair. I feel her trembling there and when I look up I see the perspiration falling off her chin.

"Don't get up," says Dee. Since I am stout it takes something of a push. You can see me trying to move a second or two before I make it. She turns, showing white heels through her sandals, and goes back to the car. Out she peeks next with a Polaroid. She stoops down quickly and lines up picture after picture of me sitting there in front of the house with Maggie cowering behind me. She never takes a shot without making sure the house is included. When a cow comes nibbling around the edge of the yard she snaps it and me and Maggie and the house. Then she puts the Polaroid in the back seat of the car, and comes up and kisses me on the forehead.

Meanwhile Asalamalakim is going through motions with Maggie's hand. Maggie's hand is as limp as a fish, and probably as cold, despite the sweat, and she keeps trying to pull it back. It looks like Asalamalakim wants to shake hands but wants to do it fancy. Or maybe he don't know how people shake hands. Anyhow, he soon gives up on Maggie.

"Well," I say. "Dee."

25   "No, Mama," she says. "Not 'Dee,' Wangero Leewanika Kemanjo!"

"What happened to 'Dee'?" I wanted to know.

"She's dead," Wangero said. "I couldn't bear it any longer, being named after the people who oppress me."

"You know as well as me you was named after your aunt Dicie," I said. Dicie is my sister. She named Dee. We called her "Big Dee" after Dee was born.

"But who was she named after?" asked Wangero.

30   "I guess after Grandma Dee," I said.

"And who was she named after?" asked Wangero.

"Her mother," I said, and saw Wangero was getting tired. "That's about as far back as I can trace it," I said. Though, in fact, I probably could have carried it back beyond the Civil War through the branches.

"Well," said Asalamalakim, "there you are."

"Uhnnnh," I heard Maggie say.

35   "There I was not," I said, "before 'Dicie' cropped up in our family, so why should I try to trace it that far back?"

He just stood there grinning, looking down on me like somebody inspecting a Model A car. Every once in a while he and Wangero sent eye signals over my head.

"How do you pronounce this name?" I asked.

"You don't have to call me by it if you don't want to," said Wangero.

"Why shouldn't I?" I asked. "If that's what you want us to call you, we'll call you."

"I know it might sound awkward at first," said Wangero.   40

"I'll get used to it," I said. "Ream it out again."

Well, soon we got the name out of the way. Asalamalakim had a name twice as long and three times as hard. After I tripped over it two or three times he told me to just call him Hakim-a-barber. I wanted to ask him was he a barber, but I didn't really think he was, so I didn't ask.

"You must belong to those beef-cattle peoples down the road," I said. They said "Asalamalakim" when they met you, too, but they didn't shake hands. Always too busy: feeding the cattle, fixing the fences, putting up salt-lick shelters, throwing down hay. When the white folks poisoned some of the herd the men stayed up all night with rifles in their hands. I walked a mile and a half just to see the sight.

Hakim-a-barber said, "I accept some of their doctrines, but farming and raising cattle is not my style." (They didn't tell me, and I didn't ask, whether Wangero (Dee) had really gone and married him.)

We sat down to eat and right away he said he didn't eat collards   45 and pork was unclean. Wangero, though, went on through the chitlins and corn bread, the greens and everything else. She talked a blue streak over the sweet potatoes. Everything delighted her. Even the fact that we still used the benches her daddy made for the table when we couldn't afford to buy chairs.

"Oh, Mama!" she cried. Then turned to Hakim-a-barber. "I never knew how lovely these benches are. You can feel the rump prints," she said, running her hands underneath her and along the bench. Then she gave a sigh and her hand closed over Grandma Dee's butter dish. "That's it!" she said. "I knew there was something I wanted to ask you if I could have." She jumped up from the table and went over in the corner where the churn stood, the milk in it clabber by now. She looked at the churn and looked at it.

"This churn top is what I need," she said. "Didn't Uncle Buddy whittle it out of a tree you all used to have?"

"Yes," I said.

"Uh huh," she said happily. "And I want the dasher, too."

"Uncle Buddy whittle that, too?" asked the barber.   50

Dee (Wangero) looked up at me.

"Aunt Dee's first husband whittled the dash," said Maggie so low you almost couldn't hear her. "His name was Henry, but they called him Stash."

"Maggie's brain is like an elephant's," Wangero said, laughing. "I can use the churn top as a centerpiece for the alcove table," she said, sliding a plate over the churn, "and I'll think of something artistic to do with the dasher."

When she finished wrapping the dasher the handle stuck out. I took it for a moment in my hands. You didn't even have to look close to see where hands pushing the dasher up and down to make butter had left a kind of sink in the wood. In fact, there were a lot of small sinks; you could see where thumbs and fingers had sunk into the wood. It was beautiful light yellow wood, from a tree that grew in the yard where Big Dee and Stash had lived.

55   After dinner Dee (Wangero) went to the trunk at the foot of my bed and started rifling through it. Maggie hung back in the kitchen over the dishpan. Out came Wangero with two quilts. They had been pieced by Grandma Dee and then Big Dee and me had hung them on the quilt frames on the front porch and quilted them. One was in the Lone Star pattern. The other was Walk Around the Mountain. In both of them were scraps of dresses Grandma Dee had worn fifty and more years ago. Bits and pieces of Grandpa Jarrell's Paisley shirts. And one teeny faded blue piece, about the size of a penny matchbox, that was from Great Grandpa Ezra's uniform that he wore in the Civil War.

"Mama," Wangero said sweet as a bird. "Can I have these old quilts?"

I heard something fall in the kitchen, and a minute later the kitchen door slammed.

"Why don't you take one or two of the others?" I asked. "These old things was just done by me and Big Dee from some tops your grandma pieced before she died."

"No," said Wangero. "I don't want those. They are stitched around the borders by machine."

60   "That'll make them last better," I said.

"That's not the point," said Wangero. "These are all pieces of dresses Grandma used to wear. She did all this stitching by hand. Imagine!" She held the quilts securely in her arms, stroking them.

"Some of the pieces, like those lavender ones, come from old clothes her mother handed down to her," I said, moving up to touch the quilts. Dee (Wangero) moved back just enough so that I couldn't reach the quilts. They already belonged to her.

"Imagine!" she breathed again, clutching them closely to her bosom.

"The truth is," I said, "I promised to give them quilts to Maggie, for when she marries John Thomas."

She gasped like a bee had stung her.   65

"Maggie can't appreciate these quilts!" she said. "She'd probably be backward enough to put them to everyday use."

"I reckon she would," I said. "God knows I been saving 'em for long enough with nobody using 'em. I hope she will!" I didn't want to bring up how I had offered Dee (Wangero) a quilt when she went away to college. Then she had told me they were old-fashioned, out of style.

"But they're *priceless!*" she was saying now, furiously; for she has a temper. "Maggie would put them on the bed and in five years they'd be in rags. Less than that!"

"She can always make some more," I said. "Maggie knows how to quilt."

Dee (Wangero) looked at me with hatred. "You just will not understand. The point is these quilts, *these* quilts!"   70

"Well," I said, stumped. "What would *you* do with them?"

"Hang them," she said. As if that was the only thing you *could* do with quilts.

Maggie by now was standing in the door. I could almost hear the sound her feet made as they scraped over each other.

"She can have them, Mama," she said, like somebody used to never winning anything, or having anything reserved for her. "I can 'member Grandma Dee without the quilts."

I looked at her hard. She had filled her bottom lip with checkerberry snuff and it gave her face a kind of dopey, hangdog look. It was 75
Grandma Dee and Big Dee who taught her how to quilt herself. She stood there with her scarred hands hidden in the folds of her skirt. She looked at her sister with something like fear but she wasn't mad at her. This was Maggie's portion. This was the way she knew God to work.

When I looked at her like that something hit me in the top of my head and ran down to the soles of my feet. Just like when I'm in church and the spirit of God touches me and I get happy and shout. I did something I never had done before: hugged Maggie to me, then dragged her on into the room, snatched the quilts out of Miss Wangero's hands and dumped them into Maggie's lap. Maggie just sat there on my bed with her mouth open.

"Take one or two of the others," I said to Dee.

But she turned without a word and went out to Hakim-a-barber.

"You just don't understand," she said, as Maggie and I came out to the car.

80   "What don't I understand?" I wanted to know.

"Your heritage," she said. And then she turned to Maggie, kissed her, and said, "You ought to try to make something of yourself, too, Maggie. It's really a new day for us. But from the way you and Mama still live you'd never know it."

She put on some sunglasses that hid everything above the tip of her nose and her chin.

Maggie smiled; maybe at the sunglasses. But a real smile, not scared. After we watched the car dust settle I asked Maggie to bring me a dip of snuff. And then the two of us sat there just enjoying, until it was time to go in the house and go to bed.

QUESTIONS

1. Characterize the speaker and evaluate her reliability as a reporter and interpreter of events. Where does she refrain from making judgments? Where does she present less than the full truth? Do these examples of reticence undercut her reliability?

2. Describe as fully as possible the lives of the mother, Dee, and Maggie prior to the events of the story. How are the following incidents from the past also reflected in the present actions: (a) Dee's hatred of the old house; (b) Dee's ability "to stare down any disaster"; (c) Maggie's burns from the fire; (d) the mother's having been "hooked in the side" while milking a cow; (e) Dee's refusal to accept a quilt when she went away to college?

3. As evidence of current social movements and as innovations that the mother responds to, what do the following have in common: (a) Dee's new name and costume; (b) Hakim's behavior and attitudes; (c) the "beef-cattle peoples down the road"; (d) Dee's concern for her "heritage"?

4. Does the mother's refusal to let Dee have the quilts indicate a permanent or temporary change of character? Why has she never done anything like it before? Why does she do it now? What details in the story prepare for and foreshadow that refusal?

5. How does the physical setting give support to the contrasting attitudes of both the mother and Dee? Does the author indicate that one or the other of them is entirely correct in her feelings about the house and yard?

6. Is Dee wholly unsympathetic? Is the mother's victory over her altogether positive? What emotional ambivalence is there in the final scene between Maggie and her mother in the yard?

Katherine Mansfield
Miss Brill

Although it was so brilliantly fine—the blue sky powdered with gold and great spots of light like white wine splashed over the Jardins Publiques—Miss Brill was glad that she had decided on her fur. The air was motionless, but when you opened your mouth there was just a faint chill, like a chill from a glass of iced water before you sip, and now and again a leaf came drifting—from nowhere, from the sky. Miss Brill put up her hand and touched her fur. Dear little thing! It was nice to feel it again. She had taken it out of its box that afternoon, shaken out the moth powder, given it a good brush, and rubbed the life back into the dim little eyes. "What has been happening to me?" said the sad little eyes. Oh, how sweet it was to see them snap at her again from the red eiderdown! . . . But the nose, which was of some black composition, wasn't at all firm. It must have had a knock, somehow. Never mind—a little dab of black sealing-wax when the time came—when it was absolutely necessary . . . Little rogue! Yes, she really felt like that about it. Little rogue biting its tail just by her left ear. She could have taken it off and laid it on her lap and stroked it. She felt a tingling in her hands and arms, but that came from walking, she supposed. And when she breathed, something light and sad—no, not sad, exactly—something gentle seemed to move in her bosom.

There were a number of people out this afternoon, far more than last Sunday. And the band sounded louder and gayer. That was because the Season had begun. For although the band played all the year round on Sundays, out of season it was never the same. It was like some one playing with only the family to listen; it didn't care how it played if there weren't any strangers present. Wasn't the conductor wearing a new coat, too? She was sure it was new. He scraped with his foot and flapped his arms like a rooster about to crow, and the bandsmen sitting in the green rotunda blew out their cheeks and glared at the music. Now there came a little "flutey" bit—very pretty!—a little chain of bright drops. She was sure it would be repeated. It was; she lifted her head and smiled.

MISS BRILL   Written in 1921; first published in 1922. "Jardins Publiques" is French for Public Gardens. Katherine Mansfield (1888–1923) was born and grew up in New Zealand but lived her adult life in London, with various sojourns on the Continent.

Only two people shared her "special" seat: a fine old man in a velvet coat, his hands clasped over a huge carved walking-stick, and a big old woman, sitting upright, with a roll of knitting on her embroidered apron. They did not speak. This was disappointing, for Miss Brill always looked forward to the conversation. She had become really quite expert, she thought, at listening as though she didn't listen, at sitting in other people's lives just for a minute while they talked round her.

She glanced, sideways, at the old couple. Perhaps they would go soon. Last Sunday, too, hadn't been as interesting as usual. An Englishman and his wife, he wearing a dreadful Panama hat and she button boots. And she'd gone on the whole time about how she ought to wear spectacles; she knew she needed them; but that it was no good getting any; they'd be sure to break and they'd never keep on. And he'd been so patient. He'd suggested everything—gold rims, the kind that curve round your ears, little pads inside the bridge. No, nothing would please her. "They'll always be sliding down my nose!" Miss Brill had wanted to shake her.

5   The old people sat on the bench, still as statues. Never mind, there was always the crowd to watch. To and fro, in front of the flower beds and the band rotunda, the couples and groups paraded, stopped to talk, to greet, to buy a handful of flowers from the old beggar who had his tray fixed to the railings. Little children ran among them, swooping and laughing; little boys with big white silk bows under their chins, little girls, little French dolls, dressed up in velvet and lace. And sometimes a tiny staggerer came suddenly rocking into the open from under the trees, stopped, stared, as suddenly sat down "flop," until its small high-stepping mother, like a young hen, rushed scolding to its rescue. Other people sat on the benches and green chairs, but they were nearly always the same, Sunday after Sunday, and—Miss Brill had often noticed—there was something funny about nearly all of them. They were odd, silent, nearly all old, and from the way they stared they looked as though they'd just come from dark little rooms or even—even cupboards!

Behind the rotunda the slender trees with yellow leaves down drooping, and through them just a line of sea, and beyond the blue sky with gold-veined clouds.

Tum-tum-tum tiddle-um! tiddle-um! tum tiddley-um tum ta! blew the band.

Two young girls in red came by and two young soldiers in blue met them, and they laughed and paired and went off arm-in-arm. Two peasant women with funny straw hats passed, gravely, leading beautiful smoke-colored donkeys. A cold, pale nun hurried by. A beautiful woman came along and dropped her bunch of violets, and a little boy ran after to hand them to her, and she took them and threw them away as if they'd been poisoned. Dear me! Miss Brill didn't know whether to admire that or not! And now an ermine toque and a gentleman in gray met just in front of her. He was tall, stiff, dignified, and she was wearing the ermine toque she'd bought when her hair was yellow. Now everything, her hair, her face, even her eyes, was the same color as the shabby ermine, and her hand, in its cleaned glove, lifted to dab her lips, was a tiny yellowish paw. Oh, she was so pleased to see him—delighted! She rather thought they were going to meet that afternoon. She described where she'd been—everywhere, here, there, along by the sea. The day was so charming—didn't he agree? And wouldn't he, perhaps? . . . But he shook his head, lighted a cigarette, slowly breathed a great deep puff into her face, and, even while she was still talking and laughing, flicked the match away and walked on. The ermine toque was alone; she smiled more brightly than ever. But even the band seemed to know what she was feeling and played more softly, played tenderly, and the drum beat, "The Brute! The Brute!" over and over. What would she do? What was going to happen now? But as Miss Brill wondered, the ermine toque turned, raised her hand as though she'd seen some one else, much nicer, just over there, and pattered away. And the band changed again and played more quickly, more gayly than ever, and the old couple on Miss Brill's seat got up and marched away, and such a funny old man with long whiskers hobbled along in time to the music and was nearly knocked over by four girls walking abreast.

Oh, how fascinating it was! How she enjoyed it! How she loved sitting here, watching it all! It was like a play. It was exactly like a play. Who could believe the sky at the back wasn't painted? But it wasn't till a little brown dog trotted on solemn and then slowly trotted off, like a little "theater" dog, a little dog that had been drugged, that Miss Brill discovered what it was that made it so exciting. They were all on stage. They weren't only the audience, not only looking on; they were acting. Even she had a part and came every Sunday. No doubt somebody would have noticed if she hadn't been there; she was part of the performance after all. How strange she'd never thought of it like that before! And yet it explained why she made such a point of starting from home at just the same time each week—so as not to be late for the performance—and it also explained why she had quite a queer, shy feeling at telling her English pupils how she spent her Sunday afternoons. No wonder! Miss Brill nearly laughed out loud. She was on the stage. She thought of the old invalid gentleman to whom she read the newspaper four afternoons a week while he slept in the garden. She had got quite used to the frail head on the cotton pillow, the hollowed eyes, the open mouth and the high pinched nose. If he'd been dead she mightn't have noticed for weeks; she wouldn't have minded. But suddenly he knew he was having the paper read to him by an actress! "An actress!" The old head lifted; two points of light quivered in the old eyes. "An actress—are ye?" And Miss Brill smoothed the newspaper as though it were the manuscript of her part and said gently: "Yes, I have been an actress for a long time."

10   The band had been having a rest. Now they started again. And what they played was warm, sunny, yet there was just a faint chill—a something, what was it?—not sadness—no, not sadness—a something that made you want to sing. The tune lifted, lifted, the light shone; and it seemed to Miss Brill that in another moment all of them, all the whole company, would begin singing. The young ones, the laughing ones who were moving together, they would begin, and the men's voices, very resolute and brave, would join them. And then she too, she too, and the others on the benches—they would come in with a kind of accompaniment—something low, that scarcely rose or fell, something so beautiful—moving . . . And Miss Brill's eyes filled with tears and she looked smiling at all the other members of the company. Yes, we understand, we understand, she thought—though what they understood she didn't know.

Just at that moment a boy and girl came and sat down where the old couple had been. They were beautifully dressed; they were in love. The hero and heroine, of course, just arrived from his father's yacht. And still soundlessly singing, still with that trembling smile, Miss Brill prepared to listen.

"No, not now," said the girl. "Not here, I can't."

"But why? Because of that stupid old thing at the end there?" asked the boy. "Why does she come here at all—who wants her? Why doesn't she keep her silly old mug at home?"

"It's her fu-fur which is so funny," giggled the girl. "It's exactly like a fried whiting."

15   "Ah, be off with you!" said the boy in an angry whisper. Then: "Tell me, ma petite chère—"

"No, not here," said the girl. "Not yet."

On her way home she usually bought a slice of honeycake at the baker's. It was her Sunday treat. Sometimes there was an almond in her slice, sometimes not. It made a great difference. If there was an almond it was like carrying home a tiny present—a surprise—something that might very well not have been there. She hurried on the almond Sundays and struck the match for the kettle in quite a dashing way.

But today she passed the baker's by, climbed the stairs, went into the little dark room—her room like a cupboard—and sat down on the red eiderdown. She sat there for a long time. The box that the fur came out of was on the bed. She unclasped the necklet quickly; quickly, without looking, laid it inside. But when she put the lid on she thought she heard something crying.

QUESTIONS

1. We view the people and events of this story almost entirely through the eyes and feelings of its protagonist. The author relies upon indirect presentation for her characterization of Miss Brill. After answering the following questions, write as full an account as you can of the nature and temperament of the story's main character.
2. What nationality is Miss Brill? What is the story's setting? Why is it important?
3. How old is Miss Brill? What are her circumstances? Why does she listen in on conversations?
4. Why does Miss Brill enjoy her Sundays in the park? Why especially this Sunday?
5. Of what importance to the story is the woman in the ermine toque?
6. What is Miss Brill's mood at the beginning of the story? What is it at the end? Why? Is she a static or a developing character?
7. What function does Miss Brill's fur serve in the story? What is the meaning of the final sentence?
8. Does Miss Brill come to a realization about her life and habits, or does she manage to suppress the truths that have been presented to her?

Mary Hood
How Far She Went

They had quarreled all morning, squalled all summer about the incidentals: how tight the girl's cut-off jeans were, the "Every Inch a Woman" T-shirt, her choice of music and how loud she played it, her practiced inattention, her sullen look. Her granny wrung out the last boiled dishcloth, pinched it to the line, giving the basin a sling and a

HOW FAR SHE WENT   First published in 1984. Born in Brunswick, Georgia, in 1946, Mary Hood has set most of her fiction in rural Georgia, where she now resides. She has taught creative writing at the University of Mississippi, Berry College, and elsewhere. Her first collection, *How Far She Went*, won the Flannery O'Connor Award for Short Fiction in 1984, and she subsequently published a second collection, *And Venus Is Blue* (1986) and a novel, *Familiar Heat* (1995).

slap, the water flying out in a scalding arc onto the Queen Anne's lace
by the path, never mind if it bloomed, that didn't make it worth anything except to chiggers, but the girl would cut it by the everlasting
armload and cherish it in the old churn, going to that much trouble for
a weed but not bending once—unbegged—to pick the nearest bean;
she was sulking now. Bored. Displaced.

"And what do you think happens to a chigger if nobody ever walks
by his weed?" her granny asked, heading for the house with that sidelong uneager unanswered glance, hoping for what? The surprise gift of
a smile? Nothing. The woman shook her head and said it. "Nothing."
The door slammed behind her. Let it.

"I hate it here!" the girl yelled then. She picked up a stick and
broke it and threw the pieces—one from each hand—at the laundry
drying in the noon. Missed. Missed.

Then she turned on her bare, haughty heel and set off high-shouldered into the heat, quick but not far, not far enough—no road was *that*
long—only as far as she dared. At the gate, a rusty chain swinging between two lichened posts, she stopped, then backed up the raw drive to
make a run at the barrier, lofting, clearing it clean, her long hair wild
in the sun. Triumphant, she looked back at the house where she caught
at the dark window her granny's face in its perpetual eclipse of disappointment, old at fifty. She stepped back, but the girl saw her.

5   "You don't know me!" the girl shouted, chin high, and ran till her
ribs ached.

As she rested in the rattling shade of the willows, the little dog
found her. He could be counted on. He barked all the way, and squealed
when she pulled the burr from his ear. They started back to the house
for lunch. By then the mailman had long come and gone in the old
ruts, leaving the one letter folded now to fit the woman's apron pocket.

If bad news darkened her granny's face, the girl ignored it. Didn't
talk at all, another of her distancings, her defiances. So it was as they
ate that the woman summarized, "Your daddy wants you to cash in the
plane ticket and buy you something. School clothes. For here."

Pale, the girl stared, defenseless only an instant before blurting out,
"You're lying."

The woman had to stretch across the table to leave her handprint
on that blank cheek. She said, not caring if it stung or not, "He's been
planning it since he sent you here."

10   "I could turn this whole house over, dump it! Leave you slobbering
over that stinking jealous dog in the dust!" The girl trembled with the
vision, with the strength it gave her. It made her laugh. "Scatter the

Holy Bible like confetti and ravel the crochet into miles of stupid string! I could! I will! I won't stay here!" But she didn't move, not until her tears rose to meet her color, and then to escape the shame of minding so much she fled. Just headed away, blind. It didn't matter, this time, how far she went.

The woman set her thoughts against fretting over their bickering, just went on unalarmed with chores, clearing off after the uneaten meal, bringing in the laundry, scattering corn for the chickens, ladling manure tea onto the porch flowers. She listened though. She always had been a listener. It gave her a cocked look. She forgot why she had gone into the girl's empty room, that ungirlish, tenuous lodging place with its bleak order, its ready suitcases never unpacked, the narrow bed, the contested radio on the windowsill. The woman drew the cracked shade down between the radio and the August sun. There wasn't anything else to do.

It was after six when she tied on her rough oxfords and walked down the drive and dropped the gate chain and headed back to the creosoted shed where she kept her tools. She took a hoe for snakes, a rake, shears to trim the grass where it grew, and seed in her pocket to scatter where it never had grown at all. She put the tools and her gloves and the bucket in the trunk of the old Chevy, its prime and rust like an Appaloosa's spots through the chalky white finish. She left the trunk open and the tool handles sticking out. She wasn't going far.

The heat of the day had broken, but the air was thick, sultry, weighted with honeysuckle in second bloom and the Nu-Grape scent of kudzu. The maple and poplar leaves turned over, quaking, silver. There wouldn't be any rain. She told the dog to stay, but he knew a trick. He stowed away when she turned her back, leaped right into the trunk with the tools, then gave himself away with exultant barks. Hearing him, her court jester, she stopped the car and welcomed him into the front seat beside her. Then they went on. Not a mile from her gate she turned onto the blue gravel of the cemetery lane, hauled the gearshift into reverse to whoa them, and got out to take the idle walk down to her buried hopes, bending all along to rout out a handful of weeds from between the markers of old acquaintance. She stood there and read, slow. The dog whined at her hem; she picked him up and rested her chin on his head, then he wriggled and whined to run free, contrary and restless as a child.

The crows called strong and bold MOM! MOM! A trick of the ear to hear it like that. She knew it was the crows, but still she looked around. No one called her that now. She was done with that. And what was it worth anyway? It all came to this: solitary weeding. The sinful fumble of flesh, the fear, the listening for a return that never came, the shamed waiting, the unanswered prayers, the perjury on the certificate—hadn't she lain there weary of the whole lie and it only beginning? And a voice telling her, "Here's your baby, here's your girl," and the swaddled package meaning no more to her than an extra anything, something store-bought, something she could take back for a refund.

15   "Tie her to the fence and give her a bale of hay," she had murmured, drugged, and they teased her, excused her for such a welcoming, blaming the anesthesia, but it went deeper than that; *she* knew, and the *baby* knew: there was no love in the begetting. That was the secret, unforgivable, that not another good thing could ever make up for, where all the bad had come from, like a visitation, a punishment. She knew that was why Sylvie had been wild, had gone to earth so early, and before dying had made this child in sudden wedlock, a child who would be just like her, would carry the hurting on into another generation. A matter of time. No use raising her hand. But she *had* raised her hand. Still wore on its palm the memory of the sting of the collision with the girl's cheek; had she broken her jaw? Her heart? Of course not. She said it aloud: "Takes more than that."

She went to work then, doing what she could with her old tools. She pecked the clay on Sylvie's grave, new-looking, unhealed after years. She tried again, scattering seeds from her pocket, every last possible one of them. Off in the west she could hear the pulpwood cutters sawing through another acre across the lake. Nearer, there was the racket of motorcycles laboring cross-country, insect-like, distracting.

She took her bucket to the well and hung it on the pump. She had half filled it when the bikers roared up, right down the blue gravel, straight at her. She let the bucket overflow, staring. On the back of one of the machines was the girl. Sylvie's girl! Her bare arms wrapped around the shirtless man riding between her thighs. They were first. The second biker rode alone. She studied their strangers' faces as they circled her. They were the enemy, all of them. Laughing. The girl was laughing too, laughing like her mama did. Out in the middle of nowhere the girl had found these two men, some moth-musk about her drawing them (too soon!) to what? She shouted it: "What in God's—" They roared off without answering her, and the bucket of water tipped over, spilling its stain blood-dark on the red dust.

The dog went wild barking, leaping after them, snapping at the tires, and there was no calling him down. The bikers made a wide circuit of the church-yard, then roared straight across the graves, leaping the ditch and landing upright on the road again, heading off toward the reservoir.

Furious, she ran to her car, past the barking dog, this time leaving him behind, driving after them, horn blowing nonstop, to get back what was not theirs. She drove after them knowing what they did not know, that all the roads beyond that point dead-ended. She surprised them, swinging the Impala across their path, cutting them off; let them hit it! They stopped. She got out, breathing hard, and said, when she could, "She's underage." Just that. And put out her claiming hand with an authority that made the girl's arms drop from the man's insolent waist and her legs tremble.

"I was just riding," the girl said, not looking up.   20

Behind them the sun was heading on toward down. The long shadows of the pines drifted back and forth in the same breeze that puffed the distant sails on the lake. Dead limbs creaked and clashed overhead like the antlers of locked and furious beasts.

"Sheeeut," the lone rider said. "I told you." He braced with his muddy boot and leaned out from his machine to spit. The man the girl had been riding with had the invading sort of eyes the woman had spent her lifetime bolting doors against. She met him now, face to face.

"Right there, missy," her granny said, pointing behind her to the car.

The girl slid off the motorcycle and stood halfway between her choices. She started slightly at the poosh! as he popped another top and chugged the beer in one uptilting of his head. His eyes never left the woman's. When he was through, he tossed the can high, flipping it end over end. Before it hit the ground he had his pistol out and, firing once, winged it into the lake.

"Freaking lucky shot," the other one grudged.   25

"I don't need luck," he said. He sighted down the barrel of the gun at the woman's head. "POW!" he yelled, and when she recoiled, he laughed. He swung around to the girl; he kept aiming the gun, here, there, high, low, all around. "Y'all settle it," he said, with a shrug.

The girl had to understand him then, had to know him, had to know better. But still she hesitated. He kept looking at her, then away.

"She's fifteen," her granny said. "You can go to jail."

"You can go to hell," he said.

"Probably will," her granny told him. "I'll save you a seat by the   30
fire." She took the girl by the arm and drew her to the car; she backed up, swung around, and headed out the road toward the churchyard for her tools and dog. The whole way the girl said nothing, just hunched against the far door, staring hard-eyed out at the pines going past.

The woman finished watering the seed in, and collected her tools. As she worked, she muttered, "It's your own kin buried here, you might have the decency to glance this way one time . . ." The girl was finger-tweezing her eyebrows in the side mirror. She didn't look around as the dog and the woman got in. Her granny shifted hard, sending the tools clattering in the trunk.

When they came to the main road, there were the men. Watching for them. Waiting for them. They kicked their machines into life and followed, close, bumping them, slapping the old fenders, yelling. The girl gave a wild glance around at the one by her door and said, "Gran'ma!" and as he drew his pistol, "Gran'ma!" just as the gun nosed into the open window. She frantically cranked the glass up between her and the weapon, and her granny, seeing, spat, "Fool!" She never had been one to pray for peace or rain. She stamped the accelerator right to the floor.

The motorcycles caught up. Now she braked, hard, and swerved off the road into an alley between the pines, not even wide enough for the school bus, just a fire scrape that came out a quarter mile from her own house, if she could get that far. She slewed on the pine straw, then righted, tearing along the dark tunnel through the woods. She had for the time being bested them; they were left behind. She was winning. Then she hit the wallow where the tadpoles were already five weeks old. The Chevy plowed in and stalled. When she got it cranked again, they were stuck. The tires spattered mud three feet up the near trunks as she tried to spin them out, to rock them out. Useless. "Get out and run!" she cried, but the trees were too close on the passenger side. The girl couldn't open her door. She wasted precious time having to crawl out under the steering wheel. The woman waited but the dog ran on.

They struggled through the dusky woods, their pace slowed by the thick straw and vines. Overhead, in the last light, the martins were reeling free and sure after their prey.

35   "Why? Why?" the girl gasped, as they lunged down the old deer trail. Behind them they could hear shots, and glass breaking as the men came to the bogged car. The woman kept on running, swatting their way clear through the shoulder-high weeds. They could see the Greer cottage, and made for it. But it was ivied-over, padlocked, the woodpile dry-rotting under its tarp, the electric meterbox empty on the pole. No help there.

The dog, excited, trotted on, yelping, his lips white-flecked. He scented the lake and headed that way, urging them on with thirsty yips. On the clay shore, treeless, deserted, at the utter limit of land, they stood defenseless, listening to the men coming on, between them and home. The woman pressed her hands to her mouth, stifling her cough. She was exhausted. She couldn't think.

"We can get under!" the girl cried suddenly, and pointed toward the Greers' dock, gap-planked, its walkway grounded on the mud. They splashed out to it, wading in, the woman grabbing up the telltale, tattle-tale dog in her arms. They waded out to the far end and ducked under. There was room between the foam floats for them to crouch neck-deep.

The dog wouldn't hush, even then; never had yet, and there wasn't time to teach him. When the woman realized that, she did what she had to do. She grabbed him whimpering; held him; held him under till the struggle ceased and the bubbles rose silver from his fur. They crouched there then, the two of them, submerged to the shoulders, feet unsteady on the slimed lake bed. They listened. The sky went from rose to ocher to violet in the cracks over their heads. The motorcycles had stopped now. In the silence there was the glissando of locusts, the dry crunch of boots on the flinty beach, their low man-talk drifting as they prowled back and forth. One of them struck a match.

"—they in these woods we could burn 'em out."

The wind carried their voices away into the pines. Some few words   40
eddied back.

"—lippy old smartass do a little work on her knees besides pray-ing—"

Laughter. It echoed off the deserted house. They were getting closer.

One of them strode directly out to the dock, walked on the planks over their heads. They could look up and see his boot soles. He was the one with the gun. He slapped a mosquito on his bare back and cursed. The carp, roused by the troubling of the waters, came nosing around the dock, guzzling and snorting. The girl and her granny held still, so still. The man fired his pistol into the shadows, and a wounded fish thrashed, dying. The man knelt and reached for it, chuffing out his beery breath. He belched. He pawed the lake for the dead fish, cursing as it floated out of reach. He shot it again, firing at it till it sank and the gun was empty. Cursed that too. He stood then and unzipped and re-lieved himself of some of the beer. They had to listen to that. To know that about him. To endure that, unprotesting.

Back and forth on shore the other one ranged, restless. He lit an-other cigarette. He coughed. He called, "Hey! They got away, man, that's all. Don't get your shorts in a wad. Let's go."

"Yeah." He finished. He zipped. He stumped back across the planks   45
and leaped to shore, leaving the dock tilting amid widening ripples. Underneath, they waited.

The bike cranked. The other ratcheted, ratcheted, then coughed, caught, roared. They circled, cut deep ruts, slung gravel, and went. Their roaring died away and away. Crickets resumed and a near frog bic-bic-bicked.

Under the dock, they waited a little longer to be sure. Then they ducked below the water, scraped out from under the pontoon, and came up into free air, slogging toward shore. It had seemed warm enough in the water. Now they shivered. It was almost night. One streak of light still stood reflected on the darkening lake, drew itself thinner, narrowing into a final cancellation of day. A plane winked its way west.

The girl was trembling. She ran her hands down her arms and legs, shedding water like a garment. She sighed, almost a sob. The woman held the dog in her arms; she dropped to her knees upon the random stones and murmured, private, haggard, "Oh, honey," three times, maybe all three times for the dog, maybe once for each of them. The girl waited, watching. Her granny rocked the dog like a baby, like a dead child, rocked slower and slower and was still.

"I'm sorry," the girl said then, avoiding the dog's inert, empty eye.

50   "It was him or you," her granny said, finally, looking up. Looking her over. "Did they mess with you? With your britches? Did they?"

"No!" Then, quieter, "No, ma'am."

When the woman tried to stand up she staggered, lightheaded, clumsy with the freight of the dog. "No, ma'am," she echoed, fending off the girl's "Let me." And she said again, "It was him or you. I know that. I'm not going to rub your face in it." They saw each other as well as they could in that failing light, in any light.

The woman started toward home, saying, "Around here, we bear our own burdens." She led the way along the weedy shortcuts. The twilight bleached the dead limbs of the pines to bone. Insects sang in the thickets, silencing at their oncoming.

"We'll see about the car in the morning," the woman said. She bore her armful toward her own moth-ridden dusk-to-dawn security light with that country grace she had always had when the earth was reliably progressing underfoot. The girl walked close behind her, exactly where *she* walked, matching her pace, matching her stride, close enough to put her hand forth (if the need arose) and touch her granny's back where the faded voile was clinging damp, the merest gauze between their wounds.

QUESTIONS

1. Describe the plot structure. How is narrative suspense initiated and maintained? Where would you locate the climactic point in the story?

2. Contrast the characterizations of the grandmother and her granddaughter. Which is the more sympathetic character, and why?
3. Discuss the use of detail in the story. How are small details used to create and enrich the characterizations?
4. What is the role of the small dog in the plot? Why is the dog an essential element in the story?
5. Are the bike riders flat or round characters? How do they conform to stereotypical notions of men who travel the countryside on motorcycles?
6. Is the granddaughter a developing character? Locate a key moment when her character undergoes a significant change.
7. What is the role of the grandmother's deceased daughter, Sylvie? What do we learn about her character, and how is this information important to the story?
8. Discuss the ending. What are the "wounds" described in the final line?

SUGGESTIONS FOR WRITING

1. Write an essay on the direct or indirect presentation of character in one of the following:
   a. Connell, "The Most Dangerous Game" (page 67).
   b. Greene, "The Destructors" (page 111).
   c. Lahiri, "Interpreter of Maladies" (page 141).
2. Considering the three criteria that are necessary for developing a convincing character, write an essay in which you determine whether one of the following characters meets these criteria:
   a. Rainsford in Connell, "The Most Dangerous Game" (page 67).
   b. Blackie in Greene, "The Destructors" (page 111).
   c. Mr. Kapasi in Lahiri, "Interpreter of Maladies" (page 141).

Chapter Four

Theme

"Daddy, the man next door kisses his wife every morning when he leaves for work. Why don't you do that?"

"Are you kidding? I don't even know the woman."

"Daughter, your young man stays until a very late hour. Hasn't your mother said anything to you about this habit of his?"

"Yes, father. Mother says men haven't altered a bit."

For readers who contemplate the two jokes above, a significant difference emerges between them. The first joke depends only upon a reversal of expectation. We expect the man to explain why he doesn't kiss his wife; instead he explains why he doesn't kiss his neighbor's wife. The second joke, though it contains a reversal of expectation, depends as much or more for its effectiveness on a truth about human life, namely, that *people tend to grow more conservative as they grow older* or that *parents often scold their children for doing exactly what they did themselves when young*. This truth, which might be stated in different ways, is the *theme* of the joke.

The **theme** of a piece of fiction is its controlling idea or its central insight. It is the unifying generalization about life stated or implied by the story. To derive the theme of a story, we must determine what its central *purpose* is: what view of life it supports or what insight into life it reveals.

Not all stories have a significant theme. The purpose of a horror story may be simply to scare readers, to give them gooseflesh. The purpose of an adventure story may be simply to carry readers through a series of exciting escapades. The purpose of a murder mystery may be simply to pose a problem for readers to try to solve (and to prevent them from solving it, if possible, until the last paragraph). The purpose of some stories may be simply to provide suspense or to make readers laugh or to surprise them with a sudden twist at the end. Theme exists only (1) when an author has seriously attempted to record life accurately or to reveal some truth about it or (2) when an author has deliberately introduced as a unifying element some concept or theory of life that the story illuminates. Theme exists in virtually all literary fiction but only in some commercial fiction. In literary fiction it is the primary purpose of the story; in commercial fiction, it is usually less important than such elements as plot and suspense.

In many stories the theme may be equivalent to the revelation of human character. If a story has as its central purpose to exhibit a certain kind of human being, our statement of theme may be no more than a concentrated description of the person revealed, with the addition, "Some people are like this." Frequently, however, a story through its portrayal of specific persons in specific situations will have something to say about the nature of all human beings or about their relationship to each other or to the universe. Whatever central generalization about life arises from the specifics of the story constitutes theme.

The theme of a story, like its plot, may be stated very briefly or at greater length. With a simple or very brief story, we may be satisfied to sum up the theme in a single sentence. With a more complex story, if it is successfully unified, we can still state the theme in a single sentence, but we may feel that a paragraph—or occasionally even an essay—is needed to state it adequately. A rich story will give us many and complex insights into life. In stating the theme in a sentence, we must pick the *central* insight, the one that explains the greatest number of elements in the story and relates them to each other. For theme is what gives a story its unity. In any story at all complex, however, we are likely to feel that a one-sentence statement of theme leaves out a great part of the story's meaning. Though the theme of *Othello* may be expressed as "Jealousy exacts a terrible cost," such a statement does not begin to suggest the range and depth of Shakespeare's play. Any successful story is a good deal more and means a good deal more than any one-sentence statement of theme that we may extract from it, for the story will modify and expand this statement in various and subtle ways.

We must never think, once we have stated the theme of a story, that the whole purpose of the story has been to yield up this abstract statement. If this were so, there would be no reason for the story: we could stop with the abstract statement. The function of literary writers is not to state a theme but to vivify it. They wish to deliver it not simply to our intellects but to our emotions, our senses, and our imaginations. The theme of a story may be little or nothing except as it is embodied and vitalized by the story. Unembodied, it is a dry backbone, without flesh or life.

Sometimes the theme of a story is explicitly stated somewhere in the story, either by the author or by one of the characters. More often, however, the theme is implied. Story writers, after all, are story writers, not essayists or philosophers. Their first business is to reveal life, not to comment on it. They may well feel that unless the story somehow expresses its own meaning, without their having to point it out, they have not told the story well. Or they may feel that if the story is to have its maximum emotional effect, they must refrain from interrupting it or making remarks about it. They are also wary of spoiling a story for perceptive readers by "explaining" it, just as some people ruin jokes by explaining them. For these reasons theme is more often left implicit than stated explicitly. Good writers do not ordinarily write a story for the sole purpose of "illustrating" a theme, as do the writers of parables or fables. They write stories to bring alive some segment of human existence. When they do so searchingly and coherently, theme arises naturally out of what they have written. Good readers may state the generalizations for themselves.

Some readers—especially inexperienced readers—look for a "moral" in everything they read, some rule of conduct that they regard as applicable to their lives. They consider the words "theme" and "moral" to be interchangeable. Sometimes the words are interchangeable. Occasionally the theme of a story may be expressed as a moral principle without doing violence to the story. More frequently, however, the word "moral" is too narrow to fit the kind of illumination provided by a first-rate story. It is hardly suitable, for instance, for the kind of story that simply displays human character. Such nouns as "moral," "lesson," and "message" are therefore best avoided in the discussion of fiction. The critical term **theme** is preferable for several reasons. First, it is less likely to obscure the fact that a story is not a preachment or a sermon: a story's *first* object is enjoyment. Second, it should keep us from trying to wring from every story a didactic pronouncement about life. The person who seeks a moral in every story is likely to oversimplify and conventionalize it—to reduce it to some dusty platitude like "Be kind to animals" or "Look before you leap" or "Crime does not pay." The purpose of literary story writers is to give us a greater awareness and a greater understanding of life, not to inculcate a code of moral rules for regulating daily conduct. In getting at the theme of the story it is better to ask not *What does this story teach?* but *What does this story reveal?* Readers who analyze Lahiri's "Interpreter of Maladies" as being simply about the danger of keeping secrets in a marriage have missed nine-tenths of the story. The theme could be stated more accurately this way: "The human search for love can result in a 'malady' when unaccompanied by honest emotion (as is the case with

Mrs. Das) or when inspired by naïve infatuation (as is the case with Mr. Kapasi). Different sets of cultural and moral values often result in comic but also poignant failures to connect meaningfully with another person." Obviously, this dry statement is a poor thing beside the living reality of the story. But it is a more faithful abstracting of the story's content than any pat, cut-and-dried "moral."

The revelation offered by a good story may be something fresh or something old. The story may bring us some insight into life that we had not had before, and thus expand our horizons, or it may make us *feel* or *feel again* some truth of which we have long been merely intellectually aware. We may know in our minds, for instance, that "War is horrible" or that "Old age is often pathetic and in need of understanding," but these are insights that need to be periodically renewed. *Emotionally* we may forget them, and if we do, we are less alive and complete as human beings. Story writers perform a service for us—interpret life for us—whether they give us new insights or refresh and extend old ones.

The themes of commercial and literary stories may be identical, but frequently they are different. Commercial stories, for the most part, confirm their readers' prejudices, endorse their opinions, ratify their feelings, and satisfy their wishes. Usually, therefore, the themes of such stories are widely accepted platitudes of experience that may or may not be supported by the life around us. They represent life as we would like it to be, not always as it is. We should certainly like to believe, for instance, that "motherhood is sacred," that "true love always wins through," that "virtue and hard work are rewarded in the end," that "cheaters never win," that "old age brings a mellow wisdom that compensates for its infirmity," and that "every human being has a soft spot in him somewhere." Literary writers, however, being thoughtful observers of life, are likely to question these beliefs and often to challenge them. Their ideas about life are not simply taken over ready-made from what they were taught in Sunday school or from the books they read as children; they are the formulations of sensitive and independent observers who have collated all that they have read and been taught by life itself. The themes of their stories therefore do not often correspond to the pretty little sentiments we find inscribed in greeting cards. They may sometimes represent rather somber truths. Much of the process of maturing as a reader lies in the discovery that there may be more nourishment and deeper enjoyment in these somber truths than in the warm and fuzzy optimism found in so-called "inspirational" fiction.

We do not, however, have to accept the theme of a literary story any more than we do that of a commercial story. Though we should never summarily dismiss it without reflection, we may find that the theme of a story represents a judgment on life with which, on examination, we cannot agree. If it is the reasoned view of a seasoned and serious artist, nevertheless, it cannot be without value to us. There is value in knowing what the world looks like to others, and we can thus use a judgment to expand our knowledge of human experience even though we cannot ourselves accept it. Genuine artists and thoughtful observers, moreover, can hardly fail to present us with partial insights along the way, although we disagree with the total view. Careful readers, therefore, will not reject a story because they reject its theme. They can enjoy any story that arises from sufficient depth of observation and reflection and is artistically composed, though they disagree with its theme; and they will prefer it to a shallower, less thoughtful, or less successfully integrated story that presents a theme they endorse.

Discovering and stating the theme of a story is often a delicate task. Sometimes we will *feel* what the story is about strongly enough and yet find it difficult to put this feeling into words. If we are skilled readers, it is perhaps unnecessary that we do so. The bare statement of the theme, so lifeless and impoverished when abstracted from the story, may seem to diminish the story to something less than it is. Often, however, the attempt to state a theme will reveal to us aspects of a story that we should otherwise not have noticed and will thereby lead to more thorough understanding. The ability to state theme, moreover, is a test of our understanding of a story. Careless readers often think they understand a story when in actuality they have misunderstood it. They understand the events but not what the events add up to. Or, in adding up the events, they arrive at an erroneous total. People sometimes miss the point of a joke. It is not surprising that they should occasionally miss the point of a good piece of fiction, which is many times more complex than a joke.

There is no prescribed method for discovering theme. Sometimes we can best get at it by asking in what way the main character has changed in the course of the story and what, if anything, the character has learned before its end. Sometimes the best approach is to explore the nature of the central conflict and its outcome. Sometimes the title will provide an important clue. At all times we should keep in mind the following principles:

1. Theme should be expressible in the form of a statement with a subject and a predicate. It is insufficient to say that the theme of a story is motherhood or loyalty to country. Motherhood and loyalty are simply subjects. Theme must be a statement *about* the subject. For instance, "Motherhood sometimes has more frustrations than rewards" or "Loyalty to country often inspires heroic self-sacrifice." If we express

the theme in the form of a phrase, the phrase must be convertible to sentence form. A phrase such as "the futility of envy," for instance, may be converted to the statement "Envy is futile": it may therefore serve as a statement of theme.

2. The theme should be stated as a *generalization* about life. In stating theme we do not use the names of the characters or refer to precise places or events, for to do so is to make a specific rather than a general statement. The theme of "The Destructors" is not that "The Wormsley Common Gang of London, in the aftermath of World War II, found a creative outlet in destroying a beautiful two-hundred-year-old house designed by Sir Christopher Wren." Rather, it is something like this: "The dislocations caused by a devastating war may produce among the young a conscious or unconscious rebellion against all the values of the reigning society—a rebellion in which the creative instincts are channeled into destructive enterprises."

3. We must be careful not to make the generalization larger than is justified by the terms of the story. Terms like *every, all, always* should be used very cautiously; terms like *some, sometimes, may* are often more accurate. The theme of "Everyday Use" is not that "Habitually compliant and tolerant mothers will eventually stand up to their bullying children," for we have only one instance of such behavior in the story. But the story does sufficiently present this event as a climactic change in a developing character. Because the story's narrator recalls precise details of her previous behavior that she brings to bear on her present decision, we can safely infer that this decision will be meaningful and lasting, and should feel that we can generalize beyond the specific situation. The theme might be expressed thus: "A person whose honesty and tolerance have long made her susceptible to the strong will of another may reach a point where she will exert her own will for the sake of justice," or more generally, "Ingrained habits can be given up if justice makes a greater demand." Notice that we have said *may* and *can*, not *will* and *must*. Only occasionally will the theme of a story be expressible as a universal generalization. The bleak, darkly humorous ending of "Hunters in the Snow" lets us know that Wolff views all three of his characters as hopelessly "lost" in both the geographical and moral senses of the word. The world contains many people who are essentially predatory, the story seems to say, entirely self-interested "hunters" in a cold universe; even when two individuals form temporary alliances, these are symbiotic relationships in which each person is simply trying to fulfill a selfish need through the other.

4. Theme is the *central* and *unifying* concept of a story. Therefore (a) it accounts for all the major details of the story. If we cannot explain

the bearing of an important incident or character on the theme, either in exemplifying it or modifying it in some way, it is probable that our interpretation is partial and incomplete, that at best we have got hold only of a subtheme. Another alternative, though it must be used with caution, is that the story itself is imperfectly constructed and lacks unity. (b) The theme is not contradicted by any detail of the story. If we have to overlook or blink at or "force" the meaning of some significant detail in order to frame our statement, we may be sure that our statement is defective. (c) The theme cannot rely upon supposed facts—facts not actually stated or clearly implied by the story. The theme exists *inside,* not *outside,* the story. The statement of it must be based on the data of the story itself, not on assumptions supplied from our own experience.

5. There is no *one* way of stating the theme of a story. The story is not a guessing game or an acrostic that is supposed to yield some magic verbal formula that won't work if a syllable is changed. It merely presents a view of life, and, as long as the above conditions are fulfilled, that view may surely be stated in more than one way. Here, for instance, are three possible ways of stating the theme of "Miss Brill": (a) A person living alone may create a protective fantasy life by dramatizing insignificant activities, but such a life can be jeopardized when she is forced to see herself as others see her. (b) Isolated elderly people, unsupported by a network of family and friends, may make a satisfying adjustment through a pleasant fantasy life, but when their fantasy is punctured by the cold claw of reality, the effect can be devastating. (c) Loneliness is a pitiable emotional state that may be avoided by refusing to acknowledge that one feels lonely, though such an avoidance may also require one to create unrealistic fantasies about oneself.

6. We should avoid any statement that reduces the theme to some familiar saying that we have heard all our lives, such as "You can't judge a book by its cover" or "A stitch in time saves nine." Although such a statement *may* express the theme accurately, too often it is simply a lazy shortcut that impoverishes the essential meaning of the story in order to save mental effort. When readers force every new experience into an old formula, they lose the chance for a fresh perception. Beware of using clichés when attempting to summarize a story's theme. To decide that "love is blind" is the theme of "How I Met My Husband" is to indulge in a reductive absurdity. When a ready-made phrase comes to mind as the theme of a story, this may be a sign that the reader should think more deeply and thoroughly about the author's central purpose.

REVIEWING CHAPTER FOUR

1. Review the definition of "theme" in fiction.
2. Describe the best way(s) in which the theme of a story may be stated.
3. Distinguish between the theme of a story and the central purpose of a story.
4. Differentiate between the typical themes of commercial vs. literary stories.
5. Review the six principles relating to theme as described in this chapter.

Toni Cade Bambara
The Lesson

Back in the days when everyone was old and stupid or young and foolish and me and Sugar were the only ones just right, this lady moved on our block with nappy hair and proper speech and no makeup. And quite naturally we laughed at her, laughed the way we did at the junk man who went about his business like he was some big-time president and his sorry-ass horse his secretary. And we kinda hated her too, hated the way we did the winos who cluttered up our parks and pissed on our handball walls and stank up our hallways and stairs so you couldn't halfway play hide-and-seek without a goddamn gas mask. Miss Moore was her name. The only woman on the block with no first name. And she was black as hell, cept for her feet, which were fish-white and spooky. And she was always planning these boring-ass things for us to do, us being my cousin, mostly, who lived on the block cause we all moved North the same time and to the same apartment then spread out gradual to breathe. And our parents would yank our heads into some kinda shape and crisp up our clothes so we'd be presentable for travel with Miss Moore, who always looked like she was going to church,

THE LESSON   First published in her collection *Gorilla, My Love* in 1972. Toni Cade Bambara (1939–1995) was born in New York City, the site of the various place-names in the story, and was raised in Harlem and Bedford-Stuyvesant. She earned a B.A. at Queens College and an M.A. at the City College of New York. She began publishing her fiction in 1960 and earned distinction as an advocate of civil rights and as an anthologist of black literature. F. A. O. Schwarz (named in paragraph 45) is a toy store located on fashionable Fifth Avenue in Manhattan.

though she never did. Which is just one of the things the grownups talked about when they talked behind her back like a dog. But when she came calling with some sachet she'd sewed up or some gingerbread she'd made or some book, why then they'd all be too embarrassed to turn her down and we'd get handed over all spruced up. She'd been to college and said it was only right that she should take responsibility for the young ones' education, and she not even related by marriage or blood. So they'd go for it. Specially Aunt Gretchen. She was the main gofer in the family. You got some ole dumb shit foolishness you want somebody to go for, you send for Aunt Gretchen. She been screwed into the go-along for so long, it's a blood-deep natural thing with her. Which is how she got saddled with me and Sugar and Junior in the first place while our mothers were in a la-de-da apartment up the block having a good ole time.

So this one day Miss Moore rounds us all up at the mailbox and it's puredee hot and she's knockin herself out about arithmetic. And school suppose to let up in summer I heard, but she don't never let up. And the starch in my pinafore scratching the shit outta me and I'm really hating this nappy-head bitch and her goddamn college degree. I'd much rather go to the pool or to the show where it's cool. So me and Sugar leaning on the mailbox being surly, which is a Miss Moore word. And Flyboy checking out what everybody brought for lunch. And Fat Butt already wasting his peanut-butter-and-jelly sandwich like the pig he is. And Junebug punchin on Q.T.'s arm for potato chips. And Rosie Giraffe shifting from one hip to the other waiting for somebody to step on her foot or ask her if she from Georgia so she can kick ass, preferably Mercedes'. And Miss Moore asking us do we know what money is, like we a bunch of retards. I mean real money, she say, like it's only poker chips or monopoly papers we lay on the grocer. So right away I'm tired of this and say so. And would much rather snatch Sugar and go to the Sunset and terrorize the West Indian kids and take their hair ribbons and their money too. And Miss Moore files that remark away for next week's lesson on brotherhood, I can tell. And finally I say we oughta get to the subway cause it's cooler and besides we might meet some cute boys. Sugar done swiped her mama's lipstick, so we ready.

So we heading down the street and she's boring us silly about what things cost and what our parents make and how much goes for rent and how money ain't divided up right in this country. And then she gets to the part about we all poor and live in the slums, which I don't feature. And I'm ready to speak on that, but she steps out in the street and hails two cabs just like that. Then she hustles half the crew in with her and hands me a five-dollar bill and tells me to calculate 10 percent tip for the driver. And we're off. Me and Sugar and Junebug and Flyboy hangin out the window and hollering to everybody, putting lipstick on each other cause Flyboy a faggot anyway, and making farts with our sweaty armpits. But I'm mostly trying to figure how to spend this money. But they all fascinated with the meter ticking and Junebug starts laying bets as to how much it'll read when Flyboy can't hold his breath no more. Then Sugar lays bets as to how much it'll be when we get there. So I'm stuck. Don't nobody want to go for my plan, which is to jump out at the next light and run off to the first bar-b-que we can find. Then the driver tells us to get the hell out cause we there already. And the meter reads eighty-five cents. And I'm stalling to figure out the tip and Sugar say give him a dime. And I decide he don't need it bad as I do, so later for him. But then he tries to take off with Junebug foot still in the door so we talk about his mama something ferocious. Then we check out that we on Fifth Avenue and everybody dressed up in stockings. One lady in a fur coat, hot as it is. White folks crazy.

"This is the place," Miss Moore say, presenting it to us in the voice she uses at the museum. "Let's look in the windows before we go in."

"Can we steal?" Sugar asks very serious like she's getting the ground rules squared away before she plays. "I beg your pardon," say Miss Moore, and we fall out. So she leads us around the windows of the toy store and me and Sugar screamin, "This is mine, that's mine, I gotta have that, that was made for me, I was born for that," till Big Butt drowns us out.

"Hey, I'm goin to buy that there."

"That there? You don't even know what it is, stupid."

"I do so," he say punchin on Rosie Giraffe. "It's a microscope."

"Whatcha gonna do with a microscope, fool?"

"Look at things."

"Like what, Ronald?" ask Miss Moore. And Big Butt ain't got the first notion. So here go Miss Moore gabbing about the thousands of bacteria in a drop of water and the somethinorother in a speck of blood and the million and one living things in the air around us is invisible to the naked eye. And what she say that for? Junebug go to town on that "naked" and we rolling. Then Miss Moore ask what it cost. So we all jam into the window smudgin it up and the price tag say $300. So then she ask how long'd take for Big Butt and Junebug to save up their allowances. "Too long," I say. "Yeh," adds Sugar, "outgrown it by that time." And Miss Moore say no, you never outgrow learning instruments. "Why, even medical students and interns and," blah, blah, blah. And we ready to choke Big Butt for bringing it up in the first damn place.

"This here costs four hundred eighty dollars," say Rosie Giraffe. So we pile up all over her to see what she pointin out. My eyes tell me it's

5

10

a chunk of glass cracked with something heavy, and different-color inks dripped into the splits, then the whole thing put into a oven or something. But for $480 it don't make sense.

"That's a paperweight made of semi-precious stones fused together under tremendous pressure," she explains slowly, with her hands doing the mining and all the factory work.

"So what's a paperweight?" asks Rosie Giraffe.

15   "To weigh paper with, dumbbell," say Flyboy, the wise man from the East.

"Not exactly," say Miss Moore, which is what she say when you warm or way off too. "It's to weigh paper down so it won't scatter and make your desk untidy." So right away me and Sugar curtsy to each other and then to Mercedes who is more the tidy type.

"We don't keep paper on top of the desk in my class," say Junebug, figuring Miss Moore crazy or lyin one.

"At home, then," she say. "Don't you have a calendar and a pencil case and a blotter and a letter-opener on your desk at home where you do your homework?" And she know damn well what our homes look like cause she nosys around in them every chance she gets.

"I don't even have a desk," say Junebug. "Do we?"

20   "No. And I don't get no homework neither," says Big Butt.

"And I don't even have a home," say Flyboy like he do at school to keep the white folks off his back and sorry for him. Send this poor kid to camp posters, is his specialty.

"I do," says Mercedes. "I have a box of stationery on my desk and a picture of my cat. My godmother bought the stationery and the desk. There's a big rose on each sheet and the envelopes smell like roses."

"Who wants to know about your smelly-ass stationery," say Rosie Giraffe fore I can get my two cents in.

"It's important to have a work area all your own so that . . ."

25   "Will you look at this sailboat, please," say Flyboy, cuttin her off and pointin to the thing like it was his. So once again we tumble all over each other to gaze at this magnificent thing in the toy store which is just big enough to maybe sail two kittens across the pond if you strap them to the posts tight. We all start reciting the price tag like we in assembly. "Handcrafted sailboat of fiberglass at one thousand one hundred ninety-five dollars."

"Unbelievable," I hear myself say and am really stunned. I read it again for myself just in case the group recitation put me in a trance. Same thing. For some reason this pisses me off. We look at Miss Moore and she lookin at us, waiting for I dunno what.

"Who'd pay all that when you can buy a sailboat set for a quarter at Pop's, a tube of glue for a dime, and a ball of string for eight cents? It must have a motor and a whole lot else besides," I say. "My sailboat cost me about fifty cents."

"But will it take water?" say Mercedes with her smart ass.

"Took mine to Alley Pond Park once," say Flyboy. "String broke. Lost it. Pity."

"Sailed mine in Central Park and it keeled over and sank. Had to   30
ask my father for another dollar."

"And you got the strap," laugh Big Butt. "The jerk didn't even have a string on it. My old man wailed on his behind."

Little Q.T. was staring hard at the sailboat and you could see he wanted it bad. But he too little and somebody'd just take it from him. So what the hell. "This boat for kids, Miss Moore?"

"Parents silly to buy something like that just to get all broke up," say Rosie Giraffe.

"That much money it should last forever," I figure.

"My father'd buy it for me if I wanted it."   35

"Your father, my ass," say Rosie Giraffe getting a chance to finally push Mercedes.

"Must be rich people shop here," say Q.T.

"You are a very bright boy," say Flyboy. "What was your first clue?" And he rap him on the head with the back of his knuckles, since Q.T. the only one he could get away with. Though Q.T. liable to come up behind you years later and get his licks in when you half expect it.

"What I want to know is," I says to Miss Moore though I never talk to her, I wouldn't give the bitch that satisfaction, "is how much a real boat costs? I figure a thousand'd get you a yacht any day."

"Why don't you check that out," she says, "and report back to the   40
group?" Which really pains my ass. If you gonna mess up a perfectly good swim day least you could do is have some answers. "Let's go in," she say like she got something up her sleeve. Only she don't lead the way. So me and Sugar turn the corner to where the entrance is, but when we get there I kinda hang back. Not that I'm scared, what's there to be afraid of, just a toy store. But I feel funny, shame. But what I got to be shamed about? Got as much right to go in as anybody. But somehow I can't seem to get hold of the door, so I step away from Sugar to lead. But she hangs back too. And I look at her and she looks at me and this is ridiculous. I mean, damn, I have never ever been shy about doing nothing or going nowhere. But then Mercedes steps up and then Rosie Giraffe and Big Butt crowd in behind and shove, and next thing we all stuffed into

the doorway with only Mercedes squeezing past us, smoothing out her jumper and walking right down the aisle. Then the rest of us tumble in like a glued-together jigsaw done all wrong. And people lookin at us. And it's like the time me and Sugar crashed into the Catholic church on a dare. But once we got in there and everything so hushed and holy and the candles and the bowin and the handkerchiefs on all the drooping heads, I just couldn't go through with the plan. Which was for me to run up to the altar and do a tap dance while Sugar played the nose flute and messed around in the holy water. And Sugar kept givin me the elbow. Then later teased me so bad I tied her up in the shower and turned it on and locked her in. And she'd be there till this day if Aunt Gretchen hadn't finally figured I was lyin about the boarder takin a shower.

Same thing in the store. We all walkin on tiptoe and hardly touchin the games and puzzles and things. And I watched Miss Moore who is steady watchin us like she waitin for a sign. Like Mama Drewery watches the sky and sniffs the air and takes note of just how much slant is in the bird formation. Then me and Sugar bump smack into each other, so busy gazing at the toys, 'specially the sailboat. But we don't laugh and go into our fat-lady bump-stomach routine. We just stare at that price tag. Then Sugar run a finger over the whole boat. And I'm jealous and want to hit her. Maybe not her, but I sure want to punch somebody in the mouth.

"Watcha bring us here for, Miss Moore?"

"You sound angry, Sylvia. Are you mad about something?" Givin me one of them grins like she tellin a grown-up joke that never turns out to be funny. And she's lookin very closely at me like maybe she plannin to do my portrait from memory. I'm mad, but I won't give her that satisfaction. So I slouch around the store bein very bored and say, "Let's go."

Me and Sugar at the back of the train watchin the tracks whizzin by large then small then gettin gobbled up in the dark. I'm thinkin about this tricky toy I saw in the store. A clown that somersaults on a bar then does chin-ups just cause you yank lightly at his leg. Cost $35. I could see me askin my mother for a $35 birthday clown. "You wanna who that costs what?" she'd say, cocking her head to the side to get a better view of the hole in my head. Thirty-five dollars could buy new bunk beds for Junior and Gretchen's boy. Thirty-five dollars and the whole household could go visit Granddaddy Nelson in the country. Thirty-five dollars would pay for the rent and the piano bill too. Who are these people that spend that much for performing clowns and $1000 for toy sailboats? What kinda work they do and how they live and how come we ain't in on it? Where we are is who we are, Miss Moore always pointin out. But it don't necessarily have to be that way, she always adds then waits for somebody to say that poor people have to wake up and demand their share of the pie and don't none of us know what kind of pie she talking about in the first damn place. But she ain't so smart cause I still got her four dollars from the taxi and she sure ain't gettin it. Messin up my day with this shit. Sugar nudges me in my pocket and winks.

Miss Moore lines us up in front of the mailbox where we started   45 from, seem like years ago, and I got a headache for thinkin so hard. And we lean all over each other so we can hold up under the draggy-ass lecture she always finishes us off with at the end before we thank her for borin us to tears. But she just looks at us like she readin tea leaves. Finally she say, "Well, what did you think of F. A. O. Schwarz?"

Rosie Giraffe mumbles, "White folks crazy."

"I'd like to go there again when I get my birthday money," says Mercedes, and we shove her out the pack so she has to lean on the mailbox by herself.

"I'd like a shower. Tiring day," say Flyboy.

Then Sugar surprises me by sayin, "You know, Miss Moore, I don't think all of us here put together eat in a year what that sailboat costs." And Miss Moore lights up like somebody goosed her. "And?" she say, urging Sugar on. Only I'm standin on her foot so she don't continue.

"Imagine for a minute what kind of society it is in which some   50 people can spend on a toy what it would cost to feed a family of six or seven. What do you think?"

"I think," say Sugar pushing me off her feet like she never done before, cause I whip her ass in a minute, "that this is not much of a democracy if you ask me. Equal chance to pursue happiness means an equal crack at the dough, don't it?" Miss Moore is besides herself and I am disgusted with Sugar's treachery. So I stand on her foot one more time to see if she'll shove me. She shuts up, and Miss Moore looks at me, sorrowfully I'm thinkin. And somethin weird is goin on, I can feel it in my chest.

"Anybody else learn anything today?" lookin dead at me. I walk away and Sugar has to run to catch up and don't even seem to notice when I shrug her arm off my shoulder.

"Well, we got four dollars anyway," she says.

"Uh hunh."

"We could go to Hascombs and get half a chocolate layer and then   55 go to the Sunset and still have plenty money for potato chips and ice cream sodas."

"Uh hunh."

"Race you to Hascombs," she say.

We start down the block and she gets ahead which is O.K. by me cause I'm going to the West End and then over to the Drive to think this day through. She can run if she want to and even run faster. But ain't nobody gonna beat me at nuthin.

QUESTIONS

1. Define the nature of the conflict between the narrator Sylvia and Miss Moore. What are the differences between that conflict and how the other children respond to Miss Moore? What conflicts exist among the children themselves?

2. What strengths and weaknesses in Sylvia's character are illuminated by her being the narrator? How is her language evidence of both strengths and weaknesses? In particular, what extremes of character are displayed in paragraph 58 when Sylvia says to herself that she will have "to think this day through" yet is determined that "nobody [is] gonna beat [her] at nuthin"? Is she a developing character?

3. What is the relationship between Sylvia and her cousin Sugar? How are they contrasted?

4. Sugar states the lesson that she has learned in paragraph 51. How does the sorrowful look that Miss Moore gives Sylvia in that paragraph suggest that there is more to the lesson? What more? Explain the effect of Sugar's definition of happiness as "an equal crack at the dough" on Miss Moore and on Sylvia.

5. State the theme of the story.

Anton Chekhov
Gooseberries

The whole sky had been overcast with rain clouds from early morning; it was a still day, not hot, but heavy, as it is in gray dull weather

GOOSEBERRIES   First published in 1898. Translated from the Russian by Constance Garnett. Anton Chekov (1860–1904) was raised in semipoverty in the town of Taganrog, on the Black Sea. A scholarship enabled him to take a medical degree from Moscow University, but writing plays, stories, and sketches was his main source of income. Partly because of ill health, he purchased in 1892 a small country estate for his family near Moscow, where he enjoyed the benefits of country life. The onset of tuberculosis sent him to the warmer climate of the seaside town Yalta, where he wrote Gooseberries." [A *note on Russian names:* In Russia a person was identified by three names—a given name (such as Ivan), a patronymic name (Ivanovitch), and a family or surname (Tchimsha-Himalaisky). The patronymic indicated one's father's given name, and for men was formed by adding the suffix -tch, -itch, or -ovitch; for women, the suffixes were -evna or -ovna. "Ivan Ivanovitch" is thus Ivan, son of Ivan Tchimsha-Himalaisky. As in English, nicknames abound.]

when the clouds have been hanging over the country for a long while, when one expects rain and it does not come. Ivan Ivanovitch, the veterinary surgeon, and Burkin, the high school teacher, were already tired from walking, and the fields seemed to them endless. Far ahead of them they could just see the windmills of the village of Mironositskoe; on the right stretched a row of hillocks which disappeared in the distance behind the village, and they both knew that this was the bank of the river, that there were meadows, green willows, homesteads there, and that if one stood on one of the hillocks one could see from it the same vast plain, telegraph wires, and a train which in the distance looked like a crawling caterpillar, and that in clear weather one could even see the town. Now, in still weather, when all nature seemed mild and dreamy, Ivan Ivanovitch and Burkin were filled with love of that countryside, and both thought how great, how beautiful a land it was.

"Last time we were in Prokofy's barn," said Burkin, "you were about to tell me a story."

"Yes; I meant to tell you about my brother."

Ivan Ivanovitch heaved a deep sigh and lighted a pipe to begin to tell his story, but just at that moment the rain began. And five minutes later heavy rain came down, covering the sky, and it was hard to tell when it would be over. Ivan Ivanovitch and Burkin stopped in hesitation; the dogs, already drenched, stood with their tails between their legs gazing at them feelingly.

"We must take shelter somewhere," said Burkin. "Let us go to   5
Alehin's; it's close by."

"Come along."

They turned aside and walked through mown fields, sometimes going straight forward, sometimes turning to the right, till they came out on the road. Soon they saw poplars, a garden, then the red roofs of barns; there was a gleam of the river, and the view opened on to a broad expanse of water with a windmill and a white bathhouse: this was Sofino, where Alehin lived.

The watermill was at work, drowning the sound of the rain; the dam was shaking. Here wet horses with drooping heads were standing near their carts, and men were walking about covered with sacks. It was damp, muddy, and desolate; the water looked cold and malignant. Ivan Ivanovitch and Burkin were already conscious of a feeling of wetness, messiness, and discomfort all over; their feet were heavy with mud, and when, crossing the dam, they went up to the barns, they were silent, as though they were angry with one another.

In one of the barns there was the sound of a winnowing machine, the door was open, and clouds of dust were coming from it. In the doorway was standing Alehin himself, a man of forty, tall and stout, with long hair, more like a professor or an artist than a landowner. He had on a white shirt that badly needed washing, a rope for a belt, drawers instead of trousers, and his boots, too, were plastered up with mud and straw. His eyes and nose were black with dust. He recognized Ivan Ivanovitch and Burkin, and was apparently much delighted to see them.

10   "Go into the house, gentlemen," he said, smiling; "I'll come directly, this minute."

It was a big two-storied house. Alehin lived in the lower story, with arched ceilings and little windows, where the bailiffs had once lived; here everything was plain, and there was a smell of rye bread, cheap vodka, and harness. He went upstairs into the best rooms only on rare occasions, when visitors came. Ivan Ivanovitch and Burkin were met in the house by a maidservant, a young woman so beautiful that they both stood still and looked at one another.

"You can't imagine how delighted I am to see you, my friends," said Alehin, going into the hall with them. "It is a surprise! Pelagea," he said, addressing the girl, "give our visitors something to change into. And, by the way, I will change too. Only I must first go and wash, for I almost think I have not washed since spring. Wouldn't you like to come into the bathhouse? and meanwhile they will get things ready here."

Beautiful Pelagea, looking so refined and soft, brought them towels and soap, and Alehin went to the bathhouse with his guests.

"It's a long time since I had a wash," he said, undressing. "I have got a nice bathhouse, as you see—my father built it—but I somehow never have time to wash."

15   He sat down on the steps and soaped his long hair and his neck, and the water round him turned brown.

"Yes, I must say," said Ivan Ivanovitch meaningly, looking at his head.

"It's a long time since I washed . . ." said Alehin with embarrassment, giving himself a second soaping, and the water near him turned dark blue, like ink.

Ivan Ivanovitch went outside, plunged into the water with a loud splash, and swam in the rain, flinging his arms out wide. He stirred the water into waves which set the white lilies bobbing up and down; he swam to the very middle of the millpond and dived, and came up a minute later in another place, and swam on, and kept on diving, trying to touch the bottom.

"Oh, my goodness!" he repeated continually, enjoying himself thoroughly. "Oh, my goodness!" He swam to the mill, talked to the peasants there, then returned and lay on his back in the middle of the pond, turning his face to the rain. Burkin and Alehin were dressed and ready to go, but he still went on swimming and diving. "Oh, my goodness! . . ." he said. "Oh, Lord, have mercy on me! . . ."

"That's enough!" Burkin shouted to him.   20

They went back to the house. And only when the lamp was lighted in the big drawing room upstairs, and Burkin and Ivan Ivanovitch, attired in silk dressing gowns and warm slippers, were sitting in armchairs; and Alehin, washed and combed, in a new coat, was walking about the drawing room, evidently enjoying the feeling of warmth, cleanliness, dry clothes, and light shoes; and when lovely Pelagea, stepped noiselessly on the carpet and smiling softly, handed tea and jam on a tray—only then Ivan Ivanovitch began on his story, and it seemed as though not only Burkin and Alehin were listening, but also the ladies, young and old, and the officers who looked down upon them sternly and calmly from their gold frames.

"There are two of us brothers," he began—"I, Ivan Ivanovitch, and my brother, Nikolay Ivanovitch, two years younger. I went in for a learned profession and became a veterinary surgeon, while Nikolay sat in a government office from the time he was nineteen. Our father, Tchimsha-Himalaisky, was a kantonist,° but he rose to be an officer and left us a little estate and the rank of nobility. After his death the little estate went in debts and legal expenses; but, anyway, we had spent our childhood running wild in the country. Like peasant children, we passed our days and nights in the fields and the woods, looked after horses, stripped the bark off the trees, fished, and so on. . . . And, you know, whoever has once in his life caught perch or has seen the migrating of the thrushes in autumn, watched how they float in flocks over the village on bright, cool days, he will never be a real townsman, and will have a yearning for freedom to the day of his death. My brother was miserable in the government office. Years passed by, and he went on sitting in the same place, went on writing the same papers and thinking of one and the same thing—how to get into the country. And this yearning by degrees passed into a definite desire, into a dream of buying himself a little farm somewhere on the banks of a river or a lake.

"He was a gentle, good-natured fellow, and I was fond of him, but I never sympathized with this desire to shut himself up for the rest of his life in a little farm of his own. It's the correct thing to say that a man needs no more than six feet of earth. But six feet is what a corpse needs,

---

kantonist: the son of a private, registered at birth in the army and trained in a military school

not a man. And they say, too, now, that if our intellectual classes are attracted to the land and yearn for a farm, it's a good thing. But these farms are just the same as six feet of earth. To retreat from town, from the struggle, from the bustle of life, to retreat and bury oneself in one's farm—it's not life, it's egoism, laziness, it's monasticism of a sort, but monasticism without good works. A man does not need six feet of earth or a farm, but the whole globe, all nature, where he can have room to display all the qualities and peculiarities of his free spirit.

"My brother Nikolay, sitting in his government office, dreamed of how he would eat his own cabbages, which would fill the whole yard with such a savory smell, take his meals on the green grass, sleep in the sun, sit for whole hours on the seat by the gate gazing at the fields and the forest. Gardening books and the agricultural hints in calendars were his delight, his favorite spiritual sustenance; he enjoyed reading newspapers, too, but the only things he read in them were the advertisements of so many acres of arable land and a grass meadow with farmhouses and buildings, a river, a garden, a mill and millponds, for sale. And his imagination pictured the garden paths, flowers and fruit, starling cotes, the carp in the pond, and all that sort of thing, you know. These imaginary pictures were of different kinds according to the advertisements which he came across, but for some reason in every one of them he had always to have gooseberries. He could not imagine a homestead, he could not picture an idyllic nook, without gooseberries.

25   "'Country life has its conveniences,' he would sometimes say. 'You sit on the verandah and you drink tea, while your ducks swim on the pond, there is a delicious smell everywhere, and . . . and the gooseberries are growing.'

"He used to draw a map of his property, and in every map there were the same things—(a) house for the family, (b) servants' quarters, (c) kitchen garden, (d) gooseberry bushes. He lived parsimoniously, was frugal in food and drink, his clothes were beyond description; he looked like a beggar, but kept on saving and putting money in the bank. He grew fearfully avaricious. I did not like to look at him, and I used to give him something and send him presents for Christmas and Easter, but he used to save that too. Once a man is absorbed by an idea there is no doing anything with him.

"Years passed: he was transferred to another province. He was over forty and he was still reading the advertisements in the papers and saving up. Then I heard he was married. Still with the same object of buying a farm and having gooseberries, he married an elderly and ugly widow without a trace of feeling for her, simply because she had filthy lucre. He went on living frugally after marrying her, and kept her short of food, while he put her money in the bank in his name.

"Her first husband had been a postmaster, and with him she was accustomed to pies and homemade wines, while with her second husband she did not get enough black bread; she began to pine away with this sort of life, and three years later she gave up her soul to God. And I need hardly say that my brother never for one moment imagined that he was responsible for her death. Money, like vodka, makes a man queer. In our town there was a merchant who, before he died, ordered a plateful of honey and ate up all his money and lottery tickets with the honey, so that no one might get the benefit of it. While I was inspecting cattle at a railway station, a cattle dealer fell under an engine and had his leg cut off. We carried him into the waiting room, the blood was flowing—it was a horrible thing—and he kept asking them to look for his leg and was very much worried about it; there were twenty rubles in the boot on the leg that had been cut off, and he was afraid they would be lost."

"That's a story from a different opera," said Burkin.

"After his wife's death," Ivan Ivanovitch went on, after thinking for half a minute, "my brother began looking out for an estate for himself. Of course, you may look about for five years and yet end by making a mistake, and buying something quite different from what you have dreamed of. My brother Nikolay bought through an agent a mortgaged estate of three hundred and thirty acres, with a house for the family, with servants' quarters, with a park, but with no orchard, no gooseberry bushes, and no duck pond; there was a river, but the water in it was the color of coffee, because on one side of the estate there was a brickyard and on the other a factory for burning bones. But Nikolay Ivanovitch did not grieve much; he ordered twenty gooseberry bushes, planted them, and began living as a country gentleman.

"Last year I went to pay him a visit. I thought I would go and see what it was like. In his letters my brother called his estate 'Tchumbaroklov Waste, alias Himalaiskoe.' I reached 'alias Himalaiskoe' in the afternoon. It was hot. Everywhere there were ditches, fences, hedges, fir trees planted in rows, and there was no knowing how to get to the yard, where to put one's horse. I went up to the house, and was met by a fat red dog that looked like a pig. It wanted to bark, but it was too lazy. The cook, a fat, barefooted woman, came out of the kitchen, and she, too, looked like a pig, and said that her master was resting after dinner. I went in to see my brother. He was sitting up in bed with a quilt over his legs; he had grown older, fatter, wrinkled; his cheeks, his nose, and his

30

mouth all stuck out—he looked as though he might begin grunting into the quilt at any moment.

"We embraced each other, and shed tears of joy and of sadness at the thought that we had once been young and now were both gray headed and near the grave. He dressed, and led me out to show me the estate.

"'Well, how are you getting on here?' I asked.

"'Oh, all right, thank God; I am getting on very well.'

35   "He was no more a poor timid clerk, but a real landowner, a gentleman. He was already accustomed to it, had grown used to it, and liked it. He ate a great deal, went to the bathhouse, was growing stout, was already at law with the village commune and both factories, and was very much offended when the peasants did not call him 'Your Honor.' And he concerned himself with the salvation of his soul in a substantial, gentlemanly manner, and performed deeds of charity, not simply, but with an air of consequence. And what deeds of charity! He treated the peasants for every sort of disease with soda and castor oil, and on his name day had a thanksgiving service in the middle of the village, and then treated the peasants to a gallon of vodka—he thought that was the thing to do. Oh, those horrible gallons of vodka! One day the fat landowner hauls the peasants up before the district captain for trespass, and next day, in honor of a holiday, treats them to a gallon of vodka, and they drink and shout 'Hurrah!' and when they are drunk bow down to his feet. A change of life for the better, and being well fed and idle develop in a Russian the most insolent self-conceit. Nikolay Ivanovitch, who at one time in the government office was afraid to have any views of his own, now could say nothing that was not gospel truth, and uttered such truths in the tone of a prime minister. 'Education is essential, but for the peasants it is premature.' 'Corporal punishment is harmful as a rule, but in some cases it is necessary and there is nothing to take its place.'

"'I know the peasants and understand how to treat them,' he would say. 'The peasants like me. I need only to hold up my little finger and the peasants will do anything I like.'

"And all this, observe, was uttered with a wise, benevolent smile. He repeated twenty times over 'We noblemen,' 'I as a noble'; obviously he did not remember that our grandfather was a peasant, and our father a soldier. Even our surname Tchimsha-Himalaisky, in reality so incongruous, seemed to him now melodious, distinguished, and very agreeable.

"But the point just now is not he, but myself. I want to tell you about the change that took place in me during the brief hours I spent at his country place. In the evening, when we were drinking tea, the cook put on the table a plateful of gooseberries. They were not bought, but his own gooseberries, gathered for the first time since the bushes were planted. Nikolay Ivanovitch laughed and looked for a minute in silence at the gooseberries, with tears in his eyes; he could not speak for excitement. Then he put one gooseberry in his mouth, looked at me with the triumph of a child who has at last received his favorite toy, and said:

"'How delicious!'

"And he ate them greedily, continually repeating, 'Ah, how deli-   40
cious! Do taste them!'

"They were sour and unripe, but, as Pushkin says:

> "'Dearer to us the falsehood that exalts
> Than hosts of baser truths.'

"I saw a happy man whose cherished dream was so obviously ful-filled, who had attained this object in life, who had gained what he wanted, who was satisfied with his fate and himself. There is always, for some reason, an element of sadness mingled with my thoughts of hu-man happiness, and, on this occasion, at the sight of a happy man I was overcome by an oppressive feeling that was close upon despair. It was particularly oppressive at night. A bed was made up for me in the room next to my brother's bedroom, and I could hear that he was awake, and that he kept getting up and going to the plate of gooseberries and tak-ing one. I reflected how many satisfied, happy people there really are! What a suffocating force it is! You look at life: the insolence and idle-ness of the strong, the ignorance and brutishness of the weak, incredi-ble poverty all about us, overcrowding, degeneration, drunkenness, hypocrisy, lying. . . . Yet all is calm and stillness in the houses and in the streets; of the fifty thousand living in a town, there is not one who would cry out, who would give vent to his indignation aloud. We see the people going to market for provisions, eating by day, sleeping by night, talking their silly nonsense, getting married, growing old, serenely escorting their dead to the cemetery; but we do not see and we do not hear those who suffer, and what is terrible in life goes on some-where behind the scenes. . . . Everything is quiet and peaceful, and noth-ing protests but mute statistics: so many people gone out of their minds, so many gallons of vodka drunk, so many children dead from malnutri-tion. . . . And this order of things is evidently necessary; evidently the happy man only feels at ease because the unhappy bear their burdens in silence, and without that silence happiness would be impossible. It's a case of general hypnotism. There ought to be behind the door of every happy, contented man someone standing with a hammer continually reminding him with a tap that there are unhappy people; that however happy he may be, life will show him her laws sooner or later, trouble will come for him—disease, poverty, losses, and no one will see or hear, just as now he neither sees nor hears others. But there is no man with a hammer; the happy man lives at his ease, and trivial daily cares faintly agitate him like the wind in the aspen tree—and all goes well.

"That night I realized that I, too, was happy and contented," Ivan Ivanovitch went on, getting up. "I too, at dinner and at the hunt liked to lay down the law on life and religion, and the way to manage the peasantry. I, too, used to say that science was light, that culture was essential, but for the simple people reading and writing was enough for the time. Freedom is a blessing, I used to say; we can no more do without it than without air, but we must wait a little. Yes, I used to talk like that, and now I ask, 'For what reason are we to wait?'" asked Ivan Ivanovitch, looking angrily at Burkin. "Why wait, I ask you? What grounds have we for waiting? I shall be told, it can't be done all at once; every idea takes shape in life gradually, in its due time. But who is it says that? Where is the proof that it's right? You will fall back upon the natural order of things, the uniformity of phenomena; but is there order and uniformity in the fact that I, a living, thinking man, stand over a chasm and wait for it to close of itself, or to fill up with mud at the very time when perhaps I might leap over it or build a bridge across it? And again, wait for the sake of what? Wait till there's no strength to live? And meanwhile one must live, and one wants to live!

"I went away from my brother's early in the morning, and ever since then it has been unbearable for me to be in town. I am oppressed by its peace and quiet; I am afraid to look at the windows, for there is no spectacle more painful to me now than the sight of a happy family sitting round the table drinking tea. I am old and am not fit for the struggle; I am not even capable of hatred; I can only grieve inwardly, feel irritated and vexed, but at night my head is hot from the rush of ideas, and I cannot sleep. . . . Ah, if I were young!"

45   Ivan Ivanovitch walked backwards and forwards in excitement, and repeated: "If I were young!"

He suddenly went up to Alehin and began pressing first one of his hands and then the other.

"Pavel Konstantinovitch," he said in an imploring voice, "don't be calm and contented, don't let yourself be put to sleep! While you are young, strong, confident, be not weary in well-doing! There is no happiness, and there ought not to be; but if there is a meaning and an object in life, that meaning and object is not our happiness, but something greater and more rational. Do good!"

And all this Ivan Ivanovitch said with a pitiful, imploring smile, as though he were asking him a personal favor.

Then all three sat in armchairs at different ends of the drawing room and were silent. Ivan Ivanovitch's story had not satisfied either Burkin or Alehin. When the generals and ladies gazed down from their gilt frames, looking in the dusk as though they were alive, it was dreary to listen to the story of the poor clerk who ate gooseberries. They felt inclined, for some reason, to talk about elegant people, about women. And their sitting in the drawing room where everything—the chandeliers in their covers, the armchairs, and the carpet under their feet—reminded them that those very people who were now looking down from their frames had once moved about, sat, drunk tea in this room, and the fact that lovely Pelagea was moving noiselessly about was better than any story.

Alehin was fearfully sleepy; he had got up early, before three 50 o'clock in the morning, to look after his work, and now his eyes were closing; but he was afraid his visitors might tell some interesting story after he had gone, and he lingered on. He did not go into the question whether what Ivan Ivanovitch had just said was right and true. His visitors did not talk of groats, nor of hay, nor of tar, but of something that had no direct bearing on his life, and he was glad and wanted them to go on.

"It's bedtime, though," said Burkin, getting up. "Allow me to wish you goodnight."

Alehin said goodnight and went downstairs to his own domain, while the visitors remained upstairs. They were both taken for the night to a big room where there stood two old wooden beds decorated with carvings, and in the corner was an ivory crucifix. The big cool beds, which had been made by the lovely Pelagea, smelt agreeably of clean linen.

Ivan Ivanovitch undressed in silence and got into bed.

"Lord forgive us sinners!" he said, and put his head under the quilt.

His pipe lying on the table smelt strongly of stale tobacco, and 55 Burkin could not sleep for a long while, and kept wondering where the oppressive smell came from.

The rain was pattering on the windowpanes all night.

QUESTIONS

1. Distinguish between the "frame story" (what happens to Ivan, Burkin, and Alehin at Alehin's estate) and the story that Ivan tells about his brother.

What are the major events and actions in each? What are the personality traits of the characters in each? What are the plot conflicts in each? What theme does each story have?

2. What correspondences exist between the frame story and Ivan's narration? What parallels are there between Nikolay's estate and Alehin's?

3. In the opening paragraph, the landscape is described this way: "overcast . . . gray dull weather . . . one expects rain and it does not come . . . mild and dreamy . . . love of that countryside . . . how beautiful a land it was." Account for these seemingly contradictory descriptions, and find other passages in the story that seem equally self-contradictory. Are such contradictions characteristic of both the frame story and the narrative?

4. What does Ivan see as the lesson to be learned from his brother's history? Why does he urge that lesson on Alehin? What does Alehin think of Ivan's story and its lesson? Is either Ivan or Alehin entirely right or wrong?

5. Explore the symbolism of (a) Ivan's swim, (b) Ivan's pipe, and (c) the gooseberries.

6. Having answered the five preceding questions, reread question 1, and use your answers to it to form a statement that combines the themes of the frame and those of the narrative into a coherent theme for Chekhov's story.

Eudora Welty

A Worn Path

It was December—a bright frozen day in the early morning. Far out in the country there was an old Negro woman with her head tied in a red rag, coming along a path through the pinewoods. Her name was Phoenix Jackson. She was very old and small and she walked slowly in the dark pine shadows, moving a little from side to side in her steps, with the balanced heaviness and lightness of a pendulum in a grandfather clock. She carried a thin, small cane made from an umbrella, and with this she kept tapping the frozen earth in front of her. This made a grave and persistent noise in the still air, that seemed meditative like the chirping of a solitary little bird.

She wore a dark striped dress reaching down to her shoe tops, and an equally long apron of bleached sugar sacks, with a full pocket: all

A WORN PATH   First published in 1941. Eudora Welty (1909–2001) was born in Jackson, Mississippi, where she was raised and to which she returned after studying at the University of Wisconsin and Columbia University. In the mid-1930s she was employed by the federal Work Projects Administration (WPA) to travel throughout Mississippi writing newspaper copy and taking photographs, a job that enabled her to observe many varieties of rural life in her native state.

neat and tidy, but every time she took a step she might have fallen over her shoelaces, which dragged from her unlaced shoes. She looked straight ahead. Her eyes were blue with age. Her skin had a pattern all its own of numberless branching wrinkles and as though a whole little tree stood in the middle of her forehead, but a golden color ran underneath, and the two knobs of her cheeks were illu- mined by a yellow burning under the dark. Under the red rag her hair came down on her neck in the frailest of ringlets, still black, and with an odor like copper.

Now and then there was a quivering in the thicket. Old Phoenix said, "Out of my way, all you foxes, owls, beetles, jack rabbits, coons, and wild animals! . . . Keep out from under these feet, little bob- whites. . . . Keep the big wild hogs out of my path. Don't let none of those come running my direction. I got a long way." Under her small black-freckled hand her cane, limber as a buggy whip, would switch at the brush as if to rouse up any hiding things.

On she went. The woods were deep and still. The sun made the pine needles almost too bright to look at, up where the wind rocked. The cones dropped as light as feathers. Down in the hollow was the mourning dove—it was not too late for him.

The path ran up a hill. "Seem like there is chains about my feet, time I get this far," she said, in the voice of argument old people keep to use with themselves. "Something always take a hold of me on this hill—pleads I should stay."   5

After she got to the top she turned and gave a full, severe look be- hind her where she had come. "Up through pines," she said at length. "Now down through oaks."

Her eyes opened their widest, and she started down gently. But before she got to the bottom of the hill a bush caught her dress.

Her fingers were busy and intent, but her skirts were full and long, so that before she could pull them free in one place they were caught in another. It was not possible to allow the dress to tear. "I in the thorny bush," she said. "Thorns, you doing your appointed work. Never want to let folks pass, no sir. Old eyes thought you was a pretty little *green* bush."

Finally, trembling all over, she stood free, and after a moment dared to stoop for her cane.

"Sun so high!" she cried, leaning back and looking, while the thick tears went over her eyes. "The time getting all gone here."   10

At the foot of this hill was a place where a log was laid across the creek.

"Now comes the trial," said Phoenix.

Putting her right foot out, she mounted the log and shut her eyes. Lifting her skirt, leveling her cane fiercely before her, like a festival figure in some parade, she began to march across. Then she opened her eyes and she was safe on the other side.

"I wasn't as old as I thought," she said.

15   But she sat down to rest. She spread her skirts on the bank around her and folded her hands over her knees. Up above her was a tree in a pearly cloud of mistletoe. She did not dare to close her eyes, and when a little boy brought her a plate with a slice of marble-cake on it she spoke to him. "That would be acceptable," she said. But when she went to take it there was just her own hand in the air.

So she left that tree, and had to go through a barbed-wire fence. There she had to creep and crawl, spreading her knees and stretching her fingers like a baby trying to climb the steps. But she talked loudly to herself: she could not let her dress be torn now, so late in the day, and she could not pay for having her arm or her leg sawed off if she got caught fast where she was.

At last she was safe through the fence and risen up out in the clearing. Big dead trees, like black men with one arm, were standing in the purple stalks of the withered cotton field. There sat a buzzard.

"Who you watching?"

In the furrow she made her way along.

20   "Glad this not the season for bulls," she said, looking sideways, "and the good Lord made his snakes to curl up and sleep in the winter. A pleasure I don't see no two-headed snake coming around that tree, where it come once. It took a while to get by him, back in the summer."

She passed through the old cotton and went into a field of dead corn. It whispered and shook and was taller than her head. "Through the maze now," she said, for there was no path.

Then there was something tall, black, and skinny there, moving before her.

At first she took it for a man. It could have been a man dancing in the field. But she stood still and listened, and it did not make a sound. It was as silent as a ghost.

"Ghost," she said sharply, "who be you the ghost of? For I have heard of nary death close by."

25   But there was no answer—only the ragged dancing in the wind.

She shut her eyes, reached out her hand, and touched a sleeve. She found a coat and inside that an emptiness, cold as ice.

"You scarecrow," she said. Her face lighted. "I ought to be shut up for good," she said with laughter. "My senses is gone. I too old. I the oldest people I ever know. Dance, old scarecrow," she said, "while I dancing with you."

She kicked her foot over the furrow, and with mouth drawn down, shook her head once or twice in a little strutting way. Some husks blew down and whirled in streamers about her skirts.

Then she went on, parting her way from side to side with the cane, through the whispering field. At last she came to the end, to a wagon track where the silver grass blew between the red ruts. The quail were walking around like pullets, seeming all dainty and unseen.

"Walk pretty," she said. "This the easy place. This the easy going."   30

She followed the track, swaying through the quiet bare fields, through the little strings of trees silver in their dead leaves, past cabins silver from weather, with the doors and windows boarded shut, all like old women under a spell sitting there. "I walking in their sleep," she said, nodding her head vigorously.

In a ravine she went where a spring was silently flowing through a hollow log. Old Phoenix bent and drank. "Sweet-gum makes the water sweet," she said, and drank more. "Nobody know who made this well, for it was here when I was born."

The track crossed a swampy part where the moss hung as white as lace from every limb. "Sleep on, alligators, and blow your bubbles." Then the track went into the road.

Deep, deep the road went down between the high green-colored banks. Overhead the live-oaks met, and it was as dark as a cave.

A black dog with a lolling tongue came up out of the weeds by the   35
ditch. She was meditating, and not ready, and when he came at her she only hit him a little with her cane. Over she went in the ditch, like a little puff of milkweed.

Down there, her senses drifted away. A dream visited her, and she reached her hand up, but nothing reached down and gave her a pull. So she lay there and presently went to talking. "Old woman," she said to herself, "that black dog come up out of the weeds to stall you off, and now there he sitting on his fine tail, smiling at you."

A white man finally came along and found her—a hunter, a young man, with his dog on a chain.

"Well, Granny!" he laughed. "What are you doing there?"

"Lying on my back like a June-bug waiting to be turned over, mister," she said, reaching up her hand.

He lifted her up, gave her a swing in the air, and set her down.   40
"Anything broken, Granny?"

"No sir, them old dead weeds is springy enough," said Phoenix, when she had got her breath. "I thank you for your trouble."

"Where do you live, Granny?" he asked, while the two dogs were growling at each other.

"Away back yonder, sir, behind the ridge. You can't even see it from here."

"On your way home?"

45   "No sir, going to town."

"Why, that's too far! That's as far as I walk when I come out my-self, and I get something for my trouble." He patted the stuffed bag he carried, and there hung down a little closed claw. It was one of the bob-whites, with its beak hooked bitterly to show it was dead. "Now you go on home, Granny!"

"I bound to go to town, mister," said Phoenix. "The time come around."

He gave another laugh, filling the whole landscape. "I know you old colored people! Wouldn't miss going to town to see Santa Claus!"

But something held old Phoenix very still. The deep lines in her face went into a fierce and different radiation. Without warning, she had seen with her own eyes a flashing nickel fall out of the man's pocket onto the ground.

50   "How old are you, Granny?" he was saying.

"There is no telling, mister," she said, "no telling."

Then she gave a little cry and clapped her hands and said, "Git on away from here, dog! Look! Look at that dog!" She laughed as if in admiration. "He ain't scared of nobody. He a big black dog." She whis-pered, "Sic him!"

"Watch me get rid of that cur," said the man. "Sic him, Pete! Sic him!"

Phoenix heard the dogs fighting, and heard the man running and throwing sticks. She even heard a gunshot. But she was slowly bending forward by that time, further and further forward, the lids stretched down over her eyes, as if she were doing this in her sleep. Her chin was lowered almost to her knees. The yellow palm of her hand came out from the fold of her apron. Her fingers slid down and along the ground under the piece of money with the grace and care they would have in lifting an egg from under a setting hen. Then she slowly straightened up, she stood erect, and the nickel was in her apron pocket. A bird flew by. Her lips moved. "God watching me the whole time. I come to stealing."

55   The man came back, and his own dog panted about them. "Well, I scared him off that time," he said, and then he laughed and lifted his gun and pointed it at Phoenix.

She stood straight and faced him.

"Doesn't the gun scare you?" he said, still pointing it.

"No, sir, I seen plenty go off closer by, in my day, and for less than what I done," she said, holding utterly still.

He smiled, and shouldered the gun. "Well, Granny," he said, "you must be a hundred years old, and scared of nothing. I'd give you a dime if I had any money with me. But you take my advice and stay home, and nothing will happen to you."

"I bound to go on my way, mister," said Phoenix. She inclined her   60
head in the red rag. Then they went in different directions, but she could hear the gun shooting again and again over the hill.

She walked on. The shadows hung from the oak trees to the road like curtains. Then she smelled wood-smoke, and smelled the river, and she saw a steeple and the cabins on their steep steps. Dozens of little black children whirled around her. There ahead was Natchez shining. Bells were ringing. She walked on.

In the paved city it was Christmas time. There were red and green electric lights strung and crisscrossed everywhere, and all turned on in the daytime. Old Phoenix would have been lost if she had not distrusted her eyesight and depended on her feet to know where to take her.

She paused quietly on the sidewalk where people were passing by. A lady came along in the crowd, carrying an armful of red-, green-, and silver-wrapped presents; she gave off perfume like the red roses in hot summer, and Phoenix stopped her.

"Please, missy, will you lace up my shoe?" She held up her foot.

"What do you want, Grandma?"   65

"See my shoe," said Phoenix. "Do all right for out in the country, but wouldn't look right to go in a big building."

"Stand still then, Grandma," said the lady. She put her packages down on the sidewalk beside her and laced and tied both shoes tightly.

"Can't lace 'em with a cane," said Phoenix. "Thank you, missy. I doesn't mind asking a nice lady to tie up my shoe, when I gets out on the street."

Moving slowly and from side to side, she went into the big building, and into a tower of steps, where she walked up and around and around until her feet knew to stop.

She entered a door, and there she saw nailed up on the wall the   70
document that had been stamped with the gold seal and framed in the gold frame, which matched the dream that was hung up in her head.

"Here I be," she said. There was a fixed and ceremonial stiffness over her body.

"A charity case, I suppose," said an attendant who sat at the desk before her.

But Phoenix only looked above her head. There was sweat on her face, the wrinkles in her skin shone like a bright net.

"Speak up, Grandma," the woman said. "What's your name? We must have your history, you know. Have you been here before? What seems to be the trouble with you?"

75   Old Phoenix only gave a twitch to her face as if a fly were bothering her.

"Are you deaf?" cried the attendant.

But then the nurse came in.

"Oh, that's just old Aunt Phoenix," she said. "She doesn't come for herself—she has a little grandson. She makes these trips just as regular as clockwork. She lives away back off the Old Natchez Trace." She bent down. "Well, Aunt Phoenix, why don't you just take a seat? We won't keep you standing after your long trip." She pointed.

The old woman sat down, bolt upright in the chair.

80   "Now, how is the boy?" asked the nurse.

Old Phoenix did not speak.

"I said, how is the boy?"

But Phoenix only waited and stared straight ahead, her face very solemn and withdrawn into rigidity.

"Is his throat any better?" asked the nurse. "Aunt Phoenix, don't you hear me? Is your grandson's throat any better since the last time you came for the medicine?"

85   With her hands on her knees, the old woman waited, silent, erect and motionless, just as if she were in armor.

"You mustn't take up our time this way, Aunt Phoenix," the nurse said. "Tell us quickly about your grandson, and get it over. He isn't dead, is he?"

At last there came a flicker and then a flame of comprehension across her face, and she spoke.

"My grandson. It was my memory had left me. There I sat and forgot why I made my long trip."

"Forgot?" The nurse frowned. "After you came so far?"

90   Then Phoenix was like an old woman begging a dignified forgiveness for waking up frightened in the night. "I never did go to school, I was too old at the Surrender," she said in a soft voice. "I'm an old woman without an education. It was my memory fail me. My little grandson, he is just the same, and I forgot it in the coming."

"Throat never heals, does it?" said the nurse, speaking in a loud, sure voice to old Phoenix. By now she had a card with something written on it, a little list. "Yes. Swallowed lye. When was it?—January—two, three years ago—?"

Phoenix spoke unasked now. "No, missy, he not dead, he just the same. Every little while his throat begin to close up again, and he not able to swallow. He not get his breath. He not able to help himself. So the time come around, and I go on another trip for the soothing medicine."

"All right. The doctor said as long as you came to get it, you could have it," said the nurse. "But it's an obstinate case."

"My little grandson, he sit up there in the house all wrapped up, waiting by himself," Phoenix went on. "We is the only two left in the world. He suffer and it don't seem to put him back at all. He got a sweet look. He going to last. He wear a little patch quilt and peep out holding his mouth open like a little bird. I remembers so plain now. I not going to forget him again, no, the whole enduring time. I could tell him from all the others in creation."

"All right." The nurse was trying to hush her now. She brought her   95
a bottle of medicine. "Charity," she said, making a check mark in a book.

Old Phoenix held the bottle close to her eyes, and then carefully put it into her pocket.

"I thank you," she said.

"It's Christmas time, Grandma," said the attendant. "Could I give you a few pennies out of my purse?"

"Five pennies is a nickel," said Phoenix stiffly.

"Here's a nickel," said the attendant.   100

Phoenix rose carefully and held out her hand. She received the nickel and then fished the other nickel out of her pocket and laid it beside the new one. She stared at her palm closely, with her head on one side.

Then she gave a tap with her cane on the floor.

"This is what come to me to do," she said. "I going to the store and buy my child a little windmill they sells, made out of paper. He going to find it hard to believe there such a thing in the world. I'll march myself back where he waiting, holding it straight up in this hand."

She lifted her free hand, gave a little nod, turned around, and walked out of the doctor's office. Then her slow step began on the stairs, going down.

QUESTIONS

1. Write a precise, well-developed sentence that states as fully as possible the theme of the story. Remember to avoid clichés or oversimplification.
2. Apart from the story's major theme, can you isolate minor themes that help give the story richness and depth? List as many as you can.

3. Discuss the way the characterization of Phoenix contributes to the theme.
4. Analyze the minor characters. What do they reveal about Phoenix and about the world in which she lives?
5. Like many classic works of literature, "A Worn Path" features a journey and a quest. Discuss the elements of plot and structure that dramatize Phoenix's journey. What are the obstacles to her quest, and how does she overcome them?
6. In answer to a student who wrote to ask her, "Is the grandson really dead?" Welty responded, "My best answer would be: *Phoenix* is alive." What might have led the student to ask that question? How can the author's remark be seen as an answer?

Nadine Gordimer

Once upon a Time

Someone has written to ask me to contribute to an anthology of stories for children. I reply that I don't write children's stories; and he writes back that at a recent congress/book fair/seminar a certain novelist said every writer ought to write at least one story for children. I think of sending a postcard saying I don't accept that I "ought" to write anything.

And then last night I woke up—or rather was awakened without knowing what had roused me.

A voice in the echo-chamber of the subconscious?

A sound.

5   A creaking of the kind made by the weight carried by one foot after another along a wooden floor. I listened. I felt the apertures of my ears distend with concentration. Again: the creaking. I was waiting for it; waiting to hear if it indicated that feet were moving from room to room, coming up the passage—to my door. I have no burglar bars, no gun under the pillow, but I have the same fears as people who do take these precautions, and my windowpanes are thin as rime, could shatter like a wineglass. A woman was murdered (how do they put it) in broad

ONCE UPON A TIME   First published in 1989. Nadine Gordimer was born in 1923 in a small town near Johannesburg, South Africa, and graduated from the University of Witwatersrand. She has taught at several American universities but continues to reside in her native country. A prolific writer, Gordimer has published more than twenty books of fiction (novels and short story collections). In addition to England's prestigious Booker Prize for Fiction, she received the Nobel Prize for literature in 1991.

daylight in a house two blocks away, last year, and the fierce dogs who guarded an old widower and his collection of antique clocks were strangled before he was knifed by a casual laborer he had dismissed without pay.

I was staring at the door, making it out in my mind rather than seeing it, in the dark. I lay quite still—a victim already—the arrhythmia of my heart was fleeing, knocking this way and that against its body-cage. How finely tuned the senses are, just out of rest, sleep! I could never listen intently as that in the distractions of the day; I was reading every faintest sound, identifying and classifying its possible threat.

But I learned that I was to be neither threatened nor spared. There was no human weight pressing on the boards, the creaking was a buckling, an epicenter of stress. I was in it. The house that surrounds me while I sleep is built on undermined ground; far beneath my bed, the floor, the house's foundations, the stopes and passages of gold mines have hollowed the rock, and when some face trembles, detaches and falls, three thousand feet below, the whole house shifts slightly, bringing uneasy strain to the balance and counterbalance of brick, cement, wood and glass that hold it as a structure around me. The misbeats of my heart tailed off like the last muffled flourishes on one of the wooden xylophones made by the Chopi and Tsonga° migrant miners who might have been down there, under me in the earth at that moment. The stope where the fall was could have been disused, dripping water from its ruptured veins; or men might now be interred there in the most profound of tombs.

I couldn't find a position in which my mind would let go of my body—release me to sleep again. So I began to tell myself a story; a bedtime story.

In a house, in a suburb, in a city, there were a man and his wife who loved each other very much and were living happily ever after. They had a little boy, and they loved him very much. They had a cat and a dog that the little boy loved very much. They had a car and a caravan trailer for holidays, and a swimming-pool which was fenced so that the little boy and his playmates would not fall in and drown. They had a housemaid who was absolutely trustworthy and an itinerant gardener who was highly recommended by the neighbors. For when they began to live happily ever after they were warned, by that wise old witch, the husband's mother, not to take on anyone off the street. They were inscribed in a medical benefit society, their pet dog was licensed, they

Chopi and Tsonga: two peoples from Mozambique, northeast of South Africa

were insured against fire, flood damage and theft, and subscribed to the local Neighborhood Watch, which supplied them with a plaque for their gates lettered YOU HAVE BEEN WARNED over the silhouette of a would-be intruder. He was masked; it could not be said if he was black or white, and therefore proved the property owner was no racist.

10   It was not possible to insure the house, the swimming-pool or the car against riot damage. There were riots, but these were outside the city, where people of another color were quartered. These people were not allowed into the suburb except as reliable housemaids and gardeners, so there was nothing to fear, the husband told the wife. Yet she was afraid that some day such people might come up the street and tear off the plaque YOU HAVE BEEN WARNED and open the gates and stream in . . . Nonsense, my dear, said the husband, there are police and soldiers and tear-gas and guns to keep them away. But to please her—for he loved her very much and buses were being burned, cars stoned, and schoolchildren shot by the police in those quarters out of sight and hearing of the suburb—he had electronically controlled gates fitted. Anyone who pulled off the sign YOU HAVE BEEN WARNED and tried to open the gates would have to announce his intentions by pressing a button and speaking into a receiver relayed to the house. The little boy was fascinated by the device and used it as a walkie-talkie in cops and robbers play with his small friends.

The riots were suppressed, but there were many burglaries in the suburb and somebody's trusted housemaid was tied up and shut in a cupboard by thieves while she was in charge of her employers' house. The trusted housemaid of the man and wife and little boy was so upset by this misfortune befalling a friend left, as she herself often was, with responsibility for the possessions of the man and his wife and the little boy that she implored her employers to have burglar bars attached to the doors and windows of the house, and an alarm system installed. The wife said, She is right, let us take heed of her advice. So from every window and door in the house where they were living happily ever after they now saw the trees and sky through bars, and when the little boy's pet cat tried to climb in by the fanlight to keep him company in his little bed at night, as it customarily had done, it set off the alarm keening through the house.

The alarm was often answered—it seemed—by other burglar alarms, in other houses, that had been triggered by pet cats or nibbling mice. The alarms called to one another across the gardens in shrills and bleats and wails that everyone soon became accustomed to, so that the din roused the inhabitants of the suburb no more than the croak of frogs and musical grating of cicadas' legs. Under cover of the electronic harpies' discourse intruders sawed the iron bars and broke into homes, taking away hi-fi equipment, television sets, cassette players, cameras and radios, jewelry and clothing, and sometimes were hungry enough to devour everything in the refrigerator or paused audaciously to drink the whiskey in the cabinets or patio bars. Insurance companies paid no compensation for single malt,° a loss made keener by the property owner's knowledge that the thieves wouldn't even have been able to appreciate what it was they were drinking.

Then the time came when many of the people who were not trusted housemaids and gardeners hung about the suburb because they were unemployed. Some importuned for a job: weeding or painting a roof; anything, *baas*,° madam. But the man and his wife remembered the warning about taking on anyone off the street. Some drank liquor and fouled the street with discarded bottles. Some begged, waiting for the man or his wife to drive the car out of the electronically operated gates. They sat about with their feet in the gutters, under the jacaranda trees that made a green tunnel of the street—for it was a beautiful suburb, spoilt only by their presence—and sometimes they fell asleep lying right before the gates in the midday sun. The wife could never see anyone go hungry. She sent the trusted housemaid out with bread and tea, but the trusted housemaid said these were loafers and *tsotsis*,° who would come and tie her and shut her in a cupboard. The husband said, She's right. Take heed of her advice. You only encourage them with your bread and tea. They are looking for their chance . . . And he brought the little boy's tricycle from the garden into the house every night, because if the house was surely secure, once locked and with the alarm set, someone might still be able to climb over the wall or the electronically closed gates into the garden.

You are right, said the wife, then the wall should be higher. And the wise old witch, the husband's mother, paid for the extra bricks as her Christmas present to her son and his wife—the little boy got a Space Man outfit and a book of fairy tales.

But every week there were more reports of intrusion: in broad daylight and the dead of night, in the early hours of the morning, and even in the lovely summer twilight—a certain family was at dinner while the bedrooms were being ransacked upstairs. The man and his wife, talking of the latest armed robbery in the suburb, were distracted by the sight of the little boy's pet cat effortlessly arriving over the seven-foot wall, descending first with a rapid bracing of extended forepaws down on the sheer vertical surface, and then a graceful launch, landing with   15

---

single malt: an expensive Scotch whiskey   ***baas:*** boss   ***tsotsis:*** hooligans

swishing tail within the property. The whitewashed wall was marked with the cat's comings and goings; and on the street side of the wall there were larger red-earth smudges that could have been made by the kind of broken running shoes, seen on the feet of unemployed loiterers, that had no innocent destination.

When the man and wife and little boy took the pet dog for its walk round the neighborhood streets they no longer paused to admire this show of roses or that perfect lawn; these were hidden behind an array of different varieties of security fences, walls and devices. The man, wife, little boy and dog passed a remarkable choice: there was the low-cost option of pieces of broken glass embedded in cement along the top of walls, there were iron grilles ending in lance-points, there were attempts at reconciling the aesthetics of prison architecture with the Spanish Villa style (spikes painted pink) and with the plaster urns of neoclassical façades (twelve-inch pikes finned like zigzags of lightning and painted pure white). Some walls had a small board affixed, giving the name and telephone number of the firm responsible for the installation of the devices. While the little boy and the pet dog raced ahead, the husband and wife found themselves comparing the possible effectiveness of each style against its appearance; and after several weeks when they paused before this barricade or that without needing to speak, both came out with the conclusion that only one was worth considering. It was the ugliest but the most honest in its suggestion of the pure concentration-camp style, no frills, all evident efficacy. Placed the length of walls, it consisted of a continuous coil of stiff and shining metal serrated into jagged blades, so that there would be no way of climbing over it and no way through its tunnel without getting entangled in its fangs. There would be no way out, only a struggle getting bloodier and bloodier, a deeper and sharper hooking and tearing of flesh. The wife shuddered to look at it. You're right, said the husband, anyone would think twice . . . And they took heed of the advice on a small board fixed to the wall: Consult DRAGON'S TEETH The People For Total Security.

Next day a gang of workmen came and stretched the razor-bladed coils all round the walls of the house where the husband and wife and little boy and pet dog and cat were living happily ever after. The sunlight flashed and slashed, off the serrations, the cornice of razor thorns encircled the home, shining. The husband said, Never mind. It will weather. The wife said, You're wrong. They guarantee it's rust-proof. And she waited until the little boy had run off to play before she said, I hope the cat will take heed . . . The husband said, Don't worry, my dear, cats always look before they leap. And it was true that from that day on the cat slept in the little boy's bed and kept to the garden, never risking a try at breaching security.

One evening, the mother read the little boy to sleep with a fairy story from the book the wise old witch had given him at Christmas. Next day he pretended to be the Prince who braves the terrible thicket of thorns to enter the palace and kiss the Sleeping Beauty back to life: he dragged a ladder to the wall, the shining coiled tunnel was just wide enough for his little body to creep in, and with the first fixing of its razor-teeth in his knees and hands and head he screamed and struggled deeper into its tangle. The trusted housemaid and the itinerant gardener, whose "day" it was, came running, the first to see and to scream with him, and the itinerant gardener tore his hands trying to get at the little boy. Then the man and his wife burst wildly into the garden and for some reason (the cat, probably) the alarm set up wailing against the screams while the bleeding mass of the little boy was hacked out of the security coil with saws, wire-cutters, choppers, and they carried it—the man, the wife, the hysterical trusted housemaid and the weeping gardener—into the house.

QUESTIONS

1. The opening section of the story is told by a writer awakened by a frightening sound in the night. What two causes for the sound does she consider? Ultimately, which is the more significant cause for fear? How do these together create an emotional background for the "children's story" she tells?
2. What stylistic devices create the atmosphere of children's stories? How is this atmosphere related to the story's theme?
3. To what extent does the story explore the motives for the behavior of the wife and husband, the husband's mother, the servants, and the people who surround the suburb and the house? What motives can you infer for these people? What ironies do they display in their actions?
4. Can you fix the blame for the calamity that befalls the child? What are the possible meanings of the repeated phrase "YOU HAVE BEEN WARNED"?
5. What details in the introductory section and in the children's story imply the nature of the social order in which both occur?
6. Analyze the story's final paragraph in detail. How does it help to elucidate the theme?

SUGGESTIONS FOR WRITING

1. Bearing in mind point 5 in the introduction to this chapter ("there is no *one* way of stating the theme of a story"), write out three alternative statements of theme for one or more of the following:
   a. Wolff, "Hunters in the Snow" (page 86).
   b. Munro, "How I Met My Husband" (page 125).
   c. Chekhov, "Gooseberries" (page 195).

2. The theme of a story often is displayed in the development of the protagonist or in the epiphany that the protagonist experiences. But in some stories, there may be more than one focal character, and the theme must therefore be inferred by examining the different experiences of more than one person. Demonstrate the validity of this statement by examining the three main characters in one of the following:

   a. Wolff, "Hunters in the Snow" (page 86).

   b. Walker, "Everyday Use" (page 166).

   c. Hurston, "The Gilded Six-Bits" (page 564).

Chapter Five

Point of View

Primitive storytellers, unbothered by considerations of form, simply spun their tales. "Once upon a time," they began, and proceeded to narrate the story to their listeners, describing the characters when necessary, telling what the characters thought and felt as well as what they did, and interjecting comments and ideas of their own. Modern fiction writers are artistically more self-conscious. They realize that there are many ways of telling a story; they decide upon a method before they begin, or discover one while in the act of writing, and may even set up rules for themselves. Instead of telling the story themselves, they may let one of the characters tell it; they may tell it by means of letters or diaries; they may confine themselves to recording the thoughts of one of the characters. With the growth of artistic consciousness, the question of **point of view**—of who tells the story, and, therefore, of how it gets told—has assumed special importance.

To determine the point of view of a story, we ask, "Who tells the story?" and "How much is this person allowed to know?" and, especially, "To what extent does the narrator look inside the characters and report their thoughts and feelings?"

1. Omniscient

2. Third-person limited
 $\begin{cases} \text{(a) Major character} \\ \text{(b) Minor character} \end{cases}$

3. First person
 $\begin{cases} \text{(a) Major character} \\ \text{(b) Minor character} \end{cases}$

4. Objective

Though many variations and combinations are possible, the basic points of view are four, as follows:

1. In the **omniscient point of view,** the story is told in the third person by a narrator whose knowledge and prerogatives are unlimited. Such narrators are free to go wherever they wish, to peer inside the minds and hearts of characters at will and tell us what they are thinking or feeling. These narrators can interpret behavior and can comment, if they wish, on the significance of their stories. They know all. They can tell us as much or as little as they please.

The following version of Aesop's fable "The Ant and the Grasshopper" is told from the omniscient point of view. Notice that in it we are told not only what both characters do and say, but also what they think and feel; notice also that the narrator comments at the end on the significance of the story. (The phrases in which the narrator enters into the thoughts or feelings of the ant and the grasshopper have been italicized; the comment by the author is printed in small capitals.)

> *Weary in every limb,* the ant tugged over the snow a piece of corn he had stored up last summer. *It would taste mighty good at dinner tonight.*
>
> A grasshopper, *cold and hungry,* looked on. *Finally he could bear it no longer.* "Please, friend ant, may I have a bite of corn?"
>
> "What were you doing all last summer?" asked the ant. He looked the grasshopper up and down. *He knew its kind.*
>
> "I sang from dawn till dark," replied the grasshopper, *happily unaware of what was coming next.*
>
> "Well," said the ant, *hardly bothering to conceal his contempt,* "since you sang all summer, you can dance all winter."
>
> HE WHO IDLES WHEN HE'S YOUNG
> WILL HAVE NOTHING WHEN HE'S OLD

Stories told from the omniscient point of view may vary widely in the amount of omniscience the narrator is allowed. In "Hunters in the Snow," we are frequently allowed into the mind of Tub, but near the end of the story the omniscient narrator takes over and gives us information none of the characters could know. In "The Destructors," though we are taken into the minds of Blackie, Mike, the gang as a group, Old Misery, and the lorry driver, we are not taken into the mind of Trevor—the most important character. In "The Most Dangerous Game," we are confined to the thoughts and feelings of Rainsford, except for the brief passage between Rainsford's leap into the sea and his waking in Zaroff's bed, during which the point of view shifts to General Zaroff.

The omniscient is the most flexible point of view and permits the widest scope. It is also the most subject to abuse. It offers constant danger that the narrator may come between the readers and the story, or that the continual shifting of viewpoint from character to character may cause a breakdown in coherence or unity. Used skillfully, it enables the author to achieve simultaneous breadth and depth. Unskillfully used, it can destroy the illusion of reality that the story attempts to create.

2. In the **third-person limited point of view,** the story is told in the third person, but from the viewpoint of one character in the story. Such point-of-view characters are filters through whose eyes and minds writers look at the events. Authors employing this perspective may move both inside and outside these characters but never leave their sides. They tell us what these characters see and hear and what they think and feel; they possibly interpret the characters' thoughts and behavior. They know everything about their point-of-view characters—often more than the characters know about themselves. But they limit themselves to these characters' perceptions and show no direct knowledge of what *other* characters are thinking or feeling or doing, except for what the point-of-view character knows or can infer about them. The chosen character may be either a major or a minor character, a participant or an observer, and this choice also will be a very important one for the story. "Interpreter of Maladies," "Miss Brill," and "A Worn Path" are told from the third-person limited point of view, from the perspective of the main character. The use of this viewpoint with a minor character is rare in the short story, and is not illustrated in this book.

Here is "The Ant and the Grasshopper" told, in the third person, from the point of view of the ant. Notice that this time we are told nothing of what the grasshopper thinks or feels. We see and hear and know of him only what the ant sees and hears and knows.

Weary in every limb, the ant tugged over the snow a piece of corn he had stored up last summer. *It would taste mighty good at dinner tonight. It was then that he noticed the grasshopper, looking cold and pinched.*

"Please, friend ant, may I have a bite of your corn?" asked the grasshopper.

He looked the grasshopper up and down. "What were you doing all last summer?" he asked. *He knew its kind.*

"I sang from dawn till dark," replied the grasshopper.

"Well," said the ant, *hardly bothering to conceal his contempt,* "since you sang all summer, you can dance all winter."

The third-person limited point of view, since it acquaints us with the world through the mind and senses of only one character, approximates more closely than the omniscient the conditions of real life; it also offers a ready-made unifying element, since all details of the story are the experience of one character. And it affords an additional device of characterization, since what a point-of-view character does or does not find noteworthy, and the inferences that such a character draws about other characters' actions and motives, may reveal biases or limitations in the observer. At the same time it offers a limited field of observation, for the readers can go nowhere except where the chosen character goes, and there may be difficulty in having the character naturally cognizant of all important events. Clumsy writers will constantly have the focal character listening at keyholes, accidentally overhearing important conversations, or coincidentally being present when important events occur.

A variant of third-person limited point of view, illustrated in this chapter by Porter's "The Jilting of Granny Weatherall," is called **stream of consciousness.** Stream of consciousness presents the apparently random thoughts going through a character's head within a certain period of time, mingling memory and present experiences, and employing transitional links that are psychological rather than strictly logical. (First-person narrators might also tell their stories through stream of consciousness, though first-person use of this technique is relatively rare.)

3. In the **first-person point of view,** the author disappears into one of the characters, who tells the story in the first person. This character, again, may be either a major or a minor character, protagonist or observer, and it will make considerable difference whether the protagonist tells the story or someone else tells it. In "How I Met My Husband" and "The Lesson," the protagonist tells the story in the first person. In "A Rose for Emily," presented in Part 4, the story is told in the unusual first-person plural, from the vantage point of the townspeople observing Emily's life through the years.

Our fable is retold below in the first person from the point of view of the grasshopper. (The whole story is italicized because it all comes out of the grasshopper's mind.)

Cold and hungry, I watched the ant tugging over the snow a piece of corn he had stored up last summer. My feelers twitched, and I was conscious of a tic in my left hind leg. Finally I could bear it no longer. "Please, friend ant," I asked, "may I have a bite of your corn?"

He looked me up and down. "What were you doing all last summer?" he asked, rather too smugly it seemed to me.

> "I sang from dawn till dark," I said innocently, remembering the happy times.
>
> "Well," he said, with a priggish sneer, "since you sang all summer, you can dance all winter."

The first-person point of view shares the virtues and limitations of the third-person limited. It offers, sometimes, a gain in immediacy and reality, since we get the story directly from a participant, the author as intermediary being eliminated. It offers no opportunity, however, for *direct* interpretation by the author, and there is constant danger that narrators may be made to transcend their own sensitivity, their knowledge, or their powers of language in telling a story. Talented authors, however, can make tremendous literary capital out of the very limitations of their narrators. The first-person point of view offers excellent opportunities for dramatic irony and for studies in limited or blunted human perceptiveness. In "How I Met My Husband," for instance, there is an increasingly clear difference between what the narrator perceives and what the reader perceives as the story proceeds. Even though Edie is clearly narrating her story from the vantage point of maturity—ultimately we know this from the ending and from the title itself—she rarely allows her mature voice to intrude or to make judgments on Edie's thoughts and feelings as a fifteen-year-old girl infatuated with a handsome pilot. The story gains in emotional power because of the poignancy of youthful romanticism that Edie's hopes and wishes represent, and because of the inevitable disillusionment she must suffer. By choosing this point of view, Munro offers an interpretation of the material *indirectly*, through her dramatization of Edie's experiences. In other stories, like "A Rose for Emily," the author intends the first-person viewpoint to suggest a conventional set of perceptions and attitudes, perhaps including those of the author and the reader. Identifications of a narrator's attitudes with the author's, however, must always be undertaken with extreme caution; they are justified only if the total material of the story supports them, or if outside evidence (for example, a statement by the author) supports such an identification. In "A Rose for Emily" the narrative detachment does reflect the author's own; nevertheless, much of the interest of the story arises from the limited viewpoint of the townspeople and the cloak of mystery surrounding Emily and her life inside the house.

4. In the **objective point of view,** the narrator disappears into a kind of roving sound camera. This camera can go anywhere but can record only what is seen and heard. It cannot comment, interpret, or enter a character's mind. With this point of view (sometimes called also

the **dramatic point of view**) readers are placed in the position of spectators at a movie or play. They see what the characters do and hear what they say but must infer what they think or feel and what they are like. Authors are not there to explain. The purest example of a story told from the objective point of view would be one written entirely in dialogue, for as soon as authors add words of their own, they begin to interpret through their very choice of words. Actually, few stories using this point of view are antiseptically pure, for the limitations it imposes on the author are severe. Shirley Jackson's "The Lottery," presented in this chapter, is essentially objective in its narration.

The following version of "The Ant and the Grasshopper" is also told from the objective point of view. (Since we are nowhere taken into the thoughts or feelings of the characters, none of this version is printed in italics.)

The ant tugged over the snow a piece of corn he had stored up last summer, perspiring in spite of the cold.

A grasshopper, his feelers twitching and with a tic in his left hind leg, looked on for some time. Finally he asked, "Please, friend ant, may I have a bite of your corn?"

The ant looked the grasshopper up and down. "What were you doing all last summer?" he snapped.

"I sang from dawn till dark," replied the grasshopper, not changing his tone.

"Well," said the ant, and a faint smile crept into his face, "since you sang all summer, you can dance all winter."

The objective point of view requires readers to draw their own inferences. But it must rely heavily on external action and dialogue, and it offers no opportunities for direct interpretation by the author.

Each of the points of view has its advantages, its limitations, and its peculiar uses. Ideally the choice of the author will depend upon the materials and the purpose of a story. Authors choose the point of view that enables them to present their particular materials most effectively in terms of their purposes. Writers of murder mysteries with suspense and thrills as the purpose will ordinarily avoid using the point of view of the murderer or the brilliant detective: otherwise they would have to reveal at the beginning the secrets they wish to conceal till the end. On the other hand, if they are interested in exploring criminal psychology, the murderer's point of view might be by far the most effective. In the Sherlock Holmes stories, A. Conan Doyle effectively uses the somewhat imperceptive Dr. Watson as his narrator, so that the reader may be kept in the dark as long as possible and then be as amazed as Watson is by Holmes's deductive powers. In Dostoevsky's *Crime and Punishment*, however, the author is interested not in mystifying and surprising but in illuminating the moral and psychological operations of the human soul in the act of taking life; he therefore tells the story from the viewpoint of a sensitive and intelligent murderer.

For readers, the examination of point of view may be important both for understanding and for evaluating the story. First, they should know whether the events of the story are being interpreted by a narrator or by one of the characters. If the latter, they must ask how this character's mind and personality affect the interpretation, whether the character is perceptive or imperceptive, and whether the interpretation can be accepted at face value or must be discounted because of ignorance, stupidity, or self-deception.

Next, readers should ask whether the writer has chosen the point of view for maximum revelation of the material or for another reason. The author may choose the point of view mainly to conceal certain information till the end of the story and thus maintain suspense and create surprise. The author may even deliberately mislead readers by presenting the events through a character who puts a false interpretation on them. Such a false interpretation may be justified if it leads eventually to more effective revelation of character and theme. If it is there merely to trick readers, it is obviously less justifiable.

Finally, readers should ask whether the author has used the selected point of view fairly and consistently. Even in commercial fiction we have a right to demand fair treatment. If the person to whose thoughts and feelings we are admitted has pertinent information that is not revealed, we legitimately feel cheated. To have a chance to solve a murder mystery, we must know what the detective learns. A writer also should be consistent in the point of view; if it shifts, it should do so for a just artistic reason. Serious literary writers choose and use point of view so as to yield ultimately the greatest possible insight, either in fullness or in intensity.

REVIEWING CHAPTER FIVE

1. Explain how to determine the point of view in a story.
2. Describe the characteristics of omniscient point of view.
3. Review the definition of third-person limited point of view.
4. Consider the virtues and limitations of first-person point of view.
5. Explore the use of objective point of view in Hemingway's "Hills Like White Elephants," presented in this chapter.

Willa Cather
Paul's Case

It was Paul's afternoon to appear before the faculty of the Pittsburgh High School to account for his various misdemeanors. He had been suspended a week ago, and his father had called at the Principal's office and confessed his perplexity about his son. Paul entered the faculty room suave and smiling. His clothes were a trifle outgrown, and the tan velvet on the collar of his open overcoat was frayed and worn; but for all that there was something of a dandy about him, and he wore an opal pin in his neatly knotted black four-in-hand, and a red carnation in his buttonhole. This latter adornment the faculty somehow felt was not properly significant of the contrite spirit befitting a boy under the ban of suspension.

Paul was tall for his age and very thin, with high, cramped shoulders and a narrow chest. His eyes were remarkable for a certain hysterical brilliancy, and he continually used them in a conscious, theatrical sort of way, peculiarly offensive in a boy. The pupils were abnormally large, as though he were addicted to belladonna, but there was a glassy glitter about them which that drug does not produce.

When questioned by the Principal as to why he was there, Paul stated, politely enough, that he wanted to come back to school. This was a lie, but Paul was quite accustomed to lying; found it, indeed, indispensable for overcoming friction. His teachers were asked to state their respective charges against him, which they did with such a rancor and aggrievedness as evinced that this was not a usual case. Disorder and impertinence were among the offences named, yet each of his instructors felt that it was scarcely possible to put into words the real cause of the trouble, which lay in a sort of hysterically defiant manner of the boy's; in the contempt which they all knew he felt for them, and which he seemingly made not the least effort to conceal. Once, when he had been making a synopsis of a paragraph at the blackboard, his English teacher had stepped to his side and attempted to guide his hand. Paul had started back with a shudder and thrust his hands violently behind him. The astonished woman could scarcely have been more hurt and embarrassed had he struck at her. The insult was so involuntary and

PAUL'S CASE   Written in 1904, first published in 1905. Willa Cather (1873–1947) was born in Virginia and grew up and was educated in Nebraska. From 1895 to 1905 she lived and worked in Pittsburgh, first as a journalist, writing drama and music criticism, later as a teacher of English and Latin in two Pittsburgh high schools. In 1902 she traveled in Europe.

definitely personal as to be unforgettable. In one way and another, he had made all his teachers, men and women alike, conscious of the same feeling of physical aversion. In one class he habitually sat with his hand shading his eyes; in another he always looked out of the window during the recitation; in another he made a running commentary on the lecture, with humorous intent.

His teachers felt this afternoon that his whole attitude was symbolized by his shrug and his flippantly red carnation flower, and they fell upon him without mercy, his English teacher leading the pack. He stood through it smiling, his pale lips parted over his white teeth. (His lips were continually twitching, and he had a habit of raising his eyebrows that was contemptuous and irritating to the last degree.) Older boys than Paul had broken down and shed tears under that ordeal, but his set smile did not once desert him, and his only sign of discomfort was the nervous trembling of the fingers that toyed with the buttons of his overcoat, and an occasional jerking of the other hand which held his hat. Paul was always smiling, always glancing about him, seeming to feel that people might be watching him and trying to detect something. This conscious expression, since it was as far as possible from boyish mirthfulness, was usually attributed to insolence or "smartness."

As the inquisition proceeded, one of his instructors repeated an   5
impertinent remark of the boy's, and the Principal asked him whether he thought that a courteous speech to make to a woman. Paul shrugged his shoulders slightly and his eyebrows twitched.

"I don't know," he replied. "I didn't mean to be polite or impolite, either. I guess it's a sort of way I have, of saying things regardless."

The Principal asked him whether he didn't think that a way it would be well to get rid of. Paul grinned and said he guessed so. When he was told that he could go, he bowed gracefully and went out. His bow was like a repetition of the scandalous red carnation.

His teachers were in despair, and his drawing-master voiced the feeling of them all when he declared there was something about the boy which none of them understood. He added: "I don't really believe that smile of his comes altogether from insolence; there's something sort of haunted about it. The boy is not strong for one thing. There is something wrong about the fellow."

The drawing-master had come to realize that, in looking at Paul, one saw only his white teeth and the forced animation of his eyes. One warm afternoon the boy had gone to sleep at his drawing-board, and his master had noted with amazement what a white, blue-veined face it was; drawn and wrinkled like an old man's about the eyes, the lips twitching even in his sleep.

10   His teachers left the building dissatisfied and unhappy; humiliated to have felt so vindictive toward a mere boy, to have uttered this feeling in cutting terms, and to have set each other on, as it were, in the gruesome game of intemperate reproach. One of them remembered having seen a miserable street cat set at bay by a ring of tormentors.

As for Paul, he ran down the hill whistling the Soldiers' Chorus from *Faust,* looking behind him now and then to see whether some of his teachers were not there to witness his light-heartedness. As it was now late in the afternoon and Paul was on duty that evening as usher at Carnegie Hall, he decided that he would not go home to supper.

When he reached the concert hall, the doors were not yet open. It was chilly outside, and he decided to go up into the picture gallery—always deserted at this hour—where there were some of Raffelli's gay studies of Paris streets and an airy blue Venetian scene or two that always exhilarated him. He was delighted to find no one in the gallery but the old guard, who sat in the corner, a newspaper on his knee, a black patch over one eye and the other closed. Paul possessed himself of the place and walked confidently up and down, whistling under his breath. After a while he sat down before a blue Rico and lost himself. When he bethought him to look at his watch, it was after seven o'clock and he rose with a start and ran downstairs, making a face at Augustus Caesar, peering out from the cast-room, and an evil gesture at the Venus of Milo as he passed her on the stairway.

When Paul reached the ushers' dressing-room, half a dozen boys were there already, and he began excitedly to tumble into his uniform. It was one of the few that at all approached fitting, and Paul thought it very becoming—though he knew the tight, straight coat accentuated his narrow chest, about which he was exceedingly sensitive. He was always excited while he dressed, twanging all over to the tuning of the strings and the preliminary flourishes of the horns in the music-room; but tonight he seemed quite beside himself, and he teased and plagued the boys until, telling him that he was crazy, they put him down on the floor and sat on him.

Somewhat calmed by his suppression, Paul dashed out to the front of the house to seat the early comers. He was a model usher. Gracious and smiling he ran up and down the aisles. Nothing was too much trouble for him; he carried messages and brought programs as though it were his greatest pleasure in life, and all the people in his section thought him a charming boy, feeling that he remembered and admired them. As the house filled, he grew more and more vivacious and animated, and the color came to his cheeks and lips. It was very much as though this were a great reception and Paul were the host. Just as the musicians came out to take their places, his English teacher arrived with checks for the seats which a prominent manufacturer had taken for the season. She betrayed some embarrassment when she handed Paul the tickets, and a *hauteur* which subsequently made her feel very foolish. Paul was startled for a moment, and had the feeling of wanting to put her out; what business had she here among all these fine people and gay colors? He looked her over and decided that she was not appropriately dressed and must be a fool to sit downstairs in such togs. The tickets had probably been sent her out of kindness, he reflected, as he put down a seat for her, and she had about as much right to sit there as he had.

When the symphony began, Paul sank into one of the rear seats   15 with a long sigh of relief, and lost himself as he had done before the Rico. It was not that symphonies, as such, meant anything in particular to Paul, but the first sight of the instruments seemed to free some hilarious spirit within him; something that struggled there like the Genius in the bottle found by the Arab fisherman. He felt a sudden zest of life; the lights danced before his eyes and the concert hall blazed into unimaginable splendor. When the soprano soloist came on, Paul forgot even the nastiness of his teacher's being there, and gave himself up to the peculiar intoxication such personages always had for him. The soloist chanced to be a German woman, by no means in her first youth, and the mother of many children; but she wore a satin gown and a tiara, and she had that indefinable air of achievement, that world-shine upon her, which always blinded Paul to any possible defects.

After a concert was over, Paul was often irritable and wretched until he got to sleep—and tonight he was even more than usually restless. He had the feeling of not being able to let down; of its being impossible to give up this delicious excitement which was the only thing that could be called living at all. During the last number he withdrew and, after hastily changing his clothes in the dressing-room, slipped out to the side door where the singer's carriage stood. Here he began pacing rapidly up and down the walk, waiting to see her come out.

Over yonder the Schenley, in its vacant stretch, loomed big and square through the fine rain, the windows of its twelve stories glowing like those of a lighted cardboard house under a Christmas tree. All the actors and singers of any importance stayed there when they were in Pittsburgh, and a number of the big manufacturers of the place lived there in the winter. Paul had often hung about the hotel, watching the people go in and out, longing to enter and leave schoolmasters and dull care behind him forever.

At last the singer came out, accompanied by the conductor, who helped her into her carriage and closed the door with a cordial *auf wiedersehen*—which set Paul to wondering whether she were not an old sweetheart of his. Paul followed the carriage over to the hotel, walking so rapidly as not to be far from the entrance when the singer alighted and disappeared behind the swinging glass doors which were opened by a Negro in a tall hat and a long coat. In the moment that the door was ajar, it seemed to Paul that he, too, entered. He seemed to feel himself go after her up the steps, into the warm, lighted building, into an exotic, a tropical world of shiny, glistening surfaces and basking ease. He reflected upon the mysterious dishes that were brought into the dining-room, the green bottles in buckets of ice, as he had seen them in the supper-party pictures of the Sunday supplement. A quick gust of wind brought the rain down with sudden vehemence, and Paul was startled to find that he was still outside in the slush of the gravel driveway; that his boots were letting in the water and his scanty overcoat was clinging wet about him; that the lights in front of the concert hall were out, and that the rain was driving in sheets between him and the orange glow of the windows above him. There it was, what he wanted—tangibly before him, like the fairy world of a Christmas pantomime; as the rain beat in his face, Paul wondered whether he were destined always to shiver in the black night outside, looking up at it.

He turned and walked reluctantly toward the car tracks. The end had to come sometime; his father in his night-clothes at the top of the stairs, explanations that did not explain, hastily improvised fictions that were forever tripping him up, his upstairs room and its horrible yellow wallpaper, the creaking bureau with the greasy plush collar-box, and over his painted wooden bed the pictures of George Washington and John Calvin, and the framed motto, "Feed my Lambs," which had been worked in red worsted by his mother, whom Paul could not remember.

20   Half an hour later, Paul alighted from the Negley Avenue car and went slowly down one of the side streets off the main thoroughfare. It was a highly respectable street, where all the houses were exactly alike, and where business men of moderate means begot and reared large families of children, all of whom went to Sabbath School and learned the shorter catechism, and were interested in arithmetic; all of whom were as exactly alike as their homes, and of a piece with the monotony in which they lived. Paul never went up Cordelia Street without a shudder of loathing. His home was next to the house of the Cumberland minister. He approached it tonight with the nerveless sense of defeat, the hopeless feeling of sinking back forever into ugliness and commonness that he had always had when he came home. The moment he turned into Cordelia Street he felt the waters close above his head. Af-

ter each of these orgies of living, he experienced all the physical depression which follows a debauch; the loathing of respectable beds, of common food, of a house permeated by kitchen odors; a shuddering repulsion for the flavorless, colorless mass of everyday existence; a morbid desire for cool things and soft lights and fresh flowers.

The nearer he approached the house, the more absolutely unequal Paul felt to the sight of it all: his ugly sleeping chamber; the old bathroom with the grimy zinc tub, the cracked mirror, the dripping spigots; his father, at the top of the stairs, his hairy legs sticking out from his nightshirt, his feet thrust into carpet slippers. He was so much later than usual that there would certainly be inquiries and reproaches. Paul stopped short before the door. He felt that he could not be accosted by his father tonight; that he could not toss again on that miserable bed. He would not go in. He would tell his father that he had no carfare, and it was raining so hard he had gone home with one of the boys and stayed all night.

Meanwhile, he was wet and cold. He went around to the back of the house and tried one of the basement windows, found it open, and raised it cautiously, and scrambled down the cellar wall to the floor. There he stood, holding his breath, terrified by the noise he had made; but the floor above him was silent, and there was no creak on the stairs. He found a soap-box, and carried it over to the soft ring of light that streamed from the furnace door, and sat down. He was horribly afraid of rats, so he did not try to sleep, but sat looking distrustfully at the dark, still terrified lest he might have awakened his father. In such reactions, after one of the experiences which made days and nights out of the dreary blanks of the calendar, when his senses were deadened, Paul's head was always singularly clear. Suppose his father had heard him getting in at the window and had come down and shot him for a burglar? Then, again, suppose his father had come down, pistol in hand, and he had cried out in time to save himself, and his father had been horrified to think how nearly he had killed him? Then again, suppose a day should come when his father would remember that night, and wish there had been no warning cry to stay his hand? With this last supposition Paul entertained himself until daybreak.

The following Sunday was fine; the sodden November chill was broken by the last flash of autumnal summer. In the morning Paul had to go to church and Sabbath School, as always. On seasonable Sunday afternoons the burghers of Cordelia Street usually sat out on their front "stoops," and talked to their neighbors on the next stoop, or called to those across the street in neighborly fashion. The men sat placidly on gay cushions placed upon the steps that led down to the sidewalk, while the women, in their Sunday "waists," sat in rockers on the cramped porches, pretending to be greatly at their ease. The children played in the streets; there were so many of them that the place resembled the recreation grounds of a kindergarten. The men on the steps—all in their shirt-sleeves, their vests unbuttoned, sat with their legs well apart, their stomachs comfortably protruding, and talked of the prices of things, or told anecdotes of the sagacity of their various chiefs and overlords. They occasionally looked over the multitude of squabbling children, listened affectionately to their high-pitched, nasal voices, smiling to see their own proclivities reproduced in their offspring, and interspersed their legends of the iron kings with remarks about their sons' progress at school, their grades in arithmetic, and the amounts they had saved in their toy banks.

On this last Sunday of November, Paul sat all afternoon on the lowest step of his "stoop," staring into the street, while his sisters, in their rockers, were talking to the minister's daughters next door about how many shirtwaists they had made in the last week, and how many waffles someone had eaten at the last church supper. When the weather was warm, and his father was in a particularly jovial frame of mind, the girls made lemonade, which was always brought out in a red-glass pitcher, ornamented with forget-me-nots in blue enamel. This the girls thought very fine, and the neighbors joked about the suspicious color of the pitcher.

25   Today Paul's father, on the top step, was talking to a young man who shifted a restless baby from knee to knee. He happened to be the young man who was daily held up to Paul as a model, and after whom it was his father's dearest hope that he would pattern. This young man was of a ruddy complexion, with a compressed, red mouth, and faded, nearsighted eyes, over which he wore thick spectacles, with gold bows that curved about his ears. He was clerk to one of the magnates of a great steel corporation, and was looked upon in Cordelia Street as a young man with a future. There was a story that, some five years ago— he was now barely twenty-six—he had been a trifle "dissipated," but in order to curb his appetites and save the loss of time and strength that a sowing of wild oats might have entailed, he had taken his chief's advice, oft reiterated to his employees, and at twenty-one had married the first woman whom he could persuade to share his fortunes. She happened to be an angular schoolmistress, much older than he, who also wore thick glasses, and who had now borne him four children, all nearsighted like herself.

The young man was relating how his chief, now cruising in the Mediterranean, kept in touch with all the details of the business, arranging his office hours on his yacht just as though he were at home, and "knocking off work enough to keep two stenographers busy." His father told, in turn, the plan his corporation was considering, of putting in an electric railway plant at Cairo. Paul snapped his teeth; he had an awful apprehension that they might spoil it all before he got there. Yet he rather liked to hear these legends of the iron kings, that were told and retold on Sundays and holidays; these stories of palaces in Venice, yachts on the Mediterranean, and high play at Monte Carlo appealed to his fancy, and he was interested in the triumphs of cash-boys who had become famous, though he had no mind for the cash-boy stage.

After supper was over, and he had helped to dry the dishes, Paul nervously asked his father whether he could go to George's to get some help in his geometry, and still more nervously asked for carfare. This latter request he had to repeat, as his father, on principle, did not like to hear requests for money, whether much or little. He asked Paul whether he could not go to some boy who lived nearer, and told him that he ought not to leave his school work until Sunday; but he gave him the dime. He was not a poor man, but he had a worthy ambition to come up in the world. His only reason for allowing Paul to usher was that he thought a boy ought to be earning a little.

Paul bounded upstairs, scrubbed the greasy odor of the dishwater from his hands with the ill-smelling soap he hated, and then shook over his fingers a few drops of violet water from the bottle he kept hidden in his drawer. He left the house with his geometry conspicuously under his arm, and the moment he got out of Cordelia Street and boarded a downtown car, he shook off the lethargy of two deadening days, and began to live again.

The leading juvenile of the permanent stock company which played at one of the downtown theaters was an acquaintance of Paul's, and the boy had been invited to drop in at the Sunday-night rehearsals whenever he could. For more than a year Paul had spent every available moment loitering about Charley Edwards's dressing-room. He had won a place among Edwards's following not only because the young actor, who could not afford to employ a dresser, often found him useful, but because he recognized in Paul something akin to what churchmen term "vocation."

It was at the theater and at Carnegie Hall that Paul really lived; the rest was but a sleep and a forgetting. This was Paul's fairy tale, and it had for him all the allurement of a secret love. The moment he inhaled the gassy, painty, dusty odor behind the scenes, he breathed like a prisoner set free, and felt within him the possibility of doing or saying splendid, brilliant things. The moment the cracked orchestra beat out

30

the overture from *Martha*, or jerked at the serenade from *Rigoletto*, all stupid and ugly things slid from him, and his senses were deliciously, yet delicately fired.

Perhaps it was because, in Paul's world, the natural nearly always wore the guise of ugliness, that a certain element of artificiality seemed to him necessary in beauty. Perhaps it was because his experience of life elsewhere was so full of Sabbath-School picnics, petty economies, wholesome advice as to how to succeed in life, and the unescapable odors of cooking, that he found this existence so alluring, these smartly clad men and women so attractive, that he was so moved by these starry apple orchards that bloomed perennially under the limelight.

It would be difficult to put it strongly enough how convincingly the stage entrance of the theater was for Paul the actual portal of Romance. Certainly none of the company ever suspected it, least of all Charley Edwards. It was very like the old stories that used to float about London of fabulously rich Jews, who had subterranean halls, with palms, and fountains, and soft lamps and richly appareled women who never saw the disenchanting light of London day. So, in the midst of that smoke-palled city, enamored of figures and grimy toil, Paul had his secret temple, his wishing-carpet, his bit of blue-and-white Mediterranean shore bathed in perpetual sunshine.

Several of Paul's teachers had a theory that his imagination had been perverted by garish fiction; but the truth was, he scarcely ever read at all. The books at home were not such as would either tempt or corrupt a youthful mind, and as for reading the novels that some of his friends urged upon him—well, he got what he wanted much more quickly from music; any sort of music, from an orchestra to a barrel-organ. He needed only the spark, the indescribable thrill that made his imagination master of his senses, and he could make plots and pictures enough of his own. It was equally true that he was not stage-struck—not, at any rate, in the usual acceptation of the expression. He had no desire to become an actor, any more than he had to become a musician. He felt no necessity to do any of these things; what he wanted was to see, to be in the atmosphere, float on the wave of it, to be carried out, blue league after league, away from everything.

After a night behind the scenes, Paul found the schoolroom more than ever repulsive; the bare floors and naked walls; the prosy men who never wore frock coats, or violets in their buttonholes; the women with their dull gowns, shrill voices, and pitiful seriousness about prepositions that govern the dative. He could not bear to have the other pupils think, for a moment, that he took these people seriously; he must convey to them that he considered it all trivial, and was there only by the way of a joke, anyway. He had autographed pictures of all the members of the stock company which he showed his classmates, telling them the most incredible stories of his familiarity with these people, of his acquaintance with the soloists who came to Carnegie Hall, his suppers with them and the flowers he sent them. When these stories lost their effect, and his audience grew listless, he would bid all the boys goodbye, announcing that he was going to travel for a while; going to Naples, to California, to Egypt. Then, next Monday, he would slip back, conscious and nervously smiling; his sister was ill, and he would have to defer his voyage until spring.

Matters went steadily worse with Paul at school. In the itch to let his instructors know how heartily he despised them, and how thoroughly he was appreciated elsewhere, he mentioned once or twice that he had no time to fool with theorems; adding—with a twitch of the eyebrows and a touch of that nervous bravado which so perplexed them—that he was helping the people down at the stock company; they were old friends of his.

The upshot of the matter was that the Principal went to Paul's father, and Paul was taken out of school and put to work. The manager at Carnegie Hall was told to get another usher in his stead; the doorkeeper at the theater was warned not to admit him to the house; and Charley Edwards remorsefully promised the boy's father not to see him again.

The members of the stock company were vastly amused when some of Paul's stories reached them—especially the women. They were hardworking women, most of them supporting indolent husbands or brothers, and they laughed rather bitterly at having stirred the boy to such fervid and florid inventions. They agreed with the faculty and with his father, that Paul's was a bad case.

The east-bound train was plowing through a January snowstorm; the dull dawn was beginning to show grey when the engine whistled a mile out of Newark. Paul started up from the seat where he had lain curled in uneasy slumber, rubbed the breath-misted window-glass with his hand, and peered out. The snow was whirling in curling eddies above the white bottom lands, and the drifts lay already deep in the fields and along the fences, while here and there the tall dead grass and dried weed stalks protruded black above it. Lights shone from the scattered houses, and a gang of laborers who stood beside the track waved their lanterns.

Paul had slept very little, and he felt grimy and uncomfortable. He had made the all-night journey in a day coach because he was afraid if he took a Pullman he might be seen by some Pittsburgh business man who had noticed him in Denny and Carson's office. When the whistle woke him, he clutched quickly at his breast pocket, glancing about him with an uncertain smile. But the little, clay-bespattered Italians were still sleeping, the slatternly women across the aisle were in open-mouthed oblivion, and even the crumby, crying babies were for the nonce stilled. Paul settled back to struggle with his impatience as best he could.

40   When he arrived at the Jersey City station, he hurried through his breakfast, manifestly ill at ease and keeping a sharp eye about him. After he reached the Twenty-third Street station, he consulted a cabman, and had himself driven to a men's furnishing establishment which was just opening for the day. He spent upward of two hours there, buying with endless reconsidering and great care. His new street suit he put on in the fitting-room; the frock coat and dress clothes he had bundled into the cab with his new shirts. Then he drove to a hatter's and a shoe house. His next errand was at Tiffany's, where he selected silver-mounted brushes and a scarf-pin. He would not wait to have his silver marked, he said. Lastly, he stopped at a trunk shop on Broadway, and had his purchases packed into various traveling-bags.

It was a little after one o'clock when he drove up to the Waldorf, and, after settling with the cabman, went into the office. He registered from Washington; said his mother and father had been abroad, and that he had come down to await the arrival of their steamer. He told his story plausibly and had no trouble, since he offered to pay for them in advance, in engaging his rooms; a sleeping-room, sitting-room, and bath.

Not once, but a hundred times Paul had planned this entry into New York. He had gone over every detail of it with Charley Edwards, and in his scrapbook at home there were pages of description about New York hotels, cut from the Sunday papers.

When he was shown to his sitting-room on the eighth floor, he saw at a glance that everything was as it should be; there was but one detail in his mental picture that the place did not realize, so he rang for the bell-boy and sent him down for flowers. He moved about nervously until the boy returned, putting away his new linen and fingering it delightedly as he did so. When the flowers came, he put them hastily into water, and then tumbled into a hot bath. Presently he came out of his white bathroom, resplendent in his new silk underwear, and playing with the tassels of his red robe. The snow was whirling so fiercely outside his windows that he could scarcely see across the street; but within, the air was deliciously soft and fragrant. He put the violets and jonquils on the taboret beside the couch, and threw himself down with a long sigh, covering himself with a Roman blanket. He was thoroughly tired; he had been in such haste, he had stood up to such a strain, covered so much ground in the last twenty-four hours, that he wanted to think how it had all come about. Lulled by the sound of the wind, the warm air, and the cool fragrance of the flowers, he sank into deep, drowsy retrospection.

It had been wonderfully simple; when they had shut him out of the theater and concert hall, when they had taken away his bone, the whole thing was virtually determined. The rest was a mere matter of opportunity. The only thing that at all surprised him was his own courage—for he realized well enough that he had always been tormented by fear, a sort of apprehensive dread which, of late years, as the meshes of the lies he had told closed about him, had been pulling the muscles of his body tighter and tighter. Until now, he could not remember a time when he had not been dreading something. Even when he was a little boy, it was always there—behind him, or before, or on either side. There had always been the shadowed corner, the dark place into which he dared not look, but from which something seemed always to be watching him—and Paul had done things that were not pretty to watch, he knew.

But now he had a curious sense of relief, as though he had at last thrown down the gauntlet to the thing in the corner.   45

Yet it was but a day since he had been sulking in the traces; but yesterday afternoon that he had been sent to the bank with Denny & Carson's deposit, as usual—but this time he was instructed to leave the book to be balanced. There was above two thousand dollars in checks, and nearly a thousand in the banknotes which he had taken from the book and quietly transferred to his pocket. At the bank he had made out a new deposit slip. His nerves had been steady enough to permit of his returning to the office, where he had finished his work and asked for a full day's holiday tomorrow, Saturday, giving a perfectly reasonable pretext. The bank book, he knew, would not be returned before Monday or Tuesday, and his father would be out of town for the next week. From the time he slipped the banknotes into his pocket until he boarded the night train for New York, he had not known a moment's hesitation.

How astonishingly easy it had all been; here he was, the thing done; and this time there would be no awakening, no figure at the top of the stairs. He watched the snowflakes whirling by his window until he fell asleep.

When he awoke, it was four o'clock in the afternoon. He bounded up with a start; one of his precious days gone already! He spent nearly an hour in dressing, watching every stage of his toilet carefully in the mirror. Everything was quite perfect; he was exactly the kind of boy he had always wanted to be.

When he went downstairs, Paul took a carriage and drove up Fifth Avenue toward the Park. The snow had somewhat abated; carriages and tradesmen's wagons were hurrying soundlessly to and fro in the winter twilight; boys in woolen mufflers were shoveling off the doorsteps; the Avenue stages made fine spots of color against the white street. Here and there on the corners whole flower gardens blooming behind glass windows, against which the snowflakes stuck and melted; violets, roses, carnations, lilies-of-the-valley—somehow vastly more lovely and alluring that they blossomed thus unnaturally in the snow. The Park itself was a wonderful stage winter-piece.

50   When he returned, the pause of the twilight had ceased, and the tune of the streets had changed. The snow was falling faster, lights streamed from the hotels that reared their many stories fearlessly up into the storm, defying the raging Atlantic winds. A long, black stream of carriages poured down the Avenue, intersected here and there by other streams, tending horizontally. There were a score of cabs about the entrance of his hotel, and his driver had to wait. Boys in livery were running in and out of the awning stretched across the sidewalk, up and down the red velvet carpet laid from the door to the street. Above, about, within it all, was the rumble and roar, the hurry and toss of thousands of human beings as hot for pleasure as himself, and on every side of him towered the glaring affirmation of the omnipotence of wealth.

The boy set his teeth and drew his shoulders together in a spasm of realization; the plot of all dramas, the text of all romances, the nerve-stuff of all sensations was whirling about him like the snowflakes. He burnt like a faggot in a tempest.

When Paul came down to dinner, the music of the orchestra floated up the elevator shaft to greet him. As he stepped into the thronged corridor, he sank back into one of the chairs against the wall to get his breath. The lights, the chatter, the perfumes, the bewildering medley of color—he had, for a moment, the feeling of not being able to stand it. But only for a moment; these were his own people, he told himself. He went slowly about the corridors, through the writing-rooms, smoking-rooms, reception-rooms, as though he were exploring the chambers of an enchanted palace, built and peopled for him alone.

When he reached the dining-room he sat down at a table near a window. The flowers, the white linen, the many-colored wine-glasses, the gay toilettes of the women, the low popping of corks, the undulating repetitions of the "Blue Danube" from the orchestra, all flooded Paul's dream with bewildering radiance. When the roseate tinge of his champagne was added—that cold, precious, bubbling stuff that creamed and foamed in his glass—Paul wondered that there were honest men in the world at all. This was what all the world was fighting for, he reflected; this was what all the struggle was about. He doubted the reality of his past. Had he ever known a place called Cordelia Street, a place where fagged-looking business men boarded the early car? Mere rivets in a machine they seemed to Paul—sickening men, with combings of children's hair always hanging to their coats, and the smell of cooking in their clothes. Cordelia Street— Ah, that belonged to another time and country! Had he not always been thus, had he not sat here night after night, from as far back as he could remember, looking pensively over just such shimmering textures, and slowly twirling the stem of a glass like this one between his thumb and middle finger? He rather thought he had.

He was not in the least abashed or lonely. He had no especial desire to meet or to know any of these people; all he demanded was the right to look on and conjecture, to watch the pageant. The mere stage properties were all he contended for. Nor was he lonely later in the evening, in his loge at the Opera. He was entirely rid of his nervous misgivings, of his forced aggressiveness, of the imperative desire to show himself different from his surroundings. He felt now that his surroundings explained him. Nobody questioned the purple; he had only to wear it passively. He had only to glance down at his dress coat to reassure himself that here it would be impossible for anyone to humiliate him.

He found it hard to leave his beautiful sitting-room to go to bed that night, and sat long watching the raging storm from his turret window. When he went to sleep, it was with the lights turned on in his bedroom; partly because of his old timidity, and partly so that, if he should wake in the night, there would be no wretched moment of doubt, no horrible suspicion of yellow wallpaper, or of Washington and Calvin above his bed. 55

On Sunday morning the city was practically snowbound. Paul breakfasted late, and in the afternoon he fell in with a wild San Francisco boy, a freshman at Yale, who said he had run down for a "little flyer" over Sunday. The young man offered to show Paul the night side of the town, and the two boys went off together after dinner, not returning to the hotel until seven o'clock the next morning. They had started out in the confiding warmth of a champagne friendship, but their parting in the elevator was singularly cool. The freshman pulled himself together to make his train, and Paul went to bed. He awoke at two o'clock in the afternoon, very thirsty and dizzy, and rang for ice-water, coffee, and the Pittsburgh papers.

On the part of the hotel management, Paul excited no suspicion. There was this to be said for him, that he wore his spoils with dignity and in no way made himself conspicuous. His chief greediness lay in his ears and eyes, and his excesses were not offensive ones. His dearest pleasures were the grey winter twilights in his sitting-room; his quiet enjoyment of his flowers, his clothes, his wide divan, his cigarette, and his sense of power. He could not remember a time when he had felt so at peace with himself. The mere release from the necessity of petty lying, lying every day and every day, restored his self-respect. He had never lied for plea-sure, even at school; but to make himself noticed and admired, to assert his difference from other Cordelia Street boys; and he felt a good deal more manly, more honest, even, now that he had no need for boastful pretensions, now that he could, as his actor friends used to say, "dress the part." It was characteristic that remorse did not occur to him. His golden days went by without a shadow, and he made each as perfect as he could.

On the eighth day after his arrival in New York, he found the whole affair exploited in the Pittsburgh papers, exploited with a wealth of detail which indicated that local news of a sensational nature was at a low ebb. The firm of Denny & Carson announced that the boy's fa-ther had refunded the full amount of his theft, and that they had no in-tention of prosecuting. The Cumberland minister had been inter-viewed, and expressed his hope of yet reclaiming the motherless lad, and Paul's Sabbath-School teacher declared that she would spare no effort to that end. The rumor had reached Pittsburgh that the boy had been seen in a New York hotel, and his father had gone East to find him and bring him home.

Paul had just come in to dress for dinner; he sank into the chair, weak in the knees, and clasped his head in his hands. It was to be worse than jail, even; the tepid waters of Cordelia Street were to close over him finally and forever. The grey monotony stretched before him in hopeless, unrelieved years;—Sabbath School, Young People's Meeting, the yellow-papered room, the damp dish-towels; it all rushed back upon him with sickening vividness. He had the old feeling that the orches-tra had suddenly stopped, the sinking sensation that the play was over. The sweat broke out on his face, and he sprang to his feet, looked about him with his white, conscious smile, and winked at himself in the mir-ror. With something of the childish belief in miracles with which he had so often gone to class, all his lessons unlearned, Paul dressed and dashed whistling down the corridor to the elevator.

He had no sooner entered the dining-room and caught the measure 60
of the music than his remembrance was lightened by his old elastic
power of claiming the moment, mounting with it, and finding it all-
sufficient. The glare and glitter about him, the mere scenic accessories
had again, and for the last time, their old potency. He would show himself that he was game, he would finish the thing splendidly. He doubted,
more than ever, the existence of Cordelia Street, and for the first time
he drank his wine recklessly. Was he not, after all, one of these fortunate beings? Was he not still himself, and in his own place? He
drummed a nervous accompaniment to the music and looked about
him, telling himself over and over that it had paid.

He reflected drowsily, to the swell of the violin and the chill sweetness of his wine, that he might have done it more wisely. He might
have caught an outbound steamer and been well out of their clutches
before now. But the other side of the world had seemed too far away
and too uncertain then; he could not have waited for it; his need had
been too sharp. If he had to choose over again, he would do the same
thing tomorrow. He looked affectionately about the dining-room, now
gilded with a soft mist. Ah, it had paid indeed!

Paul was awakened next morning by a painful throbbing in his
head and feet. He had thrown himself across the bed without undressing, and had slept with his shoes on. His limbs and hands were lead-
heavy, and his tongue and throat were parched. There came upon him
one of those fateful attacks of clear-headedness that never occurred except when he was physically exhausted and his nerves hung loose. He
lay still and closed his eyes and let the tide of realities wash over him.

His father was in New York; "stopping at some joint or other," he
told himself. The memory of successive summers on the front stoop fell
upon him like a weight of black water. He had not a hundred dollars
left; and he knew now, more than ever, that money was everything,
the wall that stood between all he loathed and all he wanted. The thing
was winding itself up; he had thought of that on his first glorious day in
New York, and had even provided a way to snap the thread. It lay on
his dressing-table now; he had got it out last night when he came
blindly up from dinner—but the shiny metal hurt his eyes, and he disliked the look of it, anyway.

He rose and moved about with a painful effort, succumbing now
and again to attacks of nausea. It was the old depression exaggerated;
all the world had become Cordelia Street. Yet somehow he was not
afraid of anything, was absolutely calm; perhaps because he had looked
into the dark corner at last, and knew. It was bad enough, what he saw
there; but somehow not so bad as his long fear of it had been. He saw

everything clearly now. He had a feeling that he had made the best of it, that he had lived the sort of life he was meant to live, and for half an hour he sat staring at the revolver. But he told himself that was not the way, so he went downstairs and took a cab to the ferry.

65   When Paul arrived at Newark, he got off the train and took another cab, directing the driver to follow the Pennsylvania tracks out of town. The snow lay heavy on the roadways and had drifted deep in the open fields. Only here and there the dead grass or dried weed stalks projected, singularly black, above it.

Once well into the country, Paul dismissed the carriage and walked, floundering along the tracks, his mind a medley of irrelevant things. He seemed to hold in his brain an actual picture of everything he had seen that morning. He remembered every feature of both his drivers, the toothless old woman from whom he had bought the red flowers in his coat, the agent from whom he had got his ticket, and all of his fellow-passengers on the ferry. His mind, unable to cope with vital matters near at hand, worked feverishly and deftly at sorting and grouping these images. They made for him a part of the ugliness of the world, of the ache in his head, and the bitter burning on his tongue. He stooped and put a handful of snow into his mouth as he walked, but that, too, seemed hot. When he reached a little hillside, where the tracks ran through a cut some twenty feet below him, he stopped and sat down.

The carnations in his coat were drooping with cold, he noticed; all their red glory over. It occurred to him that all the flowers he had seen in the show windows that first night must have gone the same way, long before this. It was only one splendid breath they had, in spite of their brave mockery at the winter outside the glass. It was a losing game in the end, it seemed, this revolt against the homilies by which the world is run. Paul took one of the blossoms carefully from his coat and scooped a little hole in the snow, where he covered it up. Then he dozed awhile, from his weak condition, seeming insensible to the cold.

The sound of an approaching train woke him and he started to his feet, remembering only his resolution, and afraid lest he should be too late. He stood watching the approaching locomotive, his teeth chattering, his lips drawn away from them in a frightened smile; once or twice he glanced nervously sidewise, as though he were being watched. When the right moment came, he jumped. As he fell, the folly of his haste occurred to him with merciless clearness, the vastness of what he had left undone. There flashed through his brain, clearer than ever before, the blue of Adriatic water, the yellow of Algerian sands.

He felt something strike his chest—his body being thrown swiftly through the air, on and on, immeasurably far and fast, while his limbs gently relaxed. Then, because the picture making mechanism was crushed, the disturbing visions flashed into black, and Paul dropped back into the immense design of things.

QUESTIONS

1. Technically we should classify the author's point of view as omniscient, for she enters into the minds of characters at will. Nevertheless, early in the story the focus changes rather abruptly. Locate the point where the change occurs. Through whose eyes do we see Paul prior to this point? Through whose eyes do we see him afterward? What is the purpose of this shift? Does it offer any clue to the purpose of the story?

2. What details of Paul's appearance and behavior, as his teachers see him, indicate that he is different from most other boys?

3. Explain Paul's behavior. Why does he lie? What does he hate? What does he want? Contrast the world of Cordelia Street with the worlds that Paul finds at Carnegie Hall, at the Schenley, at the stock theater, and in New York.

4. Is Paul artistic? Describe his reactions to music, to painting, to literature, and to the theater. What value does he find in the arts?

5. Is Paul a static or a developing character? If the latter, at what points does he change? Why?

6. What do Paul's clandestine trips to the stock theater, his trip to New York, and his suicide have in common?

7. Compare Paul and the college boy he meets in New York (paragraph 56). Are they two of a kind? If not, how do they differ?

8. What are the implications of the title? What does the last sentence of the story do to the reader's focus of vision?

9. Are there any clues to the causes of Paul's unusual personality? How many? In what is the author chiefly interested?

10. In what two cities is the story set? Does this choice of setting have any symbolic value? Could the story have been set as validly in Cleveland and Detroit? In San Francisco and Los Angeles? In New Orleans and Birmingham?

Shirley Jackson

The Lottery

The morning of June 27th was clear and sunny, with the fresh warmth of a full-summer day; the flowers were blossoming profusely and the grass was richly green. The people of the village began to gather in

THE LOTTERY   First published in 1948. Shirley Jackson (1919–1965) was born in San Francisco and spent most of her early life in California. After her marriage in 1940 she lived in a quiet rural community in Vermont.

the square, between the post office and the bank, around ten o'clock; in some towns there were so many people that the lottery took two days and had to be started on June 26th, but in this village, where there were only about three hundred people, the whole lottery took less than two hours, so it could begin at ten o'clock in the morning and still be through in time to allow the villagers to get home for noon dinner.

The children assembled first, of course. School was recently over for the summer, and the feeling of liberty sat uneasily on most of them; they tended to gather together quietly for a while before they broke into boisterous play, and their talk was still of the classroom and the teacher, of books and reprimands. Bobby Martin had already stuffed his pockets full of stones, and the other boys soon followed his example, selecting the smoothest and roundest stones; Bobby and Harry Jones and Dickie Delacroix—the villagers pronounced this name "Dellacroy"— eventually made a great pile of stones in one corner of the square and guarded it against the raids of the other boys. The girls stood aside, talking among themselves, looking over their shoulders at the boys, and the very small children rolled in the dust or clung to the hands of their older brothers or sisters.

Soon the men began to gather, surveying their own children, speaking of planting and rain, tractors and taxes. They stood together, away from the pile of stones in the corner, and their jokes were quiet and they smiled rather than laughed. The women, wearing faded house dresses and sweaters, came shortly after their menfolk. They greeted one another and exchanged bits of gossip as they went to join their husbands. Soon the women, standing by their husbands, began to call to their children, and the children came reluctantly, having to be called four or five times. Bobby Martin ducked under his mother's grasping hand and ran, laughing, back to the pile of stones. His father spoke up sharply, and Bobby came quickly and took his place between his father and his oldest brother.

The lottery was conducted—as were the square dances, the teenage club, the Halloween program—by Mr. Summers, who had time and energy to devote to civic activities. He was a round-faced, jovial man and he ran the coal business, and people were sorry for him, because he had no children and his wife was a scold. When he arrived in the square, carrying the black wooden box, there was a murmur of conversation among the villagers, and he waved and called, "Little late today, folks." The postmaster, Mr. Graves, followed him, carrying a three-legged stool, and the stool was put in the center of the square and Mr. Summers set the black box down on it. The villagers kept their distance, leaving a space between themselves and the stool, and when

Mr. Summers said, "Some of you fellows want to give me a hand?" there was a hesitation before two men, Mr. Martin and his oldest son, Baxter, came forward to hold the box steady on the stool while Mr. Summers stirred up the papers inside it.

The original paraphernalia for the lottery had been lost long ago, and the black box now resting on the stool had been put into use even before Old Man Warner, the oldest man in town, was born. Mr. Summers spoke frequently to the villagers about making a new box, but no one liked to upset even as much tradition as was represented by the black box. There was a story that the present box had been made with some pieces of the box that had preceded it, the one that had been constructed when the first people settled down to make a village here. Every year, after the lottery, Mr. Summers began talking again about a new box, but every year the subject was allowed to fade off without anything's being done. The black box grew shabbier each year; by now it was no longer completely black but splintered badly along one side to show the original wood color, and in some places faded or stained.

Mr. Martin and his oldest son, Baxter, held the black box securely on the stool until Mr. Summers had stirred the papers thoroughly with his hand. Because so much of the ritual had been forgotten or discarded, Mr. Summers had been successful in having slips of paper substituted for the chips of wood that had been used for generations. Chips of wood, Mr. Summers had argued, had been all very well when the village was tiny, but now that the population was more than three hundred and likely to keep on growing, it was necessary to use something that would fit more easily into the black box. The night before the lottery, Mr. Summers and Mr. Graves made up the slips of paper and put them in the box, and it was then taken to the safe of Mr. Summers's coal company and locked up until Mr. Summers was ready to take it to the square next morning. The rest of the year, the box was put away, sometimes one place, sometimes another; it had spent one year in Mr. Graves's barn and another year underfoot in the post office, and sometimes it was set on a shelf in the Martin grocery and left there.

There was a great deal of fussing to be done before Mr. Summers declared the lottery open. There were the lists to make up—of heads of families, heads of households in each family, members of each household in each family. There was the proper swearing-in of Mr. Summers by the postmaster, as the official of the lottery; at one time, some people remembered, there had been a recital of some sort, performed by the official of the lottery, a perfunctory, tuneless chant that had been rattled off duly each year; some people believed that the official of the lottery used to stand just so when he said or sang it,

5

others believed that he was supposed to walk among the people, but years and years ago this part of the ritual had been allowed to lapse. There had been, also, a ritual salute, which the official of the lottery had had to use in addressing each person who came up to draw from the box, but this also had changed with time, until now it was felt necessary only for the official to speak to each person approaching. Mr. Summers was very good at all this; in his clean white shirt and blue jeans, with one hand resting carelessly on the black box, he seemed very proper and important as he talked interminably to Mr. Graves and the Martins.

Just as Mr. Summers finally left off talking and turned to the assembled villagers, Mrs. Hutchinson came hurriedly along the path to the square, her sweater thrown over her shoulders, and slid into place in the back of the crowd. "Clean forgot what day it was," she said to Mrs. Delacroix, who stood next to her, and they both laughed softly. "Thought my old man was out back stacking wood," Mrs. Hutchinson went on, "and then I looked out the window and the kids were gone, and then I remembered it was the twenty-seventh and came a-running." She dried her hands on her apron, and Mrs. Delacroix said, "You're in time, though. They're still talking away up there."

Mrs. Hutchinson craned her neck to see through the crowd and found her husband and children standing near the front. She tapped Mrs. Delacroix on the arm as a farewell and began to make her way through the crowd. The people separated good-humoredly to let her through; two or three people said, in voices just loud enough to be heard across the crowd, "Here comes your Missus, Hutchinson," and "Bill, she made it after all." Mrs. Hutchinson reached her husband, and Mr. Summers, who had been waiting, said cheerfully, "Thought we were going to have to get on without you, Tessie." Mrs. Hutchinson said, grinning, "Wouldn't have me leave m'dishes in the sink, now, would you, Joe?" and soft laughter ran through the crowd as the people stirred back into position after Mrs. Hutchinson's arrival.

10   "Well, now," Mr. Summers said soberly, "guess we better get started, get this over with, so's we can go back to work. Anybody ain't here?"

"Dunbar," several people said. "Dunbar, Dunbar."

Mr. Summers consulted his list. "Clyde Dunbar," he said. "That's right. He's broke his leg, hasn't he? Who's drawing for him?"

"Me, I guess," a woman said, and Mr. Summers turned to look at her. "Wife draws for her husband," Mr. Summers said. "Don't you have a grown boy to do it for you, Janey?" Although Mr. Summers and everyone else in the village knew the answer perfectly well, it was the business of the official of the lottery to ask such questions formally.

Mr. Summers waited with an expression of polite interest while Mrs. Dunbar answered.

"Horace's not but sixteen yet," Mrs. Dunbar said regretfully. "Guess I gotta fill in for the old man this year."

"Right," Mr. Summers said. He made a note on the list he was   15
holding. Then he asked, "Watson boy drawing this year?"

A tall boy in the crowd raised his hand. "Here," he said. "I'm drawing for m'mother and me." He blinked his eyes nervously and ducked his head as several voices in the crowd said things like "Good fellow, Jack," and "Glad to see your mother's got a man to do it."

"Well," Mr. Summers said, "guess that's everyone. Old Man Warner make it?"

"Here," a voice said, and Mr. Summers nodded.

A sudden hush fell on the crowd as Mr. Summers cleared his throat and looked at the list. "All ready?" he called. "Now, I'll read the names—heads of families first—and the men come up and take a paper out of the box. Keep the paper folded in your hand without looking at it until everyone has had a turn. Everything clear?"

The people had done it so many times that they only half listened   20
to the directions; most of them were quiet, wetting their lips, not looking around. Then Mr. Summers raised one hand high and said, "Adams." A man disengaged himself from the crowd and came forward. "Hi, Steve," Mr. Summers said, and Mr. Adams said, "Hi, Joe." They grinned at one another humorlessly and nervously. Then Mr. Adams reached into the black box and took out a folded paper. He held it firmly by one corner as he turned and went hastily back to his place in the crowd, where he stood a little apart from his family, not looking down at his hand.

"Allen," Mr. Summers said. "Anderson . . . Bentham."

"Seems like there's no time at all between lotteries any more," Mrs. Delacroix said to Mrs. Graves in the back row. "Seems like we got through with the last one only last week."

"Time sure goes fast," Mrs. Graves said.

"Clark . . . Delacroix."

"There goes my old man," Mrs. Delacroix said. She held her breath   25
while her husband went forward.

"Dunbar," Mr. Summers said, and Mrs. Dunbar went steadily to the box while one of the women said, "Go on, Janey," and another said, "There she goes."

"We're next," Mrs. Graves said. She watched while Mr. Graves came around from the side of the box, greeted Mr. Summers gravely, and selected a slip of paper from the box. By now, all through the crowd there were men holding the small folded papers in their large hands, turning them over and over nervously. Mrs. Dunbar and her two sons stood together, Mrs. Dunbar holding the slip of paper.

"Harburt . . . Hutchinson."

"Get up there, Bill," Mrs. Hutchinson said, and the people near her laughed.

30   "Jones."

"They do say," Mr. Adams said to Old Man Warner, who stood next to him, "that over in the north village they're talking of giving up the lottery."

Old Man Warner snorted. "Pack of crazy fools," he said. "Listening to the young folks, nothing's good enough for *them*. Next thing you know, they'll be wanting to go back to living in caves, nobody work any more, live *that* way for a while. Used to be a saying about 'Lottery in June, corn be heavy soon.' First thing you know, we'd all be eating stewed chickweed and acorns. There's *always* been a lottery," he added petulantly. "Bad enough to see young Joe Summers up there joking with everybody."

"Some places have already quit lotteries," Mrs. Adams said.

"Nothing but trouble in *that*," Old Man Warner said stoutly. "Pack of young fools."

35   "Martin." And Bobby Martin watched his father go forward. "Overdyke . . . Percy."

"I wish they'd hurry," Mrs. Dunbar said to her older son. "I wish they'd hurry."

"They're almost through," her son said.

"You get ready to run tell Dad," Mrs. Dunbar said.

Mr. Summers called his own name and then stepped forward precisely and selected a slip from the box. Then he called, "Warner."

40   "Seventy-seventh year I been in the lottery," Old Man Warner said as he went through the crowd. "Seventy-seventh time."

"Watson." The tall boy came awkwardly through the crowd. Someone said, "Don't be nervous, Jack," and Mr. Summers said, "Take your time, son."

"Zanini."

After that, there was a long pause, a breathless pause, until Mr. Summers, holding his slip of paper in the air, said, "All right, fellows." For a minute, no one moved, and then all the slips of paper were opened. Suddenly, all the women began to speak at once, saying, "Who is it?" "Who's got it?" "Is it the Dunbars?" "Is it the Watsons?" Then the voices began to say, "It's Hutchinson. It's Bill." "Bill Hutchinson's got it."

"Go tell your father," Mrs. Dunbar said to her older son.

People began to look around to see the Hutchinsons. Bill   45
Hutchinson was standing quiet, staring down at the paper in his
hand. Suddenly, Tessie Hutchinson shouted to Mr. Summers. "You
didn't give him time enough to take any paper he wanted. I saw you.
It wasn't fair."

"Be a good sport, Tessie," Mrs. Delacroix called, and Mrs. Graves
said, "All of us took the same chance."

"Shut up, Tessie," Bill Hutchinson said.

"Well, everyone," Mr. Summers said, "that was done pretty fast,
and now we've got to be hurrying a little more to get done in time." He
consulted his next list. "Bill," he said, "you draw for the Hutchinson
family. You got any other households in the Hutchinsons?"

"There's Don and Eva," Mrs. Hutchinson yelled. "Make *them* take
their chance!"

"Daughters draw with their husband's families, Tessie," Mr. Sum-   50
mers said gently. "You know that as well as anyone else."

"It wasn't *fair*," Tessie said.

"I guess not, Joe," Bill Hutchinson said regretfully. "My daughter
draws with her husband's family, that's only fair. And I've got no other
family except the kids."

"Then, as far as drawing for families is concerned, it's you," Mr. Summers said in explanation, "and as far as drawing for households is concerned, that's you, too. Right?"

"Right," Bill Hutchinson said.

"How many kids, Bill?" Mr. Summers asked formally.   55

"Three," Bill Hutchinson said. "There's Bill, Jr., and Nancy, and
little Dave. And Tessie and me."

"All right, then," Mr. Summers said. "Harry, you got their tickets
back?"

Mr. Graves nodded and held up the slips of paper. "Put them in the
box, then," Mr. Summers directed. "Take Bill's and put it in."

"I think we ought to start over," Mrs. Hutchinson said, as quietly
as she could. "I tell you it wasn't *fair*. You didn't give him time enough
to choose. *Every*body saw that."

Mr. Graves had selected the five slips and put them in the box, and   60
he dropped all the papers but those onto the ground, where the breeze
caught them and lifted them off.

"Listen, everybody," Mrs. Hutchinson was saying to the people
around her.

"Ready, Bill?" Mr. Summers asked, and Bill Hutchinson, with one
quick glance around at his wife and children, nodded.

"Remember," Mr. Summers said, "take the slips and keep them folded until each person has taken one. Harry, you help little Dave." Mr. Graves took the hand of the little boy, who came willingly with him up to the box. "Take a paper out of the box, Davy," Mr. Summers said. Davy put his hand into the box and laughed. "Take just *one* paper," Mr. Summers said. "Harry, you hold it for him." Mr. Graves took the child's hand and removed the folded paper from the tight fist and held it while little Dave stood next to him and looked up at him wonderingly.

"Nancy next," Mr. Summers said. Nancy was twelve, and her school friends breathed heavily as she went forward, switching her skirt, and took a slip daintily from the box. "Bill, Jr.," Mr. Summers said, and Billy, his face red and his feet over-large, nearly knocked the box over as he got a paper out. "Tessie," Mr. Summers said. She hesitated for a minute, looking around defiantly, and then set her lips and went up to the box. She snatched a paper out and held it behind her.

65   "Bill," Mr. Summers said, and Bill Hutchinson reached into the box and felt around, bringing his hand out at last with the slip of paper in it.

The crowd was quiet. A girl whispered, "I hope it's not Nancy," and the sound of the whisper reached the edges of the crowd.

"It's not the way it used to be," Old Man Warner said clearly. "People ain't the way they used to be."

"All right," Mr. Summers said. "Open the papers. Harry, you open little Dave's."

Mr. Graves opened the slip of paper and there was a general sigh through the crowd as he held it up and everyone could see that it was blank. Nancy and Bill, Jr., opened theirs at the same time, and both beamed and laughed, turning around to the crowd and holding their slips of paper above their heads.

70   "Tessie," Mr. Summers said. There was a pause, and then Mr. Summers looked at Bill Hutchinson, and Bill unfolded his paper and showed it. It was blank.

"It's Tessie," Mr. Summers said, and his voice was hushed. "Show us her paper, Bill."

Bill Hutchinson went over to his wife and forced the slip of paper out of her hand. It had a black spot on it, the black spot Mr. Summers had made the night before with the heavy pencil in the coal-company office. Bill Hutchinson held it up, and there was a stir in the crowd.

"All right, folks," Mr. Summers said. "Let's finish quickly."

Although the villagers had forgotten the ritual and lost the original black box, they still remembered to use stones. The pile of stones the boys had made earlier was ready; there were stones on the ground with the blowing scraps of paper that had come out of the box. Mrs. Delacroix selected a stone so large she had to pick it up with both hands and turned to Mrs. Dunbar. "Come on," she said. "Hurry up."

Mrs. Dunbar had small stones in both hands, and she said, gasping   75
for breath, "I can't run at all. You'll have to go ahead and I'll catch up with you."

The children had stones already, and someone gave little Davy Hutchinson a few pebbles.

Tessie Hutchinson was in the center of a cleared space by now, and she held her hands out desperately as the villagers moved in on her. "It isn't fair," she said. A stone hit her on the side of the head.

Old Man Warner was saying, "Come on, come on, everyone." Steve Adams was in front of the crowd of villagers, with Mrs. Graves beside him.

"It isn't fair, it isn't right," Mrs. Hutchinson screamed, and then they were upon her.

QUESTIONS

1. What is a "lottery"? How does the title lead you to expect something very different from what the story presents?
2. What is a scapegoat? Who is the scapegoat in this story? What other examples of scapegoating can you recall?
3. What normal law of probability has been suspended in this story? Granting this initial implausibility, does the story proceed naturally?
4. What is the significance of the fact that the original box has been lost and many parts of the ritual have been forgotten? Can you find a statement in the story that most likely explains the original purpose of the ritual?
5. What different attitudes toward the ritual stoning are represented by (a) Mr. Summers, (b) Old Man Warner, (c) Mr. and Mrs. Adams, (d) Mrs. Hutchinson, (e) the villagers in general? Which attitude most closely reflects the point of the story?
6. By transporting a primitivistic ritual into a modern setting, the story reveals something about human nature and human society. What?
7. Many modern customs or rituals have developed from primitive origins (for example, the decoration of a Christmas tree). Can you identify some others? What would set them apart from the ritual stoning in this story?
8. Can you support a claim that this story is presented from the objective point of view? Why is the dispassionate, matter-of-fact tone of the story so effective?

Katherine Anne Porter

The Jilting of Granny Weatherall

She flicked her wrist neatly out of Doctor Harry's pudgy careful fingers and pulled the sheet up to her chin. The brat ought to be in knee breeches. Doctoring around the country with spectacles on his nose! "Get along now, take your schoolbooks and go. There's nothing wrong with me."

Doctor Harry spread a warm paw like a cushion on her forehead where the forked green vein danced and made her eyelids twitch. "Now, now, be a good girl, and we'll have you up in no time."

"That's no way to speak to a woman nearly eighty years old just because she's down. I'd have you respect your elders, young man."

"Well, Missy, excuse me." Doctor Harry patted her cheek. "But I've got to warn you, haven't I? You're a marvel, but you must be careful or you're going to be good and sorry."

5   "Don't tell me what I'm going to be. I'm on my feet now, morally speaking. It's Cornelia. I had to go to bed to get rid of her."

Her bones felt loose, and floated around in her skin, and Doctor Harry floated like a balloon around the foot of the bed. He floated and pulled down his waistcoat and swung his glasses on a cord. "Well, stay where you are, it certainly can't hurt you."

"Get along and doctor your sick," said Granny Weatherall. "Leave a well woman alone. I'll call for you when I want you. . . . Where were you forty years ago when I pulled through milk-leg and double pneumonia? You weren't even born. Don't let Cornelia lead you on," she shouted, because Doctor Harry appeared to float up to the ceiling and out. "I pay my own bills, and I don't throw my money away on nonsense!"

She meant to wave good-by, but it was too much trouble. Her eyes closed of themselves, it was like a dark curtain drawn around the bed. The pillow rose and floated under her, pleasant as a hammock in a light wind. She listened to the leaves rustling outside the window. No, somebody was swishing newspapers: no, Cornelia and Doctor Harry were whispering together. She leaped broad awake, thinking they whispered in her ear.

THE JILTING OF GRANNY WEATHERALL   First published in 1930. Katherine Anne Porter (1890–1980) was born and grew up in Texas, was educated at convent schools in New Orleans, and lived in Chicago, Fort Worth, Mexico, and New York City before writing this story.

"She was never like this, *never* like this!" "Well, what can we ex-pect?" "Yes, eighty years old. . . ."

Well, and what if she was? She still had ears. It was like Cornelia   10
to whisper around doors. She always kept things secret in such a public way. She was always being tactful and kind. Cornelia was dutiful; that was the trouble with her. Dutiful and good: "So good and dutiful," said Granny, "that I'd like to spank her." She saw herself spanking Cornelia and making a fine job of it.

"What'd you say, Mother?"

Granny felt her face tying up in hard knots.

"Can't a body think, I'd like to know?"

"I thought you might want something."

"I do. I want a lot of things. First off, go away and don't whisper."   15

She lay and drowsed, hoping in her sleep that the children would keep out and let her rest a minute. It had been a long day. Not that she was tired. It was always pleasant to snatch a minute now and then. There was always so much to be done, let me see: tomorrow.

Tomorrow was far away and there was nothing to trouble about. Things were finished somehow when the time came; thank God there was always a little margin over for peace: then a person could spread out the plan of life and tuck in the edges orderly. It was good to have every-thing clean and folded away, with the hair brushes and tonic bottles sitting straight on the white embroidered linen: the day started without fuss and the pantry shelves laid out with rows of jelly glasses and brown jugs and white stone-china jars with blue whirligigs and words painted on them: coffee, tea, sugar, ginger, cinnamon, allspice: and the bronze clock with the lion on top nicely dusted off. The dust that lion could collect in twenty-four hours! The box in the attic with all those letters tied up, well, she'd have to go through that tomorrow. All those letters—George's letters and John's letters and her letters to them both—lying around for the children to find afterwards made her uneasy. Yes, that would be tomorrow's business. No use to let them know how silly she had been once.

While she was rummaging around she found death in her mind and it felt clammy and unfamiliar. She had spent so much time preparing for death there was no need for bringing it up again. Let it take care of itself now. When she was sixty she had felt very old, finished, and went around making farewell trips to see her children and grandchildren, with a secret in her mind: This is the very last of your mother, children! Then she made her will and came down with a long fever. That was all just a notion like a lot of other things, but it was lucky too, for she had once for all got over the idea of dying for a long time. Now she couldn't be worried. She hoped she had better sense now. Her father had lived to be one hundred and two years old and had drunk a noggin of strong hot toddy on his last birthday. He told the reporters it was his daily habit, and he owed his long life to that. He had made quite a scandal and was very pleased about it. She believed she'd just plague Cornelia a little.

"Cornelia! Cornelia!" No footsteps, but a sudden hand on her cheek. "Bless you, where have you been?"

20   "Here, Mother."

"Well, Cornelia, I want a noggin of hot toddy."

"Are you cold, darling?"

"I'm chilly, Cornelia. Lying in bed stops the circulation. I must have told you that a thousand times."

Well, she could just hear Cornelia telling her husband that Mother was getting a little childish and they'd have to humor her. The thing that most annoyed her was that Cornelia thought she was deaf, dumb, and blind. Little hasty glances and tiny gestures tossed around her and over her head saying, "Don't cross her, let her have her way, she's eighty years old," and she sitting there as if she lived in a thin glass cage. Sometimes Granny almost made up her mind to pack up and move back to her own house where nobody could remind her every minute that she was old. Wait, wait, Cornelia, till your own children whisper behind your back!

25   In her day she had kept a better house and had got more work done. She wasn't too old yet for Lydia to be driving eighty miles for advice when one of the children jumped the track, and Jimmy still dropped in and talked things over: "Now, Mammy, you've a good business head, I want to know what you think of this? . . ." Old. Cornelia couldn't change the furniture around without asking. Little things, little things! They had been so sweet when they were little. Granny wished the old days were back again with the children young and everything to be done over. It had been a hard pull, but not too much for her. When she thought of all the food she had cooked, and all the clothes she had cut and sewed, and all the gardens she had made—well, the children showed it. There they were, made out of her, and they couldn't get away from that. Sometimes she wanted to see John again and point to them and say, Well, I didn't do so badly, did I? But that would have to wait. That was for tomorrow. She used to think of him as a man, but now all the children were older than their father, and he would be a child beside her if she saw him now. It seemed strange and there was something wrong in the idea. Why, he couldn't possibly recognize her. She had fenced in a hundred acres once, digging the post

holes herself and clamping the wires with just a negro boy to help. That changed a woman. John would be looking for a young woman with the peaked Spanish comb in her hair and the painted fan. Digging post holes changed a woman. Riding country roads in the winter when women had their babies was another thing: sitting up nights with sick horses and sick negroes and sick children and hardly ever losing one. John, I hardly ever lost one of them! John would see that in a minute, that would be something he could understand, she wouldn't have to explain anything!

It made her feel like rolling up her sleeves and putting the whole place to rights again. No matter if Cornelia was determined to be everywhere at once, there were a great many things left undone on this place. She would start tomorrow and do them. It was good to be strong enough for everything, even if all you made melted and changed and slipped under your hands, so that by the time you finished you almost forgot what you were working for. What was it I set out to do? she asked herself intently, but she could not remember. A fog rose over the valley, she saw it marching across the creek swallowing the trees and moving up the hill like an army of ghosts. Soon it would be at the near edge of the orchard, and then it was time to go in and light the lamps. Come in, children, don't stay out in the night air.

Lighting the lamps had been beautiful. The children huddled up to her and breathed like little calves waiting at the bars in the twilight. Their eyes followed the match and watched the flame rise and settle in a blue curve, then they moved away from her. The lamp was lit, they didn't have to be scared and hang on to mother any more. Never, never, never more. God, for all my life I thank Thee. Without Thee, my God, I could never have done it. Hail, Mary, full of grace.

I want you to pick all the fruit this year and see that nothing is wasted. There's always someone who can use it. Don't let good things rot for want of using. You waste life when you waste good food. Don't let things get lost. It's bitter to lose things. Now, don't let me get to thinking, not when I am tired and taking a little nap before supper. . . .

The pillow rose about her shoulders and pressed against her heart and the memory was being squeezed out of it: oh, push down the pillow, somebody: it would smother her if she tried to hold it. Such a fresh breeze blowing and such a green day with no threats in it. But he had not come, just the same. What does a woman do when she has put on the white veil and set out the white cake for a man and he doesn't come? She tried to remember. No, I swear he never harmed me but in that. He never harmed me but in that . . . and what if he did? There was the day, the day, but a whirl of dark smoke rose and covered it, crept up and over into the bright field where everything was planted so carefully in orderly rows. That was hell, she knew hell when she saw it. For sixty years she had prayed against remembering him and against losing her soul in the deep pit of hell, and now the two things were mingled in one and the thought of him was a smoky cloud from hell that moved and crept in her head when she had just got rid of Doctor Harry and was trying to rest a minute. Wounded vanity, Ellen, said a sharp voice in the top of her mind. Don't let your wounded vanity get the upper hand of you. Plenty of girls get jilted. You were jilted, weren't you? Then stand up to it. Her eyelids wavered and let in streamers of blue-gray light like tissue paper over her eyes. She must get up and pull the shades down or she'd never sleep. She was in bed again and the shades were not down. How could that happen? Better turn over, hide from the light, sleeping in the light gave you nightmares. "Mother, how do you feel now?" and a stinging wetness on her forehead. But I don't like having my face washed in cold water!

30   Hapsy? George? Lydia? Jimmy? No, Cornelia, and her features were swollen and full of little puddles. "They're coming, darling, they'll all be here soon." Go wash your face, child, you look funny.

Instead of obeying, Cornelia knelt down and put her head on the pillow. She seemed to be talking but there was no sound. "Well, are you tongue-tied? Whose birthday is it? Are you going to give a party?"

Cornelia's mouth moved urgently in strange shapes. "Don't do that, you bother me, daughter."

"Oh, no, Mother. Oh, no. . . ."

Nonsense. It was strange about children. They disputed your every word. "No what, Cornelia?"

35   "Here's Doctor Harry."

"I won't see that boy again. He just left five minutes ago."

"That was this morning, Mother. It's night now. Here's the nurse."

"This is Doctor Harry, Mrs. Weatherall. I never saw you look so young and happy!"

"Ah, I'll never be young again—but I'd be happy if they'd let me lie in peace and get rested."

40   She thought she spoke up loudly, but no one answered. A warm weight on her forehead, a warm bracelet on her wrist, and a breeze went on whispering, trying to tell her something. A shuffle of leaves in the everlasting hand of God, He blew on them and they danced and rattled. "Mother, don't mind, we're going to give you a little hypodermic." "Look here, daughter, how do ants get in this bed? I saw sugar ants yesterday." Did you send for Hapsy too?

It was Hapsy she really wanted. She had to go a long way back through a great many rooms to find Hapsy standing with a baby on her arm. She seemed to herself to be Hapsy also, and the baby on Hapsy's arm was Hapsy and himself and herself, all at once, and there was no surprise in the meeting. Then Hapsy melted from within and turned flimsy as gray gauze and the baby was a gauzy shadow, and Hapsy came up close and said, "I thought you'd never come," and looked at her very searchingly and said, "You haven't changed a bit!" They leaned forward to kiss, when Cornelia began whispering from a long way off, "Oh, is there anything you want to tell me? Is there anything I can do for you?"

Yes, she had changed her mind after sixty years and she would like to see George. I want you to find George. Find him and be sure to tell him I forgot him. I want him to know I had my husband just the same and my children and my house like any other woman. A good house too and a good husband that I loved and fine children out of him. Better than I hoped for even. Tell him I was given back everything he took away and more. Oh, no, oh, God, no, there was something else besides the house and the man and the children. Oh, surely they were not all? What was it? Something not given back. . . . Her breath crowded down under her ribs and grew into a monstrous frightening shape with cutting edges; it bored up into her head, and the agony was unbelievable: Yes, John, get the Doctor now, no more talk, my time has come.

When this one was born it should be the last. The last. It should have been born first, for it was the one she had truly wanted. Everything came in good time. Nothing left out, left over. She was strong, in three days she would be as well as ever. Better. A woman needed milk in her to have her full health.

"Mother, do you hear me?"

"I've been telling you—"

"Mother, Father Connolly's here."

"I went to Holy Communion only last week. Tell him I'm not so sinful as all that."

"Father just wants to speak to you."

He could speak as much as he pleased. It was like him to drop in and inquire about her soul as if it were a teething baby, and then stay on for a cup of tea and a round of cards and gossip. He always had a funny story of some sort, usually about an Irishman who made his little mistakes and confessed them, and the point lay in some absurd thing he would blurt out in the confessional showing his struggles between native piety and original sin. Granny felt easy about her soul. Cornelia, where are your manners? Give Father Connolly a chair. She had her

45

secret comfortable understanding with a few favorite saints who cleared
a straight road to God for her. All as surely signed and sealed as the papers for the new Forty Acres. Forever . . . heirs and assigns forever.
Since the day the wedding cake was not cut, but thrown out and
wasted. The whole bottom dropped out of the world, and there she was
blind and sweating with nothing under her feet and the walls falling
away. His hand had caught her under the breast, she had not fallen,
there was the freshly polished floor with the green rug on it, just as before. He had cursed like a sailor's parrot and said, "I'll kill him for you."
Don't lay a hand on him, for my sake leave something to God. "Now,
Ellen, you must believe what I tell you. . . ."

50   So there was nothing, nothing to worry about any more, except
sometimes in the night one of the children screamed in a nightmare,
and they both hustled out shaking and hunting for the matches and
calling, "There, wait a minute, here we are!" John, get the doctor now,
Hapsy's time has come. But there was Hapsy standing by the bed in a
white cap. "Cornelia, tell Hapsy to take off her cap. I can't see her
plain."

Her eyes opened very wide and the room stood out like a picture
she had seen somewhere. Dark colors with the shadows rising towards
the ceiling in long angles. The tall black dresser gleamed with nothing
on it but John's picture, enlarged from a little one, with John's eyes very
black when they should have been blue. You never saw him, so how do
you know how he looked? But the man insisted the copy was perfect, it
was very rich and handsome. For a picture, yes, but it's not my husband.
The table by the bed had a linen cover and a candle and a crucifix. The
light was blue from Cornelia's silk lampshades. No sort of light at all,
just frippery. You had to live forty years with kerosene lamps to appreciate honest electricity. She felt very strong and she saw Doctor Harry
with a rosy nimbus around him.

"You look like a saint, Doctor Harry, and I vow that's as near as
you'll ever come to it."

"She's saying something."

"I heard you, Cornelia. What's all this carrying-on?"

55   "Father Connolly's saying—"

Cornelia's voice staggered and bumped like a cart in a bad road. It
rounded corners and turned back again and arrived nowhere. Granny
stepped up in the cart very lightly and reached for the reins, but a man
sat beside her and she knew him by his hands, driving the cart. She did
not look in his face, for she knew without seeing, but looked instead
down the road where the trees leaned over and bowed to each other
and a thousand birds were singing a Mass. She felt like singing too, but

she put her hand in the bosom of her dress and pulled out a rosary, and Father Connolly murmured Latin in a very solemn voice and tickled her feet. My God, will you stop that nonsense? I'm a married woman. What if he did run away and leave me to face the priest by myself? I found another a whole world better. I wouldn't have exchanged my husband for anybody except St. Michael himself, and you may tell him that for me with a thank you in the bargain.

Light flashed on her closed eyelids, and a deep roaring shook her. Cornelia, is that lightning? I hear thunder. There's going to be a storm. Close all the windows. Call the children in. . . . "Mother, here we are, all of us." "Is that you, Hapsy?" "Oh, no, I'm Lydia. We drove as fast as we could." Their faces drifted above her, drifted away. The rosary fell out of her hands and Lydia put it back. Jimmy tried to help, their hands fumbled together, and Granny closed two fingers around Jimmy's thumb. Beads wouldn't do, it must be something alive. She was so amazed her thoughts ran round and round. So, my dear Lord, this is my death and I wasn't even thinking about it. My children have come to see me die. But I can't, it's not time. Oh, I always hated surprises. I wanted to give Cornelia the amethyst set—Cornelia, you're to have the amethyst set, but Hapsy's to wear it when she wants, and, Doctor Harry, do shut up. Nobody sent for you. Oh, my dear Lord, do wait a minute. I meant to do something about the Forty Acres, Jimmy doesn't need it and Lydia will later on, with that worthless husband of hers. I meant to finish the altar cloth and send six bottles of wine to Sister Borgia for her dyspepsia. I want to send six bottles of wine to Sister Borgia, Father Connolly, now don't let me forget.

Cornelia's voice made short turns and tilted over and crashed. "Oh, Mother, oh, Mother, oh, Mother. . . ."

"I'm not going, Cornelia. I'm taken by surprise. I can't go."

You'll see Hapsy again. What about her? "I thought you'd never come." Granny made a long journey outward, looking for Hapsy. What if I don't find her? What then? Her heart sank down and down, there was no bottom to death, she couldn't come to the end of it. The blue light from Cornelia's lampshade drew into a tiny point in the center of her brain, it flickered and winked like an eye, quietly it fluttered and dwindled. Granny lay curled down within herself, amazed and watchful, staring at the point of light that was herself; her body was now only a deeper mass of shadow in an endless darkness and this darkness would curl around the light and swallow it up. God, give a sign!

For the second time there was no sign. Again no bridegroom and the priest in the house. She could not remember any other sorrow because this grief wiped them all away. Oh, no, there's nothing more cruel

60

than this—I'll never forgive it. She stretched herself with a deep breath
and blew out the light.

QUESTIONS

1. Why is stream of consciousness appropriate in this story? What characteristics of Ellen Weatherall's condition does this narrative technique represent? How effectively does it reveal events of the past? How clearly does it reflect the present? What is gained by the lack of clarity?
2. The protagonist reveals herself to be in conflict with other persons, and with her physical environment, both in the past and in the present. Identify her antagonists. To what extent has she experienced conflicts within herself? To what extent is she now experiencing such conflicts?
3. What does her memory present as the major turning points in her life? Is it more than a coincidence that one of them occurs every twenty years? Considering the many major events in a woman's life that might have been climactic, how do the ones she recalls so vividly define her character?
4. What kind of life has Granny Weatherall made for herself? What have been her characteristic activities and attitudes? Can her "jilting" be seen as a partial cause for these activities and attitudes?
5. What is the significance of Hapsy? What religious symbolism is attached to the vision of her and her infant son (paragraph 41)?
6. Most critics understand the title to refer to two "jiltings," the one by her fiancé sixty years earlier, the other by God at the moment of her death. Can you justify this interpretation? Does the story have a determinate or indeterminate ending?

Ernest Hemingway

Hills Like White Elephants

The hills across the valley of the Ebro were long and white. On this side there was no shade and no trees and the station was between two lines of rails in the sun. Close against the side of the station there was the warm shadow of the building and a curtain, made of strings of bamboo beads, hung across the open door into the bar, to keep out flies. The American and the girl with him sat at a table in the shade, outside the building. It was very hot and the express from Barcelona would come

HILLS LIKE WHITE ELEPHANTS First published in 1927. Ernest Hemingway (1899–1961) was born and grew up in Oak Park, Illinois, with summer vacations in northern Michigan. By the time he wrote this story he had been wounded in Italy during World War I; had traveled extensively in Europe as a newspaper correspondent and writer; had married, fathered a son, been divorced, and remarried.

in forty minutes. It stopped at this junction for two minutes and went on to Madrid.

"What should we drink?" the girl asked. She had taken off her hat and put it on the table.

"It's pretty hot," the man said.

"Let's drink beer."

"Dos cervezas," the man said into the curtain.   5

"Big ones?" a woman asked from the doorway.

"Yes. Two big ones."

The woman brought two glasses of beer and two felt pads. She put the felt pads and beer glasses on the table and looked at the man and the girl. The girl was looking off at the line of hills. They were white in the sun and the country was brown and dry.

"They look like white elephants," she said.

"I've never seen one," the man drank his beer.   10

"No, you wouldn't have."

"I might have," the man said. "Just because you say I wouldn't have doesn't prove anything."

The girl looked at the bead curtain. "They've painted something on it," she said "What does it say?"

"Anis del Toro. It's a drink."

"Could we try it?"   15

The man called "Listen" through the curtain. The woman came out from the bar.

"Four reales."

"We want two Anis del Toro."

"With water?"

"Do you want it with water?"   20

"I don't know," the girl said. "Is it good with water?"

"It's all right."

"You want them with water?" asked the woman.

"Yes, with water."

"It tastes like licorice," the girl said and put the glass down.   25

"That's the way with everything."

"Yes," said the girl. "Everything tastes of licorice. Especially all the things you've waited so long for, like absinthe."

"Oh, cut it out."

"You started it," the girl said. "I was being amused. I was having a fine time."

"Well, let's try to have a fine time."   30

"All right. I was trying. I said the mountains looked like white elephants. Wasn't that bright?"

"That was bright."

"I wanted to try this new drink. That's all we do, isn't it—look at things and try new drinks."

"I guess so."

35   The girl looked across at the hills.

"They're lovely hills," she said. "They don't really look like white elephants. I just meant the coloring of their skin through the trees."

"Should we have another drink?"

"All right."

The warm wind blew the bead curtain against the table.

40   "The beer's nice and cool," the man said.

"It's lovely," the girl said.

"It's really an awfully simple operation, Jig," the man said. "It's not really an operation at all."

The girl looked at the ground the table legs rested on.

"I know you wouldn't mind it, Jig. It's really not anything. It's just to let the air in."

45   The girl did not say anything.

"I'll go with you and I'll stay with you all the time. They just let the air in and then it's all perfectly natural."

"Then what will we do afterward?"

"We'll be fine afterward. Just like we were before."

"What makes you think so?"

50   "That's the only thing that bothers us. It's the only thing that's made us unhappy."

The girl looked at the bead curtain, put her hand out and took hold of two strings of beads.

"And you think then we'll be all right and be happy."

"I know we will. You don't have to be afraid. I've known lots of people that have done it."

"So have I," said the girl. "And afterward they were all so happy."

55   "Well," the man said. "if you don't want to you don't have to. I wouldn't have you do it if you didn't want to. But I know it's perfectly simple."

"And you really want to?"

"I think it's the best thing to do. But I don't want you to do it if you don't really want to."

"And if I do it you'll be happy and things will be like they were and you'll love me?"

"I love you now. You know I love you."

60   "I know. But if I do it, then it will be nice again if I say things are like white elephants, and you'll like it?"

"I'll love it. I love it now but I just can't think about it. You know how I get when I worry."

"If I do it you won't ever worry."

"I won't worry about that because it's perfectly simple."

"Then I'll do it. Because I don't care about me."

"What do you mean?"   65

"I don't care about me."

"Well, I care about you."

"Oh yes. But I don't care about me. And I'll do it and then everything will be fine."

"I don't want you to do it if you feel that way."

The girl stood up and walked to the end of the station. Across, on   70
the other side, were fields of grain and trees along the banks of the Ebro. Far away, beyond the river, were mountains. The shadow of a cloud moved across the field of grain and she saw the river through the trees.

"And we could have all this," she said. "And we could have everything and every day we make it more impossible."

"What did you say?"

"I said we could have everything."

"We can have everything."

"No, we can't."   75

"We can have the whole world."

"No, we can't."

"We can go everywhere."

"No, we can't. It isn't ours any more."

"It's ours."   80

"No, it isn't. And once they take it away, you never get it back."

"But they haven't taken it away."

"We'll wait and see."

"Come on back in the shade," he said. "You mustn't feel that way."

"I don't feel any way," the girl said. "I just know things."   85

"I don't want you to do anything that you don't want to do—"

"Nor that isn't good for me," she said. "I know. Could we have another beer."

"All right. But you've got to realize—"

"I realize," the girl said. "Can't we stop talking?"

They sat down at the table and the girl looked across at the hills   90
on the dry side of the valley and the man looked at her and at the table.

"You've got to realize," he said, "that I don't want you to do it if you don't want to. I'm perfectly willing to go through with it if it means anything to you."

"Doesn't it mean anything to you? We could get along."

"Of course it does. But I don't want anybody but you. I don't want any one else. And I know it's perfectly simple."

"Yes, you know it's perfectly simple."

95   "It's all right for you to say that, but I do know it."

"Would you do something for me now?"

"I'd do anything for you."

"Would you please please please please please please please stop talking?"

He did not say anything but looked at the bags against the wall of the station. There were labels on them from all the hotels where they had spent nights.

100   "But I don't want you to," he said. "I don't care anything about it."

"I'll scream," said the girl.

The woman came out through the curtains with two glasses of beer and put them down on the damp felt pads. "The train comes in five minutes," she said.

"What did she say?" asked the girl.

"That the train is coming in five minutes."

105   The girl smiled brightly at the woman, to thank her.

"I'd better take the bags over to the other side of the station," the man said. She smiled at him.

"All right. Then come back and we'll finish the beer."

He picked up the two heavy bags and carried them around the station to the other tracks. He looked up the tracks but could not see the train. Coming back, he walked through the barroom, where people waiting for the train were drinking. He drank an Anis at the bar and looked at the people. They were all waiting reasonably for the train. He went out through the bead curtain. She was sitting at the table and smiled at him.

"Do you feel better?" he asked.

110   "I feel fine," she said. "There's nothing wrong with me. I feel fine."

QUESTIONS

1. The main topic of discussion between the man and the girl is never named. What is the "awfully simple operation"? Why is it not named? What different attitudes are taken toward it by the man and the girl? Why?

2. What is indicated about the past life of the man and the girl? How? What has happened to the quality of their relationship? Why? How do we know? How accurate is the man's judgment about their future?

3. Though the story consists mostly of dialogue, and though it contains strong emotional conflict, it is entirely without adverbs indicating the tone of the

remarks. How does Hemingway indicate tone? At what points are the characters insincere? Self-deceived? Ironic or sarcastic? To what extent do they give open expression to their feelings? Does either want an open conflict? Why or why not? Trace the various phases of emotion in the girl.

4. How sincere is the man in his insistence that he would not have the girl undergo the operation if she does not want to and that he is "perfectly willing to go through with it" if it means anything to the girl? What is "it"? How many times does he repeat these ideas? What significance has the man's drinking an Anis by himself before rejoining the girl at the end of the story?

5. Much of the conversation seems to be about trivial things (ordering drinks, the weather, and so on). What purposes does this conversation serve? What relevance has the girl's remark about absinthe?

6. What is the point of the girl's comparison of the hills to white elephants? Does the remark assume any significance for the reader beyond its significance for the characters? Why does the author use it for his title?

7. What purpose does the setting serve—the hills across the valley, the treeless railroad tracks and station? What is contributed by the precise information about time at the end of the first paragraph?

8. Which of the two characters is more "reasonable"? Which "wins" the conflict between them? The point of view is objective. Does this mean that we cannot tell whether the sympathy of the author lies more with one character than with the other? Explain your answer.

SUGGESTIONS FOR WRITING

1. Compare the effectiveness of first-person point of view in any two of the following stories. What contrasting effects do the authors achieve from the different ways they use the first person?
   a. Munro, "How I Met My Husband" (page 125).
   b. Faulkner, "A Rose for Emily" (page 556).
   c. Melville, "Bartleby the Scrivener" (page 579).
   d. Poe, "The Cask of Amontillado" (page 611).

2. Compare/contrast the use of third-person point of view in any two of the following stories. Does the author use objective, omniscient, or limited? Why is the particular point of view appropriate to each story? Focus on scenes in which the chosen point of view is especially effective.
   a. Wolff, "Hunters in the Snow" (page 86).
   b. Lahiri, "Interpreter of Maladies" (page 141).
   c. Mansfield, "Miss Brill" (page 175).
   d. Joyce, "Eveline" (page 442).
   e. Hawthorne, "Young Goodman Brown" (page 299).
   f. García Márquez, "A Very Old Man with Enormous Wings" (page 327).
   g. Oates, "Where Are You Going, Where Have You Been?" (page 311).
   h. Allen, "The Kugelmass Episode" (page 348).
   i. Jackson, "The Lottery" (page 251).

Chapter Six

Symbol, Allegory, and Fantasy

Most successful stories are characterized by compression. The writer's aim is to say as much as possible as briefly as possible. This does not mean that most good stories are brief. It means only that nothing is wasted and that the author chooses each word and detail carefully for maximum effectiveness.

Talented authors achieve compression by exercising a careful selectivity. They choose the details and incidents essential to the story they have to tell and they eliminate any that do not contribute to the unified effect of the story. Because every element in a story must do as much as possible, some details and incidents may serve a variety of purposes at once. A detail that illustrates character at the same time that it advances plot is more useful than a detail that does only one or the other.

Three of the many resources available to writers for achieving compression are symbol, allegory, and fantasy. To varying degrees, each of these techniques is a way to depart from the strict adherence to factual language and representation of the kind a journalist uses, for instance, in writing a newspaper story. By modifying, enhancing, and at times even abandoning such a factual or realistic approach to storytelling, an author can increase the emotional force and resonance of a story, suggesting a much larger and richer meaning than might be achieved with a strictly realistic approach. But such narrative strategies also require close attention on the reader's part.

A literary **symbol** is something that means *more* than what it suggests on the surface. It may be an object, a person, a situation, an action, or some other element that has a literal meaning in the story but that suggests or represents other meanings as well. A very simple illustration is that of name symbolism. Most names are simply labels. A name, for instance, does not tell much about the person to whom it is attached, except possibly the individual's nationality or, in the case of first names, the person's gender. In a story, however, authors may choose names for their characters that not only label them but also suggest something about them. In "A Worn Path," for instance, the name "Phoenix" has several meanings that are relevant to Welty's character. In Egyptian mythology, a phoenix was a bird that consumed itself by fire after five hundred years, but then rose from its own ashes. It was also employed as a Christian symbol of death and resurrection in the art and architecture of the medieval period. Authors have often used this bird to suggest magical powers of renewal and endurance, and this meaning certainly relates to Phoenix Jackson's enduring love for her grandson. More generally, a phoenix also means a person of particular excellence, a meaning also applicable to Welty's protagonist. In "Everyday Use," Dee's rejection of her name and adoption of the alternative "Wangero" symbolizes for her a changed perspective on her heritage. The name of General Zaroff in "The Most Dangerous Game" is fitting for a former "officer of the Czar" who now behaves like a czar himself. Trevor's name in Greene's "The Destructors" suggests his upper-class origins. Equally meaningful in that story is the name of the Wormsley Common Gang. First, the word "Common," here designating a small public park or green, also suggests the "common people" or the lower middle and laboring classes as opposed to the upper class. More significant, when Trevor advocates his plan for gutting the old house—"We'd do it from inside. . . . We'd be like worms, don't you see, in an apple" (paragraph 52), we see that Greene's choice of the name Wormsley was quite deliberate and that it is appropriate also (as well as perfectly natural) that Wormsley Common should have an Underground Station. (The word "apple," in Trevor's speech, also has symbolic resonances. Though it is often a mistake to push symbolism too hard, the reader may well ask whether anything would be lost if Trevor had compared the gang's activities to those of worms in a peach or a pear.)

More important than name symbolism is the symbolic use of objects and actions. In some stories these symbols will fit so naturally into the literal context that their symbolic value will not at first be apparent except to the most perceptive reader. In other stories—usually stories with a less realistic surface—they will be so central and so obvious that they will demand symbolical interpretation if the story is to yield significant meaning. In the first kind of story the symbols *reinforce* and *add* to the meaning. In the second kind of story they *carry* the meaning.

Eudora Welty's "A Worn Path" superficially concerns a very old woman who walks from the back country into the city, encountering a variety of obstacles on her trip, in order to receive a bottle of soothing medicine from a charity clinic for her chronically ill grandson. The story has the familiar structure of a journey or quest and, in the old woman's ability to overcome or avert the dangers that she faces, a kind of mythic power that might remind us of *The Odyssey* or *Pilgrim's Progress*. It is a story of valor, purposefulness, and triumph, as the abiding love of the protagonist gives her the strength and shrewdness to achieve her goal.

But the symbolic meaning is more profound and moving. There are two predominant sets of symbols in the story, one made apparent by repetition, the other gradually developed by realistic details that build by accretion. The first is initially suggested by the symbolic name of the protagonist, "Phoenix" (not uncommon for a black woman in the south at the time of the story). In this example of name symbolism the character thus embodies such qualities as great age, pertinacity, persistence, and the magical ability to renew herself and regain strength and vigor.

Name symbolism, however, is only a beginning point in interpreting "A Worn Path." It adds grandeur to an otherwise apparently insignificant person, but it also initiates the repetitive references to birds that fill the story. At the onset of her trip, Phoenix's tapping of her cane sounds like "the chirping of a solitary little bird"; as she begins her journey, she warns "little bobwhites" to avoid being underfoot; and when she hears the "mourning dove" still crying down in the hollow, she symbolically interprets it as a parallel to herself: it too has persisted into the winter season. A buzzard among "big dead trees" she interprets as a reminder of death—and she brusquely dismisses it by asking, "'Who you watching?'" When she encounters a scarecrow, she first mistakes it for a mysterious dancing man, then for a ghost. As a bird herself she is "scared" by it, then identifies it for what it is and dances with it while corn husks "whirl in streamers about her skirts," a festive dance of triumph over this enemy of birds. Immediately after, as she escapes from the "maze" of the dead cornfield into a familiar wagon track, the "quail . . . walking around like pullets, seeming all dainty and unseen" reinforce her victory over fear and confusion.

The next bird that Phoenix sees is one of those same quail, now called "bobwhite," in the hunter's bag, with "a little closed claw" and "its beak hooked bitterly to show it was dead," a symbol of the genuine dangers that all mortal birds may face—but not Phoenix, who is not frightened by the foolish, callous hunter pointing his gun at her.

Birds thus symbolize for Phoenix the dangers and the delights of her life, both past and present. They are a well-known population of her world, and all of them embody some meaning for her. She is an interpreter of symbols. She feels protective and pitying toward the vulnerable, and she scorns and dismisses the threatening. There is one bird, however, that truly disturbs her. When by her ruse of inciting a dog-fight so as to pick up the nickel dropped by the hunter (who later lies to her about having any money, pretending he wishes to be charitable), Phoenix looks up as she puts the coin in her pocket and sees "a bird [fly] by." Her interpretation links bird-life to faith and morality: "'God watching me the whole time. I come to stealing.'" What birds know and do is to her an intimation of God's commandments and love.

At the climax of the story, one final symbolic reference to birds reveals the central meaning of the story. After a momentary memory lapse at the charity clinic, Phoenix focuses again on the purpose of her trip, to relieve the suffering of her grandson. "'We is the only two left in the world,'" she says, meaning that the two of them are the last of their family but also implying their mutual need to sustain each other. She goes on, "He wear a little patch quilt and peep out holding his mouth open like a little bird." She is confident that the two of them are "going to last," the loving spirit of Phoenix ever renewing itself, and the innocent "sweet" child always needing and receiving her self-sacrifice.

There is another symbolic frame of reference in this story, not so obvious but perhaps just as important. While the bird symbolism enlarges the meaning of Phoenix's trip to embrace enduring human values that transcend time and place, the story also symbolizes the historical and cultural issue of racial division in America at the time of its writing and in the years before and since the Civil War. Phoenix, who "'was too old at the Surrender'" (1865) to attend school, and now at over 100 is the oldest person she knows about, spans in her lifetime the period of slavery, emancipation, its aftermath during the Reconstruction, and the era of Jim Crow laws in the south and prejudice and bigotry throughout the country. A diligent reading will reveal a constant recurrence of "black" and "white" as words, as implied appearances, and even as moral abstractions. Because they are not always easily associated with right and wrong, good and evil, the references do not constitute an allegorical system but rather a repeated reminder of black-white oppositions. The first of these will suggest the subtlety of this symbolism: in the initial description of Phoenix's appearance, the narrator points out that the hair of this centenarian, falling on her neck "in the frailest of ringlets . . . [is] still black." Contrary to natural expectations, her hair has not turned *white,* and her racial identity is intact. Following this implied contrast of black and white, the careful reader will discover many explicit or implicit references to these colors.

Symbolically, the most impressive and touching example occurs during Phoenix's dream as she rests after the ordeal of crossing the creek. She sits down, spreads out her skirts, and assumes a girlish posture as she looks around: "Up above her was a tree in a pearly cloud of mistletoe. She did not dare to close her eyes, and when a little boy brought her a plate with a slice of marble-cake on it she spoke to him. 'That would be acceptable,' she said. But when she went to take it there was just her hand in the air." Here, as if from heaven itself (where the "pearly" gates are as white as the garments of the angels themselves), a "little boy" (perhaps reminiscent of her grandson) offers her a delicacy that displays a perfect mixing of light and dark, a promised harmony of sweet equality—but not yet, not in real life. Phoenix's understated acceptance of it as a gift offered rather than a right demanded is characteristic of the humble gratitude for small advances that was all too common at the time of the story. As a black woman, she has endured and she will keep enduring the vicissitudes of social change, a reminder of love as a remedy for hatred.

Another example of symbolic setting and action is presented in Hemingway's "Hills Like White Elephants," in which a man and a girl sit waiting for the train to Madrid, where the girl is to have an abortion. But the girl is not fully persuaded that she wants an abortion (at the deepest levels of her being, she does not). The man is aware of this and seeks to reassure her: "It's really an awfully simple operation. . . . It's not really an operation at all. . . . But I don't want you to do it if you don't really want to." The man *does* want her to do it even if she doesn't really want to; nevertheless, the decision is not irrevocable. They are at a railroad junction, a place where one can change directions. Symbolically it represents a juncture where they can change the direction of their lives. Their bags, with "labels on them from all the hotels where they had spent nights," indicate the kind of rootless, pleasure-seeking existence without responsibility they have hitherto lived. The man wants the girl to have the abortion so that they can go on living as they have before.

The railway station is situated in a river valley between two mountain ranges. On one side of the valley there is no shade and no trees and the country is "brown and dry." It is on this side, "the dry side," that the station sits in the heat, "between two lines of rails." It is also this side that the couple see from their table and that prompts the girl's remark that the hills look "like white elephants." On the other side of the valley, which the girl can see when she walks to the end of the station, lies the river, with "fields of grain and trees" along its banks, the "shadow of a cloud" moving across a field of grain, and another range of mountains in the distance. Looking in this direction, the girl remarks, "And we could have all this." The two landscapes, on opposite sides of the valley, have symbolic meaning in relation to the decision that the girl is being asked to reconfirm. The hot arid side of the valley represents sterility; the other side, with water in the river and the cloud, a hint of coolness in the cloud's moving shadow, and growing things along the river banks, represents fertility. The girl's remark about this other side shows a conscious recognition of its symbolism.

But what does the girl mean by her remark that the mountains on the dry side of the valley look "like white elephants"? Perhaps nothing at all. It is intended as a "bright" remark, a clever if far-fetched comparison made to amuse the man, as it would have in their earlier days together. But whether or not the girl means anything by it, almost certainly Hemingway means something. Or perhaps several things. Clearly the child begun in the girl's womb is a "white elephant" for the man, who says, "I don't want anybody but you. I don't want any one else." For the girl, on the other hand, the abortion itself, the decision to continue living as they have been living, without responsibility, may be considered a "white elephant." We already know that this life has lost its savor for her. When she remarks that the Anis del Toro "tastes like licorice," the man's response—"that's the way with everything"—is probably meant to apply only to the drink and food in this section of the country, but the girl's confirmation of his observation seems to enlarge its meaning to the whole life they have been living together, which consists, she says, only of looking at things and trying new drinks. Thus the licorice flavor, suggesting tedium and disillusion, joins the "hills like white elephants," the opposed sides of the river valley, and the railroad junction in a network of symbols that intensify the meaning and impact of the story.

The ability to recognize and identify symbols requires perception and tact. The great danger facing readers when they first become aware of symbolic values is a tendency to run wild—to find symbols everywhere and to read into the details of a story all sorts of fanciful meanings not legitimately supported by it. But we need to remember that most stories operate almost wholly at the literal level and that even in highly symbolic stories, the majority of the details are purely literal. A story is not an excuse for an exercise in ingenuity. It is better, indeed, to miss the symbolic meanings of a story than to pervert its meaning by discovering symbols that are nonexistent. Better to miss the boat than to jump wildly for it and drown.

The ability to interpret symbols is nevertheless essential for a full understanding of literature. Readers should always be alert for symbolic meanings but should observe the following cautions:

1. The story itself must furnish a clue that a detail is to be taken symbolically. In Mansfield's story, Miss Brill's fur is given prominence at

the beginning of the story, when it is taken out of its box; at the climax of the story, when the girl on the bench compares it to "a fried whiting"; and at the end of the story, when Miss Brill puts it back in the box and thinks she hears it crying. The fur is clearly a symbol for Miss Brill herself. It comes out of a box like a dark little room or a cupboard, it is old and in need of repair, it is ridiculed by the boy and the girl on the park bench, and it is returned to its box at the end of the story. Symbolically, it is herself whom Miss Brill hears crying. In Welty's story, the repetition of references to birds, including the name of the protagonist, signals the need to interpret them symbolically. The title "A Worn Path" explicitly refers to Phoenix's repeated journeys, and by implication symbolizes the journeys of her race toward love and full acceptance. Both items are emphasized and significant to the meaning of the story, but neither is essential to its plot. Even greater emphasis is given to the quilts in the story by Walker. Symbols nearly always signal their existence by *emphasis, repetition,* or *position.* In the absence of such signals, we should be reluctant to identify an item as symbolic.

2. The meaning of a literary symbol must be established and supported by the entire context of the story. The symbol has its meaning *in* the story, not *outside* it. For instance, in "A Worn Path," the meaning of the "pearly cloud of mistletoe" is supported by and dependent on its relation to other references within the story establishing the correlations between black and white and the dreams that Phoenix harbors. In another context a cloud of mistletoe might connote parasitism and the death of the host tree. Here, associated as it is with a proffered gift of delight from on high, the symbol reinforces Phoenix's faith and reliance on God's will.

3. To be called a symbol, an item must suggest a meaning different in *kind* from its literal meaning; a symbol is something more than the representative of a class or type. Miss Brill, for instance, is an old, odd, silent, friendless person, set in her ways, who does not realize (until the climax of the story) that she herself is old, odd, and set in her ways— like other elderly people she observes in the park each Sunday. But to say this is to say no more than that the story has a theme. Every literary story suggests a generalization about life, is more than an accounting of the specific fortunes of specific individuals. There is no point, therefore, in calling Miss Brill a *symbol* of odd, self-deluded elderly people; she *is* an odd, self-deluded elderly person: a member of the class of odd, self-deluded elderly persons. Her fur is a symbol, but she is not. We ought not to use the phrase *is a symbol of* when we can easily use *is,* or *is an example of* or *is an evidence of.* Phoenix Jackson, in "A Worn Path," through the symbolic associations attached to her name, is clearly

meant to be something more than an *example* of any class or race of human beings, or of humanity in general; she is a symbol of something *within* the human spirit, of hidden possibilities latent in many people.

The quilts in Alice Walker's "Everyday Use" are *evidence* that the family has been enslaved and impoverished, evidence of a past that Dee is proud to have escaped. To her, they are valuable as artifacts of oppression. In the story, however, they *symbolize* a wealth beyond money in the family's linkages to an authentic heritage of craftsmanship and beauty.

4. A symbol may have more than one meaning. It may suggest a cluster of meanings. At its most effective, a symbol is like a many-faceted jewel: it flashes different colors when turned in the light. This is not to say that it can mean anything we want it to: the area of possible meanings is always controlled by the context. Nevertheless, this possibility of complex meaning plus concreteness and emotional power gives the symbol its peculiar compressive value. The path in Welty's story symbolizes life itself, including its obstacles, its habits, its occasional moments of humor, pain, and beauty, and above all its nature as a journey human beings must undertake with as much courage and dignity as possible, motivated by love. The quilts in Walker's story have an equally wide range of meaning—inherited values, family attachments, independence and self-reliance, the beauty of useful objects, the virtue of craftsmanship—all in contrast to the shallow, monetary meaning expressed in Dee's acquisitive demand for them. When she says, "But they're *priceless!*" she means that they are worth a great deal of money, but in the truer sense their symbolic values cannot be reckoned at any price. The meaning is not confined to any one of these qualities: it is all of them, and therein lies the symbol's value.

An **allegory** is a story that has a second meaning beneath the surface, endowing a cluster of characters, objects, or events with added significance; often the pattern relates each literal item to a corresponding abstract idea or moral principle. It is different from symbolism in that it puts less emphasis on the literal meanings and more on the ulterior meanings. Also, those ulterior meanings are more fixed, and they usually constitute a pre-existing system of ideas or principles. Medieval and Renaissance religious allegories, for instance, were intended to illustrate the progress of a typical Christian individual through life, as in the medieval play *Everyman* and in John Bunyan's *Pilgrim's Progress*, a seventeenth-century work in which a character named "Christian" journeys toward salvation, encountering along the way such temptations as despair, labeled "The Slough of Despond," and witnessing human hypocrisy in a town called "Fair Speech." Probably the most widely read allegorical work today is Nathaniel Hawthorne's novel *The Scarlet Letter* (1850). Although Hawthorne's novel, like most more modern allegories, eschews the mechanical, one-to-one correspondences found in older allegorical works (which were written more for religious or political than literary purposes), he does provide a coherent system that evokes and critiques the seventeenth-century Puritan world in which the novel is set. The novel's allegorical pattern includes the scarlet "A" for adultery that Hester Prynne wears on her dress; the names of her husband, Chillingworth, and her daughter, Pearl; Hester's uneasy residence on the border between the wilderness, representing natural impulses, and the "civilized" Puritan culture that ostracizes her. In this chapter, Hawthorne's story "Young Goodman Brown" has a similar allegorical pattern. The title character, as his name suggests, is a typical young and virtuous man; his surname "Brown," like "Smith" in America today, is the most common name during his era, again suggesting his identity as a representative individual. His wife, "Faith," represents the steadfast virtue he is leaving behind during his journey into the wilderness, just as her pink ribbons suggest her innocence. During a crisis point in the story, Brown shouts "My Faith is gone!" and the allegorical meaning is clear, for he is talking simultaneously about his literal wife and the abstraction of his religious faith. Other elements in the story—the old man's staff that begins "writhing" like a serpent, the wilderness itself with its suggestions of moral chaos and depravity—likewise fulfill roles in Hawthorne's allegory.

It should be stressed, however, that an author employing allegory usually does not intend simply to create two levels of reality, one literal and one abstract, which readers merely identify as though connecting a series of dots. Serious writers often introduce an element of ambiguity into their allegorical meanings, undercutting easy and simplistic interpretation. For example, in Hawthorne's story, Brown's innocent wife Faith pleads with her husband not to undertake the journey, observing, "A lone woman is troubled with such dreams and such thoughts that she's afeared of herself sometimes"—a bit of dialogue that suggests her identity as more than an abstract representation of faith but also as a flesh-and-blood woman who may well encounter her own temptations and psychological turmoil when separated from her husband.

The creation of an allegorical pattern of meaning enables an author to achieve power through economy. Reading a story, you should therefore be aware of an author's use of description and detail, for these may be present not only to create a sensual apprehension of a story's characters and settings, but also to suggest meanings—moral, intellectual, emotional—beyond that reality. This ability to compress a great deal of meaning into the relatively small canvas of a short story is part of what gives the best examples of this genre their powerful narrative impact.

While some stories use factual details to suggest additional, sometimes abstract, meanings, there is another type of story that abandons factual representation altogether. The nonrealistic story, or **fantasy,** is one that transcends the bounds of known reality. After all, truth in fiction is not the same as fidelity to fact. All fiction is essentially a game of make-believe in which the author imaginatively conceives characters and situations and sets them down on paper. The purpose of any literary artist is to communicate truths by means of imagined facts. While most authors, using realistic means, attempt to create an illusion of reality in telling their stories, careful to stay in the realm of the plausible and relate something that *could have happened,* sometimes an author chooses to go a step further and create a story that is entirely implausible or even impossible. Such stories require from the reader what the poet Samuel Taylor Coleridge called "a willing suspension of disbelief": that is, the reader is willing to accept the author's premise of a strange and marvelous world, in which a character falls down a rabbit hole or climbs up a beanstalk or finds himself in an alien spaceship. Such a fantasy story introduces human beings into a world where the ordinary laws of nature are suspended or superseded and where the landscape and its creatures are unfamiliar; or, on the other hand, it may introduce ghosts, fairies, dragons, werewolves, talking animals, Martian invaders, or miraculous occurrences into the recognizable, everyday world of human beings. A recently popular form of this second approach to fantasy has been called "magical realism," in which fantastic and magical events are woven into mundane and ordinary situations, creating striking and memorable effects unavailable to either realism or fantasy alone. Such popular forms of storytelling as fables, ghost stories, and science fiction are all types of fantasy. Like stories using symbolism and allegory, fantasy stories are often highly compressed, enabling the author to convey a richly textured, resonant vision within a relatively short narrative.

The story writer begins, then, by saying, "What if. . . ." "What if," for instance, "a young, somewhat naïve girl working in a farmhouse should meet a handsome pilot visiting the area and become infatuated with him." From this initial assumption the author goes on to develop a story ("How I Met My Husband"), which, though presumably imaginary in the sense that it never happened, nevertheless reveals convincingly to us some truths of human behavior.

But now, what if the author goes a step further and supposes not just something that might very well have happened (though it didn't) but something highly improbable—something that could happen, say, only as the result of a very surprising coincidence? What if he begins, "Let's suppose that a misogynist and a charming woman find themselves alone on a desert island"? This initial supposition causes us to stretch our imaginations a bit further, but is not this situation just as capable of revealing human truths as the former? The psychologist puts a rat in a maze (certainly an improbable situation for a rat), observes its reactions to the maze, and discovers some truth of rat behavior. The author may put imaginary characters on an imagined desert island, imaginatively study their reactions, and reveal some truth of human nature. The improbable initial situation may yield as much truth as the probable one.

From the improbable it is but one step further to the impossible (as we know it in this life). Why should our author not begin "Let's suppose that a miser and his termagant wife find themselves in hell" or "Let's suppose that a primitive scapegoat ritual still survives in contemporary America." Could not these situations also be used to exhibit human traits?

Like stories employing realistic characters and events, fantasies may be purely commercial entertainment or they may be serious literary works. A story about a spaceship on its way to a distant planet might be filled with stock characters or with richly imagined human beings; it may be designed chiefly to exhibit mechanical marvels and to provide thrills and adventures, or it may be a way of creating a setting in which human behavior can be sharply observed and studied. Fantasy, like other forms of fiction, may be employed sheerly for its own sake or as a means of communicating significant insights into the world of human beings. The important point to remember is that truth in fiction is not to be identified with a realistic method. Stories that fly on the wings of fantasy may be vehicles for truth that are as powerful in their own way as such realistic stories as "Hunters in the Snow" or "Interpreter of Maladies." Fantasy may employ the techniques of symbolism or allegory, or it may simply provide an exotic, nonrealistic setting as a way of observing human nature. Some of the world's greatest works of literature have been partly or wholly fantasy: *The Odyssey*, *The Divine Comedy*, *The Tempest*, *Pilgrim's Progress*, *Gulliver's Travels*, and *Alice in Wonderland* all offer profound and significant insights into the human condition.

Clearly, then, we must not judge a story as good or bad according to whether or not it stays within the limits of the possible. Rather, we should begin reading any story by suspending disbelief—that is, by granting every story its initial premise or assumption. The writer may begin with an ordinary, everyday situation or with a far-fetched, improbable coincidence. Or the writer may be allowed to suspend a law of nature or to create a marvelous being or machine or place. But once we have accepted an impossible reality as a premise, we have a right to demand probability and consistency in the author's treatment of it. Fantasy is not an excuse for haphazard writing or a poorly imagined story. We need to ask, too, for what reason the story employs fantasy. Is it used simply for its own strangeness, or for thrills or surprises or laughs? Or is it used to illuminate truths of the reader's own experience? What, finally, is the purpose of the author's fantastic invention? Is it, like a roller coaster, simply a machine for producing a temporary thrill? Or does it, like an observation balloon, provide a unique vantage point that may change our view of the world forever?

REVIEWING CHAPTER SIX

1. Review the definition of a literary symbol.
2. Explore the uses of symbolic names, objects, and actions.
3. Summarize the use of symbolism in Welty's "A Worn Path."
4. Distinguish between symbolism and allegory.
5. Describe the importance of ambiguity in a literary allegory.
6. Define the term "fantasy" and describe the prominent features of a fantastic story.

D. H. Lawrence

The Rocking-Horse Winner

There was a woman who was beautiful, who started with all the advantages, yet she had no luck. She married for love, and the love turned to dust. She had bonny children, yet she felt they had been thrust upon her, and she could not love them. They looked at her coldly, as if they were finding fault with her. And hurriedly she felt she must cover up some fault in herself. Yet what it was that she must cover up she never knew. Nevertheless, when her children were present, she always felt the center of her heart go hard. This troubled her, and in her manner she

THE ROCKING-HORSE WINNER   First published in 1933. D. H. Lawrence (1885–1930), son of a coal miner and a school teacher, was born and grew up in Nottinghamshire, England, was rejected for military service in World War I because of lung trouble, and lived most of his adult life abroad, including parts of three years in New Mexico.

was all the more gentle and anxious for her children, as if she loved them very much. Only she herself knew that at the center of her heart was a hard little place that could not feel love, no, not for anybody. Everybody else said of her: "She is such a good mother. She adores her children." Only she herself, and her children themselves, knew it was not so. They read it in each other's eyes.

There were a boy and two little girls. They lived in a pleasant house, with a garden, and they had discreet servants, and felt themselves superior to anyone in the neighborhood.

Although they lived in style, they felt always an anxiety in the house. There was never enough money. The mother had a small income, and the father had a small income, but not nearly enough for the social position which they had to keep up. The father went into town to some office. But though he had good prospects, these prospects never materialized. There was always the grinding sense of the shortage of money, though the style was always kept up.

At last the mother said: "I will see if I can't make something." But she did not know where to begin. She racked her brains, and tried this thing and the other, but could not find anything successful. The failure made deep lines come into her face. Her children were growing up, they would have to go to school. There must be more money, there must be more money. The father, who was always very handsome and expensive in his tastes, seemed as if he never would be able to do anything worth doing. And the mother, who had a great belief in herself, did not succeed any better, and her tastes were just as expensive.

5   And so the house came to be haunted by the unspoken phrase: There must be more money! There must be more money! The children could hear it all the time, though nobody said it aloud. They heard it at Christmas, when the expensive and splendid toys filled the nursery. Behind the shining modern rocking horse, behind the smart doll's-house, a voice would start whispering: "There must be more money! There must be more money!" And the children would stop playing, to listen for a moment. They would look into each other's eyes, to see if they had all heard. And each one saw in the eyes of the other two that they too had heard. "There must be more money! There must be more money!"

It came whispering from the springs of the still-swaying rocking horse, and even the horse, bending his wooden, champing head, heard it. The big doll, sitting so pink and smirking in her new pram, could hear it quite plainly, and seemed to be smirking all the more self-consciously because of it. The foolish puppy, too, that took the place of the Teddy bear, he was looking so extraordinarily foolish for no other reason but that he heard the secret whisper all over the house: "There must be more money!"

Yet nobody ever said it aloud. The whisper was everywhere, and therefore no one spoke it. Just as no one ever says: "We are breathing!" in spite of the fact that breath is coming and going all the time.

"Mother," said the boy Paul one day, "why don't we keep a car of our own? Why do we always use uncle's, or else a taxi?"

"Because we're the poor members of the family," said the mother.

"But why are we, mother?"   10

"Well—I suppose," she said slowly and bitterly, "it's because your father has no luck."

The boy was silent for some time.

"Is luck money, mother?" he asked, rather timidly.

"No, Paul. Not quite. It's what causes you to have money."

"Oh!" said Paul vaguely. "I thought when Uncle Oscar said filthy   15
lucker, it meant money."

"Filthy lucre° does mean money," said the mother. "But it's lucre, not luck."

"Oh!" said the boy. "Then what is luck, mother?"

"It's what causes you to have money. If you're lucky you have money. That's why it's better to be born lucky than rich. If you're rich, you may lose your money. But if you're lucky, you will always get more money."

"Oh! Will you? And is father not lucky?"

"Very unlucky, I should say," she said bitterly.   20

The boy watched her with unsure eyes.

"Why?" he asked.

"I don't know. Nobody ever knows why one person is lucky and another unlucky."

"Don't they? Nobody at all? Does nobody know?"

"Perhaps God. But He never tells."   25

"He ought to, then. And aren't you lucky either, mother?"

"I can't be, if I married an unlucky husband."

"But by yourself, aren't you?"

"I used to think I was, before I married. Now I think I am very unlucky indeed."

"Why?"   30

"Well—never mind! Perhaps I'm not really," she said.

The child looked at her, to see if she meant it. But he saw, by the lines of her mouth, that she was only trying to hide something from him.

---

filthy lucre: See New Testament, I Timothy 3:3.

"Well, anyhow," he said stoutly, "I'm a lucky person."

"Why?" said his mother, with a sudden laugh.

35   He stared at her. He didn't even know why he had said it.

"God told me," he asserted, brazening it out.

"I hope He did, dear!" she said, again with a laugh, but rather bitter.

"He did, mother!"

"Excellent!" said the mother, using one of her husband's exclamations.

40   The boy saw she did not believe him; or, rather, that she paid no attention to his assertion. This angered him somewhat, and made him want to compel her attention.

He went off by himself, vaguely, in a childish way, seeking for the clue to "luck." Absorbed, taking no heed of other people, he went about with a sort of stealth, seeking inwardly for luck. He wanted luck, he wanted it, he wanted it. When the two girls were playing dolls in the nursery, he would sit on his big rocking horse, charging madly into space, with a frenzy that made the little girls peer at him uneasily. Wildly the horse careered, the waving dark hair of the boy tossed, his eyes had a strange glare in them. The little girls dared not speak to him.

When he had ridden to the end of his mad little journey, he climbed down and stood in front of his rocking horse, staring fixedly into its lowered face. Its red mouth was slightly open, its big eye was wide and glassy-bright.

"Now!" he would silently command the snorting steed. "Now, take me to where there is luck! Now take me!"

And he would slash the horse on the neck with the little whip he had asked Uncle Oscar for. He knew the horse could take him to where there was luck, if only he forced it. So he would mount again, and start on his furious ride, hoping at last to get there. He knew he could get there.

45   "You'll break your horse, Paul!" said the nurse.

"He's always riding like that! I wish he'd leave off!" said his elder sister Joan.

But he only glared down on them in silence. Nurse gave him up. She could make nothing of him. Anyhow he was growing beyond her.

One day his mother and his Uncle Oscar came in when he was on one of his furious rides. He did not speak to them.

"Hallo, you young jockey! Riding a winner?" said his uncle.

50   "Aren't you growing too big for a rocking horse? You're not a very little boy any longer, you know," said his mother.

But Paul only gave a blue glare from his big, rather close-set eyes. He would speak to nobody when he was in full tilt. His mother watched him with an anxious expression on her face.

At last he suddenly stopped forcing his horse into the mechanical gallop, and slid down.

"Well, I got there!" he announced fiercely, his blue eyes still flaring, and his sturdy long legs straddling apart.

"Where did you get to?" asked his mother.

"Where I wanted to go," he flared back at her.   55

"That's right, son!" said Uncle Oscar. "Don't you stop till you get there. What's the horse's name?"

"He doesn't have a name," said the boy.

"Gets on without all right?" asked the uncle.

"Well, he has different names. He was called Sansovino last week."

"Sansovino, eh? Won the Ascot. How did you know his name?"   60

"He always talks about horse races with Bassett," said Joan.

The uncle was delighted to find that his small nephew was posted with all the racing news. Bassett, the young gardener, who had been wounded in the left foot in the war and got his present job through Oscar Cresswell, whose batman he had been, was a perfect blade of the "turf." He lived in the racing events, and the small boy lived with him.

Oscar Cresswell got it all from Bassett.

"Master Paul comes and asks me, so I can't do more than tell him, sir," said Bassett, his face terribly serious, as if he were speaking of religious matters.

"And does he ever put anything on a horse he fancies?"   65

"Well—I don't want to give him away—he's a young sport, a fine sport, sir. Would you mind asking him yourself? He sort of takes a pleasure in it, and perhaps he'd feel I was giving him away, sir, if you don't mind."

Bassett was serious as a church.

The uncle went back to his nephew, and took him off for a ride in the car.

"Say, Paul, old man, do you ever put anything on a horse?" the uncle asked.

The boy watched the handsome man closely.   70

"Why, do you think I oughtn't to?" he parried.

"Not a bit of it! I thought perhaps you might give me a tip for the Lincoln."

The car sped on into the country, going down to Uncle Oscar's place in Hampshire.

"Honor bright?" said the nephew.

75   "Honor bright, son!" said the uncle.
"Well, then, Daffodil."
"Daffodil! I doubt it, sonny. What about Mirza?"
"I only know the winner," said the boy. "That's Daffodil."
"Daffodil, eh?"
80   There was a pause. Daffodil was an obscure horse comparatively.
"Uncle!"
"Yes, son?"
"You won't let it go any further, will you? I promised Bassett."
"Bassett be damned, old man! What's he got to do with it?"
85   "We're partners. We've been partners from the first. Uncle, he lent
me my first five shillings, which I lost. I promised him, honor bright, it
was only between me and him; only you gave me that ten-shilling note
I started winning with, so I thought you were lucky. You won't let it go
any further, will you?"
The boy gazed at his uncle from those big, hot, blue eyes, set rather
close together. The uncle stirred and laughed uneasily.
"Right you are, son! I'll keep your tip private. Daffodil, eh? How
much are you putting on him?"
"All except twenty pounds," said the boy. "I keep that in reserve."
The uncle thought it a good joke.
90   "You keep twenty pounds in reserve, do you, you young romancer?
What are you betting, then?"
"I'm betting three hundred," said the boy gravely. "But it's between
you and me, Uncle Oscar! Honor bright?"
The uncle burst into a roar of laughter.
"It's between you and me all right, you young Nat Gould,"° he said,
laughing. "But where's your three hundred?"
"Bassett keeps it for me. We're partners."
95   "You are, are you! And what is Bassett putting on Daffodil?"
"He won't go quite as high as I do, I expect. Perhaps he'll go a hundred and fifty."
"What, pennies?" laughed the uncle.
"Pounds," said the child, with a surprised look at his uncle. "Bassett keeps a bigger reserve than I do."
Between wonder and amusement Uncle Oscar was silent. He pursued the matter no further, but he determined to take his nephew with
him to the Lincoln races.
100   "Now, son," he said, "I'm putting twenty on Mirza, and I'll put five
for you on any horse you fancy. What's your pick?"

Nat Gould: a journalist and novelist (1857–1919) who wrote about horse racing

"Daffodil, uncle."

"No, not the fiver on Daffodil!"

"I should if it was my own fiver," said the child.

"Good! Good! Right you are! A fiver for me and a fiver for you on Daffodil."

The child had never been to a race meeting before, and his eyes   105
were blue fire. He pursed his mouth tight, and watched. A Frenchman just in front had put his money on Lancelot. Wild with excitement, he flayed his arms up and down, yelling "Lancelot! Lancelot!" in his French accent.

Daffodil came in first, Lancelot second, Mirza third. The child, flushed and with eyes blazing, was curiously serene. His uncle brought him four five-pound notes, four to one.

"What am I to do with these?" he cried, waving them before the boy's eyes.

"I suppose we'll talk to Bassett," said the boy. "I expect I have fifteen hundred now; and twenty in reserve; and this twenty."

His uncle studied him for some moments.

"Look here, son!" he said. "You're not serious about Bassett and   110
that fifteen hundred, are you?"

"Yes, I am. But it's between you and me, uncle. Honor bright!"

"Honor bright all right, son! But I must talk to Bassett."

"If you'd like to be a partner, uncle, with Bassett and me, we could all be partners. Only, you'd have to promise, honor bright, uncle, not to let it go beyond us three. Bassett and I are lucky, and you must be lucky, because it was your ten shillings I started winning with . . ."

Uncle Oscar took both Bassett and Paul into Richmond Park for an afternoon, and there they talked.

"It's like this, you see, sir," Bassett said. "Master Paul would get me   115
talking about racing events, spinning yarns, you know, sir. And he was always keen on knowing if I'd made or if I'd lost. It's about a year since, now, that I put five shillings on Blush of Dawn for him—and we lost. Then the luck turned, with that ten shillings he had from you, that we put on Singhalese. And since that time, it's been pretty steady, all things considering. What do you say, Master Paul?"

"We're all right when we're sure," said Paul. "It's when we're not quite sure that we go down."

"Oh, but we're careful then," said Bassett.

"But when are you sure?" smiled Uncle Oscar.

"It's Master Paul, sir," said Bassett, in a secret, religious voice. "It's as if he had it from heaven. Like Daffodil, now, for the Lincoln. That was as sure as eggs."

120   "Did you put anything on Daffodil?" asked Oscar Cresswell.
       "Yes, sir, I made my bit."
       "And my nephew?"
       Bassett was obstinately silent, looking at Paul.
       "I made twelve hundred, didn't I, Bassett? I told uncle I was putting
three hundred on Daffodil."
125   "That's right," said Bassett, nodding.
       "But where's the money?" asked the uncle.
       "I keep it safe locked up, sir. Master Paul he can have it any minute
he likes to ask for it."
       "What, fifteen hundred pounds?"
       "And twenty! and forty, that is, with the twenty he made on the
course."
130   "It's amazing!" said the uncle.
       "If Master Paul offers you to be partners, sir, I would, if I were you;
if you'll excuse me," said Bassett.
       Oscar Cresswell thought about it.
       "I'll see the money," he said.
       They drove home again, and sure enough, Bassett came round to
the garden-house with fifteen hundred pounds in notes. The twenty
pounds reserve was left with Joe Glee, in the Turf Commission deposit.
135   "You see, it's all right, uncle, when I'm sure! Then we go strong, for
all we're worth. Don't we Bassett?"
       "We do that, Master Paul."
       "And when are you sure?" said the uncle, laughing.
       "Oh, well, sometimes I'm absolutely sure, like about Daffodil," said
the boy; "and sometimes I have an idea; and sometimes I haven't even
an idea, have I, Bassett? Then we're careful, because we mostly go
down."
       "You do, do you! And when you're sure, like about Daffodil, what
makes you sure, sonny?"
140   "Oh, well, I don't know," said the boy uneasily. "I'm sure, you
know, uncle; that's all."
       "It's as if he had it from heaven, sir," Bassett reiterated.
       "I should say so!" said the uncle.
       But he became a partner. And when the Leger was coming on, Paul
was "sure" about Lively Spark, which was a quite inconsiderable horse.
The boy insisted on putting a thousand on the horse, Bassett went for
five hundred, and Oscar Cresswell two hundred. Lively Spark came in
first, and the betting had been ten to one against him. Paul had made
ten thousand.
       "You see," he said, "I was absolutely sure of him."

Even Oscar Cresswell had cleared two thousand.   145

"Look here son," he said, "this sort of thing makes me nervous."

"It needn't, uncle! Perhaps I shan't be sure again for a long time."

"But what are you going to do with your money?" asked the uncle.

"Of course," said the boy, "I started it for mother. She said she had no luck, because father is unlucky, so I thought if I was lucky, it might stop whispering."

"What might stop whispering?"   150

"Our house. I hate our house for whispering."

"What does it whisper?"

"Why—why"—the boy fidgeted—"why, I don't know. But it's always short of money, you know, uncle."

"I know it, son, I know it."

"You know people send mother writs, don't you, uncle?"   155

"I'm afraid I do," said the uncle.

"And then the house whispers, like people laughing at you behind your back. It's awful, that is! I thought if I was lucky . . ."

"You might stop it," added the uncle.

The boy watched him with big blue eyes that had an uncanny cold fire in them, and he said never a word.

"Well, then!" said the uncle. "What are we doing?"   160

"I shouldn't like mother to know I was lucky," said the boy.

"Why not, son?"

"She'd stop me."

"I don't think she would."

"Oh!"—and the boy writhed in an odd way—"I don't want her to   165
know, uncle."

"All right, son! We'll manage it without her knowing."

They managed it very easily. Paul, at the other's suggestion, handed over five thousand pounds to his uncle, who deposited it with the family lawyer, who was then to inform Paul's mother that a relative had put five thousand pounds into his hands, which sum was to be paid out a thousand pounds at a time, on the mother's birthday, for the next five years.

"So she'll have a birthday present of a thousand pounds for five successive years," said Uncle Oscar. "I hope it won't make it all the harder for her later."

Paul's mother had her birthday in November. The house had been "whispering" worse than ever lately, and, even in spite of his luck, Paul could not bear up against it. He was very anxious to see the effect of the birthday letter telling his mother about the thousand pounds.

When there were no visitors, Paul now took his meals with his   170
parents, as he was beyond the nursery control. His mother went into

town nearly every day. She had discovered that she had an odd knack of sketching furs and dress materials, so she worked secretly in the studio of a friend who was the chief "artist" for the leading drapers. She drew the figures of ladies in furs and ladies in silk and sequins for the newspaper advertisements. This young woman artist earned several thousand pounds a year, but Paul's mother only made several hundreds, and she was again dissatisfied. She so wanted to be first in something, and she did not succeed, even in making sketches for drapery advertisements.

She was down to breakfast on the morning of her birthday. Paul watched her face as she read her letters. He knew the lawyer's letter. As his mother read it, her face hardened and became more expressionless. Then a cold, determined look came on her mouth. She hid the letter under the pile of others, and said not a word about it.

"Didn't you have anything nice in the post for your birthday, mother?" said Paul.

"Quite moderately nice," she said, her voice cold and absent.

She went away to town without saying more.

175   But in the afternoon Uncle Oscar appeared. He said Paul's mother had had a long interview with the lawyer, asking if the whole five thousand could be advanced at once, as she was in debt.

"What do you think, uncle?" said the boy.

"I leave it to you, son."

"Oh, let her have it, then! We can get some more with the other," said the boy.

"A bird in the hand is worth two in the bush, laddie!" said Uncle Oscar.

180   "But I'm sure to know for the Grand National; or the Lincolnshire; or else the Derby. I'm sure to know for one of them," said Paul.

So Uncle Oscar signed the agreement, and Paul's mother touched the whole five thousand. Then something very curious happened. The voices in the house suddenly went mad, like a chorus of frogs on a spring evening. There were certain new furnishings, and Paul had a tutor. He was really going to Eton,° his father's school, in the following autumn. There were flowers in the winter, and a blossoming of the luxury Paul's mother had been used to. And yet the voices in the house, behind the sprays of mimosa and almond blossom, and from under the piles of iridescent cushions, simply trilled and screamed in a sort of ecstasy: "There must be more money! Oh-h-h, there must be more money. Oh, now, now-w! Now-w-w—there must be more money—more than ever! More than ever!"

Eton: England's most prestigious privately supported school

It frightened Paul terribly. He studied away at his Latin and Greek with his tutor. But his intense hours were spent with Bassett. The Grand National had gone by: he had not "known," and had lost a hundred pounds. Summer was at hand. He was in agony for the Lincoln. But even for the Lincoln he didn't "know" and he lost fifty pounds. He became wild-eyed and strange, as if something were going to explode in him.

"Let it alone, son! Don't you bother about it!" urged Uncle Oscar. But it was as if the boy couldn't really hear what his uncle was saying.

"I've got to know for the Derby! I've got to know for the Derby!" the child reiterated, his big blue eyes blazing with a sort of madness.

His mother noticed how overwrought he was.   185

"You'd better go to the seaside. Wouldn't you like to go now to the seaside, instead of waiting? I think you'd better," she said, looking down at him anxiously, her heart curiously heavy because of him.

But the child lifted his uncanny blue eyes.

"I couldn't possibly go before the Derby, mother!" he said. "I couldn't possibly!"

"Why not?" she said, her voice becoming heavy when she was opposed. "Why not? You can still go from the seaside to see the Derby with your Uncle Oscar, if that's what you wish. No need for you to wait here. Besides, I think you care too much about these races. It's a bad sign. My family has been a gambling family, and you won't know till you grow up how much damage it has done. But it has done damage. I shall have to send Bassett away, and ask Uncle Oscar not to talk racing to you, unless you promise to be reasonable about it; go away to the seaside and forget it. You're all nerves!"

"I'll do what you like, mother, so long as you don't send me away   190 till after the Derby," the boy said.

"Send you away from where? Just from this house?"

"Yes," he said, gazing at her.

"Why, you curious child, what makes you care about this house so much, suddenly? I never knew you loved it."

He gazed at her without speaking. He had a secret within a secret, something he had not divulged, even to Bassett or to his Uncle Oscar.

But his mother, after standing undecided and a little bit sullen for   195 some moments, said:

"Very well, then! Don't go to the seaside till after the Derby, if you don't wish it. But promise me you won't let your nerves go to pieces. Promise you won't think so much about horse racing and events, as you call them!"

"Oh, no," said the boy casually. "I won't think much about them, mother. You needn't worry. I wouldn't worry, mother, if I were you."

"If you were me and I were you," said his mother, "I wonder what we should do!"

"But you know you needn't worry, mother, don't you?" the boy repeated.

200   "I should be awfully glad to know it," she said wearily.

"Oh, well, you can, you know. I mean, you ought to know you needn't worry," he insisted.

"Ought I? Then I'll see about it," she said.

Paul's secret of secrets was his wooden horse, that which had no name. Since he was emancipated from a nurse and a nursery-governess, he had had his rocking horse removed to his own bedroom at the top of the house.

"Surely, you're too big for a rocking horse!" his mother had remonstrated.

205   "Well, you see mother, till I can have a real horse, I like to have some sort of animal about," had been his quaint answer.

"Do you feel he keeps you company?" she laughed.

"Oh, yes! He's very good, he always keeps me company, when I'm there," said Paul.

So the horse, rather shabby, stood in an arrested prance in the boy's bedroom.

The Derby was drawing near, and the boy grew more and more tense. He hardly heard what was spoken to him, he was very frail, and his eyes were really uncanny. His mother had sudden seizures of uneasiness about him. Sometimes, for half-an-hour, she would feel a sudden anxiety about him that was almost anguish. She wanted to rush to him at once, and know he was safe.

210   Two nights before the Derby, she was at a big party in town, when one of her rushes of anxiety about her boy, her first-born, gripped her heart till she could hardly speak. She fought with the feeling, might and main, for she believed in common sense. But it was too strong. The children's nursery-governess was terribly surprised and startled at being rung up in the night.

"Are the children all right, Miss Wilmot?"

"Oh, yes, they are quite all right."

"Master Paul? Is he all right?"

"He went to bed as right as a trivet. Shall I run up and look at him?"

215   "No," said Paul's mother reluctantly. "No! Don't trouble. It's all right. Don't sit up. We shall be home fairly soon." She did not want her son's privacy intruded upon.

"Very good," said the governess.

It was about one o'clock when Paul's mother and father drove up to their house. All was still. Paul's mother went to her room and slipped off her white fur coat. She had told her maid not to wait up for her. She heard her husband downstairs, mixing a whiskey-and-soda.

And then, because of the strange anxiety at her heart, she stole upstairs to her son's room. Noiselessly she went along the upper corridor. Was there a faint noise? What was it?

She stood, with arrested muscles, outside his door listening. There was a strange, heavy, and yet not loud noise. Her heart stood still. It was a soundless noise, yet rushing and powerful. Something huge, in violent, hushed motion. What was it? What in God's name was it? She ought to know. She felt that she knew the noise. She knew what it was.

Yet she could not place it. She couldn't say what it was. And on and on it went, like madness.

Softly, frozen with anxiety and fear, she turned the door handle.

The room was dark. Yet in the space near the window, she heard and saw something plunging to and fro. She gazed in fear and amazement.

Then suddenly she switched on the light, and saw her son, in his green pajamas, madly surging on the rocking horse. The blaze of light suddenly lit him up, as he urged the wooden horse, and lit her up, as she stood, blonde, in her dress of pale green and crystal, in the doorway.

"Paul!" she cried. "Whatever are you doing?"

"It's Malabar!" he screamed, in a powerful, strange voice. "It's Malabar."

His eyes blazed at her for one strange and senseless second, as he ceased urging his wooden horse. Then he fell with a crash to the ground, and she, all her tormented motherhood flooding upon her, rushed to gather him up.

But he was unconscious, and unconscious he remained, with some brain-fever. He talked and tossed, and his mother sat stonily by his side.

"Malabar! It's Malabar! Bassett, Bassett, I know it! It's Malabar!"

So the child cried, trying to get up and urge the rocking horse that gave him his inspiration.

"What does he mean by Malabar?" asked the heart-frozen mother.

"I don't know," said his father stonily.

"What does he mean by Malabar?" she asked her brother Oscar.

"It's one of the horses running for the Derby," was the answer.

And, in spite of himself, Oscar Cresswell spoke to Bassett, and himself put a thousand on Malabar: at fourteen to one.

The third day of the illness was critical: they were waiting for a change. The boy, with his rather long, curly hair, was tossing ceaselessly on the pillow. He neither slept nor regained consciousness, and his eyes were like blue stones. His mother sat, feeling her heart had gone, turned actually into a stone.

In the evening, Oscar Cresswell did not come, but Bassett sent a message, saying could he come up for one moment, just one moment? Paul's mother was very angry at the intrusion, but on second thought she agreed. The boy was the same. Perhaps Bassett might bring him to consciousness.

The gardener, a shortish fellow with a brown mustache, and sharp little brown eyes, tiptoed into the room, touched his imaginary cap to Paul's mother, and stole to the bedside, staring with glittering, smallish eyes, at the tossing, dying child.

"Master Paul!" he whispered. "Master Paul! Malabar came in first all right, a clean win. I did as you told me. You've made over seventy thousand pounds, you have; you've got over eighty thousand. Malabar came in all right, Master Paul."

"Malabar! Malabar! Did I say Malabar, mother? Did I say Malabar? Do you think I'm lucky, mother? I knew Malabar, didn't I? Over eighty thousand pounds! I call that lucky, don't you, mother? Over eighty thousand pounds! I knew, didn't I know I knew? Malabar came in all right. If I ride my horse till I'm sure, then I tell you, Bassett, you can go as high as you like. Did you go for all you were worth, Bassett?"

240   "I went a thousand on it, Master Paul."

"I never told you, mother, that if I can ride my horse, and get there, then I'm absolutely sure—oh, absolutely! Mother, did I ever tell you? I'm lucky."

"No, you never did," said the mother.

But the boy died in the night.

And even as he lay dead, his mother heard her brother's voice saying to her: "My God, Hester, you're eighty-odd thousand to the good and a poor devil of a son to the bad. But, poor devil, poor devil, he's best gone out of a life where he rides his rocking horse to find a winner."

QUESTIONS

1. In the phraseology of its beginning ("There was a woman . . ."), its simple style, its direct characterization, and its use of the wish motif—especially that of the wish that is granted only on conditions that nullify its desirability (compare the story of King Midas)—this story has the qualities of a fairy tale. Its differences, however—in characterization, setting, and ending—are especially significant. What do they tell us about the purpose of the story?

2. Characterize the mother fully. How does she differ from the stepmothers in fairy tales like "Cinderella" and "Hansel and Gretel"? How does the boy's

mistake about *filthy lucker* (paragraph 15) clarify her thinking and her motivations? Why had her love for her husband turned to dust? Why is she "unlucky"?

3. What kind of a child is Paul? What are his motivations?
4. The initial assumptions of the story are that (a) a boy might get divinatory powers by riding a rocking horse, (b) a house can whisper. Could the second of these be accepted as little more than a metaphor? Once we have granted these initial assumptions, does the story develop plausibly?
5. It is ironic that the boy's attempt to stop the whispers should only increase them. Is this a plausible irony? Why? What does it tell us about the theme of the story? Why is it ironic that the whispers should be especially audible at Christmas time? What irony is contained in the boy's last speech?
6. In what way is the boy's furious riding on the rocking horse an appropriate symbol for materialistic pursuits?
7. How might a commercial writer have ended the story?
8. How many persons in the story are affected (or infected) by materialism?
9. What is the theme of the story?

Nathaniel Hawthorne
Young Goodman Brown

Young Goodman Brown came forth at sunset into the street of Salem village, but put his head back, after crossing the threshold, to exchange a parting kiss with his young wife. And Faith, as the wife was aptly named, thrust her own pretty head into the street, letting the wind play with the pink ribbons of her cap while she called to Goodman Brown.

"Dearest heart," whispered she softly and rather sadly when her lips were close to his ear, "prithee, put off your journey until sunrise, and sleep in your own bed tonight. A lone woman is troubled with such dreams and such thoughts that she's afeard of herself, sometimes. Pray, tarry with me this night, dear husband, of all nights in the year!"

YOUNG GOODMAN BROWN   First published in 1835. "Goodman" was a title of respect, but at a social rank lower than "gentleman." "Goody" (or "Goodwife") was the feminine equivalent. Deacon Gookin in the story is a historical personage (1612–1687), as are also Goody Cloyse, Goody Cory, and Martha Carrier, all three executed at the Salem witchcraft trials in 1692. Nathaniel Hawthorne (1804–1864) was born and grew up in Salem, Massachusetts, where Hawthornes had lived since the seventeenth century. One ancestor had been a judge at the Salem witch trials; another had been a leader in the persecution of Quakers. "Young Goodman Brown" is one of several stories in which Hawthorne explored the Puritan past of New England.

"My love and my Faith," replied young Goodman Brown, "of all nights in the year this one must I tarry away from thee. My journey, as thou callest it, forth and back again must needs be done 'twixt now and sunrise. What, my sweet, pretty wife, dost thou doubt me already, and we but three months married!"

"Then God bless you!" said Faith with the pink ribbons, "and may you find all well when you come back."

5   "Amen!" cried Goodman Brown. "Say thy prayers, dear Faith, and go to bed at dusk, and no harm will come to thee."

So they parted; and the young man pursued his way until, being about to turn the corner by the meeting-house, he looked back and saw the head of Faith still peeping after him with a melancholy air in spite of her pink ribbons.

"Poor little Faith!" thought he, for his heart smote him. "What a wretch am I, to leave her on such an errand! She talks of dreams, too. Methought, as she spoke, there was trouble in her face, as if a dream had warned her what work is to be done tonight. But no, no! 'twould kill her to think it. Well; she's a blessed angel on earth and after this one night I'll cling to her skirts and follow her to Heaven."

With this excellent resolve for the future, Goodman Brown felt himself justified in making more haste on his present evil purpose. He had taken a dreary road, darkened by all the gloomiest trees of the forest, which barely stood aside to let the narrow path creep through, and closed immediately behind. It was all as lonely as could be; and there is this peculiarity in such a solitude, that the traveler knows not who may be concealed by the innumerable trunks and the thick boughs overhead, so that with lonely footsteps he may be passing through an unseen multitude.

"There may be a devilish Indian behind every tree," said Goodman Brown to himself; and he glanced fearfully behind him as he added, "What if the devil himself should be at my very elbow!"

10   His head being turned back, he passed a crook of the road, and looking forward again beheld the figure of a man in grave and decent attire, seated at the foot of an old tree. He rose at Goodman Brown's approach and walked onward side by side with him.

"You are late, Goodman Brown," said he. "The clock of the Old South was striking as I came through Boston, and that is full fifteen minutes agone."°

---

full fifteen minutes agone: The distance from the center of Boston to the forest was over twenty miles.

"Faith kept me back awhile," replied the young man with a tremor in his voice caused by the sudden appearance of his companion, though not wholly unexpected.

It was now deep dusk in the forest, and deepest in that part of it where these two were journeying. As nearly as could be discerned, the second traveler was about fifty years old, apparently in the same rank of life as Goodman Brown, and bearing a considerable resemblance to him, though perhaps more in expression than features. Still, they might have been taken for father and son. And yet, though the elder person was as simply clad as the younger, and as simple in manner too, he had an indescribable air of one who knew the world and would not have felt abashed at the governor's dinner table or in King William's court,° were it possible that his affairs should call him thither. But the only thing about him that could be fixed upon as remarkable was his staff, which bore the likeness of a great black snake, so curiously wrought that it might almost be seen to twist and wriggle itself like a living serpent. This, of course, must have been an ocular deception, assisted by the uncertain light.

"Come, Goodman Brown!" cried his fellow-traveler, "this is a dull pace for the beginning of a journey. Take my staff if you are so soon weary."

"Friend," said the other, exchanging his slow pace for a full stop, 15 "having kept covenant by meeting thee here, it is my purpose now to return whence I came. I have scruples touching the matter thou wot'st of."

"Sayest thou so?" replied he of the serpent, smiling apart. "Let us walk on nevertheless, reasoning as we go, and if I convince thee not, thou shalt turn back. We are but a little way in the forest yet."

"Too far, too far!" exclaimed the goodman, unconsciously resuming his walk. "My father never went into the woods on such an errand, nor his father before him. We have been a race of honest men and good Christians since the days of the martyrs. And shall I be the first of the name of Brown that ever took this path and kept—"

"Such company, thou wouldst say," observed the elder person interrupting his pause. "Well said, Goodman Brown! I have been as well acquainted with your family as with ever a one among the Puritans, and that's no trifle to say. I helped your grandfather the constable when he lashed the Quaker woman so smartly through the streets of Salem. And it was I that brought your father a pitch-pine knot kindled at my own hearth, to set fire to an Indian village, in King Philip's war.° They were

King William's court: William III, King of England, 1689–1702   King Philip's war: a war between the colonists and Indians, 1675–1676

my good friends, both; and many a pleasant walk have we had along this path and returned merrily after midnight. I would fain be friends with you, for their sake."

"If it be as thou sayest," replied Goodman Brown, "I marvel they never spoke of these matters. Or, verily, I marvel not, seeing that the least rumor of the sort would have driven them from New England. We are a people of prayer, and good works to boot, and abide no such wickedness."

20   "Wickedness or not," said the traveler with twisted staff, "I have a general acquaintance here in New England. The deacons of many a church have drunk the communion wine with me, the selectmen of divers towns make me their chairman, and a majority of the Great and General Court° are firm supporters of my interest. The governor and I, too—but these are state secrets."

"Can this be so!" cried Goodman Brown with a stare of amazement at his undisturbed companion. "Howbeit, I have nothing to do with the governor and council; they have their own ways and are no rule for a simple husbandman like me. But were I to go on with thee, how should I meet the eye of that good old man, our minister, at Salem village? Oh, his voice would make me tremble, both Sabbathday and lecture-day!"

Thus far, the elder traveler had listened with due gravity but now burst into a fit of irrepressible mirth, shaking himself so violently that his snakelike staff actually seemed to wriggle in sympathy.

"Ha! ha! ha!" shouted he, again and again; then composing himself, "Well, go on, Goodman Brown, go on; but prithee, don't kill me with laughing!"

"Well, then, to end the matter at once," said Goodman Brown, considerably nettled, "there is my wife, Faith. It would break her dear little heart, and I'd rather break my own!"

25   "Nay, if that be the case," answered the other, "e'en go thy ways, Goodman Brown. I would not for twenty old women like the one hobbling before us that Faith should come to any harm."

As he spoke he pointed his staff at a female figure on the path in whom Goodman Brown recognized a very pious and exemplary dame who had taught him his catechism in youth and was still his moral and spiritual adviser, jointly with the minister and Deacon Gookin.

"A marvel, truly, that Goody Cloyse should be so far in the wilderness at nightfall!" said he. "But with your leave, friend, I shall take a cut through the woods until we have left this Christian woman behind. Be-

Great and General Court: the legislature of the Massachusetts Bay Colony

ing a stranger to you, she might ask whom I was consorting with and whither I was going."

"Be it so," said his fellow-traveler. "Betake you to the woods and let me keep the path."

Accordingly, the young man turned aside, but took care to watch his companion who advanced softly along the road until he had come within a staff's length of the old dame. She, meanwhile, was making the best of her way, with singular speed for so aged a woman, and mumbling some indistinct words, a prayer, doubtless, as she went. The traveler put forth his staff and touched her withered neck with what seemed the serpent's tail.

"The devil!" screamed the pious old lady.   30

"Then Goody Cloyse knows her old friend?" observed the traveler, confronting her and leaning on his writhing stick.

"Ah, forsooth, and is it your worship indeed?" cried the good dame. "Yea, truly is it, and in the very image of my old gossip, Goodman Brown, the grandfather of the silly fellow that now is. But would your worship believe it? my broomstick hath strangely disappeared, stolen as I suspect by that unhanged witch, Goody Cory, and that, too, when I was all anointed with the juice of smallage and cinque-foil and wolf's-bane—"

"Mingled with fine wheat and the fat of a new-born babe," said the shape of old Goodman Brown.

"Ah, your worship knows the recipe," cried the old lady, cackling aloud. "So, as I was saying, being all ready for the meeting, and no horse to ride on, I made up my mind to foot it; for they tell me there is a nice young man to be taken into communion tonight. But now your good worship will lend me your arm and we shall be there in a twinkling."

"That can hardly be," answered her friend. "I may not spare you my   35
arm, Goody Cloyse, but here is my staff, if you will."

So saying, he threw it down at her feet where, perhaps, it assumed life, being one of the rods which its owner had formerly lent to the Egyptian Magi. Of this fact, however, Goodman Brown could not take cognizance. He had cast up his eyes in astonishment, and looking down again beheld neither Goody Cloyse nor the serpentine staff, but his fellow-traveler alone, who waited for him as calmly as if nothing had happened.

"That old woman taught me my catechism!" said the young man, and there was a world of meaning in this simple comment.

They continued to walk onward while the elder traveler exhorted his companion to make good speed and persevere in the path, discoursing so aptly that his arguments seemed rather to spring up in the bosom of his auditor than to be suggested by himself. As they went he plucked a branch of maple to serve for a walking-stick, and began to strip it of the twigs and little boughs which were wet with evening dew. The moment his fingers touched them they became strangely withered and dried up, as with a week's sunshine. Thus the pair proceeded at a good free pace, until suddenly, in a gloomy hollow of the road, Goodman Brown sat himself down on the stump of a tree and refused to go any farther.

"Friend," said he stubbornly, "my mind is made up. Not another step will I budge on this errand. What if a wretched old woman do choose to go to the devil when I thought she was going to Heaven! Is that any reason why I should quit my dear Faith and go after her?"

40   "You will think better of this by and by," said his acquaintance composedly. "Sit here and rest yourself awhile, and when you feel like moving again, there is my staff to help you along."

Without more words, he threw his companion the maple stick and was as speedily out of sight as if he had vanished into the deepening gloom. The young man sat a few moments by the roadside, applauding himself greatly and thinking with how clear a conscience he should meet the minister in his morning walk, nor shrink from the eye of good old Deacon Gookin. And what calm sleep would be his that very night, which was to have been spent so wickedly, but purely and sweetly now, in the arms of Faith! Amidst these pleasant and praiseworthy meditations, Goodman Brown heard the tramp of horses along the road and deemed it advisable to conceal himself within the verge of the forest, conscious of the guilty purpose that had brought him thither, though now so happily turned from it.

On came the hoof-tramps and the voices of the riders, two grave old voices conversing soberly as they drew near. These mingled sounds appeared to pass along the road within a few yards of the young man's hiding place; but owing, doubtless, to the depth of the gloom at that particular spot, neither the travelers nor their steeds were visible. Though their figures brushed the small boughs by the wayside, it could not be seen that they intercepted even for a moment the faint gleam from the strip of bright sky athwart which they must have passed. Goodman Brown alternately crouched and stood on tiptoe, pulling aside the branches and thrusting forth his head as far as he durst, without discerning so much as a shadow. It vexed him the more because he could have sworn, were such a thing possible, that he recognized the voices of the minister and Deacon Gookin, jogging along quietly as they were wont to do when bound to some ordination or ecclesiastical council. While yet within hearing, one of the riders stopped to pluck a switch.

"Of the two, reverend Sir," said the voice like the deacon's, "I had rather miss an ordination dinner than tonight's meeting. They tell me that some of our community are to be here from Falmouth and beyond, and others from Connecticut and Rhode Island, besides several of the Indian powwows who, after their fashion, know almost as much deviltry as the best of us. Moreover, there is a goodly young woman to be taken into communion."

"Mighty well, Deacon Gookin!" replied the solemn old tones of the minister. "Spur up, or we shall be late. Nothing can be done, you know, until I get on the ground."

The hoofs clattered again, and the voices talking so strangely in   45
the empty air passed on through the forest where no church had ever been gathered nor solitary Christian prayed. Whither, then, could these holy men be journeying, so deep into the heathen wilderness? Young Goodman Brown caught hold of a tree for support, being ready to sink down on the ground, faint and over-burthened with the heavy sickness of his heart. He looked up to the sky, doubting whether there really was a Heaven above him. Yet there was the blue arch, and the stars brightening in it.

"With Heaven above, and Faith below, I will yet stand firm against the devil!" cried Goodman Brown.

While he still gazed upward into the deep arch of the firmament and had lifted his hands to pray, a cloud, though no wind was stirring, hurried across the zenith and hid the brightening stars. The blue sky was still visible except directly overhead, where this black mass of cloud was sweeping swiftly northward. Aloft in the air, as if from the depths of the cloud, came a confused and doubtful sound of voices. Once the listener fancied that he could distinguish the accents of townspeople of his own, men and women, both pious and ungodly, many of whom he had met at the communion-table, and had seen others rioting at the tavern. The next moment, so indistinct were the sounds, he doubted whether he had heard aught but the murmur of the old forest whispering without a wind. Then came a stronger swell of those familiar tones heard daily in the sunshine at Salem village, but never, until now, from a cloud at night. There was one voice, of a young woman uttering lamentations yet with an uncertain sorrow, and entreating for some favor, which, perhaps, it would grieve her to obtain. And all the unseen multitude, both saints and sinners, seemed to encourage her onward.

"Faith!" shouted Goodman Brown in a voice of agony and desperation; and the echoes of the forest mocked him, crying "Faith! Faith!" as if bewildered wretches were seeking her all through the wilderness.

The cry of grief, rage, and terror was yet piercing the night when the unhappy husband held his breath for a response. There was a scream, drowned immediately in a louder murmur of voices fading into far-off laughter as the dark cloud swept away leaving the clear and silent sky above Goodman Brown. But something fluttered lightly down through the air and caught on the branch of a tree. The young man seized it and beheld a pink ribbon.

50   "My Faith is gone!" cried he, after one stupefied moment. "There is no good on earth, and sin is but a name. Come, devil! for to thee is this world given."

And maddened with despair, so that he laughed loud and long, did Goodman Brown grasp his staff and set forth again at such a rate that he seemed to fly along the forest path rather than to walk or run. The road grew wilder and drearier and more faintly traced, and vanished at length, leaving him in the heart of the dark wilderness, still rushing onward with the instinct that guides mortal man to evil. The whole forest was peopled with frightful sounds—the creaking of the trees, the howling of wild beasts, and the yell of Indians; while sometimes the wind tolled like a distant church bell, and sometimes gave a broad roar around the traveler, as if all Nature were laughing him to scorn. But he was himself the chief horror of the scene, and shrank not from its other horrors.

"Ha! ha! ha!" roared Goodman Brown when the wind laughed at him. "Let us hear which will laugh loudest! Think not to frighten me with your deviltry! come witch, come wizard, come Indian powwow, come devil himself! and here comes Goodman Brown. You may as well fear him as he fear you!"

In truth, all through the haunted forest there could be nothing more frightful than the figure of Goodman Brown. On he flew among the black pines, brandishing his staff with frenzied gestures, now giving vent to an inspiration of horrid blasphemy, and now shouting forth such laughter as set all the echoes of the forest laughing like demons around him. The fiend in his own shape is less hideous than when he rages in the breast of man. Thus sped the demoniac on his course until, quivering among the trees, he saw a red light before him, as when the felled trunks and branches of a clearing have been set on fire and throw up their lurid blaze against the sky at the hour of midnight. He paused in a lull of the tempest that had driven him onward, and heard the swell of what seemed a hymn rolling solemnly from a distance with the weight of many voices. He knew the tune. It was a familiar one in the choir of the village meeting-house. The verse died heavily away, and was lengthened by a chorus not of human voices but of all the sounds of the benighted wilderness pealing in awful harmony together. Goodman Brown cried out, and his cry was lost to his own ear by its unison with the cry of the desert.

In the interval of silence he stole forward until the light glared full upon his eyes. At one extremity of an open space, hemmed in by the dark wall of the forest, arose a rock bearing some rude, natural resemblance either to an altar or a pulpit, and surrounded by four blazing pines, their tops aflame, their stems untouched, like candles at an evening meeting. The mass of foliage that had overgrown the summit of the rock was all on fire, blazing high into the night and fitfully illuminating the whole field. Each pendent twig and leafy festoon was in a blaze. As the red light arose and fell, a numerous congregation alternately shone forth, then disappeared in shadow, and again grew, as it were, out of the darkness, peopling the heart of the solitary woods at once.

"A grave and dark-clad company!" quoth Goodman Brown.   55

In truth they were such. Among them, quivering to and fro between gloom and splendor, appeared faces that would be seen next day at the council-board of the province, and others which Sabbath after Sabbath looked devoutly heavenward and benignantly over the crowded pews from the holiest pulpits in the land. Some affirm that the lady of the governor was there. At least, there were high dames well known to her, and wives of honored husbands, and widows a great multitude, and ancient maidens, all of excellent repute, and fair young girls who trembled lest their mothers should espy them. Either the sudden gleams of light flashing over the obscure field bedazzled Goodman Brown, or he recognized a score of the church members of Salem village famous for their especial sanctity. Good old Deacon Gookin had arrived and waited at the skirts of that venerable saint, his reverend pastor. But irreverently consorting with these grave, reputable, and pious people, these elders of the church, these chaste dames and dewy virgins, there were men of dissolute lives and women of spotted fame, wretches given over to all mean and filthy vice and suspected even of horrid crimes. It was strange to see that the good shrank not from the wicked, nor were the sinners abashed by the saints. Scattered also among their pale-faced enemies were the Indian priests or powwows who had often scared their native forest with more hideous incantations than any known to English witchcraft.

"But where is Faith?" thought Goodman Brown; and as hope came into his heart he trembled.

Another verse of the hymn arose, a slow and mournful strain such as the pious love, but joined to words which expressed all that our nature can conceive of sin, and darkly hinted at far more. Unfathomable to mere mortals is the lore of fiends. Verse after verse was sung, and still the chorus of the desert swelled between, like the deepest tone of a mighty organ. And with the final peal of that dreadful anthem, there came a sound as if the roaring wind, the rushing streams, the howling beasts, and every other voice of the unconverted wilderness were mingling and according with the voice of guilty man in homage to the prince of all. The four blazing pines threw up a loftier flame and obscurely discovered shapes and visages of horror on the smoke-wreaths above the impious assembly. At the same moment the fire on the rock shot redly forth and formed a glowing arch above its base, where now appeared a figure. With reverence be it spoken, the apparition bore no slight similitude both in garb and manner to some grave divine of the New England churches.

"Bring forth the converts!" cried a voice that echoed through the field and rolled into the forest.

60   At the word, Goodman Brown stepped forth from the shadow of the trees and approached the congregation, with whom he felt a loathful brotherhood by the sympathy of all that was wicked in his heart. He could have well-nigh sworn that the shape of his own dead father beckoned him to advance, looking downward from a smoke-wreath, while a woman with dim features of despair threw out her hand to warn him back. Was it his mother? But he had no power to retreat one step nor to resist, even in thought, when the minister and good old Deacon Gookin seized his arms and led him to the blazing rock. Thither came also the slender form of a veiled female led between Goody Cloyse, that pious teacher of the catechism, and Martha Carrier, who had received the devil's promise to be queen of hell. A rampant hag was she! And there stood the proselytes beneath the canopy of fire.

"Welcome, my children," said the dark figure, "to the communion of your race! Ye have found, thus young, your nature and your destiny. My children, look behind you!"

They turned, and flashing forth as it were in a sheet of flame, the fiend-worshippers were seen; the smile of welcome gleamed darkly on every visage.

"There," resumed the sable form, "are all whom ye have reverenced from youth. Ye deemed them holier than yourselves and shrank from your own sin, contrasting it with their lives of righteousness and prayerful aspirations heavenward. Yet here are they all in my worshipping assembly! This night it shall be granted you to know their secret deeds: how hoary-bearded elders of the church have whispered wanton words to the young maids of their households; how many a woman eager for widow's weeds has given her husband a drink at bedtime, and let him sleep his last sleep in her bosom; how beardless youths have made haste to inherit their father's wealth; and how fair damsels—blush not, sweet ones!—have dug little graves in the garden and bidden me, the sole guest, to an infant's funeral. By the sympathy of your human hearts for sin, ye shall scent out all the places—whether in church, bedchamber, street, field, or forest—where crime has been committed, and shall exult to behold the whole earth one stain of guilt, one mighty blood-spot. Far more than this! It shall be yours to penetrate in every bosom the deep mystery of sin, the fountain of all wicked arts, and which inexhaustibly supplies more evil impulses than human power—than my power, at its utmost!—can make manifest in deeds. And now, my children, look upon each other."

They did so, and by the blaze of the hell-kindled torches the wretched man beheld his Faith, and the wife her husband trembling before that unhallowed altar.

"Lo! there ye stand, my children," said the figure in a deep solemn tone, almost sad with its despairing awfulness, as if his once angelic nature could yet mourn for our miserable race. "Depending upon one another's hearts, ye had still hoped that virtue were not all a dream! Now are ye undeceived—Evil is the nature of mankind. Evil must be your only happiness. Welcome, again, my children, to the communion of your race!"   65

"Welcome!" repeated the fiend-worshippers in one cry of despair and triumph.

And there they stood, the only pair as it seemed who were yet hesitating on the verge of wickedness in this dark world. A basin was hollowed naturally in the rock. Did it contain water, reddened by the lurid light? or was it blood? or, perchance, a liquid flame? Herein did the Shape of Evil dip his hand and prepare to lay the mark of baptism upon their foreheads, that they might be partakers of the mystery of sin, more conscious of the secret guilt of others both in deed and thought than they could now be of their own. The husband cast one look at his pale wife, and Faith at him. What polluted wretches would the next glance show them to each other, shuddering alike at what they disclosed and what they saw!

"Faith! Faith!" cried the husband. "Look up to Heaven, and resist the Wicked One!"

Whether Faith obeyed he knew not. Hardly had he spoken when he found himself amid calm night and solitude, listening to a roar of the wind which died heavily away through the forest. He staggered against the rock and felt it chill and damp, while a hanging twig that had been all on fire besprinkled his cheek with the coldest dew.

70   The next morning, young Goodman Brown came slowly into the street of Salem village staring around him like a bewildered man. The good old minister was taking a walk along the graveyard to get an appetite for breakfast and meditate his sermon, and bestowed a blessing as he passed on Goodman Brown. He shrank from the venerable saint as if to avoid an anathema. Old Deacon Gookin was at domestic worship, and the holy words of his prayer were heard through the open window. "What God doth the wizard pray to?" quoth Goodman Brown. Goody Cloyse, that excellent old Christian, stood in the early sunshine at her own lattice catechizing a little girl who had brought her a pint of morning's milk. Goodman Brown snatched away the child as from the grasp of the fiend himself. Turning the corner by the meeting-house, he spied the head of Faith with the pink ribbons gazing anxiously forth, and bursting into such joy at sight of him that she skipped along the street and almost kissed her husband before the whole village. But Goodman Brown looked sternly and sadly into her face and passed on without a greeting.

Had Goodman Brown fallen asleep in the forest and only dreamed a wild dream of a witch-meeting?

Be it so, if you will. But, alas! it was a dream of evil omen for young Goodman Brown. A stern, a sad, a darkly meditative, a distrustful, if not a desperate man did he become from the night of that fearful dream. On the Sabbath-day when the congregation were singing a holy psalm, he could not listen because an anthem of sin rushed loudly upon his ear and drowned all the blessed strain. When the minister spoke from the pulpit with power and fervid eloquence and with his hand on the open Bible, of the sacred truths of our religion, and of saint-like lives and triumphant deaths, and of future bliss or misery unutterable, then did Goodman Brown turn pale, dreading lest the roof should thunder down upon the gray blasphemer and his hearers. Often awaking suddenly at midnight, he shrank from the bosom of Faith, and at morning or eventide when the family knelt down at prayer, he scowled and muttered to himself and gazed sternly at his wife and turned away. And when he had lived long and was borne to his grave a hoary corpse, followed by Faith, an aged woman, and children and grandchildren, a goodly procession, besides neighbors not a few, they carved no hopeful verse upon his tombstone, for his dying hour was gloom.

QUESTIONS

1. What does Hawthorne gain by including the names of actual persons (Goody Cloyse, Goody Cory, Deacon Gookin, Martha Carrier) and places (Salem village, Boston, Old South Church)? What religion is practiced by the townspeople?

2. What is the point of view? Where does it change, and what is the result of the change?
3. What allegorical meanings may be given to Goodman Brown? His wife? The forest? Night (as opposed to day)? Brown's journey?
4. What is Brown's motive for going into the forest? What results does he expect from his journey? What does he expect the rest of his life to be like?
5. After he keeps his appointment with the traveler in the forest, Brown announces that he plans to return home. Why does he not do so immediately, and why at each stage when he renews his intention to do so does he proceed deeper into the forest? Is there any reason to suppose he does not actually see and hear what he thinks he perceives?
6. What details of the "witch-meeting" parallel those of a church communion service? Why does the congregation include "grave, reputable, and pious people" as well as known sinners (paragraph 56)?
7. What prevents Goodman Brown from receiving baptism? What does the devil promise as the result of baptism? Is that what you usually suppose is the reward for selling your soul to the devil? Why is it an appropriate reward for Goodman Brown? Since he does not receive baptism, how do you account for his behavior when he returns to the village?
8. "Had Goodman Brown . . . only dreamed a wild dream of a witch-meeting?" (paragraph 71). How are we to answer this question? Point out other places where Hawthorne leaves the interpretation of the story ambiguous. How is such ambiguity related to the story's theme?
9. Characterize the behavior of Faith and the other townspeople after Brown's return to the village. Are Brown's attitude and behavior thereafter the result of conviction or doubt? Is he completely misanthropic?
10. Does the story demonstrate the devil's claim that "Evil is the nature of mankind" (paragraph 65)?

Joyce Carol Oates

Where Are You Going, Where Have You Been?

Her name was Connie. She was fifteen and she had a quick nervous giggling habit of craning her neck to glance into mirrors, or checking other people's faces to make sure her own was all right. Her mother,

WHERE ARE YOU GOING, WHERE HAVE YOU BEEN?   First published in 1968. Joyce Carol Oates (b. 1938), one of contemporary America's most prolific writers, is the author of more than seventy volumes of fiction, literary criticism, poetry, and drama. She grew up in rural New York and since 1978 has taught creative writing at Princeton University. Concerning "Where Are You Going, Where Have You Been?" Oates has written that "every third or fourth story of mine is probably in this mode—'realistic allegory,' it might be called. It is Hawthornean, romantic, shading into parable."

who noticed everything and knew everything and who hadn't much reason any longer to look at her own face, always scolded Connie about it. "Stop gawking at yourself, who are you? You think you're so pretty?" she would say. Connie would raise her eye-brows at these familiar complaints and look right through her mother, into a shadowy vision of herself as she was right at that moment: she knew she was pretty and that was everything. Her mother had been pretty once too, if you could believe those old snapshots in the album, but now her looks were gone and that was why she was always after Connie.

"Why don't you keep your room clean like your sister? How've you got your hair fixed—what the hell stinks? Hair spray? You don't see your sister using that junk."

Her sister June was twenty-four and still lived at home. She was a secretary in the high school Connie attended, and if that wasn't bad enough—with her in the same building—she was so plain and chunky and steady that Connie had to hear her praised all the time by her mother and her mother's sisters. June did this, June did that, she saved money and helped clean the house and cooked and Connie couldn't do a thing, her mind was all filled with trashy daydreams. Their father was away at work most of the time and when he came home he wanted supper and he read the newspaper at supper and after supper he went to bed. He didn't bother talking much to them, but around his bent head Connie's mother kept picking at her until Connie wished her mother was dead and she herself was dead and it was all over. "She makes me want to throw up sometimes," she complained to her friends. She had a high, breathless, amused voice which made everything she said sound a little forced, whether it was sincere or not.

There was one good thing: June went places with girl friends of hers, girls who were just as plain and steady as she, and so when Connie wanted to do that her mother had no objections. The father of Connie's best girl friend drove the girls the three miles to town and left them off at a shopping plaza, so that they could walk through the stores or go to a movie, and when he came to pick them up again at eleven he never bothered to ask what they had done.

5   They must have been familiar sights, walking around that shopping plaza in their shorts and flat ballerina slippers that always scuffed the sidewalk, with charm bracelets jingling on their thin wrists; they would lean together to whisper and laugh secretly if someone passed by who amused or interested them. Connie had long dark blond hair that drew anyone's eye to it, and she wore part of it pulled up on her head and puffed out and the rest of it she let fall down her back. She wore a pullover jersey blouse that looked one way when she was at home and an-

other way when she was away from home. Everything about her had two sides to it, one for home and one for anywhere that was not home: her walk that could be childlike and bobbing, or languid enough to make anyone think she was hearing music in her head, her mouth which was pale and smirking most of the time, but bright and pink on these evenings out, her laugh which was cynical and drawling at home—"Ha, ha, very funny"—but high-pitched and nervous anywhere else, like the jingling of the charms on her bracelet.

Sometimes they did go shopping or to a movie, but sometimes they went across the highway, ducking fast across the busy road, to a drive-in restaurant where older kids hung out. The restaurant was shaped like a big bottle, though squatter than a real bottle, and on its cap was a re-volving figure of a grinning boy who held a hamburger aloft. One night in mid-summer they ran across, breathless with daring, and right away someone leaned out a car window and invited them over, but it was just a boy from high school they didn't like. It made them feel good to be able to ignore him. They went up through the maze of parked and cruis-ing cars to the bright-lit, fly-infested restaurant, their faces pleased and expectant as if they were entering a sacred building that loomed out of the night to give them what haven and what blessing they yearned for. They sat at the counter and crossed their legs at the ankles, their thin shoulders rigid with excitement, and listened to the music that made everything so good: the music was always in the background like music at a church service, it was something to depend upon.

A boy named Eddie came in to talk with them. He sat backwards on his stool, turning himself jerkily around in semi-circles and then stopping and turning again, and after a while he asked Connie if she would like something to eat. She said she did and so she tapped her friend's arm on her way out—her friend pulled her face up into a brave droll look—and Connie said she would meet her at eleven, across the way. "I just hate to leave her like that," Connie said earnestly, but the boy said that she wouldn't be alone for long. So they want out to his car and on the way Connie couldn't help but let her eyes wander over the windshields and faces all around her, her face gleaming with a joy that had nothing to do with Eddie or even this place; it might have been the music. She drew her shoulders up and sucked in her breath with the pure pleasure of being alive, and just at that moment she hap-pened to glance at a face just a few feet from hers. It was a boy with shaggy black hair, in a convertible jalopy painted gold. He stared at her and then his lips widened into a grin. Connie slit her eyes at him and turned away, but she couldn't help glancing back and there he was still watching her. He wagged a finger and laughed and said, "Gonna get you, baby," and Connie turned away again without Eddie noticing anything.

She spent three hours with him, at the restaurant where they ate hamburgers and drank Cokes in wax cups that were always sweating, and then down an alley a mile or so away, and when he left her off at five to eleven only the movie house was still open at the plaza. Her girl friend was there, talking with a boy. When Connie came up the two girls smiled at each other and Connie said, "How was the movie?" and the girl said, "*You* should know." They rode off with the girl's father, sleepy and pleased, and Connie couldn't help but look at the darkened shopping plaza with its big empty parking lot and its signs that were faded and ghostly now, and over at the drive-in restaurant where cars were still circling tirelessly. She couldn't hear the music at this distance.

Next morning June asked her how the movie was and Connie said, "So-so."

10   She and that girl and occasionally another girl went out several times a week that way, and the rest of the time Connie spent around the house—it was summer vacation—getting in her mother's way and thinking, dreaming, about the boys she met. But all the boys fell back and dissolved into a single face that was not even a face, but an idea, a feeling, mixed up with the urgent insistent pounding of the music and the humid night air of July. Connie's mother kept dragging her back to the daylight by finding things for her to do or saying, suddenly, "What's this about the Pettinger girl?"

And Connie would say nervously, "Oh, her. That dope." She always drew thick clear lines between herself and such girls, and her mother was simple and kindly enough to believe her. Her mother was so simple, Connie thought, that it was maybe cruel to fool her so much. Her mother went scuffling around the house in old bedroom slippers and complained over the telephone to one sister about the other, then the other called up and the two of them complained about the third one. If June's name was mentioned her mother's tone was approving, and if Connie's name was mentioned it was disapproving. This did not really mean she disliked Connie and actually Connie thought that her mother preferred her to June because she was prettier, but the two of them kept up a pretense of exasperation, a sense that they were tugging and struggling over something of little value to either of them. Sometimes, over coffee, they were almost friends, but something would come up—some vexation that was like a fly buzzing suddenly around their heads—and their faces went hard with contempt.

One Sunday Connie got up at eleven—none of them bothered with church—and washed her hair so that it could dry all day long, in the sun. Her parents and sister were going to a barbecue at an aunt's house and Connie said no, she wasn't interested, rolling her eyes to let her mother know just what she thought of it. "Stay home alone then," her mother said sharply. Connie sat out back in a lawn chair and watched them drive away, her father quiet and bald, hunched around so that he could back the car out, her mother with a look that was still angry and not at all softened through the windshield, and in the back seat poor old June all dressed up as if she didn't know what a barbecue was, with all the running yelling kids and the flies. Connie sat with her eyes closed in the sun, dreaming and dazed with the warmth about her as if this were a kind of love, the caresses of love, and her mind slipped over onto thoughts of the boy she had been with the night before and how nice he had been, how sweet it always was, not the way someone like June would suppose but sweet, gentle, the way it was in movies and promised in songs; and when she opened her eyes she hardly knew where she was, the back yard ran off into weeds and a fence-line of trees and behind it the sky was perfectly blue and still. The asbestos "ranch house" that was now three years old startled her—it looked small. She shook her head as if to get awake.

It was too hot. She went inside the house and turned on the radio to drown out the quiet. She sat on the edge of her bed, barefoot, and listened for an hour and a half to a program called XYZ Sunday Jamboree, record after record of hard, fast, shrieking songs she sang along with, interspersed by exclamations from "Bobby King": "An' look here you girls at Napoleon's—Son and Charley want you to pay real close attention to this song coming up!"

And Connie paid close attention herself, bathed in a glow of slow-pulsed joy that seemed to rise mysteriously out of the music itself and lay languidly about the airless little room, breathed in and breathed out with each gentle rise and fall of her chest.

After a while she heard a car coming up the drive. She sat up at once, startled, because it couldn't be her father so soon. The gravel kept crunching all the way in from the road—the driveway was long—and Connie ran to the window. It was a car she didn't know. It was an open jalopy, painted a bright gold that caught the sunlight opaquely. Her heart began to pound and her fingers snatched at her hair, checking it, and she whispered "Christ. Christ," wondering how bad she looked. The car came to a stop at the side door and the horn sounded four short taps as if this were a signal Connie knew.

15

She went into the kitchen and approached the door slowly, then hung out the screen door, her bare toes curling down off the step. There were two boys in the car and now she recognized the driver: he had shaggy, shabby black hair that looked crazy as a wig and he was grinning at her.

"I ain't late, am I?" he said.

"Who the hell do you think you are?" Connie said.

"Toldja I'd be out, didn't I?"

20   "I don't even know who you are."

She spoke sullenly, careful to show no interest or pleasure, and he spoke in a fast bright monotone. Connie looked past him to the other boy, taking her time. He had fair brown hair, with a lock that fell onto his forehead. His sideburns gave him a fierce, embarrassed look, but so far he hadn't even bothered to glance at her. Both boys wore sunglasses. The driver's glasses were metallic and mirrored everything in miniature.

"You wanta come for a ride?" he said.

Connie smirked and let her hair fall loose over one shoulder.

"Don'tcha like my car? New paint job," he said. "Hey."

25   "What?"

"You're cute."

She pretended to fidget, chasing flies away from the door.

"Don'tcha believe me, or what?" he said.

"Look, I don't even know who you are," Connie said in disgust.

30   "Hey, Ellie's got a radio, see. Mine's broke down." He lifted his friend's arm and showed her the little transistor the boy was holding, and now Connie began to hear the music. It was the same program that was playing inside the house.

"Bobby King?" she said.

"I listen to him all the time. I think he's great."

"He's kind of great," Connie said reluctantly.

"Listen, that guy's *great*. He knows where the action is."

35   Connie blushed a little, because the glasses made it impossible for her to see just what this boy was looking at. She couldn't decide if she liked him or if he was just a jerk, and so she dawdled in the doorway and wouldn't come down or go back inside. She said, "What's all that stuff painted on your car?"

"Can'tcha read it?" He opened the door very carefully, as if he was afraid it might fall off. He slid out just as carefully, planting his feet firmly on the ground, the tiny metallic world in his glasses slowing down like gelatine hardening and in the midst of it Connie's bright green blouse. "This here is my name, to begin with," he said. ARNOLD

FRIEND was written in tarlike black letters on the side, with a drawing of a round grinning face that reminded Connie of a pumpkin, except it wore sunglasses. "I wanta introduce myself, I'm Arnold Friend and that's my real name and I'm gonna be your friend, honey, and inside the car's Ellie Oscar, he's kinda shy." Ellie brought his transistor radio up to his shoulder and balanced it there. "Now these numbers are a secret code, honey," Arnold Friend explained. He read off the numbers 33, 19, 17 and raised his eyebrows at her to see what she thought of that, but she didn't think much of it. The left rear fender had been smashed and around it was written, on the gleaming gold background: DONE BY CRAZY WOMAN DRIVER. Connie had to laugh at that. Arnold Friend was pleased at her laughter and looked up at her. "Around the other side's a lot more—you wanta come and see them?"

"No."

"Why not?"

"Why should I?"

"Don'tcha wanta see what's on the car? Don'tcha wanta go for a   40
ride?"

"I don't know."

"Why not?"

"I got things to do."

"Like what?"

"Things."   45

He laughed as if she had said something funny. He slapped his thighs. He was standing in a strange way, leaning back against the car as if he were balancing himself. He wasn't tall, only an inch or so taller than she would be if she came down to him. Connie liked the way he was dressed, which was the way all of them dressed: tight faded jeans stuffed into black, scuffed boots, a belt that was a little soiled and showed how lean he was, and a white pull-over shirt that was a little soiled and showed the hard small muscles of his arms and shoulders. He looked as if he probably did hard work, lifting and carrying things. Even his neck looked muscular. And his face was a familiar face, somehow: the jaw and chin and cheeks slightly darkened, because he hadn't shaved for a day or two, and the nose long and hawk-like, sniffing as if she were a treat he was going to gobble up and it was all a joke.

"Connie, you ain't telling the truth. This is your day set aside for a ride with me and you know it," he said, still laughing. The way he straightened and recovered from his fit of laughing showed that it had been all fake.

"How do you know what my name is?" she said suspiciously.

"It's Connie."

50   "Maybe and maybe not."

"I know my Connie," he said, wagging his finger. Now she remembered him even better, back at the restaurant, and her cheeks warmed at the thought of how she sucked in her breath just at the moment she passed him—how she must have looked to him. And he had remembered her. "Ellie and I come out here especially for you," he said. "Ellie can sit in back. How about it?"

"Where?"

"Where what?"

"Where're we going?"

55   He looked at her. He took off the sunglasses and she saw how pale the skin around his eyes was, like holes that were not in shadow but instead in light. His eyes were chips of broken glass that catch the light in an amiable way. He smiled. It was as if the idea of going for a ride somewhere, to some place, was a new idea to him.

"Just for a ride, Connie sweetheart."

"I never said my name was Connie," she said.

"But I know what it is. I know your name and all about you, lots of things," Arnold Friend said. He had not moved yet but stood still leaning back against the side of the jalopy. "I took a special interest in you, such a pretty girl, and found out all about you like I know your parents and sister are gone somewheres and I know where and how long they're going to be gone, and I know who you were with last night, and your best girl friend's name is Betty. Right?"

He spoke in a simple lilting voice, exactly as if he were reciting the words to a song. His smile assured her that everything was fine. In the car Ellie turned up the volume on his radio and did not bother to look around at them.

60   "Ellie can sit in the back seat," Arnold Friend said. He indicated his friend with a casual jerk of his chin, as if Ellie did not count and she should not bother with him.

"How'd you find out all that stuff?" Connie said.

"Listen: Betty Schultz and Tony Fitch and Jimmy Pettinger and Nancy Pettinger," he said, in a chant. "Raymond Stanley and Bob Hutter—"

"Do you know all those kids?"

"I know everybody."

65   "Look, you're kidding. You're not from around here."

"Sure."

"But—how come we never saw you before?"

"Sure you saw me before," he said. He looked down at his boots, as if he were a little offended. "You just don't remember."

"I guess I'd remember you," Connie said.

"Yeah?" He looked up at this, beaming. He was pleased. He began   70
to mark time with the music from Ellie's radio, tapping his fists lightly
together. Connie looked away from his smile to the car, which was
painted so bright it almost hurt her eyes to look at it. She looked at that
name, ARNOLD FRIEND. And up at the front fender was an expression that was familiar—MAN THE FLYING SAUCERS. It was an expression kids had used the year before, but didn't use this year. She
looked at it for a while as if the words meant something to her that she
did not yet know.

"What're you thinking about? Huh?" Arnold Friend demanded.
"Not worried about your hair blowing around in the car, are you?"

"No."

"Think I maybe can't drive good?"

"How do I know?"

"You're a hard girl to handle. How come?" he said. "Don't you   75
know I'm your friend? Didn't you see me put my sign in the air when
you walked by?"

"What sign?"

"My sign." And he drew an X in the air, leaning out toward her.
They were maybe ten feet apart. After his hand fell back to his side the
X was still in the air, almost visible. Connie let the screen door close
and stood perfectly still inside it, listening to the music from her radio
and the boy's blend together. She stared at Arnold Friend. He stood
there so stiffly relaxed, pretending to be relaxed, with one hand idly on
the door handle as if he were keeping himself up that way and had no
intention of ever moving again. She recognized most things about him,
the tight jeans that showed his thighs and buttocks and the greasy
leather boots and the tight shirt, and even that slippery friendly smile
of his, that sleepy dreamy smile that all the boys used to get across ideas
they didn't want to put into words. She recognized all this and also the
singsong way he talked, slightly mocking, kidding, but serious and a little melancholy, and she recognized the way he tapped one fist against
the other in homage to the perpetual music behind him. But all these
things did not come together.

She said suddenly, "Hey, how old are you?"

His smile faded. She could see then that he wasn't a kid, he was
much older—thirty, maybe more. At this knowledge her heart began to
pound faster.

"That's a crazy thing to ask. Can'tcha see I'm your own age?"   80

"Like hell you are."

"Or maybe a coupla years older, I'm eighteen."

"Eighteen?" she said doubtfully.

He grinned to reassure her and lines appeared at the corners of his mouth. His teeth were big and white. He grinned so broadly his eyes became slits and she saw how thick the lashes were, thick and black as if painted with a black tar-like material. Then he seemed to become embarrassed, abruptly, and looked over his shoulder at Ellie. "*Him*, he's crazy," he said. "Ain't he a riot, he's a nut, a real character." Ellie was still listening to the music. His sunglasses told nothing about what he was thinking. He wore a bright orange shirt unbuttoned halfway to show his chest, which was a pale, bluish chest and not muscular like Arnold Friend's. His shirt collar was turned up all around and the very tips of the collar pointed out past his chin as if they were protecting him. He was pressing the transistor radio up against his ear and sat there in a kind of daze, right in the sun.

85   "He's kinda strange," Connie said.

"Hey, she says you're kinda strange! Kinda strange!" Arnold Friend cried. He pounded on the car to get Ellie's attention. Ellie turned for the first time and Connie saw with shock that he wasn't a kid either— he had a fair, hairless face, cheeks reddened slightly as if the veins grew too close to the surface of his skin, the face of a forty-year-old baby. Connie felt a wave of dizziness rise in her at this sight and she stared at him as if waiting for something to change the shock of the moment, make it all right again. Ellie's lips kept shaping words, mumbling along with the words blasting in his ear.

"Maybe you two better go away," Connie said faintly.

"What? How come?" Arnold Friend cried. "We come out here to take you for a ride. It's Sunday." He had the voice of the man on the radio now. It was the same voice, Connie thought. "Don'tcha know it's Sunday all day and honey, no matter who you were with last night today you're with Arnold Friend and don't you forget it!—Maybe you better step out here," he said, and this last was in a different voice. It was a little flatter, as if the heat was finally getting to him.

"No. I got things to do."

90   "Hey."

"You two better leave."

"We ain't leaving until you come with us."

"Like hell I am—"

"Connie, don't fool around with me. I mean, I mean, don't fool *around*," he said, shaking his head. He laughed incredulously. He placed his sunglasses on top of his head, carefully, as if he were indeed wearing a wig, and brought the stems down behind his ears. Connie stared at him, another wave of dizziness and fear rising in her so that for a moment he wasn't even in focus but was just a blur, standing there against his gold car, and she had the idea that he had driven up the driveway all right but had come from nowhere before that and belonged nowhere and that everything about him and even about the music that was so familiar to her was only half real.

"If my father comes and sees you—"   95

"He ain't coming. He's at a barbecue."

"How do you know that?"

"Aunt Tillie's. Right now they're—uh—they're drinking. Sitting around," he said vaguely, squinting as if he were staring all the way to town and over to Aunt Tillie's backyard. Then the vision seemed to get clear and he nodded energetically. "Yeah. Sitting around. There's your sister in a blue dress, huh? And high heels, the poor sad bitch—nothing like you sweetheart! And your mother's helping some fat woman with the corn, They're cleaning the corn—husking the corn—"

"What fat woman?" Connie cried.

"How do I know what fat woman. I don't know every goddam fat   100
woman in the world!" Arnold Friend laughed.

"Oh, that's Mrs. Hornby. . . . Who invited her?" Connie said. She felt a little light-headed. Her breath was coming quickly.

"She's too fat. I don't like them fat. I like them the way you are, honey," he said, smiling sleepily at her. They stared at each other for a while, through the screen door. He said softly, "Now what you're going to do is this: you're going to come out that door. You're going to sit up front with me and Ellie's going to sit in the back, the hell with Ellie, right? This isn't Ellie's date. You're my date. I'm your lover, honey."

"What? You're crazy—"

"Yes, I'm your lover. You don't know what that is but you will," he said. "I know that too. I know all about you. But look: it's real nice and you couldn't ask for nobody better than me, or more polite. I always keep my word. I'll tell you how it is, I'm always nice at first, the first time. I'll hold you so tight you won't think you have to try to get away or pretend anything because you'll know you can't. And I'll come inside you where it's all secret and you'll give in to me and you'll love me—"

"Shut up! You're crazy!" Connie said. She backed away from the   105
door. She put her hands against her ears as if she'd heard something terrible, something not meant for her. "People don't talk like that, you're crazy," she muttered. Her heart was almost too big now for her chest and its pumping made sweat break out all over her. She looked out to see Arnold Friend pause and then take a step toward the porch lurching. He almost fell. But, like a clever drunken man, he managed to

catch his balance. He wobbled in his high boots and grabbed hold of one of the porch posts.

"Honey?" he said. "You still listening?"

"Get the hell out of here!"

"Be nice, honey. Listen."

"I'm going to call the police—"

110   He wobbled again and out of the side of his mouth came a fast spat curse, an aside not meant for her to hear. But even this "Christ!" sounded forced. Then he began to smile again. She watched this smile come, awkward as if he were smiling from inside a mask. His whole face was a mask, she thought wildly, tanned down onto his throat but then running out as if he had plastered makeup on his face but had forgotten about his throat.

"Honey—? Listen, here's how it is. I always tell the truth and I promise you this: I ain't coming in that house after you."

"You better not! I'm going to call the police if you—if you don't—"

"Honey," he said, talking right through her voice, "honey, I'm not coming in there but you are coming out here. You know why?"

She was panting. The kitchen looked like a place she had never seen before, some room she had run inside but which wasn't good enough, wasn't going to help her. The kitchen window had never had a curtain, after three years, and there were dishes in the sink for her to do—probably—and if you ran your hand across the table you'd probably feel something sticky there.

115   "You listening, honey? Hey?"

"—going to call the police—"

"Soon as you touch the phone I don't need to keep my promise and can come inside. You won't want that."

She rushed forward and tried to lock the door. Her fingers were shaking. "But why lock it," Arnold Friend said gently, talking right into her face. "It's just a screen door. It's just nothing." One of his boots was at a strange angle, as if his foot wasn't in it. It pointed out to the left, bent at the ankle. "I mean, anybody can break through a screen door and glass and wood and iron or anything else if he needs to, anybody at all and specially Arnold Friend. If the place got lit up with a fire honey you'd come running out into my arms, right into my arms and safe at home—like you knew I was your lover and'd stopped fooling around. I don't mind a nice shy girl but I don't like no fooling around." Part of those words were spoken with a slight rhythmic lilt, and Connie somehow recognized them—the echo of a song from last year, about a girl rushing into her boyfriend's arms and coming home again—

Connie stood barefoot on the linoleum floor, staring at him. "What do you want?" she whispered.

"I want you," he said.   120

"What?"

"Seen you that night and thought, that's the one, yes sir. I never needed to look any more."

"But my father's coming back. He's coming to get me. I had to wash my hair first—" She spoke in a dry, rapid voice, hardly raising it for him to hear.

"No, your daddy is not coming and yes, you had to wash your hair and you washed it for me. It's nice and shining and all for me, I thank you, sweetheart," he said, with a mock bow, but again he almost lost his balance. He had to bend and adjust his boots. Evidently his feet did not go all the way down; the boots must have been stuffed with something so that he would seem taller. Connie stared out at him and behind him Ellie in the car, who seemed to be looking off toward Connie's right, into nothing. This Ellie said, pulling the words out of the air one after another as if he were just discovering them, "You want me to pull out the phone?"

"Shut your mouth and keep it shut," Arnold Friend said, his face   125
red from bending over or maybe from embarrassment because Connie had seen his boots. "This ain't none of your business."

"What—what are you doing? What do you want?" Connie said. "If I call the police they'll get you, they'll arrest you—

"Promise was not to come in unless you touch that phone, and I'll keep that promise," he said. He resumed his erect position and tried to force his shoulders back. He sounded like a hero in a movie, declaring something important. He spoke too loudly and it was as if he were speaking to someone behind Connie. "I ain't made plans for coming in that house where I don't belong but just for you to come out to me, the way you should. Don't you know who I am?"

"You're crazy," she whispered. She backed away from the door but did not want to go into another part of the house, as if this would give him permission to come through the door. "What do you. . . . You're crazy, you . . ."

"Huh? What're you saying, honey?"

Her eyes darted everywhere in the kitchen. She could not remem-   130
ber what it was, this room.

"This is how it is, honey: you come out and we'll drive away, have a nice ride. But if you don't come out we're gonna wait till your people come home and then they're all going to get it."

"You want that telephone pulled out?" Ellie said. He held the radio away from his ear and grimaced, as if without the radio the air was too much for him.

"I toldja shut up, Ellie," Arnold Friend said, "you're deaf, get a hearing aid, right? Fix yourself up. This little girl's no trouble and's gonna be nice to me, so Ellie keep to yourself, this ain't your date— right? Don't hem in on me. Don't hog. Don't crush. Don't bird dog. Don't trail me," he said in a rapid meaningless voice, as if he were running through all the expressions he'd learned but was no longer sure which one of them was in style, then rushing on to new ones, making them up with his eyes closed, "Don't crawl under my fence, don't squeeze in my chipmunk hole, don't sniff my glue, suck my Popsicle, keep your own greasy fingers on yourself!" He shaded his eyes and peered in at Connie, who was backed against the kitchen table. "Don't mind him honey he's just a creep. He's a dope. Right? I'm the boy for you and like I said you come out here nice like a lady and give me your hand, and nobody else gets hurt, I mean, your nice old bald-headed daddy and your mummy and your sister in her high heels. Because listen: why bring them in this?"

"Leave me alone," Connie whispered.

135   "Hey, you know that old woman down the road, the one with the chickens and stuff—you know her?"

"She's dead!"

"Dead? What? You know her?" Arnold Friend said.

"She's dead—"

"Don't you like her?"

140   "She's dead—she's—she isn't here any more—"

"But don't you like her, I mean, you got something against her? Some grudge or something?" Then his voice dipped as if he were conscious of a rudeness. He touched the sunglasses perched on top of his head as if to make sure they were still there. "Now you be a good girl."

"What are you going to do?"

"Just two things, or maybe three," Arnold Friend said. "But I promise it won't last long and you'll like me that way you get to like people you're close to. You will. It's all over for you here, so come on out. You don't want your people in any trouble, do you?"

She turned and bumped against a chair or something, hurting her leg, but she ran into the back room and picked up the telephone. Something roared in her ear, a tiny roaring, and she was so sick with fear that she could do nothing but listen to it—the telephone was clammy and very heavy and her fingers groped down to the dial but were too weak to touch it. She began to scream into the phone, into the roaring. She cried out, she cried for her mother, she felt her breath start jerking back and forth in her lungs as if it were something Arnold Friend were stabbing her with again and again with no tenderness. A noisy sorrowful wailing rose all about her and she was locked inside it the way she was locked inside the house.

After a while she could hear again. She was sitting on the floor   145
with her wet back against the wall.

Arnold Friend was saying from the door, "That's a good girl. Put the phone back."

She kicked the phone away from her.

"No, honey. Pick it up. Put it back right."

She picked it up and put it back. The dial tone stopped.

"That's a good girl. Now you come outside.   150

She was hollow with what had been fear, but what was now just an emptiness. All that screaming had blasted it out of her. She sat, one leg cramped under her, and deep inside her brain was something like a pinpoint of light that kept going and would not let her relax. She thought, I'm not going to see my mother again. She thought, I'm not going to sleep in my bed again. Her bright green blouse was all wet.

Arnold Friend said, in a gentle-loud voice that was like a stage voice, "The place where you came from ain't there any more, and where you had in mind to go is cancelled out. This place you are now— inside your daddy's house—is nothing but a cardboard box I can knock down any time. You know that and always did know it. You hear me?"

She thought, I have got to think. I have to know what to do.

"We'll go out to a nice field, out in the country here where it smells so nice and it's sunny," Arnold Friend said. "I'll have my arms around you so you won't need to try to get away and I'll show you what love is like, what it does. The hell with this house! It looks solid all right," he said. He ran a fingernail down the screen and the noise did not make Connie shiver, as it would have the day before. "Now put your hand on your heart, honey. Feel that? That feels solid too but we know better, be nice to me, be sweet like you can because what else is there for a girl like you but to be sweet and pretty and give in?—and get away before her people come back?"

She felt her pounding heart. Her hand seemed to enclose it. She   155
thought for the first time in her life that it was nothing that was hers, that belonged to her, but just a pounding, living thing inside this body that wasn't really hers either.

"You don't want them to get hurt," Arnold Friend went on. "Now get up, honey. Get up all by yourself."

She stood.

"Now turn this way. That's right. Come over here to me—Ellie, put that away, didn't I tell you? You dope. You miserable creepy dope," Arnold Friend said. His words were not angry but only part of an incantation. The incantation was kindly. "Now come out through the kitchen to me honey and let's see a smile, try it, you're a brave sweet little girl and now they're eating corn and hotdogs cooked to bursting over an outdoor fire, and they don't know one thing about you and never did and honey you're better than them because not a one of them would have done this for you."

Connie felt the linoleum under her feet; it was cool. She brushed her hair back out of her eyes. Arnold Friend let go of the post tentatively and opened his arms for her, his elbows pointing in toward each other and his wrists limp, to show that this was an embarrassed embrace and a little mocking, he didn't want to make her self-conscious.

160   She put out her hand against the screen. She watched herself push the door slowly open as if she were safe back somewhere in the other doorway, watching this body and this head of long hair moving out into the sunlight where Arnold Friend waited.

"My sweet little blue-eyed girl," he said, in a half-sung sigh that had nothing to do with her brown eyes but was taken up just the same by the vast sunlit reaches of the land behind him and on all sides of him, so much land that Connie had never seen before and did not recognize except to know that she was going to it.

QUESTIONS

1. Oates has called this story a "realistic allegory." What are the allegorical elements in the story?
2. Describe the characterization of Connie. Is she a typical teenage girl of her time and place? What techniques does Oates employ to make her an individual, three-dimensional character?
3. Why is Connie's sister June included in the story? How does her characterization serve to highlight Connie's own?
4. Do the descriptions of Arnold Friend—his face, his clothing, his dialogue—have symbolic meaning? Is his name symbolic?
5. Discuss the symbolic importance of music in the story. Why is music so important to Connie and to the story as a whole?
6. What is the significance of the title? Does it point to an allegorical interpretation?
7. Describe the ways in which the story generates suspense. At which points is an increase of suspense particularly noticeable?
8. Why does Connie agree to go with Arnold Friend? Is she motivated by altruism and a love for her family, or by simple fear and hysteria? What is her ultimate fate?

9. View the film version of this story, entitled *Smooth Talk*, directed by Joyce Chopra and starring Laura Dern as Connie and Treat Williams as Arnold Friend. How is your experience of the film different from that of the story? Note in particular the different ending in the film version. Why do you suppose the director chose to change the ending?

Gabriel García Márquez

A Very Old Man with Enormous Wings

On the third day of rain they had killed so many crabs inside the house that Pelayo had to cross his drenched courtyard and throw them into the sea, because the newborn child had a temperature all night and they thought it was due to the stench. The world had been sad since Tuesday. Sea and sky were a single ash-gray thing and the sands of the beach, which on March nights glimmered like powdered light, had become a stew of mud and rotten shellfish. The light was so weak at noon that when Pelayo was coming back to the house after throwing away the crabs, it was hard for him to see what it was that was moving and groaning in the rear of the courtyard. He had to go very close to see that it was an old man, a very old man, lying face down in the mud, who, in spite of his tremendous efforts, couldn't get up, impeded by his enormous wings.

Frightened by that nightmare, Pelayo ran to get Elisenda, his wife, who was putting compresses on the sick child, and he took her to the rear of the courtyard. They both looked at the fallen body with mute stupor. He was dressed like a ragpicker. There were only a few faded hairs left on his bald skull and very few teeth in his mouth, and his pitiful condition of a drenched great-grandfather had taken away any sense of grandeur he might have had. His huge buzzard wings, dirty and half-plucked, were forever entangled in the mud. They looked at him so long and so closely that Pelayo and Elisenda very soon overcame their surprise and in the end found him familiar. Then they dared speak to him, and he answered in an incomprehensible dialect with a strong

A VERY OLD MAN WITH ENORMOUS WINGS   First published in 1955. Translated by Gregory Rabassa. Born in Colombia in 1928, Gabriel García Márquez studied law and worked as a newspaper reporter before publishing his first book of stories, *Leaf Storm* (1955). His best-known novels, which exemplify the unique blend of realistic and fantastic detail known as magical realism, include *One Hundred Years of Solitude* (1969) and *Love in the Time of Cholera* (1988). He won the Nobel Prize for literature in 1982.

sailor's voice. That was how they skipped over the inconvenience of the wings and quite intelligently concluded that he was a lonely castaway from some foreign ship wrecked by the storm. And yet, they called in a neighbor woman who knew everything about life and death to see him, and all she needed was one look to show them their mistake.

"He's an angel," she told them. "He must have been coming for the child, but the poor fellow is so old that the rain knocked him down."

On the following day everyone knew that a flesh-and-blood angel was held captive in Pelayo's house. Against the judgment of the wise neighbor woman, for whom angels in those times were the fugitive survivors of a celestial conspiracy, they did not have the heart to club him to death. Pelayo watched over him all afternoon from the kitchen, armed with his bailiff's club, and before going to bed he dragged him out of the mud and locked him up with the hens in the wire chicken coop. In the middle of the night, when the rain stopped, Pelayo and Elisenda were still killing crabs. A short time afterward the child woke up without a fever and with a desire to eat. Then they felt magnanimous and decided to put the angel on a raft with fresh water and provisions for three days and leave him to his fate on the high seas. But when they went out into the courtyard with the first light of dawn, they found the whole neighborhood in front of the chicken coop having fun with the angel, without the slightest reverence, tossing him things to eat through the openings in the wire as if he weren't a supernatural creature but a circus animal.

5   Father Gonzaga arrived before seven o'clock, alarmed at the strange news. By that time onlookers less frivolous than those at dawn had already arrived and they were making all kinds of conjectures concerning the captive's future. The simplest among them thought that he should be named mayor of the world. Others of sterner mind felt that he should be promoted to the rank of five-star general in order to win all wars. Some visionaries hoped that he could be put to stud in order to implant on earth a race of winged wise men who could take charge of the universe. But Father Gonzaga, before becoming a priest, had been a robust woodcutter. Standing by the wire, he reviewed his catechism in an instant and asked them to open the door so that he could take a close look at that pitiful man who looked more like a huge decrepit hen among the fascinated chickens. He was lying in a corner drying his open wings in the sunlight among the fruit peels and breakfast leftovers that the early risers had thrown him. Alien to the impertinences of the world, he only lifted his antiquarian eyes and murmured something in his dialect when Father Gonzaga went into the chicken

coop and said good morning to him in Latin. The parish priest had his first suspicion of an impostor when he saw that he did not understand the language of God or know how to greet His ministers. Then he noticed that seen close up he was much too human: he had an unbearable smell of the outdoors, the back side of his wings was strewn with parasites and his main feathers had been mistreated by terrestrial winds, and nothing about him measured up to the proud dignity of angels. Then he came out of the chicken coop and in a brief sermon warned the curious against the risks of being ingenuous. He reminded them that the devil had the bad habit of making use of carnival tricks in order to confuse the unwary. He argued that if wings were not the essential element in determining the difference between a hawk and an airplane, they were even less so in the recognition of angels. Nevertheless, he promised to write a letter to his bishop so that the latter would write to his primate so that the latter would write to the Supreme Pontiff in order to get the final verdict from the highest courts.

His prudence fell on sterile hearts. The news of the captive angel spread with such rapidity that after a few hours the courtyard had the bustle of a marketplace and they had to call in troops with fixed bayonets to disperse the mob that was about to knock the house down. Elisenda, her spine all twisted from sweeping up so much marketplace trash, then got the idea of fencing in the yard and charging five cents admission to see the angel.

The curious came from far away. A traveling carnival arrived with a flying acrobat who buzzed over the crowd several times, but no one paid any attention to him because his wings were not those of an angel but, rather, those of a sidereal bat. The most unfortunate invalids on earth came in search of health: a poor woman who since childhood had been counting her heartbeats and had run out of numbers; a Portuguese man who couldn't sleep because the noise of the stars disturbed him; a sleep-walker who got up at night to undo the things he had done while awake; and many others with less serious ailments. In the midst of that shipwreck disorder that made the earth tremble, Pelayo and Elisenda were happy with fatigue, for in less than a week they had crammed their rooms with money and the line of pilgrims waiting their turn to enter still reached beyond the horizon.

The angel was the only one who took no part in his own act. He spent his time trying to get comfortable in his borrowed nest, befuddled by the hellish heat of the oil lamps and sacramental candles that had been placed along the wire. At first they tried to make him eat some mothballs, which, according to the wisdom of the wise neighbor woman, were the food prescribed for angels. But he turned them down, just as he turned down the papal lunches that the penitents brought him, and they never found out whether it was because he was an angel or because he was an old man that in the end he ate nothing but egg-plant mush. His only supernatural virtue seemed to be patience. Especially during the first days, when the hens pecked at him, searching for the stellar parasites that proliferated in his wings, and the cripples pulled out feathers to touch their defective parts with, and even the most merciful threw stones at him, trying to get him to rise so they could see him standing. The only time they succeeded in arousing him was when they burned his side with an iron for branding steers, for he had been motionless for so many hours that they thought he was dead. He awoke with a start, ranting in his hermetic language and with tears in his eyes, and he flapped his wings a couple of times, which brought on a whirlwind of chicken dung and lunar dust and a gale of panic that did not seem to be of this world. Although many thought that his reaction had been one not of rage but of pain, from then on they were careful not to annoy him, because the majority understood that his passivity was not that of a hero taking his ease but that of a cataclysm in repose.

Father Gonzaga held back the crowd's frivolity with formulas of maidservant inspiration while awaiting the arrival of a final judgment on the nature of the captive. But the mail from Rome showed no sense of urgency. They spent their time finding out if the prisoner had a navel, if his dialect had any connection with Aramaic, how many times he could fit on the head of a pin, or whether he wasn't just a Norwegian with wings. Those meager letters might have come and gone until the end of time if a providential event had not put an end to the priest's tribulations.

10   It so happened that during those days, among so many other carnival attractions, there arrived in town the traveling show of the woman who had been changed into a spider for having disobeyed her parents. The admission to see her was not only less than the admission to see the angel, but people were permitted to ask her all manner of questions about her absurd state and to examine her up and down so that no one would ever doubt the truth of her horror. She was a frightful tarantula the size of a ram and with the head of a sad maiden. What was most heart-rending, however, was not her outlandish shape but the sincere affliction with which she recounted the details of her misfortune. While still practically a child she had sneaked out of her parents' house to go to a dance, and while she was coming back through the woods after having danced all night without permission, a fearful thunderclap rent the sky in two and through the crack came the lightning bolt of brimstone that changed her into a spider. Her only nourishment

came from the meatballs that charitable souls chose to toss into her mouth. A spectacle like that, full of so much human truth and with such a fearful lesson, was bound to defeat without even trying that of a haughty angel who scarcely deigned to look at mortals. Besides, the few miracles attributed to the angel showed a certain mental disorder, like the blind man who didn't recover his sight but grew three new teeth, or the paralytic who didn't get to walk but almost won the lottery, and the leper whose sores sprouted sunflowers. Those consolation miracles, which were more like mocking fun, had already ruined the angel's reputation when the woman who had been changed into a spider finally crushed him completely. That was how Father Gonzaga was cured forever of his insomnia and Pelayo's courtyard went back to being as empty as during the time it had rained for three days and crabs walked through the bedrooms.

The owners of the house had no reason to lament. With the money they saved they built a two-story mansion with balconies and gardens and high netting so that crabs wouldn't get in during the winter, and with iron bars on the windows so that angels wouldn't get in. Pelayo also set up a rabbit warren close to town and gave up his job as bailiff for good, and Elisenda bought some satin pumps with high heels and many dresses of iridescent silk, the kind worn on Sunday by the most desirable women in those times. The chicken coop was the only thing that didn't receive any attention. If they washed it down with creolin and burned tears of myrrh inside it every so often, it was not in homage to the angel but to drive away the dungheap stench that still hung everywhere like a ghost and was turning the new house into an old one. At first, when the child learned to walk, they were careful that he not get too close to the chicken coop. But then they began to lose their fears and got used to the smell, and before the child got his second teeth he'd gone inside the chicken coop to play, where the wires were falling apart. The angel was no less standoffish with him than with other mortals, but he tolerated the most ingenious infamies with the patience of a dog who had no illusions. They both came down with chicken pox at the same time. The doctor who took care of the child couldn't resist the temptation to listen to the angel's heart, and he found so much whistling in the heart and so many sounds in his kidneys that it seemed impossible for him to be alive. What surprised him most, however, was the logic of his wings. They seemed so natural on that completely human organism that he couldn't understand why other men didn't have them too.

When the child began school it had been some time since the sun and rain had caused the collapse of the chicken coop. The angel went dragging himself about here and there like a stray dying man. They would drive him out of the bedroom with a broom and a moment later find him in the kitchen. He seemed to be in so many places at the same time that they grew to think that he'd been duplicated, that he was reproducing himself all through the house, and the exasperated and unhinged Elisenda shouted that it was awful living in that hell full of angels. He could scarcely eat and his antiquarian eyes had also become so foggy that he went about bumping into posts. All he had left were the bare cannulae of his last feathers. Pelayo threw a blanket over him and extended him the charity of letting him sleep in the shed, and only then did they notice that he had a temperature at night, and was delirious with the tongue twisters of an old Norwegian. That was one of the few times they became alarmed, for they thought he was going to die and not even the wise neighbor woman had been able to tell them what to do with dead angels.

And yet he not only survived his worst winter, but seemed improved with the first sunny days. He remained motionless for several days in the farthest corner of the courtyard, where no one would see him, and at the beginning of December some large, stiff feathers began to grow on his wings, the feathers of a scarecrow, which looked more like another misfortune of decrepitude. But he must have known the reason for those changes, for he was quite careful that no one should notice them, that no one should hear the sea chanteys that he sometimes sang under the stars. One morning Elisenda was cutting some bunches of onions for lunch when a wind that seemed to come from the high seas blew into the kitchen. Then she went to the window and caught the angel in his first attempts at flight. They were so clumsy that his fingernails opened a furrow in the vegetable patch and he was on the point of knocking the shed down with the ungainly flapping that slipped on the light and couldn't get a grip on the air. But he did manage to gain altitude. Elisenda let out a sigh of relief, for herself and for him, when she saw him pass over the last houses, holding himself up in some way with the risky flapping of a senile vulture. She kept watching him even when she was through cutting the onions and she kept on watching until it was no longer possible for her to see him, because then he was no longer an annoyance in her life but an imaginary dot on the horizon of the sea.

QUESTIONS

1. At what point in the story did you first know that it included elements of fantasy? Discuss the effect of the second sentence: "The world had been sad since Tuesday."

2. What is the symbolic significance of the old man and his enormous wings? Since he's called an "angel," is there a religious significance to his physical appearance? Why does the narrator stress such details as his "dirty and half-plucked" wings and his grossly physical, animalistic traits? How is the oxymoron "flesh-and-blood angel" central to the meaning?

3. The author wrote that this was "a tale for children." In what ways is it a tale for children but also a story for adults?

4. Discuss the blend of realistic and fantastic details. Does this blend make the story more or less effective? Does it require a different way of reading than other stories you've read that contain no elements of fantasy?

5. The story contains almost no dialogue. Why is this appropriate? How does it relate to the point of view the author has chosen?

6. What is the major theme of the story? How do the fantastic elements help provide insights into the way human beings actually think and behave?

SUGGESTIONS FOR WRITING

1. Compare the use of symbolism in any two of the following stories, clarifying how each achieves compression through the use of symbols:
   a. Mansfield, "Miss Brill" (page 175).
   b. Joyce, "Eveline" (page 442).
   c. Gordimer, "Once upon a Time" (page 220).
   d. Faulkner, "A Rose for Emily" (page 556).
   e. Hurston, "The Gilded Six-Bits" (page 564).
   f. Poe, "The Cask of Amontillado" (page 611).

2. Argue that any one of the following stories does, or does not, contain elements of fantasy. Carefully support your argument.
   a. Connell, "The Most Dangerous Game" (page 67).
   b. Mansfield, "Miss Brill" (page 175).
   c. Porter, "The Jilting of Granny Weatherall" (page 260).
   d. Lawrence, "The Rocking-Horse Winner" (page 285).
   e. Hawthorne, "Young Goodman Brown" (page 299).
   f. Jackson, "The Lottery" (page 251).
   g. Poe, "The Cask of Amontillado" (page 611).

Chapter Seven

Humor and Irony

In previous chapters, we have sometimes used the term "serious" to describe a story or writer whose intentions are literary and artistic rather than primarily commercial. In this context, however, it's important to understand that a serious story is not necessarily a solemn one. In fact, many of the world's great works of serious literature have employed humor in conveying major truths about the human condition. The ancient Greek and Roman dramatists wrote raucous comic plays; Shakespeare's humor is an important dimension of his work, in tragedies such as *Hamlet* and *King Lear* as well as in his famous comedies. Writers as diverse as Geoffrey Chaucer, Jonathan Swift, Jane Austen, Charles Dickens, Mark Twain, and Flannery O'Connor have used humor as a central element in their art.

Novels and short stories that employ humor often use the technique we call **irony,** a term which has a range of meanings that all involve some sort of discrepancy or incongruity. All the above-named writers are master ironists, employing incongruous situations and characters that evoke laughter in the reader even as they express a significant insight into human nature. Irony should not be equated with mere sarcasm, which is simply language one person uses to belittle or ridicule another. Irony is far more complex, a technique used to convey a truth about human experience by exposing some incongruity of a character's behavior or a society's traditions. Operating through careful, often subtle indirection, irony helps to critique the world in which we live by laughing at the many varieties of human eccentricity and folly. It may be useful here to distinguish three distinct kinds of irony found in literary fiction.

Verbal irony, usually the simplest kind, is a figure of speech in which the speaker says the opposite of what he or she intends to say. (This form of irony is, in fact, often employed to create sarcasm.) In "Hunters in the Snow," when Kenny says to Tub, "You're just wasting away before my very eyes," he is speaking ironically—and sarcastically—for of course Tub is obese. In the opening sentence of "The Lesson," the narrator writes that "Back in the days when everyone was old and stupid or young and foolish," she and her friend Sugar "were the only ones just right." This ironic beginning immediately establishes a distance between the adult narrator and her own youthful self at a time when she and Sugar, like most kids their age, thought they knew everything. These two examples clarify the distinction between sarcasm and irony: Kenny's remark is sarcastic, intended to ridicule Tub, whereas Sylvia is speaking with irony rather than sarcasm.

In **dramatic irony** the contrast is between what a character says or thinks and what the reader knows to be true. The value of this kind of irony lies in the truth it conveys about the character or the character's expectations. In "How I Met My Husband," for instance, Loretta Bird says about Mrs. Peebles, "She wouldn't find time to lay down in the middle of the day, if she had seven kids like I got." The reader grasps the irony of this remark, since Loretta herself often "finds time" to sit gossiping at the Peebles farm instead of staying home with her children. Another effective example comes when Miss Brill, sitting in the park, thinks about the other people around her:

> Other people sat on the benches and green chairs, but they were nearly always the same, Sunday after Sunday, and—Miss Brill had often noticed—there was something funny about nearly all of them . . . from the way they stared they looked as though they'd just come from dark little rooms or even—even cupboards!

It is ironic that the judgment she makes of them is exactly the same one the story makes of her—even including the word "funny," which the young girl later uses about her beloved fur. Miss Brill is unaware that her phrase "nearly always the same, Sunday after Sunday" describes her own behavior, which she unwittingly reveals when she thinks that she "had *often* noticed" them. And of course the irony of the statement about the "cupboards" they must have come from becomes overt when she returns at the end of the story to "her room like a cupboard." Perhaps the most poignant of the dramatic ironies involving Miss Brill lies in her boastful thought, "Yes, I have been an actress for a long time," for she has indeed created a fictitious role for herself—not that of a glamorous stage actress in a romantic musical play, but that of a perceptive, happy, and self-sufficient woman. First-person stories similarly use dramatic irony to suggest that the narrator is not reliable. In Porter's "The Jilting of Granny Weatherall," for example, Granny confusedly reports that ants are biting her when she is actually receiving a hypodermic injection, and that the priest is tickling her feet when really he is administering extreme unction (the last rites in Roman Catholicism). The result is an ironic portrayal of Granny's bewildered mental state.

In **irony of situation,** usually the most important kind for the fiction writer, the discrepancy is between appearance and reality, or between expectation and fulfillment, or between what is and what would seem appropriate. In "The Most Dangerous Game," it is ironic that Rainsford, "the celebrated hunter," should become the hunted, for this is a reversal of his expected and appropriate role. In "The Destructors," it is ironic that Old Misery's horoscope should read, "Abstain from any dealings in first half of week. Danger of serious crash," for the horoscope is valid in a sense that is quite different from what the words appear to indicate. In "Interpreter of Maladies," it is ironic that Mr. Das's guidebook to India "looked as if it had been published abroad," and that the Indian tour guide Mr. Kapasi watches the American television show *Dallas* but the American-born Tina Das has never heard of the program. In "Hunters in the Snow," it is ironic that inside the diner Frank and Tub encourage one another's self-indulgent behavior—Frank's lust for a teenage babysitter, Tub's gluttony—and view themselves as forming a noble, trusting alliance, when all the while their companion Kenny is lying wounded and freezing outside in the back of their truck.

Irony, like symbol and allegory, is often a means for the author to achieve compression. By creating an ironic situation or perspective, the author can suggest complex meanings without stating them. In "Miss Brill," we do not need to be told how difficult it is for an aging, solitary woman to cope with her aloneness; we witness her plight and the incongruous means by which she attempts to deny it and therefore endure it. In "Hunters in the Snow," we do not need to be told that these three hunting buddies are not "friends" in any meaningful sense of that word; we witness their cruel, self-absorbed behavior. In these and other stories, the ironic contrast between appearances and reality generates a complex set of meanings.

One reason that irony is such an important technique is that a story, like other art forms, achieves its effects through indirection. "Tell all the truth," Emily Dickinson advised, "but tell it slant"—advice as valid for fiction writers as for poets. In art, the truth must be produced indirectly because a flat statement—as in an essay, or a dry plot summary—can have no emotional impact on the reader. We must *feel* the truth a story conveys with our whole being, not simply understand it with our intellect. If a story has no emotional impact, it has failed as a work of art.

Humor and irony are important because they help an author to achieve such an impact. A reader will not respond to a story, for instance, that contrives its emotions and attempts to "play upon" the reader's feelings directly. An ironic method can help to temper and control the emotional content of a story, evoking responses that are intellectual and emotional at once. At the end of "Interpreter of Maladies," we feel Mr. Kapasi's disillusionment even as we understand the hopelessness of his attraction to Mrs. Das. The narrator's cool, dispassionate stance, complete with its ironic observations and its undercurrent of humor, helps to keep the story's emotional content more honest, genuine, and believable.

By contrast, stories that try to elicit easy or unearned emotional responses are guilty of **sentimentality.** Sentimentality in fiction is not the same as genuine emotion; rather, it is contrived or excessive emotion. A novel such as Harriet Beecher Stowe's *Uncle Tom's Cabin* (1852), for instance, often tries to wring tears from the reader over the plight of African American slaves; for this reason, the novel is much less powerful as a work of art than Toni Morrison's *Beloved* (1987), which uses carefully restrained, artful language and a frequently biting irony in its castigation of slavery. A narrative contains genuine emotion when it treats life faithfully and perceptively. A sentimental narrative oversimplifies and exaggerates emotion in the attempt to arouse a similarly excessive emotion in the reader.

Genuine emotion, like character, is presented indirectly—it is dramatized. It cannot be produced by words that identify emotions, like *angry, sad, pathetic, heart-breaking,* or *passionate.* A writer draws forth genuine emotion by producing a character in a situation that deserves our sympathy and showing us enough about the character and the situation to make them real and convincing.

Sentimental writers are recognizable by a number of characteristics. First, they often try to make words do what the situation faithfully presented by itself will not do. They **editorialize**—that is, comment on the story and, in a manner, instruct us how to feel. Or they overwrite and **poeticize**—use an immoderately heightened and distended language to accomplish their effects. Second, they make an excessively selective use of detail. All artists, of course, must be selective in their use of detail, but good writers use representative details while sentimentalists use details that all point one way—toward producing emotion rather than conveying truth. The little child who dies will be shown as always uncomplaining and cheerful under adversity, never as naughty, querulous, or ungrateful. It will possibly be an orphan or the only child of a mother who loves it dearly; in addition, it may be lame, hungry, ragged, and possessed of one toy, from which it cannot be parted. The villain will be *all* villain, with a cruel laugh and a sharp whip, though he may reform at the end, for sentimentalists are firm believers in the heart of gold beneath the rough exterior. In short, reality will be unduly heightened and drastically oversimplified. Third, sentimentalists rely heavily on the stock response—an emotion that has its source outside the facts established by the story. In some readers certain situations and objects—babies, mothers, grandmothers, young love, patriotism, worship—produce an almost automatic response, whether the immediate situation warrants it or not. Sentimental writers, to affect such readers, have only to draw out certain stops, as on an organ, to produce an easily anticipated effect. They depend on stock materials to produce a stock response. They thus need not go to the trouble of picturing the situation in realistic and convincing detail. Finally, sentimental writers present, nearly always, a fundamentally "sweet" picture of life. They rely not only on stock characters and situations but also on stock themes. For them every cloud has its silver lining, every bad event its good side, every storm its rainbow. If the little child dies, it goes to heaven or makes some life better by its death. Virtue is characteristically triumphant: the villain is defeated, the ne'er-do-well redeemed. True love is rewarded in some fashion; it is love—never hate—that makes the world go round. In short, sentimental writers specialize in the sad but sweet. The tears called for are warm tears, never bitter. There is always sugar at the bottom of the cup.

The writers we value most are able to look at human experience in a clear-eyed, honest way and to employ literary techniques such as humor and irony as a way to enhance, not reduce, the emotional impact of their stories. Though not every first-rate story contains humor—Joyce's "Eveline," for instance, presents a relentlessly bleak portrait of its heroine's plight—there are few that do not involve some blend on the author's part of human empathy and ironic detachment. After reading "Hills Like White Elephants," "Miss Brill," and "A Rose for Emily," for example, we experience a similarly blended response to the protagonists of these stories. A complex human reality requires a complex narrative technique, and in this way the best storytellers always have attempted to portray the whole of human experience—from its most tragic misery to its most absurd folly—in a single, integrated artistic vision.

REVIEWING CHAPTER SEVEN

1. Distinguish between verbal irony and dramatic irony.
2. Define the term "irony of situation."
3. Explore the reasons why sentimentality is an undesirable trait in literary fiction.
4. List the major characteristics of sentimental writing.
5. Describe the particular types of irony found in the following stories.

Frank O'Connor
The Drunkard

It was a terrible blow to Father when Mr. Dooley on the terrace died. Mr. Dooley was a commercial traveler with two sons in the Dominicans and a car of his own, so socially he was miles ahead of us, but he had no false pride. Mr. Dooley was an intellectual, and, like all intellectuals, the thing he loved best was conversation, and in his own limited way Father was a well-read man and could appreciate an intelligent talker. Mr. Dooley was remarkably intelligent. Between business acquaintances and clerical contacts, there was very little he didn't know about what went on in town, and evening after evening he crossed the road to our gate to explain to Father the news behind the news. He had a low, palavering voice and a knowing smile, and Father would listen in astonishment, giving him a conversational lead now and again, and then stump triumphantly in to Mother with his face aglow and ask: "Do you know what Mr. Dooley is after telling me?" Ever since, when somebody has given me some bit of information off the record I have found myself on the point of asking: "Was it Mr. Dooley told you that?"

Till I actually saw him laid out in his brown shroud with the rosary beads entwined between his waxy fingers I did not take the report of his death seriously. Even then I felt there must be a catch and that some summer evening Mr. Dooley must reappear at our gate to give us the lowdown on the next world. But Father was very upset, partly because Mr. Dooley was about one age with himself, a thing that always gives a distinctly personal turn to another man's demise; partly because now he would have no one to tell him what dirty work was behind the latest scene at the Corporation.° You could count on your fingers the number of men in Blarney Lane who read the papers as Mr. Dooley did, and none of these would have overlooked the fact that Father was only a laboring man. Even Sullivan, the carpenter, a mere nobody, thought he was a cut above Father. It was certainly a solemn event.

THE DRUNKARD   First published in 1948. Frank O'Connor (1903–1966) was born Michael O'Donovan, the only child of very poor, Roman Catholic parents in Cork, Ireland. He used his mother's maiden name as a pseudonym when he began to publish. "The Drunkard" is based on an incident from his boyhood in Cork, as revealed in the first two chapters of his autobiographical volume, *An Only Son* (1961).

Corporation: the officials of the city (mayor, aldermen, councillors)

"Half past two to the Curragh," Father said meditatively, putting down the paper.

"But you're not thinking of going to the funeral?" Mother asked in alarm.

5   "'Twould be expected," Father said, scenting opposition. "I wouldn't give it to say to them."

"I think," said Mother with suppressed emotion, "it will be as much as anyone will expect if you go to the chapel with him."

("Going to the chapel," of course, was one thing, because the body was removed after work, but going to a funeral meant the loss of a half-day's pay.)

"The people hardly know us," she added.

"God between us and all harm," Father replied with dignity, "we'd be glad if it was our own turn."

10   To give Father his due, he was always ready to lose a half day for the sake of an old neighbor. It wasn't so much that he liked funerals as that he was a conscientious man who did as he would be done by, and nothing could have consoled him so much for the prospect of his own death as the assurance of a worthy funeral. And, to give Mother her due, it wasn't the half-day's pay she begrudged, badly as we could afford it.

Drink, you see, was Father's great weakness. He could keep steady for months, even for years, at a stretch, and while he did he was as good as gold. He was first up in the morning and brought the mother a cup of tea in bed, stayed home in the evenings and read the paper; saved money and bought himself a new blue serge suit and bowler hat. He laughed at the folly of men who, week in, week out, left their hard-earned money with the publicans; and sometimes, to pass an idle hour, he took pencil and paper and calculated precisely how much he saved each week through being a teetotaller. Being a natural optimist he sometimes continued this calculation through the whole span of his prospective existence and the total was breathtaking. He would die worth hundreds.

If I had only known it, this was a bad sign; a sign he was becoming stuffed up with spiritual pride and imagining himself better than his neighbors. Sooner or later, the spiritual pride grew till it called for some form of celebration. Then he took a drink—not whiskey, of course; nothing like that—just a glass of some harmless drink like lager beer. That was the end of Father. By the time he had taken the first he already realized that he had made a fool of himself, took a second to forget it and a third to forget that he couldn't forget, and at last came home reeling drunk. From this on it was "The Drunkard's Progress," as in the moral prints. Next day he stayed in from work with a sick head while Mother went off to make his excuses at the works, and inside a fortnight he was poor and savage and despondent again. Once he began he drank steadily through everything down to the kitchen clock. Mother and I knew all the phases and dreaded all the dangers. Funerals were one.

"I have to go to Dunphy's to do a half-day's work," said Mother in distress. "Who's to look after Larry?"

"I'll look after Larry," Father said graciously. "The little walk will do him good."

There was no more to be said, though we all knew I didn't need anyone to look after me, and that I could quite well have stayed home and looked after Sonny, but I was being attached to the party to act as a brake on Father. As a brake I had never achieved anything, but Mother still had great faith in me.

Next day, when I got home from school, Father was there before me and made a cup of tea for both of us. He was very good at tea, but too heavy in the hand for anything else; the way he cut bread was shocking. Afterwards, we went down the hill to the church, Father wearing his best blue serge and a bowler cocked to one side of his head with the least suggestion of the masher. To his great joy he discovered Peter Crowley among the mourners. Peter was another danger signal, as I knew well from certain experiences after Mass on Sunday morning: a mean man, as Mother said, who only went to funerals for the free drinks he could get at them. It turned out that he hadn't even known Mr. Dooley! But Father had a sort of contemptuous regard for him as one of the foolish people who wasted their good money in public-houses when they could be saving it. Very little of his own money Peter Crowley wasted!

It was an excellent funeral from Father's point of view. He had it all well studied before we set off after the hearse in the afternoon sunlight.

"Five carriages!" he exclaimed. "Five carriages and sixteen covered cars! There's one alderman, two councillors and 'tis unknown how many priests. I didn't see a funeral like this from the road since Willie Mack, the publican, died."

"Ah, he was well liked," said Crowley in his husky voice.

"My goodness, don't I know that?" snapped Father. "Wasn't the man my best friend? Two nights before he died—only two nights—he was over telling me the goings-on about the housing contract. Them fellows in the Corporation are night and day robbers. But even I never imagined he was as well connected as that."

15

20

Father was stepping out like a boy, pleased with everything: the other mourners, and the fine houses along Sunday's Well. I knew danger signals were there in full force: a sunny day, a fine funeral and a distinguished company of clerics and public men were bringing out all the natural vanity and flightiness of Father's character. It was with something like genuine pleasure that he saw his old friend lowered into the grave; with the sense of having performed a duty and the pleasant awareness that however much he would miss poor Mr. Dooley in the long summer evenings, it was he and not poor Mr. Dooley who would do the missing.

"We'll be making tracks before they break up," he whispered to Crowley as the gravediggers tossed in the first shovelfuls of clay, and away he went, hopping like a goat from grassy hump to hump. The drivers, who were probably in the same state as himself, though without months of abstinence to put an edge on it, looked up hopefully.

"Are they nearly finished, Mick?" bawled one.

"All over now bar the last prayers," trumpeted Father in the tone of one who brings news of great rejoicing.

25   The carriages passed us in a lather of dust several hundred yards from the public-house, and Father, whose feet gave him trouble in hot weather, quickened his pace, looking nervously over his shoulder for any sign of the main body of mourners crossing the hill. In a crowd like that a man might be kept waiting.

When we did reach the pub the carriages were drawn up outside, and solemn men in black ties were cautiously bringing out consolation to mysterious females whose hands reached out modestly from behind the drawn blinds of the coaches. Inside the pub there were only the drivers and a couple of shawly women. I felt if I was to act as a brake at all, this was the time, so I pulled Father by the coattails.

30   "Dadda, can't we go home now?" I asked.

"Two minutes now," he said, beaming affectionately. "Just a bottle of lemonade and we'll go home."

This was a bribe, and I knew it, but I was always a child of weak character. Father ordered lemonade and two pints. I was thirsty and swallowed my drink at once. But that wasn't Father's way. He had long months of abstinence behind him and an eternity of pleasure before. He took out his pipe, blew through it, filled it, and then lit it with loud pops, his eyes bulging above it. After that he deliberately turned his back on the pint, leaned one elbow on the counter in the attitude of a man who did not know there was a pint behind him, and deliberately brushed the tobacco from his palms. He had settled down for the evening. He was steadily working through all the important funerals he had ever attended. The carriages departed and the minor mourners drifted in till the pub was half full.

"Dadda," I said, pulling his coat again, "can't we go home now?"

"Ah, your mother won't be in for a long time yet," he said benevolently enough. "Run out in the road and play, can't you."

It struck me very cool, the way grown-ups assumed that you could play all by yourself on a strange road. I began to get bored as I had so often been bored before. I knew Father was quite capable of lingering there till nightfall. I knew I might have to bring him home, blind drunk, down Blarney Lane, with all the old women at their doors, saying: "Mick Delaney is on it again." I knew that my mother would be half crazy with anxiety; that next day Father wouldn't go out to work; and before the end of the week she would be running down to the pawn with the clock under her shawl. I could never get over the lonesomeness of the kitchen without a clock.

I was still thirsty. I found if I stood on tiptoe I could just reach Father's glass, and the idea occurred to me that it would be interesting to know what the contents were like. He had his back to it and wouldn't notice. I took down the glass and sipped cautiously. It was a terrible disappointment. I was astonished that he could even drink such stuff. It looked as if he had never tried lemonade.

I should have advised him about lemonade but he was holding forth himself in great style. I heard him say that bands were a great addition to a funeral. He put his arms in the position of someone holding a rifle in reverse and hummed a few bars of Chopin's Funeral March. Crowley nodded reverently. I took a longer drink and began to see that porter might have its advantages. I felt pleasantly elevated and philosophic. Father hummed a few bars of the Dead March in *Saul*. It was a nice pub and a very fine funeral, and I felt sure that poor Mr. Dooley in Heaven must be highly gratified. At the same time I thought they might have given him a band. As Father said, bands were a great addition.

But the wonderful thing about porter was the way it made you   35
stand aside, or rather float aloft like a cherub rolling on a cloud, and watch yourself with your legs crossed, leaning against a bar counter, not worrying about trifles but thinking deep, serious, grown-up thoughts about life and death. Looking at yourself like that, you couldn't help thinking after a while how funny you looked, and suddenly you got embarrassed and wanted to giggle. But by the time I had finished the pint, that phase too had passed; I found it hard to put back the glass, the counter seemed to have grown so high. Melancholia was supervening again.

"Well," Father said reverently, reaching behind him for his drink, "God rest the poor man's soul, wherever he is!" He stopped, looked first at the glass, and then at the people around him. "Hello," he said in a fairly good-humored tone, as if he were just prepared to consider it a joke, even if it was in bad taste, "who was at this?"

There was silence for a moment while the publican and the old women looked first at Father and then at his glass.

"There was no one at it, my good man," one of the women said with an offended air. "Is it robbers you think we are?"

"Ah, there's no one here would do a thing like that, Mick," said the publican in a shocked tone.

40   "Well, someone did it," said Father, his smile beginning to wear off.

"If they did, they were them that were nearer it," said the woman darkly, giving me a dirty look; and at the same moment the truth began to dawn on Father. I suppose I must have looked a bit starry-eyed. He bent and shook me.

"Are you all right, Larry?" he asked in alarm.

Peter Crowley looked down at me and grinned.

"Could you beat that?" he exclaimed in a husky voice.

45   I could and without difficulty. I started to get sick. Father jumped back in holy terror that I might spoil his good suit, and hastily opened the back door.

"Run! run! run!" he shouted.

I saw the sunlit wall outside with the ivy overhanging it, and ran. The intention was good but the performance was exaggerated, because I lurched right into the wall, hurting it badly, as it seemed to me. Being always very polite, I said "Pardon" before the second bout came on me. Father, still concerned for his suit, came up behind and cautiously held me while I got sick.

"That's a good boy!" he said encouragingly. "You'll be grand when you get that up."

Begor, I was not grand! Grand was the last thing I was. I gave one unmerciful wail out of me as he steered me back to the pub and put me sitting on the bench near the shawlies. They drew themselves up with an offended air, still sore at the suggestion that they had drunk his pint.

50   "God help us!" moaned one, looking pityingly at me. "Isn't it the likes of them would be fathers?"

"Mick," said the publican in alarm, spraying sawdust on my tracks, "that child isn't supposed to be in here at all. You'd better take him home quick in case a bobby would see him."

"Merciful God!" whimpered Father, raising his eyes to heaven and clapping his hands silently as he only did when distraught. "What misfortune was on me? Or what will his mother say? . . . If women might stop at home and look after their children themselves!" he added in a snarl for the benefit of the shawlies. "Are them carriages all gone, Bill?"

"The carriages are finished long ago, Mick," replied the publican.

"I'll take him home," Father said despairingly. . . . "I'll never bring you out again," he threatened me. "Here," he added, giving me the clean handkerchief from his breast pocket, "put that over your eye."

The blood on the handkerchief was the first indication I got that I   55
was cut, and instantly my temple began to throb and I set up another howl. "Whisht, whisht, whisht!" Father said testily, steering me out the door. "One'd think you were killed. That's nothing. We'll wash it when we get home."

"Steady now, old scout!" Crowley said, taking the other side of me. "You'll be all right in a minute."

I never met two men who knew less about the effects of drink. The first breath of fresh air and the warmth of the sun made me groggier than ever and I pitched and rolled between wind and tide till Father started to whimper again.

"God Almighty, and the whole road out! What misfortune was on me didn't stop at my work! Can't you walk straight?"

I couldn't. I saw plain enough that, coaxed by the sunlight, every woman old and young in Blarney Lane was leaning over her half-door or sitting on her doorstep. They all stopped gabbling to gape at the strange spectacle of two sober, middle-aged men bringing home a drunken small boy with a cut over his eye. Father, torn between the shamefast desire to get me home as quick as he could, and the neighborly need to explain that it wasn't his fault, finally halted outside Mrs. Roche's. There was a gang of old women outside a door at the opposite side of the road. I didn't like the look of them from the first. They seemed altogether too interested in me. I leaned against the wall of Mrs. Roche's cottage with my hands in my trousers pockets, thinking mournfully of poor Mr. Dooley in his cold grave on the Curragh, who would never walk down the road again, and, with great feeling, I began to sing a favorite song of Father's.

Though lost to Mononia and cold in the grave
He returns to Kincora no more.

"Wisha, the poor child!" Mrs. Roche said, "Haven't he a lovely   60
voice, God bless him!"

That was what I thought myself, so I was the more surprised when Father said "Whisht!" and raised a threatening finger at me. He didn't seem to realize the appropriateness of the song, so I sang louder than ever.

"Whisht, I tell you!" he snapped, and then tried to work up a smile for Mrs. Roche's benefit. "We're nearly home now. I'll carry you the rest of the way."

But, drunk and all as I was, I knew better than to be carried home ignominiously like that.

"Now," I said severely, "can't you leave me alone? I can walk all right. 'Tis only my head. All I want is a rest."

65 "But you can rest at home in bed," he said viciously, trying to pick me up, and I knew by the flush on his face that he was very vexed.

"Ah, Jasus," I said crossly, "what do I want to go home for? Why the hell can't you leave me alone?"

For some reason the gang of old women at the other side of the road thought this was very funny. They nearly split their sides over it. A gassy fury began to expand in me at the thought that a fellow couldn't have a drop taken without the whole neighborhood coming out to make game of him.

"Who are ye laughing at?" I shouted, clenching my fists at them. "I'll make ye laugh at the other side of yeer faces if ye don't let me pass."

They seemed to think this funnier still; I had never seen such ill-mannered people.

70 "Go away, ye bloody bitches!" I said.

"Whisht, whisht, whisht, I tell you!" snarled Father, abandoning all pretence of amusement and dragging me along behind him by the hand. I was maddened by the women's shrieks of laughter. I was maddened by Father's bullying. I tried to dig in my heels but he was too powerful for me, and I could only see the women by looking back over my shoulder.

"Take care or I'll come back and show ye!" I shouted. "I'll teach ye to let decent people pass. Fitter for ye to stop at home an wash yeer dirty faces."

"'Twill be all over the road," whimpered Father. "Never again, never again, not if I live to be a thousand!"

To this day I don't know whether he was forswearing me or the drink. By way of a song suitable to my heroic mood I bawled "The Boys of Wexford," as he dragged me in home. Crowley, knowing he was not safe, made off and Father undressed me and put me to bed. I couldn't sleep because of the whirling in my head. It was very unpleasant, and I got sick again. Father came in with a wet cloth and mopped up after me. I lay in a fever, listening to him chopping sticks to start a fire. After that I heard him lay the table.

Suddenly the front door banged open and Mother stormed in with   75
Sonny in her arms, not her usual gentle, timid self, but a wild, raging
woman. It was clear that she had heard it all from the neighbors.

"Mick Delaney," she cried hysterically, "what did you do to
my son?"

"Whisht, woman, whisht, whisht!" he hissed, dancing from one
foot to the other. "Do you want the whole road to hear?"

"Ah," she said with a horrifying laugh, "the road knows all about it
by this time. The road knows the way you filled your unfortunate innocent child with drink to make sport for you and that other rotten,
filthy brute."

"But I gave him no drink," he shouted, aghast at the horrifying interpretation the neighbors had chosen to give his misfortune. "He took
it while my back was turned. What the hell do you think I am?"

"Ah," she replied bitterly, "everyone knows what you are now. God   80
forgive you, wasting our hard-earned few ha'pence on drink, and bringing up your child to be a drunken corner-boy like yourself."

Then she swept into the bedroom and threw herself on her knees
by the bed. She moaned when she saw the gash over my eye. In the
kitchen Sonny set up a loud bawl on his own, and a moment later Father appeared in the bedroom door with his cap over his eyes, wearing
an expression of the most intense self-pity.

"That's a nice way to talk to me after all I went through," he
whined. "That's a nice accusation, that I was drinking. Not one drop of
drink crossed my lips the whole day. How could it when he drank it all?
I'm the one that ought to be pitied, with my day ruined on me, and I
after being made a show for the whole road."

But the next morning, when he got up and went out quietly to
work with his dinner-basket, Mother threw herself on me in the bed
and kissed me. It seemed it was all my doing, and I was being given a
holiday till my eye got better.

"My brave little man!" she said with her eyes shining. "It was God
did it you were there. You were his guardian angel."

QUESTIONS

1. What are the sources of humor in this story? Does the humor arise from observation of life or from distortion of life? What elements of the story seem
to you funniest?
2. Is this a purely humorous story, or are there undertones of pathos in it? If
the latter, from what does the pathos arise?
3. List what seem to you the chief insights into life and character presented by
the story.

4. Is the title seriously meant? To whom does it refer?
5. The boy's drunkenness is seen from four perspectives. What are they, and how do they differ?
6. What is the principal irony in the story?
7. The story is told in retrospect by a man recalling an incident from his boyhood. What does this removal in time do to the treatment of the material?
8. *Did* Larry's father forswear liquor? Support your answer with evidence from the story.

Woody Allen

The Kugelmass Episode

Kugelmass, a professor of humanities at City College, was unhappily married for the second time. Daphne Kugelmass was an oaf. He also had two dull sons by his first wife, Flo, and was up to his neck in alimony and child support.

"Did I know it would turn out so badly?" Kugelmass whined to his analyst one day. "Daphne had promise. Who suspected she'd let herself go and swell up like a beach ball? Plus she had a few bucks, which is not in itself a healthy reason to marry a person, but it doesn't hurt, with the kind of operating nut° I have. You see my point?"

Kugelmass was bald and as hairy as a bear, but he had soul.

"I need to meet a new woman," he went on. "I need to have an affair. I may not look the part, but I'm a man who needs romance. I need softness, I need flirtation. I'm not getting younger, so before it's too late I want to make love in Venice, trade quips at '21,'° and exchange coy glances over red wine and candlelight. You see what I'm saying?"

5   Dr. Mandel shifted in his chair and said, "An affair will solve nothing. You're so unrealistic. Your problems run much deeper."

"And also this affair must be discreet," Kugelmass continued. "I can't afford a second divorce. Daphne would really sock it to me."

"Mr. Kugelmass—"

THE KUGELMASS EPISODE   First published in 1977. This story was awarded First Prize in *Prize Stories: The O.Henry Awards 1978.* Woody Allen (b. 1935) is one of America's best-known film directors and comic actors. His essays and short stories have appeared in such publications as *The New Yorker* and *The New Republic* and have been collected in two volumes published by Random House.

operating nut: budget   **21:** a fashionable New York City nightclub and restaurant

"But it can't be anyone at City College, because Daphne also works there. Not that anyone on the faculty at C.C.N.Y. is any great shakes, but some of those coeds . . ."

"Mr. Kugelmass—"

"Help me. I had a dream last night. I was skipping through a meadow holding a picnic basket and the basket was marked 'Options.' And then I saw there was a hole in the basket."

"Mr. Kugelmass, the worst thing you could do is act out. You must simply express your feelings here, and together we'll analyze them. You have been in treatment long enough to know there is no overnight cure. After all, I'm an analyst, not a magician."

"Then perhaps what I need is a magician," Kugelmass said, rising from his chair. And with that he terminated his therapy.

A couple of weeks later, while Kugelmass and Daphne were moping around in their apartment one night like two pieces of old furniture, the phone rang.

"I'll get it," Kugelmass said. "Hello."

"Kugelmass?" a voice said. "Kugelmass, this is Persky."

"Who?"

"Persky. Or should I say The Great Persky?"

"Pardon me?"

"I hear you're looking all over town for a magician to bring a little exotica into your life? Yes or no?"

"Sh-h-h," Kugelmass whispered. "Don't hang up. Where are you calling from, Persky?"

Early the following afternoon, Kugelmass climbed three flights of stairs in a broken-down apartment house in the Bushwick section of Brooklyn. Peering through the darkness of the hall, he found the door he was looking for and pressed the bell. I'm going to regret this, he thought to himself.

Seconds later, he was greeted by a short, thin, waxy-looking man.

"*You're* Persky the Great?" Kugelmass said.

"The Great Persky. You want a tea?"

"No, I want romance. I want music. I want love and beauty."

"But not tea, eh? Amazing. O.K., sit down."

Persky went to the back room, and Kugelmass heard the sounds of boxes and furniture being moved around. Persky reappeared, pushing before him a large object on squeaky roller-skate wheels. He removed some old silk handkerchiefs that were lying on its top and blew away a bit of dust. It was a cheap-looking Chinese cabinet, badly lacquered.

"Persky," Kugelmass said, "what's your scam?"

"Pay attention," Persky said. "This is some beautiful effect. I developed it for a Knights of Pythias° date last year, but the booking fell through. Get into the cabinet."

30   "Why, so you can stick it full of swords or something?"

"You see any swords?"

Kugelmass made a face and, grunting, climbed into the cabinet. He couldn't help noticing a couple of ugly rhinestones glued onto the raw plywood just in front of his face. "If this is a joke," he said.

"Some joke. Now, here's the point. If I throw any novel into this cabinet with you, shut the doors, and tap it three times, you will find yourself projected into that book."

Kugelmass made a grimace of disbelief.

35   "It's the emess,"° Persky said. "My hand to God. Not just a novel, either. A short story, a play, a poem. You can meet any of the women created by the world's best writers. Whoever you dreamed of. You could carry on all you like with a real winner. Then when you've had enough you give a yell, and I'll see you're back here in a split second."

"Persky, are you some kind of outpatient?"

"I'm telling you it's on the level," Persky said.

Kugelmass remained skeptical. "What are you telling me—that this cheesy homemade box can take me on a ride like you're describing?"

"For a double sawbuck°."

40   Kugelmass reached for his wallet. "I'll believe this when I see it," he said.

Persky tucked the bills in his pants pocket and turned toward his bookcase. "So who do you want to meet? Sister Carrie? Hester Prynne? Ophelia?° maybe someone by Saul Bellow?° Hey, what about Temple Drake?° Although for a man your age she'd be a workout."

"French. I want to have an affair with a French lover."

"Nana?"°

"I don't want to have to pay for it."

45   "What about Natasha in 'War and Peace'?"

"I said French. I know! What about Emma Bovary?° That sounds to me perfect."

Knights of Pythias: a secretive fraternal society   **the emess:** the truth   **double sawbuck:** twenty dollars   **Sister Carrie? Hester Prynne? Ophelia?:** major characters, respectively, in Theodore Dreiser's *Sister Carrie* (1900), Nathaniel Hawthorne's *The Scarlet Letter* (1850), and William Shakespeare's *Hamlet* (1601)   **Saul Bellow:** contemporary American novelist (b. 1915)   **Temple Drake:** a character in William Faulkner's *Sanctuary* (1931)   **Nana:** a prostitute, the protagonist of Emile Zola's novel *Nana* (1880)   **Emma Bovary:** the heroine of Gustave Flaubert's novel *Madame Bovary* (1857), much of which is set in the French town of Yonville

"You got it, Kugelmass. Give me a holler when you've had enough." Persky tossed in a paperback copy of Flaubert's novel.

"You sure this is safe?" Kugelmass asked as Persky began shutting the cabinet doors.

"Safe. Is anything safe in this crazy world?" Persky rapped three times on the cabinet and then flung open the doors.

Kugelmass was gone. At the same moment, he appeared in the   50
bedroom of Charles and Emma Bovary's house at Yonville. Before him was a beautiful woman, standing alone with her back turned to him as she folded some linen. I can't believe this, thought Kugelmass, staring at the doctor's ravishing wife. This is uncanny. I'm here. It's her.

Emma turned in surprise. "Goodness, you startled me," she said. "Who are you?" She spoke in the same fine English translation as the paperback.

It's simply devastating, he thought. Then, realizing that it was he whom she had addressed, he said, "Excuse me. I'm Sidney Kugelmass. I'm from City College. A professor of humanities. C.C.N.Y.? Uptown. I—oh, boy!"

Emma Bovary smiled flirtatiously and said, "Would you like a drink? A glass of wine, perhaps?"

She is beautiful, Kugelmass thought. What a contrast with the troglodyte who shared his bed! He felt a sudden impulse to take this vision into his arms and tell her she was the kind of woman he had dreamed of all his life.

"Yes, some wine," he said hoarsely. "White. No, red. No, white.   55
Make it white."

"Charles is out for the day," Emma said, her voice full of playful implication.

After the wine, they went for a stroll in the lovely French countryside. "I've always dreamed that some mysterious stranger would appear and rescue me from the monotony of this crass rural existence," Emma said, clasping his hand. They passed a small church. "I love what you have on," she murmured. "I've never seen anything like it around here. It's so . . . so modern."

"It's called a leisure suit," he said romantically. "It was marked down." Suddenly he kissed her. For the next hour they reclined under a tree and whispered together and told each other deeply meaningful things with their eyes. Then Kugelmass sat up. He had just remembered he had to meet Daphne at Bloomingdale's. "I must go," he told her. "But don't worry, I'll be back."

"I hope so," Emma said.

60   He embraced her passionately, and the two walked back to the house. He held Emma's face cupped in his palms, kissed her again, and yelled, "O.K., Persky! I got to be at Bloomingdale's by three-thirty."

There was an audible pop, and Kugelmass was back in Brooklyn.

"So? Did I lie?" Persky asked triumphantly.

"Look, Persky, I'm right now late to meet the ball and chain at Lexington Avenue, but when can I go again? Tomorrow?"

"My pleasure. Just bring a twenty. And don't mention this to anybody."

65   "Yeah. I'm going to call Rupert Murdoch°."

Kugelmass hailed a cab and sped off to the city. His heart danced on point. I am in love, he thought, I am the possessor of a wonderful secret. What he didn't realize was that at this very moment students in various classrooms across the country were saying to their teachers, "Who is this character on page 100? A bald Jew is kissing Madame Bovary?" A teacher in Sioux Falls, South Dakota, sighed and thought, Jesus, these kids, with their pot and acid. What goes through their minds!

Daphne Kugelmass was in the bathroom-accessories department at Bloomingdale's when Kugelmass arrived breathlessly. "Where've you been?" she snapped. "It's four-thirty."

"I got held up in traffic," Kugelmass said.

Kugelmass visited Persky the next day, and in a few minutes was again passed magically to Yonville. Emma couldn't hide her excitement at seeing him. The two spent hours together, laughing and talking about their different backgrounds. Before Kugelmass left, they made love. "My God, I'm doing it with Madame Bovary!" Kugelmass whispered to himself. "Me, who failed freshman English."

70   As the months passed, Kugelmass saw Persky many times and developed a close and passionate relationship with Emma Bovary. "Make sure and always get me into the book before page 120," Kugelmass aid to the magician one day. "I always have to meet her before she hooks up with this Rodolphe character."

"Why?" Persky asked. "You can't beat his time?"

"Beat his time. He's landed gentry. Those guys have nothing better to do than flirt and ride horses. To me, he's one of those faces you see in the pages of *Women's Wear Daily*. With the Helmut Berger° hairdo. But to her he's hot stuff."

"And her husband suspects nothing?"

Rupert Murdoch: Australian newspaper tycoon who owns several New York newspapers.
Helmut Berger: a German film actor (b. 1942) popular in the 1970s

"He's out of his depth. He's a lackluster little paramedic who's thrown in his lot with a jitterbug. He's ready to go to sleep by ten, and she's putting on her dancing shoes. Oh, well . . . See you later."

And once again Kugelmass entered the cabinet and passed instantly to the Bovary estate at Yonville. "How you doing, cupcake?" he said to Emma. 75

"Oh, Kugelmass," Emma sighed. "What I have to put up with. Last night at dinner, Mr. Personality dropped off to sleep in the middle of the dessert course. I'm pouring my heart out about Maxim's° and the ballet, and out of the blue I hear snoring."

"It's O.K., darling. I'm here now," Kugelmass said, embracing her. I've earned this, he thought, smelling Emma's French perfume and burying his nose in her hair. I've suffered enough. I've paid enough analysts. I've searched till I'm weary. She's young and nubile, and I'm here a few pages after Léon and just before Rodolphe. By showing up during the correct chapters, I've got the situation knocked.

Emma, to be sure, was just as happy as Kugelmass. She had been starved for excitement, and his tales of Broadway night life, of fast cars and Hollywood and TV stars, enthralled the young French beauty.

"Tell me again about O.J. Simpson," she implored that evening, as she and Kugelmass strolled past Abbé Bournisien's church.

"What can I say? The man is great. He sets all kinds of rushing records. Such moves. They can't touch him." 80

"And the Academy Awards?" Emma said wistfully. "I'd give anything to win one."

"First you've got to be nominated."

"I know. You explained it. But I'm convinced I can act. Of course, I'd want to take a class or two. With Strasberg° maybe. Then, if I had the right agent—"

"We'll see, we'll see. I'll speak to Persky."

That night, safely returned to Persky's flat, Kugelmass brought up the idea of having Emma visit him in the big city. 85

"Let me think about it," Persky said. "Maybe I could work it. Stranger things have happened." Of course, neither of them could think of one.

"Where the hell do you go all the time?" Daphne Kugelmass barked at her husband as he returned home late that evening. "You got a chippie stashed somewhere?"

Maxim's: a chic restaurant in Paris   **Strasberg:** Lee Strasberg, the owner of a New York acting school

"Yeah, sure, I'm just the type," Kugelmass said wearily. "I was with Leonard Popkin. We were discussing Socialist agriculture in Poland. You know Popkin. He's a freak on the subject."

"Well, you've been very odd lately," Daphne said. "Distant. Just don't forget about my father's birthday. On Saturday?"

90   "Oh, sure, sure," Kugelmass said, heading for the bathroom.

"My whole family will be there. We can see the twins. And Cousin Hamish. You should be more polite to Cousin Hamish—he likes you."

"Right, the twins," Kugelmass said, closing the bathroom door and shutting out the sound of his wife's voice. He leaned against it and took a deep breath. In a few hours, he told himself, he would be back in Yonville again, back with his beloved. And this time, if all went well, he would bring Emma back with him.

At three-fifteen the following afternoon, Persky worked his wizardry again. Kugelmass appeared before Emma, smiling and eager. The two spent a few hours at Yonville with Binet and then remounted the Bovary carriage. Following Persky's instructions, they held each other tightly, closed their eyes, and counted to ten. When they opened them, the carriage was just drawing up at the side door of the Plaza Hotel, where Kugelmass had optimistically reserved a suite earlier in the day.

"I love it! It's everything I dreamed it would be," Emma said as she swirled joyously around the bedroom, surveying the city from their window, "There's F.A.O. Schwarz.° And there's Central Park, and the Sherry° is which one? Oh, there—I see. It's too divine."

95   On the bed there were boxes from Halston and Saint Laurent. Emma unwrapped a package and held up a pair of black velvet pants against her perfect body.

"The slacks suit is by Ralph Lauren," Kugelmass said. "You'll look like a million bucks in it. Come on, sugar, give us a kiss."

"I've never been so happy!" Emma squealed as she stood before the mirror. "Let's go out on the town. I want to see 'Chorus Line' and the Guggenheim and this Jack Nicholson character you always talk about. Are any of his flicks showing?"

"I cannot get my mind around this," a Stanford professor said. "First a strange character named Kugelmass, and now she's gone from the book. Well, I guess the mark of a classic is that you can reread it a thousand times and always find something new."

F.A.O. Schwarz: a famous New York toy store   **the Sherry:** the Sherry-Netherland Hotel in New York

The lovers passed a blissful weekend. Kugelmass had told Daphne he would be away at a symposium in Boston and would return Monday. Savoring each moment, he and Emma went to the movies, had dinner in Chinatown, passed two hours at a discothèque, and went to bed with a TV movie. They slept till noon on Sunday, visited SoHo,° and ogled celebrities at Elaine's.° They had caviar and champagne in their suite on Sunday night and talked until dawn. That morning, in the cab taking them to Persky's apartment, Kugelmass thought, It was hectic, but worth it. I can't bring her here too often, but now and then it will be a charming contrast with Yonville.

At Persky's, Emma climbed into the cabinet, arranged her new   100
boxes of clothes neatly around her, and kissed Kugelmass fondly. "My place next time," she said with a wink. Persky rapped three times on the cabinet. Nothing happened.

"Hmm," Persky said, scratching his head. He rapped again, but still no magic. "Something must be wrong," he mumbled.

"Persky, you're joking!" Kugelmass cried. "How can it not work?"

"Relax, relax. Are you still in the box, Emma?"

"Yes."

Persky rapped again—harder this time.   105

"I'm still here, Persky."

"I know, darling. Sit tight."

"Persky, we *have* to get her back," Kugelmass whispered. "I'm a married man, and I have a class in three hours. I'm not prepared for anything more than a cautious affair at this point."

"I can't understand it," Persky muttered. "It's such a reliable little trick."

But he could do nothing. "It's going to take a little while," he said   110
to Kugelmass. "I'm going to have to strip it down. I'll call you later."

Kugelmass bundled Emma into a cab and took her back to the Plaza. He barely made it to his class on time. He was on the phone all day, to Persky and to his mistress. The magician told him it might be several days before he got to the bottom of the trouble.

"How was the symposium?" Daphne asked him that night.

"Fine, fine," he said, lighting the filter end of a cigarette.

"What's wrong? You're as tense as a cat."

"Me? Ha, that's a laugh. I'm as calm as a summer night. I'm just going   115
to take a walk." He eased out the door, hailed a cab, and flew to the Plaza.

"This is no good," Emma said. "Charles will miss me."

SoHo: an upscale neighborhood near Greenwich Village   **Elaine's:** a New York restaurant frequented by film and literary celebrities

"Bear with me, sugar," Kugelmass said. He was pale and sweaty. He kissed her again, raced to the elevators, yelled at Persky over a pay phone in the Plaza lobby, and just made it home before midnight.

"According to Popkin, barley prices in Kraków have not been this stable since 1971," he said to Daphne, and smiled wanly as he climbed into bed.

The whole week went by like that. On Friday night, Kugelmass told Daphne there was another symposium he had to catch, this one in Syracuse. He hurried back to the Plaza, but the second weekend there was nothing like the first. "Get me back into the novel or marry me," Emma told Kugelmass. "Meanwhile, I want to get a job or go to class, because watching TV all day is the pits."

120   "Fine. We can use the money," Kugelmass said. "You consume twice your weight in room service."

"I met an Off Broadway producer in Central Park yesterday, and he said I might be right for a project he's doing," Emma said.

"Who is this clown?" Kugelmass asked.

"He's not a clown. He's sensitive and kind and cute. His name's Jeff Something-or-Other, and he's up for a Tony."

Later that afternoon, Kugelmass showed up at Persky's drunk.

125   "Relax," Persky told him. "You'll get a coronary."

"Relax. The man says relax. I've got a fictional character stashed in a hotel room, and I think my wife is having me tailed by a private shamus."

"O.K., O.K. We know there's a problem." Persky crawled under the cabinet and started banging on something with a large wrench.

"I'm like a wild animal," Kugelmass went on. "I'm sneaking around town, and Emma and I have had it up to here with each other. Not to mention a hotel tab that reads like the defense budget."

"So what should I do? This is the world of magic," Persky said. "It's

130   all nuance."

"Nuance, my foot. I'm pouring Dom Pérignon and black eggs into this little mouse, plus her wardrobe, plus she's enrolled at the Neighborhood Playhouse and suddenly needs professional photos. Also, Persky, Professor Fivish Kopkind, who teaches Comp Lit and who has always been jealous of me, has identified me as the sporadically appearing character in the Flaubert book. He's threatened to go to Daphne. I see ruin and alimony jail. For adultery with Madame Bovary, my wife will reduce me to beggary."

"What do you want me to day? I'm working on it night and day. As far as your personal anxiety goes, that I can't help you with. I'm a magician, not an analyst."

By Sunday afternoon, Emma had locked herself in the bathroom and refused to respond to Kugelmass's entreaties. Kugelmass stared out the window at the Wollman Rink° and contemplated suicide. Too bad this is a low floor, he thought, or I'd do it right now. Maybe if I ran away to Europe and started life over . . . Maybe I could sell the *International Herald Tribune*, like those young girls used to.

The phone rang. Kugelmass lifted it to his ear mechanically.

"Bring her over," Persky said. "I think I got the bugs out of it."

Kugelmass's heart leaped. "You're serious?" he said. "You got it licked?"   135

"It was something in the transmission. Go figure."

"Persky, you're a genius. We'll be there in a minute. Less than a minute."

Again the lovers hurried to the magician's apartment, and again Emma Bovary climbed into the cabinet with her boxes. This time there was no kiss. Persky shut the doors, took a deep breath, and tapped the box three times. There was the reassuring popping noise, and when Persky peered inside, the box was empty. Madame Bovary was back in her novel. Kugelmass heaved a great sigh of relief and pumped the magician's hand.

"It's over," he said. "I learned my lesson. I'll never cheat again, I swear it." He pumped Persky's hand again and made a mental note to send him a necktie.

Three weeks later, at the end of a beautiful spring afternoon, Persky   140
answered his doorbell. It was Kugelmass, with a sheepish expression on his face.

"O.K., Kugelmass," the magician said. "Where to this time?"

"It's just this once," Kugelmass said. "The weather is so lovely, and I'm not getting any younger. Listen, you've read 'Portnoy's Complaint'°? Remember The Monkey?"

"The price is now twenty-five dollars, because the cost of living is up, but I'll start you off with one freebie, due to all the trouble I caused you."

"You're good people," Kugelmass said, combing his few remaining hairs as he climbed into the cabinet again. "This'll work all right?"

"I hope. But I haven't tried it much since all that unpleasantness."   145

"Sex and romance," Kugelmass said from inside the box. "What we go through for a pretty face."

Persky tossed in a copy of "Portnoy's Complaint" and rapped three times on the box. This time, instead of a popping noise there was a dull explosion, followed by a series of crackling noises and a shower of sparks.

Wollman Rink: a famous skating rink in New York's Central Park   ***Portnoy's Complaint:*** a sexually explicit 1969 novel by Philip Roth, in which "The Monkey" is a major character

Persky leaped back, was seized by a heart attack, and dropped dead. The cabinet burst into flames, and eventually the entire house burned down.

Kugelmass, unaware of this catastrophe, had his own problems. He had not been thrust into "Portnoy's Complaint," or into any other novel, for that matter. He had been projected into an old textbook, "Remedial Spanish," and was running for his life over a barren, rocky terrain as the word "*tener*" ("to have")—a large and hairy irregular verb—raced after him on its spindly legs.

QUESTIONS

1. What are the primary sources of humor in this story? Does it use verbal irony, dramatic irony, irony of situation, or a combination of all three?
2. Describe the characterization of Kugelmass. What particular characteristics make him a suitable comic protagonist?
3. Describe the blend of fantasy and realism in the story. How does this blend add to the story's humorous effects?
4. Outline the plot structure. What plot twists and turns are particularly effective?
5. Consider the story's conclusion. Is the ending a surprise? If so, how does the ending provide a suitable and effective resolution?
6. How would you describe the tone of the story? Can it be argued that the story is "serious" in its presentation of the protagonist's midlife crisis?

Albert Camus
The Guest

The schoolmaster was watching the two men climb toward him. One was on horseback, the other on foot. They had not yet tackled the abrupt rise leading to the schoolhouse built on the hillside. They were toiling onward, making slow progress in the snow, among the stones, on the vast expanse of the high, deserted plateau. From time to time the

THE GUEST   First published in 1957. Translated into English by Justin O'Brien. Algeria, now a republic, was until midcentury a French territory with a population about 88 percent Muslim (either Arab or Berber). Daru and Balducci, in the story, are French civil servants. Algeria gained its independence as a result of the Algerian War, 1954–1962, a Muslim revolt against French rule. Albert Camus (1913–1960), though a Frenchman, was born in northeastern Algeria, was educated in Algiers, and did not see France until 1939. In 1940, with the fall of France to Germany, he returned to Algiers and taught for two years in a private school in Oran, on the seacoast. In 1942 he returned to Paris and engaged actively in the Resistance movement by writing for the underground press. He continued his residence in Paris after World War II.

horse stumbled. Without hearing anything yet, he could see the breath issuing from the horse's nostrils. One of the men, at least, knew the region. They were following the trail although it had disappeared days ago under a layer of dirty white snow. The schoolmaster calculated that it would take them half an hour to get onto the hill. It was cold; he went back into the school to get a sweater.

He crossed the empty, frigid classroom. On the blackboard the four rivers of France, drawn with four different colored chalks, had been flowing toward their estuaries for the past three days. Snow had suddenly fallen in mid-October after eight months of drought without the transition of rain, and the twenty pupils, more or less, who lived in the villages scattered over the plateau had stopped coming. With fair weather they would return. Daru now heated only the single room that was his lodging, adjoining the classroom and giving also onto the plateau to the east. Like the class windows, his window looked to the south too. On that side the school was a few kilometers from the point where the plateau began to slope toward the south. In clear weather could be seen the purple mass of the mountain range where the gap opened onto the desert.

Somewhat warmed, Daru returned to the window from which he had first seen the two men. They were no longer visible. Hence they must have tackled the rise. The sky was not so dark, for the snow had stopped falling during the night. The morning had opened with a dirty light which had scarcely become brighter as the ceiling of clouds lifted. At two in the afternoon it seemed as if the day were merely beginning. But still this was better than those three days when the thick snow was falling amidst unbroken darkness with little gusts of wind that rattled the double door of the classroom. Then Daru had spent long hours in his room, leaving it only to go to the shed and feed the chickens or get some coal. Fortunately the delivery truck from Tadjid, the nearest village to the north, had brought his supplies two days before the blizzard. It would return in forty-eight hours.

Besides, he had enough to resist a siege, for the little room was cluttered with bags of wheat that the administration left as a stock to distribute to those of his pupils whose families had suffered from the drought. Actually they had all been victims because they were all poor. Every day Daru would distribute a ration to the children. They had missed it, he knew, during these bad days. Possibly one of the fathers or big brothers would come this afternoon and he could supply them with grain. It was just a matter of carrying them over to the next harvest. Now shiploads of wheat were arriving from France and the worst was over. But it would be hard to forget that poverty, that army of ragged ghosts wandering in the sunlight, the plateaus burned to a cinder month after month, the earth shriveled up little by little, literally scorched, every stone bursting into dust under one's foot. The sheep had died then by thousands and even a few men, here and there, sometimes without anyone's knowing.

5   In contrast with such poverty, he who lived almost like a monk in his remote schoolhouse, nonetheless satisfied with the little he had and with the rough life, had felt like a lord with his whitewashed walls, his narrow couch, his unpainted shelves, his well, and his weekly provision of water and food. And suddenly this snow, without warning, without the foretaste of rain. This is the way the region was, cruel to live in, even without men—who didn't help matters either. But Daru had been born here. Everywhere else, he felt exiled.

He stepped out onto the terrace in front of the schoolhouse. The two men were now halfway up the slope. He recognized the horseman as Balducci, the old gendarme he had known for a long time. Balducci was holding on the end of a rope an Arab who was walking behind him with hands bound and head lowered. The gendarme waved a greeting to which Daru did not reply, lost as he was in contemplation of the Arab dressed in a faded blue jellaba, his feet in sandals but covered with socks of heavy raw wool, his head surmounted by a narrow, short *chèche*. They were approaching. Balducci was holding back his horse in order not to hurt the Arab, and the group was advancing slowly.

Within earshot, Balducci shouted: "One hour to do the three kilometers from El Ameur!" Daru did not answer. Short and square in his thick sweater, he watched them climb. Not once had the Arab raised his head. "Hello," said Daru when they got up onto the terrace. "Come in and warm up." Balducci painfully got down from his horse without letting go the rope. From under his bristling mustache he smiled at the schoolmaster. His little dark eyes, deep-set under a tanned forehead, and his mouth surrounded with wrinkles made him look attentive and studious. Daru took the bridle, led the horse to the shed, and came back to the two men, who were now waiting for him in the school. He led them into his room. "I am going to heat up the classroom," he said. "We'll be more comfortable there." When he entered the room again, Balducci was on the couch. He had undone the rope tying him to the Arab, who had squatted near the stove. His hands still bound, the *chèche* pushed back on his head, he was looking toward the window. At first Daru noticed only his huge lips, fat, smooth, almost Negroid; yet his nose was straight, his eyes were dark and full of fever. The *chèche* revealed an obstinate forehead and, under the weathered skin now rather discolored by the cold, the whole

face had a restless and rebellious look that struck Daru when the
Arab, turning his face toward him, looked him straight in the eyes.
"Go into the other room," said the schoolmaster, "and I'll make you
some mint tea." "Thanks," Balducci said. "What a chore! How I long
for retirement." And addressing his prisoner in Arabic: "Come on,
you." The Arab got up and, slowly, holding his bound wrists in front
of him, went into the classroom.

With the tea, Daru brought a chair. But Balducci was already en-
throned on the nearest pupil's desk and the Arab had squatted against
the teacher's platform facing the stove, which stood between the desk
and the window. When he held out the glass of tea to the prisoner,
Daru hesitated at the sight of his bound hands. "He might perhaps be
untied." "Sure," said Balducci. "That was for the trip." He started to get
to his feet. But Daru, setting the glass on the floor, had knelt beside the
Arab. Without saying anything, the Arab watched him with his fever-
ish eyes. Once his hands were free, he rubbed his swollen wrists against
each other, took the glass of tea, and sucked up the burning liquid in
swift little sips.

"Good," said Daru. "And where are you headed?"

Balducci withdrew his mustache from the tea. "Here, son."   10

"Odd pupils! And you're spending the night?"

"No. I'm going back to El Ameur. And you will deliver this fellow
to Tinguit. He is expected at police headquarters."

Balducci was looking at Daru with a friendly little smile.

"What's this story?" asked the schoolmaster. "Are you pulling
my leg?"

"No, son. Those are the orders."   15

"The orders? I'm not . . ." Daru hesitated, not wanting to hurt the
old Corsican. "I mean, that's not my job."

"What! What's the meaning of that? In wartime people do all kinds
of jobs."

"Then I'll wait for the declaration of war!"

Balducci nodded.

"O.K. But the orders exist and they concern you too. Things are   20
brewing, it appears. There is talk of a forthcoming revolt. We are mo-
bilized, in a way."

Daru still had his obstinate look.

"Listen, son," Balducci said. "I like you and you must understand.
There's only a dozen of us at El Ameur to patrol throughout the whole
territory of a small department and I must get back in a hurry. I was
told to hand this guy over to you and return without delay. He could-
n't be kept there. His village was beginning to stir; they wanted to

take him back. You must take him to Tinguit tomorrow before the day is over. Twenty kilometers shouldn't faze a husky fellow like you. After that, all will be over. You'll come back to your pupils and your comfortable life."

Behind the wall the horse could be heard snorting and pawing the earth. Daru was looking out the window. Decidedly, the weather was clearing and the light was increasing over the snowy plateau. When all the snow was melted, the sun would take over again and once more would burn the fields of stone. For days, still, the unchanging sky would shed its dry light on the solitary expanse where nothing had any connection with man.

"After all," he said, turning around toward Balducci, "what did he do?" And, before the gendarme had opened his mouth, he asked: "Does he speak French?"

25   "No, not a word. We had been looking for him for a month, but they were hiding him. He killed his cousin."

"Is he against us?"

"I don't think so. But you can never be sure."

"Why did he kill?"

"A family squabble, I think. One owed the other grain, it seems. It's not at all clear. In short, he killed his cousin with a billhook. You know, like a sheep, *kreezk!*"

30   Balducci made the gesture of drawing a blade across his throat and the Arab, his attention attracted, watched him with a sort of anxiety. Daru felt a sudden wrath against the man, against all men with their rotten spite, their tireless hates, their blood lust.

But the kettle was singing on the stove. He served Balducci more tea, hesitated, then served the Arab again, who, a second time, drank avidly. His raised arms made the jellaba fall open and the schoolmaster saw his thin, muscular chest.

"Thanks, kid," Balducci said. "And now, I'm off."

He got up and went toward the Arab, taking a small rope from his pocket.

"What are you doing?" Daru asked dryly.

35   Balducci, disconcerted, showed him the rope.

"Don't bother."

The old gendarme hesitated. "It's up to you. Of course, you are armed?"

"I have my shotgun."

"Where?"

40   "In the trunk."

"You ought to have it near your bed."

"Why? I have nothing to fear."

"You're crazy, son. If there's an uprising, no one is safe, we're all in the same boat."

"I'll defend myself. I'll have time to see them coming."

Balducci began to laugh, then suddenly the mustache covered the   45
white teeth.

"You'll have time? O.K. That's just what I was saying. You have always been a little cracked. That's why I like you, my son was like that."

At the same time he took out his revolver and put it on the desk.

"Keep it; I don't need two weapons from here to El Ameur."

The revolver shone against the black paint of the table. When the gendarme turned toward him, the schoolmaster caught the smell of leather and horseflesh.

"Listen, Balducci," Daru said suddenly, "every bit of this disgusts   50
me, and first of all your fellow here. But I won't hand him over. Fight, yes, if I have to. But not that."

The old gendarme stood in front of him and looked at him severely.

"You're being a fool," he said slowly. "I don't like it either. You don't get used to putting a rope on a man even after years of it, and you're even ashamed—yes, ashamed. But you can't let them have their way."

"I won't hand him over," Daru said again.

"It's an order, son, and I repeat it."

"That's right. Repeat to them what I've said to you: I won't hand   55
him over."

Balducci made a visible effort to reflect. He looked at the Arab and at Daru. At last he decided.

"No, I won't tell them anything. If you want to drop us, go ahead; I'll not denounce you. I have an order to deliver the prisoner and I'm doing so. And now you'll just sign this paper for me."

"There's no need. I'll not deny that you left him with me."

"Don't be mean with me. I know you'll tell the truth. You're from hereabouts and you are a man. But you must sign, that's the rule."

Daru opened his drawer, took out a little square bottle of purple   60
ink, the red wooden penholder with the "sergeant-major" pen he used for making models of penmanship, and signed. The gendarme carefully folded the paper and put it into his wallet. Then he moved toward the door.

"I'll see you off," Daru said.

"No," said Balducci. "There's no use being polite. You insulted me."

He looked at the Arab, motionless in the same spot, sniffed peevishly, and turned away toward the door. "Good-by, son," he said. The door shut behind him. Balducci appeared suddenly outside the window and then disappeared. His footsteps were muffled by the snow. The horse stirred on the other side of the wall and several chickens fluttered in fright. A moment later Balducci reappeared outside the window leading the horse by the bridle. He walked toward the little rise without turning around and disappeared from sight with the horse following him. A big stone could be heard bouncing down. Daru walked back toward the prisoner, who, without stirring, never took his eyes off him. "Wait," the schoolmaster said in Arabic and went toward the bedroom. As he was going through the door, he had a second thought, went to the desk, took the revolver, and stuck it in his pocket. Then, without looking back, he went into his room.

For some time he lay on his couch watching the sky gradually close over, listening to the silence. It was this silence that had seemed painful to him during the first days here, after the war. He had requested a post in the little town at the base of the foothills separating the upper plateaus from the desert. There, rocky walls, green and black to the north, pink and lavender to the south, marked the frontier of eternal summer. He had been named to a post farther north, on the plateau itself. In the beginning, the solitude and the silence had been hard for him on these wastelands peopled only by stones. Occasionally, furrows suggested cultivation, but they had been dug to uncover a certain kind of stone good for building. The only plowing here was to harvest rocks. Elsewhere a thin layer of soil accumulated in the hollows would be scraped out to enrich paltry village gardens. This is the way it was: bare rock covered three quarters of the region. Towns sprang up, flourished, then disappeared; men came by, loved one another or fought bitterly, then died. No one in this desert, neither he nor his guest, mattered. And yet, outside this desert neither of them, Daru knew, could have really lived.

65   When he got up, no noise came from the classroom. He was amazed at the unmixed joy he derived from the mere thought that the Arab might have fled and that he would be alone with no decision to make. But the prisoner was there. He had merely stretched out between the stove and the desk. With eyes open, he was staring at the ceiling. In that position, his thick lips were particularly noticeable, giving him a pouting look. "Come," said Daru. The Arab got up and followed him. In the bedroom, the schoolmaster pointed to a chair near the table under the window. The Arab sat down without taking his eyes off Daru.

"Are you hungry?"

"Yes," the prisoner said.

Daru set the table for two. He took flour and oil, shaped a cake in a frying-pan, and lighted the little stove that functioned on bottled gas.

While the cake was cooking, he went out to the shed to get cheese, eggs, dates, and condensed milk. When the cake was done he set it on the window sill to cool, heated some condensed milk diluted with water, and beat up the eggs into an omelette. In one of his motions he knocked against the revolver stuck in his right pocket. He set the bowl down, went into the classroom, and put the revolver in his desk drawer. When he came back to the room, night was falling. He put on the light and served the Arab. "Eat," he said. The Arab took a piece of the cake, lifted it eagerly to his mouth, and stopped short.

"And you?" he asked.

"After you. I'll eat too." 70

The thick lips opened slightly. The Arab hesitated, then bit into the cake determinedly.

The meal over, the Arab looked at the schoolmaster. "Are you the judge?"

"No, I'm simply keeping you until tomorrow."

"Why do you eat with me?"

"I'm hungry." 75

The Arab fell silent. Daru got up and went out. He brought back a folding bed from the shed, set it up between the table and the stove, perpendicular to his own bed. From a large suitcase which, upright in a corner, served as a shelf for papers, he took two blankets and arranged them on the camp bed. Then he stopped, felt useless, and sat down on his bed. There was nothing more to do or to get ready. He had to look at this man. He looked at him, therefore, trying to imagine his face bursting with rage. He couldn't do so. He could see nothing but the dark yet shining eyes and the animal mouth.

"Why did you kill him?" he asked in a voice whose hostile tone surprised him.

The Arab looked away.

"He ran away. I ran after him."

He raised his eyes to Daru again and they were full of a sort of woe- 80 ful interrogation. "Now what will they do to me?"

"Are you afraid?"

He stiffened, turning his eyes away.

"Are you sorry?"

The Arab stared at him openmouthed. Obviously he did not understand. Daru's annoyance was growing. At the same time he felt awkward and self-conscious with his big body wedged between the two beds.

"Lie down there," he said impatiently. "That's your bed." 85

The Arab didn't move. He called to Daru:

"Tell me!"

The schoolmaster looked at him.

"Is the gendarme coming back tomorrow?"

90   "I don't know."

"Are you coming with us?"

"I don't know. Why?"

The prisoner got up and stretched out on top of the blankets, his feet toward the window. The light from the electric bulb shone straight into his eyes and he closed them at once.

"Why?" Daru repeated, standing beside the bed.

95   The Arab opened his eyes under the blinding light and looked at him, trying not to blink.

"Come with us," he said.

In the middle of the night, Daru was still not asleep. He had gone to bed after undressing completely; he generally slept naked. But when he suddenly realized that he had nothing on, he hesitated. He felt vulnerable and the temptation came to him to put his clothes back on. Then he shrugged his shoulders; after all, he wasn't a child and, if need be, he could break his adversary in two. From his bed he could observe him, lying on his back, still motionless with his eyes closed under the harsh light. When Daru turned out the light, the darkness seemed to coagulate all of a sudden. Little by little, the night came back to life in the window where the starless sky was stirring gently. The schoolmaster soon made out the body lying at his feet. The Arab still did not move, but his eyes seemed open. A faint wind was prowling around the schoolhouse. Perhaps it would drive away the clouds and the sun would reappear.

During the night the wind increased. The hens fluttered a little and then were silent. The Arab turned over on his side with his back to Daru, who thought he heard him moan. Then he listened for his guest's breathing, become heavier and more regular. He listened to that breath so close to him and mused without being able to go to sleep. In this room where he had been sleeping alone for a year, this presence bothered him. But it bothered him also by imposing on him a sort of brotherhood he knew well but refused to accept in the present circumstances. Men who share the same rooms, soldiers or prisoners, develop a strange alliance as if, having cast off their armor with their clothing, they fraternized every evening, over and above their differences, in the ancient community of dream and fatigue. But Daru shook himself; he didn't like such musings, and it was essential to sleep.

A little later, however, when the Arab stirred slightly, the schoolmaster was still not asleep. When the prisoner made a second move, he stiffened, on the alert. The Arab was lifting himself slowly on his arms with almost the motion of a sleepwalker. Seated upright in bed, he waited motionless without turning his head toward Daru, as if he were listening attentively. Daru did not stir; it had just occurred to him that the revolver was still in the drawer of his desk. It was better to act at once. Yet he continued to observe the prisoner, who, with the same slithery motion, put his feet on the ground, waited again, then began to stand up slowly. Daru was about to call out to him when the Arab began to walk, in a quite natural but extraordinarily silent way. He was heading toward the door at the end of the room that opened into the shed. He lifted the latch with precaution and went out, pushing the door behind him but without shutting it. Daru had not stirred. "He is running away," he merely thought. "Good riddance!" Yet he listened attentively. The hens were not fluttering; the guest must be on the plateau. A faint sound of water reached him, and he didn't know what it was until the Arab again stood framed in the doorway, closed the door carefully, and came back to bed without a sound. Then Daru turned his back on him and fell asleep. Still later he seemed, from the depths of his sleep, to hear furtive steps around the schoolhouse. "I'm dreaming! I'm dreaming!" he repeated to himself. And he went on sleeping.

When he awoke, the sky was clear; the loose window let in a cold, 100 pure air. The Arab was asleep, hunched up under the blankets now, his mouth open, utterly relaxed. But when Daru shook him, he started dreadfully, staring at Daru with wild eyes as if he had never seen him and such a frightened expression that the schoolmaster stepped back. "Don't be afraid. It's me. You must eat." The Arab nodded his head and said yes. Calm had returned to his face, but his expression was vacant and listless.

The coffee was ready. They drank it seated together on the folding bed as they munched their pieces of the cake. Then Daru led the Arab under the shed and showed him the faucet where he washed. He went back into the room, folded the blankets and the bed, made his own bed and put the room in order. Then he went through the classroom and out onto the terrace. The sun was already rising in the blue sky; a soft, bright light was bathing the deserted plateau. On the ridge the snow was melting in spots. The stones were about to reappear. Crouched on the edge of the plateau, the schoolmaster looked at the deserted expanse. He thought of Balducci. He had hurt him, for he had sent him off in a way as if he didn't want to be associated with him. He could still hear the gendarme's farewell and, without knowing why, he felt strangely empty and vulnerable. At that moment, from the other side of the schoolhouse, the prisoner coughed. Daru listened to him almost despite himself and then, furious, threw a pebble that whistled through the air before sinking into the snow. That man's stupid crime revolted him, but to hand him over was contrary to honor. Merely thinking of it made him smart with humiliation. And he cursed at one and the same time his own people who had sent him this Arab and the Arab too who had dared to kill and not managed to get away. Daru got up, walked in a circle on the terrace, waited motionless, and then went back into the schoolhouse.

The Arab, leaning over the cement floor of the shed, was washing his teeth with two fingers. Darn looked at him and said: "Come." He went back into the room ahead of the prisoner. He slipped a hunting-jacket on over his sweater and put on walking-shoes. Standing, he waited until the Arab had put on his *chèche* and sandals. They went into the classroom and the schoolmaster pointed to the exit, saying: "Go ahead." The fellow didn't budge. "I'm coming," said Daru. The Arab went out. Daru went back into the room and made a package of pieces of rusk, dates, and sugar. In the classroom, before going out, he hesitated a second in front of his desk, then crossed the threshold and locked the door. "That's the way," he said. He started toward the east, followed by the prisoner. But, a short distance from the schoolhouse, he thought he heard a slight sound behind them. He retraced his steps and examined the surroundings of the house; there was no one there. The Arab watched him without seeming to understand. "Come on," said Daru.

They walked for an hour and rested beside a sharp peak of limestone. The snow was melting faster and faster and the sun was drinking up the puddles at once, rapidly cleaning the plateau, which gradually dried and vibrated like the air itself. When they resumed walking, the ground rang under their feet. From time to time a bird rent the space in front of them with a joyful cry. Daru breathed in deeply the fresh morning light. He felt a sort of rapture before the vast familiar expanse, now almost entirely yellow under its dome of blue sky. They walked an hour more, descending toward the south. They reached a level height made up of crumbly rocks. From there on, the plateau sloped down, eastward, toward a low plain where there were a few spindly trees and, to the south, toward outcroppings of rock that gave the landscape a chaotic look.

Daru surveyed the two directions. There was nothing but the sky on the horizon. Not a man could be seen. He turned toward the Arab, who was looking at him blankly. Daru held out the package to him. "Take it," he said. "There are dates, bread, and sugar. You can hold out for two days. Here are a thousand francs too." The Arab took the package and the money but kept his full hands at chest level as if he didn't know what to do with what was being given him. "Now look," the schoolmaster said as he pointed in the direction of the east, "there's the way to Tinguit. You have a two-hour walk. At Tinguit you'll find the administration and the police. They are expecting you." The Arab looked toward the east, still holding the package and the money against his chest. Daru took his elbow and turned him rather roughly toward the south. At the foot of the height on which they stood could be seen a faint path. "That's the trail across the plateau. In a day's walk from here you'll find pasturelands and the first nomads. They'll take you in and shelter you according to their law." The Arab had now turned toward Daru and a sort of panic was visible in his expression. "Listen," he said. Daru shook his head: "No, be quiet. Now I'm leaving you." He turned his back on him, took two long steps in the direction of the school, looked hesitantly at the motionless Arab, and started off again. For a few minutes he heard nothing but his own step resounding on the cold ground and did not turn his head. A moment later, however, he turned around. The Arab was still there on the edge of the hill, his arms hanging now, and he was looking at the schoolmaster. Daru felt something rise in his throat. But he swore with impatience, waved vaguely, and started off again. He had already gone some distance when he again stopped and looked. There was no longer anyone on the hill.

Daru hesitated. The sun was now rather high in the sky and was beginning to beat down on his head. The schoolmaster retraced his steps, at first somewhat uncertainly, then with decision. When he reached the little hill, he was bathed in sweat. He climbed it as fast as he could and stopped, out of breath, at the top. The rock-fields to the south stood out sharply against the blue sky, but on the plain to the east a steamy heat was already rising. And in that slight haze, Daru, with heavy heart, made out the Arab walking slowly on the road to prison.   105

A little later, standing before the window of the classroom, the schoolmaster was watching the clear light bathing the whole surface of the plateau, but he hardly saw it. Behind him on the blackboard, among the winding French rivers, sprawled the clumsily chalked-up words he had just read: "You handed over our brother. You will pay for this." Daru looked at the sky, the plateau, and, beyond, the invisible lands stretching all the way to the sea. In this vast landscape he had loved so much, he was alone.

QUESTIONS

1. What is the central conflict of the story? Is it external or internal? Can it be defined in terms of dilemma?

2. Compare and contrast the attitudes of Daru and Balducci toward the prisoner and the situation. What is their attitude toward each other? Is either a bad or a cruel man? How does the conflict between Daru and Balducci intensify the central conflict?

3. Why does Daru give the prisoner his freedom? What reasons are there for not giving him his freedom?

4. In what respect is the title ironic? Why does "The Guest" make a better title than "The Prisoner"? And why does the French title "L'Hôte" (which can mean either "The Guest" or "The Host") make an even better title than its English translation?

5. This story contains the materials of explosive action—a revolver, a murderer, a state of undeclared war, an incipient uprising, a revenge note—but no violence occurs in the story. In what aspect of the situation is Camus principally interested?

6. This story has as its background a specific political situation—the French Algerian crisis in the years following World War II. How does Daru reflect France's plight? Is the story's meaning limited to this situation? What does the story tell us about good and evil and the nature of moral choice? How does the story differ in its treatment of these things from the typical Western story or the patriotic editorial?

7. In what respect is the ending of the story ironic? What kind of irony is this? What does it contribute to the meaning of the story?

8. Besides the ironies of the title and the ending, there are other ironies in the story. Find and explain them. Daru uses verbal irony in paragraph 11 when he exclaims, "Odd pupils!" Is verbal irony the same thing as sarcasm?

9. Comment on the following: (a) Daru's behavior toward firearms and how it helps reveal him; (b) Camus's reason for making the Arab a murderer; (c) the Arab's reason for taking the road to prison.

SUGGESTIONS FOR WRITING

1. Write an essay exploring the use of irony in one of the following stories, or compare the use of irony in any two of the stories:
   a. Wolff, "Hunters in the Snow" (page 86).
   b. Munro, "How I Met My Husband" (page 125).
   c. Lahiri, "Interpreter of Maladies" (page 141).
   d. Walker, "Everyday Use" (page 166).
   e. O'Connor, "The Drunkard" (page 339).
   f. Allen, "The Kugelmass Episode" (page 348).
   g. O'Connor, "Good Country People" (page 468).
   h. Melville, "Bartleby the Scrivener" (page 576).

2. Discuss the effect of humor in any of the following. Apart from its entertainment value, how does the humor contribute to the theme and significance of the story?
   a. Wolff, "Hunters in the Snow" (page 86).
   b. Walker, "Everyday Use" (page 166).
   c. O'Connor, "The Drunkard" (page 339).
   d. Allen, "The Kugelmass Episode" (page 348).
   e. Hurston, "The Gilded Six-Bits" (page 564).
   f. Melville, "Bartleby the Scrivener" (page 576).
   g. Crane, "The Bride Comes to Yellow Sky" (page 546).

Chapter Eight

Evaluating Fiction

Our purpose in the preceding chapters has been to develop not literary critics but proficient readers—readers who choose wisely and read well. Yet good reading involves the ability to evaluate what we read, and making wise choices necessitates sound judgment. This does not mean that in order to read well we must decide whether Welty's "A Worn Path" or Lawrence's "The Rocking-Horse Winner" is the "better" story, or whether Willa Cather is a "better" writer than Katherine Anne Porter. Any such judgments would be unpredictable, since in both these pairings equally intelligent readers might choose one or the other based on personal tastes and preferences. We do need, however, to be able to discriminate between the genuine and the spurious, the consequential and the trivial, the significant and the merely entertaining. Where such distinct categories are the issue, good readers will almost always reach the same conclusions.

There are no simple rules for literary judgment. Such judgment depends ultimately on our sensitivity, intelligence, and experience; it is a product of how much and how alertly we have lived and how much and how well we have read. Yet there are at least two basic principles that may serve to help you form your own evaluations. First, *every story should be judged initially by how fully it achieves its central purpose.* In a first-rate story, every element works with every other element to accomplish the central purpose as economically and powerfully as possible. For this reason, no single element in a story should be judged in isolation.

In fact, isolating a single element for evaluation without considering the other fictional elements in a story can lead to a flawed evaluation. It would be a mistake, for instance, to decide that "The Lesson" is an inferior story because the narrator uses slang expressions and fails to observe the rules of standard English grammar. Because the author wishes to evoke the authentic voice of a young black girl, she allows the narrator to speak in her own idiom, and her use of language helps to enrich her characterization.

Similarly, it would be inappropriate to criticize "The Guest" for not revealing what ultimately happens to Daru, since the theme of the story involves the unpredictability of the consequences of human choices in unfriendly conditions. We cannot say that "Miss Brill" and "Eveline" are poor stories because they do not have exciting plots full of action and conflict: the effectiveness of a story's plot can be judged only in relation to the other elements in a story and to its central purpose. In "Miss Brill" and "Eveline," of course, the relatively plotless quality of the narratives reflects the uneventful nature of these two women's lives.

Every first-rate story is an organic whole. All its parts should be related and all should be essential to the central purpose. We might ask, for example, whether the plot and characterizations of "The Most Dangerous Game" help to elucidate an important theme. Near the beginning of the story, there *is* a suggestion of theme. When Whitney declares that hunting is a great sport—for the hunter, not for the jaguar—Rainsford replies, "Who cares how a jaguar feels? . . . They've no understanding." To this, Whitney counters: "I rather think they understand one thing—fear. The fear of pain and the fear of death." Evidently Rainsford has something to learn about how it feels to be hunted, and presumably during the hunt he learns it, for when General Zaroff turns back the first time—playing cat and mouse—we are told, "Then it was that Rainsford knew the full meaning of terror." Later, on the morning of the third day, Rainsford awakens to the baying of hounds—"a sound that made him know that he had new things to learn about fear." But little is made of Rainsford's terror during the hunt. The story focuses instead on Malay man-catchers, Burmese tiger pits, Ugandan knife-throwers—in short, on the colorful and entertaining action. The story ends with the physical triumph of Rainsford over Zaroff, but has Rainsford been altered by the experience? Has he learned anything significant? Has he changed his attitudes toward hunting? We cannot answer, for the author's major purpose has been not to develop these themes but to entertain the reader. There is no clear thematic connection between the final sentence—"He had never slept in a better bed, Rainsford decided"—and the question "Who cares how a jaguar feels?" Rather, the ending merely provokes a smile from the reader at Rainsford's victory and at the cleverness of the author's concluding flourish; it does not, however, encourage the reader to think further about the story as an artistic statement of any real import.

By contrast, Wolff's "Hunters in the Snow" is a far more thematically unified story. Throughout a varied group of scenes, the story develops the idea that human beings, like animals in the wild, engage constantly in a struggle for power. Tub is overweight and the more sympathetic of the three major characters, and both Frank and Kenny treat him cruelly at several key points. Once Kenny is wounded, however, and thereby becomes the "weakest" of the characters, Frank and Tub form a new alliance and Kenny becomes the odd man out. Ultimately the story makes clear that the more powerful individual in any relationship will behave in a cruel and callous way toward the weaker individual. The reader finishes this masterful story thinking not about the bleak setting or the hunting trip it depicts but about the dark complexity of human relationships.

Once you have judged a story as successful in achieving its central purpose, you may consider a second principle of judgment: *a story should also be judged by the significance of its purpose.* Once you determine that a story successfully integrates its materials into an organic unity, you should then evaluate the depth, the range, and the significance of what the story has achieved. This principle returns us to our distinction between commercial and literary fiction. If a story's chief aim is to entertain, we may judge it to have less stature and significance than a story whose aim is to reveal important truths of human experience. "The Most Dangerous Game" and "Hunters in the Snow," it could be argued, are equally successful in achieving their central purposes. But Wolff's story is far more ambitious and significant than Connell's. A critical consensus has developed that "Hunters in the Snow" is a contemporary masterpiece of short fiction, while Connell's story is less highly regarded. Using other stories from the preceding chapters, we might also argue that "Once upon a Time" has a more ambitious, significant purpose than "The Drunkard," and that "Young Goodman Brown" has a more ambitious, significant purpose than "Miss Brill." This is not to disparage either "The Drunkard" or "Miss Brill," both of which are excellent stories, but to suggest that certain stories stake out larger thematic terrain and plumb the depths of human experience more profoundly than others.

A related evaluative principle is simply one of length. Most fiction takes the form of novels, not short stories, and while all the aspects of fiction we have discussed are represented in both longer and shorter forms, there is no doubt that a novel has the room to explore more varieties of human experience than does the short story, and that it has the leisure to explore them in greater depth. Obviously, then, Hawthorne's *The Scarlet Letter* is a greater work than his short story "Young Goodman Brown," simply by virtue of its greater length and therefore its greater richness of characterization, plot, and language. It should be stressed, however, that length alone is not a significant criterion in evaluating a work of fiction. The very brief "Eveline" is a more significant literary work, of course, than any 500-page romance or horror novel found on a best-seller list. But a serious literary author practicing the long form of the novel inevitably has greater opportunities for developing varieties of characters, exploring multiple themes, and providing richer and fuller artistic visions than the short story affords.

Again, as we stressed in discussing literary versus commercial fiction, we cannot evaluate stories by placing them into artificial categories; the evaluation of individual stories and novels is an ongoing process, and even the most informed evaluations do not remain fixed in time. For instance, the finest work of Herman Melville, author of *Moby-Dick* and "Bartleby the Scrivener," received scathing critical assessments and was virtually forgotten at the time of his death; yet today he is considered one of the most significant fiction writers of his era. Conversely, a short story called "Circumstance," published by Harriet Prescott Spofford in 1860, was one of the most famous stories of the nineteenth century, highly praised by such discriminating readers as Emily Dickinson and Henry James; but today the story is seldom read except by scholars and historians. When we evaluate a work of fiction, therefore, we must be aware that we are judging it according to the aesthetic criteria of our own time and that such criteria evolve and change. Similarly, individual readers—including professional critics—may evaluate works differently at different points in their own lives. Some readers, for instance, might respond enthusiastically to a particular novel in their twenties, but in their fifties might reread the beloved novel and wonder why they rated it so highly. While evaluating what we read is essential to developing our skill and insight, we must also be aware that any evaluation of a given work—our own, or that of the culture at large—may well change over time.

Ultimately, however, we must rely on our own judgments, based on our accumulated experience with both literature and life.

REVIEWING CHAPTER EIGHT

1. Review the two basic principles required for evaluating fiction.
2. Describe the elements that make up a first-rate story.
3. Analyze the literary quality of Connell's "The Most Dangerous Game" vs. Wolff's "Hunters in the Snow."
4. Describe the importance of length in evaluating fiction.
5. Choose any two stories in this book and evaluate them comparatively.

EXERCISE

The two stories that follow have a number of plot features in common; in purpose, however, they are quite different. One attempts to reveal certain truths about aspects of human life and succeeds in doing so. The other attempts to do little more than entertain the reader, and, in achieving this end, it falsifies human life. Which story is which? Support your decision by making a thorough analysis of both.

O. Henry
A Municipal Report

> The cities are full of pride,
>   Challenging each to each—
> This from her mountainside,
>   That from her burthened beach.
> —R. KIPLING

Fancy a novel about Chicago or Buffalo, let us say, or Nashville, Tennessee! There are just three big cities in the United States that are "story cities"—New York, of course, New Orleans, and, best of the lot, San Francisco.—FRANK NORRIS

East is east,° and west is San Francisco, according to Californians. Californians are a race of people; they are not merely inhabitants of a State. They are the Southerners of the West. Now, Chicagoans are no less loyal to their city; but when you ask them why, they stammer and speak of lake fish and the new Odd Fellows Building. But Californians go into detail.

Of course they have, in the climate, an argument that is good for half an hour while you are thinking of your coal bills and heavy

---

A MUNICIPAL REPORT   First published in 1909. Rand McNally and Co. (see end of second paragraph), founded in 1856, is a well-known publisher of atlases and gazetteers. The statistical and historical notes about Nashville in the story are such as might be excerpted from one of their books. Fort Sumter, Appomattox, and Generals Hood, Thomas, Sherman, and Longstreet are all names connected with the Civil War, during which, in 1863, the slaves were emancipated. William Sydney Porter (1862–1910), who wrote under the pseudonym O. Henry, was born in North Carolina, but his immensely varied life took him to Texas, Central and South America, Mexico, Ohio, and Pittsburgh before he arrived in New York City in 1901 to become a writer very much in demand for his short stories.

East is east . . . : cf. Rudyard Kipling's poem "The Ballad of East and West"

underwear. But as soon as they come to mistake your silence for conviction, madness comes upon them, and they picture the city of the Golden Gate as the Baghdad of the New World. So far, as a matter of opinion, no refutation is necessary. But dear cousins all (from Adam and Eve descended), it is a rash one who will lay his finger on the map and say "In this town there can be no romance—what could happen here?" Yes, it is a bold and a rash deed to challenge in one sentence history, romance, and Rand and McNally.

> Nashville.—A city, port of delivery, and the capital of the State of Tennessee, is on the Cumberland River and on the N.C. & St.L. and the L. & N. railroads. This city is regarded as the most important educational center in the South.

I stepped off the train at 8 P.M. Having searched the thesaurus in vain for adjectives, I must, as a substitution, hie me to comparison in the form of a recipe.

5   Take of London fog 30 parts; malaria 10 parts; gas leaks 20 parts; dewdrops gathered in a brick yard at sunrise, 25 parts; odor of honeysuckle 15 parts. Mix.

The mixture will give you an approximate conception of a Nashville drizzle. It is not so fragrant as a moth-ball nor as thick as peasoup; but 'tis enough—'twill serve.°

I went to a hotel in a tumbril. It required strong self-suppression for me to keep from climbing to the top of it and giving an imitation of Sidney Carton.° The vehicle was drawn by beasts of a bygone era and driven by something dark and emancipated.

I was sleepy and tired, so when I got to the hotel I hurriedly paid it the fifty cents it demanded (with approximate lagniappe, I assure you). I knew its habits; and I did not want to hear it prate about its old "marster" or anything that happened "befo' de wah."

The hotel was one of the kind described as "renovated." That means $20,000 worth of new marble pillars, tiling, electric lights and brass cuspidors in the lobby, and a new L. & N. time table and a lithograph of Lookout Mountain in each one of the great rooms above. The management was without reproach, the attention full of exquisite Southern courtesy, the service as slow as the progress of a snail and as good-humored as Rip Van Winkle. The food was worth traveling a thousand miles for. There is no other hotel in the world where you can get such chicken livers en brochette.

---

not so fragrant . . . 'twill serve: cf. Mercutio's dying speech, *Romeo and Juliet*, 3.1.99–100
Sidney Carton: a dissipated character who dies nobly on the guillotine in Dickens's novel *A Tale of Two Cities* (1859)

At dinner I asked a Negro waiter if there was anything doing in   10
town. He pondered gravely for a minute, and then replied: "Well, boss,
I don't really reckon there's anything at all doin' after sundown."
Sundown had been accomplished: it had been drowned in drizzle
long before. So that spectacle was denied me. But I went forth upon the
streets in the drizzle to see what might be there.

It is built on undulating grounds; and the streets are lighted by electric-
ity at a cost of $32,470 per annum.

As I left the hotel there was a race riot. Down upon me charged a
company of freedmen, or Arabs, or Zulus, armed with—no, I saw with
relief that they were not rifles, but whips. And I saw dimly a caravan of
black, clumsy vehicles; and at the reassuring shouts, "Kyar you anywhere in the town, boss, fuh fifty cents," I reasoned that I was merely a
"fare" instead of a victim.
I walked through long streets, all leading uphill. I wondered how
those streets ever came down again. Perhaps they didn't until they were
"graded." On a few of the "main streets" I saw lights in stores here and
there; saw street cars go by conveying worthy burghers hither and yon;
saw people pass engaged in the art of conversation, and heard a burst of
semi-lively laughter issuing from a soda-water and ice-cream parlor.
The streets other than "main" seemed to have enticed upon their borders houses consecrated to peace and domesticity. In many of them
lights shone behind discreetly drawn window shades, in a few pianos
tinkled orderly and irreproachable music. There was indeed, little "doing." I wished I had come before sundown. So I returned to my hotel.

In November, 1864, the Confederate General Hood advanced against   15
Nashville, where he shut up a National force under General Thomas. The
latter then sallied forth and defeated the Confederates in a terrible conflict.

All my life I have heard of, admired, and witnessed the fine marksmanship of the South in its peaceful conflicts in the tobacco-chewing
regions. But in my hotel a surprise awaited me. There were twelve
bright, new, imposing, capacious brass cuspidors in the great lobby, tall
enough to be called urns and so wide-mouthed that the crack pitcher
of a lady baseball team should have been able to throw a ball into one
of them at five paces distant. But, although a terrible battle had raged
and was still raging, the enemy had not suffered. Bright, new, imposing,
capacious, untouched, they stood. But, shades of Jefferson Brick!° the

Jefferson Brick: an American journalist, "unwholesomely pale" from "excessive use of
[chewing] tobacco" in Dickens's novel *Martin Chuzzlewit* (1844)

tile floor—the beautiful tile floor! I could not avoid thinking of the battle of Nashville, and trying to draw, as is my foolish habit, some deductions about hereditary marksmanship.

Here I first saw Major (by misplaced courtesy) Wentworth Caswell. I knew him for a type the moment my eyes suffered from the sight of him. A rat has no geographical habitat. My old friend, A. Tennyson,° said, as he so well said almost everything:

> Prophet, curse me the blabbing lip,
> And curse me the British vermin, the rat.

Let us regard the word "British" as interchangeable *ad lib*. A rat is a rat.

This man was hunting about the hotel lobby like a starved dog that had forgotten where he had buried a bone. He had a face of great acreage, red, pulpy, and with a kind of sleepy massiveness like that of Buddha. He possessed one single virtue—he was very smoothly shaven. The mark of the beast is not indelible upon a man until he goes about with a stubble. I think that if he had not used his razor that day I would have repulsed his advances, and the criminal calendar of the world would have been spared the addition of one murder.

20   I happened to be standing within five feet of a cuspidor when Major Caswell opened fire upon it. I had been observant enough to perceive that the attacking force was using Gatlings instead of squirrel rifles, so I sidestepped so promptly that the major seized the opportunity to apologize to a noncombatant. He had the blabbing lip. In four minutes he had become my friend and had dragged me to the bar.

I desire to interpolate here that I am a Southerner. But I am not one by profession or trade. I eschew the string tie, the slouch hat, the Prince Albert, the number of bales of cotton destroyed by Sherman, and plug chewing. When the orchestra plays "Dixie" I do not cheer. I slide a little lower on the leather-cornered seat and, well, order another Würzburger and wish that Longstreet had—but what's the use?

Major Caswell banged the bar with his fist, and the first gun at Fort Sumter re-echoed. When he fired the last one at Appomattox I began to hope. But then he began on family trees, and demonstrated that Adam was only a third cousin of a collateral branch of the Caswell family. Genealogy disposed of, he took up, to my distaste, his private family matters. He spoke of his wife, traced her descent back to Eve, and profanely denied any possible rumor that she may have had relations in the land of Nod.°

A. Tennyson: The quoted lines are from Tennyson's *Maud*, part 2.5.6   **land of Nod:** where Cain, the exiled son of Adam and Eve, found a wife (Genesis 4.16ff)

By this time I began to suspect that he was trying to obscure by noise the fact that he had ordered the drinks, on the chance that I would be bewildered into paying for them. But when they were down he crashed a silver dollar loudly upon the bar. Then, of course, another serving was obligatory. And when I had paid for that I took leave of him brusquely; for I wanted no more of him. But before I had obtained my release he had prated loudly of an income that his wife received, and showed a handful of silver money.

When I got my key at the desk the clerk said to me courteously: "If that man Caswell has annoyed you, and if you would like to make a complaint, we will have him ejected. He is a nuisance, a loafer, and without any known means of support, although he seems to have some money most of the time. But we don't seem to be able to hit upon any means of throwing him out legally."

"Why, no," said I, after some reflection; "I don't see my way clear to making a complaint. But I would like to place myself on record as asserting that I do not care for his company. Your town," I continued, "seems to be a quiet one. What manner of entertainment, adventure, or excitement, have you to offer to the stranger within your gates?"° 25

"Well, sir," said the clerk, "there will be a show here next Thursday. It is—I'll look it up and have the announcement sent up to your room with the ice water. Good-night."

After I went up to my room I looked out the window. It was only about ten o'clock, but I looked upon a silent town. The drizzle continued, spangled with dim lights, as far apart as currants in a cake sold at the Ladies' Exchange.

"A quiet place," I said to myself, as my first shoe struck the ceiling of the occupant of the room beneath mine. "Nothing of the life here that gives color and good variety to the cities in the East and West. Just a good, ordinary, humdrum, business town."

Nashville occupies a foremost place among the manufacturing centers of the country. It is the fifth boot and shoe market in the United States, the largest candy and cracker manufacturing city in the South, and does an enormous wholesale drygoods, grocery, and drug business.

I must tell you how I came to be in Nashville, and I assure you the digression brings as much tedium to me as it does to you. I was traveling elsewhere on my own business, but I had a commission from a Northern literary magazine to stop over there and establish a personal 30

---

stranger within your gates: cf. Exodus 20.10

connection between the publication and one of its contributors, Azalea Adair.

Adair (there was no clue to the personality except the handwriting) had sent in some essays (lost art!) and poems that had made the editors swear approvingly over their one o'clock luncheon. So they had commissioned me to round up said Adair and corner by contract his or her output at two cents a word before some other publisher offered her ten or twenty.

At nine o'clock the next morning, after my chicken livers *en brochette* (try them if you can find that hotel), I strayed out into the drizzle, which was still on for an unlimited run. At the first corner I came upon Uncle Caesar. He was a stalwart Negro, older than the pyramids, with gray wool and a face that reminded me of Brutus,° and a second afterwards of the late King Cettiwayo.° He wore the most remarkable coat that I ever had seen or expect to see. It reached to his ankles and had once been a confederate gray in color. But rain and sun and age had so variegated it that Joseph's coat,° beside it, would have faded to a pale monochrome. I must linger with that coat, for it has to do with the story—the story that is so long in coming, because you can hardly expect anything to happen in Nashville.

Once it must have been the military coat of an officer. The cape of it had vanished, but all adown its front it had been frogged and tasseled magnificently. But now the frogs and tassels were gone. In their stead had been patiently stitched (I surmised by some surviving "black mammy") new frogs made of cunningly twisted common hempen twine. This twine was frayed and disheveled. It must have been added to the coat as a substitute for vanished splendors, with tasteless but painstaking devotion, for it followed faithfully the curves of the long-missing frogs. And, to complete the comedy and pathos of the garment, all its buttons were gone save one. The second button from the top alone remained. The coat was fastened by other twine strings tied through the buttonholes and other holes rudely pierced in the opposite side. There was never such a weird garment so fantastically bedecked and of so many mottled hues. The lone button was the size of a half-dollar, made of yellow horn and sewed on with coarse twine.

This Negro stood by a carriage so old that Ham° himself might have started a hack line with it after he left the ark with the two animals hitched to it. As I approached he threw open the door, drew out

Brutus: tragic hero of Shakespeare's *Julius Caesar*   **King Cettiwayo:** king of the Zulus (1872–1884)   **Joseph's coat:** cf. Genesis 37   **Ham:** son of Noah who, according to tradition, settled in Africa and was the ancestor of the black races

a feather duster, waved it without using it, and said in deep, rumbling tones:

"Step right in, suh; ain't a speck of dust in it—jus' got back from a   35
funeral, suh."

I inferred that on such gala occasions carriages were given an extra cleaning. I looked up and down the street and perceived that there was little choice among the vehicles for hire that lined the curb. I looked in my memorandum book for the address of Azalea Adair.

"I want to go to 861 Jessamine Street," I said, and was about to step into the hack. But for an instant the thick, long, gorilla-like arm of the Negro barred me. On his massive and saturnine face a look of sudden suspicion and enmity flashed for a moment. Then, with quickly returning conviction, he asked, blandishingly: "What are you gwine there for, boss?"

"What is that to you?" I asked, a little sharply.

"Nothin', suh, jus' nothin'. Only it's a lonesome kind of part of town and few folks ever has business out there. Step right in. The seats is clean—jus' got back from a funeral, suh."

A mile and a half it must have been to our journey's end. I could   40
hear nothing but the fearful rattle of the ancient hack over the uneven brick paving; I could smell nothing but the drizzle, now further flavored with coal smoke and something like a mixture of tar and oleander blossoms. All I could see through the streaming windows were two rows of dim houses.

The city has an area of 10 square miles; 181 miles of streets, of which 137 miles are paved; a system of waterworks that cost $2,000,000, with 77 miles of mains.

Eight-six-one Jessamine Street was a decayed mansion. Thirty yards back from the street it stood, outmerged in a splendid grove of trees and untrimmed shrubbery. A row of box bushes overflowed and almost hid the paling fence from sight; the gate was kept closed by a rope noose that encircled the gate post and the first paling of the gate. But when you got inside you saw that 861 was a shell, a shadow, a ghost of former grandeur and excellence. But in the story, I have not yet got inside.

When the hack had ceased from rattling and the weary quadrupeds came to a rest I handed my jehu° his fifty cents with an additional quarter, feeling a glow of conscious generosity as I did so. He refused it.

"It's two dollars, suh," he said.

jehu: a fast driver (cf. 2 Kings 9.20)

45   "How's that?" I asked, "I plainly heard you call at the hotel. 'Fifty cents to any part of town.'"

"It's two dollars, suh," he repeated obstinately. "It's a long ways from the hotel."

"It is within the city limits and well within them," I argued. "Don't think that you have picked up a greenhorn Yankee. Do you see those hills over there?" I went on, pointing toward the east (I could not see them, myself, for the drizzle); "well, I was born and raised on their other side. You old fool nigger, can't you tell people from other people when you see 'em?"

The grim face of King Cettiwayo softened. "Is you from the South, suh? I reckon it was them shoes of yourn' fooled me. They is somethin' sharp in the toes for a Southern gen'l'man to wear."

"Then the charge is fifty cents, I suppose?" said I, inexorably.

50   His former expression, a mingling of cupidity and hostility, returned, remained ten seconds, and vanished.

"Boss," he said, "fifty cents is right; but I *needs* two dollars, suh; I'm *obleeged* to have two dollars. I ain't *demandin'* it now, suh; after I knows whar you's from; I'm jus' sayin' that I *has* to have two dollars tonight and business is mighty po'."

Peace and confidence settled upon his heavy features. He had been luckier than he had hoped. Instead of having picked up a greenhorn, ignorant of rates, he had come upon an inheritance.

"You confounded old rascal," I said, reaching down to my pocket, "you ought to be turned over to the police."

For the first time I saw him smile. He knew; *he knew*; HE KNEW.

55   I gave him two one-dollar bills. As I handed them over I noticed that one of them had seen parlous times. Its upper right-hand corner was missing and it had been torn through in the middle, but joined again. A strip of blue tissue paper, pasted over the split, preserved its negotiability.

Enough of the African bandit for the present: I left him happy, lifted the rope, and opened the creaky gate.

The house, as I said, was a shell. A paint brush had not touched it in twenty years. I could not see why a strong wind should not have bowled it over like a house of cards until I looked again at the trees that hugged it close—the trees that saw the battle of Nashville and still drew their protecting branches around it against storm and enemy and cold.

Azalea Adair, fifty years old, white-haired, a descendant of the cavaliers, as thin and frail as the house she lived in, robed in the cheapest and cleanest dress I ever saw, with an air as simple as a queen's, received me.

The reception room seemed a mile square, because there was nothing in it except some rows of books on unpainted white-pine bookshelves, a cracked marble-topped table, a rag rug, a hairless horsehair sofa, and two or three chairs. Yes, there was a picture on the wall, a colored crayon drawing of a cluster of pansies. I looked around for the portrait of Andrew Jackson and the pine-cone hanging basket but they were not there.

Azalea Adair and I had conversation, a little of which will be repeated to you. She was a product of the old South, gently nurtured in the sheltered life. Her learning was not broad, but was deep and of splendid originality in its somewhat narrow scope. She had been educated at home, and her knowledge of the world was derived from inference and by inspiration. Of such is the precious, small group of essayists made. While she talked to me I kept brushing my fingers, trying, unconsciously, to rid them guiltily of the absent dust from the half-calf backs of Lamb, Chaucer, Hazlitt, Marcus Aurelius, Montaigne, and Hood. She was exquisite, she was a valuable discovery. Nearly everybody nowadays knows too much—oh, so much too much—of real life.

I could perceive clearly that Azalea Adair was very poor. A house and a dress she had, not much else, I fancied. So, divided between my duty to the magazine and my loyalty to the poets and essayists who fought Thomas in the valley of the Cumberland, I listened to her voice which was like a harpsichord's and found that I could not speak of contracts. In the presence of the nine Muses and the three Graces one hesitated to lower the topic to two cents. There would have to be another colloquy after I had regained my commercialism. But I spoke of my mission, and three o'clock of the next afternoon was set for the discussion of the business proposition.

"Your town," I said, as I began to make ready to depart (which is the time for smooth generalities), "seems to be a quiet, sedate place. A home town, I should say, where few things out of the ordinary ever happen."

It carries on an extensive trade in stoves and hollow ware with the West and South, and its flouring mills have a daily capacity of more than 2,000 barrels.

Azalea Adair seemed to reflect.

"I have never thought of it that way," she said, with a kind of sincere intensity that seemed to belong to her. "Isn't it in the still, quiet places that things do happen? I fancy that when God began to create the earth on the first Monday morning one could have leaned out one's window and heard the drops of mud splashing from His trowel as He built up the everlasting hills. What did the noisiest project in the world—I mean the building of the tower of Babel—result in finally? A page and a half of Esperanto in the *North American Review.*"

"Of course," said I, platitudinously, "human nature is the same everywhere; but there is more color—er—more drama and movement and—er—romance in some cities than in others."

"On the surface," said Azalea Adair. "I have traveled many times around the world in a golden airship wafted on two wings—print and dreams. I have seen (on one of my imaginary tours) the Sultan of Turkey bowstring° with his own hands one of his wives who had uncovered her face in public. I have seen a man in Nashville tear up his theater tickets because his wife was going out with her face covered—with rice powder. In San Francisco's Chinatown I saw the slave girl Sing Yee dipped slowly, inch by inch, in boiling almond oil to make her swear she would never see her American lover again. She gave in when the boiling oil had reached three inches above her knees. At a euchre party in East Nashville the other night I saw Kitty Morgan cut dead by seven of her schoolmates and lifelong friends because she had married a house painter. The boiling oil was sizzling as high as her heart; but I wish you could have seen the fine little smile that she carried from table to table. Oh, yes, it is a humdrum town. Just a few miles of red brick houses and mud and stores and lumber yards."

Someone had knocked hollowly at the back of the house. Azalea Adair breathed a soft apology and went to investigate the sound. She came back in three minutes with brightened eyes, a faint flush on her cheeks, and ten years lifted from her shoulders.

"You must have a cup of tea before you go," she said, "and a sugar cake."

70   She reached and shook a little iron bell. In shuffled a small Negro girl about twelve, barefoot, not very tidy, glowering at me with thumb in mouth and bulging eyes.

Azalea Adair opened a tiny, worn purse and drew out a dollar bill, a dollar bill with the upper right-hand corner missing, torn in two pieces and pasted together again with a strip of blue tissue paper. It was one of those bills I had given the piratical Negro—there was no doubt of it.

"Go up to Mr. Baker's store on the corner, Impy," she said, handing the girl the dollar bill, "and get a quarter pound of tea—the kind he always sends me—and ten cents' worth of sugar cakes. Now, hurry. The supply of tea in the house happens to be exhausted," she explained to me.

bowstring: strangle with a bowstring

Impy left by the back way. Before the scrape of her hard, bare feet had died away on the back porch, a wild shriek—I was sure it was hers—filled the hollow house. Then the deep, gruff tones of an angry man's voice mingled with the girl's further squeals and unintelligible words.

Azalea Adair rose without surprise or emotion and disappeared. For two minutes I heard the hoarse rumble of the man's voice; then something like an oath and a slight scuffle, and she returned calmly to her chair.

"This is a roomy house," she said, "and I have a tenant for part of it. I am sorry to have to rescind my invitation to tea. It is impossible to get the kind I always use at the store. Perhaps tomorrow Mr. Baker will be able to supply me."   75

I was sure that Impy had not had time to leave the house. I inquired concerning street-car lines and took my leave. After I was well on my way I remembered that I had not learned Azalea Adair's name. But tomorrow would do.

The same day I started in on the course of iniquity that this uneventful city forced upon me. I was in the town only two days, but in that time I managed to lie shamelessly by telegraph, and to be an accomplice—after the fact, if that is the correct legal term—to a murder.

As I rounded the corner nearest my hotel the Afrite coachman of the polychromatic, nonpareil coat seized me, swung open the dungeony door of his peripatetic sarcophagus, flirted his feather duster and began his ritual: "Step right in, boss. Carriage is clean—jus' got back from a funeral. Fifty cents to any—"

And then he knew me and grinned broadly. "'Scuse me, boss; you is de gen'l'man what rid out with me dis mawnin'. Thank you kindly, suh."

"I am going out to 861 again tomorrow afternoon at three," said I, "and if you will be here, I'll let you drive me. So you know Miss Adair?" I concluded, thinking of my dollar bill.   80

"I belonged to her father, Judge Adair, suh," he replied.

"I judge that she is pretty poor," I said. "She hasn't much money to speak of, has she?"

For an instant I looked again at the fierce countenance of King Cettiwayo, and then he changed back to an extortionate old Negro hack driver.

"She ain't gwine to starve, suh," he said. "She has reso'ces, suh; she has reso'ces."

"I shall pay you fifty cents for the trip," said I.   85

"Dat is puffeckly correct, suh," he answered, humbly. "I just *had* to have dat two dollars dis mawnin', boss."

I went to the hotel and lied by electricity. I wired the magazine: "A. Adair holds out for eight cents a word."

The answer that came back was: "Give it to her quick, you duffer."

Just before dinner "Major" Wentworth Caswell bore down upon me with greetings of a long-lost friend. I have seen few men whom I have so instantaneously hated, and of whom it was so difficult to be rid. I was standing at the bar when he invaded me; therefore I could not wave the white ribbon in his face. I would have paid gladly for the drinks, hoping thereby to escape another; but he was one of those despicable, roaring, advertising bibbers who must have brass bands and fireworks attend upon every cent that they waste in their follies.

90   With an air of producing millions he drew two one-dollar bills from a pocket and dashed one of them upon the bar. I looked once more at the dollar bill with the upper right-hand corner missing, torn through the middle, and patched with a strip of blue tissue paper. It was my dollar again. It could have been no other.

I went up to my room. The drizzle and the monotony of a dreary, eventless Southern town had made me tired and listless. I remember that just before I went to bed I mentally disposed of the mysterious dollar bill (which might have formed the clue to a tremendously fine detective story of San Francisco) by saying to myself sleepily: "Seems as if a lot of people here own stock in the Hack-Drivers' Trust. Pays dividends promptly, too. Wonder if—" Then I fell asleep.

King Cettiwayo was at his post the next day, and rattled my bones over the stones out to 861. He was to wait and rattle me back again when I was ready.

Azalea Adair looked paler and cleaner and frailer than she had looked on the day before. After she had signed the contract at eight cents per word she grew still paler and began to slip out of her chair. Without much trouble I managed to get her up on the antediluvian horsehair sofa and then I ran out to the sidewalk and yelled to the coffee-colored Pirate to bring a doctor. With a wisdom that I had not suspected in him, he abandoned his team and struck off up the street afoot, realizing the value of speed. In ten minutes he returned with a grave, gray-haired, and capable man of medicine. In a few words (worth much less than eight cents each) I explained to him my presence in the hollow house of mystery. He bowed with stately understanding, and turned to the old Negro.

"Uncle Caesar," he said, calmly, "run up to my house and ask Miss Lucy to give you a cream pitcher full of fresh milk and half a tumbler of

port wine. And hurry back. Don't drive—run. I want you to get back
sometime this week."

It occurred to me that Dr. Merriman also felt a distrust as to the   95
speeding powers of the land-pirate's steeds. After Uncle Caesar was
gone, lumberingly, but swiftly, up the street, the doctor looked me over
with great politeness and as much careful calculation until he had decided that I might do.

"It is only a case of insufficient nutrition," he said. "In other words,
the result of poverty, pride, and starvation. Mrs. Caswell has many devoted friends who would be glad to aid her, but she will accept nothing
except from that old Negro, Uncle Caesar, who was once owned by her
family."

"Mrs. Caswell!" said I, in surprise. And then I looked at the contract and saw that she had signed it "Azalea Adair Caswell."

"I thought she was Miss Adair," I said.

"Married to a drunken, worthless loafer, sir," said the doctor. "It is
said that he robs her even of the small sums that her old servant contributes toward her support."

When the milk and wine had been brought the doctor soon re-   100
vived Azalea Adair. She sat up and talked of the beauty of the autumn
leaves that were then in season and their height of color. She referred
lightly to her fainting seizure as the outcome of an old palpitation of
her heart. Impy fanned her as she lay on the sofa. The doctor was due
elsewhere, and I followed him to the door. I told him that it was within
my power and intentions to make a reasonable advance of money to
Azalea Adair on future contributions to the magazine, and he seemed
pleased.

"By the way," he said, "perhaps you would like to know that you
have had royalty for a coachman. Old Caesar's grandfather was a king
in Congo. Caesar himself has royal ways, as you may have observed."

As the doctor was moving off I heard Uncle Caesar's voice inside:
"Did he get bofe of dem two dollars from you, Mis' Zalea?"

"Yes, Caesar," I heard Azalea Adair answer, weakly. And then I
went in and concluded business negotiations with our contributor. I assumed the responsibility of advancing fifty dollars, putting it as a necessary formality in binding our bargain. And then Uncle Caesar drove
me back to the hotel.

Here ends all of the story as far as I can witness. The rest must be
only bare statements of facts.

At about six o'clock I went out for a stroll. Uncle Caesar was at his   105
corner. He threw open the door of his carriage, flourished his duster,
and began his depressing formula: "Step right in, suh. Fifty cents to

anywhere in the city—hack's puffickly clean, suh—jus' got back from a funeral—"

And then he recognized me. I think his eyesight was getting bad. His coat had taken on a few more faded shades of color, the twine strings were more frayed and ragged, the last remaining button—the button of yellow horn—was gone. A motley descendant of kings was Uncle Caesar!

About two hours later I saw an excited crowd besieging the front of the drug store. In a desert where nothing happens this was manna; so I wedged my way inside. On an extemporized couch of empty boxes and chairs was stretched the mortal corporeality of Major Wentworth Caswell. A doctor was testing him for the mortal ingredient. His decision was that it was conspicuous by its absence.

The erstwhile Major had been found dead on a dark street and brought by curious and ennuied citizens to the drug store. The late human being had been engaged in terrific battle—the details showed that. Loafer and reprobate though he had been, he had been also a warrior. But he had lost. His hands were yet clinched so tightly that his fingers could not be opened. The gentle citizens who had known him stood about and searched their vocabularies to find some good words, if it were possible, to speak of him. One kindlooking man said, after much thought: "When 'Cas' was about fo'teen he was one of the best spellers in the school."

While I stood there the fingers of the right hand of "the man that was," which hung down the side of a white pine box, relaxed, and dropped something at my feet. I covered it with one foot quietly, and a little later on I picked it up and pocketed it. I reasoned that in his last struggle his hand must have seized that object unwittingly and held it in a death grip.

110   At the hotel that night the main topic of conversation, with the possible exceptions of politics and prohibition, was the demise of Major Caswell. I heard one man say to a group of listeners:

"In my opinion, gentlemen, Caswell was murdered by some of these no-account niggers for his money. He had fifty dollars this afternoon which he showed to several gentlemen in the hotel. When he was found the money was not on his person."

I left the city the next morning at nine, and as the train was crossing the bridge over the Cumberland River I took out of my pocket a yellow horn overcoat button the size of a fifty-cent piece, with frayed ends of coarse twine hanging from it, and cast it out of the window into the slow, muddy waters below.

I wonder what's doing in Buffalo!

QUESTIONS

1. What is the narrator's attitude toward the South? What is his purpose in "quoting" the statistical data that intersperse the story? What type of humor does he employ?
2. What coincidences are required for the development of the plot?
3. Characterize Azalea Adair, Uncle Caesar, and Major Caswell. Are they round characters?
4. The central conflict of the story is resolved by a murder. What does the story offer in the way of analysis of the psychology or morality of murder? Is there a justification for Caesar's murder of Caswell?
5. One issue raised by the story is whether there can be "romance" in such a place as Nashville. Azalea Adair offers one answer in paragraph 67. Is that the same answer that the narrator comes to accept?
6. The story contains what today is considered offensively racist language. How does this element affect your evaluation of the story? Could it be argued that the racist language has a significant literary purpose?

Susan Glaspell
A Jury of Her Peers

When Martha Hale opened the storm door and got a cut of the north wind, she ran back for her big woolen scarf. As she hurriedly wound that round her head her eye made a scandalized sweep of her kitchen. It was no ordinary thing that called her away—it was probably farther from ordinary than anything that had ever happened in Dickson County. But what her eye took in was that her kitchen was in no shape for leaving: her bread all ready for mixing, half the flour sifted and half unsifted.

She hated to see things half done; but she had been at that when the team from town stopped to get Mr. Hale, and then the sheriff came running in to say his wife wished Mrs. Hale would come too—adding, with a grin, that he guessed she was getting scarey and wanted another woman along. So she had dropped everything right where it was.

"Martha!" now came her husband's impatient voice. "Don't keep folks waiting out here in the cold."

A JURY OF HER PEERS   First published in 1917, the story is based on the author's one-act play *Trifles*, written in 1916 for the Provincetown Players. Susan Glaspell (1882–1948) lived for the first thirty-two years of her life in Iowa. She said that *Trifles* (and hence this short story) was suggested to her by an experience she had while working for a Des Moines newspaper.

She again opened the storm door, and this time joined the three men and the one woman waiting for her in the big two-seated buggy.

5   After she had the robes tucked around her she took another look at the woman who sat beside her on the back seat. She had met Mrs. Peters the year before at the county fair, and the thing she remembered about her was that she didn't seem like a sheriff's wife. She was small and thin and didn't have a strong voice. Mrs. Gorman, sheriff's wife before Gorman went out and Peters came in, had a voice that somehow seemed to be backing up the law with every word. But if Mrs. Peters didn't look like a sheriff's wife, Peters made it up in looking like a sheriff. He was to a dot the kind of man who could get himself elected sheriff—a heavy man with a big voice, who was particularly genial with the law-abiding, as if to make it plain that he knew the difference between criminals and non-criminals. And right there it came into Mrs. Hale's mind, with a stab, that this man who was so pleasant and lively with all of them was going to the Wrights' now as a sheriff.

"The country's not very pleasant this time of year," Mrs. Peters at last ventured, as if she felt they ought to be talking as well as the men.

Mrs. Hale scarcely finished her reply, for they had gone up a little hill and could see the Wright place now, and seeing it did not make her feel like talking. It looked very lonesome this cold March morning. It had always been a lonesome-looking place. It was down in a hollow, and the poplar trees around it were lonesome-looking trees. The men were looking at it and talking about what had happened. The county attorney was bending to one side of the buggy, and kept looking steadily at the place as they drew up to it.

"I'm glad you came with me," Mrs. Peters said nervously, as the two women were about to follow the men in through the kitchen door.

Even after she had her foot on the doorstep, her hand on the knob, Martha Hale had a moment of feeling she could not cross the threshold. And the reason it seemed she couldn't cross it now was simply because she hadn't crossed it before. Time and time again it had been in her mind, "I ought to go over and see Minnie Foster"—she still thought of her as Minnie Foster, though for twenty years she had been Mrs. Wright. And then there was always something to do and Minnie Foster would go from her mind. But *now* she could come.

10   The men went over to the stove. The women stood close together by the door. Young Henderson, the county attorney, turned around and said, "Come up to the fire, ladies."

Mrs. Peters took a step forward, then stopped. "I'm not—cold," she said.

And so the two women stood by the door, at first not even so much as looking around the kitchen.

The men talked for a minute about what a good thing it was the sheriff had sent his deputy out that morning to make a fire for them, and then Sheriff Peters stepped back from the stove, unbuttoned his outer coat, and leaned his hands on the kitchen table in a way that seemed to mark the beginning of official business. "Now, Mr. Hale," he said in a sort of semiofficial voice, "before we move things about, you tell Mr. Henderson just what it was you saw when you came here yesterday morning."

The county attorney was looking around the kitchen.

"By the way," he said, "has anything been moved?" He turned to the sheriff. "Are things just as you left them yesterday?"   15

Peters looked from cupboard to sink; from that to a small worn rocker a little to one side of the kitchen table.

"It's just the same."

"Somebody should have been left here yesterday," said the county attorney.

"Oh—yesterday," returned the sheriff, with a little gesture as of yesterday having been more than he could bear to think of. "When I had to send Frank to Morris Center for that man who went crazy—let me tell you, I had my hands full *yesterday*. I knew you could get back from Omaha by today, George, and as long as I went over everything here myself—"

"Well, Mr. Hale," said the county attorney, in a way of letting what was past and gone go, "tell just what happened when you came here yesterday morning."   20

Mrs. Hale, still leaning against the door, had that sinking feeling of the mother whose child is about to speak a piece. Lewis often wandered along and got things mixed up in a story. She hoped he would tell this straight and plain, and not say unnecessary things that would just make things harder for Minnie Foster. He didn't begin at once, and she noticed that he looked queer—as if standing in that kitchen and having to tell what he had seen there yesterday morning made him almost sick.

"Yes, Mr. Hale?" the county attorney reminded.

"Harry and I had started to town with a load of potatoes," Mrs. Hale's husband began.

Harry was Mrs. Hale's oldest boy. He wasn't with them now, for the very good reason that those potatoes never got to town yesterday and he was taking them this morning, so he hadn't been home when the sheriff stopped to say he wanted Mr. Hale to come over to the Wright place and tell the county attorney his story there, where he could point it all out. With all Mrs. Hale's other emotions came the fear that maybe Harry wasn't dressed warm enough—they hadn't any of them realized how that north wind did bite.

25   "We come along this road," Hale was going on, with a motion of his hand to the road over which they had just come, "and as we got in sight of the house I says to Harry, 'I'm goin' to see if I can't get John Wright to take a telephone.' You see," he explained to Henderson, "unless I can get somebody to go in with me they won't come out this branch road except for a price I can't pay. I'd spoke to Wright about it once before; but he put me off, saying folks talked too much anyway, and all he asked was peace and quiet—guess you know about how much he talked himself. But I thought maybe if I went to the house and talked about it before his wife, and said all the women-folks liked the telephones, and that in this lonesome stretch of road it would be a good thing—well, I said to Harry that that was what I was going to say— though I said at the same time that I didn't know as what his wife wanted made much difference to John—"

Now, there he was!—saying things he didn't need to say. Mrs. Hale tried to catch her husband's eye, but fortunately the county attorney interrupted with:

"Let's talk about that a little later, Mr. Hale. I do want to talk about that, but I'm anxious now to get along to just what happened when you got here."

When he began this time, it was very deliberately and carefully:

"I didn't see or hear anything. I knocked at the door. And still it was all quiet inside. I knew they must be up—it was past eight o'clock. So I knocked again, louder, and I thought I heard somebody say 'Come in.' I wasn't sure—I'm not sure yet. But I opened the door—this door," jerking a hand toward the door by which the two women stood, "and there, in that rocker"—pointing to it—"sat Mrs. Wright."

30   Every one in the kitchen looked at the rocker. It came into Mrs. Hale's mind that that rocker didn't look in the least like Minnie Foster—the Minnie Foster of twenty years before. It was a dingy red, with wooden rungs up the back, and the middle rung was gone, and the chair sagged to one side.

"How did she—look?" the county attorney was inquiring.

"Well," said Hale, "she looked—queer."

"How do you mean—queer?"

As he asked it he took out a notebook and pencil. Mrs. Hale did not like the sight of that pencil. She kept her eye fixed on her husband, as if to keep him from saying unnecessary things that would go into that notebook and make trouble.

Hale did speak guardedly, as if the pencil had affected him too.   35
"Well, as if she didn't know what she was going to do next. And kind of—done up."

"How did she seem to feel about your coming?"

"Why, I don't think she minded—one way or other. She didn't pay much attention. I said, 'Ho' do, Mrs. Wright? It's cold, ain't it?' And she said, 'Is it?'—and went on pleatin' at her apron.

"Well, I was surprised. She didn't ask me to come up to the stove, or to sit down, but just set there, not even lookin' at me. And so I said: 'I want to see John.'

"And then she—laughed. I guess you would call it a laugh.   40

"I thought of Harry and the team outside, so I said, a little sharp, 'Can I see John?' 'No,' says she—kind of dull like. 'Ain't he home?' says I. Then she looked at me. 'Yes,' says she, 'he's home.' 'Then why can't I see him?' I asked her, out of patience with her now. ''Cause he's dead,' says she, just as quiet and dull—and fell to pleatin' her apron. 'Dead?' says I, like you do when you can't take in what you've heard.

"She just nodded her head, not getting a bit excited, but rockin' back and forth.

"'Why—where is he?' says I, not knowing *what* to say.

"She just pointed upstairs—like this"—pointing to the room above.

"I got up, with the idea of going up there myself. By this time I—   45
didn't know what to do. I walked from there to here; then I says: 'Why, what did he die of?'

"'He died of a rope around his neck,' says she; and just went on pleatin' at her apron."

Hale stopped speaking, and stood staring at the rocker, as if he were still seeing the woman who had sat there the morning before. Nobody spoke; it was as if every one were seeing the woman who had sat there the morning before.

"And what did you do then?" the county attorney at last broke the silence.

"I went out and called Harry. I thought I might—need help. I got Harry in, and we went upstairs." His voice fell almost to a whisper. "There he was—lying over the—"

"I think I'd rather have you go into that upstairs," the county at-   50
torney interrupted, "where you can point it all out. Just go on now with the rest of the story."

"Well, my first thought was to get that rope off. It looked—"

He stopped, his face twitching.

"But Harry, he went up to him, and he said, 'No, he's dead all right, and we'd better not touch anything.' So we went downstairs.

"She was still sitting that same way. 'Has anybody been notified?' I asked. 'No,' says she, unconcerned."

55   "'Who did this, Mrs. Wright?' said Harry. He said it businesslike, and she stopped pleatin' at her apron. 'I don't know,' she says. 'You don't *know?*' says Harry. 'Weren't you sleepin' in the bed with him?' 'Yes,' says she, 'but I was on the inside.' 'Somebody slipped a rope round his neck and strangled him, and you didn't wake up?' says Harry. 'I didn't wake up,' she said after him.

"We may have looked as if we didn't see how that could be, for after a minute she said, 'I sleep sound.'

"Harry was going to ask her more questions, but I said maybe that weren't our business; maybe we ought to let her tell her story first to the coroner or the sheriff. So Harry went fast as he could over to High Road—the Rivers's place, where there's a telephone."

"And what did she do when she knew you had gone for the coroner?" The attorney got his pencil in his hand all ready for writing.

"She moved from that chair to this one over here"—Hale pointed to a small chair in the corner—"and just sat there with her hands held together and looking down. I got a feeling that I ought to make some conversation, so I said I had come in to see if John wanted to put in a telephone; and at that she started to laugh, and then she stopped and looked at me—scared."

60   At the sound of a moving pencil the man who was telling the story looked up.

"I dunno—maybe it wasn't scared," he hastened; "I wouldn't like to say it was. Soon Harry got back, and then Dr. Lloyd came, and you, Mr. Peters, and so I guess that's all I know that you don't."

He said that last with relief, and moved a little, as if relaxing. Every one moved a little. The county attorney walked toward the stair door.

"I guess we'll go upstairs first—then out to the barn and around there."

He paused and looked around the kitchen.

65   "You're convinced there was nothing important here?" he asked the sheriff. "Nothing that would—point to any motive?"

The sheriff too looked all around, as if to re-convince himself.

"Nothing here but kitchen things," he said, with a little laugh for the insignificance of kitchen things.

The county attorney was looking at the cupboard—a peculiar, ungainly structure, half closet and half cupboard, the upper part of it being built in the wall, and the lower part just the old-fashioned kitchen cupboard. As if its queerness attracted him, he got a chair and opened the upper part and looked in. After a moment he drew his hand away sticky.

"Here's a nice mess," he said resentfully.

The two women had drawn nearer, and now the sheriff's wife   70
spoke.

"Oh—her fruit," she said, looking to Mrs. Hale for sympathetic understanding. She turned back to the county attorney and explained: "She worried about that when it turned so cold last night. She said the fire would go out and her jars might burst."

Mrs. Peters's husband broke into a laugh.

"Well, can you beat the women! Held for murder, and worrying about her preserves!"

The young attorney set his lips.

"I guess before we're through with her she may have something   75
more serious than preserves to worry about."

"Oh, well," said Mrs. Hale's husband, with good-natured superiority, "women are used to worrying over trifles."

The two women moved a little closer together. Neither of them spoke. The county attorney seemed suddenly to remember his manners—and think of his future.

"And yet," said he, with the gallantry of a young politician, "for all their worries, what would we do without the ladies?"

The women did not speak, did not unbend. He went to the sink and began washing his hands. He turned to wipe them on the roller wheel—whirled it for a cleaner place.

"Dirty towels! Not much of a housekeeper, would you say, ladies?"   80

He kicked his foot against some dirty pans under the sink.

"There's a great deal of work to be done on a farm," said Mrs. Hale stiffly.

"To be sure. And yet"—with a little bow to her—"I know there are some Dickson County farmhouses that do not have such roller towels." He gave it a pull to expose its full length again.

"Those towels get dirty awful quick. Men's hands aren't always as clean as they might be."

"Ah, loyal to your sex, I see," he laughed. He stopped and gave her   85
a keen look. "But you and Mrs. Wright were neighbors. I suppose you were friends, too."

Martha Hale shook her head.

"I've seen little enough of her of late years. I've not been in this house—it's more than a year."

"And why was that? You didn't like her?"

"I liked her well enough," she replied with spirit. "Farmers' wives have their hands full, Mr. Henderson. And then—" She looked around the kitchen.

90   "Yes?" he encouraged.

"It never seemed a very cheerful place," said she, more to herself than to him.

"No," he agreed; "I don't think any one would call it cheerful. I shouldn't say she had the homemaking instinct."

"Well, I don't know as Wright had, either," she muttered.

"You mean they didn't get on very well?" he was quick to ask.

95   "No; I don't mean anything," she answered, with decision. As she turned a little away from him, she added: "But I don't think a place would be any the cheerfuler for John Wright's bein' in it."

"I'd like to talk to you about that a little later, Mrs. Hale," he said. "I'm anxious to get the lay of things upstairs now."

He moved toward the stair door, followed by the two men.

"I suppose anything Mrs. Peters does'll be all right?" the sheriff inquired. "She was to take in some clothes for her, you know—and a few little things. We left in such a hurry yesterday."

The county attorney looked at the two women whom they were leaving alone there among the kitchen things.

100   "Yes—Mrs. Peters," he said, his glance resting on the woman who was not Mrs. Peters, the big farmer woman who stood behind the sheriff's wife. "Of course Mrs. Peters is one of us," he said, in a manner of entrusting responsibility. "And keep your eye out, Mrs. Peters, for anything that might be of use. No telling; you women might come upon a clue to the motive—and that's the thing we need."

Mr. Hale rubbed his face after the fashion of a show man getting ready for a pleasantry.

"But would the women know a clue if they did come upon it?" he said; and, having delivered himself of this, he followed the others through the stair door.

The women stood motionless and silent, listening to the footsteps, first upon the stairs, then in the room above them.

Then, as if releasing herself from something strange, Mrs. Hale began to arrange the dirty pans under the sink, which the county attorney's disdainful push of the foot had deranged.

105   "I'd hate to have men comin' into my kitchen," she said testily— "snoopin' round and criticizin'."

"Of course it's no more than their duty," said the sheriff's wife, in her manner of timid acquiescence.

"Duty's all right," replied Mrs. Hale bluffly; "but I guess that deputy sheriff that come out to make the fire might have got a little of this on." She gave the roller towel a pull. "Wish I'd thought of that sooner!

Seems mean to talk about her for not having things slicked up, when she had to come away in such a hurry."

She looked around the kitchen. Certainly it was not "slicked up." Her eye was held by a bucket of sugar on a low shelf. The cover was off the wooden bucket, and beside it was a paper bag—half full.

Mrs. Hale moved toward it.

"She was putting this in here," she said to herself—slowly.   110

She thought of the flour in her kitchen at home—half sifted, half not sifted. She had been interrupted, and had left things half done. What had interrupted Minnie Foster? Why had that work been left half done? She made a move as if to finish it,—unfinished things always bothered her,—and then she glanced around and saw that Mrs. Peters was watching her—and she didn't want Mrs. Peters to get that feeling she had got of work begun and then—for some reason—not finished.

"It's a shame about her fruit," she said, and walked toward the cupboard that the county attorney had opened, and got on the chair, murmuring: "I wonder if it's all gone."

It was a sorry enough looking sight, but "Here's one that's all right," she said at last. She held it toward the light. "This is cherries, too." She looked again. "I declare I believe that's the only one."

With a sigh, she got down from the chair, went to the sink, and wiped off the bottle.

"She'll feel awful bad, after all her hard work in the hot weather. I   115
remember the afternoon I put up my cherries last summer."

She set the bottle on the table, and, with another sigh, started to sit down in the rocker. But she did not sit down. Something kept her from sitting down in that chair. She straightened—stepped back, and, half turned away, stood looking at it, seeing the woman who sat there "pleatin' at her apron."

The thin voice of the sheriff's wife broke in upon her: "I must be getting those things from the front room closet." She opened the door into the other room, started in, stepped back. "You coming with me, Mrs. Hale?" she asked nervously. "You—you could help me get them."

They were soon back—the stark coldness of that shut-up room was not a thing to linger in.

"My!" said Mrs. Peters, dropping the things on the table and hurrying to the stove.

Mrs. Hale stood examining the clothes the woman who was being   120
detained in town had said she wanted.

"Wright was close!" she exclaimed, holding up a shabby black skirt that bore the marks of much making over. "I think maybe that's why she kept so much to herself. I s'pose she felt she couldn't do her part; and then, you don't enjoy things when you feel shabby. She used to wear pretty clothes and be lively—when she was Minnie Foster, one of the town girls, singing in the choir. But that—oh, that was twenty years ago."

With a carefulness in which there was something tender, she folded the shabby clothes and piled them at one corner of the table. She looked at Mrs. Peters, and there was something in the other woman's look that irritated her.

"She don't care," she said to herself. "Much difference it makes to her whether Minnie Foster had pretty clothes when she was a girl."

Then she looked again, and she wasn't so sure; in fact, she hadn't at any time been perfectly sure about Mrs. Peters. She had that shrinking manner, and yet her eyes looked as if they could see a long way into things.

125   "This all you was to take in?" asked Mrs. Hale.

"No," said the sheriff's wife; "she said she wanted an apron. Funny thing to want," she ventured in her nervous little way, "for there's not much to get you dirty in jail, goodness knows. But I suppose just to make her feel more natural. If you're used to wearing an apron—. She said they were in the bottom drawer of this cupboard. Yes—here they are. And then her little shawl that always hung on the stair door."

She took the small gray shawl from behind the door leading upstairs, and stood a minute looking at it.

Suddenly Mrs. Hale took a quick step toward the other woman.

"Mrs. Peters!"

130   "Yes, Mrs. Hale?"

"Do you think she—did it?"

A frightened look blurred the other things in Mrs. Peters's eyes.

"Oh, I don't know," she said, in a voice that seemed to shrink away from the subject.

"Well, I don't think she did," affirmed Mrs. Hale stoutly. "Asking for an apron, and her little shawl. Worryin' about her fruit."

135   "Mr. Peters says—." Footsteps were heard in the room above; she stopped, looked up, then went on in a lowered voice: "Mr. Peters says—it looks bad for her. Mr. Henderson is awful sarcastic in a speech, and he's going to make fun of her saying she didn't—wake up."

For a moment Mrs. Hale had no answer. Then, "Well, I guess John Wright didn't wake up—when they was slippin' that rope under his neck," she muttered.

"No, it's *strange*," breathed Mrs. Peters. "They think it was such a—funny way to kill a man."

She began to laugh; at the sound of the laugh, abruptly stopped.

"That's just what Mr. Hale said," said Mrs. Hale, in a resolutely natural voice. "There was a gun in the house. He says that's what he can't understand."

"Mr. Henderson said, coming out, that what was needed for the   140
case was a motive. Something to show anger—or sudden feeling."

"Well, I don't see any signs of anger around here," said Mrs. Hale. "I don't—"

She stopped. It was as if her mind tripped on something. Her eye was caught by a dish-towel in the middle of the kitchen table. Slowly she moved toward the table. One half of it was wiped clean, the other half messy. Her eyes made a slow, almost unwilling turn to the bucket of sugar and the half empty bag beside it. Things begun—and not finished.

After a moment she stepped back, and said, in that manner of releasing herself:

"Wonder how they're finding things upstairs? I hope she had it a little more red up° up there. You know,"—she paused, and feeling gathered,—"it seems kind of *sneaking;* locking her up in town and coming out here to get her own house to turn against her!"

"But, Mrs. Hale," said the sheriff's wife, "the law is the law."   145

"I s'pose 'tis," answered Mrs. Hale shortly.

She turned to the stove, saying something about that fire not being much to brag of. She worked with it a minute, and when she straightened up she said aggressively:

"The law is the law—and a bad stove is a bad stove. How'd you like to cook on this?"—pointing with the poker to the broken lining. She opened the oven door and started to express her opinion of the oven; but she was swept into her own thoughts, thinking of what it would mean, year after year, to have that stove to wrestle with. The thought of Minnie Foster trying to bake in that oven—and the thought of her never going over to see Minnie Foster—.

She was startled by hearing Mrs. Peters say: "A person gets discouraged—and loses heart."

The sheriff's wife had looked from the stove to the sink—to the   150
pail of water which had been carried in from outside. The two women stood there silent, above them the footsteps of the men who were looking for evidence against the woman who had worked in that kitchen. That look of seeing into things, of seeing through a thing to something

---

red up: neatened, readied (dialect)

else, was in the eyes of the sheriff's wife now. When Mrs. Hale next spoke to her, it was gently:

"Better loosen up your things, Mrs. Peters. We'll not feel them when we go out."

Mrs. Peters went to the back of the room to hang up the fur tippet she was wearing. A moment later she exclaimed, "Why, she was piecing a quilt," and held up a large sewing basket piled high with quilt pieces.

Mrs. Hale spread some of the blocks on the table.

"It's log-cabin pattern," she said, putting several of them together. "Pretty, isn't it?"

155   They were so engaged with the quilt that they did not hear the footsteps on the stairs. Just as the stair door opened Mrs. Hale was saying:

"Do you suppose she was going to quilt it or just knot it?"

The sheriff threw up his hands.

"They wonder whether she was going to quilt it or just knot it!"

There was a laugh for the ways of women, a warming of hands over the stove, and then the county attorney said briskly:

160   "Well, let's go right out to the barn and get that cleared up."

"I don't see as there's anything so strange," Mrs. Hale said resentfully, after the outside door had closed on the three men—"our taking up our time with little things while we're waiting for them to get the evidence. I don't see as it's anything to laugh about."

"Of course they've got awful important things on their minds," said the sheriff's wife apologetically.

They returned to an inspection of the blocks for the quilt. Mrs. Hale was looking at the fine, even sewing, and preoccupied with thoughts of the woman who had done that sewing, when she heard the sheriff's wife say, in a queer tone:

"Why, look at this one."

165   She turned to take the block held out to her.

"The sewing," said Mrs. Peters, in a troubled way. "All the rest of them have been so nice and even—but—this one. Why, it looks as if she didn't know what she was about!"

Their eyes met—something flashed to life, passed between them; then, as if with an effort, they seemed to pull away from each other. A moment Mrs. Hale sat there, her hands folded over that sewing which was so unlike all the rest of the sewing. Then she had pulled a knot and drawn the threads.

"Oh, what are you doing, Mrs. Hale?" asked the sheriff's wife, startled.

"Just pulling out a stitch or two that's not sewed very good," said Mrs. Hale mildly.

"I don't think we ought to touch things," Mrs. Peters said, a little helplessly.   170

"I'll just finish up this end," answered Mrs. Hale, still in that mild, matter-of-fact fashion.

She threaded a needle and started to replace bad sewing with good. For a little while she sewed in silence. Then, in that thin, timid voice, she heard:

"Mrs. Hale!"

"Yes, Mrs. Peters?"

"What do you suppose she was so—nervous about?"   175

"Oh, I don't know," said Mrs. Hale, as if dismissing a thing not important enough to spend much time on. "I don't know as she was—nervous. I sew awful queer sometimes when I'm just tired."

She cut a thread, and out of the corner of her eye looked up at Mrs. Peters. The small, lean face of the sheriff's wife seemed to have tightened up. Her eyes had that look of peering into something. But the next moment she moved, and said in her thin, indecisive way:

"Well, I must get those clothes wrapped. They may be through sooner than we think. I wonder where I could find a piece of paper—and string."

"In that cupboard, maybe," suggested Mrs. Hale, after a glance around.

One piece of the crazy sewing remained unripped. Mrs. Peters's   180 back turned, Martha Hale now scrutinized that piece, compared it with the dainty, accurate sewing of the other blocks. The difference was startling. Holding this block made her feel queer, as if the distracted thoughts of the woman who had perhaps turned to it to try and quiet herself were communicating themselves to her.

Mrs. Peters's voice roused her.

"Here's a birdcage," she said. "Did she have a bird, Mrs. Hale?"

"Why, I don't know whether she did or not." She turned to look at the cage Mrs. Peters was holding up. "I've not been here in so long." She sighed. "There was a man round last year selling canaries cheap—but I don't know as she took one. Maybe she did. She used to sing real pretty herself."

Mrs. Peters looked around the kitchen.

"Seems kind of funny to think of a bird here." She half laughed—   185 an attempt to put up a barrier. "But she must have had one—or why would she have a cage? I wonder what happened to it?"

"I suppose maybe the cat got it," suggested Mrs. Hale, resuming her sewing.

"No, she didn't have a cat. She's got that feeling some people have about cats—being afraid of them. When they brought her to our house yesterday, my cat got in the room, and she was real upset and asked me to take it out."

"My sister Bessie was like that," laughed Mrs. Hale.

The sheriff's wife did not reply. The silence made Mrs. Hale turn around. Mrs. Peters was examining the birdcage.

190 "Look at this door," she said slowly. "It's broke. One hinge has been pulled apart."

Mrs. Hale came nearer.

"Looks as if some one must have been—rough with it."

Again their eyes met—startled, questioning, apprehensive. For a moment neither spoke nor stirred. Then Mrs. Hale, turning away, said brusquely:

"If they're going to find any evidence, I wish they'd be about it. I don't like this place."

195 "But I'm awful glad you came with me, Mrs. Hale." Mrs. Peters put the birdcage on the table and sat down. "It would be lonesome for me—sitting here alone."

"Yes, it would, wouldn't it?" agreed Mrs. Hale, a certain determined naturalness in her voice. She picked up the sewing, but now it dropped in her lap, and she murmured in a different voice: "But I tell you what I *do* wish, Mrs. Peters. I wish I had come over sometimes when she was here. I wish—I had."

"But of course you were awful busy, Mrs. Hale. Your house—and your children."

"I could've come," retorted Mrs. Hale shortly. "I stayed away because it weren't cheerful—and that's why I ought to have come. I"—she looked around—"I've never liked this place. Maybe because it's down in a hollow and you don't see the road. I don't know what it is, but it's a lonesome place, and always was. I wish I had come over to see Minnie Foster sometimes. I can see now—" She did not put it into words.

"Well, you mustn't reproach yourself," counseled Mrs. Peters. "Somehow, we just don't see how it is with other folks till—something comes up."

200 "Not having children makes less work," mused Mrs. Hale, after a silence, "but it makes a quiet house—and Wright out to work all day—and no company when he did come in. Did you know John Wright, Mrs. Peters?"

"Not to know him. I've seen him in town. They say he was a good man."

"Yes—good," conceded John Wright's neighbor grimly. "He didn't drink, and kept his word as well as most, I guess, and paid his debts. But he was a hard man, Mrs. Peters. Just to pass the time of day with him—." She stopped, shivered a little. "Like a raw wind that gets to the bone." Her eye fell upon the cage on the table before her, and she added, almost bitterly: "I should think she would've wanted a bird!"

Suddenly she leaned forward, looking intently at the cage. "But what do you s'pose went wrong with it?"

"I don't know," returned Mrs. Peters; "unless it got sick and died."

But after she said it she reached over and swung the broken door.   205
Both women watched it as if somehow held by it.

"You didn't know—her?" Mrs. Hale asked, a gentler note in her voice.

"Not till they brought her yesterday," said the sheriff's wife.

"She—come to think of it, she was kind of like a bird herself. Real sweet and pretty, but kind of timid and—fluttery. How—she—did—change."

That held her for a long time. Finally, as if struck with a happy thought and relieved to get back to everyday things, she exclaimed:

"Tell you what, Mrs. Peters, why don't you take the quilt in with   210
you? It might take up her mind."

"Why, I think that's a real nice idea, Mrs. Hale," agreed the sheriff's wife, as if she too were glad to come into the atmosphere of a simple kindness. "There couldn't possibly be any objection to that, could there? Now, just what will I take? I wonder if her patches are in here—and her things."

They turned to the sewing basket.

"Here's some red," said Mrs. Hale, bringing out a roll of cloth. Underneath that was a box. "Here, maybe her scissors are in here—and her things." She held it up. "What a pretty box! I'll warrant that was something she had a long time ago—when she was a girl."

She held it in her hand a moment; then, with a little sigh, opened it.

Instantly her hand went to her nose.   215

"Why—!"

Mrs. Peters drew nearer—then turned away.

"There's something wrapped up in this piece of silk," faltered Mrs. Hale.

"This isn't her scissors," said Mrs. Peters in a shrinking voice.

220   Her hand not steady, Mrs. Hale raised the piece of silk. "Oh, Mrs. Peters!" she cried. "It's—"

Mrs. Peters bent closer.

"It's the bird," she whispered.

"But, Mrs. Peters!" cried Mrs. Hale. "*Look* at it! Its neck—look at its neck! It's all—other side *to.*"

She held the box away from her.

225   The sheriff's wife again bent closer.

"Somebody wrung its neck," said she, in a voice that was slow and deep.

And then again the eyes of the two women met—this time clung together in a look of dawning comprehension, of growing horror. Mrs. Peters looked from the dead bird to the broken door of the cage. Again their eyes met. And just then there was a sound at the outside door.

Mrs. Hale slipped the box under the quilt pieces in the basket, and sank into the chair before it. Mrs. Peters stood holding to the table. The county attorney and the sheriff came in from outside.

"Well, ladies," said the county attorney, as one turning from serious things to little pleasantries, "have you decided whether she was going to quilt it or knot it?"

230   "We think," began the sheriff's wife in a flurried voice, "that she was going to—knot it."

He was too preoccupied to notice the change that came in her voice on that last.

"Well, that's very interesting, I'm sure," he said tolerantly. He caught sight of the birdcage. "Has the bird flown?"

"We think the cat got it," said Mrs. Hale in a voice curiously even.

He was walking up and down, as if thinking something out.

235   "Is there a cat?" he asked absently.

Mrs. Hale shot a look up at the sheriff's wife.

"Well, not *now*," said Mrs. Peters. "They're superstitious, you know; they leave."

She sank into the chair.

The county attorney did not heed her. "No sign at all of any one having come in from the outside," he said to Peters, in the manner of continuing an interrupted conversation. "Their own rope. Now let's go upstairs again and go over it, piece by piece. It would have to have been some one who knew just the—"

240   The stair door closed behind them and their voices were lost.

The two women sat motionless, not looking at each other, but as if peering into something and at the same time holding back. When they spoke now it was as if they were afraid of what they were saying, but as if they could not help saying it.

"She liked the bird," said Martha Hale, low and slowly. "She was going to bury it in that pretty box."

"When I was a girl," said Mrs. Peters, under her breath, "my kitten—there was a boy took a hatchet, and before my eyes—before I could get there—" She covered her face an instant. "If they hadn't held me back I would have"—she caught herself, looked upstairs where footsteps were heard, and finished weakly—"hurt him."

Then they sat without speaking or moving.

"I wonder how it would seem," Mrs. Hale at last began, as if feeling   245
her way over strange ground—"never to have had any children around?" Her eyes made a slow sweep of the kitchen, as if seeing what that kitchen had meant through all the years. "No, Wright wouldn't like the bird," she said after that—"a thing that sang. She used to sing. He killed that too." Her voice tightened.

Mrs. Peters moved uneasily.

"Of course we don't know who killed the bird."

"I knew John Wright," was Mrs. Hale's answer.

"It was an awful thing was done in this house that night, Mrs. Hale," said the sheriff's wife. "Killing a man while he slept—slipping a thing round his neck that choked the life out of him."

Mrs. Hale's hand went out to the birdcage.   250

"His neck. Choked the life out of him."

"We don't *know* who killed him," whispered Mrs. Peters wildly. "We don't *know*."

Mrs. Hale had not moved. "If there had been years and years of—nothing, then a bird to sing to you, it would be awful—still—after the bird was still."

It was as if something within her not herself had spoken, and it found in Mrs. Peters something she did not know as herself.

"I know what stillness is," she said, in a queer, monotonous voice.   255
"When we homesteaded in Dakota, and my first baby died—after he was two years old—and me with no other then—"

Mrs. Hale stirred.

"How soon do you suppose they'll be through looking for evidence?"

"I know what stillness is," repeated Mrs. Peters, in just that same way. Then she too pulled back. "The law has got to punish crime, Mrs. Hale," she said in her tight little way.

"I wish you'd seen Minnie Foster," was the answer, "when she wore a white dress with blue ribbons, and stood up there in the choir and sang."

260   The picture of that girl, the fact that she had lived neighbor to that girl for twenty years, and had let her die for lack of life, was suddenly more than she could bear.

"Oh, I *wish* I'd come over here once in a while!" she cried. "That was a crime! That was a crime! Who's going to punish that?"

"We mustn't take on," said Mrs. Peters, with a frightened look toward the stairs.

"I might 'a' *known* she needed help! I tell you, it's *queer*, Mrs. Peters. We live close together, and we live far apart. We all go through the same things—it's all just a different kind of the same thing! If it weren't—why do you and I *understand?* Why do we *know*—what we know this minute?"

She dashed her hand across her eyes. Then, seeing the jar of fruit on the table, she reached for it and choked out:

265   "If I was you I wouldn't *tell* her her fruit was gone! Tell her it *ain't*. Tell her it's all right—all of it. Here—take this in to prove it to her! She—she may never know whether it was broke or not."

She turned away.

Mrs. Peters reached out for the bottle of fruit as if she were glad to take it—as if touching a familiar thing, having something to do, could keep her from something else. She got up, looked about for something to wrap the fruit in, took a petticoat from the pile of clothes she had brought from the front room, and nervously started winding that round the bottle.

"My!" she began, in a high, false voice, "it's a good thing the men couldn't hear us! Getting all stirred up over a little thing like a—dead canary." She hurried over that. "As if that could have anything to do with—with—My, wouldn't they *laugh?*"

Footsteps were heard on the stairs.

270   "Maybe they would," muttered Mrs. Hale—"maybe they wouldn't."

"No, Peters," said the county attorney incisively; "it's all perfectly clear, except the reason for doing it. But you know juries when it comes to women. If there was some definite thing—something to show. Something to make a story about. A thing that would connect up with this clumsy way of doing it."

In a covert way Mrs. Hale looked at Mrs. Peters. Mrs. Peters was looking at her. Quickly they looked away from each other. The outer door opened and Mr. Hale came in.

"I've got the team round now," he said. "Pretty cold out there."

"I'm going to stay here awhile by myself," the county attorney suddenly announced. "You can send Frank out for me, can't you?" he asked the sheriff. "I want to go over everything. I'm not satisfied we can't do better."

Again, for one brief moment, the two women's eyes found one   275
another.

The sheriff came up to the table.

"Did you want to see what Mrs. Peters was going to take in?"

The county attorney picked up the apron. He laughed.

"Oh, I guess they're not very dangerous things the ladies have
picked out."

Mrs. Hale's hand was on the sewing basket in which the box was   280
concealed. She felt that she ought to take her hand off the basket. She
did not seem able to. He picked up one of the quilt blocks which she
had piled on to cover the box. Her eyes felt like fire. She had a feeling
that if he took up the basket she would snatch it from him.

But he did not take it up. With another little laugh, he turned
away, saying:

"No; Mrs. Peters doesn't need supervising. For that matter, a sheriff's wife is married to the law. Ever think of it that way, Mrs. Peters?"

Mrs. Peters was standing beside the table. Mrs. Hale shot a look up
at her; but she could not see her face. Mrs. Peters had turned away.
When she spoke, her voice was muffled.

"Not—just that way," she said.

"Married to the law!" chuckled Mrs. Peters's husband. He moved   285
toward the door into the front room, and said to the county attorney:

"I just want you to come in here a minute, George. We ought to
take a look at these windows."

"Oh—windows," said the county attorney scoffingly.

"We'll be right out, Mr. Hale," said the sheriff to the farmer, who
was still waiting by the door.

Hale went to look after the horses. The sheriff followed the county
attorney into the other room. Again—for one moment—the two
women were alone in that kitchen.

Martha Hale sprang up, her hands tight together, looking at that   290
other woman, with whom it rested. At first she could not see her eyes,
for the sheriff's wife had not turned back since she turned away at that
suggestion of being married to the law. But now Mrs. Hale made her
turn back. Her eyes made her turn back. Slowly, unwillingly, Mrs.
Peters turned her head until her eyes met the eyes of the other woman.
There was a moment when they held each other in a steady, burning
look in which there was no evasion nor flinching. Then Martha Hale's
eyes pointed the way to the basket in which was hidden the thing that
would make certain the conviction of the other woman—that woman
who was not there and yet who had been there with them all through
the hour.

For a moment Mrs. Peters did not move. And then she did it. With a rush forward, she threw back the quilt pieces, got the box, tried to put it in her handbag. It was too big. Desperately she opened it, started to take the bird out. But there she broke—she could not touch the bird. She stood helpless, foolish.

There was the sound of a knob turning in the inner door. Martha Hale snatched the box from the sheriff's wife, and got it in the pocket of her big coat just as the sheriff and the county attorney came back into the kitchen.

"Well, Henry," said the county attorney facetiously, "at least we found out that she was not going to quilt it. She was going to—what is it you call it, ladies?"

Mrs. Hale's hand was against the pocket of her coat.

295   "We call it—knot it, Mr. Henderson."

QUESTIONS

1. At the time this story was published, women were not entitled to vote or sit on juries. The title alludes to the concept in common law (encoded in Magna Carta, 1215) that an accused *man* has the right to be judged by his peers. Given these facts, what ironies are suggested by the title and the decision reached by Mrs. Hale and Mrs. Peters? Do they find that Mrs. Wright killed her husband? Do they judge her guilty of murder?

2. In what various ways are Mrs. Hale and Mrs. Peters "peers" of Mrs. Wright?

3. What common assumptions about women are shared by the men in the story? How do they try to show that they do not think women to be their inferiors? How are their assumptions ironic?

4. Since no one seems to doubt that Mrs. Wright killed her husband (there are no other suspects, and she is already being held for the crime), how does this story create suspense?

5. Compare Mrs. Wright's motives for killing to Uncle Caesar's. Compare Major Caswell to Mr. Wright. Compare the decision made at the end by the narrator of "A Municipal Report" to that of Mrs. Hale and Mrs. Peters. How do these comparisons make the purposes of these two stories clearer?

EXERCISE

The two stories that follow both deal with the experiences of Americans in Europe, with social and moral standards of sexual behavior, and with contrasts between past actions and present behavior. Which story, in your estimation, deserves the higher ranking? Which gives the greater insight into significant human values? Support your decision with a reasoned and thorough analysis, using the study questions for what help they may provide.

Edith Wharton
Roman Fever

1

From the table at which they had been lunching two American ladies of ripe but well-cared-for middle age moved across the lofty terrace of the Roman restaurant and, leaning on its parapet, looked first at each other, and then down on the outspread glories of the Palatine and the Forum, with the same expression of vague but benevolent approval.

As they leaned there a girlish voice echoed up gaily from the stairs leading to the court below. "Well, come along, then," it cried, not to them but to an invisible companion, "and let's leave the young things to their knitting"; and a voice as fresh laughed back: "Oh, look here, Babs, not actually *knitting*—" "Well, I mean figuratively," rejoined the first. "After all, we haven't left our poor parents much else to do. . . ." and at that point the turn of the stairs engulfed the dialogue.

The two ladies looked at each other again, this time with a tinge of smiling embarrassment, and the smaller and paler one shook her head and colored slightly.

"Barbara!" she murmured, sending an unheard rebuke after the mocking voice in the stairway.

The other lady, who was fuller, and higher in color, with a small determined nose supported by vigorous black eyebrows, gave a good-humored laugh. "That's what our daughters think of us!"   5

Her companion replied by a deprecating gesture. "Not of us individually. We must remember that. It's just the collective modern idea of Mothers. And you see—" Half-guiltily she drew from her handsomely mounted black handbag a twist of crimson silk run through by two fine knitting needles. "One never knows," she murmured. "The new system has certainly given us a good deal of time to kill; and sometimes I get tired just looking—even at this." Her gesture was now addressed to the stupendous scene at their feet.

Roman Fever   First published in 1934. Edith Wharton (1862–1937) was born into a socially prominent New York family and was privately educated by governesses and tutors. She married in 1885 and began a financially and critically successful writing career in 1890. After frequent visits to Europe beginning in her childhood, she took up permanent residence in France. Both she and her husband had a history of adulterous affairs, and she divorced him in 1913; she had no children. "Roman fever" was the name given to a type of malaria prevalent in Rome in the nineteenth century.

The dark lady laughed again, and they both relapsed upon the view, contemplating it in silence, with a sort of diffused serenity which might have been borrowed from the spring effulgence of the Roman skies. The luncheon hour was long past, and the two had their end of the vast terrace to themselves. At its opposite extremity a few groups, detained by a lingering look at the outspread city, were gathering up guidebooks and fumbling for tips. The last of them scattered, and the two ladies were alone on the air-washed height.

"Well, I don't see why we shouldn't just stay here," said Mrs. Slade, the lady of the high color and energetic brows. Two derelict basket chairs stood near, and she pushed them into the angle of the parapet, and settled herself in one, her gaze upon the Palatine. "After all, it's still the most beautiful view in the world."

"It always will be, to me," assented her friend Mrs. Ansley, with so slight a stress on the "me" that Mrs. Slade, though she noticed it, wondered if it were not merely accidental, like the random underlinings of old-fashioned letter writers.

10 "Grace Ansley was always old-fashioned," she thought; and added aloud, with a retrospective smile: "It's a view we've both been familiar with for a good many years. When we first met here we were younger than our girls are now. You remember?"

"Oh, yes, I remember," murmured Mrs. Ansley, with the same undefinable stress. "There's that headwaiter wondering," she interpolated. She was evidently far less sure than her companion of herself and of her rights in the world.

"I'll cure him of wondering," said Mrs. Slade, stretching her hand toward a bag as discreetly opulent-looking as Mrs. Ansley's. Signing to the headwaiter, she explained that she and her friend were old lovers of Rome, and would like to spend the end of the afternoon looking down on the view—that is, if it did not disturb the service? The headwaiter, bowing over her gratuity, assured her that the ladies were most welcome, and would be still more so if they would condescend to remain for dinner. A full-moon night, they would remember. . . .

Mrs. Slade's black brows drew together, as though references to the moon were out of place and even unwelcome. But she smiled away her frown as the headwaiter retreated. "Well, why not? We might do worse. There's no knowing, I suppose, when the girls will be back. Do you even know back from *where?* I don't!"

Mrs. Ansley again colored slightly. "I think those young Italian aviators we met at the Embassy invited them to fly to Tarquinia for tea. I suppose they'll want to wait and fly back by moonlight."

"Moonlight—moonlight! What a part it still plays. Do you suppose   15
they're as sentimental as we were?"

"I've come to the conclusion that I don't in the least know what
they are," said Mrs. Ansley. "And perhaps we didn't know much more
about each other."

"No; perhaps we didn't."

Her friend gave her a shy glance. "I never should have supposed
you were sentimental, Alida."

"Well, perhaps I wasn't." Mrs. Slade drew her lids together in retrospect; and for a few moments the two ladies, who had been intimate
since childhood, reflected how little they knew each other. Each one, of
course, had a label ready to attach to the other's name; Mrs. Delphin
Slade, for instance, would have told herself, or anyone who asked her,
that Mrs. Horace Ansley, twenty-five years ago, had been exquisitely
lovely—no, you wouldn't believe it, would you? . . . though, of course,
still charming, distinguished. . . . Well, as a girl she had been exquisite;
far more beautiful than her daughter Barbara, though certainly Babs,
according to the new standards at any rate, was more effective—had
more *edge,* as they say. Funny where she got it, with those two nullities
as parents. Yes; Horace Ansley was—well, just the duplicate of his wife.
Museum specimens of old New York. Good-looking, irreproachable,
exemplary. Mrs. Slade and Mrs. Ansley had lived opposite each other—
actually as well as figuratively—for years. When the drawing-room curtains in No. 20 East 73rd Street were renewed, No. 23, across the way,
was always aware of it. And of all the movings, buyings, travels, anni-
versaries, illnesses—the tame chronicle of an estimable pair. Little of it
escaped Mrs. Slade. But she had grown bored with it by the time her
husband made his big *coup* in Wall Street, and when they bought in upper Park Avenue had already begun to think: "I'd rather live opposite a
speakeasy for a change; at least one might see it raided." The idea of
seeing Grace raided was so amusing that (before the move) she
launched it at a woman's lunch. It made a hit, and went the rounds—
she sometimes wondered if it had crossed the street, and reached Mrs.
Ansley. She hoped not, but didn't much mind. Those were the days
when respectability was at a discount, and it did the irreproachable no
harm to laugh at them a little.

A few years later, and not many months apart, both ladies lost their   20
husbands. There was an appropriate exchange of wreaths and condo-
lences, and a brief renewal of intimacy in the half-shadow of their
mourning; and now, after another interval, they had run across each
other in Rome, at the same hotel, each of them the modest appendage
of a salient daughter. The similarity of their lot had again drawn them

together, lending itself to mild jokes, and the mutual confession that, if in old days it must have been tiring to "keep up" with daughters, it was now, at times, a little dull not to.

No doubt, Mrs. Slade reflected, she felt her unemployment more than poor Grace ever would. It was a big drop from being the wife of Delphin Slade to being his widow. She had always regarded herself (with a certain conjugal pride) as his equal in social gifts, as contributing her full share to the making of the exceptional couple they were: but the difference after his death was irremediable. As the wife of the famous corporation lawyer, always with an international case or two on hand, every day brought its exciting and unexpected obligation: the impromptu entertaining of eminent colleagues from abroad, the hurried dashes on legal business to London, Paris or Rome, where the entertaining was so handsomely reciprocated; the amusement of hearing in her wake: "What, that handsome woman with the good clothes and the eyes is Mrs. Slade—*the* Slade's wife? Really? Generally the wives of celebrities are such frumps."

Yes; being *the* Slade's widow was a dullish business after that. In living up to such a husband all her faculties had been engaged; now she had only her daughter to live up to, for the son who seemed to have inherited his father's gifts had died suddenly in boyhood. She had fought through that agony because her husband was there, to be helped and to help; now, after the father's death, the thought of the boy had become unbearable. There was nothing left but to mother her daughter; and dear Jenny was such a perfect daughter that she needed no excessive mothering. "Now with Babs Ansley I don't know that I *should* be so quiet," Mrs. Slade sometimes half-enviously reflected; but Jenny, who was younger than her brilliant friend, was that rare accident, an extremely pretty girl who somehow made youth and prettiness seem as safe as their absence. It was all perplexing—and to Mrs. Slade a little boring. She wished that Jenny would fall in love—with the wrong man, even; that she might have to be watched, out-maneuvered, rescued. And instead, it was Jenny who watched her mother, kept her out of drafts, made sure that she had taken her tonic. . . .

Mrs. Ansley was much less articulate than her friend, and her mental portrait of Mrs. Slade was slighter, and drawn with fainter touches. "Alida Slade's awfully brilliant; but not as brilliant as she thinks," would have summed it up; though she would have added, for the enlightenment of strangers, that Mrs. Slade had been an extremely dashing girl; much more so than her daughter, who was pretty, of course, and clever in a way, but had none of her mother's—well, "vividness," someone had once called it. Mrs. Ansley would take up current words like this, and cite them in quotation marks, as unheard-of audacities. No; Jenny was not like her mother. Sometimes Mrs. Ansley thought Alida Slade was disappointed; on the whole she had had a sad life. Full of failures and mistakes; Mrs. Ansley had always been rather sorry for her. . . .

So these two ladies visualized each other, each through the wrong end of her little telescope.

2

For a long time they continued to sit side by side without speaking.   25
It seemed as though, to both, there was a relief in laying down their somewhat futile activities in the presence of the vast Memento Mori° which faced them. Mrs. Slade sat quite still, her eyes fixed on the golden slope of the Palace of the Caesars, and after a while Mrs. Ansley ceased to fidget with her bag, and she too sank into meditation. Like many intimate friends, the two ladies had never before had occasion to be silent together, and Mrs. Ansley was slightly embarrassed by what seemed, after so many years, a new stage in their intimacy, and one with which she did not yet know how to deal.

Suddenly the air was full of that deep clangor of bells which periodically covers Rome with a roof of silver. Mrs. Slade glanced at her wristwatch. "Five o'clock already," she said, as though surprised.

Mrs. Ansley suggested interrogatively: "There's bridge at the Embassy at five." For a long time Mrs. Slade did not answer. She appeared to be lost in contemplation, and Mrs. Ansley thought the remark had escaped her. But after a while she said, as if speaking out of a dream: "Bridge, did you say? Not unless you want to. . . . But I don't think I will, you know."

"Oh, no," Mrs. Ansley hastened to assure her. "I don't care to at all. It's so lovely here; and so full of old memories, as you say." She settled herself in her chair, and almost furtively drew forth her knitting. Mrs. Slade took sideway note of this activity, but her own beautifully cared-for hands remained motionless on her knee.

"I was just thinking," she said slowly, "what different things Rome stands for to each generation of travelers. To our grandmothers, Roman fever; to our mothers, sentimental dangers—how we used to be guarded! —to our daughters, no more dangers than the middle of Main Street. They don't know it—but how much they're missing!"

The long golden light was beginning to pale, and Mrs. Ansley lifted   30
her knitting a little closer to her eyes. "Yes; how we were guarded!"

Memento Mori: reminder of mortality (Latin: literally, "remember that you must die")

"I always used to think," Mrs. Slade continued, "that our mothers had a much more difficult job than our grandmothers. When Roman fever stalked the streets it must have been comparatively easy to gather in the girls at the danger hour; but when you and I were young, with such beauty calling us, and the spice of disobedience thrown in, and no worse risk than catching cold during the cool hour after sunset, the mothers used to be put to it to keep us in—didn't they?"

She turned again toward Mrs. Ansley, but the latter had reached a delicate point in her knitting. "One, two, three—slip two; yes, they must have been," she assented, without looking up.

Mrs. Slade's eyes rested on her with a deepened attention. "She can knit—in the face of *this!* How like her. . . ."

Mrs. Slade leaned back, brooding, her eyes ranging from the ruins which faced her to the long green hollow of the Forum, the fading glow of the church fronts beyond it, and the outlying immensity of the Colosseum. Suddenly she thought: "It's all very well to say that our girls have done away with sentiment and moonlight. But if Babs Ansley isn't out to catch that young aviator—the one who's a Marchese—then I don't know anything. And Jenny has no chance beside her. I know that too. I wonder if that's why Grace Ansley likes the two girls to go everywhere together? My poor Jenny as a foil—!" Mrs. Slade gave a hardly audible laugh, and at the sound Mrs. Ansley dropped her knitting.

35   "Yes—?"

"I—oh, nothing. I was only thinking how your Babs carries everything before her. That Campolieri boy is one of the best matches in Rome. Don't look so innocent, my dear—you know he is. And I was wondering, ever so respectfully, you understand . . . wondering how two such exemplary characters as you and Horace had managed to produce anything quite so dynamic." Mrs. Slade laughed again, with a touch of asperity.

Mrs. Ansley's hands lay inert across her needles. She looked straight out at the great accumulated wreckage of passion and splendor at her feet. But her small profile was almost expressionless. At length she said: "I think you overrate Babs, my dear."

Mrs. Slade's tone grew easier. "No; I don't. I appreciate her. And perhaps envy you. Oh, my girl's perfect; if I were a chronic invalid I'd—well, I think I'd rather be in Jenny's hands. There must be times . . . but there! I always wanted a brilliant daughter . . . and never quite understood why I got an angel instead."

Mrs. Ansley echoed her laugh in a faint murmur. "Babs is an angel too."

"Of course—of course! But she's got rainbow wings. Well, they're   40
wandering by the sea with their young men; and here we sit . . . and it
all brings back the past a little too acutely."

Mrs. Ansley had resumed her knitting. One might almost have
imagined (if one had known her less well, Mrs. Slade reflected) that, for
her also, too many memories rose from the lengthening shadows of
those august ruins. But no; she was simply absorbed in her work. What
was there for her to worry about? She knew that Babs would almost certainly come back engaged to the extremely eligible Campolieri. "And
she'll sell the New York house, and settle down near them in Rome,
and never be in their way . . . she's much too tactful. But she'll have an
excellent cook, and just the right people in for bridge and cocktails . . .
and a perfectly peaceful old age among her grandchildren."

Mrs. Slade broke off this prophetic flight with a recoil of self-disgust.
There was no one of whom she had less right to think unkindly than of
Grace Ansley. Would she never cure herself of envying her? Perhaps
she had begun too long ago.

She stood up and leaned against the parapet, filling her troubled eyes
with the tranquilizing magic of the hour. But instead of tranquilizing her
the sight seemed to increase her exasperation. Her gaze turned toward
the Colosseum. Already its golden flank was drowned in purple shadow,
and above it the sky curved crystal clear, without light or color. It was the
moment when afternoon and evening hang balanced in mid-heaven.

Mrs. Slade turned back and laid her hand on her friend's arm. The
gesture was so abrupt that Mrs. Ansley looked up, startled.

"The sun's set. You're not afraid, my dear?"   45

"Afraid—?"

"Of Roman fever or pneumonia? I remember how ill you were that
winter. As a girl you had a very delicate throat, hadn't you?"

"Oh, we're all right up here. Down below, in the Forum, it does get
deathly cold, all of a sudden . . . but not here."

"Ah, of course you know because you had to be so careful." Mrs.
Slade turned back to the parapet. She thought: "I must make one more
effort not to hate her." Aloud she said: "Whenever I look at the Forum
from up here, I remember that story about a great-aunt of yours, wasn't
she? A dreadfully wicked great-aunt?"

"Oh, yes; great-aunt Harriet. The one who was supposed to have   50
sent her young sister out to the Forum after sunset to gather a night-
blooming flower for her album. All our great-aunts and grandmothers
used to have albums of dried flowers."

Mrs. Slade nodded. "But she really sent her because they were in
love with the same man—"

"Well, that was the family tradition. They said Aunt Harriet confessed it years afterward. At any rate, the poor little sister caught the fever and died. Mother used to frighten us with the story when we were children."

"And you frightened *me* with it, that winter when you and I were here as girls. The winter I was engaged to Delphin."

Mrs. Ansley gave a faint laugh. "Oh, did I? Really frightened you? I don't believe you're easily frightened."

55   "Not often; but I was then. I was easily frightened because I was too happy. I wonder if you know what that means?"

"I—yes . . ." Mrs. Ansley faltered.

"Well, I suppose that was why the story of your wicked aunt made such an impression on me. And I thought: 'There's no more Roman fever, but the Forum is deathly cold after sunset—especially after a hot day. And the Colosseum's even colder and damper.'"

"The Colosseum—?"

"Yes. It wasn't easy to get in, after the gates were locked for the night. Far from easy. Still, in those days it could be managed; it *was* managed, often. Lovers met there who couldn't meet elsewhere. You knew that?"

60   "I—I dare say. I don't remember."

"You don't remember? You don't remember going to visit some ruins or other one evening, just after dark, and catching a bad chill? You were supposed to have gone to see the moon rise. People always said that expedition was what caused your illness."

There was a moment's silence; then Mrs. Ansley rejoined: "Did they? It was all so long ago."

"Yes. And you got well again—so it didn't matter. But I suppose it struck your friends—the reason given for your illness, I mean—because everybody knew you were so prudent on account of your throat, and your mother took such care of you. . . . You *had* been out late sightseeing, hadn't you, that night?"

"Perhaps I had. The most prudent girls aren't always prudent. What made you think of it now?"

65   Mrs. Slade seemed to have no answer ready. But after a moment she broke out: "Because I simply can't bear it any longer—!"

Mrs. Ansley lifted her head quickly. Her eyes were wide and very pale. "Can't bear what?"

"Why—your not knowing that I've always known why you went."

"Why I went—?"

"Yes. You think I'm bluffing, don't you? Well, you went to meet the man I was engaged to—and I can repeat every word of the letter that took you there."

While Mrs. Slade spoke Mrs. Ansley had risen unsteadily to her feet.   70
Her bag, her knitting and gloves, slid in a panic-stricken heap to the
ground. She looked at Mrs. Slade as though she were looking at a ghost.
"No, no—don't," she faltered out.

"Why not? Listen, if you don't believe me. 'My one darling, things
can't go on like this. I must see you alone. Come to the Colosseum immediately after dark tomorrow. There will be somebody to let you in.
No one whom you need fear will suspect'—but perhaps you've forgotten what the letter said?"

Mrs. Ansley met the challenge with an unexpected composure.
Steadying herself against the chair she looked at her friend, and replied:
"No; I know it by heart too."

"And the signature? 'Only *your* D.S.' Was that it? I'm right, am I?
That was the letter that took you out that evening after dark?"

Mrs. Ansley was still looking at her. It seemed to Mrs. Slade that a   75
slow struggle was going on behind the voluntarily controlled mask of her
small quiet face. "I shouldn't have thought she had herself so well in
hand," Mrs. Slade reflected, almost resentfully. But at this moment Mrs.
Ansley spoke. "I don't know how you knew. I burnt that letter at once."

"Yes; you would, naturally—you're so prudent!" The sneer was
open now. "And if you burnt the letter you're wondering how on earth
I know what was in it. That's it, isn't it?"

Mrs. Slade waited, but Mrs. Ansley did not speak.

"Well, my dear, I know what was in that letter because I wrote it!"

"You wrote it?"

"Yes."   80

The two women stood for a minute staring at each other in the last
golden light. Then Mrs. Ansley dropped back into her chair. "Oh," she
murmured, and covered her face with her hands.

Mrs. Slade waited nervously for another word or movement. None
came, and at length she broke out: "I horrify you."

Mrs. Ansley's hands dropped to her knee. The face they uncovered
was streaked with tears. "I wasn't thinking of you. I was thinking—it
was the only letter I ever had from him!"

"And I wrote it. Yes; I wrote it! But I was the girl he was engaged
to. Did you happen to remember that?"

Mrs. Ansley's head drooped again. "I'm not trying to excuse   85
myself . . . I remembered. . . ."

"And still you went?"

"Still I went."

Mrs. Slade stood looking down on the small bowed figure at her
side. The flame of her wrath had already sunk, and she wondered why

she had ever thought there would be any satisfaction in inflicting so purposeless a wound on her friend. But she had to justify herself.

"You do understand? I'd found out—and I hated you, hated you. I knew you were in love with Delphin—and I was afraid; afraid of you, of your quiet ways, your sweetness . . . your . . . well, I wanted you out of the way, that's all. Just for a few weeks; just till I was sure of him. So in a blind fury I wrote that letter . . . I don't know why I'm telling you now."

90 "I suppose," said Mrs. Ansley slowly, "it's because you've always gone on hating me."

"Perhaps. Or because I wanted to get the whole thing off my mind." She paused. "I'm glad you destroyed the letter. Of course I never thought you'd die."

Mrs. Ansley relapsed into silence, and Mrs. Slade, leaning above her, was conscious of a strange sense of isolation, of being cut off from the warm current of human communion. "You think me a monster!"

"I don't know. . . . It was the only letter I had, and you say he didn't write it?"

"Ah, how you care for him still!"

95 "I cared for that memory," said Mrs. Ansley.

Mrs. Slade continued to look down on her. She seemed physically reduced by the blow—as if, when she got up, the wind might scatter her like a puff of dust. Mrs. Slade's jealousy suddenly leapt up again at the sight. All these years the woman had been living on that letter. How she must have loved him, to treasure the mere memory of its ashes! The letter of the man her friend was engaged to. Wasn't it she who was the monster?

"You tried your best to get him away from me, didn't you? But you failed; and I kept him. That's all."

"Yes. That's all."

"I wish now I hadn't told you. I'd no idea you'd feel about it as you do; I thought you'd be amused. It all happened so long ago, as you say; and you must do me the justice to remember that I had no reason to think you'd ever taken it seriously. How could I, when you were married to Horace Ansley two months afterward? As soon as you could get out of bed your mother rushed you off to Florence and married you. People were rather surprised—they wondered at its being done so quickly; but I thought I knew. I had an idea you did it out of *pique*—to be able to say you'd got ahead of Delphin and me. Girls have such silly reasons for doing the most serious things. And your marrying so soon convinced me that you'd never really cared."

100 "Yes. I suppose it would," Mrs. Ansley assented.

The clear heaven overhead was emptied of all its gold. Dusk spread over it, abruptly darkening the Seven Hills. Here and there lights began to twinkle through the foliage at their feet. Steps were coming and going on the deserted terrace—waiters looking out of the doorway at the head of the stairs, then reappearing with trays and napkins and flasks of wine. Tables were moved, chairs straightened. A feeble string of electric lights flickered out. Some vases of faded flowers were carried away, and brought back replenished. A stout lady in a dust coat suddenly appeared, asking in broken Italian if anyone had seen the elastic band which held together her tattered Baedeker.° She poked with her stick under the table at which she had lunched, the waiters assisting.

The corner where Mrs. Slade and Mrs. Ansley sat was still shadowy and deserted. For a long time neither of them spoke. At length Mrs. Slade began again: "I suppose I did it as a sort of joke—"

"A joke?"

"Well, girls are ferocious sometimes, you know. Girls in love especially. And I remember laughing to myself all that evening at the idea that you were waiting around there in the dark, dodging out of sight, listening for every sound, trying to get in— Of course I was upset when I heard you were so ill afterward."

Mrs. Ansley had not moved for a long time. But now she turned   105
slowly toward her companion. "But I didn't wait. He'd arranged everything. He was there. We were let in at once," she said.

Mrs. Slade sprang up from her leaning position. "Delphin there? They let you in?— Ah, now you're lying!" she burst out with violence.

Mrs. Ansley's voice grew clearer, and full of surprise. "But of course he was there. Naturally he came—"

"Came? How did he know he'd find you there? You must be raving!"

Mrs. Ansley hesitated, as though reflecting. "But I answered the letter. I told him I'd be there. So he came."

Mrs. Slade flung her hands up to her face. "Oh, God—you an-   110
swered! I never thought of your answering. . . ."

"It's odd you never thought of it, if you wrote the letter."

"Yes. I was blind with rage."

Mrs. Ansley rose, and drew her fur scarf about her. "It is cold here. We'd better go . . . I'm sorry for you," she said, as she clasped the fur about her throat.

The unexpected words sent a pang through Mrs. Slade. "Yes; we'd better go." She gathered up her bag and cloak. "I don't know why you should be sorry for me," she muttered.

Mrs. Ansley stood looking away from her toward the dusky secret   115
mass of the Colosseum. "Well—because I didn't have to wait that night."

Baedeker: tourist guidebook (one of a series issued by the German publisher Karl Baedeker)

Mrs. Slade gave an unquiet laugh. "Yes; I was beaten there. But I oughtn't to begrudge it to you, I suppose. At the end of all these years. After all, I had everything; I had him for twenty-five years. And you had nothing but that one letter that he didn't write."

Mrs. Ansley was again silent. At length she turned toward the door of the terrace. She took a step, and turned back, facing her companion.

"I had Barbara," she said, and began to move ahead of Mrs. Slade toward the stairway.

QUESTIONS

1. Characterize Grace Ansley and Alida Slade as fully as you can. By what characterizing devices does the story imply the superiority of Mrs. Slade (what gestures, what statements, what unspoken thoughts)? At what point does Mrs. Ansley begin to seem the superior person?

2. What is the meaning of the comment about "the wrong end of [the] little telescope" (paragraph 24)? How is that comment a suitable conclusion for the first part of the story?

3. Trace the revelation of the animosity that Mrs. Slade feels for Mrs. Ansley. Is Mrs. Ansley doing anything on this evening to provoke her envy? Why has Mrs. Slade always harbored negative feelings about her friend?

4. What purpose is served by the discussion of the different meanings of Rome to mothers and daughters of different generations (paragraphs 29–31)? What standards of behavior have changed from one generation to the next? What standards have remained the same? How does this discussion expand the meaning of the title of the story?

F. Scott Fitzgerald

A New Leaf

1

It was the first day warm enough to eat outdoors in the Bois de Boulogne, while chestnut blossoms slanted down across the tables and dropped impudently into the butter and the wine. Julia Ross ate a few with her bread and listened to the big goldfish rippling in the pool and

A NEW LEAF   First published in 1931. The lines of poetry are slightly misquoted from Shelley's "Stanzas Written in Dejection—December 1818, Near Naples," lines 4–6; Shelley wrote "Blue isles and snowy mountains wear / The purple noon's transparent might, / The breath of the moist earth is light / Around its unexpanded buds" (3–6). F. Scott Fitzgerald (1896–1940) published dozens of short stories during the 1920s and 1930s. Their popularity helped him earn huge sums from such magazines as *The Saturday Evening Post*, providing Fitzgerald and his wife, Zelda, with an affluent lifestyle. Fitzgerald struggled with alcoholism for most of his adult life; he and Zelda lived for several years in France before returning permanently to the United States in 1931.

the sparrows whirring about an abandoned table. You could see every-body again—the waiters with their professional faces, the watchful Frenchwomen all heels and eyes, Phil Hoffman opposite her with his heart balanced on his fork, and the extraordinarily handsome man just coming out on the terrace.

> —the purple noon's transparent might.
> The breath of the moist air is light
> Around each unexpanded bud—

Julia trembled discreetly; she controlled herself; she didn't spring up and call, "Yi-yi-yi-yi! Isn't this grand?" and push the maître d'hôtel into the lily pond. She sat there, a well-behaved woman of twenty-one, and discreetly trembled.

Phil was rising, napkin in hand. "Hi there, Dick!"

"Hi, Phil!"

It was the handsome man; Phil took a few steps forward and they   5
talked apart from the table.

"——seen Carter and Kitty in Spain——"

"——poured on to the Bremen——"

"——so I was going to——"

The man went on, following the head waiter, and Phil sat down.

"Who is that?" she demanded.   10

"A friend of mine—Dick Ragland."

"He's without doubt the handsomest man I ever saw in my life."

"Yes, he's handsome," he agreed without enthusiasm.

"Handsome! He's an archangel, he's a mountain lion, he's some-thing to eat. Just why didn't you introduce him?"

"Because he's got the worst reputation of any American in   15
Paris."

"Nonsense; he must be maligned. It's all a dirty frame-up—a lot of jealous husbands whose wives got one look at him. Why, that man's never done anything in his life except lead cavalry charges and save children from drowning."

"The fact remains he's not received anywhere—not for one reason but for a thousand."

"What reasons?"

"Everything. Drink, women, jails, scandals, killed somebody with an automobile, lazy, worthless——"

"I don't believe a word of it," said Julia firmly. "I bet he's tremen-   20
dously attractive. And you spoke to him as if you thought so too."

"Yes," he said reluctantly, "like so many alcoholics, he has a certain charm. If he'd only make his messes off by himself somewhere—except right in people's laps. Just when somebody's taken him up and is making a big fuss over him, he pours the soup down his hostess' back, kisses the serving maid and passes out in the dog kennel. But he's done it too often. He's run through about everybody, until there's no one left."

"There's me," said Julia.

There was Julia, who was a little too good for anybody and sometimes regretted that she had been quite so well endowed. Anything added to beauty has to be paid for—that is to say, the qualities that pass as substitutes can be liabilities when added to beauty itself. Julia's brilliant hazel glance was enough, without the questioning light of intelligence that flickered in it; her irrepressible sense of the ridiculous detracted from the gentle relief of her mouth, and the loveliness of her figure might have been more obvious if she had slouched and postured rather than sat and stood very straight, after the discipline of a strict father.

Equally perfect young men had several times appeared bearing gifts, but generally with the air of being already complete, of having no space for development. On the other hand, she found that men of larger scale had sharp corners and edges in youth, and she was a little too young herself to like that. There was, for instance, this scornful young egotist, Phil Hoffman, opposite her, who was obviously going to be a brilliant lawyer and who had practically followed her to Paris. She liked him as well as anyone she knew, but he had at present all the overbearance of the son of a chief of police.

25   "Tonight I'm going to London, and Wednesday I sail," he said. "And you'll be in Europe all summer, with somebody new chewing on your ear every few weeks."

"When you've been called for a lot of remarks like that you'll begin to edge into the picture," Julia remarked. "Just to square yourself, I want you to introduce that man Ragland."

"My last few hours!" he complained.

"But I've given you three whole days on the chance you'd work out a better approach. Be a little civilized and ask him to have some coffee."

As Mr. Dick Ragland joined them, Julia drew a little breath of pleasure. He was a fine figure of a man, in coloring both tan and blond, with a peculiar luminosity to his face. His voice was quietly intense; it seemed always to tremble a little with a sort of gay despair; the way he looked at Julia made her feel attractive. For half an hour, as their sentences floated pleasantly among the scent of violets and snowdrops, forget-me-nots and pansies, her interest in him grew. She was even glad when Phil said:

"I've just thought about my English visa. I'll have to leave you two   30 incipient love birds together against my better judgment. Will you meet me at the Gare St. Lazare° at five and see me off?"

He looked at Julia hoping she'd say, "I'll go along with you now." She knew very well she had no business being alone with this man, but he made her laugh, and she hadn't laughed much lately, so she said: "I'll stay a few minutes; it's so nice and springy here."

When Phil was gone, Dick Ragland suggested a *fine* champagne.

"I hear you have a terrible reputation?" she said impulsively.

"Awful. I'm not even invited out any more. Do you want me to slip on my false mustache?"

"It's so odd," she pursued. "Don't you cut yourself off from all nour-   35 ishment? Do you know that Phil felt he had to warn me about you before he introduced you? And I might very well have told him not to."

"Why didn't you?"

"I thought you seemed so attractive and it was such a pity."

His face grew bland; Julia saw that the remark had been made so often that it no longer reached him.

"It's none of my business," she said quickly. She did not realize that his being a sort of outcast added to his attraction for her—not the dissipation itself, for never having seen it, it was merely an abstraction— but its result in making him so alone. Something atavistic in her went out to the stranger to the tribe, a being from a world with different habits from hers, who promised the unexpected—promised adventure.

"I'll tell you something else," he said suddenly. "I'm going perma-   40 nently on the wagon on June fifth, my twenty-eighth birthday. I don't have fun drinking any more. Evidently I'm not one of the few people who can use liquor."

"You sure you can go on the wagon?"

"I always do what I say I'll do. Also I'm going back to New York and go to work."

"I'm really surprised how glad I am." This was rash, but she let it stand.

"Have another *fine?*" Dick suggested. "Then you'll be gladder still."

"Will you go on this way right up to your birthday?"   45

"Probably. On my birthday I'll be on the Olympic in mid-ocean."

"I'll be on that boat too!" she exclaimed.

Gare St. Lazare: a railroad station

"You can watch the quick change; I'll do it for the ship's concert."

The tables were being cleared off. Julia knew she should go now, but she couldn't bear to leave him sitting with that unhappy look under his smile. She felt, maternally, that she ought to say something to help him keep his resolution.

50   "Tell me why you drink so much. Probably some obscure reason you don't know yourself."

"Oh, I know pretty well how it began."

He told her as another hour waned. He had gone to the war at seventeen and, when he came back, life as a Princeton freshman with a little black cap was somewhat tame. So he went up to Boston Tech and then abroad to the Beaux Arts; it was there that something happened to him.

"About the time I came into some money I found that with a few drinks I got expansive and somehow had the ability to please people, and the idea turned my head. Then I began to take a whole lot of drinks to keep going and have everybody think I was wonderful. Well, I got plastered a lot and quarreled with most of my friends, and then I met a wild bunch and for a while I was expansive with them. But I was inclined to get superior and suddenly think 'What am I doing with this bunch?' They didn't like that much. And when a taxi that I was in killed a man, I was sued. It was just a graft, but it got in the papers, and after I was released the impression remained that I'd killed him. So all I've got to show for the last five years is a reputation that makes mothers rush their daughters away if I'm at the same hotel."

An impatient waiter was hovering near and she looked at her watch.

55   "Gosh, we're to see Phil off at five. We've been here all the afternoon."

As they hurried to the Gare St. Lazare, he asked: "Will you let me see you again; or do you think you'd better not?"

She returned his long look. There was no sign of dissipation in his face, in his warm cheeks, in his erect carriage.

"I'm always fine at lunch," he added, like an invalid.

"I'm not worried," she laughed. "Take me to lunch day after tomorrow."

60   They hurried up the steps of the Gare St. Lazare, only to see the last carriage of the Golden Arrow disappearing toward the Channel. Julia was remorseful, because Phil had come so far.

As a sort of atonement, she went to the apartment where she lived with her aunt and tried to write a letter to him, but Dick Ragland intruded himself into her thoughts. By morning the effect of his good looks had faded a little; she was inclined to write him a note that she couldn't see him. Still, he had made her a simple appeal and she had brought it all on herself. She waited for him at half-past twelve on the appointed day.

Julia had said nothing to her aunt, who had company for luncheon and might mention his name—strange to go out with a man whose name you couldn't mention. He was late and she waited in the hall, listening to the echolalia of chatter from the luncheon party in the dining room. At one she answered the bell.

There in the outer hall stood a man whom she thought she had never seen before. His face was dead white and erratically shaven, his soft hat was crushed bunlike on his head, his shirt collar was dirty, and all except the band of his tie was out of sight. But at the moment when she recognized the figure as Dick Ragland she perceived a change which dwarfed the others into nothing; it was in his expression. His whole face was one prolonged sneer—the lids held with difficulty from covering the fixed eyes, the drooping mouth drawn up over the upper teeth, the chin wabbling like a madeover chin in which the paraffin had run—it was a face that both expressed and inspired disgust.

"H'lo," he muttered.

For a minute she drew back from him; then, at a sudden silence from the dining room that gave on the hall, inspired by the silence in the hall itself, she half pushed him over the threshold, stepped out herself and closed the door behind them.   65

"Oh-h-h!" she said in a single, shocked breath.

"Haven't been home since yest'day. Got involve' on a party at——"

With repugnance, she turned him around by his arm and stumbled with him down the apartment stairs, passing the concierge's wife, who peered out at them curiously from her glass room. Then they came out into the bright sunshine of the Rue Guynemer.

Against the spring freshness of the Luxembourg Gardens opposite, he was even more grotesque. He frightened her; she looked desperately up and down the street for a taxi, but one turning the corner of the Rue de Vaugirard disregarded her signal.

"Where'll we go lunch?" he asked.   70

"You're in no shape to go to lunch. Don't you realize? You've got to go home and sleep."

"I'm all right. I get a drink I'll be fine."

A passing cab slowed up at her gesture.

"You go home and go to sleep. You're not fit to go anywhere."

As he focused his eyes on her, realizing her suddenly as something fresh, something new and lovely, something alien to the smoky and   75 turbulent world where he had spent his recent hours, a faint current of reason flowed through him. She saw his mouth twist with vague awe, saw him make a vague attempt to stand up straight. The taxi yawned.

"Maybe you're right. Very sorry."

"What's your address?"

He gave it and then tumbled into a corner, his face still struggling toward reality. Julia closed the door.

When the cab had driven off, she hurried across the street and into the Luxembourg Gardens as if someone were after her.

2

80   Quite by accident, she answered when he telephoned at seven that night. His voice was strained and shaking:

"I suppose there's not much use apologizing for this morning. I didn't know what I was doing, but that's no excuse. But if you could let me see you for a while somewhere tomorrow—just for a minute—I'd like the chance of telling you in person how terribly sorry——"

"I'm busy tomorrow."

"Well, Friday then, or any day."

"I'm sorry, I'm very busy this week."

85   "You mean you don't ever want to see me again?"

"Mr. Ragland, I hardly see the use of going any further with this. Really, that thing this morning was a little too much. I'm very sorry. I hope you feel better. Good-by."

She put him entirely out of her mind. She had not even associated his reputation with such a spectacle—a heavy drinker was someone who sat up late and drank champagne and maybe in the small hours rode home singing. This spectacle at high noon was something else again. Julia was through.

Meanwhile there were other men with whom she lunched at Ciro's and danced in the Bois. There was a reproachful letter from Phil Hoffman in America. She liked Phil better for having been so right about this. A fortnight passed and she would have forgotten Dick Ragland, had she not heard his name mentioned with scorn in several conversations. Evidently he had done such things before.

Then, a week before she was due to sail, she ran into him in the booking department of the White Star Line. He was as handsome—she could hardly believe her eyes. He leaned with an elbow on the desk, his fine figure erect, his yellow gloves as stainless as his clear, shining eyes. His strong, gay personality had affected the clerk who served him with fascinated deference; the stenographers behind looked up for a minute and exchanged a glance. Then he saw Julia; she nodded, and with a quick, wincing change of expression he raised his hat.

They were together by the desk a long time and the silence was   90
oppressive.

"Isn't this a nuisance?" she said.

"Yes," he said jerkily, and then: "You going by the Olympic?"

"Oh, yes."

"I thought you might have changed."

"Of course not," she said coldly.   95

"I thought of changing; in fact, I was here to ask about it."

"That's absurd."

"You don't hate the sight of me? So it'll make you seasick when we pass each other on the deck?"

She smiled. He seized his advantage:

"I've improved somewhat since we last met."   100

"Don't talk about that."

"Well then, you have improved. You've got the loveliest costume on I ever saw."

This was presumptuous, but she felt herself shimmering a little at the compliment.

"You wouldn't consider a cup of coffee with me at the café next door, just to recover from this ordeal?"

How weak of her to talk to him like this, to let him make advances.   105
It was like being under the fascination of a snake.

"I'm afraid I can't." Something terribly timid and vulnerable came into his face, twisting a little sinew in her heart. "Well, all right," she shocked herself by saying.

Sitting at the sidewalk table in the sunlight, there was nothing to remind her of that awful day two weeks ago. Jekyll and Hyde. He was courteous, he was charming, he was amusing. He made her feel, oh, so attractive! He presumed on nothing.

"Have you stopped drinking?" she asked.

"Not till the fifth."

"Oh!"   110

"Not until I said I'd stop. Then I'll stop."

When Julia rose to go, she shook her head at his suggestion of a further meeting.

"I'll see you on the boat. After your twenty-eighth birthday."

"All right; one more thing: It fits in with the high price of crime that I did something inexcusable to the one girl I've ever been in love with in my life."

115   She saw him the first day on board, and then her heart sank into her shoes as she realized at last how much she wanted him. No matter what his past was, no matter what he had done. Which was not to say that she would ever let him know, but only that he moved her chemically more than anyone she had ever met, that all other men seemed pale beside him.

He was popular on the boat; she heard that he was giving a party on the night of his twenty-eighth birthday. Julia was not invited; when they met they spoke pleasantly, nothing more.

It was the day after the fifth that she found him stretched in his deck chair looking wan and white. There were wrinkles on his fine brow and around his eyes, and his hand, as he reached out for a cup of bouillon, was trembling. He was still there in the late afternoon, visibly suffering, visibly miserable. After three times around, Julia was irresistibly impelled to speak to him:

"Has the new era begun?"

He made a feeble effort to rise, but she motioned him not to and sat on the next chair.

120   "You look tired."

"I'm just a little nervous. This is the first day in five years that I haven't had a drink."

"It'll be better soon."

"I know," he said grimly.

"Don't weaken."

125   "I won't."

"Can't I help you in any way? Would you like a bromide?"

"I can't stand bromides," he said almost crossly. "No, thanks, I mean."

Julia stood up: "I know you feel better alone. Things will be brighter tomorrow."

"Don't go, if you can stand me."

130   Julia sat down again.

"Sing me a song—can you sing?"

"What kind of a song?"

"Something sad—some sort of blues."

She sang him Libby Holman's "This is how the story ends," in a low, soft voice.

135   "That's good. Now sing another. Or sing that again."

"All right. If you like, I'll sing to you all afternoon."

3

The second day in New York he called her on the phone. "I've missed you so," he said. "Have you missed me?"

"I'm afraid I have," she said reluctantly.

"Much?"

"I've missed you a lot. Are you better?"   140

"I'm all right now. I'm still just a little nervous, but I'm starting work tomorrow. When can I see you?"

"When you want."

"This evening then. And look—say that again."

"What?"

"That you're afraid you have missed me."   145

"I'm afraid that I have," Julia said obediently.

"Missed me," he added.

"I'm afraid I have missed you."

"All right. It sounds like a song when you say it."

"Good-by, Dick."   150

"Good-by, Julia dear."

She stayed in New York two months instead of the fortnight she had intended, because he would not let her go. Work took the place of drink in the daytime, but afterward he must see Julia.

Sometimes she was jealous of his work when he telephoned that he was too tired to go out after the theater. Lacking drink, night life was less than nothing to him—something quite spoiled and well lost. For Julia, who never drank, it was a stimulus in itself—the music and the parade of dresses and the handsome couple they made dancing together. At first they saw Phil Hoffman once in a while; Julia considered that he took the matter rather badly; then they didn't see him any more.

A few unpleasant incidents occurred. An old schoolmate, Esther Cary, came to her to ask if she knew of Dick Ragland's reputation. Instead of growing angry, Julia invited her to meet Dick and was delighted with the ease with which Esther's convictions were changed. There were other, small, annoying episodes, but Dick's misdemeanors had, fortunately, been confined to Paris and assumed here a far-away unreality. They loved each other deeply now—the memory of that morning slowly being effaced from Julia's imagination—but she wanted to be sure.

"After six months, if everything goes along like this, we'll an-   155 nounce our engagement. After another six months we'll be married."

"Such a long time," he mourned.

"But there were five years before that," Julia answered. "I trust you with my heart and with my mind, but something else says wait. Remember, I'm also deciding for my children."

Those five years—oh, so lost and gone.

In August, Julia went to California for two months to see her family. She wanted to know how Dick would get along alone. They wrote every day; his letters were by turns cheerful, depressed, weary and hopeful. His work was going better. As things came back to him, his uncle had begun really to believe in him, but all the time he missed his Julia so. It was when an occasional note of despair began to appear that she cut her visit short by a week and came East to New York.

160   "Oh, thank God you're here!" he cried as they linked arms and walked out of the Grand Central station. "It's been so hard. Half a dozen times lately I've wanted to go on a bust and I had to think of you, and you were so far away."

"Darling—darling, you're so tired and pale. You're working too hard."

"No, only that life is so bleak alone. When I go to bed my mind churns on and on. Can't we get married sooner?"

"I don't know; we'll see. You've got your Julia near you now, and nothing matters."

After a week, Dick's depression lifted. When he was sad, Julia made him her baby, holding his handsome head against her breast, but she liked it best when he was confident and could cheer her up, making her laugh and feel taken care of and secure. She had rented an apartment with another girl and she took courses in biology and domestic science in Columbia. When deep fall came, they went to football games and the new shows together, and walked through the first snow in Central Park, and several times a week spent long evenings together in front of her fire. But time was going by and they were both impatient. Just before Christmas, an unfamiliar visitor—Phil Hoffman—presented himself at her door. It was the first time in many months. New York, with its quality of many independent ladders set side by side, is unkind to even the meetings of close friends; so, in the case of strained relations, meetings are easy to avoid.

165   And they were strange to each other. Since his expressed skepticism of Dick, he was automatically her enemy; on another count, she saw that he had improved, some of the hard angles were worn off; he was now an assistant district attorney, moving around with increasing confidence through his profession.

"So you're going to marry Dick?" he said. "When?"

"Soon now. When mother comes East."

He shook his head emphatically. "Julia, don't marry Dick. This isn't jealousy—I know when I am licked—but it seems awful for a lovely girl like you to take a blind dive into a lake full of rocks. What makes you think that people change their courses? Sometimes they dry up or even flow into a parallel channel, but I've never known anybody to change."

"Dick's changed."

"Maybe so. But isn't that an enormous 'maybe'? If he was unattrac-   170
tive and you liked him, I'd say go ahead with it. Maybe I'm all wrong,
but it's so darn obvious that what fascinates you is that handsome pan
of his and those attractive manners."

"You don't know him," Julia answered loyally. "He's different with
me. You don't know how gentle he is, and responsive. Aren't you being
rather small and mean?"

"Hm." Phil thought for a moment. "I want to see you again in a few
days. Or perhaps I'll speak to Dick."

"You let Dick alone," she cried. "He has enough to worry him without your nagging him. If you were his friend you'd try to help him instead of coming to me behind his back."

"I'm your friend first."

"Dick and I are one person now."   175

But three days later Dick came to see her at an hour when he would
usually have been at the office.

"I'm here under compulsion," he said lightly, "under threat of exposure by Phil Hoffman."

Her heart dropping like a plummet. "Has he given up?" she
thought. "Is he drinking again?"

"It's about a girl. You introduced me to her last summer and told
me to be very nice to her—Esther Cary."

Now her heart was beating slowly.   180

"After you went to California I was lonesome and I ran into her.
She'd liked me that day, and for a while we saw quite a bit of each
other. Then you came back and I broke it off. It was a little difficult; I
hadn't realized that she was so interested."

"I see." Her voice was starved and aghast.

"Try and understand. Those terribly lonely evenings. I think if it
hadn't been for Esther, I'd have fallen off the wagon. I never loved
her—I never loved anybody but you—but I had to see somebody who
liked me."

He put his arm around her, but she felt cold all over and he
drew away.

"Then any woman would have done," Julia said slowly. "It didn't   185
matter who."

"No!" he cried.

"I stayed away so long to let you stand on your own feet and get
back your self-respect by yourself."

"I only love you, Julia."

"But any woman can help you. So you don't really need me,
do you?"

190   His face wore that vulnerable look that Julia had seen several times before; she sat on the arm of his chair and ran her hand over his cheek.
"Then what do you bring me?" she demanded. "I thought that there'd be the accumulated strength of having beaten your weakness. What do you bring me now?"
"Everything I have."
She shook her head. "Nothing. Just your good looks—and the head waiter at dinner last night had that."
They talked for two days and decided nothing. Sometimes she would pull him close and reach up to his lips that she loved so well, but her arms seemed to close around straw.

195   "I'll go away and give you a chance to think it over," he said despairingly. "I can't see any way of living without you, but I suppose you can't marry a man you don't trust or believe in. My uncle wanted me to go to London on some business——"
The night he left, it was sad on the dim pier. All that kept her from breaking was that it was not an image of strength that was leaving her; she would be just as strong without him. Yet as the murky lights fell on the fine structure of his brow and chin, as she saw the faces turn toward him, the eyes that followed him, an awful emptiness seized her and she wanted to say: "Never mind, dear; we'll try it together."
But try what? It was human to risk the toss between failure and success, but to risk the desperate gamble between adequacy and disaster——
"Oh, Dick, be good and be strong and come back to me. Change, change, Dick—change!"
"Good-by, Julia—good-by."

200   She last saw him on the deck, his profile cut sharp as a cameo against a match as he lit a cigarette.

4

It was Phil Hoffman who was to be with her at the beginning and the end. It was he who broke the news as gently as it could be broken. He reached her apartment at half-past eight and carefully threw away the morning paper outside. Dick Ragland had disappeared at sea.
After her first wild burst of grief, he became purposely a little cruel.
"He knew himself. His will had given out; he didn't want life any more. And, Julia, just to show you how little you can possibly blame yourself, I'll tell you this: He'd hardly gone to his office for four months— since you went to California. He wasn't fired because of his uncle; the business he went to London on was of no importance at all. After his first enthusiasm was gone he'd given up."

She looked at him sharply. "He didn't drink, did he? He wasn't drinking?"

For a fraction of a second Phil hesitated. "No, he didn't drink; he kept his promise—he held on to that." 205

"That was it," she said. "He kept his promise and he killed himself doing it."

Phil waited uncomfortably.

"He did what he said he would and broke his heart doing it," she went on chokingly. "Oh, isn't life cruel sometimes—so cruel, never to let anybody off. He was so brave—he died doing what he said he'd do."

Phil was glad he had thrown away the newspaper that hinted of Dick's gay evening in the bar—one of many gay evenings that Phil had known of in the past few months. He was relieved that was over, because Dick's weakness had threatened the happiness of the girl he loved; but he was terribly sorry for him—even understanding how it was necessary for him to turn his maladjustment to life toward one mischief or another—but he was wise enough to leave Julia with the dream that she had saved out of wreckage.

There was a bad moment a year later, just before their marriage, 210 when she said:

"You'll understand the feeling I have and always will have about Dick, won't you, Phil? It wasn't just his good looks. I believed in him—and I was right in a way. He broke rather than bent; he was a ruined man, but not a bad man. In my heart I knew when I first looked at him."

Phil winced, but he said nothing. Perhaps there was more behind it than they knew. Better let it all alone in the depths of her heart and the depths of the sea.

QUESTIONS

1. The title alludes to the familiar phrase "turning over a new leaf." What does that mean? In the story, how might it apply to both Julia Ross and Dick Ragland? To what extent does either of them live up to the meaning of the phrase? Which of them would you call the protagonist?

2. From what point of view is the story told? For what purposes does the point of view shift? Pick out several examples to support your interpretation. Compare the contribution of point of view here to that in "Roman Fever."

3. As fully as possible, explain what causes Julia to fall in love with Dick, and what causes Dick to fall in love with Julia. Does either of them have a more mature or sound basis for loving the other? Compare their emotional lives with those of Mrs. Ansley and Mrs. Slade in "Roman Fever."

4. What causes Julia to reject Dick, twice? What in his behavior causes her rejections, and what in her character causes them?

5. What is the function of Phil Hoffman in the plot? Why does Julia reject him, and why does she finally marry him?
6. What are the connotations of the settings of the story—Paris, the steamship Olympia, and New York—and how do they reinforce your understanding of the social class and attitudes of the characters? Compare the role of settings in this story to that in "Roman Fever." Which story more fully integrates the setting into its meanings and emotional effects?
7. How do we learn about the emotional reactions of the characters to each other and to their own situations? Find several examples for analysis to support your answer. How does this story differ from "Roman Fever" in the way it presents the emotional lives of its characters?
8. What is the theme of "A New Leaf"? By comparison, is it more or less significant than that of "Roman Fever"?

SUGGESTIONS FOR WRITING

1. Write an essay evaluating the relative quality of any of the following pairs of stories. Decide which is the better story, and support your argument fully:
   a. Connell, "The Most Dangerous Game" (page 67) and Wolfe, "The Child by Tiger" (page 625).
   b. Walker, "Everyday Use" (page 166) and Bambara, "The Lesson" (page 195).
   c. O'Connor, "The Drunkard" (page 339) and Cheever, "The Swimmer" (page 529).
   d. Wolff, "Hunters in the Snow" (page 86) and Wolfe, "The Child by Tiger" (page 625).
   e. O. Henry, "A Municipal Report" (page 375) and Glaspell, "A Jury of Her Peers" (page 389).
   f. Wharton, "Roman Fever" (page 409) and Fitzgerald, "A New Leaf" (page 420).
   g. Porter, "The Jilting of Granny Weatherall" (page 260) and Cofer, "American History" (page 539).
2. Write an essay in which you argue for the literary quality of any one of the following stories, detailing its successful use of the elements of fiction:
   a. Lahiri, "Interpreter of Maladies" (page 141).
   b. Joyce, "Eveline" (page 442).
   c. Gordimer, "Once upon a Time" (page 220).
   d. Hawthorne, "Young Goodman Brown" (page 299).
   e. Melville, "Bartleby the Scrivener" (page 579).
   f. Oates, "Where Are You Going, Where Have You Been?" (page 311).
   g. Wharton, "Roman Fever" (page 409).

Two Featured Writers

James Joyce
and
Flannery O'Connor

Introduction

Suggestions for Writing

James Joyce
Araby

   North Richmond Street, being blind,° was a quiet street except at the hour when the Christian Brothers' School set the boys free. An uninhabited house of two storeys stood at the blind end, detached from its neighbours in a square ground. The other houses of the street, conscious of decent lives within them, gazed at one another with brown imperturbable faces.

   The former tenant of our house, a priest, had died in the back drawing-room. Air, musty from having been long enclosed, hung in all the rooms, and the waste room behind the kitchen was littered with old useless papers. Among these I found a few paper-covered books, the pages of which were curled and damp: *The Abbot*, by Walter Scott, *The Devout Communicant* and *The Memoirs of Vidocq*.° I liked the last best because its leaves were yellow. The wild garden behind the house contained a central apple-tree and a few straggling bushes under one of which I found the late tenant's rusty bicycle-pump. He had been a very charitable priest; in his will he had left all his money to institutions and the furniture of his house to his sister.

   When the short days of winter came dusk fell before we had well eaten our dinners. When we met in the street the houses had grown somber. The space of sky above us was the colour of ever-changing violet and towards it the lamps of the street lifted their feeble lanterns. The cold air stung us and we played till our bodies glowed. Our shouts echoed in the silent street. The career of our play brought us through the dark muddy lanes behind the houses where we ran the gauntlet of the rough tribes from the cottages, to the back doors of the dark dripping gardens where odors arose from the ashpits, to the dark odorous stables where a coachman smoothed and combed the horse or shook music from the buckled harness. When we returned to the street, light from the kitchen windows had filled the areas. If my uncle was seen

ARABY   First published in 1914. James Joyce (1882-1941) was born and lived in Dublin, Ireland, until 1904 when he went to Paris, and for the rest of his life he lived abroad and wrote about Dublin. He attended Jesuit school and graduated from University College in Dublin. The short stories collected in his first book, *Dubliners*, are among the most celebrated and influential of the genre in the modern era.

blind: a dead-end street   *The Abbot:* an 1820 novel by Sir Walter Scott (1771–1834); *The Devout Communicant:* a Roman Catholic tract published in 1813; ***The Memoirs of Vidocq:*** memoirs by a French detective, Francois Vidocq (1775–1857)

turning the corner we hid in the shadow until we had seen him safely housed. Or if Mangan's sister came out on the doorstep to call her brother in to his tea we watched her from our shadow peer up and down the street. We waited to see whether she would remain or go in and, if she remained, we left our shadow and walked up to Mangan's steps resignedly. She was waiting for us, her figure defined by the light from the half-opened door. Her brother always teased her before he obeyed and I stood by the railings looking at her. Her dress swung as she moved her body and the soft rope of her hair tossed from side to side.

Every morning I lay on the floor in the front parlor watching her door. The blind was pulled down to within an inch of the sash so that I could not be seen. When she came out on the doorstep my heart leaped. I ran to the hall, seized my books and followed her. I kept her brown figure always in my eye and, when we came near the point at which our ways diverged, I quickened my pace and passed her. This happened morning after morning. I had never spoken to her, except for a few casual words, and yet her name was like a summons to all my foolish blood.

5   Her image accompanied me even in places the most hostile to romance. On Saturday evenings when my aunt went marketing I had to go to carry some of the parcels. We walked through the flaring streets, jostled by drunken men and bargaining women, amid the curses of laborers, the shrill litanies of shop-boys who stood on guard by the barrels of pigs' cheeks, the nasal chanting of street-singers, who sang a *come-all-you* about O'Donovan Rossa,° or a ballad about the troubles in our native land. These noises converged in a single sensation of life for me: I imagined that I bore my chalice safely through a throng of foes. Her name sprang to my lips at moments in strange prayers and praises which I myself did not understand. My eyes were often full of tears (I could not tell why) and at times a flood from my heart seemed to pour itself out into my bosom. I thought little of the future. I did not know whether I would ever speak to her or not or, if I spoke to her, how I could tell her of my confused adoration. But my body was like a harp and her words and gestures were like fingers running upon the wires.

One evening I went into the back drawing-room in which the priest had died. It was a dark rainy evening and there was no sound in the house. Through one of the broken panes I heard the rain impinge upon the earth, the fine incessant needles of water playing in the sodden beds. Some distant lamp or lighted window gleamed below me. I was thankful that I could see so little. All my senses seemed to desire to

come-all-you: an Irish patriotic song   O'Donovan Rossa: Jeremiah O'Donovan (1831–1915), an Irish nationalist

veil themselves and, feeling that I was about to slip from them, I pressed the palms of my hands together until they trembled, murmuring: O *love!* O *love!* many times.

At last she spoke to me. When she addressed the first words to me I was so confused that I did not know what to answer. She asked me was I going to *Araby.* I forget whether I answered yes or no. It would be a splendid bazaar, she said; she would love to go.

"And why can't you?" I asked.

While she spoke she turned a silver bracelet round and round her wrist. She could not go, she said, because there would be a retreat that week in her convent. Her brother and two other boys were fighting for their caps and I was alone at the railings. She held one of the spikes, bowing her head towards me. The light from the lamp opposite our door caught the white curve of her neck, lit up her hair that rested there and, falling, lit up the hand upon the railing. It fell over one side of her dress and caught the white border of a petticoat, just visible as she stood at ease.

"It's well for you," she said.   10

"If I go," I said, "I will bring you something."

What innumerable follies laid waste my waking and sleeping thoughts after that evening! I wished to annihilate the tedious intervening days. I chafed against the work of school. At night in my bedroom and by day in the classroom her image came between me and the page I strove to read. The syllables of the word *Araby* were called to me through the silence in which my soul luxuriated and cast an Eastern enchantment over me. I asked for leave to go to the bazaar Saturday night. My aunt was surprised and hoped it was not some Freemason° affair. I answered few questions in class. I watched my master's face pass from amiability to sternness; he hoped I was not beginning to idle. I could not call my wandering thoughts together. I had hardly any patience with the serious work of life which, now that it stood between me and my desire, seemed to me child's play, ugly monotonous child's play.

On Saturday morning I reminded my uncle that I wished to go to the bazaar in the evening. He was fussing at the hallstand, looking for the hat-brush, and answered me curtly:

"Yes, boy, I know."

As he was in the hall I could not go into the front parlor and lie at   15
the window. I left the house in bad humor and walked slowly towards the school. The air was pitilessly raw and already my heart misgave me.

Freemason: member of a highly secretive fraternal organization

When I came home to dinner my uncle had not yet been home. Still it was early. I sat staring at the clock for some time and, when its ticking began to irritate me, I left the room. I mounted the staircase and gained the upper part of the house. The high cold empty gloomy rooms liberated me and I went from room to room singing. From the front window I saw my companions playing below in the street. Their cries reached me weakened and indistinct and, leaning my forehead against the cool glass, I looked over at the dark house where she lived. I may have stood there for an hour, seeing nothing but the brown-clad figure cast by my imagination, touched discreetly by the lamplight at the curved neck, at the hand upon the railings and at the border below the dress.

When I came downstairs again I found Mrs. Mercer sitting at the fire. She was an old garrulous woman, a pawnbroker's widow, who collected used stamps for some pious purpose. I had to endure the gossip of the tea-table. The meal was prolonged beyond an hour and still my uncle did not come. Mrs. Mercer stood up to go: she was sorry she couldn't wait any longer, but it was after eight o'clock and she did not like to be out late, as the night air was bad for her. When she had gone I began to walk up and down the room, clenching my fists. My aunt said:

"I'm afraid you may put off your bazaar for this night of Our Lord."

At nine o'clock I heard my uncle's latchkey in the halldoor. I heard him talking to himself and heard the hallstand rocking when it had received the weight of his overcoat. I could interpret these signs. When he was midway through his dinner I asked him to give me the money to go to the bazaar. He had forgotten.

20   "The people are in bed and after their first sleep now," he said.

I did not smile. My aunt said to him energetically:

"Can't you give him the money and let him go? You've kept him late enough as it is."

My uncle said he was very sorry he had forgotten. He said he believed in the old saying: *All work and no play makes Jack a dull boy.* He asked me where I was going and, when I had told him a second time he asked me did I know *The Arab's Farewell to his Steed.*° When I left the kitchen he was about to recite the opening lines of the piece to my aunt.

I held a florin° tightly in my hand as I strode down Buckingham Street towards the station. The sight of the streets thronged with buyers and glaring with gas recalled to me the purpose of my journey. I took my seat in a third-class carriage of a deserted train. After an intolerable

---

"The Arab's Farewell to His Steed": a popular nineteenth-century song   **florin**: a coin worth two shillings

delay the train moved out of the station slowly. It crept onward among ruinous houses and over the twinkling river. At Westland Row Station a crowd of people pressed to the carriage doors; but the porters moved them back, saying that it was a special train for the bazaar. I remained alone in the bare carriage. In a few minutes the train drew up beside an improvised wooden platform. I passed out on to the road and saw by the lighted dial of a clock that it was ten minutes to ten. In front of me was a large building which displayed the magical name.

I could not find any sixpenny entrance and, fearing that the bazaar   25
would be closed, I passed in quickly through a turnstile, handing a shilling to a weary-looking man. I found myself in a big hall girdled at half its height by a gallery. Nearly all the stalls were closed and the greater part of the hall was in darkness. I recognized a silence like that which pervades a church after a service. I walked into the center of the bazaar timidly. A few people were gathered about the stalls which were still open. Before a curtain, over which the words *Café Chantant°* were written in colored lamps, two men were counting money on a salver. I listened to the fall of the coins.

Remembering with difficulty why I had come I went over to one of the stalls and examined porcelain vases and flowered tea-sets. At the door of the stall a young lady was talking and laughing with two young gentlemen. I remarked their English accents and listened vaguely to their conversation.

"O, I never said such a thing!"

"O, but you did!"

"O, but I didn't!"

"Didn't she say that?"   30

"Yes, I heard her."

"O, there's a . . . fib!"

Observing me the young lady came over and asked me did I wish to buy anything. The tone of her voice was not encouraging; she seemed to have spoken to me out of a sense of duty. I looked humbly at the great jars that stood like eastern guards at either side of the dark entrance to the stall and murmured:

"No, thank you."

The young lady changed the position of one of the vases and went   35
back to the two young men. They began to talk of the same subject. Once or twice the young lady glanced at me over her shoulder.

I lingered before her stall, though I knew my stay was useless, to make my interest in her wares seem the more real. Then I turned away

Café Chantant: a café with music

slowly and walked down the middle of the bazaar. I allowed the two pennies to fall against the sixpence in my pocket. I heard a voice call from one end of the gallery that the light was out. The upper part of the hall was now completely dark.

Gazing up into the darkness I saw myself as a creature driven and derided by vanity; and my eyes burned with anguish and anger.

QUESTIONS

1. Discuss the setting and the way it is described in the opening paragraphs. How is the setting related to the boy's state of mind?
2. How is the boy characterized? Roughly how old is he and how would you describe his temperament and personality?
3. Analyze the role of Mangan's sister. Why is she not given a name? How does her physical description relate to the boy's state of mind?
4. Describe the role of the boy's uncle. Can he be called the antagonist? When the uncle returns home, he is talking to himself and moving awkwardly. What are these "signs" the boy says he is able to interpret?
5. How is the bazaar described? How is it different from the reader's and the boy's expectations?
6. At the bazaar, there is an inconsequential conversation between the young salesgirl and two Englishmen. Why is this dialogue important? How does the boy react to it?
7. Why does the boy decide not to buy anything for Mangan's sister? Where in the text would you locate the moment of "epiphany"?
8. Analyze the boy's feelings as described in the story's last paragraph. Are his feelings justified? How will he be changed as a result of his experience at the bazaar?

James Joyce

Eveline

She sat at the window watching evening invade the avenue. Her head was leaned against the window curtains and in her nostrils was the odor of dusty cretonne. She was tired.

Few people passed. The man out of the last house passed on his way home; she heard his footsteps clacking along the concrete pave-

EVELINE   First published in 1904. Eveline's weekly wages working as a sales clerk in "the Stores" are the equivalent of less than ten dollars. The "night boat" that she and Frank are planning to take departed from a dock called "the North Wall" for Liverpool, England; presumably Frank has planned to take a ship from there to Argentina with her. See the note on "Araby" for information on Joyce and his career.

ment and afterwards crunching on the cinder path before the new red houses. One time there used to be a field there in which they used to play every evening with other people's children. Then a man from Belfast bought the field and built houses in it—not like their little brown houses but bright brick houses with shining roofs. The children of the avenue used to play together in that field—the Devines, the Waters, the Dunns, little Keogh the cripple, she and her brothers and sisters. Ernest, however, never played: he was too grown up. Her father used often to hunt them in out of the field with his blackthorn stick; but usually little Keogh used to keep *nix* and call out when he saw her father coming. Still they seemed to have been rather happy then. Her father was not so bad then; and besides, her mother was alive. That was a long time ago; she and her brothers and sisters were all grown up; her mother was dead. Tizzie Dunn was dead, too, and the Waters had gone back to England. Everything changes. Now she was going to go away like the others, to leave her home.

Home! She looked round the room, reviewing all its familiar objects which she had dusted once a week for so many years, wondering where on earth all the dust came from. Perhaps she would never see again those familiar objects from which she had never dreamed of being divided. And yet during all those years she had never found out the name of the priest whose yellowing photograph hung on the wall above the broken harmonium beside the colored print of the promises made to Blessed Margaret Mary Alacoque.° He had been a school friend of her father. Whenever he showed the photograph to a visitor her father used to pass it with a casual word:

"He is in Melbourne now."

She had consented to go away, to leave her home. Was that wise?   5 She tried to weigh each side of the question. In her home anyway she had shelter and food; she had those whom she had known all her life about her. Of course she had to work hard both in the house and at business. What would they say of her in the Stores when they found out that she had run away with a fellow? Say she was a fool, perhaps; and her place would be filled up by advertisement. Miss Gavan would be glad. She had always had an edge on her, especially whenever there were people listening.

"Miss Hill, don't you see these ladies are waiting?"

"Look lively, Miss Hill, please."

She would not cry many tears at leaving the Stores.

Blessed Margaret Mary Alacoque: now a saint in the Roman Catholic church (canonized in 1920), Margaret Mary Alacoque (1647–1690) reported visions of Christ and suffered much illness during her brief life

But in her new home, in a distant unknown country, it would not be like that. Then she would be married—she, Eveline. People would treat her with respect then. She would not be treated as her mother had been. Even now, though she was over nineteen, she sometimes felt herself in danger of her father's violence. She knew it was that that had given her the palpitations. When they were growing up he had never gone for her, like he used to go for Harry and Ernest, because she was a girl; but latterly he had begun to threaten her and say what he would do to her only for° her dead mother's sake. And now she had nobody to protect her. Ernest was dead and Harry, who was in the church decorating business, was nearly always down somewhere in the country. Besides, the invariable squabble for money on Saturday nights had begun to weary her unspeakably. She always gave her entire wages—seven shillings—and Harry always sent up what he could but the trouble was to get any money from her father. He said she used to squander the money, that she had no head, that he wasn't going to give her his hard-earned money to throw about the streets, and much more, for he was usually fairly bad of a Saturday night. In the end he would give her the money and ask her had she any intention of buying Sunday's dinner. Then she had to rush out as quickly as she could and do her marketing, holding her black leather purse tightly in her hand as she elbowed her way through the crowds and returning home late under her load of provisions. She had hard work to keep the house together and to see that the two young children who had been left to her charge went to school regularly and got their meals regularly. It was hard work—a hard life—but now that she was about to leave it she did not find it a wholly undesirable life.

10   She was about to explore another life with Frank. Frank was very kind, manly, open-hearted. She was to go away with him by the night-boat to be his wife and to live with him in Buenos Aires where he had a home waiting for her. How well she remembered the first time she had seen him; he was lodging in a house on the main road where she used to visit. It seemed a few weeks ago. He was standing at the gate, his peaked cap pushed back on his head and his hair tumbled forward over a face of bronze. Then they had come to know each other. He used to meet her outside the Stores every evening and see her home. He took her to see *The Bohemian Girl* ° and she felt elated as she sat in an unaccustomed part of the theater with him. He was awfully fond of music and sang a little. People knew that they were courting and, when he

only for: except for   ***The Bohemian Girl:*** an opera by the Irish composer Michael William Balfe, first produced in 1843

sang about the lass that loves a sailor, she always felt pleasantly confused. He used to call her Poppens out of fun. First of all it had been an excitement for her to have a fellow and then she had begun to like him. He had tales of distant countries. He had started as a deck boy at a pound a month on a ship of the Allan Line going out to Canada. He told her the names of the ships he had been on and the names of the different services. He had sailed through the Straits of Magellan and he told her stories of the terrible Patagonians. He had fallen on his feet in Buenos Aires, he said, and had come over to the old country just for a holiday. Of course, her father had found out the affair and had forbidden her to have anything to say to him.

"I know these sailor chaps," he said.

One day he had quarrelled with Frank and after that she had to meet her lover secretly.

The evening deepened in the avenue. The white of two letters in her lap grew indistinct. One was to Harry; the other was to her father. Ernest had been her favorite but she liked Harry too. Her father was becoming old lately, she noticed; he would miss her. Sometimes he could be very nice. Not long before, when she had been laid up for a day, he had read her out a ghost story and made toast for her at the fire. Another day, when their mother was alive, they had all gone for a picnic to the Hill of Howth.° She remembered her father putting on her mother's bonnet to make the children laugh.

Her time was running out but she continued to sit by the window, leaning her head against the window curtain, inhaling the odor of dusty cretonne. Down far in the avenue she could hear a street organ playing. She knew the air. Strange that it should come that very night to remind her of the promise to her mother, her promise to keep the home together as long as she could. She remembered the last night of her mother's illness; she was again in the close dark room at the other side of the hall and outside she heard a melancholy air of Italy. The organ-player had been ordered to go away and given sixpence. She remembered her father strutting back into the sickroom saying:

"Damned Italians! coming over here!"   15

As she mused the pitiful vision of her mother's life laid its spell on the very quick of her being—that life of commonplace sacrifices closing in final craziness. She trembled as she heard again her mother's voice saying constantly with foolish insistence:

"Derevaun Seraun! Derevaun Seraun!"°

The Hill of Howth: located nine miles northeast of Dublin, this hill overlooks Dublin Bay
Derevaun Seraun!: interpreted as a slurred Gaelic phrase meaning either "the end of pleasure is pain" or "the end of song is raving madness"

She stood up in a sudden impulse of terror. Escape! She must escape! Frank would save her. He would give her life, perhaps love, too. But she wanted to live. Why should she be unhappy? She had a right to happiness. Frank would take her in his arms, fold her in his arms. He would save her.

She stood among the swaying crowd in the station at the North Wall. He held her hand and she knew that he was speaking to her, saying something about the passage over and over again. The station was full of soldiers with brown baggages. Through the wide doors of the sheds she caught a glimpse of the black mass of the boat, lying in beside the quay wall, with illumined portholes. She answered nothing. She felt her cheek pale and cold and, out of a maze of distress, she prayed to God to direct her, to show her what was her duty. The boat blew a long mournful whistle into the mist. If she went, tomorrow she would be on the sea with Frank, steaming towards Buenos Aires. Their passage had been booked. Could she still draw back after all he had done for her? Her distress awoke a nausea in her body and she kept moving her lips in silent fervent prayer.

20   A bell clanged upon her heart. She felt him seize her hand:
"Come!"

All the seas of the world tumbled about her heart. He was drawing her into them: he would drown her. She gripped with both hands at the iron railing.
"Come!"

No! No! No! It was impossible. Her hands clutched the iron in frenzy. Amid the seas she sent a cry of anguish!
25   "Eveline! Evvy!"

He rushed beyond the barrier and called to her to follow. He was shouted at to go on but he still called to her. She set her white face to him, passive, like a helpless animal. Her eyes gave him no sign of love or farewell or recognition.

QUESTIONS

1. Analyze the first brief paragraph in detail. How does it help to introduce the story's theme? Why does the narrator use the unexpected word "invade" in the first sentence? Why is the second sentence written in passive voice?

2. What in Eveline's present circumstances makes it desirable for her to escape her home? Characterize her father and Miss Gavan, her supervisor. What does the memory of her mother contribute to her decision to leave?

3. At just about the middle of the story (end of paragraph 9), Eveline sums up her life in Dublin: "It was hard work—a hard life—but now that she was

about to leave it she did not find it a wholly undesirable life." What about it makes it attractive to her?

4. What kind of man is Frank? Why does Eveline's father forbid her to see him? Is there any evidence to support her father's suspicion about Frank?

5. Look closely at the descriptions of Eveline's life in Dublin and contrast them with Frank's destination in Buenos Aires. How do these two settings aid our understanding of Eveline's situation and her ultimate fate?

6. To what extent is Eveline's refusal to board the ship based on her judgment and will? Has she *decided* not to go?

7. Is Eveline a sympathetic or unsympathetic character? Is she a victim of her character or of circumstances beyond her control? How do these issues contribute to the major theme?

8. Joyce said that this and other stories he wrote about Dublin dealt with the "spiritual paralysis" of its citizens. What evidence in this story supports that idea as a major theme?

James Joyce
The Boarding House

Mrs. Mooney was a butcher's daughter. She was a woman who was quite able to keep things to herself: a determined woman. She had married her father's foreman and opened a butcher's shop near Spring Gardens. But as soon as his father-in-law was dead Mr. Mooney began to go to the devil. He drank, plundered the till, ran headlong into debt. It was no use making him take the pledge: he was sure to break out again a few days after. By fighting his wife in the presence of customers and by buying bad meat he ruined his business. One night he went for his wife with the cleaver and she had to sleep in a neighbor's house.

After that they lived apart. She went to the priest and got a separation from him with care of the children. She would give him neither money nor food nor house-room; and so he was obliged to enlist himself as a sheriff's man. He was a shabby stooped little drunkard with a white face and a white moustache and white eyebrows, penciled above his little eyes, which were pink-veined and raw; and all day long he sat

THE BOARDING HOUSE   First published in 1914. Hardwicke Street, where Mrs. Mooney's boarding house is located, is in the vicinity of Mountjoy Square, a formerly fashionable district that had grown shabby. "George's Church" is the Protestant church of St. George, and when Mrs. Mooney thinks of "catching short twelve at Marlborough Street," she is planning to attend the abbreviated noon mass at the chief Catholic church in Dublin, the Metropolitan Pro-Cathedral. See the note on "Araby" for information on Joyce and his career.

in the bailiff's room, waiting to be put on a job. Mrs. Mooney, who had taken what remained of her money out of the butcher business and set up a boarding house in Hardwicke Street, was a big imposing woman. Her house had a floating population made up of tourists from Liverpool and the Isle of Man and, occasionally, *artistes* from the music halls. Its resident population was made up of clerks from the city. She governed her house cunningly and firmly, knew when to give credit, when to be stern and when to let things pass. All the resident young men spoke of her as *The Madam*.

Mrs. Mooney's young men paid fifteen shillings a week for board and lodgings (beer or stout at dinner excluded). They shared in common tastes and occupations and for this reason they were very chummy with one another. They discussed with one another the chances of favorites and outsiders. Jack Mooney, the Madam's son, who was clerk to a commission agent in Fleet Street, had the reputation of being a hard case. He was fond of using soldiers' obscenities: usually he came home in the small hours. When he met his friends he had always a good one to tell them as he was always sure to be on to a good thing—that is to say, a likely horse or a likely *artiste*. He was also handy with the mitts and sang comic songs. On Sunday nights there would often be a reunion in Mrs. Mooney's front drawing-room. The music-hall *artistes* would oblige; and Sheridan played waltzes and polkas and vamped accompaniments. Polly Mooney, the Madam's daughter, would also sing. She sang:

> I'm a . . . naughty girl.
> You needn't sham:
> You know I am.

Polly was a slim girl of nineteen, she had light soft hair and a small full mouth. Her eyes, which were grey with a shade of green through them, had a habit of glancing upwards when she spoke with anyone, which made her look like a little perverse madonna. Mrs. Mooney had first sent her daughter to be a typist in a corn-factor's office but, as a disreputable sheriff's man used to come every other day to the office, asking to be allowed to say a word to his daughter, she had taken her daughter home again and set her to do housework. As Polly was very lively the intention was to give her the run of the young men. Besides, young men like to feel that there is a young woman not very far away. Polly, of course, flirted with the young men but Mrs. Mooney, who was a shrewd judge, knew that the young men were only passing the time away: none of them meant business. Things went on so for a long time and Mrs. Mooney began to think of sending Polly back to typewriting when she noticed that something was going on between Polly and one of the young men. She watched the pair and kept her own counsel.

Polly knew that she was being watched, but still her mother's persistent silence could not be misunderstood. There had been no open complicity between mother and daughter, no open understanding but, though people in the house began to talk of the affair, still Mrs. Mooney did not intervene. Polly began to grow a little strange in her manner and the young man was evidently perturbed. At last, when she judged it to be the right moment, Mrs. Mooney intervened. She dealt with moral problems as a cleaver deals with meat: and in this case she had made up her mind.

It was a bright Sunday morning of early summer, promising heat, but with a fresh breeze blowing. All the windows of the boarding house were open and the lace curtains ballooned gently towards the street beneath the raised sashes. The belfry of George's Church sent out constant peals and worshippers, singly or in groups, traversed the little circus before the church, revealing their purpose by their self-contained demeanor no less than by the little volumes in their gloved hands. Breakfast was over in the boarding house and the table of the breakfast-room was covered with plates on which lay yellow streaks of eggs with morsels of bacon-fat and bacon-rind. Mrs. Mooney sat in the straw arm-chair and watched the servant Mary remove the breakfast things. She made Mary collect the crusts and pieces of broken bread to help to make Tuesday's bread-pudding. When the table was cleared, the broken bread collected, the sugar and butter safe under lock and key, she began to reconstruct the interview which she had had the night before with Polly. Things were as she had suspected: she had been frank in her questions and Polly had been frank in her answers. Both had been somewhat awkward, of course. She had been made awkward by her not wishing to receive the news in too cavalier a fashion or to seem to have connived and Polly had been made awkward not merely because allusions of that kind always made her awkward but also because she did not wish it to be thought that in her wise innocence she had divined the intention behind her mother's tolerance.

Mrs. Mooney glanced instinctively at the little gilt clock on the mantelpiece as soon as she had become aware through her revery that the bells of George's Church had stopped ringing. It was seventeen minutes past eleven: she would have lots of time to have the matter out with Mr. Doran and then catch short twelve at Marlborough Street. She was sure she would win. To begin with she had all the weight of social opinion on her side: she was an outraged mother. She had allowed him to live beneath her roof, assuming that he was a man of honor, and he had simply abused her hospitality. He was thirty-four or thirty-five years of age, so that youth could not be pleaded as his excuse; nor could ignorance be his excuse since he was a man who had seen something of the world. He had simply taken advantage of Polly's youth and inexperience: that was evident. The question was: What reparation would he make?

There must be reparation made in such cases. It is all very well for the man: he can go his ways as if nothing had happened, having had his moment of pleasure, but the girl has to bear the brunt. Some mothers would be content to patch up such an affair for a sum of money; she had known cases of it. But she would not do so. For her only one reparation could make up for the loss of her daughter's honor: marriage.

She counted all her cards again before sending Mary up to Mr. Doran's room to say that she wished to speak with him. She felt sure she would win. He was a serious young man, not rakish or loud-voiced like the others. If it had been Mr. Sheridan or Mr. Meade or Bantam Lyons her task would have been much harder. She did not think he would face publicity. All the lodgers in the house knew something of the affair; details had been invented by some. Besides, he had been employed for thirteen years in a great Catholic wine-merchant's office and publicity would mean for him, perhaps, the loss of his sit.° Whereas if he agreed all might be well. She knew he had a good screw° for one thing and she suspected he had a bit of stuff put by.

10   Nearly the half-hour! She stood up and surveyed herself in the pier-glass. The decisive expression of her great florid face satisfied her and she thought of some mothers she knew who could not get their daughters off their hands.

Mr. Doran was very anxious indeed this Sunday morning. He had made two attempts to shave but his hand had been so unsteady that he had been obliged to desist. Three days' reddish beard fringed his jaws and every two or three minutes a mist gathered on his glasses so that he had to take them off and polish them with his pocket-handkerchief. The recollection of his confession of the night before was a cause of acute pain to him; the priest had drawn out every ridiculous detail of the affair and in the end had so magnified his sin that he was almost thankful at being afforded a loophole of reparation. The harm was done. What could he do now but marry her or run away? He could not brazen it out. The affair would be sure to be talked of and his employer would be certain to hear of it. Dublin is such a small city: everyone knows everyone else's business. He felt his heart leap warmly in his

sit: slang for "situation," job   screw: slang for salary or wages

throat as he heard in his excited imagination old Mr. Leonard calling out in his rasping voice: *Send Mr. Doran here, please.*

All his long years of service gone for nothing! All his industry and diligence thrown away! As a young man he had sown his wild oats, of course; he had boasted of his free-thinking and denied the existence of God to his companions in public-houses. But that was all passed and done with . . . nearly. He still bought a copy of *Reynolds's Newspaper* every week but he attended to his religious duties and for nine-tenths of the year lived a regular life. He had money enough to settle down on; it was not that. But the family would look down on her. First of all there was her disreputable father and then her mother's boarding house was beginning to get a certain fame. He had a notion that he was being had. He could imagine his friends talking of the affair and laughing. She *was* a little vulgar; sometimes she said *I seen* and *If I had've known.* But what would grammar matter if he really loved her? He could not make up his mind whether to like her or despise her for what she had done. Of course, he had done it too. His instinct urged him to remain free, not to marry. Once you are married you are done for, it said.

While he was sitting helplessly on the side of the bed in shirt and trousers she tapped lightly at his door and entered. She told him all, that she had made a clean breast of it to her mother and that her mother would speak with him that morning. She cried and threw her arms round his neck, saying:

"O, Bob! Bob! What am I to do? What am I to do at all?"

She would put an end to herself, she said.   15

He comforted her feebly, telling her not to cry, that it would be all right, never fear. He felt against his shirt the agitation of her bosom.

It was not altogether his fault that it had happened. He remembered well, with the curious patient memory of the celibate, the first casual caresses her dress, her breath, her fingers had given him. Then late one night as he was undressing for bed she had tapped at his door, timidly. She wanted to relight her candle at his for hers had been blown out by a gust. It was her bath night. She wore a loose open combing-jacket of printed flannel. Her white instep shone in the opening of her furry slippers and the blood glowed warmly behind her perfumed skin. From her hands and wrists too as she lit and steadied her candle a faint perfume arose.

On nights when he came in very late it was she who warmed up his dinner. He scarcely knew what he was eating, feeling her beside him alone, at night, in the sleeping house. And her thoughtfulness! If the night was anyway cold or wet or windy there was sure to be a little tumbler of punch ready for him. Perhaps they could be happy together. . . .

They used to go upstairs together on tiptoe, each with a candle, and on the third landing exchange reluctant good-nights. They used to kiss. He remembered well her eyes, the touch of her hand and his delirium. . . .

20   But delirium passes. He echoed her phrase, applying it to himself: *What am I to do?* The instinct of the celibate warned him to hold back. But the sin was there; even his sense of honor told him that reparation must be made for such a sin.

While he was sitting with her on the side of the bed Mary came to the door and said that the missus wanted to see him in the parlor. He stood up to put on his coat and waistcoat, more helpless than ever. When he was dressed he went over to her to comfort her. It would be all right, never fear. He left her crying on the bed and moaning softly: *O my God!*

Going down the stairs his glasses became so dimmed with moisture that he had to take them off and polish them. He longed to ascend through the roof and fly away to another country where he would never hear again of his trouble, and yet a force pushed him downstairs step by step. The implacable faces of his employer and of the Madam stared upon his discomfiture. On the last flight of stairs he passed Jack Mooney who was coming up from the pantry nursing two bottles of *Bass*. They saluted coldly; and the lover's eyes rested for a second or two on a thick bulldog face and a pair of thick short arms. When he reached the foot of the staircase he glanced up and saw Jack regarding him from the door of the return-room.

Suddenly he remembered the night when one of the music-hall *artistes*, a little blond Londoner, had made a rather free allusion to Polly. The reunion had been almost broken up on account of Jack's violence. Everyone tried to quiet him. The music-hall *artiste*, a little paler than usual, kept smiling and saying that there was no harm meant: but Jack kept shouting at him that if any fellow tried that sort of a game on with *his* sister he'd bloody well put his teeth down his throat, so he would.

Polly sat for a little time on the side of the bed, crying. Then she dried her eyes and went over to the looking-glass. She dipped the end of the towel in the water-jug and refreshed her eyes with the cool water. She looked at herself in profile and readjusted a hairpin above her ear. Then she went back to the bed again and sat at the foot. She regarded the pillows for a long time and the sight of them awakened in her mind secret amiable memories. She rested the nape of her neck against the cool iron bed-rail and fell into a revery. There was no longer any perturbation visible on her face.

She waited on patiently, almost cheerfully, without alarm, her   25
memories gradually giving place to hopes and visions of the future. Her
hopes and visions were so intricate that she no longer saw the white
pillows on which her gaze was fixed or remembered that she was waiting for anything.

At last she heard her mother calling. She started to her feet and
ran to the banisters.

"Polly! Polly!"

"Yes, mamma?"

"Come down, dear. Mr. Doran wants to speak to you." Then she
remembered what she had been waiting for.

QUESTIONS

1. Characterize Mrs. Mooney. What clues to her character are provided by the
   account of her first marriage? What kind of landlady does she prove to be?
   What are the connotations attached to her identity as a "butcher's daughter"? Why do her boarders refer to her as "the Madam"? What are her motivations in actions concerning her daughter?
2. Consider the role of Mrs. Mooney's son. Why is he included in the story?
3. What kind of young woman is Polly? In what ways is she like or unlike her
   mother? To what extent does she collaborate with her mother?
4. Characterize Mr. Doran. To what extent has he "taken advantage" of Polly?
   What qualities in himself and in his situation make him peculiarly vulnerable? Did you find him to be a sympathetic character?
5. What is the function of dramatic irony in this story? Point out examples,
   and discuss.

Flannery O'Connor
A Good Man Is Hard to Find

The grandmother didn't want to go to Florida. She wanted to visit some of her connections in east Tennessee and she was seizing at every chance to change Bailey's mind. Bailey was the son she lived with, her only boy. He was sitting on the edge of his chair at the table, bent over the orange sports section of the *Journal*. "Now look here, Bailey," she said, "see here, read this," and she stood with one hand on her thin hip and the other rattling the newspaper at his bald head. "Here this fellow that calls himself The Misfit is aloose from the Federal Pen and headed toward Florida and you read here what it says he did to these people. Just you read it. I wouldn't take my children in any direction with a criminal like that aloose in it. I couldn't answer to my conscience if I did."

Bailey didn't look up from his reading so she wheeled around then and faced the children's mother, a young woman in slacks, whose face was as broad and innocent as a cabbage and was tied around with a green head-kerchief that had two points on the top like a rabbit's ears. She was sitting on the sofa, feeding the baby his apricots out of a jar. "The children have been to Florida before," the old lady said. "You all ought to take them somewhere else for a change so they would see different parts of the world and be broad. They never have been to east Tennessee."

The children's mother didn't seem to hear her but the eight-year-old boy, John Wesley, a stocky child with glasses, said, "If you don't want to go to Florida, why dontcha stay at home?" He and the little girl, June Star, were reading the funny papers on the floor.

"She wouldn't stay at home to be queen for a day," June Star said without raising her yellow head.

5   "Yes and what would you do if this fellow, The Misfit, caught you?" the grandmother asked.

"I'd smack his face," John Wesley said.

"She wouldn't stay at home for a million bucks," June Star said. "Afraid she'd miss something. She has to go everywhere we go."

A GOOD MAN IS HARD TO FIND   First published in 1953. Flannery O'Connor (1925–1964) spent most of her writing life in Milledgeville, Georgia. Though a devout Roman Catholic, she wrote about the denizens of the rural South, most of whom were fundamentalist Protestants. O'Connor's people are often prideful, hardheaded southerners whose confrontation with violence and death forces them to test their capacity for grace; O'Connor insisted that her Christian vision of human life and destiny informed all her writing.

"All right, Miss," the grandmother said. "Just remember that the next time you want me to curl your hair."

June Star said her hair was naturally curly.

The next morning the grandmother was the first one in the car,   10
ready to go. She had her big black valise that looked like the head of a hippopotamus in one corner, and underneath it she was hiding a basket with Pitty Sing, the cat, in it. She didn't intend for the cat to be left alone in the house for three days because he would miss her too much and she was afraid he might brush against one of the gas burners and accidentally asphyxiate himself. Her son, Bailey, didn't like to arrive at a motel with a cat.

She sat in the middle of the back seat with John Wesley and June Star on either side of her. Bailey and the children's mother and the baby sat in front and they left Atlanta at eight forty-five with the mileage on the car at 55890. The grandmother wrote this down because she thought it would be interesting to say how many miles they had been when they got back. It took them twenty minutes to reach the outskirts of the city.

The old lady settled herself comfortably, removing her white cotton gloves and putting them up with her purse on the shelf in front of the back window. The children's mother still had on slacks and still had her head tied up in a green kerchief, but the grandmother had on a navy blue straw sailor hat with a bunch of white violets on the brim and a navy blue dress with a small white dot in the print. Her collars and cuffs were white organdy trimmed with lace and at her neckline she had pinned a purple spray of cloth violets containing a sachet. In case of an accident, anyone seeing her dead on the highway would know at once that she was a lady.

She said she thought it was going to be a good day for driving, neither too hot nor too cold, and she cautioned Bailey that the speed limit was fifty-five miles an hour and that the patrolmen hid themselves behind billboards and small clumps of trees and sped out after you before you had a chance to slow down. She pointed out interesting details of the scenery: Stone Mountain; the blue granite that in some places came up to both sides of the highway; the brilliant red clay banks slightly streaked with purple; and the various crops that made rows of green lace-work on the ground. The trees were full of silver-white sunlight and the meanest of them sparkled. The children were reading comic magazines and their mother had gone back to sleep.

"Let's go through Georgia fast so we won't have to look at it much," John Wesley said.

15   "If I were a little boy," said the grandmother, "I wouldn't talk about my native state that way. Tennessee has the mountains and Georgia has the hills."

"Tennessee is just a hillbilly dumping ground," John Wesley said, "and Georgia is a lousy state too."

"You said it," June Star said.

"In my time," said the grandmother, folding her thin veined fingers, "children were more respectful of their native states and their parents and everything else. People did right then. Oh look at the cute little pickaninny!" she said and pointed to a Negro child standing in the door of a shack. "Wouldn't that make a picture, now?" she asked and they all turned and looked at the little Negro out of the back window. He waved.

"He didn't have any britches on," June Star said.

20   "He probably didn't have any," the grandmother explained. "Little niggers in the country don't have things like we do. If I could paint, I'd paint that picture," she said.

The children exchanged comic books.

The grandmother offered to hold the baby and the children's mother passed him over the front seat to her. She set him on her knee and bounced him and told him about the things they were passing. She rolled her eyes and screwed up her mouth and stuck her leathery thin face into his smooth bland one. Occasionally he gave her a faraway smile. They passed a large cotton field with five or six graves fenced in the middle of it, like a small island. "Look at the graveyard!" the grandmother said, pointing it out. "That was the old family burying ground. That belonged to the plantation."

"Where's the plantation?" John Wesley asked.

"Gone With the Wind," said the grandmother. "Ha. Ha."

25   When the children finished all the comic books they had brought, they opened the lunch and ate it. The grandmother ate a peanut butter sandwich and an olive and would not let the children throw the box and the paper napkins out the window. When there was nothing else to do they played a game by choosing a cloud and making the other two guess what shape it suggested. John Wesley took one the shape of a cow and June Star guessed a cow and John Wesley said, no, an automobile, and June Star said he didn't play fair, and they began to slap each other over the grandmother.

The grandmother said she would tell them a story if they would keep quiet. When she told a story, she rolled her eyes and waved her head and was very dramatic. She said once when she was a maiden lady she had been courted by a Mr. Edgar Atkins Teagarden from Jasper,

Georgia. She said he was a very good-looking man and a gentleman and that he brought her a watermelon every Saturday afternoon with his initials cut in it, E. A. T. Well, one Saturday, she said, Mr. Teagarden brought the watermelon and there was nobody at home and he left it on the front porch and returned in his buggy to Jasper, but she never got the watermelon, she said, because a nigger boy ate it when he saw the initials, E. A. T.! This story tickled John Wesley's funny bone and he giggled and giggled but June Star didn't think it was any good. She said she wouldn't marry a man that just brought her a watermelon on Saturday. The grandmother said she would have done well to marry Mr. Teagarden because he was a gentleman and had bought Coca-Cola stock when it first came out and that he had died only a few years ago, a very wealthy man.

They stopped at The Tower for barbecued sandwiches. The Tower was a part stucco and part wood filling station and dance hall set in a clearing outside of Timothy. A fat man named Red Sammy Butts ran it and there were signs stuck here and there on the building and for miles up and down the highway saying, TRY RED SAMMY'S FAMOUS BARBECUE. NONE LIKE FAMOUS RED SAMMY'S! RED SAM! THE FAT BOY WITH THE HAPPY LAUGH! A VETERAN! RED SAMMY'S YOUR MAN!

Red Sammy was lying on the bare ground outside The Tower with his head under a truck while a gray monkey about a foot high, chained to a small chinaberry tree, chattered nearby. The monkey sprang back into the tree and got on the highest limb as soon as he saw the children jump out of the car and run toward him.

Inside, The Tower was a long dark room with a counter at one end and tables at the other and dancing space in the middle. They all sat down at a board table next to the nickelodeon and Red Sam's wife, a tall burnt-brown woman with hair and eyes lighter than her skin, came and took their order. The children's mother put a dime in the machine and played "The Tennessee Waltz," and the grandmother said that tune always made her want to dance. She asked Bailey if he would like to dance but he only glared at her. He didn't have a naturally sunny disposition like she did and trips made him nervous. The grandmother's brown eyes were very bright. She swayed her head from side to side and pretended she was dancing in her chair. June Star said play something she could tap to so the children's mother put in another dime and played a fast number and June Star stepped out onto the dance floor and did her tap routine.

"Ain't she cute?" Red Sam's wife said, leaning over the counter. 30 "Would you like to come be my little girl?"

"No I certainly wouldn't," June Star said. "I wouldn't live in a broken-down place like this for a million bucks!" and she ran back to the table.

"Ain't she cute?" the woman repeated, stretching her mouth politely.

"Aren't you ashamed?" hissed the grandmother.

Red Sam came in and told his wife to quit lounging on the counter and hurry up with these people's order. His khaki trousers reached just to his hip bones and his stomach hung over them like a sack of meal swaying under his shirt. He came over and sat down at a table nearby and let out a combination sigh and yodel. "You can't win," he said. "You can't win," and he wiped his sweating red face off with a gray handkerchief. "These days you don't know who to trust," he said. "Ain't that the truth?"

35   "People are certainly not nice like they used to be," said the grandmother.

"Two fellers come in here last week," Red Sammy said, "driving a Chrysler. It was a old beat-up car but it was a good one and these boys looked all right to me. Said they worked at the mill and you know I let them fellers charge the gas they bought? Now why did I do that?"

"Because you're a good man!" the grandmother said at once.

"Yes'm, I suppose so," Red Sam said as if he were struck with this answer.

His wife brought the orders, carrying the five plates all at once without a tray, two in each hand and one balanced on her arm. "It isn't a soul in this green world of God's that you can trust," she said. "And I don't count nobody out of that, not nobody," she repeated, looking at Red Sammy.

40   "Did you read about that criminal, The Misfit, that's escaped?" asked the grandmother.

"I wouldn't be a bit surprised if he didn't attact this place right here," said the woman. "If he hears about it being here, I wouldn't be none surprised to see him. If he hears it's two cent in the cash register, I wouldn't be a tall surprised if he . . ."

"That'll do," Red Sam said. "Go bring these people their Co'-Colas," and the woman went off to get the rest of the order.

"A good man is hard to find," Red Sammy said. "Everything is getting terrible. I remember the day you could go off and leave your screen door unlatched. Not no more."

He and the grandmother discussed better times. The old lady said that in her opinion Europe was entirely to blame for the way things were now. She said the way Europe acted you would think we were made of money and Red Sam said it was no use talking about it, she was exactly right. The children ran outside into the white sunlight and looked at the monkey in the lacy chinaberry tree. He was busy catching fleas on himself and biting each one carefully between his teeth as if it were a delicacy.

They drove off again into the hot afternoon. The grandmother took   45 cat naps and woke up every few minutes with her own snoring. Outside of Toombsboro she woke up and recalled an old plantation that she had visited in this neighborhood once when she was a young lady. She said the house had six white columns across the front and that there was an avenue of oaks leading up to it and two little wooden trellis arbors on either side in front where you sat down with your suitor after a stroll in the garden. She recalled exactly which road to turn off to get to it. She knew that Bailey would not be willing to lose any time looking at an old house, but the more she talked about it, the more she wanted to see it once again and find out if the little twin arbors were still standing. "There was a secret panel in this house," she said craftily, not telling the truth but wishing that she were, "and the story went that all the family silver was hidden in it when Sherman came through but it was never found . . ."

"Hey!" John Wesley said. "Let's go see it! We'll find it! We'll poke all the woodwork and find it! Who lives there? Where do you turn off at? Hey Pop, can't we turn off there?"

"We never have seen a house with a secret panel!" June Star shrieked. "Let's go to the house with the secret panel! Hey Pop, can't we go see the house with the secret panel!"

"It's not far from here, I know," the grandmother said. "It wouldn't take over twenty minutes."

Bailey was looking straight ahead. His jaw was as rigid as a horseshoe. "No," he said.

The children began to yell and scream that they wanted to see the   50 house with the secret panel. John Wesley kicked the back of the front seat and June Star hung over her mother's shoulder and whined desperately into her ear that they never had any fun even on their vacation, that they could never do what THEY wanted to do. The baby began to scream and John Wesley kicked the back of the seat so hard that his father could feel the blows in his kidney.

"All right!" he shouted and drew the car to a stop at the side of the road. "Will you all shut up? Will you all just shut up for one second? If you don't shut up, we won't go anywhere."

"It would be very educational for them," the grandmother murmured.

"All right," Bailey said, "but get this: this is the only time we're going to stop for anything like this. This is the one and only time."

"The dirt road that you have to turn down is about a mile back," the grandmother directed. "I marked it when we passed."

55   "A dirt road," Bailey groaned.

After they had turned around and were headed toward the dirt road, the grandmother recalled other points about the house, the beautiful glass over the front doorway and the candle-lamp in the hall. John Wesley said that the secret panel was probably in the fireplace.

"You can't go inside this house," Bailey said. "You don't know who lives there."

"While you all talk to the people in front, I'll run around behind and get in a window," John Wesley suggested.

"We'll all stay in the car," his mother said.

60   They turned onto the dirt road and the car raced roughly along in a swirl of pink dust. The grandmother recalled the times when there were no paved roads and thirty miles was a day's journey. The dirt road was hilly and there were sudden washes in it and sharp curves on dangerous embankments. All at once they would be on a hill, looking down over the blue tops of trees for miles around, then the next minute, they would be in a red depression with the dust-coated trees looking down on them.

"This place had better turn up in a minute," Bailey said, "or I'm going to turn around."

The road looked as if no one had traveled on it in months.

"It's not much farther," the grandmother said and just as she said it, a horrible thought came to her. The thought was so embarrassing that she turned red in the face and her eyes dilated and her feet jumped up, upsetting her valise in the corner. The instant the valise moved, the newspaper top she had over the basket under it rose with a snarl and Pitty Sing, the cat, sprang onto Bailey's shoulder.

The children were thrown to the floor and their mother, clutching the baby, was thrown out the door onto the ground; the old lady was thrown into the front seat. The car turned over once and landed right-side-up in a gulch off the side of the road. Bailey remained in the driver's seat with the cat—gray-striped with a broad white face and an orange nose—clinging to his neck like a caterpillar.

65   As soon as the children saw they could move their arms and legs, they scrambled out of the car, shouting, "We've had an ACCIDENT!" The grandmother was curled up under the dashboard, hoping she was injured so that Bailey's wrath would not come down on her all at once. The horrible thought she had had before the accident was that the house she had remembered so vividly was not in Georgia but in Tennessee.

Bailey removed the cat from his neck with both hands and flung it out the window against the side of a pine tree. Then he got out of the car and started looking for the children's mother. She was sitting against the side of the red gutted ditch, holding the screaming baby, but she only had a cut down her face and a broken shoulder. "We've had an ACCIDENT!" the children screamed in a frenzy of delight.

"But nobody's killed," June Star said with disappointment as the grandmother limped out of the car, her hat still pinned to her head but the broken front brim standing up at a jaunty angle and the violet spray hanging off the side. They all sat down in the ditch, except the children, to recover from the shock. They were all shaking.

"Maybe a car will come along," said the children's mother hoarsely.

"I believe I have injured an organ," said the grandmother, pressing her side, but no one answered her. Bailey's teeth were clattering. He had on a yellow sport shirt with bright blue parrots designed in it and his face was as yellow as the shirt. The grandmother decided that she would not mention that the house was in Tennessee.

The road was about ten feet above and they could see only the tops of the trees on the other side of it. Behind the ditch they were sitting in there were more woods, tall and dark and deep. In a few minutes they saw a car some distance away on top of a hill, coming slowly as if the occupants were watching them. The grandmother stood up and waved both arms dramatically to attract their attention. The car continued to come on slowly, disappeared around a bend and appeared again, moving even slower, on top of the hill they had gone over. It was a big black battered hearse-like automobile. There were three men in it.   70

It came to a stop just over them and for some minutes, the driver looked down with a steady expressionless gaze to where they were sitting, and didn't speak. Then he turned his head and muttered something to the other two and they got out. One was a fat boy in black trousers and a red sweat shirt with a silver stallion embossed on the front of it. He moved around on the right side of them and stood staring, his mouth partly open in a kind of loose grin. The other had on khaki pants and a blue striped coat and a gray hat pulled down very low, hiding most of his face. He came around slowly on the left side. Neither spoke.

The driver got out of the car and stood by the side of it, looking down at them. He was an older man than the other two. His hair was just beginning to gray and he wore silver-rimmed spectacles that gave him a scholarly look. He had a long creased face and didn't have on any shirt or undershirt. He had on blue jeans that were too tight for him and was holding a black hat and a gun. The two boys also had guns.

"We've had an ACCIDENT!" the children screamed.

The grandmother had the peculiar feeling that the bespectacled man was someone she knew. His face was as familiar to her as if she had known him all her life but she could not recall who he was. He moved away from the car and began to come down the embankment, placing his feet carefully so that he wouldn't slip. He had on tan and white shoes and no socks, and his ankles were red and thin. "Good afternoon," he said. "I see you all had you a little spill."

75   "We turned over twice!" said the grandmother.

"Oncet," he corrected. "We seen it happen. Try their car and see will it run, Hiram," he said quietly to the boy with the gray hat.

"What you got that gun for?" John Wesley asked. "Whatcha gonna do with that gun?"

"Lady," the man said to the children's mother, "would you mind calling them children to sit down by you? Children make me nervous. I want all you all to sit down right together there where you're at."

"What are you telling US what to do for?" June Star asked.

80   Behind them the line of woods gaped like a dark open mouth. "Come here," said their mother.

"Look here now," Bailey began suddenly, "we're in a predicament! We're in . . ."

The grandmother shrieked. She scrambled to her feet and stood staring. "You're The Misfit!" she said. "I recognized you at once!"

"Yes'm," the man said, smiling slightly as if he were pleased in spite of himself to be known, "but it would have been better for all of you, lady, if you hadn't of reckernized me."

Bailey turned his head sharply and said something to his mother that shocked even the children. The old lady began to cry and The Misfit reddened.

85   "Lady," he said, "don't you get upset. Sometimes a man says things he don't mean. I don't reckon he meant to talk to you thataway."

"You wouldn't shoot a lady, would you?" the grandmother said and removed a clean handkerchief from her cuff and began to slap at her eyes with it.

The Misfit pointed the toe of his shoe into the ground and made a little hole and then covered it up again. "I would hate to have to," he said.

"Listen," the grandmother almost screamed, "I know you're a good man. You don't look a bit like you have common blood. I know you must come from nice people!"

"Yes mam," he said, "finest people in the world." When he smiled he showed a row of strong white teeth. "God never made a finer woman than my mother and my daddy's heart was pure gold," he said. The boy with the red sweat shirt had come around behind them and was standing with his gun at his hip. The Misfit squatted down on the ground. "Watch them children, Bobby Lee," he said. "You know they make me nervous." He looked at the six of them huddled together in front of him and he seemed to be embarrassed as if he couldn't think of anything to say. "Ain't a cloud in the sky," he remarked, looking up at it. "Don't see no sun but don't see no cloud neither."

"Yes, it's a beautiful day," said the grandmother. "Listen," she said, "you shouldn't call yourself The Misfit because I know you're a good man at heart. I can just look at you and tell." 90

"Hush!" Bailey yelled. "Hush! Everybody shut up and let me handle this!" He was squatting in the position of a runner about to sprint forward but he didn't move.

"I pre-chate that, lady," The Misfit said and drew a little circle in the ground with the butt of his gun.

"It'll take a half a hour to fix this here car," Hiram called, looking over the raised hood of it.

"Well, first you and Bobby Lee get him and that little boy to step over yonder with you," The Misfit said, pointing to Bailey and John Wesley. "The boys want to ast you something," he said to Bailey. "Would you mind stepping back in them woods there with them?"

"Listen," Bailey began, "we're in a terrible predicament! Nobody realizes what this is," and his voice cracked. His eyes were as blue and intense as the parrots in his shirt and he remained perfectly still. 95

The grandmother reached up to adjust her hat brim as if she were going to the woods with him but it came off in her hand. She stood staring at it and after a second she let it fall on the ground. Hiram pulled Bailey up by the arm as if he were assisting an old man. John Wesley caught hold of his father's hand and Bobby Lee followed. They went off toward the woods and just as they reached the dark edge, Bailey turned and supporting himself against a gray naked pine trunk, he shouted, "I'll be back in a minute, Mamma, wait on me!"

"Come back this instant!" his mother shrilled but they all disappeared into the woods.

"Bailey Boy!" the grandmother called in a tragic voice but she found she was looking at The Misfit squatting on the ground in front of her. "I just know you're a good man," she said desperately. "You're not a bit common!"

"Nome, I ain't a good man," The Misfit said after a second as if he had considered her statement carefully, "but I ain't the worst in the world neither. My daddy said I was a different breed of dog from my brothers and sisters. 'You know,' Daddy said, 'it's some that can live their whole life out without asking about it and it's others has to know why it is, and this boy is one of the latters. He's going to be into everything!'" He put on his black hat and looked up suddenly and then away deep into the woods as if he were embarrassed again. "I'm sorry I don't have on a shirt before you ladies," he said, hunching his shoulders slightly. "We buried our clothes that we had on when we escaped and we're just making do until we can get better. We borrowed these from some folks we met," he explained.

100   "That's perfectly all right," the grandmother said. "Maybe Bailey has an extra shirt in his suitcase."

"I'll look and see terrectly," The Misfit said.

"Where are they taking him?" the children's mother screamed.

"Daddy was a card himself," The Misfit said. "You couldn't put anything over on him. He never got in trouble with the Authorities though. Just had the knack of handling them."

"You could be honest too if you'd only try," said the grandmother. "Think how wonderful it would be to settle down and live a comfortable life and not have to think about somebody chasing you all the time."

105   The Misfit kept scratching in the ground with the butt of his gun as if he were thinking about it. "Yes'm, somebody is always after you," he murmured.

The grandmother noticed how thin his shoulder blades were just behind his hat because she was standing up looking down on him. "Do you ever pray?" she asked.

He shook his head. All she saw was the black hat wiggle between his shoulder blades. "Nome," he said.

There was a pistol shot from the woods, followed closely by another. Then silence. The old lady's head jerked around. She could hear the wind move through the tree tops like a long satisfied insuck of breath. "Bailey Boy!" she called.

"I was a gospel singer for a while," The Misfit said. "I been most everything. Been in the arm service, both land and sea, at home and abroad, been twict married, been an undertaker, been with the railroads, plowed Mother Earth, been in a tornado, seen a man burnt alive oncet," and looked up at the children's mother and the little girl who were sitting close together, their faces white and their eyes glassy; "I even seen a woman flogged," he said.

110   "Pray, pray," the grandmother began, "pray, pray . . ."

"I never was a bad boy that I remember of," The Misfit said in an almost dreamy voice, "but somewheres along the line I done something wrong and got sent to the penitentiary. I was buried alive," and he looked up and held her attention to him by a steady stare.

"That's when you should have started to pray," she said. "What did you do to get sent to the penitentiary that first time?"

"Turn to the right, it was a wall," The Misfit said, looking up again at the cloudless sky. "Turn to the left, it was a wall. Look up it was a ceiling, look down it was a floor. I forget what I done, lady. I set there and set there, trying to remember what it was I done and I ain't recalled it to this day. Oncet in a while, I would think it was coming to me, but it never come."

"Maybe they put you in by mistake," the old lady said vaguely.

"Nome," he said. "It wasn't no mistake. They had the papers on me."   115

"You must have stolen something," she said.

The Misfit sneered slightly. "Nobody had nothing I wanted," he said. "It was a head-doctor at the penitentiary said what I had done was kill my daddy but I known that for a lie. My daddy died in nineteen ought nineteen of the epidemic flu and I never had a thing to do with it. He was buried in the Mount Hopewell Baptist churchyard and you can go there and see for yourself."

"If you would pray," the old lady said, "Jesus would help you."

"That's right," The Misfit said.

"Well then, why don't you pray?" she asked trembling with delight   120
suddenly.

"I don't want no hep," he said. "I'm doing all right by myself."

Bobby Lee and Hiram came ambling back from the woods. Bobby Lee was dragging a yellow shirt with bright blue parrots in it.

"Thow me that shirt, Bobby Lee," The Misfit said. The shirt came flying at him and landed on his shoulder and he put it on. The grandmother couldn't name what the shirt reminded her of. "No, lady," The Misfit said while he was buttoning it up, "I found out the crime don't matter. You can do one thing or you can do another, kill a man or take a tire off his car, because sooner or later you're going to forget what it was you done and just be punished for it."

The children's mother had begun to make heaving noises as if she couldn't get her breath. "Lady," he asked, "would you and that little girl like to step off yonder with Bobby Lee and Hiram and join your husband?"

"Yes, thank you," the mother said faintly. Her left arm dangled help-   125
lessly and she was holding the baby, who had gone to sleep, in the other. "Hep that lady up, Hiram," The Misfit said as she struggled to climb out of the ditch, "and Bobby Lee, you hold onto that little girl's hand."

"I don't want to hold hands with him," June Star said. "He reminds me of a pig."

The fat boy blushed and laughed and caught her by the arm and pulled her off into the woods after Hiram and her mother.

Alone with The Misfit, the grandmother found that she had lost her voice. There was not a cloud in the sky nor any sun. There was nothing around her but woods. She wanted to tell him that he must pray. She opened and closed her mouth several times before anything came out. Finally she found herself saying, "Jesus, Jesus," meaning, Jesus will help you, but the way she was saying it, it sounded as if she might be cursing.

"Yes'm," The Misfit said as if he agreed. "Jesus thown everything off balance. It was the same case with Him as with me except He hadn't committed any crime and they could prove I had committed one because they had the papers on me. Of course," he said, "they never shown me my papers. That's why I sign myself now. I said long ago, you get you a signature and sign everything you do and keep a copy of it. Then you'll know what you done and you can hold up the crime to the punishment and see do they match and in the end you'll have something to prove you ain't been treated right. I call myself The Misfit," he said, "because I can't make what all I done wrong fit what all I gone through in punishment."

130   There was a piercing scream from the woods, followed closely by a pistol report. "Does it seem right to you, lady, that one is punished a heap and another ain't punished at all?"

"Jesus!" the old lady cried. "You've got good blood! I know you wouldn't shoot a lady! I know you come from nice people! Pray! Jesus, you ought not to shoot a lady. I'll give you all the money I've got!"

"Lady," The Misfit said, looking beyond her far into the woods, "there never was a body that give the undertaker a tip."

There were two more pistol reports and the grandmother raised her head like a parched old turkey hen crying for water and called, "Bailey Boy, Bailey Boy!" as if her heart would break.

"Jesus was the only One that ever raised the dead." The Misfit continued, "and He shouldn't have done it. He thown everything off balance. If He did what He said, then it's nothing for you to do but thow away everything and follow Him, and if He didn't, then it's nothing for you to do but enjoy the few minutes you got left the best way you can— by killing somebody or burning down his house or doing some other meanness to him. No pleasure but meanness," he said and his voice had become almost a snarl.

135   "Maybe He didn't raise the dead," the old lady mumbled, not knowing what she was saying and feeling so dizzy that she sank down in the ditch with her legs twisted under her.

"I wasn't there so I can't say He didn't," The Misfit said. "I wisht I had of been there," he said, hitting the ground with his fist. "It ain't right I wasn't there because if I had of been there I would of known. Listen lady," he said in a high voice, "if I had of been there I would of known and I wouldn't be like I am now." His voice seemed about to crack and the grandmother's head cleared for an instant. She saw the man's face twisted close to her own as if he were going to cry and she murmured, "Why you're one of my babies. You're one of my own children!" She reached out and touched him on the shoulder. The Misfit sprang back as if a snake had bitten him and shot her three times through the chest. Then he put his gun down on the ground and took off his glasses and began to clean them.

Hiram and Bobby Lee returned from the woods and stood over the ditch, looking down at the grandmother who half sat and half lay in a puddle of blood with her legs crossed under her like a child's and her face smiling up at the cloudless sky.

Without his glasses, The Misfit's eyes were red-rimmed and pale and defenseless-looking. "Take her off and thow her where you thown the others," he said, picking up the cat that was rubbing itself against his leg.

"She was a talker, wasn't she?" Bobby Lee said, sliding down the ditch with a yodel.

"She would of been a good woman," The Misfit said, "if it had been   140
somebody there to shoot her every minute of her life."

"Some fun!" Bobby Lee said.

"Shut up, Bobby Lee," The Misfit said. "It's no real pleasure in life."

QUESTIONS

1. The family members surrounding the grandmother are carefully portrayed. Discuss their characterizations and the way they affect our perceptions of the grandmother.

2. Some readers have found the grandmother sympathetic and others have found her a figure of evil, portrayed with imagery often associated with witches. How can these conflicting responses be resolved? Is she more or less sympathetic than the other members of her family?

3. What is the function of the scene at Red Sammy's barbecue place? How does it advance the plot? the theme?

4. During the conversation between the grandmother and Red Sammy, they discuss the difficulty of finding a "good man" in the modern world. Is this a plain statement of the theme, or does the context of their conversation make the dialogue ironic? How does their discussion relate to the larger dramatization of good and evil in the story?

5. The story makes extensive use of animal symbolism. Find the many references to animals and discuss the overall significance of this motif.

6. Analyze The Misfit's motivation for killing the family and for his criminal behavior in general. Unlike his sidekicks, he has a philosophical temperament and carefully rationalizes his behavior. What do his remarks contribute to the theme of the story?

7. Why do the murders of the grandmother's family members take place "off-stage," out in the woods? Could it be argued that this heightens the effect of the violence?

8. At the end of the story, what does The Misfit mean when he says of the grandmother, "She would of been a good woman . . . if it had been somebody there to shoot her every minute of her life" (paragraph 140)?

9. Reread the description of the grandmother after she has been murdered and is lying in the ditch (paragraph 137). Why is she described in this way?

10. In an essay, "A Reasonable Use of the Unreasonable," O'Connor argues that just before the grandmother's death "Her head clears for an instant and she realizes, even in her limited way, that she is responsible for the man before her and joined to him by ties of kinship. . . . And at this point she does the right thing, she makes the right gesture." Compare these comments with your own initial sense of the climactic scene. Does O'Connor's "reading" of this scene differ from your own? Does her commentary change your understanding of the story?

11. In the same essay, O'Connor argues that not only is The Misfit more intelligent than the grandmother but his "capacity for grace" is greater than hers. Do you agree with this remark? Why or why not?

Flannery O'Connor
Good Country People

Besides the neutral expression that she wore when she was alone, Mrs. Freeman had two others, forward and reverse, that she used for all her human dealings. Her forward expression was steady and driving like the advance of a heavy truck. Her eyes never swerved to left or right but turned as the story turned as if they followed a yellow line down the center of it. She seldom used the other expression because it was not often necessary for her to retract a statement, but when she did, her face came to a complete stop, there was an almost imperceptible movement of her black eyes, during which they seemed to be re-

GOOD COUNTRY PEOPLE   First published in 1955. See the note on "A Good Man Is Hard to Find" for information on O'Connor and her career.

ceding, and then the observer would see that Mrs. Freeman, though she might stand there as real as several grain sacks thrown on top of each other, was no longer there in spirit. As for getting anything across to her when this was the case, Mrs. Hopewell had given it up. She might talk her head off. Mrs. Freeman could never be brought to admit herself wrong on any point. She would stand there and if she could be brought to say anything, it was something like, "Well, I wouldn't of said it was and I wouldn't of said it wasn't," or letting her gaze range over the top kitchen shelf where there was an assortment of dusty bottles, she might remark, "I see you ain't ate many of them figs you put up last summer."

They carried on their most important business in the kitchen at breakfast. Every morning Mrs. Hopewell got up at seven o'clock and lit her gas heater and Joy's. Joy was her daughter, a large blonde girl who had an artificial leg. Mrs. Hopewell thought of her as a child though she was thirty-two years old and highly educated. Joy would get up while her mother was eating and lumber into the bathroom and slam the door, and before long, Mrs. Freeman would arrive at the back door. Joy would hear her mother call, "Come on in," and then they would talk for a while in low voices that were indistinguishable in the bathroom. By the time Joy came in, they had usually finished the weather report and were on one or the other of Mrs. Freeman's daughters, Glynese or Carramae, Joy called them Glycerin and Caramel. Glynese, a redhead, was eighteen and had many admirers; Carramae, a blonde, was only fifteen but already married and pregnant. She could not keep anything on her stomach. Every morning Mrs. Freeman told Mrs. Hopewell how many times she had vomited since the last report.

Mrs. Hopewell liked to tell people that Glynese and Carramae were two of the finest girls she knew and that Mrs. Freeman was a *lady* and that she was never ashamed to take her anywhere or introduce her to anybody they might meet. Then she would tell how she had happened to hire the Freemans in the first place and how they were a godsend to her and how she had had them four years. The reason for her keeping them so long was that they were not trash. They were good country people. She had telephoned the man whose name they had given as a reference and he had told her that Mr. Freeman was a good farmer but that his wife was the nosiest woman ever to walk the earth. "She's got to be into everything," the man said. "If she don't get there before the dust settles, you can bet she's dead, that's all. She'll want to know all your business. I can stand him real good," he had said, "but me nor my wife neither could have stood that woman one more minute on this place." That had put Mrs. Hopewell off for a few days.

She had hired them in the end because there were no other ap-
plicants but she had made up her mind beforehand exactly how she
would handle the woman. Since she was the type who had to be into
everything, then, Mrs. Hopewell had decided, she would not only let
her be into everything, she would *see to it* that she was into everything—she would give her the responsibility of everything, she would
put her in charge. Mrs. Hopewell had no bad qualities of her own but
she was able to use other people's in such a constructive way that she
never felt the lack. She had hired the Freemans and she had kept
them four years.

5   Nothing is perfect. This was one of Mrs. Hopewell's favorite sayings. Another was: that is life! And still another, the most important,
was: well, other people have their opinions too. She would make these
statements, usually at the table, in a tone of gentle insistence as if no
one held them but her, and the large hulking Joy, whose constant outrage had obliterated every expression from her face, would stare just a
little to the side of her, her eyes icy blue, with the look of someone who
has achieved blindness by an act of will and means to keep it.

When Mrs. Hopewell said to Mrs. Freeman that life was like that,
Mrs. Freeman would say, "I always said so myself." Nothing had been
arrived at by anyone that had not first been arrived at by her. She was
quicker than Mr. Freeman. When Mrs. Hopewell said to her after they
had been on the place a while, "You know, you're the wheel behind the
wheel," and winked, Mrs. Freeman had said, "I know it. I've always
been quick. It's some that are quicker than others."

"Everybody is different," Mrs. Hopewell said.

"Yes, most people is," Mrs. Freeman said.

"It takes all kinds to make the world."

10   "I always said it did myself."

The girl was used to this kind of dialogue for breakfast and more of
it for dinner; sometimes they had it for supper too. When they had no
guest they ate in the kitchen because that was easier. Mrs. Freeman always managed to arrive at some point during the meal and to watch
them finish it. She would stand in the doorway if it were summer but
in the winter she would stand with one elbow on top of the refrigerator and look down on them, or she would stand by the gas heater, lifting the back of her skirt slightly. Occasionally she would stand against
the wall and roll her head from side to side. At no time was she in any
hurry to leave. All this was very trying on Mrs. Hopewell but she was a
woman of great patience. She realized that nothing is perfect and that
in the Freemans she had good country people and that if, in this day
and age, you get good country people, you had better hang onto them.

She had had plenty of experience with trash. Before the Freemans she had averaged one tenant family a year. The wives of these farmers were not the kind you would want to be around you for very long. Mrs. Hopewell, who had divorced her husband long ago, needed someone to walk over the fields with her; and when Joy had to be impressed for these services, her remarks were usually so ugly and her face so glum that Mrs. Hopewell would say, "If you can't come pleasantly, I don't want you at all," to which the girl, standing square and rigid-shouldered with her neck thrust slightly forward, would reply, "If you want me, here I am—LIKE I AM."

Mrs. Hopewell excused this attitude because of the leg (which had been shot off in a hunting accident when Joy was ten). It was hard for Mrs. Hopewell to realize that her child was thirty-two now and that for more than twenty years she had had only one leg. She thought of her still as a child because it tore her heart to think instead of the poor stout girl in her thirties who had never danced a step or had any *normal* good times. Her name was really Joy but as soon as she was twenty-one and away from home, she had had it legally changed. Mrs. Hopewell was certain that she had thought and thought until she had hit upon the ugliest name in any language. Then she had gone and had the beautiful name, Joy, changed without telling her mother until after she had done it. Her legal name was Hulga.

When Mrs. Hopewell thought the name, Hulga, she thought of the broad blank hull of a battleship. She would not use it. She continued to call her Joy to which the girl responded but in a purely mechanical way.

Hulga had learned to tolerate Mrs. Freeman who saved her from taking walks with her mother. Even Glynese and Carramae were useful when they occupied attention that might otherwise have been directed at her. At first she had thought she could not stand Mrs. Freeman for she had found that it was not possible to be rude to her. Mrs. Freeman would take on strange resentments and for days together she would be sullen but the source of her displeasure was always obscure; a direct attack, a positive leer, blatant ugliness to her face—these never touched her. And without warning one day, she began calling her Hulga.

She did not call her that in front of Mrs. Hopewell who would have been incensed but when she and the girl happened to be out of the house together, she would say something and add the name Hulga to the end of it, and the big spectacled Joy-Hulga would scowl and redden as if her privacy had been intruded upon. She considered the name her personal affair. She had arrived at it first purely on the basis of its ugly sound and then the full genius of its fitness had struck her. She had a vision of the name working like the ugly sweating Vulcan who stayed

15

in the furnace and to whom, presumably, the goddess had to come when called. She saw it as the name of her highest creative act. One of her major triumphs was that her mother had not been able to turn her dust into Joy, but the greater one was that she had been able to turn it herself into Hulga. However, Mrs. Freeman's relish for using the name only irritated her. It was as if Mrs. Freeman's beady steel-pointed eyes had penetrated far enough behind her face to reach some secret fact. Something about her seemed to fascinate Mrs. Freeman and then one day Hulga realized that it was the artificial leg. Mrs. Freeman had a special fondness for the details of secret infections, hidden deformities, assaults upon children. Of diseases, she preferred the lingering or incurable. Hulga had heard Mrs. Hopewell give her the details of the hunting accident, how the leg had been literally blasted off, how she had never lost consciousness. Mrs. Freeman could listen to it any time as if it had happened an hour ago.

When Hulga stumped into the kitchen in the morning (she could walk without making the awful noise but she made it—Mrs. Hopewell was certain—because it was ugly-sounding), she glanced at them and did not speak. Mrs. Hopewell would be in her red kimono with her hair tied around her head in rags. She would be sitting at the table, finishing her breakfast and Mrs. Freeman would be hanging by her elbow outward from the refrigerator, looking down at the table. Hulga always put her eggs on the stove to boil and then stood over them with her arms folded, and Mrs. Hopewell would look at her—a kind of indirect gaze divided between her and Mrs. Freeman—and would think that if she would only keep herself up a little, she wouldn't be so bad looking. There was nothing wrong with her face that a pleasant expression wouldn't help. Mrs. Hopewell said that people who looked on the bright side of things would be beautiful even if they were not.

Whenever she looked at Joy this way, she could not help but feel that it would have been better if the child had not taken the Ph.D. It had certainly not brought her out any and now that she had it, there was no more excuse for her to go to school again. Mrs. Hopewell thought it was nice for girls to go to school to have a good time but Joy had "gone through." Anyhow, she would not have been strong enough to go again. The doctors had told Mrs. Hopewell that with the best of care, Joy might see forty-five. She had a weak heart. Joy had made it plain that if it had not been for this condition, she would be far from these red hills and good country people. She would be in a university lecturing to people who knew what she was talking about. And Mrs. Hopewell could very well picture her there, looking like a scarecrow and lecturing to more of the same. Here she went about all day in a six-year-old skirt and a yellow sweat shirt with a faded cowboy on a horse embossed on it. She thought this was funny; Mrs. Hopewell thought it was idiotic and showed simply that she was still a child. She was brilliant but she didn't have a grain of sense. It seemed to Mrs. Hopewell that every year she grew less like other people and more like herself—bloated, rude, and squint-eyed. And she said such strange things! To her own mother she had said—without warning, without excuse, standing up in the middle of a meal with her face purple and her mouth half full—"Woman! Do you ever look inside? Do you ever look inside and see what you are *not*? God!" she had cried sinking down again and staring at her plate, "Male-branche was right: we are not our own light. We are not our own light!" Mrs. Hopewell had no idea to this day what brought that on. She had only made the remark, hoping Joy would take it in, that a smile never hurt anyone.

The girl had taken the Ph.D. in philosophy and this left Mrs. Hopewell at a complete loss. You could say, "My daughter is a nurse," or "My daughter is a schoolteacher," or even, "My daughter is a chemical engineer." You could not say, "My daughter is a philosopher." That was something that had ended with the Greeks and Romans. All day Joy sat on her neck in a deep chair, reading. Sometimes she went for walks but she didn't like dogs or cats or birds or flowers or nature or nice young men. She looked at nice young men as if she could smell their stupidity.

One day Mrs. Hopewell had picked up one of the books the girl had just put down and opening it at random, she read, "Science, on the other hand, has to assert its soberness and seriousness afresh and declare that it is concerned solely with what-is. Nothing—how can it be for science anything but a horror and a phantasm? If science is right, then one thing stands firm: science wishes to know nothing of Nothing. Such is after all the strictly scientific approach to Nothing. We know it by wishing to know nothing of Nothing." These words had been underlined with a blue pencil and they worked on Mrs. Hopewell like some evil incantation in gibberish. She shut the book quickly and went out of the room as if she were having a chill. 20

This morning when the girl came in, Mrs. Freeman was on Carramae. "She thrown up four times after supper," she said, "and was up twict in the night after three o'clock. Yesterday she didn't do nothing but ramble in the bureau drawer. All she did. Stand up there and see what she could run up on."

"She's got to eat," Mrs. Hopewell muttered, sipping her coffee, while she watched Joy's back at the stove. She was wondering what the child had said to the Bible salesman. She could not imagine what kind of a conversation she could possibly have had with him.

He was a tall gaunt hatless youth who had called yesterday to sell them a Bible. He had appeared at the door, carrying a large black suitcase that weighted him so heavily on one side that he had to brace himself against the door facing. He seemed on the point of collapse but he said in a cheerful voice. "Good morning, Mrs. Cedars!" and set the suitcase down on the mat. He was not a bad-looking young man though he had on a bright blue suit and yellow socks that were not pulled up far enough. He had prominent face bones and a streak of sticky-looking brown hair falling across his forehead.

"I'm Mrs. Hopewell," she said.

25   "Oh!" he said, pretending to look puzzled but with his eyes sparkling, "I saw it said 'The Cedars' on the mailbox so I thought you was Mrs. Cedars!" and he burst out in a pleasant laugh. He picked up the satchel and under cover of a pant, he fell forward into her hall. It was rather as if the suitcase had moved first, jerking him after it. "Mrs. Hopewell!" he said and grabbed her hand. "I hope you are well!" and he laughed again and then all at once his face sobered completely. He paused and gave her a straight earnest look and said, "Lady, I've come to speak of serious things."

"Well, come in," she muttered, none too pleased because her dinner was almost ready. He came into the parlor and sat down on the edge of a straight chair and put the suitcase between his feet and glanced around the room as if he were sizing her up by it. Her silver gleamed on the two sideboards; she decided he had never been in a room as elegant as this.

"Mrs. Hopewell," he began, using her name in a way that sounded almost intimate, "I know you believe in Chrustian service."

"Well yes," she murmured.

"I know," he said and paused, looking very wise with his head cocked on one side, "that you're a good woman. Friends have told me."

30   Mrs. Hopewell never liked to be taken for a fool. "What are you selling?" she asked.

"Bibles," the young man said and his eye raced around the room before he added, "I see you have no family Bible in your parlor, I see that is the one lack you got!"

Mrs. Hopewell could not say, "My daughter is an atheist and won't let me keep the Bible in the parlor." She said, stiffening slightly, "I keep my Bible by my bedside." This was not the truth. It was in the attic somewhere.

"Lady," he said, "the word of God ought to be in the parlor."

"Well, I think that's a matter of taste," she began. "I think . . ."

35   "Lady," he said, "for a Chrustian, the word of God ought to be in every room in the house besides in his heart. I know you're a Chrustian because I can see it in every line of your face."

She stood up and said, "Well, young man, I don't want to buy a Bible and I smell my dinner burning."

He didn't get up. He began to twist his hands and looking down at them, he said softly, "Well lady, I'll tell you the truth—not many people want to buy one nowadays and besides, I know I'm real simple. I don't know how to say a thing but to say it. I'm just a country boy." He glanced up into her unfriendly face. "People like you don't like to fool with country people like me!"

"Why!" she cried, "good country people are the salt of the earth! Besides, we all have different ways of doing, it takes all kinds to make the world go 'round. That's life!"

"You said a mouthful," he said.

"Why, I think there aren't enough good country people in the   40
world!" she said, stirred. "I think that's what's wrong with it!"

His face had brightened. "I didn't intraduce myself," he said. "I'm Manley Pointer from out in the country around Willohobie, not even from a place, just from near a place."

"You wait a minute," she said. "I have to see about my dinner." She went out to the kitchen and found Joy standing near the door where she had been listening.

"Get rid of the salt of the earth," she said, "and let's eat."

Mrs. Hopewell gave her a pained look and turned the heat down under the vegetables. "*I* can't be rude to anybody," she murmured and went back into the parlor.

He had opened the suitcase and was sitting with a Bible on each   45
knee.

"You might as well put those up," she told him. "I don't want one."

"I appreciate your honesty," he said. "You don't see any more real honest people unless you go way out in the country."

"I know," she said, "real genuine folks!" Through the crack in the door she heard a groan.

"I guess a lot of boys come telling you they're working their way through college," he said, "but I'm not going to tell you that. Somehow," he said, "I don't want to go to college. I want to devote my life to Chrustian service. See," he said, lowering his voice, "I got this heart condition. I may not live long. When you know it's something wrong with you and you may not live long, well then, lady . . ." He paused, with his mouth open, and stared at her.

He and Joy had the same condition! She knew that her eyes were   50
filling with tears but she collected herself quickly and murmured, "Won't you stay for dinner? We'd love to have you!" and was sorry the instant she heard herself say it.

"Yes mam," he said in an abashed voice, "I would sher love to do that!"

Joy had given him one look on being introduced to him and then throughout the meal had not glanced at him again. He had addressed several remarks to her, which she had pretended not to hear. Mrs. Hopewell could not understand deliberate rudeness, although she lived with it, and she felt she had always to overflow with hospitality to make up for Joy's lack of courtesy. She urged him to talk about himself and he did. He said he was the seventh child of twelve and that his father had been crushed under a tree when he himself was eight year old. He had been crushed very badly, in fact, almost cut in two and was practically not recognizable. His mother had got along the best she could by hard working and she had always seen that her children went to Sunday School and that they read the Bible every evening. He was now nineteen year old and he had been selling Bibles for four months. In that time he had sold seventy-seven Bibles and had the promise of two more sales. He wanted to become a missionary because he thought that was the way you could do most for people. "He who losest his life shall find it," he said simply and he was so sincere, so genuine and earnest that Mrs. Hopewell would not for the world have smiled. He prevented his peas from sliding onto the table by blocking them with a piece of bread which he later cleaned his plate with. She could see Joy observing sidewise how he handled his knife and fork and she saw too that every few minutes, the boy would dart a keen appraising glance at the girl as if he were trying to attract her attention.

After dinner Joy cleared the dishes off the table and disappeared and Mrs. Hopewell was left to talk with him. He told her again about his childhood and his father's accident and about various things that had happened to him. Every five minutes or so she would stifle a yawn. He sat for two hours until finally she told him she must go because she had an appointment in town. He packed his Bibles and thanked her and prepared to leave, but in the doorway he stopped and wrung her hand and said that not on any of his trips had he met a lady as nice as her and he asked if he could come again. She had said she would always be happy to see him.

Joy had been standing in the road, apparently looking at something in the distance, when he came down the steps toward her, bent to the side with his heavy valise. He stopped where she was standing and confronted her directly. Mrs. Hopewell could not hear what he said but she trembled to think what Joy would say to him. She could see that after a minute Joy said something and that then the boy began to speak again, making an excited gesture with his free hand. After a minute Joy said something else at which the boy began to speak once more. Then to her amazement, Mrs. Hopewell saw the two of them walk off together, toward the gate. Joy had walked all the way to the gate with him and Mrs. Hopewell could not imagine what they had said to each other, and she had not yet dared to ask.

Mrs. Freeman was insisting upon her attention. She had moved   55
from the refrigerator to the heater so that Mrs. Hopewell had to turn and face her in order to seem to be listening. "Glynese gone out with Harvey Hill again last night," she said. "She had this sty."

"Hill," Mrs. Hopewell said absently, "is that the one who works in the garage?"

"Nome, he's the one that goes to chiropracter school," Mrs. Freeman said. "She had this sty. Been had it two days. So she says when he brought her in the other night he says, 'Lemme get rid of that sty for you,' and she says, 'How?' and he says, 'You just lay yourself down acrost the seat of that car and I'll show you.' So she done it and he popped her neck. Kept on a-popping it several times until she made him quit. This morning," Mrs. Freeman said, "she ain't got no sty. She ain't got no traces of a sty."

"I never heard of that before," Mrs. Hopewell said.

"He ast her to marry him before the Ordinary," Mrs. Freeman went on, "and she told him she wan't going to be married in no *office*."

"Well, Glynese is a fine girl," Mrs. Hopewell said. "Glynese and   60
Carramae are both fine girls."

"Carramae said when her and Lyman was married Lyman said it sure felt sacred to him. She said he said he wouldn't take five hundred dollars for being married by a preacher."

"How much would he take?" the girl asked from the stove.

"He said he wouldn't take five hundred dollars," Mrs. Freeman repeated.

"Well we all have work to do," Mrs. Hopewell said.

"Lyman said it just felt more sacred to him," Mrs. Freeman said.   65
"The doctor wants Carramae to eat prunes. Says instead of medicine. Says them cramps is coming from pressure. You know where I think it is?"

"She'll be better in a few weeks," Mrs. Hopewell said.

"In the tube," Mrs. Freeman said. "Else she wouldn't be as sick as she is."

Hulga had cracked her two eggs into a saucer and was bringing them to the table along with a cup of coffee that she had filled too full. She sat down carefully and began to eat, meaning to keep Mrs. Freeman there by questions if for any reason she showed an inclination to leave. She could perceive her mother's eye on her. The first round-about question would be about the Bible salesman and she did not wish to bring it on. "How did he pop her neck?" she asked.

Mrs. Freeman went into a description of how he had popped her neck. She said he owned a '55 Mercury but that Glynese said she would rather marry a man with only a '36 Plymouth who would be married by a preacher. The girl asked what if he had a '32 Plymouth and Mrs. Freeman said what Glynese had said was a '36 Plymouth.

70   Mrs. Hopewell said there were not many girls with Glynese's common sense. She said what she admired in those girls was their common sense. She said that reminded her that they had had a nice visitor yesterday, a young man selling Bibles. "Lord," she said, "he bored me to death but he was so sincere and genuine I couldn't be rude to him. He was just good country people, you know," she said, "—just the salt of the earth."

"I seen him walk up," Mrs. Freeman said, "and then later—I seen him walk off," and Hulga could feel the slight shift in her voice, the slight insinuation, that he had not walked off alone, had he? Her face remained expressionless but the color rose into her neck and she seemed to swallow it down with the next spoonful of egg. Mrs. Freeman was looking at her as if they had a secret together.

"Well, it takes all kinds of people to make the world go 'round," Mrs. Hopewell said. "It's very good we aren't all alike."

"Some people are more alike than others," Mrs. Freeman said.

Hulga got up and stumped, with about twice the noise that was necessary, into her room and locked the door. She was to meet the Bible salesman at ten o'clock at the gate. She had thought about it half the night. She had started thinking of it as a great joke and then she had begun to see profound implications in it. She had lain in bed imagining dialogues for them that were insane on the surface but that reached below to depths that no Bible salesman would be aware of. Their conversation yesterday had been of this kind.

75   He had stopped in front of her and had simply stood there. His face was bony and sweaty and bright, with a little pointed nose in the center of it, and his look was different from what it had been at the dinner table. He was gazing at her with open curiosity, with fascination, like a child watching a new fantastic animal at the zoo, and he was breathing as if he had run a great distance to reach her. His gaze seemed somehow familiar but she could not think where she had been regarded with it before. For almost a minute he didn't say anything. Then on what seemed an insuck of breath, he whispered, "You ever ate a chicken that was two days old?"

The girl looked at him stonily. He might have just put this question up for consideration at the meeting of a philosophical association. "Yes," she presently replied as if she had considered it from all angles.

"It must have been mighty small!" he said triumphantly and shook all over with little nervous giggles, getting very red in the face, and subsiding finally into his gaze of complete admiration, while the girl's expression remained exactly the same.

"How old are you?" he asked softly.

She waited some time before she answered. Then in a flat voice she said, "Seventeen."

His smiles came in succession like waves breaking on the surface of a little lake. "I see you got a wooden leg," he said. "I think you're brave. I think you're real sweet."

The girl stood blank and solid and silent.

"Walk to the gate with me," he said. "You're a brave sweet little thing and I liked you the minute I seen you walk in the door."

Hulga began to move forward.

"What's your name?" he asked, smiling down on the top of her head.

"Hulga," she said.

"Hulga," he murmured, "Hulga. Hulga. I never heard of anybody name Hulga before. You're shy, aren't you, Hulga?" he asked.

She nodded, watching his large red hand on the handle of the giant valise.

"I like girls that wear glasses," he said. "I think a lot. I'm not like these people that a serious thought don't ever enter their heads. It's because I may die."

"I may die too," she said suddenly and looked up at him. His eyes were very small and brown, glittering feverishly.

"Listen," he said, "don't you think some people was meant to meet on account of what all they got in common and all? Like they both think serious thoughts and all?" He shifted the valise to his other hand so that the hand nearest her was free. He caught hold of her elbow and shook it a little. "I don't work on Saturday," he said. "I like to walk in the woods and see what Mother Nature is wearing. O'er the hills and far away. Pic-nics and things. Couldn't we go on a pic-nic tomorrow? Say yes, Hulga," he said and gave her a dying look as if he felt his insides about to drop out of him. He had even seemed to sway slightly toward her.

During the night she had imagined that she seduced him. She imagined that the two of them walked on the place until they came to the storage barn beyond the two back fields and there, she imagined, that things came to such a pass that she very easily seduced him and that

80

85

90

then, of course, she had to reckon with his remorse. True genius can get an idea across even to an inferior mind. She imagined that she took his remorse in hand and changed it into a deeper understanding of life. She took all his shame away and turned it into something useful.

She set off for the gate at exactly ten o'clock, escaping without drawing Mrs. Hopewell's attention. She didn't take anything to eat, forgetting that food is usually taken on a picnic. She wore a pair of slacks and a dirty white shirt, and as an afterthought, she had put some Vapex on the collar of it since she did not own any perfume. When she reached the gate no one was there.

She looked up and down the empty highway and had the furious feeling that she had been tricked, that he had only meant to make her walk to the gate after the idea of him. Then suddenly he stood up, very tall, from behind a bush on the opposite embankment. Smiling, he lifted his hat which was new and wide-brimmed. He had not worn it yesterday and she wondered if he had bought it for the occasion. It was toast-colored with a red and white band around it and was slightly too large for him. He stepped from behind the bush still carrying the black valise. He had on the same suit and the same yellow socks sucked down in his shoes from walking. He crossed the highway and said, "I knew you'd come!"

The girl wondered acidly how he had known this. She pointed to the valise and asked, "Why did you bring your Bibles?"

95   He took her elbow, smiling down on her as if he could not stop. "You can never tell when you'll need the word of God, Hulga," he said. She had a moment in which she doubted that this was actually happening and then they began to climb the embankment. They went down into the pasture toward the woods. The boy walked lightly by her side, bouncing on his toes. The valise did not seem to be heavy today; he even swung it. They crossed half the pasture without saying anything and then, putting his hand easily on the small of her back, he asked softly, "Where does your wooden leg join on?"

She turned an ugly red and glared at him and for an instant the boy looked abashed. "I didn't mean you no harm," he said. "I only meant you're so brave and all. I guess God takes care of you."

"No," she said, looking forward and walking fast, "I don't even believe in God."

At this he stopped and whistled. "No!" he exclaimed as if he were too astonished to say anything else.

She walked on and in a second he was bouncing at her side, fanning with his hat. "That's very unusual for a girl," he remarked, watching her out of the corner of his eye. When they reached the edge of the wood, he put his hand on her back again and drew her against him without a word and kissed her heavily.

The kiss, which had more pressure than feeling behind it, produced   100
that extra surge of adrenalin in the girl that enables one to carry a packed trunk out of a burning house, but in her, the power went at once to the brain. Even before he released her, her mind, clear and detached and ironic anyway, was regarding him from a great distance, with amusement but with pity. She had never been kissed before and she was pleased to discover that it was an unexceptional experience and all a matter of the mind's control. Some people might enjoy drain water if they were told it was vodka. When the boy, looking expectant but uncertain, pushed her gently away, she turned and walked on, saying nothing as if such business, for her, were common enough.

He came along panting at her side, trying to help her when he saw a root that she might trip over. He caught and held back the long swaying blades of thorn vine until she had passed beyond them. She led the way and he came breathing heavily behind her. Then they came out on a sunlit hillside, sloping softly into another one a little smaller. Beyond, they could see the rusted top of the old barn where the extra hay was stored.

The hill was sprinkled with small pink weeds. "Then you ain't saved?" he asked suddenly, stopping.

The girl smiled. It was the first time she had smiled at him at all. "In my economy," she said, "I'm saved and you are damned but I told you I didn't believe in God."

Nothing seemed to destroy the boy's look of admiration. He gazed at her now as if the fantastic animal at the zoo had put its paw through the bars and given him a loving poke. She thought he looked as if he wanted to kiss her again and she walked on before he had the chance.

"Ain't there somewheres we can sit down sometime?" he mur-   105
mured, his voice softening toward the end of the sentence.

"In that barn," she said.

They made for it rapidly as if it might slide away like a train. It was a large two-story barn, cool and dark inside. The boy pointed up the ladder that led into the loft and said, "It's too bad we can't go up there."

"Why can't we?" she asked.

"Yer leg," he said reverently.

The girl gave him a contemptuous look and putting both hands on   110
the ladder, she climbed it while he stood below, apparently awestruck. She pulled herself expertly through the opening and then looked down at him and said, "Well, come on if you're coming," and he began to climb the ladder, awkwardly bringing the suitcase with him.

"We won't need the Bible," she observed.

"You never can tell," he said, panting. After he had got into the loft, he was a few seconds catching his breath. She had sat down in a pile of straw. A wide sheath of sunlight, filled with dust particles, slanted over her. She lay back against a bale, her face turned away, looking out the front opening of the barn where hay was thrown from a wagon into the loft. The two pink-speckled hillsides lay back against a dark ridge of woods. The sky was cloudless and cold blue. The boy dropped down by her side and put one arm under her and the other over her and began methodically kissing her face, making little noises like a fish. He did not remove his hat but it was pushed far enough back not to interfere. When her glasses got in his way, he took them off of her and slipped them into his pocket.

The girl at first did not return any of the kisses but presently she began to and after she had put several on his cheek, she reached his lips and remained there, kissing him again and again as if she were trying to draw all the breath out of him. His breath was clear and sweet like a child's and the kisses were sticky like a child's. He mumbled about loving her and about knowing when he first seen her that he loved her, but the mumbling was like the sleepy fretting of a child being put to sleep by his mother. Her mind, throughout this, never stopped or lost itself for a second to her feelings. "You ain't said you loved me none," he whispered finally, pulling back from her. "You got to say that."

She looked away from him off into the hollow sky and then down at a black ridge and then down farther into what appeared to be two green swelling lakes. She didn't realize he had taken her glasses but this landscape could not seem exceptional to her for she seldom paid any close attention to her surroundings.

115   "You got to say it," he repeated. "You got to say you love me."

She was always careful how she committed herself. "In a sense," she began, "if you use the word loosely, you might say that. But it's not a word I use. I don't have illusions. I'm one of those people who see *through* to nothing."

The boy was frowning. "You got to say it. I said it and you got to say it," he said.

The girl looked at him almost tenderly. "You poor baby," she murmured. "It's just as well you don't understand," and she pulled him by the neck, face-down, against her. "We are all damned," she said, "but some of us have taken off our blindfolds and see that there's nothing to see. It's a kind of salvation."

The boy's astonished eyes looked blankly through the ends of her hair. "Okay," he almost whined, "but do you love me or don'tcher?"

"Yes," she said and added, "in a sense. But I must tell you some-   120
thing. There mustn't be anything dishonest between us." She lifted his
head and looked him in the eye. "I am thirty years old," she said. "I
have a number of degrees."

The boy's look was irritated but dogged. "I don't care," he said. "I
don't care a thing about what all you done. I just want to know if you
love me or don'tcher?" and he caught her to him and wildly planted her
face with kisses until she said, "Yes, yes."

"Okay then," he said, letting her go. "Prove it."

She smiled, looking dreamily out on the shifty landscape. She had
seduced him without even making up her mind to try. "How?" she
asked, feeling that he should be delayed a little.

He leaned over and put his lips to her ear. "Show me where your
wooden leg joins on," he whispered.

The girl uttered a sharp little cry and her face instantly drained of   125
color. The obscenity of the suggestion was not what shocked her. As a
child she had sometimes been subject to feelings of shame but education had removed the last traces of that as a good surgeon scrapes for
cancer; she would no more have felt it over what he was asking than
she would have believed in his Bible. But she was as sensitive about the
artificial leg as a peacock about his tail. No one ever touched it but her.
She took care of it as someone else would his soul, in private and almost with her own eyes turned away. "No," she said.

"I known it," he muttered, sitting up. "You're just playing me for a
sucker."

"Oh no no!" she cried. "It joins on at the knee. Only at the knee.
Why do you want to see it?"

The boy gave her a long penetrating look. "Because," he said, "it's
what makes you different. You ain't like anybody else."

She sat staring at him. There was nothing about her face or her
round freezing-blue eyes to indicate that this had moved her; but she felt
as if her heart had stopped and left her mind to pump her blood. She decided that for the first time in her life she was face to face with real innocence. This boy, with an instinct that came from beyond wisdom, had
touched the truth about her. When after a minute, she said in a hoarse
high voice, "All right," it was like surrendering to him completely. It was
like losing her own life and finding it again, miraculously, in his.

Very gently he began to roll the slack leg up. The artificial limb, in   130
a white sock and brown flat shoe, was bound in a heavy material like
canvas and ended in an ugly jointure where it was attached to the
stump. The boy's face and his voice were entirely reverent as he uncovered it and said, "Now show me how to take it off and on."

She took it off for him and put it back on again and then he took it off himself, handling it as tenderly as if it were a real one. "See!" he said with a delighted child's face. "Now I can do it myself!"

"Put it back on," she said. She was thinking that she would run away with him and that every night he would take the leg off and every morning put it back on again. "Put it back on," she said.

"Not yet," he murmured, setting it on its foot out of her reach. "Leave it off for a while. You got me instead."

She gave a little cry of alarm but he pushed her down and began to kiss her again. Without the leg she felt entirely dependent on him. Her brain seemed to have stopped thinking altogether and to be about some other function that it was not very good at. Different expressions raced back and forth over her face. Every now and then the boy, his eyes like two steel spikes, would glance behind him where the leg stood. Finally she pushed him off and said, "Put it back on me now."

135   "Wait," he said. He leaned the other way and pulled the valise toward him and opened it. It had a pale blue spotted lining and there were only two Bibles in it. He took one of these out and opened the cover of it. It was hollow and contained a pocket flask of whiskey, a pack of cards, and a small blue box with printing on it. He laid these out in front of her one at a time in an evenly-spaced row, like one presenting offerings at the shrine of a goddess. He put the blue box in her hand. THIS PRODUCT TO BE USED ONLY FOR THE PREVENTION OF DISEASE, she read, and dropped it. The boy was unscrewing the top of the flask. He stopped and pointed, with a smile, to the deck of cards. It was not an ordinary deck but one with an obscene picture on the back of each card. "Take a swig," he said, offering her the bottle first. He held it in front of her, but like one mesmerized, she did not move.

Her voice when she spoke had an almost pleading sound. "Aren't you," she murmured, "aren't you just good country people?"

The boy cocked his head. He looked as if he were just beginning to understand that she might be trying to insult him. "Yeah," he said, curling his lip slightly, "but it ain't held me back none. I'm as good as you any day in the week."

"Give me my leg," she said.

He pushed it farther away with his foot. "Come on now, let's begin to have us a good time," he said coaxingly. "We ain't got to know one another good yet."

140   "Give me my leg!" she screamed and tried to lunge for it but he pushed her down easily.

"What's the matter with you all of a sudden?" he asked, frowning as he screwed the top on the flask and put it quickly back inside the Bible. "You just a while ago said you didn't believe in nothing. I thought you was some girl!"

Her face was almost purple. "You're a Christian!" she hissed. "You're a fine Christian! You're just like them all—say one thing and do another. You're a perfect Christian, you're . . ."

The boy's mouth was set angrily. "I hope you don't think," he said in a lofty indignant tone, "that I believe in that crap! I may sell Bibles but I know which end is up and I wasn't born yesterday and I know where I'm going!"

"Give me my leg!" she screeched. He jumped up so quickly that she barely saw him sweep the cards and the blue box into the Bible and throw the Bible into the valise. She saw him grab the leg and then she saw it for an instant slanted forlornly across the inside of the suitcase with a Bible at either side of its opposite ends. He slammed the lid shut and snatched up the valise and swung it down the hole and then stepped through himself.

When all of him had passed but his head, he turned and regarded her with a look that no longer had any admiration in it. "I've gotten a lot of interesting things," he said. "One time I got a woman's glass eye this way. And you needn't to think you'll catch me because Pointer ain't really my name. I use a different name at every house I call at and don't stay nowhere long. And I'll tell you another thing, Hulga," he said, using the name as if he didn't think much of it, "you ain't so smart. I been believing in nothing ever since I was born!" and then the toast-colored hat disappeared down the hole and the girl was left, sitting on the straw in the dusty sunlight. When she turned her churning face toward the opening, she saw his blue figure struggling successfully over the green speckled lake.

Mrs. Hopewell and Mrs. Freeman, who were in the back pasture, digging up onions, saw him emerge a little later from the woods and head across the meadow toward the highway. "Why, that looks like that nice dull young man that tried to sell me a Bible yesterday," Mrs. Hopewell said, squinting. "He must have been selling them to the Negroes back in there. He was so simple," he said, "but I guess the world would be better off if we were all that simple."

Mrs. Freeman's gaze drove forward and just touched him before he disappeared under the hill. Then she returned her attention to the evil-smelling onion shoot she was lifting from the ground. "Some can't be that simple," she said. "I know I never could."

145

QUESTIONS

1. Consider the use of irony in this story. What different types of irony does O'Connor employ?
2. The story features a "frame narrative" involving a minor character, Mrs. Freeman. How does this structure relate to the meaning? What does Mrs. Freeman add to the story?
3. Discuss the use of name symbolism. How do the names Mrs. Hopewell, Mrs. Freeman, Joy/Hulga, and Manley Pointer relate to their respective characterizations?
4. Why does Joy/Hulga take an interest in the Bible salesman? What does she hope to gain by interacting with him?
5. How would you describe the relationship between Joy/Hulga and her mother? Do you think the relationship will change after the story's conclusion?
6. What is the symbolic meaning of Joy/Hulga's wooden leg? How does her own view of it differ from the reader's as the story proceeds?
7. How is Mrs. Hopewell characterized? Is she a sympathetic character? Does the reader's view of her change during the story?
8. Does Joy/Hulga experience an epiphany by the end of the story? Why is her face described as "churning" in the final scene? Do you think she will undergo any permanent change?

Flannery O'Connor

Greenleaf

Mrs. May's bedroom window was low and faced on the east and the bull, silvered in the moonlight, stood under it, his head raised as if he listened—like some patient god come down to woo her—for a stir inside the room. The window was dark and the sound of her breathing too light to be carried outside. Clouds crossing the moon blackened him and in the dark he began to tear at the hedge. Presently they passed and he appeared again in the same spot, chewing steadily, with a hedge-wreath that he had ripped loose for himself caught in the tips of his horns. When the moon drifted into retirement again, there was nothing to mark his place but the sound of steady chewing. Then abruptly a pink glow filled the window. Bars of light slid across him as the venetian blind was slit. He took a step backward and lowered his head as if to show the wreath across his horns.

For almost a minute there was no sound from inside, then as he raised his crowned head again, a woman's voice, guttural as if addressed

GREENLEAF   First published in 1956. See the note on "A Good Man Is Hard to Find" for information on O'Connor and her career.

to a dog, said, "Get away from here, Sir!" and in a second muttered, "Some nigger's scrub bull."

The animal pawed the ground and Mrs. May, standing bent forward behind the blind, closed it quickly lest the light make him charge into the shrubbery. For a second she waited, still bent forward, her nightgown hanging loosely from her narrow shoulders. Green rubber curlers sprouted neatly over her forehead and her face beneath them was smooth as concrete with an egg-white paste that drew the wrinkles out while she slept.

She had been conscious in her sleep of a steady rhythmic chewing as if something were eating one wall of the house. She had been aware that whatever it was had been eating as long as she had the place and had eaten everything from the beginning of her fence line up to the house and now was eating the house and calmly with the same steady rhythm would continue through the house, eating her and the boys, and then on, eating everything but the Greenleafs, on and on, eating everything until nothing was left but the Greenleafs on a little island all their own in the middle of what had been her place. When the munching reached her elbow, she jumped up and found herself, fully awake, standing in the middle of her room. She identified the sound at once: a cow was tearing at the shrubbery under the window. Mr. Greenleaf had left the lane gate open and she didn't doubt that the entire herd was on her lawn. She turned on the dim pink table lamp and then went to the window and slit the blind. The bull, gaunt and long-legged, was standing about four feet from her, chewing calmly like an uncouth country suitor.

For fifteen years, she thought as she squinted at him fiercely, 5 she had been having shiftless people's hogs root up her oats, their mules wallow on her lawn, their scrub bulls breed her cows. If this one was not put up now, he would be over the fence, ruining her herd before morning—and Mr. Greenleaf was soundly sleeping a half mile down the road in the tenant house. There was no way to get him unless she dressed and got in her car and rode down there and woke him up. He would come but his expression, his whole figure, his every pause, would say: "Hit looks to me like one or both of them boys would not make their maw ride out in the middle of the night thisaway. If hit was my boys, they would have got the bull up theirself."

The bull lowered his head and shook it and the wreath slipped down to the base of his horns where it looked like a menacing prickly crown. She had closed the blind then; in a few seconds she heard him move off heavily.

Mr. Greenleaf would say, "If hit was my boys they would never have allowed their maw to go after the hired help in the middle of the night. They would have did it theirself."

Weighing it, she decided not to bother Mr. Greenleaf. She returned to bed thinking that if the Greenleaf boys had risen in the world it was because she had given their father employment when no one else would have him. She had had Mr. Greenleaf fifteen years but no one else would have had him five minutes. Just the way he approached an object was enough to tell anybody with eyes what kind of a worker he was. He walked with a high-shouldered creep and he never appeared to come directly forward. He walked on the perimeter of some invisible circle and if you wanted to look him in the face, you had to move and get in front of him. She had not fired him because she had always doubted she could do better. He was too shiftless to go out and look for another job; he didn't have the initiative to steal, and after she had told him three or four times to do a thing, he did it; but he never told her about a sick cow until it was too late to call the veterinarian and if her barn had caught fire, he would have called his wife to see the flames before he began to put them out. And of the wife, she didn't even like to think. Beside the wife, Mr. Greenleaf was an aristocrat.

"If hit had been my boys," he would have said, "they would have cut off their right arm before they would have allowed their maw to . . ."

10   "If your boys had any pride, Mr. Greenleaf," she would like to say to him some day, "there are many things that they would not *allow* their mother to do."

The next morning as soon as Mr. Greenleaf came to the back door, she told him there was a stray bull on the place and that she wanted him penned up at once.

"Done already been here three days," he said, addressing his right foot which he held forward, turned slightly as if he were trying to look at the sole. He was standing at the bottom of the three back steps while she leaned out the kitchen door, a small woman with pale near-sighted eyes and grey hair that rose on top like the crest of some disturbed bird.

"Three days!" she said in the restrained screech that had become habitual with her.

Mr. Greenleaf, looking into the distance over the near pasture, removed a package of cigarets from his shirt pocket and let one fall into his hand. He put the package back and stood for a while looking at the cigaret. "I put him in the bull pen but he torn out of there," he said presently. "I didn't see him none after that." He bent over the cigaret and lit it and then turned his head briefly in her direction. The upper part of his face sloped gradually into the lower which was long and narrow, shaped like a rough chalice. He had deep-set fox-colored eyes shadowed under a grey felt hat that he wore slanted forward following the line of his nose. His build was insignificant.

"Mr. Greenleaf," she said, "get the bull up this morning before you   15
do anything else. You know he'll ruin the breeding schedule. Get him up and keep him up and the next time there's a stray bull on this place, tell me at once. Do you understand?"

"Where do you want him put at?" Mr. Greenleaf asked.

"I don't care where you put him," she said. "You are supposed to have some sense. Put him where he can't get out. Whose bull is he?"

For a moment Mr. Greenleaf seemed to hesitate between silence and speech. He studied the air to the left of him. "He must be somebody's bull," he said after a while.

"Yes, he must!" she said and shut the door with a precise little slam.

She went into the dining room where the two boys were eating   20
breakfast and sat down on the edge of her chair at the head of the table. She never ate breakfast but she sat with them to see that they had what they wanted. "Honestly!" she said, and began to tell about the bull, aping Mr. Greenleaf saying, "It must be *somebody's* bull."

Wesley continued to read the newspaper folded beside his plate but Scofield interrupted his eating from time to time to look at her and laugh. The two boys never had the same reaction to anything. They were as different, she said, as night and day. The only thing they did have in common was neither of them cared what happened on the place. Scofield was a business type and Wesley was an intellectual.

Wesley, the younger child, had had rheumatic fever when he was seven and Mrs. May thought that this was what had caused him to be an intellectual. Scofield, who had never had a day's sickness in his life, was an insurance salesman. She would not have minded his selling insurance if he had sold a nicer kind but he sold the kind that only Negroes buy. He was what Negroes call a "policy man." He said there was more money in nigger-insurance than any other kind, and before company, he was very loud about it. He would shout, "Mama don't like to hear me say it but I'm the best nigger-insurance salesman in this county!"

Scofield was thirty-six and he had a broad pleasant face but he was not married. "Yes," Mrs. May would say, "and if you sold decent insurance, some *nice* girl would be willing to marry you. What nice girl wants to marry a nigger-insurance man? You'll wake up some day and it'll be too late."

And at this Scofield would yodel and say, "Why Mamma, I'm not going to marry until you're dead and gone and then I'm going to marry me some nice fat girl that can take over this place!" And once he had added, "—some nice lady like Mrs. Greenleaf." When he had said this Mrs. May had risen from her chair, her back stiff as a rake handle, and had gone to her room. There she had sat down on the edge of her bed for some time with her small face drawn. Finally she had whispered, "I work and slave, I struggle and sweat to keep this place for them and as soon as I'm dead, they'll marry trash and bring it in here and ruin everything. They'll marry trash and ruin everything I've done," and she had made up her mind at that moment to change her will. The next day she had gone to her lawyer and had had the property entailed so that if they married, they could not leave it to their wives.

25   The idea that one of them might marry a woman even remotely like Mrs. Greenleaf was enough to make her ill. She had put up with Mr. Greenleaf for fifteen years, but the only way she had endured his wife had been by keeping entirely out of her sight. Mrs. Greenleaf was large and loose. The yard around her house looked like a dump and her five girls were always filthy; even the youngest one dipped snuff. Instead of making a garden or washing their clothes, her preoccupation was what she called "prayer healing."

Every day she cut all the morbid stories out of the newspaper—the accounts of women who had been raped and criminals who had escaped and children who had been burned and of train wrecks and plane crashes and the divorces of movie stars. She took these to the woods and dug a hole and buried them and then she fell on the ground over them and mumbled and groaned for an hour or so, moving her huge arms back and forth under her and out again and finally just lying down flat and, Mrs. May suspected, going to sleep in the dirt.

She had not found out about this until the Greenleafs had been with her a few months. One morning she had been out to inspect a field that she wanted planted in rye but that had come up in clover because Mr. Greenleaf had used the wrong seeds in the grain drill. She was returning through a wooded path that separated two pastures, muttering to herself and hitting the ground methodically with a long stick she carried in case she saw a snake. "Mr. Greenleaf," she was saying in a low voice, "I cannot afford to pay for your mistakes. I am a poor woman and this place is all I have. I have two boys to educate. I cannot . . ."

Out of nowhere a guttural agonized voice groaned, "Jesus! Jesus!" In a second it came again with a terrible urgency. "Jesus! Jesus!"

Mrs. May stopped still, one hand lifted to her throat. The sound was so piercing that she felt as if some violent unleashed force had broken out of the ground and was charging toward her. Her second thought was more reasonable: somebody had been hurt on the place and would sue her for everything she had. She had no insurance. She rushed forward and turning a bend in the path, she saw Mrs. Greenleaf sprawled on her hands and knees off the side of the road, her head down.

"Mrs. Greenleaf!" she shrilled, "what's happened?"   30

Mrs. Greenleaf raised her head. Her face was a patchwork of dirt and tears and her small eyes, the color of two field peas, were red-rimmed and swollen, but her expression was as composed as a bulldog's. She swayed back and forth on her hands and knees and groaned, "Jesus, Jesus."

Mrs. May winced. She thought the word, Jesus, should be kept inside the church building like other words inside the bedroom. She was a good Christian woman with a large respect for religion, though she did not, of course, believe any of it was true. "What is the matter with you?" she asked sharply.

"You broke my healing," Mrs. Greenleaf said, waving her aside. "I can't talk to you until I finish."

Mrs. May stood, bent forward, her mouth open and her stick raised off the ground as if she were not sure what she wanted to strike with it.

"Oh, Jesus, stab me in the heart!" Mrs. Greenleaf shrieked. "Jesus,   35 stab me in the heart!" and she fell back flat in the dirt, a huge human mound, her legs and arms spread out as if she were trying to wrap them around the earth.

Mrs. May felt as furious and helpless as if she had been insulted by a child. "Jesus," she said, drawing herself back, "would be *ashamed* of you. He would tell you to get up from there this instant and go wash your children's clothes!" and she had turned and walked off as fast as she could.

Whenever she thought of how the Greenleaf boys had advanced in the world, she had only to think of Mrs. Greenleaf sprawled obscenely on the ground, and say to herself, "Well, no matter how far they go, they *came* from that."

She would like to have been able to put in her will that when she died, Wesley and Scofield were not to continue to employ Mr. Greenleaf. She was capable of handling Mr. Greenleaf; they were not. Mr. Greenleaf had pointed out to her once that her boys didn't know hay from silage. She had pointed out to him that they had other talents, that Scofield was a successful businessman and Wesley a successful intellectual. Mr. Greenleaf did not comment, but he never lost an opportunity of letting her see, by his expression or some simple gesture, that he held the two of them in infinite contempt. As scrub-human as the Greenleafs were, he never hesitated to let her know that in any like circumstance in which his own boys might have been involved, they—O. T. and E. T. Greenleaf—would have acted to better advantage.

The Greenleaf boys were two or three years younger than the May boys. They were twins and you never knew when you spoke to one of them whether you were speaking to O. T. or E. T., and they never had the politeness to enlighten you. They were long-legged and raw-boned and red-skinned, with bright grasping fox-colored eyes like their father's. Mr. Greenleaf's pride in them began with the fact that they were twins. He acted, Mrs. May said, as if this were something smart they had thought of themselves. They were energetic and hard-working and she would admit to anyone that they had come a long way—and that the Second World War was responsible for it.

40   They had both joined the service and, disguised in their uniforms, they could not be told from other people's children. You could tell, of course, when they opened their mouths but they did that seldom. The smartest thing they had done was to get sent overseas and there to marry French wives. They hadn't married French trash either. They had married nice girls who naturally couldn't tell that they murdered the king's English or that the Greenleafs were who they were.

Wesley's heart condition had not permitted him to serve his country but Scofield had been in the army for two years. He had not cared for it and at the end of his military service, he was only a Private First Class. The Greenleaf boys were both some kind of sergeants, and Mr. Greenleaf, in those days, had never lost an opportunity of referring to them by their rank. They had both managed to get wounded and now they both had pensions. Further, as soon as they were released from the army, they took advantage of all the benefits and went to the school of agriculture at the university—the taxpayers meanwhile supporting their French wives. The two of them were living now about two miles down the highway on a piece of land that the government had helped them to buy and in a brick duplex bungalow that the government had helped to build and pay for. If the war had made anyone, Mrs. May said, it had made the Greenleaf boys. They each had three little children apiece, who spoke Greenleaf English and French, and who, on account of their mothers' background, would be sent to the convent school and brought up with manners. "And in twenty years," Mrs. May asked Scofield and Wesley, "do you know what those people will be?

"*Society*," she said blackly.

She had spent fifteen years coping with Mr. Greenleaf and, by now, handling him had become second nature with her. His disposition on any particular day was as much a factor in what she could and couldn't do as the weather was, and she had learned to read his face the way real country people read the sunrise and sunset.

She was a country woman only by persuasion. The late Mr. May, a businessman, had bought the place when land was down, and when he died it was all he had to leave her. The boys had not been happy to move to the country to a broken-down farm, but there was nothing else for her to do. She had the timber on the place cut and with the proceeds had set herself up in the dairy business after Mr. Greenleaf had answered her ad. "i seen yor add and i will come have 2 boys," was all his letter said, but he arrived the next day in a pieced-together truck, his wife and five daughters sitting on the floor in the back, himself and the two boys in the cab.

Over the years they had been on her place, Mr. and Mrs. Greenleaf   45 had aged hardly at all. They had no worries, no responsibilities. They lived like the lilies of the field, off the fat that she struggled to put into the land. When she was dead and gone from overwork and worry, the Greenleafs, healthy and thriving, would be just ready to begin draining Scofield and Wesley.

Wesley said the reason Mrs. Greenleaf had not aged was because she released all her emotions in prayer healing. "You ought to start praying, Sweetheart," he had said in the voice that, poor boy, he could not help making deliberately nasty.

Scofield only exasperated her beyond endurance but Wesley caused her real anxiety. He was thin and nervous and bald and being an intellectual was a terrible strain on his disposition. She doubted if he would marry until she died but she was certain that then the wrong woman would get him. Nice girls didn't like Scofield but Wesley didn't like nice girls. He didn't like anything. He drove twenty miles every day to the university where he taught and twenty miles back every night, but he said he hated the twenty-mile drive and he hated the second-rate university and he hated the morons who attended it. He hated the country and he hated the life he lived; he hated living with his mother and his idiot brother and he hated hearing about the damn dairy and the damn help and the damn broken machinery. But in spite of all he said, he never made any move to leave. He talked about Paris and Rome but he never went even to Atlanta.

"You'd go to those places and you'd get sick," Mrs. May would say. "Who in Paris is going to see that you get a salt-free diet? And do you think if you married one of those odd numbers you take out that *she* would cook a salt-free diet for you? No indeed, she would not!" When she took this line, Wesley would turn himself roughly around in his chair and ignore her. Once when she had kept it up too long, he had snarled, "Well, why don't you do something practical, Woman? Why don't you pray for me like Mrs. Greenleaf would?"

"I don't like to hear you boys make jokes about religion," she had said. "If you would go to church, you would meet some nice girls."

50   But it was impossible to tell them anything. When she looked at the two of them now, sitting on either side of the table, neither one caring the least if a stray bull ruined her herd—which was their herd, their future—when she looked at the two of them, one hunched over a paper and the other teetering back in his chair, grinning at her like an idiot, she wanted to jump up and beat her fist on the table and shout, "You'll find out one of these days, you'll find out what *Reality* is when it's too late!"

"Mamma," Scofield said, "don't you get excited now but I'll tell you whose bull that is." He was looking at her wickedly. He let his chair drop forward and he got up. Then with his shoulders bent and his hands held up to cover his head, he tiptoed to the door. He backed into the hall and pulled the door almost to so that it hid all of him but his face. "You want to know, Sugar-pie?" he asked.

Mrs. May sat looking at him coldly.

"That's O. T. and E. T.'s bull," he said. "I collected from their nigger yesterday and he told me they were missing it," and he showed her an exaggerated expanse of teeth and disappeared silently.

Wesley looked up and laughed.

55   Mrs. May turned her head forward again, her expression unaltered. "I am the only *adult* on this place," she said. She leaned across the table and pulled the paper from the side of his plate. "Do you see how it's going to be when I die and you boys have to handle him?" she began. "Do you see why he didn't know whose bull that was? Because it was theirs. Do you see what I have to put up with? Do you see that if I hadn't kept my foot on his neck all these years, you boys might be milking cows every morning at four o'clock?"

Wesley pulled the paper back toward his plate and staring at her full in the face, he murmured, "I wouldn't milk a cow to save your soul from hell."

"I know you wouldn't," she said in a brittle voice. She sat back and began rapidly turning her knife over at the side of her plate. "O. T. and E. T. are fine boys," she said. "They ought to have been my sons." The thought of this was so horrible that her vision of Wesley was blurred at once by a wall of tears. All she saw was his dark shape, rising quickly from the table. "And you two," she cried, "you two should have belonged to that woman!"

He was heading for the door.

"When I die," she said in a thin voice, "I don't know what's going to become of you."

"You're always yapping about when-you-die," he growled as he rushed out, "but you look pretty healthy to me." 60

For some time she sat where she was, looking straight ahead through the window across the room into a scene of indistinct grays and greens. She stretched her face and her neck muscles and drew in a long breath but the scene in front of her flowed together anyway into a watery gray mass. "They needn't think I'm going to die any time soon," she muttered, and some more defiant voice in her added: I'll die when I get good and ready.

She wiped her eyes with the table napkin and got up and went to the window and gazed at the scene in front of her. The cows were grazing on two pale green pastures across the road and behind them, fencing them in, was a black wall of trees with a sharp sawtooth edge that held off the indifferent sky. The pastures were enough to calm her. When she looked out any window in her house, she saw the reflection of her own character. Her city friends said she was the most remarkable woman they knew, to go, practically penniless and with no experience, out to a rundown farm and make a success of it. "Everything is against you," she would say, "the weather is against you and the dirt is against you and the help is against you. They're all in league against you. There's nothing for it but an iron hand!"

"Look at Mamma's iron hand!" Scofield would yell and grab her arm and hold it up so that her delicate blue-veined little hand would dangle from her wrist like the head of a broken lily. The company always laughed.

The sun, moving over the black and white grazing cows, was just a little brighter than the rest of the sky. Looking down, she saw a darker shape that might have been its shadow cast at an angle, moving among them. She uttered a sharp cry and turned and marched out of the house.

Mr. Greenleaf was in the trench silo, filling a wheelbarrow. She stood on the edge and looked down at him. "I told you to get up that bull. Now he's in with the milk herd." 65

"You can't do two thangs at oncet," Mr. Greenleaf remarked.

"I told you to do that first."

He wheeled the barrow out of the open end of the trench toward the barn and she followed close behind him. "And you needn't think, Mr. Greenleaf," she said, "that I don't know exactly whose bull that is or why you haven't been in any hurry to notify me he was here. I might as well feed O. T. and E. T.'s bull as long as I'm going to have him here ruining my herd."

Mr. Greenleaf paused with the wheelbarrow and looked behind him. "Is that them boys' bull?" he asked in an incredulous tone.

70   She did not say a word. She merely looked away with her mouth taut.

"They told me their bull was out but I never known that was him," he said.

"I want that bull put up now," she said, "and I'm going to drive over to O. T. and E. T.'s and tell them they'll have to have to come get him today. I ought to charge for the time he's been here—then it wouldn't happen again."

"They didn't pay but seventy-five dollars for him," Mr. Greenleaf offered.

"I wouldn't have had him as a gift," she said.

75   "They was just going to beef him," Mr. Greenleaf went on, "but he got loose and run his head into their pickup truck. He don't like cars and trucks. They had a time getting his horn out the fender and when they finally got him loose, he took off and they was too tired to run after him—but I never known that was him there."

"It wouldn't have paid you to know, Mr. Greenleaf," she said. "But you know now. Get a horse and get him."

In a half hour, from her front window she saw the bull, squirrel-colored, with jutting hips and long light horns, ambling down the dirt road that ran in front of the house. Mr. Greenleaf was behind him on the horse. "That's a Greenleaf bull if I ever saw one," she muttered. She went out on the porch and called, "Put him where he can't get out."

"He likes to bust loose," Mr. Greenleaf said, looking with approval at the bull's rump. "This gentleman is a sport."

"If those boys don't come for him, he's going to be a dead sport," she said. "I'm just warning you."

80   He heard her but he didn't answer.

"That's the awfullest looking bull I ever saw," she called but he was too far down the road to hear.

It was mid-morning when she turned into O. T. and E. T.'s driveway. The house, a new red-brick, low-to-the-ground building that looked like a warehouse with windows, was on top of a treeless hill. The sun was beating down directly on the white roof of it. It was the kind of house that everybody built now and nothing marked it as belonging to Greenleafs except three dogs, part hound and part spitz, that rushed out from behind it as soon as she stopped her car. She reminded herself that you could always tell the class of people by the class of dog, and honked her horn. While she sat waiting for someone to come, she continued to study the house. All the windows were down and she wondered if the government could have air-conditioned the thing. No one came and she honked again. Presently a door opened and several children appeared in it and stood looking at her, making no move to come forward. She recognized this as a true Greenleaf trait—they could hang in the door, looking at you for hours.

"Can't one of you children come here?" she called.

After a minute they all began to move forward, slowly. They had on overalls and were barefooted but they were not as dirty as she might have expected. There were two or three that looked distinctly like Greenleafs; the others not so much so. The smallest child was a girl with untidy black hair. They stopped about six feet from the automobile and stood looking at her.

"You're mighty pretty," Mrs. May said, addressing herself to the   85
smallest girl.

There was no answer. They appeared to share one dispassionate expression between them.

"Where's your Mamma?" she asked.

There was no answer to this for some time. Then one of them said something in French. Mrs. May did not speak French.

"Where's your daddy?" she asked.

After a while, one of the boys said, "He ain't hyar neither."   90

"Ahhhh," Mrs. May said as if something had been proven. "Where's the colored man?"

She waited and decided no one was going to answer. "The cat has six little tongues," she said. "How would you like to come home with me and let me teach you how to talk?" She laughed and her laugh died on the silent air. She felt as if she were on trial for her life, facing a jury of Greenleafs. "I'll go down and see if I can find the colored man," she said.

"You can go if you want to," one of the boys said.

"Well, thank you," she murmured and drove off.

The barn was down the lane from the house. She had not seen it   95
before but Mr. Greenleaf had described it in detail for it had been built according to the latest specifications. It was a milking parlor arrangement where the cows are milked from below. The milk ran in pipes from the machines to the milk house and was never carried in no bucket, Mr. Greenleaf said, by no human hand. "When you gonter get you one?" he had asked.

"Mr. Greenleaf," she had said, "I have to do for myself. I am not assisted hand and foot by the government. It would cost me $20,000 to install a milking parlor. I barely make ends meet as it is."

"My boys done it," Mr. Greenleaf had murmured and then—"but all boys ain't alike."

"No indeed!" she had said. "I thank God for that!"

"I thank Gawd for ever-thang," Mr. Greenleaf had drawled.

100   You might as well, she had thought in the fierce silence that followed; you've never done anything for yourself.

She stopped by the side of the barn and honked but no one appeared. For several minutes she sat in the car, observing the various machines parked around, wondering how many of them were paid for. They had a forage harvester and a rotary hay baler. She had those too. She decided that since no one was here, she would get out and have a look at the milking parlor and see if they kept it clean.

She opened the milking room door and stuck her head in and for the first second she felt as if she were going to lose her breath. The spotless white concrete room was filled with sunlight that came from a row of windows head-high along both walls. The metal stanchions gleamed ferociously and she had to squint to be able to look at all. She drew her head out the room quickly and closed the door and leaned against it, frowning. The light outside was not so bright but she was conscious that the sun was directly on top of her head, like a silver bullet ready to drop into her brain.

A Negro carrying a yellow calf-feed bucket appeared from around the corner of the machine shed and came toward her. He was a light yellow boy dressed in the cast-off army clothes of the Greenleaf twins. He stopped at a respectable distance and set the bucket on the ground.

"Where's Mr. O. T. and Mr. E. T.?" she asked.

105   "Mist O. T. he in town, Mist E. T. he off yonder in the field," the Negro said, pointing first to the left and then to the right as if he were naming the position of two planets.

"Can you remember a message?" she asked, looking as if she thought this doubtful.

"I'll remember it if I don't forget it," he said with a touch of sullenness.

"Well, I'll write it down then," she said. She got in her car and took a stub of pencil from her pocket book and began to write on the back of an empty envelope. The Negro came and stood at the window. "I'm Mrs. May," she said as she wrote. "Their bull is on my place and I want him off *today*. You can tell them I'm furious about it."

"That bull lef here Sareday," the Negro said, "and none of us ain't seen him since. We ain't knowed where he was."

110   "Well, you know now," she said, "and you can tell Mr. O. T. and Mr. E. T. that if they don't come get him today, I'm going to have their

daddy shoot him the first thing in the morning. I can't have that bull ruining my herd." She handed him the note.

"If I knows Mist O. T. and Mist E. T.," he said, taking it, "they goin to say go ahead on and shoot him. He done busted up one of our trucks already and we be glad to see the last of him."

She pulled her head back and gave him a look from slightly bleared eyes. "Do they expect me to take my time and my worker to shoot their bull?" she asked. "They don't want him so they just let him loose and expect somebody else to kill him? He's eating my oats and ruining my herd and I'm expected to shoot him too?"

"I speck you is," he said softly. "He done busted up . . ."

She gave him a very sharp look and said, "Well, I'm not surprised. That's just the way some people are," and after a second she asked, "Which is boss, Mr. O. T. or Mr. E. T. ?" She had always suspected that they fought between themselves secretly.

"They never quarls," the boy said. "They like one man in two skins."   115

"Hmp. I expect you just never heard them quarrel."

"Nor nobody else heard them neither," he said, looking away as if this insolence were addressed to someone else.

"Well," she said, "I haven't put up with their father for fifteen years not to know a few things about Greenleafs."

The Negro looked at her suddenly with a gleam of recognition. "Is you my policy man's mother?" he asked.

"I don't know who your policy man is," she said sharply. "You give   120
them that note and tell them if they don't come for that bull today, they'll be making their father shoot it tomorrow," and she drove off.

She stayed at home all afternoon waiting for the Greenleaf twins to come for the bull. They did not come. I might as well be working for them, she thought furiously. They are simply going to use me to the limit. At the supper table, she went over it again for the boys' benefit because she wanted them to see exactly what O. T. and E. T. would do. "They don't want that bull," she said, "—pass the butter—so they simply turn him loose and let somebody else worry about getting rid of him for them. How do you like that? I'm the victim. I've always been the victim."

"Pass the butter to the victim," Wesley said. He was in a worse humor than usual because he had had a flat tire on the way home from the university.

Scofield handed her the butter and said, "Why, Mamma, ain't you ashamed to shoot an old bull that ain't done nothing but give you a little scrub strain in your herd? I declare," he said, "with the Mamma I got it's a wonder I turned out to be such a nice boy!"

"You ain't her boy, Son," Wesley said.

125   She eased back in her chair, her fingertips on the edge of the table. "All I know is," Scofield said, "I done mighty well to be as nice as I am seeing what I come from."

When they teased her they spoke Greenleaf English but Wesley made his own particular tone come through it like a knife edge. "Well lemme tell you one thang, Brother," he said, leaning over the table, "that if you had half a mind you would already know."

"What's that, Brother?" Scofield asked, his broad face grinning into the thin constricted one across from him.

"That is," Wesley said, "that neither you nor me is her boy. . . . ," but he stopped abruptly as she gave a kind of hoarse wheeze like an old horse lashed unexpectedly. She reared up and ran from the room.

130   "Oh, for God's sake," Wesley growled, "what did you start her off for?"

"I never started her off," Scofield said. "You started her off."

"Hah."

"She's not as young as she used to be and she can't take it."

"She can only give it out," Wesley said. "I'm the one that takes it."

135   His brother's pleasant face had changed so that an ugly family resemblance showed between them. "Nobody feels sorry for a lousy bastard like you," he said and grabbed across the table for the other's shirtfront.

From her room she heard a crash of dishes and she rushed back through the kitchen into the dining room. The hall door was open and Scofield was going out of it. Wesley was lying like a large bug on his back with the edge of the over-turned table cutting him across the middle and broken dishes scattered on top of him. She pulled the table off him and caught his arm to help him rise but he scrambled up and pushed her off with a furious charge of energy and flung himself out the door after his brother.

She would have collapsed but a knock on the door stiffened her and she swung around. Across the kitchen and back porch, she could see Mr. Greenleaf peering eagerly through the screenwire. All her resources returned in full strength as if she had only needed to be challenged by the devil himself to regain them. "I heard a thump," he called, "and I thought the plastering might have fell on you."

If he had been wanted someone would have had to go on a horse to find him. She crossed the kitchen and the porch and stood inside the screen and said, "No, nothing happened but the table turned over. One of the legs was weak," and without pausing, "the boys didn't come for the bull so tomorrow you'll have to shoot him."

The sky was crossed with thin red and purple bars and behind them the sun was moving down slowly as if it were descending a ladder.

Mr. Greenleaf squatted down on the step, his back to her, the top of his hat on a level with her feet. "Tomorrow I'll drive him home for you," he said.

"Oh no, Mr. Greenleaf," she said in a mocking voice, "you drive him home tomorrow and next week he'll be back here. I know better than that." Then in a mournful tone, she said, "I'm surprised at O. T. and E. T. to treat me this way. I thought they'd have more gratitude. Those boys spent some mighty happy days on this place, didn't they, Mr. Greenleaf?"

Mr. Greenleaf didn't say anything.

"I think they did," she said. "I think they did. But they've forgotten all the nice little things I did for them now. If I recall, they wore my boys' old clothes and played with my boys' old toys and hunted with my boys' old guns. They swam in my pond and shot my birds and fished in my stream and I never forgot their birthday and Christmas seemed to roll around very often if I remember it right. And do they think of any of those things now?" she asked. "NOOOOO," she said.

For a few seconds she looked at the disappearing sun and Mr. Greenleaf examined the palms of his hands. Presently as if it had just occurred to her, she asked, "Do you know the real reason they didn't come for that bull?"

"Naw I don't," Mr. Greenleaf said in a surly voice.

"They didn't come because I'm a woman," she said. "You can get away with anything when you're dealing with a woman. If there were a man running this place . . ."

Quick as a snake striking Mr. Greenleaf said, "You got two boys. They know you got two men on the place."

The sun had disappeared behind the tree line. She looked down at the dark crafty face, upturned now, and at the wary eyes, bright under the shadow of the hatbrim. She waited long enough for him to see that she was hurt and then she said, "Some people learn gratitude too late, Mr. Greenleaf, and some never learn it at all," and she turned and left him sitting on the steps.

Half the night in her sleep she heard a sound as if some large stone were grinding a hole on the outside wall of her brain. She was walking on the inside, over a succession of beautiful rolling hills, planting her stick in front of each step. She became aware after a time that the noise was the sun trying to burn through the tree line and she stopped to watch, safe in the knowledge that it couldn't, that it had to sink the way it always did outside of her property. When she first stopped it was a swollen red ball, but as she stood watching it began to narrow and pale

140

145

until it looked like a bullet. Then suddenly it burst through the tree line and raced down the hill toward her. She woke up with her hand over her mouth and the same noise, diminished but distinct, in her ear. It was the bull munching under her window. Mr. Greenleaf had let him out.

She got up and made her way to the window in the dark and looked out through the slit blind, but the bull had moved away from the hedge and at first she didn't see him. Then she saw a heavy form some distance away, paused as if observing her. This is the last night I am going to put up with this, she said, and watched until the iron shadow moved away in the darkness.

150   The next morning she waited until exactly eleven o'clock. Then she got in her car and drove to the barn. Mr. Greenleaf was cleaning milk cans. He had seven of them standing up outside the milk room to get the sun. She had been telling him to do this for two weeks. "All right, Mr. Greenleaf," she said, "go get your gun. We're going to shoot that bull."

"I thought you wanted theseyer cans . . ."

"Go get your gun, Mr. Greenleaf," she said. Her voice and face were expressionless.

"That gentleman torn out of there last night," he murmured in a tone of regret and bent again to the can he had his arm in.

"Go get your gun, Mr. Greenleaf," she said in the same triumphant toneless voice. "The bull is in the pasture with the dry cows. I saw him from my upstairs window. I'm going to drive you up to the field and you can run him into the empty pasture and shoot him there."

155   He detached himself from the can slowly. "Ain't nobody ever ast me to shoot my boys' own bull!" he said in a high rasping voice. He removed a rag from his back pocket and began to wipe his hands violently, then his nose.

She turned as if she had not heard this and said, "I'll wait for you in the car. Go get your gun."

She sat in the car and watched him stalk off toward the harness room where he kept a gun. After he had entered the room, there was a crash as if he had kicked something out of his way. Presently he emerged again with the gun, circled behind the car, opened the door violently and threw himself onto the seat beside her. He held the gun between his knees and looked straight ahead. He'd like to shoot me instead of the bull, she thought, and turned her face away so that he could not see her smile.

The morning was dry and clear. She drove through the woods for a quarter of a mile and then out into the open where there were fields on either side of the narrow road. The exhilaration of carrying her point had sharpened her senses. Birds were screaming everywhere, the grass was almost too bright to look at, the sky was an even piercing blue. "Spring is here!" she said gaily. Mr. Greenleaf lifted one muscle somewhere near his mouth as if he found this the most asinine remark ever made. When she stopped at the second pasture gate, he flung himself out of the car door and slammed it behind him. Then he opened the gate and she drove through. He closed it and flung himself back in, silently, and she drove around the rim of the pasture until she spotted the bull, almost in the center of it, grazing peacefully among the cows.

"The gentleman is waiting on you," she said and gave Mr. Greenleaf's furious profile a sly look. "Run him into that next pasture and when you get him in, I'll drive in behind you and shut the gate myself."

He flung himself out again, this time deliberately leaving the car door open so that she had to lean across the seat and close it. She sat smiling as she watched him make his way across the pasture toward the opposite gate. He seemed to throw himself forward at each step and then pull back as if he were calling on some power to witness that he was being forced. "Well," she said aloud as if he were still in the car, "it's your own boys who are making you do this, Mr. Greenleaf." O. T. and E. T. were probably splitting their sides laughing at him now. She could hear their identical nasal voices saying, "Made Daddy shoot our bull for us. Daddy don't know no better than to think that's a fine bull he's shooting. Gonna kill Daddy to shoot that bull!"

"If those boys cared a thing about you, Mr. Greenleaf," she said, "they would have come for that bull. I'm surprised at them."

He was circling around to open the gate first. The bull, dark among the spotted cows, had not moved. He kept his head down, eating constantly. Mr. Greenleaf opened the gate and then began circling back to approach him from the rear. When he was about ten feet behind him, he flapped his arms at his sides. The bull lifted his head indolently and then lowered it again and continued to eat. Mr. Greenleaf stooped again and picked up something and threw it at him with a vicious swing. She decided it was a sharp rock for the bull leapt and then began to gallop until he disappeared over the rim of the hill. Mr. Greenleaf followed at his leisure.

"You needn't think you're going to lose him!" she cried and started the car straight across the pasture. She had to drive slowly over the terraces and when she reached the gate, Mr. Greenleaf and the bull were nowhere in sight. This pasture was smaller than the last, a green arena, encircled almost entirely by woods. She got out and closed the gate and stood looking for some sign of Mr. Greenleaf but he had disappeared completely. She knew at once that his plan was to lose the bull in the

160

woods. Eventually, she would see him emerge somewhere from the circle of trees and come limping toward her and when he finally reached her, he would say, "If you can find that gentleman in them woods, you're better than me."

She was going to say, "Mr. Greenleaf, if I have to walk into those woods with you and stay all afternoon, we are going to find that bull and shoot him. You are going to shoot him if I have to pull the trigger for you." When he saw she meant business, he would return and shoot the bull quickly himself.

165   She got back into the car and drove to the center of the pasture where he would not have so far to walk to reach her when he came out of the woods. At this moment she could picture him sitting on a stump, making lines in the ground with a stick. She decided she would wait exactly ten minutes by her watch. Then she would begin to honk. She got out of the car and walked around a little and then sat down on the front bumper to wait and rest. She was very tired and she lay her head back against the hood and closed her eyes. She did not understand why she should be so tired when it was only mid-morning. Through her closed eyes, she could feel the sun, red-hot overhead. She opened her eyes slightly but the white light forced her to close them again.

For some time she lay back against the hood, wondering drowsily why she was so tired. With her eyes closed, she didn't think of time as divided into days and nights but into past and future. She decided she was tired because she had been working continuously for fifteen years. She decided she had every right to be tired, and to rest for a few minutes before she began working again. Before any kind of judgment seat, she would be able to say: I've worked, I have not wallowed. At this very instant while she was recalling a lifetime of work, Mr. Greenleaf was loitering in the woods and Mrs. Greenleaf was probably flat on the ground, asleep over her holeful of clippings. The woman had got worse over the years and Mrs. May believed that now she was actually demented. "I'm afraid your wife has let religion warp her," she said once tactfully to Mr. Greenleaf. "Everything in moderation, you know."

"She cured a man oncet that half his gut was eat out with worms," Mr. Greenleaf said, and she had turned away, half-sickened. Poor souls, she thought now, so simple. For a few seconds she dozed.

When she sat up and looked at her watch, more than ten minutes had passed. She had not heard any shot. A new thought occurred to her; suppose Mr. Greenleaf had aroused the bull chunking stones at him and the animal had turned on him and run him up against a tree and gored him? The irony of it deepened: O. T. and E. T. would then get a shyster lawyer and sue her. It would be the fitting end to her fifteen years with the Greenleafs. She thought of it almost with pleasure as if she had hit on the perfect ending for a story she was telling her friends. Then she dropped it, for Mr. Greenleaf had a gun with him and she had insurance.

She decided to honk. She got up and reached inside the car window and gave three sustained honks and two or three shorter ones to let him know she was getting impatient. Then she went back and sat down on the bumper again.

In a few minutes something emerged from the tree line, a black heavy shadow that tossed its head several times and then bounded forward. After a second she saw it was the bull. He was crossing the pasture toward her at a slow gallop, a gay almost rocking gait as if he were overjoyed to find her again. She looked beyond him to see if Mr. Greenleaf was coming out of the woods too but he was not. "Here he is, Mr. Greenleaf!" she called and looked on the other side of the pasture to see if he could be coming out there but he was not in sight. She looked back and saw that the bull, his head lowered, was racing toward her. She remained perfectly still, not in fright, but in a freezing disbelief. She stared at the violent black streak bounding toward her as if she had no sense of distance, as if she could not decide at once what his intention was, and the bull had buried his head in her lap, like a wild tormented lover, before her expression changed. One of his horns sank until it pierced her heart and the other curved around her side and held her in an unbreakable grip. She continued to stare straight ahead but the entire scene in front of her had changed—the tree line was a dark wound in a world that was nothing but sky—and she had the look of a person whose sight has been suddenly restored but who finds the light unbearable.

Mr. Greenleaf was running toward her from the side with his gun raised and she saw him coming though she was not looking in his direction. She saw him approaching on the outside of some invisible circle, the tree line gaping behind him and nothing under his feet. He shot the bull four times through the eye. She did not hear the shots but she felt the quake in the huge body as it sank, pulling her forward on its head, so that she seemed, when Mr. Greenleaf reached her, to be bent over whispering some last discovery into the animal's ear.

170

QUESTIONS

1. The characters and events of the story are almost entirely reflected through Mrs. May's mind. How objective are her evaluations? How far are they reliable testimony and how far only an index of her own mind?

2. What is Mrs. May's mental image of herself? How does it compare with the image her sons have of her? How does it compare with the reader's image?

3. What is Mrs. May's dominant emotion? What is the consuming preoccupation of her mind? Are there any occasions on which she feels joy? What are they?

4. Describe the behavior of Mrs. May and Greenleaf toward each other. Why does Mrs. May keep Greenleaf on when she despises him so?

5. The two families—the Mays and the Greenleafs—are obviously contrasted. Describe this contrast as fully as possible, considering especially the following: (a) their social and economic status—past, present, and future; (b) their religious attitudes; (c) the attitudes of Mrs. May and Greenleaf respectively toward their children; (d) Wesley and Scofield versus O. T. and E. T. What are the reasons for Mrs. May's feelings toward the Greenleafs?

6. The turning point of the story comes when Mrs. May commands Greenleaf to get his gun. What emotional reversal takes place at this point? What are Mrs. May's motivations in having the bull shot?

7. "[S]uppose [thinks Mrs. May in paragraph 168] Mr. Greenleaf had aroused the bull chunking stones at him and the animal had turned on him and run him up against a tree and gored him? . . . She thought of it almost with pleasure as if she had hit on the perfect ending for a story she was telling her friends." From what perspective is the actual ending of the story a perfect ending? Is the ending of the story purely chance, or is there a sense in which Mrs. May has brought this on herself?

8. What symbolic implications, if any, have the following: (a) the name Greenleaf; (b) the bull; (c) the sun; (d) Mrs. May's two dreams (paragraphs 4 and 148); and (e) the name May? How important is symbolism to the final effect of the story?

9. What kinds of irony predominate in the story? Identify examples of each of the three kinds of irony. How important is irony to the final effect of the story?

SUGGESTIONS FOR WRITING

The following are suggestions for essays on the featured authors. Use of secondary sources, widely available for both authors, should assist you in developing your ideas.

1. Compare the characterizations of Joy/Hulga in "Good Country People" and Eveline in "Eveline." In what ways are they typical women of their era? How do they differ?

2. Study the use of settings in "Greenleaf" and in "The Boarding House." How do the authors employ the settings differently in each story? How are the characters related to the settings of each?

3. Analyze and compare the plot structures of each of the three O'Connor stories. How are the plots similar? How do the main characters' fates elucidate a common theme?

4. Discuss the depiction of the intergenerational relationships in the three O'Connor stories, focusing on Bailey and the grandmother, Mrs. May and her sons Scofield and Wesley, and Joy/Hulga and her mother, Mrs. Hopewell. What are the primary similarities and differences in these relationships in the three stories?

5. Write an essay on family dysfunction as dramatized in O'Connor's "A Good Man Is Hard to Find" and Joyce's "Eveline." What do these stories say about family interactions and the relationship of the family to the larger world? What comparisons and contrasts can you identify between the depictions of family in the two stories?

6. Discuss the theme of romantic love in Joyce's "Araby" and "Eveline." What do these stories say about the satisfactions and frustrations of romantic relationships? How are healthy and unhealthy forms of love contrasted and dramatized?

7. Write an essay on one of the following characters, elucidating his or her significance within the story.
   a. Mangan's sister in "Araby"
   b. Frank in "Eveline"
   c. The Misfit in "A Good Man Is Hard to Find"
   d. Red Sammy in "A Good Man Is Hard to Find"
   e. Mrs. Greenleaf in "Greenleaf"
   f. Mr. Greenleaf in "Greenleaf"
   g. Mrs. Freeman in "Good Country People"

8. Compare/contrast the use of irony in any two of the O'Connor stories. In addition to providing humor, how does the use of irony help clarify the theme in each story? How do the characters' stated opinions and judgments and the narrators' implied judgments differ in each?

9. Discuss the use of the following symbols: religious symbolism in "Araby"; the boarding house in "The Boarding House"; the bull in "Greenleaf"; animal symbolism in "A Good Man Is Hard to Find"; the Bible in "Good Country People."

Stories for Further Reading

Chinua Achebe
Civil Peace

Jonathan Iwegbu counted himself extraordinarily lucky. "Happy survival!" meant so much more to him than just a current fashion of greeting old friends in the first hazy days of peace. It went deep to his heart. He had come out of the war with five inestimable blessings—his head, his wife Maria's head, and the heads of three out of their four children. As a bonus he also had his old bicycle—a miracle too but naturally not to be compared to the safety of five human heads.

The bicycle had a little history of its own. One day at the height of the war it was commandeered "for urgent military action." Hard as its loss would have been to him he would still have let it go without a thought had he not had some doubts about the genuineness of the officer. It wasn't his disreputable table rags, nor the toes peeping out of one blue and one brown canvas shoes, nor yet the two stars of his rank done obviously in a hurry in biro,° that troubled Jonathan; many good and heroic soldiers looked the same or worse. It was rather a certain lack of grip and firmness in his manner. So Jonathan, suspecting he might be amenable to influence, rummaged in his raffia bag° and produced the two pounds with which he had been going to buy firewood which his wife, Maria, retailed to camp officials for extra stock-fish and corn meal, and got his bicycle back. That night he buried it in the little clearing in the bush where the dead of the camp, including his own youngest son, were buried. When he dug it up again a year later after the surrender all it needed was a little palm-oil greasing. "Nothing puzzles God," he said in wonder.

He put it to immediate use as a taxi and accumulated a small pile of Biafran money ferrying camp officials and their families across the four-mile stretch to the nearest tarred road. His standard charge per trip was six pounds and those who had the money were only glad to be rid

CIVIL PEACE   First published in 1972. Chinua Achebe (b. 1930) grew up in eastern Nigeria. From early childhood he was bilingual, speaking both English and Igbo, the language of the Ibo tribe. He studied at London University and earned a B.A. degree from the University College of Ibadan. During the violent seven-year Nigerian Civil War, he served for two years (1967–69) on diplomatic missions for Biafra. Achebe is best known for his 1958 novel, *Things Fall Apart*. He has taught at Nigerian universities and at the University of Massachusetts (Amherst), the University of Connecticut, and UCLA.

biro: ball-point pen   **raffia bag:** bag made from palm tree leaves

of some of it in this way. At the end of a fortnight he had made a small fortune of one hundred and fifteen pounds.

Then he made the journey to Enugu and found another miracle waiting for him. It was unbelievable. He rubbed his eyes and looked again and it was still standing there before him. But, needless to say, even that monumental blessing must be accounted also totally inferior to the five heads in the family. This newest miracle was his little house in Ogui Overside. Indeed nothing puzzles God! Only two houses away a huge concrete edifice some wealthy contractor had put up just before the war was a mountain of rubble. And here was Jonathan's little zinc house of no regrets built with mud blocks quite intact! Of course the doors and windows were missing and five sheets off the roof. But what was that? And anyhow he had returned to Enugu early enough to pick up bits of old zinc and wood and soggy sheets of cardboard lying around the neighborhood before thousands more came out of their forest holes looking for the same things. He got a destitute carpenter with one old hammer, a blunt plane, and a few bent and rusty nails in his tool bag to turn this assortment of wood, paper, and metal into door and window shutters for five Nigerian shillings or fifty Biafran pounds. He paid the pounds, and moved in with his overjoyed family carrying five heads on their shoulders.

5   His children picked mangoes near the military cemetery and sold them to soldiers' wives for a few pennies—real pennies this time—and his wife started making breakfast akara balls° for neighbors in a hurry to start life again. With his family earnings he took his bicycle to the villages around and bought fresh palm-wine which he mixed generously in his rooms with the water which had recently started running again in the public tap down the road, and opened up a bar for soldiers and other lucky people with good money.

At first he went daily, then every other day, and finally once a week, to the offices of the Coal Corporation where he used to be a miner, to find out what was what. The only thing he did find out in the end was that that little house of his was even a greater blessing than he had thought. Some of his fellow ex-miners who had nowhere to return at the end of the day's waiting just slept outside the doors of the offices and cooked what meal they could scrounge together in Bournvita° tins. As the weeks lengthened and still nobody could say what was what Jonathan discontinued his weekly visits altogether and faced his palm-wine bar.

---

akara balls: made from ground black beans fried in oil   Bournvita: a type of candy

But nothing puzzles God. Came the day of the windfall when after five days of endless scuffles in queues and counter-queues in the sun outside the Treasury he had twenty pounds counted into his palms as ex-gratia award° for the rebel money he had turned in. It was like Christmas for him and for many others like him when the payments began. They called it (since few could manage its proper official name) *egg-rasher.*

As soon as the pound notes were placed in his palm Jonathan simply closed it tight over them and buried fist and money inside his trouser pocket. He had to be extra careful because he had seen a man a couple of days earlier collapse into near-madness in an instant before that oceanic crowd because no sooner had he got his twenty pounds than some heartless ruffian picked it off him. Though it was not right that a man in such an extremity of agony should be blamed yet many in the queues that day were able to remark quietly on the victim's carelessness, especially after he pulled out the innards of his pocket and revealed a hole in it big enough to pass a thief's head. But of course he had insisted that the money had been in the other pocket, pulling it out too to show its comparative wholeness. So one had to be careful.

Jonathan soon transferred the money to his left hand and pocket so as to leave his right free for shaking hands should the need arise, though by fixing his gaze at such an elevation as to miss all approaching human faces he made sure that the need did not arise, until he got home.

He was normally a heavy sleeper but that night he heard all the   10
neighborhood noises die down one after another. Even the night watchman who knocked the hour on some metal somewhere in the distance had fallen silent after knocking one o'clock. That must have been the last thought in Jonathan's mind before he was finally carried away himself. He couldn't have been gone for long, though, when he was violently awakened again.

"Who is knocking?" whispered his wife lying beside him on the floor.

"I don't know," he whispered back breathlessly.

The second time the knocking came it was so loud and imperious that the rickety old door could have fallen down.

"Who is knocking?" he asked then, his voice parched and trembling.

"Na tief-man and him people," came the cool reply. "Make you   15
hopen de door." This was followed by the heaviest knocking of all.

---

ex-gratia award: monetary reward given freely rather than required by law

Maria was the first to raise the alarm, then he followed and all their children.

"Police-o! Thieves-o! Neighbors-o! Police-o! We are lost! We are dead! Neighbors, are you asleep? Wake up! Police-o!"

This went on for a long time and then stopped suddenly. Perhaps they had scared the thief away. There was total silence. But only for a short while.

"You done finish?" asked the voice outside. "Make we help you small.° Oya, everybody!"

20   *"Police-o! Tief-man-o! Neighbors-o! we done loss-o! Police-o! . . ."*

There were at least five other voices besides the leader's.

Jonathan and his family were now completely paralyzed by terror. Maria and the children sobbed inaudibly like lost souls. Jonathan groaned continuously.

The silence that followed the thieves' alarm vibrated horribly. Jonathan all but begged their leader to speak again and be done with it.

"My frien," said he at long last, "we don try our best for call dem but I tink say dem all done sleep-o . . . So wetin we go do now? Sometaim you wan call soja? Or you wan make we call dem for you? Soja better pass police. No be so?"

25   "Na so!" replied his men. Jonathan thought he heard even more voices now than before and groaned heavily. His legs were sagging under him and his throat felt like sandpaper.

"My frien, why you no de talk again. I de ask you say you wan make we call soja?"

"No."

"Awrighto. Now make we talk business. We no be bad tief. We no like for make trouble. Trouble done finish. War done finish and all the katakata wey de for inside. No Civil War again. This time na Civil Peace. No be so?"

"Na so!" answered the horrible chorus.

30   "What do you want from me? I am a poor man. Everything I had went with this war. Why do you come to me? You know people who have money. We . . . "

"Awright! We know say you no get plenty money. But we sef no get even anini. So derefore make you open dis window and give us one hundred pound and we go commot. Orderwise we de come for inside now to show you guitar-boy like dis . . . "

"Make we help you small": "Let us help you a little" (spoken sarcastically)

A volley of automatic fire rang through the sky. Maria and the children began to weep aloud again.

"Ah, missisi de cry again. No need for dat. We done talk say we na good tief. We just take our small money and go nwayorly. No molest. Abi we de molest?"

"At all!" sang the chorus.

"My friends," began Jonathan hoarsely. "I hear what you say and I thank you. If I had one hundred pounds . . ."   35

"Lookia my frien, no be play we come play for your house. If we make mistake and step for inside you no go like am-o. So derefore . . ."

"To God who made me; if you come inside and find one hundred pounds, take it and shoot me and shoot my wife and children. I swear to God. The only money I have in this life is this twenty pounds *egg-rasher* they gave me today . . ."

"OK. Time de go. Make you open dis window and bring the twenty pound. We go manage am like dat."

There were now loud murmurs of dissent among the chorus: "Na lie de man de lie; e get plenty money . . . Make we go inside and search properly well . . . Wetin be twenty pound? . . ."

"Shurrup!" rang the leader's voice like a lone shot in the sky and silenced the murmuring at once. "Are you dere? Bring the money quick!"   40

"I am coming," said Jonathan fumbling in the darkness with the key of the small wooden box he kept by his side on the mat.

At the first sign of light as neighbors and others assembled to commiserate with him he was already strapping his five-gallon demijohn° to his bicycle carrier and his wife, sweating in the open fire, was turning over akara balls in a wide clay bowl of boiling oil. In the corner his eldest son was rinsing out dregs of yesterday's palm-wine from old beer bottles.

"I count it as nothing," he told his sympathizers, his eyes on the rope he was tying. "What is *egg-rasher*? Did I depend on it last week? Or is it greater than other things that went with the war? I say, let *egg-rasher* perish in the flames! Let it go where everything else has gone. Nothing puzzles God."

demijohn: a large, narrow-necked bottle

Raymond Carver

Cathedral

This blind man, an old friend of my wife's, he was on his way to spend the night. His wife had died. So he was visiting the dead wife's relatives in Connecticut. He called my wife from his in-laws'. Arrangements were made. He would come by train, a five-hour trip, and my wife would meet him at the station. She hadn't seen him since she worked for him one summer in Seattle ten years ago. But she and the blind man had kept in touch. They made tapes and mailed them back and forth. I wasn't enthusiastic about his visit. He was no one I knew. And his being blind bothered me. My idea of blindness came from the movies. In the movies, the blind moved slowly and never laughed. Sometimes they were led by seeing-eye dogs. A blind man in my house was not something I looked forward to.

That summer in Seattle she had needed a job. She didn't have any money. The man she was going to marry at the end of the summer was in officers' training school. He didn't have any money, either. But she was in love with the guy, and he was in love with her, etc. She'd seen something in the paper: HELP WANTED—*Reading to Blind Man*, and a telephone number. She phoned and went over, was hired on the spot. She'd worked with this blind man all summer. She read stuff to him, case studies, reports, that sort of thing. She helped him organize his little office in the county social-service department. They'd become good friends, my wife and the blind man. How do I know these things? She told me. And she told me something else. On her last day in the office, the blind man asked if he could touch her face. She agreed to this. She told me he touched his fingers to every part of her face, her nose—even her neck! She never forgot it. She even tried to write a poem about it. She was always trying to write a poem. She wrote a poem or two every year, usually after something really important had happened to her.

When we first started going out together, she showed me the poem. In the poem, she recalled his fingers and the way they had moved around over her face. In the poem, she talked about what she had felt

CATHEDRAL   First published in 1981. Raymond Carver (1938–1988) was born in Oregon, attended college in California, and earned an M.F.A. from the University of Iowa. During the 1970s and 1980s his spare, carefully crafted short stories brought him wide acclaim, and he is now considered one of the American masters of the short story in the twentieth century. During Carver's last months, before succumbing to lung cancer in 1988, he married his longtime companion, the poet Tess Gallagher.

at the time, about what went through her mind when the blind man touched her nose and lips. I can remember I didn't think much of the poem. Of course, I didn't tell her that. Maybe I just don't understand poetry. I admit it's not the first thing I reach for when I pick up something to read.

Anyway, this man who'd first enjoyed her favors, the officer-to-be, he'd been her childhood sweetheart. So okay. I'm saying that at the end of the summer she let the blind man run his hands over her face, said good-bye to him, married her childhood etc., who was now a commissioned officer, and she moved away from Seattle. But they'd kept in touch, she and the blind man. She made the first contact after a year or so. She called him up one night from an Air Force base in Alabama. She wanted to talk. They talked. He asked her to send him a tape and tell him about her life. She did this. She sent the tape. On the tape, she told the blind man about her husband and about their life together in the military. She told the blind man she loved her husband but she didn't like it where they lived and she didn't like it that he was a part of the military-industrial thing. She told the blind man she'd written a poem and he was in it. She told him that she was writing a poem about what it was like to be an Air Force officer's wife. The poem wasn't finished yet. She was still writing it. The blind man made a tape. He sent her the tape. She made a tape. This went on for years. My wife's officer was posted to one base and then another. She sent tapes from Moody AFB, McGuire, McConnell, and finally Travis, near Sacramento, where one night she got to feeling lonely and cut off from people she kept losing in that moving-around life. She got to feeling she couldn't go it another step. She went in and swallowed all the pills and capsules in the medicine chest and washed them down with a bottle of gin. Then she got into a hot bath and passed out.

But instead of dying, she got sick. She threw up. Her officer—why   5
should he have a name? he was the childhood sweetheart, and what more does he want?—came home from somewhere, found her, and called the ambulance. In time, she put it all on a tape and sent the tape to the blind man. Over the years, she put all kinds of stuff on tapes and sent the tapes off lickety-split. Next to writing a poem every year, I think it was her chief means of recreation. On one tape, she told the blind man she'd decided to live away from her officer for a time. On another tape, she told him about her divorce. She and I began going out, and of course she told her blind man about it. She told him everything, or so it seemed to me. Once she asked me if I'd like to hear the latest tape from the blind man. This was a year ago. I was on the tape, she said. So I said okay, I'd listen to it. I got us drinks and we settled down

in the living room. We made ready to listen. First she inserted the tape into the player and adjusted a couple of dials. Then she pushed a lever. The tape squeaked and someone began to talk in this loud voice. She lowered the volume. After a few minutes of harmless chitchat, I heard my own name in the mouth of this stranger, this blind man I didn't even know! And then this: "From all you've said about him, I can only conclude—" But we were interrupted, a knock at the door, something, and we didn't ever get back to the tape. Maybe it was just as well. I'd heard all I wanted to.

Now this same blind man was coming to sleep in my house.

"Maybe I could take him bowling," I said to my wife. She was at the draining board doing scalloped potatoes. She put down the knife she was using and turned around.

"If you love me," she said, "you can do this for me. If you don't love me, okay. But if you had a friend, any friend, and the friend came to visit, I'd make him feel comfortable." She wiped her hands with the dish towel.

"I don't have any blind friends," I said.

10   "You don't have *any* friends," she said. "Period. Besides," she said, "goddamn it, his wife's just died! Don't you understand that? The man's lost his wife!"

I didn't answer. She'd told me a little about the blind man's wife. Her name was Beulah. Beulah! That's a name for a colored woman.

"Was his wife a Negro?" I asked.

"Are you crazy?" my wife said. "Have you just flipped or something?" She picked up a potato. I saw it hit the floor, then roll under the stove. "What's wrong with you?" she said. "Are you drunk?"

"I'm just asking," I said.

15   Right then my wife filled me in with more detail than I cared to know. I made a drink and sat at the kitchen table to listen. Pieces of the story began to fall into place.

Beulah had gone to work for the blind man the summer after my wife had stopped working for him. Pretty soon Beulah and the blind man had themselves a church wedding. It was a little wedding—who'd want to go to such a wedding in the first place?—just the two of them, plus the minister and the minister's wife. But it was a church wedding just the same. It was what Beulah had wanted, he'd said. But even then Beulah must have been carrying the cancer in her glands. After they had been inseparable for eight years—my wife's word, *inseparable*—Beulah's health went into a rapid decline. She died in a Seattle hospital room, the blind man sitting beside the bed and holding on to her hand. They'd married, lived and worked together, slept together—had sex, sure—and then the blind man had to bury her. All this without his having ever seen what the goddamned woman looked like. It was beyond my understanding. Hearing this, I felt sorry for the blind man for a little bit. And then I found myself thinking what a pitiful life this woman must have led. Imagine a woman who could never see herself as she was seen in the eyes of her loved one. A woman who could go on day after day and never receive the smallest compliment from her beloved. A woman whose husband could never read the expression on her face, be it misery or something better. Someone who could wear makeup or not—what difference to him? She could, if she wanted, wear green eye-shadow around one eye, a straight pin in her nostril, yellow slacks, and purple shoes, no matter. And then to slip off into death, the blind man's hand on her hand, his blind eyes streaming tears—I'm imagining now—her last thought maybe this: that he never even knew what she looked like, and she on an express to the grave. Robert was left with a small insurance policy and half of a twenty-peso Mexican coin. The other half of the coin went into the box with her. Pathetic.

So when the time rolled around, my wife went to the depot to pick him up. With nothing to do but wait—sure, I blamed him for that—I was having a drink and watching the TV when I heard the car pull into the drive. I got up from the sofa with my drink and went to the window to have a look.

I saw my wife laughing as she parked the car. I saw her get out of the car and shut the door. She was still wearing a smile. Just amazing. She went around to the other side of the car to where the blind man was already starting to get out. This blind man, feature this, he was wearing a full beard! A beard on a blind man! Too much, I say. The blind man reached into the backseat and dragged out a suitcase. My wife took his arm, shut the car door, and, talking all the way, moved him down the drive and then up the steps to the front porch. I turned off the TV. I finished my drink, rinsed the glass, dried my hands. Then I went to the door.

My wife said, "I want you to meet Robert. Robert, this is my husband. I've told you all about him." She was beaming. She had this blind man by his coat sleeve.

The blind man let go of his suitcase and up came his hand.   20

I took it. He squeezed hard, held my hand, and then he let it go.

"I feel like we've already met," he boomed.

"Likewise," I said. I didn't know what else to say. Then I said, "Welcome. I've heard a lot about you." We began to move then, a little group, from the porch into the living room, my wife guiding him by the arm. The blind man was carrying his suitcase in his other hand. My wife said things like, "To your left here, Robert. That's right. Now watch it, there's a chair. That's it. Sit down right here. This is the sofa. We just bought this sofa two weeks ago."

I started to say something about the old sofa. I'd liked that old sofa. But I didn't say anything. Then I wanted to say something else, small-talk, about the scenic ride along the Hudson. How going *to* New York, you should sit on the right-hand side of the train, and coming *from* New York, the left-hand side.

25 "Did you have a good train ride?" I said. "Which side of the train did you sit on, by the way?"

"What a question, which side!" my wife said. "What's it matter which side?" she said.

"I just asked," I said.

"Right side," the blind man said. "I hadn't been on a train in nearly forty years. Not since I was a kid. With my folks. That's been a long time. I'd nearly forgotten the sensation. I have winter in my beard now," he said. "So I've been told, anyway. Do I look distinguished, my dear?" the blind man said to my wife.

"You look distinguished, Robert," she said. "Robert," she said. "Robert, it's just so good to see you."

30 My wife finally took her eyes off the blind man and looked at me. I had the feeling she didn't like what she saw. I shrugged.

I've never met, or personally known, anyone who was blind. This blind man was late forties, a heavy-set, balding man with stooped shoulders, as if he carried a great weight there. He wore brown slacks, brown shoes, a light-brown shirt, a tie, a sports coat. Spiffy. He also had this full beard. But he didn't use a cane and he didn't wear dark glasses. I'd always thought dark glasses were a must for the blind. Fact was, I wished he had a pair. At first glance, his eyes looked like anyone else's eyes. But if you looked close, there was something different about them. Too much white in the iris, for one thing, and the pupils seemed to move around in the sockets without his knowing it or being able to stop it. Creepy. As I stared at his face, I saw the left pupil turn in toward his nose while the other made an effort to keep in one place. But it was only an effort, for that eye was on the roam without his knowing it or wanting it to be.

I said, "Let me get you a drink. What's your pleasure? We have a little of everything. It's one of our pastimes."

"Bub, I'm a Scotch man myself," he said fast enough in this big voice.

"Right," I said. Bub! "Sure you are. I knew it."

35 He let his fingers touch his suitcase, which was sitting alongside the sofa. He was taking his bearings. I didn't blame him for that.

"I'll move that up to your room," my wife said.

"No, that's fine," the blind man said loudly. "It can go up when I go up."

"A little water with the Scotch?" I said.

"Very little," he said.

"I knew it," I said.   40

He said, "Just a tad. The Irish actor, Barry Fitzgerald? I'm like that fellow. When I drink water, Fitzgerald said, I drink water. When I drink whiskey, I drink whiskey." My wife laughed. The blind man brought his hand up under his beard. He lifted his beard slowly and let it drop.

I did the drinks, three big glasses of Scotch with a splash of water in each. Then we made ourselves comfortable and talked about Robert's travels. First the long flight from the West Coast to Connecticut, we covered that. Then from Connecticut up here by train. We had another drink concerning that leg of the trip.

I remembered having read somewhere that the blind didn't smoke because, as speculation had it, they couldn't see the smoke they exhaled. I thought I knew that much and that much only about blind people. But this blind man smoked his cigarette down to the nubbin and then lit another one. This blind man filled his ashtray and my wife emptied it.

When we sat down at the table for dinner, we had another drink. My wife heaped Robert's plate with cube steak, scalloped potatoes, green beans. I buttered him up two slices of bread. I said, "Here's bread and butter for you." I swallowed some of my drink. "Now let us pray," I said, and the blind man lowered his head. My wife looked at me, her mouth agape. "Pray the phone won't ring and the food doesn't get cold," I said.

We dug in. We ate everything there was to eat on the table. We ate   45
like there was no tomorrow. We didn't talk. We ate. We scarfed. We grazed that table. We were into serious eating. The blind man had right away located his foods, he knew just where everything was on his plate. I watched with admiration as he used his knife and fork on the meat. He'd cut two pieces of meat, fork the meat into his mouth, and then go all out for the scalloped potatoes, the beans next, and then he'd tear off a hunk of buttered bread and eat that. He'd follow this up with a big drink of milk. It didn't seem to bother him to use his fingers once in a while, either.

We finished everything, including half a strawberry pie. For a few moments, we sat as if stunned. Sweat beaded on our faces. Finally, we got up from the table and left the dirty plates. We didn't look back. We took ourselves into the living room and sank into our places again.

Robert and my wife sat on the sofa. I took the big chair. We had us two or three more drinks while they talked about the major things that had come to pass for them in the past ten years. For the most part, I just listened. Now and then I joined in. I didn't want him to think I'd left the room, and I didn't want her to think I was feeling left out. They talked of things that had happened to them—to them!—these past ten years. I waited in vain to hear my name on my wife's sweet lips: "And then my dear husband came into my life"—something like that. But I heard nothing of the sort. More talk of Robert. Robert had done a little of everything, it seemed, a regular blind jack-of-all-trades. But most recently he and his wife had had an Amway distributorship, from which, I gathered, they'd earned their living, such as it was. The blind man was also a ham radio operator. He talked in his loud voice about conversations he'd had with fellow operators in Guam, in the Philippines, in Alaska, and even in Tahiti. He said he'd have a lot of friends there if he ever wanted to go visit those places. From time to time, he'd turn his blind face toward me, put his hand under his beard, ask me something. How long had I been in my present position? (Three years.) Did I like my work? (I didn't.) Was I going to stay with it? (What were the options?) Finally, when I thought he was beginning to run down, I got up and turned on the TV.

My wife looked at me with irritation. She was heading toward a boil. Then she looked at the blind man and said, "Robert, do you have a TV?"

The blind man said, "My dear, I have two TVs. I have a color set and a black-and-white thing, an old relic. It's funny, but if I turn the TV on, and I'm always turning it on, I turn on the color set. It's funny, don't you think?"

I didn't know what to say to that. I had absolutely nothing to say to that. No opinion. So I watched the news program and tried to listen to what the announcer was saying.

50   "This is a color TV," the blind man said. "Don't ask me how, but I can tell."

"We traded up a while ago," I said.

The blind man had another taste of his drink. He lifted his beard, sniffed it, and let it fall. He leaned forward on the sofa. He positioned his ashtray on the coffee table, then put the lighter to his cigarette. He leaned back on the sofa and crossed his legs at the ankles.

My wife covered her mouth, and then she yawned. She stretched. She said, "I think I'll go upstairs and put on my robe. I think I'll change into something else. Robert, you make yourself comfortable," she said.

"I'm comfortable," the blind man said.

"I want you to feel comfortable in this house," she said.   55
"I am comfortable," the blind man said.

After she'd left the room, he and I listened to the weather report and then to the sports roundup. By that time, she'd been gone so long I didn't know if she was going to come back. I thought she might have gone to bed. I wished she'd come back downstairs. I didn't want to be left alone with a blind man. I asked him if he wanted another drink, and he said sure. Then I asked if he wanted to smoke some dope with me. I said I'd just rolled a number. I hadn't, but I planned to do so in about two shakes.

"I'll try some with you," he said.

"Damn right," I said. "That's the stuff."

I got our drinks and sat down on the sofa with him. Then I rolled   60
us two fat numbers. I lit one and passed it. I brought it to his fingers. He took it and inhaled.

"Hold it as long as you can," I said. I could tell he didn't know the first thing.

My wife came back downstairs wearing her pink robe and her pink slippers.

"What do I smell?" she said.

"We thought we'd have us some cannabis," I said.

My wife gave me a savage look. Then she looked at the blind man   65
and said, "Robert, I didn't know you smoked."

He said, "I do now, my dear. There's a first time for everything. But I don't feel anything yet."

"This stuff is pretty mellow," I said. "This stuff is mild. It's dope you can reason with," I said. "It doesn't mess you up."

"Not much it doesn't, bub," he said, and laughed.

My wife sat on the sofa between the blind man and me. I passed her the number. She took it and toked and then passed it back to me. "Which way is this going?" she said. Then she said, "I shouldn't be smoking this. I can hardly keep my eyes open as it is. That dinner did me in. I shouldn't have eaten so much."

"It was the strawberry pie," the blind man said. "That's what did it,"   70
he said, and he laughed his big laugh. Then he shook his head.

"There's more strawberry pie," I said.

"Do you want some more, Robert?" my wife said.

"Maybe in a little while," he said.

We gave our attention to the TV. My wife yawned again. She said, "Your bed is made up when you feel like going to bed, Robert. I know you must have had a long day. When you're ready to go to bed, say so." She pulled his arm. "Robert?"

75   He came to and said, "I've had a real nice time. This beats tapes, doesn't it?"
          I said, "Coming at you," and I put the number between his fingers. He inhaled, held the smoke, and then let it go. It was like he'd been doing it since he was nine years old.
          "Thanks, bub," he said. "But I think this is all for me. I think I'm beginning to feel it," he said. He held the burning roach out for my wife.
          "Same here," she said. "Ditto. Me, too." She took the roach and passed it to me. "I may just sit here for a while between you two guys with my eyes closed. But don't let me bother you, okay? Either one of you. If it bothers you, say so. Otherwise, I may just sit here with my eyes closed until you're ready to go to bed," she said. "Your bed's made up, Robert, when you're ready. It's right next to our room at the top of the stairs. We'll show you up when you're ready. You wake me up now, you guys, if I fall asleep." She said that and then she closed her eyes and went to sleep.
          The news program ended. I got up and changed the channel. I sat back down on the sofa. I wished my wife hadn't pooped out. Her head lay across the back of the sofa, her mouth open. She'd turned so that her robe had slipped away from her legs, exposing a juicy thigh. I reached to draw her robe back over her, and it was then that I glanced at the blind man. What the hell! I flipped the robe open again.
80   "You say when you want some strawberry pie," I said.
          "I will," he said.
          I said, "Are you tired? Do you want me to take you up to your bed? Are you ready to hit the hay?"
          "Not yet," he said. "No, I'll stay up with you, bub. If that's all right. I'll stay up until you're ready to turn in. We haven't had a chance to talk. Know what I mean? I feel like me and her monopolized the evening." He lifted his beard and he let it fall. He picked up his cigarettes and his lighter.
          "That's all right," I said. Then I said, "I'm glad for the company."
85   And I guess I was. Every night I smoked dope and stayed up as long as I could before I fell asleep. My wife and I hardly ever went to bed at the same time. When I did go to sleep, I had these dreams. Sometimes I'd wake up from one of them, my heart going crazy.
          Something about the church and the Middle Ages was on the TV. Not your run-of-the-mill TV fare. I wanted to watch something else. I turned to the other channels. But there was nothing on them, either. So I turned back to the first channel and apologized.

"Bub, it's all right," the blind man said. "It's fine with me. Whatever you want to watch is okay. I'm always learning something. Learning never ends. It won't hurt me to learn something tonight. I got ears,"
he said.

We didn't say anything for a time. He was learning forward with his
head turned at me, his right ear aimed in the direction of the set. Very
disconcerting. Now and then his eyelids drooped and then they
snapped open again. Now and then he put his fingers into his beard and
tugged, like he was thinking about something he was hearing on the
television.

On the screen, a group of men wearing cowls was being set upon
and tormented by men dressed in skeleton costumes and men dressed
as devils. The men dressed as devils wore devil masks, horns, and long
tails. This pageant was part of a procession. The Englishman who was
narrating the thing said it took place in Spain once a year. I tried to explain to the blind man what was happening.

"Skeletons," he said. "I know about skeletons," he said, and he   90
nodded.

The TV showed this one cathedral. Then there was a long, slow
look at another one. Finally, the picture switched to the famous one in
Paris, with its flying buttresses and its spires reaching up to the clouds.
The camera pulled away to show the whole of the cathedral rising
above the skyline.

There were times when the Englishman who was telling the thing
would shut up, would simply let the camera move around over the
cathedrals. Or else the camera would tour the countryside, men in fields
walking behind oxen. I waited as long as I could. Then I felt I had to
say something. I said, "They're showing the outside of this cathedral
now. Gargoyles. Little statues carved to look like monsters. Now I guess
they're in Italy. Yeah, they're in Italy. There's paintings on the walls of
this one church."

"Are those fresco paintings, bub?" he asked, and he sipped from his
drink.

I reached for my glass. But it was empty. I tried to remember what
I could remember. "You're asking me are those frescoes?" I said. "That's
a good question. I don't know."

The camera moved to a cathedral outside Lisbon. The differences   95
in the Portuguese cathedral compared with the French and Italian were
not that great. But they were there. Mostly the interior stuff. Then
something occurred to me, and I said, "Something has occurred to me.
Do you have any idea what a cathedral is? What they look like, that is?

Do you follow me? If somebody says cathedral to you, do you have any notion what they're talking about? Do you know the difference between that and a Baptist church, say?"

He let the smoke dribble from his mouth. "I know they took hundreds of workers fifty or a hundred years to build," he said. "I just heard the man say that, of course. I know generations of the same families worked on a cathedral. I heard him say that, too. The men who began their life's work on them, they never lived to see the completion of their work. In that wise, bub, they're no different from the rest of us, right?" He laughed. Then his eyelids drooped again. His head nodded. He seemed to be snoozing. Maybe he was imagining himself in Portugal. The TV was showing another cathedral now. This one was in Germany. The Englishman's voice droned on. "Cathedrals," the blind man said. He sat up and rolled his head back and forth. "If you want the truth, bub, that's about all I know. What I just said. What I heard him say. But maybe you could describe one to me? I wish you'd do it. I'd like that. If you want to know, I really don't have a good idea."

I stared hard at the shot of the cathedral on the TV. How could I even begin to describe it? But say my life depended on it. Say my life was being threatened by an insane guy who said I had to do it or else.

I stared some more at the cathedral before the picture flipped off into the countryside. There was no use. I turned to the blind man and said, "To begin with, they're very tall." I was looking around the room for clues. "They reach way up. Up and up. Toward the sky. They're so big, some of them, they have to have these supports. To help them up, so to speak. These supports are called buttresses. They remind me of viaducts, for some reason. But maybe you don't know viaducts, either? Sometimes the cathedrals have devils and such carved into the front. Sometimes lords and ladies. Don't ask me why this is," I said.

He was nodding. The whole upper part of his body seemed to be moving back and forth.

100   "I'm not doing so good, am I?" I said.

He stopped nodding and leaned forward on the edge of the sofa. As he listened to me, he was running his fingers through his beard. I wasn't getting through to him, I could see that. But he waited for me to go on just the same. He nodded, like he was trying to encourage me. I tried to think what else to say. "They're really big," I said. "They're massive. They're built of stone. Marble, too, sometimes. In those olden days, when they built cathedrals, men wanted to be close to God. In those olden days, God was an important part of everyone's life. You could tell this from their cathedral-building. I'm sorry," I said, "but it looks like that's the best I can do for you. I'm just no good at it."

"That's all right, bub," the blind man said. "Hey, listen. I hope you don't mind my asking you. Can I ask you something? Let me ask you a simple question, yes or no. I'm just curious and there's no offense. You're my host. But let me ask if you are in any way religious? You don't mind my asking?"

I shook my head. He couldn't see that, though. A wink is the same as a nod to a blind man. "I guess I don't believe in it. In anything. Sometimes it's hard. You know what I'm saying?"

"Sure, I do," he said.

"Right," I said.   105

The Englishman was still holding forth. My wife sighed in her sleep. She drew a long breath and went on with her sleeping.

"You'll have to forgive me," I said. "But I can't tell you what a cathedral looks like. It just isn't in me to do it. I can't do any more than I've done."

The blind man sat very still, his head down, as he listened to me.

I said, "The truth is, cathedrals don't mean anything special to me. Nothing. Cathedrals. They're something to look at on late-night TV. That's all they are."

It was then that the blind man cleared his throat. He brought   110
something up. He took a handkerchief from his back pocket. Then he said, "I get it, bub. It's okay. It happens. Don't worry about it," he said. "Hey, listen to me. Will you do me a favor? I got an idea. Why don't you find us some heavy paper? And a pen. We'll do something. We'll draw one together. Get us a pen and some heavy paper. Go on, bub, get the stuff," he said.

So I went upstairs. My legs felt like they didn't have any strength in them. They felt like they did after I'd done some running. In my wife's room, I looked around. I found some ballpoints in a little basket on her table. And then I tried to think where to look for the kind of paper he was talking about.

Downstairs, in the kitchen, I found a shopping bag with onion skins in the bottom of the bag. I emptied the bag and shook it. I brought it into the living room and sat down with it near his legs. I moved some things, smoothed the wrinkles from the bag, spread it out on the coffee table.

The blind man got down from the sofa and sat next to me on the carpet.

He ran his fingers over the paper. He went up and down the sides of the paper. The edges, even the edges. He fingered the corners.

115   "All right," he said. "All right, let's do her."

He found my hand, the hand with the pen. He closed his hand over my hand. "Go ahead, bub, draw," he said. "Draw. You'll see. I'll follow along with you. It'll be okay. Just begin now like I'm telling you. You'll see. Draw," the blind man said.

So I began. First I drew a box that looked like a house. It could have been the house I lived in. Then I put a roof on it. At either end of the roof, I drew spires. Crazy.

"Swell," he said. "Terrific. You're doing fine," he said. "Never thought anything like this could happen in your lifetime, did you, bub? Well, it's a strange life, we all know that. Go on now. Keep it up."

I put in windows with arches. I drew flying buttresses. I hung great doors. I couldn't stop. The TV station went off the air. I put down the pen and closed and opened my fingers. The blind man felt around over the paper. He moved the tips of his fingers over the paper, all over what I had drawn, and he nodded.

120   "Doing fine," the blind man said.

I took up the pen again, and he found my hand. I kept at it. I'm no artist. But I kept drawing just the same.

My wife opened up her eyes and gazed at us. She sat up on the sofa, her robe hanging open. She said, "What are you doing? Tell me, I want to know."

I didn't answer her.

The blind man said, "We're drawing a cathedral. Me and him are working on it. Press hard," he said to me. "That's right. That's good," he said. "Sure. You got it, bub. I can tell. You didn't think you could. But you can, can't you? You're cooking with gas now. You know what I'm saying? We're going to really have us something here in a minute. How's the old arm?" he said. "Put some people in there now. What's a cathedral without people?"

125   My wife said, "What's going on? Robert, what are you doing? What's going on?"

"It's all right," he said to her. "Close your eyes now," the blind man said to me.

I did it. I closed them just like he said.

"Are they closed?" he said. "Don't fudge."

"They're closed," I said.

130   "Keep them that way," he said. He said, "Don't stop now. Draw."

So we kept on with it. His fingers rode my fingers as my hand went over the paper. It was like nothing else in my life up to now.

Then he said, "I think that's it. I think you got it," he said. "Take a look. What do you think?"

But I had my eyes closed. I thought I'd keep them that way for a little longer. I thought it was something I ought to do.

"Well?" he said. "Are you looking?"

My eyes were still closed. I was in my house. I knew that. But I   135
didn't feel like I was inside anything.

"It's really something," I said.

John Cheever
The Swimmer

It was one of those midsummer Sundays when everyone sits around saying "I *drank* too much last night." You might have heard it whispered by the parishioners leaving church, heard it from the lips of the priest himself, struggling with his cassock in the *vestiarium,* heard it from the golf links and the tennis courts, heard it from the wildlife preserve where the leader of the Audubon group was suffering from a terrible hangover. "I *drank* too much," said Donald Westerhazy. "We all *drank* too much," said Lucinda Merrill. "It must have been the wine," said Helen Westerhazy. "I *drank* too much of that claret."

This was at the edge of the Westerhazys' pool. The pool, fed by an artesian well with a high iron content, was a pale shade of green. It was a fine day. In the west there was a massive stand of cumulus clouds so like a city seen from a distance—from the bow of an approaching ship—that it might have had a name. Lisbon. Hackensack. The sun was hot. Neddy Merrill sat by the green water, one hand in it, one around a glass of gin. He was a slender man—he seemed to have the especial slenderness of youth—and while he was far from young he had slid down his banister that morning and given the bronze backside of Aphrodite on the hall table a smack, as he jogged toward the smell of coffee in his dining room. He might have been compared to a summer's day, particularly the last hours of one, and while he lacked a tennis racket or a sail bag the impression was definitely one of youth, sport, and clement weather. He had been swimming and now he was breathing deeply, stertorously as if he could gulp into his lungs the

THE SWIMMER   First published in 1964. John Cheever (1912–1982) was born in Quincy, Massachusetts. After being expelled from a private school at seventeen, he went to New York City and published his first story later that year. He lived in various New England and New York towns, especially in commuter towns near New York City.

components of that moment, the heat of the sun, the intenseness of his pleasure. It all seemed to flow into his chest. His own house stood in Bullet Park, eight miles to the south, where his four beautiful daughters would have had their lunch and might be playing tennis. Then it occurred to him that by taking a dogleg to the southwest he could reach his home by water.

His life was not confining and the delight he took in this observation could not be explained by its suggestion of escape. He seemed to see, with a cartographer's eye, that string of swimming pools, that quasi-subterranean stream that curved across the county. He had made a discovery, a contribution to modern geography; he would name the stream Lucinda after his wife. He was not a practical joker nor was he a fool but he was determinedly original and had a vague and modest idea of himself as a legendary figure. The day was beautiful and it seemed to him that a long swim might enlarge and celebrate its beauty.

He took off a sweater that was hung over his shoulders and dove in. He had an inexplicable contempt for men who did not hurl themselves into pools. He swam a choppy crawl, breathing either with every stroke or every fourth stroke and counting somewhere well in the back of his mind the one-two one-two of a flutter kick. It was not a serviceable stroke for long distances but the domestication of swimming had saddled the sport with some customs and in his part of the world a crawl was customary. To be embraced and sustained by the light green water was less a pleasure, it seemed, than the resumption of a natural condition, and he would have liked to swim without trunks, but this was not possible, considering his project. He hoisted himself up on the far curb—he never used the ladder—and started across the lawn. When Lucinda asked where he was going he said he was going to swim home.

5   The only maps and charts he had to go by were remembered or imaginary but these were clear enough. First there were the Grahams, the Hammers, the Lears, the Howlands, and the Crosscups. He would cross Ditmar Street to the Bunkers and come, after a short portage, to the Levys, the Welchers, and the public pool in Lancaster. Then there were the Hallorans, the Sachses, the Biswangers, Shirley Adams, the Gilmartins, and the Clydes. The day was lovely, and that he lived in a world so generously supplied with water seemed like a clemency, a beneficence. His heart was high and he ran across the grass. Making his way home by an uncommon route gave him the feeling that he was a pilgrim, an explorer, a man with a destiny, and he knew that he would find friends all along the way; friends would line the banks of the Lucinda River.

He went through a hedge that separated the Westerhazys' land from the Grahams', walked under some flowering apple trees, passed the shed that housed their pump and filter, and came out at the Grahams' pool. "Why, Neddy," Mrs. Graham said, "what a marvelous surprise. I've been trying to get you on the phone all morning. Here, let me get you a drink." He saw then, like any explorer, that the hospitable customs and traditions of the natives would have to be handled with diplomacy if he was ever going to reach his destination. He did not want to mystify or seem rude to the Grahams nor did he have the time to linger there. He swam the length of their pool and joined them in the sun and was rescued, a few minutes later, by the arrival of two carloads of friends from Connecticut. During the uproarious reunions he was able to slip away. He went down by the front of the Grahams' house, stepped over a thorny hedge, and crossed a vacant lot to the Hammers'. Mrs. Hammer, looking up from her roses, saw him swim by although she wasn't quite sure who it was. The Lears heard him splashing past the open windows of their living room. The Howlands and the Crosscups were away. After leaving the Howlands' he crossed Ditmar Street and started for the Bunkers', where he could hear, even at that distance, the noise of a party.

The water refracted the sound of voices and laughter and seemed to suspend it in midair. The Bunkers' pool was on a rise and he climbed some stairs to a terrace where twenty-five or thirty men and women were drinking. The only person in the water was Rusty Towers, who floated there on a rubber raft. Oh, how bonny and lush were the banks of the Lucinda River! Prosperous men and women gathered by the sapphire-colored waters while caterer's men in white coats passed them cold gin. Overhead a red de Haviland trainer was circling around and around and around in the sky with something like the glee of a child in a swing. Ned felt a passing affection for the scene, a tenderness for the gathering, as if it was something he might touch. In the distance he heard thunder. As soon as Enid Bunker saw him she began to scream: "Oh, look who's here! What a marvelous surprise! When Lucinda said that you couldn't come I thought I'd *die*." She made her way to him through the crowd, and when they had finished kissing she led him to the bar, a progress that was slowed by the fact that he stopped to kiss eight or ten other women and shake the hands of as many men. A smiling bartender he had seen at a hundred parties gave him a gin and tonic and he stood by the bar for a moment, anxious not to get stuck in any conversation that would delay his voyage. When he seemed about to be surrounded he dove in and swam close to the side to avoid colliding with Rusty's raft. At the far end of the pool he bypassed the Tomlinsons with a broad smile and jogged up the garden path. The gravel cut his feet but this was the only unpleasantness. The party was confined to the pool, and as he went toward the house he heard the brilliant, watery sound of voices fade, heard the noise of a radio from the Bunkers' kitchen, where someone was listening to a ball game. Sunday afternoon. He made his way through the parked cars and down the grassy border of their driveway to Alewives Lane. He did not want to be seen on the road in his bathing trunks but there was no traffic and he made the short distance to the Levys' driveway, marked with a PRIVATE PROPERTY sign and a green tube for *The New York Times*. All the doors and windows of the big house were open but there were no signs of life; not even a dog barked. He went around the side of the house to the pool and saw that the Levys had only recently left. Glasses and bottles and dishes of nuts were on a table at the deep end, where there was a bathhouse or gazebo, hung with Japanese lanterns. After swimming the pool he got himself a glass and poured a drink. It was his fourth or fifth drink and he had swum nearly half the length of the Lucinda River. He felt tired, clean, and pleased at that moment to be alone; pleased with everything.

It would storm. The stand of cumulus cloud—that city—had risen and darkened, and while he sat there he heard the percussiveness of thunder again. The de Haviland trainer was still circling overhead and it seemed to Ned that he could almost hear the pilot laugh with pleasure in the afternoon; but when there was another peal of thunder he took off for home. A train whistle blew and he wondered what time it had gotten to be. Four? Five? He thought of the provincial station at that hour, where a waiter, his tuxedo concealed by a raincoat, a dwarf with some flowers wrapped in newspaper, and a woman who had been crying would be waiting for the local. It was suddenly growing dark; it was that moment when the pinheaded birds seem to organize their song into some acute and knowledgeable recognition of the storm's approach. Then there was a fine noise of rushing water from the crown of an oak at his back, as if a spigot there had been turned. Then the noise of fountains came from the crowns of all the tall trees. Why did he love storms, what was the meaning of his excitement when the door sprang open and the rain wind fled rudely up the stairs, why had the simple task of shutting the windows of an old house seemed fitting and urgent, why did the first watery notes of a storm wind have for him the unmistakable sound of good news, cheer, glad tidings? Then there was an explosion, a smell of cordite, and rain lashed the Japanese lanterns that Mrs. Levy had bought in Kyoto the year before last, or was it the year before that?

He stayed in the Levys' gazebo until the storm had passed. The rain had cooled the air and he shivered. The force of the wind had stripped a maple of its red and yellow leaves and scattered them over the grass and the water. Since it was midsummer the tree must be blighted, and yet he felt a peculiar sadness at this sign of autumn. He braced his shoulders, emptied his glass, and started for the Welchers' pool. This meant crossing the Lindleys' riding ring and he was surprised to find it overgrown with grass and all the jumps dismantled. He wondered if the Lindleys had sold their horses or gone away for the summer and put them out to board. He seemed to remember having heard something about the Lindleys and their horses but the memory was unclear. On he went, barefoot through the wet grass, to the Welchers', where he found their pool was dry.

This breach in his chain of water disappointed him absurdly, and   10
he felt like some explorer who seeks a torrential headwater and finds a dead stream. He was disappointed and mystified. It was common enough to go away for the summer but no one ever drained his pool. The Welchers had definitely gone away. The pool furniture was folded, stacked, and covered with a tarpaulin. The bathhouse was locked. All the windows of the house were shut, and when he went around to the driveway in front he saw a FOR SALE sign nailed to a tree. When had he last heard from the Welchers—when, that is, had he and Lucinda last regretted an invitation to dine with them? It seemed only a week or so ago. Was his memory failing or had he so disciplined it in the repression of unpleasant facts that he had damaged his sense of the truth? Then in the distance he heard the sound of a tennis game. This cheered him, cleared away all his apprehensions and let him regard the overcast sky and the cold air with indifference. This was the day that Neddy Merrill swam across the county. That was the day! He started off then for his most difficult portage.

Had you gone for a Sunday afternoon ride that day you might have seen him, close to naked, standing on the shoulders of Route 424, waiting for a chance to cross. You might have wondered if he was the victim of foul play, had his car broken down, or was he merely a fool. Standing barefoot in the deposits of the highway—beer cans, rags, and blowout patches—exposed to all kinds of ridicule, he seemed pitiful. He had known when he started that this was a part of his journey—it had been on his maps—but confronted with the lines of traffic, worming through the summery light, he found himself unprepared. He was laughed at, jeered at, a beer can was thrown at him, and he had no dignity or humor to bring to the situation. He could have gone back, back to the Westerhazys', where Lucinda would still be sitting in the sun. He had signed nothing, vowed nothing, pledged nothing, not even to himself. Why, believing as he did, that all human obduracy was susceptible to common sense, was he unable to turn back? Why was he determined to complete his journey even if it meant putting his life in danger? At what point had this prank, this joke, this piece of horseplay become serious? He could not go back, he could not even recall with any clearness the green water at the Westerhazys', the sense of inhaling the day's components, the friendly and relaxed voices saying that they had *drunk* too much. In the space of an hour, more or less, he had covered a distance that made his return impossible.

An old man, tooling down the highway at fifteen miles an hour, let him get to the middle of the road, where there was a grass divider. Here he was exposed to the ridicule of the northbound traffic, but after ten or fifteen minutes he was able to cross. From here he had only a short walk to the Recreation Center at the edge of the village of Lancaster, where there were some handball courts and a public pool.

The effect of the water on voices, the illusion of brilliance and suspense, was the same here as it had been at the Bunkers' but the sounds here were louder, harsher, and more shrill, and as soon as he entered the crowded enclosure he was confronted with regimentation. "ALL SWIMMERS MUST TAKE A SHOWER BEFORE USING THE POOL. ALL SWIMMERS MUST USE THE FOOTBATH. ALL SWIMMERS MUST WEAR THEIR IDENTIFICATION DISKS." He took a shower, washed his feet in a cloudy and bitter solution, and made his way to the edge of the water. It stank of chlorine and looked to him like a sink. A pair of lifeguards in a pair of towers blew police whistles at what seemed to be regular intervals and abused the swimmers through a public address system. Neddy remembered the sapphire water at the Bunkers' with longing and thought that he might contaminate himself—damage his own prosperousness and charm—by swimming in this murk, but he reminded himself that he was an explorer, a pilgrim, and that this was merely a stagnant bend in the Lucinda River. He dove, scowling with distaste, into the chlorine and had to swim with his head above water to avoid collisions, but even so he was bumped into, splashed, and jostled. When he got to the shallow end both lifeguards were shouting at him: "Hey, you, you without the identification disk, get outa the water." He did, but they had no way of pursuing him and he went through the reek of suntan oil and chlorine out through the hurricane fence and passed the handball courts. By crossing the road he entered the wooded part of the Halloran estate. The woods were not cleared and the footing was treacherous and difficult until he reached the lawn and the clipped beech hedge that encircled their pool.

The Hallorans were friends, an elderly couple of enormous wealth who seemed to bask in the suspicion that they might be Communists. They were zealous reformers but they were not Communists, and yet when they were accused, as they sometimes were, of subversion, it seemed to gratify and excite them. Their beech hedge was yellow and he guessed this had been blighted like the Levys' maple. He called hullo, hullo, to warn the Hallorans of his approach, to palliate his invasion of their privacy. The Hallorans, for reasons that had never been explained to him, did not wear bathing suits. No explanations were in order, really. Their nakedness was a detail in their uncompromising zeal for reform and he stepped politely out of his trunks before he went through the opening in the hedge.

Mrs. Halloran, a stout woman with white hair and a serene face,   15
was reading the *Times*. Mr. Halloran was taking beech leaves out of the water with a scoop. They seemed not surprised or displeased to see him. Their pool was perhaps the oldest in the county, a fieldstone rectangle, fed by a brook. It had no filter or pump and its waters were the opaque gold of the stream.

"I'm swimming across the county," Ned said.

"Why, I didn't know one could," exclaimed Mrs. Halloran.

"Well, I've made it from the Westerhazys'," Ned said. "That must be about four miles."

He left his trunks at the deep end, walked to the shallow end, and swam this stretch. As he was pulling himself out of the water he heard Mrs. Halloran say, "We've been *terribly* sorry to hear about all your misfortunes, Neddy."

"My misfortunes?" Ned asked. "I don't know what you mean."   20

"Why, we heard that you'd sold the house and that your poor children . . ."

"I don't recall having sold the house," Ned said, "and the girls are at home."

"Yes," Mrs. Halloran sighed. "Yes . . ." Her voice filled the air with an unseasonable melancholy and Ned spoke briskly. "Thank you for the swim."

"Well, have a nice trip," said Mrs. Halloran.

Beyond the hedge he pulled on his trunks and fastened them. They   25
were loose and he wondered if, during the space of an afternoon, he could have lost some weight. He was cold and he was tired and the naked Hallorans and their dark water had depressed him. The swim was too much for his strength but how could he have guessed this, sliding down the banister that morning and sitting in the Westerhazys' sun? His arms were lame. His legs felt rubbery and ached at the joints. The

worst of it was the cold in his bones and the feeling that he might never
be warm again. Leaves were falling down around him and he smelled
wood smoke on the wind. Who would be burning wood at this time of
year?

He needed a drink. Whiskey would warm him, pick him up, carry
him through the last of his journey, refresh his feeling that it was original and valorous to swim across the county. Channel swimmers took
brandy. He needed a stimulant. He crossed the lawn in front of the
Hallorans' house and went down a little path to where they had built a
house for their only daughter, Helen, and her husband, Eric Sachs. The
Sachses' pool was small and he found Helen and her husband there.

"Oh, *Neddy*," Helen said. "Did you lunch at Mother's?"

"Not *really*," Ned said. "I *did* stop to see your parents." This seemed
to be explanation enough. "I'm terribly sorry to break in on you like
this but I've taken a chill and I wonder if you'd give me a drink."

"Why, I'd *love* to," Helen said, "but there hasn't been anything in
this house to drink since Eric's operation. That was three years ago."

30   Was he losing his memory, had his gift for concealing painful
facts let him forget that he had sold his house, that his children were in
trouble, and that his friend had been ill? His eyes slipped from Eric's
face to his abdomen, where he saw three pale, sutured scars, two of
them at least a foot long. Gone was his navel, and what, Neddy
thought, would the roving hand, bed-checking one's gifts at 3 A.M.,
make of a belly with no navel, no link to birth, this breach in the succession?

"I'm sure you can get a drink at the Biswangers'," Helen said.
"They're having an enormous do. You can hear it from here. Listen!"

She raised her head and from across the road, the lawns, the gardens, the woods, the fields, he heard again the brilliant noise of voices
over water. "Well, I'll get wet," he said, still feeling that he had no freedom of choice about his means of travel. He dove into the Sachses' cold
water and, gasping, close to drowning, made his way from one end of
the pool to the other. "Lucinda and I want *terribly* to see you," he said
over his shoulder, his face set toward the Biswangers'. "We're sorry it's
been so long and we'll call you *very* soon."

He crossed some fields to the Biswangers' and the sounds of revelry
there. They would be honored to give him a drink, they would be
happy to give him a drink. The Biswangers invited him and Lucinda for
dinner four times a year, six weeks in advance. They were always rebuffed and yet they continued to send out their invitations, unwilling
to comprehend the rigid and undemocratic realities of their society.
They were the sort of people who discussed the price of things at

cocktails, exchanged market tips during dinner, and after dinner told dirty stories to mixed company. They did not belong to Neddy's set—they were not even on Lucinda's Christmas card list. He went toward their pool with feelings of indifference, charity, and some unease, since it seemed to be getting dark and these were the longest days of the year. The party when he joined it was noisy and large. Grace Biswanger was the kind of hostess who asked the optometrist, the veterinarian, the real-estate dealer, and the dentist. No one was swimming and the twilight, reflected on the water of the pool, had a wintry gleam. There was a bar and he started for this. When Grace Biswanger saw him she came toward him, not affectionately as he had every right to expect, but bellicosely.

"Why, this party has everything," she said loudly, "including a gate crasher."

She could not deal him a social blow—there was no question about this and he did not flinch. "As a gate crasher," he asked politely, "do I rate a drink?"   35

"Suit yourself," she said. "You don't seem to pay much attention to invitations."

She turned her back on him and joined some guests, and he went to the bar and ordered a whiskey. The bartender served him but he served him rudely. His was a world in which the caterer's men kept the social score, and to be rebuffed by a part-time barkeep meant that he had suffered some loss of social esteem. Or perhaps the man was new and uninformed. Then he heard Grace at his back say: "They went for broke overnight—nothing but income—and he showed up drunk one Sunday and asked us to loan him five thousand dollars. . . ." She was always talking about money. It was worse than eating your peas off a knife. He dove into the pool, swam its length and went away.

The next pool on his list, the last but two, belonged to his old mistress, Shirley Adams. If he had suffered any injuries at the Biswangers' they would be cured here. Love—sexual roughhouse in fact—was the supreme elixir, the pain killer, the brightly colored pill that would put the spring back into his step, the joy of life in his heart. They had had an affair last week, last month, last year. He couldn't remember. It was he who had broken it off, his was the upper hand, and he stepped through the gate of the wall that surrounded her pool with nothing so considered as self-confidence. It seemed in a way to be his pool, as the lover, particularly the illicit lover, enjoys the possessions of his mistress with an authority unknown to holy matrimony. She was there, her hair the color of brass, but her figure, at the edge of the lighted, cerulean water, excited in him no profound memories. It had been, he thought, a lighthearted affair, although she had wept when he broke it off. She seemed confused to see him and he wondered if she was still wounded. Would she, God forbid, weep again?

"What do you want?" she asked.

40   "I'm swimming across the county."

"Good Christ. Will you ever grow up?"

"What's the matter?"

"If you've come here for money," she said, "I won't give you another cent."

"You could give me a drink."

45   "I could but I won't. I'm not alone."

"Well, I'm on my way."

He dove in and swam the pool, but when he tried to haul himself up onto the curb he found that the strength in his arms and shoulders had gone, and he paddled to the ladder and climbed out. Looking over his shoulder he saw, in the lighted bathhouse, a young man. Going out onto the dark lawn he smelled chrysanthemums or marigolds—some stubborn autumnal fragrance—on the night air, strong as gas. Looking overhead he saw that the stars had come out, but why should he seem to see Andromeda, Cepheus, and Cassiopeia? What had become of the constellations of midsummer? He began to cry.

It was probably the first time in his adult life that he had ever cried, certainly the first time in his life that he had ever felt so miserable, cold, tired, and bewildered. He could not understand the rudeness of the caterer's barkeep or the rudeness of a mistress who had come to him on her knees and showered his trousers with tears. He had swum too long, he had been immersed too long, and his nose and his throat were sore from the water. What he needed then was a drink, some company, and some clean, dry clothes, and while he could have cut directly across the road to his home he went on to the Gilmartins' pool. Here, for the first time in his life, he did not dive but went down the steps into the icy water and swam a hobbled sidestroke that he might have learned as a youth. He staggered with fatigue on his way to the Clydes' and paddled the length of their pool, stopping again and again with his hand on the curb to rest. He climbed up the ladder and wondered if he had the strength to get home. He had done what he wanted, he had swum the county, but he was so stupefied with exhaustion that his triumph seemed vague. Stooped, holding on to the gateposts for support, he turned up the driveway of his own house.

The place was dark. Was it so late that they had all gone to bed? Had Lucinda stayed at the Westerhazys' for supper? Had the girls joined her there or gone someplace else? Hadn't they agreed, as they usually did on Sunday, to regret all their invitations and stay at home? He tried the garage doors to see what cars were in but the doors were locked and rust came off the handles onto his hands. Going toward the house, he saw that the force of the thunderstorm had knocked one of the rain gutters loose. It hung down over the front door like an umbrella rib, but it could be fixed in the morning. The house was locked, and he thought that the stupid cook or the stupid maid must have locked the place up until he remembered that it had been some time since they had employed a maid or a cook. He shouted, pounded on the door, tried to force it with his shoulder, and then, looking in at the windows, saw the place was empty.

Judith Ortiz Cofer
American History

I once read in a "Ripley's Believe It or Not" column that Paterson, New Jersey, is the place where the Straight and Narrow (streets) intersect. The Puerto Rican tenement known as El Building was one block up from Straight. It was, in fact, the corner of Straight and Market; not "at" the corner, but *the* corner. At almost any hour of the day, El Building was like a monstrous jukebox, blasting out *salsas* from open windows as the residents, mostly new immigrants just up from the island, tried to drown out whatever they were currently enduring with loud music. But the day President Kennedy was shot there was a profound silence in El Building, even the abusive tongues of *viragoes*, the cursing of the unemployed, and the screeching of small children had been somehow muted. President Kennedy was a saint to these people. In fact, soon his photograph would be hung alongside the Sacred Heart and over the spiritist altars that many women kept in their apartments. He would become part of the hierarchy of martyrs they prayed to for favors that only one who had died for a cause would understand.

On the day that President Kennedy was shot, my ninth-grade class had been out in the fenced playground of Public School Number 13. We had been given "free" exercise time and had been ordered by our

AMERICAN HISTORY   First published in 1991. Judith Ortiz Cofer (b. 1952) was born in Puerto Rico and grew up in New Jersey. She is the author of several volumes of fiction, poetry, and essays, and is the recipient of fellowships from the Witter Bynner Foundation for Poetry and the National Endowment for the Arts. She now resides in Georgia, where she is a professor of English at the University of Georgia.

P.E. teacher, Mr. DePalma, to "keep moving." That meant that the girls should jump rope and the boys toss basketballs through a hoop at the far end of the yard. He in the meantime would "keep an eye" on us from just inside the building.

It was a cold gray day in Paterson. The kind that warns of early snow. I was miserable since I had forgotten my gloves and my knuckles were turning red and raw from the jump rope. I was also taking a lot of abuse from the black girls for not turning the rope hard and fast enough for them.

"Hey, Skinny Bones, pump it, girl. Ain't you got no energy today?" Gail, the biggest of the black girls, who had the other end of the rope, yelled. "Didn't you eat your rice and beans and pork chops for breakfast today?"

5   The other girls picked up the "pork chop" and made it into a refrain: "pork chop, pork chop, did you eat your pork chop?" They entered the double ropes in pairs and exited without tripping or missing a beat. I felt a burning on my cheeks and then my glasses fogged up so that I could not manage to coordinate the jump rope with Gail. The chill was doing to me what it always did; entering my bones, making me cry, humiliating me. I hated the city, especially in winter. I hated Public School Number 13. I hated my skinny flat-chested body, and I envied the black girls who could jump rope so fast that their legs became a blur. They always seemed to be warm while I froze.

There was only one source of beauty and light for me that school year. The only thing I had anticipated at the start of the semester. That was seeing Eugene. In August, Eugene and his family had moved into the only house on the block that had a yard and trees. I could see his place from my window in El Building. In fact, if I sat on the fire escape I was literally suspended above Eugene's backyard. It was my favorite spot to read my library books in the summer. Until that August the house had been occupied by an old Jewish couple. Over the years I had become part of their family, without their knowing it, of course. I had a view of their kitchen and their backyard, and though I could not hear what they said, I knew when they were arguing, when one of them was sick, and many other things. I knew all this by watching them at mealtimes. I could see their kitchen table, the sink and the stove. During good times, he sat at the table and read his newspapers while she fixed the meals. If they argued, he would leave and the old woman would sit and stare at nothing for a long time. When one of them was sick, the other would come and get things from the kitchen and carry them out on a tray. The old man had died in June. The last week of school I had not seen him at the table at all. Then one day I saw that there was a crowd in the kitchen. The old woman had finally emerged from the house on the arm of a stocky middle-aged woman, whom I had seen there a few times before, maybe her daughter. Then a man had carried out suitcases. The house had stood empty for weeks. I had had to resist the temptation to climb down into the yard and water the flowers the old lady had taken such good care of.

By the time Eugene's family moved in, the yard was a tangled mass of weeds. The father had spent several days mowing, and when he finished I didn't see the red, yellow, and purple clusters that meant flowers to me from where I sat. I didn't see this family sit down at the kitchen table together. It was just the mother, a red-headed tall woman who wore a white uniform—a nurse's, I guessed it was; the father was gone before I got up in the morning and was never there at dinner time. I saw him only on weekends when they sometimes sat on lawn chairs under the oak tree, each hidden behind a section of the newspaper; and there was Eugene. He was tall and blond, and he wore glasses. I liked him right away because he sat at the kitchen table and read books for hours. That summer, before we had even spoken one word to each other, I kept him company on my fire escape.

Once school started I looked for him in all my classes, but P.S. 13 was a huge, overpopulated place and it took me days and many discreet questions to discover that Eugene was in honors classes for all his subjects; classes that were not open to me because English was not my first language, though I was a straight-A student. After much maneuvering I managed "to run into him" in the hallway where his locker was—on the other side of the building from mine—and in study hall at the library where he first seemed to notice me, but did not speak; and finally, on the way home after school one day when I decided to approach him directly, though my stomach was doing somersaults.

I was ready for rejection, snobbery, the worst. But when I came up to him, practically panting in my nervousness, and blurted out: "You're Eugene. Right?" he smiled, pushed his glasses up on his nose, and nodded. I saw then that he was blushing deeply. Eugene liked me, but he was shy. I did most of the talking that day. He nodded and smiled a lot. In the weeks that followed, we walked home together. He would linger at the corner of El Building for a few minutes then walk down to his two-story house. It was not until Eugene moved into that house that I noticed that El Building blocked most of the sun, and that the only spot that got a little sunlight during the day was the tiny square of earth the old woman had planted with flowers.

I did not tell Eugene that I could see inside his kitchen from my bedroom. I felt dishonest, but I liked my secret sharing of his evenings,   10 especially now that I knew what he was reading since we chose our books together at the school library.

One day my mother came into my room as I was sitting on the window sill staring out. In her abrupt way she said: "Elena, you are acting 'moony.'" *Enamorada* was what she really said, that is—like a girl stupidly infatuated. Since I had turned fourteen and started menstruating my mother had been more vigilant than ever. She acted as if I was going to go crazy or explode or something if she didn't watch me and nag me all the time about being a *señorita* now. She kept talking about virtue, morality, and other subjects that did not interest me in the least. My mother was unhappy in Paterson, but my father had a good job at the blue jeans factory in Passaic and soon, he kept assuring us, we would be moving to our own house there. Every Sunday we drove out to the suburbs of Paterson, Clifton, and Passaic, out to where people mowed grass on Sundays in the summer, and where children made snowmen in the winter from pure white snow, not like the gray slush of Paterson, which seemed to fall from the sky in that hue. I had learned to listen to my parents' dreams, which were spoken in Spanish, as fairy tales, like the stories about life in the island-paradise of Puerto Rico before I was born. I had been to the island once as a little girl, to grandmother's funeral, and all I remembered was wailing women in black, my mother becoming hysterical and being given a pill that made her sleep two days, and me feeling lost in a crowd of strangers all claiming to be my aunts, uncles, and cousins. I had actually been glad to return to the city. We had not been back there since then, though my parents talked constantly about buying a house on the beach someday, retiring on the island—that was a common topic among the residents of El Building. As for me, I was going to go to college and become a teacher.

But after meeting Eugene I began to think of the present more than of the future. What I wanted now was to enter that house I had watched for so many years. I wanted to see the other rooms where the old people had lived, and where the boy I liked spent his time. Most of all, I wanted to sit at the kitchen table with Eugene like two adults, like the old man and his wife had done, maybe drink some coffee and talk about books. I had started reading *Gone with the Wind*. I was enthralled by it, with the daring and the passion of the beautiful girl living in a mansion, and with her devoted parents and the slaves who did everything for them. I didn't believe such a world had ever really existed, and I wanted to ask Eugene some questions since he and his parents, he had told me, had come up from Georgia, the same place where the novel was set. His father worked for a company that had transferred him to Paterson. His mother was very unhappy, Eugene said, in his beautiful voice that rose and fell over words in a strange, lilting way. The kids at school called him "the hick" and made fun of the way he talked. I knew I was his only friend so far, and I liked that, though I felt sad for him sometimes. "Skinny Bones" and "Hick" was what they called us at school when we were seen together.

The day Mr. DePalma came out into the cold and asked us to line up in front of him was the day that President Kennedy was shot. Mr. DePalma, a short, muscular man with slicked-down black hair, was the science teacher, P.E. coach, and disciplinarian at P.S. 13. He was the teacher to whose homeroom you got assigned if you were a trouble-maker, and the man called out to break up playground fights, and to escort violently angry teenagers to the office. And Mr. DePalma was the man who called your parents in for "a conference."

That day, he stood in front of two rows of mostly black and Puerto Rican kids, brittle from their efforts to "keep moving" on a November day that was turning bitter cold. Mr. DePalma, to our complete shock, was crying. Not just silent adult tears, but really sobbing. There were a few titters from the back of the line where I stood shivering.

"Listen," Mr. DePalma raised his arms over his head as if he were about to conduct an orchestra. His voice broke, and he covered his face with his hands. His barrel chest was heaving. Someone giggled behind me.

"Listen," he repeated, "something awful has happened." A strange 15 gurgling came from his throat, and he turned around and spit on the cement behind him.

"Gross," someone said, and there was a lot a laughter.

"The President is dead, you idiots. I should have known that wouldn't mean anything to a bunch of losers like you kids. Go home." He was shrieking now. No one moved for a minute or two, but then a big girl let out a "Yeah!" and ran to get her books piled up with the others against the brick wall of the school building. The others followed in a mad scramble to get to their things before somebody caught on. It was still an hour to the dismissal bell.

A little scared, I headed for El Building. There was an eerie feeling on the streets. I looked into Mario's drugstore, a favorite hangout for the high-school crowd, but there were only a couple of old Jewish men at the soda-bar talking with the short-order cook in tones that sounded almost angry, but they were keeping their voices low. Even the traffic on one of the busiest intersections in Paterson—Straight Street and Park Avenue—seemed to be moving slower. There were no horns blasting that day. At El Building, the usual little group of unemployed men was not hanging out on the front stoop making it difficult for women to enter the front door. No music spilled out from open doors in the hallway. When I walked into our apartment, I found my mother sitting in front of the grainy picture of the television set.

20   She looked up at me with a tear-streaked face and just said: "*Dios mio*," turning back to the set as if it were pulling at her eyes. I went into my room.

Though I wanted to feel the right thing about President Kennedy's death, I could not fight the feeling of elation that stirred in my chest. Today was the day I was to visit Eugene in his house. He had asked me to come over after school to study for an American history test with him. We had also planned to walk to the public library together. I looked down into his yard. The oak tree was bare of leaves and the ground looked gray with ice. The light through the large kitchen window of his house told me that El Building blocked the sun to such an extent that they had to turn lights on in the middle of the day. I felt ashamed about it. But the white kitchen table with the lamp hanging just above it looked cozy and inviting. I would soon sit there, across from Eugene, and I would tell him about my perch just above his house. Maybe I would.

In the next thirty minutes I changed clothes, put on a little pink lipstick and got my books together. Then I went in to tell my mother that I was going to a friend's house to study. I did not expect her reaction.

"You are going out *today*?" The way she said *today* sounded as if a storm warning had been issued. It was said in utter disbelief. Before I could answer, she came toward me and held my elbows as I clutched my books.

"*Hija*,° the President has been killed. We must show respect. He was a great man. Come to church with me tonight."

25   She tried to embrace me, but my books were in the way. My first impulse was to comfort her, she seemed so distraught, but I had to meet Eugene in fifteen minutes.

"I have a test to study for, Mamá. I will be home by eight."

"You are forgetting who you are, *niña*. I have seen you staring down at that boy's house. You are heading for humiliation and pain." My mother said this in Spanish and in a resigned tone that surprised me, as if she had no intention of stopping me from "heading for humiliation and pain." I started for the door. She sat in front of the TV holding a white handkerchief to her face.

I walked out to the street and around the chain-link fence that separated El Building from Eugene's house. The yard was neatly edged

hija: daughter

around the little walk that led to the door. It always amazed me how Paterson, the inner core of the city, had no apparent logic to its architecture. Small, neat, single residences like this one could be found right next to huge, dilapidated apartment buildings like El Building. My guess was that the little houses had been there first, then the immigrants had come in droves, and the monstrosities had been raised for them—the Italians, the Irish, the Jews, and now us, the Puerto Ricans and the blacks. The door was painted a deep green: *verde*, the color of hope, I had heard my mother say it: *Verde-Esperanza*.

I knocked softly. A few suspenseful moments later the door opened just a crack. The red, swollen face of a woman appeared. She had a halo of red hair floating over a delicate ivory face—the face of a doll—with freckles on the nose. Her smudged eye makeup made her look unreal to me, like a mannequin seen through a warped store window.

"What do you want?" Her voice was tiny and sweet-sounding, like   30
a little girl's, but her tone was not friendly.

"I'm Eugene's friend. He asked me over. To study." I thrust out my books, a silly gesture that embarrassed me almost immediately.

"You live there?" She pointed up to El Building, which looked particularly ugly, like a gray prison with its many dirty windows and rusty fire escapes. The woman had stepped halfway out and I could see that she wore a white nurse's uniform with St. Joseph's Hospital on the nametag.

"Yes. I do."

She looked intently at me for a couple of heartbeats, then said as if to herself, "I don't know how you people do it." Then directly to me: "Listen, honey. Eugene doesn't want to study with you. He is a smart boy. Doesn't need help. You understand me. I am truly sorry if he told you you could come over. He cannot study with you. It's nothing personal. You understand? We won't be in this place much longer, no need for him to get close to people—it'll just make it harder for him later. Run back home now."

I couldn't move. I just stood there in shock at hearing these things   35
said to me in such a honey-drenched voice. I had never heard an accent like hers, except for Eugene's softer version. It was as if she were singing me a little song.

"What's wrong? Didn't you hear what I said?" She seemed very angry, and I finally snapped out of my trance. I turned away from the green door and heard her close it gently.

Our apartment was empty when I got home. My mother was in someone else's kitchen, seeking the solace she needed. Father would come in from his late shift at midnight. I would hear them talking softly in the kitchen for hours that night. They would not discuss their dreams for the future, or life in Puerto Rico, as they often did; that night they would talk sadly about the young widow and her two children, as if they were family. For the next few days, we would observe *luto* in our apartment; that is, we would practice restraint and silence— no loud music or laughter. Some of the women of El Building would wear black for weeks.

That night, I lay in my bed trying to feel the right thing for our dead president. But the tears that came up from a deep source inside me were strictly for me. When my mother came to the door, I pretended to be sleeping. Sometime during the night, I saw from my bed the streetlight come on. It had a pink halo around it. I went to my window and pressed my face to the cool glass. Looking up at the light I could see the white snow falling like a lace veil over its face. I did not look down to see it turning gray as it touched the ground below.

Stephen Crane
The Bride Comes to Yellow Sky

1

The great Pullman was whirling onward with such dignity of motion that a glance from the window seemed simply to prove that the plains of Texas were pouring eastward. Vast flats of green grass, dull-hued spaces of mesquite and cactus, little groups of frame houses, woods of light and tender trees, all were sweeping into the east, sweeping over the horizon, a precipice.

A newly married pair had boarded this coach at San Antonio. The man's face was reddened from many days in the wind and sun, and a direct result of his new black clothes was that his brick-colored hands were constantly performing in a most conscious fashion. From time to time he looked down respectfully at his attire. He sat with a hand on each knee, like a man waiting in a barber's shop. The glances he devoted to other passengers were furtive and shy.

THE BRIDE COMES TO YELLOW SKY   First published in 1898. Stephen Crane (1871–1900), son of a Methodist minister, grew up in New Jersey and New York State and did his early writing in New York City. A newspaper assignment in the West (including Texas, Arizona, Nevada, and Mexico) in the early months of 1895 provided background for this story.

The bride was not pretty, nor was she very young. She wore a dress of blue cashmere, with small reservations of velvet here and there, and with steel buttons abounding. She continually twisted her head to regard her puff sleeves, very stiff, straight, and high. They embarrassed her. It was quite apparent that she had cooked, and that she expected to cook, dutifully. The blushes caused by the careless scrutiny of some passengers as she had entered the car were strange to see upon this plain, underclass countenance, which was drawn in placid, almost emotionless lines.

They were evidently very happy. "Ever been in a parlor car before?" he asked, smiling with delight.

"No," she answered, "I never was. It's fine, ain't it?"   5

"Great! And then after a while we'll go forward to the diner, and get a big lay-out. Finest meal in the world. Charge a dollar."

"Oh, do they?" cried the bride. "Charge a dollar? Why, that's too much—for us—ain't it, Jack?"

"Not this trip, anyhow," he answered bravely. "We're going to go the whole thing."

Later he explained to her about the trains. "You see, it's a thousand miles from one end of Texas to the other; and this train runs right across it, and never stops but four times." He had the pride of an owner. He pointed out to her the dazzling fittings of the coach; and in truth her eyes opened wider as she contemplated the sea-green figured velvet, the shining brass, silver, and glass, the wood that gleamed as darkly brilliant as the surface of a pool of oil. At one end a bronze figure sturdily held a support for a separated chamber, and at convenient places on the ceiling were frescos in olive and silver.

To the minds of the pair, their surroundings reflected the glory of   10
their marriage that morning in San Antonio; this was the environment of their new estate; and the man's face in particular beamed with an elation that made him appear ridiculous to the Negro porter. This individual at times surveyed them from afar with an amused and superior grin. On other occasions he bullied them with skill in ways that did not make it exactly plain to them that they were being bullied. He subtly used all the manners of the most unconquerable kind of snobbery. He oppressed them; but of this oppression they had small knowledge, and they speedily forgot that infrequently a number of travelers covered them with stares of derisive enjoyment. Historically there was supposed to be something infinitely humorous in their situation.

"We are due in Yellow Sky at 3:42," he said, looking tenderly into her eyes.

"Oh, are we?" she said, as if she had not been aware of it. To evince surprise at her husband's statement was part of her wifely amiability. She took from a pocket a little silver watch; and as she held it before her, and stared at it with a frown of attention, the new husband's face shone.

"I bought it in San Anton' from a friend of mine," he told her gleefully.

"It's seventeen minutes past twelve," she said, looking up at him with a kind of shy and clumsy coquetry. A passenger, noting this play, grew excessively sardonic, and winked at himself in one of the numerous mirrors.

15   At last they went to the dining car. Two rows of Negro waiters, in glowing white suits, surveyed their entrance with the interest, and also the equanimity, of men who had been forewarned. The pair fell to the lot of a waiter who happened to feel pleasure in steering them through their meal. He viewed them with the manner of a fatherly pilot, his countenance radiant with benevolence. The patronage, entwined with the ordinary deference, was not plain to them. And yet, as they returned to their coach, they showed in their faces a sense of escape.

To the left, miles down a long purple slope, was a little ribbon of mist where moved the keening Rio Grande. The train was approaching it at an angle, and the apex was Yellow Sky. Presently it was apparent that, as the distance from Yellow Sky grew shorter, the husband became commensurately restless. His brick-red hands were more insistent in their prominence. Occasionally he was even rather absent-minded and faraway when the bride leaned forward and addressed him.

As a matter of truth, Jack Potter was beginning to find the shadow of a deed weigh upon him like a leaden slab. He, the town marshal of Yellow Sky, a man known, liked, and feared in his corner, a prominent person, had gone to San Antonio to meet a girl he believed he loved, and there, after the usual prayers, had actually induced her to marry him, without consulting Yellow Sky for any part of the transaction. He was now bringing his bride before an innocent and unsuspecting community.

Of course people in Yellow Sky married as it pleased them, in accordance with a general custom; but such was Potter's thought of his duty to his friends, or of their idea of his duty, or of an unspoken form which does not control men in these matters, that he felt he was heinous. He had committed an extraordinary crime. Face to face with this girl in San Antonio, and spurred by his sharp impulse, he had gone headlong over all the social hedges. At San Antonio he was like a man hidden in the dark. A knife to sever any friendly duty, any form, was easy to his hand in that remote city. But the hour of Yellow Sky—the hour of daylight—was approaching.

He knew full well that his marriage was an important thing to his town. It could only be exceeded by the burning of the new hotel. His friends could not forgive him. Frequently he had reflected on the advisability of telling them by telegraph, but a new cowardice had been upon him. He feared to do it. And now the train was hurrying him toward a scene of amazement, glee, and reproach. He glanced out of the window at the line of haze swinging slowly in toward the train.

Yellow Sky had a kind of brass band, which played painfully, to the   20
delight of the populace. He laughed without heart as he thought of it. If the citizens could dream of his prospective arrival with his bride, they would parade the band at the station and escort them, amid cheers and laughing congratulations, to his adobe home.

He resolved that he would use all the devices of speed and plainscraft in making the journey from the station to his house. Once within that safe citadel, he could issue some sort of vocal bulletin, and then not go among the citizens until they had time to wear off a little of their enthusiasm.

The bride looked anxiously at him. "What's worrying you, Jack?"

He laughed again. "I'm not worrying, girl; I'm only thinking of Yellow Sky."

She flushed in comprehension.

A sense of mutual guilt invaded their minds and developed a finer   25
tenderness. They looked at each other with eyes softly aglow. But Potter often laughed the same nervous laugh; the flush upon the bride's face seemed quite permanent.

The traitor to the feelings of Yellow Sky narrowly watched the speeding landscape. "We're nearly there," he said.

Presently the porter came and announced the proximity of Potter's home. He held a brush in his hand, and, with all his airy superiority gone, he brushed Potter's new clothes as the latter slowly turned this way and that way. Potter fumbled out a coin and gave it to the porter, as he had seen others do. It was a heavy and muscle-bound business, as that of a man shoeing his first horse.

The porter took their bag, and as the train began to slow they moved forward to the hooded platform of the car. Presently the two engines and their long string of coaches rushed into the station of Yellow Sky.

"They have to take water here," said Potter, from a constricted throat and in mournful cadence, as one announcing death. Before the train stopped, his eye had swept the length of the platform, and he was glad and astonished to see there was none upon it but the station agent, who, with a slightly hurried and anxious air, was walking toward the water tanks. When the train had halted, the porter alighted first, and placed in position a little temporary step.

30   "Come on, girl," said Potter, hoarsely. As he helped her down they each laughed on a false note. He took the bag from the Negro, and bade his wife cling to his arm. As they slunk rapidly away, his hangdog glance perceived that they were unloading the two trunks, and also that the station agent, far ahead near the baggage car, had turned and was running toward him, making gestures. He laughed, and groaned as he laughed, when he noted the first effect of his marital bliss upon Yellow Sky. He gripped his wife's arm firmly to his side, and they fled. Behind them the porter stood, chuckling fatuously.

2

The California Express on the Southern Railway was due at Yellow Sky in twenty-one minutes. There were six men at the bar of the Weary Gentleman saloon. One was a drummer° who talked a great deal and rapidly; three were Texans who did not care to talk at that time; and two were Mexican sheepherders, who did not talk as a general practice in the Weary Gentleman saloon. The barkeeper's dog lay on the boardwalk that crossed in front of the door. His head was on his paws, and he glanced drowsily here and there with the constant vigilance of a dog that is kicked on occasion. Across the sandy street were some vivid green grass-plots, so wonderful in appearance, amid the sands that burned near them in a blazing sun, that they caused a doubt in the mind. They exactly resembled the grass mats used to represent lawns on the stage. At the cooler end of the railway station, a man without a coat sat in a tilted chair and smoked his pipe. The fresh-cut bank of the Rio Grande circled near the town, and there could be seen beyond it a great plum-colored plain of mesquite.

Save for the busy drummer and his companions in the saloon, Yellow Sky was dozing. The newcomer leaned gracefully upon the bar, and recited many tales with the confidence of a bard who has come upon a new field.

"—and at the moment that the old man fell downstairs with the bureau in his arms, the old woman was coming up with two scuttles of coal, and of course—"

The drummer's tale was interrupted by a young man who suddenly appeared in the open door. He cried: "Scratchy Wilson's drunk, and has

drummer: traveling salesman

turned loose with both hands." The two Mexicans at once set down their glasses and faded out of the rear entrance of the saloon.

The drummer, innocent and jocular, answered: "All right, old man.   35 S'pose he has? Come in and have a drink, anyhow."

But the information had made such an obvious cleft in every skull in the room that the drummer was obliged to see its importance. All had become instantly solemn. "Say," said he, mystified, "what is this?" His three companions made the introductory gesture of eloquent speech; but the young man at the door forestalled them.

"It means, my friend," he answered, as he came into the saloon, "that for the next two hours this town won't be a health resort."

The barkeeper went to the door, and locked and barred it; reaching out of the window, he pulled in heavy wooden shutters, and barred them. Immediately a solemn, chapel-like gloom was upon the place. The drummer was looking from one to another.

"But say," he cried, "what is this anyhow? You don't mean there is going to be a gun fight?"

"Don't know whether there'll be a fight or not," answered one man,   40 grimly, "but there'll be some shootin'—some good shootin'."

The young man who had warned them waved his hand. "Oh, there'll be a fight fast enough, if anyone wants it. Anybody can get a fight out there in the street. There's a fight just waiting."

The drummer seemed to be swayed between the interest of a foreigner and a perception of personal danger.

"What did you say his name was?" he asked.

"Scratchy Wilson," they answered in chorus.

"And will he kill anybody? What are you going to do? Does this   45 happen often? Does he rampage around like this once a week or so? Can he break in that door?"

"No, he can't break down that door," replied the barkeeper. "He's tried it three times. But when he comes you'd better lay down on the floor, stranger. He's dead sure to shoot at it, and a bullet may come through."

Thereafter the drummer kept a strict eye upon the door. The time had not yet been called for him to hug the floor, but, as a minor precaution, he sidled near to the wall. "Will he kill anybody?" he said again.

The men laughed low and scornfully at the question.

"He's out to shoot, and he's out for trouble. Don't see any good in experimentin' with him."

"But what do you do in a case like this? What do you do?"   50

A man responded: "Why, he and Jack Potter—"

"But," in chorus the other men interrupted, "Jack Potter's in San Anton'."

"Well, who is he? What's he got to do with it?"

"Oh, he's the town marshal. He goes out and fights Scratchy when he gets on one of these tears."

55   "Wow!" said the drummer, mopping his brow. "Nice job he's got."

The voices had toned away to mere whisperings. The drummer wished to ask further questions, which were born of an increasing anxiety and bewilderment; but when he attempted them, the men merely looked at him in irritation and motioned him to remain silent. A tense waiting hush was upon them. In the deep shadows of the room their eyes shone as they listened for sounds from the street. One man made three gestures at the barkeeper; and the latter, moving like a ghost, handed him a glass and a bottle. The man poured a full glass of whisky, and set down the bottle noiselessly. He gulped the whisky in a swallow, and turned again toward the door in immovable silence. The drummer saw that the barkeeper, without a sound, had taken a Winchester from beneath the bar. Later he saw this individual beckoning to him, so he tip-toed across the room.

"You better come with me back of the bar."

"No, thanks," said the drummer, perspiring; "I'd rather be where I can make a break for the back door."

Whereupon the man of bottles made a kindly but peremptory gesture. The drummer obeyed it, and, finding himself seated on a box with his head below the level of the bar, balm was laid upon his soul at sight of various zinc and copper fittings that bore a resemblance to armor plate. The barkeeper took a seat comfortably upon an adjacent box.

60   "You see," he whispered, "this here Scratchy Wilson is a wonder with a gun—a perfect wonder; and when he goes on the war-trail, we hunt our holes—naturally. He's about the last one of the old gang that used to hang out along the river here. He's a terror when he's drunk. When he's sober he's all right—kind of simple—wouldn't hurt a fly— nicest fellow in town. But when he's drunk—whoo!"

There were periods of stillness. "I wish Jack Potter was back from San Anton'," said the barkeeper. "He shot Wilson up once—in the leg—and he would sail in and pull out the kinks in this thing."

Presently they heard from a distance the sound of a shot, followed by three wild yowls. It instantly removed a bond from the men in the darkened saloon. There was a shuffling to feet. They looked at each other. "Here he comes," they said.

3

A man in a maroon-colored flannel shirt, which had been purchased for purposes of decoration, and made principally by some Jewish women on the east side of New York, rounded a corner and walked into the middle of the main street of Yellow Sky. In either hand the man held a long, heavy, blue-black revolver. Often he yelled, and these cries rang through a semblance of a deserted village, shrilly flying over the roofs in a volume that seemed to have no relation to the ordinary vocal strength of a man. It was as if the surrounding stillness formed the arch of a tomb over him. These cries of ferocious challenge rang against walls of silence. And his boots had red tops with gilded imprints, of the kind beloved in winter by little sledding boys on the hillsides of New England.

The man's face flamed in a rage begot of whisky. His eyes, rolling, and yet keen for ambush, hunted the still doorways and windows. He walked with the creeping movement of the midnight cat. As it occurred to him, he roared menacing information. The long revolvers in his hands were as easy as straws; they were moved with an electric swiftness. The little fingers of each hand played sometimes in a musician's way. Plain from the low collar of the shirt, the cords of his neck straightened and sank, straightened and sank, as passion moved him. The only sounds were his terrible invitations. The calm adobes preserved their demeanor at the passing of this small thing in the middle of the street.

There was no offer of fight—no offer of fight. The man called to the sky. There were no attractions. He bellowed and fumed and swayed his revolvers here and everywhere.   65

The dog of the barkeeper of the Weary Gentleman saloon had not appreciated the advance of events. He yet lay dozing in front of his master's door. At sight of the dog, the man paused and raised his revolver humorously. At sight of the man, the dog sprang up and walked diagonally away, with a sullen head, and growling. The man yelled, and the dog broke into a gallop. As it was about to enter an alley, there was a loud noise, a whistling, and something spat the ground directly before it. The dog screamed, and, wheeling in terror, galloped headlong in a new direction. Again there was a noise, a whistling, and sand was kicked viciously before it. Fear-stricken, the dog turned and flurried like an animal in a pen. The man stood laughing, his weapons at his hips.

Ultimately the man was attracted by the closed door of the Weary Gentleman saloon. He went to it and, hammering with a revolver, demanded drink.

The door remaining imperturbable, he picked a bit of paper from the walk, and nailed it to the framework with a knife. He then turned his back contemptuously upon this popular resort and, walking to the opposite side of the street and spinning there on his heel quickly and lithely, fired at the bit of paper. He missed it by a half-inch. He swore at himself, and went away. Later he comfortably fusilladed the windows of his most intimate friend. The man was playing with this town; it was a toy for him.

But still there was no offer of fight. The name of Jack Potter, his ancient antagonist, entered his mind, and he concluded that it would be a glad thing if he should go to Potter's house, and by bombardment induce him to come out and fight. He moved in the direction of his desire, chanting Apache scalp-music.

70   When he arrived at it, Potter's house presented the same still, calm front as had the other adobes. Taking up a strategic position, the man howled a challenge. But this house regarded him as might a great stone god. It gave no sign. After a decent wait, the man howled further challenges, mingling with them wonderful epithets.

Presently there came the spectacle of a man churning himself into deepest rage over the immobility of a house. He fumed at it as the winter wind attacks a prairie cabin in the North. To the distance there should have gone the sound of a tumult like the fighting of two hundred Mexicans. As necessity bade him, he paused for breath or to reload his revolvers.

4

Potter and his bride walked sheepishly and with speed. Sometimes they laughed together shamefacedly and low.

"Next corner, dear," he said finally.

They put forth the efforts of a pair walking bowed against a strong wind. Potter was about to raise a finger to point the first appearance of the new home when, as they circled the corner, they came face to face with a man in a maroon-colored shirt, who was feverishly pushing cartridges into a large revolver. Upon the instant the man dropped this revolver to the ground and, like lightning, whipped another from its holster. The second weapon was aimed at the bridegroom's chest.

75   There was a silence. Potter's mouth seemed to be merely a grave for his tongue. He exhibited an instinct to at once loosen his arm from the woman's grip, and he dropped the bag to the sand. As for the bride, her face had gone as yellow as old cloth. She was a slave to hideous rites, gazing at the apparitional snake.

The two men faced each other at a distance of three paces. He of the revolver smiled with a new and quiet ferocity.

"Tried to sneak up on me," he said. "Tried to sneak up on me!" His eyes grew more baleful. As Potter made a slight movement, the man thrust his revolver venomously forward. "No, don't you do it, Jack Potter. Don't you move a finger toward a gun just yet. Don't you move an eyelash. The time has come for me to settle with you, and I'm goin' to do it my own way, and loaf along with no interferin'. So if you don't want a gun bent on you, just mind what I tell you."

Potter looked at his enemy. "I ain't got a gun on me, Scratchy," he said. "Honest, I ain't." He was stiffening and steadying, but yet somewhere at the back of his mind a vision of the Pullman floated, the sea-green figured velvet, the shining brass, silver, and glass, the wood that gleamed as darkly brilliant as the surface of a pool of oil—all the glory of the marriage, the environment of the new estate. "You know I fight when it comes to fighting, Scratchy Wilson, but I ain't got a gun on me. You'll have to do all the shootin' yourself."

His enemy's face went livid. He stepped forward and lashed his weapon to and fro before Potter's chest. "Don't you tell me you ain't got no gun on you, you whelp. Don't tell me no lie like that. There ain't a man in Texas ever seen you without no gun. Don't take me for no kid." His eyes blazed with light, and his throat worked like a pump.

"I ain't takin' you for no kid," answered Potter. His heels had not moved an inch backward. "I'm takin' you for a damn fool. I tell you I ain't got a gun, and I ain't. If you're goin' to shoot me up, you better begin now; you'll never get a chance like this again."   80

So much enforced reasoning had told on Wilson's rage; he was calmer. "If you ain't got a gun, why ain't you got a gun?" he sneered. "Been to Sunday school?"

"I ain't got a gun because I've just come from San Anton' with my wife. I'm married," said Potter. "And if I'd thought there was going to be any galoots like you prowling around when I brought my wife home, I'd had a gun, and don't you forget it."

"Married!" said Scratchy, not at all comprehending.

"Yes, married. I'm married," said Potter, distinctly.

"Married?" said Scratchy. Seemingly for the first time, he saw the   85 drooping, drowning woman at the other man's side. "No!" he said. He was like a creature allowed a glimpse of another world. He moved a pace backward, and his arm with the revolver dropped to his side. "Is this—is this the lady?" he asked.

"Yes, this is the lady," answered Potter.

There was another period of silence.

90   "Well," said Wilson at last, slowly, "I s'pose it's all off now."
          "It's all off if you say so, Scratchy. You know I didn't make the
          trouble." Potter lifted his valise.
          "Well, I 'low it's off Jack," said Wilson. He was looking at the
          ground. "Married!" He was not a student of chivalry; it was merely that
          in the presence of this foreign condition he was a simple child of the
          earlier plains. He picked up his starboard revolver, and, placing both
          weapons in their holsters, he went away. His feet made funnel-shaped
          tracks in the heavy sand.

William Faulkner
A Rose for Emily

1

        When Miss Emily Grierson died, our whole town went to her fu-
neral: the men through a sort of respectful affection for a fallen monument, the women mostly out of curiosity to see the inside of her house,
which no one save an old manservant—a combined gardener and
cook—had seen in at least ten years.
        It was a big, squarish frame house that had once been white, deco-
rated with cupolas and spires and scrolled balconies in the heavily
lightsome style of the seventies, set on what had once been our most
select street. But garages and cotton gins had encroached and obliterated even the august names of that neighborhood; only Miss Emily's
house was left, lifting its stubborn and coquettish decay above the cotton wagons and the gasoline pumps—an eyesore among eyesores. And
now Miss Emily had gone to join the representatives of those august
names where they lay in the cedar-bemused cemetery among the
ranked and anonymous graves of Union and Confederate soldiers who
fell at the battle of Jefferson.
        Alive, Miss Emily had been a tradition, a duty, and a care; a sort of
hereditary obligation upon the town, dating from that day in 1894
when Colonel Sartoris, the mayor—he who fathered the edict that no

A ROSE FOR EMILY.   First published in 1930. William Faulkner (1897–1962) spent
most of his life in Oxford, Mississippi, the small town he mythologized as "Jefferson" in his fiction. Faulkner's novels and stories often portray small-town southerners isolated psychologically—sometimes to an extreme degree—from the modern world. He won the Nobel Prize for literature in 1950.

Negro woman should appear on the streets without an apron—remitted her taxes, the dispensation dating from the death of her father on into perpetuity. Not that Miss Emily would have accepted charity. Colonel Sartoris invented an involved tale to the effect that Miss Emily's father had loaned money to the town, which the town, as a matter of business, preferred this way of repaying. Only a man of Colonel Sartoris' generation and thought could have invented it, and only a woman could have believed it.

When the next generation, with its more modern ideas, became mayors and aldermen, this arrangement created some little dissatisfaction. On the first of the year they mailed her a tax notice. February came, and there was no reply. They wrote her a formal letter, asking her to call at the sheriff's office at her convenience. A week later the mayor wrote her himself, offering to call or to send his car for her, and received in reply a note on paper of an archaic shape, in a thin, flowing calligraphy in faded ink, to the effect that she no longer went out at all. The tax notice was also enclosed, without comment.

They called a special meeting of the Board of Aldermen. A deputation waited upon her, knocked at the door through which no visitor had passed since she ceased giving china-painting lessons eight or ten years earlier. They were admitted by the old Negro into a dim hall from which a stairway mounted into still more shadow. It smelled of dust and disuse—a close, dank smell. The Negro led them into the parlor. It was furnished in heavy, leather-covered furniture. When the Negro opened the blinds of one window, a faint dust rose sluggishly about their thighs, spinning with slow motes in the single sun-ray. On a tarnished gilt easel before the fireplace stood a crayon portrait of Miss Emily's father.

They rose when she entered—a small, fat woman in black, with a thin gold chain descending to her waist and vanishing into her belt, leaning on an ebony cane with a tarnished gold head. Her skeleton was small and spare; perhaps that was why what would have been merely plumpness in another was obesity in her. She looked bloated, like a body long submerged in motionless water, and of that pallid hue. Her eyes, lost in the fatty ridges of her face, looked like two small pieces of coal pressed into a lump of dough as they moved from one face to another while the visitors stated their errand.

She did not ask them to sit. She just stood in the door and listened quietly until the spokesman came to a stumbling halt. Then they could hear the invisible watch ticking at the end of the gold chain.

Her voice was dry and cold. "I have no taxes in Jefferson. Colonel Sartoris explained it to me. Perhaps one of you can gain access to the city records and satisfy yourselves."

5

"But we have. We are the city authorities, Miss Emily. Didn't you get a notice from the sheriff, signed by him?"

10   "I received a paper, yes," Miss Emily said. "Perhaps he considers himself the sheriff. . . . I have no taxes in Jefferson."

"But there is nothing on the books to show that, you see. We must go by the—"

"See Colonel Sartoris. I have no taxes in Jefferson."

"But, Miss Emily—"

"See Colonel Sartoris." (Colonel Sartoris had been dead almost ten years.) "I have no taxes in Jefferson. Tobe!" The Negro appeared. "Show these gentlemen out."

2

15   So she vanquished them, horse and foot, just as she had vanquished their fathers thirty years before about the smell. That was two years after her father's death and a short time after her sweetheart—the one we believed would marry her—had deserted her. After her father's death she went out very little; after her sweetheart went away, people hardly saw her at all. A few of the ladies had the temerity to call, but were not received, and the only sign of life about the place was the Negro man—a young man then—going in and out with a market basket.

"Just as if a man—any man—could keep a kitchen properly," the ladies said; so they were not surprised when the smell developed. It was another link between the gross, teeming world and the high and mighty Griersons.

A neighbor, a woman, complained to the mayor, Judge Stevens, eighty years old.

"But what will you have me do about it, madam?" he said.

"Why, send her word to stop it," the woman said. "Isn't there a law?"

20   "I'm sure that won't be necessary," Judge Stevens said. "It's probably just a snake or a rat that nigger of hers killed in the yard. I'll speak to him about it."

The next day he received two more complaints, one from a man who came in diffident deprecation. "We really must do something about it, Judge. I'd be the last one in the world to bother Miss Emily, but we've got to do something." That night the Board of Aldermen met— three gray-beards and one younger man, a member of the rising generation.

"It's simple enough," he said. "Send her word to have her place cleaned up. Give her a certain time to do it in, and if she don't . . ."

"Dammit, sir," Judge Stevens said, "will you accuse a lady to her face of smelling bad?"

So the next night, after midnight, four men crossed Miss Emily's lawn and slunk about the house like burglars, sniffing along the base of the brickwork and at the cellar openings while one of them performed a regular sowing motion with his hand out of a sack slung from his shoulder. They broke open the cellar door and sprinkled lime there, and in all the outbuildings. As they recrossed the lawn, a window that had been dark was lighted and Miss Emily sat in it, the light behind her, and her upright torso motionless as that of an idol. They crept quietly across the lawn and into the shadow of the locusts that lined the street. After a week or two the smell went away.

That was when people had begun to feel really sorry for her. People in our town, remembering how old lady Wyatt, her great-aunt, had gone completely crazy at last, believed that the Griersons held themselves a little too high for what they really were. None of the young men were quite good enough for Miss Emily and such. We had long thought of them as a tableau; Miss Emily a slender figure in white in the background, her father a spraddled silhouette in the foreground, his back to her and clutching a horsewhip, the two of them framed by the back-flung front door. So when she got to be thirty and was still single, we were not pleased exactly, but vindicated; even with insanity in the family she wouldn't have turned down all of her chances if they had really materialized.   25

When her father died, it got about that the house was all that was left to her; and in a way, people were glad. At last they could pity Miss Emily. Being left alone, and a pauper, she had become humanized. Now she too would know the old thrill and the old despair of a penny more or less.

The day after his death all the ladies prepared to call at the house and offer condolence and aid, as is our custom. Miss Emily met them at the door, dressed as usual and with no trace of grief on her face. She told them that her father was not dead. She did that for three days, with the ministers calling on her, and the doctors, trying to persuade her to let them dispose of the body. Just as they were about to resort to law and force, she broke down, and they buried her father quickly.

We did not say she was crazy then. We believed she had to do that. We remembered all the young men her father had driven away, and we knew that with nothing left, she would have to cling to that which had robbed her, as people will.

3

She was sick for a long time. When we saw her again, her hair was cut short, making her look like a girl, with a vague resemblance to those angels in colored church windows—sort of tragic and serene.

30   The town had just let the contracts for paving the sidewalks, and in the summer after her father's death they began to work. The construction company came with niggers and mules and machinery, and a foreman named Homer Barron, a Yankee—a big, dark, ready man, with a big voice and eyes lighter than his face. The little boys would follow in groups to hear him cuss the niggers, and the niggers singing in time to the rise and fall of picks. Pretty soon he knew everybody in town. Whenever you heard a lot of laughing anywhere about the square, Homer Barron would be in the center of the group. Presently we began to see him and Miss Emily on Sunday afternoons driving in the yellow-wheeled buggy and the matched team of bays from the livery stable.

At first we were glad that Miss Emily would have an interest, because the ladies all said, "Of course a Grierson would not think seriously of a Northerner, a day laborer." But there were still others, older people, who said that even grief could not cause a real lady to forget *noblesse oblige*—without calling it *noblesse oblige*. They just said, "Poor Emily. Her kinsfolk should come to her." She had some kin in Alabama; but years ago her father had fallen out with them over the estate of old lady Wyatt, the crazy woman, and there was no communication between the two families. They had not even been represented at the funeral.

And as soon as the old people said, "Poor Emily," the whispering began. "Do you suppose it's really so?" they said to one another. "Of course it is. What else could . . . " This behind their hands; rustling of craned silk and satin behind jalousies closed upon the sun of Sunday afternoon as the thin, swift clop-clop-clop of the matched team passed: "Poor Emily."

She carried her head high enough—even when we believed that she was fallen. It was as if she demanded more than ever the recognition of her dignity as the last Grierson; as if it had wanted that touch of earthiness to reaffirm her imperviousness. Like when she bought the rat poison, the arsenic. That was over a year after they had begun to say "Poor Emily," and while the two female cousins were visiting her.

"I want some poison," she said to the druggist. She was over thirty then, still a slight woman, though thinner than usual, with cold, haughty black eyes in a face the flesh of which was strained across the temples and about the eyesockets as you imagine a lighthouse-keeper's face ought to look. "I want some poison," she said.

"Yes, Miss Emily. What kind? For rats and such? I'd recom—"   35

"I want the best you have. I don't care what kind."

The druggist named several. "They'll kill anything up to an elephant. But what you want is—"

"Arsenic," Miss Emily said. "Is that a good one?"

"Is . . . arsenic? Yes ma'am. But what you want—"

"I want arsenic."   40

The druggist looked down at her. She looked back at him, erect, her face like a strained flag. "Why, of course," the druggist said. "If that's what you want. But the law requires you to tell what you are going to use it for."

Miss Emily just stared at him, her head tilted back in order to look him eye for eye, until he looked away and went and got the arsenic and wrapped it up. The Negro delivery boy brought her the package; the druggist didn't come back. When she opened the package at home there was written on the box, under the skull and bones: "For rats."

4

So the next day we all said, "She will kill herself"; and we said it would be the best thing. When she had first begun to be seen with Homer Barron, we had said, "She will marry him." Then we said, "She will persuade him yet," because Homer himself had remarked—he liked men, and it was known that he drank with the younger men in the Elk's Club—that he was not a marrying man. Later we said, "Poor Emily," behind the jalousies as they passed on Sunday afternoon in the glittering buggy, Miss Emily with her head high and Homer Barron with his hat cocked and a cigar in his teeth, reins and whip in a yellow glove.

Then some of the ladies began to say that it was a disgrace to the town and a bad example to the young people. The men did not want to interfere, but at last the ladies forced the Baptist minister— Miss Emily's people were Episcopal—to call upon her. He would never divulge what happened during that interview, but he refused to go back again. The next Sunday they again drove about the streets, and the following day the minister's wife wrote to Miss Emily's relations in Alabama.

So she had blood-kin under her roof again and we sat back to   45 watch developments. At first nothing happened. Then we were sure that they were to be married. We learned that Miss Emily had been to the jeweler's and ordered a man's toilet set in silver, with the letters

H. B. on each piece. Two days later we learned that she had bought a complete outfit of men's clothing, including a nightshirt, and we said, "They are married." We were really glad. We were glad because the two female cousins were even more Grierson than Miss Emily had ever been.

So we were not surprised when Homer Barron—the streets had been finished some time since—was gone. We were a little disappointed that there was not a public blowing-off, but we believed that he had gone on to prepare for Miss Emily's coming, or to give her a chance to get rid of the cousins. (By that time it was a cabal, and we were all Miss Emily's allies to help circumvent the cousins.) Sure enough, after another week they departed. And, as we had expected all along, within three days Homer Barron was back in town. A neighbor saw the Negro man admit him at the kitchen door at dusk one evening.

And that was the last we saw of Homer Barron. And of Miss Emily for some time. The Negro man went in and out with the market basket, but the front door remained closed. Now and then we would see her at a window for a moment, as the men did that night when they sprinkled the lime, but for almost six months she did not appear on the streets. Then we knew that this was to be expected too; as if that quality of her father which had thwarted her woman's life so many times had been too virulent and too furious to die.

When we next saw Miss Emily, she had grown fat and her hair was turning gray. During the next few years it grew grayer and grayer until it attained an even pepper-and-salt iron-gray, when it ceased turning. Up to the day of her death at seventy-four it was still that vigorous iron-gray, like the hair of an active man.

From that time on her front door remained closed, save for a period of six or seven years, when she was about forty, during which she gave lessons in china-painting. She fitted up a studio in one of the downstairs rooms, where the daughters and grand-daughters of Colonel Sartoris' contemporaries were sent to her with the same regularity and in the same spirit that they were sent on Sundays with a twenty-five cent piece for the collection plate. Meanwhile her taxes had been remitted.

50   Then the newer generation became the backbone and the spirit of the town, and the painting pupils grew up and fell away and did not send their children to her with boxes of color and tedious brushes and pictures cut from the ladies' magazines. The front door closed upon the last one and remained closed for good. When the town got free postal delivery Miss Emily alone refused to let them fasten the metal numbers above her door and attach a mailbox to it. She would not listen to them.

Daily, monthly, yearly we watched the Negro grow grayer and more stooped, going in and out with the market basket. Each December we sent her a tax notice, which would be returned by the post office a week later, unclaimed. Now and then we would see her in one of the downstairs windows—she had evidently shut up the top floor of the house—like the carven torso of an idol in a niche, looking or not looking at us, we could never tell which. Thus she passed from generation to generation—dear, inescapable, impervious, tranquil, and perverse.

And so she died. Fell ill in the house filled with dust and shadows, with only a doddering Negro man to wait on her. We did not even know she was sick; we had long since given up trying to get any information from the Negro. He talked to no one, probably not even to her, for his voice had grown harsh and rusty, as if from disuse.

She died in one of the downstairs rooms, in a heavy walnut bed with a curtain, her gray head propped on a pillow yellow and moldy with age and lack of sunlight.

5

The Negro met the first of the ladies at the front door and let them in, with their hushed, sibilant voices and their quick, curious glances, and then he disappeared. He walked right through the house and out the back and was not seen again.

The two female cousins came at once. They held the funeral on the second day, with the town coming to look at Miss Emily beneath a mass of bought flowers, with the crayon face of her father musing profoundly above the bier and the ladies sibilant and macabre; and the very old men—some in their brushed Confederate uniforms—on the porch and the lawn, talking of Miss Emily as if she had been a contemporary of theirs, believing that they had danced with her and courted her perhaps, confusing time with its mathematical progression, as the old do, to whom all the past is not a diminishing road, but, instead, a huge meadow which no winter ever quite touches, divided from them now by the narrow bottleneck of the most recent decade of years.

Already we knew that there was one room in that region above stairs which no one had seen in forty years, and which would have to be forced. They waited until Miss Emily was decently in the ground before they opened it.

The violence of breaking down the door seemed to fill this room with pervading dust. A thin, acrid pall as of the tomb seemed to lie everywhere upon this room decked and furnished as for a bridal: upon the valance curtains of faded rose color, upon the rose-shaded lights, upon the dressing table, upon the delicate array of crystal and the man's toilet things backed with tarnished silver, silver so tarnished that the monogram was obscured. Among them lay a collar and tie, as if they had just been removed, which, lifted, left upon the surface a pale crescent in the dust. Upon a chair hung the suit, carefully folded; beneath it the two mute shoes and the discarded socks.

The man himself lay in the bed.

For a long while we just stood there, looking down at the profound and fleshless grin. The body had apparently once lain in the attitude of an embrace, but now the long sleep that outlasts love, that conquers even the grimace of love, had cuckolded him. What was left of him, rotted beneath what was left of the nightshirt, had become inextricable from the bed in which he lay; and upon him and upon the pillow beside him lay that even coating of the patient and biding dust.

60   Then we noticed that in the second pillow was the indentation of a head. One of us lifted something from it, and leaning forward, that faint and invisible dust dry and acrid in the nostrils, we saw a long strand of iron-gray hair.

Zora Neale Hurston

The Gilded Six-Bits

It was a Negro yard around a Negro house in a Negro settlement that looked to the payroll of the G and G Fertilizer works for its support.

But there was something happy about the place. The front yard was parted in the middle by a sidewalk from gate to door-step, a sidewalk edged on either side by quart bottles driven neck down into the ground on a slant. A mess of homey flowers planted without a plan but blooming cheerily from their helter-skelter places. The fence and house were whitewashed. The porch and steps scrubbed white.

THE GILDED SIX-BITS   First published in 1933. Zora Neale Hurston (1891–1960), the daughter of a preacher and of a teacher who died when Hurston was thirteen, was raised in Eatonville, Florida, the setting of this story. Her schooling was repeatedly interrupted, but included a high school diploma in 1918 and college studies at Howard University in Washington, D.C., and Barnard College in New York. She did extensive field research in the folkways of African Americans in the south and in the Caribbean; by the time she wrote this story, she had married and divorced her first husband. In slang, a "bit" was twelve and a half cents, but was used only in multiples of two; "six-bits" refers to the two gilded coins used for ornaments by Mr. Slemmons, his twenty-five-cent stickpin and the fifty-cent coin on his watch chain.

The front door stood open to the sunshine so that the floor of the front room could finish drying after its weekly scouring. It was Saturday. Everything clean from the front gate to the privy house. Yard raked so that the strokes of the rake would make a pattern. Fresh newspaper cut in fancy edge on the kitchen shelves.

Missie May was bathing herself in the galvanized washtub in the bedroom. Her dark-brown skin glistened under the soapsuds that skittered down from her wash rag. Her stiff young breasts thrust forward aggressively like broad-based cones with the tips lacquered in black.

She heard men's voices in the distance and glanced at the dollar clock on the dresser. 5

"Humph! Ah'm way behind time t'day! Joe gointer be heah 'fore Ah git mah clothes on if Ah don't make haste."

She grabbed the clean meal sack at hand and dried herself hurriedly and began to dress. But before she could tie her slippers, there came the ring of singing metal on wood. Nine times.

Missie May grinned with delight. She had not seen the big tall man come stealing in the gate and creep up the walk grinning happily at the joyful mischief he was about to commit. But she knew that it was her husband throwing silver dollars in the door for her to pick up and pile beside her plate at dinner. It was this way every Saturday afternoon. The nine dollars hurled into the open door, he scurried to a hiding place behind the cape jasmine bush and waited.

Missie May promptly appeared at the door in mock alarm.

"Who dat chunkin' money in mah do'way?" she demanded. No answer from the yard. She leaped off the porch and began to search the shrubbery. She peeped under the porch and hung over the gate to look up and down the road. While she did this, the man behind the jasmine darted to the chinaberry tree. She spied him and gave chase. 10

"Nobody ain't gointer be chunkin' money at me and Ah not do 'em nothin'," she shouted in mock anger. He ran around the house with Missie May at his heels. She overtook him at the kitchen door. He ran inside but could not close it after him before she crowded in and locked with him in a rough and tumble. For several minutes the two were a furious mass of male and female energy. Shouting, laughing, twisting, turning, tussling, tickling each other in the ribs; Missie May clutching onto Joe and Joe trying, but not too hard, to get away.

"Missie May, take yo' hand out mah pocket!" Joe shouted out between laughs.

"Ah ain't, Joe, not lessen you gwine gimme whateve' it is good you got in yo' pocket. Turn it go, Joe, do Ah'll tear yo' clothes."

"Go on tear 'em. You de one dat pushes de needles round heah. Move yo' hand Missie May."

15   "Lemme git dat paper sack out yo' pocket. Ah bet its candy kisses."

"Tain't. Move yo' hand. Woman ain't got no business in a man's clothes nohow. Go way."

Missie May gouged way down and gave an upward jerk and triumphed.

"Unhhunh! Ah got it. It 'tis so candy kisses. Ah knowed you had somethin' for me in yo' clothes. Now Ah got to see whut's in every pocket you got."

Joe smiled indulgently and let his wife go through all of his pockets and take out the things that he had hidden there for her to find. She bore off the chewing gum, the cake of sweet soap, the pocket handkerchief as if she had wrested them from him, as if they had not been bought for the sake of this friendly battle.

20   "Whew! dat play-fight done got me all warmed up," Joe exclaimed. "Got me some water in de kittle?"

"Yo' water is on de fire and yo' clean things is cross de bed. Hurry up and wash yo'self and git changed so we kin eat. Ah'm hongry." As Missie said this, she bore the steaming kettle into the bedroom.

"You ain't hongry, sugar," Joe contradicted her. "Youse jes' a little empty. Ah'm de one whut's hongry. Ah could eat up camp meetin', back off 'ssociation, and drink Jurdan dry. Have it on de table when Ah git out de tub."

"Don't you mess wid mah business, man. You git in yo' clothes. Ah'm a real wife, not no dress and breath. Ah might not look lak one, but if you burn me, you won't git a thing but wife ashes."

Joe splashed in the bedroom and Missie May fanned around in the kitchen. A fresh red and white checked cloth on the table. Big pitcher of buttermilk beaded with pale drops of butter from the churn. Hot fried mullet, crackling bread, ham hock atop a mound of string beans and new potatoes, and perched on the window-sill a pone of spicy potato pudding.

25   Very little talk during the meal but that little consisted of banter that pretended to deny affection but in reality flaunted it. Like when Missie May reached for a second helping of the tater pone. Joe snatched it out of her reach.

After Missie May had made two or three unsuccessful grabs at the pan, she begged, "Aw, Joe gimme some mo' dat tater pone."

"Nope, sweetenin' is for us men-folks. Y'all pritty lil frail eels don't need nothin' lak dis. You too sweet already."

"Please, Joe."

"Naw, naw. Ah don't want you to git no sweeter than whut you is already. We goin' down de road a lil piece t'night so you go put on yo' Sunday-go-to-meetin' things."

Missie May looked at her husband to see if he was playing some   30 prank. "Sho nuff, Joe?"

"Yeah. We goin' to de ice cream parlor."

"Where de ice cream parlor at, Joe?"

"A new man done come heah from Chicago and he done got a place and took and opened it up for a ice cream parlor, and bein' as it's real swell, Ah wants you to be one de first ladies to walk in dere and have some set down."

"Do Jesus, Ah ain't knowed nothin' 'bout it. Who de man done it?"

"Mister Otis D. Slemmons, of spots and places—Memphis, Chi-   35 cago, Jacksonville, Philadelphia and so on."

"Dat heavy-set man wid his mouth full of gold teethes?"

"Yeah. Where did you see 'im at?"

"Ah went down to de sto' tuh git a box of lye and Ah seen 'im standin' on de corner talkin' to some of de mens, and Ah come on back and went to scrubbin' de floor, and he passed and tipped his hat whilst Ah was scourin' de steps. Ah thought Ah never seen *him* befo'."

Joe smiled pleasantly. "Yeah, he's up to date. He got de finest clothes Ah ever seen on a colored man's back."

"Aw, he don't look no better in his clothes than you do in yourn.   40 He got a puzzlegut on 'im and he so chuckle-headed, he got a pone behind his neck."

Joe looked down at his own abdomen and said wistfully, "Wisht Ah had a build on me lak he got. He ain't puzzlegutted, honey. He jes' got a corperation. Dat make 'm look lak a rich white man. All rich mens is got some belly on 'em."

"Ah seen de pitchers of Henry Ford and he's a spare-built man and Rockefeller look lak he ain't got but one gut. But Ford and Rockefeller and dis Slemmons and all de rest kin be as many-gutted as dey please, Ah'm satisfied wid you jes' lak you is, baby. God took pattern after a pine tree and built you noble. Youse a pritty man, and if Ah knowed any way to make you mo' pritty still Ah'd take and do it."

Joe reached over gently and toyed with Missie May's ear. "You jes' say dat cause you love me, but Ah know Ah can't hold no light to Otis D. Slemmons. Ah ain't never been nowhere and Ah ain't got nothin' but you."

Missie May got on his lap and kissed him and he kissed back in kind. Then he went on. "All de womens is crazy 'bout 'im everywhere he go."

45   "How you know dat, Joe?"
       "He tole us so hisself."
       "Dat don't make it so. His mouf is cut cross-ways, ain't it? Well, he kin lie jes' lak anybody else."
       "Good Lawd, Missie! You womens sho is hard to sense into things. He's got a five-dollar gold piece for a stick-pin and he got a ten-dollar gold piece on his watch chain and his mouf is jes' crammed full of gold teethes. Sho wisht it wuz mine. And whut make it so cool, he got money 'cumulated. And womens give it all to 'im."
       "Ah don't see whut de womens see on 'im. Ah wouldn't give 'im a wink if de sheriff wuz after 'im."

50   "Well, he tole us how de white womens in Chicago give 'im all dat gold money. So he don't 'low nobody to touch it at all. Not even put dey finger on it. Dey tole 'im not to. You kin make 'miration at it, but don't tetch it."
       "Whyn't he stay up dere where dey so crazy 'bout 'im?"
       "Ah reckon dey done made 'im vast-rich and he wants to travel some. He say dey wouldn't leave 'im hit a lick of work. He got mo' lady people crazy 'bout him than he kin shake a stick at."
       "Joe, Ah hates to see you so dumb. Dat stray nigger jes' tell y'all anything and y'all b'lieve it."
       "Go 'head on now, honey and put on yo' clothes. He talkin' 'bout his pritty womens—Ah want 'im to see *mine*."

55   Missie May went off to dress and Joe spent the time trying to make his stomach punch out like Slemmons' middle. He tried the rolling swagger of the stranger, but found that his tall bone-and-muscle stride fitted ill with it. He just had time to drop back into his seat before Missie May came in dressed to go.
       On the way home that night Joe was exultant. "Didn't Ah say ole Otis was swell? Can't he talk Chicago talk? Wuzn't dat funny whut he said when great big fat ole Ida Armstrong come in? He asted me, 'Who is dat broad wid de forte shake?' Dat's a new word. Us always thought forty was a set of figgers but he showed us where it means a whole heap of things. Sometimes he don't say forty, he jes' say thirty-eight and two and dat mean de same thing. Know whut he tole me when Ah wuz payin' for our ice cream? He say, 'Ah have to hand it to you, Joe. Dat wife of yours is jes' thirty-eight and two. Yessuh, she's forte!' Ain't he killin'?"
       "He'll do in case of a rush. But he sho is got uh heap uh gold on 'im. Dat's de first time Ah ever seed gold money. It lookted good on him sho nuff, but it'd look a whole heap better on you."
       "Who, me? Missie May youse crazy! Where would a po' man lak me git gold money from?"

Missie May was silent for a minute, then she said, "Us might find some goin' long de road some time. Us could."

"Who would be losin' gold money round heah? We ain't even seen   60
none dese white folks wearin' no gold money on dey watch chain. You must be figgerin' Mister Packard or Mister Cadillac goin' pass through heah."

"You don't know whut been lost 'round heah. Maybe somebody way back in memorial times lost they gold money and went on off and it ain't never been found. And then if we wuz to find it, you could wear some 'thout havin' no gang of womens lak dat Slemmons say he got."

Joe laughed and hugged her. "Don't be so wishful 'bout me. Ah'm satisfied de way Ah is. So long as Ah be yo' husband, Ah don't keer 'bout nothin' else. Ah'd ruther all de other womens in de world to be dead than for you to have de toothache. Less we go to bed and git our night rest."

It was Saturday night once more before Joe could parade his wife in Slemmons' ice cream parlor again. He worked the night shift and Saturday was his only night off. Every other evening around six o'clock he left home, and dying dawn saw him hustling home around the lake where the challenging sun flung a flaming sword from east to west across the trembling water.

That was the best part of life—going home to Missie May. Their whitewashed house, the mock battle on Saturday, the dinner and ice cream parlor afterwards, church on Sunday nights when Missie out-dressed any woman in town—all, everything was right.

One night around eleven the acid ran out at the G and G. The   65
foreman knocked off the crew and let the steam die down. As Joe rounded the lake on his way home, a lean moon rode the lake in a silver boat. If anybody had asked Joe about the moon on the lake, he would have said he hadn't paid it any attention. But he saw it with his feelings. It made him yearn painfully for Missie. Creation obsessed him. He thought about children. They had been married more than a year now. They had money put away. They ought to be making little feet for shoes. A little boy child would be about right.

He saw a dim light in the bedroom and decided to come in through the kitchen door. He could wash the fertilizer dust off himself before presenting himself to Missie May. It would be nice for her not to know that he was there until he slipped into his place in bed and hugged her back. She always liked that.

He eased the kitchen door open slowly and silently, but when he went to set his dinner bucket on the table he bumped it into a pile of dishes, and something crashed to the floor. He heard his wife gasp in fright and hurried to reassure her.

"Iss me, honey. Don't git skeered."

There was a quick, large movement in the bedroom. A rustle, a thud, and a stealthy silence. The light went out.

70   What? Robbers? Murderers? Some varmint attacking his helpless wife, perhaps. He struck a match, threw himself on guard and stepped over the door-sill into the bedroom.

The great belt on the wheel of Time slipped and eternity stood still. By the match light he could see the man's legs fighting with his breeches in his frantic desire to get them on. He had both chance and time to kill the intruder in his helpless condition—half in and half out of his pants—but he was too weak to take action. The shapeless enemies of humanity that live in the hours of Time had waylaid Joe. He was assaulted in his weakness. Like Samson awakening after his haircut. So he just opened his mouth and laughed.

The match went out and he struck another and lit the lamp. A howling wind raced across his heart, but underneath its fury he heard his wife sobbing and Slemmons pleading for his life. Offering to buy it with all that he had. "Please, suh, don't kill me. Sixty-two dollars at de sto'. Gold money."

Joe just stood. Slemmons looked at the window, but it was screened. Joe stood out like a rough-backed mountain between him and the door. Barring him from escape, from sunrise, from life.

He considered a surprise attack upon the big clown that stood there laughing like a chessy cat. But before his fist could travel an inch, Joe's own rushed out to crush him like a battering ram. Then Joe stood over him.

75   "Git into yo' damn rags, Slemmons, and dat quick."

Slemmons scrambled to his feet and into his vest and coat. As he grabbed his hat, Joe's fury overrode his intentions and he grabbed at Slemmons with his left hand and struck at him with his right. The right landed. The left grazed the front of his vest. Slemmons was knocked a somersault into the kitchen and fled through the open door. Joe found himself alone with Missie May, with the golden watch charm clutched in his left fist. A short bit of broken chain dangled between his fingers.

Missie May was sobbing. Wails of weeping without words. Joe stood, and after awhile he found out that he had something in his hand. And then he stood and felt without thinking and without seeing with his natural eyes. Missie May kept on crying and Joe kept on feeling so much and not knowing what to do with all his feelings, he put Slem-

mons' watch charm in his pants pocket and took a good laugh and went
to bed.

"Missie May, whut you cryin' for?"

"Cause Ah love you so hard and Ah know you don't love *me* no mo'."

Joe sank his face into the pillow for a spell then he said huskily,   80
"You don't know de feelings of dat yet, Missie May."

"Oh Joe, honey, he said he wuz gointer give me dat gold money and
he jes' kept on after me——"

Joe was very still and silent for a long time. Then he said, "Well,
don't cry no mo', Missie May. Ah got yo' gold piece for you."

The hours went past on their rusty ankles. Joe still and quiet on
one bed-rail and Missie May wrung dry of sobs on the other. Finally the
sun's tide crept upon the shore of night and drowned all its hours.
Missie May with her face stiff and streaked towards the window saw the
dawn come into her yard. It was day. Nothing more. Joe wouldn't be
coming home as usual. No need to fling open the front door and sweep
off the porch, making it nice for Joe. Never no more breakfast to cook;
no more washing and starching of Joe's jumper-jackets and pants. No
more nothing. So why get up?

With this strange man in her bed, she felt embarrassed to get up
and dress. She decided to wait till he had dressed and gone. Then she
would get up, dress quickly and be gone forever beyond reach of Joe's
looks and laughs. But he never moved. Red light turned to yellow, then
white.

From beyond the no-man's land between them came a voice. A   85
strange voice that yesterday had been Joe's.

"Missie May, ain't you gonna fix me no breakfus'?"

She sprang out of bed. "Yeah, Joe. Ah didn't reckon you wuz
hongry."

No need to die today. Joe needed her for a few more minutes
anyhow.

Soon there was a roaring fire in the cook stove. Water bucket full
and two chickens killed. Joe loved fried chicken and rice. She didn't
deserve a thing and good Joe was letting her cook him some breakfast.
She rushed hot biscuits to the table as Joe took his seat.

He ate with his eyes in his plate. No laughter, no banter.   90

"Missie May, you ain't eatin' yo' breakfus'."

"Ah don't choose none, Ah thank yuh."

His coffee cup was empty. She sprang to refill it. When she turned
from the stove and bent to set the cup beside Joe's plate, she saw the
yellow coin on the table between them.

She slumped into her seat and wept into her arms.

95   Presently Joe said calmly, "Missie May, you cry too much. Don't look back lak Lot's wife and turn to salt."

The sun, the hero of every day, the impersonal old man that beams as brightly on death as on birth, came up every morning and raced across the blue dome and dipped into the sea of fire every evening. Water ran down hill and birds nested.

Missie knew why she didn't leave Joe. She couldn't. She loved him too much, but she could not understand why Joe didn't leave her. He was polite, even kind at times, but aloof.

There were no more Saturday romps. No ringing silver dollars to stack beside her plate. No pockets to rifle. In fact the yellow coin in his trousers was like a monster hiding in the cave of his pockets to destroy her.

She often wondered if he still had it, but nothing could have induced her to ask nor yet to explore his pockets to see for herself. Its shadow was in the house whether or no.

100   One night Joe came home around midnight and complained of pains in the back. He asked Missie to rub him down with liniment. It had been three months since Missie had touched his body and it all seemed strange. But she rubbed him. Grateful for the chance. Before morning, youth triumphed and Missie exulted. But the next day, as she joyfully made up their bed, beneath her pillow she found the piece of money with the bit of chain attached.

Alone to herself, she looked at the thing with loathing, but look she must. She took it into her hands with trembling and saw first thing that it was no gold piece. It was a gilded half dollar. Then she knew why Slemmons had forbidden anyone to touch his gold. He trusted village eyes at a distance not to recognize his stick-pin as a gilded quarter, and his watch charm as a four-bit piece.

She was glad at first that Joe had left it there. Perhaps he was through with her punishment. They were man and wife again. Then another thought came clawing at her. He had come home to buy from her as if she were any woman in the long house. Fifty cents for her love. As if to say that he could pay as well as Slemmons. She slid the coin into his Sunday pants pocket and dressed herself and left his house.

Half way between her house and the quarters she met her husband's mother, and after a short talk she turned and went back home. Never would she admit defeat to that woman who prayed for it nightly. If she had not the substance of marriage she had the outside show. Joe must leave *her*. She let him see she didn't want his gold four-bits too.

She saw no more of the coin for some time though she knew that Joe could not help finding it in his pocket. But his health kept poor, and he came home at least every ten days to be rubbed.

The sun swept around the horizon, trailing its robes of weeks and days. One morning as Joe came in from work, he found Missie May chopping wood. Without a word he took the ax and chopped a huge pile before he stopped.

"You ain't got no business choppin' wood, and you know it."

"How come? Ah been choppin' it for de last longest."

"Ah ain't blind. You makin' feet for shoes."

"Won't you be glad to have a lil baby chile, Joe?"

"You know dat 'thout astin' me."

"Iss gointer be a boy chile and de very spit of you."

"You reckon, Missie May?"

"Who else could it look lak?"

Joe said nothing, but he thrust his hand deep into his pocket and fingered something there.

It was almost six months later Missie May took to bed and Joe went and got his mother to come wait on the house.

Missie May was delivered of a fine boy. Her travail was over when Joe came in from work one morning. His mother and the old women were drinking great bowls of coffee around the fire in the kitchen.

The minute Joe came into the room his mother called him aside.

"How did Missie May make out?" he asked quickly.

"Who, dat gal? She strong as a ox. She gointer have plenty mo'. We done fixed her wid de sugar and lard to sweeten her for de nex' one."

Joe stood silent awhile.

"You ain't ast 'bout de baby, Joe. You oughter be mighty proud cause he sho is de spittin' image of yuh, son. Dat's yourn all right, if you never git another one, dat un is yourn. And you know Ah'm mighty proud too, son, cause Ah never thought well of you marryin' Missie May cause her ma used tuh fan her foot round° right smart and Ah been mighty skeered dat Missie May wuz gointer git misput on her road."

Joe said nothing. He fooled around the house till late in the day then just before he went to work, he went and stood at the foot of the bed and asked his wife how she felt. He did this every day during the week.

On Saturday he went to Orlando to make his market. It had been a long time since he had done that.

fan . . . round: run around on her husband

Meat and lard, meal and flour, soap and starch. Cans of corn and tomatoes. All the staples. He fooled around town for awhile and bought bananas and apples. Way after while he went around to the candy store.

125   "Hello, Joe," the clerk greeted him. "Ain't seen you in a long time."

"Nope, Ah ain't been heah. Been round in spots and places."

"Want some of them molasses kisses you always buy?"

"Yessuh." He threw the gilded half dollar on the counter. "Will dat spend?"

"Whut is it, Joe? Well, I'll be doggone! A gold-plated four-bit piece. Where'd you git it, Joe?"

130   "Offen a stray nigger dat come through Eatonville. He had it on his watch chain for a charm—goin' round making out iss gold money. Ha ha! He had a quarter on his tie pin and it wuz all golded up too. Tryin' to fool people. Makin' out he so rich and everything. Ha! Ha! Tryin' to tole off folkses wives from home."

"How did you git it, Joe? Did he fool you, too?"

"Who, me? Naw suh! He ain't fooled me none. Know whut Ah done? He come round me wid his smart talk. Ah hauled off and knocked 'im down and took his old four-bits way from 'im. Gointer buy my wife some good ole lasses kisses wid it. Gimme fifty cents worth of dem candy kisses."

"Fifty cents buys a mighty lot of candy kisses, Joe. Why don't you split it up and take some chocolate bars, too. They eat good, too."

"Yessuh, dey do, but Ah wants all dat in kisses. Ah got a lil boy chile home now. Tain't a week old yet, but he kin suck a sugar tit and maybe eat one them kisses hisself."

135   Joe got his candy and left the store. The clerk turned to the next customer. "Wisht I could be like these darkies. Laughin' all the time. Nothin' worries 'em."

Back in Eatonville, Joe reached his own front door. There was the ring of singing metal on wood. Fifteen times. Missie May couldn't run to the door, but she crept there as quickly as she could.

"Joe Banks, Ah hear you chunkin' money in mah do'way. You wait till Ah got mah strength back and Ah'm gointer fix you for dat."

Ha Jin
A Contract

Since the new soldiers came to my squad in February, Gu Gong had never stopped bullying them. Though it was an unstated rule that an older soldier could demand small services from a new soldier, Gu went too far—he would have the two boys wash his bowls and clothes, take his mail to the post office, and even fetch water for him in the morning, as if they had been his orderlies. The new soldiers complained to me twice, and I promised them that I would talk Gu out of his lording over the new comrades, but I didn't have a chance to speak to him before I found myself resorting to force.

It happened one night in early April. After studying the documents issued by the Central Committee on the Ninth Chinese Communist Party Congress, we were preparing to go to bed. Some men went to the washroom down the hall to bathe their feet, while others were taking off their clothes and spreading their quilts.

"Feng Dong," Gu said from the top of the bunk bed, "you forgot to dump the water in my basin."

Sitting beneath Gu, Feng didn't reply and kept unlacing his boots. I hung my hat on a hook on the wall and turned to Gu, who lay on his bed smoking.

"Feng Dong, you bastard of a new soldier." Gu's body jerked up.   5
"Why don't you dump the water?"

"I've never looked after my grandfather that way," Feng said, as if to himself.

"I am your great-grandpa in this squad!"

"Stop it, Gu Gong," I said. "You've gone too far. It's unreasonable to ask others to dump the water you washed your own feet with."

"Oh yeah? I want him to get rid of the water, or somebody will step on it going out to the latrine at night."

"Then it's your duty to dispose of it."   10

Gu's face turned red. "Who are you, Cheng Zhi? A big squad leader? So what? Do you think you're an officer? How big are you anyway? As big as one of my balls?"

A CONTRACT   First published in 1996. Ha Jin (b. 1956) was born in Liaoning, China. At age fourteen he joined the Chinese army and spent six years as a soldier. The author of several novels and story collections—including *Waiting*, which won the National Book Award in 1999—Ha Jin now lives in Boston and teaches creative writing at Boston University.

The men around laughed. Enraged, I went up to Gu and pulled him off his bed, together with his quilt and sheet. He fell on the cement floor. Before he could get up, I gave him a kick in the jaw. He jumped to his feet and scuffled toward me, but a few pairs of hands restrained him.

"You beat me," he yelled. "You, a squad leader, beat your soldier." He was struggling to get loose. "Let me go! Let me settle it with him!"

Without a word I walked to the door. I thought it was better for me to stay out of this mess for a moment.

15   "Cheng Zhi," Gu shouted, "I screw your ancestors one by one! If you are your father's son, don't leave. Let's fight it out."

The sky over Hutou was glimmering with thin mist pierced by stars. The chilly spring wind was rubbing my burning forehead as I went across the drill ground and reached the stream behind our barracks. The thawing ice sent out small noises on the water surface, while some birds were chirping and quacking in the dark. I was grateful to Liu Sheng, the vice squad leader, who had held Gu back before the whole thing could turn ugly. Whatever the reason, as a leader I shouldn't have used force first. Besides, Gu was a stout man and the best fighter in my squad. He came from Shandong Province and had practiced kung fu since childhood. That was why nobody dared confront him. To tell the truth, I was not his match if we fought bare-handed.

I wandered along the stream and through the birch woods until the chilly air began making my skin tingle in my cotton-padded clothes.

When I returned to our room, it was quiet except for several men snoring away. Everybody was fast asleep. I undressed myself and slipped into my bed. Gu stirred, gnashed his teeth, then resumed snoring.

The next day everything went as usual. In the morning we practiced throwing antitank grenades; in the afternoon we worked in our company's vegetable cellar, peeling off rotten cabbage leaves. Gu remained rather placid. I knew the matter was not over, so for an entire day I racked my brain for a solution. Though I did not have a definite idea how to resolve the issue, without doubt it would be better to talk it out than fight it out.

20   To my surprise, Gu proposed a talk. That evening, when I returned to our room with newspapers and mail, he came to me and said, "Squad Leader Cheng, I need to chat with you."

"All right." I tried to remain calm. "When do you think we should talk?"

"Now." He smiled awkwardly. "Can we go outside?"

"Sure."

All the men watched us in silence as we walked out. Since I had agreed, I had to follow him to any place he thought suitable. The dark evening was a little warm, and the smoky air was motionless. We crossed two rows of poplars and reached the area for gymnastic exercises. He stopped, resting one hand on a parallel bar.

"Cheng Zhi, I never thought you were so fierce." A mysterious grin spread on his egg-shaped face.   25

"Gu Gong, we joined the army in the same year, and I didn't mean to embarrass you in front of the new soldiers—"

"You beat me! Damn you, even my parents never kicked me like that."

"Listen to me—"

"You were so wild last night. Now, let yourself run wild again."

"What do you want?"   30

"I want to settle it with you now. Let's go a few rounds." His small eyes were shimmering in the dark while his hands were rubbing each other, as if he were preparing himself for a wrestling contest.

I tried hard to stay coolheaded. "Listen, Gu Gong, we are revolutionary soldiers and don't play games like hooligans. I'm not good at doing things in your style and can only fight in the soldier's way, so I refuse to 'play' with you."

"You chicken. All right then, let your grandpa teach you manners." He was moving toward me.

"Halt!" a few voices shouted. Vice Squad Leader Liu Sheng, Zhao Min, and Wang Longyun emerged. They stopped Gu, pacifying him and hauling him back to the quarters. Though his elbows were struggling, Gu's legs seemed ready to give in as he followed them away.

Meanwhile he kept cursing, "Chicken, chicken. You dare not fight.   35
All you dare do is steal a blow when others are unprepared. Chicken, how come you lead us men?"

They were out of the drill ground now. I stood there alone, feeling my blood boil. What should I do? Fight bare-handed with him? If I could not beat him, what was the use of fighting that way? They had all seen us just now and must have believed I was afraid of him. What should I do? I had to find a way to stop him. How?

Ten minutes later I rejoined my squad. When I entered the room, the men suddenly stopped talking. Feng Dong was gaping at Gu Gong, who smirked silently while exhaling smoke, I picked up a poker, drilled a few holes through the cinders in the stove, and added three shovels of coal to the flames, which began crackling. Raising my head, I saw Gu standing erect against the pillar of his bed, his chin up and his eyes peering at me. Nobody had made a sound since I came in.

I sat down at the desk, took out a sheet of paper, and started writing. I wrote as follows:

> This evening, Soldier Gu Gong challenged Cheng Zhi, Leader of the Eighth Squad of the First Company, to fight bare-handed with him. All having been considered, we realized that a melee does not suit the style of revolutionary soldiers, so we have decided to do it with weapons. Also having considered bullets must be saved for the Russians, we have chosen to use bayonets. When we begin, the whole squad will be present, and we will not stop until one of us cannot resist anymore. If either of us gets wounded or killed in this practice, the victim himself is solely responsible for such a mishap. This contract, drawn on April 15, is here signed by both
>
> Cheng Zhi   Gu Gong

I signed my name but couldn't find red ink paste for a fingerprint, so I used a black ink stick instead and put my thumbprint beneath my name. Then I handed the sheet to Liu Sheng. "Read it out to the whole squad."

While Liu was reading in a metallic voice, I went to the gun rack and picked up a semiautomatic rifle. The bayonet was pressed down between my forefinger and thumb. Its blade drew a semicircle in the air, and with a clatter it settled firmly on the muzzle. Wiping the bluish bayonet with a rag, I looked at Gu Gong, whose face had turned sallow. Tiny beads of sweat were breaking out on his forehead, and his eyes fixed on the floor. My heart was fluttering.

40   "I'll wait for you fellows on the drill ground." I opened the door and went out.

Once in the hall, I heard Gu cry out inside the room, "He's an orphan, but I have my old parents at home!" What he said was true.

The gun seemed weightless on my back as I paced about under the poplars, rolling cigarettes and smoking. The breeze was fanning my face and hair. It was good to feel and smell the approach of the spring, which day and night was creeping from the south to the north—to us, and then to Siberia. The purple sky, so vast, curved in every direction toward the serrated hilltops in both China and Russia. I waited at the drill ground for half an hour, until Vice Squad Leader Liu appeared from the dark.

"Gu Gong has buried his head in his quilt," he said with a smile.

"I'd better not go in now. You stay with the squad. If you want me, go to the study room for me. All right?"

45   "Sure."

I thought that our company leaders would reprimand me and order me to write out self-criticism for impairing our solidarity, but when I reported the incident the next day, they didn't look worried at all. Secretary Ling Ping screwed up one of his eyes and said, "Comrade Cheng Zhi, remember: Never strike the first blow."

Two months later, I was promoted to command the Second Platoon.

Herman Melville
Bartleby the Scrivener

A Story of Wall Street

I am a rather elderly man. The nature of my avocations for the last thirty years has brought me into more than ordinary contact with what would seem an interesting and somewhat singular set of men of whom as yet nothing that I know of has ever been written—I mean the law-copyists or scriveners. I have known very many of them, professionally and privately, and if I pleased could relate diverse histories at which good-natured gentlemen might smile and sentimental souls might weep. But I waive the biographies of all other scriveners for a few passages in the life of Bartleby, who was a scrivener the strangest I ever saw or heard of. While of other law-copyists I might write the complete life, of Bartleby nothing of that sort can be done. I believe that no materials exist for a full and satisfactory biography of this man. It is an irreparable loss to literature. Bartleby was one of those beings of whom nothing is ascertainable except from the original sources, and in his case those are very small. What my own astonished eyes saw of Bartleby, *that* is all I know of him except, indeed, one vague report which will appear in the sequel.

BARTLEBY THE SCRIVENER   First published in 1853. Herman Melville (1819–1891) was born in New York City. After working as a farmhand, clerk, bookkeeper, and teacher, he went to sea in 1837, where his adventures and observations supplied him with the material for several novels of the sea including *Moby-Dick* (1851). The lack of financial success of that book and later works of fiction, including *Piazza Tales*, which reprinted "Bartleby the Scrivener," led Melville eventually to write poetry instead. By the time of the story, Wall Street had become the financial and business center of New York City. In the days before the invention of the typewriter, official documents and legal papers had to be copied by hand—the job of a "scrivener." "The Tombs" (paragraph 11 and thereafter) was the vivid nickname of the city prison, properly called the Halls of Justice.

Ere introducing the scrivener as he first appeared to me, it is fit I make some mention of myself, my employees, my business, my chambers, and general surroundings, because some such description is indispensable to an adequate understanding of the chief character about to be presented.

Imprimis: I am a man who from his youth upwards has been filled with a profound conviction that the easiest way of life is the best. Hence, though I belong to a profession proverbially energetic and nervous, even to turbulence at times, yet nothing of that sort have I ever suffered to invade my peace. I am one of those unambitious lawyers who never addresses a jury or in any way draws down public applause, but in the cool tranquility of a snug retreat do a snug business among rich men's bonds and mortgages and title-deeds. All who know me consider me an eminently *safe* man. The late John Jacob Astor, a personage little given to poetic enthusiasm, had no hesitation in pronouncing my first grand point to be prudence; my next, method. I do not speak it in vanity but simply record the fact that I was not unemployed in my profession by the late John Jacob Astor, a name which, I admit, I love to repeat, for it hath a rounded and orbicular sound to it and rings like unto bullion. I will freely add that I was not insensible to the late John Jacob Astor's good opinion.

Sometime prior to the period at which this little history begins, my avocations had been largely increased. The good old office now extinct in the State of New York of a Master in Chancery had been conferred upon me. It was not a very arduous office but very pleasantly remunerative. I seldom lose my temper; much more seldom indulge in dangerous indignation at wrongs and outrages; but I must be permitted to be rash here and declare that I consider the sudden and violent abrogation of the office of Master in Chancery by the new Constitution as a —— premature act, inasmuch as I had counted upon a life-lease of the profits, whereas I only received those of a few short years. But this is by the way.

5   My chambers were upstairs at No. —— Wall Street. At one end they looked upon the white wall of the interior of a spacious skylight shaft penetrating the building from top to bottom. This view might have been considered rather tame than otherwise, deficient in what landscape painters call "life." But if so, the view from the other end of my chambers offered at least a contrast, if nothing more. In that direction my windows commanded an unobstructed view of a lofty brick wall, black by age and everlasting shade, which wall required no spy-glass to bring out its lurking beauties, but for the benefit of all near-sighted spectators was pushed up to within ten feet of my window panes. Ow-

ing to the great height of the surrounding buildings, and my chambers being on the second floor, the interval between this wall and mine not a little resembled a huge square cistern.

At the period just preceding the advent of Bartleby, I had two persons as copyists in my employment and a promising lad as an office boy. First, Turkey; second, Nippers; third, Ginger Nut. These may seem names the like of which are not usually found in the Directory. In truth they were nicknames mutually conferred upon each other by my three clerks, and were deemed expressive of their respective persons or characters. Turkey was a short, pursy Englishman of about my own age, that is, somewhere not far from sixty. In the morning, one might say, his face was of a fine florid hue, but after twelve o'clock, meridian—his dinner hour—it blazed like a grate full of Christmas coals, and continued blazing—but as it were with a gradual wane—till 6 o'clock P.M. or thereabouts, after which I saw no more of the proprietor of the face, which gaining its meridian with the sun, seemed to set with it, to rise, culminate, and decline the following day, with the like regularity and undiminished glory. There are many singular coincidences I have known in the course of my life, not the least among which was the fact that exactly when Turkey displayed his fullest beams from his red and radiant countenance, just then, too, at the critical moment began the daily period when I considered his business capacities as seriously disturbed for the remainder of the twenty-four hours. Not that he was absolutely idle or averse to business then; far from it. The difficulty was, he was apt to be altogether too energetic. There was a strange, inflamed, flurried, flighty recklessness of activity about him. He would be incautious in dipping his pen into his inkstand. All his blots upon my documents were dropped there after twelve o'clock, meridian. Indeed not only would he be reckless and sadly given to making blots in the afternoon, but some days he went further and was rather noisy. At such times, too, his face flamed with augmented blazonry, as if cannel coal had been heaped on anthracite. He made an unpleasant racket with his chair; spilled his sand-box°; in mending his pens, impatiently split them all to pieces, and threw them on the floor in a sudden passion; stood up and leaned over his table, boxing his papers about in a most indecorous manner, very sad to behold in an elderly man like him. Nevertheless, as he was in many ways a most valuable person to me, and all the time before twelve o'clock, meridian, was the quickest, steadiest creature too, accomplishing a great deal of work in a style not easy to be matched—for these reasons, I was willing to overlook his

---

sand-box: sand kept in a shaker and used for blotting wet ink

eccentricities, though indeed occasionally I remonstrated with him. I did this very gently, however, because though the civilest, nay, the blandest and most reverential of men in the morning, yet in the afternoon he was disposed upon provocation to be slightly rash with his tongue, in fact insolent. Now valuing his morning services as I did, and resolved not to lose them; yet at the same time made uncomfortable by his inflamed ways after twelve o'clock; and being a man of peace, unwilling by my admonitions to call forth unseemly retorts from him, I took upon me one Saturday noon (he was always worse on Saturdays) to hint to him very kindly that perhaps now that he was growing old, it might be well to abridge his labors; in short, he need not come to my chambers after twelve o'clock but, dinner over, had best go home to his lodgings and rest himself till tea-time. But no; he insisted upon his afternoon devotions. His countenance became intolerably fervid as he oratorically assured me—gesticulating with a long ruler at the other end of the room—that if his services in the morning were useful, how indispensable, then, in the afternoon?

"With submission, sir," said Turkey on this occasion. "I consider myself your right-hand man. In the morning I but marshal and deploy my columns, but in the afternoon I put myself at their head and gallantly charge the foe, thus!"—and he made a violent thrust with the ruler.

"But the blots, Turkey," intimated I.

"True,—but, with submission, sir, behold these hairs! I am getting old. Surely, sir, a blot or two of a warm afternoon is not to be severely urged against gray hairs. Old age—even if it blot the page—is honorable. With submission, sir, we *both* are getting old."

10   This appeal to my fellow-feeling was hardly to be resisted. At all events, I saw that go he would not. So I made up my mind to let him stay, resolving nevertheless to see to it that during the afternoon he had to do with my less important papers.

Nippers, the second on my list, was a whiskered, sallow, and upon the whole rather piratical-looking young man of about five and twenty. I always deemed him the victim of two evil powers—ambition and indigestion. The ambition was evinced by a certain impatience of the duties of a mere copyist, an unwarrantable usurpation of strictly professional affairs such as the original drawing up of legal documents. The indigestion seemed betokened in an occasional nervous testiness and grinning irritability causing the teeth to audibly grind together over mistakes committed in copying; unnecessary maledictions hissed rather than spoken in the heat of business; and especially by a continual discontent with the height of the table where he worked. Though of a very ingenious mechanical turn, Nippers could never get this table to suit him. He put chips under it, blocks of various sorts, bits of pasteboard, and at last went so far as to attempt an exquisite adjustment by final pieces of folded blotting-paper. But no invention would answer. If for the sake of easing his back he brought the table lid at a sharp angle well up towards his chin, and wrote there like a man using the steep roof of a Dutch house for his desk, then he declared that it stopped the circulation in his arms. If now he lowered the table to his waistbands and stooped over it in writing, then there was a sore aching in his back. In short, the truth of the matter was Nippers knew not what he wanted. Or if he wanted anything, it was to be rid of a scrivener's table altogether. Among the manifestations of his diseased ambition was a fondness he had for receiving visits from certain ambiguous-looking fellows in seedy coats, whom he called his clients. Indeed I was aware that not only was he at times considerable of a ward-politician, but he occasionally did a little business at the Justices' courts and was not unknown on the steps of the Tombs. I have good reason to believe however that one individual who called upon him at my chambers and who with a grand air he insisted was his client was no other than a dun, and the alleged title-deed, a bill. But with all his failings, and the annoyances he caused me, Nippers, like his compatriot Turkey, was a very useful man to me; wrote a neat, swift hand; and, when he chose, was not deficient in a gentlemanly sort of deportment. Added to this, he always dressed in a gentlemanly sort of way, and so incidentally reflected credit upon my chambers. Whereas with respect to Turkey, I had much ado to keep him from being a reproach to me. His clothes were apt to look oily and smell of eating-houses. He wore his pantaloons very loose and baggy in the summer. His coats were execrable, his hat not to be handled. But while the hat was a thing of indifference to me inasmuch as his natural civility and deference as a dependent Englishman always led him to doff it the moment he entered the room, yet his coat was another matter. Concerning his coats, I reasoned with him, but with no effect. The truth was I suppose that a man with so small an income could not afford to sport such a lustrous face and a lustrous coat at one and the same time. As Nippers once observed, Turkey's money went chiefly for red ink. One winter day I presented Turkey with a highly respectable looking coat of my own, a padded gray coat of a most comfortable warmth and which buttoned straight up from the knee to the neck. I thought Turkey would appreciate the favor and abate his rashness and obstreperousness of afternoons. But no. I verily believe that buttoning himself up in so downy and blanket-like a coat had a pernicious effect upon him, upon the same principle that too much oats are bad for horses. In fact, precisely as a rash, restive horse is said to feel his oats, so Turkey felt his coat. It made him insolent. He was a man whom prosperity harmed.

Though concerning the self-indulgent habits of Turkey I had my own private surmises, yet touching Nippers I was well persuaded that whatever might be his faults in other respects, he was at least a temperate young man. But indeed, nature herself seemed to have been his vintner and at his birth charged him so thoroughly with an irritable, brandy-like disposition that all subsequent potations were needless. When I consider how amid the stillness of my chambers Nippers would sometimes impatiently rise from his seat and stooping over his table spread his arms wide apart, seize the whole desk, and move it, and jerk it, with a grim, grinding motion on the floor, as if the table were a perverse voluntary agent intent on thwarting and vexing him, I plainly perceive that for Nippers, brandy and water were altogether superfluous.

It was fortunate for me that, owing to its peculiar cause—indigestion—the irritability and consequent nervousness of Nippers were mainly observable in the morning, while in the afternoon he was comparatively mild. So that Turkey's paroxysms only coming on about twelve o'clock, I never had to do with their eccentricities at one time. Their fits relieved each other like guards. When Nippers's was on, Turkey's was off, and vice versa. This was a good natural arrangement under the circumstances.

Ginger Nut, the third on my list, was a lad some twelve years old. His father was a carman,° ambitious of seeing his son on the bench instead of a cart before he died. So he sent him to my office as student at law, errand boy, and cleaner and sweeper, at the rate of one dollar a week. He had a little desk to himself but he did not use it much. Upon inspection, the drawer exhibited a great array of the shells of various sorts of nuts. Indeed, to this quick-witted youth the whole noble science of the law was contained in a nutshell. Not the least among the employments of Ginger Nut, as well as one which he discharged with the most alacrity, was his duty as cake and apple purveyor for Turkey and Nippers. Copying law papers being proverbially a dry, husky sort of business, my two scriveners were fain to moisten their mouths very often with Spitzenbergs° to be had at the numerous stalls nigh the Custom House and Post Office. Also, they sent Ginger Nut very frequently for that peculiar cake—small, flat, round, and very spicy—after which he had been named by them. Of a cold morning when business was but

carman: a cart driver   **Spitzenbergs:** a variety of apple

dull, Turkey would gobble up scores of these cakes as if they were mere wafers—indeed they sell them at the rate of six or eight for a penny—the scrape of his pen blending with the crunching of the crisp particles in his mouth. Of all the fiery afternoon blunders and flurried rashnesses of Turkey was his once moistening a ginger cake between his lips and clapping it on to a mortgage for a seal. I came within an ace of dismissing him then. But he mollified me by making an oriental bow and saying—"With submission, sir, it was generous of me to find you in stationery on my own account."

Now my original business—that of a conveyancer and title hunter, and drawer-up of recondite documents of all sorts—was considerably increased by receiving the master's office. There was now great work for scriveners. Not only must I push the clerks already with me, but I must have additional help. In answer to my advertisement, a motionless young man one morning stood upon my office threshold, the door being open, for it was summer. I can see that figure now—pallidly neat, pitiably respectable, incurably forlorn! It was Bartleby. 15

After a few words touching his qualifications I engaged him, glad to have among my corps of copyists a man of so singularly sedate an aspect, which I thought might operate beneficially upon the flighty temper of Turkey and the fiery one of Nippers.

I should have stated before that ground glass folding doors divided my premises into two parts, one of which was occupied by my scriveners, the other by myself. According to my humor I threw open these doors, or closed them. I resolved to assign Bartleby a corner by the folding doors, but on my side of them so as to have this quiet man within easy call in case any trifling thing was to be done. I placed his desk close up to a small side window in that part of the room, a window which originally had afforded a lateral view of certain grimy backyards and bricks, but which owing to subsequent erections commanded at present no view at all, though it gave some light. Within three feet of the panes was a wall, and the light came down from far above between two lofty buildings as from a very small opening in a dome. Still further to a satisfactory arrangement, I procured a high green folding screen which might entirely isolate Bartleby from my sight though not remove him from my voice. And thus, in a manner privacy and society were conjoined.

At first Bartleby did an extraordinary quantity of writing. As if long famishing for something to copy, he seemed to gorge himself on my documents. There was no pause for digestion. He ran a day and night line, copying by sunlight and by candlelight. I should have been quite delighted with his application had he been cheerfully industrious. But he wrote on silently, palely, mechanically.

It is of course an indispensable part of a scrivener's business to verify the accuracy of his copy, word by word. Where there are two or more scriveners in an office, they assist each other in this examination, one reading from the copy, the other holding the original. It is a very dull, wearisome, and lethargic affair. I can readily imagine that to some sanguine temperaments it would be altogether intolerable. For example, I cannot credit that the mettlesome poet Byron would have contentedly sat down with Bartleby to examine a law document of, say, five hundred pages closely written in a crimpy hand.

20   Now and then in the haste of business, it had been my habit to assist in comparing some brief document myself, calling Turkey or Nippers for this purpose. One object I had in placing Bartleby so handy to me behind the screen was to avail myself of his services on such trivial occasions. It was on the third day, I think, of his being with me, and before any necessity had arisen for having his own writing examined, that being much hurried to complete a small affair I had in hand, I abruptly called to Bartleby. In my haste and natural expectancy of instant compliance, I sat with my head bent over the original on my desk and my right hand sideways and somewhat nervously extended with the copy, so that immediately upon emerging from his retreat Bartleby might snatch it and proceed to business without the least delay.

In this very attitude did I sit when I called to him, rapidly stating what it was I wanted him to do—namely, to examine a small paper with me. Imagine my surprise, nay my consternation, when without moving from his privacy Bartleby in a singularly mild, firm voice replied, "I would prefer not to."

I sat awhile in perfect silence, rallying my stunned faculties. Immediately it occurred to me that my ears had deceived me, or Bartleby had entirely misunderstood my meaning. I repeated my request in the clearest tone I could assume. But in quite as clear a one came the previous reply, "I would prefer not to."

"Prefer not to," echoed I, rising in high excitement and crossing the room with a stride, "What do you mean? Are you moonstruck? I want you to help me compare this sheet here—take it," and I thrust it towards him.

"I would prefer not to," said he.

25   I looked at him steadfastly. His face was leanly composed, his gray eye dimly calm. Not a wrinkle of agitation rippled him. Had there been the least uneasiness, anger, impatience or impertinence in his manner, in other words had there been anything ordinarily human about him, doubtless I should have violently dismissed him from the premises. But as it was, I should have as soon thought of turning my pale plaster-of-

paris bust of Cicero out of doors. I stood gazing at him awhile as he went on with his own writing, and then reseated myself at my desk. This is very strange, thought I. What had one best do? But my business hurried me. I concluded to forget the matter for the present, reserving it for my future leisure. So calling Nippers from the other room, the paper was speedily examined.

A few days after this Bartleby concluded four lengthy documents, being quadruplicates of a week's testimony taken before me in my High Court of Chancery. It became necessary to examine them. It was an important suit and great accuracy was imperative. Having all things arranged I called Turkey, Nippers and Ginger Nut from the next room, meaning to place the four copies in the hands of my four clerks while I should read from the original. Accordingly Turkey, Nippers and Ginger Nut had taken their seats in a row, each with his document in hand, when I called to Bartleby to join this interesting group.

"Bartleby! quick, I am waiting."

I heard a slow scrape of his chair legs on the unscraped floor, and soon he appeared standing at the entrance of his hermitage.

"What is wanted?" said he mildly.

"The copies, the copies," said I hurriedly. "We are going to examine them. There"—and I held towards him the fourth quadruplicate.   30

"I would prefer not to," he said, and gently disappeared behind the screen.

For a few moments I was turned into a pillar of salt° standing at the head of my seated column of clerks. Recovering myself, I advanced towards the screen and demanded the reason for such extraordinary conduct.

"Why do you refuse?"

"I would prefer not to."

With any other man I should have flown outright into a dreadful   35 passion, scorned all further words, and thrust him ignominiously from my presence. But there was something about Bartleby that not only strangely disarmed me, but in a wonderful manner touched and disconcerted me. I began to reason with him.

"These are your own copies we are about to examine. It is labor saving to you, because one examination will answer for your four papers. It is common usage. Every copyist is bound to help examine his copy. Is it not so? Will you not speak? Answer!"

"I prefer not to," he replied in a flute-like tone. It seemed to me that while I had been addressing him, he carefully revolved every

pillar of salt: See Genesis 19.26.

statement that I made, fully comprehended the meaning, could not gainsay the irresistible conclusion, but at the same time some paramount consideration prevailed with him to reply as he did.

"You are decided, then, not to comply with my request—a request made according to common usage and common sense?"

He briefly gave me to understand that on that point my judgment was sound. Yes: his decision was irreversible.

40   It is not seldom the case that when a man is browbeaten in some unprecedented and violently unreasonable way he begins to stagger in his own plainest faith. He begins, as it were, vaguely to surmise that wonderful as it may be, all the justice and all the reason is on the other side. Accordingly, if any disinterested persons are present he turns to them for some reinforcement for his own faltering mind.

"Turkey," said I, "what do you think of this? Am I not right?"

"With submission, sir," said Turkey with his blandest tone, "I think that you are."

"Nippers," said I, "what do *you* think of it?"

"I think I should kick him out of the office."

45   (The reader of nice perceptions will here perceive that, it being morning, Turkey's answer is couched in polite and tranquil terms, but Nippers replies in ill-tempered ones. Or, to repeat a previous sentence, Nippers's ugly mood was on duty, and Turkey's off.)

"Ginger Nut," said I, willing to enlist the smallest suffrage in my behalf, "what do *you* think of it?"

"I think, sir, he's a little *loony*," replied Ginger Nut, with a grin.

"You hear what they say," said I, turning towards the screen, "come forth and do your duty."

But he vouchsafed no reply. I pondered a moment in sore perplexity. But once more business hurried me. I determined again to postpone the consideration of this dilemma to my future leisure. With a little trouble we made out to examine the papers without Bartleby, though at every page or two, Turkey deferentially dropped his opinion that this proceeding was quite out of the common, while Nippers, twitching in his chair with a dyspeptic nervousness, ground out between his set teeth occasional hissing maledictions against the stubborn oaf behind the screen. And for his (Nippers's) part, this was the first and the last time he would do another man's business without pay.

50   Meanwhile Bartleby sat in his hermitage, oblivious to everything but his own peculiar business there.

Some days passed, the scrivener being employed upon another lengthy work. His late remarkable conduct led me to regard his way narrowly. I observed that he never went to dinner, indeed that he never went anywhere. As yet I had never of my personal knowledge known him to be outside of my office. He was a perpetual sentry in the corner. At about eleven o'clock though, in the morning, I noticed that Ginger Nut would advance toward the opening in Bartleby's screen as if silently beckoned thither by a gesture invisible to me where I sat. That boy would then leave the office jingling a few pence and reappear with a handful of ginger nuts which he delivered in the hermitage, receiving two of the cakes for his trouble.

He lives then on ginger nuts, thought I; never eats a dinner, properly speaking; he must be a vegetarian then, but no, he never eats even vegetables, he eats nothing but ginger nuts. My mind then ran on in reveries concerning the probable effects upon the human constitution of living entirely on ginger nuts. Ginger nuts are so called because they contain ginger as one of their peculiar constituents, and the final flavoring one. Now what was ginger? A hot, spicy thing. Was Bartleby hot and spicy? Not at all. Ginger, then, had no effect upon Bartleby. Probably he preferred it should have none.

Nothing so aggravates an earnest person as a passive resistance. If the individual so resisted be of a not inhumane temper, and the resisting one perfectly harmless in his passivity, then in the better moods of the former, he will endeavor charitably to construe to his imagination what proves impossible to be solved by his judgment. Even so for the most part I regarded Bartleby and his ways. Poor fellow! thought I, he means no mischief; it is plain he intends no insolence; his aspect sufficiently evinces that his eccentricities are involuntary. He is useful to me. I can get along with him. If I turn him away, the chances are he will fall in with some less indulgent employer, and then he will be rudely treated and perhaps driven forth miserably to starve. Yes. Here I can cheaply purchase a delicious self-approval. To befriend Bartleby, to humor him in his strange wilfulness, will cost me little or nothing, while I lay up in my soul what will eventually prove a sweet morsel for my conscience. But this mood was not invariable with me. The passiveness of Bartleby sometimes irritated me. I felt strangely goaded on to encounter him in new opposition, to elicit some angry spark from him answerable to my own. But indeed I might as well have essayed to strike fire with my knuckles against a bit of Windsor soap. But one afternoon the evil impulse in me mastered me, and the following little scene ensued:

"Bartleby," said I, "when those papers are all copied I will compare them with you."

"I would prefer not to."   55

"How? Surely you do not mean to persist in that mulish vagary?"

No answer.

I threw open the folding doors nearby, and turning upon Turkey and Nippers, exclaimed in an excited manner—

"He says, a second time, he won't examine his papers. What do you think of it, Turkey?"

60   It was afternoon, be it remembered. Turkey sat glowing like a brass boiler, his bald head steaming, his hands reeling among his blotted papers.

"Think of it?" roared Turkey, "I think I'll just step behind his screen and black his eyes for him!"

So saying, Turkey rose to his feet and threw his arms into a pugilistic position. He was hurrying away to make good his promise when I detained him, alarmed at the effect of incautiously rousing Turkey's combativeness after dinner.

"Sit down, Turkey," said I, "and hear what Nippers has to say. What do you think of it, Nippers? Would I not be justified in immediately dismissing Bartleby?"

"Excuse me, that is for you to decide, sir. I think his conduct quite unusual, and indeed unjust as regards Turkey and myself. But it may only be a passing whim."

65   "Ah," exclaimed I, "you have strangely changed your mind then— you speak very gently of him now."

"All beer," cried Turkey, "gentleness is effects of beer—Nippers and I dined together today. You see how gentle *I* am, sir. Shall I go and black his eyes?"

"You refer to Bartleby, I suppose. No, not today, Turkey," I replied, "pray, put up your fists."

I closed the doors, and again advanced towards Bartleby. I felt additional incentives tempting me to my fate. I burned to be rebelled against again. I remembered that Bartleby never left the office.

"Bartleby," said I, "Ginger Nut is away; just step round to the post office, won't you? (it was but a three minutes walk) and see if there is anything for me."

70   "I would prefer not to."

"You *will* not?"

"I *prefer* not."

I staggered to my desk and sat there in a deep study. My blind inveteracy returned. Was there any other thing in which I could procure myself to be ignominiously repulsed by this lean, penniless wight?—my hired clerk? What added thing is there, perfectly reasonable, that he will be sure to refuse to do?

"Bartleby!"

No answer.   75

"Bartleby," in a louder tone.

No answer.

"Bartleby," I roared.

Like a very ghost, agreeably to the laws of magical invocation, at the third summons he appeared at the entrance of his hermitage.

"Go to the next room, and tell Nippers to come to me."   80

"I prefer not to," he respectfully and slowly said, and mildly disappeared.

"Very good, Bartleby," said I, in a quiet sort of serenely severe self-possessed tone, intimating the unalterable purpose of some terrible retribution very close at hand. At the moment I half intended something of the kind. But upon the whole, as it was drawing towards my dinner hour, I thought it best to put on my hat and walk home for the day, suffering much from perplexity and distress of mind.

Shall I acknowledge it? The conclusion of this whole business was that it soon became a fixed fact of my chambers that a pale young scrivener by the name of Bartleby had a desk there; that he copied for me at the usual rate of four cents a folio (one hundred words); but he was permanently exempt from examining the work done by him, that duty being transferred to Turkey and Nippers, one of compliment doubtless to their superior acuteness; moreover, said Bartleby was never on any account to be dispatched on the most trivial errand of any sort, and that even if entreated to take upon him such a matter, it was generally understood that he would prefer not to—in other words, that he would refuse point-blank.

As days passed on, I became considerably reconciled to Bartleby. His steadiness, his freedom from all dissipation, his incessant industry (except when he chose to throw himself into a standing revery behind his screen), his great stillness, his unalterableness of demeanor under all circumstances, made him a valuable acquisition. One prime thing was this—*he was always there*—first in the morning, continually through the day, and the last at night. I had a singular confidence in his honesty. I felt my most precious papers perfectly safe in his hands. Sometimes to be sure I could not for the very soul of me avoid falling into sudden spasmodic passions with him. For it was exceeding difficult to bear in mind all the time those strange peculiarities, privileges, and unheard of exemptions forming the tacit stipulations on Bartleby's part under which he remained in my office. Now and then in the eagerness of dispatching pressing business, I would inadvertently summon Bartleby, in a short rapid tone, to put his finger, say, on the incipient tie of a bit of red tape with which I was about compressing some papers. Of course, from behind the screen the usual answer, "I prefer not to," was sure to come, and then how could a human creature with the common infirmities of our nature, refrain from bitterly exclaiming upon such perverseness—such unreasonableness? However, every added repulse of this sort which I received only tended to lessen the probability of my repeating the inadvertence.

85   Here it must be said that according to the custom of most legal gentlemen occupying chambers in densely populated law buildings, there were several keys to my door. One was kept by a woman residing in the attic, which person weekly scrubbed and daily swept and dusted my apartments. Another was kept by Turkey for convenience sake. The third I sometimes carried in my own pocket. The fourth I knew not who had.

Now one Sunday morning I happened to go to Trinity Church° to hear a celebrated preacher, and finding myself rather early on the ground I thought I would walk round to my chambers for a while. Luckily I had my key with me, but upon applying it to the lock, I found it resisted by something inserted from the inside. Quite surprised, I called out, when to my consternation a key was turned from within, and thrusting his lean visage at me and holding the door ajar, the apparition of Bartleby appeared, in his shirt sleeves, and otherwise in a strangely tattered dishabille, saying quietly that he was sorry but he was deeply engaged just then and—preferred not admitting me at present. In a brief word or two, he moreover added that perhaps I had better walk round the block two or three times, and by that time he would probably have concluded his affairs.

Now, the utterly unsurmised appearance of Bartleby tenanting my law-chambers of a Sunday morning with his cadaverously gentlemanly nonchalance, yet withal firm and self-possessed, had such a strange effect upon me that incontinently I slunk away from my own door and did as desired. But not without sundry twinges of impotent rebellion against the mild effrontery of this unaccountable scrivener. Indeed it was his wonderful mildness chiefly which not only disarmed me but unmanned me, as it were. For I consider that one, for the time, is a sort of unmanned when he tranquilly permits his hired clerk to dictate to him and order him away from his own premises. Furthermore, I was full of uneasiness as to what Bartleby could possibly be doing in my office in his shirt sleeves and in an otherwise dismantled condition of a Sunday morning. Was anything amiss going on? Nay, that was out of the question. It was not to be thought of for a moment that Bartleby was an im-

Trinity Church: located at the corner of Broadway and Wall Street

moral person. But what could he be doing there?—copying? Nay again, whatever might be his eccentricities, Bartleby was an eminently decorous person. He would be the last man to sit down to his desk in any state approaching to nudity. Besides, it was Sunday, and there was something about Bartleby that forbade the supposition that he would by any secular occupation violate the proprieties of the day.

Nevertheless, my mind was not pacified; and full of a restless curiosity, at last I returned to the door. Without hindrance I inserted my key, opened it, and entered. Bartleby was not to be seen. I looked round anxiously, peeped behind his screen, but it was very plain that he was gone. Upon more closely examining the place, I surmised that for an indefinite period Bartleby must have ate, dressed, and slept in my office, and that too without plate, mirror, or bed. The cushioned seat of a rickety old sofa in one corner bore the faint impress of a lean, reclining form. Rolled away under his desk I found a blanket; under the empty grate, a blacking box and brush; on a chair, a tin basin with soap and a ragged towel; in a newspaper a few crumbs of ginger nuts and a morsel of cheese. Yes, thought I, it is evident enough that Bartleby has been making his home here, keeping bachelor's hall all by himself. Immediately then the thought came sweeping across me, what miserable friendlessness and loneliness are here revealed! His poverty is great; but his solitude, how horrible! Think of it. Of a Sunday, Wall Street is deserted as Petra, and every night of every day it is an emptiness. This building too which of weekdays hums with industry and life at nightfall echoes with sheer vacancy, and all through Sunday is forlorn. And here Bartleby makes his home, sole spectator of a solitude which he has seen all populous—a sort of innocent and transformed Marius brooding among the ruins of Carthage!

For the first time in my life a feeling of overpowering stinging melancholy seized me. Before I had never experienced aught but a not unpleasing sadness. The bond of a common humanity now drew me irresistibly to gloom. A fraternal melancholy! For both I and Bartleby were sons of Adam. I remembered the bright silks and sparkling faces I had seen that day in gala trim, swan-like sailing down the Mississippi of Broadway; and I contrasted them with the pallid copyist, and thought to myself, Ah, happiness courts the light, so we deem the world is gay; but misery hides aloof, so we deem that misery there is none. These sad fancyings—chimeras doubtless of a sick and silly brain—led on to other and more special thoughts concerning the eccentricities of Bartleby. Presentiments of strange discoveries hovered round me. The scrivener's pale form appeared to me laid out, among uncaring strangers, in its shivering winding sheet.

90   Suddenly I was attracted by Bartleby's closed desk, the key in open
         sight left in the lock.
            I mean no mischief, seek the gratification of no heartless curiosity,
         thought I; besides, the desk is mine, and its contents too, so I will make
         bold to look within. Everything was methodically arranged, the papers
         smoothly placed. The pigeon holes were deep, and removing the files
         of documents, I groped into their recesses. Presently I felt something
         there and dragged it out. It was an old bandanna handkerchief, heavy
         and knotted. I opened it, and saw it was a savings bank.
            I now recalled all the quiet mysteries which I had noted in the
         man. I remembered that he never spoke but to answer; that though at
         intervals he had considerable time to himself, yet I had never seen him
         reading—no, not even a newspaper; that for long periods he would
         stand looking out, at his pale window behind the screen, upon the dead
         brick wall; I was quite sure he never visited any refectory or eating
         house, while his pale face clearly indicated that he never drank beer
         like Turkey, or tea and coffee even, like other men; that he never went
         anywhere in particular that I could learn, never went out for a walk,
         unless indeed that was the case at present; that he had declined telling
         who he was or whence he came or whether he had any relatives in the
         world; that though so thin and pale, he never complained of ill health.
         And more than all, I remembered a certain unconscious air of pallid—
         how shall I call it?—of pallid haughtiness, say, or rather an austere re-
         serve about him, which had positively awed me into my tame compli-
         ance with his eccentricities when I had feared to ask him to do the
         slightest incidental thing for me, even though I might know from his
         long-continued motionlessness that behind his screen he must be
         standing in one of those dead-wall reveries of his.
            Revolving all these things, and coupling them with the recently
         discovered fact that he made my office his constant abiding place and
         home, and not forgetful of his morbid moodiness; revolving all these
         things, a prudential feeling began to steal over me. My first emotions
         had been those of pure melancholy and sincerest pity; but just in pro-
         portion as the forlornness of Bartleby grew and grew to my imagination,
         did that same melancholy merge into fear, that pity into repulsion. So
         true it is, and so terrible too, that up to a certain point the thought or
         sight of misery enlists our best affections; but in certain special cases,
         beyond that point it does not. They err who would assert that invari-
         ably this is owing to the inherent selfishness of the human heart. It
         rather proceeds from a certain hopelessness of remedying excessive and
         organic ill. To a sensitive being, pity is not seldom pain. And when at
         last it is perceived that such pity cannot lead to effectual succor, com-

mon sense bids the soul be rid of it. What I saw that morning persuaded me that the scrivener was the victim of innate and incurable disorder. I might give alms to his body, but his body did not pain him; it was his soul that suffered, and his soul I could not reach.

I did not accomplish the purpose of going to Trinity Church that morning. Somehow, the things I had seen disqualified me for the time from church-going. I walked homeward, thinking what I would do with Bartleby. Finally I resolved upon this:—I would put certain calm questions to him the next morning, touching his history, &c., and if he declined to answer them openly and unreservedly (and I supposed he would prefer not), then to give him a twenty dollar bill over and above whatever I might owe him, and tell him his services were no longer required; but that if in any other way I could assist him, I would be happy to do so, especially if he desired to return to his native place, wherever that might be, I would willingly help to defray the expenses. Moreover, if after reaching home he found himself at any time in want of aid, a letter from him would be sure of a reply.

The next morning came.   95

"Bartleby," said I, gently calling to him behind his screen.

No reply.

"Bartleby," said I, in a still gentler tone, "come here; I am not going to ask you to do anything you would prefer not to do—I simply wish to speak to you."

Upon this he noiselessly slid into view.

"Will you tell me, Bartleby, where you were born?"   100

"I would prefer not to."

"Will you tell me *anything* about yourself?"

"I would prefer not to."

"But what reasonable objection can you have to speak to me? I feel friendly towards you."

He did not look at me while I spoke, but kept his glance fixed upon   105
my bust of Cicero, which as I then sat was directly behind me, some six inches above my head.

"What is your answer, Bartleby?" said I, after waiting a considerable time for a reply, during which his countenance remained immovable, only there was the faintest conceivable tremor of the white attenuated mouth.

"At present I prefer to give no answer," he said, and retired into his hermitage.

It was rather weak in me I confess, but his manner on this occasion nettled me. Not only did there seem to lurk in it a certain disdain, but his perverseness seemed ungrateful, considering the undeniable good usage and indulgence he had received from me.

Again I sat ruminating what I should do. Mortified as I was at his behavior, and resolved as I had been to dismiss him when I entered my office, nevertheless I strangely felt something superstitious knocking at my heart, and forbidding me to carry out my purpose, and denouncing me for a villain if I dared to breathe one bitter word against this forlornest of mankind. At last, familiarly drawing my chair behind his screen, I sat down and said: "Bartleby, never mind then about revealing your history; but let me entreat you, as a friend, to comply as far as may be with the usages of this office. Say now you will help to examine papers tomorrow or next day: in short, say now that in a day or two you will begin to be a little reasonable:—say so, Bartleby."

110   "At present I would prefer not to be a little reasonable," was his mildly cadaverous reply.

Just then the folding doors opened, and Nippers approached. He seemed suffering from an unusually bad night's rest, induced by severer indigestion than common. He overheard those final words of Bartleby.

"*Prefer not*, eh?" gritted Nippers—"I'd *prefer* him, if I were you, sir," addressing me—"I'd *prefer* him; I'd give him preferences, the stubborn mule! What is it, sir, pray, that he *prefers* not to do now?"

Bartleby moved not a limb.

"Mr. Nippers," said I, "I'd prefer that you would withdraw for the present."

115   Somehow, of late I had got into the way of involuntarily using this word "prefer" upon all sorts of not exactly suitable occasions. And I trembled to think that my contact with the scrivener had already and seriously affected me in a mental way. And what further and deeper aberration might it not yet produce? This apprehension had not been without efficacy in determining me to summary means.

As Nippers, looking very sour and sulky, was departing, Turkey blandly and deferentially approached.

"With submission, sir," said he, "yesterday I was thinking about Bartleby here, and I think that if he would but prefer to take a quart of good ale every day, it would do much towards mending him and enabling him to assist in examining his papers."

"So you have got the word too," said I, slightly excited.

"With submission, what word, sir?" asked Turkey, respectfully crowding himself into the contracted space behind the screen, and by so doing making me jostle the scrivener. "What word, sir?"

120   "I would prefer to be left alone here," said Bartleby, as if offended at being mobbed in his privacy.

"*That's* the word, Turkey," said I—"*that's* it."

"Oh, *prefer?* oh yes—queer word. I never use it myself. But, sir, as I was saying, if he would but prefer—"

"Turkey," interrupted I, "you will please withdraw."

"Oh certainly, sir, if you prefer that I should."

As he opened the folding door to retire, Nippers at his desk caught a glimpse of me and asked whether I would prefer to have a certain paper copied on blue paper or white. He did not in the least roguishly accent the word prefer. It was plain that it involuntarily rolled from his tongue. I thought to myself, surely I must get rid of a demented man who already has in some degree turned the tongues if not the heads of myself and clerks. But I thought it prudent not to break the dismission at once. 125

The next day I noticed that Bartleby did nothing but stand at his window in his dead-wall revery. Upon my asking him why he did not write, he said that he had decided upon doing no more writing.

"Why, how now? what next?" exclaimed I, "do no more writing?"

"No more."

"And what is the reason?"

"Do you not see the reason for yourself?" he indifferently replied. 130

I looked steadfastly at him, and perceived that his eyes looked dull and glazed. Instantly it occurred to me that his unexampled diligence in copying by his dim window for the first few weeks of his stay with me might have temporarily impaired his vision.

I was touched. I said something in condolence with him. I hinted that of course he did wisely in abstaining from writing for a while, and urged him to embrace that opportunity of taking wholesome exercise in the open air. This, however, he did not do. A few days after this, my other clerks being absent, and being in a great hurry to dispatch certain letters by the mail, I thought that, having nothing else earthly to do, Bartleby would surely be less inflexible than usual and carry these letters to the post office. But he blankly declined. So, much to my inconvenience, I went myself.

Still added days went by. Whether Bartleby's eyes improved or not, I could not say. To all appearance, I thought they did. But when I asked him if they did, he vouchsafed no answer. At all events, he would do no copying. At last, in reply to my urgings, he informed me that he had permanently given up copying.

"What!" exclaimed I; "suppose your eyes should get entirely well—better than ever before—would you not copy then?"

"I have given up copying," he answered, and slid aside. 135

He remained as ever, a fixture in my chamber. Nay—if that were possible—he became still more of a fixture than before. What was to be done? He would do nothing in the office: why should he stay there? In plain fact, he had now become a millstone to me, not only useless as a necklace but afflictive to bear. Yet I was sorry for him. I speak less than truth when I say that on his own account, he occasioned me uneasiness. If he would but have named a single relative or friend, I would instantly have written and urged their taking the poor fellow away to some convenient retreat. But he seemed alone, absolutely alone in the universe. A bit of wreck in the mid-Atlantic. At length, necessities connected with my business tyrannized over all other considerations. Decently as I could, I told Bartleby that in six days' time he must unconditionally leave the office. I warned him to take measures, in the interval, for procuring some other abode. I offered to assist him in this endeavor, if he himself would but take the first step towards a removal. "And when you finally quit me, Bartleby," added I, "I shall see that you go not away entirely unprovided. Six days from this hour, remember."

At the expiration of that period I peeped behind the screen, and lo! Bartleby was there.

I buttoned up my coat, balanced myself, advanced slowly towards him, touched his shoulder, and said, "The time has come; you must quit this place; I am sorry for you; here is money; but you must go."

"I would prefer not," he replied, with his back still towards me.

140   "You *must.*"

He remained silent.

Now I had an unbounded confidence in this man's common honesty. He had frequently restored to me six pences and shillings carelessly dropped upon the floor, for I am apt to be very reckless in such shirt-button affairs. The proceeding then which followed will not be deemed extraordinary.

"Bartleby," said I, "I owe you twelve dollars on account; here are thirty-two; the odd twenty are yours. Will you take it?" and I handed the bills towards him.

But he made no motion.

145   "I will leave them here then," putting them under a weight on the table. Then taking my hat and cane and going to the door I tranquilly turned and added, "After you have removed your things from these offices, Bartleby, you will of course lock the door—since every one is now gone for the day but you—and if you please, slip your key underneath the mat so that I may have it in the morning. I shall not see you again, so good-bye to you. If hereafter in your new place of abode I can be of any service to you, do not fail to advise me by letter. Good-bye, Bartleby, and fare you well."

But he answered not a word; like the last column of some ruined temple, he remained standing mute and solitary in the middle of the otherwise deserted room.

As I walked home in a pensive mood, my vanity got the better of my pity. I could not but highly plume myself on my masterly management in getting rid of Bartleby. Masterly I call it, and such it must appear to any dispassionate thinker. The beauty of my procedure seemed to consist in its perfect quietness. There was no vulgar bullying, no bravado of any sort, no choleric hectoring and striding to and fro across the apartment, jerking out vehement commands for Bartleby to bundle himself off with his beggarly traps.° Nothing of the kind. Without loudly bidding Bartleby depart—as an inferior genius might have done—I *assumed* the ground that depart he must, and upon the assumption built all I had to say. The more I thought over my procedure, the more I was charmed with it. Nevertheless, next morning, upon awakening, I had my doubts—I had somehow slept off the fumes of vanity. One of the coolest and wisest hours a man has is just after he awakes in the morning. My procedure seemed as sagacious as ever—but only in theory. How it would prove in practice—there was the rub. It was truly a beautiful thought to have assumed Bartleby's departure; but after all, that assumption was simply my own, and none of Bartleby's. The great point was not whether I had assumed that he would quit me, but whether he would prefer so to do. He was more a man of preferences than assumptions.

After breakfast, I walked downtown, arguing the probabilities *pro* and *con*. One moment I thought it would prove a miserable failure, and Bartleby would be found all alive at my office as usual; the next moment it seemed certain that I should see his chair empty. And so I kept veering about. At the corner of Broadway and Canal Street, I saw quite an excited group of people standing in earnest conversation.

"I'll take odds he doesn't," said a voice as I passed.

"Doesn't go?—done!" said I, "put up your money."   150

I was instinctively putting my hand in my pocket to produce my own, when I remembered that this was an election day. The words I had overheard bore no reference to Bartleby, but to the success or non-success of some candidate for the mayoralty. In my intent frame of mind, I had, as it were, imagined that all Broadway shared in my excitement and were debating the same question with me. I passed on, very thankful that the uproar of the street screened my momentary absent-mindedness.

traps: belongings

As I had intended, I was earlier than usual at my office door. I stood listening for a moment. All was still. He must be gone. I tried the knob. The door was locked. Yes, my procedure had worked to a charm; he indeed must be vanished. Yet a certain melancholy mixed with this: I was almost sorry for my brilliant success. I was fumbling under the door mat for the key which Bartleby was to have left there for me when accidentally my knee knocked against a panel, producing a summoning sound, and in response a voice came to me from within—"Not yet; I am occupied."

It was Bartleby.

I was thunderstruck. For an instant I stood like the man who, pipe in mouth, was killed one cloudless afternoon long ago in Virginia, by summer lightning; at his own warm open window he was killed, and remained leaning out there upon the dreamy afternoon till someone touched him, when he fell.

155   "Not gone!" I murmured at last. But again obeying that wondrous ascendancy which the inscrutable scrivener had over me, and from which ascendancy, for all my chafing, I could not completely escape, I slowly went downstairs and out into the street, and while walking round the block, considered what I should next do in this unheard of perplexity. Turn the man out by an actual thrusting I could not; to drive him away by calling him hard names would not do; calling in the police was an unpleasant idea; and yet, permit him to enjoy his cadaverous triumph over me?—this too I could not think of. What was to be done? or if nothing could be done, was there anything further that I could *assume* in the matter? Yes, as before I had prospectively assumed that Bartleby would depart, so now I might retrospectively assume that departed he was. In the legitimate carrying out of this assumption, I might enter my office in a great hurry, and pretending not to see Bartleby at all, walk straight against him as if he were air. Such a proceeding would in a singular degree have the appearance of a home-thrust. It was hardly possible that Bartleby could withstand such an application of the doctrine of assumptions. But upon second thoughts the success of the plan seemed rather dubious. I resolved to argue the matter over with him again.

"Bartleby," said I, entering the office with a quietly severe expression, "I am seriously displeased. I am pained, Bartleby. I had thought better of you. I had imagined you of such a gentlemanly organization that in my delicate dilemma a slight hint would suffice—in short, an assumption. But it appears I am deceived. Why," I added, unaffectedly starting, "you have not even touched that money yet," pointing to it just where I had left it the evening previous.

He answered nothing.

"Will you, or will you not, quit me?" I now demanded in a sudden passion, advancing close to him.

"I would prefer *not* to quit you," he replied, gently emphasizing the not.

"What earthly right have you to stay here? Do you pay any rent?   160
Do you pay my taxes? Or is this property yours?"

He answered nothing.

"Are you ready to go on and write now? Are your eyes recovered? Could you copy a small paper for me this morning? or help examine a few lines? or step round to the post office? In a word, will you do anything at all to give a coloring to your refusal to depart the premises?"

He silently retired into his hermitage.

I was now in such a state of nervous resentment that I thought it but prudent to check myself at present from further demonstrations. Bartleby and I were alone. I remembered the tragedy of the unfortunate Adams and the still more unfortunate Colt° in the solitary office of the latter; and how poor Colt, being dreadfully incensed by Adams, and imprudently permitting himself to get wildly excited, was at unawares hurried into his fatal act—an act which certainly no man could possibly deplore more than the actor himself. Often it had occurred to me in my ponderings upon the subject that had that altercation taken place in the public street, or at a private residence, it would not have terminated as it did. It was the circumstance of being alone in a solitary office, upstairs, of a building entirely unhallowed by humanizing domestic associations—an uncarpeted office, doubtless, of a dusty haggard sort of appearance—this it must have been which greatly helped to enhance the irritable desperation of the hapless Colt.

But when this old Adam of resentment rose in me and tempted me   165
concerning Bartleby, I grappled him and threw him. How? Why, simply by recalling the divine injunction: "A new commandment° give I unto you, that ye love one another." Yes, this it was that saved me. Aside from higher considerations, charity often operates as a vastly wise and prudent principle—a great safeguard to its possessor. Men have committed murder for jealousy's sake, and anger's sake, and hatred's sake, and selfishness' sake, and spiritual pride's sake; but no man that ever I heard of ever committed a diabolical murder for sweet charity's sake. Mere self-interest, then, if no better motive can be enlisted, should, especially with high-tempered men, prompt all beings to charity and

---

Colt: In a famous murder case in 1841, John Colt used a hatchet to kill Samuel Adams, who owed him money.   **commandment:** See John 15.12.

philanthropy. At any rate, upon the occasion in question, I strove to drown my exasperated feelings towards the scrivener by benevolently construing his conduct. Poor fellow, poor fellow! thought I, he don't mean anything; and besides, he has seen hard times, and ought to be indulged.

I endeavored also immediately to occupy myself, and at the same time to comfort my despondency. I tried to fancy that in the course of the morning, at such time as might prove agreeable to him, Bartleby of his own free accord would emerge from his hermitage and take up some decided line of march in the direction of the door. But no. Half-past twelve o'clock came; Turkey began to glow in the face, overturn his inkstand, and become generally obstreperous; Nippers abated down into quietude and courtesy; Ginger Nut munched his noon apple; and Bartleby remained standing at his window in one of his profoundest dead-wall reveries. Will it be credited? Ought I to acknowledge it? That afternoon I left the office without saying one further word to him.

Some days now passed, during which at leisure intervals I looked a little into "Edwards on the Will," and "Priestly on Necessity."° Under the circumstances, those books induced a salutary feeling. Gradually I slid into the persuasion that these troubles of mine touching the scrivener had been all predestinated from eternity, and Bartleby was billeted upon me for some mysterious purpose of an all-wise Providence which it was not for a mere mortal like me to fathom. Yes, Bartleby, stay there behind your screen, thought I; I shall persecute you no more; you are harmless and noiseless as any of these old chairs; in short, I never feel so private as when I know you are here. At least I see it, I feel it; I penetrate to the predestinated purpose of my life. I am content. Others may have loftier parts to enact; but my mission in this world, Bartleby, is to furnish you with office-room for such period as you may see fit to remain.

I believe that this wise and blessed frame of mind would have continued with me had it not been for the unsolicited and uncharitable remarks obtruded upon me by my professional friends who visited the rooms. But thus it often is, that the constant friction of illiberal minds wears out at last the best resolves of the more generous. Though to be sure, when I reflected upon it, it was not strange that people entering my office should be struck by the peculiar aspect of the unaccountable Bartleby, and so be tempted to throw out some sinister observations concerning him. Sometimes an attorney having business with me, and

---

"Edwards . . . Necessity": writings by eighteenth-century philosophers who took the position that free will does not exist

calling at my office, and finding no one but the scrivener there, would undertake to obtain some sort of precise information from him touching my whereabouts; but without heeding his idle talk, Bartleby would remain standing immovable in the middle of the room. So after contemplating him in that position for a time, the attorney would depart, no wiser than he came.

Also, when a reference was going on, and the room full of lawyers and witnesses and business was driving fast, some deeply occupied legal gentleman present seeing Bartleby wholly unemployed would request him to run round to his (the legal gentleman's) office and fetch some papers for him. Thereupon, Bartleby would tranquilly decline, and remain idle as before. Then the lawyer would give a great stare and turn to me. And what could I say? At last I was made aware that all through the circle of my professional acquaintance, a whisper of wonder was running round having reference to the strange creature I kept at my office. This worried me very much. And as the idea came upon me of his possibly turning out a long-lived man, and keep occupying my chambers, and denying my authority, and perplexing my visitors, and scandalizing my professional reputation, and casting a general gloom over the premises, keeping soul and body together to the last upon his savings (for doubtless he spent but half a dime a day), and in the end perhaps outliving me, and claiming possession of my office by right of his perpetual occupancy: as all these dark anticipations crowded upon me more and more, and my friends continually intruded their relentless remarks upon the apparition in my room, a great change was wrought in me. I resolved to gather all my faculties together, and forever rid me of this intolerable incubus.

Ere revolving any complicated project, however, adapted to this end, I first simply suggested to Bartleby the propriety of his permanent departure. In a calm and serious tone, I commended the idea to his careful and mature consideration. But having taken three days to meditate upon it, he apprised me that his original determination remained the same, in short, that he still preferred to abide with me.   170

What shall I do? I now said to myself, buttoning up my coat to the last button. What shall I do? what ought I do? what does conscience say I *should* do with this man, or rather ghost? Rid myself of him, I must; go, he shall. But how? You will not thrust him, the poor, pale, passive mortal—you will not thrust such a helpless creature out of your door? you will not dishonor yourself by such cruelty? No, I will not, I cannot do that. Rather would I let him live and die here, and then mason up his remains in the wall. What then will you do? For all your coaxing, he will not budge. Bribes he leaves under your own paperweight on your table; in short, it is quite plain that he prefers to cling to you.

Then something severe, something unusual must be done. What! surely you will not have him collared by a constable, and commit his innocent pallor to the common jail? And upon what ground could you procure such a thing to be done?—a vagrant, is he? What! he a vagrant, a wanderer, who refuses to budge? It is because he will *not* be a vagrant, then, that you seek to count him *as* a vagrant. That is too absurd. No visible means of support: there I have him. Wrong again: for indubitably he *does* support himself, and that is the only unanswerable proof that any man can show of his possessing the means so to do. No more then. Since he will not quit me, I must quit him. I will change my offices; I will move elsewhere, and give him fair notice that if I find him on my new premises I will then proceed against him as a common trespasser.

Acting accordingly, next day I thus addressed him: "I find these chambers too far from the City Hall; the air is unwholesome. In a word, I propose to remove my offices next week, and shall no longer require your services. I tell you this now, in order that you may seek another place."

He made no reply, and nothing more was said.

175   On the appointed day I engaged carts and men, proceeded to my chambers, and having but little furniture, everything was removed in a few hours. Throughout, the scrivener remained standing behind the screen, which I directed to be removed the last thing. It was withdrawn, and being folded up like a huge folio, left him the motionless occupant of a naked room. I stood in the entry watching him a moment, while something from within me upbraided me.

I re-entered, with my hand in my pocket—and—and my heart in my mouth.

"Good-bye, Bartleby; I am going—good-bye, and God some way bless you; and take that," slipping something in his hand. But it dropped upon the floor, and then—strange to say—I tore myself from him whom I had so longed to be rid of.

Established in my new quarters, for a day or two I kept the door locked, and started at every footfall in the passages. When I returned to my rooms after any little absence, I would pause at the threshold for an instant, and attentively listen ere applying my key. But these fears were needless. Bartleby never came nigh me.

I thought all was going well, when a perturbed looking stranger visited me inquiring whether I was the person who had recently occupied rooms at No.— Wall Street.

180   Full of forebodings, I replied that I was.

"Then sir," said the stranger, who proved a lawyer, "you are responsible for the man you left there. He refuses to do any copying; he refuses to do anything; he says he prefers not to; and he refuses to quit the premises."

"I am very sorry, sir," said I, with assumed tranquility, but an inward tremor, "but, really, the man you allude to is nothing to me—he is no relation or apprentice of mine, that you should hold me responsible for him."

"In mercy's name, who is he?"

"I certainly cannot inform you. I know nothing about him. Formerly I employed him as a copyist, but he has done nothing for me now for some time past."

"I shall settle him then—good morning, sir."   185

Several days passed, and I heard nothing more; and though I often felt a charitable prompting to call at the place and see poor Bartleby, yet a certain squeamishness of I know not what withheld me.

All is over with him by this time, thought I at last, when through another week no further intelligence reached me. But coming to my room the day after, I found several persons waiting at my door in a high state of nervous excitement.

"That's the man—here he comes," cried the foremost one, whom I recognized as the lawyer who had previously called upon me alone.

"You must take him away, sir, at once," cried a portly person among them, advancing upon me, and whom I knew to be the landlord of No.— Wall Street. "These gentlemen, my tenants, cannot stand it any longer; Mr. B—" pointing to the lawyer, "has turned him out of his room, and he now persists in haunting the building generally, sitting upon the banisters of the stairs by day, and sleeping in the entry by night. Everybody is concerned; clients are leaving the offices; some fears are entertained of a mob; something you must do, and that without delay."

Aghast at this torrent, I fell back before it, and would fain have   190
locked myself in my new quarters. In vain I persisted that Bartleby was nothing to me—no more than to anyone else. In vain—I was the last person known to have anything to do with him, and they held me to the terrible account. Fearful then of being exposed in the papers (as one person present obscurely threatened), I considered the matter, and at length said that if the lawyer would give me a confidential interview with the scrivener, in his (the lawyer's) own room, I would that afternoon strive my best to rid them of the nuisance they complained of.

Going upstairs to my old haunt, there was Bartleby silently sitting upon the banister at the landing.

"What are you doing here, Bartleby?" said I.

"Sitting upon the banister," he mildly replied.

I motioned him into the lawyer's room, who then left us.

195   "Bartleby," said I, "are you aware that you are the cause of great tribulation to me, by persisting in occupying the entry after being dismissed from the office?"

No answer.

"Now one of two things must take place. Either you must do something or something must be done to you. Now what sort of business would you like to engage in? Would you like to re-engage in copying for someone?"

"No; I would prefer not to make any change."

"Would you like a clerkship in a dry-goods store?"

200   "There is too much confinement about that. No, I would not like a clerkship; but I am not particular."

"Too much confinement," I cried, "why you keep yourself confined all the time!"

"I would prefer not to take a clerkship," he rejoined, as if to settle that little item at once.

"How would a bar-tender's business° suit you? There is no trying of the eyesight in that."

"I would not like it at all; though, as I said before, I am not particular."

205   His unwonted wordiness inspirited me. I returned to the charge.

"Well then, would you like to travel through the country collecting bills for the merchants? That would improve your health."

"No, I would prefer to be doing something else."

"How then would going as a companion to Europe, to entertain some young gentleman with your conversation—how would that suit you?"

"Not at all. It does not strike me that there is anything definite about that. I like to be stationary. But I am not particular."

210   "Stationary you shall be then," I cried, now losing all patience, and for the first time in all my exasperating connection with him fairly flying into a passion. "If you do not go away from these premises before night, I shall feel bound—indeed I *am* bound—to—to—to quit the premises myself!" I rather absurdly concluded, knowing not with what possible threat to try to frighten his immobility into compliance. Despairing of all further efforts, I was precipitately leaving him, when a final thought occurred to me—one which had not been wholly unindulged before.

"Bartleby," said I, in the kindest tone I could assume under such exciting circumstances, "will you go home with me now—not to my

bar-tender's business: work as an attendant in a courtroom

office, but my dwelling—and remain there till we can conclude upon some convenient arrangement for you at our leisure? Come, let us start now, right away."

"No: at present I would prefer not to make any change at all."

I answered nothing, but effectually dodging everyone by the suddenness and rapidity of my flight, rushed from the building, ran up Wall Street towards Broadway, and jumping into the first omnibus was soon removed from pursuit. As soon as tranquility returned I distinctly perceived that I had now done all that I possibly could, both in respect to the demands of the landlord and his tenants, and with regard to my own desire and sense of duty, to benefit Bartleby and shield him from rude persecution. I now strove to be entirely carefree and quiescent; and my conscience justified me in the attempt though indeed it was not so successful as I could have wished. So fearful was I of being again hunted out by the incensed landlord and his exasperated tenants that, surrendering my business to Nippers, for a few days I drove about the upper part of the town and through the suburbs in my rockaway; crossed over to Jersey City and Hoboken, and paid fugitive visits to Manhattanville and Astoria. In fact I almost lived in my rockaway for the time.

When again I entered my office, lo, a note from the landlord lay upon the desk. I opened it with trembling hands. It informed me that the writer had sent to the police and had Bartleby removed to the Tombs as a vagrant. Moreover, since I knew more about him than anyone else, he wished me to appear at that place and make a suitable statement of the facts. These tidings had a conflicting effect upon me. At first I was indignant, but at last almost approved. The landlord's energetic, summary disposition had led him to adopt a procedure which I do not think I would have decided upon myself; and yet as a last resort, under such peculiar circumstances, it seemed the only plan.

As I afterwards learned, the poor scrivener, when told that he must be conducted to the Tombs, offered not the slightest obstacle, but in his pale unmoving way, silently acquiesced.   215

Some of the compassionate and curious bystanders joined the party; and headed by one of the constables arm in arm with Bartleby, the silent procession filed its way through all the noise, and heat, and joy of the roaring thoroughfares at noon.

The same day I received the note I went to the Tombs or, to speak more properly, the Halls of Justice. Seeking the right officer, I stated the purpose of my call, and was informed that the individual I described was indeed within. I then assured the functionary that Bartleby was a perfectly honest man, and greatly to be compassionated, however unaccountably eccentric. I narrated all I knew, and closed by suggesting the idea of letting him remain in as indulgent confinement as possible till something less harsh might be done—though indeed I hardly knew what. At all events, if nothing else could be decided upon, the alms-house must receive him. I then begged to have an interview.

Being under no disgraceful charge, and quite serene and harmless in all his ways, they had permitted him freely to wander about the prison, and especially in the inclosed grass-platted yards thereof. And so I found him there, standing all alone in the quietest of the yards, his face towards a high wall, while all around, from the narrow slits of the jail windows, I thought I saw peering out upon him the eyes of murderers and thieves.

"Bartleby!"

"I know you," he said, without looking around—"and I want nothing to say to you."

"It was not I that brought you here, Bartleby," said I, keenly pained at his implied suspicion. "And to you, this should not be so vile a place. Nothing reproachful attaches to you by being here. And see, it is not so sad a place as one might think. Look, there is the sky, and here is the grass."

"I know where I am," he replied, but would say nothing more, and so I left him.

As I entered the corridor again, a broad meat-like man in an apron accosted me, and jerking his thumb over his shoulder said—"Is that your friend?"

"Yes."

"Does he want to starve? If he does, let him live on the prison fare, that's all."

"Who are you?" asked I, not knowing what to make of such an unofficially speaking person in such a place.

"I am the grub-man. Such gentlemen as have friends here, hire me to provide them with something good to eat."

"Is this so?" said I, turning to the turnkey.

He said it was.

"Well, then," said I, slipping some silver into the grub-man's hands (for so they called him), "I want you to give particular attention to my friend there; let him have the best dinner you can get. And you must be as polite to him as possible."

"Introduce me, will you?" said the grub-man, looking at me with an expression which seemed to say he was all impatience for an opportunity to give a specimen of his breeding.

220

225

230

Thinking it would prove of benefit to the scrivener, I acquiesced, and asking the grub-man his name, went up with him to Bartleby.

"Bartleby, this is a friend; you will find him very useful to you."

"Your sarvant, sir, your sarvant," said the grub-man making a low salutation behind his apron. "Hope you find it pleasant here, sir—spacious grounds—cool apartments, sir—hope you'll stay with us some time—try to make it agreeable. What will you have for dinner today?"

"I prefer not to dine today," said Bartleby, turning away. "It would   235 disagree with me; I am unused to dinners." So saying he slowly moved to the other side of the enclosure, and took up a position fronting the dead wall.

"How's this?" said the grub-man, addressing me with a stare of astonishment. "He's odd, ain't he?"

"I think he is a little deranged," said I, sadly.

"Deranged? deranged is it? Well now, upon my word, I thought that friend of yourn was a gentleman forger; they are always pale and genteel-like, them forgers. I can't help pity 'em—can't help it, sir. Did you know Monroe Edwards?" he added touchingly, and paused. Then, laying his hand pityingly on my shoulder, sighed, "he died of consumption at Sing-Sing. So you weren't acquainted with Monroe?"

"No, I was never socially acquainted with any forgers. But I cannot stop longer. Look to my friend yonder. You will not lose by it. I will see you again."

Some few days after this, I again obtained admission to the Tombs,   240 and went through the corridors in quest of Bartleby, but without finding him.

"I saw him coming from his cell not long ago," said a turnkey, "maybe he's gone to loiter in the yards."

So I went in that direction.

"Are you looking for the silent man?" said another turnkey passing me. "Yonder he lies—sleeping in the yard there. 'Tis not twenty minutes since I saw him lie down."

The yard was entirely quiet. It was not accessible to the common prisoners. The surrounding walls, of amazing thickness, kept off all sound behind them. The Egyptian character of the masonry weighed upon me with its gloom. But a soft imprisoned turf grew under foot. The heart of the eternal pyramids, it seemed, wherein, by some strange magic, through the clefts, grass-seed dropped by birds had sprung.

Strangely huddled at the base of the wall, his knees drawn up,   245 and lying on his side, his head touching the cold stones, I saw the wasted Bartleby. But nothing stirred. I paused; then went close up to him; stooped over, and saw that his dim eyes were open; otherwise he seemed profoundly sleeping. Something prompted me to touch him. I felt his hand, when a tingling shiver ran up my arm and down my spine to my feet.

The round face of the grub-man peered upon me now. "His dinner is ready. Won't he dine today, either? Or does he live without dining?"

"Lives without dining," said I, and closed the eyes.

"Eh!—He's asleep, ain't he?"

"With kings and counselors,"° murmured I.

250   There would seem little need for proceeding further in this history. Imagination will readily supply the meager recital of poor Bartleby's interment. But ere parting with the reader, let me say that if this little narrative has sufficiently interested him to awaken curiosity as to who Bartleby was, and what manner of life he led prior to the present narrator's making his acquaintance, I can only reply that in such curiosity I fully share, but am wholly unable to gratify it. Yet here I hardly know whether I should divulge one little item of rumor which came to my ear a few months after the scrivener's decease. Upon what basis it rested, I could never ascertain; and hence how true it is I cannot now tell. But inasmuch as this vague report has not been without a certain strange suggestive interest to me, however sad, it may prove the same with some others; and so I will briefly mention it. The report was this: that Bartleby had been a subordinate clerk in the Dead Letter Office at Washington, from which he had been suddenly removed by a change in the administration. When I think over this rumor, I cannot adequately express the emotions which seize me. Dead letters! does it not sound like dead men? Conceive a man by nature and misfortune prone to a pallid hopelessness, can any business seem more fitted to heighten it than that of continually handling these dead letters and assorting them for the flames? For by the cart-load they are annually burned. Sometimes from out the folded paper the pale clerk takes a ring—the finger it was meant for, perhaps, moulders in the grave; a bank note sent in swiftest charity—he whom it would relieve, nor eats nor hungers any more; pardon for those who died despairing; hope for those who died unhoping; good tidings for those who died stifled by unrelieved calamities. On errands of life, these letters speed to death.

Ah, Bartleby! Ah, humanity!

"With . . . counselors": Job 3.14

Edgar Allan Poe
The Cask of Amontillado

The thousand injuries of Fortunato I had borne as I best could; but when he ventured upon insult, I vowed revenge. You, who so well know the nature of my soul, will not suppose, however, that I gave utterance to a threat. *At length* I would be avenged; this was a point definitively settled—but the very definitiveness with which it was resolved precluded the idea of risk. I must not only punish, but punish with impunity. A wrong is unredressed when retribution overtakes its redresser. It is equally unredressed when the avenger fails to make himself felt as such to him who has done the wrong.

It must be understood, that neither by word nor deed had I given Fortunato cause to doubt my good will. I continued, as was my wont, to smile in his face, and he did not perceive that my smile *now* was at the thought of his immolation.

He had a weak point—this Fortunato—although in other regards he was a man to be respected and even feared. He prided himself on his connoisseurship in wine. Few Italians have the true virtuoso spirit. For the most part their enthusiasm is adopted to suit the time and opportunity—to practice imposture upon the British and Austrian *millionaires*. In painting and gemmary Fortunato, like his countrymen, was a quack—but in the matter of old wines he was sincere. In this respect I did not differ from him materially: I was skillful in the Italian vintages myself, and bought largely whenever I could.

It was about dusk, one evening during the supreme madness of the carnival season, that I encountered my friend. He accosted me with excessive warmth, for he had been drinking much. The man wore motley. He had on a tight-fitting parti-striped dress, and his head was surmounted by the conical cap and bells. I was so pleased to see him, that I thought I should never have done wringing his hand.

THE CASK OF AMONTILLADO   First published in 1846. Edgar Allan Poe (1809–1849) was one of the first modern practitioners and theorists of the short story as a literary form, prescribing as its highest goal the creation of "a certain unique or single effect." His own achievement best matches his theory in his horror tales, of which this is an example. Poe was born in Boston, abandoned at the age of three by his father after the death of his mother, and raised by adoptive parents in Virginia. As a young man he failed in attempts at education at the University of Virginia and at West Point. Difficulty with alcohol combined with nervous sensitivity led to continuing health problems and perhaps to his early death. "Amontillado" is a dry Spanish sherry wine; "carnival" is the festive season preceding Lent.

5   I said to him—"My dear Fortunato, you are luckily met. How remarkably well you are looking today! But I have received a pipe of what
passes for Amontillado, and I have my doubts."

"How?" said he. "Amontillado? A pipe? Impossible! And in the
middle of the carnival!"

"I have my doubts," I replied; "and I was silly enough to pay the full
Amontillado price without consulting you in the matter. You were not
to be found, and I was fearful of losing a bargain."

"Amontillado!"

"I have my doubts."

10   "Amontillado!"

"And I must satisfy them."

"Amontillado!"

"As you are engaged, I am on my way to Luchesi. If anyone has a
critical turn, it is he. He will tell me—"

"Luchesi cannot tell Amontillado from Sherry."

15   "And yet some fools will have it that his taste is a match for
your own."

"Come, let us go."

"Whither?"

"To your vaults."

"My friend, no; I will not impose upon your good nature. I perceive
you have an engagement. Luchesi—"

20   "I have no engagement;—come."

"My friend, no. It is not the engagement, but the severe cold with
which I perceive you are afflicted. The vaults are insufferably damp.
They are encrusted with niter."

"Let us go, nevertheless. The cold is merely nothing. Amontillado!
You have been imposed upon. And as for Luchesi, he cannot distinguish Sherry from Amontillado."

Thus speaking, Fortunato possessed himself of my arm. Putting on
a mask of black silk, and drawing a *roquelaire*° closely about my person,
I suffered him to hurry me to my palazzo.

There were no attendants at home; they had absconded to make
merry in honor of the time. I had told them that I should not return until the morning, and had given them explicit orders not to stir from the
house. These orders were sufficient, I well knew, to insure their immediate disappearance, one and all, as soon as my back was turned.

---

roquelaire: a knee-length cloak worn in the eighteenth century

I took from their sconces two flambeaux, and giving one to Fortu-   25
nato, bowed him through several suites of rooms to the archway that
led into the vaults. I passed down a long and winding staircase, requesting him to be cautious as he followed. We came at length to the
foot of the descent, and stood together on the damp ground of the catacombs of the Montresors.

The gait of my friend was unsteady, and the bells upon his cap
jingled as he strode.

"The pipe," said he.

"It is farther on," said I; "but observe the white web-work which
gleams from these cavern walls."

He turned towards me, and looked into my eyes with two filmy orbs
that distilled the rheum of intoxication.

"Niter?" he asked, at length.   30

"Niter," I replied. "How long have you had that cough?"

"Ugh! ugh! ugh!—ugh! ugh! ugh!—ugh! ugh! ugh!—ugh! ugh!
ugh!—ugh! ugh! ugh!"

My poor friend found it impossible to reply for many minutes.

"It is nothing," he said, at last.

"Come," I said, with decision, "we will go back; your health is pre-   35
cious. You are rich, respected, admired, beloved; you are happy, as once I
was. You are a man to be missed. For me it is no matter. We will go back;
you will be ill, and I cannot be responsible. Beside, there is Luchesi—"

"Enough," he said; "the cough is a mere nothing; it will not kill me.
I shall not die of a cough."

"True—true," I replied; "and, indeed, I had no intention of alarm-
ing you unnecessarily—but you should use all proper caution. A
draught of this Medoc will defend us from the damps."

Here I knocked off the neck of a bottle which I drew from a long
row of its fellows that lay upon the mold.

"Drink," I said, presenting him the wine.

He raised it to his lips with a leer. He paused and nodded to me fa-   40
miliarly, while his bells jingled.

"I drink," he said, "to the buried that repose around us."

"And I to your long life."

He again took my arm, and we proceeded.

"These vaults," he said, "are extensive."

"The Montresors," I replied, "were a great and numerous family."   45

"I forget your arms."

"A huge human foot d'or, in a field azure; the foot crushes a serpent
rampant whose fangs are imbedded in the heel."

"And the motto?"

"*Nemo me impune lacessit.*"°

50   "Good!" he said.

The wine sparkled in his eyes and the bells jingled. My own fancy grew warm with the Medoc. We had passed through walls of piled bones, with casks and puncheons intermingling, into the inmost recesses of the catacombs. I paused again, and this time I made bold to seize Fortunato by an arm above the elbow.

"The niter!" I said; "see, it increases. It hangs like moss upon the vaults. We are below the river's bed. The drops of moisture trickle among the bones. Come, we will go back ere it is too late. Your cough—"

"It is nothing," he said; "let us go on. But first, another draught of the Medoc."

I broke and reached him a flacon of De Grâve. He emptied it at a breath. His eyes flashed with a fierce light. He laughed and threw the bottle upwards with a gesticulation I did not understand.

55   I looked at him in surprise. He repeated the movement—a grotesque one.

"You do not comprehend?" he said.

"Not I," I replied.

"Then you are not of the brotherhood."

"How?"

60   "You are not of the masons."

"Yes, yes," I said, "yes, yes."

"You? Impossible! A mason?"

"A mason," I replied.

"A sign," he said.

65   "It is this," I answered, producing a trowel from beneath the folds of my *roquelaire*.

"You jest," he exclaimed, recoiling a few paces. "But let us proceed to the Amontillado."

"Be it so," I said, replacing the tool beneath the cloak, and again offering him my arm. He leaned upon it heavily. We continued our route in search of the Amontillado. We passed through a range of low arches, descended, passed on, and descending again, arrived at a deep crypt, in which the foulness of the air caused our flambeaux rather to glow than flame.

At the most remote end of the crypt there appeared another less spacious. Its walls had been lined with human remains, piled to the vault overhead, in the fashion of the great catacombs of Paris. Three sides of

Nemo . . . lacessit: No one can provoke me and get away with it.

this interior crypt were still ornamented in this manner. From the fourth the bones had been thrown down, and lay promiscuously upon the earth, forming at one point a mound of some size. Within the wall thus exposed by the displacing of the bones, we perceived a still interior recess, in depth about four feet, in width three, in height six or seven. It seemed to have been constructed for no especial use within itself, but formed merely the interval between two of the colossal supports of the roof of the catacombs, and was backed by one of their circumscribing walls of solid granite.

It was in vain that Fortunato, uplifting his dull torch, endeavored to pry into the depth of the recess. Its termination the feeble light did not enable us to see.

"Proceed," I said; "herein is the Amontillado. As for Luchesi—"   70

"He is an ignoramus," interrupted my friend, as he stepped unsteadily forward, while I followed immediately at his heels. In an instant he had reached the extremity of the niche, and finding his progress arrested by the rock, stood stupidly bewildered. A moment more and I had fettered him to the granite. In its surface were two iron staples, distant from each other about two feet, horizontally. From one of these depended a short chain, from the other a padlock. Throwing the links about his waist, it was but the work of a few seconds to secure it. He was too much astounded to resist. Withdrawing the key I stepped back from the recess.

"Pass your hand," I said, "over the wall; you cannot help feeling the niter. Indeed it is *very* damp. Once more let me *implore* you to return. No? Then I must positively leave you. But I must first render you all the little attentions in my power."

"The Amontillado!" ejaculated my friend, not yet recovered from his astonishment.

"True," I replied; "the Amontillado."

As I said these words, I busied myself among the pile of bones of   75 which I have before spoken. Throwing them aside, I soon uncovered a quantity of building stone and mortar. With these materials and with the aid of my trowel, I began vigorously to wall up the entrance of the niche.

I had scarcely laid the first tier of the masonry when I discovered that the intoxication of Fortunato had in a great measure worn off. The earliest indication I had of this was a low moaning cry from the depth of the recess. It was *not* the cry of a drunken man. There was then a long and obstinate silence. I laid the second tier, and the third, and the fourth; and then I heard the furious vibrations of the chain. The noise lasted for several minutes, during which, that I might harken to it with the more satisfaction, I ceased my labors and sat down upon the bones. When at last the clanking subsided, I resumed the trowel, and finished without interruption the fifth, the sixth, and the seventh tier. The wall was now nearly upon a level with my breast. I again paused, and holding the flambeaux over the masonwork, threw a few feeble rays upon the figure within.

A succession of loud and shrill screams, bursting suddenly from the throat of the chained form, seemed to thrust me violently back. For a brief moment I hesitated—I trembled. Unsheathing my rapier, I began to grope with it about the recess: but the thought of an instant reassured me. I placed my hand upon the solid fabric of the catacombs, and felt satisfied. I reapproached the wall. I replied to the yells of him who clamored. I re-echoed—I aided—I surpassed them in volume and in strength. I did this, and the clamorer grew still.

It was now midnight, and my task was drawing to a close. I had completed the eighth, the ninth, and the tenth tier. I had finished a portion of the last and the eleventh; there remained but a single stone to be fitted and plastered in. I struggled with its weight; I placed it partially in its destined position. But now there came from out the niche a low laugh that erected the hairs upon my head. It was succeeded by a sad voice, which I had difficulty in recognising as that of the noble Fortunato. The voice said—

"Ha! ha! ha!—he! he!—a very good joke indeed—an excellent jest. We will have many a rich laugh about it at the palazzo—he! he! he!—over our wine—he! he! he!"

80   "The Amontillado!" I said.

"He! he! he!—he! he! he!—yes, the Amontillado. But is it not getting late? Will not they be awaiting us at the palazzo, the Lady Fortunato and the rest? Let us be gone."

"Yes," I said, "let us be gone."

"*For the love of God, Montresor!*"

"Yes," I said, "for the love of God!"

85   But to these words I harkened in vain for a reply. I grew impatient. I called aloud—

"Fortunato!"

No answer. I called again—

"Fortunato!"

No answer still. I thrust a torch through the remaining aperture and let it fall within. There came forth in return only a jingling of the bells. My heart grew sick—on account of the dampness of the catacombs. I hastened to make an end of my labor. I forced the last stone into its position; I plastered it up. Against the new masonry I re-erected the old rampart of bones. For the half of a century no mortal has disturbed them. *In pace requiescat!*°

In pace requiescat: May he rest in peace!

Elizabeth Tallent
No One's a Mystery

For my eighteenth birthday Jack gave me a five-year diary with a latch and a little key, light as a dime. I was sitting beside him scratching at the lock, which didn't want to work, when he thought he saw his wife's Cadillac in the distance, coming toward us. He pushed me down onto the dirty floor of the pickup and kept one hand on my head while I inhaled the musk of his cigarettes in the dashboard ashtray and sang along with Rosanne Cash on the tape deck. We'd been drinking tequila and the bottle was between his legs, resting up against his crotch, where the seam of his Levi's was bleached linen-white, though the Levi's were nearly new. I don't know why his Levi's always bleached like that, along the seams and at the knees. In a curve of cloth his zipper glinted, gold.

"It's her," he said. "She keeps the lights on in the daytime. I can't think of a single habit in a woman that irritates me more than that." When he saw that I was going to stay still he took his hand from my head and ran it through his own dark hair.

"Why does she?" I said.

"She thinks it's safe. Why does she need to be safer? She's driving exactly fifty-five miles an hour. She believes in those signs: 'Speed Monitored by Aircraft.' It doesn't matter that you can look up and see that the sky is empty."

"She'll see your lips move, Jack. She'll know you're talking to   5 someone."

"She'll think I'm singing along with the radio."

He didn't lift his hand, just raised the fingers in salute while the pressure of his palm steadied the wheel, and I heard the Cadillac honk twice, musically; he was driving easily eighty miles an hour. I studied his boots. The elk heads stitched into the leather were bearded with frayed thread, the toes were scuffed, and there was a compact wedge of muddy manure between the heel and the sole—the same boots he'd been wearing for the two years I'd known him. On the tape deck Rosanne Cash sang, "Nobody's into me, no one's a mystery."

"Do you think she's getting famous because of who her daddy is or for herself?" Jack said.

No One's a Mystery   First published in 1987. Elizabeth Tallent (b. 1955) is the author of a novel, *Museum Pieces*, and three collections of short stories. She has taught at the University of California at Irvine and the Iowa Writers Workshop, and currently teaches creative writing at Stanford University.

"There are about a hundred pop tops on the floor, did you know that? Some little kid could cut a bare foot on one of these, Jack."

10   "No little kids get into this truck except for you."

"How come you let it get so dirty?"

"'How come,'" he mocked. "You even sound like a kid. You can get back into the seat now, if you want. She's not going to look over her shoulder and see you."

"How do you know?"

"I just know," he said. "Like I know I'm going to get meat loaf for supper. It's in the air. Like I know what you'll be writing in that diary."

15   "What will I be writing?" I knelt on my side of the seat and craned around to look at the butterfly of dust printed on my jeans. Outside the window Wyoming was dazzling in the heat. The wheat was fawn and yellow and parted smoothly by the thin dirt road. I could smell the water in the irrigation ditches hidden in the wheat.

"Tonight you'll write, 'I love Jack. This is my birthday present from him. I can't imagine anybody loving anybody more than I love Jack.'"

"I can't."

"In a year you'll write, 'I wonder what I ever really saw in Jack. I wonder why I spent so many days just riding around in his pickup. It's true he taught me something about sex. It's true there wasn't ever much else to do in Cheyenne.'"

"I won't write that."

20   "In two years you'll write, 'I wonder what that old guy's name was, the one with the curly hair and the filthy dirty pickup truck and time on his hands.'"

"I won't write that."

"No?"

"Tonight I'll write, 'I love Jack. This is my birthday present from him. I can't imagine anybody loving anybody more than I love Jack.'"

"No, you can't," he says. "You can't imagine it."

25   "In a year I'll write, 'Jack should be home any minute now. The table is set—my grandmother's linen and her old silver and the yellow candles left over from the wedding—but I don't know if I can wait until after the trout à la Navarra to make love to him.'"

"It must have been a fast divorce."

"In two years I'll write, 'Jack should be home by now. Little Jack is hungry for his supper. He said his first word today besides "Mama" and "Papa." He said, "Caca."'"

Jack laughed. "He was probably trying to fingerpaint with caca on the bathroom wall when you heard him say it."

"In three years I'll write, 'My nipples are a little sore from nursing   30 Eliza Rosamund.'"

"Rosamund. Every little girl should have a middle name she hates."

"'Her breath smells like vanilla and her eyes are just Jack's color of blue.'"

"That's nice," Jack said.

"So? Which one do you like?"

"I like yours," he said. "But I believe mine."

"It doesn't matter. I believe mine."   35

"Not in your heart of hearts, you don't."

"You're wrong."

"I'm not wrong," he said. "And her breath would smell like your milk, and it's kind of a bittersweet smell, if you want to know the truth."

John Updike
A & P

In walks these three girls in nothing but bathing suits. I'm in the third check-out slot, with my back to the door, so I don't see them until they're over by the bread. The one that caught my eye first was the one in the plaid green two-piece. She was a chunky kid, with a good tan and a sweet broad soft-looking can with those two crescents of white just under it, where the sun never seems to hit, at the top of the backs of her legs. I stood there with my hand on a box of HiHo crackers trying to remember if I rang it up or not. I ring it up again and the customer starts giving me hell. She's one of these cash-register-watchers, a witch about fifty with rouge on her cheekbones and no eyebrows, and I know it made her day to trip me up. She'd been

A & P   First published in 1960. John Updike (b. 1932) is one of America's most celebrated contemporary writers and a highly prolific, equally adept practitioner in many genres: the novel, the short story, poetry, and criticism. Born in Shillington, Pennsylvania, he attended Harvard University and shortly after his graduation began publishing short stories in *The New Yorker,* the magazine with which his work is strongly identified. In his most characteristic fiction, he portrays the anxieties of middle-class life in a style of luminous clarity and realism.

watching cash registers for fifty years and probably never seen a mistake before.

By the time I got her feathers smoothed and her goodies into a bag—she gives me a little snort in passing, if she'd been born at the right time they would have burned her over in Salem—by the time I get her on her way the girls had circled around the bread and were coming back, without a push-cart, back my way along the counters, in the aisle between the check-outs and the Special bins. They didn't even have shoes on. There was this chunky one, with the two-piece—it was bright green and the seams on the bra were still sharp and her belly was still pretty pale so I guessed she just got it (the suit)—there was this one, with one of those chubby berry-faces, the lips all bunched together under her nose, this one, and a tall one, with black hair that hadn't quite frizzed right, and one of these sun-burns right across under the eyes, and a chin that was too long—you know, the kind of girl other girls think is very "striking" and "attrac-tive" but never quite makes it, as they very well know, which is why they like her so much—and then the third one, that wasn't quite so tall. She was the queen. She kind of led them, the other two peeking around and making their shoulders round. She didn't look around, not this queen, she just walked straight on slowly, on these long white prima-donna legs. She came down a little hard on her heels, as if she didn't walk in her bare feet that much, putting down her heels and then letting the weight move along to her toes as if she was testing the floor with every step, putting a little deliberate extra action into it. You never know for sure how girls' minds work (do you really think it's a mind in there or just a little buzz like a bee in a glass jar?) but you got the idea she had talked the other two into coming in here with her, and now she was showing them how to do it, walk slow and hold yourself straight.

She had on a kind of dirty-pink—beige maybe, I don't know—bathing suit with a little nubble all over it and, what got me, the straps were down. They were off her shoulders looped loose around the cool tops of her arms, and I guess as a result the suit had slipped a little on her, so all around the top of the cloth there was this shining rim. If it hadn't been there you wouldn't have known there could have been anything whiter than those shoulders. With the straps pushed off, there was nothing between the top of the suit and the top of her head except just *her,* this clean bare plane of the top of her chest down from the shoulder bones like a dented sheet of metal tilted in the light. I mean, it was more than pretty.

She had sort of oaky hair that the sun and salt had bleached, done up in a bun that was unraveling, and a kind of prim face. Walking into the A&P with your straps down, I suppose it's the only kind of face you *can* have. She held her head so high her neck, coming up out of those white shoulders, looked kind of stretched, but I didn't mind. The longer her neck was, the more of her there was.

She must have felt in the corner of her eye me and over my shoulder Stokesie in the second slot watching, but she didn't tip. Not this queen. She kept her eyes moving across the racks, and stopped, and turned so slow it made my stomach rub the inside of my apron, and buzzed to the other two, who kind of huddled against her for relief, and they all three of them went up the cat-and-dog-food-breakfast-cereal-macaroni-rice-raisins-seasonings-spreads-spaghetti-soft-drinks-crackers-and-cookies aisle. Form the third slot I look straight up this aisle to the meat counter, and I watched them all the way. The fat one with the tan sort of fumbled with the cookies, but on second thought she put the packages back. The sheep pushing their carts down the aisle—the girls were walking against the usual traffic (not that we have one-way signs or anything)—were pretty hilarious. You could see them, when Queenie's white shoulders dawned on them, kind of jerk, or hop, or hiccup, but their eyes snapped back to their own baskets and on they pushed. I bet you could set off dynamite in an A&P and the people would by and large keep reaching and checking oatmeal off their lists and muttering "Let me see, there was a third thing, began with A, asparagus, no, ah, yes, applesauce!" or whatever it is they do mutter. But there was no doubt, this jiggled them. A few houseslaves in pin curlers even looked around after pushing their carts to make sure what they had seen was correct.

You know, it's one thing to have a girl in a bathing suit down on the beach, where what with the glare nobody can look at each other much anyway, and another thing in the cool of the A&P, under the fluorescent lights, against all those stacked packages, with her feet paddling along naked over our checkerboard green-and-cream rubber-tile floor.

"Oh Daddy," Stokesie said beside me. "I feel so faint."

"Darling," I said. "Hold me tight." Stokesie's married, with two babies chalked up on his fuselage already, but as far as I can tell that's the only difference. He's twenty-two, and I was nineteen this April.

"Is it done?" he asks, the responsible married man finding his voice. I forgot to say he thinks he's going to be manager some sunny day, maybe in 1990 when it's called the Great Alexandrov and Petrooshki Tea Company or something.

10   What he meant was, our town is five miles from a beach, with a big
summer colony out on the Point, but we're right in the middle of town,
and the women generally put on a shirt or shorts or something before
they get out of the car into the street. And anyway these are usually
women with six children and varicose veins mapping their legs and nobody, including them, could care less. As I say, we're right in the middle of town, and if you stand at our front doors you can see two banks
and the Congregational church and the newspaper store and three real-
estate offices and about twenty-seven old freeloaders tearing up Central
Street because the sewer broke again. It's not as if we're on the Cape;
we're north of Boston and there's people in this town haven't seen the
ocean for twenty years.

        The girls had reached the meat counter and were asking McMahon
something. He pointed, they pointed, and they shuffled out of sight behind a pyramid of Diet Delight peaches. All that was left for us to see was
old McMahon patting his mouth and looking after them sizing up their
joints. Poor kids, I began to feel sorry for them, they couldn't help it.

        Now here comes the sad part of the story, at least my family says it's
sad but I don't think it's sad myself. The store's pretty empty, it being
Thursday afternoon, so there was nothing much to do except lean on
the register and wait for the girls to show up again. The whole store was
like a pinball machine and I didn't know which tunnel they'd come out
of. After a while they come around out of the far aisle, around the light
bulbs, records at discount of the Caribbean Six or Tony Martin Sings
or some such gunk you wonder they waste the wax on, sixpacks of
candy bars, and plastic toys done up in cellophane that fall apart when
a kid looks at them anyway. Around they come, Queenie still leading
the way, and holding a little gray jar in her hand. Slots Three through
Seven are unmanned and I could see her wondering between Stokes
and me, but Stokesie with his usual luck draws an old party in baggy
gray pants who stumbles up with four giant cans of pineapple juice
(what do these bums *do* with all that pineapple juice? I've often asked
myself) so the girls come to me. Queenie puts down the jar and I take
it into my fingers icy cold. Kingfish Fancy Herring Snacks in Pure Sour
Cream: 49. Now her hands are empty, not a ring or a bracelet, bare as
God made them, and I wonder where the money's coming from. Still
with that prim look she lifts a folded dollar bill out of the hollow at the
center of her nubbled pink top. The jar went heavy in my hand. Really,
I thought that was so cute.

        Then everybody's luck begins to run out. Lengel comes in from
haggling with a truck full of cabbages on the lot and is about to scuttle

into that door marked MANAGER behind which he hides all day when the girls touch his eye. Lengel's pretty dreary, teaches Sunday school and the rest, but he doesn't miss that much. He comes over and says, "Girls, this isn't the beach."

Queenie blushes, though maybe it's just a brush of sunburn I was noticing for the first time, now that she was so close. "My mother asked me to pick up a jar of herring snacks." Her voice kind of startled me, the way voices do when you see the people first, coming out so flat and dumb yet kind of tony, too, the way it ticked over "pick up" and "snacks." All of a sudden I slid right down her voice into her living room. Her father and the other men were standing around in ice-cream coats and bow ties and the women were in sandals picking up herring snacks on toothpicks off a big plate and they were all holding drinks the color of water with olives and sprigs of mint in them. When my parents have somebody over they get lemonade and if it's a real racy affair Schlitz in tall glasses with "They'll Do It Every Time" cartoons stencilled on.

"That's all right," Lengel said. "But this isn't the beach." His re-   15
peating this struck me as funny, as if it had just occurred to him, and he had been thinking all these years the A&P was a great big dune and he was the head lifeguard. He didn't like my smiling—as I say he doesn't miss much—but he concentrates on giving the girls that sad Sunday-school-superintendent stare.

Queenie's blush is no sunburn now, and the plump one in plaid, that I liked better from the back—a really sweet can—pipes up, "We weren't doing any shopping. We just came in for the one thing."

"That makes no difference," Lengel tells her, and I could see from the way his eyes went that he hadn't noticed she was wearing a two-piece before. "We want you decently dressed when you come in here."

"We *are* decent," Queenie says suddenly, her lower lip pushing, getting sore now that she remembers her place, a place from which the crowd that runs the A&P must look pretty crummy. Fancy Herring Snacks flashed in her very blue eyes.

"Girls, I don't want to argue with you. After this come in here with your shoulders covered. It's our policy." He turns his back. That's policy for you. Policy is what the kingpins want. What the others want is juvenile delinquency.

All this while, the customers had been showing up with their carts   20
but, you know, sheep, seeing a scene, they had all bunched up on Stokesie, who shook open a paper bag as gently as peeling a peach, not wanting to miss a word. I could feel in the silence everybody getting nervous, most of all Lengel, who asks me, "Sammy, have you rung up this purchase?"

I thought and said "No" but it wasn't about that I was thinking. I go through the punches, 4, 9, GROC, TOT—it's more complicated than you think, and after you do it often enough, it begins to make a little song, that you hear words to, in my case "Hello *(bing)* there, you *(gung)* hap-py *pee-*pul *(splat)*!"—the *splat* being the drawer flying out. I increase the bill, tenderly as you may imagine, it just having come from between the two smoothest scoops of vanilla I had ever known were there, and pass a half and a penny into her narrow pink palm, and nestle the herrings in a bag and twist its neck and hand it over, all the time thinking.

The girls, and who'd blame them, are in a hurry to get out, so I say "I quit" to Lengel quick enough for them to hear, hoping they'll stop and watch me, their unsuspected hero. They keep right on going, into the electric eye; the door flies open and they flicker across the lot to their car, Queenie and Plaid and Big Tall Goony-Goony (not that as raw material she was so bad), leaving me with Lengel and a kink in his eyebrow.

"Did you say something, Sammy?"

"I said I quit."

25   "I thought you did."

"You didn't have to embarrass them."

"It was they who were embarrassing us."

I started to say something that came out "Fiddle-de-doo." It's a saying of my grandmother's, and I know she would have been pleased.

"I don't think you know what you're saying," Lengel said.

30   "I know you don't," I said. "But I do." I pull the bow at the back of my apron and start shrugging it off my shoulders. A couple customers that had been heading for my slot begin to knock against each other, like scared pigs in a chute.

Lengel sighs and begins to look very patient and old and gray. He's been a friend of my parents for years. "Sammy, you don't want to do this to your Mom and Dad," he tells me. It's true, I don't. But it seems to me that once you begin a gesture it's fatal not to go through with it. I fold the apron, "Sammy" stitched in red on the pocket, and put it on the counter, and drop the bow tie on top of it. The bow tie is theirs, if you've ever wondered. "You'll feel this for the rest of your life," Lengel says, and I know that's true, too, but remembering how he made that pretty girl blush makes me so scrunchy inside I punch the No Sale tab and the machine whirs "pee-pul" and the drawer splats out. One advantage to this scene taking place in summer, I can follow this up with a clean exit, there's no fumbling around getting your coat and galoshes, I just saunter into the electric eye in my white shirt that my mother ironed the night before, and the door heaves itself open, and outside the sunshine is skating around the asphalt.

I look around for my girls, but they're gone, of course. There wasn't anybody but some young married screaming with her children about some candy they didn't get by the door of a powder-blue Falcon station wagon. Looking back in the big windows, over the bags of peat moss and aluminum lawn furniture stacked on the pavement, I could see Lengel in my place in the slot, checking the sheep through. His face was dark gray and his back stiff, as if he'd just had an injection of iron, and my stomach kind of fell as I felt how hard the world was going to be to me hereafter.

Thomas Wolfe
The Child by Tiger

> Tiger, tiger, burning bright
> In the forests of the night,
> What immortal hand or eye
> Could frame thy fearful symmetry?

One day after school, twenty-five years ago, several of us were playing with a football in the yard at Randy Shepperton's. Randy was calling signals and handling the ball. Nebraska Crane was kicking it. Augustus Potterham was too clumsy to run or kick or pass, so we put him at center, where all he'd have to do would be to pass the ball back to Randy when he got the signal.

It was late in October and there was a smell of smoke, of leaves, of burning in the air. Nebraska had just kicked to us. It was a good kick, too—a high, soaring punt that spiraled out above my head, behind me. I ran back and tried to get it, but it was far and away "over the goal line"—that is to say, out in the street. It hit the street and bounded back and forth with that peculiarly erratic bounce a football has.

The ball rolled away from me down toward the corner. I was running out to get it when Dick Prosser, Shepperton's new Negro man, came along, gathered it up neatly in his great black paw and tossed it to me. He turned in then, and came on down the alleyway, greeting us as he

THE CHILD BY TIGER   First published in 1937. Thomas Wolfe (1900–1938) was born and grew up in Asheville, North Carolina. An altered, expanded version of this story was included in chapter 8 of his posthumously published novel *The Web and the Rock* (1939).

did. He called all of us "Mister" except Randy, and Randy was always "Cap'n"—"Cap'n Shepperton." This formal address—"Mr." Crane, "Mr." Potterham, "Mr." Spangler, "Cap'n" Shepperton—pleased us immensely, gave us a feeling of mature importance and authority.

"Cap'n Shepperton" was splendid! It had a delightful military association, particularly when Dick Prosser said it. Dick had served a long enlistment in the United States Army. He had been a member of a regiment of crack Negro troops upon the Texas border, and the stamp of the military man was evident in everything he did. It was a joy, for example, just to watch him split up kindling. He did it with a power, a kind of military order, that was astounding. Every stick he cut seemed to be exactly the same length and shape as every other one. He had all of them neatly stacked against the walls of the Shepperton basement with such regimented faultlessness that it almost seemed a pity to disturb their symmetry for the use for which they were intended.

5   It was the same with everything else he did. His little whitewashed basement room was as spotless as a barracks room. The bare board floor was always cleanly swept, a plain bare table and a plain straight chair were stationed exactly in the center of the room. On the table there was always just one object: an old Bible almost worn out by constant use, for Dick was a deeply religious man. There was a little cast-iron stove and a little wooden box with a few lumps of coal and a neat stack of kindling in it. And against the wall, to the left, there was an iron cot, always precisely made and covered cleanly with a coarse gray blanket.

The Sheppertons were delighted with him. He had come there looking for work just a month or two before, and modestly presented his qualifications. He had, he said, only recently received his discharge from the Army and was eager to get employment, at no matter what wage. He could cook, he could tend the furnace, he knew how to drive a car—in fact, it seemed to us boys that there was very little that Dick Prosser could not do. He could certainly shoot. He gave a modest demonstration of his prowess one afternoon, with Randy's .22, that left us gasping. He just lifted that little rifle in his powerful black hands as if it were a toy, without seeming to take aim, pointed it toward a strip of tin on which we had crudely marked out some bull's-eye circles, and he simply peppered the center of the bull's-eye, putting twelve holes through a space one inch square, so fast we could not even count the shots.

He knew how to box too. I think he had been a regimental champion. At any rate, he was as cunning and crafty as a cat. He never boxed with us, of course, but Randy had two sets of gloves, and Dick used to coach us while we sparred. There was something amazingly tender and watchful about him. He taught us many things—how to lead, to hook, to counter and to block—but he was careful to see that we did not hurt each other.

He knew about football, too, and today he paused, a powerful, respectable-looking Negro man of thirty years or more, and watched us for a moment as we played.

Randy took the ball and went up to him. "How do you hold it, Dick?" he said. "Is this right?"

Dick watched him attentively as he gripped the ball, and held it   10 back above his shoulder. The Negro nodded approvingly and said, "That's right, Cap'n Shepperton. You've got it. Only," he said gently, and now took the ball in his own powerful hand, "when you gits a little oldah yo' handses gits biggah and you gits a bettah grip."

His own great hand, in fact, seemed to hold the ball as easily as if it were an apple. And, holding it so a moment, he brought it back, aimed over his outstretched left hand as if he were pointing a gun, and rifled it in a beautiful, whizzing spiral thirty yards or more to Gus. He then showed us how to kick, how to get the ball off of the toe in such a way that it would rise and spiral cleanly. He knew how to do this too. He must have got off kicks there, in the yard at Shepperton's, that traveled fifty yards.

He showed us how to make a fire, how to pile the kindling so that the flames shot up cone-wise, cleanly, without smoke or waste. He showed us how to strike a match with the thumbnail of one hand and keep and hold the flame in the strongest wind. He showed us how to lift a weight, how to tote a burden on our shoulders in the easiest way. There was nothing that he did not know. We were all so proud of him. Mr. Shepperton himself declared that Dick was the best man he'd ever had, the smartest darky that he'd ever known.

And yet? He went too softly, at too swift a pace. He was there upon you sometimes like a cat. Looking before us, sometimes, seeing nothing but the world before us, suddenly we felt a shadow at our backs and, looking up, would find that Dick was there. And there was something moving in the night. We never saw him come or go. Sometimes we would waken, startled, and feel that we had heard a board creak, and the soft clicking of a latch, a shadow passing swiftly. All was still.

"Young white fokes, oh, young white gent'mun,"—his soft voice ending in a moan, a kind of rhythm in his hips—"oh, young white fokes, Ise tellin' *you*"—that soft low moan again—"you gotta love each othah like a brothah." He was deeply religious and went to church three times a week. He read his Bible every night. It was the only object on his square board table.

15   Sometimes Dick would come out of his little basement room, and his eyes would be red, as if he had been weeping. We would know, then, that he had been reading his Bible. There would be times when he would almost moan when he talked to us, a kind of hymnal chant that came from some deep and fathomless intoxication of the spirit, and that transported him. For us, it was a troubling and bewildering experience. We tried to laugh it off and make jokes about it. But there was something in it so dark and strange and full of a feeling that we could not fathom that our jokes were hollow, and the trouble in our minds and in our hearts remained.

Sometimes on these occasions his speech would be made up of some weird jargon of Biblical phrases, of which he seemed to have hundreds, and which he wove together in this strange pattern of his emotion in a sequence that was meaningless to us, but to which he himself had the coherent clue. "Oh, young white fokes," he would begin, moaning gently, "de dry bones in de valley. I tell you, white fokes, de day is comin' when He's comin' on dis earth again to sit in judgment. He'll put de sheep upon de right hand and de goats upon de left. Oh, white fokes, white fokes, de Armageddon day's a-comin', white fokes, an' de dry bones in de valley."

Or again, we could hear him singing as he went about his work, in his deep rich voice, so full of warmth and strength, so full of Africa, singing hymns that were not only of his own race but familiar to us all. I don't know where he learned them. Perhaps they were remembered from his Army days. Perhaps he had learned them in the service of former masters. He drove the Sheppertons to church on Sunday morning, and would wait for them throughout the morning service. He would come up to the side door of the church while the service was going on, neatly dressed in his good dark suit, holding his chauffeur's hat respectfully in his hand, and stand there humbly and listen during the course of the entire sermon.

And then, when the hymns were sung and the great rich sound would swell and roll out into the quiet air of Sunday, Dick would stand and listen, and sometimes he would join in quietly in the song. A number of these favorite Presbyterian hymns we heard him singing many times in a low rich voice as he went about his work around the house. He would sing Who Follows in His Train? or Alexander's Glory Song, or Rock of Ages, or Onward, Christian Soldiers!

And yet? Well, nothing happened—there was just "a flying hint from here and there," and the sense of something passing in the night. Turning into the square one day as Dick was driving Mr. Shepperton to town, Lon Everett skidded murderously around the corner, sideswiped

Dick and took the fender off. The Negro was out of the car like a cat and got his master out. Shepperton was unhurt. Lon Everett climbed out and reeled across the street, drunk as a sot at three o'clock. He swung viciously, clumsily, at the Negro, smashed him in the face. Blood trickled from the flat black nostrils and from the thick liver-colored lips. Dick did not move. But suddenly the whites of his eyes were shot with red, his bleeding lips bared for a moment over the white ivory of his teeth. Lon smashed at him again. The Negro took it full in the face again; his hands twitched slightly, but he did not move. They collared the drunken sot and hauled him off and locked him up. Dick stood there for a moment, then he wiped his face and turned to see what damage had been done to the car. No more now, but there were those who saw it who remembered later how the eyes went red.

Another thing: Sheppertons had a cook named Pansy Harris. She   20
was a comely Negro wench, young, plump, black as the ace of spades, a good-hearted girl with a deep dimple in her cheeks and faultless teeth, bared in the most engaging smile. No one ever saw Dick speak to her. No one ever saw her glance at him, or him at her, and yet that smilingly good-natured wench became as mournful-silent and as silent-sullen as midnight pitch. She went about her work as mournfully as if she were going to a funeral. The gloom deepened all about her. She answered sullenly now when spoken to.

One night toward Christmas she announced that she was leaving. In response to all entreaties, all efforts to find the reason for her sudden and unreasonable decision, she had no answer except a sullen repetition of the assertion that she had to leave. Repeated questionings did finally wring from her a sullen statement that her husband needed her at home. More than this she would not say, and even this excuse was highly suspect, because her husband was a Pullman porter, only home two days a week and well accustomed to do himself such housekeeping tasks as she might do for him.

The Sheppertons were fond of her. They tried again to find the reason for her leaving. Was she dissatisfied? "No'm" —an implacable monosyllable, mournful, unrevealing as the night. Had she been offered a better job elsewhere? "No'm" —as untelling as before. If they offered her more wages, would she stay with them? "No'm," again and again, sullen and unyielding, until finally the exasperated mistress threw her hands up in a gesture of defeat and said, "All right then, Pansy. Have it your own way, if that's the way you feel. Only for heaven's sake don't leave us in the lurch until we get another cook."

This, at length, with obvious reluctance, the girl agreed to. Then, putting on her hat and coat and taking the paper bag of "leavings" she was allowed to take home with her at night, she went out the kitchen door and made her sullen and morose departure.

This was on Saturday night, a little after eight o'clock. That afternoon Randy and I had been fooling around the basement and, seeing that Dick's door was slightly ajar, we looked in to see if he was there. The little room was empty, swept and spotless, as it had always been.

25   But we did not notice that! We saw it! At the same moment, our breaths caught sharply in a gasp of startled wonderment. Randy was the first to speak. "Look!" he whispered. "Do you see it?"

See it! My eyes were glued upon it. Squarely across the bare board table, blue-dull, deadly in its murderous efficiency, lay a modern repeating rifle. Beside it was a box containing one hundred rounds of ammunition, and behind it, squarely in the center, face downward on the table, was the familiar cover of Dick's worn old Bible.

Then he was on us like a cat. He was there like a great dark shadow before we knew it. We turned, terrified. He was there above us, his thick lips bared above his gums, his eyes gone small and red as rodents'.

"Dick!" Randy gasped, and moistened his dry lips. "Dick!" he fairly cried now.

It was all over like a flash. Dick's mouth closed. We could see the whites of his eyes again. He smiled and said softly, affably, "Yes, suh, Cap'n Shepperton. Yes, suh! You gent'mun lookin' at my rifle?" he said, and moved into the room.

30   I gulped and nodded my head and couldn't say a word, and Randy whispered, "Yes." And both of us still stared at him, with an expression of appalled and fascinated interest.

Dick shook his head and chuckled. "Can't do without my rifle, white fokes. No, suh!" he shook his head good-naturedly again. "Ole Dick, he's—he's—he's an ole Ahmy man, you know. If they take his rifle away from him, why, that's jest lak takin' candy from a little baby. Yes, suh!" he chuckled, and picked the weapon up affectionately. "Ole Dick felt Christmas comin' on—he-he—I reckon he must have felt it in his bones"—he chuckled—"so I been savin' up my money. I just thought I'd hide this heah and keep it as a big supprise fo' the young white fokes untwil Christmas morning. Then I was gonna take the young white fokes out and show 'em how to shoot."

We had begun to breathe more easily now and, almost as if we had been under the spell of the Pied Piper of Hamelin, we had followed him, step by step, into the room.

"Yes, suh," Dick chuckled, "I was just fixin' to hide this gun away twill Christmas Day, but Cap'n Shepperton—hee!" He chuckled heartily and slapped his thigh. "You can't fool ole Cap'n Shepperton. He just must've smelled this ole gun right out. He comes right in and sees it befo' I has a chance to tu'n around. . . . Now, white fokes"— Dick's voice fell to a tone of low and winning confidence—"now that you's found out, I'll tell you what I'll do. If you'll just keep it a suprise from the other white fokes twill Christmas Day, I'll take all you gent'mun out and let you shoot it. Now, cose," he went on quietly, with a shade of resignation, "if you want to tell on me, you can, but"—here his voice fell again, with just the faintest, yet most eloquent shade of sorrowful regret—"old Dick was looking fahwad to this; hopin' to give all the white fokes a suprise Christmas Day."

We promised earnestly that we would keep his secret as if it were our own. We fairly whispered our solemn vow. We tiptoed away out of the little basement room as if we were afraid our very footsteps might betray the partner of our confidence.

This was four o'clock on Saturday afternoon. Already, there was a somber moaning of the wind, gray storm clouds sweeping over. The threat of snow was in the air. 35

Snow fell that night. It came howling down across the hills. It swept in on us from the Smokies. By seven o'clock the air was blind with sweeping snow, the earth was carpeted, the streets were numb. The storm howled on, around houses warm with crackling fires and shaded light. All life seemed to have withdrawn into thrilling isolation. A horse went by upon the streets with muffled hoofs. Storm shook the houses. The world was numb. I went to sleep upon this mystery, lying in the darkness, listening to that exultancy of storm, to that dumb wonder, that enormous and attentive quietness of snow, with something dark and jubilant in my soul I could not utter.

A little after one o'clock that morning I was awakened by the ringing of a bell. It was the fire bell of the city hall, and it was beating an alarm—a hard fast stroke that I had never heard before. Bronze with peril, clangorous through the snow-numbed silence of the air, it had a quality of instancy and menace I had never known before. I leaped up and ran to the window to look for the telltale glow against the sky. But almost before I looked, those deadly strokes beat in upon my brain the message that this was no alarm for fire. It was a savage clangorous alarm to the whole town, a brazen tongue to warn mankind against the menace of some peril, secret, dark, unknown, greater than fire or flood could ever be.

I got instantly, in the most overwhelming and electric way, the sense that the whole town had come to life. All up and down the street the houses were beginning to light up. Next door, the Shepperton house was ablaze with light from top to bottom. Even as I looked, Mr. Shepperton, wearing an overcoat over his pajamas, ran down the snow-covered steps and padded out across the snow-covered walk toward the street.

People were beginning to run out of doors. I heard excited shouts and questions everywhere. I saw Nebraska Crane come pounding down the middle of the street. I knew that he was coming for me and Randy. As he ran by Shepperton's, he put his fingers to his mouth and whistled piercingly. It was a signal we all knew.

40   I was all ready by the time he came running down the alley toward our cottage. He hammered at the door; I was already there.

"Come on!" he said, panting with excitement, his black eyes burning with an intensity I'd never seen before. "Come on!" he cried. We were halfway out across the yard by now. "It's that nigger. He's gone crazy and is running wild."

"Wh-wh-what nigger?" I gasped, pounding at his heels.

Even before he spoke, I had the answer. Mr. Crane had already come out of his house, buttoning his heavy policeman's overcoat as he came. He had paused to speak for a moment to Mr. Shepperton, and I heard Shepperton say quickly, in a low voice, "Which way did he go?"

Then I heard somebody cry, "It's that nigger of Shepperton's!"

45   Mr. Shepperton turned and went quickly back across his yard toward the house. His wife and two girls stood huddled in the open doorway, white, trembling, holding themselves together, their arms thrust into the wide sleeves of their kimonos.

The telephone in Shepperton's house was ringing like mad, but no one was paying any attention to it. I heard Mrs. Shepperton say quickly, as he ran up the steps, "Is it Dick?" He nodded and passed her brusquely, going toward the phone.

At this moment, Nebraska whistled piercingly again upon his fingers and Randy Shepperton ran past his mother and down the steps. She called sharply to him. He paid no attention to her. When he came up, I saw that his fine thin face was white as a sheet. He looked at me and whispered, "It's—it's Dick!" And in a moment, "They say he's killed four people."

"With—" I couldn't finish.

Randy nodded dumbly, and we both stared there for a minute, aware now of the murderous significance of the secret we had kept, with a sudden sense of guilt and fear, as if somehow the crime lay on our shoulders.

50   Across the street a window banged up in the parlor of Suggs' house, and Old Man Suggs appeared in the window, clad only in his night-

gown, his brutal old face inflamed with excitement, his shock of silvery white hair awry, his powerful shoulders, and his thick hands gripping his crutches.

"He's coming this way!" he bawled to the world in general. "They say he lit out across the square! He's heading out in this direction!"

Mr. Crane paused to yell back impatiently over his shoulder, "No, he went down South Dean Street! He's heading for Wilton and the river! I've already heard from headquarters!"

Automobiles were beginning to roar and sputter all along the street. Across the street I could hear Mr. Potterham sweating over his. He would whirl the crank a dozen times or more; the engine would catch for a moment, cough and sputter, and then die again. Gus ran out-of-doors with a kettle of boiling water and began to pour it feverishly down the radiator spout.

Mr. Shepperton was already dressed. We saw him run down the back steps toward the carriage house. All three of us, Randy, Nebraska, and myself, streaked down the alleyway to help him. We got the old wooden doors open. He went in and cranked the car. It was a new one, and started up at once. Mr. Shepperton backed out into the snowy drive. We all clambered up on the running board. He spoke absently, saying, "You boys stay here. . . . Randy, your mother's calling you," but we all tumbled in and he didn't say a word.

He came backing down the alleyway at top speed. We turned into   55
the street and picked up Mr. Crane at the corner. We lit out for town, going at top speed. Cars were coming out of alleys everywhere. We could hear people shouting questions and replies at one another. I heard one man shout, "He's killed six men!"

I don't think it took us over five minutes to reach the square, but when we got there, it seemed as if the whole town was there ahead of us. Mr. Shepperton pulled the car up and parked in front of the city hall. Mr. Crane leaped out and went pounding away across the square without another word to us.

From every corner, every street that led into the square, people were streaking in. One could see the dark figures of running men across the white carpet of the square. They were all rushing in to one focal point.

The southwest corner of the square where South Dean Street came into it was like a dog fight. Those running figures streaking toward that dense crowd gathered there made me think of nothing else so much as a fight between two boys upon the playgrounds of the school at recess time. The way the crowd was swarming in was just the same.

But then I *heard* a difference. From that crowd came a low and growing mutter, an ugly and insistent growl, of a tone and quality I had never heard before. But I knew instantly what it meant. There was no mistaking the blood note in that foggy growl. And we looked at one another with the same question in the eyes of all.

60   Only Nebraska's coal-black eyes were shining now with a savage sparkle even they had never had before. "Come on," he said in a low tone, exultantly. "They mean business this time, sure. Let's go." And he darted away toward the dense and sinister darkness of the crowd.

Even as we followed him we heard coming toward us now, growing, swelling at every instant, one of the most savagely mournful and terrifying sounds that night can know. It was the baying of the hounds as they came up upon the leash from Niggertown. Full-throated, howling deep, the savagery of blood was in it, and the savagery of man's guilty doom was in it too.

They came up swiftly, fairly baying at our heels as we sped across the snow-white darkness of the square. As we got up to the crowd, we saw that it had gathered at the corner where my uncle's hardware store stood. Cash Eager had not yet arrived, but, facing the crowd which pressed in on them so close and menacing that they were almost flattened out against the glass, three or four men were standing with arms stretched out in a kind of chain, as if trying to protect with the last resistance of their strength and eloquence the sanctity of private property.

Will Hendershot was mayor at that time, and he was standing there, arm to arm with Hugh McNair. I could see Hugh, taller by half a foot than anyone around him, his long gaunt figure, the gaunt passion of his face, even the attitude of his outstretched bony arms, strangely, movingly Lincolnesque, his one good eye blazing in the cold glare of the corner lamp with a kind of cold inspired Scotch passion.

"Wait a minute! You men wait a minute!" he cried. His words cut out above the clamor of the mob like an electric spark. "You'll gain nothing, you'll help nothing if you do this thing!"

65   They tried to drown him out with an angry and derisive roar. He shot his big fist up into the air and shouted at them, blazed at them with that cold single eye, until they had to hear. "Listen to me!" he cried. "This is no time for mob law! This is no case for lynch law! This is a time for law and order! Wait till the sheriff swears you in! Wait until Cash Eager comes! Wait—"

He got no farther. "Wait, hell!" cried someone. "We've waited long enough! We're going to get that nigger!"

The mob took up the cry. The whole crowd was writhing angrily now, like a tormented snake. Suddenly there was a flurry in the crowd, a scattering. Somebody yelled a warning at Hugh McNair. He ducked quickly, just in time. A brick whizzed past him, smashing the plate-glass window into fragments.

And instantly a bloody roar went up. The crowd surged forward, kicked the fragments of jagged glass away. In a moment the whole mob was storming into the dark store. Cash Eager got there just too late. He arrived in time to take out his keys and open the front doors, but as he grimly remarked it was like closing the barn doors after the horse had been stolen.

The mob was in and helped themselves to every rifle they could find. They smashed open cartridge boxes and filled their pockets with the loose cartridges. Within ten minutes they had looted the store of every rifle, every cartridge in the stock. The whole place looked as if a hurricane had hit it. The mob was streaming out into the street, was already gathering round the dogs a hundred feet or so away, who were picking up the scent at that point, the place where Dick had halted last before he had turned and headed south, downhill along South Dean Street toward the river.

The hounds were scampering about, tugging at the leash, moaning   70
softly with their noses pointed to the snow, their long ears flattened down. But in that light and in that snow it almost seemed no hounds were needed to follow Dick. Straight as a string right down the center of the sheeted car tracks, the Negro's footsteps led away until they vanished downhill in the darkness.

But now, although the snow had stopped, the wind was swirling through the street and making drifts and eddies in the snow. The footprints were fading rapidly. Soon they would be gone.

The dogs were given their head. They went straining on softly, sniffing at the snow; behind them the dark masses of the mob closed in and followed. We stood there watching while they went. We saw them go on down the street and vanish. But from below, over the snownumbed stillness of the air, the vast low mutter of the mob came back to us.

Men were clustered now in groups. Cash Eager stood before his shattered window, ruefully surveying the ruin. Other men were gathered around the big telephone pole at the corner, pointing out two bullet holes that had been drilled cleanly through it.

And swiftly, like a flash, running from group to group, like a powder train of fire, the full detail of that bloody chronicle of night was pieced together.

This was what had happened. Somewhere between nine and ten   75
o'clock that night, Dick Prosser had gone to Pansy Harris's shack in

Niggertown. Some said he had been drinking when he went there. At any rate, the police had later found the remnants of a gallon jug of raw corn whisky in the room. What happened, what passed between them, was never known. And, besides, no one was greatly interested. It was a crazy nigger with "another nigger's woman."

Shortly after ten o'clock that night, the woman's husband appeared upon the scene. The fight did not start then. According to the woman, the real trouble did not come until an hour or more after his return.

The men drank together. Each was in an ugly temper. Shortly before midnight, they got into a fight. Harris slashed at Dick with a razor. In a second they were locked together, rolling about and fighting like two madmen on the floor. Pansy Harris went screaming out-of-doors and across the street into a dingy little grocery store.

A riot call was telephoned at once to police headquarters on the public square. The news came in that a crazy nigger had broken loose on Gulley Street in Niggertown, and to send help at once. Pansy Harris ran back across the street toward her little shack.

As she got there, her husband, with blood streaming from his face, staggered out into the street, with his hands held up protectively behind his head in a gesture of instinctive terror. At the same moment, Dick Prosser appeared in the doorway of the shack, deliberately took aim with his rifle and shot the fleeing Negro squarely through the back of the head. Harris dropped forward on his face into the snow. He was dead before he hit the ground. A huge dark stain of blood-soaked snow widened out around him. Dick Prosser seized the terrified Negress by the arm, hurled her into the shack, bolted the door, pulled down the shades, blew out the lamp and waited.

80   A few minutes later, two policemen arrived from town. They were a young constable named Willis, and John Grady, a lieutenant of police. The policemen took one look at the bloody figure in the snow, questioned the frightened keeper of the grocery store and, after consulting briefly, produced their weapons and walked out into the street.

Young Willis stepped softly down on to the snow-covered porch of the shack, flattened himself against the wall between the window and the door, and waited. Grady went around to the side and flashed his light through the window, which, on this side, was shadeless. Grady said in a loud tone: "Come out of there!"

Dick's answer was to shoot him cleanly through the wrist. At the same moment Willis kicked the door in and, without waiting, started in with pointed revolver. Dick shot him just above the eyes. The policeman fell forward on his face.

Grady came running out around the house, rushed into the grocery store, pulled the receiver of the old-fashioned telephone off the hook, rang frantically for headquarters and yelled out across the wire that a crazy nigger had killed Sam Willis and a Negro man, and to send help.

At this moment Dick stepped out across the porch into the street, aimed swiftly through the dirty window of the little store and shot John Grady as he stood there at the phone. Grady fell dead with a bullet that entered just below his left temple and went out on the other side.

Dick, now moving in a long, unhurried stride that covered the ground with catlike speed, turned up the long snow-covered slope of Gulley Street and began his march toward town. He moved right up the center of the street, shooting cleanly from left to right as he went. Halfway up the hill, the second-story window of a two-story Negro tenement flew open. An old Negro man stuck out his ancient head of cotton wool. Dick swiveled and shot casually from his hip. The shot tore the top of the old Negro's head off.

By the time Dick reached the head of Gulley Street, they knew he was coming. He moved steadily along, leaving his big tread cleanly in the middle of the sheeted street, shifting a little as he walked, swinging his gun crosswise before him. This was the Negro Broadway of the town, but where those poolrooms, barbershops, drugstores and fried-fish places had been loud with dusky life ten minutes before, they were now silent as the ruins of Egypt. The word was flaming through the town that a crazy nigger was on the way. No one showed his head.

Dick moved on steadily, always in the middle of the street, reached the end of Gulley Street and turned into South Dean—turned right, uphill, in the middle of the car tracks, and started toward the square. As he passed the lunchroom on the left, he took a swift shot through the window at the counter man. The fellow ducked behind the counter. The bullet crashed into the wall above his head.

Meanwhile, at police headquarters, the sergeant had sent John Chapman out across the square to head Dick off. Mr. Chapman was perhaps the best-liked man upon the force. He was a pleasant florid-faced man of forty-five, with curling brown mustaches, congenial and good-humored, devoted to his family, courageous, but perhaps too kindly and too gentle for a good policeman.

John Chapman heard the shots and ran. He came up to the corner by Eager's hardware store just as Dick's last shot went crashing through the lunchroom window. Mr. Chapman took up his post there at the corner behind the telephone post that stood there at that time. Mr.

85

Chapman, from his vantage point behind this post, took out his revolver and shot directly at Dick Prosser as he came up the street.

90   By this time Dick was not more than thirty yards away. He dropped quietly upon one knee and aimed. Mr. Chapman shot again and missed. Dick fired. The high-velocity bullet bored through the post a little to one side. It grazed the shoulder of John Chapman's uniform and knocked a chip out of the monument sixty yards or more behind him in the center of the square.

Mr. Chapman fired again and missed. And Dick, still coolly poised upon his knee, as calm and steady as if he were engaging in a rifle practice, fired again, drilled squarely through the center of the post and shot John Chapman through the heart. Then Dick rose, pivoted like a soldier in his tracks and started down the street, straight as a string, right out of town.

This was the story as we got it, pieced together like a train of fire among the excited groups of men that clustered there in trampled snow before the shattered glass of Eager's store.

But now, save for these groups of talking men, the town again was silent. Far off in the direction of the river, we could hear the mournful baying of the hounds. There was nothing more to see or do. Cash Eager stopped, picked up some fragments of the shattered glass and threw them in the window. A policeman was left on guard, and presently all five of us—Mr. Shepperton, Cash Eager and we three boys—walked back across the square and got into the car and drove home again.

But there was no more sleep, I think, for anyone that night. Black Dick had murdered sleep. Toward daybreak, snow began to fall again. The snow continued through the morning. It was piled deep in gusting drifts by noon. All footprints were obliterated; the town waited, eager, tense, wondering if the man could get away.

95   They did not capture him that day, but they were on his trail. From time to time throughout the day, news would drift back to us. Dick had turned east along the river and gone out for some miles along the Fairchilds road. There, a mile or two from Fairchilds, he crossed the river at the Rocky Shallows.

Shortly after daybreak, a farmer from the Fairchilds section had seen him cross a field. They picked the trail up there again and followed it across the field and through a wood. He had come out on the other side and got down into the Cane Creek section, and there, for several hours, they lost him. Dick had gone right down into the icy water of the creek and walked upstream a mile or so. They brought the dogs down to the creek, to where he broke the trail, took them over to the other side and scented up and down.

Toward five o'clock that afternoon they picked the trail up on the other side, a mile or more upstream. From that point on, they began to close in on him. The dogs followed him across the fields, across the Lester road, into a wood. One arm of the posse swept around the wood to head him off. They knew they had him. Dick, freezing, hungry and unsheltered, was hiding in that wood. They knew he couldn't get away. The posse ringed the wood and waited until morning.

At 7:30 the next morning he made a break for it. He got through the line without being seen, crossed the Lester road and headed back across the field in the direction of Cane Creek. And there they caught him. They saw him plunging through the snowdrift of a field. A cry went up. The posse started after him.

Part of the posse were on horseback. The men rode in across the field. Dick halted at the edge of the wood, dropped deliberately upon one knee and for some minutes held them off with rapid fire. At two hundred yards he dropped Doc Lavender, a deputy, with a bullet through the throat.

The posse came in slowly, in an encircling, flankwise movement.   100 Dick got two more of them as they closed in, and then, as deliberately as a trained soldier retreating in good order, still firing as he went, he fell back through the wood. At the other side he turned and ran down through a sloping field that bordered on Cane Creek. At the creek edge, he turned again, knelt once more in the snow and aimed.

It was Dick's last shot. He didn't miss. The bullet struck Wayne Foraker, a deputy, dead center in the forehead and killed him in his saddle. Then the posse saw the Negro aim again, and nothing happened. Dick snapped the breech open savagely, then hurled the gun away. A cheer went up. The posse came charging forward. Dick turned, stumblingly, and ran the few remaining yards that separated him from the cold and rock-bright waters of the creek.

And here he did a curious thing—a thing that no one ever wholly understood. It was thought that he would make one final break for freedom, that he would wade the creek and try to get away before they got to him. Instead, he sat down calmly on the bank and, as quietly as if he were seated on his cot in an Army barracks, he unlaced his shoes, took them off, placed them together neatly at his side, and then stood up like a soldier, erect, in his bare bleeding feet, and faced the mob.

The men on horseback reached him first. They rode up around him and discharged their guns into him. He fell forward in the snow, riddled with bullets. The men dismounted, turned him over on his back, and all the other men came in and riddled him. They took his lifeless body, put a rope around his neck and hung him to a tree. Then the mob exhausted all their ammunition on the riddled carcass.

By nine o'clock that morning the news had reached town. Around eleven o'clock, the mob came back along the river road. A good crowd had gone out to meet it at the Wilton Bottoms. The sheriff rode ahead. Dick's body had been thrown like a sack and tied across the saddle of the horse of one of the deputies he had killed.

105   It was in this way, bullet-riddled, shot to pieces, open to the vengeful and the morbid gaze of all, that Dick came back to town. The mob came back right to its starting point in South Dean Street. They halted there before an undertaking parlor, not twenty yards away from where Dick knelt to kill John Chapman. They took that ghastly mutilated thing and hung it in the window of the undertaker's place, for every woman, man, and child in town to see.

And it was so we saw him last. We said we wouldn't look. But in the end we went. And I think it has always been the same with people. They protest. They shudder. And they say they will not go. But in the end they always have their look.

At length we went. We saw it, tried wretchedly to make ourselves believe that once this thing had spoken to us gently, had been partner to our confidence, object of our affection and respect. And we were sick with nausea and fear, for something had come into our lives we could not understand.

We looked and whitened to the lips, craned our necks and looked away, and brought unwilling, fascinated eyes back to the horror once again, and craned and turned again, and shuffled in the slush uneasily, but could not go. And we looked up at the leaden reek of day, the dreary vapor of the sky, and, bleakly, at these forms and faces all around us—the people come to gape and stare, the poolroom loafers, the town toughs, the mongrel conquerors of earth—and yet, familiar to our lives and to the body of our whole experience, all known to our landscape, all living men.

And something had come into life—into our lives—that we had never known about before. It was a kind of shadow, a poisonous blackness filled with bewildered loathing. The snow would go, we knew; the reeking vapors of the sky would clear away. The leaf, the blade, the bud, the bird, then April, would come back again, and all of this would be as it had ever been. The homely light of day would shine again familiarly. And all of this would vanish as an evil dream. And yet not wholly so. For we would still remember the old dark doubt and loathing of our kind, of something hateful and unspeakable in the souls of men. We knew that we should not forget.

110   Beside us, a man was telling the story of his own heroic accomplishments to a little group of fascinated listeners. I turned and looked

at him. It was Ben Pounders of the ferret face, the furtive and uneasy eye, Ben Pounders of the mongrel mouth, the wiry muscles of the jaw, Ben Pounders, the collector of usurious lendings to the blacks, the nigger hunter. And now Ben Pounders boasted of another triumph. He was the proud possessor of another scalp.

"I was the first one to git in a shot," he said. "You see that hole there?" He pointed with a dirty finger. "That big hole right above the eye?" They turned and goggled with a drugged and feeding stare.

"That's mine," the hero said, turned briefly to the side and spat tobacco juice into the slush. "That's where I got him. Hell, after that he didn't know what hit him. He was dead before he hit the ground. We all shot him full of holes then. We sure did fill him full of lead. Why, hell, yes," he declared, with a decisive movement of his head, "we counted up to two hundred and eighty-seven. We must have put three hundred holes in him."

And Nebraska, fearless, blunt, outspoken as he always was, turned abruptly, put two fingers to his lips and spat between them, widely and contemptuously.

"Yeah—*we!*" he grunted. "*We* killed a big one! We—we killed a b'ar, we did! . . . Come on, boys," he said gruffly. "Let's be on our way!"

And, fearless and unshaken, untouched by any terror or any doubt, he moved away. And two white-faced, nauseated boys went with him. 115

A day or two went by before anyone could go into Dick's room again. I went in with Randy and his father. The little room was spotless, bare and tidy as it had always been. But even the very austerity of that little room now seemed terribly alive with the presence of its black tenant. It was Dick's room. We all knew that. And somehow we all knew that no one else could ever live there again.

Mr. Shepperton went over to the table, picked up Dick's old Bible that still lay there, open and face downward, held it up to the light and looked at it, at the place that Dick had marked when he last read in it. And in a moment, without speaking to us, he began to read in a quiet voice:

"The Lord is my shepherd; I shall not want.

"2. He maketh me to lie down in green pastures: he leadeth me beside the still waters.

"3. He restoreth my soul: he leadeth me in the paths of righteousness for his name's sake. 120

"4. Yea, though I walk through the valley of the shadow of death, I will fear no evil: for thou art with me—"

Then Mr. Shepperton closed the book and put it down upon the table, the place where Dick had left it. And we went out the door, he locked it, and we went back into that room no more forever.

The years passed, and all of us were given unto time. We went our ways. But often they would turn and come again, these faces and these voices of the past, and burn there in my memory again, upon the muted and immortal geography of time.

And all would come again—the shout of the young voices, the hard thud of the kicked ball, and Dick moving, moving steadily, Dick moving, moving silently, a storm-white world and silence, and something moving, moving in the night. Then I would hear the furious bell, the crowd a-clamor and the baying of the dogs, and feel the shadow coming that would never disappear. Then I would see again the little room that we would see no more, the table and the book. And the pastoral holiness of that old psalm came back to me and my heart would wonder with perplexity and doubt.

125   For I had heard another song since then, and one that Dick, I know, had never heard, and one perhaps he might not have understood, but one whose phrases and whose imagery it seemed to me would suit him better:

> What the hammer? What the chain?
> In what furnace was thy brain?
> What the anvil? What dread grasp
> Dare its deadly terrors clasp?
>
> When the stars threw down their spears,
> And water'd heaven with their tears,
> Did He smile His work to see?
> Did He who made the lamb make thee?

"*What* the hammer? *What* the chain?" No one ever knew. It was a mystery and a wonder. There were a dozen stories, a hundred clues and rumors; all came to nothing in the end. Some said that Dick had come from Texas, others that his home had been in Georgia. Some said that it was true that he had been enlisted in the Army, but that he had killed a man while there and served a term at Leavenworth. Some said he had served in the Army and had received an honorable discharge, but had later killed a man and had served a term in a state prison in Louisiana. Others said that he had been an Army man, but that he had gone crazy, that he had served a period in an asylum, that he had escaped from prison, that he was a fugitive from justice at the time he came to us.

But all these stories came to nothing. Nothing was ever proved. Men debated and discussed these things a thousand times—who and what he had been, what he had done, where he had come from—and all of it came to nothing. No one knew the answer. But I think that I have found the answer. I think I know from where he came.

He came from darkness. He came out of the heart of darkness, from the dark heart of the secret and undiscovered South. He came by night, just as he passed by night. He was night's child and partner, a token of the other side of man's dark soul, a symbol of those things that pass by darkness and that still remain, a symbol of man's evil innocence, and the token of his mystery, a projection of his own unfathomed quality, a friend, a brother and a mortal enemy, an unknown demon, two worlds together—a tiger and a child.

Poetry

Elements of Poetry

Chapter One

What Is Poetry?

Poetry is as universal as language and almost as ancient. The most primitive peoples have used it, and the most civilized have cultivated it. In all ages and in all countries, poetry has been written, and eagerly read or listened to, by all kinds and conditions of people—by soldiers, statesmen, lawyers, farmers, doctors, scientists, clergy, philosophers, kings, and queens. In all ages it has been especially the concern of the educated, the intelligent, and the sensitive, and it has appealed, in its simpler forms, to the uneducated and to children. Why? First, because it has given pleasure. People have read it, listened to it, or recited it because they liked it—because it gave them enjoyment. But this is not the whole answer. Poetry in all ages has been regarded as important, not simply as one of several alternative forms of amusement, as one person might choose bowling, another chess, and another poetry. Rather, it has been regarded as something central to existence, something having unique value to the fully realized life, something that we are better off for having and without which we are spiritually impoverished. To understand the reasons for this, we need to have at least a provisional understanding of what poetry is—provisional, because people have always been more successful at appreciating poetry than at defining it.

Initially, poetry might be defined as a kind of language that says *more* and says it *more intensely* than does ordinary language. To understand this fully, we need to understand what poetry "says." For language is employed on different occasions to say quite different kinds of things; in other words, language has different uses.

Perhaps the commonest use of language is to communicate *information*. We say that it is nine o'clock, that we liked a certain movie, that George Washington was the first president of the United States, that bromine and iodine are members of the halogen group of chemical elements. This we might call the *practical* use of language; it helps us with the ordinary business of living.

But it is not primarily to communicate information that novels, short stories, plays, and poems are written. These exist to bring us a sense and a perception of life, to widen and sharpen our contacts with existence. Their concern is with *experience*. We all have an inner need to live more deeply and fully and with greater awareness, to know the experience of others, and to understand our own experience better. Poets, from their own store of felt, observed, or imagined experiences, select, combine, and reorganize. They create significant new experiences for their readers—significant because focused and formed—in which readers can participate and from which they may gain a greater awareness and understanding of their world. Literature, in other words, can be used as a gear for stepping up the intensity and increasing the range of our experience and as a glass for clarifying it. This is the *literary* use of language, for literature is not only an aid to living but a means of living.

In advertisements, sermons, political speeches, and even some poems we find a third use of language: as an instrument of *persuasion*, or argument. But the distinctions among these three uses—the practical, the literary, and the argumentative—are not always clear-cut, since some written language simultaneously performs two or even all three functions. For example, an excellent poem we consider "literary" may convey information, and may also try to persuade us to share a particular point of view. Effectiveness in communicating experience, however, is the one essential criterion for any poem aspiring to the condition of literature.

Suppose, for instance, that we are interested in eagles. If we want simply to acquire information about eagles, we may turn to an encyclopedia or a book of natural history. We would find that there are about fifty-five species of eagles and that most have hooked bills, curved claws, broad wings, and powerfully developed breast muscles. We would also learn that eagles vary in length from about sixteen inches to as long as forty inches; that most hunt while flying, though some await their prey on a high perch; that they nest in tall trees or on inaccessible cliffs; that they lay only one or two eggs; and that for human beings eagles "symbolize power, courage, freedom, and immortality and have long been used as national, military, and heraldic emblems and as symbols in religion."*

But unless we are interested in this information only for practical purposes, we are likely to feel a little disappointed, as though we had grasped the feathers of the eagle but not its soul. True, we have learned many facts about the eagle, but we have missed somehow its lonely majesty, its power, and the wild grandeur of its surroundings that would make the eagle a living creature rather than a mere museum specimen. For the living eagle we must turn to literature.

Encyclopedia Americana, International Edition, Vol. 9 (1995) 520–22.

The Eagle

He clasps the crag with crooked hands;
Close to the sun in lonely lands,
Ringed with the azure world, he stands.

The wrinkled sea beneath him crawls;
He watches from his mountain walls,   5
And like a thunderbolt he falls.

Alfred, Lord Tennyson (1809–1892)

QUESTIONS

1. What is peculiarly effective about the expressions "crooked hands," "Close to the sun," "Ringed with the azure world," "wrinkled," "crawls," and "like a thunderbolt"?
2. Notice the formal pattern of the poem, particularly the contrast of "he stands" in the first stanza and "he falls" in the second. Is there any other contrast between the two stanzas?

When "The Eagle" has been read well, readers will feel that they have enjoyed a significant experience and understand eagles better, though in a different way, than they did from the encyclopedia article alone. For while the article *analyzes* our experience of eagles, the poem in some sense *synthesizes* such an experience. Indeed, we may say the two approaches to experience—the scientific and the literary—complement each other. And we may contend that the kind of understanding we get from the second is at least as valuable as the kind we get from the first.

Literature, then, exists to communicate significant experience—significant because it is concentrated and organized. Its function is not to tell us *about* experience but to allow us imaginatively to *participate* in it. It is a means of allowing us, through the imagination, to live more fully, more deeply, more richly, and with greater awareness. It can do this in two ways: by *broadening* our experience—that is, by making us acquainted with a range of experience with which in the ordinary course of events we might have no contact, or by *deepening* our experience—that is, by making us feel more poignantly and more understandingly the everyday experiences all of us have. It enlarges our perspectives and breaks down some of the limits we may feel.

We can avoid two limiting approaches to poetry if we keep this conception of literature firmly in mind. The first approach always looks for a lesson or a bit of moral instruction. The second expects to find poetry always beautiful. Let us consider one of the songs from Shakespeare's *Love's Labor's Lost* (5.2).

Winter

When icicles hang by the wall,
And Dick the shepherd blows his nail,
And Tom bears logs into the hall,
And milk comes frozen home in pail,
When blood is nipped and ways be foul,   5
Then nightly sings the staring owl,
"Tu-whit, tu-who!"
    A merry note,
    While greasy Joan doth keel° the pot.   skim

When all aloud the wind doth blow,   10
And coughing drowns the parson's saw,
And birds sit brooding in the snow,
And Marian's nose looks red and raw,
When roasted crabs° hiss in the bowl,   crab apples
Then nightly sings the staring owl,   15
"Tu-whit, tu-who!"
    A merry note,
    While greasy Joan doth keel the pot.

William Shakespeare (1564–1616)

QUESTIONS

1. Vocabulary: *saw* (11), *brooding* (12).
2. Is the owl's cry really a "merry" note? How are this adjective and the verb "sings" employed?
3. In what way does the owl's cry contrast with the other details of the poem?

In this poem Shakespeare communicates the quality of winter life around a sixteenth-century English country house. But he does not do so by telling us flatly that winter in such surroundings is cold and in many respects unpleasant, though with some pleasant features too (the adjectives *cold, unpleasant,* and *pleasant* are not even used in the poem). Instead, he provides a series of concrete, homely details that suggest these qualities and enable us, imaginatively, to experience this winter life ourselves. The shepherd blows on his fingernails to warm his hands; the milk freezes in the pail between the cowshed and the kitchen; the cook is slovenly and unclean, "greasy" either from spattered cooking fat or from her own sweat as she leans over the hot fire; the roads are muddy; the folk listening to the parson have colds; the birds "sit brooding in the snow"; and the servant girl's nose is raw from cold. But pleasant things are in prospect. Tom is bringing in logs for the fire, the hot cider or ale is ready for drinking, and the soup or stew will soon be ready. In contrast to all these familiar details of country life is the mournful and eerie note of the owl.

Obviously the poem contains no moral. If we limit ourselves to looking in poetry for some lesson, message, or noble truth about life, we are bound to be disappointed. This limited approach sees poetry as a kind of sugarcoated pill—a wholesome truth or lesson made palatable by being put into pretty words. What this narrow approach really wants is a sermon—not a poem, but something inspirational. Yet "Winter," which has appealed to readers for more than four centuries, is not inspirational and contains no moral preachment.

Neither is the poem "Winter" beautiful. Though it is appealing in its way and contains elements of beauty, there is little that is really beautiful in red, raw noses, coughing in chapel, nipped blood, foul roads, and greasy cooks. Yet the second limiting approach may lead us to feel that poetry deals exclusively with beauty—with sunsets, flowers, butterflies, love, God—and that the one appropriate response to any poem is, after a moment of awed silence, "Isn't that beautiful!" But this narrow approach excludes a large proportion of poetry. The function of poetry is sometimes to be ugly rather than beautiful. And poetry may deal with common colds and greasy cooks as legitimately as with sunsets and flowers. Consider another example:

Dulce et Decorum Est

Bent double, like old beggars under sacks,
Knock-kneed, coughing like hags, we cursed through sludge,
Till on the haunting flares we turned our backs,
And towards our distant rest began to trudge.
Men marched asleep. Many had lost their boots,   5
But limped on, blood-shod. All went lame, all blind;
Drunk with fatigue; deaf even to the hoots
Of gas-shells dropping softly behind.

Gas! GAS! Quick, boys!—An ecstasy of fumbling,
Fitting the clumsy helmets just in time,   10
But someone still was yelling out and stumbling
And flound'ring like a man in fire or lime.—

Dim through the misty panes and thick green light,
As under a green sea, I saw him drowning.
In all my dreams before my helpless sight   15
He plunges at me, guttering, choking, drowning.

If in some smothering dreams, you too could pace
Behind the wagon that we flung him in,
And watch the white eyes writhing in his face,
His hanging face, like a devil's sick of sin,   20
If you could hear, at every jolt, the blood
Come gargling from the froth-corrupted lungs
Bitter as the cud
Of vile, incurable sores on innocent tongues,—
My friend, you would not tell with such high zest   25
To children ardent for some desperate glory,
The old lie: *Dulce et decorum est*
Pro patria mori.

                                    Wilfred Owen (1893–1918)

QUESTIONS

1. The Latin quotation, from the Roman poet Horace, means "It is sweet and
   becoming to die for one's country." What is the poem's comment on this
   statement?
2. List the elements of the poem that seem not beautiful and therefore "unpo-
   etic." Are there any elements of beauty in the poem?
3. How do the comparisons in lines 1, 14, 20, and 23–24 contribute to the effectiveness of the poem?
4. What does the poem gain by moving from plural pronouns and the past
   tense to singular pronouns and the present tense?

    Poetry takes all life as its province. Its primary concern is not
with beauty, not with philosophical truth, not with persuasion, but
with experience. Beauty and philosophical truth are aspects of experience, and the poet is often engaged with them. But poetry as a
whole is concerned with all kinds of experience—beautiful or ugly,
strange or common, noble or ignoble, actual or imaginary. Paradoxi-
cally, an artist can transform even the most unpleasant or painful experiences into works of great beauty and emotional power. Encountered in real life, pain and death are not pleasurable for most people;
but we might read and reread poems about these subjects because of
their ability to enlighten and move us. A real-life experience that

makes us cry is usually an unhappy one; but if we cry while reading a great novel or poem it is because we are deeply moved, our humanity affirmed. Similarly, we do not ordinarily like to be frightened in real life, but we sometimes seek out books or movies that will terrify us. Works of art focus and organize experiences of all kinds, conveying the broad spectrum of human life and evoking a full range of emotional and intellectual responses. Even the most tragic literature, through its artistry of language, can help us to see and feel the significance of life, appealing to our essential humanity in a way that can be intensely pleasurable and affirming.

There is no sharp distinction between poetry and other forms of imaginative literature. Although some inexperienced readers may believe that poetry can be recognized by the arrangement of its lines on the page or by its use of rhyme and meter, such superficial signs are of little worth. The Book of Job in the Bible and Melville's *Moby-Dick* are highly poetical, but the familiar verse that begins "Thirty days hath September, / April, June, and November . . ." is not. The difference between poetry and other literature is one of degree. Poetry is the most condensed and concentrated form of literature. It is language whose individual lines, either because of their own brilliance or because they focus so powerfully on what has gone before, have a higher voltage than most language. It is language that grows frequently incandescent, giving off both light and heat.

Ultimately, therefore, poetry can be recognized only by the response made to it by a practiced reader, someone who has acquired some sensitivity to poetry. But there is a catch here. We are not all equally experienced readers. To some readers, poetry may often seem dull and boring, a fancy way of writing something that could be said more simply. So might a color-blind person deny that there is such a thing as color.

The act of communication involved in reading poetry is like the act of communication involved in receiving a message by radio. Two devices are required: a transmitting station and a receiving set. The completeness of the communication depends on both the power and clarity of the transmitter and the sensitivity and tuning of the receiver. When a person reads a poem and no experience is received, either the poem is not a good poem or the reader is not properly tuned. With new poetry, we cannot always be sure which is at fault. With older poetry, if it has acquired critical acceptance—has been enjoyed by generations of good readers—we may assume that the receiving set is at fault. Fortunately, the fault is not irremediable. Though we cannot all become expert readers, we can become good enough to find both pleasure and value in much good poetry, or we can increase the amount of pleasure we already find in poetry and the number of kinds of poetry in which we find it. The purpose of this book is to help you increase your sensitivity and range as a receiving set.

Poetry, finally, is a kind of multidimensional language. Ordinary language—the kind that we use to communicate information—is one-dimensional. It is directed at only part of the listener, the understanding. Its one dimension is intellectual. Poetry, which is language used to communicate experience, has at least four dimensions. If it is to communicate experience, it must be directed at the *whole* person, not just at your understanding. It must involve not only your intelligence but also your senses, emotions, and imagination. To the intellectual dimension, poetry adds a sensuous dimension, an emotional dimension, and an imaginative dimension.

Poetry achieves its extra dimensions—its greater pressure per word and its greater tension per poem—by drawing more fully and more consistently than does ordinary language on a number of language resources, none of which is peculiar to poetry. These various resources form the subjects of a number of the following chapters. Among them are connotation, imagery, metaphor, symbol, paradox, irony, allusion, sound repetition, rhythm, and pattern. Using these resources and the materials of life, the poet shapes and makes a poem. Successful poetry is never effusive language. If it is to come alive it must be as cunningly put together and as efficiently organized as a tree. It must be an organism whose every part serves a useful purpose and cooperates with every other part to preserve and express the life that is within it.

REVIEWING CHAPTER ONE

1. Differentiate between ordinary language and poetic language.
2. Describe the uses of language: information, experience, persuasion.
3. Consider how looking for moral instruction or beauty are limiting approaches.
4. Explain the distinctions between poetry and other imaginative literature.
5. Review the four dimensions of experience that poetry involves.
6. Determine which ideas in this chapter are exemplified in the following poems.

Understanding and Evaluating Poetry

Most of the poems in this book are accompanied by study questions that are by no means exhaustive. The following is a list of questions that you may apply to any poem. You may be unable to answer many of them until you have read further into the book.

1. Who is the speaker? What kind of person is the speaker?
2. Is there an identifiable audience for the speaker? What can we know about it (her, him, or them)?
3. What is the occasion?
4. What is the setting in time (hour, season, century, and so on)?
5. What is the setting in place (indoors or out, city or country, land or sea, region, nation, hemisphere)?
6. What is the central purpose of the poem?
7. State the central idea or theme of the poem in a sentence.
8. a. Outline the poem to show its structure and development, or
   b. Summarize the events of the poem.
9. Paraphrase the poem.
10. Discuss the diction of the poem. Point out words that are particularly well chosen and explain why.
11. Discuss the imagery of the poem. What kinds of imagery are used? Is there a structure of imagery?
12. Point out examples of metaphor, simile, personification, and metonymy, and explain their appropriateness.
13. Point out and explain any symbols. If the poem is allegorical, explain the allegory.
14. Point out and explain examples of paradox, overstatement, understatement, and irony. What is their function?
15. Point out and explain any allusions. What is their function?
16. What is the tone of the poem? How is it achieved?
17. Point out significant examples of sound repetition and explain their function.
18. a. What is the meter of the poem?
    b. Copy the poem and mark its scansion.
19. Discuss the adaptation of sound to sense.
20. Describe the form or pattern of the poem.
21. Criticize and evaluate the poem.

Shall I compare thee to a summer's day?*

Shall I compare thee to a summer's day?
Thou art more lovely and more temperate:
Rough winds do shake the darling buds of May,
And summer's lease hath all too short a date.
Sometimes too hot the eye of heaven shines,   5
And often is his gold complexion dimmed;
And every fair° from fair sometimes declines   beauty
By chance of nature's changing course untrimmed°;   stripped bare
But thy eternal summer shall not fade
Nor lose possession of that fair thou ow'st°,   own 10
Nor shall death brag thou wand'rest in his shade
When in eternal lines to time thou grow'st.
So long as men can breathe or eyes can see,
So long lives this°, and this gives life to thee.   this poem

William Shakespeare (1564–1616)

QUESTIONS

1. Vocabulary: *temperate* (2), *shade* (11). What different meanings does "temperate" have when used to describe a person or "a summer's day"?
2. What details show that "a summer's day" is lacking in loveliness and is intemperate?
3. What are "the eye of heaven" (5) and "his gold complexion" (6)?
4. The poem begins more or less literally comparing the person being addressed to "a summer's day," but at line 9 it departs from what is literally possible into what is impossible. What does the poem gain by this shift in meaning?
5. Explain the logic behind lines 13–14. Is this a valid proof? Why or why not?

The Whipping

The old woman across the way
is whipping the boy again
and shouting to the neighborhood
her goodness and his wrongs.

Wildly he crashes through elephant-ears,   5
pleads in dusty zinnias,

*Whenever a heading duplicates the first line of the poem or a substantial portion thereof, with typically only the first word capitalized, it is probable that the poet left the poem untitled and that the anthologist has substituted the first line or part of it as an editorial convenience. Such a heading is not referred to as the title of the poem.

while she in spite of crippling fat
    pursues and corners him.

She strikes and strikes the shrilly circling
    boy till the stick breaks   10
in her hand. His tears are rainy weather
    to woundlike memories:

My head gripped in bony vise
    of knees, the writhing struggle
to wrench free, the blows, the fear   15
    worse than blows that hateful

Words could bring, the face that I
    no longer knew or loved . . .
Well, it is over now, it is over,
    and the boy sobs in his room,   20

And the woman leans muttering against
    a tree, exhausted, purged—
avenged in part for lifelong hidings
    she has had to bear.

Robert Hayden (1913–1980)

QUESTIONS

1. What similarities connect the old woman, the boy, and the speaker? Can you say that one of them is the main subject of the poem?
2. Does this poem express any beauty? What human truth does it embody? Could you argue against the claim that "it is over now, it is over" (19)?

The last Night that She lived

The last Night that She lived
It was a Common Night
Except the Dying—this to Us
Made Nature different

We noticed smallest things—   5
Things overlooked before
By this great light upon our Minds
Italicized—as 'twere.

As We went out and in
Between Her final Room   10
And Rooms where Those to be alive
Tomorrow were, a Blame

That Others could exist
While She must finish quite
A Jealousy for Her arose   15
So nearly infinite—

We waited while She passed—
It was a narrow time—
Too jostled were Our Souls to speak
At length the notice came.   20

She mentioned, and forgot—
Then lightly as a Reed
Bent to the Water, struggled scarce—
Consented, and was dead—

And We–We placed the Hair—   25
And drew the Head erect—
And then an awful leisure was
Belief to regulate—

Emily Dickinson (1830–1886)

QUESTIONS

1. Vocabulary: *Italicized* (8), *awful* (27).
2. Lines 11–12 and 12–15 depart from common word order and grammar. Rephrase them so that their plain sense is clear (e.g., "Rooms where Those to be alive / Tomorrow were" means "Rooms in which there were people who would be alive tomorrow"). Notice that both "a Blame" (12) and "A Jealousy" (15) are subjects of the verb "arose" (15).
3. What do the images of "a narrow time" (18) and "Too jostled" (19) contribute to the emotions of the poem?
4. Why is the comparison in lines 22–23 particularly effective?
5. Explain the emotional and spiritual adjustments expressed in the last four lines.

Ballad of Birmingham

(On the bombing of a church in Birmingham, Alabama, 1963)

"Mother dear, may I go downtown
Instead of out to play,

And march the streets of Birmingham
In a Freedom March today?"

"No, baby, no, you may not go,   5
For the dogs are fierce and wild,
And clubs and hoses, guns and jails
Aren't good for a little child."

"But, mother, I won't be alone.
Other children will go with me,   10
And march the streets of Birmingham
To make our country free."

"No, baby, no, you may not go,
For I fear those guns will fire.
But you may go to church instead   15
And sing in the children's choir."

She has combed and brushed her night-dark hair,
And bathed rose petal sweet,
And drawn white gloves on her small brown hands,
And white shoes on her feet.   20

The mother smiled to know her child
Was in the sacred place,
But that smile was the last smile
To come upon her face.

For when she heard the explosion,   25
Her eyes grew wet and wild.
She raced through the streets of Birmingham
Calling for her child.

She clawed through bits of glass and brick,
Then lifted out a shoe.   30
"O, here's the shoe my baby wore,
But, baby, where are you?"

Dudley Randall (1914–2000)

QUESTIONS

1. This poem is based on a historical incident. Throughout 1963, Birmingham, Alabama, was the site of demonstrations and marches protesting the
   racial segregation of schools and other public facilities. Although they were

intended as peaceful protests, these demonstrations often erupted in violence as police attempted to disperse them with fire hoses and police dogs.
On the morning of September 15, 1963, a bomb exploded during Sunday
School at the 16th Street Baptist Church, killing four children and injur-
ing fourteen. How does the poem differ from what you would expect to find
in a newspaper account of such an incident? In an encyclopedia entry? In a
speech calling for the elimination of racial injustice?

2. What do the details in the fifth stanza (17–20) contribute to the effect of
   the poem? Is "She" (17) the mother or the child?
3. In form, this poem shares certain characteristics with the folk ballad (see
   Glossary of Terms, page 1659). Why do you think this twentieth-century
   poet chose to write in a form that recalls the ballad tradition?
4. What purpose does the poem have beyond simply telling a story? How does
   the irony help achieve that purpose?

Kitchenette Building

We are things of dry hours and the involuntary plan,
Grayed in, and gray. "Dream" makes a giddy sound, not strong
Like "rent," "feeding a wife," "satisfying a man."

But could a dream send up through onion fumes
Its white and violet, fight with fried potatoes   5
And yesterday's garbage ripening in the hall,
Flutter, or sing an aria down these rooms

Even if we were willing to let it in,
Had time to warm it, keep it very clean,
Anticipate a message, let it begin?   10

We wonder. But not well! not for a minute!
Since Number Five is out of the bathroom now,
We think of lukewarm water, hope to get in it.

Gwendolyn Brooks (1917–2000)

QUESTIONS

1. Vocabulary: *aria* (7). A "kitchenette" (title) is a small kitchen or an alcove
   or part of a room fitted as a kitchen. What, then, is a "kitchenette building"? Who do you suppose is "Number Five" (12)?
2. Who is the "We" of the poem? Why is the use of plural speakers effective?

3. Why would these speakers refer to themselves as "things" (1)? If a dream rose through the cooking fumes and smell of garbage, why might these people not be "willing to let it in" (8)?

The Red Wheelbarrow

so much depends
upon

a red wheel
barrow

glazed with rain   5
water

beside the white
chickens.

William Carlos Williams (1883–1963)

QUESTIONS

1. The speaker asserts that "so much depends upon" the objects he refers to, leading the reader to ask: *How much* and *why?* This glimpse of a farm scene implies one kind of answer. What is the importance of the wheelbarrow, rain, and chicken to a farmer? To all of us?
2. What further importance can you infer from the references to color, shape, texture, and the juxtaposition of objects? Does the poem itself have a shape? What two ways of observing and valuing the world does the poem imply?
3. What are the possible reasons for "experimental" qualities in this poem— for instance, its lack of capitalization, its very short lines, and its plain, even homely images? Do these qualities give the poem a greater emotional power than a more conventional and decorative poem on the same topic might have achieved?

Suicide's Note

The calm,
Cool face of the river
Asked me for a kiss.

Langston Hughes (1902–1967)

QUESTIONS

1. How is the speaker's desire for death like the desire expressed in the comparison of the river to a person? How are they unlike? Explore the frame of mind that would create this comparison.
2. Does the repeated "k" sound seem beautiful to you? Can you explain the repetition in terms that reflect the speaker's frame of mind?

Terence, this is stupid stuff

"Terence, this is stupid stuff:
You eat your victuals fast enough;
There can't be much amiss, 'tis clear,
To see the rate you drink your beer.
But oh, good Lord, the verse you make,   5
It gives a chap the belly-ache.
The cow, the old cow, she is dead;
It sleeps well, the horned head:
We poor lads, 'tis our turn now
To hear such tunes as killed the cow.   10
Pretty friendship 'tis to rhyme
Your friends to death before their time
Moping melancholy mad:
Come, pipe a tune to dance to, lad."

Why, if 'tis dancing you would be,   15
There's brisker pipes than poetry.
Say, for what were hop-yards meant,
Or why was Burton built on Trent?
Oh many a peer of England brews
Livelier liquor than the Muse,   20
And malt does more than Milton can
To justify God's ways to man.
Ale, man, ale's the stuff to drink
For fellows whom it hurts to think:
Look into the pewter pot   25
To see the world as the world's not.
And faith, 'tis pleasant till 'tis past:
The mischief is that 'twill not last.
Oh I have been to Ludlow fair
And left my necktie God knows where,   30
And carried half-way home, or near,

Pints and quarts of Ludlow beer:
Then the world seemed none so bad,
And I myself a sterling lad;
And down in lovely muck I've lain,   35
Happy till I woke again.
Then I saw the morning sky:
Heigho, the tale was all a lie;
The world, it was the old world yet,
I was I, my things were wet,   40
And nothing now remained to do
But begin the game anew.

    Therefore, since the world has still
Much good, but much less good than ill,
And while the sun and moon endure   45
Luck's a chance, but trouble's sure,
I'd face it as a wise man would,
And train for ill and not for good.
'Tis true, the stuff I bring for sale
Is not so brisk a brew as ale: 50
Out of a stem that scored the hand
I wrung it in a weary land.
But take it: if the smack is sour,
The better for the embittered hour;
It should do good to heart and head   55
When your soul is in my soul's stead;
And I will friend you, if I may,
In the dark and cloudy day.

    There was a king reigned in the East:
There, when kings will sit to feast,   60
They get their fill before they think
With poisoned meat and poisoned drink.
He gathered all that springs to birth
From the many-venomed earth;
First a little, thence to more,   65
He sampled all her killing store;
And easy, smiling, seasoned sound,
Sate the king when healths went round.
They put arsenic in his meat
And stared aghast to watch him eat;   70
They poured strychnine in his cup

And shook to see him drink it up:
They shook, they stared as white's their shirt:
Them it was their poison hurt.
—I tell the tale that I heard told.   75
Mithridates, he died old.

A. E. Housman (1859–1936)

QUESTIONS

1. The poem opens with the speaker quoting another person whose remarks he then refutes. What is the relationship between the two? Of what is the other person complaining? What request does he make of the speaker?
2. Hops (17) and "malt" (21) are principal ingredients of beer and ale. Burton-upon-Trent (18) is an English city famous for its breweries. Milton (21), in the invocation of his epic poem *Paradise Lost*, declares that his purpose is to "justify the ways of God to men." What, in Terence's eyes, is the efficacy of liquor in helping one live a difficult life? What is the "stuff" *he* brings "for sale" (49)?
3. "Mithridates" (76) was a king of Pontus and a contemporary of Julius Caesar; his "tale" is told in Pliny's *Natural History*. The poem is structured by its line spacing into four verse paragraphs. What is the connection of this last verse paragraph with the rest of the poem? What is the function of each of the other three?
4. Essentially, Terence assesses the value of three possible aids for worthwhile living. What are they? Which does Terence consider the best? What six lines of the poem best sum up his philosophy?
5. Many people like reading material that is cheerful and optimistic; they argue that "there's enough suffering and unhappiness in the world already." What, for Housman, is the value of pessimistic and tragic literature?

Poetry: I

Someone at a table under a brown metal lamp
is studying the history of poetry.
Someone in the library at closing-time
has learned to say *modernism*,
trope, vatic, text.   5
She is listening for shreds of music.
He is searching for his name
back in the old country.
They cannot learn without teachers.
They are like us   what we were   10
if you remember.

In a corner of night a voice
is crying in a kind of whisper:
More!

Can you remember?   when we thought   15
the poets taught   how to live?
That is not the voice of a critic
nor a common reader
it is someone young   in anger
hardly knowing what to ask   20
who finds our lines   our glosses
wanting   in this world.

Adrienne Rich (b. 1929)

Ars Poetica

A poem should be palpable and mute
As a globed fruit,

Dumb
As old medallions to the thumb,

Silent as the sleeve-worn stone   5
Of casement ledges where the moss has grown—

A poem should be wordless
As the flight of birds.

*

A poem should be motionless in time
As the moon climbs,   10

Leaving, as the moon releases
Twig by twig the night-entangled trees,

Leaving, as the moon behind the winter leaves,
Memory by memory the mind—

A poem should be motionless in time   15
As the moon climbs.

*

A poem should be equal to:
Not true.

For all the history of grief
An empty doorway and a maple leaf.   20

For love
The leaning grasses and two lights above the sea—

A poem should not mean
But be.

Archibald MacLeish (1892–1982)

QUESTIONS
1. How can a poem be "wordless" (7)? How can it be "motionless in time" (15)?
2. The Latin title, literally translated "The Art of Poetry," is a traditional title for works on the philosophy of poetry. What is *this* poet's philosophy of poetry? What does he mean by saying that a poem should not "mean" (23) and should not be "true" (18)?

SUGGESTIONS FOR WRITING
"Writing about Literature," the first section of this book, offers practical advice about the formal requirements and style that are usually expected in student papers. While many of the suggestions presented there may be familiar to you, reviewing them when you prepare to complete these writing assignments should help you to write more effectively.
1. The following pairs of poems deal with similar subject matter treated in very different ways. Yet in each case the two poems employ the multidimensional language that is one criterion of poetic excellence. Choose one pair and discuss the ways in which both poems qualify as poetry, even though they take different approaches to similar topics.
   a. Tennyson, "The Eagle" (page 649) and Hardy, "The Darkling Thrush" (page 969).
   b. Owen, "Dulce et Decorum Est" (page 651) and Stevens, "The Death of a Soldier" (page 1007).
   c. Hopkins, "Spring" (page 703) and Dickinson, "A Light exists in Spring" (page 955).
   d. Angelou, "Woman Work" (page 832) and Wright, "Portrait" (page 1020).
   e. Hayden, "The Whipping" (page 656) and Roethke, "My Papa's Waltz" (page 997).
   f. Hughes, "Suicide's Note" (page 661) and Robinson, "Richard Cory" (page 996).

2. According to "Ars Poetica" by Archibald MacLeish, "A poem should not mean / But be" (23–24). Relate this assertion to one or more of the following:
   a. Williams, "The Red Wheelbarrow" (page 661).
   b. Keats, "Ode on a Grecian Urn" (page 918).
   c. Blake, "The Tiger" (page 947).
   d. Hughes, "Thistles" (page 974).
   e. Shapiro, "The Fly" (page 1001).
   f. Stevens, "Disillusionment of Ten O'Clock" (page 1008).
   g. Williams, "Poem" (page 1016).
   h. Wordsworth, "I wandered lonely as a cloud" (page 1019).

Chapter Two

Reading the Poem

How can you develop your understanding and appreciation of poetry? Here are some preliminary suggestions:

1. Read a poem more than once. A good poem will no more yield its full meaning on a single reading than will a Beethoven symphony on a single hearing. Two readings may be necessary simply to let you get your bearings. And if the poem is a work of art, it will repay repeated and prolonged examination. One does not listen to a good piece of music once and forget it; one does not look at a good painting once and throw it away. A poem is not like a newspaper, to be hastily read and cast into the wastebasket. It is to be hung on the wall of one's mind.

2. Keep a dictionary by you and use it. It is futile to try to understand poetry without troubling to learn the meanings of the words of which it is composed. You might as well attempt to play tennis without a ball. One of the benefits of studying literature is an enlarged vocabulary, and the study of poetry offers an excellent opportunity. A few other reference books also will be invaluable, particularly a good book on mythology (your instructor may recommend one) and a Bible.

3. Read so as to hear the sounds of the words in your mind. Poetry is written to be heard: its meanings are conveyed through sound as well as through print. Every word is therefore important. The best way to read a poem may be just the opposite of the best way to read a newspaper. One might read a newspaper article rapidly, and probably only once, before putting the paper into the recycling bag; but a poem should be read slowly, and most poems must be read many times before their full complexity and meaning can be experienced. When you cannot read a poem aloud so as to hear its sounds, lip-read it: form the words with your tongue and mouth even though you do not utter sounds. With ordinary reading material, lip-reading is a bad habit; with poetry, it is a good habit.

4. Always pay careful attention to what the poem is saying. Though you should be conscious of the sounds of the poem, you should never be so exclusively conscious of them that you pay no attention to what the poem means. For some readers, reading a poem is like getting on board a rhythmical roller coaster. The car starts and off they go, up and down, paying no

attention to the landscape flashing past them, arriving at the end of the poem breathless, with no idea of what it has been about. This is the wrong way to read a poem. One should make the utmost effort to follow the thought continuously and to grasp the full implications and suggestions. Because a poem says so much, several readings may be necessary, but on the very first reading you should determine the subjects of the verbs, the antecedents of the pronouns, and other normal grammatical facts.

5. Practice reading poems aloud. When you find one you especially like, have friends listen to your reading of it. Try to read it to them in such a way that they will like it too. (a) Read it affectionately, but not affectedly. The two extremes that oral readers often fall into are equally deadly: one is to read as if one were reading a tax report or a railroad timetable, unexpressively, in a monotone; the other is to elocute, with artificial flourishes and vocal histrionics. It is not necessary to put emotion into reading a poem. The emotion is already there. It wants only a fair chance to get out. It will express *itself* if the poem is read naturally and sensitively. (b) Of the two extremes, reading too fast offers greater danger than reading too slow. Read slowly enough that each word is clear and distinct and that the meaning has time to sink in. Remember that your friends do not have the advantage, as you do, of having the text before them. Your ordinary rate of reading will probably be too fast. (c) Read the poem so that the rhythmical pattern is felt but not exaggerated. Remember that poetry, with few exceptions, is written in sentences, just as prose is, and that punctuation is a signal as to how it should be read. Give all grammatical pauses their full due. Do not distort the natural pronunciation of words or a normal accentuation of the sentence to fit into what you have decided is its metrical pattern. One of the worst ways to read a poem is to read it ta-DUM ta-DUM ta-DUM, with an exaggerated emphasis on every other syllable. On the other hand, it should not be read as if it were prose. An important test of your reading will be how you handle the end of a line that lacks line-ending punctuation. A frequent mistake of the beginning reader is to treat each line as if it were a complete thought, whether grammatically complete or not, and to drop the voice at the end of it. A frequent mistake of the sophisticated reader is to take a running start upon approaching the end of a line and fly over it as if it were not there. The line is a rhythmical unit, and its end should be observed whether there is punctuation or not. If there is no punctuation, you ordinarily should observe the end of the line by the slightest of pauses or by holding on to the last word in the line just a little longer than usual, without dropping your voice. In line 12 of the following poem, you should hold on to the word "although" longer than if it occurred elsewhere in the line. But do not lower your voice on it: it is part of the clause that follows in the next stanza.

The Man He Killed

Had he and I but met
By some old ancient inn,
We should have sat us down to wet
Right many a nipperkin!°   half-pint cup

But ranged as infantry,   5
And staring face to face,
I shot at him as he at me,
And killed him in his place.

I shot him dead because—
Because he was my foe,   10
Just so: my foe of course he was;
That's clear enough; although

He thought he'd 'list, perhaps,
Off-hand-like—just as I—
Was out of work—had sold his traps—°   belongings 15
No other reason why.

Yes; quaint and curious war is!
You shoot a fellow down
You'd treat, if met where any bar is,
Or help to half-a-crown.   20

Thomas Hardy (1840–1928)

QUESTIONS
1. Vocabulary: *half-a-crown* (20).
2. In informational prose the repetition of a word like "because" (9–10) would be an error. What purpose does the repetition serve here? Why does the speaker repeat to himself his "clear" reason for killing a man (10–11)? The word "although" (12) gets more emphasis than it would ordinarily because it comes not only at the end of a line but at the end of a stanza. What purpose does this emphasis serve? Can the redundancy of "old ancient" (2) be poetically justified?
3. Poetry has been defined as "the expression of elevated thought in elevated language." Comment on the adequacy of this definition in the light of Hardy's poem.

One starting point for understanding a poem at the simplest level, and for clearing up misunderstanding, is to paraphrase its content or part of its content. To **paraphrase** a poem means to restate it in different language, so as to make its prose sense as plain as possible. The paraphrase may be longer or shorter than the poem, but it should contain all the ideas in the poem in such a way as to make them clear and to make the central idea, or **theme,** of the poem more accessible.

A Study of Reading Habits

When getting my nose in a book
Cured most things short of school,
It was worth ruining my eyes
To know I could still keep cool,
And deal out the old right hook   5
To dirty dogs twice my size.

Later, with inch-thick specs,
Evil was just my lark:
Me and my cloak and fangs
Had ripping times in the dark.   10
The women I clubbed with sex!
I broke them up like meringues.

Don't read much now: the dude
Who lets the girl down before
The hero arrives, the chap   15
Who's yellow and keeps the store,
Seem far too familiar. Get stewed:
Books are a load of crap.

Philip Larkin (1922–1985)

QUESTIONS
1. The three stanzas delineate three stages in the speaker's life. Describe each.
2. What kind of person is the speaker? What kinds of books does he read? May we identify him with the poet?
3. Contrast the speaker's advice in stanza 3 with Terence's counsel in "Terence, this is stupid stuff" (page 662). Are A. E. Housman and Philip Larkin at odds in their attitudes toward drinking and reading? Discuss.

Larkin's poem may be paraphrased as follows:

There was a time when reading was one way I could avoid almost all my troubles—except for school. It seemed worth the danger of ruining my eyes to read stories in which I could imagine myself maintaining my poise in the face of threats and having the boxing skill and experience needed to defeat bullies who were twice my size.

Later, already having to wear thick glasses because my eyesight had become so poor, I found my delight in stories of sex and evil: imagining myself with Dracula cloak and fangs, I relished vicious nocturnal adventures. I identified myself with sexual marauders whose inexhaustible potency was like a weapon wielded against women who were sweet and fragile.

I don't read much any more because now I can identify myself only with the flawed secondary characters, such as the flashy dresser who wins the heroine's confidence and then betrays her in a moment of crisis before the cowboy hero comes to her rescue, or the cowardly storekeeper who cringes behind the counter at the first sign of danger. Getting drunk is better than reading—books are just full of useless lies.

Notice that in a paraphrase, figurative language gives way to literal language (similes replace metaphors) and normal word order supplants inverted syntax. But a paraphrase retains the speaker's use of first, second, and third person, and the tenses of verbs. Though it is neither necessary nor possible to avoid using some of the words found in the original, a paraphrase should strive for plain, direct diction. And since a paraphrase is prose, it does not maintain the length and position of poetic lines.

A paraphrase is useful only if you understand that it is the barest, most inadequate approximation of what the poem really "says" and is no more equivalent to the poem than a corpse is to a person. After you have paraphrased a poem, you should endeavor to see how far short of the poem it falls, and why. In what respects does Larkin's poem say more, and say it more memorably, than the paraphrase? Does the phrase "full of useless lies" capture the impact of "a load of crap"? Furthermore, a paraphrase may fall far short of revealing the theme of a poem. "A Study of Reading Habits" represents a man summing up his reading experience and evaluating it—but in turn the poem itself evaluates *him* and his defects. A statement of the theme of the poem might be this: A person who turns to books as a source of self-gratifying fantasies may, in the course of time, discover that escapist reading no longer protects him from his awareness of his own reality, and he may out of habit have to find other, more potent, and perhaps more self-destructive means of escaping. Notice that in stating a theme, we should be careful not to phrase it as a moral or lesson—not "you shouldn't" but "a person may."

To aid us in the understanding of a poem, we may ask ourselves a number of questions about it. Two of the most important are *Who is the speaker?* and *What is the occasion?* A cardinal error of some readers is to assume that a speaker who uses the first-person pronouns (*I, my, mine, me*) is always the poet. A less risky course would be to assume always that the speaker is someone other than the poet. Poems, like short stories, novels, and plays, belong to the world of fiction, an imaginatively conceived world that at its best is "truer" than the factually "real" world that it reflects. When poets put themselves or their thoughts into a poem, they present a *version* of themselves; that is, they present a person who in many ways is *like* themselves but who, consciously or unconsciously, is shaped to fit the needs of the poem. We must be very careful, therefore, about identifying anything in a poem with the biography of the poet.

However, caution is not prohibition. Sometimes events or ideas in a poem will help us to understand some episodes in the poet's life. More importantly for us, knowledge of the poet's life may help us understand a poem. There can be little doubt, when all the evidence is in, that "Terence, this is stupid stuff" (page 662) is Housman's defense of the kind of poetry he writes, and that the six lines in which Terence sums up his beliefs about life and the function of poetry closely echo Housman's own beliefs. On the other hand, it would be folly to suppose that Housman ever got drunk at "Ludlow fair" and once lay down in "lovely muck" and slept all night in a roadside ditch. It may seem paradoxical that Philip Larkin, a poet and novelist and for many years the chief administrator of a university library, would end a poem with the line, "Books are a load of crap." But poems often feature a persona, or speaker, who expresses a viewpoint the poet presumably does not share.

We may well think of every poem, therefore, as being to some degree *dramatic*—that is, the utterance not of the person who wrote the poem but of a fictional character in a particular situation that may be inferred. Many poems are expressly dramatic.

In "The Man He Killed" the speaker is a soldier; the occasion is his having been in battle and killed a man—obviously for the first time in his life. We can tell a good deal about him. He is not a career soldier: he enlisted only because he was out of work. He is a workingman: he speaks a simple and colloquial language ("nipperkin," "'list," "off-hand-like," "traps"). He is a friendly, kindly sort who enjoys a neighborly drink of ale in a bar and will gladly lend a friend a half-a-crown when he has it. He has known what it is to be poor. In any other circum-

674 Chapter Two / Reading the Poem

stances he would have been horrified at taking a human life. It gives him pause even now. He is trying to figure it out. But he is not a deep thinker and thinks he has supplied a reason when he has only supplied a name: "I killed the man . . . because he was my foe." The critical question, of course, is *why* was the man his "foe"? Even the speaker is left unsatisfied by his answer, though he is not analytical enough to know what is wrong with it. Obviously this poem is expressly dramatic. We need know nothing about Thomas Hardy's life (he was never a soldier and never killed a man) to realize that the poem is dramatic. The internal evidence of the poem tells us so.

A third important question that we should ask ourselves upon reading any poem is *What is the central purpose of the poem?** The purpose may be to tell a story, to reveal human character, to impart a vivid impression of a scene, to express a mood or an emotion, or to convey vividly some idea or attitude. Whatever the purpose is, we must determine it for ourselves and define it mentally as precisely as possible. Only by relating the various details in the poem to the central purpose or theme can we fully understand their function and meaning. Only then can we begin to assess the value of the poem and determine whether it is a good one or a poor one. In "The Man He Killed" the central purpose is quite clear: it is to make us realize more keenly the irrationality of war. The puzzlement of the speaker may be our puzzlement. But even if we are able to give a more sophisticated answer than his as to why men kill each other, we ought still to have a greater awareness, after reading the poem, of the fundamental irrationality in war that makes men kill who have no grudge against each other and who might under different circumstances show each other considerable kindness.

Is my team plowing

"Is my team plowing,
That I was used to drive
And hear the harness jingle
When I was man alive?"

---

*Our only reliable evidence of the poem's purpose, of course, is the poem itself. External evidence, when it exists, though often helpful, may also be misleading. Some critics have objected to the use of such terms as "purpose" and "intention" altogether; we cannot know, they maintain, what was *attempted* in the poem; we can only know what was *done*. We are concerned, however, not with the *poet's* purpose, but with the *poem's* purpose; that is, with the theme (if it has one), and this is determinable from the poem itself.

Aye, the horses trample,   5
The harness jingles now;
No change though you lie under
The land you used to plow.

"Is football playing
Along the river shore,   10
With lads to chase the leather,
Now I stand up no more?"

Aye, the ball is flying,
The lads play heart and soul;
The goal stands up, the keeper   15
Stands up to keep the goal.

"Is my girl happy,
That I thought hard to leave,
And has she tired of weeping
As she lies down at eve?"   20

Aye, she lies down lightly,
She lies not down to weep:
Your girl is well contented.
Be still, my lad, and sleep.

"Is my friend hearty,   25
Now I am thin and pine;
And has he found to sleep in
A better bed than mine?"

Yes, lad, I lie easy,
I lie as lads would choose;   30
I cheer a dead man's sweetheart,
Never ask me whose.

A. E. Housman (1859–1936)

QUESTIONS

1. How many actual speakers are there in this poem? What is meant by "whose" in line 32?
2. Is this poem cynical in its observation of human nature?
3. The word *sleep* in the concluding stanzas suggests three different meanings. What are they? How many meanings are suggested by the word *bed*?

Once we have answered the question *What is the central purpose of the poem?* we can consider another question, equally important to full understanding: *By what means is that purpose achieved?* It is important to distinguish means from ends. A student on an examination once used the poem "Is my team plowing" as evidence that A. E. Housman believed in immortality because in it a man speaks from the grave. This is as much a misconstruction as to say that Thomas Hardy joined the army because he was out of work. The purpose of Housman's poem is to communicate poignantly a certain truth about human life: life goes on after our deaths pretty much as it did before—our dying does not disturb the universe. Further, it dramatizes that irrational sense of betrayal and guilt that may follow the death of a friend. The poem achieves this purpose by means of a fanciful dramatic framework in which a dead man converses with his still-living friend. The framework tells us nothing about whether Housman believed in immortality (as a matter of fact, he did not). It is simply an effective means by which we *can* learn how Housman felt a man's death affected the life he left behind. The question *By what means is that purpose achieved?* is partially answered by describing the poem's dramatic framework, if it has any. The complete answer requires an accounting of various resources of communication that we will discuss in this book.

The most important preliminary advice we can give for reading poetry is to maintain always, while reading it, the utmost mental alertness. The most harmful idea one can get about poetry is that its purpose is to soothe and relax and that the best place to read it is lying in a hammock with a cool drink while low music plays in the background. You *can* read poetry lying in a hammock, but only if you refuse to put your mind in the same attitude as your body. Its purpose is not to soothe and relax but to arouse and awake, to shock us into life, to make us more alive.

An analogy can be drawn between reading poetry and playing tennis. Both offer great enjoyment if the game is played hard. Good tennis players must be constantly on the tips of their toes, concentrating on their opponent's every move. They must be ready for a drive to the right or left, a lob overhead, or a drop shot barely over the net. They must be ready for topspin or underspin, a ball that bounces crazily to the left or right. They must jump for the high ones and run for the long ones. And they will enjoy the game almost exactly in proportion to the effort they put into it. The same is true of reading poetry. Great enjoyment is there, but this enjoyment demands a mental effort equivalent to the physical effort one puts into tennis.

The reader of poetry has one advantage over the tennis player: poets are not trying to win matches. They may expect the reader to stretch for their shots, but they *want* the reader to return them.

REVIEWING CHAPTER TWO

1. Review the five preliminary suggestions for reading poems.
2. List steps in paraphrasing, and create paraphrases of several poems, showing how paraphrase helps to clarify the theme.
3. Explain how identifying the speaker and the occasion of the poem shows the dramatic quality of poetry.
4. Explore the concept of a "central purpose" of a poem.
5. Consider the difference between the means and the ends in determining the central purpose of a poem.
6. Determine which ideas in this chapter are exemplified in the following poems.

Break of Day

'Tis true, 'tis day; what though it be?
Oh, wilt thou therefore rise from me?
Why should we rise because 'tis light?
Did we lie down because 'twas night?
Love which in spite of darkness brought us hither   5
Should, in despite of light, keep us together.

Light hath no tongue, but is all eye;
If it could speak as well as spy,
This were the worst that it could say:
That, being well, I fain would stay,   10
And that I loved my heart and honor so,
That I would not from him that had them go.

Must business thee from hence remove?
Oh, that's the worst disease of love;
The poor, the foul, the false, love can   15
Admit, but not the busied man.
He which hath business and makes love, doth do
Such wrong as when a married man doth woo.

John Donne (1572–1631)

QUESTIONS

1. Who is the speaker? Who is addressed? What is the situation? Can the speaker be identified with the poet?

2. Explain the comparison in line 7. To whom does "I" (10–12) refer? Is "love" (15) the subject or object of "can admit"?
3. Summarize the arguments used by the speaker to keep the person addressed from leaving. What does the speaker value most?
4. Are the two persons married or unmarried? Justify your answer.

There's been a Death, in the Opposite House

There's been a Death, in the Opposite House,
As lately as Today—
I know it, by the numb look
Such Houses have—alway—

The Neighbors rustle in and out—   5
The Doctor—drives away—
A Window opens like a Pod—
Abrupt—mechanically—

Somebody flings a Mattress out—
The Children hurry by—   10
They wonder if it died—on that—
I used to—when a Boy—

The Minister—goes stiffly in—
As if the House were His—
And He owned all the Mourners—now—   15
And little Boys—besides—

And then the Milliner—and the Man
Of the Appalling Trade—
To take the measure of the House—

There'll be that Dark Parade—   20

Of Tassels—and of Coaches—soon—
It's easy as a Sign—
The Intuition of the News—
In just a Country Town—

Emily Dickinson (1830–1886)

QUESTIONS

1. What can we know about the speaker in the poem?
2. By what signs does the speaker "intuit" that a death has occurred? Explain them stanza by stanza. What does it mean that the speaker must intuit rather than simply *know* that death has taken place?

3. Comment on the words "Appalling" (18) and "Dark" (20).
4. What shift in the poem is signaled by the separation of line 20 from the end of stanza 5?
5. What is the speaker's attitude toward death?

When in Rome

Mattie dear
the box is full
take
whatever you like
to eat   5
     (an egg
     or soup
     . . . there ain't no meat.)
there's endive there
and   10
cottage cheese
     (whew! If I had some
     black-eyed peas . . .)
there's sardines
on the shelves   15
and such
but
don't
get my anchovies
they cost   20
too much!
     (me get the
     anchovies indeed!
     what she think, she got—
     a bird to feed?)   25
there's plenty in there
to fill you up.
     (yes'm. just the
     sight's
     enough!   30

     Hope I lives till I get
     home
     I'm tired of eatin'
     what they eats in Rome . . .)

Mari Evans (b. 1923)

QUESTIONS
1. Who are the two speakers? What is the situation? Why are the second speaker's words enclosed in parentheses?
2. What are the attitudes of the two speakers toward one another? What is the attitude of each to herself?
3. What implications have the title and the last two lines?

Mirror

I am silver and exact. I have no preconceptions.
Whatever I see I swallow immediately
Just as it is, unmisted by love or dislike.
I am not cruel, only truthful—
The eye of a little god, four-cornered.   5
Most of the time I meditate on the opposite wall.
It is pink, with speckles. I have looked at it so long
I think it is a part of my heart. But it flickers.
Faces and darkness separate us over and over.

Now I am a lake. A woman bends over me,   10
Searching my reaches for what she really is.
Then she turns to those liars, the candles or the moon.
I see her back, and reflect it faithfully.
She rewards me with tears and an agitation of hands.
I am important to her. She comes and goes.   15
Each morning it is her face that replaces the darkness.
In me she has drowned a young girl, and in me an old woman
Rises toward her day after day, like a terrible fish.

                                          Sylvia Plath (1932–1963)

QUESTIONS
1. Who is the speaker? What is the central purpose of the poem, and by what means is it achieved?
2. In what ways is the mirror like and unlike a person (stanza 1)? In what ways is it like a lake (stanza 2)?
3. What is the meaning of the last two lines?

The Clod and the Pebble

"Love seeketh not Itself to please,
Nor for itself hath any care;
But for another gives its ease,
And builds a Heaven in Hell's despair."

So sang a little Clod of Clay,   5
Trodden with the cattle's feet;
But a Pebble of the brook,
Warbled out these meters meet:

"Love seeketh only Self to please,
To bind another to its delight,   10
Joys in another's loss of ease,
And builds a Hell in Heaven's despite."

William Blake (1757–1827)

QUESTIONS

1. Vocabulary: *Clod* (title). Explore the literal physical contrasts between a clod and a pebble. Why are these suitable "characters" to carry out this debate?
2. Paraphrase lines 4 and 12. What do "Heaven" and "Hell" have to do with this debate? Are they to be taken literally?
3. The Pebble gets the last word here. Does that mean that its philosophy is the poet's?

Facing It

My black face fades,
hiding inside the black granite.
I said I wouldn't,
dammit: No tears.
I'm stone. I'm flesh.   5
My clouded reflection eyes me
like a bird of prey, the profile of night
slanted against morning. I turn
this way—the stone lets me go.
I turn that way—I'm inside   10
the Vietnam Veterans Memorial
again, depending on the light
to make a difference.
I go down the 58,022 names,
half-expecting to find   15
my own in letters like smoke.
I touch the name Andrew Johnson;
I see the booby trap's white flash.
Names shimmer on a woman's blouse

but when she walks away   20
the names stay on the wall.
Brushstrokes flash, a red bird's
wings cutting across my stare.
The sky. A plane in the sky.
A white vet's image floats   25
closer to me, then his pale eyes
look through mine. I'm a window.
He's lost his right arm
inside the stone. In the black mirror
a woman's trying to erase names: 30
No, she's brushing a boy's hair.

Yusef Komunyakaa (b. 1947)

QUESTIONS

1. As the title suggests, this poem evokes the speaker's personal confrontation with the Vietnam Veterans Memorial. Why does the speaker focus throughout the poem on his own "clouded reflection" (6) in the granite surface of the memorial?

2. The speaker emphasizes the contrast between the fixed identity of the memorial and the shifting reflections of human beings who are paying their respects. Identify the lines that evoke this contrast.

3. Much of the poem's vividness comes from its use of colors. How do the various colors add significance and depth to the poem?

4. Some of what the speaker sees in the memorial is literal and physical, while some of what he sees is part of an imaginative vision the memorial inspires. Identify lines that describe these two kinds of vision.

Eros Turannos

She fears him, and will always ask
    What fated her to choose him;
She meets in his engaging mask
    All reasons to refuse him;
But what she meets and what she fears   5
Are less than are the downward years,
Drawn slowly to the foamless weirs
    Of age, were she to lose him.

Between a blurred sagacity
    That once had power to sound him,   10
And Love, that will not let him be

The Judas that she found him,
Her pride assuages her almost,
As if it were alone the cost.
He sees that he will not be lost,   15
    And waits and looks around him.

A sense of ocean and old trees
    Envelops and allures him;
Tradition, touching all he sees,
    Beguiles and reassures him;   20
And all her doubts of what he says
Are dimmed with what she knows of days—
Till even prejudice delays
    And fades, and she secures him.

The falling leaf inaugurates   25
    The reign of her confusion;
The pounding wave reverberates
    The dirge of her illusion;
And home, where passion lived and died,
Becomes a place where she can hide,   30
While all the town and harbor side
    Vibrate with her seclusion.

We tell you, tapping on our brows,
    The story as it should be,
As if the story of a house   35
    Were told, or ever could be;
We'll have no kindly veil between
Her visions and those we have seen,
As if we guessed what hers have been,
    Or what they are or would be.   40

Meanwhile we do no harm; for they
    That with a god have striven,
Not hearing much of what we say,
    Take what the god has given;
Though like waves breaking it may be,   45
Or like a changed familiar tree,
Or like a stairway to the sea
    Where down the blind are driven.

Edwin Arlington Robinson (1869–1935)

QUESTIONS

1. The Greek title may be translated "the tyrannical god of love"; it echoes the title of Sophocles's tragedy *Oedipos Turannos* (called *Oedipus Rex* in Latin), which told another story of the destruction of a family. What does this verbal reference add to the poem?
2. The poem tells a story of courtship, marriage, and disillusionment, from three distinct perspectives: that of the woman (lines 1–14, 21–32), the man (15–20), and the townspeople (33–48). As clearly as you can, determine the motives of each of them.
3. Although a narrative, this poem omits details of actions, presenting instead definitions of the emotions that fed the actions. Can you deduce what some of those actions might have been? What does the poem gain by this indirect method? How does the concluding stanza help to answer this question?

Storm Warnings

The glass has been falling all the afternoon,
And knowing better than the instrument
What winds are walking overhead, what zone
Of gray unrest is moving across the land,
I leave the book upon a pillowed chair   5
And walk from window to closed window, watching
Boughs strain against the sky

And think again, as often when the air
Moves inward toward a silent core of waiting,
How with a single purpose time has traveled   10
By secret currents of the undiscerned
Into this polar realm. Weather abroad
And weather in the heart alike come on
Regardless of prediction.

Between foreseeing and averting change   15
Lies all the mastery of elements
Which clocks and weatherglasses cannot alter.
Time in the hand is not control of time,
Nor shattered fragments of an instrument
A proof against the wind; the wind will rise,   20
We can only close the shutters.

I draw the curtains as the sky goes black
And set a match to candles sheathed in glass

Against the keyhole draught, the insistent whine
Of weather through the unsealed aperture.   25
This is our sole defense against the season;
These are the things that we have learned to do
Who live in troubled regions.

Adrienne Rich (b. 1929)

SUGGESTIONS FOR WRITING

1. Here are four definitions of poetry, all framed by poets themselves. Which definition best fits the poems you have so far read?

   a. I wish our clever young poets would remember my homely definitions of prose and poetry: that is, prose = words in their best order; poetry = the *best* words in the best order.   *Samuel Taylor Coleridge*

   b. It is not meters, but a meter-making argument, that makes a poem—a thought so passionate and alive that, like the spirit of a plant or an animal, it has an architecture of its own, and adorns nature with a new thing.   *Ralph Waldo Emerson*

   c. If I read a book and it makes my whole body so cold no fire can warm me, I know that is poetry. If I feel physically as if the top of my head were taken off, I know that is poetry. These are the only ways I know it. Is there any other way?   *Emily Dickinson*

   d. A poem begins in delight, it inclines to the impulse, it assumes a direction with the first line laid down, it runs a course of lucky events, and ends in a clarification of life—not necessarily a great clarification, such as sects and cults are founded on, but in a momentary stay against confusion.   *Robert Frost*

2. Using two or three poems from this chapter, or poems from the following list, write an essay that supports the definition you have chosen.
   a. Atwood, "Siren Song" (page 943).
   b. Clifton, "good times" (page 950).
   c. Dickinson, "A narrow Fellow in the Grass" (page 955).
   d. Donne, "The Triple Fool" (page 959).
   e. Joseph, "Warning" (page 974).
   f. Olds, "The Victims" (page 984).

Chapter Three

Denotation and Connotation

A primary distinction between the practical use of language and the literary use is that in literature, especially in poetry, a *fuller* use is made of individual words. To understand this, we need to examine the composition of a word.

The average word has three component parts: sound, denotation, and connotation. It begins as a combination of tones and noises, uttered by the lips, tongue, and throat, for which the written word is a notation. But it differs from a musical tone or a noise in that it has a meaning attached to it. The basic part of this meaning is its **denotation** or denotations: that is, the dictionary meaning or meanings of the word. Beyond its denotations, a word may also have connotations. The **connotations** are what it suggests beyond what it expresses: its overtones of meaning. It acquires these connotations from its past history and associations, from the way and the circumstances in which it has been used. The word *home*, for instance, by denotation means only a place where one lives, but by connotation it suggests security, love, comfort, and family. The words *childlike* and *childish* both mean "characteristic of a child," but *childlike* suggests meekness, innocence, and wide-eyed wonder, while *childish* suggests pettiness, willfulness, and temper tantrums. If we list the names of different coins—nickel, peso, lira, shilling, sen, doubloon—the word *doubloon*, to four out of five readers, immediately will suggest pirates, though a dictionary definition includes nothing about pirates. Pirates are part of its connotation.

Connotation is very important in poetry, for it is one of the means by which the poet can concentrate or enrich meaning—say more in fewer words. Consider, for instance, the following short poem:

There is no Frigate like a Book

> There is no Frigate like a Book
> To take us Lands away
> Nor any Coursers like a Page
> Of prancing Poetry—
> This Traverse may the poorest take

Without oppress of Toll—
How frugal is the Chariot
That bears the Human soul.

Emily Dickinson (1830–1886)

In this poem Emily Dickinson is considering the power of a book or of poetry to carry us away, to take us from our immediate surroundings into a world of the imagination. To do this she has compared literature to various means of transportation: a boat, a team of horses, a wheeled land vehicle. But she has been careful to choose kinds of transportation and names for them that have romantic connotations. "Frigate" suggests exploration and adventure; "coursers," beauty, spirit, and speed; "chariot," speed and the ability to go through the air as well as on land. (Compare "Swing Low, Sweet Chariot" and the myth of Phaëthon, who tried to drive the chariot of Apollo, and the famous painting of Aurora with her horses, once hung in almost every school.) How much of the meaning of the poem comes from this selection of vehicles and words is apparent if we substitute *steamship* for "frigate," *horses* for "coursers," and *streetcar* for "chariot."

QUESTIONS

1. What is lost if *miles* is substituted for "Lands" (2) or *cheap* for "frugal" (7)?
2. How is "prancing" (4) peculiarly appropriate to poetry as well as to coursers? Could the poet without loss have compared a book to coursers and poetry to a frigate?
3. Is this account appropriate to all kinds of poetry or just to certain kinds? That is, was the poet thinking of poems like Wilfred Owen's "Dulce et Decorum Est" (page 651) or of poems like Coleridge's "Kubla Khan" (page 951) and Keats's "La Belle Dame sans Merci" (page 975)?

Just as a word has a variety of connotations, so may it have more than one denotation. If we look up the word *spring* in the dictionary, for instance, we will find that it has between twenty-five and thirty distinguishable meanings: it may mean (1) a pounce or leap, (2) a season of the year, (3) a natural source of water, (4) a coiled elastic wire, and so forth. This variety of denotation, complicated by additional tones of connotation, makes language confusing and difficult to use. Any person using words must be careful to define precisely by context the denotation that is intended. But the difference between the writer using language to communicate and the poet is this: the practical writer will usually attempt to confine words to one denotation at a time; the poet will often take advantage of the fact that the word has more than one meaning by using it to mean more than one thing at the same time. Thus, when Edith Sitwell in one of her poems writes, "this is the time of the wild spring and the mating of the tigers,"* she uses the word "spring" to denote both a season of the year and a sudden leap (and she uses the word "tigers" rather than *deer* or *birds* because it has a connotation of fierceness and wildness that the others lack). The two denotations of "spring" are also appropriately possessed of contrasting connotations: the season is positive in its implications, while a sudden leap may connote the pouncing of a beast of prey. Similarly, in "Mirror" (page 680), the word "swallow" in line 2 denotes both accepting without question and consuming or devouring, and so connotes both an inability to think and an obliteration or destruction.

When my love swears that she is made of truth

When my love swears that she is made of truth,
I do believe her, though I know she lies,
That she might think me some untutored youth,
Unlearnèd in the world's false subtleties.
Thus vainly thinking that she thinks me young,   5
Although she knows my days are past the best,
Simply I credit her false-speaking tongue;
On both sides thus is simple truth supprest.
But wherefore says she not she is unjust?°   unfaithful
And wherefore say not I that I am old?   10
Oh, love's best habit is in seeming trust,
And age in love loves not to have years told:
Therefore I lie with her and she with me,
And in our faults by lies we flattered be.

William Shakespeare (1564–1616)

QUESTIONS

1. How old is the speaker? How old is his beloved? What is the nature of their relationship?
2. How is the contradiction in line 2 to be resolved? In lines 5–6? Who is lying to whom?
3. How do "simply" (7) and "simple" (8) differ in meaning? The words "vainly" (5), "habit" (11), "told" (12), and "lie" (13) all have double denotative meanings. What are they?
4. What is the tone of the poem—that is, the attitude of the speaker toward his situation? Should line 11 be taken as an expression of (a) wisdom,

Collected Poems (New York: Vanguard, 1968) 392.

(b) conscious rationalization, or (c) self-deception? In answering these questions, consider both the situation and the connotations of all the important words beginning with "swears" (1) and ending with "flattered" (14).

A frequent misconception of poetic language is that poets seek always the most beautiful or noble-sounding words. What they really seek are the most *meaningful* words, and these vary from one context to another. Language has many levels and varieties, and poets may choose from all of them. Their words may be grandiose or humble, fanciful or matter-of-fact, romantic or realistic, archaic or modern, technical or everyday, monosyllabic or polysyllabic. Usually a poem will be pitched pretty much in one key: the words in Emily Dickinson's "There is no Frigate like a Book" (page 686) and those in Thomas Hardy's "The Man He Killed" (page 670) are chosen from quite different areas of language, but both poets have chosen the words most meaningful for their own poetic context. It is always important to determine the level of diction employed in a poem, for it may provide clear insight into the purpose of the poem by helping to characterize the speaker. Sometimes a poet may import a word from one level or area of language into a poem composed mostly of words from a different level or area. If this is done clumsily, the result will be incongruous and sloppy; if it is done skillfully, the result will be a shock of surprise and an increment of meaning for the reader. In fact, the many varieties of language open to poets provide their richest resource. Their task is one of constant exploration and discovery. They search always for the secret affinities of words that allow them to be brought together with soft explosions of meaning.

Pathedy of Manners

> At twenty she was brilliant and adored,
> Phi Beta Kappa, sought for every dance;
> Captured symbolic logic and the glance
> Of men whose interest was their sole reward.
>
> She learned the cultured jargon of those bred   5
> To antique crystal and authentic pearls,
> Scorned Wagner, praised the Degas dancing girls,
> And when she might have thought, conversed instead.
>
> She hung up her diploma, went abroad,
> Saw catalogues of domes and tapestry,   10
> Rejected an impoverished marquis,
> And learned to tell real Wedgwood from a fraud.

Back home her breeding led her to espouse
A bright young man whose pearl cufflinks were real.
They had an ideal marriage, and ideal   15
But lonely children in an ideal house.

I saw her yesterday at forty-three,
Her children gone, her husband one year dead,
Toying with plots to kill time and re-wed
Illusions of lost opportunity.   20

But afraid to wonder what she might have known
With all that wealth and mind had offered her,
She shuns conviction, choosing to infer
Tenets of every mind except her own.

A hundred people call, though not one friend,   25
To parry a hundred doubts with nimble talk.
Her meanings lost in manners, she will walk
Alone in brilliant circles to the end.

Ellen Kay (b. 1931)

QUESTIONS

1. The title alludes to the type of drama called "comedy of manners" and coins a word combining the suffix -edy with the Greek root path- (as in pathetic, sympathy, pathology). How does the poem narrate a story with both comic and pathetic implications? For what might the central character be blamed? What arouses our pity for her?

2. Explore the multiple denotations and the connotations attached to each denotation of "brilliant" (both in 1 and 28), "interest" and "reward" (4), "cultured" and "jargon" (5), "circles" (28).

3. Why are the poet's words more effective than these possible synonyms: "captured" (3) rather than *learned*; "conversed" (8) rather than *chatted, gossiped,* or *talked*; "catalogues" (10) rather than *volumes* or *multitudes*; "espouse" (13) rather than *marry*? Discuss the momentary ambiguity presented by the word "re-wed" (19).

4. At what point in the poem does the speaker shift from language that represents the way the woman might have talked about herself to language that reveals how the speaker judges her? Point out examples of both kinds of language.

People using language only to convey information are usually indifferent to the sounds of the words and may feel frustrated by their connotations and multiple denotations. They would rather confine each word to a single, exact meaning. They use, one might say, a fraction of the word and throw away the rest. Poets, on the other hand, use as much of the word as possible. They are interested in connotation and use it to enrich and convey meaning. And they may rely on more than one denotation.

Perhaps the purest form of practical language is scientific language. Scientists need a precise language to convey information precisely. The existence of multiple denotations and various overtones of meaning may interfere with this purpose. As a result of this, scientists have even devised special "languages" such as the following:

$$SO_2 + H_2O = H_2SO_3$$

In such a statement the symbols are entirely unambiguous; they have been stripped of all connotation and of all denotations but one. The word *sulfurous*, if it occurred in poetry, might have all kinds of connotations: fire, smoke, brimstone, hell, damnation. But H_2SO_3 means one thing and one thing only: sulfurous acid.

The ambiguity and multiplicity of meanings possessed by words might be an obstacle to the scientist, but they are an advantage for the poet who seeks richness of meaning. One resource for that is a multidimensional language using a multidimensional vocabulary, in which the dimensions of connotation and sound are added to the dimension of denotation.

The poet, we may say, plays on a many-stringed instrument and sounds more than one note at a time.

The first task in reading poetry, therefore, as in reading any kind of literature, is to develop a sense of language, a feeling for words. One needs to become acquainted with their shape, their color, and their flavor. Two of the ways of doing this are extensive use of the dictionary and extensive reading.

EXERCISES

1. Which word in each group has the most "romantic" connotations: (a) horse, steed, nag; (b) king, ruler, tyrant, autocrat; (c) Chicago, Pittsburgh, Samarkand, Detroit?
2. Which word in each group is the most emotionally connotative: (a) female parent, mother, dam; (b) offspring, children, progeny; (c) brother, sibling?
3. Arrange the words in each of the following groups from most positive to most negative in connotation: (a) skinny, thin, gaunt, slender; (b) prosperous, loaded, moneyed, affluent; (c) brainy, intelligent, eggheaded, smart.
4. Of the following, which should you be less offended at being accused of: (a) having acted foolishly, (b) having acted like a fool?

5. In any competent piece of writing, the possible multiple denotations and connotations of the words used are controlled by context. The context screens out irrelevant meanings while allowing the relevant meanings to pass through. What denotation has the word *fast* in the following contexts: fast runner, fast color, fast living, fast day? What are the varying connotations of these four denotations of *fast?*

6. Explain how in the following examples the denotation of the word *white* remains the same, but the connotations differ: (a) The young princess had blue eyes, golden hair, and a breast as white as snow; (b) Confronted with the evidence, the false princess turned as white as a sheet.

REVIEWING CHAPTER THREE

1. Distinguish between connotation and denotation as components of words.
2. Explain how words accumulate their connotations.
3. Explore the ways in which a word may have multiple denotations, and multiple connotations, showing that different denotations may have different connotations.
4. Explore the ways in which the context will determine which denotations and which connotations are relevant in a poem.
5. Show how levels of diction may characterize the speaker in a poem.

Naming of Parts

Today we have naming of parts. Yesterday,
We had daily cleaning. And tomorrow morning,
We shall have what to do after firing. But today,
Today we have naming of parts. Japonica
Glistens like coral in all of the neighboring gardens,   5
    And today we have naming of parts.

This is the lower sling swivel. And this
Is the upper sling swivel, whose use you will see,
When you are given your slings. And this is the piling swivel,
Which in your case you have not got. The branches   10
Hold in the gardens their silent, eloquent gestures,
    Which in our case we have not got.

This is the safety-catch, which is always released
With an easy flick of the thumb. And please do not let me
See anyone using his finger. You can do it quite easy   15
If you have any strength in your thumb. The blossoms
Are fragile and motionless, never letting anyone see
    Any of them using their finger.

And this you can see is the bolt. The purpose of this
Is to open the breech, as you see. We can slide it   20
Rapidly backwards and forwards: we call this
Easing the spring. And rapidly backwards and forwards
The early bees are assaulting and fumbling the flowers:
    They call it easing the Spring.

They call it easing the Spring: it is perfectly easy   25
If you have any strength in your thumb: like the bolt,
And the breech, and the cocking-piece, and the point of balance,
Which in our case we have not got; and the almond-blossom
Silent in all of the gardens and the bees going backwards and forwards,
    For today we have naming of parts.   30

Henry Reed (1914–1986)

QUESTIONS

1. Who is the speaker (or speakers) in the poem, and what is the situation?
2. What basic contrasts are represented by the trainees and by the gardens?
3. What is it that trainees "have not got" (28)? How many meanings have the phrases "easing the spring" (22) and "point of balance" (27)?
4. What differences in language and rhythm do you find between the lines that involve the "naming of parts" and those that describe the gardens?
5. Does the repetition of certain phrases throughout the poem have any special function or does it merely create a kind of refrain?
6. What statement does the poem make about war as it affects men and their lives?

Cross

    My old man's a white old man
    And my old mother's black.
    If ever I cursed my white old man
    I take my curses back.

If ever I cursed my black old mother   5
And wished she were in hell,
I'm sorry for that evil wish
And now I wish her well.

My old man died in a fine big house.
My ma died in a shack.   10
I wonder where I'm gonna die,
Being neither white nor black?

Langston Hughes (1902–1967)

QUESTIONS

1. What different denotations does the title have? What connotations are linked to each of them?
2. The language in this poem, such as "old man" (1, 3, 9), "ma" (10), and "gonna" (11), is plain, and even colloquial. Is it appropriate to the subject? Why or why not?

The world is too much with us

The world is too much with us; late and soon,
Getting and spending, we lay waste our powers:
Little we see in nature that is ours;
We have given our hearts away, a sordid boon!
This sea that bares her bosom to the moon,   5
The winds that will be howling at all hours,
And are up-gathered now like sleeping flowers,
For this, for everything, we are out of tune;
It moves us not. —Great God! I'd rather be
A pagan suckled in a creed outworn;   10
So might I, standing on this pleasant lea,
Have glimpses that would make me less forlorn;
Have sight of Proteus rising from the sea;
Or hear old Triton blow his wreathèd horn.

William Wordsworth (1770–1850)

QUESTIONS

1. Vocabulary: *boon* (4), *Proteus* (13), *Triton* (14). What two relevant denotations has "wreathèd" (14)?
2. Explain why the poet's words are more effective than these possible alternatives: *earth* for "world" (1); *selling and buying* for "getting and spending"

(2); *exposes* for "bares" (5); *dozing* for "sleeping" (7); *posies* for "flowers" (7); *nourished* for "suckled" (10); *visions* for "glimpses" (12); *sound* for "blow" (14).
3. Is "Great God!" (9) a vocative (term of address) or an expletive (exclamation)? Or something of both?
4. State the theme (central idea) of the poem in a sentence.

"I Am in Danger—Sir—"

"Half-cracked" to Higginson, living,
afterward famous in garbled versions,
your hoard of dazzling scraps a battlefield,
now your old snood

mothballed at Harvard   5
and you in your variorum monument
equivocal to the end—
who are you?

Gardening the day-lily,
wiping the wine-glass stems,   10
your thought pulsed on behind
a forehead battered paper-thin,

you, woman, masculine
in single-mindedness,
for whom the word was more   15
than a symptom—

a condition of being.
Till the air buzzing with spoiled language
sang in your ears
of Perjury   20

and in your half-cracked way you chose
silence for entertainment,
chose to have it out at last
on your own premises.

Adrienne Rich (b. 1929)

NOTE: "Higginson" (1) refers to Thomas Wentworth Higginson, the *Atlantic Monthly* editor to whom Emily Dickinson sent poems and letters between 1862 and 1886, the year of her death. The poem's title is a quotation from one of these letters. In 1955 a complete "variorum" (6) edition of Dickinson's poems was published providing the variant readings from her manuscripts.

Desert Places

Snow falling and night falling fast, oh, fast
In a field I looked into going past,
And the ground almost covered smooth in snow,
But a few weeds and stubble showing last.

The woods around it have it—it is theirs.   5
All animals are smothered in their lairs.
I am too absent-spirited to count;
The loneliness includes me unawares.

And lonely as it is that loneliness
Will be more lonely ere it will be less—   10
A blanker whiteness of benighted snow
With no expression, nothing to express.

They cannot scare me with their empty spaces
Between stars—on stars where no human race is.
I have it in me so much nearer home   15
To scare myself with my own desert places.

Robert Frost (1874–1963)

QUESTIONS

1. Examine the poem for examples of words or phrases with negative or positive connotations. Which stanza is most negative? Considering its possible
   synonyms, how emotionally powerful is the word "scare" (13 and 16)?
2. What multiple denotations of the word "benighted" (11) are functional
   in the poem? How does the etymology of "blanker" add to its force in this
   context?
3. "Absent-spirited" (7) is coined from the common phrase "absent-minded."
   What denotations of "spirit" are relevant here?
4. Who are "They" (13) who can create fear by talking about the emptiness of
   space? Fear of what? What are the "desert places" (16) within the speaker
   that may be compared to literal emptiness of space?
5. In the first publication of the poem, line 14 concluded "on stars void of human races." Frost's final version calls attention to the potentially comic effect of rhyming *spaces/race is/places,* a device called feminine rhyme often
   used in humorous verse (see pages 825, 829). Is the speaker feeling comical?
   Can you relate this effect to what you determined about the word "scare" in
   question 1?

A Hymn to God the Father

Wilt thou forgive that sin where I begun,
  Which is my sin, though it were done before?
Wilt thou forgive those sins through which I run,°   ran
  And do them still, though still I do deplore?
    When thou hast done, thou hast not done,   5
      For I have more.

Wilt thou forgive that sin by which I won
  Others to sin, and made my sin their door?
Wilt thou forgive that sin which I did shun
  A year or two, but wallowed in a score?   10
    When thou hast done, thou hast not done,
      For I have more.

I have a sin of fear, that when I have spun
  My last thread, I shall perish on the shore;
Swear by thyself that at my death thy Sun   15
  Shall shine as it shines now, and heretofore;
    And having done that, thou hast done.
      I have no more.

John Donne (1572–1631)

QUESTIONS

1. In 1601, John Donne at 29 secretly married Anne More, age 17, infuriating her upper-class father, who had him imprisoned for three days. Because of the marriage, Donne lost his job as private secretary to an important official at court, and probably ruined his chances for the career at court that he desired. It was, however, a true love match. In 1615 Donne entered the church. In 1617 his wife, then 33, died after bearing twelve children. In 1621 he was appointed Dean of St. Paul's Cathedral in London and quickly won a reputation for his eloquent sermons. His religious poems differ markedly in tone from the often cynical, sometimes erotic poems of his youth. The foregoing poem was probably written during a severe illness in 1623. Is this information of any value to a reader of the poem?
2. What sin is referred to in lines 1–2? What is meant by "when I have spun / My last thread" (13–14)? By "I shall perish on the shore" (14)?
3. How do the puns on "done" (5, 11, 17) and "Sun" (15) give structure and meaning to the poem? Explain the relevance of the meanings generated by the puns.

One Art

The art of losing isn't hard to master;
so many things seem filled with the intent
to be lost that their loss is no disaster.

Lose something every day. Accept the fluster
of lost door keys, the hour badly spent.   5
The art of losing isn't hard to master.

Then practice losing farther, losing faster:
places, and names, and where it was you meant
to travel. None of these will bring disaster.

I lost my mother's watch. And look! my last, or   10
next-to-last, of three loved houses went.
The art of losing isn't hard to master.

I lost two cities, lovely ones. And, vaster,
some realms I owned, two rivers, a continent.
I miss them, but it wasn't a disaster.   15

—Even losing you (the joking voice, a gesture
I love) I shan't have lied. It's evident
the art of losing's not too hard to master
though it may look like (*Write* it!) like disaster.

Elizabeth Bishop (1911–1979)

QUESTIONS

1. What various denotations of "lose" and its derivative forms are relevant to the context? What connotations are attached to the separate denotative meanings?
2. Explain how "owned" (14) and "lost" (13) shift the meanings of possessing and losing.
3. What seems to be the purpose of the speaker in the first three tercets (three-line units)? How is the advice given there supported by the personal experiences related in the next two tercets?
4. The concluding quatrain (four-line unit) contains direct address to a person, as well as a command the speaker addresses to herself. How do these details reveal the real purpose of the poem? *Can* all kinds of losses be mastered with one "art of losing"?

SUGGESTIONS FOR WRITING

Consider the denotative meaning(s) of the following titles. Then read each poem carefully and note the multiple connotations that attach to the title phrase as the poem progresses. Choose two or three titles, then write a short essay comparing the denotative and connotative meanings of each.

1. Williams, "The Red Wheelbarrow" (page 661).
2. Frost, "Fire and Ice" (page 746).
3. Piercy, "Barbie Doll" (page 761).
4. Bottoms, "Sign for My Father, Who Stressed the Bunt" (page 948).
5. Donne, "The Good-Morrow" (page 957).
6. Phillips, "Wish You Were Here" (page 985).
7. Roethke, "My Papa's Waltz" (page 997).
8. Soto, "Small Town with One Road" (page 1005).
9. Wordsworth, "The Solitary Reaper" (page 1019).

Chapter Four

Imagery

Experience comes to us largely through the senses. Our experiences of a spring day, for instance, may consist partly of certain emotions we feel and partly of certain thoughts we think, but most of it will be a cluster of sense impressions. It will consist of *seeing* blue sky and white clouds, budding leaves and daffodils; of *hearing* robins and bluebirds singing in the early morning; of *smelling* damp earth and blossoming hyacinths; and of *feeling* a fresh wind against one's cheek. A poet seeking to express the experience of a spring day therefore provides a selection of sense impressions. Similarly, to present a winter day (page 650), Shakespeare gives us hanging "icicles," milk "frozen," blood "nipped," and Marian's "red and raw" nose as well as the melancholy "'Tu-whit, tu-who'" of the owl. Had he not done so, he might have failed to evoke the emotions that accompany these sensations. The poet's language, then, is more *sensuous* than ordinary language. It is richer in imagery.

Imagery may be defined as the representation through language of sense experience. Poetry appeals directly to our senses, of course, through its music and rhythms, which we actually hear when it is read aloud. But indirectly it appeals to our senses through imagery, the representation to the imagination of sense experience. The word *image* perhaps most often suggests a mental picture, something seen in the mind's eye—and *visual* imagery is the kind of imagery that occurs most frequently in poetry. But an image may also represent a sound (*auditory imagery*); a smell (*olfactory imagery*); a taste (*gustatory imagery*); touch, such as hardness, softness, wetness, or heat and cold (*tactile imagery*); an internal sensation, such as hunger, thirst, fatigue, or nausea (*organic imagery*); or movement or tension in the muscles or joints (*kinesthetic imagery*). If we wish to be scientific, we could extend this list further, for psychologists no longer confine themselves to five or even six senses, but for purposes of discussing poetry the preceding classification should ordinarily be sufficient.

Meeting at Night

The gray sea and the long black land;
And the yellow half-moon large and low;
And the startled little waves that leap
In fiery ringlets from their sleep,
As I gain the cove with pushing prow,   5
And quench its speed i' the slushy sand.

Then a mile of warm sea-scented beach;
Three fields to cross till a farm appears;
A tap at the pane, the quick sharp scratch
And blue spurt of a lighted match,   10
And a voice less loud, through its joys and fears,
Than the two hearts beating each to each!

Robert Browning (1812–1889)

"Meeting at Night" is a poem about love. It makes, one might say, a number of statements about love: being in love is a sweet and exciting experience; when one is in love everything seems beautiful, and the most trivial things become significant; when one is in love one's beloved seems the most important thing in the world. But the poet actually *tells* us none of these things directly. He does not even use the word *love* in his poem. His business is to communicate experience, not information. He does this largely in two ways. First, he presents us with a specific situation, in which a lover goes to meet his love. Second, he describes the lover's journey so vividly in terms of sense impressions that the reader virtually sees and hears what the lover saw and heard and seems to share his anticipation and excitement.

Every line in the poem contains some image, some appeal to the senses: the gray sea, the long black land, the yellow half-moon, the startled little waves with their fiery ringlets, the blue spurt of the lighted match—all appeal to our sense of sight and convey not only shape but also color and motion. The warm sea-scented beach appeals to the senses of both smell and touch. The pushing prow of the boat on the slushy sand, the tap at the pane, the quick scratch of the match, the low speech of the lovers, and the sound of their hearts beating—all appeal to the sense of hearing.

Parting at Morning

Round the cape of a sudden came the sea,
And the sun looked over the mountain's rim:
And straight was a path of gold for him,
And the need of a world of men for me.

Robert Browning (1812–1889)

QUESTIONS

1. This poem is a sequel to "Meeting at Night." "[H]im" (3) refers to the sun.
   Does the last line mean that the lover needs the world of men or that the
   world of men needs the lover? Or both?
2. Does the sea *actually* come suddenly around the cape or *appear* to? Why does
   Browning mention the *effect* before its *cause* (the sun looking over the
   mountain's rim)?
3. Do these two poems, taken together, suggest any larger truths about love?
   Browning, in answer to a question, said that the second poem is the man's
   confession of "how fleeting is the belief (implied in the first part) that such
   raptures are self-sufficient and enduring—as for the time they appear."

   The sharpness and vividness of any image will ordinarily depend
on how specific it is and on the poet's use of effective detail. The word
hummingbird, for instance, conveys a more definite image than does
bird, and *ruby-throated hummingbird* is sharper and more specific still.
However, to represent something vividly a poet need not describe it
completely. One or two especially sharp and representative details will
often serve, inviting the reader's imagination to fill in the rest.
Tennyson in "The Eagle" (page 649) gives only one visual detail about
the eagle itself—that he clasps the crag with "crooked hands"—but this
detail is an effective and memorable one. Brooks in "Kitchenette Building" (page 660) offers no visual description of the tenement, but the
smells of "onion fumes," "fried potatoes," and "garbage ripening in the
hall" speak volumes about the conditions of life there. Browning, in
"Meeting at Night," calls up a whole scene with "A tap at the pane, the
quick sharp scratch / And blue spurt of a lighted match."
   Since imagery is a peculiarly effective way of evoking vivid experience, and since it may be used to convey emotion and suggest ideas as
well as to cause a mental reproduction of sensations, it is an invaluable
resource for the poet. In general, the poet will seek concrete or image-
bearing words in preference to abstract or nonimage-bearing words. We
cannot evaluate a poem, however, by the amount or quality of its imagery alone. Sense impression is only one of the elements of experi-

ence. Poetry may attain its ends by other means. We should never judge any single element of a poem except in reference to the total intent of that poem.

EXERCISES

In the following images, what sense is being evoked, and what does the image contribute to its context?

1. "Dulce et Decorum Est" (page 651): "deaf even to the hoots / Of gas-shells" (7-8); "He plunges at me, guttering, choking, drowning" (16); "gargling from the froth-corrupted lungs" (22).
2. "Shall I compare thee to a summer's day?" (page 656): "Rough winds do shake the darling buds of May" (3); "Sometimes too hot the eye of heaven shines" (5); "often is his gold complexion dimmed" (6).
3. "Ballad of Birmingham" (page 658): "her night-dark hair" (17); "rose petal sweet" (18); "clawed through bits of glass and brick" (29).
4. "Eros Turannos" (page 682): "foamless weirs" (7); "pounding wave" (27); "stairway to the sea" (47).

REVIEWING CHAPTER FOUR

1. State the definition of poetic imagery.
2. Relate imagery to its uses in conveying emotion, suggesting ideas, and mentally evoking sense experience.
3. Select individual images that demonstrate these three uses of imagery, and explain how they work.
4. Show that specificity in an image contributes to its sharpness and vividness.
5. Draw the distinction between abstract statements and concrete, image-bearing statements, providing examples.
6. Demonstrate that ambiguity and multiplicity of meanings contribute to the richness of poetic language.

Spring

Nothing is so beautiful as spring—
　　When weeds, in wheels, shoot long and lovely and lush;
　　Thrush's eggs look little low heavens, and thrush
Through the echoing timber does so rinse and wring
The ear, it strikes like lightnings to hear him sing;　　　5

The glassy peartree leaves and blooms, they brush
The descending blue; that blue is all in a rush
With richness; the racing lambs too have fair their fling.

What is all this juice and all this joy?
    A strain of the earth's sweet being in the beginning   10
In Eden garden. —Have, get, before it cloy,

    Before it cloud, Christ, lord, and sour with sinning,
Innocent mind and Mayday in girl and boy,
    Most, O maid's child, thy choice and worthy the winning.

Gerard Manley Hopkins (1844–1889)

QUESTIONS

1. The first line makes an abstract statement. How is this statement brought to carry conviction?
2. The sky is described as being "all in a rush / With richness" (7–8). In what other respects is the poem "rich"?
3. To what two things does the speaker compare the spring in lines 9–14? In what ways are the comparisons appropriate?
4. Lines 11–14 might be made clearer by paraphrasing them thus: "Christ, lord, child of the Virgin: save the innocent mind of girl and boy before sin taints it, since it is most like yours and worth saving." Why are Hopkins's lines more effective, both in imagery and in syntax?

The Widow's Lament in Springtime

Sorrow is my own yard
where the new grass
flames as it has flamed
often before but not
with the cold fire   5
that closes round me this year.
Thirtyfive years
I lived with my husband.
The plumtree is white today
with masses of flowers.   10
Masses of flowers
load the cherry branches
and color some bushes

yellow and some red
but the grief in my heart   15
is stronger than they
for though they were my joy
formerly, today I notice them
and turned away forgetting.
Today my son told me   20
that in the meadows,
at the edge of the heavy woods
in the distance, he saw
trees of white flowers.
I feel that I would like   25
to go there
and fall into those flowers
and sink into the marsh near them.

William Carlos Williams (1883–1963)

QUESTIONS

1. Why is springtime so poignant a time for this lament? What has been the speaker's previous experience at this time of year?
2. Why does the speaker's son tell her of the flowering trees "in the distance" (23)? What does he want her to do? Contrast the two locations in the poem—"yard" versus "meadows" (21), "woods" (22), and "marsh" (28). What does the widow desire?
3. Imagery may have degrees of vividness, depending on its particularity, concreteness, and specific detail. What is the result of the contrast between the vividness of lines 2–3 and the relative flatness of lines 13–14? How does the fact that "masses" (10, 11) appeals to two senses relate to the speaker's emotional condition?

I felt a Funeral, in my Brain

I felt a Funeral, in my Brain,
And Mourners to and fro
Kept treading—treading—till it seemed
That Sense was breaking through—

And when they all were seated,   5
A Service, like a Drum—
Kept beating—beating—till I thought
My Mind was going numb—

And then I heard them lift a Box
And creak across my Soul   10
With those same Boots of Lead, again,
Then Space—began to toll,

As all the Heavens were a Bell,
And Being, but an Ear,
And I, and Silence, some strange Race   15
Wrecked, solitary, here—

And then a Plank in Reason, broke,
And I dropped down, and down—
And hit a World, at every plunge,
And Finished knowing—then—   20

Emily Dickinson (1830–1886)

QUESTIONS

1. What senses are being evoked by the imagery? Can you account for the fact that one important sense is absent from the poem?
2. In sequence, what aspects of a funeral and burial are represented in the poem? Is it possible to define the sequence of mental events that are being compared to them?
3. With respect to the funeral activities in stanzas 1–3, where is the speaker imaginatively located?
4. What finally happens to the speaker?

Living in Sin

She had thought the studio would keep itself,
no dust upon the furniture of love.
Half heresy, to wish the taps less vocal,
the panes relieved of grime. A plate of pears,
a piano with a Persian shawl, a cat   5
stalking the picturesque amusing mouse
had risen at his urging.
Not that at five each separate stair would writhe
under the milkman's tramp; that morning light
so coldly would delineate the scraps   10
of last night's cheese and three sepulchral bottles;
that on the kitchen shelf among the saucers
a pair of beetle-eyes would fix her own—

envoy from some village in the moldings . . .
Meanwhile, he, with a yawn,   15
sounded a dozen notes upon the keyboard,
declared it out of tune, shrugged at the mirror,
rubbed at his beard, went out for cigarettes;
while she, jeered by the minor demons,
pulled back the sheets and made the bed and found   20
a towel to dust the table-top,
and let the coffee-pot boil over on the stove.
By evening she was back in love again,
though not so wholly but throughout the night
she woke sometimes to feel the daylight coming   25
like a relentless milkman up the stairs.

Adrienne Rich (b. 1929)

The Forge

All I know is a door into the dark.
Outside, old axles and iron hoops rusting;
Inside, the hammered anvil's short-pitched ring,
The unpredictable fantail of sparks
Or hiss when a new shoe toughens in water.   5
The anvil must be somewhere in the center,
Horned as a unicorn, at one end square,
Set there immovable: an altar
Where he expends himself in shape and music.
Sometimes, leather-aproned, hairs in his nose,   10
He leans out on the jamb, recalls a clatter
Of hoofs where traffic is flashing in rows;
Then grunts and goes in, with a slam and flick
To beat real iron out, to work the bellows.

Seamus Heaney (b. 1939)

QUESTIONS

1. What does the speaker mean when he says that "all" he knows is "a door into the dark" (1)? What more does he know, and how does he make his knowledge evident?

2. How do the images describing the blacksmith (10–11) relate to his attitude toward his work and toward the changing times?

3. The speaker summarizes the smith's world as "shape and music" (9), terms
   that suggest visual and auditory imagery. What do the contrasts between visual images contribute? The contrasts between auditory images?

After Apple-Picking

My long two-pointed ladder's sticking through a tree
Toward heaven still,
And there's a barrel that I didn't fill
Beside it, and there may be two or three
Apples I didn't pick upon some bough.   5
But I am done with apple-picking now.
Essence of winter sleep is on the night,
The scent of apples: I am drowsing off.
I cannot rub the strangeness from my sight
I got from looking through a pane of glass   10
I skimmed this morning from the drinking trough
And held against the world of hoary grass.
It melted, and I let it fall and break.
But I was well
Upon my way to sleep before it fell,   15
And I could tell
What form my dreaming was about to take.
Magnified apples appear and disappear,
Stem end and blossom end,
And every fleck of russet showing clear.   20
My instep arch not only keeps the ache,
It keeps the pressure of a ladder-round.
I feel the ladder sway as the boughs bend.
And I keep hearing from the cellar bin
The rumbling sound   25
Of load on load of apples coming in.
For I have had too much
Of apple-picking: I am overtired
Of the great harvest I myself desired.
There were ten thousand thousand fruit to touch,   30
Cherish in hand, lift down, and not let fall.
For all
That struck the earth,
No matter if not bruised or spiked with stubble,
Went surely to the cider-apple heap   35
As of no worth.

One can see what will trouble
This sleep of mine, whatever sleep it is.
Were he not gone,
The woodchuck could say whether it's like his   40
Long sleep, as I describe its coming on,
Or just some human sleep.

Robert Frost (1874–1963)

QUESTIONS

1. How does the poet convey so vividly the experience of "apple-picking"? Point out effective examples of each kind of imagery used. What emotional responses do the images evoke?
2. How does the speaker regard his work? Has he done it well or poorly? Does he find it enjoyable or tedious? Is he dissatisfied with its results?
3. The speaker predicts what he will dream about in his sleep. Why does he shift to the present tense (18) when he begins describing a dream he has not yet had? How sharply are real experience and dream experience differentiated in the poem?
4. The poem uses the word *sleep* six times. Does it, through repetition, come to suggest a meaning beyond the purely literal? If so, what attitude does the speaker take toward this second signification? Does he fear it? Does he look forward to it? What does he expect of it?
5. If sleep is symbolic (both literal and metaphorical), other details also may take on additional meaning. If so, how would you interpret (a) the ladder, (b) the season of the year, (c) the harvesting, (d) the "pane of glass" (10)? What denotations has the word "Essence" (7)?
6. How does the woodchuck's sleep differ from "just some human sleep" (42)?

Those Winter Sundays

Sundays too my father got up early
and put his clothes on in the blueblack cold,
then with cracked hands that ached
from labor in the weekday weather made
banked fires blaze. No one ever thanked him.   5

I'd wake and hear the cold splintering, breaking.
When the rooms were warm, he'd call,
and slowly I would rise and dress,
fearing the chronic angers of that house,

Speaking indifferently to him,   10
who had driven out the cold

and polished my good shoes as well.
What did I know, what did I know
of love's austere and lonely offices?

Robert Hayden (1913–1980)

QUESTIONS

1. Vocabulary: *offices* (14).
2. What kind of imagery is central to the poem? How is this imagery related to the emotional concerns of the poem?
3. How do the subsidiary images relate to the central images?
4. From what point in time does the speaker view the subject matter of the poem? What has happened to him in the interval?

Reapers

Black reapers with the sound of steel on stones
Are sharpening scythes. I see them place the hones
In their hip-pockets as a thing that's done,
And start their silent swinging, one by one.
Black horses drive a mower through the weeds,   5
And there, a field rat, startled, squealing bleeds,
His belly close to ground. I see the blade,
Blood-stained, continue cutting weeds and shade.

Jean Toomer (1894–1967)

QUESTIONS

1. The poem presents two examples of cutting down vegetation. What contrasts are drawn between reaping and mowing? How does imagery reinforce those contrasts?
2. What is signified by the speaker's stating that the "horses drive" (5) the mowing machine rather than that a man is driving the team of horses?
3. For whom (or what) would the weeds represent "shade" (8)? Are the connotations of *shade* positive or negative in this context? How are the usual connotations of "rat" (6) altered in the poem? Characterize the speaker.

The Destruction of Sennacherib

The Assyrian came down like the wolf on the fold,
And his cohorts were gleaming in purple and gold;
And the sheen of their spears was like stars on the sea,
When the blue wave rolls nightly on deep Galilee.

Like the leaves of the forest when summer is green,   5
That host with their banners at sunset were seen:
Like the leaves of the forest when autumn hath blown,
That host on the morrow lay withered and strown.

For the Angel of Death spread his wings on the blast,
And breathed in the face of the foe as he passed;   10
And the eyes of the sleepers waxed deadly and chill,
And their hearts but once heaved—and for ever grew still!

And there lay the steed with his nostril all wide,
But through it there rolled not the breath of his pride;
And the foam of his gasping lay white on the turf,   15
And cold as the spray of the rock-beating surf.

And there lay the rider distorted and pale,
With the dew on his brow, and the rust on his mail;
And the tents were all silent, the banners alone,
The lances unlifted, the trumpet unblown.   20

And the widows of Ashur° are loud in their wail,   Assyria
And the idols are broke in the temple of Baal;
And the might of the Gentile, unsmote by the sword,
Hath melted like snow in the glance of the Lord!

George Gordon, Lord Byron (1788–1824)

QUESTIONS

1. Vocabulary: *host* (6), *blown* (7), *strown* (8), *steed* (13), *mail* (18), *Baal* (22).
2. Read the biblical story on which this poem is based (II Kings, 19:31–36). How do the rhythm and imagery of the poem convey the spirit of the biblical account?
3. Identify significant images in the poem. How do they deepen and enrich the poem's meaning?

To Autumn

Season of mists and mellow fruitfulness,
    Close bosom-friend of the maturing sun;
Conspiring with him how to load and bless
    With fruit the vines that round the thatch-eaves run;

To bend with apples the mossed cottage-trees,   5
  And fill all fruit with ripeness to the core;
    To swell the gourd, and plump the hazel shells
With a sweet kernel; to set budding more,
  And still more, later flowers for the bees,
    Until they think warm days will never cease,   10
      For summer has o'er-brimmed their clammy cells.

Who hath not seen thee oft amid thy store?
  Sometimes whoever seeks abroad may find
Thee sitting careless on a granary floor,
  Thy hair soft-lifted by the winnowing wind;   15
Or on a half-reaped furrow sound asleep,
  Drowsed with the fume of poppies, while thy hook
    Spares the next swath and all its twinèd flowers:
And sometimes like a gleaner thou dost keep
  Steady thy laden head across a brook;   20
  Or by a cider-press, with patient look,
    Thou watchest the last oozings hours by hours.

Where are the songs of spring? Ay, where are they?
  Think not of them, thou hast thy music too,—
While barred clouds bloom the soft-dying day,   25
  And touch the stubble-plains with rosy hue;
Then in a wailful choir the small gnats mourn
  Among the river sallows, borne aloft
    Or sinking as the light wind lives or dies;
And full-grown lambs loud bleat from hilly bourn;   30
  Hedge-crickets sing; and now with treble soft
  The red-breast whistles from a garden-croft;
    And gathering swallows twitter in the skies.

John Keats (1795–1821)

QUESTIONS

1. Vocabulary: *hook* (17), *barred* (25), *sallows* (28), *bourn* (30), *croft* (32).
2. How many kinds of imagery do you find in the poem? Give examples of each.
3. Are the images arranged haphazardly or are they carefully organized? In answering this question, consider (a) what aspect of autumn each stanza particularly concerns, (b) what kind of imagery dominates each stanza, and (c) what time of the season each stanza presents. Is there any progression in time of day?

4. What is autumn personified as in stanza 2? Is there any suggestion of personification in the other two stanzas?
5. Although the poem is primarily descriptive, what attitude toward transience and passing beauty is implicit in it?

SUGGESTIONS FOR WRITING

Analyze the imagery in one of the following poems, drawing some conclusions as to whether individual images function primarily to evoke vivid experience, convey emotion, or suggest ideas (see page 702). Be sure in each case to identify the sense reference of the imagery—visual, auditory, and so forth.

1. Berry, "On Reading Poems to a Senior Class at South High" (page 945).
2. Dickinson, "A narrow Fellow in the Grass" (page 955).
3. Forché, "The Colonel" (page 961).
4. Hardy, "The Darkling Thrush" (page 969).
5. Hughes, "Thistles" (page 974).
6. Kumin, "The Sound of Night" (page 979).
7. Plath, "Spinster" (page 987).
8. Roethke, "My Papa's Waltz" (page 997).
9. Shapiro, "The Fly" (page 1001).
10. Stevens, "The Snow Man" (page 1008).
11. Yeats, "The Wild Swans at Coole" (page 1023).

Chapter Five

Figurative Language I
Simile, Metaphor, Personification, Apostrophe, Metonymy

*Poetry provides the one permissible way
of saying one thing and meaning another.*

Robert Frost

Let us assume that your brother has just come in out of a rainstorm and you say to him, "Well, you're a pretty sight! Got slightly wet, didn't you?" And he replies, "Wet? I'm drowned! It's raining cats and dogs, and my raincoat's like a sieve!"

You and your brother probably understand each other well enough; yet if you examine this conversation literally, that is to say unimaginatively, you will find that you have been speaking nonsense. Actually you have been speaking figuratively. You have been saying less than what you mean, or more than what you mean, or the opposite of what you mean, or something other than what you mean. You did not mean that your brother was a pretty sight but that he was a wretched sight. You did not mean that he got slightly wet but that he got very wet. Your brother did not mean that he got drowned but that he got drenched. It was not raining cats and dogs; it was raining water. And your brother's raincoat is so unlike a sieve that not even a child would confuse them.

If you are familiar with Molière's play *Le Bourgeois Gentilhomme*, you will remember how delighted M. Jourdain is to discover that he has been speaking prose all his life. Many people might be equally surprised to learn that they have been speaking a kind of subpoetry all their lives. The difference between their figures of speech and the poet's is that theirs are probably worn and trite, the poet's fresh and original.

On first examination, it might seem absurd to say one thing and mean another. But we all do it—and with good reason. We do it because we can say what we want to say more vividly and forcefully by figures of speech than we can by saying it directly. And we can say more by figurative statement than we can by literal statement. Figures of speech offer another way of adding extra dimensions to language.

Broadly defined, a **figure of speech** is any way of saying something other than the ordinary way, and some rhetoricians have classified as many as 250 separate figures. For our purposes, however, a figure of speech is more narrowly definable as a way of saying one thing and meaning another, and we need to be concerned with no more than a dozen. **Figurative language**—language using figures of speech—is language that cannot be taken literally (or should not be taken literally only).

Simile and **metaphor** are both used as a means of comparing things that are essentially unlike. The only distinction between them is that in simile the comparison is *expressed* by the use of some word or phrase, such as *like, as, than, similar to, resembles,* or *seems*; in metaphor, the comparison is not expressed but is created when a figurative term is *substituted for* or *identified with* the literal term.

The Guitarist Tunes Up

With what attentive courtesy he bent
Over his instrument;
Not as a lordly conqueror who could
Command both wire and wood,
But as a man with a loved woman might,   5
Inquiring with delight
What slight essential things she had to say
Before they started, he and she, to play.

Frances Cornford (1886–1960)

QUESTIONS
1. Explore the comparisons. Do they principally illuminate the guitarist, the conquering lord, or the lovers?
2. What one word brings the figurative and literal terms together?

The Hound

Life the hound
Equivocal
Comes at a bound

Either to rend me
Or to befriend me.   5
I cannot tell
The hound's intent
Till he has sprung
At my bare hand
With teeth or tongue.   10
Meanwhile I stand
And wait the event.

Robert Francis (1901–1987)

QUESTIONS

1. What does "Equivocal" (2) mean? Show how this is a key word in the poem.
2. What is the effect of "Equivocal" constituting a line by itself?

Metaphors may take one of four forms, depending on whether the literal and figurative terms are respectively *named* or *implied*. In the first form of metaphor, as in simile, *both* the literal *and* figurative terms are *named*. In Francis's poem, for example, the literal term is "life" and the figurative term is "hound." In the second form, the literal term is *named* and the figurative term is *implied*.

Bereft

Where had I heard this wind before
Change like this to a deeper roar?
What would it take my standing there for,
Holding open a restive door,
Looking down hill to a frothy shore?   5
Summer was past and day was past.
Somber clouds in the west were massed.
Out in the porch's sagging floor,
Leaves got up in a coil and hissed,
Blindly struck at my knee and missed.   10
Something sinister in the tone
Told me my secret must be known:
Word I was in the house alone
Somehow must have gotten abroad,
Word I was in my life alone,   15
Word I had no one left but God.

Robert Frost (1874–1963)

QUESTIONS

1. Describe the situation precisely. What time of day and year is it? Where is the speaker? What is happening to the weather?
2. How does the comparison in lines 9–10 reflect the state of mind of the speaker?
3. The word "hissed" (9) is onomatopoetic (see Glossary of Terms). How is its effect reinforced in the lines following?
4. Though lines 9–10 present the clearest example of the second form of metaphor, there are others. To what is the wind ("it") compared in line 3? Why is the door "restive" (4) and what does this do (figuratively) to the door? To what is the speaker's "life" (15) compared?
5. What is the tone of the poem? How reassuring is the last line?

In the third form of metaphor, the literal term is *implied* and the figurative term is *named*. In the fourth form, *both* the literal *and* figurative terms are *implied*. The following poem exemplifies both forms:

It sifts from Leaden Sieves

It sifts from Leaden Sieves—
It powders all the Wood.
It fills with Alabaster Wool
The Wrinkles of the Road—

It makes an Even Face   5
Of Mountain, and of Plain—
Unbroken Forehead from the East
Unto the East again—

It reaches to the Fence—
It wraps it Rail by Rail   10
Till it is lost in Fleeces—
It deals Celestial Veil

To Stump, and Stack—and Stem—
A Summer's empty Room—
Acres of Joints, where Harvests were,   15
Recordless,° but for them—   unrecorded

> It Ruffles Wrists of Posts
> As Ankles of a Queen—
> Then stills its Artisans—like Ghosts—
> Denying they have been—   20

Emily Dickinson (1830–1886)

QUESTIONS

1. This poem consists essentially of a series of metaphors with the same literal term identified only as "It." What is "It"?
2. In several of these metaphors the figurative term is named—"Alabaster Wool" (3), "Fleeces" (11), "Celestial Veil" (12). In two of them, however, the figurative term as well as the literal term is left unnamed. To what is "It" compared in lines 1–2? In lines 17–18?
3. Comment on the additional metaphorical expressions or complications contained in "Leaden Sieves" (1), "Alabaster Wool" (3), "Even Face" (5), "Unbroken Forehead" (7), "A Summer's empty Room" (14), "Artisans" (19).

Metaphors of the fourth form, as one might guess, are comparatively rare. An extended example, however, is provided by Dickinson's "I like to see it lap the Miles" (page 911).

Using some examples from the previous four poems, the chart below provides a visual demonstration of the figures of comparison (simile and the four forms of metaphor).

		Poet	Literal Term	Figurative Term
Similes (*like, as, seems*, etc.)		Cornford	named guitarist guitarist	named conqueror man with woman
Metaphors (*is, are*, etc.)	**Form 1**	Francis	named life	named hound
	Form 2	Frost	named leaves	implied [snake] hissed
	Form 3	Dickinson	implied it [snow]	named wool
	Form 4	Dickinson	implied it [snow]	implied [flour] sifts

Personification consists in giving the attributes of a human being to an animal, an object, or a concept. It is really a subtype of metaphor, an implied comparison in which the figurative term of the comparison is always a human being. When Sylvia Plath makes a mirror speak and think (page 680), she is personifying an object. When Keats describes autumn as a harvester "sitting careless on a granary floor" or "on a half-reaped furrow sound asleep" (page 712), he is personifying a season. Personifications differ in the degree to which they ask the reader actually to visualize the literal term in human form. In Keats's comparison, we are asked to make a complete identification of autumn with a human being. In Sylvia Plath's, though the mirror speaks and thinks, we continue to visualize it as a mirror; similarly, in Frost's "Bereft" (page 716), the "restive" door remains in appearance a door tugged by the wind. In Browning's reference to "the startled little waves" (page 701), a personification is barely suggested; we would make a mistake if we tried to visualize the waves in human form or even, really, to think of them as having human emotions.*

Song of the Powers

Mine, said the stone,
mine is the hour.
I crush the scissors,
such is my power.
Stronger than wishes,   5
my power, alone.

Mine, said the paper,
mine are the words
that smother the stone
with imagined birds,   10
reams of them, flown
from the mind of the shaper.

Mine, said the scissors,
mine all the knives
gashing through paper's   15
ethereal lives;
nothing's so proper
as tattering wishes.

*The various figures of speech blend into each other, and it is sometimes difficult to classify a specific example as definitely metaphor or symbol, symbol or allegory, understatement or irony, irony or paradox. Often a given example may exemplify two or more figures at once. In "The Guitarist Tunes Up" (page 715), "wire and wood" are metonymies (see page 721) for a guitar and are personified as subjects, slaves, or soldiers who could be commanded by a lordly conqueror. In "The world is too much with us" (page 694), when the winds are described as calm, "like sleeping flowers," the flowers function as part of a simile and are personified as something that can sleep. The important consideration in reading poetry is not that we classify figures definitively but that we construe them correctly.

As stone crushes scissors,
as paper snuffs stone   20
and scissors cut paper,
all end alone.
So heap up your paper
and scissor your wishes
and uproot the stone   25
from the top of the hill.
They all end alone
as you will, you will.

David Mason (b. 1954)

QUESTIONS

1. Vocabulary: *reams* (11), *ethereal* (16).
2. The poem is based on a children's game but is entitled "Song of the Powers." Why is this title appropriate?
3. In stanzas 1 through 3 the poem employs personification to convey the attitude of each element—stone, paper, and scissors—to its own unique power. Why is having the elements speak in their own voices more effective than if their viewpoints were merely described? Does the speaker of the poem agree with what the individual elements say?
4. What does the final stanza say about the nature of power? Is physical power finally destructive or affirmative?

Closely related to personification is **apostrophe,** which consists in addressing someone absent or dead or something nonhuman as if that person or thing were present and alive and could reply to what is being said. The speaker in A. E. Housman's "To an Athlete Dying Young" (page 971) apostrophizes a dead runner. William Blake apostrophizes a tiger throughout his famous poem (page 947) but does not otherwise personify it. In the poem printed below, Keats apostrophizes *and* personifies a star, as he does with autumn in "To Autumn" (page 711).

Personification and apostrophe are both ways of giving life and immediacy to one's language, but since neither requires great imaginative power on the part of the poet—apostrophe especially does not—they may degenerate into mere mannerisms and occur as often in bad and mediocre poetry as in good, a fact that Shakespeare parodies in Bottom's apostrophe to night in *A Midsummer Night's Dream* (5.1):

O grim-looked night! O night with hue so black!
O night, which ever art when day is not!
O night, O night! Alack, alack, alack.

We need to distinguish between their effective use and their merely conventional use.

Bright Star

Bright star, would I were steadfast as thou art—
   Not in lone splendor hung aloft the night,
And watching, with eternal lids apart,
   Like nature's patient, sleepless Eremite,°   hermit
The moving waters at their priestlike task   5
   Of pure ablution° round earth's human shores,   cleansing
Or gazing on the new soft fallen mask
   Of snow upon the mountains and the moors—
No—yet still steadfast, still unchangeable,
   Pillowed upon my fair love's ripening breast,   10
To feel forever its soft fall and swell,
   Awake forever in a sweet unrest,
Still, still to hear her tender-taken breath,
And so live ever—or else swoon to death.

John Keats (1795–1821)

QUESTIONS

1. The speaker longs to be as "steadfast" (1) as the star, yet lines 2–8 express his wish to be unlike the star in important ways. What are the qualities of the star that he would not want to emulate? Why would these be wrong for him in his situation?
2. Explore the apparent contradictions in the phrase "sweet unrest" (12). How do they anticipate the final line?
3. The speaker repeats "still" (13). What relevant denotations does the word evoke, and how does the repetition add intensity and meaning to this apostrophe?
4. Why is an apostrophe more effective here than a description of the star that does not address it?

In contrast to the preceding figures that compare *unlike* things are two figures that rest on congruences or correspondences. **Synecdoche** (the use of the part for the whole) and **metonymy** (the use of something closely related for the thing actually meant) are alike in that both substitute some significant detail or quality of an experience for the experience itself. Thus Randall uses metonymy when he says "those guns will fire" (page 659), for he means "the police will fire their guns." Kay uses synecdoche when she refers to "catalogues of domes" (page 689), because what she means is "enough domed buildings to fill a catalogue," and Housman's Terence (page 662) uses synecdoche when he declares that "malt does more than Milton can / To justify God's ways to man," for "malt" means beer or ale, of which malt is an essential ingredient. On the other hand, when Terence advises "fellows whom it hurts to think" to "Look into the pewter pot / To see the world as the world's not," he is using metonymy, for by "pewter pot" he means the ale *in* the pot, not the pot itself, and by "world" he means human life and the conditions under which it is lived. Robert Frost uses metonymy in "'Out, Out—'" (page 779) when he describes an injured boy holding up his cut hand "as if to keep / The life from spilling," for literally he means to keep the blood from spilling. In each case, however, the poem gains in compactness, vividness, or meaning. Kay, by substituting one architectural detail for whole buildings, suggests the superficiality and boredom of a person who looks at many but appreciates none. Frost tells us both that the boy's hand is bleeding and that his life is in danger.

Many synecdoches and metonymies, of course, like many metaphors, have become so much a part of the language that they no longer strike us as figurative; this is the case with *redhead* for a red-haired person, *hands* for manual workers, *highbrow* for a sophisticate, *tongues* for languages, and a boiling *kettle* for the water *in* the kettle. Such figures are often called *dead metaphors* (where the word *metaphor* is itself a metonymy for all figurative speech). Synecdoche and metonymy are so much alike that it is hardly worthwhile to distinguish between them, and the latter term is increasingly used for both. In this book *metonymy* will be used for both figures—that is, for any figure in which a part or something closely related is substituted for the thing literally meant.

We said at the beginning of this chapter that figurative language often provides a more effective means of saying what we mean than does direct statement. What are some of the reasons for that effectiveness?

First, figurative language affords us imaginative pleasure. Imagination might be described in one sense as that faculty or ability of the mind that proceeds by sudden leaps from one point to another, that goes up a stair by leaping in one jump from the bottom to the top rather than by climbing up one step at a time.* The mind takes delight in these sudden leaps, in seeing likenesses between unlike things. We have all probably taken pleasure in staring into a fire and seeing castles and cities and armies in it, or in looking into the clouds and shaping them into animals or faces, or in seeing a man in the moon. We name our plants and flowers after fancied resemblances: jack-in-the-pulpit, baby's breath, Queen Anne's lace. Figures of speech are therefore satisfying in themselves, providing us with a source of pleasure in the exercise of the imagination.

---

*It is also the faculty of mind that is able to "picture" or "image" absent objects as if they were present. It was with imagination in this sense that we were concerned in the chapter on imagery.

Second, figures of speech are a way of bringing additional imagery into verse, of making the abstract concrete, of making poetry more sensuous. When Tennyson's eagle falls "like a thunderbolt" (page 649), his swooping down for his prey is charged with energy, speed, and power; the simile also recalls that the Greek god Zeus was accompanied by an eagle and armed with lightning. When Emily Dickinson compares poetry to prancing coursers (page 686), she objectifies imaginative and rhythmical qualities by presenting them in visual terms. When Robert Browning compares the crisping waves to "fiery ringlets" (page 701), he starts with one image and transforms it into three. Figurative language is a way of augmenting the sense appeal of poetry.

Third, figures of speech are a way of adding emotional intensity to otherwise merely informative statements and of conveying attitudes along with information. If we say, "So-and-so is a rat" or "My feet are killing me," our meaning is as much emotional as informative. When Philip Larkin's pathetic escapist metaphorically compares books to "a load of crap" (page 671), the vulgar language not only expresses his distaste for reading, but intensifies the characterization of him as a man whose intellectual growth was stunted. As this example shows, the use of figures may be a poet's means of revealing the characteristics of a speaker—*how* he or she expresses a thought will define the attitudes or qualities as much as *what* that thought is. When Frost's speaker in "Bereft" (page 716) sees a striking snake in an eddy of leaves he shows that he is fearful. When Wilfred Owen compares a soldier caught in a gas attack to a man drowning under a green sea (page 651), he conveys a feeling of despair and suffocation as well as a visual image.

Fourth, figures of speech are an effective means of concentration, a way of saying much in brief compass. Like words, they may be multidimensional. Consider, for instance, the merits of comparing life to a candle, as Shakespeare does in a passage from *Macbeth* (page 780). Life is like a candle in that it begins and ends in darkness; in that while it burns, it gives off light and energy, is active and colorful; in that it gradually consumes itself, gets shorter and shorter; in that it can be snuffed out at any moment; in that it is brief at best, burning only for a short duration. Possibly your imagination can suggest other similarities. But at any rate, Macbeth's compact, metaphorical description of life as a "brief candle" suggests certain truths about life that would require dozens of words to state in literal language. At the same time it makes the abstract concrete, provides imaginative pleasure, and adds a degree of emotional intensity.

It is as important, when analyzing and discussing a poem, to decide what it is that the figures accomplish as it is to identify them. Seeing a personification or a simile should lead to analytical questions: *What use is being made of this figure? How does it contribute to the experience of the poem?*

If we are to read poetry well, we must be able to respond to figurative language. Every use of figurative language involves a risk of misinterpretation, though the risk is well worth taking. For the person who can interpret the figure, the dividends are immense. Fortunately all people have imagination to some degree, and imagination can be cultivated. Through practice, one's ability to interpret figures of speech can be enhanced.

EXERCISE

Decide whether the following quotations are literal or figurative. If figurative, identify the figure, explain what is being compared to what, and explain the appropriateness of the comparison. EXAMPLE: "Talent is a cistern; genius is a fountain." ANSWER: Metaphor. Talent = cistern; genius = fountain. Talent exists in finite supply, and can be used up. Genius is inexhaustible, ever renewing.

1. O tenderly the haughty day
   Fills his blue urn with fire.   *Ralph Waldo Emerson*
2. It is with words as with sunbeams—the more
   they are condensed, the deeper they burn.   *Robert Southey*
3. Joy and Temperance and Repose
   Slam the door on the doctor's nose.   *Anonymous*
4. The pen is mightier than the sword.   *Edward Bulwer-Lytton*
5. The strongest oaths are straw
   To the fire i' the blood.   *William Shakespeare*
6. The Cambridge ladies . . . live in furnished souls.   *e. e. cummings*
7. Dorothy's eyes, with their long brown lashes,
   looked very much like her mother's.   *Laetitia Johnson*
8. The tawny-hided desert crouches watching her.   *Francis Thompson*
9. Let us eat and drink, for tomorrow we shall die.   *Isaiah 22.13*
10. Let us eat and drink, for tomorrow we may die.
                                        Common misquotation of the above

---

REVIEWING CHAPTER FIVE

1. Distinguish between language used literally and language used figuratively, and consider why poetry is often figurative.
2. Define the figures of comparison (simile and metaphor, personification and apostrophe), and rank them in order of their emotional effectiveness.
3. Define the figures of congruence or correspondence (synecdoche and metonymy).
4. Review the four major contributions of figurative language.

Mind

Mind in its purest play is like some bat
That beats about in caverns all alone,
Contriving by a kind of senseless wit
Not to conclude against a wall of stone.

It has no need to falter or explore;   5
Darkly it knows what obstacles are there,
And so may weave and flitter, dip and soar
In perfect courses through the blackest air.

And has this simile a like perfection?
The mind is like a bat. Precisely. Save   10
That in the very happiest intellection
A graceful error may correct the cave.

Richard Wilbur (b. 1921)

QUESTIONS

1. A poet may use a variety of metaphors and similes in developing a subject or may, as Wilbur does here, develop a single figure at length (this poem is an example of an **extended simile**). Identify in this chapter a poem containing a variety of figures and define the advantages of each type of development.
2. Explore the similarities between the two things compared in this poem. In line 12, what is meant by "A graceful error" and by "correct the cave"?

I taste a liquor never brewed

I taste a liquor never brewed—
From Tankards scooped in Pearl—
Not all the Vats upon the Rhine
Yield such an Alcohol!

Inebriate of Air—am I—   5
And Debauchee of Dew—
Reeling—thro endless summer days—
From inns of Molten Blue—

When "Landlords" turn the drunken Bee
Out of the Foxglove's door—   10

When Butterflies—renounce their "drams"—
I shall but drink the more!

Till Seraphs swing their snowy Hats—
And Saints—to windows run—
To see the little Tippler   15
Leaning against the—Sun—

Emily Dickinson (1830–1886)

QUESTIONS

1. Vocabulary: *debauchee* (6), *foxglove* (10).
2. In this **extended metaphor,** what is being compared to alcoholic intoxication? The clues are given in the variety of "liquors" named or implied—
   "Air" (5), "Dew" (6), and the nectar upon which birds and butterflies feed.
3. What figurative meanings have the following details: "Tankards scooped in
   Pearl" (2), "inns of Molten Blue" (8), "snowy Hats" (13)?
4. The last stanza creates a stereotypical street scene in which neighbors observe the behavior of a drunkard. What do comic drunks lean against in the
   street? What unexpected attitude do the seraphs and saints display?

Metaphors

I'm a riddle in nine syllables,
An elephant, a ponderous house,
A melon strolling on two tendrils.
O red fruit, ivory, fine timbers!
This loaf's big with its yeasty rising.   5
Money's new-minted in this fat purse.
I'm a means, a stage, a cow in calf.
I've eaten a bag of green apples,
Boarded the train there's no getting off.

Sylvia Plath (1932–1963)

QUESTIONS

1. Like its first metaphor, this poem is a riddle to be solved by identifying the literal terms of its metaphors. After you have identified the speaker ("riddle,"
   "elephant," "house," "melon," "stage," "cow"), identify the literal meanings of
   the related metaphors ("syllables," "tendrils," "fruit," "ivory," "timbers," "loaf,"
   "yeasty rising," "money," "purse," "train"). How do you interpret line 8?
2. How does the form of the poem relate to its content? Is this poem a complaint?

Toads

Why should I let the toad *work*
    Squat on my life?
Can't I use my wit as a pitchfork
    And drive the brute off?

Six days of the week it soils   5
    With its sickening poison—
Just for paying a few bills!
    That's out of proportion.

Lots of folk live on their wits:
    Lecturers, lispers,   10
Losels,° loblolly-men,° louts—   scoundrels; bumpkins
    They don't end as paupers;

Lots of folk live up lanes
    With fires in a bucket,
Eat windfalls and tinned sardines—   15
    They seem to like it.

Their nippers° have got bare feet,   children
    Their unspeakable wives
Are skinny as whippets—and yet
    No one actually *starves*.   20

Ah, were I courageous enough
    To shout *Stuff your pension!*
But I know, all too well, that's the stuff
    That dreams are made on;

For something sufficiently toad-like   25
    Squats in me, too;
Its hunkers° are heavy as hard luck,   haunches
    And cold as snow,

And will never allow me to blarney
    My way to getting   30
The fame and the girl and the money
    All at one sitting.

I don't say, one bodies the other
   One's spiritual truth;
But I do say it's hard to lose either,   35
   When you have both.

                     Philip Larkin (1922–1985)

QUESTIONS

1. The poem describes two "toads." Where is each located? How are they described? What are the antecedents of the pronouns "one" and "the other / One's" (33–34) respectively?
2. What characteristics in common have the people mentioned in lines 9–12? Those mentioned in lines 13–20?
3. Explain the pun in lines 22–23 and the literary allusion it leads into. (If you don't recognize the allusion, check Shakespeare's *The Tempest*, Act 4, scene 1, lines 156–58.)
4. The first "toad" is explicitly identified as *"work"* (1). The literal term for the second "toad" is not named. Why not? What do you take it to be?
5. What kind of person is the speaker? What are his attitudes toward work?

Ghost of a Chance

You see a man
trying to think.

You want to say
to everything:
Keep off! Give him room!   5
But you only watch,
terrified
the old consolations
will get him at last
like a fish   10
half-dead from flopping
and almost crawling
across the shingle,°   gravel beach
almost breathing
the raw, agonizing   15
air
till a wave
pulls it back blind into the triumphant
sea.

                     Adrienne Rich (b. 1929)

A Valediction: Forbidding Mourning

As virtuous men pass mildly away,
  And whisper to their souls to go,
While some of their sad friends do say,
  The breath goes now, and some say, no:

So let us melt, and make no noise,   5
  No tear-floods, nor sigh-tempests move;
'Twere profanation of our joys
  To tell the laity our love.

Moving of th' earth brings harms and fears,
  Men reckon what it did and meant,   10
But trepidation of the spheres,
  Though greater far, is innocent.

Dull sublunary lovers' love
  (Whose soul is sense) cannot admit
Absence, because it doth remove   15
  Those things which elemented it.

But we by a love so much refined,
  That ourselves know not what it is,
Inter-assurèd of the mind,
  Care less, eyes, lips, and hands to miss.   20

Our two souls therefore, which are one,
  Though I must go, endure not yet
A breach, but an expansion,
  Like gold to airy thinness beat.

If they be two, they are two so   25
  As stiff twin compasses are two;
Thy soul, the fixed foot, makes no show
  To move, but doth, if th' other do.

And though it in the center sit,
  Yet when the other far doth roam,   30
It leans, and hearkens after it,
  And grows erect, as that comes home.

Such wilt thou be to me, who must
  Like th' other foot, obliquely run;

Thy firmness makes my circle just,   35
And makes me end, where I begun.

John Donne (1572–1631)

QUESTIONS

1. Vocabulary: *valediction* (title), *mourning* (title), *profanation* (7), *laity* (8), *trepidation* (11), *innocent* (12), *sublunary* (13), *elemented* (16). Line 11 is a reference to the spheres of the Ptolemaic cosmology, whose movements caused no such disturbance as does a movement of the earth—that is, an earthquake.
2. Is the speaker in the poem about to die? Or about to leave on a journey? (The answer may be found in a careful analysis of the simile in the last three stanzas and by noticing that the idea of dying in stanza 1 is introduced in a simile.)
3. The poem is organized around a contrast of two kinds of lovers: the "laity" (8) and, as their implied opposite, the priesthood. Are these terms literal or metaphorical? What is the essential difference between their two kinds of love? How, according to the speaker, does their behavior differ when they must separate from each other? What is the motivation of the speaker in this "valediction"?
4. Find and explain three similes and one metaphor used to describe the parting of true lovers. The figure in the last three stanzas is one of the most famous in English literature. Demonstrate its appropriateness by obtaining a drawing compass or by using two pencils to imitate the two legs.

To His Coy Mistress

Had we but world enough, and time,
This coyness, lady, were no crime.
We would sit down, and think which way
To walk, and pass our long love's day.
Thou by the Indian Ganges' side   5
Shouldst rubies find; I by the tide
Of Humber would complain. I would
Love you ten years before the Flood,
And you should, if you please, refuse
Till the conversion of the Jews.   10
My vegetable love should grow
Vaster than empires, and more slow;
An hundred years should go to praise
Thine eyes, and on thy forehead gaze;
Two hundred to adore each breast,   15
But thirty thousand to the rest;
An age at least to every part,

And the last age should show your heart.
For, lady, you deserve this state,
Nor would I love at lower rate.   20
    But at my back I always hear
Time's wingèd chariot hurrying near;
And yonder all before us lie
Deserts of vast eternity.
Thy beauty shall no more be found,   25
Nor, in thy marble vault, shall sound
My echoing song; then worms shall try
That long-preserved virginity,
And your quaint honor turn to dust,
And into ashes all my lust: 30
The grave's a fine and private place,
But none, I think, do there embrace.
    Now therefore, while the youthful hue
Sits on thy skin like morning dew,
And while thy willing soul transpires   35
At every pore with instant fires,
Now let us sport us while we may,
And now, like amorous birds of prey,
Rather at once our time devour
Than languish in his slow-chapped power.   40
Let us roll all our strength and all
Our sweetness up into one ball,
And tear our pleasures with rough strife
Thorough° the iron gates of life.   through
Thus, though we cannot make our sun   45
Stand still, yet we will make him run.

Andrew Marvell (1621–1678)

QUESTIONS

1. Vocabulary: *coy* (title), *Humber* (7), *transpires* (35). "Mistress" (title) has the now archaic meaning of *sweetheart*; "slow-chapped" (40) derives from *chap*, meaning *jaw*.
2. What is the speaker urging his sweetheart to do? Why is she being "coy"?
3. Outline the speaker's argument in three sentences that begin with the words *If*, *But*, and *Therefore*. Is the argument valid?
4. Explain the appropriateness of "vegetable love" (11). What simile in the third section contrasts with it and how? What image in the third section contrasts with the distance between the Ganges and the Humber? Of what would the speaker be "complaining" by the Humber (7)?

5. Explain the figures in lines 22, 24, and 40 and their implications.
6. Explain the last two lines. For what is "sun" a metonymy?
7. Is this poem principally about love or about time? If the latter, what might making love represent? What philosophy is the poet advancing here?

Dream Deferred

What happens to a dream deferred?

Does it dry up
like a raisin in the sun?
Or fester like a sore—
And then run?   5
Does it stink like rotten meat?
Or crust and sugar over—
like a syrupy sweet?

Maybe it just sags
like a heavy load.   10

Or does it explode?

Langston Hughes (1902–1967)

QUESTIONS
1. Of the six images, five are similes. Which is a metaphor? Comment on its position and its effectiveness.
2. Since the dream could be any dream, the poem is general in its implication. What happens to your understanding of it on learning that its author was a black American?

Introduction to Poetry

I ask them to take a poem
and hold it up to the light
like a color slide

or press an ear against its hive.

I say drop a mouse into a poem   5
and watch him probe his way out,

or walk inside the poem's room
and feel the walls for a light switch.

I want them to water-ski
across the surface of a poem   10
waving at the author's name on the shore.

But all they want to do
is tie the poem to a chair with rope
and torture a confession out of it.

They begin beating it with a hose   15
to find out what it really means.

Billy Collins (b. 1941)

QUESTIONS

1. What is the basic situation of the poem? Who are "I" (1) and "them" (1)?
2. Explain the simile in line 3. From that point onward through line 11, the speaker invents a series of metaphors. For each of them, define what a poem is being compared to and how the metaphor expresses some characteristic quality of poetry. For example, how is a poem like a "hive" (4) full of buzzing bees?
3. The last five lines present a single extended metaphor to express what "they want to do" when they encounter a poem. What are "they" and "the poem" compared to, and how do these comparisons reflect a different attitude toward poetry from the ones expressed in the first 11 lines? What, ultimately, does this poem express about poetry and its readers?

SUGGESTIONS FOR WRITING

1. Robert Frost has said that "poetry is what evaporates from all translations." Why might this be true? How much of a word can be translated?
2. Ezra Pound has defined great literature as "simply language charged with meaning to the utmost possible degree." Would this be a good definition of poetry? The word "charged" is roughly equivalent to *filled*. Why is "charged" a better word in Pound's definition?
3. In each of the following the title announces a metaphor that dominates the poem. Write an essay describing the pair of objects and/or concepts compared in one of these poems. How does the figurative language help to communicate an idea with greater vividness or force than an ordinary, prosaic description could have achieved?
   a. Frost, "A Considerable Speck" (page 770).
   b. Atwood, "Landcrab" (page 876).
   c. Wilbur, "A Fire-Truck" (page 880).
   d. Herbert, "The Pulley" (page 884).
   e. Stevens, "The Snow Man" (page 1008).
   f. Updike, "Telephone Poles" (page 1013).

Chapter Six

Figurative Language 2

Symbol, Allegory

The Road Not Taken

Two roads diverged in a yellow wood,
And sorry I could not travel both
And be one traveler, long I stood
And looked down one as far as I could
To where it bent in the undergrowth;   5

Then took the other, as just as fair,
And having perhaps the better claim,
Because it was grassy and wanted wear;
Though as for that the passing there
Had worn them really about the same,   10

And both that morning equally lay
In leaves no step had trodden black.
Oh, I kept the first for another day!
Yet knowing how way leads on to way,
I doubted if I should ever come back.   15

I shall be telling this with a sigh
Somewhere ages and ages hence:
Two roads diverged in a wood, and I—
I took the one less traveled by,
And that has made all the difference.   20

Robert Frost (1874–1963)

QUESTIONS

1. Does the speaker feel that he has made the wrong choice in taking the road "less traveled by" (19)? If not, why will he "sigh" (16)? What does he regret?

2. Why will the choice between two roads that seem very much alike make such a big difference many years later?

A **symbol** may be roughly defined as something that means *more* than what it is. "The Road Not Taken," for instance, concerns a choice made between two roads by a person out walking in the woods. He would like to explore both roads. He tells himself that he will explore one and then come back and explore the other, but he knows that he will probably be unable to do so. By the last stanza, however, we realize that the poem is about something more than the choice of paths in a wood, for that choice would be relatively unimportant, whereas this choice, the speaker believes, is one that will make a great difference in his life and is one that he will remember "with a sigh . . . ages and ages hence." We must interpret his choice of a road as a symbol for any choice in life between alternatives that appear almost equally attractive but will result through the years in a large difference in the kind of experience one knows.

Image, metaphor, and symbol shade into each other and are sometimes difficult to distinguish. In general, however, an image means only what it is; the figurative term in a metaphor means something other than what it is; and a symbol means what it is and something more, too. A symbol, that is, functions literally and figuratively at the same time.* If I say that a shaggy brown dog was rubbing its back against a white picket fence, I am talking about nothing but a dog (and a picket fence) and am therefore presenting an image. If I say, "Some dirty dog stole my wallet at the party," I am not talking about a dog at all and am therefore using a metaphor. But if I say, "You can't teach an old dog new tricks," I am talking not only about dogs but about living creatures of any species and am therefore speaking symbolically. Images, of course, do not cease to be images when they become incorporated in metaphors or symbols. If we are discussing the sensuous qualities of "The Road Not Taken," we should refer to the two leaf-strewn roads in the yellow wood as an image; if we are discussing the significance of the poem, we talk about the roads as symbols.

The symbol is the richest and at the same time the most difficult of the poetic figures. Both its richness and its difficulty result from its imprecision. Although the poet may pin down the meaning of a symbol to something fairly definite and precise, more often the symbol is so general

---

*This account does not hold for nonliterary symbols such as the letters of the alphabet and algebraic signs (the symbol ∞ for infinity or = for equals). With these, the symbol is meaningless except as it stands for something else, and the connection between the sign and what it stands for is purely arbitrary.

in its meaning that it can suggest a great variety of specific meanings. It is like an opal that flashes out different colors when slowly turned in the light. "The Road Not Taken," for instance, concerns some choice in life, but what choice? Was it a choice of profession? A choice of residence? A choice of mate? It might be any, all, or none of these. We cannot determine what particular choice the poet had in mind, if any, and it is not important that we do so. It is enough if we see in the poem an expression of regret that the possibilities of life experience are so sharply limited. The speaker in the poem would have liked to explore both roads, but he could explore only one. The person with a craving for life, whether satisfied or dissatisfied with the choices he has made, will always long for the realms of experience that he had to forgo. Because the symbol is a rich one, the poem suggests other meanings too. It affirms a belief in the possibility of choice and says something about the nature of choice—how each choice narrows the range of possible future choices, so that we make our lives as we go, both freely choosing and being determined by past choices. Though not a philosophical poem, it obliquely comments on the issue of free will and determinism and indicates the poet's own position. It can do all these things, concretely and compactly, by its use of an effective symbol.

Symbols vary in the degree of identification and definition given them by their authors. In this poem Frost forces us to interpret the choice of roads symbolically by the degree of importance he gives it in the last stanza. Sometimes poets are much more specific in identifying their symbols. Sometimes they do not identify them at all. Consider, for instance, the next two poems.

A Noiseless Patient Spider

A noiseless patient spider,
I marked where on a little promontory it stood isolated,
Marked how to explore the vacant vast surrounding,
It launched forth filament, filament, filament, out of itself,
Ever unreeling them, ever tirelessly speeding them.   5

And you, O my soul where you stand,
Surrounded, detached, in measureless oceans of space,
Ceaselessly musing, venturing, throwing, seeking the spheres to
    connect them,
Till the bridge you will need be formed, till the ductile anchor hold,
Till the gossamer thread you fling catch somewhere, O my soul.   10

Walt Whitman (1819–1892)

In the first stanza the speaker describes a spider's apparently tireless effort to attach its thread to some substantial support so that it can begin constructing a web. The speaker reveals his attentive interest by the hinted personification of the spider, and his sympathy with it is expressed in the overstatement of size and distance—he is trying to perceive the world as a spider sees it from a "promontory" surrounded by vast space. He even attributes a human motive to the spider: exploration, rather than instinctive web-building. Nevertheless, the first stanza is essentially literal—the close observation of an actual spider at its task. In the second stanza the speaker explicitly interprets the symbolic meaning of what he has observed: his soul (personified by apostrophe and by the capabilities assigned to it) is like the spider in its constant striving. But the soul's purpose is to find spiritual or intellectual certainties in the vast universe it inhabits. The symbolic meaning is richer than a mere comparison; while a spider's actual purpose is limited to its instinctive drives, the human soul strives for much more, in a much more complex "surrounding." And, of course, the result of the soul's symbolized striving is much more open-ended than is the attempt of a spider to spin a web, as the paradoxical language ("Surrounded, detached," "ductile anchor") implies. *Can* the human soul connect the celestial spheres?

QUESTIONS

1. In "The Hound" (page 715) Robert Francis compares unpredictable human life to a hound. Whitman compares the striving human soul to a spider. Why is Francis's comparison a metaphor and Whitman's a symbol? What additional comparison does Whitman make to the soul's quest? What figure of speech is it?
2. In what ways are the spider and the soul contrasted? What do the contrasts contribute to the meaning of the symbol?
3. Can the questing soul represent human actions other than the search for spiritual certainties?

The Sick Rose

O Rose, thou art sick!
The invisible worm
That flies in the night,
In the howling storm,

Has found out thy bed   5
Of crimson joy,

And his dark secret love
Does thy life destroy.

William Blake (1757–1827)

QUESTIONS

1. What figures of speech do you find in the poem in addition to symbol? How do they contribute to its force or meaning?
2. Several symbolic interpretations of this poem are given below. Can you think of others?
3. Should symbolic meanings be sought for the night and the storm? If so, what meanings would you suggest?

In "A Noiseless Patient Spider" the symbolic meaning of the spider is identified and named. By contrast, in "The Sick Rose" no meanings are explicitly indicated for the rose and the worm. Indeed, we are not *compelled* to assign them specific meanings. The poem might literally be read as being about a rose that has been attacked on a stormy night by a cankerworm.

The organization of "The Sick Rose" is so rich, however, and its language so powerful that the rose and the worm refuse to remain *merely* a flower and an insect. The rose, apostrophized and personified in the first line, has traditionally been a symbol of feminine beauty and love, as well as of sensual pleasures. "Bed" can refer to a woman's bed as well as to a flower bed. "Crimson joy" suggests the intense pleasure of passionate lovemaking as well as the brilliant beauty of a red flower. The "dark secret love" of the "invisible worm" is more strongly suggestive of a concealed or illicit love affair than of the feeding of a cankerworm on a plant, though it fits that too. For all these reasons the rose almost immediately suggests a woman and the worm her secret lover— and the poem suggests the corruption of innocent but physical love by concealment and deceit. But the possibilities do not stop there. The worm is a common symbol or metonymy for death; and for readers steeped in Milton (as Blake was) it recalls the "undying worm" of *Paradise Lost*, Milton's metaphor for the snake (or Satan in the form of a snake) that tempted Eve. Meanings multiply also for the reader who is familiar with Blake's other writings. Thus "The Sick Rose" has been variously interpreted as referring to the destruction of joyous physical love by jealousy, deceit, concealment, or the possessive instinct; of innocence by experience; of humanity by Satan; of imagination and joy by analytic reason; of life by death. We cannot say what specifically the poet had in mind, nor need we do so. A symbol defines an *area* of meaning, and any interpretation that falls within that area is permissible. In

Blake's poem the rose stands for something beautiful, or desirable, or good. The worm stands for some corrupting agent. Within these limits, the meaning is largely "open." And because the meaning is open, the reader is justified in bringing personal experience to its interpretation. Blake's poem, for instance, might remind someone of a gifted friend whose promise has been destroyed by drug addiction.

Between the extremes exemplified by "A Noiseless Patient Spider" and "The Sick Rose" a poem may exercise all degrees of control over the range and meaning of its symbolism. Consider another example.

Digging

Between my finger and my thumb
The squat pen rests; snug as a gun.

Under my window, a clean rasping sound
When the spade sinks into gravelly ground:
My father, digging. I look down   5

Till his straining rump among the flowerbeds
Bends low, comes up twenty years away
Stooping in rhythm through potato drills
Where he was digging.

The coarse boot nestled on the lug, the shaft   10
Against the inside knee was levered firmly.
He rooted out tall tops, buried the bright edge deep
To scatter new potatoes that we picked
Loving their cool hardness in our hands.

By God, the old man could handle a spade.   15
Just like his old man.

My grandfather cut more turf in a day
Than any other man on Toner's bog.
Once I carried him milk in a bottle
Corked sloppily with paper. He straightened up   20
To drink it, then fell to right away

Nicking and slicing neatly, heaving sods
Over his shoulder, going down and down
For the good turf. Digging.

The cold smell of potato mould, the squelch and slap   25
Of soggy peat, the curt cuts of an edge
Through living roots awaken in my head.
But I've no spade to follow men like them.

Between my finger and my thumb
The squat pen rests.   30
I'll dig with it.

                                        Seamus Heaney (b. 1939)

QUESTIONS

1. Vocabulary: *drills* (8), *fell to* (21). In Ireland, "turf" (17) is a block of peat dug from a bog; when dried, it is used as fuel.
2. What emotional responses are evoked by the imagery?

On the literal level, this poem presents a writer who interrupts himself to have a look at his father digging in a flower garden below his window. He is reminded of his father twenty years earlier digging potatoes for harvesting, and by that memory he is drawn farther back to his grandfather digging peat from a bog for fuel. The memories are vivid and appealing and rich in imagery, but the writer is not like his forebears; he has "no spade to follow" their examples. And so, with a trace of regret, he decides that his writing will have to be his substitute for their manual tasks.

But the title and the emphasis on varieties of the same task carried out in several different ways over a span of generations alert the reader to the need to discover the further significance of this literal statement. The last line is metaphorical, comparing digging to writing (and thus is itself not symbolic, for on a literal level one cannot dig with a pen). The metaphor, however, suggesting that the writer will commit himself to exploring the kinds of memories in this poem, invites an interpretation of the literal forms of digging. We notice then that the father has been involved in two sorts—the practical, backbreaking task of digging up potatoes to be gathered by the children, and twenty years later the relatively easy chore of digging in flowerbeds so as to encourage the growth of ornamental plants. There is a progression represented in the father's activities, from the necessary and arduous earlier life to the leisurely growing of flowers. Farther back in time, the grandfather's labors were deeper, heavier, and more essential, cutting and digging the material that would be used for heating and cooking—cooking potatoes, we should assume. The grandfather digs deeper and deeper, always in quest of the best peat, "the good turf."

Symbolically, then, digging has meanings that relate to basic needs—for warmth, for sustenance, for beauty, and for the personal satisfaction of doing a job well. In the concluding metaphor, another basic need is implied, the need to remember and confront one's origins, to find oneself in a continuum of meaningful activities, to assert the relevance and importance of one's vocation. And it is not coincidental that an Irish poet should find symbolic meanings in a confluence of Irish materials—from peat bogs to potatoes to poets and writers, that long-beleaguered island has asserted its special and distinct identity. Nor is it coincidental that Heaney selected this to be the opening poem in his first book of poetry: "Digging" is what his poetry does.

Meanings ray out from a symbol, like the corona around the sun or like connotations around a richly suggestive word. But the very fact that a symbol may be so rich in meanings requires that we use the greatest tact in its interpretation. Although Blake's "The Sick Rose" might, because of personal association, remind us of a friend destroyed by drug addiction, it would be unwise to say that Blake uses the rose to symbolize a gifted person succumbing to drug addiction, for this interpretation is private, idiosyncratic, and narrow. The poem allows it, but does not itself suggest it.

Moreover, we should never assume that because the meaning of a symbol is more or less open, we may make it mean anything we choose. We would be wrong, for instance, in interpreting the choice in "The Road Not Taken" as some choice between good and evil, for the poem tells us that the two roads are much alike and that both lie "In leaves no step had trodden black." Whatever the choice is, it is a choice between two goods. Whatever our interpretation of a symbolic poem, it must be tied firmly to the facts of the poem. We must not let loose of the string and let our imaginations go ballooning up among the clouds. Because the symbol is capable of adding so many dimensions to a poem, it is a peculiarly effective resource for the poet, but it is also peculiarly susceptible to misinterpretation by the incautious reader.

Accurate interpretation of the symbol requires delicacy, tact, and good sense. The reader must maintain balance while walking a tightrope between too little and too much—between underinterpretation and overinterpretation. If the reader falls off, however, it is much more desirable to fall off on the side of too little. Someone who reads "The Road Not Taken" as being only about a choice between two roads in a wood has at least understood part of the experience that the poem communicates, but the reader who reads into it anything imaginable might as well discard the poem and simply daydream.

Above all, we should avoid the tendency to indulge in symbol-hunting and to see virtually anything in a poem as symbolic. It is preferable to miss a symbol than to try to find one in every line of a poem.

To the Virgins, to Make Much of Time

Gather ye rosebuds while ye may,
    Old Time is still a-flying;
And this same flower that smiles today
    Tomorrow will be dying.

The glorious lamp of heaven, the Sun,   5
    The higher he's a-getting,
The sooner will his race be run,
    And nearer he's to setting.

That age is best which is the first,
    When youth and blood are warmer;   10
But being spent, the worse, and worst
    Times still succeed the former.

Then be not coy, but use your time;
    And while ye may, go marry;
For having lost but once your prime,   15
    You may forever tarry.

Robert Herrick (1591–1674)

QUESTIONS

1. The first two stanzas might be interpreted literally if the third and fourth stanzas did not force us to interpret them symbolically. What do the "rosebuds" symbolize (stanza 1)? What does the course of a day symbolize (stanza 2)? Does the poet narrow the meaning of the rosebud symbol in the last stanza or merely name *one* of its specific meanings?

2. How does the title help us interpret the meaning of the symbol? Why is "virgins" a more meaningful word than, for example, *maidens*?

3. Why is such haste necessary in gathering the rosebuds? True, the blossoms die quickly, but others will replace them. Who *really* is dying?

4. What are "the worse, and worst" times (11)? Why?

5. Why is the wording of the poem better than these possible alternatives: *blooms* for "smiles" (3); *course* for "race" (7); *used* for "spent" (11); *spend* for "use" (13)?

Allegory is a narrative or description that has a second meaning beneath the surface. Although the surface story or description may have its own interest, the author's major interest is in the ulterior meaning. When Pharoah in the Bible, for instance, has a dream in which seven fat kine are devoured by seven lean kine, the story does not really become significant until Joseph interprets its allegorical meaning: that Egypt is to enjoy seven years of fruitfulness and prosperity followed by seven years of famine. Allegory has been defined sometimes as an extended metaphor and sometimes as a series of related symbols. But it is usually distinguishable from both of these. It is unlike extended metaphor in that it involves a *system* of related comparisons rather than one comparison drawn out. It differs from symbolism in that it puts less emphasis on the images for their own sake and more on their ulterior meanings. Also, these meanings are more fixed. In allegory there is usually a one-to-one correspondence between the details and a single set of ulterior meanings. In complex allegories the details may have more than one meaning, but these meanings tend to be definite. Meanings do not ray out from allegory as they do from a symbol.

Allegory is less popular in modern literature than it was in medieval and Renaissance writing, and it is much less often found in short poems than in long narrative works such as *The Faerie Queene*, *Everyman*, and *Pilgrim's Progress*. It has sometimes, especially with political allegory, been used to disguise meaning rather than reveal it (or, rather, to disguise it from some people while revealing it to others). Though less rich than the symbol, allegory is an effective way of making the abstract concrete and has occasionally been used effectively even in fairly short poems.

Peace

Sweet Peace, where dost thou dwell? I humbly crave,
Let me once know.
I sought thee in a secret cave,
And asked if Peace were there.
A hollow wind did seem to answer, "No,   5
Go seek elsewhere."

I did, and going did a rainbow note.
"Surely," thought I,
"This is the lace of Peace's coat;
I will search out the matter."   10

But while I looked, the clouds immediately
    Did break and scatter.

Then went I to a garden, and did spy
    A gallant flower,
The Crown Imperial. "Sure," said I,   15
    "Peace at the root must dwell."
But when I digged, I saw a worm devour
    What showed so well.

At length I met a reverend good old man,
    Whom when for Peace   20
    I did demand, he thus began:
        "There was a prince of old
At Salem dwelt, who lived with good increase
    Of flock and fold.

"He sweetly lived; yet sweetness did not save   25
    His life from foes.
    But after death out of his grave
        There sprang twelve stalks of wheat;
Which many wondering at, got some of those
    To plant and set.   30

"It prospered strangely, and did soon disperse
    Through all the earth,
    For they that taste it do rehearse°   declare
        That virtue lies therein,
A secret virtue, bringing peace and mirth   35
    By flight of sin.

"Take of this grain, which in my garden grows,
    And grows for you;
    Make bread of it; and that repose
        And peace, which everywhere   40
With so much earnestness you do pursue,
    Is only there."

George Herbert (1593–1633)

QUESTIONS

1. Vocabulary: *gallant* (14), *virtue* (34). "Crown Imperial" (15) is a garden flower, fritillary; "Salem" (23) is Jerusalem.

2. Identify the "prince" (22), his "flock and fold" (24), the "twelve stalks of wheat" (28), the "grain" (37), and the "bread" (39).
3. Should the "secret cave" (stanza 1), the "rainbow" (stanza 2), and the flower "garden" (stanza 3) be understood merely as places where the speaker searched or do they have more precise meanings?
4. Who is the "reverend good old man" (19), and what is *his* garden (37)?

EXERCISES

1. Determine whether "sleep" in the following poems is literal, a symbol, or a metaphor (or simile).
   a. "Stopping by Woods on a Snowy Evening" (page 793)
   b. "The Chimney Sweeper" (page 763)
   c. "Is my team plowing" (page 674)
   d. "The Second Coming" (page 1022)
   e. "Women Who Love Angels" (page 950)
2. Shapiro's "The Fly" (page 1001) and Dickinson's "I heard a Fly buzz—when I died" (page 871) deal with a common subject. Which of them is symbolic? Explain your choice.
3. What does Blake's tiger symbolize (page 947)?
4. Determine whether the following poems are predominantly symbolic or literal.
   a. "Because I could not stop for Death" (page 752)
   b. "The Snow Man" (page 1008)
   c. "The Darkling Thrush" (page 969)
   d. "Song: Go and catch a falling star" (page 958)
   e. "Blackberry Eating" (page 879)
   f. "Musée des Beaux Arts" (page 944)
   g. "Richard Cory" (page 996)
   h. "The Wild Swans at Coole" (page 1023)
   i. "Poem: As the cat" (page 1016)
   j. "Desert Places" (page 696)
   k. "Never Again Would Birds' Song Be the Same" (page 965)
   l. "Constantly risking absurdity" (page 860)

REVIEWING CHAPTER SIX

1. Using examples from the poems that follow, explore how symbols must read both literally and figuratively.
2. Show that the context of a poem determines the limits of its symbolic meanings (as an exercise, you might want to examine the multiple possible meanings of a particular symbol, and eliminate those that are ruled out by the context).
3. Discuss the difference between symbol and allegory, if possible accounting for the fact that allegory is no longer as popular a figure as it once was.

Fire and Ice

Some say the world will end in fire,
Some say in ice.
From what I've tasted of desire
I hold with those who favor fire.
But if it had to perish twice,   5
I think I know enough of hate
To say that for destruction ice
Is also great
And would suffice.

Robert Frost (1874–1963)

QUESTIONS

1. Who are "Some" (1–2)? To which two theories do lines 1–2 refer? (In answering, it might help you to know that the poem was published in 1920.)
2. What do "fire" and "ice" respectively symbolize? What two meanings has "the world"?
3. The poem ends with an *understatement* (see Chapter 7). How does it affect the tone of the poem?

Ulysses

It little profits that an idle king,
By this still hearth, among these barren crags,
Matched with an agèd wife, I mete and dole
Unequal laws unto a savage race,
That hoard, and sleep, and feed, and know not me.   5
I cannot rest from travel; I will drink
Life to the lees. All times I have enjoyed
Greatly, have suffered greatly, both with those
That loved me, and alone; on shore, and when
Through scudding drifts the rainy Hyades   10
Vext the dim sea. I am become a name;
For always roaming with a hungry heart
Much have I seen and known,—cities of men,
And manners, climates, councils, governments,
Myself not least, but honored of them all;   15
And drunk delight of battle with my peers,
Far on the ringing plains of windy Troy.

I am a part of all that I have met;
Yet all experience is an arch wherethrough
Gleams that untraveled world, whose margin fades   20
For ever and for ever when I move.
How dull it is to pause, to make an end,
To rust unburnished, not to shine in use!
As though to breathe were life! Life piled on life
Were all too little, and of one to me   25
Little remains; but every hour is saved
From that eternal silence, something more,
A bringer of new things; and vile it were
For some three suns to store and hoard myself,
And this gray spirit yearning in desire   30
To follow knowledge like a sinking star,
Beyond the utmost bound of human thought.

This is my son, mine own Telemachus,
To whom I leave the scepter and the isle—
Well-loved of me, discerning to fulfil   35
This labor, by slow prudence to make mild
A rugged people, and through soft degrees
Subdue them to the useful and the good.
Most blameless is he, centered in the sphere
Of common duties, decent not to fail   40
In offices of tenderness, and pay
Meet adoration to my household gods,
When I am gone. He works his work, I mine.

There lies the port; the vessel puffs her sail:
There gloom the dark, broad seas. My mariners,   45
Souls that have toiled, and wrought, and thought with me—
That ever with a frolic welcome took
The thunder and the sunshine, and opposed
Free hearts, free foreheads—you and I are old;
Old age hath yet his honor and his toil.   50
Death closes all; but something ere the end,
Some work of noble note, may yet be done,
Not unbecoming men that strove with Gods.
The lights begin to twinkle from the rocks;
The long day wanes; the slow moon climbs; the deep   55
Moans round with many voices. Come, my friends,
'Tis not too late to seek a newer world.

Push off, and sitting well in order smite
The sounding furrows; for my purpose holds
To sail beyond the sunset, and the baths   60
Of all the western stars, until I die.
It may be that the gulfs will wash us down;
It may be we shall touch the Happy Isles,
And see the great Achilles, whom we knew.
Though much is taken, much abides; and though   65
We are not now that strength which in old days
Moved earth and heaven, that which we are, we are:
One equal temper of heroic hearts,
Made weak by time and fate, but strong in will
To strive, to seek, to find, and not to yield.   70

Alfred, Lord Tennyson (1809–1892)

QUESTIONS

1. Vocabulary: *lees* (7), *Hyades* (10), *meet* (42).
2. Ulysses, king of Ithaca, is a legendary Greek hero, a major figure in Homer's *Iliad*, the hero of Homer's *Odyssey*, and a minor figure in Dante's *Divine Comedy*. After ten years at the siege of Troy, Ulysses set sail for home but, having incurred the wrath of the god of the sea, he was subjected to storms and vicissitudes and was forced to wander for another ten years, having many adventures and seeing most of the Mediterranean world before again reaching Ithaca, his wife, and his son. Once back home, according to Dante, he still wished to travel and "to follow virtue and knowledge." In Tennyson's poem, Ulysses is represented as about to set sail on a final voyage from which he will not return. Locate Ithaca on a map. Where exactly, in geographical terms, does Ulysses intend to sail (59–64)? (The Happy Isles were the Elysian fields, or Greek paradise; Achilles was another Greek prince, the hero of the *Iliad*, who was killed at the siege of Troy.)
3. Ulysses's speech is divided into three sections, beginning at lines 1, 33, and 44. What is the topic or purpose of each section? To whom, specifically, is the third section addressed? To whom, would you infer, are sections 1 and 2 addressed? Where do you visualize Ulysses as standing during his speech?
4. Characterize Ulysses. What kind of person is he as Tennyson represents him?
5. What way of life is symbolized by Ulysses? Find as many evidences as you can that Ulysses's desire for travel represents something more than mere wanderlust and wish for adventure.
6. Give two symbolic implications of the westward direction of Ulysses's journey.
7. Interpret lines 18–21 and 26–29. What metaphor is implied in line 23? What is symbolized by "The thunder and the sunshine" (48)? What do the two metonymies in line 49 stand for?

Curiosity

may have killed the cat; more likely
the cat was just unlucky, or else curious
to see what death was like, having no cause
to go on licking paws, or fathering
litter on litter of kittens, predictably.   5

Nevertheless, to be curious
is dangerous enough. To distrust
what is always said, what seems,
to ask odd questions, interfere in dreams,
leave home, smell rats, have hunches   10
do not endear cats to those doggy circles
where well-smelt baskets, suitable wives, good lunches
are the order of things, and where prevails
much wagging of incurious heads and tails.

Face it. Curiosity   15
will not cause us to die—
only lack of it will.
Never to want to see
the other side of the hill
or that improbable country   20
where living is an idyll
(although a probable hell)
would kill us all.
Only the curious
have, if they live, a tale   25
worth telling at all.

Dogs say cats love too much, are irresponsible,
are changeable, marry too many wives,
desert their children, chill all dinner tables
with tales of their nine lives.   30
Well, they are lucky. Let them be
nine-lived and contradictory,
curious enough to change, prepared to pay
the cat price, which is to die
and die again and again,   35
each time with no less pain.
A cat minority of one
is all that can be counted on

to tell the truth. And what cats have to tell
on each return from hell   40
is this: that dying is what the living do,
that dying is what the loving do,
and that dead dogs are those who do not know
that dying is what, to live, each has to do.

Alastair Reid (b. 1926)

QUESTIONS

1. On the surface this poem is a dissertation on cats. What deeper comments
   does it make? Of what are cats and dogs, in this poem, symbols?
2. In what different senses are the words *death*, *die*, and *dying* here used?
3. Compare and contrast this poem in meaning and manner with "Ulysses."

The Writer

In her room at the prow of the house
Where light breaks, and the windows are tossed with linden,
My daughter is writing a story.

I pause in the stairwell, hearing
From her shut door a commotion of typewriter-keys   5
Like a chain hauled over a gunwale.

Young as she is, the stuff
Of her life is a great cargo, and some of it heavy:
I wish her a lucky passage.

But now it is she who pauses,   10
As if to reject my thought and its easy figure.
A stillness greatens, in which

The whole house seems to be thinking,
And then she is at it again with a bunched clamor
Of strokes, and again is silent.   15

I remember the dazed starling
Which was trapped in that very room, two years ago;
How we stole in, lifted a sash

And retreated, not to affright it;
And how for a helpless hour, through the crack of the door,   20
We watched the sleek, wild, dark

And iridescent creature
Batter against the brilliance, drop like a glove
To the hard floor, or the desk-top,

And wait then, humped and bloody,   25
For the wits to try it again; and how our spirits
Rose when, suddenly sure,

It lifted off from a chair-back,
Beating a smooth course for the right window
And clearing the sill of the world.   30

It is always a matter, my darling,
Of life or death, as I had forgotten. I wish
What I wished you before, but harder.

Richard Wilbur (b. 1921)

QUESTIONS

1. What "easy figure" (11) of speech is presented by such language as "prow"
   (1), "chain hauled over a gunwale" (6), "cargo" (8), "passage" (9)? What is
   being compared to what? Why would "the writer"—either the daughter or
   the speaker—be justified in rejecting that figure?
2. The daughter seems to be rejecting both the figure of speech and the
   thought that it represents (11). Why might the thought be as unacceptable
   as the figure that expresses it?
3. Lines 16 through 30 develop the image of the trapped starling. Why should
   it be interpreted as a symbol? How is its meaning more complex than that
   of the figure developed in lines 1–15?
4. The poem symmetrically divides into two 15-line units, each developing a
   different figure of speech. What is the function of the additional three lines
   with which the poem ends?

Power

Living   in the earth-deposits   of our history

Today a backhoe divulged   out of a crumbling flank of earth
one bottle   amber   perfect   a hundred-year-old
cure for fever   or melancholy   a tonic
for living on this earth   in the winters of this climate   5

Today I was reading about Marie Curie:
she must have known she suffered   from radiation sickness

her body bombarded for years   by the element
she had purified
It seems she denied to the end   10
the source of the cataracts on her eyes
the cracked and suppurating skin   of her finger-ends
till she could no longer hold   a test-tube or a pencil

She died   a famous woman   denying
her wounds   15
denying
her wounds   came   from the same source as her power

Adrienne Rich (b. 1929)

NOTE: Marie Curie (6) was a Polish-born scientist (1867–1934) who studied in Paris, married the French chemist Pierre Curie, pioneered the study of radioactivity, and received two Nobel Prizes, in physics and in chemistry.

Because I could not stop for Death

Because I could not stop for Death—
He kindly stopped for me—
The Carriage held but just Ourselves—
And Immortality.

We slowly drove—He knew no haste   5
And I had put away
My labor and my leisure too,
For His Civility—

We passed the School, where Children strove
At Recess—in the Ring—   10
We passed the Fields of Gazing Grain—
We passed the Setting Sun—

Or rather—He passed Us—
The Dews drew quivering and chill—
For only Gossamer, my Gown—   15
My Tippet—only Tulle—

We paused before a House that seemed
A Swelling of the Ground—

The Roof was scarcely visible—
The Cornice—in the Ground—   20

Since then—'tis Centuries—and yet
Feels shorter than the Day
I first surmised the Horses' Heads
Were toward Eternity—

Emily Dickinson (1830–1886)

QUESTIONS

1. Vocabulary: *Gossamer* (15); *Tippet, Tulle* (16); *surmised* (23).
2. Define the stages of this journey—where it begins, what events occur on the way, and its destination. Where is the speaker *now*? What is her present emotional condition?
3. To what is "Death" (1) being compared?
4. Identify the allegorical implications of the events. For example, what aspects of human life are implied by the three items that are "passed" in stanza 3? What is the "House" (17) before which the carriage pauses, and why does it pause there?
5. Explore the three time references in the concluding stanza. Can you explain why the passage of "Centuries" "Feels shorter than the Day" the speaker guessed that her journey was proceeding "toward Eternity"? For what is "Eternity" a metonymy? Has the carriage reached that destination yet?

Hymn to God My God, in My Sickness

Since I am coming to that holy room
    Where, with thy choir of saints for evermore,
I shall be made thy music, as I come
    I tune the instrument here at the door,
    And what I must do then, think now before.   5

Whilst my physicians by their love are grown
    Cosmographers, and I their map, who lie
Flat on this bed, that by them may be shown
    That this is my southwest discovery,
    Per fretum febris,° by these straits to die,   through the 10
                        raging of fever

I joy that in these straits I see my west;
    For though those currents yield return to none,
What shall my west hurt me? As west and east
    In all flat maps (and I am one) are one,
    So death doth touch the resurrection.   15

Is the Pacific Sea my home? Or are
The eastern riches? Is Jerusalem?
Anyan° and Magellan and Gibraltar,   Bering Strait
    All straits, and none but straits, are ways to them,
    Whether where Japhet dwelt, or Cham, or Shem.   20

We think that Paradise and Calvary,
    Christ's cross and Adam's tree, stood in one place;
Look, Lord, and find both Adams met in me;
    As the first Adam's sweat surrounds my face,
    May the last Adam's blood my soul embrace.   25

So, in his purple wrapped receive me, Lord;
    By these his thorns give me his other crown;
And as to others' souls I preached thy word,
    Be this my text, my sermon to mine own:
    Therefore that he may raise, the Lord throws down.   30

John Donne (1572–1631)

QUESTIONS

1. Vocabulary: *Cosmographers* (7).
2. What is the speaker doing in stanza 1? What are "that holy room" (1) and "the instrument" (4)? For what is the speaker preparing himself?
3. In Donne's time explorers were seeking a Northwest Passage to Asia to match discovery of a southwest passage, the Straits of Magellan. Why is "southwest" more appropriate to the speaker's condition than "northwest"? In what ways is his fever like a strait? What denotations of "straits" (10) are relevant? What do the straits symbolize?
4. In what ways does the speaker's body resemble a map? Although the map is metaphorical, its parts are symbolic. What do west and east symbolize? Explain how the west and east "are one" (14).
5. Japhet, Cham (or Ham), and Shem (20)—sons of Noah—were in Christian legend the ancestors of the races of man, roughly identified as European, African, and Asian. In what ways are the Pacific Ocean, the East Indies, and Jerusalem (16–17) fitting symbols for the speaker's destination?
6. According to early Christian thinking, the Garden of Eden and Calvary were located in the same place. How does this tie in with the poem's geographical symbolism? Because Adam is said to prefigure Christ (Romans 5:12–21), Christ is called the second Adam. What connection is there between Adam's "sweat" (24) and Christ's "blood" (25)? How do the two Adams meet in the speaker? What do blood and sweat (together and separately) symbolize?

7. For what are "eastern riches" (17), "his purple" (26), and "his thorns" (27) metonymies? What do "purple" and "thorns" symbolize? What is Christ's "other crown" (27)?
8. How does this poem explain human suffering and give it meaning?

SUGGESTIONS FOR WRITING

The following poems may be regarded as character sketches, but in each case the richness and suggestiveness of the presentation point to the symbolic nature of the sketch. Of what are the characters symbolic, and what clues does the poem present that make a symbolic interpretation valid?

1. Kay, "Pathedy of Manners" (page 689).
2. Frost, "After Apple-Picking" (page 708).
3. Dickinson, "I died for Beauty—but was scarce" (page 956).
4. Joseph, "Warning" (page 974).
5. Plath, "Spinster" (page 987).
6. Ríos, "Nani" (page 993).
7. Robinson, "Richard Cory" (page 996).

Chapter Seven

Figurative Language 3

Paradox, Overstatement, Understatement, Irony

  Aesop tells the tale of a traveler who sought refuge with a Satyr on a bitter winter night. On entering the Satyr's lodging, he blew on his fingers, and was asked by the Satyr why he did it. "To warm them up," he explained. Later, on being served a piping-hot bowl of porridge, he blew also on it, and again was asked why he did it. "To cool it off," he explained. The Satyr thereupon thrust him out of doors, for he would have nothing to do with a man who could blow hot and cold with the same breath.

  A **paradox** is an apparent contradiction that is nevertheless somehow true. It may be either a situation or a statement. Aesop's tale of the traveler illustrates a paradoxical situation. As a figure of speech, paradox is a statement. When Alexander Pope wrote that a literary critic of his time would "damn with faint praise," he was using a verbal paradox, for how can a man damn by praising?

  When we understand all the conditions and circumstances involved in a paradox, we find that what at first seemed impossible is actually entirely plausible and not strange at all. The paradox of the cold hands and hot porridge is not strange to anyone who knows that a stream of air directed upon an object of different temperature will tend to bring that object closer to its own temperature. And Pope's paradox is not strange when we realize that *damn* is being used figuratively, and that Pope means only that a too reserved praise may damage an author with the public almost as much as adverse criticism. In a paradoxical statement the contradiction usually stems from one of the words being used figuratively or with more than one denotation.

  The value of paradox is its shock value. Its seeming impossibility startles the reader into attention and, by the fact of its apparent absurdity, underscores the truth of what is being said.

Much Madness is divinest Sense

Much Madness is divinest Sense—
To a discerning Eye—
Much Sense—the starkest Madness—
'Tis the Majority
In this, as All, prevail—   5
Assent—and you are sane—
Demur—you're straightway dangerous—
And handled with a Chain—

Emily Dickinson (1830–1886)

QUESTIONS

1. This poem presents the two sides of a paradoxical proposition: that insanity is good sense, and that good sense is insane. How do the concepts implied by the words "discerning" (2) and "Majority" (4) provide the resolution of this paradox?
2. How do we know that the speaker does not believe that the majority is correct? How do the last five lines extend the subject beyond a contrast between sanity and insanity?

Overstatement, understatement, and verbal irony form a continuous series, for they consist, respectively, of saying more, saying less, and saying the opposite of what one really means.

Overstatement, or *hyperbole,* is simply exaggeration, but exaggeration in the service of truth. It is not the same as a fish story. If you say, "I'm starved!" or "You could have knocked me over with a feather!" or "I'll die if I don't pass this course!" you do not expect to be taken literally; you are merely adding emphasis to what you really mean. (And if you say, "There were literally millions of people at the beach!" you are merely piling one overstatement on top of another, for you really mean, "There were figuratively millions of people at the beach," or, literally, "The beach was very crowded.") Like all figures of speech, overstatement may be used with a variety of effects. It may be humorous or grave, fanciful or restrained, convincing or unconvincing. When Tennyson says of his eagle (page 649) that it is "*Close* to the sun in lonely lands," he says what appears to be literally true, though we know from our study of astronomy that it is not. When Kay reports that her character in "Pathedy of Manners" (page 689) "Saw *catalogues* of domes" on her European trip, she implies the superficiality of a person for whom visiting a few churches and palaces seemed like enough

architecture to fill catalogues. When Frost says, at the conclusion of
"The Road Not Taken" (page 734),

> I shall be telling this with a sigh
> Somewhere *ages and ages hence*

we are scarcely aware of the overstatement, so quietly is the assertion
made. Unskillfully used, however, overstatement may seem strained
and ridiculous, leading us to react as Gertrude does to the player-
queen's speeches in *Hamlet:* "The lady doth protest too much."

It is paradoxical that one can emphasize a truth either by over-
stating it or by understating it. **Understatement,** or saying less than
one means, may exist in what one says or merely in how one says it.
If, for instance, upon sitting down to a loaded dinner plate, you say,
"This looks like a nice snack," you are actually stating less than the
truth; but if you say, with the humorist Artemus Ward, that a man
who holds his hand for half an hour in a lighted fire will experience
"a sensation of excessive and disagreeable warmth," you are stating
what is literally true but with a good deal less force than the situation warrants.

The Sun Rising

> Busy old fool, unruly sun,
> Why dost thou thus
> Through windows and through curtains call on us?
> Must to thy motions lovers' seasons run?
> Saucy pedantic wretch, go chide   5
> Late schoolboys and sour 'prentices,
> Go tell court-huntsmen that the king will ride,
> Call country ants to harvest offices;
> Love, all alike, no season knows, nor clime,
> Nor hours, days, months, which are the rags of time.   10
>
> Thy beams so reverend and strong
> Why shouldst thou think?
> I could eclipse and cloud them with a wink,
> But that I would not lose her sight so long;
> If her eyes have not blinded thine,   15
> Look, and tomorrow late tell me
> Whether both th' Indias of spice and mine
> Be where thou left'st them, or lie here with me.

Ask for those kings whom thou saw'st yesterday,
And thou shalt hear, "All here in one bed lay."   20

  She's all states, and all princes I;
    Nothing else is.
Princes do but play us; compared to this,
All honor's mimic, all wealth alchemy.
    Thou, sun, art half as happy as we,   25
      In that the world's contracted thus;
    Thine age asks ease, and since thy duties be
    To warm the world, that's done in warming us.
Shine here to us, and thou art everywhere;
This bed thy center is, these walls thy sphere.   30

John Donne (1572–1631)

QUESTIONS

1. Vocabulary: *offices* (8), *alchemy* (24).
2. As precisely as possible, identify the time of day and the locale. What three "persons" does the poem involve?
3. What is the speaker's attitude toward the sun in stanzas 1 and 2? How and why does it change in stanza 3?
4. Does the speaker understate or overstate the actual qualities of the sun? Point out specific examples. Identify the overstatements in lines 9–10, 13, 15, 16–20, 21–24, 29–30. What do these overstatements achieve?
5. Line 17 introduces a geographical image referring to the East and West Indies, sources respectively of spices and gold. What relationship between the lovers and the rest of the world is expressed in lines 15–22?
6. Who is actually the intended listener for this extended apostrophe? What is the speaker's purpose? What is the poem's purpose?

Incident

Once riding in old Baltimore
  Heart-filled, head-filled with glee,
I saw a Baltimorean
  Keep looking straight at me.

Now I was eight and very small,   5
  And he was no whit bigger,
And so I smiled, but he poked out
  His tongue, and called me, "Nigger."

I saw the whole of Baltimore
From May until December;   10
Of all the things that happened there
That's all that I remember.

Countee Cullen (1903–1946)

QUESTION

What accounts for the effectiveness of the last stanza? Comment on the title. Is it in key with the meaning of the poem?

Like paradox, **irony** has meanings that extend beyond its use merely as a figure of speech.

Verbal irony, saying the opposite of what one means, is often confused with sarcasm and with satire, and for that reason it may be well to look at the meanings of all three terms. Sarcasm and satire both imply ridicule, one on the colloquial level, the other on the literary level. **Sarcasm** is simply bitter or cutting speech, intended to wound the feelings (it comes from a Greek word meaning to tear flesh). **Satire** is a more formal term, usually applied to written literature rather than to speech and ordinarily implying a higher motive: it is ridicule (either bitter or gentle) of human folly or vice, with the purpose of bringing about reform or at least of keeping other people from falling into similar folly or vice. Irony, on the other hand, is a literary device or figure that may be used in the service of sarcasm or ridicule or may not. It is popularly confused with sarcasm and satire because it is so often used as their tool; but irony may be used without either sarcastic or satirical intent, and sarcasm and satire may exist (though they do not usually) without irony. If, for instance, one of the members of your class raises his hand on the discussion of this point and says, "I don't understand," and your instructor replies, with a tone of heavy disgust in his voice, "Well, I wouldn't expect *you* to," he is being sarcastic but not ironic; he means exactly what he says. But if, after you have done particularly well on an examination, your instructor brings your test papers into the classroom saying, "Here's some *bad* news for you: you all got A's and B's!" he is being ironic but not sarcastic. Sarcasm, we may say, is cruel, as a bully is cruel: it intends to give hurt. Satire is both cruel and kind, as a surgeon is cruel and kind: it gives hurt in the interest of the patient or of society. Irony is neither cruel nor kind: it is simply a device, like a surgeon's scalpel, for performing any operation more skillfully.

Though verbal irony always implies the opposite of what is said, it has many gradations, and only in its simplest forms does it mean *only* the opposite of what is said. In more complex forms it means both what is said and the opposite of what is said, at once, though in different ways and with different degrees of emphasis. When Terence's critic, in Housman's "Terence, this is stupid stuff" (page 662) says, "'*Pretty* friendship 'tis to rhyme / Your friends to death before their time'" (11–12), we may substitute the literal *sorry* for the ironic "pretty" with little or no loss of meaning. When Terence speaks in reply, however, of the pleasure of drunkenness—"And down in *lovely* muck I've lain, / Happy till I woke again" (35–36)—we cannot substitute *loathsome* for "lovely" without considerable loss of meaning, for while muck is actually extremely unpleasant to lie in, it may *seem* lovely to an intoxicated person. Thus two meanings—one the opposite of the other—operate at once.

Like all figures of speech, verbal irony runs the danger of being misunderstood. With irony, the risks are perhaps greater than with other figures, for if metaphor is misunderstood, the result may be simply bewilderment; but if irony is misunderstood, the reader goes away with an idea exactly the opposite of what the user meant to convey. The results of misunderstanding if, for instance, you ironically called someone a numbskull might be calamitous. For this reason the user of irony must be very skillful in its use, conveying by an altered tone, or by a wink of the eye or pen, that irony is intended; and the reader of literature must be always alert to recognize the subtle signs of irony.

No matter how broad or obvious the irony, a number of people in any large audience always will misunderstand. Artemus Ward used to protect himself against these people by writing at the bottom of his newspaper column, "This is writ ironical." But irony is most delightful and most effective when it is subtlest. It sets up a special understanding between writer and reader that may add either grace or force. If irony is too obvious, it sometimes seems merely crude. But if effectively used, it, like all figurative language, is capable of adding extra dimensions to meaning.

Barbie Doll

> This girlchild was born as usual
> and presented dolls that did pee-pee
> and miniature GE stoves and irons
> and wee lipsticks the color of cherry candy.
> Then in the magic of puberty, a classmate said: 5
> You have a great big nose and fat legs.

She was healthy, tested intelligent,
possessed strong arms and back,
abundant sexual drive and manual dexterity.
She went to and fro apologizing.   10
Everyone saw a fat nose on thick legs.

She was advised to play coy,
exhorted to come on hearty,
exercise, diet, smile and wheedle.
Her good nature wore out   15
like a fan belt.
So she cut off her nose and her legs
and offered them up.

In the casket displayed on satin she lay
with the undertaker's cosmetics painted on,   20
a turned-up putty nose,
dressed in a pink and white nightie.
Doesn't she look pretty? everyone said.
Consummation at last.
To every woman a happy ending.   25

Marge Piercy (b. 1936)

QUESTIONS

1. In what ways is the girl described in this poem different from a Barbie doll? Discuss the poem's contrast of the living girl, a human being with intelligence and healthy appetites, and the doll, an inanimate object.
2. The poem contains a surprising but apt simile: "Her good nature wore out / like a fan belt" (15–16). Why is the image of the fan belt appropriate here?
3. Why does the speaker mention the girl's "strong arms and back" (8) and her "manual dexterity" (9)? How do these qualities contribute to her fate?
4. Discuss the verbal irony in the phrase "the magic of puberty" (5) and in the last three lines. What is the target of this satire?

The term *irony* always implies some sort of discrepancy or incongruity. In verbal irony the discrepancy is between what is said and what is meant. In other forms the discrepancy may be between appearance and reality or between expectation and fulfillment. These other forms of irony are, on the whole, more important resources for the poet than is verbal irony. Two types are especially important.

In **dramatic irony** the discrepancy is not between what the speaker says and what the speaker means but between what the speaker says and what the poem means. The speaker's words may be perfectly straightforward, but the author, by putting these words in a particular speaker's mouth, may be indicating to the reader ideas or attitudes quite opposed to those the speaker is voicing. This form of irony is more complex than verbal irony and demands a more complex response from the reader. It may be used not only to convey attitudes but also to illuminate character, for the author who uses it is indirectly commenting not only upon the value of the ideas uttered but also upon the nature of the person who utters them. Such comment may be harsh, gently mocking, or sympathetic.

The Chimney Sweeper

When my mother died I was very young,
And my father sold me while yet my tongue
Could scarcely cry "'weep! 'weep! 'weep! 'weep!"
So your chimneys I sweep, and in soot I sleep.

There's little Tom Dacre, who cried when his head,   5
That curled like a lamb's back, was shaved; so I said,
"Hush, Tom! never mind it, for, when your head's bare,
You know that the soot cannot spoil your white hair."

And so he was quiet, and that very night,
As Tom was asleeping, he had such a sight!   10
That thousands of sweepers, Dick, Joe, Ned, and Jack,
Were all of them locked up in coffins of black.

And by came an Angel who had a bright key,
And he opened the coffins and set them all free;
Then down a green plain leaping, laughing, they run,   15
And wash in a river, and shine in the sun.

Then naked and white, all their bags left behind,
They rise upon clouds and sport in the wind;
And the Angel told Tom, if he'd be a good boy,
He'd have God for his father, and never want joy.   20

And so Tom awoke, and we rose in the dark,
And got with our bags and our brushes to work.
Though the morning was cold, Tom was happy and warm;
So if all do their duty they need not fear harm.

William Blake (1757–1827)

QUESTIONS

1. In the eighteenth century small boys, sometimes no more than four or five years old, were employed to climb up the narrow chimney flues and clean them, collecting the soot in bags. Such boys, sometimes sold to the master sweepers by their parents, were miserably treated by their masters and often suffered disease and physical deformity. Characterize the boy who speaks in this poem. How do his and the poet's attitudes toward his lot in life differ? How, especially, are the meanings of the poet and the speaker different in lines 3, 7–8, and 24?

2. The dream in lines 11–20, besides being a happy dream, can be interpreted allegorically. Point out possible significances of the sweepers' being "locked up in coffins of black" (12) and the Angel's releasing them with a bright key to play upon green plains.

A third type of irony, **irony of situation,** occurs when a discrepancy exists between the actual circumstances and those that would seem appropriate or between what one anticipates and what actually comes to pass. If a man and his second wife, on the first night of their honeymoon, are accidentally seated at the theater next to the man's first wife, we should call the situation ironic. When, in O. Henry's famous short story "The Gift of the Magi," a poor young husband pawns his gold watch, in order to buy his wife a set of combs for her hair for Christmas, and his wife sells her long brown hair, in order to buy a fob for her husband's watch, the situation is ironic. When King Midas in the famous fable is granted his wish that anything he touch turn to gold, and then finds that he cannot eat because even his food turns to gold, the situation is ironic. When Coleridge's Ancient Mariner finds himself in the middle of the ocean with "Water, water, everywhere" but not a "drop to drink," the situation is ironic. In each case the circumstances are not what would seem appropriate or what we would expect.

Dramatic irony and irony of situation are powerful devices for poetry, for, like symbol, they enable a poem to suggest meanings without stating them—to communicate a great deal more than is said. We have seen one effective use of irony of situation in "The Widow's Lament in Springtime" (page 704). Another is in "Ozymandias," which follows.

Ozymandias

I met a traveler from an antique land
Who said: Two vast and trunkless legs of stone
Stand in the desert . . . Near them, on the sand,

Half sunk, a shattered visage lies, whose frown,
And wrinkled lip, and sneer of cold command,   5
Tell that its sculptor well those passions read
Which yet survive, stamped on these lifeless things,
The hand that mocked them, and the heart that fed;
And on the pedestal these words appear:
"My name is Ozymandias, king of kings;   10
Look on my works, ye Mighty, and despair!"
Nothing beside remains. Round the decay
Of that colossal wreck, boundless and bare
The lone and level sands stretch far away.

Percy Bysshe Shelley (1792–1822)

QUESTIONS

1. "[S]urvive" (7) is a transitive verb with "hand" and "heart" as direct objects. Whose hand? Whose heart? What figure of speech is exemplified in "hand" and "heart"?
2. Characterize Ozymandias.
3. Ozymandias was an ancient Egyptian tyrant. This poem was first published in 1817. Of what is Ozymandias a *symbol*? What contemporary reference might the poem have had in Shelley's time?
4. What is the theme of the poem and how is it "stated"?

Irony and paradox may be trivial or powerful devices, depending on their use. At their worst they may degenerate into mere mannerism and mental habit. At their best they may greatly extend the dimensions of meaning in a work of literature. Because irony and paradox demand an exercise of critical intelligence, they are particularly valuable as safeguards against sentimentality.

EXERCISE

Identify the figure in each of the following quotations as paradox, overstatement, understatement, or irony—and explain the use to which the figure is put (emotional emphasis, humor, satire, etc.).

1. Poetry is a language that tells us, through a more or less emotional reaction, something that cannot be said.   *Edwin Arlington Robinson*
2. Christians have burnt each other, quite persuaded
   That all the Apostles would have done as they did.   *Lord Byron*
3. A man who could make so vile a pun would not scruple to pick a pocket.
                                                                  John Dennis
4. Last week I saw a woman flayed, and you will hardly believe how much it altered her person for the worse.   *Jonathan Swift*

5. . . . Where ignorance is bliss, / 'Tis folly to be wise.   *Thomas Gray*
6. All night I made my bed to swim; with my tears I dissolved my couch.
                                                                    Psalms 6.6
7. Believe him, he has known the world too long,
   And seen the death of much immortal song.   *Alexander Pope*
8. Cowards die many times before their deaths;
   The valiant never taste of death but once.   *William Shakespeare*
9. . . . all men would be cowards if they durst.   *John Wilmot, Earl of Rochester*

REVIEWING CHAPTER SEVEN

1. Distinguish between paradoxical actions and paradoxical statements, and explain how paradoxical statements may usually be resolved—that is, how their underlying validity is determined.
2. Define overstatement and understatement, and draw the distinction between stating what is less than is true and underemphasizing what is true.
3. Review the definitions of sarcasm and satire.
4. Using examples from the poems that follow in this chapter, define the three principal forms of irony and demonstrate how the ironies contribute meaning or forcefulness to the poems.

Batter my heart, three-personed God

Batter my heart, three-personed God; for you
As yet but knock, breathe, shine, and seek to mend;
That I may rise and stand, o'erthrow me, and bend
Your force to break, blow, burn, and make me new.
I, like an usurped town, to another due,   5
Labor to admit you, but oh, to no end;
Reason, your viceroy in me, me should defend,
But is captived, and proves weak or untrue.
Yet dearly I love you and would be lovèd fain,°   gladly
But am betrothed unto your enemy;   10
Divorce me, untie or break that knot again,
Take me to you, imprison me, for I,
Except° you enthrall me, never shall be free,   unless
Nor ever chaste, except you ravish me.

John Donne (1572–1631)

QUESTIONS

1. In this sonnet (one in a group called "Holy Sonnets") the speaker addresses God in a series of metaphors and paradoxes. What is the paradox in the first quatrain? To what is the "three-personed God" metaphorically compared? To what is the speaker compared? Can the first three verbs of the parallel lines 2 and 4 be taken as addressed to specific "persons" of the Trinity (Father, Son, Holy Spirit)? If so, to which are "knock" and "break" addressed? "breathe" and "blow"? "shine" and "burn"? (What concealed pun helps in the attribution of the last pair? What etymological pun in the attribution of the second pair?)
2. To what does the speaker compare himself in the second quatrain? To what is God compared? Who is the usurper? What role does "Reason" (7) play in this political metaphor, and why is it a weak one?
3. To what does the speaker compare himself in the sestet (lines 9–14)? To what does he compare God? Who is the "enemy" (10)? Resolve the paradox in lines 12–13 by explaining the double meaning of "enthrall." Resolve the paradox in line 14 by explaining the double meaning of "ravish."

Sorting Laundry

Folding clothes,
I think of folding you
into my life.

Our king-sized sheets
like tablecloths   5
for the banquets of giants,

pillowcases, despite so many
washings, seams still
holding our dreams.

Towels patterned orange and green,   10
flowered pink and lavender,
gaudy, bought on sale,

reserved, we said, for the beach,
refusing, even after years,
to bleach into respectability.   15

So many shirts and skirts and pants
recycling week after week, head over heels
recapitulating themselves.

All those wrinkles
to be smoothed, or else   20
ignored; they're in style.

Myriad uncoupled socks
which went paired into the foam
like those creatures in the ark.

And what's shrunk   25
is tough to discard
even for Goodwill.

In pockets, surprises:
forgotten matches,
lost screws clinking on enamel;   30

paper clips, whatever they held
between shiny jaws, now
dissolved or clogging the drain;

well-washed dollars, legal tender
for all debts public and private,   35
intact despite agitation;

and, gleaming in the maelstrom,
one bright dime,
broken necklace of good gold

you brought from Kuwait,   40
the strangely tailored shirt
left by a former lover. . . .

If you were to leave me,
if I were to fold
only my own clothes,   45

the convexes and concaves
of my blouses, panties, stockings, bras
turned upon themselves,

a mountain of unsorted wash
could not fill   50
the empty side of the bed.

Elisavietta Ritchie (b. 1932)

QUESTIONS

1. Explain the metaphor in the first stanza. Where does the poem explicitly return to it? What psychological association connects lines 41–42 to line 43?
2. Explain how the length of the poem supports the overstatement in line 49. What is the speaker's attitude toward the "you" in the poem, and toward her role as housekeeper?

The History Teacher

Trying to protect his students' innocence
he told them the Ice Age was really just
the Chilly Age, a period of a million years
when everyone had to wear sweaters.

And the Stone Age became the Gravel Age,   5
named after the long driveways of the time.

The Spanish Inquisition was nothing more
than an outbreak of questions such as
"How far is it from here to Madrid?"
"What do you call the matador's hat?"   10

The War of the Roses took place in a garden,
and the Enola Gay dropped one tiny atom
on Japan.

The children would leave his classroom
for the playground to torment the weak   15
and the smart,
mussing up their hair and breaking their glasses,

while he gathered up his notes and walked home
past flower beds and white picket fences,
wondering if they would believe that soldiers   20
in the Boer War told long, rambling stories
designed to make the enemy nod off.

Billy Collins (b. 1941)

QUESTIONS

1. Vocabulary: *Spanish Inquisition* (7), *War of the Roses* (11) (usually with the plural "Wars"), *Boer War* (21). Enola Gay (12) was the name of the mother

of the pilot who dropped the atomic bomb on Hiroshima and who named his plane in her honor.

2. The first two references are to extended periods of prehistory, both of them made humorous by the anachronistic references to "sweaters" (4) and "driveways" (6). What do the remaining four historical references have in common? How does the speaker bring humor to them?

3. This poem employs a particular kind of understatement called "euphemism," the substitution of a less offensive or severe term for one that might give offense. In the first line, the speaker explains why the teacher uses this device. What situational irony is revealed in lines 14–17? Considering lines 18–19, who is actually innocent in this poem?

4. Beyond the humor of the poem, what serious meanings can you discern?

A Considerable Speck

(Microscopic)

A speck that would have been beneath my sight
On any but a paper sheet so white
Set off across what I had written there.
And I had idly poised my pen in air
To stop it with a period of ink   5
When something strange about it made me think.
This was no dust speck by my breathing blown,
But unmistakably a living mite
With inclinations it could call its own.
It paused as with suspicion of my pen,   10
And then came racing wildly on again
To where my manuscript was not yet dry;
Then paused again and either drank or smelt—
With loathing, for again it turned to fly.
Plainly with an intelligence I dealt.   15
It seemed too tiny to have room for feet,
Yet must have had a set of them complete
To express how much it didn't want to die.
It ran with terror and with cunning crept.
It faltered: I could see it hesitate;   20
Then in the middle of the open sheet
Cower down in desperation to accept
Whatever I accorded it of fate.
I have none of the tenderer-than-thou
Collectivistic regimenting love   25
With which the modern world is being swept.

But this poor microscopic item now!
Since it was nothing I knew evil of
I let it lie there till I hope it slept.

I have a mind myself and recognize   30
Mind when I meet with it in any guise.
No one can know how glad I am to find
On any sheet the least display of mind.

Robert Frost (1874–1963)

QUESTIONS

1. Who is the speaker in this poem?
2. How would you describe the speaker's attitude toward the "speck" he sees on his manuscript sheet? How do lines 24–29 help clarify his attitude? At what is the irony in these lines directed?
3. Analyze the connotations of the following phrases: "beneath my sight" (1), "a period of ink" (5), "a living mite" (8), "On any sheet the least display of mind" (33).
4. What does the poem finally suggest is the significance of the mite? How does the irony in the last four lines articulate the larger theme of the poem?

The Unknown Citizen
(To JS/07/M/378 This Marble Monument Is Erected by the State)

He was found by the Bureau of Statistics to be
One against whom there was no official complaint,
And all the reports on his conduct agree
That, in the modern sense of an old-fashioned word, he was a saint,
For in everything he did he served the Greater Community.   5
Except for the War till the day he retired
He worked in a factory and never got fired,
But satisfied his employers, Fudge Motors Inc.
Yet he wasn't a scab or odd in his views,
For his Union reports that he paid his dues
(Our report on his Union shows it was sound),   10
And our Social Psychology workers found
That he was popular with his mates and liked a drink.
The Press are convinced that he bought a paper every day
And that his reactions to advertisements were normal in every way.
Policies taken out in his name prove that he was fully insured,   15
And his Health-card shows he was once in hospital but left it cured.

Both Producers Research and High-Grade Living declare
He was fully sensible to the advantages of the Installment Plan
And had everything necessary to the Modern Man,
A phonograph, a radio, a car and a frigidaire.   20
Our researchers into Public Opinion are content
That he held the proper opinions for the time of year;
When there was peace, he was for peace; when there was war, he went.
He was married and added five children to the population,
Which our Eugenist says was the right number for a parent of his   25
    generation,
And our teachers report that he never interfered with their education.
Was he free? Was he happy? The question is absurd:
Had anything been wrong, we should certainly have heard.

W. H. Auden (1907–1973)

QUESTIONS

1. Vocabulary: *scab* (9), *Eugenist* (26).
2. Explain the allusion and the irony in the title. Why was the citizen "unknown"?
3. This obituary of an unknown state "hero" was apparently prepared by a functionary of the state. Give an account of the citizen's life and character from Auden's own point of view.
4. What trends in modern life and social organization does the poem satirize?

American Holiday

Military New Year's Eve!
Jets bombarding the sky with confetti!

Heroes' welcome-homecoming
plummeting out of the sky!

Bugles brassy with being right,   5
flares reddening peasant hills!

After the first of the explosions
thousands of unidentified birds scattered skyward.
The air darkened with shrieks.
Here below our nostrils were impacted   10
with hair, or wet ashes.

Only Monday.
A long week ahead.

Joyce Carol Oates (b. 1938)

QUESTIONS
1. This poem employs verbal irony in the service of social satire. Identify specific lines and images that use verbal irony.
2. Discuss the significance of the following verb choices: "bombarding" (2), "plummeting" (4), "reddening" (6), and "darkened" (9). How do these words help create the ironic meaning of the poem?
3. The second stanza describes "Bugles brassy with being right" (5). What is the double meaning of "brassy"?
4. In the third stanza, the speaker contrasts the patriotic fanfare described in the first two stanzas with its effect on ordinary citizens "Here below" (10). Identify the irony implicit in this contrast.
5. Analyze the final stanza. Why does the speaker suggest that there is a "long week ahead" (13)?

in the inner city

in the inner city
or
like we call it
home
we think a lot about uptown   5
and the silent nights
and the houses straight as
dead men
and the pastel lights
and we hang on to our no place   10
happy to be alive
and in the inner city
or
like we call it
home   15

Lucille Clifton (b. 1936)

QUESTIONS
1. In what contexts is the term "inner city" most often used, and what is it usually meant to imply?

2. What are the connotations of "silent nights" (6), "straight as / dead men" (7–8), and "pastel lights" (9)? By implication, what contrasting qualities might be found in the life of the inner city?
3. Is the irony in this poem verbal or dramatic?

Mr. Z

Taught early that his mother's skin was the sign of error,
He dressed and spoke the perfect part of honor;
Won scholarships, attended the best schools,
Disclaimed kinship with jazz and spirituals;
Chose prudent, raceless views of each situation,   5
Or when he could not cleanly skirt dissension,
Faced up to the dilemma, firmly seized
Whatever ground was Anglo-Saxonized.

In diet, too, his practice was exemplary:
Of pork in its profane forms he was wary;   10
Expert in vintage wines, sauces and salads,
His palate shrank from cornbread, yams and collards.

He was as careful whom he chose to kiss:
His bride had somewhere lost her Jewishness,
But kept her blue eyes; an Episcopalian   15
Prelate proclaimed them matched chameleon.
Choosing the right addresses, here, abroad,
They shunned those places where they might be barred;
Even less anxious to be asked to dine
Where hosts catered to kosher accent or exotic skin.   20

And so he climbed, unclogged by ethnic weights,
An airborne plant, flourishing without roots.
Not one false note was struck—until he died:
His subtly grieving widow could have flayed   24
The obit writers, ringing crude changes on a clumsy phrase:
"One of the most distinguished members of his race."

M. Carl Holman (1919–1988)

QUESTIONS

1. Vocabulary: *profane* (10), *kosher* (20), *exotic* (20), *ethnic* (21), *obit* (25).
2. Explain Mr. Z's motivation and the strategies he used to achieve his goal.

3. What is the author's attitude toward Mr. Z? Is he satirizing him or the society that produced him? Why does he not give Mr. Z a name?
4. What judgments on Mr. Z are implied by the metaphors in lines 16 and 22? Explain them.
5. What kind of irony is operating in the last line? As you reread the poem, where else do you detect ironic overtones?
6. What is Mr. Z's color?

Afterward

Now that your hopes are shamed, you stand
At last believing and resigned,
And none of us who touch your hand
Know how to give you back in kind
The words you flung when hopes were proud: 5
Being born to happiness
Above the asking of the crowd,
You would not take a finger less.
We who know limits now give room
To one who grows to fit her doom.   10

Adrienne Rich (b. 1929)

My Last Duchess
Ferrara

That's my last duchess painted on the wall,
Looking as if she were alive. I call
That piece a wonder, now; Fra Pandolf's hands
Worked busily a day, and there she stands.
Will 't please you sit and look at her? I said   5
"Fra Pandolf" by design, for never read
Strangers like you that pictured countenance,
The depth and passion of its earnest glance,
But to myself they turned (since none puts by
The curtain I have drawn for you, but I)   10
And seemed as they would ask me, if they durst,
How such a glance came there; so, not the first
Are you to turn and ask thus. Sir, 'twas not
Her husband's presence only, called that spot
Of joy into the Duchess' cheek; perhaps   15
Fra Pandolf chanced to say, "Her mantle laps

Over my lady's wrist too much," or, "Paint
Must never hope to reproduce the faint
Half-flush that dies along her throat." Such stuff
Was courtesy, she thought, and cause enough   20
For calling up that spot of joy. She had
A heart—how shall I say?—too soon made glad,
Too easily impressed; she liked whate'er
She looked on, and her looks went everywhere.
Sir, 'twas all one! My favor at her breast,   25
The dropping of the daylight in the West,
The bough of cherries some officious fool
Broke in the orchard for her, the white mule
She rode with round the terrace—all and each
Would draw from her alike the approving speech,   30
Or blush, at least. She thanked men—good! but thanked
Somehow—I know not how—as if she ranked
My gift of a nine-hundred-years-old name
With anybody's gift. Who'd stoop to blame
This sort of trifling? Even had you skill   35
In speech—which I have not—to make your will
Quite clear to such an one, and say, "Just this
Or that in you disgusts me; here you miss,
Or there exceed the mark"—and if she let
Herself be lessoned so, nor plainly set   40
Her wits to yours, forsooth, and made excuse,
—E'en then would be some stooping; and I choose
Never to stoop. Oh, sir, she smiled, no doubt,
Whene'er I passed her; but who passed without
Much the same smile? This grew; I gave commands;   45
Then all smiles stopped together. There she stands
As if alive. Will 't please you rise? We'll meet
The company below, then. I repeat,
The Count your master's known munificence
Is ample warrant that no just pretense   50
Of mine for dowry will be disallowed;
Though his fair daughter's self, as I avowed
At starting, is my object. Nay, we'll go
Together down, sir. Notice Neptune, though,
Taming a sea-horse, thought a rarity,   55
Which Claus of Innsbruck cast in bronze for me!

Robert Browning (1812–1889)

QUESTIONS

1. Vocabulary: *favor* (25), *officious* (27), *munificence* (49).
2. Ferrara is in Italy. The time is during the Renaissance, probably the six-teenth century. To whom is the Duke speaking? What is the occasion? Are the Duke's remarks about his last Duchess a digression, or do they have some relation to the business at hand?
3. Characterize the Duke as fully as you can. How does your characterization differ from the Duke's opinion of himself? What kind of irony is this?
4. Why was the Duke dissatisfied with his last Duchess? Was it sexual jealousy? What opinion do you get of the Duchess's personality, and how does it dif-fer from the Duke's opinion?
5. What characteristics of the Italian Renaissance appear in the poem (mar-riage customs, social classes, art)? What is the Duke's attitude toward art? Is it insincere?
6. What happened to the Duchess? Should Browning have told us?

SUGGESTIONS FOR WRITING

1. Discuss the irony in one of the following poems. Does the poem employ ver-bal irony, dramatic irony, or irony of situation? How does the ironic content of the poem heighten its impact?
   a. Kumin, "Woodchucks" (page 899).
   b. Crane, "War Is Kind" (page 952).
   c. Cullen, "For a Lady I Know" (page 955).
   d. Dickinson, "I died for Beauty—but was scarce" (page 956).
   e. Larkin, "Aubade" (page 980).
   f. Sexton, "Her Kind" (page 999).
2. Each of the following poems deals, at least in part, with the relationship be-tween the individual human being and a society that imposes a dehuman-izing conformity. Choose any two of the poems and compare their use(s) of irony in conveying this theme.
   a. Dickinson, "Much Madness is divinest Sense" (page 757).
   b. Auden, "The Unknown Citizen" (page 771).
   c. Piercy, "Barbie Doll" (page 761).
   d. Holman, "Mr. Z" (page 774).
   e. Atwood, "Siren Song" (page 943).
   f. Hughes, "Theme for English B" (page 972).
   g. Soyinka, "Telephone Conversation" (page 1006).

Chapter Eight

Allusion

The famous English diplomat and letter writer Lord Chesterfield once was invited to a great dinner given by the Spanish ambassador. At the conclusion of the meal the host rose and proposed a toast to his master, the king of Spain, whom he compared to the sun. The French ambassador followed with a health to the king of France, whom he likened to the moon. It was then Lord Chesterfield's turn. "Your excellencies have taken from me," he said, "all the greatest luminaries of heaven, and the stars are too small for me to make a comparison of my royal master; I therefore beg leave to give your excellencies—Joshua!"*

A reader familiar with the Bible—that is, one who recognizes the biblical allusion—will recognize the witty point of Lord Chesterfield's story. For an **allusion**—a reference to something in history or previous literature—is, like a richly connotative word or a symbol, a means of suggesting far more than it says. The one word "Joshua," in the context of Chesterfield's toast, calls up in the reader's mind the whole biblical story of how the Israelite captain stopped the sun and the moon in order that the Israelites might finish a battle and conquer their enemies before nightfall (Josh. 10.12–14). The force of the toast lies in its extreme economy; it says so much in so little, and it exercises the mind of the reader to make the connection for himself.

The effect of Chesterfield's allusion is chiefly humorous or witty, but allusions also may have a powerful emotional effect. The essayist William Hazlitt writes of addressing a fashionable audience about the lexicographer Samuel Johnson. Speaking of Johnson's great heart and of his charity to the unfortunate, Hazlitt recounted how, finding a drunken prostitute lying in Fleet Street late at night, Johnson carried her on his broad back to the address she managed to give him. The audience, unable to face the picture of the famous dictionary-maker doing such a thing, broke out in titters and expostulations, whereupon Hazlitt simply said: "I remind you, ladies and gentlemen, of the parable of the Good Samaritan." The audience was promptly silenced.†

---

*Samuel Shellabarger, *Lord Chesterfield and His World* (Boston: Little, Brown, 1951) 132.

†Jacques Barzun, *Teacher in America* (Boston: Little, Brown, 1945) 160.

Allusions are a means of reinforcing the emotion or the ideas of one's own work with the emotion or ideas of another work or occasion. Because they may compact so much meaning in so small a space, they are extremely useful to the poet.

"Out, Out—"

The buzz-saw snarled and rattled in the yard
And made dust and dropped stove-length sticks of wood,
Sweet-scented stuff when the breeze drew across it.
And from there those that lifted eyes could count
Five mountain ranges one behind the other   5
Under the sunset far into Vermont.
And the saw snarled and rattled, snarled and rattled,
As it ran light, or had to bear a load.
And nothing happened: day was all but done.
Call it a day, I wish they might have said   10
To please the boy by giving him the half hour
That a boy counts so much when saved from work.
His sister stood beside them in her apron
To tell them "Supper." At the word, the saw,
As if to prove saws knew what supper meant,   15
Leaped out at the boy's hand, or seemed to leap—
He must have given the hand. However it was,
Neither refused the meeting. But the hand!
The boy's first outcry was a rueful laugh,
As he swung toward them holding up the hand   20
Half in appeal, but half as if to keep
The life from spilling. Then the boy saw all—
Since he was old enough to know, big boy
Doing a man's work, though a child at heart—
He saw all spoiled. "Don't let him cut my hand off—   25
The doctor, when he comes. Don't let him, sister!"
So. But the hand was gone already.
The doctor put him in the dark of ether.
He lay and puffed his lips out with his breath.
And then—the watcher at his pulse took fright.   30
No one believed. They listened at his heart.
Little—less—nothing!—and that ended it.
No more to build on there. And they, since they
Were not the one dead, turned to their affairs.

Robert Frost (1874–1963)

QUESTIONS

1. How does this poem differ from a newspaper account that might have dealt with the same incident?
2. To whom does "they" (33) refer? The boy's family? The doctor and medical attendants? Casual onlookers? Need we assume that all these people—whoever they are—turned immediately "to their affairs" (34)? Does the ending of this poem seem to you callous or merely realistic? Would a more tearful and sentimental ending have made the poem better or worse?
3. What is the figure of speech in lines 21–22?

Allusions vary widely in the burden put on them by the poet to convey meaning. Lord Chesterfield risked his whole meaning on his hearers' recognizing his allusion. Robert Frost in " 'Out, Out—' " makes his meaning entirely clear even for the reader who does not recognize the allusion contained in the poem's title. His theme is the uncertainty and unpredictability of life, which may end accidentally at any moment, and the tragic waste of human potentiality that takes place when such premature deaths occur. A boy who is already "Doing a man's work" and gives every promise of having a useful life ahead of him is suddenly wiped out. There seems no rational explanation for either the accident or the death. The only comment to be made is, "No more to build on there."

Frost's title, however, is an allusion to one of the most famous passages in all English literature, and it offers a good illustration of how a poet may use allusion not only to reinforce emotion but also to help define his theme. The passage is that in *Macbeth* in which Macbeth has just been informed of his wife's death. A good many readers will recall the key phrase, "Out, out, brief candle!" with its underscoring of the tragic brevity and uncertainty of life. For some readers, however, the allusion will summon up the whole passage in Act 5, scene 5, in which Macbeth uses this phrase:

> She should have died hereafter;
> There would have been a time for such a word.
> Tomorrow, and tomorrow, and tomorrow
> Creeps in this petty pace from day to day
> To the last syllable of recorded time;   5
> And all our yesterdays have lighted fools
> The way to dusty death. Out, out, brief candle!
> Life's but a walking shadow, a poor player,
> That struts and frets his hour upon the stage
> And then is heard no more. It is a tale   10
> Told by an idiot, full of sound and fury,
> Signifying nothing.

William Shakespeare (1564–1616)

Macbeth's first words underscore the theme of premature death. The boy also "should have died hereafter." The rest of the passage, with its marvelous evocation of the vanity and meaninglessness of life, expresses neither Shakespeare's philosophy nor, ultimately, Frost's, but it is Macbeth's philosophy at the time of his bereavement, and it is likely to express the feelings of us all when such tragic accidents occur. Life does indeed seem cruel and meaningless, "a tale / Told by an idiot, . . . / Signifying nothing," when human life and potentiality are thus without explanation so suddenly ended.

QUESTION

Examine Macbeth's speech for examples of personification, apostrophe, and metonymy. How many metaphors for an individual human life does it present?

Allusions also vary widely in the number of readers to whom they will be familiar. Poets, in using an allusion, as in using a figure of speech, are always in danger of being misunderstood. What appeals powerfully to one reader may lose another reader altogether. But poets must assume a certain fund of common experience in readers. They could not even write about the ocean unless they could assume that readers have seen the ocean or pictures of it. In the same way poets assume a certain common fund of literary experience, most frequently of classical mythology, Shakespeare, or the Bible—particularly the King James Version. Poets are often justified in expecting a rather wide range of literary experience in readers, for the people who read poetry for pleasure are generally intelligent and well-read. But, obviously, beginning readers will not have this range, just as they will not know the meanings of as many words as will more experienced readers. Students should therefore be prepared to look up certain allusions, just as they should look up in their dictionaries the meanings of unfamiliar words. They will find that every increase in knowledge broadens their base for understanding both literature and life.

REVIEWING CHAPTER EIGHT

1. Show how allusion is similar in its effect to connotative language as well as to symbolism.
2. Using examples from the poems that follow in this chapter, draw clear distinctions between allusions that reinforce the ideas in a poem and allusions that intensify the emotions being expressed—and note those allusions that carry both intellectual and emotional meanings.

in Just—

in Just-
spring   when the world is mud-
luscious the little
lame balloonman

whistles   far   and wee   5

and eddieandbill come
running from marbles and
piracies and it's
spring

when the world is puddle-wonderful   10

the queer
old balloonman whistles
far   and   wee
and bettyandisbel come dancing

from hop-scotch and jump-rope and   15

it's
spring
and
     the

          goat-footed   20

balloonMan   whistles
far
and
wee

e. e. cummings (1894–1962)

QUESTION
Why is the balloonman called "goat-footed" (20)? How does the identification
made by this mythological allusion enrich the meaning of the poem?

Yet Do I Marvel

I doubt not God is good, well-meaning, kind,
And did He stoop to quibble could tell why
The little buried mole continues blind,
Why flesh that mirrors Him must some day die,
Make plain the reason tortured Tantalus   5
Is baited by the fickle fruit, declare
If merely brute caprice dooms Sisyphus
To struggle up a never-ending stair.
Inscrutable His ways are, and immune
To catechism by a mind too strewn   10
With petty cares to slightly understand
What awful brain compels His awful hand.
Yet do I marvel at this curious thing:
To make a poet black and bid him sing!

Countee Cullen (1903–1946)

QUESTIONS

1. Vocabulary: *quibble* (2), *caprice* (7), *catechism* (10), *awful* (12). If you are unfamiliar with the allusions to Tantalus (5) and Sisyphus (7), consult a reference book on Greek mythology.
2. The poem presents a series of indirect questions about God's reasons and purposes. Restate them as direct questions, and determine the order of their relative importance. Why does the poet use the last of these questions as the conclusion of the poem?
3. Identify the ironies in the poem. What is the effect of the understated phrase "curious thing" (13)?

On His Blindness

When I consider how my light is spent
    Ere half my days in this dark world and wide,
    And that one talent which is death to hide
    Lodged with me useless, though my soul more bent
To serve therewith my Maker, and present   5
    My true account, lest he returning chide,
    "Doth God exact day-labor, light denied?"
    I fondly ask. But Patience, to prevent

That murmur, soon replies, "God doth not need
   Either man's work or his own gifts. Who best   10
Bear his mild yoke, they serve him best. His state
Is kingly: thousands at his bidding speed,
   And post o'er land and ocean without rest;
   They also serve who only stand and wait."

John Milton (1608–1674)

QUESTIONS

1. Vocabulary: *spent* (1), *fondly* (8), *prevent* (8), *post* (13).
2. What two meanings has "talent" (3)? What is Milton's "one talent"?
3. The poem is unified and expanded in its dimensions by a biblical allusion
   that Milton's original readers would have recognized immediately. What is
   it? If you do not know, look up Matthew 25.14–30. In what ways is the situation in the poem similar to that in the parable? In what ways is it different?
4. What is the point of the poem?

Hazel Tells LaVerne

last night
im cleanin out my
howard johnsons ladies room
when all of a sudden
up pops this frog   5
musta come from the sewer
swimmin aroun an tryin ta
climb up the sida the bowl
so i goes ta flushm down
but sohelpmegod he starts talkin   10
bout a golden ball
an how i can be a princess
me a princess
well my mouth drops
all the way to the floor   15
an he says
kiss me just kiss me
once on the nose
well i screams
ya little green pervert   20

an i hitsm with my mop
an has ta flush
the toilet down three times
me
a princess   25

Katharyn Howd Machan (b. 1952)

QUESTIONS
1. What is the fairy tale to which this poem alludes?
2. The speaker does not use standard, correct English. How does her use of
   language make the poem more effective? Why doesn't the poet use standard
   capitalization and punctuation?
3. Discuss the poem's use of irony.

Miniver Cheevy

Miniver Cheevy, child of scorn,
   Grew lean while he assailed the seasons;
He wept that he was ever born,
   And he had reasons.

Miniver loved the days of old   5
   When swords were bright and steeds were prancing;
The vision of a warrior bold
   Would set him dancing.

Miniver sighed for what was not,
   And dreamed, and rested from his labors;   10
He dreamed of Thebes and Camelot,
   And Priam's neighbors.

Miniver mourned the ripe renown
   That made so many a name so fragrant;
He mourned Romance, now on the town,   15
   And Art, a vagrant.

Miniver loved the Medici,
   Albeit he had never seen one;
He would have sinned incessantly
   Could he have been one.   20

Miniver cursed the commonplace
    And eyed a khaki suit with loathing;
He missed the medieval grace
    Of iron clothing.

Miniver scorned the gold he sought,   25
    But sore annoyed was he without it;
Miniver thought, and thought, and thought,
    And thought about it.

Miniver Cheevy, born too late,
    Scratched his head and kept on thinking;   30
Miniver coughed, and called it fate,
    And kept on drinking.

Edwin Arlington Robinson (1869–1935)

QUESTIONS

1. Vocabulary: *khaki* (22). The phrase "on the town" (15) means "on charity" or "down and out."
2. Identify Thebes (11), Camelot (11), Priam (12), and the Medici (17). What names and what sort of life does each call up? What does Miniver's love of these names tell about him?
3. Discuss the phrase "child of scorn" (1). What does it mean? In how many ways is it applicable to Miniver?
4. What is Miniver's attitude toward material wealth?
5. The phrase "rested from his labors" (10) alludes to the Bible *and* to Greek mythology. Explore the ironic effect of comparing Miniver to the Creator (Genesis 2.2) and to Hercules. Point out other examples of irony in the poem and discuss their importance.
6. Can we call this a poem about a man whose "fate" was to be "born too late"? Explain your answer.

Journey of the Magi

"A cold coming we had of it,
Just the worst time of the year
For a journey, and such a long journey:
The ways deep and the weather sharp,
The very dead of winter."   5
And the camels galled, sore-footed, refractory,
Lying down in the melting snow.
There were times we regretted
The summer palaces on slopes, the terraces,

And the silken girls bringing sherbet.   10
Then the camel men cursing and grumbling
And running away, and wanting their liquor and women,
And the night-fires going out, and the lack of shelters,
And the cities hostile and the towns unfriendly
And the villages dirty and charging high prices: 15
A hard time we had of it.
At the end we preferred to travel all night,
Sleeping in snatches,
With the voices singing in our ears, saying
That this was all folly.   20

Then at dawn we came down to a temperate valley,
Wet, below the snow line, smelling of vegetation;
With a running stream and a water-mill beating the darkness,
And three trees on the low sky,
And an old white horse galloped away in the meadow.   25
Then we came to a tavern with vine-leaves over the lintel,
Six hands at an open door dicing for pieces of silver,
And feet kicking the empty wine-skins.
But there was no information, and so we continued
And arrived at evening, not a moment too soon   30
Finding the place; it was (you may say) satisfactory.

All this was a long time ago, I remember,
And I would do it again, but set down
This set down
This: were we led all that way for   35
Birth or Death? There was a Birth, certainly,
We had evidence and no doubt. I had seen birth and death,
But had thought they were different; this Birth was
Hard and bitter agony for us, like Death, our death.
We returned to our places, these Kingdoms,   40
But no longer at ease here, in the old dispensation,
With an alien people clutching their gods.
I should be glad of another death.

T. S. Eliot (1888–1965)

QUESTIONS

1. The biblical account of the journey of the Magi, or wise men, to Bethlehem is given in Matthew 2:1–12 and has since been elaborated by numerous legendary accretions. It has been made familiar through countless pageants

and Christmas cards. How does this account differ from the familiar one? Compare it with the biblical account. What has been added? What has been left out? What is the poet doing? (Lines 1–5 are in quotation marks because they are taken, with very slight modification, from a Christmas sermon [1622] by the Anglican bishop Lancelot Andrewes.)

2. Who is the speaker? Where and when is he speaking? What is the "old dispensation" (41) to which he refers, and why are the people "alien" (42)? Why does he speak of the "Birth" (38) as being "like Death" (39)? Of whose "Birth" and "Death" is he speaking? How does his life differ from the life he lived before his journey? What does he mean by saying that he would be "glad of another death" (43)?

3. This poem was written while the poet was undergoing religious conversion. (Eliot published it in 1927, the year he was confirmed in the Anglican Church.) Could the poem be considered a parable of the conversion experience? If so, how does this account differ from popular conceptions of this experience?

4. How do the images in the second section differ from those of the first? Do any of them suggest connections with the life of Christ?

Leda and the Swan

A sudden blow: the great wings beating still
Above the staggering girl, her thighs caressed
By the dark webs, her nape caught in his bill,
He holds her helpless breast upon his breast.

How can those terrified vague fingers push   5
The feathered glory from her loosening thighs?
And how can body, laid in that white rush,
But feel the strange heart beating where it lies?

A shudder in the loins engenders there
The broken wall, the burning roof and tower   10
And Agamemnon dead.
                            Being so caught up,
So mastered by the brute blood of the air,
Did she put on his knowledge with his power
Before the indifferent beak could let her drop?

William Butler Yeats (1865–1939)

QUESTIONS

1. What is the connection between Leda and "The broken wall, the burning roof and tower / And Agamemnon dead" (10–11)? If you do not know, look up the myth of Leda and the story of Agamemnon.

2. How does this poem do more than evoke an episode out of mythology? What is the significance of the question asked in the last two lines? How would you answer it?

I Dream I'm the Death of Orpheus

I am walking rapidly through striations of light
    and dark thrown under an arcade.

I am a woman in the prime of life, with certain powers
and those powers severely limited
by authorities whose faces I rarely see.
I am a woman in the prime of life   5
driving her dead poet in a black Rolls-Royce
through a landscape of twilight and thorns.
A woman with a certain mission
which if obeyed to the letter will leave her intact.
A woman with the nerves of a panther   10
a woman with contacts among Hell's Angels
a woman feeling the fullness of her powers
at the precise moment when she must not use them
a woman sworn to lucidity
who sees through the mayhem, the smoky fires   15
of these underground streets
her dead poet learning to walk backward against the wind
on the wrong side of the mirror

Adrienne Rich (b. 1929)

NOTE: Orpheus (title) was the legendary poet-singer who journeyed to the underworld to re- trieve his dead wife Eurydice. In a modernized form, Orpheus was the subject of a 1950 film by the French playwright-director Jean Cocteau (1889–1963). In the film, Death is personi- fied as a mysterious woman riding in a Rolls-Royce, accompanied by black-leather-jacketed motorcyclists, who takes the dead poet through a mirror into the underworld.

SUGGESTIONS FOR WRITING

An allusion may present a comparison or parallel, or it may create an ironic contrast. Choosing one or more of the following examples, write an essay demonstrating that the poem(s) use allusion positively, to enrich the theme, or ironically, to undercut the speaker's ideas.
1. Larkin, "A Study of Reading Habits" (page 671) (allusions to types of cheap fiction).
2. Keats, "On the Sonnet" (page 798) (allusions to Andromeda and Midas).
3. Collins, "Sonnet" (page 798) (allusion to Petrarch and Laura).

4. Dickinson, "One dignity delays for all" (page 812, line 15) (allusion to Matthew 5.5).

5. Ferlinghetti, "Constantly risking absurdity" (page 860, line 29) (allusion to Charlie Chaplin).

6. Atwood, "Siren Song" (page 943) (allusion to Greek mythology).

7. Frost, "Never Again Would Birds' Song Be the Same" (page 965) (allusion to events in the Garden of Eden).

8. Hardy, "Channel Firing" (page 968) (historical and legendary allusions).

9. Keats, "Ode to a Nightingale" (page 978, line 66) (allusion to the Book of Ruth).

Chapter Nine

Meaning and Idea

Little Jack Horner

Little Jack Horner
Sat in a corner
Eating a Christmas pie.
He stuck in his thumb
And pulled out a plum   5
And said, "What a good boy am I!"

Anonymous

The meaning of a poem is the experience it expresses—nothing less. But readers who, baffled by a particular poem, ask perplexedly, "What does it *mean?*" are usually after something more specific than this. They want something they can grasp entirely with their minds. We may therefore find it useful to distinguish the **total meaning** of a poem—the experience it communicates (and which can be communicated in no other way)—from its **prose meaning**—the ingredient that can be separated out in the form of a prose paraphrase (see chapter 2). If we make this distinction, however, we must be careful not to confuse the two kinds of meaning. The prose meaning is no more the poem than a plum is a pie or a prune is a plum.

The prose meaning will not necessarily or perhaps even usually be an idea. It may be a story, a description, a statement of emotion, a presentation of human character, or some combination of these. "Eros Turannos" (page 682) tells a story; "The Eagle" (page 649) is primarily descriptive; "The Widow's Lament in Springtime" (page 704) is an expression of emotion; "My Last Duchess" (page 775) is an account of human character. None of these poems is directly concerned with ideas. Message-hunters will be baffled and disappointed by poetry of this kind because they will not find what they are looking for, and they may attempt to read some idea into the poem that is really not there. Yet ideas are also part of human experience, and therefore many poems are concerned, at least partially, with presenting ideas. But with these poems message-hunting is an even more dangerous activity, for the message-hunters are likely to think that the whole object of reading the poem is to find the message—that the idea is really the only important thing in it. Like Little Jack Horner, they will reach in and pluck out the idea and say, "What a good boy am I!" as if the pie existed for the plum.

The idea in a poem is only part of the total experience that it communicates. The value and worth of the poem are determined by the value of the total experience, not by the truth or the nobility of the idea itself. This is not to say that the truth of the idea is unimportant, or that its validity should not be examined and appraised. But a good idea alone will not make a good poem, nor need an idea with which the reader does not agree ruin one. Good readers of poetry are receptive to all kinds of experience. They are able to make that "willing suspension of disbelief" that Coleridge characterized as constituting poetic faith. When one attends a performance of *Hamlet,* one is willing to forget for the time being that such a person as Hamlet never existed and that the events on the stage are fictions. Likewise, poetry readers should be willing to entertain imaginatively, for the time being, ideas they objectively regard as untrue. It is one way of better understanding these ideas and of enlarging the reader's own experience. The person who believes in God should be able to enjoy a good poem expressing atheistic ideas, just as the atheist should be able to appreciate a good poem in praise of God. The optimist should be able to find pleasure in pessimistic poetry, and the pessimist in optimistic poetry. The teetotaler should be able to enjoy *The Rubáiyát of Omar Khayyám,* and the winebibber a good poem in praise of abstinence. The primary value of a poem depends not so much on the truth of the idea presented as on the power with which it is communicated and on its being made a convincing part of a meaningful total experience. We must feel that the idea has been truly and deeply *felt* by the poet, and that the poet is doing something more than merely moralizing. The plum must be made part of a pie. If the plum is properly combined with other ingredients and if the pie is well baked, it should be enjoyable even for persons who do not care for the type of plums from which it is made. Consider, for instance, the following two poems.

Loveliest of Trees

> Loveliest of trees, the cherry now
> Is hung with bloom along the bough,
> And stands about the woodland ride
> Wearing white for Eastertide.

Now, of my threescore years and ten,   5
Twenty will not come again,
And take from seventy springs a score,
It only leaves me fifty more.

And since to look at things in bloom
Fifty springs are little room,   10
About the woodlands I will go
To see the cherry hung with snow.

A. E. Housman (1859–1936)

QUESTIONS

1. Very briefly, this poem presents a philosophy of life. In a sentence, what is it?
2. How old is the speaker? Why does he assume that his life will be seventy years in length? What is surprising about the words "only" (8) and "little" (10)?
3. A good deal of ink has been spilt over whether "snow" (12) is literal or figurative. What do you say? Justify your answer.

Stopping by Woods on a Snowy Evening

Whose woods these are I think I know.
His house is in the village though;
He will not see me stopping here
To watch his woods fill up with snow.

My little horse must think it queer   5
To stop without a farmhouse near
Between the woods and frozen lake
The darkest evening of the year.

He gives his harness bells a shake
To ask if there is some mistake.   10
The only other sound's the sweep
Of easy wind and downy flake.

The woods are lovely, dark and deep,
But I have promises to keep,
And miles to go before I sleep,   15
And miles to go before I sleep.

Robert Frost (1874–1963)

QUESTIONS

1. How do these two poems differ in idea?
2. What contrasts are suggested between the speaker in the second poem and (a) his horse and (b) the owner of the woods?

Both of these poems present ideas, the first more or less explicitly, the second symbolically. Perhaps the best way to get at the idea of the second poem is to ask two questions. First, why does the speaker stop? Second, why does he go on? He stops, we answer, to watch the woods fill up with snow—to observe a scene of natural beauty. He goes on, we answer, because he has "promises to keep"—that is, he has obligations to fulfill. He is momentarily torn between his love of beauty and these other various and complex claims that life has upon him. The small conflict in the poem is symbolic of a larger conflict in life. One part of the sensitive, thinking person would like to give up his life to the enjoyment of beauty and art. But another part is aware of larger duties and responsibilities— responsibilities owed, at least in part, to other human beings. The speaker in the poem would like to satisfy both impulses. But when the two conflict, he seems to suggest, the "promises" must take precedence.

The first poem also presents a philosophy but it is an opposing one. For the twenty-year-old speaker, the appreciation of beauty is of such importance that he will make it his lifelong dedication, filling his time with enjoying whatever the seasons bring. The metaphor comparing white cherry blossoms to snow suggests that each season has its own special beauty, though the immediate season is spring. In a limited life, one should seek out and delight in whatever beauty is present. Thoughtful readers will have to choose between these two philosophies—to commit themselves to one or the other—but this commitment should not destroy for them their enjoyment of either poem. If it does, they are reading for plums and not for pies.

Nothing we have said so far in this chapter should be construed as meaning that the truth or falsity of the idea in a poem is a matter of no importance. *Other things being equal,* good readers naturally will, and properly should, value more highly the poem whose idea they feel to be more mature and nearer to the heart of human experience. Some ideas, moreover, may seem so vicious or so foolish or so beyond the pale of normal human decency as to discredit *by themselves* the poems in which they are found. A rotten plum may spoil a pie. But good readers strive for intellectual flexibility and tolerance, and are able to entertain sympathetically ideas other than their own. They often will like a poem whose idea they disagree with better than one with an idea they accept. And, above all, they will not confuse the prose meaning of any poem with its total meaning. They will not mistake plums for pies.

REVIEWING CHAPTER NINE

1. The second paragraph of this chapter identifies four poems as not being "directly concerned with ideas"; reexamine those poems and demonstrate that while that statement is true of the prose meaning of each, the total meaning does in fact express an idea.
2. Explain how a poem that expresses an idea with which you do not agree may nevertheless be a source of appreciation and enjoyment.
3. The poems that follow in this chapter are paired in terms of their contrasted ideas; as you read them, practice discriminating between their ideas as we have done with the pair of poems by Housman and Frost, and determine which of the contrasted ideas more closely reflects your own beliefs.
4. Having determined where your beliefs are reflected, explain how the contrasting poem nevertheless has qualities you can admire.

The Rhodora:
On Being Asked, Whence Is the Flower?

In May, when sea-winds pierced our solitudes,
I found the fresh Rhodora in the woods,
Spreading its leafless blooms in a damp nook,
To please the desert and the sluggish brook.
The purple petals, fallen in the pool,   5
Made the black water with their beauty gay;
Here might the red-bird come his plumes to cool,
And court the flower that cheapens his array.
Rhodora! if the sage's ask thee why
This charm is wasted on the earth and sky,   10
Tell them, dear, that if eyes were made for seeing,
Then Beauty is its own excuse for being:
Why thou wert there, O rival of the rose!
I never thought to ask, I never knew;
But, in my simple ignorance, suppose   15
The self-same Power that brought me there brought you.

Ralph Waldo Emerson (1803–1882)

QUESTIONS

1. Vocabulary: *Whence* (subtitle), *desert* (4), *cheapens* (8), *array* (8). The rhodora (title) is a shrub that bears its rose-purple flowers before its leaves appear.
2. Notice that the rhyme pattern of the first eight lines is repeated in the second eight, providing an implied break after line 8. What else creates a break or shift at that point?
3. The speaker credits himself with "simple ignorance." Why is that phrase ironic?

Design

I found a dimpled spider, fat and white,
On a white heal-all, holding up a moth
Like a white piece of rigid satin cloth—
Assorted characters of death and blight
Mixed ready to begin the morning right,   5
Like the ingredients of a witches' broth—
A snow-drop spider, a flower like a froth,
And dead wings carried like a paper kite.

What had that flower to do with being white,
The wayside blue and innocent heal-all?   10
What brought the kindred spider to that height,
Then steered the white moth thither in the night?
What but design of darkness to appall?—
If design govern in a thing so small.

Robert Frost (1874–1963)

QUESTIONS

1. Vocabulary: *characters* (4), *snow-drop* (7).
2. The heal-all is a wildflower, usually blue or violet but occasionally white, found blooming along roadsides in the summer. It was once supposed to have healing qualities, hence its name. Of what significance, scientific and poetic, is the fact that the spider, the heal-all, and the moth are all white? Of what poetic significance is the fact that the spider is "dimpled" and "fat" and like a "snow-drop," and that the flower is "innocent" and named "heal-all"?
3. The "argument from design"—that the manifest existence of design in the universe implies the existence of a Great Designer—was a favorite eighteenth-century argument for the existence of God. What twist does Frost give the argument? What answer does he suggest to the question in lines 11–12? How comforting is the apparent concession in line 14?

4. Contrast Frost's poem in content and emotional effect with "The Rhodora."
   Is it possible to like both?

I never saw a Moor

I never saw a Moor—
I never saw the Sea—
Yet know I how the Heather looks
And what a Billow be.

I never spoke with God   5
Nor visited in Heaven—
Yet certain am I of the spot
As if the Checks° were given—   tickets

Emily Dickinson (1830–1886)

QUESTIONS

1. If the speaker never saw the moors or the ocean, how might she still know
   what they look like? What enables her to be "certain" (7) of heaven as her
   eventual destination?
2. Dickinson did not title her poems, but if you were to give a title to this one,
   what would it be? Discuss the appropriateness of your choice.

"Faith" is a fine invention

"Faith" is a fine invention
When Gentlemen can *see*—
But *Microscopes* are prudent
In an Emergency.

Emily Dickinson (1830–1886)

QUESTIONS

1. Discuss the images of vision in this poem. What different kinds of "seeing"
   do these images encompass?
2. To what kind of an "Emergency" (4) might this speaker be referring?
3. Though dealing with a serious subject, the poem has a humorous tone. Discuss the effectiveness and appropriateness of the poem's wit and humor.
4. How does the assertion here compare with that in the preceding poem? Must
   the reader assume that Dickinson is employing a fictitious persona in one of
   the poems? How could both poems represent one person's point of view?

On the Sonnet

If by dull rhymes our English must be chained,
And like Andromeda, the sonnet sweet
Fettered, in spite of painéd loveliness,
Let us find, if we must be constrained,
Sandals more interwoven and complete   5
To fit the naked foot of Poesy:
Let us inspect the lyre, and weigh the stress
Of every chord, and see what may be gained
By ear industrious, and attention meet;
Misers of sound and syllable, no less   10
Than Midas of his coinage, let us be
Jealous of dead leaves in the bay-wreath crown;
So, if we may not let the Muse be free,
She will be bound with garlands of her own.

John Keats (1795–1821)

QUESTIONS

1. Vocabulary: *Andromeda* (2), *meet* (9), *Midas* (11).
2. The poem prescribes a specific approach to writing sonnets. What qualities does the speaker suggest a good sonnet should have?
3. The speaker compares poetry to a foot and the sonnet form to a sandal. What does he mean by suggesting that the sonnet-sandals should be "more interwoven and complete" (5)?
4. What negative qualities does the poem imply that bad sonnets display?

Sonnet

All we need is fourteen lines, well, thirteen now,
and after this one just a dozen
to launch a little ship on love's storm-tossed seas,
then only ten more left like rows of beans.
How easily it goes unless you get Elizabethan   5
and insist the iambic bongos must be played
and rhymes positioned at the ends of lines,
one for every station of the cross.
But hang on here while we make the turn
into the final six where all will be resolved,   10
where longing and heartache will find an end,
where Laura will tell Petrarch to put down his pen,

take off those crazy medieval tights,
blow out the lights, and come at last to bed.

Billy Collins (b. 1941)

QUESTIONS

1. In line 12, "Laura will tell Petrarch to put down his pen," the poem alludes to the Italian poet Francesco Petrarch (1304–1374), who wrote a sequence of sonnets to his idealized lady-love, Laura. What attitude does the speaker take toward Petrarch and the Petrarchan sonnet?
2. The phrase "love's storm-tossed seas" (3) is a deliberate cliché. Why is the cliché appropriate here?
3. What is the effect of images such as "rows of beans" (4) and "iambic bongos" (6)? How do they help create the speaker's distinctive voice?
4. While this and the preceding poem differ greatly in language and emotion, they may be compared as statements about the sonnet. What are their essential ideas about this poetic form?

The Indifferent

"I can love both fair and brown,
Her whom abundance melts, and her whom want betrays,
Her who loves loneness best, and her who masks and plays,
    Her whom the country formed, and whom the town,
        Her who believes, and her who tries,°   tests 5
        Her who still weeps with spongy eyes,
    And her who is dry cork and never cries;
    I can love her, and her, and you, and you;
    I can love any, so she be not true.°   faithful

"Will no other vice content you?   10
Will it not serve your turn to do as did your mothers?
Or have you all old vices spent, and now would find out others?
    Or doth a fear that men are true torment you?
        Oh, we are not; be not you so.
        Let me, and do you, twenty know.   15
    Rob me, but bind me not, and let me go.
    Must I, who came to travail thorough° you,   through
    Grow your fixed subject because you are true?"

    Venus heard me sigh this song,
And by love's sweetest part, variety, she swore   20

She heard not this till now, and that it should be so no more.
  She went, examined, and returned ere long,
    And said, "Alas, some two or three
    Poor heretics in love there be,
  Which think to 'stablish dangerous constancy,   25
  But I have told them, 'Since you will be true,
  You shall be true to them who are false to you.'"

John Donne (1572–1631)

QUESTIONS

1. Vocabulary: *Indifferent* (title), *know* (15), *travail* (17).
2. Who is the speaker? To whom is he speaking? About what is he "indifferent"? What one qualification does he insist on in a lover? Why?
3. Of what vice does he accuse the women of his generation in line 10? How, in his opinion, do they differ from their mothers? Why?
4. Why does Venus investigate the speaker's complaint? Does her investigation confirm or refute his accusation? Who are the "heretics in love" (24) whom she discovers? What punishment does she decree for them?

Love's Deity

I long to talk with some old lover's ghost
  Who died before the god of love was born.
I cannot think that he who then loved most
  Sunk so low as to love one which did scorn.
But since this god produced a destiny,   5
And that vice-nature, custom, lets it be,
    I must love her that loves not me.

Sure, they which made him god meant not so much,
  Nor he in his young godhead practiced it.
But when an even flame two hearts did touch,   10
  His office was indulgently to fit
Actives to passives. Correspondency
Only his subject was. It cannot be
    Love till I love her that loves me.

But every modern god will° now extend   wants to   15
  His vast prerogative as far as Jove.
To rage, to lust, to write to, to commend,
  All is the purlieu of the god of love.

Oh, were we wakened by this tyranny
To ungod this child again, it could not be   20
       I should love her who loves not me.

Rebel and atheist too, why murmur I
    As though I felt the worst that Love could do?
Love might make me leave loving, or might try
    A deeper plague, to make her love me too,   25
Which, since she loves before, I am loath to see.
Falsehood is worse than hate, and that must be
       If she whom I love should love me.

John Donne (1572–1631)

QUESTIONS

1. Vocabulary: *vice-* (6), *even* (10), *purlieu* (18).
2. Who is the modern "god of love" (2)? Why is he called a "child" (20)? What did "they which made him god" (8) intend to be his duties? How has he gone beyond these duties? Why does the speaker long to talk with some lover's ghost who died before this god was born (1–2)?
3. What is the speaker's situation? Whom does the speaker call "Rebel and atheist" (22)? Why?
4. Why does the speaker rebuke himself for "murmuring" in the final stanza? What two things could Love do to him that have not been done already? Why are they worse? Explain the words "before" (26) and "Falsehood" (27). To which word in the first stanza does "hate" (27) correspond?
5. How does the speaker define "love" in this poem? Is he consistent in his use of the term? How does he differ from the speaker in "The Indifferent" in his conception of love?
6. How do you explain the fact that "Love's Deity" and "The Indifferent," though both by the same poet, express opposite opinions about the value of fidelity in love?

My Number

Is Death miles away from this house,
reaching for a widow in Cincinnati
or breathing down the neck of a lost hiker
in British Columbia?

Is he too busy making arrangements,   5
tampering with air brakes,

scattering cancer cells like seeds,
loosening the wooden beams of roller coasters

to bother with my hidden cottage
that visitors find so hard to find?   10

Or is he stepping from a black car
parked at the dark end of the lane,
shaking open the familiar cloak,
its hood raised like the head of a crow;
and removing the scythe from the trunk?   15

Did you have any trouble with the directions?
I will ask, as I start talking my way out of this.

Billy Collins (b. 1941)

QUESTIONS

1. What human characteristics does the poem ascribe to the personified
   "Death"? Are some references more frightening than others?
2. How do the two two-line stanzas cope with the idea of dying? Are these defenses against death reassuring? To what common phrase does the title allude?
3. What does the poem have to say about fear and apprehension of death?

I had heard it's a fight

I had heard it's a fight. At the first clammy touch
You yell, you wrestle with it, it kicks you
In the stomach, squeezes your eyes, in agony you clutch
At a straw, you rattle, and that will fix you.

I don't know. The afternoon it touched me   5
It sneaked up like it was a sweet thrill
Inside my arms and back so I let it come just a wee
Mite closer, though I knew what it was, hell.

Was it sweet! Then like a cute schoolkid
Who does it the first time, I decided it was bad,   10
Cut out the liquor, went to the gym, and did
What a man naturally does, as I mostly had.

The crazy thing, so crazy it gives me a kick:
I can't get over that minute of dying so quick.

Edwin Denby (1903–1983)

QUESTIONS

1. Vocabulary: multiple denotations of *quick* (14).
2. What does the colloquial and slangy diction add to the poem? Does this diction imply that the topic of one's death is not so serious?
3. In line 8 the word "hell" grammatically might be an emphatic exclamation, or it might be a definition of "it" in the preceding phrase. Does the third stanza help you to decide between these possibilities—or to decide that both are appropriate?
4. Compare the attitude toward one's death as expressed here with that in the preceding poem. Does one poem have more "meaning" than the other?

SUGGESTIONS FOR WRITING

Explore the contrasting ideas in the following pairs or groups of poems:

1. Brooks, "Kitchenette Building" (page 660) and Clifton, "good times" (page 950).
2. Hayden, "Those Winter Sundays" (page 709) and Roethke, "My Papa's Waltz" (page 997).
3. Hopkins, "Spring" (page 703), Housman, "Loveliest of Trees" (page 792), and Williams, "Spring and All" (page 1017).
4. Hadas, "The Red Hat" (page 967), Pastan, "To a Daughter Leaving Home" (page 858), and Wilbur, "The Writer" (page 750).
5. Clifton, "in the inner city" (page 773), Brooks, "a song in the front yard" (page 949), and Levis, "L. A., Loiterings" (page 981).
6. Angelou, "Woman Work" (page 832) and Piercy, "A Work of Artifice" (page 985).
7. Owen, "Anthem for Doomed Youth" (page 875), Cross, "Rice Will Grow Again" (page 953), Douglas, "Vergissmeinnicht" (page 959), and Stevens, "The Death of a Soldier" (page 1007).

Chapter Ten

Tone

Tone, in literature, may be defined as the writer's or speaker's attitude toward the subject, the reader, or herself or himself. It is the emotional coloring, or the emotional meaning, of the work and is an extremely important part of the full meaning. In spoken language it is indicated by the inflections of the speaker's voice. If, for instance, a friend tells you, "I'm going to get married today," the facts of the statement are entirely clear. But the emotional meaning of the statement may vary widely according to the tone of voice with which it is uttered. The tone may be ecstatic ("Hooray! I'm going to get married today!"); it may be incredulous ("I can't believe it! I'm going to get married today"); it may be despairing ("Horrors! I'm going to get married today"); it may be resigned ("Might as well face it. I'm going to get married today"). Obviously, a correct interpretation of the tone will be an important part of understanding the full meaning. It may even have rather important consequences. If someone calls you a fool, your interpretation of the tone may determine whether you take it as an insult or as playful banter. If a person says "No" to your proposal of marriage, your interpretation of the tone may determine whether you ask again or start going with someone else.

In poetry tone is likewise important. We have not really understood a poem unless we have accurately sensed whether the attitude it manifests is playful or solemn, mocking or reverent, calm or excited. But the correct determination of tone in literature is a much more delicate matter than it is in spoken language, for we do not have the speaker's voice to guide us. We must learn to recognize tone by other means. Almost all of the elements of poetry help to indicate its tone: connotation, imagery, and metaphor; irony and understatement; rhythm, sentence construction, and formal pattern. There is therefore no simple formula for recognizing tone. It is an end product of all the elements in a poem. The best we can do is illustrate.

Robert Frost's "Stopping by Woods on a Snowy Evening" (page 793) seems a simple poem, but it has always afforded trouble to beginning readers. A very good student, asked to interpret it, once wrote this: "The poem means that we are forever passing up pleasures to go onward to what we wrongly consider our obligations. We would like to watch the snow fall on the peaceful countryside, but we always have to rush home to supper and other engagements. Frost feels that the average person considers life too short to stop and take time to appreciate true pleasures." This student did a good job in recognizing the central conflict of the poem but went astray in recognizing its tone. Let's examine why.

In the first place, the fact that the speaker in the poem *does* stop to watch the snow fall in the woods immediately establishes him as a human being with more sensitivity and feeling for beauty than most. He is not one of the people of Wordsworth's sonnet (page 694) who, "Getting and spending," have laid waste their powers and lost the capacity to be stirred by nature. Frost's speaker is contrasted with his horse, who, as a creature of habit and an animal without esthetic perception, cannot understand the speaker's reason for stopping. There is also a suggestion of contrast with the "owner" of the woods, who, if he saw the speaker stopping, might be as puzzled as the horse. (Who most truly "profits" from the woods—its absentee owner or the person who can enjoy its beauty?) The speaker goes on because he has "promises to keep." But the word "promises," though it may here have a wry ironic undertone of regret, has a favorable connotation: people almost universally agree that promises ought to be kept. If the poet had used a different term, say, "things to do," or "business to attend to," or "financial affairs to take care of," or "money to make," the connotations would have been quite different. As it is, the tone of the poem tells us that the poet is sympathetic to the speaker; Frost is endorsing rather than censuring the speaker's action. Perhaps we may go even further. In the concluding two lines, because of their climactic position, because they are repeated, and because "sleep" in poetry often figuratively refers to death, there is a suggestion of symbolic interpretation: "and many years to live before I die." If we accept this interpretation, it poses a parallel between giving oneself up to contemplation of the woods and dying. The poet's total implication would seem to be that beauty is a distinctively human value that deserves its place in a full life, but to devote one's life to its pursuit, at the expense of other obligations and duties, is tantamount to one's death as a responsible being. The poet therefore accepts the choice the speaker makes, though not without a touch of regret.

Differences in tone, and their importance, are most apparent in poems with similar content. Consider, for instance, the following pair.

For a Lamb

I saw on the slant hill a putrid lamb,
Propped with daisies. The sleep looked deep,
The face nudged in the green pillow
But the guts were out for crows to eat.

Where's the lamb? whose tender plaint   5
Said all for the mute breezes.
Say he's in the wind somewhere,
Say, there's a lamb in the daisies.

Richard Eberhart (b. 1904)

QUESTION

What connotative force do these words possess: "putrid" (1), "guts" (4), "mute"
(6), "lamb" (1), "daisies" (2), "pillow" (3), "tender" (5)? Give two relevant denotations of "a lamb in the daisies" (8).

Apparently with no surprise

Apparently with no surprise
To any happy Flower
The Frost beheads it at its play—
In accidental power—
The blonde Assassin passes on—   5
The Sun proceeds unmoved
To measure off another Day
For an Approving God.

Emily Dickinson (1830–1886)

QUESTIONS

1. What is the "blonde Assassin" (5)?
2. What ironies are involved in this poem?

Both of these poems are concerned with natural process; both use
contrast as their basic organizing principle—a contrast between life and
death, innocence and destruction, joy and tragedy. But in tone the two
poems are sharply different. The first is realistic and resigned; its tone
is wistful but not pessimistic. The second, though superficially fanciful,
is basically grim, almost savage; its tone is horrified. Let's examine the
difference.

The title, "For a Lamb," invites associations of innocent, frolicsome youthfulness, with the additional force of traditional Christian usage. These expectations are shockingly halted by the word "putrid." Though the speaker tries to overcome the shock with the more comforting personification implied in "face" and "pillow," the truth is undeniable: the putrefying animal is food for scavengers. The second stanza comes to grips with this truth, and also with the speaker's desire that the lamb might still represent innocence and purity in nature. It mingles fact and desire by hoping that what the lamb represented is still "somewhere" in the wind, that the lamb is both lying in the daisy field and will, in nature's processes, be transformed into the daisies. The reader shares the speaker's sad acceptance of reality.

The second poem makes the same contrast between joyful innocence ("happy Flower . . . at its play") and fearful destruction ("beheads it"). The chief difference would seem to be that the cause of destruction—"the blonde Assassin"—is specifically identified, while the lamb seems to have died in its sleep, pillowed as it is in grass and surrounded by flowers. But the metaphorical sleep is no less a death than that delivered by an assassin—lambs *do* die, and frost actually *does* destroy flowers. In the second poem, what makes the horror of the killing worse is that nothing else in nature is disturbed by it or seems even to notice it. The sun "proceeds unmoved / To measure off another Day." Nothing in nature stops or pauses. The flower itself is not surprised. And even God—the God who we have been told is benevolent and concerned over the least sparrow's fall—seems to approve of what has happened, for He shows no displeasure, and He supposedly created the frost as well as the flower. Further irony lies in the fact that the "Assassin" (the word's connotations are of terror and violence) is not dark but "blonde," or white (the connotations here are of innocence and beauty). The destructive agent, in other words, is among God's most exquisite creations. The speaker suggests a random, amoral universe in which a flower's premature beheading may be "accidental" (4); but the beheading is witnessed by a "Sun" who is "unmoved" (6) and by an "Approving God" (8) who is satisfied with the flower's fate. And if we think that the speaker is unduly disturbed over the death of a flower, we may consider that what is true for the flower is true throughout nature. Death—even early or accidental death, in terrible juxtaposition with beauty—is its constant condition; the fate that befalls the flower befalls us all. In Dickinson's poem, that is the end of the process. In Eberhart's, the potentially terrible irony is directed into a bittersweet acceptance of both death and beauty as natural.

These two poems, then, though superficially similar, are completely different. And the difference is primarily one of tone.

We have been discussing tone as if every poem could be distinguished by a single tone. But varying or shifting tones in a single poem are often a valuable means for achieving the poet's purpose, and indeed may create the dramatic structure of a poem. Consider the following.

Since there's no help

Since there's no help, come let us kiss and part;
Nay, I have done, you get no more of me,
And I am glad, yea, glad with all my heart
That thus so cleanly I myself can free;
Shake hands forever, cancel all our vows,   5
And when we meet at any time again,
Be it not seen in either of our brows
That we one jot of former love retain.
Now, at the last gasp of Love's latest breath,
When, his pulse failing, Passion speechless lies,   10
When Faith is kneeling by his bed of death,
And Innocence is closing up his eyes,
Now, if thou wouldst, when all have given him over,
From death to life thou mightst him yet recover.

Michael Drayton (1563–1631)

QUESTIONS

1. What difference in tone do you find between the first eight lines and the last six? In which part is the speaker more sincere? What differences in rhythm and language help to establish the difference in tone?
2. How many figures are there in the allegorical scene in lines 9–12? What do the pronouns "his" and "him" in lines 10–14 refer to? What is dying? Why? How might the person addressed still restore it from death to life?
3. Define the dramatic situation as precisely as possible, taking into consideration both the man's attitude and the woman's.

Accurately determining tone, whether it be the tone of a rejected marriage proposal or of an insulting remark, is extremely important when interpreting language in poetry as well as in everyday conversations. For the experienced reader it will be instinctive and automatic. For the inexperienced reader it will require study. But beyond the general suggestions for reading that we already have made, there are no specific instructions we can give. Recognition of tone requires an increasing familiarity with the meanings and connotations of words, alertness to the presence of irony and other figures, and, above all, careful reading.

REVIEWING CHAPTER TEN

1. Consider the ways in which tone is part of the total meaning of a poem (you might think of the total meaning as a compound of the intellectual and the emotional).

2. The second paragraph of this chapter lists many of the elements of poetry that contribute to tone; as you examine the first two poems presented in the chapter, try to identify which of the elements are particularly significant in each of them.

3. Tone is customarily identified by an adjective (*wistful, pessimistic, horrified* in the discussion of the first two poems). Choose adjectives to identify the two contrasting tones in "Since there's no help." (Do not settle for the first adjective that pops into mind—this is good opportunity to exercise your vocabulary and strive for precision.)

My mistress' eyes

My mistress' eyes are nothing like the sun;
Coral is far more red than her lips' red;
If snow be white, why then her breasts are dun;
If hairs be wires, black wires grow on her head.
I have seen roses damasked,° red and white,   of different colors
But no such roses see I in her cheeks;   6
And in some perfumes is there more delight
Than in the breath that from my mistress reeks.°   exhales
I love to hear her speak, yet well I know
That music hath a far more pleasing sound;   10
I grant I never saw a goddess go,—
My mistress, when she walks, treads on the ground.
And yet, by heaven, I think my love as rare
As any she belied with false compare.

William Shakespeare (1564–1616)

QUESTIONS

1. The speaker draws a contrast between the qualities often praised in exaggerated love poetry and the reality of his mistress' physical attributes. Construct the series of "false compar[isons]" that this poem implies that other poets have used (eyes as bright as the sun, hair like spun gold, etc.).

2. What is the speaker's tone in lines 1–12? Is there anything about those lines that his mistress might find pleasing? (In Shakespeare's time the word "reeks" did not have its modern denotation of "stinks.")
3. The tone clearly shifts with line 13—signaled by the simple phrase "And yet." What is the tone of the last two lines? The last line might be paraphrased "as any woman who has been lied to with false comparisons." How important are truth and lies as subjects in the poem?

Miracle Ice Cream

Miracle's truck comes down the little avenue,
Scott Joplin ragtime strewn behind it like pearls,
and, yes, you can feel happy
with one piece of your heart.

Take what's still given: in a room's rich shadow   5
a woman's breasts swinging lightly as she bends.
Early now the pearl of dusk dissolves.
Late, you sit weighing the evening news,
fast-food miracles, ghostly revolutions,
the rest of your heart.   10

Adrienne Rich (b. 1929)

NOTE: Scott Joplin (2), an African American musician and composer (1868–1917), was an originator of ragtime music; his jaunty tune "The Entertainer" (1902) is widely used by neighborhood ice-cream trucks to attract their young customers.

Crossing the Bar

Sunset and evening star,
    And one clear call for me!
And may there be no moaning of the bar
    When I put out to sea,

But such a tide as moving seems asleep,   5
    Too full for sound and foam,
When that which drew from out the boundless deep
    Turns again home.

Twilight and evening bell,
    And after that the dark!   10
And may there be no sadness of farewell
    When I embark;

For though from out our bourne of Time and Place
    The flood may bear me far,
I hope to see my Pilot face to face   15
    When I have crossed the bar.

Alfred, Lord Tennyson (1809–1892)

QUESTIONS

1. Vocabulary: *bourne* (13).
2. What two sets of figures does Tennyson use for approaching death? What is the precise moment of death in each set?
3. In troubled weather the wind and waves above the sandbar across a harbor's mouth make a moaning sound. What metaphorical meaning has the "moaning of the bar" (3) here? For what kind of death is the speaker wishing? Why does he want "no sadness of farewell" (11)?
4. What is "that which drew from out the boundless deep" (7)? What is "the boundless deep"? To what is it opposed in the poem? Why is "Pilot" (15) capitalized?

The Oxen

Christmas Eve, and twelve of the clock.
    "Now they are all on their knees,"
An elder said as we sat in a flock
    By the embers in hearthside ease.

We pictured the meek mild creatures where   5
    They dwelt in their strawy pen,
Nor did it occur to one of us there
    To doubt they were kneeling then.

So fair a fancy few would weave
    In these years! Yet, I feel,   10
If someone said on Christmas Eve,
    "Come; see the oxen kneel

"In the lonely barton° by yonder coomb°   *farm; valley*
    Our childhood used to know,"
I should go with him in the gloom,   15
    Hoping it might be so.

Thomas Hardy (1840–1928)

QUESTIONS

1. Is the simple superstition referred to in this poem opposed to, or identified with, religious faith? With what implications for the meaning of the poem?
2. What are "these years" (10), and how do they contrast with the years of the poet's boyhood? What event in intellectual history between 1840 and 1915 (the date Hardy composed this poem) was most responsible for the change?
3. Both "Crossing the Bar" and "The Oxen" in their last lines use a form of the verb *hope*. By fully discussing tone, establish the precise meaning of hope in each poem. What degree of expectation does it imply? How should the word be handled in reading Tennyson's poem aloud?

One dignity delays for all

One dignity delays for all—
One mitred Afternoon—
None can avoid this purple—
None evade this Crown!

Coach, it insures, and footmen—   5
Chamber, and state, and throng—
Bells, also, in the village
As we ride grand along!

What dignified Attendants!
What service when we pause!   10
How loyally at parting
Their hundred hats they raise!

How pomp surpassing ermine
When simple You, and I,
Present our meek escutcheon   15
And claim the rank to die!

Emily Dickinson (1830–1886)

QUESTIONS

1. Vocabulary: *mitred* (2), *state* (6), *escutcheon* (15).
2. What is the "dignity" that delays for all? What is its nature? What is being described in stanzas 2 and 3?
3. What figures of speech are combined in "our meek escutcheon" (15)? What does it represent metaphorically?

'Twas warm—at first—like Us

'Twas warm—at first—like Us—
Until there crept upon
A Chill—like frost upon a Glass—
Till all the scene—be gone.

The Forehead copied Stone—   5
The Fingers grew too cold
To ache—and like a Skater's Brook—
The busy eyes—congealed—

It straightened—that was all—
It crowded Cold to Cold—   10
It multiplied indifference—
As Pride were all it could—

And even when with Cords—
'Twas lowered, like a Weight—
It made no Signal, nor demurred,   15
But dropped like Adamant.

Emily Dickinson (1830–1886)

QUESTIONS

1. Vocabulary: *Adamant* (16).
2. What is "It" in the opening line? What is being described in the poem and between which points in time?
3. How would you describe the tone of this poem? How does it contrast with that of the preceding poem?

The Apparition

When by thy scorn, O murderess, I am dead,
        And that thou thinkst thee free
From all solicitation from me,
Then shall my ghost come to thy bed,
And thee, feigned vestal, in worse arms shall see;   5
Then thy sick taper° will begin to wink,   candle
And he, whose thou art then, being tired before,
Will, if thou stir, or pinch to wake him, think
        Thou call'st for more,

And in false sleep will from thee shrink.   10
And then, poor aspen wretch, neglected, thou,
Bathed in a cold quicksilver sweat, wilt lie
    A verier° ghost than I.   truer
What I will say, I will not tell thee now,
Lest that preserve thee; and since my love is spent,   15
I had rather thou shouldst painfully repent,
Than by my threatenings rest still innocent.

John Donne (1572–1631)

QUESTIONS

1. Vocabulary: *feigned* (5), *aspen* (11), *quicksilver* (12). Are the latter two words
   used literally or figuratively? Explain.
2. What has been the past relationship between the speaker and the woman
   addressed? How does a "solicitation" (3) differ from a proposal?
3. In line 15 the speaker proclaims that his love for the woman "is spent."
   Does the tone of the poem support this contention? Discuss.
4. In line 5 why does the speaker use the word "vestal" instead of *virgin*? Does
   he believe her not to be a virgin? Of what is he accusing her? (In ancient
   Rome the vestal virgins tended the perpetual fire in the temple of Vesta.
   They entered this service between the ages of six and ten, and served for a
   term of thirty years, during which they were bound to virginity.)
5. The implied metaphor in line 1—that a woman who will not satisfy her
   lover's desires is "killing" him—was a cliché of Renaissance poetry. What
   original twist does Donne give it to make it fresh and new?
6. In the scene imagined by the speaker of his ghost's visit to the woman's bed,
   he finds her "in worse arms" (5)—worse than whose? In what respect? By
   what will this other man have been "tired before" (7)? Of what will he
   think she is calling "for more" (9)? What is the speaker implying about himself and the woman in these lines?
7. What will the ghost say to her that he will not now reveal lest his telling it
   "preserve" (15) her? Can we know? Does *he* know? Why does he make this
   undefined threat?
8. For what does the speaker say he wants the woman to "painfully repent"
   (16)? Of what crime or sin would she remain "innocent" (17) if he revealed
   now what his ghost would say? What is the speaker's real objective?

The Flea

Mark but this flea, and mark in this
How little that which thou deny'st me is;
It sucked me first, and now sucks thee,
And in this flea our two bloods mingled be;

Thou know'st that this cannot be said   5
A sin, nor shame, nor loss of maidenhead;
   Yet this enjoys before it woo,
   And pampered swells with one blood made of two,
   And this, alas, is more than we would do.

Oh stay, three lives in one flea spare,   10
Where we almost, yea more than married are.
This flea is you and I, and this
Our marriage bed and marriage temple is;
Though parents grudge, and you, we are met
And cloistered in these living walls of jet.   15
   Though use° make you apt to kill me,   habit
   Let not to that, self-murder added be,
   And sacrilege, three sins in killing three.

Cruel and sudden, hast thou since
Purpled° thy nail in blood of innocence?   crimsoned   20
Wherein could this flea guilty be,
Except in that drop which it sucked from thee?
Yet thou triumph'st and say'st that thou
Find'st not thyself, nor me, the weaker now.
   'Tis true. Then learn how false fears be: 25
   Just so much honor, when thou yield'st to me,
   Will waste, as this flea's death took life from thee.

John Donne (1572–1631)

QUESTIONS

1. In many respects this poem is like a miniature play: it has two characters, dramatic conflict, dialogue (though we hear only one speaker), and stage action. The action is indicated by stage directions embodied in the dialogue. What has happened just *preceding* the first line of the poem? What happens *between* the first and second stanzas? What happens *between* the second and third? How does the female character behave and what does she say *during* the third stanza?

2. What has been the past relationship of the speaker and the woman? What has she denied him (2)? How has she habitually "kill[ed]" him (16)? Why has she done so? How does it happen that he is still alive? What is his objective in the poem?

3. According to a traditional Renaissance belief, the blood of lovers "mingled" during sexual intercourse. What is the speaker's argument in stanza 1? Reduce it to paraphrase. How logical is it?

4. What do "parents grudge, and you" in stanza 2? What are the "living walls of jet" (15)? What three things will the woman kill by crushing the flea? What three sins will she commit (18)?
5. Why and how does the woman "triumph" in stanza 3? What is the speaker's response? How logical is his concluding argument?
6. What action, if any, would you infer follows the conclusion of the poem?
7. "The Apparition" and "The Flea" may both be classified as "seduction poems." How do they differ in tone?

Dover Beach

The sea is calm tonight,
The tide is full, the moon lies fair
Upon the straits;—on the French coast the light
Gleams and is gone; the cliffs of England stand,
Glimmering and vast, out in the tranquil bay.   5
Come to the window, sweet is the night-air!
Only, from the long line of spray
Where the sea meets the moon-blanched land,
Listen! you hear the grating roar
Of pebbles which the waves draw back, and fling,   10
At their return, up the high strand,
Begin, and cease, and then again begin,
With tremulous cadence slow, and bring
The eternal note of sadness in.

Sophocles long ago   15
Heard it on the Aegean, and it brought
Into his mind the turbid ebb and flow
Of human misery; we
Find also in the sound a thought,
Hearing it by this distant northern sea.   20

The Sea of Faith
Was once, too, at the full, and round earth's shore
Lay like the folds of a bright girdle furled.
But now I only hear
Its melancholy, long, withdrawing roar,   25
Retreating, to the breath
Of the night-wind, down the vast edges drear
And naked shingles° of the world.   pebbled beaches

Ah, love, let us be true
To one another! for the world, which seems 30
To lie before us like a land of dreams,
So various, so beautiful, so new,
Hath really neither joy, nor love, nor light,
Nor certitude, nor peace, nor help for pain;
And we are here as on a darkling plain 35
Swept with confused alarms of struggle and flight,
Where ignorant armies clash by night.

Matthew Arnold (1822–1888)

QUESTIONS

1. Vocabulary: *strand* (11), *girdle* (23), *darkling* (35). Identify the physical locale of the cliffs of Dover and their relation to the French coast; identify
   Sophocles and the Aegean.
2. As precisely as possible, define the implied scene: What is the speaker's
   physical location? Whom is he addressing? What is the time of day and the
   state of the weather?
3. Discuss the visual and auditory images of the poem and their relation to illusion and reality.
4. The speaker is lamenting the decline of religious faith in his time. Is he
   himself a believer? Does he see any medicine for the world's maladies?
5. Discuss in detail the imagery in the last three lines. Are the "armies" figurative or literal? What makes these lines so effective?
6. What term or terms would you choose to describe the overall tone of the
   poem?

Church Going

Once I am sure there's nothing going on
I step inside, letting the door thud shut.
Another church: matting, seats, and stone,
And little books; sprawlings of flowers, cut
For Sunday, brownish now; some brass and stuff 5
Up at the holy end; the small neat organ;
And a tense, musty, unignorable silence,
Brewed God knows how long. Hatless, I take off
My cycle-clips in awkward reverence,

Move forward, run my hand around the font. 10
From where I stand, the roof looks almost new—

Cleaned, or restored? Someone would know: I don't.
Mounting the lectern, I peruse a few
Hectoring large-scale verses, and pronounce
"Here endeth" much more loudly than I'd meant.   15
The echoes snigger briefly. Back at the door
I sign the book, donate an Irish sixpence,
Reflect the place was not worth stopping for.

Yet stop I did: in fact I often do,
And always end much at a loss like this,   20
Wondering what to look for, wondering, too,
When churches fall completely out of use
What we shall turn them into, if we shall keep
A few cathedrals chronically on show,
Their parchment, plate and pyx in locked cases,   25
And let the rest rent-free to rain and sheep.
Shall we avoid them as unlucky places?

Or, after dark, will dubious women come
To make their children touch a particular stone;
Pick simples for a cancer; or on some   30
Advised night see walking a dead one?
Power of some sort or other will go on
In games, in riddles, seemingly at random;
But superstition, like belief, must die,
And what remains when disbelief has gone?   35
Grass, weedy pavement, brambles, buttress, sky,

A shape less recognizable each week,
A purpose more obscure. I wonder who
Will be the last, the very last, to seek
This place for what it was; one of the crew   40
That tap and jot and know what rood-lofts were?
Some ruin-bibber, randy for antique,
Or Christmas-addict, counting on a whiff
Of gown-and-bands and organ-pipes and myrrh?
Or will he be my representative,   45

Bored, uninformed, knowing the ghostly silt
Dispersed, yet tending to this cross of ground
Through suburb scrub because it held unspilt
So long and equably what since is found
Only in separation—marriage, and birth,   50

And death, and thoughts of these—for whom was built
This special shell? For though I've no idea
What this accoutered frowsty barn is worth,
It pleases me to stand in silence here;

A serious house on serious earth it is,   55
In whose blent air all our compulsions meet,
Are recognized, and robed as destinies.
And that much never can be obsolete,
Since someone will forever be surprising
A hunger in himself to be more serious,   60
And gravitating with it to this ground,
Which, he once heard, was proper to grow wise in,
If only that so many dead lie round.

Philip Larkin (1922–1985)

QUESTIONS

1. Vocabulary: *Hectoring* (14), *pyx* (25), *dubious* (28), *simples* (30), *accoutered* (53), *frowsty* (53), *blent* (56). *Large-scale* (14) indicates a print size suited to oral reading; an *Irish sixpence* (17) was a small coin not legal tender in England, the scene of the poem; *rood-lofts* (41) are architectural features found in many early Christian churches; *bibber* and *randy* (42) are figurative, literally meaning "drunkard" and "lustful"; *gown-and-bands* (44) are ornate robes worn by church officials in religious ceremonies.
2. Like "Dover Beach" (first published in 1867), "Church Going" (1954) is concerned with belief and disbelief. In modern England the landscape is dotted with small churches, often charming in their combination of stone (outside) and intricately carved wood (inside). Some are in ruins, some are badly in need of repair, and some are well tended by parishioners who keep them dusted and provide fresh flowers for the diminishing attendance at Sunday services. These churches invariably have by the entrance a book that visitors can sign as a record of their having been there and a collection box with a sign urging them to drop in a few coins for upkeep, repair, or restoration. In small towns and villages the church is often the chief or only building of architectural or historical interest, and tourist visitors may outnumber parishioners. To which of the three categories of churches mentioned here does Larkin's poem refer?
3. What different denotations does the title contain?
4. In what activity has the speaker been engaging when he stops to see the church? How is it revealed? Why does he stop? Is he a believer? How involved is he in inspecting this church building?
5. Compare the language used by the speakers in "Dover Beach" and "Church Going." Which speaker is more eloquent? Which is more informal and conversational? Without looking back at the texts, try to assign the following

words to one poem or the other: *moon-blanched, cycle-clips, darkling, hath, snigger, whiff, drear, brownish, tremulous, glimmering, frowsty, stuff.* Then go back and check your success.

6. Define the tone of "Church Going" as precisely as possible. Compare this tone with that of "Dover Beach."

Ending

The love we thought would never stop
now cools like a congealing chop.
The kisses that were hot as curry
are bird-pecks taken in a hurry.
The hands that held electric charges   5
now lie inert as four moored barges.
The feet that ran to meet a date
are running slow and running late.
The eyes that shone and seldom shut
are victims of a power cut.   10
The parts that then transmitted joy
are now reserved and cold and coy.
Romance, expected once to stay,
has left a note saying GONE AWAY.

Gavin Ewart (1916–1995)

QUESTIONS

1. Love poetry is often characterized by a heavy reliance on figurative language. Examine this poem for examples of simile, metaphor, metonymy, overstatement, paradox, and personification (almost every line contains an example).
2. The tone established in each of the odd-numbered lines is ironically deflated by its rhyming line. What, finally, is the tone of the poem?

Love

There's the wonderful love of a beautiful maid,
And the love of a staunch true man,
And the love of a baby that's unafraid—
All have existed since time began.
But the most wonderful love, the Love of all loves,   5
Even greater than the love for Mother,
Is the infinite, tenderest, passionate love
Of one dead drunk for another.

Anonymous

QUESTIONS

1. Where does the tone shift and how does that shift make the poem successful?
2. What characteristics of the diction create the tonal shift?
3. What is the ironic target of this poem?

SUGGESTIONS FOR WRITING

1. Marvell's "To His Coy Mistress" (page 730), Herrick's "To the Virgins, to Make Much of Time" (page 742), and Housman's "Loveliest of Trees" (page 792) all treat a traditional poetic theme known as **carpe diem** ("seize the day"). They differ sharply in tone. Pointing out the differences in poetic technique among them, characterize the tone of each.
2. Describe and account for the differences in tone between the following pairs:
   a. Hayden, "The Whipping" (page 656) and Randall, "Ballad of Birmingham" (page 658).
   b. Komunyakaa, "Facing It" (page 681) and Cross, "Rice Will Grow Again" (page 953).
   c. Rich, "Living in Sin" (page 706) and Gwynn, "Snow White and the Seven Deadly Sins" (page 965).
   d. Hardy, "The Ruined Maid" (page 896) and Brooks, "Sadie and Maud" (page 948).
   e. Frost, "Nothing Gold Can Stay" (page 837) and Frost, "Never Again Would Birds' Song Be the Same" (page 965).
   f. Blake, "The Lamb" (page 946) and Blake, "The Tiger" (page 947).

Chapter Eleven

Musical Devices

Poetry obviously makes a greater use of the "music" of language than does language that is not poetry. The poet, unlike the person who uses language to convey only information, chooses words for sound as well as for meaning, and uses the sound as a means of reinforcing meaning. So prominent is this musical quality of poetry that some writers have made it the distinguishing term in their definitions of poetry. Edgar Allan Poe, for instance, describes poetry as "music . . . combined with a pleasurable idea." Whether or not it deserves this much importance, verbal music, like connotation, imagery, and figurative language, is one of the important resources that enable the poet to do more than communicate mere information. The poet may indeed sometimes pursue verbal music for its own sake; more often, at least in first-rate poetry, it is an adjunct to the total meaning or communication of the poem.

The poet achieves musical quality in two broad ways: by the choice and arrangement of sounds and by the arrangement of accents. In this chapter we will consider the first of these.

An essential element in all music is repetition. In fact, we might say that all art consists of giving structure to two elements: repetition and variation. All things we enjoy greatly and lastingly have these two elements. We enjoy the sea endlessly because it is always the same yet always different. We enjoy a baseball game because it contains the same complex combination of pattern and variation. Our love of art, then, is rooted in human psychology. We like the familiar, we like variety, but we like them combined. If we get too much sameness, the result is monotony and tedium; if we get too much variety, the result is bewilderment and confusion. The composer of music, therefore, repeats certain musical tones; repeats them in certain combinations, or chords; and repeats them in certain patterns, or melodies. The poet likewise repeats certain sounds in certain combinations and arrangements, and thus adds musical meaning to verse. Consider the following short example.

The Turtle

> The turtle lives 'twixt plated decks
> Which practically conceal its sex.
> I think it clever of the turtle
> In such a fix to be so fertile.

Ogden Nash (1902–1971)

Here is a little joke, a paradox of animal life to which the author has cleverly drawn our attention. An experiment will show us, however, that much of its appeal lies not so much in what it says as in the manner in which it says it. If, for instance, we recast the verse as prose: "The turtle lives in a shell that almost conceals its sex. It is ingenious of the turtle, in such a situation, to be so prolific," the joke falls flat. Some of its appeal must lie in its metrical form. So now we cast it in unrhymed verse:

> Because he lives between two decks,
> It's hard to tell a turtle's gender.
> The turtle is a clever beast
> In such a plight to be so fertile.

Here, perhaps, is *some* improvement over the prose version, but still the piquancy of the original is missing. Much of that appeal must have consisted in the use of rhyme—the repetition of sound in "decks" and "sex," "turtle" and "fertile." So we try once more.

> The turtle lives 'twixt plated decks
> Which practically conceal its sex.
> I think it clever of the turtle
> In such a plight to be so fertile.

But for perceptive readers there is still something missing—they may not at first see what—but some little touch that makes the difference between a good piece of verse and a little masterpiece of its kind. And then they see it: "plight" has been substituted for "fix."

But why should "fix" make such a difference? Its meaning is little different from that of "plight"; its only important difference is in sound. But there we are. The final *x* in "fix" catches up the concluding consonant sound in "sex," and its initial *f* is repeated in the initial consonant sound of "fertile." Not only do these sound recurrences provide a subtle gratification to the ear, but they also give the verse structure; they emphasize and draw together the key words of the piece: "sex," "fix," and "fertile."

Poets may repeat any unit of sound from the smallest to the largest. They may repeat individual vowel and consonant sounds, whole syllables, words, phrases, lines, or groups of lines. In each instance, in a good poem, the repetition will serve several purposes: it will please the ear, it will emphasize the words in which the repetition occurs, and it will give structure to the poem. The popularity and initial impressiveness of such repetitions are evidenced by their becoming in many instances embedded in the language as clichés like "wild and woolly," "first and foremost," "footloose and fancy-free," "penny-wise, pound-foolish," "dead as a doornail," "might and main," "sink or swim," "do or die," "pell-mell," "helter-skelter," "harum-scarum," "hocus-pocus." Some of these kinds of repetition have names, as we will see.

A syllable consists of a vowel sound that may be preceded or followed by consonant sounds. Any of these sounds may be repeated. The repetition of initial consonant sounds, as in "tried and true," "safe and sound," "fish or fowl," "rhyme or reason," is **alliteration**. The repetition of vowel sounds, as in "mad as a hatter," "time out of mind," "free and easy," "slapdash," is **assonance**. The repetition of final consonant sounds, as in "first and last," "odds and ends," "short and sweet," "a stroke of luck," or Shakespeare's "struts and frets" (page 780) is **consonance.***

Repetitions may be used alone or in combination. Alliteration and assonance are combined in such phrases as "time and tide," "thick and thin," "kith and kin," "alas and alack," "fit as a fiddle," and Edgar Allan Poe's famous line, "The viol, the violet, and the vine." Alliteration and consonance are combined in such phrases as "crisscross," "last but not least," "lone and lorn," "good as gold," Housman's "malt does more than Milton can" (page 662), and Kay's "meanings lost in manners" (page 690).

Rhyme is the repetition of the accented vowel sound and any succeeding consonant sounds. It is called **masculine** when the rhyme sounds involve only one syllable, as in *decks* and *sex* or *support* and *re-*

---

*Different writers have defined these repetitions in various ways. *Alliteration* is used by some writers to mean any repetition of consonant sounds. *Assonance* has been used to mean the similarity as well as the identity of vowel sounds, or even the similarity of any sounds whatever. *Consonance* has often been reserved for words in which both the initial *and* final consonant sounds correspond, as in *green* and *groan*, *moon* and *mine*. *Rhyme* has been used to mean any sound repetition, including alliteration, assonance, and consonance. In the absence of clear agreement on the meanings of these terms, the terminology chosen here has appeared most useful, with support in usage. Labels are useful in analysis. However, the student should learn to recognize the devices and, more important, should learn to see their function, without worrying too much over nomenclature.

tort. It is **feminine** when the rhyme sounds involve two or more sylla-bles, as in *turtle* and *fertile* or *spitefully* and *delightfully.* It is referred to as **internal rhyme** when one or more rhyming words are *within* the line and as **end rhyme** when the rhyming words are at the *ends* of lines. End rhyme is probably the most frequently used and most consciously sought sound repetition in English poetry. Because it comes at the end of the line, it receives emphasis as a musical effect and perhaps con-tributes more than any other musical resource except rhythm to give poetry its musical effect as well as its structure. There exists, however, a large body of poetry that does not employ rhyme and for which rhyme would not be appropriate. Also, there has always been a tendency, es-pecially noticeable in modern poetry, to substitute approximate rhymes for perfect rhymes at the ends of lines. **Approximate rhymes** (also called slant rhymes) include words with any kind of sound similarity, from close to fairly remote. Under approximate rhyme we include allit-eration, assonance, and consonance or their combinations when used at the end of the line; half-rhyme (feminine rhymes in which only half of the word rhymes—the accented half, as in *lightly* and *frightful,* or the unaccented half, as in *yellow* and *willow*; and other similarities too elu-sive to name. "'Twas warm—at first—like Us" (page 813), "Toads" (page 727), and "Mr. Z" (page 774), to different degrees, all employ var-ious kinds of approximate end rhyme.

That night when joy began

That night when joy began
Our narrowest veins to flush,
We waited for the flash
Of morning's leveled gun.

But morning let us pass,   5
And day by day relief
Outgrows his nervous laugh,
Grown credulous of peace,

As mile by mile is seen
No trespasser's reproach,   10
And love's best glasses reach
No fields but are his own.

W. H. Auden (1907–1973)

QUESTIONS

1. What has been the past experience with love of the two people in the poem? What is their present experience? What precisely is the tone of the poem?
2. What basic metaphor underlies the poem? Work it out stanza by stanza. What is "the flash / Of morning's leveled gun" (3–4)? Does line 10 mean that no trespasser reproaches the lovers or that no one reproaches the lovers for being trespassers? Does "glasses" (11) refer to spectacles, tumblers, mirrors, or field glasses? Point out three personifications.
3. The rhyme pattern in the poem is intricate and exact. Work it out, considering alliteration, assonance, and consonance.

In addition to the repetition of individual sounds and syllables, the poet may repeat whole words, phrases, lines, or groups of lines. When such repetition is done according to some fixed pattern, it is called a **refrain.** The refrain is especially common in songlike poetry. Shakespeare's "Winter" (page 650) furnishes an example of a refrain.

The Waking

I wake to sleep, and take my waking slow.
I feel my fate in what I cannot fear.
I learn by going where I have to go.

We think by feeling. What is there to know?
I hear my being dance from ear to ear.   5
I wake to sleep, and take my waking slow.

Of those so close beside me, which are you?
God bless the Ground! I shall walk softly there,
And learn by going where I have to go.

Light takes the Tree; but who can tell us how?   10
The lowly worm climbs up a winding stair;
I wake to sleep, and take my waking slow.

Great Nature has another thing to do
To you and me; so take the lively air,
And, lovely, learn by going where to go.   15

This shaking keeps me steady. I should know.
What falls away is always. And is near.

I wake to sleep, and take my waking slow.
I learn by going where I have to go.

Theodore Roethke (1908–1963)

QUESTIONS

1. The refrains in lines 1 and 3 occur at patterned intervals in this example of the form called "villanelle" (see page 888 for a definition of the form). Even without the definition, you can work out the repetitive pattern—but the key question is, what do these two lines *mean*, as statements both within the first stanza and in each subsequent repetition? Starting with line 1, for what is "sleep" a common metaphor? What would be the meaning if the first phrase were "I was born to die"?

2. Paraphrase the third line, in light of the idea that the first line presents an attitude toward the fact that all living things must die. Where does the speaker "have to go" ultimately? What is the process of his present "going"?

3. Explain the clear-cut attitude toward emotive experience versus intellectual knowledge expressed in line 4. How is that attitude a basis for the ideas in the refrain lines? How does it support line 10?

4. What is it that "Great Nature has . . . to do" (13) to people? How should they live their lives, according to the speaker?

5. Explain the paradox that "shaking keeps [the speaker] steady" (16). Consider the possibility that the speaker is personifying "the Tree" (10) as himself—what then is "fall[ing] away," and how near is it (17)?

6. Is the tone of this poem melancholy? resigned? joyous? Explain.

We have not nearly exhausted the possibilities of sound repetition by giving names to a few of the more prominent kinds. The complete study of possible kinds of sound repetition in poetry would be so complex, however, that it would exceed the scope of this introductory text.

Some of the subtlest and loveliest effects escape our net of names. In as short a phrase as this from the prose of John Ruskin—"ivy as light and lovely as the vine"—we notice alliteration in *light* and *lovely*, assonance in *ivy*, *light*, and *vine*, and consonance in *ivy* and *lovely*, but we have no name to connect the *v* in *vine* with the *v*s in *ivy* and *lovely*, or the second *l* in *lovely* with the first *l*, or the final syllables of *ivy* and *lovely* with each other; yet these are all an effective part of the music of the line. Also contributing to the music of poetry is the linking of related rather than identical sounds, such as *m* and *n*, or *p* and *b*, or the vowel sounds in *boat*, *boot*, and *book*.

These various musical repetitions, for trained readers, will ordinarily make an almost subconscious contribution to their reading of the poem: readers will feel their effect without necessarily being aware of what has caused it. There is value, however, in occasionally analyzing a poem for these devices in order to increase awareness of them. A few words of caution are necessary. First, the repetitions are entirely a matter of sound; spelling is irrelevant. *Bear* and *pair* are rhymes, but *through* and *rough* are not. *Cell* and *sin*, *folly* and *philosophy* alliterate, but *sin* and *sugar*, *gun* and *gem* do not. Second, alliteration, assonance, consonance, and masculine rhyme are matters that ordinarily involve only stressed or accented syllables; for only such syllables ordinarily make enough impression on the ear to be significant in the sound pattern of the poem. For instance, we should hardly consider *which* and *its* in the second line of "The Turtle" an example of assonance, for neither word is stressed enough in the reading to make it significant as a sound. Third, the words involved in these repetitions must be close enough together that the ear retains the sound, consciously or subconsciously, from its first occurrence to its second. This distance varies according to circumstances, but for alliteration, assonance, and consonance the words ordinarily have to be in the same line or adjacent lines. End rhyme bridges a longer gap.

God's Grandeur

The world is charged with the grandeur of God.
    It will flame out, like shining from shook foil;
    It gathers to a greatness, like the ooze of oil
Crushed. Why do men then now not reck his rod?
Generations have trod, have trod, have trod;   5
    And all is seared with trade; bleared, smeared with toil;
    And wears man's smudge and shares man's smell: the soil
Is bare now, nor can foot feel, being shod.

And for all this, nature is never spent;
    There lives the dearest freshness deep down things;   10
And though the last lights off the black West went
    Oh, morning, at the brown brink eastward, springs—
Because the Holy Ghost over the bent
    World broods with warm breast and with ah! bright wings.

Gerard Manley Hopkins (1844–1889)

QUESTIONS

1. What is the theme of this sonnet?
2. The image in lines 3–4 possibly refers to olive oil being collected in great vats from crushed olives, but the image is much disputed. Explain the simile in line 2 and the symbols in lines 7–8 and 11–12.
3. Explain "reck his rod" (4), "spent" (9), "bent" (13).
4. Using different-colored pencils, encircle and connect examples of alliteration, assonance, consonance, and internal rhyme. Do these help to carry the meaning?

We should not leave the impression that the use of these musical devices is necessarily or always valuable. Like the other resources of poetry, they can be judged only in the light of the poem's total intention. Many of the greatest works of English poetry—for instance, *Hamlet* and *King Lear* and *Paradise Lost*—do not employ end rhyme. Both alliteration and rhyme, especially feminine rhyme, become humorous or silly if used excessively or unskillfully. If the intention is humorous, the result is delightful; if not, fatal. Shakespeare, who knew how to use all these devices to the utmost advantage, parodied their unskillful use in lines like "The preyful princess pierced and pricked a pretty pleasing prickett" in *Love's Labor's Lost* and

> Whereat with blade, with bloody, blameful blade,
> He bravely broached his boiling bloody breast

in *A Midsummer Night's Dream*. Swinburne parodied his own highly alliterative style in "Nephelidia" with lines like "Life is the lust of a lamp for the light that is dark till the dawn of the day when we die." Used skillfully and judiciously, however, musical devices provide a palpable and delicate pleasure to the ear and, even more important, add dimension to meaning.

EXERCISE

Discuss the various ways in which the following poems make use of refrain.
1. Shakespeare, "Winter" (page 650).
2. Shakespeare, "Blow, blow, thou winter wind" (page 830).
3. cummings, "in Just—" (page 782).
4. Donne, "A Hymn to God the Father" (page 697).
5. Blake, "The Lamb" (page 946).
6. Crane, "War Is Kind" (page 952).
7. Shakespeare, "Fear no more" (page 1000).
8. Clifton, "good times" (page 950).

REVIEWING CHAPTER ELEVEN

1. Review the terms printed in boldface, and as you read on in this chapter take note of the examples that you find (that is, make a conscious search for the materials that normally would not rise above the subconscious in their effects).
2. Musical devices do not convey meaning but reinforce meanings that are established by the other aspects of language; as you explore these musical devices, identify the ways in which emotional and intellectual meanings are conveyed so as to make it clear what the music is reinforcing and supporting.

Blow, blow, thou winter wind

Blow, blow, thou winter wind.
Thou art not so unkind
   As man's ingratitude.
Thy tooth is not so keen,
Because thou art not seen,   5
   Although thy breath be rude.°   rough
Heigh-ho, sing heigh-ho, unto the green holly.
Most friendship is feigning, most loving mere folly.
   Then heigh-ho, the holly!
     This life is most jolly.   10

Freeze, freeze, thou bitter sky,
That dost not bite so nigh°   near the heart
   As benefits forgot.
Though thou the waters warp,
Thy sting is not so sharp   15
   As friend remembered not.
Heigh-ho, sing heigh-ho, unto the green holly.
Most friendship is feigning, most loving mere folly.
   Then heigh-ho, the holly!
     This life is most jolly.   20

William Shakespeare (1564–1616)

QUESTIONS

1. Vocabulary: *Heigh-ho* (7) is an expression of melancholy or disappointment; *holly* (7) is an emblem of cheerfulness (as at Christmas); *warp* (14) implies freezing into ridges.
2. This song from *As You Like It*, 2.7, contrasts the social and natural worlds and is sung to celebrate living freely in the forest. What essential qualities does it ascribe to the two environments displayed in the behavior of people and the actions of nature? What paradox does the poem create by presenting the expression "heigh-ho" linked with "the holly"? Are we to take "heigh-ho" at its literal meaning?
3. What musical devices help to create the songlike quality of this poem?

We Real Cool

The Pool Players.
Seven At The Golden Shovel.

We real cool. We
Left school. We

Lurk late. We
Strike straight. We

Sing sin. We   5
Thin gin. We

Jazz June. We
Die soon.

Gwendolyn Brooks (1917–2000)

QUESTIONS

1. In addition to end rhyme, what other musical devices does this poem employ?
2. Try reading this poem with the pronouns at the beginning of the lines instead of at the end. What is lost?
3. English teachers in a certain urban school were once criticized for having their students read this poem: it was said to be immoral. What essential poetic device did the critics misunderstand?

Woman Work

I've got the children to tend
The clothes to mend
The floor to mop
The food to shop
Then the chicken to fry   5
The baby to dry
I got company to feed
The garden to weed
I've got the shirts to press
The tots to dress   10
The cane to be cut
I gotta clean up this hut
Then see about the sick
And the cotton to pick.

Shine on me, sunshine   15
Rain on me, rain
Fall softly, dewdrops
And cool my brow again.

Storm, blow me from here
With your fiercest wind   20
Let me float across the sky
'Til I can rest again.

Fall gently, snowflakes
Cover me with white
Cold icy kisses and   25
Let me rest tonight.

Sun, rain, curving sky
Mountain, oceans, leaf and stone
Star shine, moon glow
You're all that I can call my own.   30

Maya Angelou (b. 1928)

QUESTIONS

1. What is the pattern of rhymes in lines 1–14? What does it shift to in lines
   15–30? Whom is the speaker addressing in the first 14 lines? What figurative address characterizes the rest of the poem?

2. The phrases "I've got . . . gotta" (1–12) produce a type of refrain called **anaphora,** the repetition of an opening word or phrase in a series of lines. What feeling is expressed by this repetition here? How do the varying forms of the phrase characterize the speaker?
3. Most of the chores in the first 14 lines are associated popularly with "woman['s] work," but two are not. What do these exceptions reveal about the situation of the speaker?
4. What kinds of release from "work" are presented in lines 15–30? Metaphorically, what does the speaker desire in lines 19–26?
5. Explain the statement in the last four lines.

Rite of Passage

As the guests arrive at my son's party
they gather in the living room—
short men, men in first grade
with smooth jaws and chins.
Hands in pockets, they stand around   5
jostling, jockeying for place, small fights
breaking out and calming. One says to another
How old are you? Six. I'm seven. So?
They eye each other, seeing themselves
tiny in the other's pupils. They clear their   10
throats a lot, a room of small bankers,
they fold their arms and frown. *I could beat you
up,* a seven says to a six,
the dark cake, round and heavy as a
turret, behind them on the table. My son,   15
freckles like specks of nutmeg on his cheeks,
chest narrow as the balsa keel of a
model boat, long hands
cool and thin as the day they guided him
out of me, speaks up as a host   20
for the sake of the group.
We could easily kill a two-year-old,
he says in his clear voice. The other
men agree, they clear their throats
like Generals, they relax and get down to   25
playing war, celebrating my son's life.

Sharon Olds (b. 1942)

QUESTIONS

1. Vocabulary: *Rite of Passage* (title).

2. What is the implication of the metaphor comparing the boys to "bankers" (11) clearing their throats? of that comparing them to "Generals" (25) doing the same thing? Is there a "rite of passage" implied in the shift from one comparison to the other?
3. What tones of voice would be appropriate for the phrase *"I'm seven"* and the reply *"So?"* (8)? Explain the image in the next sentence.
4. How are the similes in lines 14–15 and 16–17 linked? How do they function in the progress from bankers to Generals?
5. What is the speaker's tone as she describes the children's violent impulses?
6. The poem displays a considerable amount of musicality—alliteration, assonance, and consonance—through line 21. Identify these devices, and discuss the implication of their absence in the remainder of the poem.

As imperceptibly as Grief

As imperceptibly as Grief
The Summer lapsed away—
Too imperceptible at last
To seem like Perfidy—
A Quietness distilled   5
As Twilight long begun,
Or Nature spending with herself
Sequestered Afternoon—
The Dusk drew earlier in—
The Morning foreign shone—   10
A courteous, yet harrowing Grace,
As Guest, that would be gone—
And thus, without a Wing
Or service of a Keel
Our Summer made her light escape   15
Into the Beautiful.

Emily Dickinson (1830–1886)

QUESTIONS

1. What are the subject and tone of the poem? Explain its opening simile.
2. Discuss the ways in which approximate rhymes, alliteration, and the consonant sounds in the last four lines contribute to the meaning and tone.
3. What possible meanings have the last two lines?

Traveling through the dark

Traveling through the dark I found a deer
dead on the edge of the Wilson River road.
It is usually best to roll them into the canyon:
that road is narrow; to swerve might make more dead.

By glow of the tail-light I stumbled back of the car   5
and stood by the heap, a doe, a recent killing;
she had stiffened already, almost cold.
I dragged her off; she was large in the belly.

My fingers touching her side brought me the reason —
her side was warm; her fawn lay there waiting,   10
alive, still, never to be born.
Beside that mountain road I hesitated.

The car aimed ahead its lowered parking lights;
under the hood purred the steady engine.
I stood in the glare of the warm exhaust turning red;   15
around our group I could hear the wilderness listen.

I thought hard for us all — my only swerving —,
then pushed her over the edge into the river.

William Stafford (1914–1993)

QUESTIONS

1. State precisely the speaker's dilemma. What kind of person is he? Does he make the right decision? Why does he call his hesitation "my only swerving" (17), and how does this connect with the word "swerve" in line 4?
2. What different kinds of imagery and of image contrasts give life to the poem? Do any of the images have symbolic overtones?
3. At first glance this poem may appear to be without end rhyme. Looking closer, do you find any correspondences between lines 2 and 4 in each four-line stanza? between lines 1 and 3 of stanzas 2 and 3? between the final words of the concluding couplet? What one line end in the poem has no connection in sound to another line end in its stanza?

In Those Years

In those years, people will say, we lost track
of the meaning of *we*, of *you*
we found ourselves
reduced to *I*
and the whole thing became   5
silly, ironic, terrible:
we were trying to live a personal life
and, yes, that was the only life
we could bear witness to

But the great dark birds of history screamed and plunged   10
into our personal weather
They were headed somewhere else but their beaks
        and pinions drove
along the shore, through the rags of fog
where we stood, saying *I*

Adrienne Rich (b. 1929)

1973

"I'm pregnant," I wrote to her in delight
from London, thirty, married, in print. A foolscap sheet scrawled slantwise with one minuscule
sentence came back. "I hope your child is white."
I couldn't tear the pieces small enough.   5
I hoped she'd be black as the ace of spades,
though hybrid beige heredity had made
that as unlikely as the spun-gold stuff
sprouted after her neonatal fur.
I grudgingly acknowledged her "good hair,"   10
which wasn't, very, from my point of view.
"No tar brush left," her father's mother said.
"She's Jewish and she's white," from her cranked bed
mine smugly snapped.
                    She's Black. She is a Jew.

Marilyn Hacker (b. 1942)

QUESTIONS

1. Vocabulary: *foolscap* (2–3), *hybrid* (7), *neonatal* (9).

2. What is the family situation this poem describes? What is the speaker's emotional reaction to her situation?
3. In what fixed form is the poem written? How does the form help to contain and clarify the poem's emotional content?
4. Why is it important for the speaker to racially define her baby, as she does in the last line?

Nothing Gold Can Stay

Nature's first green is gold,
Her hardest hue to hold.
Her early leaf's a flower;
But only so an hour.
Then leaf subsides to leaf.   5
So Eden sank to grief,
So dawn goes down to day.
Nothing gold can stay.

Robert Frost (1874–1963)

QUESTIONS

1. Explain the paradoxes in lines 1 and 3.
2. Discuss the poem as a series of symbols. What are the symbolic meanings of "gold" in the final line of the poem?
3. Discuss the contributions of alliteration, assonance, consonance, rhyme, and other repetitions to the effectiveness of the poem.

SUGGESTIONS FOR WRITING

1. Write an essay analyzing the use and effectiveness of alliteration and/or assonance in one of the following:
   a. Shakespeare, "Shall I compare thee to a summer's day?" (page 656).
   b. Dickinson, "There's a certain Slant of light" (page 920).
   c. Donne, "The Good-Morrow" (page 957).
   d. Hardy, "The Darkling Thrush" (page 969).
   e. Shapiro, "The Fly" (page 1001).
2. Discuss the rhymes in one of the following. Does the poem employ exact rhymes or approximate rhymes? How do the kind and pattern of rhyme contribute to the poem's effect?
   a. MacLeish, "Ars Poetica" (page 665).
   b. Robinson, "Eros Turannos" (page 682).
   c. Browning, "My Last Duchess" (page 775).
   d. Dickinson, "A narrow Fellow in the Grass" (page 955).
   e. Plath, "Spinster" (page 987).

Chapter Twelve

Rhythm and Meter

Our love of rhythm is rooted even more deeply in us than our love of musical repetition. It is related to the beat of our hearts, the pulse of our blood, the intake and outflow of air from our lungs. Everything that we do naturally and gracefully we do rhythmically. There is rhythm in the way we walk, the way we swim, the way we ride a horse, the way we swing a golf club or a baseball bat. So native is rhythm to us that we read it, when we can, into the mechanical world around us. Our clocks go tick-tick-tick, but we hear tick-tock, tick-tock. The click of railway wheels beneath us patterns itself into a tune in our heads. There is a strong appeal for us in language that is rhythmic.

The term **rhythm** refers to any wavelike recurrence of motion or sound. In speech it is the natural rise and fall of language. All language is to some degree rhythmic, for all language involves alternations between accented and unaccented syllables. Language varies considerably, however, in the degree to which it exhibits rhythm. Sometimes in speech the rhythm is so unobtrusive or so unpatterned that we are scarcely aware of it. Sometimes, as in rap or in oratory, the rhythm is so pronounced that we may be tempted to tap our feet to it.

In every word of more than one syllable, one or more syllables are **accented** or **stressed**; that is, given more prominence in pronunciation than the rest.* We say toDAY, toMORrow, YESterday, interVENE. These accents within individual words are indicated by stress marks in dictionaries, and with many words of more than two syllables primary and secondary stresses are shown (in′-ter-vene″). When words are arranged into a sentence, we give certain words or syllables more prominence in pronunciation than the rest. We say: "He WENT to the

---

*Though the words *accent* and *stress* generally are used interchangeably, as here, a distinction is sometimes made between them in technical discussions. **Accent,** the relative prominence given a syllable in relation to its neighbors, is then said to result from one or more of four causes: *stress,* or force of utterance, producing loudness; *duration*; *pitch*; and *juncture,* the manner of transition between successive sounds. Of these, *stress,* in verse written in English, is the most important.

STORE" or "ANN is DRIVing her CAR." There is nothing mysterious about this; it is the normal process of language. The major difference between prose and verse is that in prose these accents occur more or less haphazardly; in verse the poet may arrange them to occur at regular intervals.

In poetry as in prose, the rhythmic effects depend almost entirely on what a statement means, and different intended meanings will produce different rhythms even in identical statements. If I say "I don't believe YOU," I mean something different from "*I* don't believe you" or from "I don't beLIEVE you." In speech, these are **rhetorical stresses**, which we use to make our intentions clear. Stressing "I" separates me from others who *do* believe you; stressing "you" separates you from others whom I believe; stressing "believe" intensifies my statement of disbelief. Such rhetorical stressing comes as naturally to us as language itself, and is at least as important in poetry as it is in expressive speaking. It is also basic to understanding the rhythm of poetry, for poetic rhythm depends on the plain, rhetorical stresses to communicate its meaning. We must be able to recognize the meaning of a line of poetry before we can determine its rhythm.

In addition to accent or stress, rhythm is based on pauses. In poetry, as in prose or speech, pauses are the result of natural speech rhythms and the structure of sentences. Periods and commas create pauses, but so does the normal flow of phrases and clauses. Poetry, however, adds another kind of pause arising from the fact that poetry is written in lines. The poetic line is a unit that creates pauses in the flow of speech, sometimes slight and sometimes large. Poets have at their disposal a variety of possibilities when ending a line. An **end-stopped line** is one in which the end of the line corresponds with a natural speech pause; a **run-on line** is one in which the sense of the line moves on without pause into the next line. (There are of course all degrees of end-stop and run-on. A line ending with a period or semicolon is heavily end-stopped. A line without punctuation at the end is normally considered a run-on line, but it is less forcibly run-on if it ends at a natural speech pause—as between subject and predicate—than if it ends, say, between an article and its noun, between an auxiliary and its verb, or between a preposition and its object.) In addition there are pauses that occur within lines, either grammatical or rhetorical. These are called **caesuras**, and they are another resource for varying the rhythm of lines.

The poetic line is the basic rhythmic unit in **free verse**, the predominating type of poetry now being written. Except for its line arrangement there are no necessary differences between the rhythms of free verse and the rhythms of prose, so our awareness of the line as a rhythmic unit is essential. Consider the rhythmic contrast between end-stopped lines and run-on lines in these two excerpts from poems presented earlier, and notice how the caesuras (marked ||) help to vary the rhythms:

> A noiseless patient spider,
> I marked where on a little promontory it stood isolated,
> Marked how to explore the vacant vast surrounding,
> It launched forth filament, || filament, || filament, || out of itself,
> Ever unreeling them, || ever tirelessly speeding them.
>
> (page 736)

> Sorrow is my own yard
> where the new grass
> flames || as it has flamed
> often before || but not
> with the cold fire
> that closes round me this year.
> (page 704)

There is another sort of poetry that depends entirely on ordinary prose rhythms—the **prose poem,** exemplified by Carolyn Forché's "The Colonel" (page 961). Having dispensed even with the line as a unit of rhythm, the prose poem lays its claim to being poetry by its attention to many of the poetic elements presented earlier in this book: connotation, imagery, figurative language, and the concentration of meaning in evocative language.

But most often, when people think of poetry they think of the two broad branches, free verse and metrical verse, which are distinguished mainly by the absence or presence of meter. **Meter** is the identifying characteristic of rhythmic language that we can tap our feet to. When verse is metrical, the accents of language are so arranged as to occur at apparently equal intervals of time, and it is this interval we mark off with the tap of a foot.

The study of meter is fascinating but highly complex. It is by no means an absolute prerequisite to an enjoyment, even a rich enjoyment, of poetry, any more than is the ability to identify by name the multiplicity of figures of speech. But a knowledge of the fundamentals of meter does have value. It can make the beginning reader more aware of the rhythmic effects of poetry and of how poetry should be read. It can enable the more advanced reader to analyze how certain effects are achieved, to see how rhythm interacts with meaning, and to explain what makes one poem (in this respect) better than another. The beginning student ought to have at least an elementary knowledge of the subject. And it is not so difficult as its traditional terminology might suggest.

Even for the beginner, one essential distinction must be understood: although the terms *rhythm* and *meter* are sometimes used interchangeably, they mean different things. Rhythm designates the flow of actual, pronounced sound (or sound heard in the mind's ear), whereas meter refers to the patterns that sounds follow when a poet has arranged them into metrical verse. This may be illustrated by an analogy of a well-designed building and the architect's blueprint for its construction. The building, like rhythmic sound, is actual and real; the blueprint for it is an abstract, idealized pattern, like metrical form. When we look at a building, we see the actuality, but we also recognize that it is based on a pattern. The actuality of the building goes beyond the idealized blueprint in a number of ways—it presents us with texture, with color, with varying effects depending on light and shade, with contrasts of building materials. In poetry, the actuality is language arranged in sentences, with a progression through time, with varying emotions, dramatic contrasts of meaning and tone, the revelation of the speaker's situation, and so forth. All these are expressed through the sounds of language, which are constantly shifting to create meanings and implications.

The word *meter* comes from a word meaning "measure" (the word *rhythm* from a word meaning "flow," as in waves). To measure something we must have a unit of measurement. For measuring length we use the inch, foot, yard; for measuring time we use the second, minute, hour. For measuring verse we use the foot, the line, and (sometimes) the stanza.

One basic unit of meter, the **foot,** consists normally of one accented syllable plus one or two unaccented syllables, though occasionally there may be no unaccented syllables. To determine which syllable in a foot is accented, we compare its sound with that of the other syllables *within the foot*, not with the sounds of syllables in other feet within a line. In fact, because of the varying stresses on syllables in a spoken sentence, it is very unusual for all of the stressed syllables in a line to be equally stressed.

For diagramming the metrical form of verse, various systems of visual symbols have been devised. In this book we shall use a breve (◡) to indicate an unstressed syllable, an ictus (ʹ) to indicate a stressed syllable, and a vertical bar to indicate the division between feet. The basic kinds of feet are as follows:

Examples	Name of Foot	Adjectival Form	
ŭ ′ ŭ ′ to-day, the sun	Iamb	Iambic	⎤ ⎟ Duple meters
′ ŭ ′ ŭ dai-ly, went to	Trochee	Trochaic	⎦
ŭ ŭ ′ ŭ ŭ ′ in-ter-vene, in the dark	Anapest	Anapestic	⎤ ⎟ Triple meters
′ ŭ ŭ ′ ŭ ŭ mul-ti-ple, col-or of	Dactyl	Dactylic	⎦
′ ′ true-blue	Spondee*	Spondaic	

Two kinds of examples are given here, whole words and phrases, to indicate the fact that one must not assume that every individual word will be a foot, nor that divisions between feet necessarily fall between words. In actual lines, one might for example find the word *intervene* constituting parts of two different feet:

ŭ ′ | ŭ ′ | ŭ ′
I want | to in- | ter-vene.

As this example demonstrates, in diagramming meters we must sometimes acknowledge the primary and secondary stresses provided by dictionaries: the word *intervene* provides the stresses for two consecutive feet.

The other basic unit of measurement in metrical verse is the line, which has the same properties as in free verse—it may be end-stopped or run-on, and its phrasing and punctuation will create caesuras. The difference between metrical and free-verse lines is that metrical lines

---

*In the spondee the accent is thought of as being distributed equally or almost equally over the two syllables and is sometimes referred to as a hovering accent. No whole poems are written in spondees. Hence there are only four basic meters: iambic, trochaic, anapestic, and dactylic. Iambic and trochaic are called duple because they employ two-syllable feet, anapestic and dactylic triple because they employ three-syllable feet. Of the four standard meters, iambic is by far the most common, followed by anapestic. Trochaic occurs relatively infrequently as the meter of poems, and dactylic is so rare as to be almost a museum specimen.

are measured by naming the number of feet in them. The following names indicate number:

Monometer	one foot	Tetrameter	four feet
Dimeter	two feet	Pentameter	five feet
Trimeter	three feet	Hexameter	six feet

The third unit of measurement, the **stanza**, consists of a group of lines whose metrical pattern is repeated throughout the poem. Since much verse is not written in stanzas, we shall save our discussion of this unit till a later chapter.

Although metrical form is potentially uniform in its regularity, the poet may introduce **metrical variations**, which call attention to some of the sounds because they depart from what is regular. Three means for varying meter are **substitution** (replacing the regular foot with another one), **extrametrical syllables** added at the beginnings or endings of lines, and **truncation** (the omission of an unaccented syllable at either end of a line). Because these represent clear changes in the pattern, they are usually obvious and striking. But even metrical regularity rarely creates a monotonous rhythm because rhythm is the actuality in sound, not the pattern or blueprint of meter. The rhythm of a line of poetry, like the actuality of a building, depends on the components of sound mentioned above—stress, duration, pitch, and juncture—as these are presented in rhetorically stressed sentences. We may diagram the metrical form of a line, but because no two sentences in English are identical in sound, there can be no formulas or mechanical systems for indicating rhythm. Rhythm must be described rather than formulated.

The process of defining the metrical form of a poem is called **scansion**. To *scan* any specimen of verse, we do three things: (1) we identify the prevailing foot; (2) we name the number of feet in a line—if this length follows any regular pattern; and (3) we describe the stanzaic pattern—if there is one. We may try out our skill on the following poem:

Virtue

Sweet day, so cool, so calm, so bright,
   The bridal of the earth and sky;
The dew shall weep thy fall to night,
   For thou must die.

Sweet rose, whose hue, angry and brave,   5
   Bids the rash gazer wipe his eye;

Thy root is ever in its grave,
    And thou must die.

Sweet spring, full of sweet days and roses,
    A box where sweets compacted lie;   10
My music shows ye have your closes,
    And all must die.

Only a sweet and virtuous soul,
    Like seasoned timber, never gives;
But though the whole world turn to coal,   15
    Then chiefly lives.

                              George Herbert (1593–1633)

QUESTIONS
1. Vocabulary: *bridal* (2), *brave* (5), *closes* (11), *coal* (15).
2. How are the four stanzas interconnected? How do they build to a climax?
   How does the fourth contrast with the first three?

    The first step in scanning a poem is to read it normally, according to
its prose meaning, listening to where the accents fall naturally, and perhaps beating time with the hand. If we have any doubt about how a line
should be marked, we should skip it temporarily and go on to lines where
we feel greater confidence; that is, to those lines that seem most regular,
with accents that fall unmistakably at regular intervals—for we are seeking the poem's pattern, which will be revealed by what is regular in it. In
"Virtue" lines 3, 10, and 14 clearly fall into this category, as do the short
lines 4, 8, and 12. Lines 3, 10, and 14 may be marked as follows.

The dew ˘ shall weep ˘ thy fall ˘ to night,   3

A box ˘ where sweets ˘ com-pact-ed lie;   10

Like sea-soned tim-ber, nev-er gives   14

Lines 4, 8, and 12 are so nearly identical that we may use line 4 to represent all three.

For thou must die.   4

Surveying what we have done so far, we may with some confidence say that the prevailing metrical foot of the poem is iambic; and we may reasonably hypothesize that the second and third lines of each stanza are tetrameter (four-foot) lines and the fourth line dimeter. What about the first lines? Line 1 contains eight syllables, and since the poem is iambic, we may mark them into four feet. The last six syllables clearly constitute three iambic feet (as a general rule, the last few feet in a line tend to reflect the prevailing meter of a poem).

Sweet dáy, | so cóol, | so cálm, | so bríght | 1

This too, then, is a tetrameter line, and the only question is whether to mark the first foot as another iamb or as a spondee—that is, whether it conforms to the norm established by the iambic meter, or is a substituted foot. The adjective "Sweet" is certainly more important in the line than the repeated adverb "so," and ought to receive more stress than the adverbs on the principle of *rhetorical stress*, by which the plain prose sense governs the pronunciation. But we must remember that in marking metrical stresses, we are only comparing the syllables *within a foot*, so the comparison with the repeated "so" is irrelevant. The real question is whether "Sweet" receives as much emphasis as "day."

As another general rule (but by no means an absolute one), a noun usually receives more stress than an adjective that modifies it, a verb more than its adverbs, and an adjective more than an adverb that modifies it—except when the modifying word points to an unusual or unexpected condition. If the phrase were "fat day" or "red day," we would probably feel that those adjectives were odd enough to warrant stressing them. "Sweet day" does not strike us as particularly unusual, so the noun ought to receive stress. Further, as we notice that each of the first three stanzas begins with "Sweet" modifying different nouns, we recognize that the statement of the poem is drawing attention to the similarities (and differences) of three things that can be called *sweet*—"day," "rose," and "spring." By its repetition before those three nouns, the word *sweet* may come to seem formulaic, and the nouns the object of attention. On the other hand, the repetition of "Sweet" may seem emphatic, and lead us to give approximately equal stress to both the noun and its adjective. As our purpose is to detect the *pattern* of sounds in the poem, the most likely result of this study will be to mark it iambic. However, judging it to be spondaic would not be incorrect, for ultimately we are reporting what we *hear*, and there is room for subjective differences.

The first feet of lines 5 and 9 raise the same problem as line 1 and should be marked in the same way. Choices of a similar sort occur in other lines (15 and 16). Many readers will quite legitimately perceive line 16 as parallel to lines 4, 8, and 12. Others, however, may argue that the word "Then"—emphasizing what happens to the virtuous soul when everything else has perished—has an importance that should be reflected in both the reading and the scansion, and will therefore mark the first foot of this line as a spondee:

$$\acute{\text{Then}} \ \acute{\text{chief-}} \mid \breve{\text{ly}} \ \acute{\text{lives.}} \mid \qquad \qquad 16$$

These readers also will hear the third foot in line 15 as a spondee:

$$\breve{\text{But}} \ \acute{\text{though}} \mid \breve{\text{the}} \ \acute{\text{whole}} \mid \acute{\text{world}} \ \acute{\text{turn}} \mid \breve{\text{to}} \ \acute{\text{coal}} \mid \qquad \qquad 15$$

Lines 2 and 7 introduce a different problem. Most readers, if they encountered these lines in a paragraph of prose, would read them thus:

The BRIdal of the EARTH and SKY   2

Thy ROOT is EVer in its GRAVE   7

But this reading leaves us with an anomalous situation. First, we have only three stresses where our pattern calls for four. Second, we have three unaccented syllables occurring together, which is almost never found in verse of duple meter. From this situation we may learn an important principle. Though normal reading of the sentences in a poem establishes its metrical pattern, the metrical pattern so established in turn influences the reading. An interactive process is at work. In this poem the pressure of the pattern will cause most practiced readers to stress the second of the three unaccented syllables in both lines slightly more than those on either side of it. In scansion, comparing the syllables within the individual foot, we acknowledge that slight increase of stress by marking those syllables as stressed (remember, the marking of the accent does not indicate a *degree* of stress in comparison with other accents in the line). We mark them thus:

$$\breve{\text{The}} \ \acute{\text{bri-}} \mid \breve{\text{dal}} \ \acute{\text{of}} \mid \breve{\text{the}} \ \acute{\text{earth}} \mid \breve{\text{and}} \ \acute{\text{sky}} \mid \qquad \qquad 2$$

$$\breve{\text{Thy}} \ \acute{\text{root}} \mid \breve{\text{is}} \ \acute{\text{ev-}} \mid \breve{\text{er}} \ \acute{\text{in}} \mid \breve{\text{its}} \ \acute{\text{grave}} \mid \qquad \qquad 7$$

Line 5 presents a situation about which there can be no dispute. The word "angry," though it occurs in a position where we would expect an iamb, by virtue of its normal pronunciation *must* be accented on the first syllable, and thus must be marked a trochee:

$$\breve{\text{Sweet}} \ \acute{\text{rose,}} \mid \breve{\text{whose}} \ \acute{\text{hue,}} \mid \acute{\text{an-}} \ \breve{\text{gry}} \mid \breve{\text{and}} \ \acute{\text{brave}} \mid \qquad \qquad 5$$

There is little question also that the following line begins with a trochee, but the second foot ("rash gaz-") must be examined, for we may wonder whether the adjective *rash* presents an unexpected modification for the noun *gazer*. Since the possibilities seem about equal, we prefer to let the pattern again take precedence, although a spondee would be acceptable:

$$\text{Bids the}\ |\ \text{rash gaz-}\ |\ \text{er wipe}\ |\ \text{his eye}\ |$$

6

Similarly, the word "Only," beginning line 13, must be accented on the first syllable, thus introducing a trochaic substitution in the first foot of the line. Line 13 also presents another problem. A modern reader perceives the word "virtuous" as a three-syllable word, but the poet writing in the seventeenth century, when metrical requirements were stricter than they are today, would probably have meant the word to be pronounced as two syllables: *ver-tyus*. Following the tastes of this century, we mark it as three syllables, so introducing an anapest instead of the expected iamb in the last foot:

$$\text{On-ly}\ |\ \text{a sweet}\ |\ \text{and vir-}\ |\ \text{tu-ous soul}\ |$$

13

In doing this, however, we are consciously modernizing—altering the probable practice of the poet for the sake of a contemporary audience.

One problem of scansion remains: in the third stanza, lines 9 and 11 differ from the other lines of the poem in two respects—(a) they contain an uneven number of syllables (nine rather than the expected eight); (b) they end on unaccented syllables:

$$\text{Sweet spring,}\ |\ \text{full of}\ |\ \text{sweet days}\ |\ \text{and ros-}\ |\ \text{es,}$$

9

$$\text{My mu-}\ |\ \text{sic shows}\ |\ \text{ye have}\ |\ \text{your clos-}\ |\ \text{es}$$

11

Such leftover unaccented syllables at line ends are examples of extrametrical syllables and are not counted in identifying and naming the meter. These lines are both tetrameter, and if we tap our feet when reading them, we shall tap four times. Metrical verse will often have one and sometimes two leftover unaccented syllables. In iambic and anapestic verse they will come at the end of the lines; in trochaic and dactylic, at the beginning. They never occur in the middle of a line.

Our metrical analysis of "Virtue" is completed. Though (mainly for ease of discussion) we have skipped about, we have indicated a scansion for all its lines. "Virtue" is written in iambic meter (meaning that most of its feet are iambs), and is composed of four-line stanzas, the first three lines tetrameter, the final line dimeter. We are now ready to make a few generalizations about scansion.

1. Good readers will not ordinarily stop to scan a poem they are reading, and they certainly will not read a poem aloud with the exaggerated emphasis on accented syllables that we sometimes give them in order to make the metrical pattern more apparent. However, occasional scansion of a poem has value, as will be indicated in the next chapter, which discusses the relation of sound and meter to sense. Just one example here. The structure of meaning of "Virtue" is unmistakable; three parallel stanzas concerning things that die are followed by a contrasting fourth stanza concerning the one thing that does not die. The first three stanzas all begin with the word "Sweet" preceding a noun, and the first metrical foot in these stanzas is either an iamb or a spondee. The contrasting fourth stanza, however, begins with a trochee, thus departing both from the previous pattern and from the basic meter of the poem. This departure is significant, for the word *only* is the hinge upon which the structure of the poem turns, and the metrical reversal gives it emphasis. Thus meter serves meaning.

2. Scansion only begins to reveal the rhythmic quality of a poem. It simply involves classifying all syllables as either accented or unaccented and ignores the sometimes considerable differences between degrees of accent. Whether we call a syllable accented or unaccented depends only on its degree of accent relative to the other syllable(s) in its foot. In lines 2 and 7 of "Virtue," the accents on "of" and "in" are obviously much lighter than on the other accented syllables in the line. Further, unaccented syllables also vary in weight. In line 5 "whose" is clearly heavier than "-gry" or "and," and is arguably even heavier than the accented "of" and "in" of lines 2 and 7. It is not unusual, either, to find the unaccented syllable of a foot receiving more stress than the accented syllable immediately preceding it in another foot, as in this line by Gerard Manley Hopkins (page 828):

It will | flame out | like shin- | ing from | shook foil

The last four syllables of the line, two perfectly regular iambs, are actually spoken as a sequence of four increasingly stressed accents. A similar sequence of increasing accents occurs in lines 4, 8, and 12 of "Virtue,"

For thou | must die   4

since the necessity expressed in the word "must" makes it more heavily stressed than the pronoun "thou." The point is that metrical scansion is incapable of describing subtle rhythmic effects in poetry. It is never-theless a useful and serviceable tool, for by showing us the metrical *pat-tern*, it draws attention to the way in which the actuality of sound fol-lows the pattern even while departing from it; that is, recognizing the meter, we can more clearly hear rhythms. The *idea* of regularity helps us be aware of the *actuality* of sounds.

3. Notice that the divisions between feet have no meaning except to help us identify the meter. They do not correspond to the speech rhythms in the line. In the third foot of line 14 of "Virtue," a syntacti-cal pause occurs *within* the foot; and, indeed, feet divisions often fall in the middle of a word. It is sometimes a mistake of beginners to expect the word and the foot to be identical units. We mark the feet divisions only to reveal regularity or pattern, not to indicate rhythm. But in "Virtue," if we examine all of the two-syllable words, we find that all eleven of them as isolated words removed from their lines would be called *trochaic*. Yet only two of them—"angry" (5) and "only" (13)—actually occur as trochaic feet. All the rest are divided in the middle be-tween two iambic feet. This calls for two observations: (a) the rhythm of the poem, the *heard* sound, often runs counter to the meter—iambic feet have what is called a "rising" pattern, yet these words individually and as they are spoken have a "falling" rhythm; and (b) the trochaic hinge word "only" thus has rhythmic echoes throughout the poem, those preceding it yielding a kind of predictive power, and those follow-ing it reinforcing the fact that the sense of the poem turns at that word. This rhythmic effect is especially pronounced in the simile of line 14:

Like sea-│soned tim-│ber, nev-│er gives│   14

Echoing the key word "only," this line contains three disyllabic words, each of them having a falling rhythm running counter to the iambic meter.

4. Finally—and this is the most important generalization of all—perfect regularity of meter is no criterion of merit. Inexperienced read-ers sometimes get the notion that it is. If the meter is regular and the rhythm mirrors that regularity in sound, they may feel that the poet has handled the meter successfully and deserves all credit for it. Actually there is nothing easier for any moderately talented versifier than to make language go ta-DUM ta-DUM ta-DUM. But there are two rea-sons why this is not generally desirable. The first is that, as we have said, all art consists essentially of repetition and variation. If a rhythm alternates too regularly between light and heavy beats, the result is to banish variation; the rhythm mechanically follows the meter and be-

comes monotonous. But used occasionally or emphatically, a monotonous rhythm can be very effective, as in the triumphant last line of Tennyson's "Ulysses" (page 747):

To strive, | to seek, | to find, | and not | to yield. |

The second reason is that once a basic meter has been established, deviations from it become highly significant and are a means by which the poet can reinforce meaning. If a meter is too regular and the rhythm shows little deviation from it, the probability is that the poet, instead of adopting rhythm to meaning, has simply forced the meaning into a metrical straitjacket.

Actually what gives the skillful use of meter its greatest effectiveness is to be found in the distinction between meter and rhythm. Once we have determined the basic meter of a poem, say iambic tetrameter, we have an expectation that the rhythm will coincide with it—that the pattern will be identical to the actual sound. Thus a silent drumbeat is set up in our minds, and this drumbeat constitutes an expected rhythm. But the actual rhythm of the words—the heard rhythm—will sometimes confirm this expected rhythm and sometimes not. Thus the two—meter and rhythm—are counterpointed, and the appeal of the verse is magnified, just as when two melodies are counterpointed in music, or when we see two swallows flying together and around each other, following the same general course but with individual variations and so making a more eye-catching pattern than one swallow flying alone. If the heard rhythm conforms too closely to the expected rhythm (meter), the poem becomes dull and uninteresting rhythmically. If it departs too far from the meter, there ceases to be an expected rhythm and the result is likely to be a muddle.

There are several ways by which variation can be introduced into a poem's rhythm. The most obvious way, as we have said, is by the substitution of other kinds of feet for the basic foot. Such metrical variation will always be reflected as a rhythmic variation. In our scansion of line 13 of "Virtue," for instance, we found a trochee and an anapest substituted for the expected iambs in the first and last feet. A less obvious but equally important means of variation is through varying degrees of accent arising from the prose meaning of phrases—from the rhetorical stressing. Though we began our scansion of "Virtue" by marking lines 3, 10, and 14 as perfectly regular metrically, there is actually a considerable rhythmic difference between them. Line 3 is quite regular because the rhythmic phrasing corresponds to the metrical pattern, and the line can be read: ta DUM ta DUM ta DUM ta DUM (The

DEW shall WEEP thy FALL to NIGHT). Line 10 is less regular, for the three-syllable word "compacted" cuts across the division between two feet. This should be read: ta DUM ta DUM ta-DUM-ta DUM (a BOX where SWEETS comPACTed LIE). Line 14 is the least regular of these three because here there is no correspondence between rhythmic phrasing and metrical division. This should be read: ta DUM-ta DUM-ta DUM-ta DUM (Like SEAsoned TIMber, NEVer GIVES). Finally, variation can be introduced by **grammatical** and **rhetorical pauses,** whether or not signaled by punctuation (punctuated pauses are usually of longer duration than those occasioned only by syntax and rhetoric, and pauses for periods are longer than those for commas). The comma in line 14, by introducing a grammatical pause (in the middle of a foot), provides an additional variation from its perfect regularity. Probably the most violently irregular line in the poem is line 5,

$$\text{Sweet rose,} \mid \text{whose hue,} \mid \text{an-gry} \mid \text{and brave,} \mid \qquad 5$$

for here the unusual trochaic substitution in the second from last foot of an iambic line (a rare occurrence) is set off and emphasized by the grammatical pause; and also, as we have noted, the unaccented "whose" is considerably heavier than the other unaccented syllables in the line. This trochee "angry" is the first unquestionable metrical substitution in the poem. It occurs in a line which, because it opens a stanza, is subconsciously compared to the first line of the first stanza—an example of regularity with its grammatical pauses separating all four of its feet. Once we have noticed that the first line of the second stanza contains a metrical variation, our attention is called to the fact that after the first, each stanza opens with a line containing a trochee—and that these trochees are moved forward one foot in each of the successive stanzas, from the third position in stanza two, to the second in four, and finally to the first in the concluding stanza. This pattern itself tends to add even more emphasis to the climactic change signaled by the final trochee, "only." Again, meter and rhythm serve meaning.

The effects of rhythm and meter are several. Like the musical repetitions of sound, the musical repetitions of accent can be pleasing for their own sake. In addition, rhythm works as an emotional stimulus and heightens our awareness of what is going on in a poem. Finally, a poet can adapt the sound of the verse to its content and thus make meter a powerful reinforcement of meaning. We should avoid, however, the notion that there is any mystical correspondence between certain meters or rhythms and certain emotions. There are no "happy" meters and no "melancholy" meters. The "falling" rhythm of line 14 of

"Virtue," counterpointed against its "rising" meter, does not indicate a depression of mood or feeling—the line has quite the opposite emotional tone. Poets' choice of meter is probably less important than how they handle it after they have chosen it. In most great poetry, meter and rhythm work intimately with the other elements of the poem to produce the total effect.

And because of the importance of free verse today, we must not forget that poetry need not be metrical at all. Like alliteration and rhyme, like metaphor and irony, like even imagery, meter is simply *one* resource poets may or may not use. Their job is to employ their resources to the best advantage for the object they have in mind—the kind of experience they wish to express. And on no other basis should they be judged.

EXERCISES

1. A term that every student of poetry should know (and should be careful not to confuse with *free verse*) is blank verse. **Blank verse** has a very specific meter: it is *iambic pentameter, unrhymed*. It has a special name because it is the principal English meter; that is, the meter that has been used for a large proportion of the greatest English poetry, including the plays of Shakespeare and the epics of Milton. Iambic pentameter in English seems especially suitable for the serious treatment of serious themes. The natural movement of the English language tends to be iambic. Lines shorter than pentameter tend to be songlike, or at least less suited to sustained treatment of serious material. Lines longer than pentameter tend to break up into shorter units, the hexameter line being read as two three-foot units. Rhyme, while highly appropriate to many short poems, often proves a handicap for a long and lofty work. (The word *blank* indicates that the end of the line is bare of rhyme.)

   Of the following poems, four are in blank verse, two are in other meters, and four are in free verse. Determine in which category each belongs.
   a. Frost, "Birches" (page 962).
   b. Donne, "Break of Day" (page 677).
   c. Hughes, "Thistles" (page 974).
   d. Plath, "Mirror" (page 680).
   e. Tennyson, "Ulysses" (page 746).
   f. Arnold, "Dover Beach" (page 816).
   g. Auden, "The Unknown Citizen" (page 771).
   h. Yeats, "The Second Coming" (page 1022).
   i. Frost, "'Out, Out—'" (page 779).
   j. Atwood, "Siren Song" (page 943).

2. Examine Browning, "My Last Duchess" (page 775) and Pope, "Sound and Sense" (page 867). Both are in the same meter, iambic pentameter rhymed in couplets, but their general rhythmic effect is markedly different. What accounts for the difference? How does the contrast support our statement

that the way poets handle meter is more important than their choice of a meter?

3. Examine Williams, "The Widow's Lament in Springtime" (page 704), Francis, "The Hound" (page 715), and Williams, "The Dance" (page 881). Which is the most forcibly run-on in the majority of its lines? Describe the differences in effect.

REVIEWING CHAPTER TWELVE

1. Review the terms printed in boldface, and as you read on in this chapter take note of the examples that you find; identify the poems as free verse or metrical, and write out scansions of the metrical verse.
2. Using examples from the poems that follow in this chapter, draw clear distinctions between rhythm and meter; and using appropriate adjectives, describe the rhythmic effects (jolly, somber, playful, etc.).
3. When possible, explain how the rhythms of a poem reinforce emotional or intellectual meanings.

"Introduction" to *Songs of Innocence*

Piping down the valleys wild,
Piping songs of pleasant glee,
On a cloud I saw a child,
And he laughing said to me:

"Pipe a song about a Lamb."   5
So I piped with merry cheer.
"Piper, pipe that song again."
So I piped; he wept to hear.

"Drop thy pipe, thy happy pipe;
Sing thy songs of happy cheer."   10
So I sung the same again
While he wept with joy to hear.

"Piper, sit thee down and write
In a book that all may read."

So he vanished from my sight,   15
And I plucked a hollow reed,

And I made a rural pen,
And I stained the water clear,
And I wrote my happy songs
Every child may joy to hear.   20

William Blake (1757–1827)

QUESTIONS

1. Poets have traditionally been thought of as inspired by one of the Muses
   (Greek female divinities whose duties were to nurture the arts). Blake's
   Songs of Innocence, a book of poems about childhood and the state of innocence, includes "The Chimney Sweeper" (page 763) and "The Lamb" (page
   946). In this introductory poem to the book, what function is performed by
   the child upon a cloud?
2. What is symbolized by "a Lamb" (5)?
3. What three stages of poetic composition are suggested in stanzas 1–2, 3, and
   4–5 respectively?
4. What features of the poems in his book does Blake hint at in this "Introduction"? Name at least four.
5. Mark the stressed and unstressed syllables in lines 1–2 and 9–10. Do they
   establish the basic meter of the poem? If so, is that meter iambic or trochaic?
   Or could it be either? Some metrists have discarded the distinction between
   iambic and trochaic, and between anapestic and dactylic, as being artificial.
   The important distinction, they feel, is between duple and triple meters.
   Does this poem support their claim?

Had I the Choice

Had I the choice to tally greatest bards,
To limn their portraits, stately, beautiful, and emulate at will,
Homer with all his wars and warriors—Hector, Achilles, Ajax,
Or Shakespeare's woe-entangled Hamlet, Lear, Othello—Tennyson's
    fair ladies,
Meter or wit the best, or choice conceit to wield in perfect rhyme,   5
    delight of singers;
These, these, O sea, all these I'd gladly barter,
Would you the undulation of one wave, its trick to me transfer,
Or breathe one breath of yours upon my verse,
And leave its odor there.

Walt Whitman (1819–1892)

QUESTIONS

1. Vocabulary: *tally* (1), *limn* (2), *conceit* (5).
2. What poetic qualities does the speaker propose to barter in exchange for what? What qualities do the sea and its waves symbolize?
3. Is this free verse, or metrical verse in duple meter? In what way might this be taken as an imitation of the rhythms of the sea?

The Aim Was Song

Before man came to blow it right
   The wind once blew itself untaught,
And did its loudest day and night
   In any rough place where it caught.

Man came to tell it what was wrong: 5
   It hadn't found the place to blow;
It blew too hard—the aim was song.
   And listen—how it ought to go!

He took a little in his mouth,
   And held it long enough for north   10
To be converted into south,
   And then by measure blew it forth.

By measure. It was word and note,
   The wind the wind had meant to be—
A little through the lips and throat.   15
   The aim was song—the wind could see.

Robert Frost (1874–1963)

QUESTIONS

1. Frost invents a myth about the origin of poetry. What implications does it suggest about the relation of man to nature and of poetry to nature?
2. Contrast the thought and form of this poem with Whitman's.
3. Scan the poem and identify its meter. How does the poet give variety to a regular metrical pattern?

The Knight

A knight rides into the noon,
and his helmet points to the sun,
and a thousand splintered suns

are the gaiety of his mail.
The soles of his feet glitter   5
and his palms flash in reply,
and under his crackling banner
he rides like a ship in sail.

A knight rides into the noon,
And only his eye is living,   10
a lump of bitter jelly
set in a metal mask,
betraying rags and tatters
that cling to the flesh beneath
and wear his nerves to ribbons   15
under the radiant casque.

Who will unhorse this rider
and free him from between
the walls of iron, the emblems
crushing his chest with their weight?   20
Will they defeat him gently,
or leave him hurled on the green,
his rags and wounds still hidden
under the great breastplate?

Adrienne Rich (b. 1929)

Old Ladies' Home

Sharded in black, like beetles,
Frail as antique earthenware
One breath might shiver to bits,
The old women creep out here
To sun on the rocks or prop   5
Themselves up against the wall
Whose stones keep a little heat.

Needles knit in a bird-beaked
Counterpoint to their voices:
Sons, daughters, daughters and sons,   10
Distant and cold as photos,
Grandchildren nobody knows.
Age wears the best black fabric
Rust-red or green as lichens.

At owl-call the old ghosts flock   15
To hustle them off the lawn.
From beds boxed-in like coffins
The bonneted ladies grin.
And Death, that bald-head buzzard,
Stalls in halls where the lamp wick   20
Shortens with each breath drawn.

Sylvia Plath (1932–1963)

QUESTIONS

1. Vocabulary: *Sharded* (1), *Stalls* (20).
2. Discuss the significance of these natural images: "beetles" (1), "bird-beaked /
   Counterpoint" (8–9), "Rust-red or green as lichens" (14), "owl-call" (15),
   "bald-head buzzard" (19). These are all metaphors or similes; in each case,
   what is being compared to what?
3. What is the speaker's tone?
4. This poem is an example of **syllabic verse,** which counts only the number
   of syllables per line, regardless of accents. (Plath's "Metaphors" [page 726] is
   another example.) In this case, the poem is constructed of seven-syllable
   lines in seven-line stanzas—but there is one line that contains only six syllables. What is the significance of the shortening of that line?
5. The poem contains some rhyme (particularly slant rhyme), and some of the
   lines contain duple metrical feet. Are these musical effects regular enough
   to call this a metrical poem?

The Tropics in New York

Bananas ripe and green and ginger-root,
   Cocoa in pods and alligator pears,
And tangerines and mangoes and grape fruit,
   Fit for the highest prize at parish fairs,

Set in the window, bringing memories   5
   Of fruit trees laden by low-singing rills,
And dewy dawns and mystical blue skies
   In benediction over nun-like hills.

Mine eyes grew dim and I could no more gaze,
   A wave of longing through my body swept,   10
And, hungry for the old, familiar ways,
   I turned aside and bowed my head and wept.

Claude McKay (1890–1948)

QUESTIONS

1. This poem economically establishes a setting and situation. Where is the speaker and what is he doing?
2. What is the tone of the poem? How do the metrical pattern and the rhymed lines help to establish the tone?
3. What are the "old, familiar ways" mentioned in line 11, and how does the description of the fruit display help to evoke them?
4. At the end of the poem, why is the speaker weeping? What is the source of his emotion?

To a Daughter Leaving Home

When I taught you
at eight to ride
a bicycle, loping along
beside you
as you wobbled away   5
on two round wheels,
my own mouth rounding
in surprise when you pulled
ahead down the curved
path of the park,   10
I kept waiting
for the thud
of your crash as I
sprinted to catch up,
while you grew   15
smaller, more breakable
with distance,
pumping, pumping
for your life, screaming
with laughter,   20
the hair flapping
behind you like a
handkerchief waving
goodbye.

Linda Pastan (b. 1932)

QUESTIONS

1. How does the discrepancy between the title and the event create meaning? Which details of the poem take on symbolic meaning?

2. Write out this poem as prose, ignoring line ends. What poetic effect has been lost? Which of the original line ends are particularly important to meaning and feeling?

Quinceañera

My dolls have been put away like dead
children in a chest I will carry
with me when I marry.
I reach under my skirt to feel
a satin slip bought for this day. It is soft   5
as the inside of my thighs. My hair
has been nailed back with my mother's
black hairpins to my skull. Her hands
stretched my eyes open as she twisted
braids into a tight circle at the nape   10
of my neck. I am to wash my own clothes
and sheets from this day on, as if
the fluids of my body were poison, as if
the little trickle of blood I believe
travels from my heart to the world were   15
shameful. Is not the blood of saints and
men in battle beautiful? Do Christ's hands
not bleed into your eyes from His cross?
At night I hear myself growing and wake
to find my hands drifting of their own will   20
to soothe skin stretched tight
over my bones.
I am wound like the guts of a clock,
waiting for each hour to release me.

Judith Ortiz Cofer (b. 1952)

QUESTIONS

1. The poem's title refers to a party marking a fifteen-year-old girl's birthday in Latin cultures. According to the poem, what is the significance of this particular birthday?
2. Some of the poem's images might be described as negative and painful: "My dolls have been put away like dead / children" (1–2); "My hair / has been nailed back" (6–7); "she twisted / braids into a tight circle" (9–10). What do these images contribute to the poem?

3. The speaker compares her incipient menstruation to "the blood of saints and / men in battle" (16–17) and to the pierced hands of Christ during the crucifixion. How are these images relevant to the larger meaning of the poem?
4. Discuss the simile near the end of the poem, "I am wound like the guts of a clock" (23). Why is the word "guts" particularly appropriate? What do the final two lines reveal about the speaker's emotional state?

Constantly risking absurdity

Constantly risking absurdity
                        and death
        whenever he performs
                    above the heads
                            of his audience   5
    the poet like an acrobat
            climbs on rime
                    to a high wire of his own making
and balancing on eyebeams
                    above a sea of faces   10
        paces his way
                to the other side of day
performing entrechats
            and sleight-of-foot tricks
and other high theatrics   15
            and all without mistaking
        any thing
            for what it may not be
    For he's the super realist
                    who must perforce perceive   20
        taut truth
            before the taking of each stance or step
in his supposed advance
                    toward that still higher perch
where Beauty stands and waits   25
                with gravity
                    to start her death-defying leap
    And he
        a little charleychaplin man
                    who may or may not catch   30
        her fair eternal form
                    spreadeagled in the empty air
        of existence

                            Lawrence Ferlinghetti (b. 1919)

QUESTIONS

1. Vocabulary: *entrechats* (13). Explain the meanings of "above the heads" (4), "sleight-of-foot tricks" (14), "high theatrics" (15), and "with gravity" (26).
2. The poet "climbs on rime" (7), the poem asserts. To what extent does this poem utilize rhyme and other musical devices?
3. What statement does the poem make about poetry, truth, and beauty?
4. How do the rhythms created by the length and placement of lines reinforce the meanings of the poem? Does this poem take poets and poetry seriously? solemnly?

A Blessing

Just off the highway to Rochester, Minnesota,
Twilight bounds softly forth on the grass.
And the eyes of those two Indian ponies
Darken with kindness.
They have come gladly out of the willows   5
To welcome my friend and me.
We step over the barbed wire into the pasture
Where they have been grazing all day, alone.
They ripple tensely, they can hardly contain their happiness
That we have come.   10
They bow shyly as wet swans. They love each other.
There is no loneliness like theirs.
At home once more,
They begin munching the young tufts of spring in the darkness.
I would like to hold the slenderer one in my arms,   15
For she has walked over to me
And nuzzled my left hand.
She is black and white,
Her mane falls wild on her forehead,
And the light breeze moves me to caress her long ear   20
That is delicate as the skin over a girl's wrist.
Suddenly I realize
That if I stepped out of my body I would break
Into blossom.

James Wright (1927–1980)

QUESTIONS

1. How does the first line persuade the reader to accept the reality of the poem? What nonrealistic figure of speech predominates in the description of the ponies? What is the actual reality of lines 9–10?

2. What is so attractive to the speaker in the ponies' behavior? As he begins to describe "the slenderer one" (15), what implicit comparison does his language create?
3. What is the meaning of the sudden realization of lines 22–24?
4. In this example of free verse, the poem mostly fits complete phrase to line length. But there are exceptions, when the meaning requires you to ignore the end of a line. Where do these exceptions occur, and what do they contribute to the effect of the poem?

Break, break, break

Break, break, break,
    On thy cold gray stones, O sea!
And I would that my tongue could utter
    The thoughts that arise in me.

O, well for the fisherman's boy,   5
    That he shouts with his sister at play!
O, well for the sailor lad,
    That he sings in his boat on the bay!

And the stately ships go on
    To their haven under the hill;   10
But O for the touch of a vanished hand,
    And the sound of a voice that is still!

Break, break, break,
    At the foot of thy crags, O sea!
But the tender grace of a day that is dead   15
    Will never come back to me.

Alfred, Lord Tennyson (1809–1892)

QUESTIONS

1. In lines 3–4 the speaker wishes he could put his thoughts into words. Does he make those thoughts explicit in the course of the poem?
2. What aspects of life are symbolized by the two images in stanza 2? By the image in lines 9–10? How do lines 11–12 contrast with those images?
3. The basic meter of this poem is anapestic, and all but two lines are trimeter. Which two? What other variations from a strict anapestic trimeter do you find? How many lines (and which ones) display a strict anapestic pattern? With this much variation, would you be justified in calling the poem free verse? Do the departures from a strict metrical norm contribute to the meaning?

SUGGESTIONS FOR WRITING

The following suggestions are for brief writing exercises, not for full critical essays. The suggestions here could constitute a part of a full essay that includes some discussion of the contribution of rhythm and meter to the total meaning of a poem.

1. Scan one of the following metrical poems, and indicate how the rhythmic effects (including substitutions and variations from the metrical norm) contribute to meaning:
   a. Dickinson, "Because I could not stop for Death" (page 752).
   b. Shelley, "Ozymandias" (page 764); consider regular and irregular meters in lines 10–14.
   c. Frost, "Nothing Gold Can Stay" (page 837); consider how the first and last lines depart from metrical regularity.
   d. Blake, "Introduction" to *Songs of Innocence* (page 853; see question 5).
   e. Tennyson, "Break, break, break" (page 862; see question 3).
2. In the following free-verse poems, discuss how the line forms a rhythmic unit, paying particular attention to run-on and end-stopped lines:
   a. Williams, "The Widow's Lament in Springtime" (page 704; particularly examine lines 20–24).
   b. Pastan, "To a Daughter Leaving Home" (page 858; see question 2, and particularly examine lines 12–14, 15–16, 19–20, 21–24).
   c. Ferlinghetti, "Constantly risking absurdity" (page 860; see question 4).
   d. Hughes, "Theme for English B" (page 972).
   e. Piercy, "A Work of Artifice" (page 985).

Chapter Thirteen

Sound and Meaning

Rhythm and sound cooperate to produce what we call the music of poetry. This music, as we have pointed out, may serve two general functions: it may be enjoyable in itself, or it may reinforce meaning and intensify the communication.

Pure pleasure in sound and rhythm exists from a very early age in the human being—probably from the age the baby first starts cooing in its cradle, certainly from the age that children begin chanting nursery rhymes and skipping rope. The appeal of the following verse, for instance, depends almost entirely on its "music":

> Pease porridge hot,
>   Pease porridge cold,
> Pease porridge in the pot
>   Nine days old.

There is very little sense here; the attraction comes from the emphatic rhythm, the emphatic rhymes (with a strong contrast between the short vowel and short final consonant of *hot–pot* and the long vowel and long final consonant combination of *cold–old*), and the heavy alliteration (exactly half the words begin with *p*). From nonsense rhymes such as this, many of us graduate to a love of more meaningful poems whose appeal resides largely in the sounds they make. Much of the pleasure that we find in poems like Vachel Lindsay's "The Congo" and Edgar Allan Poe's "The Bells" derives from their musical qualities.

The peculiar function of poetry as distinguished from music, however, is to convey not sounds but meaning or experience *through* sounds. In first-rate poetry, sound exists neither for its own sake nor for mere decoration, but to enhance the meaning. Its function is to support the leading player, not to steal the scene.

The poet may reinforce meaning through sound in numerous ways. Without claiming to exhaust them, we can include most of the chief means under four general headings.

First, the poet can choose words whose sound in some degree suggests their meaning. In its narrowest sense this is called onomatopoeia.

Onomatopoeia, strictly defined, means the use of words that, at least supposedly, sound like what they mean, such as *hiss, snap,* and *bang.* Animal noises offer many examples—*bow-wow, cock-a-doodle-do, oink*—and sometimes poets may even invent words to represent them, as Shakespeare does in "Winter" (page 650) when the owl sings "Tu-whit, tu-who!" Poetry, of course, does not usually present the vocalized sounds made by animals, but onomatopoeia often expresses the sounds of movements or actions, as in the following examples: "The harness *jingles*" in Housman's "Is my team plowing" (page 674); "Neighbors *rustle* in and out" in Dickinson's "There's been a Death, in the Opposite House" (page 678); the mourners "*creak* across" in Dickinson's "I felt a Funeral, in my Brain" (page 705); and in Heaney's "The Forge" (page 707) we hear *ring, hiss, clatter, grunts,* and *slam.* Generally, we can detect the presence of onomatopoetic words simply by sounding them, but you can also use your dictionary to verify your discovery: most have the term "imitative" as part of the information about word origins.

The usefulness of onomatopoeia, of course, is strictly limited, because it occurs only where the poet is describing sound, and most poems do not describe sound. But by combining onomatopoeia with other devices that help convey meaning, the poet can achieve subtle or bold emotional effects.

In addition to onomatopoetic words there is another group of words, sometimes called **phonetic intensives**, whose sound, by a process as yet obscure, to some degree connects with their meaning. An initial *fl* sound, for instance, is often associated with the idea of moving light, as in *flame, flare, flash, flicker, flimmer.* An initial *gl* also frequently accompanies the idea of light, usually unmoving, as in *glare, gleam, glint, glow, glisten.* An initial *sl* often introduces words meaning "smoothly wet," as in *slippery, slick, slide, slime, slop, slosh, slobber, slushy.* An initial *st* often suggests strength, as in *staunch, stalwart, stout, sturdy, stable, steady, stocky, stern, strong, stubborn, steel.* Short *i* often goes with the idea of smallness, as in *inch, imp, thin, slim, little, bit, chip, sliver, chink, slit, sip, whit, tittle, snip, wink, glint, glimmer, flicker, pigmy, midge, chick, kid, kitten, minikin, miniature.* Long *o* or *oo* may suggest melancholy or sorrow, as in *moan, groan, woe, mourn, forlorn, toll, doom, gloom, moody.* Final *are* sometimes goes with the idea of a big light or noise, as *flare, glare, stare, blare.* Medial *att* suggests some kind of particled movement as in *spatter, scatter, shatter, chatter, rattle, prattle, clatter, batter.* Final *er* and *le* indicate repetition, as in *glitter, flutter, shimmer, whisper, jabber, chatter, clatter, sputter, flicker, twitter, mutter,* and *ripple, bubble, twinkle, sparkle, rattle, rumble, jingle.*

None of these various sounds is invariably associated with the idea that it seems to suggest and, in fact, a short *i* is found in *thick* as well as *thin*, in *big* as well as *little*. Language is a complex phenomenon. But there is enough association between these sounds and ideas to suggest some sort of intrinsic if obscure relationship. A word like *flicker*, though not onomatopoetic (because it does not refer to sound) would seem somehow to suggest its sense, with the *fl* suggesting moving light, the *i* suggesting smallness, the *ck* suggesting sudden cessation of movement (as in *crack*, *peck*, *pick*, *hack*, and *flick*), and the *er* suggesting repetition. The preceding list of sound-idea correspondences is only a very partial one. A complete list, though it would involve only a small proportion of words in the language, would probably be longer than that of the more strictly onomatopoetic words, to which they are related.

Eight O'Clock

He stood, and heard the steeple
    Sprinkle the quarters on the morning town.
One, two, three, four, to market-place and people
    It tossed them down.

Strapped, noosed, nighing his hour,   5
    He stood and counted them and cursed his luck;
And then the clock collected in the tower
    Its strength, and struck.

A. E. Housman (1859–1936)

QUESTIONS

1. Vocabulary: *quarters* (2).
2. Eight A.M. was the traditional hour in England for putting condemned criminals to death. Discuss the force of "morning" (2) and "struck" (8). Discuss the appropriateness of the image of the clock collecting its strength. Can you suggest any reason for the use of "nighing" (5) rather than *nearing*?
3. Consider the contribution to meaning of the following phonetic intensives: "steeple" and "Sprinkle" (1, 2), "stood" (1, 6), "Strapped" (5), "strength" and "struck" (8). Comment on the frequent *k* sounds leading up to "struck" in the second stanza.

    A second and far more important way that the poet can reinforce meaning through sound is to choose sounds and group them so that the effect is smooth and pleasant sounding (*euphonious*) or rough and harsh sounding (*cacophonous*). Vowels are in general more pleasing than consonants, for vowels are musical tones, whereas consonants are merely noises. A line with a high percentage of vowel sounds in proportion to consonant sounds will therefore tend to be more melodious than one in which the proportion is low. The vowels and consonants themselves differ considerably in quality. The "long" vowels, such as those in *fate, reed, rhyme, coat, food,* and *dune* are fuller and more resonant than the "short" vowels, as in *fat, red, rim, cot, foot,* and *dun.* Of the consonants, some are fairly mellifluous, such as the "liquids," *l, m, n,* and *r;* the soft *v* and *f* sounds; the semivowels *w* and *y;* and such combinations as *th* and *wh.* Others, such as the "plosives," *b, d, g, k, p,* and *t,* are harsher and sharper in their effect. These differences in sound are the poet's materials. Good poets, however, will not necessarily seek out the sounds that are pleasing and attempt to combine them in melodious combinations. Rather, they will use **euphony** and **cacophony** as they are appropriate to content. Consider, for instance, the following lines.

Sound and Sense

True ease in writing comes from art, not chance,
As those move easiest who have learned to dance.
'Tis not enough no harshness gives offense,
The sound must seem an echo to the sense:
Soft is the strain when Zephyr gently blows,   5
And the smooth stream in smoother numbers flows;
But when loud surges lash the sounding shore,
The hoarse, rough verse should like the torrent roar;
When Ajax strives some rock's vast weight to throw,
The line too labors, and the words move slow;   10
Not so, when swift Camilla scours the plain,
Flies o'er the unbending corn, and skims along the main.
Hear how Timotheus' varied lays surprise,
And bid alternate passions fall and rise!

Alexander Pope (1688–1744)

QUESTIONS

1. Vocabulary: *numbers* (6), *lays* (13).
2. This excerpt is from a long poem (called *An Essay on Criticism*) on the arts of writing and judging poetry. Which line states the thesis of the passage?
3. There are four classical allusions: Zephyr (5) was god of the west wind; Ajax (9), a Greek warrior noted for his strength; Camilla (11), a legendary queen

reputedly so fleet of foot that she could run over a field of grain without bending the blades or over the sea without wetting her feet; Timotheus (13), a famous Greek rhapsodic poet. How do these allusions enable Pope to achieve greater economy?

4. Copy the passage and scan it. Then, considering both meter and sounds, show how Pope practices what he preaches. (Incidentally, on which syllable should "alternate" in line 14 be accented? Does the meter help you to know the pronunciation of "Timotheus" in line 13?)

There are no strictly onomatopoetic words in this passage, and yet the sound seems marvelously adapted to the sense. When the poem is about soft, smooth effects (lines 5–6), there is an abundance of alliteration (s in soft, strain, smooth stream, smoother) and consonance (the voiced s or z sound in Zephyr, blows, numbers flows; the voiced th of smooth and smoother). When harshness and loudness are the subject, the lines become cacophonous and even the pleasant smoothness of s-alliteration when coupled with sh evokes angry hissing: "surges lash the sounding shore, / The hoarse, rough verse should. . . ." Heavy labor is expressed in cacophony ("Ajax strives some rock's vast weight to throw"), while lightness and speed are expressed with euphonious short i sounds ("swift Camilla . . . skims"). Throughout the passage there is a remarkable correspondence between the pleasant-sounding and the pleasant in idea, the unpleasant-sounding and the unpleasant in idea.

As the excerpt from Alexander Pope also demonstrates, a third way in which a poet can reinforce meaning through sound is by controlling the speed and movement of the lines by the choice and use of meter, by the choice and arrangement of vowel and consonant sounds, and by the disposition of pauses. In meter the unaccented syllables usually go faster than the accented syllables; hence the triple meters are swifter than the duple. But the poet can vary the tempo of any meter by the use of substitute feet. Generally, whenever two or more unaccented syllables come together, the effect will be to speed up the pace of the line; when two or more accented syllables come together, the effect will be to slow it down. This pace will also be affected by the vowel lengths and by whether the sounds are easily run together. The long vowels take longer to pronounce than the short ones. Some words are easily run together, while others demand that the position of the mouth be re-formed before the next word is uttered. It takes much longer, for instance, to say "Watch dogs catch much meat" than to say "My aunt is away," though the number of syllables is the same. And finally the poet can slow down the speed of a line through the introduction of grammatical and rhetorical pauses. Consider lines 54–56 from Tennyson's "Ulysses" (page 747):

> The lights be-gin to twin-kle from the rocks;
>
> The long day wanes; the slow moon climbs; the deep   55
>
> Moans round with man-y voi-ces. . . .

In these lines Tennyson wished the movement to be slow, in accordance with the slow waning of the long day and the slow climbing of the moon. His meter is iambic pentameter. This is not a swift meter, but in lines 55–56 he slows it down further, by (a) introducing three spondaic feet, thus bringing three accented syllables together in two separate places; (b) choosing for his accented syllables words that have long vowel sounds or dipthongs that the voice hangs onto: "long," "day," "wanes," "slow," "moon," "climbs," "deep," "Moans," "round"; (c) choosing words that are not easily run together (except for "day" and "slow," each of these words begins and ends with consonant sounds that require varying degrees of readjustment of the mouth before pronunciation can continue); and (d) introducing two grammatical pauses, after "wanes" and "climbs," and a rhetorical pause after "deep." The result is an extremely effective use of the movement of the verse to accord with the movement suggested by the words.

A fourth way for a poet to fit sound to sense is to control both sound and meter in such a way as to emphasize words that are important in meaning. This can be done by highlighting such words through alliteration, assonance, consonance, or rhyme; by placing them before a pause; or by skillfully placing or displacing them in the metrical scheme. We have already seen how Ogden Nash uses alliteration and consonance to emphasize and link the three major words ("sex," "fix," and "fertile") in his little verse "The Turtle" (page 823), and how George Herbert pivots the structure of meaning in "Virtue" (page 843) on a trochaic substitution in the initial foot of his final stanza. For an additional example, let us look again at Drayton's "Since there's no help" (page 808). This poem is a sonnet—fourteen lines of iambic pentameter—in which a lover threatens to abandon his courtship if the woman he desires will not go to bed with him. In the first eight lines he pretends to be *glad* that they are parting so cleanly. In the last six lines, however, he paints a vivid picture of the death of his personified Love/Passion for her but intimates that even at this last moment ("Now") she could restore it to life—by satisfying his sexual desires:

> Now, at the last gasp of Love's la-test breath,
>
> When, his pulse failing, Passion speechless lies,   10
>
> When Faith is kneeling by his bed of death,
>
> And In-no-cence is clos-ing up his eyes,
>
> Now, if thou wouldst, when all have given him o-ver,*
>
> From death to life thou mightst him yet re-cov-er.

The emphasis is on *Now*. In a matter of seconds, the speaker indicates, it will be too late: his Love/Passion will be dead, and he himself will be gone. The word "Now" begins line 9. It also begins a new sentence and a new direction in the poem. It is separated from what has gone before by a period at the end of the preceding line. Metrically it initiates a trochee, thus breaking away from the poem's basic iambic meter (line 8 is perfectly regular). In all these ways—its initial position in line, sentence, and thought, and its metrical irregularity—the word "Now" is given extraordinary emphasis appropriate to its importance in the context. Its repetition in line 13 reaffirms this importance, and there again it is given emphasis by its positional and metrical situation. It begins both a line and the final rhyming couplet, is separated by punctuation from the line before, and participates in a metrical inversion. (The lines before and after are metrically regular.)

While Herbert and Drayton use metrical deviation to give emphasis to important words, Tennyson, in the concluding line of "Ulysses," uses marked regularity, plus skillful use of grammatical pauses, to achieve the same effect.

> We are not now that strength which in old days
>
> Moved earth and heav-en, that which we are, we are:
>
> One e-qual tem-per of he-ro-ic hearts,

---

*Drayton probably intended "given" to be pronounced as one syllable (*giv'n*), and most sixteenth-century readers would have pronounced it thus in this poem.

Made weak by time and fate, but strong in will

To strive, to seek, to find, and not to yield.   70

The blank-verse rhythm throughout "Ulysses" is remarkably subtle and varied, but the last line is not only regular in its scansion but heavily regular, for a number of reasons. First, all the words are monosyllables. Second, the unaccented syllables are all very small and unimportant words—four *tos* and one *and*—whereas the accented syllables consist of four important verbs and a very important *not*. Third, each of the verbs is followed by a grammatical pause pointed off by a mark of punctuation. The result is to cause a pronounced alternation between light and heavy syllables that brings the accent down on the four verbs and the *not* with sledgehammer blows. The line rings out like a challenge, which it is.

I heard a Fly buzz—when I died

I heard a Fly buzz—when I died—
The Stillness in the Room
Was like the Stillness in the Air—
Between the Heaves of Storm—

The Eyes around—had wrung them dry—   5
And Breaths were gathering firm
For that last Onset—when the King
Be witnessed—in the Room—

I willed my Keepsakes—Signed away
What portion of me be   10
Assignable—and then it was
There interposed a Fly—

With Blue—uncertain stumbling Buzz—
Between the light—and me—
And then the Windows failed—and then   15
I could not see to see—

Emily Dickinson (1830–1886)

QUESTIONS

1. It is important to understand the sequence of events in this deathbed scene. Arrange the following events in correct chronological order: (a) the willing

of keepsakes, (b) the weeping of mourners, (c) the appearance of the fly, (d) the preternatural stillness in the room.

2. What or who are the "Eyes" and the "Breaths" in lines 5–6? What figures of speech are involved in these lines? Is the speaker making out her will in lines 9–11? What *is* she doing?

3. What sort of expectation is set up by phrases like "last Onset" (7), "the King" (7), and "Be witnessed" (8)?

4. Explain "the Windows failed" (15) and "I could not see to see" (16).

We may well conclude our discussion of the adaptation of sound to sense by analyzing this poem. It consists of four four-line stanzas of alternating iambic tetrameter (first and third lines) and iambic trimeter (second and fourth); the first and third lines are unrhymed, the second and fourth display approximate rhymes in the first three stanzas. The fourth stanza uses an exact rhyme that echoes the last word in line 3 of the preceding stanza. The poem depicts a speaker's recollection of her own deathbed scene, focusing on the suspenseful interval during which she and her loved ones await the arrival of death—ironically symbolized in the closing lines as a common housefly. But the poem does not move chronologically. Surprisingly, it begins with its conclusion, the apparently trivial fact that the last conscious perception was hearing the buzzing fly; then it proceeds to summarize the events leading up to that moment.

How is the poem's sound fitted to its sense? In the opening stanzas, the pace is slow and even solemn, the rhythm perfectly matching the meter, as befits this apparently momentous occasion with its "Stillness," its quiet, breathless awaiting of "the King"—death itself. The approximate rhymes provide a formal unity even as they convey an atmosphere of unease, an uncertainty and fear in the face of imminent death; and the dashes contribute to the poem's measured, stately rhythm. Then the poem returns to the insignificant topic of its opening line and invests it with enormous meaning.

The one onomatopoetic word in the poem is *Buzz*, introduced abruptly in line 1 without capitalization and then reintroduced with intensity in line 13. In line 11, the final word, *was*, though unrhymed in its own stanza and unrhymed in the formal rhyme scheme, nevertheless is an exact rhyme for *Buzz* in the first line of the final stanza. In line 12, the word *interposed* continues the buzzing into the final stanza. In line 13 the vowel sound of *Buzz* is preceded by the identical vowel sounds in "uncertain" and "stumbling," making three *u* sounds in close succession. Finally, the *b* sound in *Buzz* is preceded in line 13 by the *b*s in "Blue" and "stumbling." Thus *all* the sounds in *Buzz*—its initial and final consonants and its vowel—are heard at least three times in lines 11–13. This outburst of onomatopoetic effect consummates the aural imagery promised in the opening line, "I *heard* a Fly buzz."

But line 13 combines images of color and motion as well as sound. Though the sound imagery is the most important, the poem concludes with a reference to the speaker's dimming eyesight, and we may infer that she *saw* a blur of the bluebottle's deep metallic blue as well as hearing its buzz. This image is an example of **synesthesia,** the stimulation of two or more senses simultaneously, especially as here, where one sense perception is described in terms of another (as in a "Blue . . . Buzz"). The images of motion between "Blue" and "Buzz" also belong to both the visual and aural modes of sensing. The speaker hears and imperfectly sees the "uncertain" flight of the fly as it bumbles from one pane of glass to another, its buzzing now louder, now softer. Furthermore, the exact rhymes in the last stanza that pick up on "was" in the preceding one underscore the abrupt finality of the speaker's confrontation with death, and thus the sudden end of her human perception.

In analyzing verse for correspondence between sound and sense, we need to be very cautious not to make exaggerated claims. A great deal of nonsense has been written about the moods of certain meters and the effects of certain sounds, and it is easy to suggest correspondences that exist only in our imaginations. Nevertheless, the first-rate poet has nearly always an instinctive tact about handling sound so that it in some degree supports meaning. One of the few absolute rules that applies to the judgment of poetry is that the form should be adequate to the content. This rule does not mean that there must always be a close and easily demonstrable correspondence. It does mean that there will be no glaring discrepancies.

The selection that introduces this chapter ("Pease porridge hot") illustrates the use of sound in verse almost purely for its own sake, and it is, as significant poetry, among the most trivial passages in the whole book. But beyond this there is an abundant range of poetic possibilities where sound is pleasurable for itself without violating meaning and where sound to varying degrees corresponds with and corroborates meaning; and in this rich middle range lie many of the great pleasures of reading poetry.

EXERCISE

In each of the following paired quotations, the named poet wrote the version that more successfully adapts sound to sense. As specifically as possible, account for the superiority of the better version.

1. a. Go forth—and Virtue, ever in your sight,
        Shall be your guide by day, your guard by night.

   b. Go forth—and Virtue, ever in your sight,
      Shall point your way by day, and keep you safe at night.

Charles Churchill

2. a. How charming is divine philosophy!
     Not harsh and rough as foolish men suppose
     But musical as is the lute of Phoebus.
  b. How charming is divine philosophy!
     Not harsh and crabbed as dull fools suppose
     But musical as is Apollo's lute.

John Milton

3. a. All day the fleeing crows croak hoarsely over the snow.
  b. All day the out-cast crows croak hoarsely across the whiteness.

Elizabeth Coatsworth

4. a. Your talk attests how bells of singing gold
     Would sound at evening over silent water.
  b. Your low voice tells how bells of singing gold
     Would sound at twilight over silent water.   *Edwin Arlington Robinson*

5. a. A thousand streamlets flowing through the lawn,
     The moan of doves in gnarled ancient oaks,
     And quiet murmuring of countless bees.
  b. Myriads of rivulets hurrying through the lawn,
     The moan of doves in immemorial elms,
     And murmuring of innumerable bees.   *Alfred, Lord Tennyson*

6. a. It is the lark that sings so out of tune,
     Straining harsh discords and unpleasing sharps.
  b. It is the lark that warbles out of tune
     In harsh discordant tones with doleful flats.   *William Shakespeare*

7. a. "Artillery" and "armaments" and "implements of war"
     Are phrases too severe to please the gentle Muse.
  b. Bombs, drums, guns, bastions, batteries, bayonets, bullets,—
     Hard words, which stick in the soft Muses' gullets.   *Lord Byron*

8. a. The hands of the sisters Death and Night incessantly softly
       wash again, and ever again, this soiled world.
  b. The hands of the soft twins Death and Night repeatedly
       wash again, and ever again, this dirty world.   *Walt Whitman*

9. a. The curfew sounds the knell of parting day,
     The lowing cattle slowly cross the lea,
     The plowman goes wearily plodding his homeward way,
     Leaving the world to the darkening night and me.
  b. The curfew tolls the knell of parting day,
     The lowing herd wind slowly o'er the lea,

The plowman homeward plods his weary way,
And leaves the world to darkness and to me.   *Thomas Gray*

10. a. Let me chastise this odious, gilded bug,
       This painted son of dirt, that smells and bites.
    b. Yet let me flap this bug with gilded wings,
       This painted child of dirt, that stinks and stings.   *Alexander Pope*

REVIEWING CHAPTER THIRTEEN

1. Review the terms in the chapter presented in boldface.
2. The chapter presents four important means by which sound reinforces meaning; in reviewing them, decide whether the meaning being reinforced is intellectual or emotional, or both.
3. In the following poems, identify any of the devices by which sound reinforces meaning, being sure to define the meaning that is being reinforced—and identifying any elements of poetry that are employed in creating that meaning.

Anthem for Doomed Youth

What passing-bells for these who die as cattle?
Only the monstrous anger of the guns.
Only the stuttering rifles' rapid rattle
Can patter out their hasty orisons.
No mockeries now for them; no prayers nor bells,   5
Nor any voice of mourning save the choirs—
The shrill, demented choirs of wailing shells;
And bugles calling for them from sad shires.

What candles may be held to speed them all?
Not in the hands of boys, but in their eyes   10
Shall shine the holy glimmers of good-byes.
The pallor of girls' brows shall be their pall;
Their flowers the tenderness of patient minds,
And each slow dusk a drawing-down of blinds.

Wilfred Owen (1893–1918)

QUESTIONS

1. Vocabulary: *passing-bells* (1), *orisons* (4), *shires* (8), *pall* (12). It was the custom during World War I to draw down the blinds in homes where a son had been lost (14).
2. How do the octave and the sestet of this sonnet differ in (a) geographical setting, (b) subject matter, (c) kind of imagery used, and (d) tone? Who are the "boys" (10) and "girls" (12) referred to in the sestet?
3. What central metaphorical image runs throughout the poem? What secondary metaphors build up the central one?
4. Why are the "doomed youth" said to die "as cattle" (1)? Why would prayers, bells, and so on, be "mockeries" for them (5)?
5. Show how sound is adapted to sense throughout the poem.

Landcrab

A lie, that we come from water.
The truth is we were born
from stones, dragons, the sea's
teeth, as you testify,
with your crust and jagged scissors.   5

Hermit, hard socket
for a timid eye
you're a soft gut scuttling
sideways, a bone skull,
round bone on the prowl.   10
Wolf of treeroots and gravelly holes,
a mount on stilts,
the husk of a small demon.

Attack, voracious
eating, and flight: 15
it's a sound routine
for staying alive on edges.
Then there's the tide, and that dance
you do for the moon
on wet sand, claws raised   20
to fend off your mate,
your coupling a quick
dry clatter of rocks.
For mammals
with their lobes and bulbs,   25

scruples and warm milk,
you've nothing but contempt.

Here you are, a frozen scowl
targeted in flashlight,
then gone: a piece of what   30
we are, not all,
my stunted child, my momentary
face in the mirror,
my tiny nightmare.

Margaret Atwood (b. 1939)

QUESTIONS

1. What theory of the origin of human life is alluded to in line 1? Line 3 alludes to two Greek myths, of Deucalion strewing stones and Cadmus sowing dragon's teeth. If these are unfamiliar, look them up. What do theories about the origins of humankind have to do with the speaker's description of the landcrab? How do lines 30–34 return to that subject?

2. What do the free-verse rhythms contribute to the experience of the poem? Discuss the cacophony and euphony in lines 22–25. Where do you find other examples?

Recital

Roger Bobo Gives
Recital on Tuba
—Headline in the Times

Eskimos in Manitoba,
    Barracuda off Aruba,
Cock an ear when Roger Bobo
    Starts to solo on the tuba.

Men of every station—Pooh-Bah,   5
    Nabob, bozo, toff, and hobo—
Cry in unison, "Indubi-
    Tably, there is simply nobo-

Dy who oompahs on the tubo,
Solo, quite like Roger Bubo!"   10

John Updike (b. 1932)

QUESTIONS

1. Vocabulary: *Pooh-Bah* (5), *Nabob* (6), *bozo* (6), *toff* (6).
2. The tuba is a large wind instrument with a deep, brassy sound. It is rarely played in solo recitals. How do the diction and rhyme scheme help convey the sound of a tuba? Identify the one onomatopoetic word that imitates the tuba's sound.
3. How would you describe the tone of the poem? Account for the purposeful misspellings at the ends of lines 9–10. Do you think the poet would have written a poem about a tuba player named Roger Smith?

Aunt Jennifer's Tigers

Aunt Jennifer's tigers prance across a screen,
Bright topaz denizens of a world of green.
They do not fear the men beneath the tree;
They pace in sleek chivalric certainty.

Aunt Jennifer's fingers fluttering through her wool   5
Find even the ivory needle hard to pull.
The massive weight of Uncle's wedding band
Sits heavily upon Aunt Jennifer's hand.

When Aunt is dead, her terrified hands will lie
Still ringed with ordeals she was mastered by.   10
The tigers in the panel that she made
Will go on prancing, proud and unafraid.

Adrienne Rich (b. 1929)

At the round earth's imagined corners

At the round earth's imagined corners, blow
Your trumpets, angels; and arise, arise
From death, you numberless infinities
Of souls, and to your scattered bodies go:
All whom the flood did, and fire shall, o'erthrow,   5
All whom war, dearth, age, agues, tyrannies,
Despair, law, chance hath slain, and you whose eyes
Shall behold God and never taste death's woe.
But let them sleep, Lord, and me mourn a space;
For if above all these, my sins abound,   10

'Tis late to ask abundance of thy grace
When we are there. Here on this lowly ground,
Teach me how to repent; for that's as good
As if thou hadst sealed my pardon with thy blood.

John Donne (1572–1631)

QUESTIONS

1. The poem refers to the Christian doctrine of the resurrection of the body, according to which after the destruction of the world the soul will be reunited with the body—not the imperfect body of mortal life, but a perfected, glorified body. Several lines contain biblical allusions: Revelation 7.1 (1), Job 19. 25–26 (2–4), Romans 6.1 (10–11). What is the speaker calling for in lines 1–8? Why does he change his plea in lines 9–12? Where is "there" (12)?
2. Scan lines 1–8. How do the rhythms reinforce the meanings in these lines? What is the effect of the placement of "blow" (1)? Scan lines 11–12. What do the lack of a caesura in line 11 and the emphatic caesura in line 12 contribute to meaning? Comment on the trochaic substitution in line 12.

Blackberry Eating

I love to go out in late September
among fat, overripe, icy, black blackberries
to eat blackberries for breakfast,
the stalks very prickly, a penalty
they earn for knowing the black art   5
of blackberry-making; and as I stand among them
lifting the stalks to my mouth, the ripest berries
fall almost unbidden to my tongue,
as words sometimes do, certain peculiar words
like *strengths* or *squinched*,   10
many-lettered, one-syllabled lumps,
which I squeeze, squinch open, and splurge well
in the silent, startled, icy, black language
of blackberry-eating in late September.

Galway Kinnell (b. 1927)

QUESTIONS

1. Vocabulary: *black art* (5), *squinched* (10).
2. What comparison does the poet find between "certain peculiar words" (9) and blackberries? How appropriate is it?

3. Is the poem free verse or metrical? How do various musical devices reinforce its meaning?

Golden Retrievals

Fetch? Balls and sticks capture my attention
seconds at a time. Catch? I don't think so.
Bunny, tumbling leaf, a squirrel who's—oh
joy—actually scared. Sniff the wind, then

I'm off again: muck, pond, ditch, residue   5
of any thrillingly dead thing. And you?
Either you're sunk in the past, half our walk,
thinking of what you never can bring back,

or else you're off in some fog concerning
—tomorrow, is that what you call it? My work: 10
to unsnare time's warp (and woof!), retrieving,
my haze-headed friend, you. This shining bark,

a Zen master's bronzy gong, calls you here,
entirely, now: bow-wow, bow-wow, bow-wow.

Mark Doty (b. 1953)

QUESTIONS

1. Vocabulary: *warp* (11), *woof* (11).
2. You should have no difficulty identifying the speaker. How do the attitudes in the poem reflect what a dog *might* think about a walk with its owner? Select a few of the most vivid details to answer this question.
3. Explain why the dog seems to feel superior to its owner. Who is in charge?
4. The last line obviously contains onomatopoeia. Are there other examples?
5. Point out places in which the rhythm of the poem seems to imitate a dog's movements.
6. The dramatic situation of the poem, presenting a talking dog, is not the total meaning. What does the poem really say about the relationship between a dog and its owner?

A Fire-Truck

Right down the shocked street with a siren-blast
That sends all else skittering to the curb,
Redness, brass, ladders and hats hurl past,
    Blurring to sheer verb,

Shift at the corner into uproarious gear   5
And make it around the turn in a squall of traction,
The headlong bell maintaining sure and clear,
    Thought is degraded action!

Beautiful, heavy, unweary, loud, obvious thing!
I stand here purged of nuance, my mind a blank.   10
All I was brooding upon has taken wing,
    And I have you to thank.

As you howl beyond hearing I carry you into my mind,
Ladders and brass and all, there to admire
Your phoenix-red simplicity, enshrined   15
    In that not extinguished fire.

Richard Wilbur (b. 1921)

QUESTIONS

1. Vocabulary: *squall* (6), *nuance* (10). At one time, most fire trucks in America were painted bright red (see lines 3, 15).
2. Why is "Blurring to sheer verb" (4) an effective description of the truck?
3. The speaker interprets the fire truck's bell as the message *"Thought is degraded action!"* (8). In the third stanza, how has this exclamation affected the speaker's state of mind? Is the phrase "I have you to thank" (12) ironic or sincere?
4. Discuss the meaning of the phrase "phoenix-red simplicity" (15). What is "that not extinguished fire" (16)?
5. Examine the poem for such musical devices as assonance, consonance, and alliteration.

The Dance

In Breughel's great picture, The Kermess,
the dancers go round, they go round and
around, the squeal and the blare and the
tweedle of bagpipes, a bugle and fiddles
tipping their bellies (round as the thick-   5
sided glasses whose wash they impound)
their hips and their bellies off balance
to turn them. Kicking and rolling about
the Fair Grounds, swinging their butts, those
shanks must be sound to bear up under such   10

rollicking measures, prance as they dance
in Breughel's great picture, The Kermess.

William Carlos Williams (1883–1963)

QUESTIONS

1. Peter Breughel the Elder was a sixteenth-century Flemish painter of peasant life. A *kermess* is an annual outdoor festival or fair. How would you characterize the mood of the people depicted in this poem?
2. Examine the poem for alliteration, consonance, assonance, and onomatopoeia. When you pronounce the syllable *ound* (lines 2, 3, 5, 6, 9, 10), how does the shape your mouth makes seem to intensify the effect?
3. Scan the poem. (Notice that the initial syllable in lines 2, 3, and 8 has the effect of completing the rhythm of the preceding line.) What one word in the poem echoes the prevailing metrical foot, describes the rhythm of the poem, and defines the mood of the picture?
4. How does sound reinforce content in this poem? What is the attitude of the speaker to the activities shown in the picture?

SUGGESTIONS FOR WRITING

Write a short essay discussing the relationship of the poem's sound to its meaning in one of the following.
1. Dickinson, "I felt a Funeral, in my Brain" (page 705).
2. Atwood, "Landcrab" (page 876).
3. Wilbur, "A Fire-Truck" (page 880).
4. Keats, "Ode on a Grecian Urn" (page 918).
5. Hardy, "Channel Firing" (page 968).
6. Kumin, "The Sound of Night" (page 979).
7. Stevens, "The Snow Man" (page 1008).
8. Yeats, "Sailing to Byzantium" (page 1021).

Chapter Fourteen

Pattern

Art, ultimately, is organization. It is a searching after order and significance. Most artists seek to transform the chaotic nature of experience into a meaningful and coherent pattern, largely by means of selection and arrangement. For this reason we evaluate a poem partially by the same criteria that an English instructor uses to evaluate an essay theme—by its unity, its coherence, and its proper placing of emphasis. A well-constructed poem contains neither too little nor too much; every part of the poem belongs where it is and could be placed nowhere else; any interchanging of two stanzas, two lines, or even two words, would to some extent damage the poem and make it less effective. We come to feel, with a truly first-rate poem, that the choice and placement of every word are inevitable, that they could not be otherwise.

In addition to the internal ordering of the materials—the arrangement of ideas, images, thoughts, sentences, which we refer to as the poem's **structure**—the poet may impose some external pattern on a poem, may give it not only its internal order of materials but an external shape or **form.** Such formality appeals to the human instinct for design, the instinct that has prompted people, at various times, to tattoo and paint their bodies, to decorate their swords and armor with beautiful and complex tracery, and to choose patterned fabrics for their clothing, carpets, curtains, and wallpapers. The poet appeals to our love of the shapely.

In general, a poem may be cast in one of the three broad kinds of form: continuous form, stanzaic form, and fixed form. In **continuous form,** as illustrated by "The Widow's Lament in Springtime" (page 704), "After Apple-Picking" (page 708), "Ulysses" (page 746), and "My Last Duchess" (page 775), the element of design is slight. The lines follow each other without formal grouping, the only breaks being dictated by units of meaning, as paragraphs are in prose. But even here there are degrees of pattern. "The Widow's Lament in Springtime" has neither regular meter nor rhyme. "After Apple-Picking," on the other hand, is metrical; it has no regularity of length of line, but the meter is predominantly iambic; in addition, every line rhymes with another, though not according to any fixed pattern. "Ulysses" is regular in both meter and length of line: it is unrhymed iambic pentameter, or blank verse. And to these regularities "My Last Duchess" adds regularity of rhyme, for it is written in rhyming pentameter couplets. Thus, in increasing degrees, the authors of "After Apple-Picking," "Ulysses," and "My Last Duchess" have chosen a predetermined pattern in which to cast their work.

In **stanzaic form** the poet writes in a series of **stanzas**; that is, repeated units having the same number of lines, usually the same metrical pattern, and often an identical rhyme scheme. The poet may choose some traditional stanza pattern or invent an original one. The traditional stanza patterns (for example, terza rima, ballad meter, rhyme royal, Spenserian stanza) are many, and the student specializing in literature will wish to become familiar with some of them; the general student should know that they exist. Often the use of one of these traditional stanza forms constitutes a kind of literary allusion. When we are aware of the traditional use of a stanza form, or of its previous use by a great poet for a particular subject or experience, we may find additional subtleties of meaning in its later use. Robert Frost employs the same verse form for his poem about a moral quest as Dante uses for his great poem about moral truth, *The Divine Comedy*, with meaningful results (see "Acquainted with the Night," page 897).

Stanzaic form, like continuous form, exhibits degrees of formal pattern. The poem "in Just—" (page 782) is divided into alternating stanzas of four lines and one line, but the four-line stanzas have no formal resemblance to each other except for the number of lines, and the one-line stanzas are similarly disparate. In "Naming of Parts" (page 692) the stanzas are alike in number of lines and in meter, but they have no rhyme pattern. In "The Aim Was Song" (page 855) a rhyme scheme is added to a metrical pattern. In "Winter" (page 650) and "Blow, blow, thou winter wind" (page 830) Shakespeare employs a refrain in addition to the patterns of meter and rhyme. The following poem illustrates additional elements of design.

The Pulley

When God at first made man,
Having a glass of blessings standing by,
   "Let us," said he, "pour on him all we can:
Let the world's riches, which dispersèd lie,
   Contract into a span."   5

So Strength first made a way;
Then Beauty flowed; then Wisdom, Honor, Pleasure.
    When almost all was out, God made a stay,
Perceiving that alone of all his treasure
        Rest in the bottom lay.   10

    "For if I should," said he,
"Bestow this jewel also on my creature,
    He would adore my gifts instead of me,
And rest in Nature, not the God of Nature;
        So both should losers be.   15

    "Yet let him keep the rest,
But keep them with repining restlessness:
    Let him be rich and weary, that at least,
If goodness lead him not, yet weariness
        May toss him to my breast."   20

George Herbert (1593–1633)

QUESTIONS

1. Vocabulary: *span* (5, archaic meaning).
2. The words "riches" (4), "treasure" (9), "jewel" (12), and "gifts" (13) create an extended metaphor. What is being compared to things of material value? Does the word "rich" in line 18 refer to the same thing as "riches" in line 4?
3. The title "The Pulley" refers to a simple mechanical device for lifting weights. How does a pulley work? How does it metaphorically express the meaning of the last stanza?
4. To what does "both" (15) refer? What are God's final intentions?

A stanza form may be described by designating four things: the rhyme scheme (if there is one), the position of the refrain (if there is one), the prevailing metrical foot, and the number of feet in each line. Rhyme scheme is traditionally designated by using letters of the alphabet to indicate the rhyming lines, and *x* for unrhymed lines. Refrain lines may be indicated by a capital letter, and the number of feet in the line by a numerical exponent after the letter. Thus the stanza pattern of Browning's "Meeting at Night" (page 701) is iambic tetrameter *abccba* (or iambic $abccba^4$); that of Donne's "A Hymn to God the Father" (page 697) is iambic $abab^5A^4B^2$; that of "The Pulley" is iambic $a^3bab^5a^3$.

A **fixed form** is a traditional pattern that applies to a whole poem. In French poetry many fixed forms have been widely used: rondeaus, rondels, villanelles, triolets, sestinas, ballades, double ballades, and others. In English poetry, though most of the fixed forms have been experimented with, perhaps only two—the sonnet and the villanelle—have really taken hold.

Although it is classified as a fixed form, through centuries of practice the **sonnet** has attained a degree of flexibility. It must be fourteen lines in length, and it almost always is iambic pentameter, but in structure and rhyme scheme there may be considerable leeway. Most sonnets, however, conform more or less closely to one of two general models or types: the Italian and the English.

The **Italian** or *Petrarchan* **sonnet** (so-called because the Italian poet Petrarch practiced it so extensively) is divided usually between eight lines called the **octave**, using two rhymes arranged *abbaabba*, and six lines called the **sestet**, using any arrangement of either two or three rhymes: *cdcdcd* and *cdecde* are common patterns. The division between octave and sestet in the Italian sonnet (indicated by the rhyme scheme and sometimes marked off in printing by a space) usually corresponds to a division of thought. The octave may, for instance, present a situation and the sestet a comment, or the octave an idea and the sestet an example, or the octave a question and the sestet an answer. Thus the form reflects the structure.

On First Looking into Chapman's Homer

Much have I traveled in the realms of gold,
  And many goodly states and kingdoms seen;
  Round many western islands have I been
Which bards in fealty to Apollo hold.
Oft of one wide expanse had I been told   5
  That deep-browed Homer ruled as his demesne;
  Yet did I never breathe its pure serene
Till I heard Chapman speak out loud and bold:
Then felt I like some watcher of the skies
  When a new planet swims into his ken;   10
Or like stout Cortez when with eagle eyes
  He stared at the Pacific—and all his men
Looked at each other with a wild surmise—
  Silent, upon a peak in Darien.

John Keats (1795–1821)

QUESTIONS

1. Vocabulary: *fealty* (4), *Apollo* (4), *demesne* (6), *ken* (10). *Darien* (14) is an ancient name for the Isthmus of Panama.
2. John Keats, at twenty-one, could not read Greek and was probably acquainted with Homer's *Iliad* and *Odyssey* only through the translations of Alexander Pope, which to him very likely seemed prosy and stilted. Then one day he and a friend found a vigorous poetic translation by the Elizabethan poet George Chapman. Keats and his friend, enthralled, sat up late at night excitedly reading aloud to each other from Chapman's book. Toward morning Keats walked home and, before going to bed, wrote the above sonnet and sent it to his friend. What common ideas underlie the three major figures of speech in the poem?
3. What is the rhyme scheme? What division of thought corresponds to the division between octave and sestet?
4. Balboa, not Cortez, discovered the Pacific. How seriously does this mistake detract from the value of the poem?

The **English** or *Shakespearean* **sonnet** (invented by the English poet Surrey and made famous by Shakespeare) consists of three quatrains and a concluding couplet, rhyming *abab cdcd efef gg*. Again, the units marked off by the rhymes and the development of the thought often correspond. The three quatrains, for instance, may present three examples and the couplet a conclusion, or (as in the following example) the quatrains three metaphorical statements of one idea and the couplet an application.

That time of year

That time of year thou mayst in me behold
When yellow leaves, or none, or few, do hang
Upon those boughs which shake against the cold,
Bare ruined choirs where late the sweet birds sang.
In me thou see'st the twilight of such day   5
As after sunset fadeth in the west,
Which by and by black night doth take away,
Death's second self, that seals up all in rest.
In me thou see'st the glowing of such fire,
That on the ashes of his youth doth lie   10
As the deathbed whereon it must expire,
Consumed with that which it was nourished by.
This thou perceivest, which makes thy love more strong,
To love that well which thou must leave ere long.

William Shakespeare (1564–1616)

QUESTIONS

1. What are the three major images introduced by the three quatrains? What do they have in common? Can you see any reason for presenting them in this particular order, or might they be rearranged without loss?
2. Each of the images is to some degree complicated rather than simple. For instance, what additional image is introduced by "Bare ruined choirs" (4)? Explain its appropriateness.
3. What additional comparisons are introduced in the second and third quatrains? Explain line 12.
4. Whom does the speaker address? What assertion does he make in the concluding couplet, and with what degree of confidence? Paraphrase these lines so as to state their meaning as clearly as possible.

The tradition of the sonnet has proved useful because it seems effective or appropriate for certain types of subject matter and treatment. By its history as the vehicle for love poetry in the sixteenth century, the sonnet is particularly effective when used for the serious treatment of love. But it has also been used for the discussion of death, religion, political situations, and various other serious subjects. There is, of course, no magical or mysterious identity between certain forms and certain types of content, but there may be more or less correspondence. A form may seem appropriate or inappropriate. Excellent sonnets have been written outside the traditional areas.

The **villanelle**, with its complex pattern of repetition and rhyme, has become a significant form in English only in the past hundred years or so, but of the fixed forms it probably now ranks second to the sonnet. The form requires only two rhyme sounds, and its nineteen lines are divided into five three-line stanzas (tercets) and a four-line concluding quatrain. The first and third lines of the first stanza serve as refrain lines entwined with the rhyme pattern—the first line repeated at the ends of the second and fourth stanzas, and the third repeated at the ends of the third and fifth stanzas. In the concluding stanza, the refrains are repeated as lines 18 and 19. We can express the pattern thus: A^1bA^2 abA^1 abA^2 abA^1 abA^2 abA^1A^2.

Poets have been attracted to villanelles partly because they are notoriously difficult to compose effectively, thus posing a challenge to a poet's technical skill, and partly because the varying emphases given to repeated lines, along with the repetition itself, can achieve haunting, unforgettable effects. The original French models were usually light-hearted and witty, exploiting the potential for cleverness and humor inherent in the form, but modern poets often have employed the villanelle for serious subject matter. The following example, composed when the poet's father was near death, is perhaps the most famous villanelle in English.

Do Not Go Gentle into That Good Night

Do not go gentle into that good night,
Old age should burn and rave at close of day;
Rage, rage against the dying of the light.

Though wise men at their end know dark is right,
Because their words had forked no lightning they   5
Do not go gentle into that good night.

Good men, the last wave by, crying how bright
Their frail deeds might have danced in a green bay,
Rage, rage against the dying of the light.

Wild men who caught and sang the sun in flight,   10
And learn, too late, they grieved it on its way,
Do not go gentle into that good night.

Grave men, near death, who see with blinding sight
Blind eyes could blaze like meteors and be gay,
Rage, rage against the dying of the light.   15

And you, my father, there on the sad height,
Curse, bless, me now with your fierce tears, I pray.
Do not go gentle into that good night.
Rage, rage against the dying of the light.

Dylan Thomas (1914–1953)

QUESTIONS

1. Discuss the various meanings in this poem of the common phrase "good night."
2. Apart from the fixed form, the poem creates another structural principle in stanzas two through six by describing in turn "wise men" (4), "Good men" (7), "Wild men" (10), and "Grave men" (13). How does the speaker view these various types of men in their differing stances toward both life and death?
3. There are several paradoxical expressions in the poem: "dark is right" (4), "blinding sight" (13), "the sad height" (16), and "Curse, bless, me now" (17). How do these contribute to the poem's meaning?

   A good villanelle avoids the potentially monotonous effects of repetition by varying the stress patterns and the meaning of the repeated lines. In Thomas's poem, for example, the third line is a direct address by the speaker to his father, while the repetition in line 9 describes the rage "Good men" feel just before their deaths. Similarly, the poem deftly alternates lines containing grammatical pauses, such as line 7, with lines having no pauses, such as line 8; the blend of run-on and end-stopped lines likewise helps to vary the rhythm. The fixed form also serves the poem's meaning, since the repetition and the circular quality of the villanelle, its continued reiteration of the same two lines, emphasizes the speaker's emotional treadmill, his desperate and perhaps hopeless prayer that his father might rage against death. As in all good poetry, a fixed form like the villanelle does not merely display the poet's technical ability but appropriately supports the tone and meaning of the poem.

Initially, it may seem absurd that poets should choose to confine themselves in an arbitrary formal mold with prescribed meter and rhyme scheme. They do so partly from the desire to carry on a tradition, as all of us carry out certain traditions for their own sake, else why should we bring a tree indoors at Christmas time? Traditional forms are also useful because they have provided a challenge to the poet, and good poets are inspired by the challenge: it will call forth ideas and images that might not otherwise have come. They will subdue the form rather than be subdued by it; they will make it do what they require. There is no doubt that the presence of a net makes good tennis players more precise in their shots than they otherwise might be. And finally, for the poet and for the reader, there is the pleasure of form itself.

EXERCISE

The typographical shape of a poem on the page (whether, for example, printed with a straight left-hand margin or with a system of indentations) is determined sometimes by the poet, sometimes by the printer, sometimes by an editor. Examine each of the following poems and try to deduce what *principle* (if any) determined its typographical design:

1. Shakespeare, "Winter" (page 650).
2. Marvell, "To His Coy Mistress" (page 730).
3. Hughes, "Dream Deferred" (page 732).
4. Evans, "When in Rome" (page 679).
5. cummings, "in Just—" (page 782).
6. Wilbur, "The Writer" (page 750).
7. Yeats, "Leda and the Swan" (page 788).
8. Donne, "The Flea" (page 814).
9. Ferlinghetti, "Constantly risking absurdity" (page 860).
10. Blake, "The Lamb" (page 946).

REVIEWING CHAPTER FOURTEEN

1. Distinguish between structure and form, and review the definitions of the three broad types of form in poetry; using examples from the following poems in the chapter, define both the form and the structure of the poem.
2. Examine the definitions of the two types of sonnet, and explore the way in which the form of each seems to promote the structure of materials in the poem.
3. The villanelle also suggests the structure of the poem's materials; using examples from the following poems, define that implied structure.
4. Poetic forms may rely on the reader's familiarity with the subjects customarily presented in such forms—and poets may employ a form either to fulfill a reader's expectations or ironically to play against them. Find examples of both uses of the forms of the sonnet and the villanelle.

From *Romeo and Juliet*

ROMEO	If I profane with my unworthiest hand	
	This holy shrine, the gentle sin is this:	
	My lips, two blushing pilgrims, ready stand	
	To smooth that rough touch with a tender kiss.	
JULIET	Good pilgrim, you do wrong your hand too much,	5
	Which mannerly devotion shows in this;	
	For saints have hands that pilgrims' hands do touch,	
	And palm to palm is holy palmers' kiss.	
ROMEO	Have not saints lips, and holy palmers too?	
JULIET	Ay, pilgrim, lips that they must use in prayer.	10
ROMEO	O! then, dear saint, let lips do what hands do;	
	They pray, "Grant thou, lest faith turn to despair."	
JULIET	Saints do not move,° though grant for prayer's sake.	propose,
ROMEO	Then move not, while my prayer's effect I take.	instigate

William Shakespeare (1564–1616)

QUESTIONS

1. These fourteen lines occur in Act 1, scene 5, of Shakespeare's play. They are the first words exchanged between Romeo and Juliet, who are meeting, for the first time, at a masquerade ball given by her father. Struck by Juliet's beauty, Romeo has come up to greet her. What stage action accompanies this passage?
2. What is the basic metaphor created by such religious terms as "profane" (1), "shrine" (2), "pilgrims" (3), "holy palmers" (8)? How does this metaphor affect the tone of the relationship between Romeo and Juliet?
3. What play on words do you find in lines 8 and 13–14? What two meanings has line 11?
4. By meter and rhyme scheme, these lines form a sonnet. Do you think this was coincidental or intentional on Shakespeare's part? Discuss.

Death, be not proud

Death, be not proud, though some have callèd thee
Mighty and dreadful, for thou art not so;
For those whom thou think'st thou dost overthrow
Die not, poor death, nor yet canst thou kill me.
From rest and sleep, which but thy pictures be,   5
Much pleasure—then, from thee much more must flow;
And soonest° our best men with thee do go,   readiest
Rest of their bones and soul's delivery.
Thou art slave to fate, chance, kings, and desperate men,
And dost with poison, war, and sickness dwell;   10
And poppy or charms can make us sleep as well,
And better than thy stroke. Why swell'st thou then?
One short sleep passed, we wake eternally,
And death shall be no more; death, thou shalt die.

John Donne (1572–1631)

QUESTIONS

1. What two figures of speech dominate the poem?
2. Why should death not be proud? List the speaker's major reasons. Are they consistent? Logical? Persuasive?
3. Discuss the tone of the poem. Is the speaker (a) a man of assured faith with a firm conviction that death is not to be feared or (b) a man desperately trying to convince himself that there is nothing to fear in death?
4. In form, this sonnet blends the English and Italian models. Explain. Is its organization of thought closer to the Italian or the English sonnet?

The White City

I will not toy with it nor bend an inch.
Deep in the secret chambers of my heart
I muse my life-long hate, and without flinch
I bear it nobly as I live my part.
My being would be a skeleton, a shell,   5
If this dark Passion that fills my every mood,
And makes my heaven in the white world's hell,
Did not forever feed me vital blood.
I see the mighty city through a mist—
The strident trains that speed the goaded mass,   10
The poles and spires and towers vapor-kissed,
The fortressed port through which the great ships pass,
The tides, the wharves, the dens I contemplate,
Are sweet like wanton loves because I hate.

Claude McKay (1890–1948)

QUESTIONS

1. Claude McKay was a native black Jamaican who as an adult lived in New York. Why does the speaker "hate" (3) the city?
2. Traditionally, sonnets originated as love poems. Why might McKay have cast this poem in sonnet form?
3. How does the city feed the speaker with "vital blood" (8)?
4. Why are the elements of the New York landscape described in the last line as "sweet like wanton loves" (14)?

Final Notations

it will not be simple, it will not be long
it will take little time, it will take all your thought
it will take all your heart, it will take all your breath
it will be short, it will not be simple

it will touch through your ribs, it will take all your heart   5
it will not be long, it will occupy your thought
as a city is occupied, as a bed is occupied
it will take all your flesh, it will not be simple

You are coming into us who cannot withstand you
you are coming into us who never wanted to withstand you   10

you are taking parts of us into places never planned
you are going far away with pieces of our lives

it will be short, it will take all your breath
it will not be simple, it will become your will

Adrienne Rich (b. 1929)

The Story We Know

The way to begin is always the same. Hello,
Hello. Your hand, your name. So glad, Just fine,
and Good-bye at the end. That's every story we know,

and why pretend? But lunch tomorrow? No?
Yes? An omelette, salad, chilled white wine?   5
The way to begin is simple, sane, Hello,

and then it's Sunday, coffee, the *Times*, a slow
day by the fire, dinner at eight or nine
and Good-bye. In the end, this is a story we know

so well we don't turn the page, or look below   10
the picture, or follow the words to the next line:
The way to begin is always the same Hello.

But one night, through the latticed window, snow
begins to whiten the air, and the tall white pine.
Good-bye is the end of every story we know   15

that night, and when we close the curtains, oh,
we hold each other against that cold white sign
of the way we all begin and end. *Hello*,
Good-bye is the only story. We know, we know.

Martha Collins (b. 1940)

QUESTIONS

1. "The *Times*" (7) refers to the *New York Times*, the Sunday edition of which
   may run to hundreds of pages in a variety of sections. Through the first four
   stanzas this villanelle adopts the tone of most French models—a light,
   slightly detached description of a routine of social life, cleverly varying the
   two refrain lines for ironic purposes. What patterns of modern behavior are
   represented in these stanzas?

2. What is the reason for the change in tone in line 13? What does the "snow" (13) symbolize?
3. Ultimately, what broader meanings do "Hello" (1), "Good-bye" (3), and "we know" (3) take on? How is the theme of this poem similar to that of "Dover Beach" (page 816)?

Lonely Hearts

Can someone make my simple wish come true?
Male biker seeks female for touring fun.
Do you live in North London? Is it you?

Gay vegetarian whose friends are few,
I'm into music, Shakespeare and the sun,   5
Can someone make my simple wish come true?

Executive in search of something new—
Perhaps bisexual woman, arty, young.
Do you live in North London? Is it you?

Successful, straight and solvent? I am too—   10
Attractive Jewish lady with a son.
Can someone make my simple wish come true?

I'm Libran, inexperienced and blue—
Need slim non-smoker, under twenty-one.
Do you live in North London? Is it you?   15

Please write (with photo) to Box 152.
Who knows where it may lead once we've begun?
Can someone make my simple wish come true?
Do you live in North London? Is it you?

Wendy Cope (b. 1945)

QUESTIONS

1. The title refers to the "Personals" advertising section in a newspaper or magazine in which people solicit companionship from others. Each of the five tercets represents a different ad. Explore the variety of needs that they display.
2. Why is the form of the villanelle so appropriate for the subject matter and structure of this poem?

The Ruined Maid

"O 'Melia, my dear, this does everything crown!
Who could have supposed I should meet you in Town?°   London
And whence such fair garments, such prosperi-ty?"
"O didn't you know I'd been ruined?" said she.

"You left us in tatters, without shoes or socks,   5
Tired of digging potatoes, and spudding up docks;
And now you've gay bracelets and bright feathers three!"
"Yes: that's how we dress when we're ruined," said she.

"At home in the barton you said 'thee' and 'thou,'
And 'thik oon,' and 'theäs oon,' and 't'other'; but now   10
Your talking quite fits 'ee for high compa-ny!"
"Some polish is gained with one's ruin," said she.

"Your hands were like paws then, your face blue and bleak
But now I'm bewitched by your delicate cheek,
And your little gloves fit as on any la-dy!"   15
"We never do work when we're ruined," said she.

"You used to call home-life a hag-ridden dream,
And you'd sigh, and you'd sock; but at present you seem
To know not of megrims or melancho-ly!"
"True. One's pretty lively when ruined," said she.   20

"I wish I had feathers, a fine sweeping gown,
And a delicate face, and could strut about Town!"
"My dear—a raw country girl, such as you be,
Cannot quite expect that. You ain't ruined," said she.

Thomas Hardy (1840–1928)

QUESTIONS

1. This poem contains dialect terms from the countryside of southwestern England: "spudding up docks" (6) means spading weeds; "barton" (9), barnyard; "'thik oon,' and 'theäs oon'" (10), that one and this one; "'ee" (11), thee; "sock" (18), sigh; "megrims" (19), depression or unhappiness. Which speaker is characterized by her use of these terms?
2. This poem in the form of a dialogue presents a conversation between two former acquaintances. What are their situations? What is the first speaker's attitude toward "'Melia" (Amelia)? What expectations does she reveal about the status of a "ruined maid"?

3. What is a "ruined maid"? How does 'Melia not fit the stereotype? What kind of irony is this?
4. Scan the poem. What does its metrical form contribute to its effect? How does the insertion of hyphens in some words—for example, "prosperi-ty" (3), "compa-ny" (11)—emphasize that effect? Although they do not constitute a true refrain, how do the fourth lines of the stanzas resemble a refrain?

Acquainted with the Night

I have been one acquainted with the night.
I have walked out in rain—and back in rain.
I have outwalked the furthest city light.

I have looked down the saddest city lane.
I have passed by the watchman on his beat   5
And dropped my eyes, unwilling to explain.

I have stood still and stopped the sound of feet
When far away an interrupted cry
Came over houses from another street,

But not to call me back or say good-by;   10
And further still at an unearthly height,
One luminary clock against the sky

Proclaimed the time was neither wrong nor right.
I have been one acquainted with the night.

Robert Frost (1874–1963)

QUESTIONS

1. How does the speaker reveal the strength of his purpose in his night-walking? Can you specify what that purpose is? What symbolic meanings does the night hold?
2. How is the poem structured into sentences? What is the effect of repeating the phrase "I have"? of repeating line 1 at the conclusion? How do these repetitions affect the tone of the poem?
3. Some critics have interpreted the "luminary clock" (12) literally—as the illuminated dial of a tower clock; others have interpreted it figuratively as the full moon. Of what, in either case, is it a symbol? Does the clock tell accurate chronometric time? What kind of "time" is it proclaiming in line 13? Is knowing *that* kind of time the speaker's quest?
4. The poem contains 14 lines—like a sonnet. But its rhyme scheme is **terza rima,** an interlocking scheme with the pattern *aba bcb cdc,* etc., a formal

arrangement that implies continual progression. How does Frost bring the progression to an end? Terza rima was the form memorably employed by Dante for his *Divine Comedy*, of which the *Inferno* is the best-known section. In what ways does Frost's poem allude to the subject and framework of that poem?

These are the days when Birds come back

These are the days when Birds come back—
A very few—a Bird or two—
To take a backward look.

These are the days when skies resume
The old—old sophistries of June—   5
A blue and gold mistake.

Oh fraud that cannot cheat the Bee—
Almost thy plausibility
Induces my belief.

Till ranks of seeds their witness bear—   10
And softly thro' the altered air
Hurries a timid leaf.

Oh Sacrament of summer days,
Oh Last Communion in the Haze—
Permit a child to join.   15

Thy sacred emblems to partake—
Thy consecrated bread to take
And thine immortal wine!

Emily Dickinson (1830–1886)

QUESTIONS

1. Vocabulary: *sophistries* (5). The "fraud that cannot cheat the Bee" (7) is probably an allusion to one of the apocryphal tales of Solomon, who distinguished between real and artificial flowers by putting a bee into the room; the bee of course flew to the real.

2. The time of year represented in the poem is "Indian summer" (if you are unfamiliar with the term, consult a dictionary). How is the identity of this time period implied by the terms "backward" (3) and "resume" (4), and by the evidence of "seeds" and "leaf" (10–12)? Why is that time of year a "fraud" (7)? What is it pretending to be? In the final metaphor, how is Indian summer like a "Last Communion" (14)?

3. The rhyme scheme, although complicated by an inconsistency in the first stanza and approximate rhymes throughout, divides the poem into three two-stanza units. The device of repeating the opening phrase in lines 1 and 4, as well as the pattern of repeated first words in stanzas 5 and 6, reinforce this division into two-stanza units. How is the *structure* of the poem linked to the formal division into three two-stanza units?

4. What three distinct tones do you observe in the three two-stanza units? What in the development of ideas accounts for the shifts in tone?

Woodchucks

Gassing the woodchucks didn't turn out right.
The knockout bomb from the Feed and Grain Exchange
was featured as merciful, quick at the bone
and the case we had against them was airtight,
both exits shoehorned shut with puddingstone,   5
but they had a sub-sub-basement out of range.

Next morning they turned up again, no worse
for the cyanide than we for our cigarettes
and state-store Scotch, all of us up to scratch.
They brought down the marigolds as a matter of course   10
and then took over the vegetable patch
nipping the broccoli shoots, beheading the carrots.

The food from our mouths, I said, righteously thrilling
to the feel of the .22, the bullets' neat noses.
I, a lapsed pacifist fallen from grace   15
puffed with Darwinian pieties for killing,
now drew a bead on the littlest woodchuck's face.
He died down in the everbearing roses.

Ten minutes later I dropped the mother. She
flipflopped in the air and fell, her needle teeth   20
still hooked in a leaf of early Swiss chard.
Another baby next. O one-two-three
the murderer inside me rose up hard,
the hawkeye killer came on stage forthwith.

There's one chuck left. Old wily fellow, he keeps   25
me cocked and ready day after day after day.
All night I hunt his humped-up form. I dream

I sight along the barrel in my sleep.
If only they'd all consented to die unseen
gassed underground the quiet Nazi way.   30

Maxine Kumin (b. 1925)

QUESTIONS

1. Vocabulary: *puddingstone* (5), *Darwinian* (16), *chard* (21).
2. Describe the rhyme scheme of the poem. How is it effective in conveying the poem's meaning?
3. The speaker's attitude toward the woodchucks is complex. Discuss the implications of the following lines: "The food from our mouths, I said, righteously thrilling / to the feel of the .22" (13–14); "I, a lapsed pacifist fallen from grace / puffed with Darwinian pieties for killing" (15–16); "the murderer inside me rose up hard" (23).
4. In what ways is the speaker sympathetic toward the woodchucks? Which lines and images suggest this sympathy?
5. What are the implications of the last two lines? Why does the speaker wish the woodchucks had "consented to die unseen" (29)?

Delight in Disorder

A sweet disorder in the dress
Kindles in clothes a wantonness.
A lawn° about the shoulders thrown   linen scarf
Into a fine distraction;
An erring lace, which here and there   5
Enthralls the crimson stomacher;
A cuff neglected, and thereby
Ribbons to flow confusedly;
A winning wave, deserving note,
In the tempestuous petticoat;   10
A careless shoestring, in whose tie
I see a wild civility;
Do more bewitch me than when art
Is too precise in every part.

Robert Herrick (1591–1674)

QUESTIONS

1. Vocabulary: *wantonness* (2), *stomacher* (6).
2. The phrase "wild civility" (12) is an example of **oxymoron,** a compact paradox in which two successive words seemingly contradict each other. Discuss

the effectiveness of this device in this phrase and examine the poem for other examples.

3. Consider the relationship of form to structure in this poem. How does this contribute to the meaning?

In Medias Res

His waist,
like the plot,
thickens, wedding
pants now breathtaking,
belt no longer the cinch   5
it once was, belly's cambium
expanding to match each birthday,
his body a wad of anonymous tissue
swung in the same centrifuge of years
that separates a house from its foundation,   10
undermining sidewalks grim with joggers
and loose-filled graves and families
and stars collapsing on themselves,
no preservation society capable
of plugging entropy's dike,   15
under the zipper's sneer
a belly hibernation-
soft, ready for
the kill.

Michael McFee (b. 1954)

QUESTIONS

1. The Latin phrase *in medias res* (title) means "in the middle of things," and is famously associated with dramas and narratives that begin in the midst of an action and then go back to describe or imply events in the plot that caused the present situation. Why is this an appropriate title here?

2. What assumptions can we make about the age and outlook of the man described in the poem? What do the puns "thickens" (3), "breathtaking" (4), and "cinch" (5) contribute to the tone? Explain the metaphor "entropy's dike" (15).

3. Discuss the relationship of formal pattern to meaning.

SUGGESTIONS FOR WRITING

Following are two lists, one of sonnets and the other of villanelles. Using one or two examples of either form, explore the effectiveness of the relationship of structure to form. In particular, be alert for variations or departures from the form and what these contribute to meaning and emotional effect.

Sonnets
Wordsworth, "The world is too much with us" (page 694)
Shelley, "Ozymandias" (page 764)
Donne, "Batter my heart, three-personed God" (page 766)
Yeats, "Leda and the Swan" (page 788)
Frost, "Design" (page 796)
Drayton, "Since there's no help" (page 808)
Shakespeare, "My mistress' eyes" (page 809)
Owen, "Anthem for Doomed Youth" (page 875)

Villanelles
Bishop, "One Art" (page 698)
Roethke, "The Waking" (page 826)
Plath, "Mad Girl's Love Song" (page 986)

Chapter Fifteen

Evaluating Poetry I
Sentimental, Rhetorical, Didactic Verse

The attempt to evaluate a poem should never be made before the poem is understood; and, unless one has developed the capacity to experience poetry intellectually and emotionally, any judgments one makes will be of little worth. A person who likes no wines can hardly be a judge of them. But the ability to make judgments, to discriminate between good and bad, great and good, good and half-good, is surely a primary object of all liberal education, and one's appreciation of poetry is incomplete unless it includes discrimination.

In judging a poem, as in judging any work of art, we need to ask three basic questions: (1) *What is its central purpose?* (2) *How fully has this purpose been accomplished?* (3) *How important is this purpose?* We need to answer the first question in order to understand the poem. Questions 2 and 3 are those by which we evaluate it. Question 2 judges the poem on a scale of perfection. Question 3 judges it on a scale of significance.

For answering the first of our evaluative questions, *How fully has the poem's purpose been accomplished?* there are no easy yardsticks that we can apply. We cannot ask: Is the poem melodious? Does it have smooth rhythm? Does it use good grammar? Does it contain figures of speech? Are the rhymes perfect? Excellent poems exist without any of these attributes. We can judge any element in a poem only as it contributes or fails to contribute to the achievement of the central purpose; and we can judge the total poem only as these elements work together to form an integrated whole. But we can at least attempt a few generalizations. A wholly successful poem contains no excess words, no words that do not bear their full weight in contributing to the total experience, and no words that are used just to fill out the meter. Each word is the best word for expressing the total meaning: there are no inexact words forced by the rhyme scheme or the metrical pattern. The word order is the best order for expressing the author's total meaning; distortions or departures from normal order are for emphasis or some other meaningful purpose. The diction, the images, and the figures of speech are fresh, not trite (except, of course, when the poet uses trite language deliberately for purposes of irony). The sound of the poem does not clash with its sense, or the form with its content; and in general both sound and pattern are used to support meaning. The organization of the poem is the best possible organization: images and ideas are so effectively arranged that any rearrangement would be harmful to the poem. Always remember, however, that a good poem may have flaws. We should never damn a poem for its flaws if these flaws are amply compensated for by positive excellence.

What constitutes excellence in poetry? One criterion is that its combination of thought, emotion, language, and sound must be fresh and original. As the poet and critic Ezra Pound insisted, good writing must "make it new." An excellent poem will neither be merely imitative of previous literature nor appeal to stock, pre-established ways of thinking and feeling. The following discussion highlights three particular ways in which a poem can fail to achieve excellence: if a poem is sentimental, excessively rhetorical, or purely didactic, in fact, we would probably call it "verse" rather than true poetry.

Sentimentality is indulgence in emotion for its own sake, or expression of more emotion than an occasion warrants. Sentimentalists are gushy, stirred to tears by trivial or inappropriate causes; they weep at all weddings and all funerals; they are made ecstatic by manifestations of young love; they clip locks of hair, gild baby shoes, and talk baby talk. Sentimental *literature* is "tear-jerking" literature. It aims primarily at stimulating the emotions directly rather than at communicating experience truly and freshly; it depends on trite and well-tried formulas for exciting emotion; it revels in old oaken buckets, rocking chairs, mother love, and the pitter-patter of little feet; it oversimplifies; it is unfaithful to the full complexity of human experience. In this book the best example of sentimental verse is the first seven lines of the anonymous poem "Love" (page 820). If this verse had ended as it began, it would have been pure sentimentalism. The eighth line redeems it by making us realize that the writer is not serious and thus transfers the piece from the classification of sentimental verse to that of humorous verse. In fact, the poem is poking fun at sentimentality by showing that in its most maudlin form it is a characteristic of drunks.

Rhetorical poetry uses a language more glittering and high-flown than its substance warrants. It offers a spurious vehemence of language—language without a corresponding reality of emotion or thought underneath. It is oratorical, overelegant, artificially eloquent. It is superficial and, again, often basically trite. It loves rolling phrases like "from the rocky coast of Maine to the sun-washed shores of California" and "our heroic dead" and "Old Glory." It deals in generalities. At its worst it is bombast. In this book an example is offered by the two lines quoted from the play within a play in the fifth act of Shakespeare's *A Midsummer Night's Dream:*

> Whereat with blade, with bloody, blameful blade,
> He bravely broached his boiling bloody breast.

Another example may be found in the player's recitation in *Hamlet* (in Act 2, scene 2):

> Out, out, thou strumpet Fortune! All you gods,
> In general synod take away her power,
> Break all the spokes and fellies from her wheel,
> And bowl the round nave down the hill of heaven
> As low as to the fiends!

Didactic poetry has as a primary purpose to teach or preach. It is probable that all the very greatest poetry teaches in subtle ways, without being expressly didactic; and much expressly didactic poetry ranks high in poetic excellence: that is, it accomplishes its teaching without ceasing to be poetry. But when the didactic purpose supersedes the poetic purpose, when the poem communicates information or moral instruction only, then it ceases to be didactic poetry and becomes didactic verse. Such verse appeals to people who read poetry primarily for noble thoughts or inspiring lessons and like them prettily expressed. It is recognizable often by its lack of any specific situation, the flatness of its diction, the poverty of its imagery and figurative language, its emphasis on moral platitudes, its lack of poetic freshness. It is either very trite or has little to distinguish it from informational prose except rhyme or meter. Emerson's "The Rhodora" (page 795) is an example of didactic *poetry*. The familiar couplet

> Early to bed and early to rise,
> Makes a man healthy, wealthy, and wise

is more aptly characterized as didactic *verse*.

Undoubtedly, so far in this chapter, we have spoken too categorically, have made our distinctions too sharp and definite. All poetic excellence is a matter of degree. There are no absolute lines between sentimentality and true emotion, artificial and genuine eloquence, didactic verse and didactic poetry. Though the difference between extreme examples is easy to recognize, subtler discriminations are harder to make.

A final caution to students: when making judgments on literature, always be honest. Do not pretend to like what you do not like. Do not be afraid to admit a liking for what you do like. A genuine enthusiasm for the second-rate is much better than false enthusiasm or no enthusiasm at all. Be neither hasty nor timorous in making your judgments. When you have attentively read a poem and thoroughly considered it, decide what you think. Do not hedge, equivocate, or try to find out others' opinions before forming your own. But, having formed an opinion and expressed it, do not allow it to harden into a narrow-minded bias. Compare your opinion *then* with the opinions of others; allow yourself to change it when convinced of its error: in this way you learn.

In the pairs of poems for comparison that follow in this chapter, the distinction to be made is not always between bad and good; it may be between varying degrees of poetic merit.

REVIEWING CHAPTER FIFTEEN

1. Review the three basic questions to be answered in evaluating a poem.
2. Explore the three weaknesses that may lead us to judge a poem less than excellent, finding examples of each in the poems that follow in this chapter.

God's Will for You and Me

Just to be tender, just to be true,
Just to be glad the whole day through,
Just to be merciful, just to be mild,
Just to be trustful as a child,
Just to be gentle and kind and sweet,   5
Just to be helpful with willing feet,
Just to be cheery when things go wrong,
Just to drive sadness away with a song,
Whether the hour is dark or bright,
Just to be loyal to God and right,   10
Just to believe that God knows best,
Just in his promises ever to rest—
Just to let love be our daily key,
That is God's will for you and me.

Pied Beauty

Glory be to God for dappled things—
   For skies of couple-color as a brinded cow;
      For rose-moles all in stipple upon trout that swim;
Fresh-firecoal chestnut-falls; finches' wings;
   Landscape plotted and pieced—fold, fallow and plow;   5
      And all trades, their gear and tackle and trim.
All things counter, original, spare, strange;
   Whatever is fickle, freckled (who knows how?)
      With swift, slow; sweet, sour; adazzle, dim;
He fathers-forth whose beauty is past change: 10
        Praise him.

QUESTION
Which is the superior poem? Explain in full.

A Poison Tree

I was angry with my friend:
I told my wrath, my wrath did end.
I was angry with my foe:
I told it not, my wrath did grow.

And I watered it in fears,   5
Night and morning with my tears;
And I sunnèd it with smiles,
And with soft deceitful wiles.

And it grew both day and night
Till it bore an apple bright;   10
And my foe beheld it shine,
And he knew that it was mine,

And into my garden stole
When the night had veiled the pole:°   sky
In the morning glad I see   15
My foe outstretched beneath the tree.

The Most Vital Thing in Life

When you feel like saying something
    That you know you will regret,
Or keenly feel an insult
    Not quite easy to forget,
That's the time to curb resentment   5
    And maintain a mental peace,
For when your mind is tranquil
    All your ill-thoughts simply cease.

It is easy to be angry
    When defrauded or defied,   10
To be peeved and disappointed
    If your wishes are denied;
But to win a worthwhile battle
    Over selfishness and spite,
You must learn to keep strict silence   15
    Though you know you're in the right.

So keep your mental balance
    When confronted by a foe,
Be it enemy in ambush
    Or some danger that you know.   20
If you are poised and tranquil
    When all around is strife,
Be assured that you have mastered
    The most vital thing in life.

QUESTION

Which poem has more poetic merit? Explain.

Pitcher

His art is eccentricity, his aim
How not to hit the mark he seems to aim at,

His passion how to avoid the obvious,
His technique how to vary the avoidance.

The others throw to be comprehended. He   5
Throws to be a moment misunderstood.

Yet not too much. Not errant, arrant, wild,
But every seeming aberration willed.

Not to, yet still, still to communicate
Making the batter understand too late.   10

The Old-Fashioned Pitcher

How dear to my heart was the old-fashioned hurler
    Who labored all day on the old village green.
He did not resemble the up-to-date twirler
    Who pitches four innings and ducks from the scene.
The up-to-date twirler I'm not very strong for;   5
    He has a queer habit of pulling up lame.
And that is the reason I hanker and long for
    The pitcher who started and finished the game.

        The old-fashioned pitcher,
          The iron-armed pitcher,   10
        The stout-hearted pitcher
          Who finished the game.

QUESTION
Which poem is the more interesting and more meaningful? Why?

The Long Voyage

Not that the pines were darker there,
nor mid-May dogwood brighter there,
nor swifts more swift in summer air;
    it was my own country,

having its thunderclap of spring,   5
its long midsummer ripening,
its corn hoar-stiff at harvesting,
    almost like any country,

yet being mine; its face, its speech,
its hills bent low within my reach,   10
its river birch and upland beech
    were mine, of my own country.

Now the dark waters at the bow
fold back, like earth against the plow;
foam brightens like the dogwood now   15
    at home, in my own country.

Breathes there the man

Breathes there the man, with soul so dead,
Who never to himself hath said,
   This is my own, my native land!
Whose heart hath ne'er within him burned,
As home his footsteps he hath turned,   5
   From wandering on a foreign strand?
If such there breathe, go, mark him well;
For him no minstrel raptures swell;
High though his titles, proud his name,
Boundless his wealth as wish can claim—   10
Despite those titles, power, and pelf,
The wretch, concentered all in self,
Living, shall forfeit fair renown,
And, doubly dying, shall go down
To the vile dust from whence he sprung,   15
Unwept, unhonored, and unsung.

QUESTION

Which poem communicates the more genuine poetic emotion? Which is more
rhetorical? Justify your answer.

The Engine

Into the gloom of the deep, dark night,
   With panting breath and a startled scream,
Swift as a bird in sudden flight
   Darts this creature of steel and steam.

Awful dangers are lurking nigh,   5
   Rocks and chasms are near the track,
But straight by the light of its great white eye
   It speeds through the shadows, dense and black.

Terrible thoughts and fierce desires
    Trouble its mad heart many an hour,   10
Where burn and smoulder the hidden fires,
    Coupled ever with might and power.

It hates, as a wild horse hates the rein,
    The narrow track by vale and hill,
And shrieks with a cry of startled pain,   15
    And longs to follow its own wild will.

I like to see it lap the Miles

I like to see it lap the Miles—
And lick the Valleys up—
And stop to feed itself at Tanks—
And then—prodigious step

Around a Pile of Mountains—   5
And supercilious peer
In Shanties—by the sides of Roads—
And then a Quarry pare

To fit its Ribs
And crawl between
Complaining all the while   10
In horrid—hooting stanza—
Then chase itself down Hill—

And neigh like Boanerges—
Then—punctual as a Star
Stop—docile and omnipotent   15
At its own stable door—

QUESTION
Which of these poems is more rhetorical in its language?

The Toys

My little Son, who looked from thoughtful eyes
And moved and spoke in quiet grown-up wise,
Having my law the seventh time disobeyed,
I struck him, and dismissed

With hard words and unkissed,   5
His Mother, who was patient, being dead.
Then, fearing lest his grief should hinder sleep,
I visited his bed,
But found him slumbering deep,
With darkened eyelids, and their lashes yet   10
From his late sobbing wet.
And I, with moan,
Kissing away his tears, left others of my own;
For, on a table drawn beside his head,
He had put, within his reach,   15
A box of counters and a red-veined stone,
A piece of glass abraded by the beach,
And six or seven shells,
A bottle with bluebells,
And two French copper coins, ranged there with careful art,   20
To comfort his sad heart.
So when that night I prayed
To God, I wept, and said:
Ah, when at last we lie with trancèd breath,
Not vexing Thee in death,   25
And thou rememberest of what toys
We made our joys,
How weakly understood
Thy great commanded good,
Then, fatherly not less   30
Than I whom Thou has moulded from the clay,
Thou'lt leave Thy wrath, and say,
"I will be sorry for their childishness."

Little Boy Blue

The little toy dog is covered with dust,
    But sturdy and staunch he stands;
And the little toy soldier is red with rust,
    And his musket moulds in his hands.
Time was when the little toy dog was new,   5
    And the soldier was passing fair;

And that was the time when our Little Boy Blue
    Kissed them and put them there.
"Now, don't you go till I come," he said,
    "And don't you make any noise!"   10
So, toddling off to his trundle-bed,
    He dreamt of the pretty toys;
And, as he was dreaming, an angel song
    Awakened our Little Boy Blue—
Oh! the years are many, the years are long,   15
    But the little toy friends are True!

Ay, faithful to Little Boy Blue they stand
    Each in the same old place—
Awaiting the touch of a little hand,
    The smile of a little face;   20
And they wonder, as waiting the long years through
    In the dust of that little chair,
What has become of our Little Boy Blue,
    Since he kissed them and put them there.

QUESTION

One of these poems has an obvious appeal for the beginning reader. The other is likely to have more meaning for the mature reader. Try to explain in terms of sentimentality and honesty.

When I have fears that I may cease to be

When I have fears that I may cease to be
    Before my pen has gleaned my teaming brain,
Before high-pilèd books, in charactery,°   written symbols
    Hold like rich garners the full-ripened grain;
When I behold, upon the night's starred face,   5
    Huge cloudy symbols of a high romance,
And think that I may never live to trace
    Their shadows, with the magic hand of chance;
And when I feel, fair creature of an hour,
    That I shall never look upon thee more,   10
Never have relish in the faery power
    Of unreflecting love—then on the shore
Of the wide world I stand alone, and think
    Till love and fame to nothingness do sink.

O Solitude!

O Solitude! if I must with thee dwell,
    Let it not be among the jumbled heap
    Of murky buildings; climb with me the steep—
Nature's observatory—whence the dell,
Its flowery slopes, its river's crystal swell,   5
    May seem a span; let me thy vigils keep
    'Mongst boughs pavilioned, where the deer's swift leap
Startles the wild bee from the fox-glove bell.
But though I'll gladly trace these scenes with thee,
    Yet the sweet converse of an innocent mind,   10
    Whose words are images of thoughts refined,
Is my soul's pleasure; and it sure must be
    Almost the highest bliss of human-kind,
When to thy haunts two kindred spirits flee.

QUESTION

Both poems are by John Keats (1795–1821). Which of them displays true excellence? Explain.

SUGGESTIONS FOR WRITING

In each of the following pairs, both poems have literary merit, but one is clearly a more ambitious and more successful poem. Choose one pair and write a short essay in which you argue which is the better of the two poems, and why.

1. Owen, "Dulce et Decorum Est" (page 651) and Ehrhart, "Guns" (page 960).
2. Williams, "The Red Wheelbarrow" (page 661) and Twichell, "Blurry Cow" (page 1012).
3. Dickinson, "I felt a Funeral, in my Brain" (page 705) and Plath, "Mad Girl's Love Song" (page 986).
4. Clifton, "good times" (page 950) and Hughes, "Theme for English B" (page 972).
5. Joseph, "Warning" (page 974) and Yeats, "Sailing to Byzantium" (page 1021).

Chapter Sixteen

Evaluating Poetry 2
Poetic Excellence

If a poem has successfully met the test of the question, *How fully has it accomplished its purpose?* we are ready to subject it to our second evaluative question: *How important is its purpose?*

Great poetry must, of course, be good poetry. Noble intent alone cannot redeem a work that does not measure high on the scale of accomplishment; otherwise the sentimental and purely didactic verse of much of the preceding chapter would stand with the world's masterpieces. But once a work has been judged as successful on the scale of execution, its final standing will depend on its significance of purpose.

Suppose, for instance, we consider three poems in our text: the anonymous verse "Love" (page 820); the poem "It sifts from Leaden Sieves" by Emily Dickinson (page 717); and Shakespeare's sonnet "That time of year" (page 887). Each of these would probably be judged by critics as successful in what it sets out to do. The author of "Love" has created a joke by piling on a list of sentimental references to types of love, then bursting this inflated bubble by claiming that maudlin drunkenness is the best type. The joke is delightful, satirizing the excesses of sentimentality as well as the artificially induced mawkishness of the toper. But what is this verse *about?* Virtually nothing. Indeed, we should hardly call it poetry at all; it is just clever verse. Dickinson's poem, in contrast, *is* poetry, and very good poetry. It appeals richly to our senses and to our imaginations, and it succeeds excellently in its purpose: to convey the appearance and the quality of falling and newly fallen snow as well as a sense of the magic and the mystery of nature. Yet, when we compare this excellent poem with Shakespeare's, we again see important differences. Although Dickinson's poem engages the senses and the imagination and may affect us with wonder and cause us to meditate on nature, it does not deeply engage the emotions or the intellect. It does not come as close to the core of human living and suffering as does Shakespeare's sonnet. In fact, it is concerned primarily with that staple of small talk, the weather. On the other hand, Shakespeare's sonnet evokes the universal human concerns of growing old, approaching death, and love. Of these three selections, then, Shakespeare's is the greatest. It "says" more than Dickinson's poem or the little joke; it communicates a richer experience; it successfully accomplishes a more significant purpose. The reader will get from it a deeper enjoyment because it is nourishing as well as delightful.

Great poetry engages the whole person—senses, imagination, emotion, intellect; it does not touch us merely on one or two sides of our nature. Great poetry seeks not merely to entertain us but to bring us—along with pure pleasure—fresh insights, or renewed insights, and important insights, into the nature of human experience. Great poetry, we might say, gives us a broader and deeper understanding of life, of other people, and of ourselves, always with the qualification, of course, that the kind of insight literature gives is not necessarily the kind that can be summed up in a simple "lesson" or "moral." It is *knowledge—felt* knowledge, *new* knowledge—of the complexities of human nature and of the tragedies and sufferings, the excitements and joys, that characterize human experience.

Yet, after all, we have provided no easy yardsticks or rule-of-thumb measures for literary judgment. There are no mechanical tests. The final measuring rod can be only the responsiveness, the taste, and the discernment of the reader. Such taste and discernment are partly a native endowment, partly the product of experience, partly the achievement of conscious study, training, and intellectual effort. They cannot be achieved suddenly or quickly; they can never be achieved in perfection. The pull is a long and a hard one. But success, even relative success, brings enormous personal and aesthetic rewards.

The Canonization

For God's sake, hold your tongue, and let me love!
    Or chide my palsy or my gout,
My five gray hairs or ruined fortune flout;
With wealth your state, your mind with arts improve,
    Take you a course,° get you a place,   career 5
      Observe his honor° or his grace,°   judge; bishop
Or the king's real or his stamped face°   on a coin
    Contemplate; what you will, approve,°   try out
      So you will let me love.

Alas, alas, who's injured by my love?   10
    What merchant ships have my sighs drowned?

Who says my tears have overflowed his ground?
When did my colds a forward° spring remove?   early
   When did the heats which my veins fill
     Add one more to the plaguy bill?   15
Soldiers find wars, and lawyers find out still
   Litigious men which quarrels move,
      Though she and I do love.

Call us what you will, we are made such by love.
   Call her one, me another fly;°   moth   20
We are tapers too, and at our own cost die;
And we in us find the eagle and the dove;
   The phoenix riddle hath more wit°   meaning
     By us; we two, being one, are it.
So to one neutral thing both sexes fit.   25
   We die and rise the same, and prove
     Mysterious by this love.

We can die by it, if not live by love,
   And if unfit for tombs and hearse
Our legend be, it will be fit for verse;   30
And if no piece of chronicle° we prove,   history
   We'll build in sonnets pretty rooms:
     As well a well-wrought urn becomes
The greatest ashes as half-acre tombs,
   And by these hymns all shall approve°   confirm   35
     Us canonized for love,

And thus invoke us: "You whom reverend love
   Made one another's hermitage,
You to whom love was peace, that now is rage,
Who did the whole world's soul contract, and drove   40
   Into the glasses of your eyes
     (So made such mirrors and such spies
That they did all to you epitomize)
   Countries, towns, courts: beg from above
     A pattern of your love!"   45

John Donne (1572–1631)

QUESTIONS

1. Vocabulary: *Canonization* (title), *tapers* (21), *phoenix* (23), *invoke* (37), *epit-*
   omize (43). "[R]eal" (7), pronounced as two syllables, puns on *royal*. The

"plaguy bill" (15) is a list of plague victims. The word "die" (21, 26, 28) in seventeenth-century slang meant to experience the sexual climax. To understand lines 21 and 28, one also needs to be familiar with the Renaissance superstition that every act of sexual intercourse shortened one's life by one day. The "eagle" and the "dove" (22) are symbols for strength and mildness. "[P]attern" (45) is a model that one can copy.

2. Who is the speaker and what is his condition? How old is he? To whom is he speaking? What has his auditor been saying to him before the opening of the poem? What sort of values can we ascribe to the auditor by inference from the first stanza? What value does the speaker oppose to these? How does the stanzaic pattern of the poem emphasize this value?

3. The sighs, tears, fevers, and chills in the second stanza were commonplace in the love poetry of Donne's time. How does Donne make them fresh? What is the speaker's argument in this stanza? How does it begin to turn from pure defense to offense in the last three lines of the stanza?

4. How are the things to which the lovers are compared in the third stanza *arranged*? Does their ordering reflect in any way the arrangement of the whole poem? Elucidate line 21. Interpret or paraphrase lines 23–27.

5. Explain the first line of the fourth stanza. What status does the speaker claim for himself and his beloved in the last line of this stanza?

6. In what sense is the last stanza an invocation? Who speaks in it? To whom? What powers are ascribed to the lovers in it?

7. What do the following words from the poem have in common: "Mysterious" (27), "hymns" (35), "canonized" (36), "reverend" (37), "hermitage" (38)? What judgment about love does the speaker make by the use of these words?

Ode on a Grecian Urn

Thou still unravished bride of quietness,
    Thou foster-child of silence and slow time,
Sylvan historian, who canst thus express
    A flowery tale more sweetly than our rhyme:
What leaf-fringed legend haunts about thy shape   5
    Of deities or mortals, or of both,
        In Tempe or the dales of Arcady?
    What men or gods are these? What maidens loth?
What mad pursuit? What struggle to escape?
        What pipes and timbrels? What wild ecstasy?   10

Heard melodies are sweet, but those unheard
    Are sweeter; therefore, ye soft pipes, play on;
Not to the sensual ear, but, more endeared,
    Pipe to the spirit ditties of no tone:
Fair youth, beneath the trees, thou canst not leave   15

Thy song, nor ever can those trees be bare;
   Bold lover, never, never canst thou kiss,
Though winning near the goal—yet, do not grieve;
   She cannot fade, though thou hast not thy bliss,
For ever wilt thou love, and she be fair!   20

Ah, happy, happy boughs! that cannot shed
   Your leaves, nor ever bid the spring adieu;
And, happy melodist, unwearièd,
   For ever piping songs for ever new;
More happy love! more happy, happy love!   25
   For ever warm and still to be enjoyed,
      For ever panting and for ever young;
All breathing human passion far above,
   That leaves a heart high-sorrowful and cloyed,
      A burning forehead, and a parching tongue.   30

Who are these coming to the sacrifice?
   To what green altar, O mysterious priest,
Lead'st thou that heifer lowing at the skies,
   And all her silken flanks with garlands drest?
What little town by river or sea shore,   35
   Or mountain-built with peaceful citadel,
      Is emptied of its folk, this pious morn?
And, little town, thy streets for evermore
   Will silent be; and not a soul to tell
      Why thou are desolate, can e'er return.   40

O Attic shape! Fair attitude! with brede
   Of marble men and maidens overwrought,
With forest branches and the trodden weed;
   Thou, silent form, dost tease us out of thought
As doth eternity: Cold Pastoral!   45
   When old age shall this generation waste,
      Thou shalt remain, in midst of other woe
Than ours, a friend to man, to whom thou say'st,
Beauty is truth, truth beauty,—that is all
   Ye know on earth, and all ye need to know.   50

John Keats (1795–1821)

NOTE: (49–50) In the 1820 edition of Keats's poems the words "Beauty is truth, truth beauty" were enclosed in quotation marks, and the poem is often reprinted that way. It is now generally agreed, however, on the basis of contemporary transcripts of Keats's poem, that Keats intended the entire last two lines to be spoken by the urn.

QUESTIONS

1. The poem is an extended apostrophe addressed to a painted vase from ancient Greece. There are two separate scenes on the urn; the speaker summarizes their subjects in lines 5–10, and then specifically addresses them in 11–30 and 31–40. As completely as you can, describe what each of the scenes depicts.

2. What three denotations of "still" (1) are appropriate to the metaphorical identities ascribed to the urn in lines 1–4? What modes of sensory experience and of knowledge are evoked in those lines?

3. The structure of the poem includes the speaker's shifting motivations in the spaces *between* the stanzas. For example, lines 5–10 request information about the actions depicted on the urn, but lines 11–14 dismiss the need for answers. What do you suppose motivates that change?

4. Lines 15–28 celebrate the scene because it has captured in a still moment the intensity of pursuit and desire. Explain. How is that permanence contrasted to the reality of "breathing human passion" (28)?

5. In the fourth stanza the speaker turns to the second scene, again with a series of questions requesting specific information. How do the concluding lines of the third stanza motivate this shift of subject? Lines 31–34 are questions about what the speaker *sees* on the urn; lines 34–40 refer to something he cannot see—and are expressed in a tone of desolation. What is it that leads the speaker to that tone? What has *he* done to cause it?

6. In the final stanza, the speaker does not engage himself with the subjects of the scenes but with "shape" (41), "form" (44), and "attitude" (41—in its older meaning, the posture of a painted figure). What at the end of the preceding stanza might cause the speaker to withdraw his imagination from the scenes and to comment in general on the "form" of the urn? Explain lines 44–45 and the culminating oxymoron "Cold Pastoral."

7. The footnote bases its deduction—that the last two lines in their entirety are claimed by the speaker to be the urn's advice to "man" (48)—on external evidence. Can you find internal support for this in the obsolete grammatical usage in line 50? How is the urn's message suited to the experience that the speaker has undergone?

There's a certain Slant of light

There's a certain Slant of light,
Winter Afternoons—
That oppresses, like the Heft
Of Cathedral Tunes—

Heavenly Hurt, it gives us—   5
We can find no scar,
But internal difference,
Where the Meanings, are—

None may teach it—Any—
'Tis the Seal Despair—
An imperial affliction   10
Sent us of the Air—

When it comes, the Landscape listens—
Shadows—hold their breath—
When it goes, 'tis like the Distance   15
On the look of Death—

Emily Dickinson (1830–1886)

QUESTIONS

1. This is one of Dickinson's most famous poems dealing with human psychological states. Here the speaker calls her state of mind "Despair" (10), but many today would consider it "clinical depression." What particular images help convey the speaker's depressed state of mind?
2. The scene is carefully set: a winter afternoon, a speaker attempting to describe what she feels. How does the poem relate a possibly fleeting psychological state to such issues as religious faith, self-examination, and death?
3. Could it be argued that this experience, however painful, is ultimately a positive one for the speaker? What is the significance of the oxymorons "Heavenly Hurt" (5) and "imperial affliction" (11)?
4. Discuss the use of abstractions in this poem: "Hurt" (5), "Meanings" (8), "Despair" (10), "Death" (16). How do these abstractions work to enlarge the poem's meaning beyond a mere depiction of a specific person's temporary mood?
5. The final stanza describes the moment of great tension when the "Seal" (10) of despair falls upon the speaker. Why does she imagine that the entire landscape participates in this personal crisis? Does this suggest a self-absorbed projection onto the landscape or an honest attempt to understand and describe her mental state?
6. Discuss the concluding simile, "like the Distance / On the look of Death—" Do any specific visual images come to mind as you ponder this abstract phrase? Could "Death" here be interpreted as meaning "a dead person"?

Home Burial

He saw her from the bottom of the stairs
Before she saw him. She was starting down,
Looking back over her shoulder at some fear.
She took a doubtful step and then undid it
To raise herself and look again. He spoke   5

Advancing toward her: "What is it you see
From up there always—for I want to know."
She turned and sank upon her skirts at that,
And her face changed from terrified to dull.
He said to gain time: "What is it you see,"   10
Mounting until she cowered under him.
"I will find out now—you must tell me, dear."
She, in her place, refused him any help
With the least stiffening of her neck and silence.
She let him look, sure that he wouldn't see,   15
Blind creature; and awhile he didn't see.
But at last he murmured, "Oh," and again, "Oh."

"What is it—what?" she said.

                "Just that I see."

"You don't," she challenged. "Tell me what it is."

"The wonder is I didn't see at once.   20
I never noticed it from here before.
I must be wonted to it—that's the reason.
The little graveyard where my people are!
So small the window frames the whole of it.
Not so much larger than a bedroom, is it?   25
There are three stones of slate and one of marble,
Broad-shouldered little slabs there in the sunlight
On the sidehill. We haven't to mind *those*.
But I understand: it is not the stones,
But the child's mound—"

                "Don't, don't, don't, don't,"
    she cried.   30

She withdrew, shrinking from beneath his arm
That rested on the banister, and slid downstairs;
And turned on him with such a daunting look,
He said twice over before he knew himself:
"Can't a man speak of his own child he's lost?"   35

"Not you! Oh, where's my hat? Oh, I don't need it!
I must get out of here. I must get air.
I don't know rightly whether any man can."

"Amy! Don't go to someone else this time.
Listen to me. I won't come down the stairs."   40
He sat and fixed his chin between his fists.
"There's something I should like to ask you, dear."

"You don't know how to ask it."

                                        "Help me, then."

Her fingers moved the latch for all reply.

"My words are nearly always an offense.   45
I don't know how to speak of anything
So as to please you. But I might be taught,
I should suppose. I can't say I see how.
A man must partly give up being a man
With women-folk. We could have some arrangement   50
By which I'd bind myself to keep hands off
Anything special you're a-mind to name.
Though I don't like such things 'twixt those that love.
Two that don't love can't live together without them.
But two that do can't live together with them."   55
She moved the latch a little. "Don't—don't go.
Don't carry it to someone else this time.
Tell me about it if it's something human.
Let me into your grief. I'm not so much
Unlike other folks as your standing there   60
Apart would make me out. Give me my chance.
I do think, though, you overdo it a little.
What was it brought you up to think it the thing
To take your mother-loss of a first child
So inconsolably—in the face of love.   65
You'd think his memory might be satisfied—"

"There you go sneering now!"

                        "I'm not, I'm not!
You make me angry. I'll come down to you.
God, what a woman! And it's come to this,
A man can't speak of his own child that's dead."   70

"You can't because you don't know how to speak.
If you had any feelings, you that dug

With your own hand—how could you?—his little grave;
I saw you from that very window there,
Making the gravel leap and leap in air,   75
Leap up, like that, like that, and land so lightly
And roll back down the mound beside the hole.
I thought, Who is that man? I didn't know you.
And I crept down the stairs and up the stairs
To look again, and still your spade kept lifting.   80
Then you came in. I heard your rumbling voice
Out in the kitchen, and I don't know why,
But I went near to see with my own eyes.
You could sit there with the stains on your shoes
Of the fresh earth from your own baby's grave   85
And talk about your everyday concerns.
You had stood the spade up against the wall
Outside there in the entry, for I saw it."

"I shall laugh the worst laugh I ever laughed.
I'm cursed. God, if I don't believe I'm cursed."   90
"I can repeat the very words you were saying:
'Three foggy mornings and one rainy day
Will rot the best birch fence a man can build.'
Think of it, talk like that at such a time!
What had how long it takes a birch to rot   95
To do with what was in the darkened parlor?
You *couldn't* care! The nearest friends can go
With anyone to death, comes so far short
They might as well not try to go at all.
No, from the time when one is sick to death,   100
One is alone, and he dies more alone.
Friends make pretense of following to the grave,
But before one is in it, their minds are turned
And making the best of their way back to life
And living people, and things they understand.   105
But the world's evil. I won't have grief so
If I can change it. Oh, I won't, I won't!"

"There, you have said it all and you feel better.
You won't go now. You're crying. Close the door.
The heart's gone out of it: why keep it up?   110
Amy! There's someone coming down the road!"

"*You*—oh, you think the talk is all. I must go—
Somewhere out of this house. How can I make you—"

"If—you—do!" She was opening the door wider.
"Where do you mean to go? First tell me that.   115
I'll follow and bring you back by force. I *will!*—"

Robert Frost (1874–1963)

QUESTIONS

1. Vocabulary: *wonted* (22).
2. The poem centers on a conflict between husband and wife. What causes the conflict? Why does Amy resent her husband? What is *his* dissatisfaction with Amy?
3. Characterize the husband and wife respectively. What is the chief difference between them? Does the poem take sides? Is either presented more sympathetically than the other?
4. The poem does not say how long the couple have been married or how long the child has been buried. Does it contain suggestions from which we may make rough inferences?
5. The husband and wife both generalize on the other's faults during the course of the poem, attributing them to all men or to all women or to people in general. Point out these generalizations. Are they valid?
6. Finish the unfinished sentences in lines 30, 66, 113, 114.
7. Comment on the function of lines 25, 39, 92–93.
8. Following are three paraphrased and abbreviated versions of statements made in published discussions of the poem. Which would you support? Why?
   a. The young wife is gradually persuaded by her husband's kind yet firm reasonableness to express her feelings in words and to recognize that human nature is limited and cannot sacrifice everything to sorrow. Though she still suffers from excess grief, the crisis is past, and she will eventually be brought back to life.
   b. At the end, the whole poem is epitomized by the door that is neither open nor shut. The wife cannot really leave; the husband cannot really make her stay. Neither husband nor wife is capable of decisive action, of either self-liberation or liberation of the other.
   c. Her husband's attempt to talk, since it is the wrong kind of talk, only leads to her departure at the poem's end.

The Love Song of J. Alfred Prufrock

S'io credesse che mia risposta fosse
A persona che mai tornasse al mondo,
Questa fiamma staria senza piu scosse.
Ma perciocche giammai di questo fondo

Non torno vivo alcun, s'i'odo il vero,
Senza tema d'infamia ti rispondo.

Let us go then, you and I,
When the evening is spread out against the sky
Like a patient etherized upon a table;
Let us go, through certain half-deserted streets,
The muttering retreats   5
Of restless nights in one-night cheap hotels
And sawdust restaurants with oyster-shells:
Streets that follow like a tedious argument
Of insidious intent
To lead you to an overwhelming question. . . .   10
Oh, do not ask, "What is it?"
Let us go and make our visit.

In the room the women come and go
Talking of Michelangelo.

The yellow fog that rubs its back upon the window-panes,   15
The yellow smoke that rubs its muzzle on the window-panes
Licked its tongue into the corners of the evening,
Lingered upon the pools that stand in drains,
Let fall upon its back the soot that falls from chimneys,
Slipped by the terrace, made a sudden leap,   20
And seeing that it was a soft October night,
Curled once about the house, and fell asleep.

And indeed there will be time
For the yellow smoke that slides along the street,
Rubbing its back upon the window-panes;   25
There will be time, there will be time
To prepare a face to meet the faces that you meet;
There will be time to murder and create,
And time for all the works and days of hands
That lift and drop a question on your plate;   30
Time for you and time for me,
And time yet for a hundred indecisions,
And for a hundred visions and revisions,
Before the taking of a toast and tea.

In the room the women come and go   35
Talking of Michelangelo.

And indeed there will be time
To wonder, "Do I dare?" and "Do I dare?"
Time to turn back and descend the stair,
With a bald spot in the middle of my hair—   40
(They will say: "How his hair is growing thin!")
My morning coat, my collar mounting firmly to the chin,
My necktie rich and modest, but asserted by a simple pin—
(They will say: "But how his arms and legs are thin!")
Do I dare   45
Disturb the universe?
In a minute there is time
For decisions and revisions which a minute will reverse.

For I have known them all already, known them all—
Have known the evenings, mornings, afternoons,   50
I have measured out my life with coffee spoons;
I know the voices dying with a dying fall
Beneath the music from a farther room.
    So how should I presume?

And I have known the eyes already, known them all—   55
The eyes that fix you in a formulated phrase,
And when I am formulated, sprawling on a pin,
When I am pinned and wriggling on the wall,
Then how should I begin
To spit out all the butt-ends of my days and ways?   60
    And how should I presume?

And I have known the arms already, known them all—
Arms that are braceleted and white and bare
(But in the lamplight, downed with light brown hair!)
Is it perfume from a dress   65
That makes me so digress?
Arms that lie along a table, or wrap about a shawl.
    And should I then presume?
    And how should I begin?

                    *   *   *

Shall I say, I have gone at dusk through narrow streets   70
And watched the smoke that rises from the pipes
Of lonely men in shirt-sleeves, leaning out of windows? . . .

I should have been a pair of ragged claws
Scuttling across the floors of silent seas.

*   *   *

And the afternoon, the evening, sleeps so peacefully!   75
Smoothed by long fingers,
Asleep . . . tired . . . or it malingers,
Stretched on the floor, here beside you and me.
Should I, after tea and cakes and ices,
Have the strength to force the moment to its crisis?   80
But though I have wept and fasted, wept and prayed,
Though I have seen my head (grown slightly bald) brought in
    upon a platter,
I am no prophet—and here's no great matter;
I have seen the moment of my greatness flicker,
And I have seen the eternal Footman hold my coat, and snicker, 85
And in short, I was afraid.

And would it have been worth it, after all,
After the cups, the marmalade, the tea,
Among the porcelain, among some talk of you and me,
Would it have been worth while,   90
To have bitten off the matter with a smile,
To have squeezed the universe into a ball
To roll it toward some overwhelming question,
To say: "I am Lazarus, come from the dead,
Come back to tell you all, I shall tell you all"—   95
If one, settling a pillow by her head,
    Should say: "That is not what I meant at all.
    That is not it, at all."

And would it have been worth it, after all,
Would it have been worth while,   100
After the sunsets and the dooryards and the sprinkled streets,
After the novels, after the teacups, after the skirts that trail along
    the floor—
And this, and so much more?—
It is impossible to say just what I mean!
But as if a magic lantern threw the nerves in patterns   105
    on a screen:
Would it have been worth while
If one, settling a pillow or throwing off a shawl,
And turning toward the window, should say:
    "That is not it at all,
    That is not what I meant, at all."   110

*   *   *

No! I am not Prince Hamlet, nor was meant to be;
Am an attendant lord, one that will do
To swell a progress, start a scene or two,
Advise the prince; no doubt, an easy tool,
Deferential, glad to be of use,   115
Politic, cautious, and meticulous;
Full of high sentence, but a bit obtuse;
At times, indeed, almost ridiculous—
Almost, at times, the Fool.

I grow old . . . I grow old . . .   120
I shall wear the bottoms of my trousers rolled.°   cuffed

Shall I part my hair behind? Do I dare to eat a peach?
I shall wear white flannel trousers, and walk upon the beach.
I have heard the mermaids singing, each to each.

I do not think that they will sing to me.   125

I have seen them riding seaward on the waves
Combing the white hair of the waves blown back
When the wind blows the water white and black.

We have lingered in the chambers of the sea
By sea-girls wreathed with seaweed red and brown   130
Till human voices wake us, and we drown.

T. S. Eliot (1888–1965)

QUESTIONS

1. Vocabulary: *insidious* (9), *Michelangelo* (14, 36), *muzzle* (16), *malingers* (77), *progress* (113), *Deferential* (115), *Politic* (116), *meticulous* (116), *sentence* (117).
2. This poem may be for some readers the most difficult in the book because it uses a "stream of consciousness" technique (that is, it presents the apparently random thoughts going through a person's head within a certain time interval), in which the transitional links are psychological rather than logical, and also because it uses allusions you may be unfamiliar with. Even if you do not at first understand the poem in detail, you should be able to get from it a quite accurate picture of Prufrock's character and personality. What kind of person is he (answer this as fully as possible)? From what class of society does he come? What one line especially well sums up the nature of his past life? A brief initial orientation may be helpful: Prufrock is appar-

ently on his way, at the beginning of the poem, to a late afternoon tea, at which he wishes (or does he?) to make a declaration of love to some lady who will be present. The "you and I" of the first line are divided parts of Prufrock's own nature, for he is experiencing internal conflict. Does he or does he not make the declaration? Where does the climax of the poem come? If the portion leading up to the climax is devoted to Prufrock's effort to prepare himself psychologically to make the declaration (or to postpone such effort), what is the portion after the climax devoted to?

3. The poem contains a number of striking or unusual figures of speech. Most of them in some way reflect Prufrock's own nature or his desires or fears. From this point of view discuss lines 2–3; 15–22 and 75–78; 57–58; 73–74; and 124–131. What figure of speech is lines 73–74? In what respect is the title ironic?

4. The poem makes extensive use of literary allusion. The Italian epigraph is a passage from Dante's *Inferno* in which a man in Hell tells a visitor that he would never tell his story if there were a chance that it would get back to living ears. In line 29 the phrase "works and days" is the title of a long poem—a description of agricultural life and a call to toil—by the early Greek poet Hesiod. Line 52 echoes the opening speech of Shakespeare's *Twelfth Night*. The prophet of lines 81–83 is John the Baptist, whose head was delivered to Salome by Herod as a reward for her dancing (Matthew 14.1–11, and Oscar Wilde's play *Salome*). Line 92 echoes the closing six lines of Marvell's "To His Coy Mistress" (page 730). Lazarus (94–95) may be either the beggar Lazarus (of Luke 16) who was not permitted to return from the dead to warn a rich man's brothers about Hell, the Lazarus (of John 11) whom Christ raised from death, or both. Lines 111–119 allude to a number of characters from Shakespeare's *Hamlet*: Hamlet himself, the chamberlain Polonius, and various minor characters including probably Rosencrantz, Guildenstern, and Osric. "Full of high sentence" (117) echoes Chaucer's description of the Clerk of Oxford in the Prologue to *The Canterbury Tales*. Relate as many of these allusions as you can to the character of Prufrock. How is Prufrock particularly like Hamlet, and how is he unlike him? Contrast Prufrock with the speaker in "To His Coy Mistress."

Sunday Morning

1

Complacencies of the peignoir, and late
Coffee and oranges in a sunny chair,
And the green freedom of a cockatoo
Upon a rug mingle to dissipate
The holy hush of ancient sacrifice.   5
She dreams a little, and she feels the dark
Encroachment of that old catastrophe,
As a calm darkens among water-lights.

The pungent oranges and bright, green wings
Seem things in some procession of the dead,   10
Winding across wide water, without sound.
The day is like wide water, without sound,
Stilled for the passing of her dreaming feet
Over the seas, to silent Palestine,
Dominion of the blood and sepulchre.   15

2

Why should she give her bounty to the dead?
What is divinity if it can come
Only in silent shadows and in dreams?
Shall she not find in comforts of the sun,
In pungent fruit and bright, green wings, or else   20
In any balm or beauty of the earth,
Things to be cherished like the thought of heaven?
Divinity must live within herself:
Passions of rain, or moods in falling snow;
Grievings in loneliness, or unsubdued   25
Elations when the forest blooms; gusty
Emotions on wet roads on autumn nights;
All pleasures and all pains, remembering
The bough of summer and the winter branch.
These are the measures destined for her soul.   30

3

Jove in the clouds had his inhuman birth.
No mother suckled him, no sweet land gave
Large-mannered motions to his mythy mind.
He moved among us, as a muttering king,
Magnificent, would move among his hinds,   35
Until our blood, commingling, virginal,
With heaven, brought such requital to desire
The very hinds discerned it, in a star.
Shall our blood fail? Or shall it come to be
The blood of paradise? And shall the earth   40
Seem all of paradise that we shall know?
The sky will be much friendlier then than now,
A part of labor and a part of pain,
And next in glory to enduring love,
Not this dividing and indifferent blue.   45

4

She says, "I am content when wakened birds,
Before they fly, test the reality
Of misty fields, by their sweet questionings;
But when the birds are gone, and their warm fields
Return no more, where, then, is paradise?"   50
There is not any haunt of prophecy,
Nor any old chimera of the grave,
Neither the golden underground, nor isle
Melodious, where spirits gat them home,
Nor visionary south, nor cloudy palm   55
Remote on heaven's hill, that has endured
As April's green endures; or will endure
Like her remembrance of awakened birds,
Or her desire for June and evening, tipped
By the consummation of the swallow's wings.   60

5

She says, "But in contentment I still feel
The need of some imperishable bliss."
Death is the mother of beauty; hence from her,
Alone, shall come fulfillment to our dreams
And our desires. Although she strews the leaves   65
Of sure obliteration on our paths,
The path sick sorrow took, the many paths
Where triumph rang its brassy phrase, or love
Whispered a little out of tenderness,
She makes the willow shiver in the sun   70
For maidens who were wont to sit and gaze
Upon the grass, relinquished to their feet.
She causes boys to pile new plums and pears
On disregarded plate. The maidens taste
And stray impassioned in the littering leaves.   75

6

Is there no change of death in paradise?
Does ripe fruit never fall? Or do the boughs
Hang always heavy in that perfect sky,
Unchanging, yet so like our perishing earth,
With rivers like our own that seek for seas   80

They never find, the same receding shores
That never touch with inarticulate pang?
Why set the pear upon those river-banks
Or spice the shores with odors of the plum?
Alas, that they should wear our colors there,   85
The silken weavings of our afternoons,
And pick the strings of our insipid lutes!
Death is the mother of beauty, mystical,
Within whose burning bosom we devise
Our earthly mothers waiting, sleeplessly.   90

7

Supple and turbulent, a ring of men
Shall chant in orgy on a summer morn
Their boisterous devotion to the sun,
Not as a god, but as a god might be,
Naked among them, like a savage source.   95
Their chant shall be a chant of paradise,
Out of their blood, returning to the sky;
And in their chant shall enter, voice by voice,
The windy lake wherein their lord delights,
The trees, like serafin, and echoing hills,   100
That choir among themselves long afterward.
They shall know well the heavenly fellowship
Of men that perish and of summer morn.
And whence they came and whither they shall go
The dew upon their feet shall manifest.   105

8

She hears, upon that water without sound,
A voice that cries, "The tomb in Palestine
Is not the porch of spirits lingering.
It is the grave of Jesus, where he lay."
We live in an old chaos of the sun,   110
Or old dependency of day and night,
Or island solitude, unsponsored, free,
Of that wide water, inescapable.
Deer walk upon our mountains, and the quail
Whistle about us their spontaneous cries;   115
Sweet berries ripen in the wilderness;
And, in the isolation of the sky,

At evening, casual flocks of pigeons make
Ambiguous undulations as they sink,
Downward to darkness, on extended wings.   120

Wallace Stevens (1879–1955)

QUESTIONS

1. Vocabulary: *peignoir* (1), *hinds* (35, 38), *requital* (37), *chimera* (52), *consummation* (60), *obliteration* (66), *serafin* (seraphim) (100). "[G]at" (54) is an obsolete past tense of "get."
2. The poem presents a woman meditating on questions of death, mutability, and permanence, beginning with a stanza that sets the stage and shows her being drawn to these questions beyond her conscious will. The meditation proper is structured as a series of questions and answers stated in direct or indirect quotations, with the answer to a preceding question suggesting a further question, and so forth. In reading through the poem, paraphrase the sequence of implied or stated questions, and the answers to them.
3. The opening scene (stanza 1), in a collection of images and details, indicates the means the woman has chosen to avoid thinking of the typical "Sunday morning" topic, the Christian religion. Define the means she employs. Trace the further references to fruits and birds throughout the poem, and explain the ordering principle that ties them together (for example, what development of idea or attitude is implied in the sequence oranges/plums and pears/wild berries?).
4. What symbolic meanings are implied by the images of (a) water, (b) the sun, and (c) birds and other animals?
5. Why does the woman give up her desire for unchanging permanence? With what does she replace it? What is her final attitude toward a world that includes change and death? What is meant by "Death is the mother of beauty" (63, 88)?
6. The poet wrote, "This is not essentially a woman's meditation on religion and the meaning of life. It is anybody's meditation" (*Letters of Wallace Stevens*, ed. Holly Stevens [New York: Knopf, 1966], 250). Can you justify that claim?

The Weary Blues

Droning a drowsy syncopated tune,
Rocking back and forth to a mellow croon,
   I heard a Negro play.
Down on Lenox Avenue the other night
By the pale dull pallor of an old gas light   5
   He did a lazy sway. . . .
   He did a lazy sway. . . .
To the tune o' those Weary Blues.

With his ebony hands on each ivory key
He made that poor piano moan with melody.   10
    O Blues!
Swaying to and fro on his rickety stool
He played that sad raggy tune like a musical fool.
    Sweet Blues!
Coming from a black man's soul.   15
    O Blues!
In a deep song voice with a melancholy tone
I heard that Negro sing, that old piano moan—
    "Ain't got nobody in all this world,
    Ain't got nobody but ma self.   20
    I's gwine to quit ma frownin'
    And put ma troubles on the shelf."
Thump, thump, thump, went his foot on the floor.
He played a few chords then he sang some more—
    "I got the Weary Blues   25
    And I can't be satisfied.
    Got the Weary Blues
    And can't be satisfied—
    I ain't happy no mo'
    And I wish that I had died."   30
And far into the night he crooned that tune.
The stars went out and so did the moon.
The singer stopped playing and went to bed
While the Weary Blues echoed through his head.
He slept like a rock or a man that's dead.   35

Langston Hughes (1902–1967)

QUESTIONS

1. Vocabulary: *syncopated* (1), *raggy* (13)
2. What kind of music is the blues? Why is the form of "The Weary Blues" appropriate to a poem about this music?
3. The poem makes frequent use of repetition. What effect does this have on the reader?
4. Who is the speaker, and why does he respond so intensely to the piano player's "sad raggy tune" (13)?
5. The two quoted lyrics from the piano player's song (19–22 and 25–30) convey quite different messages and emotions. Describe these contrasting lyrics. What is the effect of this contrast on the reader's understanding of the song?
6. The piano player sings and plays "far into the night" (31). How is the music beneficial to him? Does the speaker derive a similar benefit?

7. Analyze the final line. How does the simile form an appropriate closure to the poem?

The Fish

I caught a tremendous fish
and held him beside the boat
half out of water, with my hook
fast in a corner of his mouth.
He didn't fight.   5
He hadn't fought at all.
He hung a grunting weight,
battered and venerable
and homely. Here and there
his brown skin hung in strips   10
like ancient wallpaper,
and its pattern of darker brown
was like wallpaper:
shapes like full-blown roses
stained and lost through age.   15
He was speckled with barnacles,
fine rosettes of lime,
and infested
with tiny white sea-lice,
and underneath two or three   20
rags of green weed hung down.
While his gills were breathing in
the terrible oxygen
—the frightening gills,
fresh and crisp with blood,   25
that can cut so badly—
I thought of the coarse white flesh
packed in like feathers,
the big bones and the little bones,
the dramatic reds and blacks   30
of his shiny entrails,
and the pink swim-bladder
like a big peony.
I looked into his eyes
which were far larger than mine   35
but shallower, and yellowed,

the irises backed and packed
with tarnished tinfoil
seen through the lenses
of old scratched isinglass.   40
They shifted a little, but not
to return my stare.
—It was more like the tipping
of an object toward the light.
I admired his sullen face,   45
the mechanism of his jaw,
and then I saw
that from his lower lip
—if you could call it a lip—
grim, wet, and weaponlike,   50
hung five old pieces of fish-line,
or four and a wire leader
with the swivel still attached,
with all their five big hooks
grown firmly in his mouth.   55
A green line, frayed at the end
where he broke it, two heavier lines,
and a fine black thread
still crimped from the strain and snap
when it broke and he got away.   60
Like medals with their ribbons
frayed and wavering,
a five-haired beard of wisdom
trailing from his aching jaw.
I stared and stared   65
and victory filled up
the little rented boat,
from the pool of bilge
where oil had spread a rainbow
around the rusted engine   70
to the bailer rusted orange,
the sun-cracked thwarts,
the oarlocks on their strings,
the gunnels—until everything
was rainbow, rainbow, rainbow!   75
And I let the fish go.

Elizabeth Bishop (1911–1979)

QUESTIONS

1. Explore the multiple denotations of "tremendous" (1) and the connotations attached to them. How does the richness of that word prepare you for the complexity of the poem?
2. In what ways are many of the images paradoxical in their emotional evocations? Where does the poem create imagery out of the speaker's imagination rather than her present observation?
3. Much of the imagery is elucidated by figurative comparisons or is itself figurative. Find examples of both uses of figures, and trace what they convey in the way of ideas and/or emotions.
4. Whose "victory" fills the boat (66–67)? What is the nature of that victory? Might the term apply to more than one kind of victory?
5. What literally is the "rainbow" (69)? To what is it transformed in lines 74–75? What accounts for the transformation?
6. Explain how the tone of the poem shifts and develops. What is happening to the speaker as she observes and comments upon the physical aspects of the fish?
7. Why does the speaker "let the fish go" (76)? Is the fish symbolic?

Diving into the Wreck

First having read the book of myths,
and loaded the camera,
and checked the edge of the knife-blade,
I put on
the body-armor of black rubber   5
the absurd flippers
the grave and awkward mask.
I am having to do this
not like Cousteau   with his
assiduous team   10
aboard the sun-flooded schooner
but here alone.

There is a ladder.
The ladder is always there
hanging innocently   15
close to the side of the schooner.
We know what it is for,
we who have used it.
Otherwise
it's a piece of maritime floss   20
some sundry equipment.

I go down.
Rung after rung and still
the oxygen immerses me
the blue light   25
the clear atoms
of our human air.
I go down.
My flippers cripple me,
I crawl like an insect down the ladder   30
and there is no one
to tell me when the ocean
will begin.

First the air is blue and then
it is bluer and then green and then   35
black I am blacking out and yet
my mask is powerful
it pumps my blood with power
the sea is another story
the sea is not a question of power   40
I have to learn alone
to turn my body without force
in the deep element.

And now: it is easy to forget
what I came for   45
among so many who have always
lived here
swaying their crenellated   fans
between the reefs
and besides   50
you breathe differently down here.

I came to explore the wreck.
The words are purposes.
The words are maps.
I came to see the damage that was done   55
and the treasures that prevail.
I stroke the beam of my lamp
slowly along the flank
of something more permanent
than fish or weed   60

the thing I came for:
the wreck and not the story of the wreck
the thing itself and not the myth
the drowned face always staring
toward the sun   65
the evidence of damage
worn by salt and sway into this threadbare beauty
the ribs of the disaster
curving their assertion
among the tentative haunters.   70

This is the place.
And I am here, the mermaid whose dark hair
streams black, the merman in his armored body
We circle silently
about the wreck   75
we dive into the hold.
I am she: I am he

whose drowned face sleeps with open eyes
whose breasts still bear the stress
whose silver, copper, vermeil cargo lies   80
obscurely inside barrels
half-wedged and left to rot
we are the half-destroyed instruments
that once held to a course
the water-eaten log   85
the fouled compass

We are, I am, you are
by cowardice or courage
the one who find our way
back to this scene   90
carrying a knife, a camera
a book of myths
in which
our names do not appear.

Adrienne Rich (b. 1929)

NOTE: Jacques Cousteau (9) (1910–1997) was a French marine scientist who led underwater exploring expeditions.

Poems for
Further Reading

To Marguerite

Yes! In the sea of life enisled,
With echoing straits between us thrown,
Dotting the shoreless watery wild,
We mortal millions live *alone*.
The islands feel the enclasping flow   5
And then their endless bounds they know.

But when the moon their hollows lights,
And they are swept by balms of spring,
And in their glens, on starry nights,
The nightingales divinely sing;   10
And lovely notes, from shore to shore,
Across the sounds and channels pour—

Oh! then a longing like despair
Is to their farthest caverns sent;
For surely once, they feel, we were   15
Parts of a single continent!
Now round us spreads the watery plain—
Oh might our marges meet again!

Who ordered that their longing's fire
Should be, as soon as kindled, cooled?   20
Who renders vain their deep desire—
A God, a God their severance ruled!
And bade betwixt their shores to be
The unplumbed, salt, estranging sea.

Matthew Arnold (1822–1888)

Siren Song

This is the one song everyone
would like to learn: the song
that is irresistible:

the song that forces men
to leap overboard in squadrons   5
even though they see the beached skulls

the song nobody knows
because anyone who has heard it
is dead, and the others can't remember.

Shall I tell you the secret   10
and if I do, will you get me
out of this bird suit?

I don't enjoy it here
squatting on this island
looking picturesque and mythical   15

with these two feathery maniacs,
I don't enjoy singing
this trio, fatal and valuable.

I will tell the secret to you,
to you, only to you.   20
Come closer. This song

is a cry for help: Help me!
Only you, only you can,
you are unique

at last. Alas   25
it is a boring song
but it works every time.

Margaret Atwood (b. 1939)

Siren (title): In Greek mythology, the sirens (sometimes pictured as birds with women's heads)
were creatures whose beautiful singing lured sailors to their deaths.

Musée des Beaux Arts

About suffering they were never wrong,
The Old Masters: how well they understood
Its human position; how it takes place
While someone else is eating or opening a window or just
    walking dully along;
How, when the aged are reverently, passionately waiting   5
For the miraculous birth, there always must be

Children who did not specially want it to happen, skating
On a pond at the edge of the wood:
They never forgot
That even the dreadful martyrdom must run its course   10
Anyhow in a corner, some untidy spot
Where the dogs go on with their doggy life and the
    torturer's horse
Scratches its innocent behind on a tree.

In Brueghel's *Icarus*, for instance: how everything
    turns away
Quite leisurely from the disaster; the plowman may   15
Have heard the splash, the forsaken cry,
But for him it was not an important failure; the sun shone
As it had to on the white legs disappearing into the green
Water; and the expensive delicate ship that must have seen
Something amazing, a boy falling out of the sky,   20
Had somewhere to get to and sailed calmly on.

W. H. Auden (1907–1973)

On Reading Poems to a Senior Class
at South High

Before
I opened my mouth
I noticed them sitting there
as orderly as frozen fish
in a package.   5

Slowly water began to fill the room
though I did not notice it
till it reached
my ears

and then I heard the sounds   10
of fish in an aquarium
and I knew that though I had
tried to drown them
with my words

that they had only opened up   15
like gills for them
and let me in.

Together we swam around the room
like thirty tails whacking words
till the bell rang   20
puncturing
a hole in the door

where we all leaked out

They went to another class
I suppose and I home   25

where Queen Elizabeth
my cat met me
and licked my fins
till they were hands again.

                                                        D. C. Berry (b. 1942)

The Lamb

    Little Lamb, who made thee?
    Dost thou know who made thee?
Gave thee life and bid thee feed
By the stream and o'er the mead;
Gave thee clothing of delight,   5
Softest clothing wooly bright;
Gave thee such a tender voice,
Making all the vales rejoice!
    Little Lamb, who made thee?
    Dost thou know who made thee?   10

    Little Lamb, I'll tell thee,
    Little Lamb, I'll tell thee!
He is callèd by thy name,
For he calls himself a Lamb;
He is meek and he is mild,   15

He became a little child;
I a child and thou a lamb,
We are callèd by his name.
    Little Lamb, God bless thee.
    Little Lamb, God bless thee.   20

William Blake (1757–1827)

The Tiger

Tiger! Tiger! burning bright
In the forests of the night,
What immortal hand or eye
Could frame thy fearful symmetry?

In what distant deeps or skies   5
Burnt the fire of thine eyes?
On what wings dare he aspire?
What the hand dare seize the fire?

And what shoulder, and what art,
Could twist the sinews of thy heart?   10
And when thy heart began to beat,
What dread hand forged thy dread feet?

What the hammer? what the chain?
In what furnace was thy brain?
What the anvil? what dread grasp   15
Dare its deadly terrors clasp?

When the stars threw down their spears,
And watered heaven with their tears,
Did he smile his work to see?
Did he who made the Lamb make thee?   20

Tiger! Tiger! burning bright
In the forests of the night,
What immortal hand or eye
Dare frame thy fearful symmetry?

William Blake (1757–1827)

Sign for My Father, Who Stressed the Bunt

On the rough diamond,
the hand-cut field below the dog lot and barn,
we rehearsed the strict technique
of bunting. I watched from the infield,
the mound, the backstop   5
as your left hand climbed the bat, your legs
and shoulders squared toward the pitcher.
You could drop it like a seed
down either base line. I admired your style,
but not enough to take my eyes off the bank   10
that served as our center-field fence.

Years passed, three leagues of organized ball,
no few lives. I could homer
into the garden beyond the bank,
into the left-field lot of Carmichael Motors,   15
and still you stressed the same technique,
the crouch and spring, the lead arm absorbing
just enough impact. That whole tiresome pitch
about basics never changing,
and I never learned what you were laying down.   20

Like a hand brushed across the bill of a cap,
let this be the sign
I'm getting a grip on the sacrifice.

David Bottoms (b. 1949)

Sadie and Maud

Maud went to college.
Sadie stayed at home.
Sadie scraped life
With a fine-tooth comb.

She didn't leave a tangle in.   5
Her comb found every strand.
Sadie was one of the livingest chits
In all the land.

Sadie bore two babies
Under her maiden name.   10
Maud and Ma and Papa
Nearly died of shame.

When Sadie said her last so-long
Her girls struck out from home.
(Sadie had left as heritage   15
Her fine-tooth comb.)

Maud, who went to college,
Is a thin brown mouse.
She is living all alone
In this old house.   20

Gwendolyn Brooks (1917–2000)

a song in the front yard

I've stayed in the front yard all my life.
I want a peek at the back
Where it's rough and untended and hungry weed grows.
A girl gets sick of a rose.

I want to go in the back yard now   5
And maybe down the alley,
To where the charity children play.
I want a good time today.

They do some wonderful things.
They have some wonderful fun.   10
My mother sneers, but I say it's fine
How they don't have to go in at quarter to nine.
My mother, she tells me that Johnnie Mae
Will grow up to be a bad woman.
That George'll be taken to Jail soon or late   15
(On account of last winter he sold our back gate).

But I say it's fine. Honest, I do.
And I'd like to be a bad woman, too,
And wear the brave stockings of night-black lace
And strut down the streets with paint on my face.   20

Gwendolyn Brooks (1917–2000)

good times

My Daddy has paid the rent
and the insurance man is gone
and the lights is back on
and my uncle Brud has hit
for one dollar straight   5
and they is good times
good times
good times

My Mama has made bread
and Grampaw has come   10
and everybody is drunk
and dancing in the kitchen
and singing in the kitchen
oh these is good times
good times   15
good times

oh children think about the
good times

Lucille Clifton (b. 1936)

Women Who Love Angels

They are thin
and rarely marry, living out
their long lives
in spacious rooms, French doors
giving view to formal gardens   5
where aromatic flowers
grow in profusion.
They play their pianos
in the late afternoon
tilting their heads   10
at a gracious angle
as if listening
to notes pitched above

the human range.
Age makes them translucent;   15
each palpitation of their hearts
visible at temple or neck.
When they die, it's in their sleep,
their spirits shaking gently loose
from a hostess too well bred   20
to protest.

Judith Ortiz Cofer (b. 1952)

Kubla Khan

In Xanadu did Kubla Khan
A stately pleasure-dome decree:
Where Alph, the sacred river, ran
Through caverns measureless to man
   Down to a sunless sea.   5
So twice five miles of fertile ground
With walls and towers were girdled round:
And here were gardens bright with sinuous rills,
Where blossomed many an incense-bearing tree;
And here were forests ancient as the hills,   10
Enfolding sunny spots of greenery.

But oh! that deep romantic chasm which slanted
Down the green hill athwart a cedarn cover!
A savage place! as holy and enchanted
As e'er beneath a waning moon was haunted   15
By woman wailing for her demon-lover!
And from this chasm, with ceaseless turmoil seething,
As if this earth in fast thick pants were breathing,
A mighty fountain momently was forced:
Amid whose swift half-intermitted burst   20
Huge fragments vaulted like rebounding hail,
Or chaffy grain beneath the thresher's flail:
And 'mid these dancing rocks at once and ever
It flung up momently the sacred river.
Five miles meandering with a mazy motion   25
Through wood and dale the sacred river ran,

Then reached the caverns measureless to man,
And sank in tumult to a lifeless ocean:
And 'mid this tumult Kubla heard from far
Ancestral voices prophesying war!   30

   The shadow of the dome of pleasure
   Floated midway on the waves;
   Where was heard the mingled measure
   From the fountain and the caves.
It was a miracle of rare device,   35
A sunny pleasure-dome with caves of ice!

   A damsel with a dulcimer
   In a vision once I saw:
   It was an Abyssinian maid,
   And on her dulcimer she played,   40
   Singing of Mount Abora.
   Could I revive within me
   Her symphony and song,
   To such a deep delight, 'twould win me,
That with music loud and long,   45
I would build that dome in air,
That sunny dome! those caves of ice!
And all who heard should see them there,
And all should cry, Beware! Beware!
His flashing eyes, his floating hair!   50
Weave a circle round him thrice,
And close your eyes with holy dread,
For he on honey-dew hath fed,
And drunk the milk of Paradise.

Samuel Taylor Coleridge (1772–1834)

War Is Kind

Do not weep, maiden, for war is kind.
Because your lover threw wild hands toward the sky
And the affrighted steed ran on alone,
Do not weep.
War is kind.   5

Hoarse, booming drums of the regiment,
Little souls who thirst for fight,
These men were born to drill and die.
The unexplained glory flies above them,
Great is the battle god, great, and his kingdom   10
A field where a thousand corpses lie.

Do not weep, babe, for war is kind.
Because your father tumbled in the yellow trenches,
Raged at his breast, gulped and died,
Do not weep.   15
War is kind.

Swift blazing flag of the regiment,
Eagle with crest of red and gold,
These men were born to drill and die.
Point for them the virtue of slaughter,   20
Make plain for them the excellence of killing
And a field where a thousand corpses lie.

Mother whose heart hung humble as a button
On the bright splendid shroud of your son,
Do not weep.   25
War is kind.

Stephen Crane (1871–1900)

Rice Will Grow Again

We were walking
On the dikes
Like damn fools—
Steppin over dud rounds.

Mitch was steppin light   5
When he saw the farmer.
    The farmer:
    With black shirt
    And shorts.
    Up to his knees   10

In the muck
Rice shoots in one hand,
The other darting
Under the water
And into the muck   15
To plant new life.

Mitch saw the farmer's hand
Going down again
With another
         Shoot   20
           But the hand
           Never came up
           Again—
After Mitch
Ripped the farmer up the middle   25
With a burst of sixteen.
We passed the farmer,
As we walked
Along the dike, and
I saw rice shoots   30
Still clutched in one hand.
He bubbled strange words
Through the blood
In his mouth.
Bong, the scout,   35
Told us the farmer
Said:
    "Damn you
    The rice will
    Grow again!"   40

Sometimes,
On dark nights
In Kansas,
The farmer comes to
        Mitch's bed: 45
And plants rice shoots
        all around.

Frank A. Cross, Jr. (b. 1945)

For a Lady I Know

She even thinks that up in heaven
    Her class lies late and snores,
While poor black cherubs rise at seven
    To do celestial chores.

Countee Cullen (1903–1946)

A Light exists in Spring

A Light exists in Spring
Not present on the Year
At any other period—
When March is scarcely here

A Color stands abroad   5
On Solitary Fields
That Science cannot overtake
But Human Nature feels.

It waits upon the Lawn,
It shows the furthest Tree
Upon the furthest Slope you know   10
It almost speaks to you.

Then as Horizons step
Or Noons report away,
Without the Formula of sound   15
It passes and we stay—

A quality of loss
Affecting our Content
As Trade had suddenly encroached
Upon a Sacrament.   20

Emily Dickinson (1830–1886)

A narrow Fellow in the Grass

A narrow Fellow in the Grass
Occasionally rides—

You may have met him? Did you not
His notice sudden is—

The Grass divides as with a Comb—   5
A spotted shaft is seen—
And then it closes at your feet
And opens further on—

He likes a Boggy Acre
A Floor too cool for Corn—   10
Yet when a Boy, and Barefoot—
I more than once at Noon

Have passed, I thought, a Whip lash—
Unbraiding in the Sun
When stooping to secure it   15
It wrinkled, and was gone—

Several of Nature's People
I know, and they know me—
I feel for them a transport
Of cordiality—   20

But never met this Fellow
Attended, or alone
Without a tighter breathing
And Zero at the Bone.

Emily Dickinson (1830–1886)

I died for Beauty—but was scarce

I died for Beauty—but was scarce
Adjusted in the Tomb
When One who died for Truth, was lain
In an adjoining Room—

He questioned softly "Why I failed"?   5
"For Beauty", I replied—
"And I—for Truth—Themself are One—
We Brethren, are", He said—

And so, as Kinsmen, met a Night—
We talked between the Rooms—   10
Until the Moss had reached our lips—
And covered up—our names—

                                Emily Dickinson (1830–1886)

I like a look of Agony

I like a look of Agony,
Because I know it's true—
Men do not sham Convulsion,
Nor simulate, a Throe—

The Eyes glaze once—and that is Death—   5
Impossible to feign
The Beads upon the Forehead
By homely Anguish strung.

                                Emily Dickinson (1830–1886)

The Good-Morrow

I wonder, by my troth, what thou and I
Did till we loved? were we not weaned till then,
But sucked on country pleasures childishly?
Or snorted we in the seven sleepers' den?
'Twas so; but this, all pleasures fancies be.   5
If ever any beauty I did see,
Which I desired, and got, 'twas but a dream of thee.

And now good-morrow to our waking souls,
Which watch not one another out of fear;
For love all love of other sights controls,   10
And makes one little room an everywhere.
Let sea-discoverers to new worlds have gone;
Let maps to other,° worlds on worlds have shown;   others
Let us possess one world; each hath one, and is one.

My face in thine eye, thine in mine appears,   15
And true plain hearts do in the faces rest;
Where can we find two better hemispheres
Without sharp north, without declining west?

Whatever dies was not mixed equally;
If our two loves be one, or thou and I   20
Love so alike that none can slacken, none can die.

John Donne (1572–1631)

(4) *seven sleepers' den:* a cave where, according to Christian legend, seven youths escaped persecution and slept for two centuries.

Song: Go and catch a falling star

Go and catch a falling star,
   Get with child a mandrake root,
Tell me where all past years are,
   Or who cleft the devil's foot,
Teach me to hear mermaids singing,   5
   Or to keep off envy's stinging,
       And find
       What wind
Serves to advance an honest mind.

If thou be'st born to strange sights,   10
   Things invisible to see,
Ride ten thousand days and nights,
   Till age snow white hairs on thee;
Thou, when thou return'st, wilt tell me
   All strange wonders that befell thee,   15
       And swear
       No where
Lives a woman true and fair.

If thou find'st one, let me know;
   Such a pilgrimage were sweet.   20
Yet do not; I would not go,
   Though at next door we might meet.
Though she were true when you met her,
   And last till you write your letter,
       Yet she   25
       Will be
False, ere I come, to two or three.

John Donne (1572–1631)

(2) *mandrake:* supposed to resemble a human being because of its forked root.

The Triple Fool

I am two fools, I know,
  For loving, and for saying so
    In whining poetry.
But where's the wiseman that would not be I
    If she would not deny?   5
Then, as the earth's inward, narrow, crooked lanes
Do purge sea water's fretful salt away,
  I thought if I could draw my pains
Through rhyme's vexations, I should them allay.
Grief brought to numbers° cannot be so fierce,   verse   10
For he tames it that fetters it in verse.

But when I have done so,
  Some man, his art and voice to show,
    Doth set and sing my pain,
And by delighting many, frees again   15
    Grief, which verse did restrain.
To love and grief tribute of verse belongs,
But not of such as pleases when 'tis read;°   read aloud
  Both are increasèd by such songs,
For both their triumphs so are publishèd.   20
And I, which was two fools, do so grow three.
Who are a little wise, the best fools be.

John Donne (1572–1631)

Vergissmeinnicht

Three weeks gone and the combatants gone,
returning over the nightmare ground
we found the place again, and found
the soldier sprawling in the sun.

The frowning barrel of his gun   5
overshadowing. As we came on
that day, he hit my tank with one
like the entry of a demon.

Look. Here in the gunpit spoil
the dishonored picture of his girl   10

who has put: *Steffi.*° *Vergissmeinnicht*   a girl's name
in a copybook gothic script.

We see him almost with content
abased, and seeming to have paid
and mocked at by his own equipment   15
that's hard and good when he's decayed.

But she would weep to see today
how on his skin the swart flies move;
the dust upon the paper eye
and the burst stomach like a cave.   20

For here the lover and killer are mingled
who had one body and one heart.
And death who had the soldier singled
has done the lover mortal hurt.

Keith Douglas (1920–1944)

The German title means "Forget me not." The author, an English poet, fought with a tank
battalion in World War II.

Guns

Again we pass that field
green artillery piece squatting
by the Legion Post on Chelten Avenue,
its ugly little pointed snout
ranged against my daughter's school.   5

"Did you ever use a gun
like that?" my daugher asks,
and I say, "No, but others did.
I used a smaller gun. A rifle."
She knows I've been to war.   10

"That's dumb," she says,
and I say, "Yes," and nod
because it was, and nod again
because she doesn't know.
How do you tell a four-year-old   15

what steel can do to flesh?
How vivid do you dare to get?
How to explain a world where men
kill other men deliberately
and call it love of country?   20

Just eighteen, I killed
a ten-year-old. I didn't know.
He spins across the marketplace
all shattered chest, all eyes and arms.
Do I tell her that? Not yet,   25

though one day I will have
no choice except to tell her
or to send her into the world
wide-eyed and ignorant.
The boy spins across the years   30

till he lands in a heap
in another war in another place
where yet another generation
is rudely about to discover
what their fathers never told them.   35

W. D. Ehrhart (b. 1948)

The Colonel

What you have heard is true. I was in his house. His wife carried a tray of coffee and sugar. His daughter filed her nails, his son went out for the night. There were daily papers, pet dogs, a pistol on the cushion beside him. The moon swung bare on its black cord over the house. On the television was a cop show. It was in English. Broken bottles were embedded in the walls around the house to scoop the kneecaps from a man's legs or cut his hands to lace. On the windows there were gratings like those in liquor stores. We had dinner, rack of lamb, good wine, a gold bell was on the table for calling the maid. The maid brought green mangoes, salt, a type of bread. I was asked how I enjoyed the country. There was a brief commercial in Spanish. His wife took everything away. There was some talk then of how difficult it had become to govern. The parrot said hello on the terrace. The colonel told it to shut up, and pushed himself from the table. My friend said to me with his eyes: say nothing. The colonel

returned with a sack used to bring groceries home. He spilled many human ears on the table. They were like dried peach halves. There is no
other way to say this. He took one of them in his hands, shook it in our
faces, dropped it into a water glass. It came alive there. I am tired of fooling around he said. As for the rights of anyone, tell your people they can
go fuck themselves. He swept the ears to the floor with his arm and held
the last of his wine in the air. Something for your poetry, no? he said.
Some of the ears on the floor caught this scrap of his voice. Some of the
ears on the floor were pressed to the ground.

May 1978

Carolyn Forché (b. 1950)

Birches

When I see birches bend to left and right
Across the lines of straighter darker trees,
I like to think some boy's been swinging them.
But swinging doesn't bend them down to stay
As ice-storms do. Often you must have seen them   5
Loaded with ice a sunny winter morning
After a rain. They click upon themselves
As the breeze rises, and turn many-colored
As the stir cracks and crazes their enamel.
Soon the sun's warmth makes them shed crystal shells   10
Shattering and avalanching on the snow-crust—
Such heaps of broken glass to sweep away
You'd think the inner dome of heaven had fallen.
They are dragged to the withered bracken by the load,
And they seem not to break; though once they are bowed   15
So low for long, they never right themselves:
You may see their trunks arching in the woods
Years afterwards, trailing their leaves on the ground
Like girls on hands and knees that throw their hair
Before them over their heads to dry in the sun.   20
But I was going to say when Truth broke in
With all her matter-of-fact about the ice-storm
I should prefer to have some boy bend them
As he went out and in to fetch the cows—
Some boy too far from town to learn baseball,   25
Whose only play was what he found himself,

Summer or winter, and could play alone.
One by one he subdued his father's trees
By riding them down over and over again
Until he took the stiffness out of them,   30
And not one but hung limp, not one was left
For him to conquer. He learned all there was
To learn about not launching out too soon
And so not carrying the tree away
Clear to the ground. He always kept his poise   35
To the top branches, climbing carefully
With the same pains you use to fill a cup
Up to the brim, and even above the brim.
Then he flung outward, feet first, with a swish,
Kicking his way down through the air to the ground.   40
So was I once myself a swinger of birches.
And so I dream of going back to be.
It's when I'm weary of considerations,
And life is too much like a pathless wood
Where your face burns and tickles with the cobwebs   45
Broken across it, and one eye is weeping
From a twig's having lashed across it open.
I'd like to get away from earth awhile
And then come back to it and begin over.
May no fate willfully misunderstand me   50
And half grant what I wish and snatch me away
Not to return. Earth's the right place for love:
I don't know where it's likely to go better.
I'd like to go by climbing a birch tree,
And climb black branches up a snow-white trunk   55
Toward heaven, till the tree could bear no more,
But dipped its top and set me down again.
That would be good both going and coming back.
One could do worse than be a swinger of birches.

Robert Frost (1874–1963)

Mending Wall

Something there is that doesn't love a wall,
That sends the frozen-ground-swell under it,
And spills the upper boulders in the sun;
And makes gaps even two can pass abreast.

The work of hunters is another thing: 5
I have come after them and made repair
Where they have left not one stone on a stone,
But they would have the rabbit out of hiding,
To please the yelping dogs. The gaps I mean,
No one has seen them made or heard them made,   10
But at spring mending-time we find them there.
I let my neighbor know beyond the hill;
And on a day we meet to walk the line
And set the wall between us once again.
We keep the wall between us as we go.   15
To each the boulders that have fallen to each.
And some are loaves and some so nearly balls
We have to use a spell to make them balance:
"Stay where you are until our backs are turned!"
We wear our fingers rough with handling them.   20
Oh, just another kind of outdoor game,
One on a side. It comes to little more:
There where it is we do not need the wall:
He is all pine and I am apple orchard.
My apple trees will never get across   25
And eat the cones under his pines, I tell him.
He only says, "Good fences make good neighbors."
Spring is the mischief in me, and I wonder
If I could put a notion in his head:
"*Why* do they make good neighbors? Isn't it   30
Where there are cows? But here there are no cows.
Before I built a wall I'd ask to know
What I was walling in or walling out,
And to whom I was like to give offense.
Something there is that doesn't love a wall,   35
That wants it down." I could say "Elves" to him,
But it's not elves exactly, and I'd rather
He said it for himself. I see him there,
Bringing a stone grasped firmly by the top
In each hand, like an old-stone savage armed.   40
He moves in darkness as it seems to me,
Not of woods only and the shade of trees.
He will not go behind his father's saying,
And he likes having thought of it so well
He says again, "Good fences make good neighbors."   45

Robert Frost (1874–1963)

Never Again Would Birds' Song Be the Same

He would declare and could himself believe
That the birds there in all the garden round
From having heard the daylong voice of Eve
Had added to their own an oversound,
Her tone of meaning but without the words.   5
Admittedly an eloquence so soft
Could only have had an influence on birds
When call or laughter carried it aloft.
Be that as may be, she was in their song.
Moreover her voice upon their voices crossed   10
Had now persisted in the woods so long
That probably it never would be lost.
Never again would birds' song be the same.
And to do that to birds was why she came.

Robert Frost (1874–1963)

The Oven Bird

There is a singer everyone has heard,
Loud, a mid-summer and a mid-wood bird,
Who makes the solid tree trunks sound again.
He says that leaves are old and that for flowers
Mid-summer is to spring as one to ten.   5
He says the early petal-fall is past,
When pear and cherry blooms went down in showers
On sunny days a moment overcast;
And comes that other fall we name the fall.
He says the highway dust is over all.   10
The bird would cease and be as other birds
But that he knows in singing not to sing.
The question that he frames in all but words
Is what to make of a diminished thing.

Robert Frost (1874–1963)

Snow White and the Seven Deadly Sins

Good Catholic girl, she didn't mind the cleaning.
All of her household chores, at first, were small

And hardly labors one could find demeaning.
One's duty was one's refuge, after all.

And if she had her doubts at certain moments   5
And once confessed them to the Father, she
Was instantly referred to texts in Romans
And Peter's First Epistle, chapter III.

Years passed. More sinful every day, the *Seven*
Breakfasted, grabbed their pitchforks, donned their horns,   10
And sped to contravene the hopes of heaven,
Sowing the neighbors' lawns with tares and thorns.

She set to work. *Pride*'s wall of looking glasses
Ogled her dimly, smeared with prints of lips;
Lust's magazines lay strewn, bare tits and asses   15
Weighted by his "devices"—chains, cuffs, whips.

Gluttony's empties covered half the table,
Mingling with *Avarice*'s cards and chips,
And she'd been told to sew a Bill Blass label
Inside the blazer *Envy*'d bought at Gyp's.   20

She knelt to the cold master bathroom floor as
If a petitioner before the Pope,
Retrieving several pairs of *Sloth*'s soiled drawers,
A sweat-sock and a cake of hairy soap.

Then, as she wiped the Windex from the mirror   25
She noticed, and the vision made her cry,
How much she'd grayed and paled, and how much
        clearer
Festered the bruise of *Wrath* beneath her eye.

"No poisoned apple needed for this Princess,"
She murmured, making X's with her thumb.   30
A car door slammed, bringing her to her senses:
Ho-hum. Ho-hum. It's home from work we come.

And she was out the window in a second,
In time to see a *Handsome Prince*, of course,
Who, spying her distressed condition, beckoned   35
For her to mount (What else?) his snow-white horse.

Impeccably he spoke. His smile was glowing.
So debonair! So charming! And so *Male*.
She took a step, reversed and without slowing
Beat it to St. Anne's where she took the veil.   40

R. S. Gwynn (b. 1948)

The Red Hat

It started before Christmas. Now our son
officially walks to school alone.
Semi-alone, it's accurate to say;
I or his father track him on the way.
He walks up on the east side of West End,   5
we on the west side. Glances can extend
(and do) across the street; not eye contact.
Already ties are feeling and not fact.
Straus Park is where these parallel paths part;
he goes alone from there. The watcher's heart   10
stretches, elastic in its love and fear,
toward him as we see him disappear,
striding briskly. Where two weeks ago,
holding a hand, he'd dawdle, dreamy, slow,
he now is hustled forward by the pull   15
of something far more powerful than school.

The mornings we turn back to are no more
than forty minutes longer than before,
but they feel vastly different—flimsy, strange,
wavering in the eddies of this change,   20
empty, unanchored, perilously light
since the red hat vanished from our sight.

Rachel Hadas (b. 1948)

My Son, My Executioner

My son, my executioner,
    I take you in my arms,
Quiet and small and just astir,
    And whom my body warms.

Sweet death, small son, our instrument   5
    Of immortality,
Your cries and hungers document
    Our bodily decay.

We twenty-five and twenty-two,
    Who seemed to live forever,   10
Observe enduring life in you
    And start to die together.

                                    Donald Hall (b. 1928)

Channel Firing

That night your great guns, unawares,
Shook all our coffins as we lay,
And broke the chancel window-squares,
We thought it was the Judgment-day

And sat upright. While drearisome   5
Arose the howl of wakened hounds:
The mouse let fall the altar-crumb,
The worms drew back into the mounds,

The glebe cow drooled. Till God called, "No;
It's gunnery practice out at sea   10
Just as before you went below;
The world is as it used to be:

"All nations striving strong to make
Red war yet redder. Mad as hatters
They do no more for Christès sake   15
Than you who are helpless in such matters.

"That this is not the judgment-hour
For some of them's a blessed thing,
For if it were they'd have to scour
Hell's floor for so much threatening. . . .   20

"Ha, ha. It will be warmer when
I blow the trumpet (if indeed
I ever do; for you are men,
and rest eternal sorely need)."

So down we lay again. "I wonder,   25
Will the world ever saner be,"
Said one, "than when He sent us under
In our indifferent century!"

And many a skeleton shook his head.
"Instead of preaching forty year,"   30
My neighbor Parson Thirdly said,
"I wish I had stuck to pipes and beer."

Again the guns disturbed the hour,
Roaring their readiness to avenge,
As far inland as Stourton Tower,   35
And Camelot, and starlit Stonehenge.

April 1914

Thomas Hardy (1840–1928)

(35–36) *Stourton Tower:* memorial at the spot where Alfred the Great resisted the invading
Danes in 879; *Camelot:* legendary capital of Arthur's kingdom; *Stonehenge:* mysterious circle
of huge stones erected in Wiltshire by very early inhabitants of Britain. The three references
move backward in time through the historic, the legendary, and the prehistoric.

The Darkling Thrush

I leant upon a coppice gate
   When Frost was specter-gray,
And Winter's dregs made desolate
   The weakening eye of day.
The tangled bine-stems scored the sky   5
   Like strings of broken lyres,
And all mankind that haunted nigh
   Had sought their household fires.

The land's sharp features seemed to be
   The Century's corpse outleant,   10
His crypt the cloudy canopy,
   The wind his death-lament.
The ancient pulse of germ and birth
   Was shrunken hard and dry,
And every spirit upon earth   15
   Seemed fervorless as I.

At once a voice arose among
   The bleak twigs overhead

In a full-hearted evensong
   Of joy illimited;   20
An aged thrush, frail, gaunt, and small,
   In blast-beruffled plume,
Had chosen thus to fling his soul
   Upon the growing gloom.

So little cause for carolings   25
   Of such ecstatic sound
Was written on terrestrial things
   Afar or nigh around,
That I could think there trembled through
   His happy good-night air   30
Some blessed Hope, whereof he knew
   And I was unaware.

31 December 1900

Thomas Hardy (1840–1928)

Hap

If but some vengeful god would call to me
From up the sky, and laugh: 'Thou suffering thing,
Know that thy sorrow is my ecstasy,
That thy love's loss is my hate's profiting!'

Then would I bear it, clench myself, and die,   5
Steeled by the sense of ire unmerited;
Half-eased in that a Powerfuller than I
Had willed and meted me the tears I shed.

But not so. How arrives it joy lies slain,
And why unblooms the best hope ever sown?   10
—Crass Casualty obstructs the sun and rain,
And dicing Time for gladness casts a moan. . . .
These purblind Doomsters had as readily strown
Blisses about my pilgrimage as pain.

Thomas Hardy (1840–1928)

To an Athlete Dying Young

The time you won your town the race
We chaired you through the market-place;
Man and boy stood cheering by,
And home we brought you shoulder-high.

Today, the road all runners come,   5
Shoulder-high, we bring you home,
And set you at your threshold down,
Townsman of a stiller town.

Smart lad, to slip betimes away
From fields where glory does not stay   10
And early though the laurel grows
It withers quicker than the rose.

Eyes the shady night has shut
Cannot see the record cut,
And silence sounds no worse than cheers   15
After earth has stopped the ears:

Now you will not swell the rout
Of lads that wore their honors out,
Runners whom renown outran
And the name died before the man.   20

So set, before its echoes fade,
The fleet foot on the sill of shade,
And hold to the low lintel up
The still-defended challenge-cup.

And round that early-laureled head   25
Will flock to gaze the strengthless dead,
And find unwithered on its curls
The garland briefer than a girl's.

                                        A. E. Housman (1859–1936)

Aunt Sue's Stories

Aunt Sue has a head full of stories.
Aunt Sue has a whole heart full of stories.
Summer nights on the front porch
Aunt Sue cuddles a brown-faced child to her bosom
And tells him stories.   5

Black slaves
Working in the hot sun,
And black slaves
Walking in the dewy night,
And black slaves   10
Singing sorrow songs on the banks of a mighty river
Mingle themselves softly
In the flow of old Aunt Sue's voice,
Mingle themselves softly
In the dark shadows that cross and recross   15
Aunt Sue's stories.

And the dark-faced child, listening,
Knows that Aunt Sue's stories are real stories.
He knows that Aunt Sue
Never got her stories out of any book at all,   20
But that they came
Right out of her own life.

And the dark-faced child is quiet
Of a summer night
Listening to Aunt Sue's stories.   25

Langston Hughes (1902–1967)

Theme for English B

The instructor said,

> *Go home, and write*
> *a page tonight.*
> *And let that page come out of you—*
> *Then, it will be true.*   5

I wonder if it's that simple?
I am twenty-two, colored, born in Winston-Salem.
I went to school there, then Durham, then here
to this college on the hill above Harlem.
I am the only colored student in my class.   10
The steps from the hill lead down into Harlem,
through a park, then I cross St. Nicholas,
Eighth Avenue, Seventh, and I come to the Y,
the Harlem Branch Y, where I take the elevator
up to my room, sit down, and write this page: 15

It's not easy to know what is true for you or me
at twenty-two, my age. But I guess I'm what
I feel and see and hear, Harlem, I hear you:
hear you, hear me—we two—you, me, talk on this page.
(I hear New York, too.) Me—who?   20
Well, I like to eat, sleep, drink, and be in love.
I like to work, read, learn, and understand life.
I like a pipe for a Christmas present,
or records—Bessie, bop, or Bach.
I guess being colored doesn't make me *not* like   25
the same things other folks like who are other races.
So will my page be colored that I write?
Being me, it will not be white.
But it will be
a part of you, instructor.   30
You are white—
yet a part of me, as I am a part of you.
That's American.
Sometimes perhaps you don't want to be a part of me.
Nor do I often want to be a part of you.   35
But we are, that's true!
As I learn from you,
I guess you learn from me—
although you're older—and white—
and somewhat more free.   40

This is my page for English B.

Langston Hughes (1902–1967)

(24) Bessie Smith: African American blues singer (1898?–1937).

Thistles

Against the rubber tongues of cows and the hoeing hands of men
Thistles spike the summer air
Or crackle open under a blue-black pressure.

Every one a revengeful burst
Of resurrection, a grasped fistful   5
Of splintered weapons and Icelandic frost thrust up

From the underground stain of a decayed Viking.
They are like pale hair and the gutturals of dialects.
Every one manages a plume of blood.

Then they grow grey, like men.   10
Mown down, it is a feud. Their sons appear,
Stiff with weapons, fighting back over the same ground.

Ted Hughes (1930–1998)

The Death of the Ball Turret Gunner

From my mother's sleep I fell into the State,
And I hunched in its belly till my wet fur froze.
Six miles from earth, loosed from its dream of life,
I woke to black flak and the nightmare fighters.
When I died they washed me out of the turret with a hose.   5

Randall Jarrell (1914–1965)

(Title) *Ball Turret:* the poet wrote, "A ball turret was a plexiglass sphere set into the belly of a B-17 or B-24 [bomber during World War II], and inhabited by two .50 caliber machine-guns and one man, a short small man. When this gunner tracked with his machine-guns a fighter [plane] attacking from below, he revolved with the turret; hunched in his little sphere, he looked like the fetus in the womb."

Warning

When I am an old woman I shall wear purple
With a red hat which doesn't go, and doesn't suit me.
And I shall spend my pension on brandy and summer gloves

And satin sandals, and say we've no money for butter.
I shall sit down on the pavement when I'm tired   5
And gobble up samples in shops and press alarm bells
And run my stick along the public railings
And make up for the sobriety of my youth.
I shall go out in my slippers in the rain
And pick the flowers in other people's gardens   10
And learn to spit.

You can wear terrible shirts and grow more fat
And eat three pounds of sausages at a go
Or only bread and pickle for a week
And hoard pens and pencils and beermats and things in boxes.   15

But now we must have clothes that keep us dry
And pay our rent and not swear in the street
And set a good example for the children.
We must have friends to dinner and read the papers.

But maybe I ought to practice a little now?   20
So people who know me are not too shocked and surprised
When suddenly I am old, and start to wear purple.

                                        Jenny Joseph (b. 1932)

La Belle Dame sans Merci

A Ballad

> O, what can ail thee, knight-at-arms,
>   Alone and palely loitering?
> The sedge has withered from the lake,
>   And no birds sing.
>
> O, what can ail thee, knight-at-arms,   5
>   So haggard and so woe-begone?
> The squirrel's granary is full,
>   And the harvest's done.
>
> I see a lily on thy brow,
>   With anguish moist and fever dew;   10
> And on thy cheeks a fading rose
>   Fast withereth too.

I met a lady in the meads,
    Full beautiful—a faery's child,
Her hair was long, her foot was light,   15
    And her eyes were wild.

I made a garland for her head,
    And bracelets too, and fragrant zone;
She looked at me as she did love,
    And made sweet moan.   20

I set her on my pacing steed,
    And nothing else saw all day long;
For sidelong would she bend, and sing
    A faery's song.

She found me roots of relish sweet,   25
    And honey wild, and manna dew,
And sure in language strange she said—
    "I love thee true."

She took me to her elfin grot,
    And there she wept and sighed full sore,   30
And there I shut her wild wild eyes
    With kisses four.

And there she lullèd me asleep
    And there I dreamed—Ah! woe betide!
The latest dream I ever dreamed   35
    On the cold hill side.

I saw pale kings and princes too,
    Pale warriors, death-pale were they all;
They cried—"La Belle Dame sans Merci
    Hath thee in thrall!"   40

I saw their starved lips in the gloam
    With horrid warning gapèd wide,
And I awoke and found me here
    On the cold hill's side.

And this is why I sojourn here   45
    Alone and palely loitering,

Though the sedge has withered from the lake,
    And no birds sing.

John Keats (1795–1821)

The title means "The beautiful lady without pity."

Ode to a Nightingale

My heart aches, and a drowsy numbness pains
    My sense, as though of hemlock° I had drunk,   a poison
Or emptied some dull opiate to the drains
    One minute past, and Lethe-wards had sunk:
'Tis not through envy of thy happy lot,   5
    But being too happy in thine happiness,—
        That thou, light-wingèd Dryad° of the trees,   wood nymph
            In some melodious plot
Of beechen green, and shadows numberless,
    Singest of summer in full-throated ease.   10

O for a draught of vintage! that hath been
    Cooled a long age in the deep-delved earth,
Tasting of Flora° and the country green,   goddess of flowers
    Dance, and Provençal song, and sunburnt mirth!
O for a beaker full of the warm South,   15
    Full of the true, the blushful Hippocrene,
        With beaded bubbles winking at the brim,
            And purple-stainèd mouth;
    That I might drink, and leave the world unseen,
        And with thee fade away into the forest dim: 20

Fade far away, dissolve, and quite forget
    What thou among the leaves hast never known,
The weariness, the fever, and the fret
    Here, where men sit and hear each other groan;
Where palsy shakes a few, sad, last gray hairs,   25
    Where youth grows pale, and specter-thin, and dies,
        Where but to think is to be full of sorrow
            And leaden-eyed despairs,
    Where Beauty cannot keep her lustrous eyes,
        Or new Love pine at them beyond tomorrow.   30

Away! away! for I will fly to thee,
    Not charioted by Bacchus and his pards,
But on the viewless° wings of Poesy,   invisible
    Though the dull brain perplexes and retards:
Already with thee! tender is the night,   35
      And haply the Queen-Moon is on her throne,
         Clustered around by all her starry Fays;
           But here there is no light,
      Save what from heaven is with the breezes blown
         Through verdurous glooms and winding mossy ways.   40

I cannot see what flowers are at my feet,
    Nor what soft incense hangs upon the boughs,
But, in embalmèd° darkness, guess each sweet   perfumed
    Wherewith the seasonable month endows
The grass, the thicket, and the fruit-tree wild;   45
      White hawthorn, and the pastoral eglantine;
         Fast fading violets covered up in leaves;
           And mid-May's eldest child,
      The coming musk-rose, full of dewy wine,
         The murmurous haunt of flies on summer eves.   50

Darkling° I listen; and, for many a time   in darkness
    I have been half in love with easeful Death,
Called him soft names in many a musèd rhyme,
    To take into the air my quiet breath;
Now more than ever seems it rich to die,   55
      To cease upon the midnight with no pain,
         While thou art pouring forth thy soul abroad
           In such an ecstasy!
      Still wouldst thou sing, and I have ears in vain—
         To thy high requiem become a sod.   60

Thou wast not born for death, immortal Bird!
    No hungry generations tread thee down;
The voice I hear this passing night was heard
    In ancient days by emperor and clown:
Perhaps the self-same song that found a path   65
      Through the sad heart of Ruth, when, sick for home,
         She stood in tears amid the alien corn;
           The same that oft-times hath

Charmed magic casements, opening on the foam
Of perilous seas, in faery lands forlorn.   70

Forlorn! the very word is like a bell
    To toll me back from thee to my sole self!
Adieu! the fancy cannot cheat so well
    As she is famed to do, deceiving elf.
Adieu! adieu! thy plaintive anthem fades   75
    Past the near meadows, over the still stream,
        Up the hill-side; and now 'tis buried deep
            In the next valley-glades:
    Was it a vision, or a waking dream?
        Fled is that music:—Do I wake or sleep?   80

John Keats (1795–1821)

(4) *Lethe:* river of forgetfulness in the Greek underworld. (14) *Provençal:* Provence, a wine-growing region in southern France famous, in the Middle Ages, for troubadours. (16) *Hippocrene:* fountain of the Muses on Mt. Helicon in Greece. (32) *Bacchus . . . pards:* Bacchus, god of wine, had a chariot drawn by leopards. (66) *Ruth:* see Bible, Ruth 2.

The Sound of Night

And now the dark comes on, all full of chitter noise.
Birds huggermugger crowd the trees,
the air thick with their vesper cries,
and bats, snub seven-pointed kites,
skitter across the lake, swing out,   5
squeak, chirp, dip, and skim on skates
of air, and the fat frogs wake and prink
wide-lipped, noisy as ducks, drunk
on the boozy black, gloating chink-chunk.

And now on the narrow beach we defend ourselves from dark.   10
The cooking done, we build our firework
bright and hot and less for outlook
than for magic, and lie in our blankets
while night nickers around us. Crickets
chorus hallelujahs; paws, quiet   15
and quick as raindrops, play on the stones
expertly soft, run past and are gone;
fish pulse in the lake; the frogs hoarsen.

Now every voice of the hour—the known, the supposed, the strange,
the mindless, the witted, the never seen—   20
sing, thrum, impinge, and rearrange
endlessly; and debarred from sleep we wait
for the birds, importantly silent,
for the crease of first eye-licking light,
for the sun, lost long ago and sweet.   25
By the lake, locked black away and tight,
we lie, day creatures, overhearing night.

Maxine Kumin (b. 1925)

Aubade

I work all day, and get half drunk at night.
Waking at four to soundless dark, I stare.
In time the curtain-edges will grow light.
Till then I see what's really always there:
Unresting death, a whole day nearer now,   5
Making all thought impossible but how
And where and when I shall myself die.
Arid interrogation: yet the dread
Of dying, and being dead,
Flashes afresh to hold and horrify.   10

The mind blanks at the glare. Not in remorse
—The good not done, the love not given, time
Torn off unused—nor wretchedly because
An only life can take so long to climb
Clear of its wrong beginnings, and may never;   15
But at the total emptiness for ever,
The sure extinction that we travel to
And shall be lost in always. Not to be here,
Not to be anywhere,
And soon; nothing more terrible, nothing more true.   20

This is a special way of being afraid
No trick dispels. Religion used to try,
That vast moth-eaten musical brocade
Created to pretend we never die,

And specious stuff that says *No rational being*   25
Can fear a thing it will not feel, not seeing
That this is what we fear—no sight, no sound,
No touch or taste or smell, nothing to think with,
Nothing to love or link with,
The anaesthetic from which none come round.   30

And so it stays just on the edge of vision,
A small unfocused blur, a standing chill
That slows each impulse down to indecision.
Most things may never happen: this one will,
And realization of it rages out   35
In furnace-fear when we are caught without
People or drink. Courage is no good:
It means not scaring others. Being brave
Lets no one off the grave.
Death is no different whined at than withstood.   40

Slowly light strengthens, and the room takes shape.
It stands plain as a wardrobe, what we know,
Have always known, know that we can't escape,
Yet can't accept. One side will have to go.
Meanwhile telephones crouch, getting ready to ring   45
In locked-up offices, and all the uncaring
Intricate rented world begins to rouse.
The sky is white as clay, with no sun.
Work has to be done.
Postmen like doctors go from house to house.   50

Philip Larkin (1922–1985)

L.A., Loiterings

1. Convalescent Home

High on painkillers,
the old don't hear
their bones hollering
anything tonight.
       They turn   5

harmless and furry, licking
themselves good-bye

They are the small animals vanishing
at the road's edge everywhere

2. **The Myth**

The go-go girl yawns.   10
The cheap dye
her mother swiped from
a five-and-ten has turned
her hair green,
but her eyes are flat   15
and still as thumbprints, or
the dead presidents pressed
into coins.
                        She glints
                    She is like
the screen flickering in   20
an empty movie house
far into the night.

                                    Larry Levis (1946–1996)

Pity me not

Pity me not because the light of day
At close of day no longer walks the sky;
Pity me not for beauties passed away
From field and thicket as the year goes by;
Pity me not the waning of the moon,   5
Nor that the ebbing tide goes out to sea,
Nor that a man's desire is hushed so soon,
And you no longer look with love on me.
This have I known always: Love is no more
Than the wide blossom which the wind assails,   10
Than the great tide that treads the shifting shore,
Strewing fresh wreckage gathered in the gales:
Pity me that the heart is slow to learn
What the swift mind beholds at every turn.

                            Edna St. Vincent Millay (1892–1950)

Loves of the Parrots

Giant parrots of Yucatán perching
splendid in the sun! Bright green,
bright yellow, bright
arterial red!

Ruffling their beauty in tireless   5
search of lice! Picking
their toenails with imperial beaks!

Desire galvanizes the male
like an electric shock,
and there's the shriek   10
all females fear—
You! or *Here!* or *Now!* or
Why did you think you could escape me!

Such throes of love!
Mad eyes ringed in white!   15
Giant beaks hook
and crack,
bloody breast feathers go flying!
Bright green, bright yellow,
bright arterial red!   20

Love, not death, is the bitter thing.

Joyce Carol Oates (b. 1938)

I Go Back to May 1937

I see them standing at the formal gates of their colleges,
I see my father strolling out
under the ochre sandstone arch, the
red tiles glinting like bent
plates of blood behind his head, I   5
see my mother with a few light books at her hip
standing at the pillar made of tiny bricks with the
wrought-iron gate still open behind her, its

sword-tips black in the May air,
they are about to graduate, they are about to get married,   10
they are kids, they are dumb, all they know is they are
innocent, they would never hurt anybody.
I want to go up to them and say Stop,
don't do it—she's the wrong woman,
he's the wrong man, you are going to do things   15
you cannot imagine you would ever do,
you are going to do bad things to children,
you are going to suffer in ways you never heard of,
you are going to want to die. I want to go
up to them there in the late May sunlight and say it,   20
her hungry pretty blank face turning to me,
her pitiful beautiful untouched body,
his arrogant handsome blind face turning to me,
his pitiful beautiful untouched body,
but I don't do it. I want to live. I   25
take them up like the male and female
paper dolls and bang them together
at the hips like chips of flint as if to
strike sparks from them, I say
Do what you are going to do, and I will tell about it.   30

Sharon Olds (b. 1942)

The Victims

When Mother divorced you, we were glad. She took it and
took it, in silence, all those years and then
kicked you out, suddenly, and her
kids loved it. Then you were fired, and we
grinned inside, the way people grinned when   5
Nixon's helicopter lifted off the South
Lawn for the last time. We were tickled
to think of your office taken away,
your secretaries taken away,
your luncheons with three double bourbons,   10
your pencils, your reams of paper. Would they take your
suits back, too, those dark
carcasses hung in your closet, and the black
noses of your shoes with their large pores?
She had taught us to take it, to hate you and take it   15
until we pricked with her for your

annihilation, Father. Now I
pass the bums in doorways, the white
slugs of their bodies gleaming through slits in their
suits of compressed silt, the stained   20
flippers of their hands, the underwater
fire of their eyes, ships gone down with the
lanterns lit, and I wonder who took it and
took it from them in silence until they had
given it all away and had nothing   25
left but this.

Sharon Olds (b. 1942)

Wish You Were Here

As a top slows, teeters, falls on its side,
vacation stalls to a halt. Rain six days
running, newspapers limp, sand underfoot,
kids frantic—too young for Trivial Pursuit.

TV's broken. The multi-movie house   5
had something new, but rain drew the tourists:
I circled for miles, there was just no way
to park. Back again, she takes up macrame.

I undertake the unnecessary: shave again,
sort hardware I don't even own.   10
Cocktails at five, too much looked forward to.
Phone-boothed one night, I call my old flame.

The inadequate mattress receives the blame
for dreams I comprehend in the morning.
My bearded boss fires me without warning.   15
I drop the ball, lose the JV game.

Robert Phillips (b. 1938)

A Work of Artifice

The bonsai tree
in the attractive pot
could have grown eighty feet tall
on the side of a mountain

till split by lightning.   5
But a gardener
carefully pruned it.
It is nine inches high.
Every day as he
whittles back the branches   10
the gardener croons,
It is your nature
to be small and cozy,
domestic and weak;
how lucky, little tree,   15
to have a pot to grow in.
With living creatures
one must begin very early
to dwarf their growth:
the bound feet,   20
the crippled brain,
the hair in curlers,
the hands you
love to touch.

Marge Piercy (b. 1936)

Mad Girl's Love Song

I shut my eyes and all the world drops dead;
I lift my lids and all is born again.
(I think I made you up inside my head.)

The stars go waltzing out in blue and red,
And arbitrary blackness gallops in: 5
I shut my eyes and all the world drops dead.

I dreamed that you bewitched me into bed
And sung me moon-struck, kissed me quite insane.
(I think I made you up inside my head.)

God topples from the sky, hell's fires fade: 10
Exit seraphim and Satan's men:
I shut my eyes and all the world drops dead.

I fancied you'd return the way you said,
But I grow old and I forget your name.
(I think I made you up inside my head.)   15

I should have loved a thunderbird instead;
At least when spring comes they roar back again.
I shut my eyes and all the world drops dead.
(I think I made you up inside my head.)

Sylvia Plath (1932–1963)

Spinster

Now this particular girl
During a ceremonious April walk
With her latest suitor
Found herself, of a sudden, intolerably struck
By the birds' irregular babel   5
And the leaves' litter.

By this tumult afflicted, she
Observed her lover's gestures unbalance the air,
His gait stray uneven
Through a rank wilderness of fern and flower.   10
She judged petals in disarray,
The whole season, sloven.

How she longed for winter then!—
Scrupulously austere in its order
Of white and black   15
Ice and rock, each sentiment within border,
And heart's frosty discipline
Exact as a snowflake.

But here—a burgeoning
Unruly enough to pitch her five queenly wits   20
Into vulgar motley—
A treason not to be borne. Let idiots
Reel giddy in bedlam spring:
She withdrew neatly.

And round her house she set   25
Such a barricade of barb and check
Against mutinous weather
As no mere insurgent man could hope to break
With curse, fist, threat
Or love, either.   30

Sylvia Plath (1932–1963)

Wuthering Heights

The horizons ring me like faggots,
Tilted and disparate, and always unstable.
Touched by a match, they might warm me,
And their fine lines singe
The air to orange   5
Before the distances they pin evaporate,
Weighting the pale sky with a solider color.
But they only dissolve and dissolve
Like a series of promises, as I step forward.

There is no life higher than the grasstops   10
Or the hearts of sheep, and the wind
Pours by like destiny, bending
Everything in one direction.
I can feel it trying
To funnel my heat away.   15
If I pay the roots of the heather
Too close attention, they will invite me
To whiten my bones among them.

The sheep know where they are,
Browsing in their dirty wool-clouds,   20
Gray as the weather.
The black slots of their pupils take me in.
It is like being mailed into space,
A thin, silly message.
They stand about in grandmotherly disguise,   25
All wig curls and yellow teeth
And hard, marbly baas.

I come to wheel ruts, and water
Limpid as the solitudes
That flee through my fingers.   30
Hollow doorsteps go from grass to grass;
Lintel and sill have unhinged themselves.
Of people the air only
Remembers a few odd syllables.
It rehearses them moaningly: 35
Black stone, black stone.

The sky leans on me, me, the one upright
Among all horizontals.
The grass is beating its head distractedly.
It is too delicate   40
For a life in such company;
Darkness terrifies it.
Now, in valleys narrow
And black as purses, the house lights
Gleam like small change.   45

Sylvia Plath (1932–1963)

To the Mercy Killers

If ever mercy move you murder me,
I pray you, kindly killers, let me live.
Never conspire with death to set me free,
but let me know such life as pain can give.
Even though I be a clot, an aching clench,   5
a stub, a stump, a butt, a scab, a knob,
a screaming pain, a putrefying stench,
still let me live, so long as life shall throb.
Even though I turn such traitor to myself
as beg to die, do not accomplice me.   10
Even though I seem not human, a mute shelf
of glucose, bottled blood, machinery
to swell the lung and pump the heart—even so,
do not put out my life. Let me still glow.

Dudley Randall (1914–2000)

Bells for John Whiteside's Daughter

There was such speed in her little body,
And such lightness in her footfall,
It is no wonder her brown study
Astonishes us all.

Her wars were bruited in our high window.   5
We looked among orchard trees and beyond,
Where she took arms against her shadow,
Or harried unto the pond,

The lazy geese, like a snow cloud
Dripping their snow on the green grass,   10
Tricking and stopping, sleepy and proud,
Who cried in goose, Alas,

For the tireless heart within the little
Lady with rod that made them rise
From their noon apple-dreams, and scuttle   15
Goose-fashion under the skies!

But now go the bells, and we are ready;
In one house we are sternly stopped
To say we are vexed at her brown study,
Lying so primly propped.   20

John Crowe Ransom (1888–1974)

Delta

If you have taken this rubble for my past
raking through it for fragments you could sell
know that I long ago moved on
deeper into the heart of the matter

If you think you can grasp me, think again: 5
my story flows in more than one direction
a delta springing from the riverbed
with its five fingers spread

Adrienne Rich (b. 1929)

Dreamwood

In the old, scratched, cheap wood of the typing stand
there is a landscape, veined, which only a child can see
or the child's older self,
a woman dreaming when she should by typing
the last report of the day.   If this were a map,   5
she thinks, a map laid down to memorize
because she might be walking it, it shows
ridge upon ridge fading into hazed desert,
here and there a sign of aquifers
and one possible watering-hole.   If this were a map   10
it would be the map of the last age of her life,
not a map of choices but a map of variations
on the one great choice. It would be the map by which
she could see the end of touristic choices,
of distances blued and purpled by romance,   15
by which she would recognize that poetry
isn't revolution but a way of knowing
why it must come.   If this cheap, massproduced
wooden stand from the Brooklyn Union Gas Co.,
massproduced yet durable, being here now,   20
is what it is yet a dream-map
so obdurate, so plain,
she thinks, the material and the dream can join
and that is the poem and that is the late report.

Adrienne Rich (b. 1929)

The Fact of a Doorframe

means there is something to hold
onto with both hands
while slowly thrusting my forehead against the wood
and taking it away
one of the oldest motions of suffering   5
as Makeba sings
a courage-song for warriors
music is suffering made powerful

I think of the story
of the goose-girl who passed through the high gate   10
where the head of her favorite mare

was nailed to the arch
and in a human voice
If she could see thee now, thy mother's heart would break
said the head   15
of Falada

Now, again, poetry,
violent, arcane, common,
hewn of the commonest living substance
into archway, portal, frame   20
I grasp for you, your bloodstained splinters, your
ancient and stubborn poise
—as the earth trembles—
burning out from the grain

Adrienne Rich (b. 1929)

Our Whole Life

Our whole life a translation
the permissible fibs

and now a knot of lies
eating at itself to get undone

Words bitten thru words   5

meanings burnt-off like paint
under the blowtorch

All those dead letters
rendered into the oppressor's language

Trying to tell the doctor where it hurts   10
like the Algerian
who walked from his village, burning

his whole body a cloud of pain
and there are no words for this

except himself   15

Adrienne Rich (b. 1929)

Nani

Sitting at her table, she serves
the sopa de arroz° to me   rice soup
instinctively, and I watch her,
the absolute *mamá,* and eat words
I might have had to say more   5
out of embarrassment. To speak,
now-foreign words I used to speak,
too, dribble down her mouth as she serves
me albóndigas.° No more   spiced meatballs
than a third are easy to me.   10
By the stove she does something with words
and looks at me only with her
back. I am full. I tell her
I taste the mint, and watch her speak
smiles at the stove. All my words   15
make her smile. Nani° never serves   granny
herself, she only watches me
with her skin, her hair. I ask for more.

I watch the *mamá* warming more
tortillas for me. I watch her   20
fingers in the flame for me.
Near her mouth, I see a wrinkle speak
of a man whose body serves
the ants like she serves me, then more words
from more wrinkles about children, words   25
about this and that, flowing more
easily from these other mouths. Each serves
as a tremendous string around her,
holding her together. They speak
nani was this and that to me   30
and I wonder just how much of me
will die with her, what were the words
I could have been, was. Her insides speak
through a hundred wrinkles, now, more
than she can bear, steel around her,   35
shouting, then, What is this thing she serves?

She asks me if I want more.
I own no words to stop her.
Even before I speak, she serves.

Alberto Ríos (b. 1952)

The Mill

The miller's wife had waited long,
    The tea was cold, the fire was dead;
And there might yet be nothing wrong
    In how he went and what he said:
"There are no millers any more,"   5
    Was all that she had heard him say;
And he had lingered at the door
    So long that it seemed yesterday.

Sick with a fear that had no form
    She knew that she was there at last;   10
And in the mill there was a warm
    And mealy fragrance of the past.
What else there was would only seem
    To say again what he had meant;
And what was hanging from a beam   15
    Would not have heeded where she went.

And if she thought it followed her,
    She may have reasoned in the dark
That one way of the few there were
    Would hide her and would leave no mark: 20
Black water, smooth above the weir
    Like starry velvet in the night,
Though ruffled once, would soon appear
    The same as ever to the sight.

Edwin Arlington Robinson (1869–1935)

Mr. Flood's Party

Old Eben Flood, climbing alone one night
Over the hill between the town below
And the forsaken upland hermitage
That held as much as he should ever know
On earth again of home, paused warily.   5
The road was his with not a native near;
And Eben, having leisure, said aloud,
For no man else in Tilbury Town to hear:

"Well, Mr. Flood, we have the harvest moon
Again, and we may not have many more;   10
The bird is on the wing, the poet says,
And you and I have said it here before.
Drink to the bird." He raised up to the light
The jug that he had gone so far to fill,
And answered huskily: "Well, Mr. Flood,   15
Since you propose it, I believe I will."

Alone, as if enduring to the end
A valiant armor of scarred hopes outworn,
He stood there in the middle of the road
Like Roland's ghost winding a silent horn.   20
Below him, in the town among the trees,
Where friends of other days had honored him,
A phantom salutation of the dead
Rang thinly till old Eben's eyes were dim.

Then, as a mother lays her sleeping child   25
Down tenderly, fearing it may awake,
He set the jug down slowly at his feet
With trembling care, knowing that most things break;
And only when assured that on firm earth
It stood, as the uncertain lives of men   30
Assuredly did not, he paced away,
And with his hand extended, paused again:

"Well, Mr. Flood, we have not met like this
In a long time; and many a change has come
To both of us, I fear, since last it was   35
We had a drop together. Welcome home!"
Convivially returning with himself,
Again he raised the jug up to the light;
And with an acquiescent quaver said:
"Well, Mr. Flood, if you insist, I might.   40

"Only a very little, Mr. Flood—
For auld lang syne. No more, sir; that will do."
So, for the time, apparently it did,
And Eben evidently thought so too;
For soon amid the silver loneliness   45
Of night he lifted up his voice and sang,

Secure, with only two moons listening,
Until the whole harmonious landscape rang—

"For auld lang syne." The weary throat gave out,
The last word wavered, and the song was done.   50
He raised again the jug regretfully
And shook his head, and was again alone.
There was not much that was ahead of him,
And there was nothing in the town below—
Where strangers would have shut the many doors   55
That many friends had opened long ago.

Edwin Arlington Robinson (1869–1935)

(11) *bird:* Mr. Flood is quoting from *The Rubáiyát of Omar Khayyám,* "The bird of Time . . . is on the wing." (20) *Roland:* hero of the French epic poem *The Song of Roland.* He died fighting a rearguard action for Charlemagne against the Moors in Spain; before his death he sounded a call for help on his famous horn, but the king's army arrived too late.

Richard Cory

Whenever Richard Cory went down town,
We people on the pavement looked at him:
He was a gentleman from sole to crown,
Clean favored, and imperially slim.

And he was always quietly arrayed,   5
And he was always human when he talked;
But still he fluttered pulses when he said,
"Good-morning," and he glittered when he walked.

And he was rich—yes, richer than a king—
And admirably schooled in every grace: 10
In fine, we thought that he was everything
To make us wish that we were in his place.

So on we worked, and waited for the light,
And went without the meat, and cursed the bread;
And Richard Cory, one calm summer night,   15
Went home and put a bullet through his head.

Edwin Arlington Robinson (1869–1935)

I knew a woman

I knew a woman, lovely in her bones,
When small birds sighed, she would sigh back at them;
Ah, when she moved, she moved more ways than one:
The shapes a bright container can contain!
Of her choice virtues only gods should speak,   5
Or English poets who grew up on Greek
(I'd have them sing in chorus, cheek to cheek).

How well her wishes went! She stroked my chin,
She taught me Turn, and Counter-turn, and Stand;
She taught me Touch, that undulant white skin;   10
I nibbled meekly from her proffered hand;
She was the sickle; I, poor I, the rake,
Coming behind her for her pretty sake
(But what prodigious mowing we did make).

Love likes a gander, and adores a goose: 15
Her full lips pursed, the errant note to seize;
She played it quick, she played it light and loose;
My eyes, they dazzled at her flowing knees;
Her several parts could keep a pure repose,
Or one hip quiver with a mobile nose   20
(She moved in circles, and those circles moved).

Let seed be grass, and grass turn into hay:
I'm martyr to a motion not my own;
What's freedom for? To know eternity.
I swear she cast a shadow white as stone.   25
But who would count eternity in days?
These old bones live to learn her wanton ways:
(I measure time by how a body sways).

Theodore Roethke (1908–1963)

My Papa's Waltz

The whiskey on your breath
Could make a small boy dizzy;
But I hung on like death:
Such waltzing was not easy.

We romped until the pans   5
Slid from the kitchen shelf;
My mother's countenance
Could not unfrown itself.

The hand that held my wrist
Was battered on one knuckle;   10
At every step you missed
My right ear scraped a buckle.

You beat time on my head
With a palm caked hard by dirt,
Then waltzed me off to bed   15
Still clinging to your shirt.

                                   Theodore Roethke (1908–1963)

Driftwood

Tumbled from the backwash of a fishing boat,
laved in salt and damascened with worm-
loops scrolling the long arm's length of it,
it rehearsed in our son's storied hands
a history of fells and sail-roads, of flare-ups,   5
strongholds, the terror-monger at last laid low
and the gold hoard hauled from its barrow.

Stripped from the tree of reckoning, arrayed
against the world's unpunished harms,
may it still serve in the coming years to bolster   10
the peacemaker's heart in him, to steer him
around whatever new perils must now
precede that homecoming folktales tell us
is the end-all meaning of our journeying.

                                   Sherod Santos (b. 1948)

The Abortion

Somebody who should have been born
is gone.

Just as the earth puckered its mouth,
each bud puffing out from its knot,
I changed my shoes, and then drove south.   5

Up past the Blue Mountains, where
Pennsylvania humps on endlessly,
wearing, like a crayoned cat, its green hair,

its roads sunken in like a gray washboard;
where, in truth, the ground cracks evilly,   10
a dark socket from which the coal has poured,

Somebody who should have been born
is gone.

the grass as bristly and stout as chives,
and me wondering when the ground would break,   15
and me wondering how anything fragile survives;

up in Pennsylvania, I met a little man,
not Rumpelstiltskin, at all, at all . . .
he took the fullness that love began.

Returning north, even the sky grew thin   20
like a high window looking nowhere.
The road was as flat as a sheet of tin.

Somebody who should have been born
is gone.

Yes, woman, such logic will lead   25
to loss without death. Or say what you meant,
you coward . . . this baby that I bleed.

Anne Sexton (1928–1974)

Her Kind

I have gone out, a possessed witch,
haunting the black air, braver at night;
dreaming evil, I have done my hitch

over the plain houses, light by light:
lonely thing, twelve-fingered, out of mind.   5
A woman like that is not a woman, quite.
I have been her kind.

I have found the warm caves in the woods,
filled them with skillets, carvings, shelves,
closets, silks, innumerable goods;   10
fixed the suppers for the worms and the elves:
whining, rearranging the disaligned.
A woman like that is misunderstood.
I have been her kind.

I have ridden in your cart, driver,   15
waved my nude arms at villages going by,
learning the last bright routes, survivor
where your flames still bite my thigh
and my ribs crack where your wheels wind.
A woman like that is not ashamed to die.   20
I have been her kind.

Anne Sexton (1928–1974)

Fear no more

Fear no more the heat o' the sun,
    Nor the furious winter's rages;
Thou thy worldly task hast done,
    Home art gone, and ta'en thy wages.
Golden lads and girls all must,   5
As chimney-sweepers, come to dust.

Fear no more the frown o' the great;
    Thou art past the tyrant's stroke;
Care no more to clothe and eat;
    To thee the reed is as the oak.   10
The scepter, learning, physic,° must   art of healing
All follow this, and come to dust.

Fear no more the lightning-flash,
    Nor the all-dreaded thunder-stone;°   thunderbolt
Fear not slander, censure rash;   15
    Thou hast finished joy and moan.

All lovers young, all lovers must
Consign to thee,° and come to dust.   yield to your condition

William Shakespeare (1564–1616)

Let me not to the marriage of true minds

Let me not to the marriage of true minds
Admit impediments. Love is not love
Which alters when it alteration finds,
Or bends with the remover to remove.
O no! it is an ever-fixèd mark   5
That looks on tempests and is never shaken;
It is the star to every wandering bark,
Whose worth's unknown, although his height be taken.
Love's not Time's fool, though rosy lips and cheeks
Within his bending sickle's compass come;   10
Love alters not with his brief hours and weeks,
But bears it out even to the edge of doom.
If this be error and upon me proved,
I never writ, nor no man ever loved.

William Shakespeare (1564–1616)

The Fly

O hideous little bat, the size of snot,
With polyhedral eye and shabby clothes,
To populate the stinking cat you walk
The promontory of the dead man's nose,
Climb with the fine leg of a Duncan-Phyfe   5
    The smoking mountains of my food
        And in a comic mood
    In mid-air take to bed a wife.

Riding and riding with your filth of hair
On gluey foot or wing, forever coy,   10
Hot from the compost and green sweet decay,
Sounding your buzzer like an urchin toy—
You dot all whiteness with diminutive stool,
    In the tight belly of the dead
        Burrow with hungry head   15
    And inlay maggots like a jewel.

At your approach the great horse stomps and paws
Bringing the hurricane of his heavy tail;
Shod in disease you dare to kiss my hand
Which sweeps against you like an angry flail;   20
Still you return, return, trusting your wing
   To draw you from the hunter's reach
     That learns to kill to teach
   Disorder to the tinier thing.

My peace is your disaster. For your death   25
Children like spiders cup their pretty hands
And wives resort to chemistry of war.
In fens of sticky paper and quicksands
You glue yourself to death. Where you are stuck
   You struggle hideously and beg,   30
     You amputate your leg
   Imbedded in the amber muck.

But I, a man, must swat you with my hate,
Slap you across the air and crush your flight,
Must mangle with my shoe and smear your blood,   35
Expose your little guts pasty and white,
Knock your head sidewise like a drunkard's hat,
   Pin your wings under like a crow's,
     Tear off your flimsy clothes,
   And beat you as one beats a rat.   40

Then like Gargantua I stride among
The corpses strewn like raisins in the dust,
The broken bodies of the narrow dead
That catch the throat with fingers of disgust.
I sweep. One gyrates like a top and falls   45
   And stunned, stone blind, and deaf
     Buzzes its frightful F
   And dies between three cannibals.

Karl Shapiro (1913–2000)

Little Ode to the Wheelchair Boys

Passing the school where midmorning sun casts crossfiring
   Spears through oak leaves, I stop my car to watch

Three boys in wheelchairs, bodies the kind we used to make
     With pipecleaners, heads bobbing as each scopes
The line they race for but cannot see. Before them the gold   5
     Hair of the special-ed teacher, like Psyche, swirls,
Gold bangles electric, orbiting the wand of her hand. They
     Can't win, she knows, hearts badly handicapped,
Unless she gives them something like courage. Faces in shade,

They lunge when her skirt lifts, her fine legs part and flex up,   10
     Her young woman's breast dares them with Go! I
Watch how each brain pounds and is geared by desire no
     Man explains, no girl ignores. But what blood's
Heat will ask these to move a chest of drawers, while love
     Lays out a room, her gaze a mare's scent leaping   15
The edges of fields? What chance have these wheel-grippers
     With those who run and jump and shriek to win
Before these can find the line? Still, sucking breath, spit flying,

They hump the rutted school courts fearless as men who give
     Their one life for a cause. Fate's done something   20
Wrong enough to each they may fall, dumped by stone, or crack,
     And who's to blame? All day they give what they have.
Maybe it's her smell. Or the faint, last desire we put into them.
     Or the way next-hour's waddlers and water-heads
Light up for wheelies, the proud high-fives these charioteers   25
     Chain around this tall gold girl who always calls
The winner *Lover*, the one who'll go inside first, as a man does.

Dave Smith (b. 1942)

The Youngest Daughter

The sky has been dark
for many years.
My skin has become as damp
and pale as rice paper
and feels the way   5
mother's used to before the drying sun
parched it out there in the fields.

Lately, when I touch my eyelids,
my hands react as if
I had just touched something   10

hot enough to burn.
My skin, aspirin colored,
tingles with migraine. Mother
has been massaging the left side of my face
especially in the evenings   15
when the pain flares up.

This morning
her breathing was graveled,
her voice gruff with affection
when I wheeled her into the bath.   20
She was in a good humor,
making jokes about her great breasts,
floating in the milky water
like two walruses,
flaccid and whiskered around the nipples.   25
I scrubbed them with a sour taste
in my mouth, thinking:
six children and an old man
have sucked from these brown nipples.

I was almost tender   30
when I came to the blue bruises
that freckle her body,
places where she has been injecting insulin
for thirty years. I soaped her slowly,
she sighed deeply, her eyes closed.   35
It seems it has always
been like this: the two of us
in this sunless room,
the splashing of the bathwater.

In the afternoons   40
when she has rested,
she prepares our ritual of tea and rice,
garnished with a shred of gingered fish,
a slice of pickled turnip,
a token for my white body.   45
We eat in the familiar silence.
She knows I am not to be trusted,
even now planning my escape.

As I toast to her health
with the tea she has poured,   50
a thousand cranes curtain the window,
fly up in a sudden breeze.

                                        Cathy Song (b. 1955)

Small Town with One Road

We could be here. This is the valley
And its black strip of highway, big-eyed
With rabbits that won't get across.
Kids could make it, though.
They leap barefoot to the store—   5
Sweetness on their tongues, red stain of laughter.
They are the spectators of fun.
Hot dimes fall from their palms,
Chinks of light, and they eat
Candies all the way home   10
Where there's a dog for each hand,
Cats, chickens in the yard.
A pot bangs and water runs in the kitchen.
Beans, they think, and beans it will be,
Brown soup that's muscle for the field   15
And crippled steps to a ladder.
Okie or Mexican, Jew that got lost,
It's a hard life where the sun looks.
The cotton gin stands tall in the money dream
And the mill is a paycheck for   20
A wife—and perhaps my wife
Who, when she was a girl,
Boxed peaches and plums, hoed
Papa's field that wavered like a mirage
That wouldn't leave. We could go back.   25
I could lose my job, this easy one
That's only words, and pick up a shovel,
Hoe, broom that takes it away.
Worry is my daughter's story.
She touches my hand. We suck roadside   30
Snowcones in the shade
And look about. Behind sunglasses

I see where I stood: a brown kid
Getting across. "He's like me,"
I tell my daughter, and she stops her mouth.   35
He looks both ways and then leaps
Across the road where riches
Happen on a red tongue.

Gary Soto (b. 1952)

Telephone Conversation

The price seemed reasonable, location
Indifferent. The landlady swore she lived
Off premises. Nothing remained
But self-confession. "Madam," I warned,
"I hate a wasted journey—I am African."   5
Silence. Silenced transmission of
Pressurized good-breeding. Voice, when it came,
Lipstick-coated, long gold-rolled
Cigarette-holder tipped. Caught I was, foully.
"HOW DARK?" . . . I had not misheard . . . "ARE YOU LIGHT   10
OR VERY DARK?" Button B. Button A. Stench
Of rancid breath of public hide-and-speak.
Red booth. Red pillar box. Red double-tiered
Omnibus squelching tar. It *was* real! Shamed
By ill-mannered silence, surrender   15
Pushed dumbfounded to beg simplification.
Considerate she was, varying the emphasis—
"ARE YOU DARK? OR VERY LIGHT?" Revelation came.
"You mean—like plain or mild chocolate?"
Her assent was clinical, crushing in its light   20
Impersonality. Rapidly, wave-length adjusted,
I chose. "West African sepia" —and as afterthought,
"Down in my passport." Silence for spectroscopic
Flight of fancy, till truthfulness clanged her accent
Hard on the mouthpiece. "WHAT'S THAT?" conceding   25
"DON'T KNOW WHAT THAT IS." "Like brunette."
"THAT'S DARK, ISN'T IT?" "Not altogether.
Facially, I am brunette, but madam, you should see
The rest of me. Palm of my hand, soles of my feet
Are a peroxide blonde. Friction, caused—   30
Foolishly madam—by sitting down, has turned

My bottom raven black—One moment, madam!—sensing
Her receiver rearing on the thunderclap
About my ears—"Madam," I pleaded, "wouldn't you rather
See for yourself?"   35

Wole Soyinka (b. 1934)

(11-14) *Button . . . Omnibus:* Public telephones in England once required the pushing of buttons to make connections and deposit coins. Telephone booths, mailboxes (called pillar boxes), and buses are painted red. (19) *plain chocolate:* dark chocolate.

One day I wrote her name upon the strand

One day I wrote her name upon the strand,°   beach
But came the waves and washèd it away:
Again I wrote it with a second hand,
But came the tide, and made my pains his prey.
"Vain man," said she, "that dost in vain assay°   attempt 5
A mortal thing so to immortalize.
For I myself shall, like to this, decay,
And eek° my name be wipèd out likewise."   also
"Not so," quoth I, "let baser things devise
To die in dust, but you shall live by fame: 10
My verse your virtues rare shall eternize,
And in the heavens write your glorious name,
Where whenas death shall all the world subdue
Our love shall live, and later life renew."

Edmund Spenser (1552–1599)

The Death of a Soldier

Life contracts and death is expected,
As in a season of autumn.
The soldier falls.
He does not become a three-days personage,
Imposing his separation,   5
Calling for pomp.

Death is absolute and without memorial,
As in a season of autumn,
When the wind stops,

When the wind stops and, over the heavens,   10
The clouds go, nevertheless,
In their direction.

Wallace Stevens (1879–1955)

Disillusionment of Ten O'Clock

The houses are haunted
By white night-gowns.
None are green,
Or purple with green rings,
Or green with yellow rings,   5
Or yellow with blue rings.
None of them are strange,
With socks of lace
And beaded ceintures.°   sashes
People are not going   10
To dream of baboons and periwinkles.
Only, here and there, an old sailor,
Drunk and asleep in his boots,
Catches tigers
In red weather.   15

Wallace Stevens (1879–1955)

The Snow Man

One must have a mind of winter
To regard the frost and the boughs
Of the pine-trees crusted with snow;

And have been cold a long time
To behold the junipers shagged with ice,   5
The spruces rough in the distant glitter
Of the January sun; and not to think
Of any misery in the sound of the wind,
In the sound of a few leaves,

Which is the sound of the land   10
Full of the same wind
That is blowing in the same bare place

For the listener, who listens in the snow,
And, nothing himself, beholds
Nothing that is not there and the nothing that is.   15

Wallace Stevens (1879–1955)

Listening to My Mother's Comic Banter
with Sackboys and Servers

It is in brief moments such as these
that I know there is no god.
And I do not suppose that,
in even one of her seventy-
some-odd years, it has entered   5
my mother's mind that the look
in this young man's eyes, adrift
somewhere between shock and shame,
might ever be anything except
kindred and reciprocal laughter.   10
In his attempts at ascertaining
her desire to supersize her fries
or seeing her apples and Oreos
safely stowed, the server seems
caught off guard, and vaguely amazed   15
by my mother's grins and gab.
She, however, sees only a co-
conspirator, one who also gets
the joke with no name, her palaver
often beginning with something   20
along the lines of "working hard,"
then straight to "hardly working." Then,
if she perceives what she conceives
to be consent, the proper glance
or repartee, silence giving consent,   25
it eggs her on to escalate to snickers,
then, perhaps, to "Lord, it's hot! I'm
just a-sweatin!" Graduating quick
enough from there to comments
maybe on the constant rise in   30
cost of things: "Shit fire to save
matches!" and beyond. Now, I

have borne witness to this bizarre
ascension many times. And always
at its end, I observe my mother's eyes   35
shifting from her daily dull to a fine
acetylene shine: opaque proof
perhaps, of linkage to some
living thing outside herself. For
long ago I think somehow   40
my mother must have caught
a glimpse of some immense
and empty ought, a vacant
maw. And although she never
said so, would not even know   45
how to say so, it seems that,
ever since that time, she reaches
out to any sign, relying even on
the fantasized response of this
poor teenaged boy, as some bleak   50
buffer piled against confronting
that sad chasm once again, any
line to keep that zap of night
at bay, depending on any bray
of mindless blather, his requesting   55
now her preference for paper over
plastic, lilt, any semblance
of communion, the kindness
of strangers on any blessed day.

Leon Stokesbury (b. 1945)

Fern Hill

Now as I was young and easy under the apple boughs
About the lilting house and happy as the grass was green,
   The night above the dingle starry,
    Time let me hail and climb
   Golden in the heydays of his eyes,   5
And honored among wagons I was prince of the apple towns
And once below a time I lordly had the trees and leaves
   Trail with daisies and barley
   Down the rivers of the windfall light.

And as I was green and carefree, famous among the barns   10
About the happy yard and singing as the farm was home,
    In the sun that is young once only,
       Time let me play and be
    Golden in the mercy of his means,
And green and golden I was huntsman and herdsman, the calves   15
Sang to my horn, the foxes on the hills barked clear and cold,
      And the sabbath rang slowly
    In the pebbles of the holy streams.

All the sun long it was running, it was lovely, the hay
Fields high as the house, the tunes from the chimneys, it was air   20
    And playing, lovely and watery
      And fire green as grass.
    And nightly under the simple stars
As I rode to sleep the owls were bearing the farm away,
All the moon long I heard, blessed among stables, the nightjars   25
    Flying with the ricks, and the horses
      Flashing into the dark.

And then to awake, and the farm, like a wanderer white
With the dew, come back, the cock on his shoulder: it was all
    Shining, it was Adam and maiden,   30
      The sky gathered again
    And the sun grew round that very day.
So it must have been after the birth of the simple light
In the first, spinning place, the spellbound horses walking warm
    Out of the whinnying green stable   35
      On to the fields of praise.

And honored among foxes and pheasants by the gay house
Under the new made clouds and happy as the heart was long,
    In the sun born over and over,
      I ran my heedless ways,   40
    My wishes raced through the house high hay
And nothing I cared, at my sky blue trades, that time allows
In all his tuneful turning so few and such morning songs
    Before the children green and golden
      Follow him out of grace,   45

Nothing I cared, in the lamb white days, that time would take me
Up to the swallow thronged loft by the shadow of my hand,
   In the moon that is always rising,
     Nor that riding to sleep
   I should hear him fly with the high fields   50
And wake to the farm forever fled from the childless land.
Oh as I was young and easy in the mercy of his means,
    Time held me green and dying
  Though I sang in my chains like the sea.

Dylan Thomas (1914–1953)

Blurry Cow

Two cows stand transfixed
by a trough of floating leaves,
facing as if into the camera,
black and white. One stamps
at the hot sting of a deerfly.   5

Seen from the window of a train,
the hoof lifts forever
over hay crosshatched by speed,
and the scales of the haunches
balance. The rest is lost: 10
the head a sudden slur of light,
the dog loping along the tracks
toward a farm yard
where a woman wavers
in her mirage of laundry.   15
A blurry cow, of all things,
strays into the mind's eye,
the afterimage
of this day on earth.

Chase Twichell (b. 1950)

Telephone Poles

They have been with us a long time.
They will outlast the elms.
Our eyes, like the eyes of a savage sieving the trees
In his search for game,
Run through them. They blend along small-town streets   5
Like a race of giants that have faded into mere mythology.
Our eyes, washed clean of belief,
Lift incredulous to their fearsome crowns of bolts, trusses,
struts, nuts, insulators, and such
Barnacles as compose
These weathered encrustations of electrical debris—   10
Each a Gorgon's head, which, seized right,
Could stun us to stone.

                    . . .

Yet they are ours. We made them.
See here, where the cleats of linemen
Have roughened a second bark   15
Onto the bald trunk. And these spikes
Have been driven sideways at intervals handy for human legs.
The Nature of our construction is in every way
A better fit than the Nature it displaces.
What other tree can you climb where the birds' twitter,   20
Unscrambled, is English? True, their thin shade is negligible,
But then again there is not that tragic autumnal
Casting-off of leaves to outface annually.
These giants are more constant than evergreens
By being never green.   25

                    John Updike (b. 1932)

What the Motorcycle Said

Br-r-r-am-m-m, rackety-am-m, OM, *Am:*
All—r-r-room, r-r-ram, ala-bas-ter—
Am, the world's my oyster.

I hate plastic, wear it black and slick,
hate hardhats, wear one on my head,   5
that's what the motorcycle said.

Passed phonies in Fords, knocked down billboards, landed
on the other side of The Gap, and Whee,
bypassed history.

When I was born (The Past), baby knew best.   10
They shook when I bawled, took Freud's path,
threw away their wrath.
R-r-rackety-am-m. *Am*. War, rhyme,
soap, meat, marriage, the Phantom Jet
are shit, and like that.   15

Hate pompousness, punishment, patience, am into Love,
hate middle-class moneymakers, live on Dad,
that's what the motorcycle said.

Br-r-r-am-m-m. It's Nowsville, man. Passed Oldies, Uglies,
Straighties, Honkies. I'll never be   20
mean, tired or unsexy.

Passed cigarette suckers, souses, mother-fuckers,
losers, went back to Nature and found
how to get VD, stoned.

Passed a cow, too fast to hear her moo, "*I* rolled   25
our leaves of grass into one ball.
I am the grassy All."

Br-r-r-am-m-m, rackety-am-m, OM, *Am:*
All—gr-r-rin, oooohgah, gl-l-utton—
Am, the world's my smilebutton.   30

Mona Van Duyn (1921–2004)

The Virgins

Down the dead streets of sun-stoned Frederiksted,
the first free port to die for tourism,
strolling at funeral pace, I am reminded
of life not lost to the American dream;
but my small-islander's simplicities   5
can't better our new empire's civilized

exchange of cameras, watches, perfumes, brandies
for the good life, so cheaply underpriced
that only the crime rate is on the rise
in streets blighted with sun, stone arches   10
and plazas blown dry by the hysteria
of rumor. A condominium drowns
in vacancy; its bargains are dusted,
but only a jeweled housefly drones
over the bargains. The roulettes spin   15
rustily to the wind—the vigorous trade
that every morning would begin afresh
by revving up green water round the pierhead
heading for where the banks of silver thresh.

Derek Walcott (b. 1930)

(1) *Frederiksted*: chief port of St. Croix, largest of the American Virgin Islands, a free port where goods can be bought without payment of customs duties and therefore at bargain prices. The economy of St. Croix, once based on sugar cane, is now chiefly dependent on tourism. Like the other American Virgin Islands, St. Croix has suffered from uncontrolled growth, building booms, unevenly distributed prosperity, destruction of natural beauty, and pollution. (5) *my . . . simplicities*: The poet is a native of St. Lucia in the West Indies. (16) *trade*: cf. trade wind.

When I Heard the Learn'd Astronomer

When I heard the learn'd astronomer,
When the proofs, the figures, were ranged in columns before me,
When I was shown the charts and diagrams, to add,
    divide, and measure them,
When I sitting heard the astronomer where he
    lectured with much applause in the lecture-room,
How soon unaccountable I became tired and sick,   5
Till rising and gliding out I wandered off by myself,
In the mystical moist night-air, and from time to time,
Looked up in perfect silence at the stars.

Walt Whitman (1819–1892)

Danse Russe

If when my wife is sleeping
and the baby and Kathleen

are sleeping
and the sun is a flame-white disc
in silken mists   5
above shining trees, —
if I in my north room
dance naked, grotesquely
before my mirror
waving my shirt round my head   10
and singing softly to myself:
"I am lonely, lonely.
I was born to be lonely,
I am best so!"
If I admire my arms, my face,   15
my shoulders, flanks, buttocks
against the yellow drawn shades,—

Who shall say I am not
the happy genius of my household?

William Carlos Williams (1883–1963)

Poem

As the cat
climbed over
the top of

the jamcloset
first the right   5
forefoot

carefully
then the hind
stepped down

into the pit of   10
the empty
flowerpot

William Carlos Williams (1883–1963)

Spring and All

By the road to the contagious hospital
under the surge of the blue
mottled clouds driven from the
northeast—a cold wind. Beyond, the
waste of broad, muddy fields   5
brown with dried weeds, standing and fallen

patches of standing water
the scattering of tall trees

All along the road the reddish
purplish, forked, upstanding, twiggy   10
stuff of bushes and small trees
with dead, brown leaves under them
leafless vines—

Lifeless in appearance, sluggish
dazed spring approaches—   15

They enter the new world naked,
cold, uncertain of all
save that they enter. All about them
the cold, familiar wind—

Now the grass, tomorrow   20
the stiff curl of wildcarrot leaf
One by one objects are defined—
It quickens: clarity, outline of leaf

But now the stark dignity of
entrance—Still, the profound change   25
has come upon them: rooted they
grip down and begin to awaken

William Carlos Williams (1883–1963)

Henzey's Pond

memory, after Brueghel's *Hunters in the Snow*

Arch, ankle, the scintillant hiss and chatter
of blades whetted with midwinter sun

inscribing the smooth stone disc of the pond.
School figures, phonics worksheets, thumbed copies
of Baltimore catechism stashed inside   5
vinyl bookbags set out to mark the netless
posts of the goals. And the long bandaged sticks
like flattened bishop's crooks to slap hell
out of the nun-dark puck. No parents,
nor penguins afloat in their chaste whispering   10
raiment whipped faintly by loops of dangled
rosary beads. *Hail Mary! Dog-damn!*
Playing, in the heat of moments, at the edge
of blasphemy with hell's own bells, the childish
knockers of our tongues. Named for saints,   15
we wore them at our throats, sometimes knotting
the parochial tie embossed with Paraclete
like rude coronals around our heads
to appear more convincingly heathen.
Our pressed white shirts, moist and steaming   20
with sweat, were unbuttoned, unlaced
into billowing wings rising in the created wind
of our bodies as we raced across the sheening
glass outbrightened, without reflection.

Ralph Tejeda Wilson (b. 1955)

Composed upon Westminster Bridge, September 3, 1802

Earth has not anything to show more fair:
Dull would he be of soul who could pass by
A sight so touching in its majesty:
This City now doth, like a garment, wear
The beauty of the morning; silent, bare,   5
Ships, towers, domes, theaters, and temples lie
Open unto the fields, and to the sky,
All bright and glittering in the smokeless air.
Never did sun more beautifully steep
In his first splendor, valley, rock, or hill;   10
Ne'er saw I, never felt, a calm so deep!
The river glideth at his own sweet will:

Dear God! the very houses seem asleep,
And all that mighty heart is lying still!

William Wordsworth (1770–1850)

I wandered lonely as a cloud

I wandered lonely as a cloud
That floats on high o'er vales and hills,
When all at once I saw a crowd,
A host, of golden daffodils;
Beside the lake, beneath the trees,   5
Fluttering and dancing in the breeze.

Continuous as the stars that shine
And twinkle on the milky way,
They stretched in never-ending line
Along the margin of a bay: 10
Ten thousand saw I at a glance,
Tossing their heads in sprightly dance.

The waves beside them danced; but they
Outdid the sparkling waves in glee;
A poet could not but be gay,   15
In such a jocund company;
I gazed—and gazed—but little thought
What wealth the show to me had brought:

For oft, when on my couch I lie
In vacant or in pensive mood,   20
They flash upon that inward eye
Which is the bliss of solitude;
And then my heart with pleasure fills,
And dances with the daffodils.

William Wordsworth (1770–1850)

The Solitary Reaper

Behold her, single in the field,
Yon solitary Highland lass!

Reaping and singing by herself;
Stop here, or gently pass!
Alone she cuts and binds the grain,   5
And sings a melancholy strain;
O listen! for the vale profound
Is overflowing with the sound.

No nightingale did ever chant
More welcome notes to weary bands   10
Of travelers in some shady haunt
Among Arabian sands.
A voice so thrilling ne'er was heard
In springtime from the cuckoo-bird,
Breaking the silence of the seas   15
Among the farthest Hebrides.

Will no one tell me what she sings?—
Perhaps the plaintive numbers° flow   measures
For old, unhappy, far-off things,
And battles long ago.   20
Or is it some more humble lay,°   song
Familiar matter of today?
Some natural sorrow, loss, or pain
That has been, and may be again?

Whate'er the theme, the maiden sang   25
As if her song could have no ending;
I saw her singing at her work,
And o'er the sickle bending—
I listened, motionless and still;
And, as I mounted up the hill,   30
The music in my heart I bore
Long after it was heard no more.

William Wordsworth (1770–1850)

Portrait

It was a heartfelt game, when it began—
polish and cook and sew and mend, contrive,
move between sink and stove, keep flower-beds weeded—
all her love needed was that it was needed,
and merely living kept the blood alive.   5

Now an old habit leads from sink to stove,
mends and keeps clean the house that looks like home,
and waits in hunger dressed to look like love
for the calm return of those who, when they come,
remind her: this was a game, when it began.   10

Judith Wright (1915–2000)

Sailing to Byzantium

That is no country for old men. The young
In one another's arms, birds in the trees
—Those dying generations—at their song,
The salmon-falls, the mackerel-crowded seas,
Fish, flesh, or fowl, commend all summer long   5
Whatever is begotten, born, and dies.
Caught in that sensual music all neglect
Monuments of unaging intellect.

An aged man is but a paltry thing,
A tattered coat upon a stick, unless   10
Soul clap its hands and sing, and louder sing
For every tatter in its mortal dress,
Nor is there singing school but studying
Monuments of its own magnificence;
And therefore I have sailed the seas and come   15
To the holy city of Byzantium.

O sages standing in God's holy fire
As in the gold mosaic of a wall,
Come from the holy fire, perne° in a gyre,   spin
And be the singing-masters of my soul.   20
Consume my heart away; sick with desire
And fastened to a dying animal
It knows not what it is; and gather me
Into the artifice of eternity.

Once out of nature I shall never take   25
My bodily form from any natural thing,
But such a form as Grecian goldsmiths make
Of hammered gold and gold enameling
To keep a drowsy Emperor awake;
Or set upon a golden bough to sing   30

To lords and ladies of Byzantium
Of what is past, or passing, or to come.

William Butler Yeats (1865–1939)

(Title) *Byzantium*: Ancient eastern capital of the Roman Empire; in this poem symbolically a holy city of the imagination. (1) *That*: Ireland, or the ordinary sensual world. (27–31) *such . . . Byzantium*: The Byzantine emperor Theophilus had made for himself mechanical golden birds that sang upon the branches of a golden tree.

The Second Coming

Turning and turning in the widening gyre
The falcon cannot hear the falconer;
Things fall apart; the center cannot hold;
Mere anarchy is loosed upon the world,
The blood-dimmed tide is loosed, and everywhere   5
The ceremony of innocence is drowned;
The best lack all conviction, while the worst
Are full of passionate intensity.

Surely some revelation is at hand;
Surely the Second Coming is at hand.   10
The Second Coming! Hardly are those words out
When a vast image out of *Spiritus Mundi*
Troubles my sight: somewhere in sands of the desert
A shape with lion body and the head of a man,
A gaze blank and pitiless as the sun,   15
Is moving its slow thighs, while all about it
Reel shadows of the indignant desert birds.
The darkness drops again; but now I know
That twenty centuries of stony sleep
Were vexed to nightmare by a rocking cradle,   20
And what rough beast, its hour come round at last,
Slouches towards Bethlehem to be born?

William Butler Yeats (1865–1939)

(Title) In Christian legend the prophesied Second Coming may refer either to Christ or to Antichrist. Yeats believed in a cyclical theory of history in which one historical era would be replaced by an opposite kind of era every two thousand years. Here, the anarchy in the world following World War I (the poem was written in 1919) heralds the end of the Christian era. (12) *Spiritus Mundi*: the racial memory or collective unconscious mind of mankind (literally, world spirit).

The Wild Swans at Coole

The trees are in their autumn beauty,
The woodland paths are dry,
Under the October twilight the water
Mirrors a still sky;
Upon the brimming water among the stones   5
Are nine-and-fifty swans.

The nineteenth autumn has come upon me
Since I first made my count;
I saw, before I had well finished,
All suddenly mount   10
And scatter wheeling in great broken rings
Upon their clamorous wings.

I have looked upon those brilliant creatures,
And now my heart is sore,
All's changed since I, hearing at twilight,   15
The first time on this shore,
The bell-beat of their wings above my head,
Trod with a lighter tread.

Unwearied still, lover by lover,
They paddle in the cold   20
Companionable streams or climb the air;
Their hearts have not grown old;
Passion or conquest, wander where they will,
Attend upon them still.

But now they drift on the still water,   25
Mysterious, beautiful;
Among what rushes will they build,
By what lake's edge or pool
Delight men's eyes when I awake some day
To find they have flown away?   30

William Butler Yeats (1865–1939)

(Title) Coole Park, in County Galway, Ireland, was the estate of Lady Augusta Gregory, Yeats's patroness and friend. Beginning in 1897, Yeats regularly summered there.

Drama

The Elements
of Drama

Chapter One

The Nature of Drama

Drama, like prose fiction, makes use of plot and characters, develops themes, arouses emotional responses, and may be either literary or commercial in its representation of reality.* Like poetry, it may draw upon all the resources of language, including verse. Much drama *is* poetry. But drama has one characteristic peculiar to itself. It is written primarily to be *performed,* not read. It normally presents its action (a) *through* actors, (b) *on* a stage, and (c) *before* an audience. Each of these conditions has important consequences for the nature of drama. Each presents an author with a potentially enormous source of power, and each imposes limitations on the directions a work may take.

Because a play presents its action *through* actors, its impact is direct, immediate, and heightened by the actors' skills. Instead of responding to words on a printed page, spectators see what is done and hear what is said. The experience of the play is registered directly upon their senses. It may therefore be both fuller and more compact. Where the work of prose fiction may tell us what a man looks like in one paragraph, how he moves or speaks in a second, what he says in a third, and how his auditors respond in a fourth, the acted play presents this material all at once. Simultaneous impressions are not temporally separated. Moreover, this experience is interpreted by actors who may be highly skilled in rendering nuances of meaning and strong emotion. Through facial expression, gesture, speech rhythm, and intonation, they may be able to make a speaker's words more expressive than can the reader's unaided imagination. Thus, the performance of a play by skilled actors expertly directed gives the playwright† a tremendous source of power.

But playwrights pay a price for this increased power. Of the four major points of view open to the fiction writer, dramatists are

---

*Plot, character, theme, symbol, irony, and other elements of literature have been discussed in the Fiction section and the Poetry section.

†The word *wright*—as in *playwright, shipwright, wheelwright, cartwright,* and the common surname *Wright*—comes from an Anglo-Saxon word meaning a workman or craftsman. It is related to the verb *wrought* (a past-tense form of *work*) and has nothing whatever to do with the verb *write*.

practically limited to one—the *objective*, or *dramatic*. They cannot directly comment on the action or the characters. They cannot enter the minds of their characters and tell us what is going on there. Although there are ways around them, each has its own limitations. Authorial commentary may be placed in the mouth of a character, but only at the risk of distorting characterization and of leaving the character's reliability uncertain. (Does the character speak for the author or only for herself or himself?) Entry can be made into a character's mind through the conventions of the **soliloquy** and the **aside**. In soliloquies, characters are presented as speaking to themselves—that is, they think out loud. In asides, characters turn from the persons with whom they are conversing to speak directly to (or for the benefit of) the audience, thus letting the audience know what they are really thinking or feeling as opposed to what they pretend to be thinking or feeling. Characters speaking in soliloquy or in asides are always presumed to be telling the truth, to the extent that they know the truth. Both devices can be used very effectively in the theater, but they interrupt the action and are therefore used sparingly. Also, they are inappropriate if the playwright is working in a strictly realistic mode.

Because a play presents its action *on* a stage, it can forcefully command the spectator's attention. The stage is lighted; the theater is dark; extraneous noises are shut out; spectators are almost literally pinned to their seats; there is nowhere they can go; there is nothing else to look at; there is nothing to distract. The playwright has extraordinary means by which to command the undivided attention of the audience. Unlike the fiction writer or the poet, the playwright is not dependent on the power of words alone.

But the necessity to confine the action to a stage, rather than to the imagination's vast arena, limits the kind of materials playwrights can easily and effectively present. For the most part, they must present human beings in spoken interaction with each other. They cannot easily use materials in which the main interest is in unspoken thoughts and reflections. They cannot present complex actions that involve nonhuman creatures such as attacking lions or charging bulls. They find it more difficult to shift scenes rapidly than writers of prose fiction do. The latter may whisk their readers from heaven to earth and back again in the twinkling of an eye, but playwrights must usually stick to one setting for an extended period of time and may feel constrained to do so for the whole play. Moreover, the events they depict must be of a magnitude appropriate to the stage. They cannot present the movements of armies and warfare on the vast scale that Tolstoy uses in *War and Peace*. They cannot easily present adventures at sea or action on a ski slope. Conversely, they cannot depict a fly crawling around the rim of a saucer or falling into a cup of milk. At best they can present a general on a hilltop reporting the movements of a battle, or two persons bending over a cup of milk reacting to a fly that the members of the audience cannot see.

The ease, and therefore the rapidity, with which a playwright can change from one scene to another depends, first, on the elaborateness of the stage setting and, second, on the means by which one scene is separated from another. In ancient plays and in many modern ones, stage settings have been extremely simple, depending only on a few easily moved properties or even entirely on the actors' words and the spectators' imaginations. In such cases, change of scenes is made fairly easily, especially if the actors themselves are allowed to carry on and off any properties that may be needed. Various means have been used to separate scenes from each other. In Greek plays, dancing and chanting by a chorus served as a scene divider. More recently, the closing and opening or dropping and raising of a curtain has been the means used. In contemporary theater, with its command of electrical technology, increased reliance has been placed on darkening and illuminating the stage or on darkening one part of it while lighting up another. But even where there is no stage scenery and where the shift of scene is made only by a change in lighting, the playwright can seldom change the setting as rapidly as the writer of prose fiction. On the stage, too-frequent shifts of scene make a play seem jerky. A reader's imagination, on the other hand, can change from one setting to another without even shifting gears.

Because a play presents its action *before* an audience, the experience it creates is communal, and its impact is intensified. Reading a short story or a novel is a private transaction between the reader and a book, but the performance of a play is public. The spectator's response is affected by the presence of other spectators. A comedy becomes funnier when one hears others laughing, a tragedy more moving when others are present to carry the current of feeling. A dramatic experience, in fact, becomes more intense almost exactly to the extent that it is shared and the individual spectator becomes aware that others are having the same experience. This intensification is partly dependent on the size of the audience, but more on their sense of community with each other. A play will be more successful performed before a small audience in a packed auditorium than before a large audience in a half-filled hall.

But, again, the advantage given playwrights by the fact of theatrical performance is paid for by limitations on the material they can present. A play must be able to hold the attention of a group audience. A higher premium than in prose fiction is placed on a well-defined plot, swift exposition, strong conflict, dramatic confrontations. Unless the play is very brief, it is usually divided into parts separated by an intermission or intermissions, and each part works up to its own climax or point of suspense. It is written so that its central meanings may be grasped in a single performance. Spectators at a play cannot back up and rerun a passage whose import they have missed; they cannot, in one night, sit through the whole performance a second time. In addition, playwrights usually avoid extensive use of materials that are purely narrative or lyrical. Long narrative passages are usually interrupted, descriptive passages kept short or eliminated altogether. Primarily, human beings are presented in spoken interaction with each other. Clearly, many of the world's literary masterpieces—stories and poems that enthrall the reader of a book—would not hold the attention of a group audience in a theater.

Drama, then, imposes sharp limitations on its writer but holds out the opportunity for extraordinary force. The successful playwright combines the power of words, the power of fiction, and the power of dramatic technique to make possible the achievement of that force.

REVIEWING CHAPTER ONE

1. Identify the three unique qualities that drama possesses (in contrast to literature written to be read).
2. Explore the advantages and disadvantages of having actors as the medium for the presentation of the dramatic experience.
3. Review the gains and losses imposed by having a drama acted on a stage rather than being presented on the page.
4. Explain how sharing the experience of drama with other audience members is an advantage over viewing it alone, and how the presence of an audience also can impose limitations on what the dramatist can include.

Understanding and Evaluating Drama

As drama may combine the literary resources of both prose fiction and poetry, many of the "Understanding and Evaluating" exercises provided for those two genres (pages 100–102 and 655) may be applicable to drama—except for those directed toward the study of point of view in fiction, since drama always employs the objective or dramatic point of view. Even if a drama is not written in verse, the general questions about diction and figurative language supplied for the elements of poetry may be applicable to drama.

In addition, the variety of dramatic forms and the special nature of drama as a theatrical as well as a literary experience require a set of supplementary questions. Many of these questions will become more meaningful as you read further in the drama section of this book. (Some terms printed in boldface are not defined in this section but are included in the Glossary of Terms, pages 1659–1671.)

1. Does the play employ **realistic** or **nonrealistic** conventions? On the spectrum from literalistic imitation of reality to stylized or surrealistic representation, where is the play situated? Are there breaks from the conventions established as a norm in the play? If so, what is the dramatic effect of these departures? Are they meaningful?

2. Is the play a **tragedy** or a **comedy,** a **melodrama** or a **farce?** If a comedy, is it primarily **romantic** or **satiric?** Does it mingle aspects of these types of drama? How important to experiencing the drama is the audience's awareness of the classification of the play?

3. Identify the **protagonist(s)** and **antagonist(s).** Are there any **foil characters?** What dramatic functions are served by the various minor characters? Do they shed light on the actions or motives of the major characters? Do they advance the **plot** by eliciting actions by others? Do they embody ideas or feelings that illuminate the major characters or the movement of the plot?

4. How is dramatic **suspense** created? Contrast the amount of information possessed by the audience as the play proceeds with the knowledge that various individual characters have: what is the effect of such a contrast?

5. What **themes** does the play present? To what extent do the thematic materials of the play have an effect on the dramatic experience? Does the power of the ideas increase or decrease the pleasure of the theatrical experience? Does the play seem either too **didactic** or insufficient in its presentation of important human concerns?

6. How do the various physical effects—theatrical components such as sets, lights, costuming, makeup, gestures, stage movements, musical effects of song or dance, and so forth—reinforce the meanings and contribute to the emotional effects? By what means does the playwright indicate the nature of these physical effects—explicitly, through stage directions and set descriptions, or implicitly, through dialogue between characters?

7. What amount of time is covered in the action? How much of the action is presented as a report rather than dramatized on stage? Is there a meaning behind the selection of events to be dramatized and those to be reported? Does the play feel loose or tight in its construction? Is that feeling appropriate to the themes and dramatic effects of the play?

8. To what extent does the play employ narration as a means of **dramatic exposition?** What other expository methods does it use? Does the exposition have a function beyond communicating information about prior events? What effects on the audience do the expository methods have?

Susan Glaspell
Trifles

Characters

GEORGE HENDERSON, *the county attorney*
HENRY PETERS, *the sheriff*
MRS. PETERS, *the sheriff's wife*
MRS. HALE, *a neighbor*
MR. HALE, *her husband, a farmer*

The kitchen in the now abandoned farmhouse of John Wright, a gloomy kitchen, and left without having been put in order—unwashed pans under the sink, a loaf of bread outside the bread-box, a dish-towel on the table—other signs of incompleted work. At the rear the outer door opens and the SHERIFF *comes in followed by the* COUNTY ATTORNEY *and* HALE. *The* SHERIFF *and* HALE *are men in middle life, the* COUNTY ATTORNEY *is a young man; all are much bundled up and go at once to the stove. They are followed by the two women—the* SHERIFF'S *wife first; she is a slight wiry woman, with a thin nervous face.* MRS. HALE *is larger and would ordinarily be called more comfortable looking, but she is disturbed now and looks fearfully about as she enters. The women have come in slowly, and stand close together near the door.*

COUNTY ATTORNEY (*rubbing his hands*).   This feels good. Come up to the fire, ladies.

MRS. PETERS (*after taking a step forward*).   I'm not—cold.

SHERIFF (*unbuttoning his overcoat and stepping away from the stove as if to mark the beginning of official business*).   Now, Mr. Hale, before we move things about, you explain to Mr. Henderson just what you saw when you came here yesterday morning.

COUNTY ATTORNEY.   By the way, has anything been moved? Are things just as you left them yesterday?

SHERIFF (*looking about*).   It's just the same. When it dropped below zero last night I thought I'd send Frank out this morning to make

TRIFLES   First performed in 1916. Susan Glaspell (1882–1948) was born and lived in Davenport, Iowa, earned a degree from Drake University, and worked as a reporter on a newspaper in Des Moines. In that capacity, she had occasion once to visit the kitchen of a woman who was in jail awaiting trial in a murder case. In her early thirties Glaspell moved to the East Coast to concentrate on writing fiction and plays. *Trifles* was produced at Provincetown on Cape Cod, Massachusetts, and a year later Glaspell adapted it as the short story "A Jury of Her Peers" (page 389).

a fire for us—no use getting pneumonia with a big case on, but I told him not to touch anything except the stove—and you know Frank.

COUNTY ATTORNEY.   Somebody should have been left here yesterday.

SHERIFF.   Oh—yesterday. When I had to send Frank to Morris Center for that man who went crazy—I want you to know I had my hands full yesterday. I knew you could get back from Omaha by today and as long as I went over everything here myself—

COUNTY ATTORNEY.   Well, Mr. Hale, tell just what happened when you came here yesterday morning.

HALE.   Harry and I had started to town with a load of potatoes. We came along the road from my place and as I got here I said, "I'm going to see if I can't get John Wright to go in with me on a party telephone." I spoke to Wright about it once before and he put me off, saying folks talked too much anyway, and all he asked was peace and quiet—I guess you know about how much he talked himself; but I thought maybe if I went to the house and talked about it before his wife, though I said to Harry that I didn't know as what his wife wanted made much difference to John—

COUNTY ATTORNEY.   Let's talk about that later, Mr. Hale. I do want to talk about that, but tell now just what happened when you got to the house.

HALE.   I didn't hear or see anything; I knocked at the door, and still it was all quiet inside. I knew they must be up, it was past eight o'clock. So I knocked again, and I thought I heard somebody say "Come in." I wasn't sure, I'm not sure yet, but I opened the door—this door (*indicating the door by which the two women are still standing*) and there in that rocker—(*pointing to it*) sat Mrs. Wright. (*They all look at the rocker.*)

COUNTY ATTORNEY.   What—was she doing?

HALE.   She was rockin' back and forth. She had her apron in her hand and was kind of—pleating it.

COUNTY ATTORNEY.   And how did she—look?

HALE.   Well, she looked queer.

COUNTY ATTORNEY.   How do you mean—queer?

HALE.   Well, as if she didn't know what she was going to do next. And kind of done up.

COUNTY ATTORNEY.   How did she seem to feel about your coming?

HALE.   Why, I don't think she minded—one way or other. She didn't pay much attention. I said, "How do, Mrs. Wright, it's cold, ain't it?" And she said "Is it?"—and went on kind of pleating at her apron. Well, I was surprised; she didn't ask me to come up to the stove, or to set down, but just sat there, not even looking at me, so I said, "I want to see John." And then she—laughed. I guess you would call it a laugh.

I thought of Harry and the team outside, so I said a little sharp: "Can't I see John?" "No," she says, kind o' dull like. "Ain't he home?" says I. "Yes," says she, "he's home." "Then why can't I see him?" I asked her out of patience. "'Cause he's dead," says she. *"Dead?"* says I. She just nodded her head, not getting a bit excited, but rockin' back and forth. "Why—where is he?" says I, not knowing what to say. She just pointed upstairs—like that (*himself pointing to the room above*). I got up, with the idea of going up there. I walked from there to here—then I says, "Why, what did he die of?" "He died of a rope round his neck," says she, and just went on pleatin' at her apron. Well, I went out and called Harry. I thought I might—need help. We went upstairs and there he was lyin'—

COUNTY ATTORNEY.   I think I'd rather have you go into that upstairs, where you can point it all out. Just go on now with the rest of the story.

HALE.   Well, my first thought was to get that rope off. It looked . . . (*Stops, his face twitches.*) . . . but Harry, he went up to him, and he said, "No, he's dead all right, and we'd better not touch anything." So we went back downstairs. She was still sitting that same way. "Has anybody been notified?" I asked. "No," says she, unconcerned. "Who did this, Mrs. Wright?" said Harry. He said it business-like—and she stopped pleatin' of her apron. "I don't know," she says. "You don't *know?*" says Harry. "No," says she. "Weren't you sleepin' in the bed with him?" says Harry. "Yes," says she, "but I was on the inside." "Somebody slipped a rope round his neck and strangled him and you didn't wake up?" says Harry. "I didn't wake up," she said after him. We must 'a looked as if we didn't see how that could be, for after a minute she said, "I sleep sound." Harry was going to ask her more questions, but I said maybe we ought to let her tell her story first to the coroner, or the sheriff, so Harry went fast as he could to Rivers's place, where there's a telephone.

COUNTY ATTORNEY.   And what did Mrs. Wright do when she knew that you had gone for the coroner?

HALE.   She moved from that chair to this over here . . . (*pointing to a small chair in the corner*) . . . and just sat there with her hands held together and looking down. I got a feeling that I ought to make some conversation, so I said I had come in to see if John wanted to put in a telephone, and at that she started to laugh, and then she stopped and looked at me—scared. (*The* COUNTY ATTORNEY, *who has had his notebook out, makes a note.*) I dunno; maybe it wasn't scared. I wouldn't like to say it was. Soon Harry got back, and then Dr. Lloyd came and you, Mr. Peters, and so I guess that's all I know that you don't.

COUNTY ATTORNEY (*looking around*).   I guess we'll go upstairs first —and then out to the barn and around there. (*To the* SHERIFF) You're convinced that there was nothing important here—nothing that would point to any motive?

SHERIFF. Nothing here but kitchen things. (*The* COUNTY ATTOR-NEY, *after again looking around the kitchen, opens the door of a cupboard closet. He gets up on a chair and looks on a shelf. Pulls his hand away, sticky.*)

COUNTY ATTORNEY. Here's a nice mess. (*The women draw nearer.*)

MRS. PETERS (*to the other woman*). Oh, her fruit; it did freeze. (*To the* ATTORNEY) She worried about that when it turned so cold. She said the fire'd go out and her jars would break.

SHERIFF. Well, can you beat the woman! Held for murder and worryin' about her preserves.

COUNTY ATTORNEY. I guess before we're through she may have something more serious than preserves to worry about.

HALE. Well, women are used to worrying over trifles. (*The two women move a little closer together.*)

COUNTY ATTORNEY (*with the gallantry of a young politician*). And yet, for all their worries, what would we do without the ladies? (*The women do not unbend. He goes to the sink, takes a dipperful of water from the pail and, pouring it into a basin, washes his hands. Starts to wipe them on the roller-towel, turns it for a cleaner place.*) Dirty towels! (*Kicks his foot against the pans under the sink.*) Not much of a housekeeper, would you say, ladies?

MRS. HALE (*stiffly*). There's a great deal of work to be done on a farm.

COUNTY ATTORNEY. To be sure. And yet . . . (*with a little bow to her*) . . . I know there are some Dickson County farmhouses which do not have such roller towels. (*He gives it a pull to expose its full length again.*)

MRS. HALE. Those towels get dirty awful quick. Men's hands aren't always as clean as they might be.

COUNTY ATTORNEY. Ah, loyal to your sex, I see. But you and Mrs. Wright were neighbors. I suppose you were friends, too.

MRS. HALE (*shaking her head*). I've not seen much of her of late years. I've not been in this house—it's more than a year.

COUNTY ATTORNEY. And why was that? You didn't like her?

MRS. HALE (*shaking her head*). I liked her all well enough. Farmers' wives have their hands full, Mr. Henderson. And then—

COUNTY ATTORNEY. Yes—?

MRS. HALE (*looking about*). It never seemed a very cheerful place.

COUNTY ATTORNEY. No—it's not cheerful. I shouldn't say she had the homemaking instinct.

MRS. HALE. Well, I don't know as Wright had, either.

COUNTY ATTORNEY. You mean that they didn't get on very well?

MRS. HALE. No, I don't mean anything. But I don't think a place'd be any cheerfuler for John Wright's being in it.

COUNTY ATTORNEY. I'd like to talk more of that a little later. I want to get the lay of things upstairs now. (*He goes to the left, where three steps lead to a stair door.*)

SHERIFF. I suppose anything Mrs. Peters does'll be all right. She was to take in some clothes for her, you know, and a few little things. We left in such a hurry yesterday.

COUNTY ATTORNEY. Yes, but I would like to see what you take, Mrs. Peters, and keep an eye out for anything that might be of use to us.

MRS. PETERS. Yes, Mr. Henderson. (*The women listen to the men's steps on the stairs, then look about the kitchen.*)

MRS. HALE. I'd hate to have men coming into my kitchen, snooping around and criticizing. (*She arranges the pans under the sink which the* ATTORNEY *had shoved out of place.*)

MRS. PETERS. Of course it's no more than their duty.

MRS. HALE. Duty's all right, but I guess that deputy sheriff that came out to make the fire might have got a little of this on. (*Gives the roller towel a pull.*) Wish I'd thought of that sooner. Seems mean to talk about her for not having things slicked up when she had to come away in such a hurry.

MRS. PETERS (*who has gone to a small table in the left corner of the room, and lifted one end of a towel that covers a pan*). She had bread set. (*Stands still.*)

MRS. HALE (*eyes fixed on a loaf of bread beside the bread-box, which is on a low shelf at the other side of the room. Moves slowly toward it*). She was going to put this in there. (*Picks up loaf, then abruptly drops it. In a manner of returning to familiar things*) It's a shame about her fruit. I wonder if it's all gone. (*Gets up on the chair and looks.*) I think there's some here that's all right, Mrs. Peters. Yes—here; (*holding it toward the window*) this is cherries, too. (*Looking again*) I declare I believe that's the only one. (*Gets down, bottle in her hand. Goes to the sink and wipes it off on the outside.*) She'll feel awful bad after all her hard work in the hot weather. I remember the afternoon I put up my cherries last summer. (*She puts the bottle on the big kitchen table, center of the room, front table. With a sigh, is about to sit down in the rocking chair. Before she is seated realizes what chair it is: with a slow look at it, steps back. The chair which she has touched rocks back and forth.*)

MRS. PETERS. Well, I must get those things from the front room closet. (*She goes to the door at the right, but after looking into the other room, steps back.*) You coming with me, Mrs. Hale? You could help me carry them. (*They go in the other room; reappear;* MRS. PETERS *carrying a dress and skirt,* MRS. HALE *following with a pair of shoes.*)

MRS. PETERS. My, it's cold in there. (*She puts the clothes on the big table and hurries to the stove.*)

Mrs. Hale (*examining the skirt*).   Wright was close. I think maybe that's why she kept so much to herself. She didn't even belong to the Ladies' Aid. I suppose she felt she couldn't do her part, and then you don't enjoy things when you feel shabby. She used to wear pretty clothes and be lively, when she was Minnie Foster, one of the town girls singing in the choir. But that—oh, that was thirty years ago. This all you was to take in?

Mrs. Peters.   She said she wanted an apron. Funny thing to want, for there isn't much to get you dirty in jail, goodness knows. But I suppose just to make her feel more natural. She said they was in the top drawer in this cupboard. Yes, here. And then her little shawl that always hung behind the door. (*Opens stair door and looks.*) Yes, here it is. (*Quickly shuts door leading upstairs.*)

Mrs. Hale (*abruptly moving toward her*).   Mrs. Peters?

Mrs. Peters.   Yes, Mrs. Hale?

Mrs. Hale.   Do you think she did it?

Mrs. Peters (*in a frightened voice*).   Oh, I don't know.

Mrs. Hale.   Well, I don't think she did. Asking for an apron and her little shawl. Worrying about her fruit.

Mrs. Peters (*starts to speak, glances up, where footsteps are heard in the room above. In a low voice*).   Mr. Peters says it looks bad for her. Mr. Henderson is awful sarcastic in a speech and he'll make fun of her sayin' she didn't wake up.

Mrs. Hale.   Well, I guess John Wright didn't wake up when they was slipping that rope under his neck.

Mrs. Peters.   No, it's strange. It must have been done awful crafty and still. They say it was such a—funny way to kill a man, rigging it all up like that.

Mrs. Hale.   That's just what Mr. Hale said. There was a gun in the house. He says that's what he can't understand.

Mrs. Peters.   Mr. Henderson said coming out that what was needed for the case was a motive; something to show anger, or—sudden feeling.

Mrs. Hale (*who is standing by the table*).   Well, I don't see any signs of anger around here. (*She puts her hand on the dish towel which lies on the table, stands looking down at table, one half of which is clean, the other half messy.*) It's wiped here. (*Makes a move as if to finish work, then turns and looks at loaf of bread outside the bread-box. Drops towel. In that voice of coming back to familiar things*) Wonder how they are finding things upstairs? I hope she had it a little more red-up° up there. You know, it seems kind of *sneaking*. Locking her up in town and then coming out here and trying to get her own house to turn against her!

red-up: neatened, readied (dialectal)

MRS. PETERS.   But, Mrs. Hale, the law is the law.

MRS. HALE.   I s'pose 'tis. (*Unbuttoning her coat.*) Better loosen up your things, Mrs. Peters. You won't feel them when you go out. (MRS. PETERS *takes off her fur tippet, goes to hang it on hook at back of room, stands looking at the under part of the small corner table.*)

MRS. PETERS.   She was piecing a quilt. (*She brings the large sewing basket and they look at the bright pieces.*)

MRS. HALE.   It's log cabin pattern. Pretty, isn't it? I wonder if she was goin' to quilt it or just knot it? (*Footsteps have been heard coming down the stairs. The* SHERIFF *enters, followed by* HALE *and the* COUNTY ATTORNEY.)

SHERIFF.   They wonder if she was going to quilt it or just knot it. (*The men laugh, the women look abashed.*)

COUNTY ATTORNEY (*rubbing his hands over the stove*).   Frank's fire didn't do much up there, did it? Well, let's go out to the barn and get that cleared up. (*The men go outside.*)

MRS. HALE (*resentfully*).   I don't know as there's anything so strange, our takin' up our time with little things while we're waiting for them to get the evidence. (*She sits down at the big table smoothing out a block with decision.*) I don't see as it's anything to laugh about.

MRS. PETERS (*apologetically*).   Of course they've got awful important things on their minds. (*Pulls up a chair and joins* MRS. HALE *at the table.*)

MRS. HALE (*examining another block*).   Mrs. Peters, look at this one. Here, this is the one she was working on, and look at the sewing! All the rest of it has been so nice and even. And look at this! It's all over the place! Why, it looks as if she didn't know what she was about! (*After she has said this they look at each other, then start to glance at the door. After an instant* MRS. HALE *has pulled at a knot and ripped the sewing.*)

MRS. PETERS.   Oh, what are you doing, Mrs. Hale?

MRS. HALE (*mildly*).   Just pulling out a stitch or two that's not sewed very good. (*Threading a needle.*) Bad sewing always made me fidgety.

MRS. PETERS (*nervously*).   I don't think we ought to touch things.

MRS. HALE.   I'll just finish up this end. (*Suddenly stopping and leaning forward*) Mrs. Peters?

MRS. PETERS.   Yes, Mrs. Hale?

MRS. HALE.   What do you suppose she was so nervous about?

MRS. PETERS.   Oh—I don't know. I don't know as she was nervous. I sometimes sew awful queer when I'm just tired. (MRS. HALE *starts to say something, looks at* MRS. PETERS, *then goes on sewing.*) Well, I must get these things wrapped up. They may be through sooner than we think. (*Putting apron and other things together.*) I wonder where I can find a piece of paper, and string.

MRS. HALE.   In that cupboard, maybe.

MRS. PETERS (*looking in cupboard*).   Why, here's a bird-cage. (*Holds it up.*) Did she have a bird, Mrs. Hale?

MRS. HALE.   Why, I don't know whether she did or not—I've not been here for so long. There was a man around last year selling canaries cheap, but I don't know as she took one; maybe she did. She used to sing real pretty herself.

MRS. PETERS (*glancing around*).   Seems funny to think of a bird here. But she must have had one, or why should she have a cage? I wonder what happened to it?

MRS. HALE.   I s'pose maybe the cat got it.

MRS. PETERS.   No, she didn't have a cat. She's got that feeling some people have about cats—being afraid of them. My cat got in her room and she was real upset and asked me to take it out.

MRS. HALE.   My sister Bessie was like that. Queer, ain't it?

MRS. PETERS (*examining the cage*).   Why, look at this door. It's broke. One hinge is pulled apart.

MRS. HALE (*looking too*).   Looks as if some one must have been rough with it.

MRS. PETERS.   Why, yes. (*She brings the cage forward and puts it on the table.*)

MRS. HALE.   I wish if they're going to find any evidence they'd be about it. I don't like this place.

MRS. PETERS.   But I'm awful glad you came with me, Mrs. Hale. It would be lonesome for me sitting here alone.

MRS. HALE.   It would, wouldn't it? (*Dropping her sewing.*) But I tell you what I do wish, Mrs. Peters. I wish I had come over sometimes when *she* was here. I—(*Looking around the room*)—wish I had.

MRS. PETERS.   But of course you were awful busy, Mrs. Hale—your house and your children.

MRS. HALE.   I could've come. I stayed away because it weren't cheerful—and that's why I ought to have come. I—I've never liked this place. Maybe because it's down in a hollow and you don't see the road. I dunno what it is, but it's a lonesome place and always was. I wish I had come over to see Minnie Foster sometimes. I can see now— (*Shakes her head.*)

MRS. PETERS.   Well, you mustn't reproach yourself, Mrs. Hale. Somehow we just don't see how it is with other folks until—something comes up.

MRS. HALE.   Not having children makes less work—but it makes a quiet house, and Wright out to work all day, and no company when he did come in. Did you know John Wright, Mrs. Peters?

MRS. PETERS.   Not to know him; I've seen him in town. They say he was a good man.

MRS. HALE.   Yes—good; he didn't drink, and kept his word as well as most, I guess, and paid his debts. But he was a hard man, Mrs. Peters. Just to pass the time of day with him. (*Shivers.*) Like a raw wind that gets to the bone. (*Pauses, her eye falling on the cage.*) I should think she would'a wanted a bird. But what do you suppose went wrong with it?

MRS. PETERS.   I don't know, unless it got sick and died. (*She reaches over and swings the broken door, swings it again, both women watch it.*)

MRS. HALE.   You weren't raised round here, were you? (MRS. PETERS *shakes her head.*) You didn't know—her?

MRS. PETERS.   Not till they brought her yesterday.

MRS. HALE.   She—come to think of it, she was kind of like a bird herself—real sweet and pretty, but kind of timid and—fluttery. How—she—did—change. (*Silence; then as if struck by a happy thought and relieved to get back to everyday things.*) Tell you what, Mrs. Peters, why don't you take the quilt in with you? It might take up her mind.

MRS. PETERS.   Why, I think that's a real nice idea, Mrs. Hale. There couldn't possibly be any objection to it, could there? Now, just what would I take? I wonder if her patches are in here—and her things. (*They look in the sewing basket.*)

MRS. HALE.   Here's some red. I expect this has got sewing things in it. (*Brings out a fancy box.*) What a pretty box. Looks like something somebody would give you. Maybe her scissors are in here. (*Opens box. Suddenly puts her hand to her nose.*) Why—(MRS. PETERS *bends nearer, then turns her face away.*) There's something wrapped up in this piece of silk.

MRS. PETERS.   Why, this isn't her scissors.

MRS. HALE (*lifting the silk*).   Oh, Mrs. Peters—it's— (MRS. PETERS *bends closer.*)

MRS. PETERS.   It's the bird.

MRS. HALE (*jumping up*).   But, Mrs. Peters—look at it. Its neck! Look at its neck! It's all—other side *to.*

MRS. PETERS.   Somebody—wrung—its neck. (*Their eyes meet. A look of growing comprehension, of horror. Steps are heard outside.* MRS. HALE *slips box under quilt pieces, and sinks into her chair. Enter* SHERIFF *and* COUNTY ATTORNEY. MRS. PETERS *rises.*)

COUNTY ATTORNEY (*as one turning from serious things to little pleasantries*).   Well, ladies, have you decided whether she was going to quilt it or knot it?

MRS. PETERS.   We think she was going to—knot it.

COUNTY ATTORNEY.   Well, that's interesting, I'm sure. (*Seeing the bird-cage*) Has the bird flown?

MRS. HALE (*putting more quilt pieces over the box*).   We think the—cat got it.

COUNTY ATTORNEY (*preoccupied*).   Is there a cat? (MRS. HALE *glances in a quick covert way at* MRS. PETERS.)

MRS. PETERS.   Well, not now. They're superstitious, you know. They leave.

COUNTY ATTORNEY (*to* SHERIFF PETERS, *continuing an interrupted conversation*).   No sign at all of anyone having come in from the outside. Their own rope. Now let's go up again and go over it piece by piece. (*They start upstairs.*) It would have to have been some one who knew just the—(MRS. PETERS *sits down. The two women sit there not looking at one another, but as if peering into something and at the same time holding back. When they talk now it is in the manner of feeling their way over strange ground, as if afraid of what they are saying, but as if they cannot help saying it.*)

MRS. HALE.   She liked the bird. She was going to bury it in that pretty box.

MRS. PETERS (*in a whisper*).   When I was a girl—my kitten—there was a boy took a hatchet, and before my eyes—and before I could get there—(*Covers her face an instant.*) If they hadn't held me back I would have—(*Catches herself, looks upstairs where steps are heard, falters weakly*)—hurt him.

MRS. HALE (*with a slow look around her*).   I wonder how it would seem never to have any children around. (*Pause*) No, Wright wouldn't like the bird—a thing that sang. She used to sing. He killed that, too.

MRS. PETERS (*moving uneasily*).   We don't know who killed the bird.

MRS. HALE.   I knew John Wright.

MRS. PETERS.   It was an awful thing was done in this house that night, Mrs. Hale. Killing a man while he slept, slipping a rope around his neck that choked the life out of him.

MRS. HALE.   His neck. Choked the life out of him. (*Her hand goes out and rests on the bird-cage.*)

MRS. PETERS (*with rising voice*).   We don't know who killed him. We don't *know*.

MRS. HALE (*her own feeling not interrupted*).   If there'd been years and years of nothing, then a bird to sing to you, it would be awful—still, after the bird was still.

MRS. PETERS (*something within her speaking*).   I know what stillness is. When we homesteaded in Dakota, and my first baby died—after he was two years old, and me with no other then—

MRS. HALE (*moving*). How soon do you suppose they'll be through, looking for the evidence?

MRS. PETERS. I know what stillness is. (*Pulling herself back*) The law has got to punish crime, Mrs. Hale.

MRS. HALE (*not as if answering that*). I wish you'd seen Minnie Foster when she wore a white dress with blue ribbons and stood up there in the choir and sang. (*A look around the room.*) Oh, I *wish* I'd come over here once in a while. That was a crime! That was a crime! Who's going to punish that?

MRS. PETERS (*looking upstairs*). We mustn't—take on.

MRS. HALE. I might have known she needed help! I know how things can be—for women. I tell you, it's queer, Mrs. Peters. We live close together and we live far apart. We all go through the same things—it's all just a different kind of the same thing. (*Brushes her eyes, noticing the bottle of fruit, reaches out for it.*) If I was you I wouldn't tell her her fruit was gone. Tell her it *ain't*. Tell her it's all right. Take this in to prove it to her. She—she may never know whether it was broke or not.

MRS. PETERS (*takes the bottle, looks about for something to wrap it in; takes petticoat from the clothes brought from the other room, very nervously begins winding this around the bottle. In a false voice*). My, it's a good thing the men couldn't hear us. Wouldn't they just laugh. Getting all stirred up over a little thing like a—dead canary. As if that could have anything to do with—with—wouldn't they *laugh*! (*The men are heard coming downstairs.*)

MRS. HALE (*under her breath*). Maybe they would—maybe they wouldn't.

COUNTY ATTORNEY. No, Peters, it's all perfectly clear except a reason for doing it. But you know juries when it comes to women. If there was some definite thing. Something to show—something to make a story about—a thing that would connect up with this strange way of doing it. (*The women's eyes meet for an instant. Enter HALE from outer door.*)

HALE. Well, I've got the team around. Pretty cold out there.

COUNTY ATTORNEY. I'm going to stay here a while by myself. (*To the SHERIFF*) You can send Frank out for me, can't you? I want to go over everything. I'm not satisfied that we can't do better.

SHERIFF. Do you want to see what Mrs. Peters is going to take in? (*The ATTORNEY goes to the table, picks up the apron, laughs.*)

COUNTY ATTORNEY. Oh, I guess they're not very dangerous things the ladies have picked out. (*Moves a few things about, disturbing the quilt pieces which cover the box. Steps back.*) No, Mrs. Peters doesn't need supervising. For that matter, a sheriff's wife is married to the law. Ever think of it that way, Mrs. Peters?

MRS. PETERS.   Not—just that way.

SHERIFF (*chuckling*).   Married to the law. (*Moves toward the other room.*) I just want you to come in here a minute, George. We ought to take a look at these windows.

COUNTY ATTORNEY (*scoffingly*).   Oh, windows!

SHERIFF.   We'll be right out, Mr. Hale. (HALE *goes outside. The* SHERIFF *follows the* COUNTY ATTORNEY *into the other room. Then* MRS. HALE *rises, hands tight together, looking intensely at* MRS. PETERS, *whose eyes make a slow turn, finally meeting* MRS. HALE'S. *A moment* MRS. HALE *holds her, then her own eyes point the way to where the box is concealed. Suddenly* MRS. PETERS *throws back quilt pieces and tries to put the box in the handbag she is carrying. It is too big. She opens box, starts to take bird out, cannot touch it, goes to pieces, stands there helpless. Sound of a knob turning in the other room.* MRS. HALE *snatches the box and puts it in the pocket of her big coat. Enter* COUNTY ATTORNEY *and* SHERIFF.)

COUNTY ATTORNEY (*facetiously*).   Well, Henry, at least we found out that she was not going to quilt it. She was going to—what is it you call it, ladies?

MRS. HALE (*her hand against her pocket*).   We call it—knot it, Mr. Henderson.

QUESTIONS

1. What individualizing characteristics do you find in the five people in the play? What contrasts are drawn between the men as a group, and the women? In what sense does the title contribute to these contrasts?
2. What contrasts exist between the two women? Is one of them clearly the protagonist? Identify the antagonist.
3. Describe the life that Mrs. Wright must have lived. What is the importance of her having been a singer?
4. Was the murder in any way justified? Why do the women conceal the evidence?
5. It is a common practice for plays to be made out of novels or stories, but unusual for the play to precede the story. Compare this play with the story "A Jury of Her Peers" (page 389). Which is clearer in its presentation of action and feelings? Which has a more direct emotional impact on the audience or reader? Discuss the differences between hearing the short story read aloud by an experienced performer and seeing the play acted by experienced actors.

Joyce Carol Oates
The Interview

Characters

THE IMMORTAL, *an elderly, white-haired aristocratic gentleman*
THE INTERVIEWER, *a youngish man, in his thirties*
KIMBERLY, *a young woman, in her twenties*

Setting

A contemporary hotel room with a suggestion of luxury. Minimal furnishings: a sofa, a table, a pitcher, and a glass of water. An elegant Mozart string quartet is issuing from a cabinet.

Lights up. Lighting is subdued at the start of the play, then gradually increases in intensity. By the end, it is as bright and pitiless as possible.

THE IMMORTAL *is seated on an antique sofa, head high, hands clasped on his knees, in a posture of imperturbable dignity. His eyes are half shut as if he is contemplating a higher reality. He is dressed with Old World formality—a dark suit with a vest, a white flower in his lapel. Brilliantly polished black shoes.*

A rapping at the door. IMMORTAL *serenely ignores it.*

INTERVIEWER.   Hello? Hello? Is anybody there? It's—me.
(*Frantic rapping.* IMMORTAL *takes no heed.*)
INTERVIEWER (*Voice, desperate*).   It's the eleven o'clock interviewer—am I late—? (*On the word "late"* INTERVIEWER *pushes open the door, which is unexpectedly unlocked. He stumbles inside the room dropping his heavy duffel bag out of which spill a tape recorder, a camera, and several books.* INTERVIEWER *is casually dressed in jeans, jacket, jogging shoes; hair in a pony- or pigtail. He is breathless and apologetic.*) Oh!–oh, my God!

THE INTERVIEW   Commissioned and first performed at McCarter Theatre, Princeton, NJ, in 1994. Joyce Carol Oates was born in upstate New York in 1938 and educated at Syracuse University and the University of Wisconsin, and is on the faculty of Princeton University. She is the author of many novels, short stories, poems, essays, and plays.

Membership in the "French Academy" (Académie Française), a group of distinguished French writers, is limited to forty; its members are called "the Immortals."

It's—you. (*Approaching* IMMORTAL *reverently*) I—I'm—jeez, excuse me! (*Staring*) It *is*—you?

> (IMMORTAL *remains unperturbed. Music continues.*)

> INTERVIEWER (*nervous chattering as he fumblingly picks up his things*). I c-can't tell you, sir, what an honor this is. The honor of a lifetime. And here I am late! (*Angry, incredulous laughter at himself.*) Held up in traffic for half an hour—plus my assistant Kimberly screwed up on the time—not that there's any excuse to be late for an interview with you, sir. I hope you will—forgive me? (*Craven.*)

> (IMMORTAL *remains unperturbed. Music continues.*)

> INTERVIEWER (*awkward, nodding*). I, um—well, yes. Right. (*Fussing with tape recorder; drops a cassette, retrieves it.*) That's right, sir. (*Nervous laugh.*) That music—it's real high class. I—sort of thought—listening out in the hall—you might be playing it, yourself. You were trained as a classical musician, sir—in addition to your other talents—weren't you?

> (IMMORTAL *remains unperturbed. Music continues.*)

> INTERVIEWER (*first hint of his self-importance*). Your publisher explained who *I* am, sir, I hope? (*Pause.*) I began with a modest Sunday books column for the *Detroit News*—within eighteen months was promoted to the editorial page—where my column HEAR THIS! ran the gamut from high culture to low controversy! (*Laughs.*) No, seriously, I never shrank from any subject. I ran my own photos, interviewed both "big" and "little" folks, soon became syndicated in over a hundred dailies—whiz bang zap zolly!—here I am: lead columnist for *America Today*, circulation fifty-seven million daily. (*Breathless.*) Interviewing, in depth, men and women of the stature, sir, of you.

> (IMMORTAL *remains unperturbed, unimpressed. Music continues.*)

> INTERVIEWER (*smiles, rubs hands, ebullient*). Well, now! The editors of *America Today* are asking five hundred of the world's leading men and women in all the creative arts—at the cutting edge of science—politics—culture: What do you prophecize for the year 2000? (*Pause, jokes*) *Will we make it?* (*Laughs.*)

> (IMMORTAL *remains as before.*)

> INTERVIEWER (*respectfully*). You, sir, having been born in 1798— Oops! (*Checks notes*)—1898—have lived through virtually the entire twentieth century—so my first question will be—Will you *make it*? (*Laughs.*)

> (IMMORTAL *remains as before, stiff and unresponsive;* INTERVIEWER *ceases laughing, embarrassed.*)

INTERVIEWER.   Umm—just a little joke. I'm known for my, um—sense of humor. *(Pause.)* "Irreverent"—"refreshing"—"wacko in all the right ways"— *(Pause.)* Bill Clinton said that, sir. About my column. *(Pause.)* What Hilary said, I don't know. *(Awkward laugh.)*

(IMMORTAL *as before.*)

INTERVIEWER *(slightly abashed, but taking a new tack).*   Well, now! Here we go in earnest! *(With tape recorder.)* You don't mind these, sir, I hope? *(Punching buttons.)* Jeez if I tried to take notes the old, literate way, I'd really screw up. My handwriting's like Helen Keller's in an earthquake. *(Laughs.)*

(IMMORTAL *as before.*)

INTERVIEWER *(slightly abashed, defensive).*   Helen Keller was an old blind deaf dumb *genius*—I guess. You'd've gotten along real well together, sir. (INTERVIEWER *fusses with his recorder, muttering under his breath. Voices emerge squealing and squawking, unintelligible.*)

FEMALE VOICE *(high-pitched squeal).*   No no no no no you stop that!

INTERVIEWER.   Oops! *(Punches a button, fast-forwarding.)* That's an oldie—Barbara Bush.

INTERVIEWER'S VOICE *(on tape, volume loud).*   —prophecize for the year 2000, sir?

MALE VOICE *(evangelical-sounding).*   The Second Coming—the Resurrection of the Body—"And all ye shall rejoice, and see God"— (INTERVIEWER *abruptly cuts off cassette, rewinds.*) We'll just tape over that. *(Condescending.)* One of those nuts—hitting all the TV talk shows last week—his book's a number one bestseller—real lowbrow crapola, not highbrow, sir, like you. *(Kneeling at IMMORTAL's feet, fussing with the recorder.)* You, sir—I reverence you. First time I read your work, sir, I was in sixth grade. Yeah, I was precocious! *(Chuckles.)* That sure does bring problems, sir, doesn't it?—precocity?—peers get God-damned *jealous*. As you'd know, sir, eh?—your first book was published when you were eighteen? Wow. *(Pause.)* Or am I thinking of—whosis—Rambo?° *(Pause.)* Hey, before we get going— *(Brings over a stack of books for IMMORTAL to sign.)* Would you sign these, please, sir? I know it's a nuisance—being so renowned—autograph seekers hounding you constantly—but I'd appreciate it so much, sir! Here's my card, sir, so you get the name right.

Rambo: presumably a reference to Arthur Rimbaud (1854–1891), French poet who published his first book in 1870 at the age of 17.

(IMMORTAL *signs books in a pompous manner, his head still held stiffly high.* INTERVIEWER *gives him a pen, opens books and positions them on his lap, chatting all the while.*)

INTERVIEWER.   Here, sir—please use this pen. It's a Mont Blanc—a little token from Samuel Beckett° when I interviewed him. Last interview that great man gave. We really hit it off, Sam and me. I may be from Detroit but I can sure yuk it up with you immortals! (*Chuckles, then peers at books.*) Um, sir—excuse me—would you date your signature, please? And, um—you might say "New York City" below, too—Thank you! Immensely! (*Checks the signatures, chuckles.*) *Your* hand-writing's like Helen Keller's in an earthquake, sir! (*Nudges* IMMORTAL *in the ribs.*)

(*The flower falls from* IMMORTAL'S *lapel.* IMMORTAL *"comes alive" though retaining, at least intermittently, certain of his pompous mannerisms.*)

IMMORTAL.   Qu'est-ce que c'est? Qui êtes vous? (*What? Who are you?*)

INTERVIEWER.   Say what? (*Atrocious accent*) Non parlez-vous français here, sir! Nossir!

IMMORTAL (*stiff alarm, distaste*).   Vous êtes—americain?

INTERVIEWER (*loudly, as if* IMMORTAL *is deaf*).   Weewee! I zetes americain!

IMMORTAL (*elderly confusion*).   Mais, pourquoi— (*But why—*)

INTERVIEWER.   Sir, parlez English, eh! (*Checks PR sheet.*) It says here you're "septo-lingual"—speak seven languages with equal fluency—so let's have it for English, eh! (*Joking.*) I didn't know there were seven languages left in Europe.

IMMORTAL (*now in Italian, haltingly*).   Non capisco . . . Che cosè? Mi sono perso . . .? (*I don't understand. What is it? Am I lost?*)

INTERVIEWER (*loudly*).   Ing-lese, sir! ING-LESE! You know it, for sure. You're in the U.S. of A. now.

IMMORTAL.   Per favore—aiuto! Mi sento male . . . (*Please, help! I feel ill.*)

INTERVIEWER.   C'mon, sir! ING-LESE! AMER-I-CAN!

IMMORTAL.   Who are you? Have you come to help me?

INTERVIEWER.   Terrifico!—English. (*Starts recorder.*) You had me worried there for a minute, sir!

IMMORTAL (*dazed, tragic voice*).   I want—to live again. (*Pause.*) I want to die.

Samuel Beckett (1906–1989): Nobel laureate in literature, Irish-born playwright who lived in Paris.

INTERVIEWER (*cheerfully, holding microphone*).   Can't do both, sir! Not at the same time. Comment, sir what do you prophecize for the upcoming millennium?

IMMORTAL.   My beloved Marguerite, where are you—

INTERVIEWER (*rattling off choices*).   "End of the world"—"things better than ever"—"more of the same?"

IMMORTAL (*wildly*).   Marguerite! Help me—

INTERVIEWER (*as if humanly struck*).   That's touching, sir. My goodness. Could you expand upon—?

IMMORTAL (*squinting at* INTERVIEWER, *tragic "classical" voice*). Please help me, have you been sent to help me? I am in pain. Where is the light?

INTERVIEWER.   Light? Nah, there's plenty of light in here, it's pouring through the window. Plus I got a flash camera. (*Pause.*) Enough of this, though— (*Strides over to a cabinet, switches off the Mozart abruptly.*) That artsy stuff gets on your nerves after a while.

IMMORTAL.   Marguerite, my dear one—

INTERVIEWER (*peering at PR sheet*).   Um— "Marguerite"—"wife of"—"deceased, 1923"—"Christiane"—"wife of"—"deceased 1939"— "Pilar"—"wife of"—"deceased 1961"—"Claudia"—"wife of"—"deceased 1979"—"Chantal"—"wife of"—"deceased 1987"— Wow, sir! I mean— *wow.* I hate to tell you, though—you got some catching up to do.

IMMORTAL.   Why am I—alone?

INTERVIEWER (*reading from sheet of paper*).   Let's move on, sir, to more provocative issues. What's your frank opinion of American civilization, as viewed from your side of the Atlantic are we a nation of coarse philistines, illiterates, and wannabee capitalist swine, or a "Brave New World?"

IMMORTAL (*confused*).   "Brave New World?"

INTERVIEWER (*enthusiastically*).   Right! I think so, too. One thing pisses me off it's that hypocritical bullshit, we Americans are crass and uncultured. Screw that! Every God-damn country in the world including your homeland, excuse me, sir, emulates us, and wants our dough. Any comment?

IMMORTAL.   I—feel such cold. Where is this terrible place?

INTERVIEWER (*consulting notes briskly*).   Um-hum—moving right along now— Sir, in your Nobel Prize acceptance speech you stated: "As a youth I had wished to emulate—"

IMMORTAL (*overlapping with unexpected passion, clarity; hand gestures*).   "As a youth I had wished to emulate Homer—Dante— Goethe—Balzac—setting myself the task of creating a great epic commensurate with the spirit of mankind. Immortalizing the heritage of the West. The most ambitious work of the twentieth century. The tragedy of Nazism unleashed the terror that history and civilization could be annihilated—and so it remains for *us* to bear witness—unflinchingly."

INTERVIEWER *(clapping).*   Wow! That's telling 'em, sir!

IMMORTAL *(continuing, gesturing).*   "The future of humankind is legislated by its spiritual leaders—its artists—"

INTERVIEWER *(cutting right in).*   Um-hum! Well, my editor's gonna make me cut all this back pretty much. *America Today* is reader-friendly—our paragraphs are never more than a single sentence. *(Briefest of pauses, no transition, abruptly and brightly)* Changing the subject somewhat, sir, moving from the lugubrious to the calumnious—is it true that you plagiarized your early dramas from Pirandello?°

IMMORTAL *(shocked, agitated).*   What! I! Plagiarize!

INTERVIEWER.   *America Today's* readers just want the simple truth, sir: *yes* or *no?*

IMMORTAL.   H-He—stole from *me*—

INTERVIEWER *(checking notes).*   One of you is the author of the immortal classic *Five Characters in Search of an Author* and the other is the author of the immortal classic *Six Characters in Search of an Author*—so, which came first?

IMMORTAL *(spitting gesture).*   Pirandello!—a shallow, meretricious talent! A mere mimicry of—

INTERVIEWER *(consulting notes).*   You had a scandalous love affair with—Colette?° Who threw you over publicly for—Franz Liszt?° Wow!

IMMORTAL *(incensed).*   How dare you! Whoever you are, how— *(*IMMORTAL *is so agitated, his hearing aid falls from his ear.)*

INTERVIEWER.   Uh-oh! We're getting a little hyper, sir, are we? *(Retrieves the hearing aid which has fallen to the floor.)* What's it—oh, a hearing aid. Jeez, you scared me, I thought it was part of your *brain* falling out. *(Laughs.)* That'd be weird, eh? Terrific story, but weird. Let me—*(Tries to fit the hearing aid into* IMMORTAL's *ear, but it slips back out.)* Damn! *(Tries again, jamming it in;* IMMORTAL *flinches with pain, but the hearing aid slips out anyway.)* Fuck it! These "miracles of modern technology!" *(Tries other ear.)* Uh-oh! There's already one in this ear. *(Hear-*

Luigi Pirandello (1867–1936): avant-garde Italian playwright, Nobel laureate in literature in 1934, author of *Six Characters in Search of an Author* (1920).   **Colette** (1873–1954): French novelist.   **Franz Liszt** (1811–1886): Hungarian composer.

ing aid falls to the floor and is apparently broken; INTERVIEWER *picks it up, chagrined.)* Ooops! Looks like it's, um, a little cracked. Shit, am I sorry! (IMMORTAL *reaches for the hearing aid, but* INTERVIEWER *stuffs it into* IMMORTAL's *pocket.)*

INTERVIEWER.   For safekeeping, sir! Wouldn't want you to lose the damn thing. *(Consulting notes.)* Ummm, yes: how does it feel, sir, to be a great artist?—a "classic?"— the oldest living "immortal" of the French Academy *and* the oldest living Nobel Prize laureate since what's-his-name, that Bulgarian, croaked last year? Our audience yearns to know, sir: how does it feel to have "made it?"

IMMORTAL *(high, quavering voice).*   So lonely. My loved ones, my friends—gone. My enemies—gone. *(Clutching at* INTERVIEWER's *arm)* I had wanted to outlive my enemies—and I have.

INTERVIEWER.   Terrific! That's sure candid stuff. *(Takes up camera.)* Lemme take a few quick shots, and we can wrap this up. *(Blinding flash.)* Little smile, sir? C'mon, little smile? You can do better than that, sir, come *on. (Aggressively close, as* IMMORTAL *flinches.)*

IMMORTAL.   What—place is this? Who are you?

INTERVIEWER *(taking photos).*   Tell our audience about your friendship with the great Nabokov,° sir. He plagiarized *you*—that's the scuttlebutt, eh?

IMMORTAL.   Why am I—here?

INTERVIEWER *(chuckling).*   You "esthetes"—any truth to the rumor you and Nabokov, um, got it on together upon occasion?

IMMORTAL.   Nabokov?

INTERVIEWER.   Those were the days, eh?—"Gay Nineties"— "Roaring Twenties"—"Lost Generation"—no "safe sex" for you, eh? *(Suddenly realizing, strikes forehead and consults notes.)* Uh-oh! Shit! You *are* Nabokov!

IMMORTAL *(trying to escape but falling back weakly onto the sofa in terror).*   I know you! I know you! Go away!

INTERVIEWER *(incensed).*   What the hell, Mr. Nabokov, I'm slotted in for thirty minutes! That's bottomline *rude.*

IMMORTAL.   I know your face—you are Death. *(Pause.* INTERVIEWER *is standing rigid, camera in hand.)*

INTERVIEWER.   Excuse me, Mr. Nabokov, but that's insulting.

IMMORTAL.   Death! Come for me! But I am not ready! My soul is not ready! Go away! (IMMORTAL *lunges suddenly at* INTERVIEWER, *trying to snatch*

Vladimir Nabokov (1898-1977): Russian-born novelist who lived in Germany, England, the United States, and Switzerland, neither elected to the French Academy nor a Nobel laureate.

his camera from him. The flash goes off.) Oh! *(As if the flashbulb has been a gunshot,* IMMORTAL *collapses onto the sofa and lies limp.* INTERVIEWER's *hair has come loose in the struggle, altering his appearance. He stands straight and tall and does indeed have the frightening aura of an agent of Death.)*

INTERVIEWER. You Immortals—all alike. Guys like me, we got your numbers. *(Packs up his things into duffel bag, muttering to himself)* Where's he get off, calling me Death! Me with a syndicated readership of fifty-seven million!—second only to "Dear Abby."

(Flurried knocking at the door. KIMBERLY *runs in, aghast.)*

KIMBERLY *(biting thumbnail)*.   Oh! oh God! oh you're going to be mad at me, oh I just know it!

INTERVIEWER.   What?

KIMBERLY *(little-girl, pleading)*.   Oh I just know you are! I know you are!

INTERVIEWER.   Kimberly, what the hell—? I've had it up to here with fucking obfuscation this morning!

KIMBERLY.   Promise you won't be mad at me . . .

INTERVIEWER *(shouting)*.   I promise! I won't be mad at you!

KIMBERLY.   I, uh—um—this is the wrong hotel. This is the Plaza, and you're supposed to be at the Saint Regis. Whoever *he* is—he's the wrong person.

INTERVIEWER *(louder)*.   What? Wrong hotel? Wrong person? *What?*

KIMBERLY *(little-girl manner, softly)*.   You promised you wouldn't get mad.

INTERVIEWER.   You're responsible for me wasting my entire morning? And I'm not supposed to be *mad?*

KIMBERLY *(pleading)*.   It wasn't my fault—the FAX from the office is so smudged. See— *(She shows him the FAX, which he snatches from her fingers.)*

INTERVIEWER *(peering at it)*.   Holy shit! I *am* supposed to be at the Saint Regis! I'm twenty minutes late already! *(In a fury, takes out his recorder, erases cassette.)* There! ERASE! Goddamn. *(As* INTERVIEWER *moves to exit,* KIMBERLY *notices* IMMORTAL *whom she approaches with concern.)*

KIMBERLY.   Oh! This gentleman! Is he—?

INTERVIEWER *(breezy, sarcastic)*.   He says he's Nabokov.

KIMBERLY *(impressed)*.   Oh!—"Nab-o-kov"—that famous dancer?° The one who deflected from the Soviet Union when it was still Communist?

---

famous dancer: presumably referring to Rudolf Nureyev (1939–1993), Russian ballet dancer who received political asylum in Paris in 1961.

INTERVIEWER *(exiting)*.   Defected.

*(*KIMBERLY *approaches* IMMORTAL. *A strain of romantic music might be used here.)*

KIMBERLY.   Mr. Nabokov? Are you—alive? *(Pause.)* I never saw you dance, but—my grandmother did, I think. She said you were— *(Pause.)*—fantastic. Mr. Nabokov? (IMMORTAL *begins to stir, moaning.* KIMBERLY *helps him sit up; unbuttons his collar, loosens his tie, etc. She dips a handkerchief or scarf into the glass of water and presses it against his forehead.)* Mr. Nabokov, I guess you had a little fainting spell! I'd better call the hotel doctor.

IMMORTAL *(reviving slowly)*.   No—no, please.

KIMBERLY *(thumb to mouth)*.   You're sure? You look kind of— pale.

IMMORTAL *(staring at* KIMBERLY*)*.   My dear one! Is it—*you?*

KIMBERLY.   Who?

IMMORTAL *(hoarse whisper)*.   Not Marguerite, but—Chantal? Returned to me?

KIMBERLY.   "Chantal"—?

IMMORTAL *(with elderly eagerness)*.   My dear! Darling! Don't ever leave me again!

KIMBERLY.   Gosh, Mr. Nabokov, I'm afraid I—

IMMORTAL.   I will die in this terrible place if you leave me. *(Takes her wrist.)*

KIMBERLY.   —afraid there's been some—

IMMORTAL.   My darling, I'm so lonely. They call me a "living classic"—an "immortal"—but without *you,* I am nothing.

KIMBERLY.   But you're so famous, Mr. Nabokov!

IMMORTAL.   Chantal, please—don't leave me again, ever. I seem to have grown old, I know—but it's only an illusion.

KIMBERLY *(embarrassed)*.   Gee, I hate to say this but you're a little . . . confused, Mr. Nabokov. I'd better call the doctor—

IMMORTAL.   *You're* still young, and I, in my heart, in my soul—I am unchanged.

KIMBERLY.   You are? *(Pause, sees flower on floor.)* Oh!—is this yours? *(Picks it up, restores it to his lapel.)* There!

IMMORTAL.   Chantal, my dear one—you won't leave me, will you? Say you won't!

KIMBERLY.   I'm, uh, not "Chantal" but "Kimberly." I'm the assistant of that man who just—

IMMORTAL *(pleading)*.   My "Chantal *des fleurs*"—my dear one? You won't abandon me in this terrible place?

KIMBERLY.   I—don't know. How long do you want me to stay, Mr. Nabokov? (*Checks watch.*) I guess I could skip lunch. (IMMORTAL *pulls at* KIMBERLY'*s arm; she sits beside him on the sofa.*)

IMMORTAL (*reverently*).   You are—Life. Restored to me. My Chantal! The only woman I ever loved. (*Pause.*) You can order up from room service anything you want, dear. This is America—all my expenses are being paid.

KIMBERLY (*a new idea*).   Oh!—Mr. Nabokov, can *I* interview you? Nobody ever gives me a chance but I know I'm a thousand times more emphatic—empathetic?—than *he* is.

IMMORTAL.   Of course, my darling. Anything! Only don't ever leave me again. (KIMBERLY *takes out her tape recorder, sets it going briskly.*)

KIMBERLY.   Oh, Mr. Nabokov, I sure won't. I promise. (*Sudden professional tone*). Mr. Nabokov, will you share with our readers your reflections on the imminent year 2000? When you defected from the Soviet Union, did you ever guess *all this would be coming to pass?*

(*Lights very bright then fade rapidly. Lights out.*)

QUESTIONS

1. Who is the protagonist, "the Interviewer" or "the Immortal"? Support your choice.
2. Characterize the Interviewer, paying close attention not only to speeches but also to gestures, stage actions, and stage directions. What is his chief motivation? Does he display secondary motivations as well?
3. What makes the motivations of the Immortal more difficult to determine? What inconsistencies does he present?
4. The Interviewer has a "PR [public relations] sheet" that presumably contains facts about the Immortal's life, including his birth year, a passage from his Nobel prize oration, a list of his wives, his membership in the French Academy, and so forth. But he learns when Kimberly arrives that he is not interviewing the man described in the fact sheet. Can you account for this apparent inconsistency?
5. The Interviewer decides that the Immortal is Vladimir Nabokov, yet Nabokov was not elected to the French Academy, did not win the Nobel Literature Prize, and was married only once. In fact, no writer has ever been one of the Academy "Immortals" and won the Nobel Prize. Furthermore, as the footnotes reveal, it would have been impossible for Colette to have had an affair with Franz Liszt. What can you deduce from these violations of literal truth? Do they reveal more about the Immortal or about the Interviewer?
6. What is the dramatic function of Kimberly? Which traits of her boss the Interviewer does she show? Compare her misunderstanding of the identity of the Immortal to the Interviewer's. Can you believe that the fax was so

smudged that the name of the Saint Regis Hotel could be mistaken for the Plaza?

7. Explore the irony of a member of a literary society being called "immortal." Considering what an interviewer is expected to do, how is this an ironic portrait of that activity? State the theme of this play by exploring misunderstandings and faulty purposes.

Edward Albee
The Sandbox

A Brief Play, in Memory of My Grandmother (1876–1959)

Players

THE YOUNG MAN, *25, a good-looking, well-built boy in a bathing suit*
MOMMY, *55, a well-dressed, imposing woman*
DADDY, *60, a small man; gray, thin*
GRANDMA, *86, a tiny, wizened woman with bright eyes*
THE MUSICIAN, *no particular age, but young would be nice*

NOTE. *When, in the course of the play,* MOMMY *and* DADDY *call each other by these names, there should be no suggestion of regionalism. These names are of empty affection and point up the pre-senility and vacuity of their characters.*

The Scene. A bare stage, with only the following: Near the footlights, far stage-right, two simple chairs set side by side, facing the audience; near the footlights, far stage-left, a chair facing stage-right with a music stand before it; farther back, and stage-center, slightly elevated and raked, a large child's sandbox with a toy pail and shovel; the background is the sky, which alters from brightest day to deepest night.

At the beginning, it is brightest day; the YOUNG MAN *is alone on stage to the rear of the sandbox, and to one side. He is doing calisthenics; he does calisthenics until quite at the very end of the play. These calisthenics, em-*

THE SANDBOX   Written in 1959. Edward Albee, abandoned by his natural parents, was adopted two weeks after birth in 1928 by a wealthy couple in Westchester County, New York, and named after his adoptive grandfather, part owner of the Keith-Albee string of movie-and-vaudeville theaters. His early schooling frequently interrupted by family vacations, Albee attended a variety of private schools. Dismissed from Trinity College (Connecticut) after three semesters, he went to Greenwich Village, against his foster parents' wishes, determined to write. For about ten years he tried poetry and fiction while working at various odd jobs to supplement a weekly allowance from a trust fund established by his grandmother. After the success of his first play, *Zoo Story* (1959), and the completion of a second, Albee interrupted work on *The American Dream* when commissioned to do a short play for an international theatrical festival. For this play (*The Sandbox*) he used characters from the work in progress placed in a different situation and setting. Despite its overlap of characters and themes with *The American Dream* (1961), it is a separate play, and Albee in 1966 declared it his favorite among his plays.

ploying the arms only, should suggest the beating and fluttering of wings. The YOUNG MAN *is, after all, the Angel of Death.*
MOMMY *and* DADDY *enter from stage-left,* MOMMY *first.*

MOMMY (*motioning to* DADDY).   Well, here we are; this is the beach.
DADDY (*whining*).   I'm cold.
MOMMY (*dismissing him with a little laugh*).   Don't be silly; it's as warm as toast. Look at that nice young man over there: he doesn't think it's cold. (*Waves to the* YOUNG MAN.) Hello.
YOUNG MAN (*with an endearing smile*).   Hi!
MOMMY (*looking about*).   This will do perfectly . . . don't you think so, Daddy? There's sand there . . . and the water beyond. What do you think, Daddy?
DADDY (*vaguely*).   Whatever you say, Mommy.
MOMMY (*with the same little laugh*).   Well, of course . . . whatever I say. Then, it's settled, is it?
DADDY (*shrugs*).   She's *your* mother, not mine.
MOMMY.   *I* know she's my mother. What do you take me for? (*A pause.*) All right, now; let's get on with it. (*She shouts into the wings, stage-left.*) You! Out there! You can come in now. (*The* MUSICIAN *enters, seats himself in the chair, stage-left, places music on the music stand, is ready to play.* MOMMY *nods approvingly.*) Very nice; very nice. Are you ready, Daddy? Let's go get Grandma.
DADDY.   Whatever you say, Mommy.
MOMMY (*leading the way out, stage-left*).   Of course, whatever I say. (*To the* MUSICIAN) You can begin now. (*The* MUSICIAN *begins playing;* MOMMY *and* DADDY *exit; the* MUSICIAN, *all the while playing, nods to the* YOUNG MAN.)
YOUNG MAN (*with the same endearing smile*).   Hi! (*After a moment,* MOMMY *and* DADDY *re-enter, carrying* GRANDMA. *She is borne in by their hands under her armpits; she is quite rigid; her legs are drawn up; her feet do not touch the ground; the expression on her ancient face is that of puzzlement and fear.*)
DADDY.   Where do we put her?
MOMMY (*with the same little laugh*).   Wherever I say, of course. Let me see . . . well . . . all right, over there . . . in the sandbox. (*Pause.*) Well, what are you waiting for, Daddy? . . . The sandbox! (*Together they carry* GRANDMA *over to the sandbox and more or less dump her in.*)
GRANDMA (*righting herself to a sitting position; her voice a cross between a baby's laugh and cry*).   Ahhhhh! Graaaaa!
DADDY (*dusting himself*).   What do we do now?

MOMMY (*to the* MUSICIAN). You can stop now. (*The* MUSICIAN *stops.*) (*Back to* DADDY) What do you mean, what do we do now? We go over there and sit down, of course. (*To the* YOUNG MAN) Hello there.

YOUNG MAN (*again smiling*). Hi! (MOMMY *and* DADDY *move to the chairs, stage-right, and sit down. A pause.*)

GRANDMA (*same as before*). Ahhhhhh! Ah-haaaaaa! Graaaaaa!

DADDY. Do you think . . . do you think she's . . . comfortable?

MOMMY (*impatiently*). How would I know?

DADDY (*pause*). What do we do now?

MOMMY (*as if remembering*). We . . . wait. We . . . sit here . . . and we wait . . . that's what we do.

DADDY (*after a pause*). Shall we talk to each other?

MOMMY (*with that little laugh; picking something off her dress*). Well, you can talk, if you want to . . . if you can think of anything to say . . . if you can think of anything *new*.

DADDY (*thinks*). No . . . I suppose not.

MOMMY (*with a triumphant laugh*). Of course not!

GRANDMA (*banging the toy shovel against the pail*). Haaaaaa! Ah-haaaaaa!

MOMMY (*out over the audience*). Be quiet, Grandma . . . just be quiet, and wait. (GRANDMA *throws a shovelful of sand at* MOMMY. *Still out over the audience*) She's throwing sand at me! You stop that, Grandma; you stop throwing sand at Mommy! (*To* DADDY) She's throwing sand at me. (DADDY *looks around at* GRANDMA, *who screams at him.*)

GRANDMA. GRAAAAAA!

MOMMY. Don't look at her. Just . . . sit here . . . be very still . . . and wait. (*To the* MUSICIAN) You . . . uh . . . you go ahead and do whatever it is you do. (*The* MUSICIAN *plays.* MOMMY *and* DADDY *are fixed, staring out beyond the audience.* GRANDMA *looks at them, looks at the* MUSICIAN, *looks at the sandbox, throws down the shovel.*)

GRANDMA. Ah-haaaaaa! Graaaaaa! (*Looks for reaction; gets none. Now . . . directly to the audience*) Honestly! What a way to treat an old woman! Drag her out of the house . . . stick her in a car . . . bring her out here from the city . . . dump her in a pile of sand . . . and leave her here to set. I'm eighty-six years old! I was married when I was seventeen. To a farmer. He died when I was thirty. (*To the* MUSICIAN) Will you stop that, please? (*The* MUSICIAN *stops playing.*) I'm a feeble old woman . . . how do you expect anybody to hear me over that peep! peep! peep! (*To herself*) There's no respect around here. (*To the* YOUNG MAN) There's no respect around here!

YOUNG MAN (*same smile*). Hi!

GRANDMA (*after a pause, a mild double-take, continues, to the audience*).   My husband died when I was thirty (*indicates* MOMMY), and I had to raise that big cow over there all by my lonesome. You can imagine what *that was like*. Lordy! (*To the* YOUNG MAN) Where'd they get *you*?

YOUNG MAN.   Oh . . . I've been around for a while.

GRANDMA.   I'll bet you have! Heh, heh, heh. Will you look at you!

YOUNG MAN (*flexing his muscles*).   Isn't that something? (*Continues his calisthenics.*)

GRANDMA.   Boy, oh boy; I'll say. Pretty good.

YOUNG MAN (*sweetly*).   I'll say.

GRANDMA.   Where ya from?

YOUNG MAN.   Southern California.

GRANDMA (*nodding*).   Figgers; figgers. What's your name, honey?

YOUNG MAN.   I don't know . . .

GRANDMA (*to the audience*).   Bright, too!

YOUNG MAN.   I mean . . . I mean, they haven't given me one yet . . . the studio . . .

GRANDMA (*giving him the once-over*).   You don't say . . . you don't say. Well . . . uh, I've got to talk some more . . . don't you go 'way.

YOUNG MAN.   Oh, no.

GRANDMA (*turning her attention back to the audience*).   Fine; fine. (*Then, once more, back to the* YOUNG MAN) You're . . . you're an actor, hunh?

YOUNG MAN (*beaming*).   Yes. I am.

GRANDMA (*to the audience again; shrugs*).   I'm smart that way. *Anyhow*, I had to raise . . . *that* over there all by my lonesome; and what's next to her there . . . that's what she married. Rich? I tell you . . . money, money, money. They took me off the *farm* . . . which was real decent of them . . . fixed a nice place for me under the stove . . . gave me an army blanket . . . and my own dish . . . my very own dish! So, what have I got to complain about? Nothing, of course. I'm not complaining. (*She looks up at the sky, shouts to someone off stage.*) Shouldn't it be getting dark now, dear? (*The lights dim; night comes on. The* MUSICIAN *begins to play; it becomes deepest night. There are spots on all the players, including the* YOUNG MAN, *who is, of course, continuing his calisthenics.*)

DADDY (*stirring*).   It's nighttime.

MOMMY.   Shhhh. Be still . . . wait.

DADDY (*whining*).   It's so hot.

MOMMY.   Shhhhhh. Be still . . . wait.

GRANDMA (*to herself*).   That's better. Night. (*To the* MUSICIAN) Honey, do you play all through this part? (*The* MUSICIAN *nods.*) Well, keep it nice and soft; that's a good boy. (*The* Musician *nods again; plays softly.*) That's nice. (*There is an off-stage rumble.*)

Daddy (*starting*).   What was that?

Mommy (*beginning to weep*).   It was nothing.

Daddy.   It was . . . it was . . . thunder . . . or a wave breaking . . . or something.

Mommy (*whispering, through her tears*).   It was an off-stage rumble . . . and you know what *that* means . . .

Daddy.   I forget . . .

Mommy (*barely able to talk*).   It means the time has come for poor Grandma . . . and I can't bear it!

Daddy (*vacantly*).   I . . . I suppose you've got to be brave.

Grandma (*mocking*).   That's right, kid; be brave. You'll bear up, you'll get over it. (*Another off-stage rumble . . . louder.*)

Mommy.   Ohhhhhhhhhh . . . poor Grandma . . . poor Grandma . . .

Grandma (*to* Mommy).   I'm fine! I'm all right! It hasn't happened yet! (*A violent off-stage rumble. All the lights go out, save the spot on the* Young Man; *the* Musician *stops playing.*)

Mommy.   Ohhhhhhhhh . . . Ohhhhhhhhh . . . (*Silence.*)

Grandma.   Don't put the lights up yet . . . I'm not ready; I'm not quite ready. (*Silence.*) All right, dear . . . I'm about done. (*The lights come up again, to brightest day; the* Musician *begins to play.* Grandma *is discovered, still in the sandbox, lying on her side, propped up on an elbow, half covered, busily shoveling sand over herself.*)

Grandma (*muttering*).   I don't know how I'm supposed to do anything with this goddam toy shovel . . .

Daddy.   Mommy! It's daylight!

Mommy (*brightly*).   So it is! Well! Our long night is over. We must put away our tears, take off our mourning . . . and face the future. It's our duty.

Grandma (*still shoveling; mimicking*).   . . . take off our mourning . . . face the future . . . Lordy! (Mommy *and* Daddy *rise, stretch.* Mommy *waves to the* Young Man.)

Young Man (*with that smile*).   Hi! (Grandma *plays dead.* [!] Mommy *and* Daddy *go over to look at her; she is a little more than half buried in the sand; the toy shovel is in her hands, which are crossed on her breast.*)

Mommy (*before the sandbox; shaking her head*).   Lovely! It's . . . it's hard to be sad . . . she looks . . . so happy. (*With pride and conviction*) It pays to do things well. (*To the* Musician) All right, you can stop now, if you want to. I mean, stay around for a swim, or something; it's all right with us. (*She sighs heavily*) Well, Daddy . . . off we go.

DADDY.   Brave Mommy!

MOMMY.   Brave Daddy! (*They exit, stage left.*)

GRANDMA (*after they leave; lying quite still*).   It pays to do things well . . . Boy, oh boy! (*She tries to sit up.*) . . . well, kids . . . (*But she finds she can't.*) . . . I . . . I can't get up. I . . . I can't move . . . (*The* YOUNG MAN *stops his calisthenics, nods to the* MUSICIAN, *walks over to* GRANDMA, *kneels down by the sandbox.*)

GRANDMA.   I . . . can't move . . .

YOUNG MAN.   Shhhhh . . . be very still . . .

GRANDMA.   I . . . I can't move . . .

YOUNG MAN.   Uh . . . ma'am; I . . . I have a line here.

GRANDMA.   Oh, I'm sorry, sweetie; you go right ahead.

YOUNG MAN.   I am . . . uh . . .

GRANDMA.   Take your time, dear.

YOUNG MAN (*prepares; delivers the line like a real amateur*).   I am the Angel of Death. I am . . . uh . . . I am come for you.

GRANDMA.   What . . . wha . . . (*then, with resignation*) . . . ohhhh . . . ohhhh, I see. (*The* YOUNG MAN *bends over, kisses* GRANDMA *gently on the forehead.*)

GRANDMA (*her eyes closed, her hands folded on her breast again, the shovel between her hands, a sweet smile on her face*).   Well . . . that was very nice, dear . . .

YOUNG MAN (*still kneeling*).   Shhhhh . . . be still . . .

GRANDMA.   What I meant was . . . you did that very well, dear . . .

YOUNG MAN (*blushing*).   . . . oh . . .

GRANDMA.   No; I mean it. You've got that . . . you've got a quality.

YOUNG MAN (*with his endearing smile*).   Oh . . . thank you; thank you very much . . . ma'am.

GRANDMA (*slowly; softly—as the* YOUNG MAN *puts his hands on top of* GRANDMA's).   You're . . . you're welcome . . . dear.

(*Tableau. The* MUSICIAN *continues to play as the curtain slowly comes down.*)

QUESTIONS

1. On the face of it, this little play is absurd—absurd both in the way it is presented and in what happens in it. Is it therefore simply horseplay, or does it have a serious subject? What is its subject?

2. The word **absurd,** used above, itself demands attention, since it has been much used with reference to modern drama. The word suggests two dif-

ferent meanings: (a) funny, (b) meaningless. Do both meanings function here? Does either meaning predominate?

3. Characterize Mommy and Daddy. In what ways are they alike? In what ways are they foils? Two of Daddy's speeches are repeated. What do they tell us about his relationship to Mommy?

4. Discuss the treatment by Mommy and Daddy, especially Mommy, of Grandma and her death and burial. What discrepancy exists between appearance and reality? Is their treatment of her in death similar to or different from their treatment of her in life? What metaphor is submerged in Grandma's account of their fixing her a place under the stove with an army blanket and her own dish? What is the function of the Musician?

5. How does the treatment accorded the Young Man by most of the characters (Mommy, the Musician, Grandma) contrast with their treatment of Grandma? What accounts for the difference? What kind of person is the Young Man?

6. What aspects of modern American life are presented in the play? In answering this question, consider your answers to Questions 3, 4, and 5. What judgment does the play make on American life?

7. Contrast Grandma with the Young Man and with Mommy and Daddy. What admirable qualities does she have? What disagreeable qualities does she have? Why? On the whole, is she presented as more, or less, worthy of respect than the other characters in the play? Why?

8. Both in the notes and in the dialogue, the Young Man is identified as the Angel of Death. How is he a very unusual Angel of Death? Is he a simple or a multiple symbol? What other meanings does he suggest?

9. What symbolic meanings are suggested by the following: (a) the bareness of the stage, (b) the sandbox, (c) the toy pail and shovel, (d) the dimming and extinguishing of the lights, (e) Grandma's burying herself with sand, (f) the fact that Grandma is buried before she is dead, (g) the Young Man's kissing Grandma? Which of them, like the Young Man, are multiple symbols?

10. At various points in the action the characters seem aware that they are performers in a play. What effect does this have on the audience's response?

David Ives
Time Flies

Characters

HORACE
MAY
DAVID ATTENBOROUGH
A FROG

SCENE: *Evening. A pond. The chirr of treetoads, and the buzz of a huge swarm of insects. Upstage, a thicket of tall cattails. Downstage, a deep green loveseat. Overhead, an enormous full moon.*

A loud cuckoo sounds, like the mechanical "cuckoo" of a clock.

Lights come up on two mayflies: HORACE *and* MAY, *buzzing as they "fly" in. They are dressed like singles on an evening out, he in a jacket and tie, she in a party dress—but they have insect-like antennae; long tube-like tails; and on their backs, translucent wings. Outsized hornrim glasses give the impression of very large eyes.* MAY *has distinctly hairy legs.*

HORACE and MAY.   Bzzzzzzzzzzzzzzzzzzz . . . (*Their wings stop fluttering, as they "settle."*)

MAY.   Well here we are. This is my place.

HORACE.   Already? That was fast.

MAY.   Swell party, huh.

HORACE.   Yeah. Quite a swarm.

MAY.   Thank you for flying me home.

HORACE.   No. Sure. I'm happy to. Absolutely. My pleasure. I mean—you're very, very, very welcome. (*Their eyes lock and they near each other as if for a kiss, their wings fluttering a little.*) Bzzzzzzzz . . .

MAY.   Bzzzzzzzz . . . (*Before their jaws can meet:* "CUCKOO!"—and HORACE *breaks away.*)

TIME FLIES   One of three one-act plays presented together as *Mere Mortals*, the play was first performed Off-Broadway in New York in 1998. David Ives was born in Chicago in 1951 and educated at Northwestern University and the Yale School of Drama, and in 1995 received a Guggenheim Fellowship for play writing. David Attenborough is the host of nature programs created for British television and broadcast in the United States. The phrase *carpe diem*, used several times in the play, is Latin for "seize the day," an admonition to live life fully because it is so brief—or, paraphrased, "time flies."

HORACE. It's that late, is it. Anyway, it was very nice meeting you—I'm sorry, is it April?

MAY. May.

HORACE. May. Yes. Later than I thought, huh. (*They laugh politely.*)

MAY. That's very funny, Vergil.

HORACE. It's Horace, actually.

MAY. I'm sorry. The buzz at that party was so loud.

HORACE. So you're "May the mayfly."

MAY. Yeah. Guess my parents didn't have much imagination. May, mayfly.

HORACE. You don't, ah, live with your parents, do you, May?

MAY. No, my parents died around dawn this morning.

HORACE. Isn't that funny. Mine died around dawn too.

MAY. Maybe it's fate.

HORACE. Is that what it izzzzzzzz . . . ?

MAY. Bzzzzzzzz . . .

HORACE. Bzzzzzzzzzzzzz . . . (*They near for a kiss, but* HORACE *breaks away.*) Well I'd better be going now. Good night.

MAY. Do you want a drink?

HORACE. I'd love a drink, actually . . .

MAY. Let me just turn on a couple of fireflies. (MAY *tickles the underside of a couple of two foot-long fireflies hanging like a chandelier, and the fireflies light up.*)

HORACE. Wow. Great pond! (*Indicating the loveseat.*) I love the lilypad.

MAY. The lilypad was here. It kinda grew on me. (*Polite laugh.*) Care to take the load off your wings?

HORACE. That's all right. I'll just—you know—hover. But will you look at that . . . ! (*Turning,* HORACE *bats* MAY *with his wings.*)

MAY. Oof!

HORACE. I'm sorry. Did we collide?

MAY. No. No. It's fine.

HORACE. I've only had my wings about six hours.

MAY. Really! So have I . . . ! Wasn't molting disgusting?

HORACE. Eugh. I'm glad that's over.

MAY. Care for some music? I've got The Beatles, The Byrds, The Crickets . . .

HORACE. I love the Crickets.

MAY. Well so do I . . . (*She kicks a large, insect-shaped coffee table, and we hear the buzz of crickets.*)

HORACE. *(as they boogie to that).*   So are you going out with any— I mean, are there any other mayflies in the neighborhood?

MAY.   No, it's mostly wasps.

HORACE.   So, you live here by your, um, all by yourself? Alone?

MAY.   All by my lonesome.

HORACE.   And will you look at that moon.

MAY.   You know that's the first moon I've ever seen?

HORACE.   That's the first moon *I've* ever seen . . . !

MAY.   Isn't that funny.

HORACE.   When were you born?

MAY.   About 7:30 this morning.

HORACE.   So was I! Seven thirty-three!

MAY.   Isn't that funny.

HORACE.   Or maybe it's fate. *(They near each other again, as if for a kiss.)* Bzzzzzzz . . .

MAY.   Bzzzzzzzzz . . . I think that moon is having a very emotional effect on me.

HORACE.   Me too.

MAY.   It must be nature.

HORACE.   Me too.

MAY.   Or maybe it's fate.

HORACE.   Me too . . .

MAY.   Bzzzzzzzzzz . . .

HORACE.   Bzzzzzzzzzzzzz . . . *(They draw their tails very close. Suddenly)*

A FROG *(amplified, over loudspeaker).*   Ribbit, ribbit!

HORACE.   A frog!

MAY.   A frog!

HORACE and MAY.   The frogs are coming, the frogs are coming! *(They "fly" around the stage in a panic. Ad lib)* A frog, a frog! The frogs are coming, the frogs are coming! *(They finally stop, breathless.)*

MAY.   It's okay. It's okay.

HORACE.   Oh my goodness.

MAY.   I think he's gone now.

HORACE.   Oh my goodness, that scared me.

MAY.   That is the only drawback to living here. The frogs.

HORACE.   You know I like frog films and frog literature. I just don't like frogs.

MAY.   And they're so rude if you're not a frog yourself.

HORACE.   Look at me. I'm shaking.

MAY.   Why don't I fix you something. Would you like a grasshopper? Or a stinger?

HORACE.   Just some stagnant water would be fine.

MAY.   A little duckweed in that? Some algae?

HORACE.   Straight up is fine.

MAY (*as she pours his drink*).   Sure I couldn't tempt you to try the lily pad?

HORACE.   Well, maybe for just a second. (HORACE *flutters down onto the love seat.*) Zzzzzzz . . .

MAY (*handing him a glass*).   Here you go. Cheers, Horace.

HORACE.   Long life, May. (*They clink glasses.*)

MAY.   Do you want to watch some tube?

HORACE.   Sure. What's on?

MAY.   Let's see. (*She checks a green TV Guide.*) There is . . . *The Love Bug, M. Butterfly, The Spider's Stratagem, Travels With My Ant, Angels and Insects, The Fly* . . .

HORACE.   The original, or Jeff Goldblum?

MAY.   Jeff Goldblum.

HORACE.   Euch. Too gruesome.

MAY.   *Born Yesterday* and *Life On Earth.*

HORACE.   What's on that?

MAY.   "Swamp Life," with Sir David Attenborough.

HORACE.   That sounds good.

MAY.   Shall we try it?

HORACE.   Carpe diem.

MAY.   Carpe diem? What's that?

HORACE.   I don't know. It's Latin.

MAY.   What's Latin?

HORACE.   I don't know. I'm just a mayfly. (*"Cuckoo!"*) And we're right on time for it. (MAY *presses a remote control and* DAVID ATTENBOROUGH *appears, wearing a safari jacket.*)

DAVID ATTENBOROUGH.   Hello, I'm David Attenborough. Welcome to "Swamp Life."

MAY.   Isn't this comfy.

HORACE.   Is my wing in your way?

MAY.   No. It's fine.

DAVID ATTENBOROUGH.   You may not believe it, but within this seemingly lifeless puddle, there thrives a teeming world of vibrant life.

HORACE.   May, look—isn't that your pond?

MAY.   I think that is my pond!

HORACE.   He said "puddle."

DAVID ATTENBOROUGH.   This puddle is only several inches across, but its stagnant water plays host to over 14 gazillion different species.

MAY.   It is my pond!

DAVID ATTENBOROUGH.   Every species here is engaged in a constant, desperate battle for survival. Feeding—meeting—mating—breeding—dying. And mating. And meeting. And mating. And feeding. And dying. Mating. Mating. Meeting. Breeding. Brooding. Braiding—those that can braid. Feeding. Mating.

MAY.   All right, Sir Dave!

DAVID ATTENBOROUGH.   Mating, mating, mating, and mating.

HORACE.   Only one thing on his mind.

MAY.   The filth on television these days.

DAVID ATTENBOROUGH.   Tonight we start off with one of the saddest creatures of this environment.

HORACE.   The dung beetle.

MAY.   The toad.

DAVID ATTENBOROUGH.   The lowly mayfly.

HORACE.   Did he say "the mayfly?"

MAY.   I think he said the lowly mayfly.

DAVID ATTENBOROUGH.   Yes. The lowly mayfly. Like these two mayflies, for instance.

HORACE.   May—I think that's us!

MAY.   Oh my God . . .

HORACE and MAY (together).   We're on television!

HORACE.   I don't believe it!

MAY.   I wish my mother was here to see this!

HORACE.   This is amazing!

MAY.   Oh God, I look terrible!

HORACE.   You look very good.

MAY.   I can't look at this.

DAVID ATTENBOROUGH.   As you can see, the lowly mayfly is not one of nature's most attractive creatures.

MAY.   At least we don't wear safari jackets.

HORACE.   I wish he'd stop saying "lowly mayfly."

DAVID ATTENBOROUGH.   The lowly mayfly has a very distinctive khkhkhkhkhkhkhkhkhkkh . . . (the sound of TV static)

MAY.   I think there's something wrong with my antenna . . . (She adjusts the antenna on her head.)

HORACE.   You don't have cable?

MAY.   Not on this pond.

DAVID ATTENBOROUGH (stops the static sound).   . . . and sixty tons of droppings.

HORACE.   That fixed it.

MAY.   Can I offer you some food? I've got some plankton in the pond. And some very nice gnat.

HORACE.   I do love good gnat.

MAY.   I'll set it out, you can pick. (*She rises and gets some food.*)

DAVID ATTENBOROUGH.   The lowly mayfly first appeared some 350 million years ago . . .

MAY.   That's impressive.

DAVID ATTENBOROUGH.   . . . and is of the order Ephemeroptera, meaning, "living for a single day."

MAY.   I did not know that!

HORACE.   "Living for a single day." Huh . . .

MAY (*setting out a tray on the coffee table*).   There you go.

HORACE.   Gosh, May. That's beautiful.

MAY.   There's curried gnat, salted gnat, Scottish smoked gnat . . .

HORACE.   I love that.

MAY.   . . . . gnat with pesto, gnat au naturelle, and Gnat King Cole.

HORACE.   I don't think I could finish a whole one.

MAY.   "Gnat" to worry. (*They laugh politely.*) That's larva dip there in the center. Just dig in.

DAVID ATTENBOROUGH.   As for the life of the common mayfly . . .

HORACE.   Oh. We're "common" now.

DAVID ATTENBOROUGH.   . . . it is a simple round of meeting, mating, meeting, mating—

MAY.   Here we go again.

DAVID ATTENBOROUGH.   —breeding, feeding, feeding . . .

HORACE.   This dip is fabulous.

DAVID ATTENBOROUGH.   . . . and dying.

MAY.   Leaf?

HORACE.   Thank you. (MAY *breaks a leaf off a plant and hands it to* HORACE.)

DAVID ATTENBOROUGH.   Mayflies are a major food source for trout and salmon.

MAY.   Will you look at that savagery?

HORACE.   That poor, poor mayfly.

DAVID ATTENBOROUGH.   Fishermen like to bait hooks with mayfly look-alikes.

MAY.   Bastards!—Excuse me.

DAVID ATTENBOROUGH.   And then there is the giant bullfrog.

FROG (*amplified, over loudspeaker*).   Ribbit, ribbit!

HORACE and MAY.   The frogs are coming, the frogs are coming! (*They "fly" around the stage in a panic—and end up "flying" right into each other's arms.*)

HORACE.   Well there.

MAY.   Hello.

DAVID ATTENBOROUGH.   Welcome to "Swamp Life." *(Exits)*

MAY *(hypnotized by* HORACE*).*   Funny how we flew right into each other's wings.

HORACE.   It is funny.

MAY.   Or fate.

HORACE.   Do you think he's gone?

MAY.   David Attenborough?

HORACE.   The frog.

MAY.   What frog? Bzzzz . . .

HORACE.   Bzzzzz . . .

DAVID ATTENBOROUGH'S VOICE.   As you see, mayflies can be quite affectionate . . .

HORACE and MAY.   Bzzzzzzzzzzz . . .

DAVID ATTENBOROUGH'S VOICE.   . . . mutually palpating their proboscises.

HORACE.   You know I've been wanting to palpate your proboscis all evening?

MAY.   I think it was larva at first sight.

HORACE and MAY *(rubbing proboscises together).*   Zzzzzzzzzz zzzzzzzzzzzzzzzzzz . . .

MAY *(very British, "Brief Encounter").*   Oh darling, darling.

HORACE.   Oh do darling do let's always be good to each other, shall we?

MAY.   Let's do do that, darling, always, always.

HORACE.   Always?

MAY.   Always.

HORACE and MAY.   Zzzzzzzzzzzzzzzzzzzzzzzzzzzzzzz!

MAY.   Rub my antennae. Rub my antennae. (HORACE *rubs* MAY's *antennae with his hands.)*

DAVID ATTENBOROUGH'S VOICE.   Sometimes mayflies rub antennae together.

MAY.   Oh yes. Yes. Just like that. Yes. Keep going. Harder. Rub harder.

HORACE.   Rub mine now. Rub my antennae. Oh yes. Yes. Yes. Yes. There's the rub. There's the rub. Go. Go. Go!

DAVID ATTENBOROUGH'S VOICE.   Isn't that a picture. Now get a load of mating. (HORACE *gets into mounting position, behind* MAY. *He rubs her antennae while she wolfs down the gnat-food in front of her.)*

HORACE and MAY.   Bzzzzzzzzzzzzzzzzzzzzzzzzzzzzzzzzzzzzz!

DAVID ATTENBOROUGH'S VOICE.   Unfortunately for this insect, the mayfly has a lifespan of only one day. (HORACE *and* MAY *stop buzzing, abruptly.)*

HORACE.   What was that . . . ?

DAVID ATTENBOROUGH'S VOICE.   The mayfly has a lifespan of only one day—living just long enough to meet, mate, have offspring, and die.

MAY.   Did he say "meet, mate, have offspring, and DIE"—?

DAVID ATTENBOROUGH'S VOICE.   I did. In fact, mayflies born at 7:30 in the morning will die by the next dawn. (HORACE *whimpers softly at the thought*) But so much for the lowly mayfly. Let's move on to the newt. (*"Cuckoo!"*)

HORACE and MAY.   We're going to die . . . We're going to die! Mayday, mayday! We're going to die, we're going to die! (*Weeping and wailing, they kneel, beat their breasts, cross themselves, and tear their hair: "Cuckoo!"*)

HORACE.   What time is it? What time is it?

MAY.   I don't wear a watch. I'm a lowly mayfly!

HORACE. (*weeping*).   Wah-ha-ha-ha!

MAY (*suddenly sober*).   Well isn't this beautiful.

HORACE (*gasping for breath*).   Oh my goodness. I think I'm having an asthma attack. Can mayflies have asthma?

MAY.   I don't know. Ask Mr. Safari Jacket.

HORACE.   Maybe if I put a paper bag over my head . . .

MAY.   So this is my sex life?

HORACE.   Do you have a paper bag?

MAY.   One bang, a bambino, and boom—that's it?

HORACE.   Do you have a paper bag?

MAY.   For the common mayfly, foreplay segues right into funeral.

HORACE.   Do you have a paper bag?

MAY.   I don't have time to look for a paper bag, I'm going to be dead very shortly, all right? (*"Cuckoo!"*)

HORACE.   Oh come on! That wasn't a whole hour! (*"Cuckoo!"*) Time is moving so fast now. (*"Cuckoo!"*)

HORACE and MAY.   Shut up! (*"Cuckoo!"*)

HORACE (*suddenly sober*).   This explains everything. We were born this morning, we hit puberty in mid-afternoon, our biological clocks went BONG, and here we are. Hot to copulate.

MAY.   For the one brief miserable time we get to do it.

HORACE.   Yeah.

MAY.   Talk about a quickie.

HORACE.   Wait a minute, wait a minute.

MAY.   Talk fast.

HORACE.   What makes you think it would be so brief?

MAY.   Oh, I'm sorry. Did I insult your vast sexual experience?

HORACE.   Are you more experienced than I am, Dr. Ruth? Luring me here to your pad?

MAY.   I see. I see. Blame me!

HORACE.   Can I remind you we only get one shot at this?

MAY.   So I can rule out multiple orgasms, is that it?

HORACE.   I'm just saying there's not a lot of time to hone one's erotic technique, okay?

MAY.   Hmp!

HORACE.   And I'm trying to sort out some very big entomontological questions here rather quickly, do you mind?

MAY.   And I'm just the babe here, is that it? I'm just a piece of tail.

HORACE.   I'm not the one who suggested TV.

MAY.   I'm not the one who wanted to watch *Life on Earth*. "Oh— Swamp Life. That sounds interesting."

FROG.   Ribbit, ribbit.

HORACE *(calmly)*.   There's a frog up there.

MAY.   Oh, I'm really scared. I'm terrified.

FROG.   Ribbit, ribbit!

HORACE *(calling to the frog)*.   We're right down here! Come and get us!

MAY.   Breeding. Dying. Breeding. Dying. So this is the whole purpose of mayflies? To make more mayflies?

HORACE.   Does the world *need* more mayflies?

MAY.   We're a major food source for trout and salmon.

HORACE.   How nice for the salmon.

MAY.   Do you want more food?

HORACE.   I've lost a bit of my appetite, all right?

MAY.   Oh. Excuse me.

HORACE.   I'm sorry. Really, May.

MAY *(starts to cry)*.   Males!

HORACE.   Leaf? *(He plucks another leaf and hands it to her.)*

MAY.   Thank you.

HORACE.   Really. I didn't mean to snap at you.

MAY.   Oh, you've been very nice. *("CUCKOO!" They jump.)* Under the circumstances.

HORACE.   I'm sorry.

MAY.   No, I'm sorry.

HORACE.   No, I'm sorry.

MAY.   No, I'm sorry.

HORACE.   No, I'm sorry.

MAY.   We'd better stop apologizing, we're going to be dead soon.

HORACE.   I'm sorry.

MAY.   Oh Horace, I had such plans. I had such wonderful plans. I wanted to see Paris.

HORACE.   What's Paris?

MAY.   I have no fucking idea.

HORACE.   Maybe we'll come back as caviar and find out. (*They laugh a little at that.*) I was just hoping to live till Tuesday.

MAY (*making a small joke*).   What's a Tuesday? (*They laugh a little more at that.*) The sun's going to be up soon. I'm scared, Horace. I'm so scared.

HORACE.   You know, May, we don't have much time, and really, we hardly know each other—but I'm going to say it. I think you're swell. I think you're divine. From your buggy eyes to the thick raspy hair on your legs to the intoxicating scent of your secretions.

MAY.   Eeeuw.

HORACE.   Eeeuw? No. I say *woof*. And I say who cares if life is a swamp and we're just a couple of small bugs in a very small pond. I say live, May! I say . . . darn it . . . live!

MAY.   But how?

HORACE.   Well I don't honestly know that . . . (ATTENBOROUGH *appears.*)

DAVID ATTENBOROUGH.   You could fly to Paris.

MAY.   We could fly to Paris!

HORACE.   Do we have time to fly to Paris?

MAY.   Carpe diem!

HORACE.   What is carpe diem?

DAVID ATTENBOROUGH.   It means "bon voyage."

HORACE and MAY.   And we're outta here!

[*They fly off to Paris as . . . Blackout.*]

QUESTIONS

1. Although Horace and May are insects, the dialogue is distinctly human. Point out examples of contemporary social conversation. To what are these mayflies being compared?

2. Mayflies do live only one day. How does that fact become symbolic of some human relationships?

3. What is the function of the voice of David Attenborough? At what points does it shift away from what you expect of the TV host of a nature program? Why?

4. Much of the humor of the play arises from insects behaving like people. In addition, there are many puns and verbal jokes. Make a list of these, and show how they distance the audience from involvement in the emotions felt by the characters. For example, "frog" is a derogatory term for the

French, and May and Horace have a bit of conversation about what they do and don't like about frogs. Translate that into trite comments on the French—and juxtapose it to the conclusion of the play. Does it matter that the audience cannot empathize with the serious emotions that the characters share?

5. Explain the pun in the title of the play. Would "carpe diem" have been as suitable as this title?

SUGGESTIONS FOR WRITING

1. Works written as short stories, novels, or poems have sometimes been dramatized for stage production. In light of the advantages and limitations discussed in this chapter, however, some are clearly more easily adapted for the stage than others. Select one or two from the following list, and explain the relative ease or difficulty—or impossibility—of a stage adaptation: "Eveline" (page 442), "Miss Brill" (page 175), "The Lottery" (page 251), "A Very Old Man with Enormous Wings" (page 327), "To Autumn" (page 711), "Home Burial" (page 921), "The Love Song of J. Alfred Prufrock" (page 925).

2. Movie and broadcast (TV and radio) productions are in many ways more flexible than stage productions and are more easily brought to a mass audience. What limitations of stage performance discussed in this chapter can be minimized or eliminated in a movie or broadcast production? Conversely, what advantages of stage performances are unavailable to media productions?

3. In view of the greater flexibility of movies and broadcasting media in dramatic representation, what accounts for the continuing popularity of stage plays?

4. If plays are written to be *performed*, what justification is there for reading them?

Chapter Two

Realistic and Nonrealistic Drama

Literary truth in drama (as in fiction and in poetry) is not the same as fidelity to fact. Fantasy is as much the property of the theater as of poetry or the prose tale. In *A Midsummer Night's Dream* and *The Tempest*, Shakespeare has fairies and spirits and monsters as characters, and in *Hamlet* and *Macbeth* he introduces ghosts and witches. These supernatural characters, nevertheless, serve as a vehicle for truth. When Bottom, in *A Midsummer Night's Dream*, is given an ass's head, the enchantment is a visual metaphor. The witches in *Macbeth* truthfully prefigure a tragic destiny.

Because it is written to be performed, however, drama adds still another dimension of possible unreality. It may be **realistic** or **nonrealistic** in mode of production as well as in content. Staging, makeup, costuming, and acting may all be handled in such a way as to emphasize the realistic or the fanciful.

It must be recognized, however, that all stage production, no matter how realistic, involves a certain necessary artificiality. If an indoor scene is presented on a picture-frame proscenium stage, the spectator is asked to imagine that a room with only three walls is actually a room with four walls. In a thrust-stage or arena theater, in which audiences are in a semicircle around the playing area, the spectator must imagine three of the four walls, while theater-in-the-round has the audience seated on all sides of the action and spectators have to imagine all four walls—while imaginatively shutting their minds to the presence of spectators facing them from the other side of the action. All of these types of stage presentation, moreover, require adjustments in the acting. In a proscenium theater the actors must be facing the missing fourth wall most of the time. In arena or round stagings, they must not turn their backs too long on any "wall." Both types of staging, in the interests of effective presentation, require the actors to depart from an absolute realism.

Beyond these basic requirements of artificiality in stagecraft, the departure from the appearance of reality may be slight or considerable. In many late-nineteenth- and early-twentieth-century productions, an effort was made to make stage sets as realistic as possible. If the play called for a setting in a study, there had to be real bookshelves on the wall and real books on the shelves. If the room contained a wash basin, real water had to flow from the taps. On the other hand, plays have been performed on bare stages with little more than platforms and a few props.

In between these two extremes, all degrees of realism are possible. The scenery may consist of painted flats, with painted bookshelves and painted books and painted pictures on the wall, and these paintings may strive for photographic faithfulness or for an impressionistic effect. Or, instead of scenery, a play may use only a few movable properties to suggest the required setting. Thornton Wilder's *Our Town* (1938) utilized a bare stage, without curtain, with exposed ropes and backstage equipment, and with a few chairs, two ladders, and a couple of trellises as the only properties. For a scene at a soda fountain, a plank was laid across the backs of two chairs. In fact, provision of elaborately realistic stage sets has been the exception rather than the rule in the long history of the theater. Neither in Greek nor in Shakespearean theater was setting much more than suggested.

The choice of realistic or nonrealistic stage sets, costuming, and makeup may, in fact, lie with the producer rather than the playwright, and a producer may choose to disregard a playwright's directions for the sake of novelty or emphasis. When we move to the realm of language and the management of dialogue, the choice is entirely the playwright's. Here again all degrees of realism and nonrealism are possible. In the realistic theater of the last hundred years, some playwrights have made an elaborate effort to reproduce the flat quality of ordinary speech, with all its stumblings and inarticulateness, its slang and its mispronunciations. Others go even further in imitating reality, even at the risk of offending some members of the audience, and reproduce the vulgarities of the language of the streets and the contemporary habit of using obscene terms simply to add force to a statement. In real life, of course, few lovers speak with the eloquence of Romeo and Juliet, and many people, in daily conversation, have difficulty getting through a grammatically correct sentence of any length or complexity. They break off, they begin again, they repeat themselves, and sometimes, like the Young Man in "The Sandbox," they are barely articulate ("I am . . . uh . . . I am the Angel of Death. I am . . . uh . . . I am come for you."). Such unimaginative and inadequate speech, skillfully used by the playwright, may faithfully render the quality of human life at some levels, yet its limitations for expressing the heights and depths of human experience are obvious. Most dramatic dialogue, even when most realistic, is more coherent and expressive than speech in actual life. Art is always a heightening or an intensification of reality; else it would have no value. The heightening may be little or great. It is greatest in poetic drama. The love exchanges of Romeo and Juliet, spoken in rhymed iambic pentameter and at one point taking the form of a perfect sonnet (see page 891), are absurdly nonrealistic if judged as an imitation of actual speech, but they vividly express the emotional truth of passionate, idealistic young love. It is no criticism of Shakespearean tragedy, therefore, to say that in real life people do not speak in blank verse. The deepest purpose of the playwright is not to imitate actual human speech but to give accurate and powerful expression to human thought and emotion.

The term **nonrealistic** used in the previous paragraph to describe the dialogue of Romeo and Juliet should not be confused with the term "unrealistic." Nonrealistic and **realistic** describe qualities of dramatic presentation; "unrealistic" is a term that judges people's actions on a scale of good sense, practicality, and insight. It is useful in discussing drama only when you are considering a character's grasp on reality—for example, a drama (whether realistic or nonrealistic) might portray a character who is unrealistic in outlook, such as a hopeless optimist or an incorrigible sentimentalist. The Immortal in Oates's "The Interview" is an unrealistic character in a realistic play. In drama, realism is the attempt to reproduce or imitate the sights and sounds of real life, insofar as these can be represented on a stage. In life, realism is looking at the world with good judgment and clear vision.

All drama asks us to accept certain departures from reality— certain **dramatic conventions.** That a room with three walls or fewer may represent one with four walls, that the actors speak in the language of the audience whatever the nationality of the persons they play, that the actors stand or sit so as to face the audience most of the time— these are all necessary conventions. Other conventions are optional— for example, that the characters may reveal their inner thoughts through soliloquies and asides or may speak in the heightened language of poetry. Playwrights working in a strictly realistic mode will avoid the optional conventions, for these conflict with the realistic method that they have chosen to achieve their purposes. Playwrights working in a freer mode may choose to use any or all of them, for they make possible the revelation of dimensions of reality unreachable by a strictly realistic method. The famous speech of Hamlet that begins "To be, or not to be," in which he debates the merits of onerous life and untimely death, is nonrealistic on two counts: (1) it is spoken as a soliloquy, and (2) it is in blank verse. But despite the nonrealistic conventions, it presents Hamlet's introspective mind, his clear rationality, and his profound emotions in a powerful way. The characteristic device of Greek drama, a **chorus**—a group of actors speaking in unison, often in a chant, while going through the steps of an elaborate formalized dance—is another nonrealistic device but a useful one for conveying communal or group emotion. It has been revived, in different forms, in many modern plays. The use of a **narrator,** as in *The Glass Menagerie* (page 1143), is a related nonrealistic device that has served playwrights as a vehicle for dramatic truth.

The history of drama might be told in a history of conventions that have arisen, flourished, and been replaced; and those readers and audiences who experience plays most fully are those who have learned to understand the main conventions of its various periods and major dramatists. The less experienced reader or spectator may judge a play defective because it makes use of conventions other than those in common current acceptance (whether or not consciously recognized as such). Most contemporary audiences, for example, have been trained by their experience with movies and television, two media based on the realistic conventions of photography. Few people pause to consider that looking at a photograph, whether filmed by a still camera or a movie camera, requires the acceptance of the simple convention that three-dimensional reality is being represented two-dimensionally, or that the full spectrum of color may be represented by shades of white, gray, or black. We accept these conventions without question, as we also accept in cinema and television the emotional reinforcement that comes with a musical background even though there is no justification for the presence of an orchestra in a living room or on a beach. The study of drama requires the purposeful learning of its conventions, both realistic and nonrealistic.

In most plays, the world into which we are taken—however unreal it may be—is treated as self-contained, and we are asked to regard it temporarily as a real world. Thus David Ives's puddle of mayflies in "Time Flies" is real to us while we watch the play. We quite willingly make that "temporary suspension of disbelief" that, according to Coleridge, "constitutes poetic faith." And the step from accepting May and Horace as real insects, though we know in fact that they are only costumed actors, is an easy one because they think and talk like human beings in a fleeting romance as they erotically rub antennae and enjoy gnat snacks. But some playwrights abandon even this much attempt to give their work an illusion of reality. They deliberately violate the self-containment of the fictional world and keep reminding us that we are only seeing a play.

Thus Edward Albee, in "The Sandbox," not only presents as his main character a Grandma who buries herself alive and speaks after she is presumably dead, but he also systematically breaks down the barriers between his fictional world and the real one. The Musician, instead of being concealed in an orchestra pit, is summoned onstage and told by Mommy and Grandma when to play and when not to play. Grandma addresses herself much of the time directly to the audience and at one time shouts to the electricians offstage, instructing them to dim the lights. The Young Man reminds us that he is an actor by telling Grandma that he has "a line here" and by delivering the line "like a real amateur." When Mommy and Daddy hear a noise offstage, Daddy thinks it may be thunder or a breaking wave, but Mommy says, with literal accuracy, "It was an off-stage rumble." In short, Albee keeps reminding us that this is a play—not reality—and not even an imitation of reality, but a symbolic representation of it. The effects he gains thereby are various: partly comic, partly antisentimental, partly intellectual; and the play that results is both theatrically effective and dramatically significant.

The adjective *realistic*, then, as applied to literature, must be regarded as a descriptive, not an evaluative, term. When we call a play realistic, we are saying something about its mode of presentation, not praising nor dispraising it. Realism indicates fidelity to the outer appearances of life. Serious dramatists are interested in life's inner meanings, which they may approach through either realistic or nonrealistic presentation. Great plays have been written in both the realistic and nonrealistic modes. It is not without significance, however, that the greatest plays in this book are probably *Oedipus Rex*, *Tartuffe*, and *Othello*—originally written in quantitative Greek verse, rhymed French hexameters, and English blank verse, respectively. Human truth, rather than fidelity to superficial fact, is the highest achievement of literary art.

REVIEWING CHAPTER TWO

1. Distinguish between realistic and nonrealistic conventions, and between the terms "nonrealistic" and "unrealistic."
2. List the important realistic conventions that may be reflected in physical appearances and in language, and consider what they may contribute to an audience's experience of a play.
3. Define the advantages gained by playwrights who employ nonrealistic conventions, both in production values and in spoken dialogue, and consider any disadvantages that may result from them.

Henrik Ibsen
A Doll House

Characters

TORVALD HELMER, *a lawyer*
NORA, *his wife*
DR. RANK
MRS. LINDE
KROGSTAD

THE HELMERS' THREE SMALL
    CHILDREN
ANNE-MARIE, *the children's nurse*
A HOUSEMAID
A PORTER

SCENE. *The Helmers' living room.*

ACT 1

A pleasant, tastefully but not expensively furnished, living room. A door on the rear wall, right, leads to the front hall, another door, left, to HELMER'S *study. Between the two doors a piano. A third door in the middle of the left wall; further front a window. Near the window a round table and a small couch. Towards the rear of the right wall a fourth door; further front a tile stove with a rocking chair and a couple of armchairs in front of it. Between the stove and the door a small table. Copperplate etchings on the walls. A whatnot with porcelain figurines and other small objects. A small bookcase with deluxe editions. A rug on the floor; fire in the stove. Winter day.*

The doorbell rings, then the sound of the front door opening. NORA *dressed for outdoors, enters, humming cheerfully. She carries several packages, which she puts down on the table, right. She leaves the door to the front hall open; there a* PORTER *is seen holding a Christmas tree and a basket. He gives them to the* MAID *who has let them in.*

A DOLL HOUSE   First published and then performed in 1879. English translation by Otto Reinert. Henrik Ibsen (1828–1906), widely regarded as one of the founders of modern drama, was born in Norway. Between 1851 and 1864, while employed at theaters in Bergen and Christiana (now Oslo), Ibsen gained experience but little financial success (he had known little but poverty since his early childhood, when his extravagant father went bankrupt). As a consequence of his promising achievement as a poet and playwright, a traveling grant and then a small annual stipend from the Norwegian government permitted him to move with his family to Rome, where he took up permanent residence in 1864. By the time he wrote this play, Ibsen had long been interested in women's rights.

NORA.   Be sure to hide the Christmas tree, Helene. The children mustn't see it before tonight when we've trimmed it. (*Opens her purse; to the* PORTER) How much?

PORTER.   Fifty øre.

NORA.   Here's a crown.° No, keep the change. (*The* PORTER *thanks her, leaves.* NORA *closes the door. She keeps laughing quietly to herself as she takes off her coat, etc. She takes a bag of macaroons from her pocket and eats a couple. She walks cautiously over to the door to the study and listens.*) Yes, he's home. (*Resumes her humming, walks over to the table, right.*)

HELMER (*in his study*).   Is that my little lark twittering out there?

NORA (*opening some packages*).   That's right.

HELMER.   My squirrel bustling about?

NORA.   Yes.

HELMER.   When did squirrel come home?

NORA.   Just now. (*Puts the bag of macaroons back in her pocket, wipes her mouth.*) Come out here, Torvald. I want to show you what I've bought.

HELMER.   I'm busy! (*After a little while he opens the door and looks in, pen in hand.*) Bought, eh? All that? So little wastrel has been throwing money around again?

NORA.   Oh but Torvald, this Christmas we can be a little extravagant, can't we? It's the first Christmas we don't have to scrimp.

HELMER.   I don't know about that. We certainly don't have money to waste.

NORA.   Yes, Torvald, we do. A little, anyway. Just a tiny little bit? Now that you're going to get that big salary and make lots and lots of money.

HELMER.   Starting at New Year's, yes. But payday isn't till the end of the quarter.

NORA.   That doesn't matter. We can always borrow.

HELMER.   Nora! (*Goes over to her and playfully pulls her ear.*) There you go being irresponsible again. Suppose I borrowed a thousand crowns today and you spent it all for Christmas and on New Year's Eve a tile hit me in the head and laid me out cold?

NORA (*putting her hand over his mouth*).   I won't have you say such horrid things.

HELMER.   But suppose it happened. Then what?

NORA.   If it did, I wouldn't care whether we owed money or not.

HELMER.   But what about the people I had borrowed from?

NORA.   Who cares about them! They are strangers.

Fifty øre . . . a crown: A crown was 100 øre.

HELMER.   Nora, Nora, you *are* a woman! No, really! You know how I feel about that. No debts! A home in debt isn't a free home, and if it isn't free it isn't beautiful. We've managed nicely so far, you and I, and that's the way we'll go on. It won't be for much longer.

NORA (*walks over toward the stove*).   All right, Torvald. Whatever you say.

HELMER (*follows her*).   Come, come, my little songbird mustn't droop her wings. What's this? Can't have a pouty squirrel in the house, you know. (*Takes out his wallet.*) Nora, what do you think I have here?

NORA (*turns around quickly*).   Money!

HELMER.   Here. (*Gives her some bills.*) Don't you think I know Christmas is expensive?

NORA (*counting*).   Ten—twenty—thirty—forty. Thank you, thank you, Torvald. This helps a lot.

HELMER.   I certainly hope so.

NORA.   It does, it does. But I want to show you what I got. It was cheap, too. Look. New clothes for Ivar. And a sword. And a horse and trumpet for Bob. And a doll and a little bed for Emmy. It isn't any good, but it wouldn't last, anyway. And here's some dress material and scarves for the maids. I feel bad about old Anne-Marie, though. She really should be getting much more.

HELMER.   And what's in here?

NORA (*cries*).   Not till tonight!

HELMER.   I see. But now what does my little prodigal have in mind for herself?

NORA.   Oh, nothing. I really don't care.

HELMER.   Of course you do. Tell me what you'd like. Within reason.

NORA.   Oh, I don't know. Really, I don't. The only thing—

HELMER.   Well?

NORA (*fiddling with his buttons, without looking at him*).   If you really want to give me something, you might—you could—

HELMER.   All right, let's have it.

NORA (*quickly*).   Some money, Torvald. Just as much as you think you can spare. Then I'll buy myself something one of these days.

HELMER.   No, really Nora—

NORA.   Oh yes, please, Torvald. Please? I'll wrap the money in pretty gold paper and hang it on the tree. Won't that be nice?

HELMER.   What's the name for little birds that are always spending money?

NORA.   Wastrels, I know. But please let's do it my way, Torvald. Then I'll have time to decide what I need most. Now that's sensible, isn't it?

HELMER (*smiling*).   Oh, very sensible. That is, if you really bought yourself something you could use. But it all disappears in the household expenses or you buy things you don't need. And then you come back to me for more.

NORA.   Oh, but Torvald—

HELMER.   That's the truth, dear little Nora, and you know it. (*Puts his arm around her.*) My wastrel is a little sweetheart, but she *does* go through an awful lot of money awfully fast. You've no idea how expensive it is for a man to keep a wastrel.

NORA.   That's not fair, Torvald. I really save all I can.

HELMER (*laughs*).   Oh, I believe that. All you can. Meaning, exactly nothing!

NORA (*hums, smiles mysteriously*).   You don't know all the things we songbirds and squirrels need money for, Torvald.

HELMER.   You know, you're funny. Just like your father. You're always looking for ways to get money, but as soon as you do it runs through your fingers and you can never say what you spent it for. Well, I guess I'll just have to take you the way you are. It's in your blood. Yes, that sort of thing is hereditary, Nora.

NORA.   In that case, I wish I had inherited many of Daddy's qualities.

HELMER.   And I don't want you any different from just what you are—my own sweet little songbird. Hey!—I think I just noticed something. Aren't you looking—what's the word?—a little—sly—?

NORA.   I am?

HELMER.   You definitely are. Look at me.

NORA (*looks at him*).   Well?

HELMER (*wagging a finger*).   Little sweet-tooth hasn't by any chance been on a rampage today, has she?

NORA.   Of course not. Whatever makes you think that?

HELMER.   A little detour by the pastry shop maybe?

NORA.   No, I assure you, Torvald—

HELMER.   Nibbled a little jam?

NORA.   Certainly not!

HELMER.   Munched a macaroon or two?

NORA.   No, really, Torvald, I honestly—

HELMER.   All right. Of course I was only joking.

NORA (*walks toward the table, right*).   You know I wouldn't do anything to displease you.

HELMER.   I know. And I have your promise. (*Over to her.*) All right, keep your little Christmas secrets to yourself, Nora darling. They'll all come out tonight, I suppose, when we light the tree.

NORA.   Did you remember to invite Rank?

HELMER.   No, but there's no need to. He knows he'll have dinner with us. Anyway, I'll see him later this morning. I'll ask him then. I did order some good wine. Oh Nora, you've no idea how much I'm looking forward to tonight!

NORA.   Me, too. And the children, Torvald! They'll have such a good time!

HELMER.   You know it *is* nice to have a good, safe job and a comfortable income. Feels good just thinking about it. Don't you agree?

NORA.   Oh, it's wonderful.

HELMER.   Remember last Christmas? For three whole weeks you shut yourself up every evening till long after midnight making ornaments for the Christmas tree and I don't know what else. Some big surprise for all of us, anyway. I'll be damned if I've ever been so bored in my whole life!

NORA.   I wasn't bored at all!

HELMER (*smiling*).   But you've got to admit you didn't have much to show for it in the end.

NORA.   Oh, don't tease me again about that! Could I help it that the cat got in and tore up everything?

HELMER.   Of course you couldn't, my poor little Nora. You just wanted to please the rest of us, and that's the important thing. But I *am* glad the hard times are behind us. Aren't you?

NORA.   Oh yes. I think it's just wonderful.

HELMER.   This year, I won't be bored and lonely. And you won't have to strain your dear eyes and your delicate little hands—

NORA (*claps her hands*).   No I won't, will I Torvald? Oh, how wonderful, how lovely, to hear you say that! (*Puts her arm under his.*) Let me tell you how I think we should arrange things, Torvald. Soon as Christmas is over—(*The doorbell rings.*) Someone's at the door. (*Straightens things up a bit.*) A caller, I suppose. Bother!

HELMER.   Remember, I'm not home for visitors.

MAID (*in the door to the front hall*).   Ma'am, there's a lady here—

NORA.   All right. Ask her to come in.

MAID (*to* HELMER).   And the Doctor just arrived.

HELMER.   Is he in the study?

MAID.   Yes, sir. (HELMER *exits into his study. The* MAID *shows* MRS. LINDE *in and closes the door behind her as she leaves.* MRS. LINDE *is in travel dress.*)

MRS. LINDE (*timid and a little hesitant*).   Good morning, Nora.

NORA (*uncertainly*).   Good morning.

MRS. LINDE.   I don't believe you know who I am.

NORA.   No— I'm not sure— Though I know I should— Of course! Kristine! It's you!

MRS. LINDE.   Yes, it's me.

NORA.   And I didn't even recognize you! I had no idea! (*In a lower voice.*) You've changed, Kristine.

MRS. LINDE.   I'm sure I have. It's been nine or ten long years.

NORA.   Has it really been that long? Yes, you're right. I've been so happy these last eight years. And now you're here. Such a long trip in the middle of winter. How brave!

MRS. LINDE.   I got in on the steamer this morning.

NORA.   To have some fun over the holidays, of course. That's lovely. For we are going to have fun. But take off your coat! You aren't cold, are you? (*Helps her.*) There, now! Let's sit down here by the fire and just relax and talk. No, you sit there. I want the rocking chair. (*Takes her hands.*) And now you've got your old face back. It was just for a minute, right at first— Though you are a little more pale, Kristine. And maybe a little thinner.

MRS. LINDE.   And much, much older, Nora.

NORA.   Maybe a little older. Just a teeny-weeny bit, not much. (*Interrupts herself, serious.*) Oh, but how thoughtless of me, chatting away like this! Sweet, good Kristine, can you forgive me?

MRS. LINDE.   Forgive you what, Nora?

NORA (*in a low voice*).   You poor dear, you lost your husband, didn't you?

MRS. LINDE.   Three years ago, yes.

NORA.   I know. I saw it in the paper. Oh please believe me, Kristine, I really meant to write you, but I never got around to it. Something was always coming up.

MRS. LINDE.   Of course, Nora. I understand.

NORA.   No, that wasn't very nice of me. You poor thing, all you must have been through. And he didn't leave you much, either, did he?

MRS. LINDE.   No.

NORA.   And no children?

MRS. LINDE.   No.

NORA.   Nothing at all, in other words?

MRS. LINDE.   Not so much as a sense of loss—a grief to live on—

NORA (*incredulous*).   But Kristine, how can that be?

MRS. LINDE (*with a sad smile, strokes* NORA's *hair*).   That's the way it sometimes is, Nora.

NORA.   All alone. How awful for you. I have three darling children. You can't see them right now, though; they're out with their nurse. But now you must tell me everything—

MRS. LINDE.   No, no; I'd rather listen to you.

NORA.   No, you begin. Today I won't be selfish. Today I'll think only of you. Except there's one thing I've just got to tell you first. Something marvelous that's happened to us just these last few days. You haven't heard, have you?

MRS. LINDE.   No; tell me.

NORA.   Just think. My husband's been made manager of the Mutual Bank.

MRS. LINDE.   Your husband—! Oh, I'm so glad!

NORA.   Yes, isn't that great? You see, private law practice is so uncertain, especially when you won't have anything to do with cases that aren't—you know—quite nice. And of course Torvald won't do that and I quite agree with him. Oh, you've no idea how delighted we are! He takes over at New Year's, and he'll be getting a big salary and all sorts of extras. From now on we'll be able to live in quite a different way—exactly as we like. Oh, Kristine! I feel so carefree and happy! It's lovely to have lots and lots of money and not have to worry about a thing! Don't you agree?

MRS. LINDE.   It would be nice to have enough at any rate.

NORA.   No, I don't mean just enough. I mean lots and lots!

MRS. LINDE (smiles).   Nora, Nora, when are you going to be sensible? In school you spent a great deal of money.

NORA (quietly laughing).   Yes, and Torvald says I still do. (Raising her finger at MRS. LINDE.) But "Nora, Nora" isn't so crazy as you all think. Believe me, we've had nothing to be extravagant with. We've both had to work.

MRS. LINDE.   You too?

NORA.   Yes. Oh, it's been little things, mostly—sewing, crocheting, embroidery—that sort of thing. (Casually) And other things too. You know of course, that Torvald left government service when we got married? There was no chance of promotion in his department, and of course he had to make more money than he had been making. So for the first few years he worked altogether too hard. He had to take jobs on the side and work night and day. It turned out to be too much for him. He became seriously ill. The doctors told him he needed to go south.

MRS. LINDE.   That's right, you spent a year in Italy, didn't you?

NORA.   Yes, we did. But you won't believe how hard it was to get away. Ivar had just been born. But of course we had to go. Oh, it was a wonderful trip. And it saved Torvald's life. But it took a lot of money, Kristine.

MRS. LINDE.   I'm sure it did.

NORA.   Twelve hundred specie dollars. Four thousand eight hundred crowns. That's a lot of money.

MRS. LINDE.   Yes. So it's lucky you have it when something like that happens.

NORA.   Well, actually we got the money from Daddy.

MRS. LINDE.   I see. That was about the time your father died, I believe.

NORA.   Yes, just about then. And I couldn't even go and take care of him. I was expecting little Ivar any day. And I had poor Torvald to look after, desperately sick and all. My dear, good Daddy! I never saw him again, Kristine. That's the saddest thing that's happened to me since I got married.

MRS. LINDE.   I know you were very fond of him. But then you went to Italy?

NORA.   Yes, for now we had the money and the doctors urged us to go. So we left about a month later.

MRS. LINDE.   And when you came back your husband was well again?

NORA.   Healthy as a horse!

MRS. LINDE.   But—the doctor?

NORA.   What do you mean?

MRS. LINDE.   I thought the maid said it was the doctor, that gentleman who came the same time I did.

NORA.   Oh, that's Dr. Rank. He doesn't come as a doctor. He's our closest friend. He looks in at least once every day. No, Torvald hasn't been sick once since then. And the children are strong and healthy, too, and so am I. (*Jumps up and claps her hands.*) Oh God, Kristine! Isn't it wonderful to be alive and happy! Isn't it just lovely!—But now I'm being mean again, talking only about myself and my things. (*Sits down on a footstool close to* MRS. LINDE *and puts her arms on her lap.*) Please don't be angry with me! Tell me, is it really true that you didn't care for your husband? Then why did you marry him?

MRS. LINDE.   Mother was still alive then, but she was bedridden and helpless. And I had my two younger brothers to look after. I didn't think I had the right to turn him down.

NORA.   No, I suppose not. So he had money then?

MRS. LINDE.   He was quite well off, I think. But it was an uncertain business, Nora. When he died, the whole thing collapsed and there was nothing left.

NORA.   And then—?

MRS. LINDE.   Well, I had to manage as best I could. With a little store and a little school and anything else I could think of. The last three years have been one long workday for me, Nora, without any rest. But now it's over. My poor mother doesn't need me any more. She's passed away. And the boys are on their own too. They've both got jobs and support themselves.

NORA.   What a relief for you—

MRS. LINDE.   No, not relief. Just a great emptiness. Nobody to live for any more. (*Gets up restlessly.*) That's why I couldn't stand it any longer in that little hole. Here in town it has to be easier to find something to keep me busy and occupy my thoughts. With a little luck I should be able to find a permanent job, something in an office—

NORA.   Oh but Kristine, that's exhausting work, and you look worn out already. It would be much better for you to go to a resort.

MRS. LINDE (*walks over to the window*).   I don't have a Daddy who can give me the money, Nora.

NORA (*getting up*).   Oh, don't be angry with me.

MRS. LINDE (*over to her*).   Dear Nora, don't *you* be angry with *me*. That's the worst thing about my kind of situation: you become so bitter. You've nobody to work for, and yet you have to look out for yourself, somehow. You've got to keep on living, and so you become selfish. Do you know—when you told me about your husband's new position I was delighted not so much for your sake as for my own.

NORA.   Why was that? Oh, I see. You think maybe Torvald can give you a job?

MRS. LINDE.   That's what I had in mind.

NORA.   And he will too, Kristine. Just leave it to me. I'll be ever so subtle about it. I'll think of something nice to tell him, something he'll like. Oh I so much want to help you.

MRS. LINDE.   That's very good of you, Nora—making an effort like that for me. Especially since you've known so little trouble and hardship in your own life.

NORA.   I—?—have known so little—?

MRS. LINDE (*smiling*).   Oh well, a little sewing or whatever it was. You're still a child, Nora.

NORA (*with a toss of her head, walks away*).   You shouldn't sound so superior.

MRS. LINDE.   I shouldn't?

NORA.   You're just like all the others. None of you think I'm good for anything really serious.

MRS. LINDE.   Well, now—

NORA.   That I've never been through anything difficult.

MRS. LINDE.   But Nora! You just told me all your troubles!

NORA.   That's nothing! (*Lowers her voice*) I haven't told you about *it*.

MRS. LINDE.   It? What's that? What do you mean?

NORA.   You patronize me, Kristine, and that's not fair. You're proud that you worked so long and so hard for your mother.

MRS. LINDE.   I don't think I patronize anyone. But it *is* true that I'm both proud and happy that I could make mother's last years comparatively easy.

NORA.   And you're proud of all you did for your brothers.

MRS. LINDE.   I think I have a right to be.

NORA.   And so do I. But now I want to tell you something, Kristine. I have something to be proud and happy about too.

MRS. LINDE.   I don't doubt that for a moment. But what exactly do you mean?

NORA.   Not so loud! Torvald mustn't hear—not for anything in the world. Nobody must know about this, Kristine. Nobody but you.

MRS. LINDE.   But what is it?

NORA.   Come here. (*Pulls her down on the couch beside her.*) You see, I *do* have something to be proud and happy about. I've saved Torvald's life.

MRS. LINDE.   Saved—? How do you mean—"saved"?

NORA.   I told you about our trip to Italy. Torvald would have died if he hadn't gone.

MRS. LINDE.   I understand that. And so your father gave you the money you needed.

NORA (*smiles*).   Yes, that's what Torvald and all the others think. But—

MRS. LINDE.   But what?

NORA.   Daddy didn't give us a penny. *I* raised that money.

MRS. LINDE.   *You* did? That whole big amount?

NORA.   Twelve hundred specie dollars. Four thousand eight hundred crowns. *Now* what do you say?

MRS. LINDE.   But Nora, how could you? Did you win in the state lottery?

NORA (*contemptuously*).   State lottery! (*Snorts.*) What is so great about that?

MRS. LINDE.   Where did it come from then?

NORA (*humming and smiling, enjoying her secret*).   Hmmm. Tra-la-la-la-la!

MRS. LINDE.   You certainly couldn't have borrowed it.

NORA.   Oh? And why not?

MRS. LINDE.   A wife can't borrow money without her husband's consent.

NORA (*with a toss of her head*).   Oh, I don't know—take a wife with a little bit of a head for business—a wife who knows how to manage things—

MRS. LINDE.   But Nora, I don't understand at all—

NORA.   You don't have to. I didn't say I borrowed the money, did I? I could have gotten it some other way. (*Leans back.*) An admirer may have given it to me. When you're as tolerably good-looking as I am—

MRS. LINDE.   Oh, you're crazy.

NORA.   I think you're dying from curiosity, Kristine.

MRS. LINDE.   I'm beginning to think you've done something very foolish, Nora.

NORA (*sits up*).   Is it foolish to save your husband's life?

MRS. LINDE.   I say it's foolish to act behind his back.

NORA.   But don't you see: he couldn't be told! You're missing the whole point, Kristine. We couldn't even let him know how seriously ill he was. The doctors came to *me* and told me his life was in danger, that nothing could save him but a stay in the south. Don't you think I tried to work on him? I told him how lovely it would be if I could go abroad like other young wives. I cried and begged. I said he'd better remember what condition I was in, that he had to be nice to me and do what I wanted. I even hinted he could borrow the money. But that almost made him angry with me. He told me I was being irresponsible and that it was his duty as my husband not to give in to my moods and whims— I think that's what he called it. All right, I said to myself, you've got to be saved somehow, and so I found a way—

MRS. LINDE.   And your husband never learned from your father that the money didn't come from him?

NORA.   Never. Daddy died that same week. I thought of telling him all about it and asking him not to say anything. But since he was so sick—It turned out I didn't have to—

MRS. LINDE.   And you've never told your husband?

NORA.   Of course not! Good heavens, how could I? He, with his strict principles! Besides, you know how men are. Torvald would find it embarrassing and humiliating to learn that he owed me anything. It would upset our whole relationship. Our happy, beautiful home would no longer be what it is.

MRS. LINDE.   Aren't you ever going to tell him?

NORA (*reflectively, half smiling*).   Yes—one day, maybe. Many, many years from now, when I'm no longer young and pretty. Don't laugh! I mean when Torvald no longer feels about me the way he does now, when he no longer thinks it's fun when I dance for him and put on costumes and recite for him. Then it will be good to have something in reserve—(*Interrupts herself.*) Oh, I'm just being silly! That day will never come.—Well, now, Kristine, what do you think of my great secret? Don't you think I'm good for something too?—By the way, you wouldn't believe all the worry I've had because of it. It's been very hard to meet my obligations on schedule. You see, in business there's something called quarterly interest and something called installments on the principal, and those are terribly hard to come up with. I've had to save a little here and a little there, whenever I could. I couldn't use much of the housekeeping money, for Torvald has to eat well. And I couldn't use what I got for clothes for the children. They have to look nice, and I didn't think it would be right to spend less than I got—the sweet little things!

Mrs. Linde.   Poor Nora! So you had to take it from your allowance!

Nora.   Yes, of course. After all, it was my affair. Every time Torvald gave me money for a new dress and things like that, I never used more than half of it. I always bought the cheapest, simplest things for myself. Thank God, everything looks good on me, so Torvald never noticed. But it was hard many times, Kristine, for it's fun to have pretty clothes. Don't you think?

Mrs. Linde.   Certainly.

Nora.   Anyway, I had other ways of making money too. Last winter I was lucky enough to get some copying work. So I locked the door and sat up writing every night till quite late. God! I often got so tired—! But it was great fun, too, working and making money. It was almost like being a man.

Mrs. Linde.   But how much have you been able to pay off this way?

Nora.   I couldn't tell you exactly. You see, it's very difficult to keep track of business like that. All I know is I have been paying off as much as I've been able to scrape together. Many times I just didn't know what to do. (*Smiles.*) Then I used to imagine a rich old gentleman had fallen in love with me—

Mrs. Linde.   What! What old gentleman?

Nora.   Phooey! And now he was dead and they were reading his will, and there it said in big letters, "All my money is to be paid in cash immediately to the charming Mrs. Nora Helmer."

Mrs. Linde.   But dearest Nora—who *was* this old gentleman?

Nora.   For heaven's sake, Kristine, don't you see? There *was* no old gentleman. He was just somebody I made up when I couldn't think of any way to raise the money. But never mind him. The old bore can be anyone he likes to for all I care. I have no use for him or his last will, for now I don't have a single worry in the world. (*Jumps up.*) Dear God, what a lovely thought this is! To be able to play and have fun with the children, to have everything nice and pretty in the house, just the way

Torvald likes it! Not a care! And soon spring will be here, and the air will be blue and high. Maybe we can travel again. Maybe I'll see the ocean again! Oh, yes, yes!—it's wonderful to be alive and happy! (*The doorbell rings.*)

MRS. LINDE (*getting up*).   There's the doorbell. Maybe I better be going.

NORA.   No, please stay. I'm sure it's just someone for Torvald—

MAID (*in the hall door*).   Excuse me, ma'am. There's a gentleman here who'd like to see Mr. Helmer.

NORA.   You mean the bank manager.

MAID.   Sorry, ma'am; the bank manager. But I didn't know—since the Doctor is with him—

NORA.   Who is the gentleman?

KROGSTAD (*appearing in the door*).   It's just me, Mrs. Helmer. (MRS. LINDE *starts, looks, turns away toward the window.*)

NORA (*takes a step toward him, tense, in a low voice*).   You? What do you want? What do you want with my husband?

KROGSTAD.   Bank business—in a way. I have a small job in the Mutual, and I understand your husband is going to be our new boss—

NORA.   So it's just—

KROGSTAD.   Just routine business, ma'am. Nothing else.

NORA.   All right. In that case, why don't you go through the door to the office. (*Dismisses him casually as she closes the door. Walks over to the stove and tends the fire.*)

MRS. LINDE.   Nora—who was that man?

NORA.   His name is Krogstad. He's a lawyer.

MRS. LINDE.   So it *was* him.

NORA.   Do you know him?

MRS. LINDE.   I used to—many years ago. For a while he clerked in our part of the country.

NORA.   Right. He did.

MRS. LINDE.   He has changed a great deal.

NORA.   I believe he had a very unhappy marriage.

MRS. LINDE.   And now he's a widower, isn't he?

NORA.   With many children. There now; it's burning nicely again. (*Closes the stove and moves the rocking chair a little to the side.*)

MRS. LINDE.   They say he's into all sorts of business.

NORA.   Really? Maybe so. I wouldn't know. But let's not think about business. It's such a bore.

DR. RANK (*appears in the door to* HELMER's *study*).   No, I don't want to be in the way. I'd rather talk to your wife a bit. (*Closes the door and notices* MRS. LINDE.) Oh, I beg your pardon. I believe I'm in the way here, too.

NORA.   No, not at all. (*Introduces them.*) Dr. Rank, Mrs. Linde.

RANK.   Aha. A name often heard in this house. I believe I passed you on the stairs coming up.

MRS. LINDE.   Yes. I'm afraid I climb stairs very slowly. They aren't good for me.

RANK.   I see. A slight case of inner decay, perhaps?

MRS. LINDE.   Overwork, rather.

RANK.   Oh, is that all? And now you've come to town to relax at all the parties?

MRS. LINDE.   I have come to look for a job.

RANK.   A proven cure for overwork, I take it?

MRS. LINDE.   One has to live, Doctor.

RANK.   Yes, that seems to be the common opinion.

NORA.   Come on, Dr. Rank—you want to live just as much as the rest of us.

RANK.   Of course I do. Miserable as I am, I prefer to go on being tortured as long as possible. All my patients feel the same way. And that's true of the moral invalids too. Helmer is talking with a specimen right this minute.

MRS. LINDE (*in a low voice*).   Ah!

NORA.   What do you mean?

RANK.   Oh, this lawyer, Krogstad. You don't know him. The roots of his character are decayed. But even he began by saying something about having *to live*—as if it were a matter of the highest importance.

NORA.   Oh? What did he want with Torvald?

RANK.   I don't really know. All I heard was something about the bank.

NORA.   I didn't know that Krog—that this Krogstad had anything to do with the Mutual Bank.

RANK.   Yes, he seems to have some kind of job there. (*To* MRS. LINDE) I don't know if you are familiar in your part of the country with the kind of person who is always running around trying to sniff out cases of moral decrepitude and as soon as he finds one puts the individual under observation in some excellent position or other. All the healthy ones are left out in the cold.

MRS. LINDE.   I should think it's the sick who need looking after the most.

RANK (*shrugs his shoulders*).   There we are. That's the attitude that turns society into a hospital. (NORA, *absorbed in her own thoughts, suddenly starts giggling and clapping her hands.*) What's so funny about that? Do you even know what society is?

NORA.   What do I care about your stupid society! I laughed at something entirely different—something terribly amusing. Tell me, Dr. Rank—all the employees in the Mutual Bank, from now on they'll all be dependent on Torvald, right?

RANK.   Is that what you find so enormously amusing?

NORA (*smiles and hums*).   That's my business, that's my business! (*Walks around.*) Yes, I do think it's fun that we—that Torvald is going to have so much influence on so many people's lives. (*Brings out the bag of macaroons.*) Have a macaroon, Dr. Rank.

RANK.   Well, well—macaroons. I thought they were banned around here.

NORA.   Yes, but these were some Kristine gave me.

MRS. LINDE.   What! I?

NORA.   That's all right. Don't look so scared. You couldn't know that Torvald won't let me have them. He's afraid they'll ruin my teeth. But who cares! Just once in a while—! Right, Dr. Rank? Have one! (*Puts a macaroon into his mouth.*) You too, Kristine. And one for me. A very small one. Or at most two. (*Walks around again.*) Yes, I really feel very, very happy. Now there's just one thing I'm dying to do.

RANK.   Oh? And what's that?

NORA.   Something I'm dying to say so Torvald could hear.

RANK.   And why can't you?

NORA.   I don't dare to, for it's not nice.

MRS. LINDE.   Not nice?

RANK.   In that case, I guess you'd better not. But surely to the two of us—? What is it you'd like to say for Helmer to hear?

NORA.   I want to say, "Goddammit!"

RANK.   Are you out of your mind!

MRS. LINDE.   For heaven's sakes, Nora!

RANK.   Say it. Here he comes.

NORA (*hiding the macaroons*).   Shhh! (HELMER *enters from his study, carrying his hat and overcoat.* NORA *goes to him.*) Well, dear, did you get rid of him?

HELMER.   Yes, he just left.

NORA.   Torvald, I want you to meet Kristine. She's just come to town.

HELMER.   Kristine—? I'm sorry; I don't think—

NORA.   Mrs. Linde, Torvald dear. Mrs. Kristine Linde.

HELMER.   Ah, yes. A childhood friend of my wife's, I suppose.

MRS. LINDE.   Yes, we've known each other for a long time.

NORA.   Just think; she has come all this way just to see you.

HELMER.   I'm not sure I understand—

MRS. LINDE.   Well, not really—

NORA.   You see, Kristine is an absolutely fantastic secretary, and she would so much like to work for a competent executive and learn more than she knows already—

HELMER.   Very sensible, I'm sure, Mrs. Linde.

NORA.   So when she heard about your appointment—there was a wire—she came here as fast as she could. How about it, Torvald? Couldn't you do something for Kristine? For my sake. Please?

HELMER.   Quite possibly. I take it you're a widow, Mrs. Linde?

MRS. LINDE.   Yes.

HELMER.   And you've had office experience?

MRS. LINDE.   Some—yes.

HELMER.   In that case I think it's quite likely that I'll be able to find you a position.

NORA (*claps her hands*).   I knew it! I knew it!

HELMER.   You've arrived at a most opportune time, Mrs. Linde.

MRS. LINDE.   Oh, how can I ever thank you—

HELMER.   Not at all, not at all. (*Puts his coat on.*) But today you'll have to excuse me—

RANK.   Wait a minute; I'll come with you. (*Gets his fur coat from the front hall, warms it by the stove.*)

NORA.   Don't be long, Torvald.

HELMER.   An hour or so; no more.

NORA.   Are you leaving, too, Kristine?

MRS. LINDE (*putting on her things*).   Yes, I'd better go and find a place to stay.

HELMER.   Good. Then we'll be going the same way.

NORA (*helping her*).   I'm sorry this place is so small, but I don't think we very well could—

MRS. LINDE.   Of course! Don't be silly, Nora. Goodbye, and thank you for everything.

NORA.   Goodbye. We'll see you soon. You'll be back this evening, of course. And you too, Dr. Rank; right? If you feel well enough? Of course you will. Just wrap yourself up. (*General small talk as all exit into the hall.* CHILDREN'*s voices are heard on the stairs.*) There they are! There they are! (*She runs and opens the door. The nurse* ANNE-MARIE *enters with the* CHILDREN.)

NORA.   Come in! Come in! (*Bends over and kisses them.*) Oh, you sweet, sweet darlings! Look at them, Kristine! Aren't they beautiful?

RANK.   No standing around in the draft!

HELMER.   Come along, Mrs. Linde. This place isn't fit for anyone but mothers right now. (DR. RANK, HELMER, *and* MRS. LINDE *go down the stairs. The* NURSE *enters the living room with the children.* NORA *follows, closing the door behind her.*)

NORA. My, how nice you all look! Such red cheeks! Like apples and roses. (*The* CHILDREN *all talk at the same time.*) You've had so much fun? I bet you have. Oh, isn't that nice! You pulled both Emmy and Bob on your sleigh? Both at the same time? That's very good, Ivar. Oh, let me hold her for a minute, Anne-Marie. My sweet little doll baby! (*Takes the smallest of the children from the* NURSE *and dances with her.*) Yes, yes, of course; Mama'll dance with you too, Bob. What? You threw snowballs? Oh, I wish I'd been there! No, no; *I* want to take their clothes off, Anne-Marie. Please let me; I think it's so much fun. You go on in. You look frozen. There's hot coffee on the stove. (*The* NURSE *exits into the room to the left.* NORA *takes the* CHILDREN's *wraps off and throws them all around. They all keep telling her things at the same time.*)

NORA. Oh, really? A big dog ran after you? But it didn't bite you. Of course not. Dogs don't bite sweet little doll babies. Don't peek at the packages, Ivar! What's in them? Wouldn't you like to know! No, no; that's something terrible! Play? You want to play? What do you want to play? Okay, let's play hide-and-seek. Bob hides first. You want *me* to? All right. I'll go first. (*Laughing and shouting,* NORA *and the* CHILDREN *play in the living room and in the adjacent room, right. Finally,* NORA *hides herself under the table; the* CHILDREN *rush in, look for her, can't find her. They hear her low giggle, run to the table, lift the rug that covers it, see her. General hilarity. She crawls out, pretends to scare them. New delight. In the meantime there has been a knock on the door between the living room and the front hall, but nobody has noticed. Now the door is opened halfway;* KROGSTAD *appears. He waits a little. The play goes on.*)

KROGSTAD. Pardon me, Mrs. Helmer—

NORA (*with a muted cry turns around, jumps up*). Ah! What do you want?

KROGSTAD. I'm sorry. The front door was open. Somebody must have forgotten to close it—

NORA (*standing up*). My husband isn't here, Mr. Krogstad.

KROGSTAD. I know.

NORA. So what do you want?

KROGSTAD. I'd like a word with you.

NORA. With—? (*To the* CHILDREN) Go in to Anne-Marie. What? No, the strange man won't do anything bad to Mama. When he's gone we'll play some more. (*She takes the* CHILDREN *into the room to the left and closes the door. She turns—tense, troubled.*) You want to speak with me?

KROGSTAD. Yes I do.

NORA. Today—? It isn't the first of the month yet.

KROGSTAD.   No, it's Christmas Eve. It's up to you what kind of holiday you'll have.

NORA.   What do you want? I can't possibly—

KROGSTAD.   Let's not talk about that just yet. There's something else. You do have a few minutes, don't you?

NORA.   Yes. Yes, of course. That is,—

KROGSTAD.   Good. I was sitting in Olsen's restaurant when I saw your husband go by.

NORA.   Yes—?

KROGSTAD.   —with a lady.

NORA.   What of it?

KROGSTAD.   May I be so free as to ask: wasn't that lady Mrs. Linde?

NORA.   Yes.

KROGSTAD.   Just arrived in town?

NORA.   Yes, today.

KROGSTAD.   She's a good friend of yours, I understand?

NORA.   Yes, she is. But I fail to see—

KROGSTAD.   I used to know her myself.

NORA.   I know that.

KROGSTAD.   So you know about that. I thought as much. In that case, let me ask you a simple question. Is Mrs. Linde going to be employed in the bank?

NORA.   What makes you think you have the right to cross-examine me like this, Mr. Krogstad—you, one of my husband's employees? But since you ask, I'll tell you. Yes, Mrs. Linde is going to be working in the bank. And it was I who recommended her, Mr. Krogstad. Now you know.

KROGSTAD.   So I was right.

NORA (*walks up and down*).   After all, one does have a little influence, you know. Just because you're a woman, it doesn't mean that— Really, Mr. Krogstad, people in a subordinate position should be careful not to offend someone who—oh well—

KROGSTAD.   —has influence?

NORA.   Exactly.

KROGSTAD (*changing his tone*).   Mrs. Helmer, I must ask you to be good enough to use your influence on my behalf.

NORA.   What do you mean?

KROGSTAD.   I want you to make sure that I am going to keep my subordinate position in the bank.

NORA.   I don't understand. Who is going to take your position away from you?

KROGSTAD.   There's no point in playing ignorant with me, Mrs. Helmer. I can very well appreciate that your friend will find it unpleasant to run into me. So now I know who I can thank for my dismissal.

NORA.   But I assure you—

KROGSTAD.   Never mind. Just want to say you still have time. I advise you to use your influence to prevent it.

NORA.   But Mr. Krogstad, I don't have any influence—none at all.

KROGSTAD.   No? I thought you just said—

NORA.   Of course I didn't mean it that way. I! Whatever makes you think that I have any influence of that kind on my husband?

KROGSTAD.   I went to law school with your husband. I have no reason to think that the bank manager is less susceptible than other husbands.

NORA.   If you're going to insult my husband, I'll ask you to leave.

KROGSTAD.   You're brave, Mrs. Helmer.

NORA.   I'm not afraid of you any more. After New Year's I'll be out of this thing with you.

KROGSTAD (*more controlled*).   Listen, Mrs. Helmer. If necessary I'll fight as for my life to keep my little job in the bank.

NORA.   So it seems.

KROGSTAD.   It isn't just the money; that's really the smallest part of it. There is something else— Well, I guess I might as well tell you. It's like this. I'm sure you know, like everybody else, that some years ago I committed—an impropriety.

NORA.   I believe I've heard it mentioned.

KROGSTAD.   The case never came to court, but from that moment all doors were closed to me. So I took up the kind of business you know about. I had to do something, and I think I can say about myself that I have not been among the worst. But now I want to get out of all that. My sons are growing up. For their sake I must get back as much of my good name as I can. This job in the bank was like the first rung on the ladder. And now your husband wants to kick me down and leave me back in the mud again.

NORA.   But I swear to you, Mr. Krogstad; it's not at all in my power to help you.

KROGSTAD.   That's because you don't want to. But I have the means to force you.

NORA.   You don't mean you're going to tell my husband I owe you money?

KROGSTAD.   And if I did?

NORA.   That would be a mean thing to do. (*Almost crying.*) That secret, which is my joy and my pride—for him to learn about it in such a coarse and ugly manner—to learn it from *you*—! It would be terribly unpleasant for me.

KROGSTAD.   Just unpleasant?

NORA (*heatedly*).   But go ahead! Do it! It will be worse for you than for me. When my husband realizes what a bad person you are you'll be sure to lose your job.

KROGSTAD.   I asked you if it was just domestic unpleasantness you were afraid of?

NORA.   When my husband finds out, of course he'll pay off the loan, and then we won't have anything more to do with you.

KROGSTAD (*stepping closer*).   Listen, Mrs. Helmer—either you have a very bad memory, or you don't know much about business. I think I had better straighten you out on a few things.

NORA.   What do you mean?

KROGSTAD.   When your husband was ill, you came to me to borrow twelve hundred dollars.

NORA.   I knew nobody else.

KROGSTAD.   I promised to get you the money on certain conditions. At the time you were so anxious about your husband's health and so set on getting him away that I doubt very much that you paid much attention to the details of our transaction. That's why I remind you of them now. Anyway, I promised to get you the money if you would sign an I.O.U., which I drafted.

NORA.   And which I signed.

KROGSTAD.   Good. But below your signature I added a few lines making your father security for the loan. Your father was supposed to put his signature to those lines.

NORA.   Supposed to—? He did.

KROGSTAD.   I had left the date blank. That is, your father was to date his own signature. You recall that, don't you, Mrs. Helmer?

NORA.   I guess so—

KROGSTAD.   I gave the note to you. You were to mail it to your father. Am I correct?

NORA.   Yes.

KROGSTAD.   And of course you did so right away, for no more than five or six days later you brought the paper back to me, signed by your father. Then I paid you the money.

NORA.   Well? And haven't I been keeping up with the payments?

KROGSTAD.   Fairly well, yes. But to get back to what we were talking about—those were difficult days for you, weren't they, Mrs. Helmer?

NORA.   Yes, they were.

KROGSTAD.   Your father was quite ill, I believe.

NORA.   He was dying.

KROGSTAD.   And died shortly afterwards?

NORA.   That's right.

KROGSTAD.   Tell me, Mrs. Helmer; do you happen to remember the date of your father's death? I mean the exact day of the month?

NORA.   Daddy died on September 29.

KROGSTAD.   Quite correct. I have ascertained that fact. That's why there is something peculiar about this (*takes out a piece of paper*), which I can't account for.

NORA.   Peculiar? How? I don't understand—

KROGSTAD.   It seems very peculiar, Mrs. Helmer, that your father signed this promissory note three days after his death.

NORA.   How so? I don't see what—

KROGSTAD.   Your father died on September 29. Now look. He has dated his signature October 2. Isn't that odd? (NORA *remains silent.*) Can you explain it? (NORA *is still silent.*) I also find it striking that the date and the month and the year are not in your father's handwriting but in a hand I think I recognize. Well, that might be explained. Your father may have forgotten to date his signature and somebody else may have done it here, guessing at the date before he had learned of your father's death. That's all right. It's only the signature itself that matters. And that is genuine, isn't it, Mrs. Helmer? Your father *did* put his name to this note?

NORA (*after a brief silence tosses her head back and looks defiantly at him*).   No, he didn't. *I* wrote Daddy's name.

KROGSTAD.   Mrs. Helmer—do you realize what a dangerous admission you just made?

NORA.   Why? You'll get your money soon.

KROGSTAD.   Let me ask you something. Why didn't you mail this note to your father?

NORA.   Because it was impossible. Daddy was sick—you know that. If I had asked him to sign it, I would have had to tell him what the money was for. But I couldn't tell him, as sick as he was, that my husband's life was in danger. That was impossible. Surely you can see that.

KROGSTAD.   Then it would have been better for you if you had given up your trip abroad.

NORA.   No, that was impossible! That trip was to save my husband's life. I couldn't give it up.

KROGSTAD.   But didn't you realize that what you did amounted to fraud against me?

NORA.   I couldn't let that make any difference. I didn't care about you at all. I hated the way you made all those difficulties for me, even though you knew the danger my husband was in. I thought you were cold and unfeeling.

KROGSTAD.   Mrs. Helmer, obviously you have no clear idea of what you have done. Let me tell you that what I did that time was no more and no worse. And it ruined my name and reputation.

NORA.   You! Are you trying to tell me that you did something brave once in order to save your wife's life?

KROGSTAD.   The law doesn't ask motives.

NORA.   Then it's a bad law.

KROGSTAD.   Bad or not—if I produce this note in court you'll be judged according to the law.

NORA.   I refuse to believe you. A daughter shouldn't have the right to spare her dying old father worry and anxiety? A wife shouldn't have the right to save her husband's life? I don't know the laws very well, but I'm sure that somewhere they make allowances for cases like that. And you, a lawyer, don't know that? I think you must be a bad lawyer, Mr. Krogstad.

KROGSTAD.   That may be. But business—the kind of business you and I have with one another—don't you think I know something about that? Very well. Do what you like. But let me tell you this: if I'm going to be kicked out again, you'll keep me company. (*He bows and exits through the front hall.*)

NORA (*pauses thoughtfully; then, with a defiant toss of her head*). Oh, nonsense! Trying to scare me like that! I'm not all that silly. (*Starts picking up the* CHILDREN's *clothes; soon stops.*) But—? No! That's impossible! I did it for love!

THE CHILDREN (*in the door to the left*).   Mama, the strange man just left. We saw him.

NORA.   Yes, yes; I know. But don't tell anybody about the strange man. Do you hear? Not even Daddy.

CHILDREN.   We won't. But now you'll play with us again, won't you, mama?

NORA.   No, not right now.

CHILDREN.   But Mama—you promised.

NORA.   I know, but I can't just now. Go to your own room. I've so much to do. Be nice now, my little darlings. Do as I say. (*She nudges them gently into the other room and closes the door. She sits down on the couch, picks up a piece of embroidery, makes a few stitches, then stops.*) No! (*Throws the embroidery down, goes to the hall door and calls out.*) Helene! Bring the Christmas tree in here, please! (*Goes to the table, left, opens the drawer, halts.*) No—that's impossible!

MAID (*with the Christmas tree*).   Where do you want it, ma'am?

NORA.   There. The middle of the floor.

MAID.   You want anything else?

NORA.   No, thanks. I have everything I need. (*The* MAID *goes out.* NORA *starts trimming the tree.*) I want candles—and flowers— That awful man! Oh nonsense! There's nothing wrong. This will be a lovely tree. I'll do everything you want me to, Torvald. I'll sing for you—dance for you—(HELMER, *a bundle of papers under his arm, enters from outside.*) Ah—you're back already?

HELMER.   Yes. Has anybody been here?

NORA.   Here? No.

HELMER.   That's funny. I saw Krogstad leaving just now.

NORA.   Oh? Oh yes, that's right. Krogstad was here for just a moment.

HELMER.   I can tell from your face that he came to ask you to put in a word for him.

NORA.   Yes.

HELMER.   And it was supposed to be your own idea, wasn't it? You were not to tell me he'd been here. He asked you that too, didn't he?

NORA.   Yes, Torvald, but—

HELMER.   Nora, Nora, how could you! Talk to a man like that and make him promises! And lying to me about it afterward—!

NORA.   Lying—?

HELMER.   Didn't you say nobody had been here? (*Shakes his finger at her.*) My little songbird must never do that again. Songbirds are supposed to have clean beaks to chirp with—no false notes. (*Puts his arm around her waist.*) Isn't that so? Of course it is. (*Lets her go.*) And that's enough about that. (*Sits down in front of the fireplace.*) Ah, it's nice and warm in here. (*Begins to leaf through his papers.*)

NORA (*busy with the tree; after a brief pause*).   Torvald.

HELMER.   Yes.

NORA.   I'm looking forward so much to the Stenborgs' costume party day after tomorrow.

HELMER.   And I can't wait to find out what you're going to surprise me with.

NORA.   Oh, that silly idea!

HELMER.   Oh?

NORA.   I can't think of anything. It all seems so foolish and pointless.

HELMER.   Ah, my little Nora admits that?

NORA (*behind his chair, her arms on the back of the chair*).   Are you very busy, Torvald?

HELMER.   Well—

NORA.   What are all those papers?

HELMER.   Bank business.

NORA.   Already?

HELMER.   I've asked the board to give me the authority to make certain changes in organization and personnel. That's what I'll be doing over the holidays. I want it all settled before New Year's.

NORA.   So that's why this poor Krogstad—

HELMER.   Hm.

NORA (*leisurely playing with the hair on his neck*).   If you weren't so busy, Torvald, I'd ask you for a great big favor.

HELMER.   Let's hear it, anyway.

NORA.   I don't know anyone with better taste than you, and I want so much to look nice at the party. Couldn't you sort of take charge of me, Torvald, and decide what I'll wear— Help me with my costume?

HELMER.   Aha! Little Lady Obstinate is looking for someone to rescue her?

NORA.   Yes, Torvald. I won't get anywhere without your help.

HELMER.   All right. I'll think about it. We'll come up with something.

NORA.   Oh, you *are* nice! (*Goes back to the Christmas tree. A pause.*) Those red flowers look so pretty.— Tell me, was it really all that bad what this Krogstad fellow did?

HELMER.   He forged signatures. Do you have any idea what that means?

NORA.   Couldn't it have been because he felt he had to?

HELMER.   Yes, or like so many others he may simply have been thoughtless. I'm not so heartless as to condemn a man absolutely because of a single imprudent act.

NORA.   Of course not, Torvald!

HELMER.   People like him can redeem themselves morally by openly confessing their crime and taking their punishment.

NORA.   Punishment—?

HELMER.   But that was not the way Krogstad chose. He got out of it with tricks and evasions. That's what has corrupted him.

NORA.   So you think that if—?

HELMER.   Can't you imagine how a guilty person like that has to lie and fake and dissemble wherever he goes—putting on a mask before everybody he's close to, even his own wife and children. It's the thing with the children that's the worst part of it, Nora.

NORA.   Why is that?

HELMER.   Because when a man lives inside such a circle of stinking lies he brings infection into his own home and contaminates his whole family. With every breath of air his children inhale the germs of something ugly.

NORA (*moving closer behind him*).   Are you so sure of that?

HELMER.   Of course I am. I have seen enough examples of that in my work. Nearly all young criminals have had mothers who lied.

NORA.   Why mothers—particularly?

HELMER.   Most often mothers. But of course fathers tend to have the same influence. Every lawyer knows that. And yet, for years this Krogstad has been poisoning his own children in an atmosphere of lies and deceit. That's why I call him a lost soul morally. (*Reaches out for her hands.*) And that's why my sweet little Nora must promise me never to take his side again. Let's shake on that.— What? What's this? Give me your hand. There! Now that's settled. I assure you, I would find it impossible to work in the same room with that man. I feel literally sick when I'm around people like that.

NORA (*withdraws her hand and goes to the other side of the Christmas tree*).   It's so hot in here. And I have so much to do.

HELMER (*gets up and collects his papers*).   Yes, and I really should try to get some of this reading done before dinner. I must think about your costume too. And maybe just possibly I'll have something to wrap in gilt paper and hang on the Christmas tree. (*Puts his hand on her head.*) Oh my adorable little songbird! (*Enters his study and closes the door.*)

NORA (*after a pause, in a low voice*).   It's all a lot of nonsense. It's not that way at all. It's impossible. It has to be impossible.

NURSE (*in the door, left*).   The little ones are asking ever so nicely if they can't come in and be with their mamma.

NORA.   No, no, no! Don't let them in here! You stay with them, Anne-Marie.

NURSE.   If you say so, ma'am. (*Closes the door.*)

NORA (*pale with terror*).   Corrupt my little children—! Poison my home—? (*Brief pause; she lifts her head.*) That's not true. Never. Never in a million years.

ACT 2

The same room. The Christmas tree is in the corner by the piano, stripped shabby-looking, with burnt-down candles. NORA's outside clothes are on the couch. NORA is alone. She walks around restlessly. She stops by the couch and picks up her coat.

NORA (*drops the coat again*).   There's somebody now! (*Goes to the door, listens.*) No. Nobody. Of course not—not on Christmas. And not tomorrow either.*— But perhaps— (*Opens the door and looks.*) No, nothing in the mailbox. All empty. (*Comes forward.*) How silly I am! Of course he isn't serious. Nothing like that could happen. After all, I have three small children. (*The* NURSE *enters from the room, left, carrying a big carton.*)

NURSE.   Well, at last I found it—the box with your costume.

NORA.   Thanks. Just put it on the table.

NURSE (*does so*).   But it's all a big mess, I'm afraid.

NORA.   Oh, I wish I could tear the whole thing to little pieces!

NURSE.   Heavens! It's not as bad as all that. It can be fixed all right. All it takes is a little patience.

NORA.   I'll go over and get Mrs. Linde to help me.

NURSE.   Going out again? In this awful weather? You'll catch a cold.

NORA.   That might not be such a bad thing. How are the children?

NURSE.   The poor little dears are playing with their presents, but—

NORA.   Do they keep asking for me?

NURSE.   Well, you know, they're used to being with their mamma.

NORA.   I know. But Anne-Marie, from now on I can't be with them as much as before.

NURSE.   Oh well. Little children get used to everything.

NORA.   You think so? Do you think they'd forget their mamma if I were gone altogether?

NURSE.   Goodness me—gone altogether?

NORA.   Listen, Anne-Marie—something I've wondered about. How could you bring yourself to leave your child with strangers?

NURSE.   But I had to, if I were to nurse you.

NORA.   Yes, but how could you *want* to?

NURSE.   When I could get such a nice place? When something like that happens to a poor young girl, she'd better be grateful for whatever she gets. For *he* didn't do a thing for me—the louse!

NORA.   But your daughter has forgotten all about you, hasn't she?

NURSE.   Oh no! Not at all! She wrote to me both when she was confirmed and when she got married.

NORA (*putting her arms around her neck*).   You dear old thing—you were a good mother to me when I was little.

NURSE.   Poor little Nora had no one else, you know.

NORA.   And if my little ones didn't, I know you'd—oh, I'm being silly! (*Opens the carton.*) Go in to them, please. I really should—. Tomorrow you'll see how pretty I'll be.

*In Norway both Christmas and the day after are legal holidays.

NURSE.   I know. There won't be anybody at that party half as pretty as you, ma'am. (*Goes out, left.*)

NORA (*begins to take clothes out of the carton; in a moment she throws it all down*).   If only I dared to go out. If only I knew nobody would come. That nothing would happen while I was gone.— How silly! Nobody'll come. Just don't think about it. Brush the muff. Beautiful gloves. Beautiful gloves. Forget it. Forget it. One, two, three, four, five, six—(*Cries out.*) There they are! (NORA *moves toward the door, stops irresolutely.* MRS. LINDE *enters from the hall. She has already taken off her coat.*) Oh, it's you, Kristine. There's no one else out there, is there? I'm so glad you're here.

MRS. LINDE.   They told me you'd asked for me.

NORA.   I just happened to walk by. I need your help with something—badly. Let's sit here on the couch. Look. Torvald and I are going to a costume party tomorrow night—at Consul Stenborg's upstairs—and Torvald wants me to go as a Neapolitan fisher girl and dance the tarantella. I learned it when we were on Capri.

MRS. LINDE.   Well, well! So you'll be putting on a whole show?

NORA.   Yes. Torvald thinks I should. Look, here's the costume. Torvald had it made for me while we were there. But it's all torn and everything. I just don't know—

MRS. LINDE.   Oh, that can be fixed. It's not that much. The trimmings have come loose in a few places. Do you have needle and thread? Ah, here we are. All set.

NORA.   I really appreciate it, Kristine.

MRS. LINDE (*sewing*).   So you'll be in disguise tomorrow night, eh? You know—I may come by for just a moment, just to look at you.— Oh dear. I haven't even thanked you for the nice evening last night.

NORA (*gets up, moves around*).   Oh, I don't know. I don't think last night was as nice as it usually is.— You should have come to town a little earlier, Kristine.— Yes, Torvald knows how to make it nice and pretty around here.

MRS. LINDE.   You too, I should think. After all, you're your father's daughter. By the way, is Dr. Rank always as depressed as he was last night?

NORA.   No, last night was unusual. He's a very sick man, you know—very sick. Poor Rank, his spine is rotting away. Tuberculosis, I think. You see, his father was a nasty old man with mistresses and all that sort of thing. Rank has been sickly ever since he was a little boy.

MRS. LINDE (*dropping her sewing to her lap*).   But dearest Nora, where have you learned about things like that?

NORA (*still walking about*).   Oh, you know—with three children you sometimes get to talk with—other wives. Some of them know quite a bit about medicine. So you pick up a few things.

MRS. LINDE (*resumes her sewing; after a brief pause*).   Does Dr. Rank come here every day?

NORA.   Every single day. He's Torvald's oldest and best friend, after all. And my friend too, for that matter. He's part of the family, almost.

MRS. LINDE.   But tell me, is he quite sincere? I mean, isn't he the kind of man who likes to say nice things to people?

NORA.   No, not at all. Rather the opposite, in fact. What makes you say that?

MRS. LINDE.   When you introduced me yesterday, he told me he'd often heard my name mentioned in the house. But later on it was quite obvious your husband really had no idea who I was. So how could Dr. Rank—?

NORA.   You're right, Kristine, but I can explain that. You see, Torvald loves me so very much that he wants me all to himself. That's what he says. When we were first married he got almost jealous when I as much as mentioned anybody from back home that I was fond of. So of course I soon stopped doing that. But with Dr. Rank I often talk about home. You see, he likes to listen to me.

MRS. LINDE.   Look here, Nora. In many ways you're still a child. After all, I'm quite a bit older than you and have had more experience. I want to give you a piece of advice. I think you should get out of this thing with Dr. Rank.

NORA.   Get out of what thing?

MRS. LINDE.   Several things in fact, if you want my opinion. Yesterday you said something about a rich admirer who was going to give you money—

NORA.   One who doesn't exist, unfortunately. What of it?

MRS. LINDE.   Does Dr. Rank have money?

NORA.   Yes, he does.

MRS. LINDE.   And no dependents?

NORA.   No. But—?

MRS. LINDE.   And he comes here every day?

NORA.   Yes, I told you that already.

MRS. LINDE.   But how can that sensitive man be so tactless?

NORA.   I haven't the slightest idea what you're talking about.

MRS. LINDE.   Don't play games with me, Nora. Don't you think I know who you borrowed the twelve hundred dollars from?

NORA.   Are you out of your mind! The very idea—! A friend of both of us who sees us every day—! What a dreadfully uncomfortable position that would be!

MRS. LINDE.   So it really isn't Dr. Rank?

NORA.   Most certainly not! I would never have dreamed of asking him—not for a moment. Anyway, he didn't have any money then. He inherited it afterwards.

MRS. LINDE.   Well, I still think it may have been lucky for you, Nora dear.

NORA.   The idea! It would never have occurred to me to ask Dr. Rank—. Though I'm sure that if I *did* ask him—

MRS. LINDE.   But of course you wouldn't.

NORA.   Of course not. I can't imagine that that would ever be necessary. But I am quite sure that if I told Dr. Rank—

MRS. LINDE.   Behind your husband's back?

NORA.   I must get out of—this other thing. That's also behind his back. I *must* get out of it.

MRS. LINDE.   That's what I told you yesterday. But—

NORA (*walking up and down*).   A man manages these things so much better than a woman—

MRS. LINDE.   One's husband, yes.

NORA.   Silly, silly! (*Stops.*) When you've paid off all you owe, you get your I.O.U. back; right?

MRS. LINDE.   Yes, of course.

NORA.   And you can tear it into a hundred thousand little pieces and burn it—that dirty, filthy, paper!

MRS. LINDE (*looks hard at her, puts down her sewing, rising slowly*). Nora—you're hiding something from me.

NORA.   Can you tell?

MRS. LINDE.   Something's happened to you, Nora, since yesterday morning. What is it?

NORA (*going to her*).   Kristine! (*Listens.*) Shhh. Torvald just came back. Listen. Why don't you go in to the children for a while. Torvald can't stand having sewing around. Get Anne-Marie to help you.

MRS. LINDE (*gathers some of the sewing things together*).   All right, but I'm not leaving here till you and I have talked. (*She goes out left, just as* HELMER *enters from the front hall.*)

NORA (*towards him*).   I have been waiting and waiting for you, Torvald.

HELMER.   Was that the dressmaker?

NORA.   No, it was Kristine. She's helping me with my costume. Oh Torvald, just wait till you see how nice I'll look!

HELMER.   I told you. Pretty good idea I had, wasn't it?

NORA.   Lovely! And wasn't it nice of me to go along with it?

HELMER (*his hand under her chin*).   Nice? To do what your husband tells you? All right, you little rascal; I know you didn't mean it that way. But don't let me interrupt you. I suppose you want to try it on.

NORA.   And you'll be working?

HELMER.   Yes. (*Shows her a pile of papers.*) Look. I've been down to the bank. (*Is about to enter his study.*)

NORA.   Torvald.

HELMER (*halts*).   Yes?

NORA.   What if your little squirrel asked you ever so nicely—

HELMER.   For what?

NORA.   Would you do it?

HELMER.   Depends on what it is.

NORA.   Squirrel would run around and do all sorts of fun tricks if you'd be nice and agreeable.

HELMER.   All right. What is it?

NORA.   Lark would chirp and twitter in all the rooms, up and down—

HELMER.   So what? Lark does that anyway.

NORA.   I'll be your elfmaid and dance for you in the moonlight, Torvald.

HELMER.   Nora, don't tell me it's the same thing you mentioned this morning?

NORA (*closer to him*).   Yes, Torvald. I beg you!

HELMER.   You really have the nerve to bring that up again?

NORA.   Yes. You've just got to do as I say. You *must* let Krogstad keep his job.

HELMER.   My dear Nora. It's his job I intend to give to Mrs. Linde.

NORA.   I know. And that's ever so nice of you. But can't you just fire someone else?

HELMER.   This is incredible! You just don't give up do you? Because you make some foolish promise, *I* am supposed to—!

NORA.   That's not the reason, Torvald. It's for your own sake. That man writes for the worst newspapers. You've said so yourself. There's no telling what he may do to you. I'm scared to death of him.

HELMER.   Ah, I understand. You're afraid because of what happened before.

NORA.   What do you mean?

HELMER.   You're thinking of your father, of course.

NORA.   Yes. You're right. Remember the awful things they wrote about Daddy in the newspapers. I really think they might have forced him to resign if the ministry hadn't sent you to look into the charges and if you hadn't been so helpful and understanding.

HELMER.   My dear little Nora, there is a world of difference be-tween your father and me. Your father's official conduct was not above reproach. Mine is, and I intend for it to remain that way as long as I hold my position.

NORA.   Oh, but you don't know what vicious people like that may think of. Oh, Torvald! Now all of us could be so happy together here in our own home, peaceful and carefree. Such a good life, Torvald, for you and me and the children! That's why I implore you—

HELMER.   And it's exactly because you plead for him that you make it impossible for me to keep him. It's already common knowledge in the bank that I intend to let Krogstad go. If it gets out that the new manager has changed his mind because of his wife—

NORA.   Yes? What then?

HELMER.   No, of course, that wouldn't matter at all as long as little Mrs. Pighead here got her way! Do you want me to make myself look ridiculous before my whole staff—make people think I can be swayed by just anybody—by outsiders? Believe me, I would soon enough find out what the consequences would be! Besides, there's an-other thing that makes it absolutely impossible for Krogstad to stay on in the bank now that I'm in charge.

NORA.   What's that?

HELMER.   I suppose in a pinch I could overlook his moral short-comings—

NORA.   Yes, you could; couldn't you, Torvald?

HELMER.   And I understand he's quite a good worker, too. But we've known each other for a long time. It's one of those imprudent re-lationships you get into when you're young that embarrass you for the rest of your life. I guess I might as well be frank with you: he and I are on a first-name basis. And that tactless fellow never hides the fact even when other people are around. Rather, he seems to think it entitles him to be familiar with me. Every chance he gets he comes out with his damn "Torvald, Torvald." I'm telling you, I find it most awkward. He would make my position in the bank intolerable.

NORA.   You don't really mean any of this, Torvald.

HELMER.   Oh? I don't? And why not?

NORA.   No, for it's all so petty.

HELMER.   What! Petty? You think I'm being petty!

NORA.   No, I *don't* think you are petty, Torvald dear. That's ex-actly why I—

HELMER.   Never mind. You think my reasons are petty, so it fol-lows that I must be petty too. Petty! Indeed! By God, I'll put an end

to this right now! (*Opens the door to the front hall and calls out.*)
Helene!

NORA. What are you doing?

HELMER (*searching among his papers*). Making a decision. (*The
MAID enters.*) Here. Take this letter. Go out with it right away. Find
somebody to deliver it. But quick. The address is on the envelope.
Wait. Here's money.

MAID. Very good sir. (*She takes the letter and goes out.*)

HELMER (*collecting his papers*). There now, little Mrs. Obstinate!

NORA (*breathless*). Torvald—what was that letter?

HELMER. Krogstad's dismissal.

NORA. Call it back, Torvald! There's still time! Oh Torvald,
please—call it back! For my sake, for your own sake, for the sake of the
children! Listen to me, Torvald! Do it! You don't know what you're doing to all of us!

HELMER. Too late.

NORA. Yes. Too late.

HELMER. Dear Nora, I forgive you this fear you're in, although it
really is an insult to me. Yes, it is! It's an insult to think that I am
scared of a shabby scrivener's revenge. But I forgive you, for it's such a
beautiful proof of how much you love me. (*Takes her in his arms.*) And
that's the way it should be, my sweet darling. Whatever happens you'll
see that when things get really rough I have both strength and
courage. You'll find out that I am man enough to shoulder the whole
burden.

NORA (*terrified*). What do you mean by that?

HELMER. All of it, I tell you—

NORA (*composed*). You'll never have to do that.

HELMER. Good. Then we'll share the burden, Nora—like husband and wife, the way it ought to be. (*Caresses her.*) Now are you satisfied? There, there, there. Not that look in your eyes—like a frightened
dove. It's all your own foolish imagination.— Why don't you practice
the tarantella—and your tambourine, too. I'll be in the inner office and
close both doors, so I won't hear you. You can make as much noise as
you like. (*Turning in the doorway.*) And when Rank comes, tell him
where to find me. (*He nods to her, enters his study carrying his papers, and
closes the door.*)

NORA (*transfixed by terror, whispers*). He would do it. He'll do
it. He'll do it in spite of the whole world.— No, this mustn't happen.
Anything rather than that! There must be a way—! (*The doorbell
rings.*) Dr. Rank! Anything rather than that! Anything—anything at
all! (*She passes her hand over her face, pulls herself together, and opens the
door to the hall. DR. RANK is out there, hanging up his coat. Darkness be-

gins to fall during the following scene.) Hello there, Dr. Rank. I recognized your ringing. Don't go in to Torvald yet. I think he's busy.

RANK.   And you?

NORA (*as he enters and she closes the door behind him*).   You know I always have time for you.

RANK.   Thanks. I'll make use of that as long as I can.

NORA.   What do you mean by that— As long as you can?

RANK.   Does that frighten you?

NORA.   Well, it's a funny expression. As if something was going to happen.

RANK.   Something is going to happen that I've long been expecting. But I admit I hadn't thought it would come quite so soon.

NORA (*seizes his arm*).   What is it you've found out? Dr. Rank— tell me!

RANK (*sits down by the stove*).   I'm going downhill fast. There's nothing to do about that.

NORA (*with audible relief*).   So it's you—

RANK.   Who else? No point in lying to myself. I'm in worse shape than any of my other patients, Mrs. Helmer. These last few days I've been making up my inner status. Bankrupt. Chances are that within a month I'll be rotting up in the cemetery.

NORA.   Shame on you! Talking that horrid way!

RANK.   The thing itself is horrid—damn horrid. The worst of it, though, is all that other horror that comes first. There is only one more test I need to make. After that I'll have a pretty good idea when I'll start coming apart. There is something I want to say to you. Helmer's refined nature can't stand anything hideous. I don't want him in my sick room.

NORA.   Oh, but Dr. Rank—

RANK.   I don't want him there. Under no circumstance. I'll close my door to him. As soon as I have full certainty that the worst is about to begin I'll give you my card with a black cross on it. Then you'll know the last horror of destruction has started.

NORA.   Today you're really quite impossible. And I had hoped you'd be in a particularly good mood.

RANK.   With death on my hands? Paying for someone else's sins? Is there justice in that? And yet there isn't a single family that isn't ruled by the same law of ruthless retribution, in one way or another.

NORA (*puts her hands over her ears*).   Poppycock! Be fun! Be fun!

RANK.   Well, yes. You may just as well laugh at the whole thing. My poor, innocent spine is suffering from my father's frolics as a young lieutenant.

NORA (*over by the table, left*).   Right. He was addicted to asparagus and goose liver paté, wasn't he?

RANK.   And truffles.

NORA.   Of course. Truffles. And oysters too, I think.

RANK.   And oysters. Obviously.

NORA.   And all the port and champagne that go with it. It's really too bad that goodies like that ruin your backbone.

RANK.   Particularly an unfortunate backbone that never enjoyed any of it.

NORA.   Ah yes, that's the saddest part of all.

RANK (*looks searchingly at her*).   Hm—

NORA (*after a brief pause*).   Why did you smile just then?

RANK.   No, it was you that laughed.

NORA.   No, it was you that smiled, Dr. Rank!

RANK (*gets up*).   You're more of a mischief-maker than I thought.

NORA.   I feel in the mood for mischief today.

RANK.   So it seems.

NORA (*with both her hands on his shoulders*).   Dear, dear Dr. Rank, don't you go and die and leave Torvald and me.

RANK.   Oh, you won't miss me for very long. Those who go away are soon forgotten.

NORA (*with an anxious look*).   Do you believe that?

RANK.   You'll make new friends, and then—

NORA.   Who'll make new friends?

RANK.   Both you and Helmer, once I'm gone. You yourself seem to have made a good start already. What was this Mrs. Linde doing here last night?

NORA.   Aha—Don't tell me you're jealous of poor Kristine?

RANK.   Yes, I am. She'll be my successor in this house. As soon as I have made my excuses, that woman is likely to—

NORA.   Shh—not so loud. She's in there.

RANK.   Today too? There you are!

NORA.   She's mending my costume. My God, you really *are* unreasonable. (*Sits down on the couch.*) Now be nice, Dr. Rank. Tomorrow you'll see how beautifully I'll dance, and then you are to pretend I'm dancing just for you—and for Torvald too, of course. (*Takes several items out of the carton.*) Sit down, Dr. Rank; I want to show you something.

RANK (*sitting down*).   What?

NORA.   Look.

RANK.   Silk stockings.

NORA.   Flesh-colored. Aren't they lovely? Now it's getting dark in here, but tomorrow— No, no. You only get to see the foot. Oh well, you might as well see all of it.

RANK.   Hmm.

NORA.   Why do you look so critical? Don't you think they'll fit?

RANK.   That's something I can't possibly have a reasoned opinion about.

NORA (*looks at him for a moment*).   Shame on you. (*Slaps his ear lightly with the stocking.*) That's what you get. (*Puts the things back in the carton.*)

RANK.   And what other treasures are you going to show me?

NORA.   Nothing at all, because you're naughty. (*She hums a little and rummages in the carton.*)

RANK (*after a brief silence*).   When I sit here like this, talking confidently with you, I can't imagine—I can't possibly imagine what would have become of me if I hadn't had you and Helmer.

NORA (*smiles*).   Well, yes—I do believe you like being with us.

RANK (*in a lower voice, lost in thought*).   And then to have to go away from it all—

NORA.   Nonsense. You are not going anywhere.

RANK (*as before*).   —and not to leave behind as much as a poor little token of gratitude, hardly a brief memory of someone missed, nothing but a vacant place that anyone can fill.

NORA.   And what if I were to ask you—? No—

RANK.   Ask me what?

NORA.   For a great proof of your friendship—

RANK.   Yes, yes—?

NORA.   No, I mean—for an enormous favor—

RANK.   Would you really for once make me as happy as all that?

NORA.   But you don't even know what it is.

RANK.   Well, then; tell me.

NORA.   Oh, but I can't, Dr. Rank. It's altogether too much to ask —It's advice and help and a favor—

RANK.   So much the better. I can't even begin to guess what it is you have in mind. So for heaven's sake tell me! Don't you trust me?

NORA.   Yes, I trust you more than anyone else I know. You are my best and most faithful friend. I know that. So I will tell you. All right, Dr. Rank. There is something you can help me prevent. You know how much Torvald loves me—beyond all words. Never for a moment would he hesitate to give his life for me.

RANK (*leaning over to her*).   Nora—do you really think he's the only one?

NORA (*with a slight start*).   Who—?

RANK.   —would gladly give his life for you.

NORA (*heavily*).   I see.

RANK.   I have sworn an oath to myself to tell you before I go. I'll never find a better occasion.— All right, Nora; now you know. And now you also know that you can confide in me more than in anyone else.

NORA (*gets up; in a calm, steady voice*).   Let me get by.

RANK (*makes room for her but remains seated*).   Nora—

NORA (*in the door to the front hall*).   Helene, bring the lamp in here, please. (*Walks over to the stove.*) Oh, dear Dr. Rank. That really wasn't very nice of you.

RANK (*gets up*).   That I have loved you as much as anybody—was that not nice?

NORA.   No; not that. But that you told me. There was no need for that.

RANK.   What do you mean? Have you known—? (*The* MAID *enters with the lamp, puts it on the table, and goes out.*) Nora—Mrs. Helmer —I'm asking you: did you know?

NORA.   Oh, how can I tell what I knew and didn't know! I really can't say— But that you could be so awkward, Dr. Rank! Just when everything was so comfortable.

RANK.   Well, anyway, now you know that I'm at your service with my life and soul. And now you must speak.

NORA (*looks at him*).   After what just happened?

RANK.   I beg of you—let me know what it is.

NORA.   There is nothing I can tell you now.

RANK.   Yes, yes. You mustn't punish me this way. Please let me do for you whatever anyone *can* do.

NORA.   Now there is nothing you can do. Besides, I don't think I really need any help, anyway. It's probably just my imagination. Of course that's all it is. I'm sure of it! (*Sits down in the rocking chair, looks at him, smiles.*) Well, well, well, Dr. Rank! What a fine gentleman you turned out to be! Aren't you ashamed of yourself, now that we have light?

RANK.   No, not really. But perhaps I ought to leave—and not come back?

NORA.   Don't be silly; of course not! You'll come here exactly as you have been doing. You know perfectly well that Torvald can't do without you.

RANK.   Yes, but what about you?

NORA.   Oh, I always think it's perfectly delightful when you come.

RANK.   That's the very thing that misled me. You are a riddle to me. It has often seemed to me that you'd just as soon be with me as with Helmer.

NORA.   Well, you see, there are people you love, and then there are other people you'd almost rather be with.

RANK.   Yes, there is something in that.

NORA.   When I lived at home with Daddy, of course I loved him most. But I always thought it was so much fun to sneak off down to the maids' room, for they never gave me advice and they always talked about such fun things.

RANK.   Aha! So it's *their* place I have taken.

NORA (*jumps up and goes over to him*).   Oh dear, kind Dr. Rank, you know very well I didn't mean it that way. Can't you see that with Torvald it is the way it used to be with Daddy? (*The* MAID *enters from the front hall.*)

MAID.   Ma'am! (*Whispers to her and gives her a caller's card.*)

NORA (*glances at the card*).   Ah! (*Puts it in her pocket.*)

RANK.   Anything wrong?

NORA.   No, no; not at all. It's nothing—just my new costume—

RANK.   But your costume is lying right there!

NORA.   Oh yes, that one. But this is another one. I ordered it. Torvald mustn't know—

RANK.   Aha. So that's the great secret.

NORA.   That's it. Why don't you go in to him, please. He's in the inner office. And keep him there for a while—

RANK.   Don't worry. He won't get away. (*Enters* HELMER's *study.*)

NORA (*to the* MAID).   You say he's waiting in the kitchen?

MAID.   Yes. He came up the back stairs.

NORA.   But didn't you tell him there was somebody with me?

MAID.   Yes, but he wouldn't listen.

NORA.   He won't leave?

MAID.   No, not till he's had a word with you, ma'am.

NORA.   All right. But try not to make any noise. And, Helene— don't tell anyone he's here. It's supposed to be a surprise for my husband.

MAID.   I understand ma'am— (*She leaves.*)

NORA.   The terrible is happening. It's happening after all. No, no, no. It can't happen. It won't happen. (*She bolts the study door. The* MAID *opens the front hall door for* KROGSTAD *and closes the door behind him. He wears a fur coat for traveling, boots, and a fur hat.* NORA *goes toward him.*) Keep your voice down. My husband's home.

KROGSTAD.   That's all right.

NORA.   What do you want?

KROGSTAD.   To find out something.

NORA.   Be quick, then. What is it?

KROGSTAD.   I expect you know I've been fired.

NORA. I couldn't prevent it, Mr. Krogstad. I fought for you as long and as hard as I could but it didn't do any good.

KROGSTAD. Your husband doesn't love you any more than that? He knows what I can do to you, and yet he runs the risk—

NORA. Surely you didn't think I'd tell him?

KROGSTAD. No, I really didn't. It wouldn't be like Torvald Helmer to show that kind of guts—

NORA. Mr. Krogstad, I insist that you show respect for my husband.

KROGSTAD. By all means. All due respect. But since you're so anxious to keep this a secret, may I assume that you are a little better informed than yesterday about exactly what you have done?

NORA. Better than *you* could ever teach me.

KROGSTAD. Of course. Such a bad lawyer as I am—

NORA. What do you want of me?

KROGSTAD. I just wanted to find out how you are, Mrs. Helmer. I've been thinking about you all day. You see, even a bill collector, a pen pusher, a—anyway, someone like me—even he has a little of what they call a heart.

NORA. Then show it. Think of my little children.

KROGSTAD. Have you and your husband thought of mine? Never mind. All I want to tell you is that you don't need to take this business too seriously. I have no intentions of bringing charges right away.

NORA. Oh no, you wouldn't; would you? I knew you wouldn't.

KROGSTAD. The whole thing can be settled quite amiably. Nobody else needs to know anything. It will be between the three of us.

NORA. My husband must never find out about this.

KROGSTAD. How are you going to prevent that? Maybe you can pay me the balance of your loan?

NORA. No, not right now.

KROGSTAD. Or do you have a way of raising the money one of these next few days?

NORA. None I intend to make use of.

KROGSTAD. It wouldn't do you any good anyway. Even if you had the cash in your hand right this minute, I wouldn't give you your note back. It wouldn't make any difference *how* much money you offered me.

NORA. Then you'll have to tell what you plan to use the note *for.*

KROGSTAD. Just keep it; that's all. Have it on hand, so to speak. I won't say a word to anybody else. So if you've been thinking about doing something desperate—

NORA. I have.

KROGSTAD.   —like leaving house and home—

NORA.   I have.

KROGSTAD.   —or even something worse—

NORA.   How did you know?

KROGSTAD.   —then: don't.

NORA.   How did you know I was thinking of *that*?

KROGSTAD.   Most of us do, right at first. I did, too, but when it came down to it I didn't have the courage—

NORA (*tonelessly*).   Nor do I.

KROGSTAD (*relieved*).   See what I mean? I thought so. You don't either.

NORA.   I don't. I don't.

KROGSTAD.   Besides, it would be very silly of you. Once that first domestic blowup is behind you—. Here in my pocket is a letter for your husband.

NORA.   Telling him everything?

KROGSTAD.   As delicately as possible.

NORA (*quickly*).   He mustn't get that letter. Tear it up. I'll get you the money somehow.

KROGSTAD.   Excuse me, Mrs. Helmer, I thought I just told you—

NORA.   I'm not talking about the money I owe you. Just let me know how much money you want from my husband, and I'll get it for you.

KROGSTAD.   I want no money from your husband.

NORA.   Then, what *do* you want?

KROGSTAD.   I'll tell you, Mrs. Helmer. I want to rehabilitate myself; I want to get up in the world; and your husband is going to help me. For a year and a half I haven't done anything disreputable. All that time I have been struggling with the most miserable circumstances. I was content to work my way up step by step. Now I've been kicked out, and I'm no longer satisfied just getting my old job back. I want more than that; I want to get to the top. I'm being quite serious. I want the bank to take me back but in a higher position. I want your husband to create a new job for me—

NORA.   He'll never do that!

KROGSTAD.   He will. I know him. He won't dare not to. And once I'm back inside and he and I are working together, you'll see! Within a year I'll be the manager's right hand. It will be Nils Krogstad and not Torvald Helmer who'll be running the Mutual Bank!

NORA.   You'll never see that happen!

KROGSTAD.   Are you thinking of—?

NORA.   Now I *do* have the courage.

KROGSTAD.   You can't scare me. A fine, spoiled lady like you—
NORA.   You'll see, you'll see!
KROGSTAD.   Under the ice, perhaps? Down into that cold, black water? Then spring comes and you float up again—hideous, can't be identified, hair all gone—
NORA.   You don't frighten me.
KROGSTAD.   Nor you me. One doesn't do that sort of thing, Mrs. Helmer. Besides, what good would it do? He'd still be in my power.
NORA.   Afterwards? When I'm no longer—?
KROGSTAD.   Aren't you forgetting that your reputation would be in my hands? (NORA *stares at him, speechless.*) All right; now I've told you what to expect. So don't do anything foolish. When Helmer gets my letter I expect to hear from him. And don't you forget that it's your husband himself who forces me to use such means again. That I'll never forgive him. Goodbye, Mrs. Helmer. (*Goes out through the hall.*)
NORA (*at the door, opens it a little, listens*).   He's going. And no letter. Of course not! That would be impossible! (*Opens the door more.*) What's he doing? He's still there. Doesn't go down. Having second thoughts—? Will he—? (*The sound of a letter dropping into the mailbox. Then* KROGSTAD's *steps are heard going down the stairs, gradually dying away. With a muted cry* NORA *runs forward to the table by the couch; brief pause.*) In the mailbox. (*Tiptoes back to the door to the front hall.*) There it is. Torvald, Torvald—now we're lost!
MRS. LINDE (*enters from the left, carrying* NORA's *Capri costume*). There now. I think it's all fixed. Why don't we try it on you—
NORA (*in a low, hoarse voice*).   Kristine, come here.
MRS. LINDE.   What's wrong with you? You look quite beside yourself.
NORA.   Come over here. Do you see that letter? There, look—through the glass in the mailbox.
MRS. LINDE.   Yes, yes; I see it.
NORA.   That letter is from Krogstad.
MRS. LINDE.   Nora—it was Krogstad who lent you the money!
NORA.   Yes, and now Torvald will find out about it.
MRS. LINDE.   Oh believe me, Nora. That's the best thing for both of you.
NORA.   There's more to it than you know. I forged a signature—
MRS. LINDE.   Oh my God—!
NORA.   I just want to tell you this, Kristine, that you must be my witness.
MRS. LINDE.   Witness? How? Witness to what?
NORA.   If I lose my mind—and that could very well happen—
MRS. LINDE.   Nora!

NORA.   —or if something were to happen to me—something that made it impossible for me to be here—

MRS. LINDE.   Nora, Nora! You're not yourself!

NORA.   —and if someone were to take all the blame, assume the whole responsibility— Do you understand—?

MRS. LINDE.   Yes, yes; but how can you think—!

NORA.   Then you are to witness that that's not so, Kristine. I am not beside myself. I am perfectly rational, and what I'm telling you is that nobody else has known about this. I've done it all by myself, the whole thing. Just remember that.

MRS. LINDE.   I will. But I don't understand any of it.

NORA.   Oh, how could you! For it's the wonderful that's about to happen.

MRS. LINDE.   The wonderful?

NORA.   Yes, the wonderful. But it's so terrible, Kristine. It mustn't happen for anything in the whole world.

MRS. LINDE.   I'm going over to talk to Krogstad right now.

NORA.   No, don't. Don't go to him. He'll do something bad to you.

MRS. LINDE.   There was a time when he would have done anything for me.

NORA.   He!

MRS. LINDE.   Where does he live?

NORA.   Oh, I don't know— Yes, wait a minute— (Reaches into her pocket.) Here's his card.— But the letter, the letter—!

HELMER (in his study, knocks on the door).   Nora!

NORA (cries out in fear).   Oh, what is it? What do you want?

HELMER.   That's all right. Nothing to be scared about. We're not coming in. For one thing, you've bolted the door, you know. Are you modeling your costume?

NORA.   Yes, yes; I am. I'm going to be so pretty, Torvald!

MRS. LINDE (having looked at the card).   He lives just around the corner.

NORA.   Yes, but it's no use. Nothing can save us now. The letter is in the mailbox.

MRS. LINDE.   And your husband has the key?

NORA.   Yes. He always keeps it with him.

MRS. LINDE.   Krogstad must ask for his letter back, unread. He's got to think up some pretext or other—

NORA.   But this is just the time of day when Torvald—

MRS. LINDE.   Delay him. Go in to him. I'll be back as soon as I can. (She hurries out through the hall door.)

NORA (walks over to HELMER's door, opens it, and peeks in). Torvald.

HELMER (*still offstage*).   Well, well! So now one's allowed in one's own living room again. Come on, Rank. Now we'll see— (*In the doorway.*) But what's this?

NORA.   What, Torvald dear?

HELMER.   Rank prepared me for a splendid metamorphosis.

RANK (*in the doorway*).   That's how I understood it. Evidently I was mistaken.

NORA.   Nobody gets to admire me in my costume before tomorrow.

HELMER.   But, dearest Nora—you look all done in. Have you been practicing too hard?

NORA.   No, I haven't practiced at all.

HELMER.   But you'll have to, you know.

NORA.   I know it, Torvald. I simply must. But I can't do a thing unless you help me. I have forgotten everything.

HELMER.   Oh it will all come back. We'll work on it.

NORA.   Oh yes, please, Torvald. You just have to help me. Promise? I am so nervous. That big party—. You mustn't do anything else tonight. Not a bit of business. Don't even touch a pen. Will you promise, Torvald?

HELMER.   I promise. Tonight I'll be entirely at your service—you helpless little thing.— Just a moment, though. First I want to— (*Goes to the door to the front hall.*)

NORA.   What are you doing out there?

HELMER.   Just looking to see if there's any mail.

NORA.   No, no! Don't, Torvald!

HELMER.   Why not?

NORA.   Torvald, I beg you. There is no mail.

HELMER.   Let me just look, anyway. (*Is about to go out. NORA by the piano, plays the first bars of the tarantella dance. HELMER halts at the door.*) Aha!

NORA.   I won't be able to dance tomorrow if I don't get to practice with you.

HELMER (*goes to her*).   Are you really all that scared, Nora dear?

NORA.   Yes, so terribly scared. Let's try it right now. There's still time before we eat. Oh please sit down and play for me, Torvald. Teach me, coach me, the way you always do.

HELMER.   Of course I will, my darling, if that's what you want. (*Sits down at the piano. NORA takes the tambourine out of the carton, as well as a long, many-colored shawl. She quickly drapes the shawl around herself, then leaps into the middle of the floor.*)

NORA.   Play for me! I want to dance! (HELMER *plays and* NORA *dances.* DR. RANK *stands by the piano behind* HELMER *and watches.*)

HELMER (*playing*).   Slow down, slow down!

NORA.   Can't!

HELMER.   Not so violent, Nora!

NORA.   It has to be this way.

HELMER (*stops playing*).   No, no. This won't do at all.

NORA (*laughing, swinging her tambourine*).   What did I tell you?

RANK.   Why don't you let me play?

HELMER (*getting up*).   Good idea. Then I can direct her better. (RANK *sits down at the piano and starts playing.* NORA *dances more and more wildly.* HELMER *stands over by the stove, repeatedly correcting her. She doesn't seem to hear. Her hair comes loose and falls down over her shoulders. She doesn't notice but keeps on dancing.* MRS. LINDE *enters.*)

MRS. LINDE (*stops by the door, dumbfounded*).   Ah—!

NORA (*dancing*).   We're having such fun, Kristine!

HELMER.   My dearest Nora, you're dancing as if it were a matter of life and death!

NORA.   It is! It is!

HELMER.   Rank, stop. This is sheer madness. Stop I say! (RANK *stops playing;* NORA *suddenly stops dancing.* HELMER *goes over to her.*) If I hadn't seen it I wouldn't have believed it. You've forgotten every single thing I ever taught you.

NORA (*tosses away the tambourine*).   See? I told you.

HELMER.   Well! You certainly need coaching.

NORA.   Didn't I tell you I did? Now you've seen for yourself. I'll need your help till the very minute we're leaving for the party. Will you promise, Torvald?

HELMER.   You can count on it.

NORA.   You're not to think of anything except me—not tonight and not tomorrow. You're not to read any letters—not to look in the mailbox—

HELMER.   Ah, I see. You're still afraid of that man.

NORA.   Yes—yes, that too.

HELMER.   Nora, I can tell from looking at you. There's a letter from him out there.

NORA.   I don't know. I think so. But you're not to read it now. I don't want anything ugly to come between us before it's all over.

RANK (*to* HELMER *in a low voice*).   Better not argue with her.

HELMER (*throws his arm around her*).   The child shall have her way. But tomorrow night, when you've done your dance—

NORA. Then you'll be free.

MAID (*in the door, right*).   Dinner can be served any time, ma'am.

NORA. We want champagne, Helene.

MAID. Very good, ma'am. (*Goes out.*)

HELMER. Aha! Having a party, eh?

NORA. Champagne from now till sunrise! (*Calls out.*) And some macaroons, Helene. Lots!—just this once.

HELMER (*taking her hands*).   There, there—I don't like this wild— frenzy— Be my own sweet little lark again, the way you always are.

NORA. Oh, I will. But you go on in. You too, Dr. Rank. Kristine, please help me put up my hair.

RANK (*in a low voice to* HELMER *as they go out*).   You don't think she is—you know—expecting—?

HELMER. Oh no. Nothing like that. It's just this childish fear I was telling you about. (*They go out, right.*)

NORA. Well?

MRS. LINDE. Left town.

NORA. I saw it in your face.

MRS. LINDE. He'll be back tomorrow night. I left him a note.

NORA. You shouldn't have. I don't want you to try to stop anything. You see, it's kind of ecstasy, too, this waiting for the wonderful.

MRS. LINDE. But what is it you're waiting *for*?

NORA. You wouldn't understand. Why don't you go in to the others. I'll be there in a minute. (MRS. LINDE *enters the dining room, right.* NORA *stands still for a little while, as if collecting herself; she looks at her watch.*) Five o'clock. Seven hours till midnight. Twenty-four more hours till next midnight. Then the tarantella is over. Twenty-four plus seven—thirty-one more hours to live.

HELMER (*in the door, right*).   What's happening to my little lark?

NORA (*to him, with open arms*).   Here's your lark!

ACT 3

The same room. The table by the couch and the chairs around it have been moved to the middle of the floor. A lighted lamp is on the table. The door to the front hall is open. Dance music is heard from upstairs.

MRS. LINDE is seated by the table, idly leafing through the pages of a book. She tries to read but seems unable to concentrate. Once or twice she turns her head in the direction of the door, anxiously listening.

MRS. LINDE (*looks at her watch*).   Not yet. It's almost too late. If only he hasn't— (*Listens again.*) Ah! There he is. (*She goes to the hall and opens the front door carefully. Quiet footsteps on the stairs. She whispers.)* Come in. There's nobody here.

KROGSTAD *(in the door).*   I found your note when I got home. What's this all about?

MRS. LINDE.   I've got to talk to you.

KROGSTAD.   Oh? And it has to be here?

MRS. LINDE.   It couldn't be at my place. My room doesn't have a separate entrance. Come in. We're quite alone. The maid is asleep and the Helmers are at a party upstairs.

KROGSTAD *(entering).*   Really? The Helmers are dancing tonight, are they?

MRS. LINDE.   And why not?

KROGSTAD.   You're right. Why not, indeed.

MRS. LINDE.   All right, Krogstad. Let's talk, you and I.

KROGSTAD.   I didn't know we had anything to talk about.

MRS. LINDE.   We have much to talk about.

KROGSTAD.   I didn't think so.

MRS. LINDE.   No, because you've never really understood me.

KROGSTAD.   What was there to understand? What happened was perfectly commonplace. A heartless woman jilts a man when she gets a more attractive offer.

MRS. LINDE.   Do you think I'm all that heartless? And do you think it was easy for me to break with you?

KROGSTAD.   No?

MRS. LINDE.   You really thought it was?

KROGSTAD.   If it wasn't, why did you write the way you did that time?

MRS. LINDE.   What else could I do? If I had to make a break, I also had the duty to destroy whatever feelings you had for me.

KROGSTAD *(clenching his hands).*   So that's the way it was. And you did—*that*—just for money!

MRS. LINDE.   Don't forget I had a helpless mother and two small brothers. We couldn't wait for you, Krogstad. You know yourself how uncertain your prospects were then.

KROGSTAD.   All right. But you still didn't have the right to throw me over for somebody else.

MRS. LINDE.   I don't know. I have asked myself that question many times. Did I have that right?

KROGSTAD *(in a lower voice).*   When I lost you I lost my footing. Look at me now. A shipwrecked man on a raft.

MRS. LINDE.   Rescue may be near.

KROGSTAD.   It *was* near. Then you came between.

MRS. LINDE.   I didn't know that, Krogstad. Only today did I find out it's your job I'm taking over in the bank.

KROGSTAD.   I believe you when you say so. But now that you *do* know, aren't you going to step aside?

MRS. LINDE.   No, for it wouldn't do you any good.

KROGSTAD.   Whether it would or not—I would do it.

MRS. LINDE.   I have learned common sense. Life and hard necessity have taught me that.

KROGSTAD.   And life has taught me not to believe in pretty speeches.

MRS. LINDE.   Then life has taught you a very sensible thing. But you do believe in actions, don't you?

KROGSTAD.   How do you mean?

MRS. LINDE.   You referred to yourself just now as a shipwrecked man.

KROGSTAD.   It seems to me I had every reason to do so.

MRS. LINDE.   And I am a shipwrecked woman. No one to grieve for, no one to care for.

KROGSTAD.   You made your choice.

MRS. LINDE.   I had no other choice that time.

KROGSTAD.   Let's say you didn't. What then?

MRS. LINDE.   Krogstad, how would it be if we two shipwrecked people got together?

KROGSTAD.   What's this!

MRS. LINDE.   Two on one wreck are better off than each on his own.

KROGSTAD.   Kristine!

MRS. LINDE.   Why do you think I came to town?

KROGSTAD.   Surely not because of me?

MRS. LINDE.   If I'm going to live at all I must work. All my life, for as long as I can remember, I have worked. That's been my one and only pleasure. But now that I'm all alone in the world I feel nothing but this terrible emptiness and desolation. There is no joy in working just for yourself. Krogstad—give me someone and something to work for.

KROGSTAD.   I don't believe this. Only hysterical females go in for that kind of high-minded self-sacrifice.

MRS. LINDE.   Did you ever know me to be hysterical?

KROGSTAD.   You really could do this? Listen—do you know about my past? All of it?

MRS. LINDE.   Yes, I do.

KROGSTAD.   Do you also know what people think of me around here?

MRS. LINDE.   A little while ago you sounded as if you thought that together with me you might have become a different person.

KROGSTAD.   I'm sure of it.

MRS. LINDE.   Couldn't that still be?

KROGSTAD.   Kristine—do you know what you are doing? Yes, I see you do. And you think you have the courage—?

MRS. LINDE.   I need someone to be a mother to, and your children need a mother. You and I need one another. Nils, I believe in you—in the real you. Together with you I dare to do anything.

KROGSTAD (*seizes her hands*).   Thanks, thanks, Kristine—now I know I'll raise myself in the eyes of others— Ah, but I forget—!

MRS. LINDE (*listening*).   Shhh!— There's the tarantella. You must go; hurry!

KROGSTAD.   Why? What is it?

MRS. LINDE.   Do you hear what they're playing up there? When that dance is over they'll be down.

KROGSTAD.   All right. I'm leaving. The whole thing is pointless, anyway. Of course you don't know what I'm doing to the Helmers.

MRS. LINDE.   Yes, Krogstad; I do know.

KROGSTAD.   Still, you're brave enough—?

MRS. LINDE.   I very well understand to what extremes despair can drive a man like you.

KROGSTAD.   If only it could be undone!

MRS. LINDE.   It could, for your letter is still out there in the mailbox.

KROGSTAD.   Are you sure?

MRS. LINDE.   Quite sure. But—

KROGSTAD (*looks searchingly at her*).   Maybe I'm beginning to understand. You want to save your friend at any cost. Be honest with me. That's it, isn't it.

MRS. LINDE.   Krogstad, you may sell yourself once for somebody else's sake, but you don't do it twice.

KROGSTAD.   I'll demand my letter back.

MRS. LINDE.   No, no.

KROGSTAD.   Yes, of course. I'll wait here till Helmer comes down. Then I'll ask him for my letter. I'll tell him it's just about my dismissal—that he shouldn't read it.

MRS. LINDE.   No, Krogstad. You are not to ask for that letter back.

KROGSTAD.   But tell me—wasn't that the real reason you wanted to meet me here?

MRS. LINDE.   At first it was, because I was so frightened. But that was yesterday. Since then I have seen the most incredible things going on in this house. Helmer must learn the whole truth. This miserable secret must come out in the open; those two must come to a full understanding. They simply can't continue with all this concealment and evasion.

KROGSTAD.   All right; if you want to take that chance. But there is one thing I *can* do, and I'll do that right now.

MRS. LINDE (*listening*).   But hurry! Go! The dance is over. We aren't safe another minute.

KROGSTAD.   I'll be waiting for you downstairs.

MRS. LINDE.   Yes, do. You must see me home.

KROGSTAD.   I've never been so happy in my whole life. (*He leaves through the front door. The door between the living room and the front hall remains open.*)

MRS. LINDE (*straightens up the room a little and gets her things ready*). What a change! Oh yes!—what a change! People to work for—to live for—a home to bring happiness to. I can't wait to get to work—! If only they'd come soon— (*Listens.*) Ah, there they are. Get my coat on— (*Puts on her coat and hat.* HELMER's *and* NORA's *voices are heard outside. A key is turned in the lock, and* HELMER *almost forces* NORA *into the hall. She is dressed in her Italian costume, with a big black shawl over her shoulders. He is in evening dress under an open black cloak.*)

NORA (*in the door, still resisting*).   No, no, no! I don't want to! I want to go back upstairs. I don't want to leave so early.

HELMER.   But dearest Nora—

NORA.   Oh please, Torvald—please! I'm asking you as nicely as I can—just another hour!

HELMER.   Not another minute, sweet. You know we agreed. There now. Get inside. You'll catch a cold out here. (*She still resists, but he guides her gently into the room.*)

MRS. LINDE.   Good evening.

NORA.   Kristine!

HELMER.   Ah, Mrs. Linde. Still here?

MRS. LINDE.   I know. I really should apologize, but I so much wanted to see Nora in her costume.

NORA.   You've been waiting up for me?

MRS. LINDE.   Yes, unfortunately I didn't get here in time. You were already upstairs, but I just didn't feel like leaving till I had seen you.

HELMER (*removing* NORA's *shawl*).   Yes, do take a good look at her, Mrs. Linde. I think I may say she's worth looking at. Isn't she lovely?

MRS. LINDE.   She certainly is—

HELMER.   Isn't she a miracle of loveliness, though? That was the general opinion at the party, too. But dreadfully obstinate—that she is, the sweet little thing. What can we do about that? Will you believe it—I practically had to use force to get her away.

NORA.   Oh Torvald, you're going to be sorry you didn't give me even half an hour more.

HELMER.   See what I mean, Mrs. Linde? She dances the tarantella—she is a tremendous success—quite deservedly so, though perhaps her performance was a little too natural—I mean, more than could be reconciled with the rules of art. But all right! The point is: she's a success, a tremendous success. So should I let her stay after that? Weaken the effect? Of course not. So I take my lovely little Capri girl—I might say, my capricious little Capri girl—under my arm—a quick turn around the room—a graceful bow in all directions, and—as they say in the novels—the beautiful apparition is gone. A finale should always be done for effect, Mrs. Linde, but there doesn't seem to be any way of getting that into Nora's head. Poooh—! It's hot in here. (*Throws his cloak down on a chair and opens the door to his room.*) Why, it's dark in here! Of course. Excuse me— (*Goes inside and lights a couple of candles.*)

NORA (*in a hurried, breathless whisper*).   Well?

MRS. LINDE (*in a low voice*).   I have talked to him.

NORA.   And—?

MRS. LINDE.   Nora—you've got to tell your husband everything.

NORA (*no expression in her voice*).   I knew it.

MRS. LINDE.   You have nothing to fear from Krogstad. But you must speak.

NORA.   I'll say nothing.

MRS. LINDE.   Then the letter will.

NORA.   Thank you, Kristine. Now I know what I have to do. Shh!

HELMER (*returning*).   Well, Mrs. Linde, have you looked your fill?

MRS. LINDE.   Yes. And now I'll say goodnight.

HELMER.   So soon? Is that your knitting?

MRS. LINDE (*takes it*).   Yes, thank you. I almost forgot.

HELMER.   So you knit, do you?

MRS. LINDE.   Oh yes.

HELMER.   You know—you ought to take up embroidery instead.

MRS. LINDE.   Oh? Why?

HELMER.   Because it's so much more beautiful. Look. You hold the embroidery so—in your left hand. Then with your right you move the needle—like this—in an easy, elongated arc—you see?

MRS. LINDE.   Maybe you're right—

HELMER.   Knitting, on the other hand, can never be anything but ugly. Look here: arms pressed close to the sides—the needles going up and down—there's something Chinese about it somehow—. That really was an excellent champagne they served us tonight.

MRS. LINDE.   Well, goodnight, Nora. And don't be obstinate any more.

HELMER.   Well said, Mrs. Linde!

MRS. LINDE.   Goodnight, sir.

HELMER (*sees her to the front door*).   Goodnight, goodnight. I hope you'll get home all right? I'd be very glad to—but of course you don't have far to walk, do you? Goodnight, goodnight. (*She leaves. He closes the door behind her and returns to the living room.*) There! At last we got rid of her. She really is an incredible bore, that woman.

NORA.   Aren't you very tired, Torvald?

HELMER.   No, not in the least.

NORA.   Not sleepy either?

HELMER.   Not at all. Quite the opposite. I feel enormously—animated. How about you? Yes, you do look tired and sleepy.

NORA.   Yes, I am very tired. Soon I'll be asleep.

HELMER.   What did I tell you? I was right, wasn't I? Good thing I didn't let you stay any longer.

NORA.   Everything you do is right.

HELMER (*kissing her forehead*).   Now my little lark is talking like a human being. But did you notice what splendid spirits Rank was in tonight?

NORA.   Was he? I didn't notice. I didn't get to talk with him.

HELMER.   Nor did I—hardly. But I haven't seen him in such a good mood for a long time. (*Looks at her, comes closer to her.*) Ah! It does feel good to be back in our own home again, to be quite alone with you— my young, lovely, ravishing woman!

NORA.   Don't look at me like that, Torvald!

HELMER.   Am I not to look at my most precious possession? All that loveliness that is mine, nobody's but mine, all of it mine.

NORA (*walks to the other side of the table*).   I won't have you talk to me like that tonight.

HELMER (*follows her*).   The tarantella is still in your blood. I can tell. That only makes you all the more alluring. Listen! The guests are beginning to leave. (*Softly.*) Nora—soon the whole house will be quiet.

NORA.   Yes, I hope so.

HELMER.   Yes, don't you, my darling? Do you know—when I'm at a party with you, like tonight—do you know why I hardly ever talk to you, why I keep away from you, only look at you once in a while—a few stolen glances—do you know why I do that? It's because I pretend that you are my secret love, my young, secret bride-to-be, and nobody has the slightest suspicion that there is anything between us.

NORA.   Yes, I know. All your thoughts are with me.

HELMER.   Then when we're leaving and I lay your shawl around your delicate young shoulders—around that wonderful curve of your neck—then I imagine you're my young bride, that we're coming away from the wedding, that I am taking you to my home for the first time—that I am alone with you for the first time—quite alone with you, you young, trembling beauty! I have desired you all evening—there hasn't been a longing in me that hasn't been for you. When you were dancing the tarantella, chasing, inviting—my blood was on fire; I couldn't stand it any longer—that's why I brought you down so early—

NORA.   Leave me now, Torvald. Please! I don't want all this.

HELMER.   What do you mean? You're only playing your little teasing bird game with me; aren't you, Nora? Don't want to? I'm your husband, aren't I? (*There is a knock on the front door.*)

NORA (*with a start*).   Did you hear that—?

HELMER (*on his way to the hall*).   Who is it?

RANK (*outside*).   It's me. May I come in for a moment?

HELMER (*in a low voice, annoyed*).   Oh, what does he want now? (*Aloud*) Just a minute. (*Opens the door.*) Well! How good of you not to pass by our door.

RANK.   I thought I heard your voice, so I felt like saying hello. (*Looks around.*) Ah yes—this dear, familiar room. What a cozy, comfortable place you have here, you two.

HELMER.   Looked to me as if you were quite comfortable upstairs too.

RANK.   I certainly was. Why not? Why not enjoy all you can in this world? As much as you can for as long as you can, anyway. Excellent wine.

HELMER.   The champagne, particularly.

RANK.   You noticed that too? Incredible how much I managed to put away.

NORA.   Torvald drank a lot of champagne tonight, too.

RANK.   Did he?

NORA.   Yes, he did, and then he's always so much fun afterwards.

RANK.   Well, why not have some fun in the evening after a well spent day?

HELMER.   Well spent? I'm afraid I can't claim that.

RANK (*slapping him lightly on the shoulder*).   But you see, I can!

NORA.   Dr. Rank, I believe you must have been conducting a scientific test today.

RANK.   Exactly.

HELMER.   What do you know—little Nora talking about scientific tests.

NORA.   May I congratulate you on the result?

RANK.   You may indeed.

NORA.   It was a good one?

RANK.   The best possible for both doctor and patient—certainty.

NORA (*a quick query*).   Certainty?

RANK.   Absolute certainty. So why shouldn't I have myself an enjoyable evening afterwards?

NORA.   I quite agree with you, Dr. Rank. You should.

HELMER.   And so do I. If only you don't pay for it tomorrow.

RANK.   Oh well—you get nothing for nothing in this world.

NORA.   Dr. Rank—you are fond of costume parties, aren't you?

RANK.   Yes, particularly when there is a reasonable number of amusing disguises.

NORA.   Listen—what are the two of us going to be the next time?

HELMER.   You frivolous little thing? Already thinking about the next party!

RANK.   You and I? That's easy. You'll be Fortune's Child.

HELMER.   Yes, but what is a fitting costume for that?

RANK.   Let your wife appear just the way she always is.

HELMER.   Beautiful. Very good indeed. But how about yourself? Don't you know what you'll go as?

RANK.   Yes, my friend. I know precisely what I'll be.

HELMER.   Yes?

RANK.   At the next masquerade I'll be invisible.

HELMER.   That's a funny idea.

RANK.   There's a certain black hat—you've heard about the hat that makes you invisible, haven't you? You put that on, and nobody can see you.

HELMER (*suppressing a smile*).   I guess that's right.

RANK.   But, I'm forgetting what I came for. Helmer, give me a cigar—one of your dark Havanas.

HELMER.   With the greatest pleasure. (*Offers him his case.*)

RANK (*takes one and cuts off the tip*).   Thanks.

NORA (*striking a match*).   Let me give you a light.

RANK.   Thanks. (*She holds the match; he lights his cigar.*) And now goodbye!

HELMER.   Goodbye, goodbye, my friend.

NORA.   Sleep well, Dr. Rank.

RANK.   I thank you.

NORA.   Wish me the same.

RANK. You? Well, if you really want me to—. Sleep well. And thanks for the light. (*He nods to both of them and goes out.*)

HELMER (*in a low voice*). He had had quite a bit to drink.

NORA (*absently*). Maybe so. (HELMER *takes out his keys and goes out into the hall.*) Torvald—what are you doing out there?

HELMER. Emptying the mailbox. It is quite full. There wouldn't be room for the newspapers in the morning—

NORA. Are you going to work tonight?

HELMER. You know very well I won't— Say! What's this? Somebody's been at the lock.

NORA. The lock—?

HELMER. Yes. Why, I wonder. I hate to think that any of the maids—. Here's a broken hairpin. It's one of yours, Nora.

NORA (*quickly*). Then it must be one of the children.

HELMER. You better make damn sure they stop that. Hm, hm.— There! I got it open, finally. (*Gathers up the mail, calls out to the kitchen.*) Helene— Oh Helene—turn out the light here in the hall, will you? (*He comes back into the living room and closes the door.*) Look how it's been piling up. (*Shows her the bundle of letters. Starts leafing through it.*) What's this?

NORA (*by the window*). The letter! Oh no, no, Torvald!

HELMER. Two calling cards—from Rank.

NORA. From Dr. Rank?

HELMER (*looking at them*). "Doctor medicinae Rank." They were on top. He must have put them there when he left just now.

NORA. Anything written on them?

HELMER. A black cross above the name. What a macabre idea. Like announcing his own death.

NORA. That's what it is.

HELMER. Hm? You know about this? Has he said anything to you?

NORA. That card means he has said goodbye to us. He'll lock himself up to die.

HELMER. My poor friend. I knew of course he wouldn't be with me very long. But so soon—. And hiding himself away like a wounded animal—

NORA. When it has to be, it's better it happens without words. Don't you think so, Torvald?

HELMER (*walking up and down*). He'd grown so close to us. I find it hard to think of him as gone. With his suffering and loneliness he was like a clouded background for our happy sunshine. Well, it may be better this way. For him, at any rate. (*Stops.*) And perhaps for us, too, Nora. For now we have nobody but each other. (*Embraces her.*) Oh you—my beloved wife! I feel I just can't hold you close enough. Do you know, Nora—many times I have wished some great danger threatened you, so I could risk my life and blood and everything—everything, for your sake.

NORA (*frees herself and says in a strong and firm voice*).   I think you should go and read your letters now, Torvald.

HELMER.   No, no—not tonight. I want to be with you, my darling.

NORA.   With the thought of your dying friend—?

HELMER.   You are right. This has shaken both of us. Something not beautiful has come between us. Thoughts of death and dissolution. We must try to get over it—out of it. Till then—we'll each go to our own room.

NORA (*her arms around his neck*).   Torvald—goodnight! Goodnight!

HELMER (*kisses her forehead*).   Goodnight, my little songbird. Sleep well, Nora. Now I'll read my letters. (*He goes into his room, carrying the mail. Closes the door.*)

NORA (*her eyes desperate, her hands groping, finds* HELMER'S *black cloak and throws it around her; she whispers, quickly, brokenly, hoarsely*). Never see him again. Never. Never. Never. (*Puts her shawl over her head.*) And never see the children again, either. Never; never.— The black, icy water—fathomless—this—! If only it was all over.— Now he has it. Now he's reading it. No, no; not yet. Torvald—goodbye— you—the children— (*She is about to hurry through the hall, when* HELMER *flings open the door to his room and stands there with an open letter in his hand.*)

HELMER.   Nora!

NORA (*cries out*).   Ah—!

HELMER.   What is it? You know what's in this letter?

NORA.   Yes, I do! Let me go! Let me out!

HELMER (*holds her back*).   Where do you think you're going?

NORA (*trying to tear herself loose from him*).   I won't let you save me, Torvald!

HELMER (*tumbles back*).   True! Is it true what he writes? Oh my God! No, no—this can't possibly be true.

NORA.   It is true. I have loved you more than anything else in the whole world.

HELMER.   Oh, don't give me any silly excuses.

NORA (*taking a step towards him*).   Torvald—!

HELMER.   You wretch! What have you done! .

NORA.   Let me go. You are not to sacrifice yourself for me. You are not to take the blame.

HELMER.   No more playacting. (*Locks the door to the front hall.*) You'll stay here and answer me. Do you understand what you have done? Answer me! Do you understand?

NORA (*gazes steadily at him with an increasingly frozen expression*). Yes. Now I'm beginning to understand.

HELMER (*walking up and down*).   What a dreadful awakening. All these years—all these eight years—she, my pride and my joy—a hypocrite, a liar—oh worse! worse!—a criminal! Oh, the bottomless ugliness in all this! Damn! Damn! Damn! (NORA, *silent, keeps gazing at him.* HELMER *stops in front of her.*) I ought to have guessed that something like this would happen. I should have expected it. All your father's loose principles— Silence! You have inherited every one of your father's loose principles. No religion, no morals, no sense of duty—. Now I am being punished for my leniency with him. I did it for your sake, and this is how you pay me back.

NORA.   Yes. This is how.

HELMER.   You have ruined all my happiness. My whole future— that's what you have destroyed. Oh, it's terrible to think about. I am at the mercy of an unscrupulous man. He can do with me whatever he likes, demand anything of me, command me and dispose of me just as he pleases— I dare not say a word! To go down so miserably, to be destroyed—all because of an irresponsible woman!

NORA.   When I am gone from the world, you'll be free.

HELMER.   No noble gestures, please. Your father was always full of such phrases too. What good would it do me if you were gone from the world, as you put it? Not the slightest good at all. He could still make the whole thing public, and if he did, people would be likely to think I had been your accomplice. They might even think it was my idea— that it was I who urged you to do it! And for all this I have you to thank—you, whom I've borne on my hands through all the years of our marriage. *Now* do you understand what you've done to me?

NORA (*with cold calm*).   Yes.

HELMER.   I just can't get it into my head that this is happening; it's all so incredible. But we have to come to terms with it somehow. Take your shawl off. Take it off, I say! I have to satisfy him one way or another. The whole affair must be kept quiet at whatever cost.— And as far as you and I are concerned, nothing must seem to have changed. I'm talking about appearances, of course. You'll go on living here; that goes without saying. But I won't let you bring up the children; I dare not trust you with them.— Oh! Having to say this to one I have loved so much, and whom I still—! But all that is past. It's not a question of happiness any more but of hanging on to what can be salvaged—

pieces, appearances— (*The doorbell rings.* HELMER *jumps.*) What's that? So late. Is the worst—? Has he—! Hide, Nora! Say you're sick. (NORA *doesn't move.* HELMER *opens the door to the hall.*)

MAID (*half dressed, out in the hall*).   A letter for your wife, sir.

HELMER.   Give it to me. (*Takes the letter and closes the door.*) Yes, it's from him. But I won't let you have it. I'll read it myself.

NORA.   Yes—you read it.

HELMER (*by the lamp*).   I hardly dare. Perhaps we're lost, both you and I. No; I've got to know. (*Tears the letter open, glances through it, looks at an enclosure; a cry of joy.*) Nora! (NORA *looks at him with a question in her eyes.*) Nora!—No, I must read it again.—Yes, yes; it is so! I'm saved! Nora, I'm saved!

NORA.   And I?

HELMER.   You too, of course; we're both saved, both you and I. Look! He's returning your note. He writes that he's sorry, he regrets, a happy turn in his life—oh, it doesn't matter what he writes. We're saved, Nora! Nobody can do anything to you now. Oh Nora, Nora—. No, I want to get rid of this disgusting thing first. Let me see— (*Looks at the signature.*) No, I don't want to see it. I don't want it to be more than a bad dream, the whole thing. (*Tears up the note and both letters, throws the pieces in the stove, and watches them burn.*) There! Now it's gone.— He wrote that ever since Christmas Eve—. Good God, Nora, these must have been three terrible days for you.

NORA.   I have fought a hard fight these last three days.

HELMER.   And been in agony and seen no other way out than—. No, we won't think of all that ugliness. We'll just rejoice and tell ourselves it's over, it's all over! Oh, listen to me, Nora. You don't seem to understand. It's over. What *is* it? Why do you look like that—that frozen expression on your face? Oh my poor little Nora, don't you think I know what it is? You can't make yourself believe that I have forgiven you. But I have, Nora; I swear to you, I have forgiven you for everything. Of course I know that what you did was for love of me.

NORA.   That is true.

HELMER.   You have loved me the way a wife ought to love her husband. You just didn't have the wisdom to judge the means. But do you think I love you any less because you don't know how to act on your own? Of course not. Just lean on me. I'll advise you; I'll guide you. I wouldn't be a man if I didn't find you twice as attractive because of your womanly helplessness. You mustn't pay any attention to the hard words I said to you right at first. It was just that first shock when I thought everything was collapsing all around me. I have forgiven you, Nora. I swear to you—I really have forgiven you.

NORA.   I thank you for your forgiveness. (*She goes out through the door, right.*)

HELMER.   No, stay— (*Looks into the room she entered.*) What are you doing in there?

NORA (*within*).   Getting out of my costume.

HELMER (*by the open door*).   Good, good. Try to calm down and compose yourself, my poor little frightened songbird. Rest safely; I have broad wings to cover you with. (*Walks around near the door.*) What a nice and cozy home we have, Nora. Here's shelter for you. Here I'll keep you safe like a hunted dove I have rescued from the hawk's talons. Believe me: I'll know how to quiet your beating heart. It will happen by and by, Nora; you'll see. Why, tomorrow you'll look at all this in quite a different light. And soon everything will be just the way it was before. I won't need to keep reassuring you that I have forgiven you; you'll feel it yourself. Did you really think I could have abandoned you, or even reproached you? Oh, you don't know a real man's heart, Nora. There is something unspeakably sweet and satisfactory for a man to know deep in himself that he has forgiven his wife—forgiven her in all the fullness of his honest heart. You see, that way she becomes his very own all over again—in a double sense, you might say. He has, so to speak, given her a second birth; it is as if she had become his wife and his child, both. From now on that's what you'll be to me, you lost and helpless creature. Don't worry about a thing, Nora. Only be frank with me, and I'll be your will and your conscience.— What's this? You're not in bed? You've changed your dress—!

NORA (*in everyday dress*).   Yes, Torvald. I have changed my dress.

HELMER.   But why—now—this late?

NORA.   I'm not going to sleep tonight.

HELMER.   But my dear Nora—

NORA (*looks at her watch*).   It isn't all that late. Sit down here with me, Torvald. You and I have much to talk about. (*Sits down at the table.*)

HELMER.   Nora—what is this all about? That rigid face—

NORA.   Sit down. This will take a while. I have much to say to you.

HELMER (*sits down, facing her across the table*).   You worry me, Nora. I don't understand you.

NORA.   No, that's just it. You don't understand me. And I have never understood you—not till tonight. No, don't interrupt me. Just listen to what I have to say.— This is a settling of accounts, Torvald.

HELMER.   What do you mean by that?

NORA (*after a brief silence*).   Doesn't one thing strike you, now that we are sitting together like this?

HELMER.   What would that be?

NORA.   We have been married for eight years. Doesn't it occur to you that this is the first time that you and I, husband and wife, are having a serious talk?

HELMER.   Well—serious—. What do you mean by that?

NORA.   For eight whole years—longer, in fact—ever since we first met we have never talked seriously to each other about a single serious thing.

HELMER.   You mean I should forever have been telling you about worries you couldn't have helped me with anyway?

NORA.   I am not talking about worries. I'm saying we have never tried seriously to get to the bottom of anything together.

HELMER.   But dearest Nora, I hardly think that would have been something *you*—

NORA.   That's the whole point. You have never understood me. Great wrong has been done to me, Torvald. First by Daddy and then by you.

HELMER.   What! By us two? We who have loved you more deeply than anyone else?

NORA (*shakes her head*).   You never loved me—neither Daddy nor you. You only thought it was fun to be in love with me.

HELMER.   But, Nora—what an expression to use!

NORA.   That's the way it has been, Torvald. When I was home with Daddy, he told me all his opinions, and so they became my opinions too. If I disagreed with him I kept it to myself, for he wouldn't have liked that. He called me his little doll baby, and he played with me the way I played with my dolls. Then I came to your house—

HELMER.   What a way to talk about our marriage!

NORA (*imperturbably*).   I mean that I passed from Daddy's hands into yours. You arranged everything according to your taste, and so I came to share it—or I pretended to; I'm not sure which. I think it was a little of both, now one and now the other. When I look back on it now, it seems to me I've been living here like a pauper—just a hand-to-mouth kind of existence. I have earned my keep by doing tricks for you, Torvald. But that's the way you wanted it. You have great sins against me to answer for, Daddy and you. It's your fault that nothing has become of me.

HELMER.   Nora, you're being both unreasonable and ungrateful. Haven't you been happy here?

NORA.   No, never. I thought I was, but I wasn't.

HELMER.   Not—not happy!

NORA.   No; just having fun. And you have always been very good to me. But our home has never been more than a playroom. I have been your doll wife here, just the way I used to be Daddy's doll child.

And the children have been my dolls. I thought it was fun when you played with me, just as they thought it was fun when I played with them. That's been our marriage, Torvald.

HELMER.   There is something in what you are saying—exaggerated and hysterical though it is. But from now on things will be different. Playtime is over; it's time for growing up.

NORA.   Whose growing up—mine or the children's?

HELMER.   Both yours and the children's, Nora darling.

NORA.   Oh Torvald, you're not the man to bring me up to be the right kind of wife for you.

HELMER.   How can you say that?

NORA.   And I—? What qualifications do I have for bringing up the children?

HELMER.   Nora!

NORA.   You said so yourself a minute ago—that you didn't dare to trust me with them.

HELMER.   In the first flush of anger, yes. Surely, you're not going to count that.

NORA.   But you were quite right. I am *not* qualified. Something else has to come first. Somehow I have to grow up myself. And you are not the man to help me do that. That's a job I have to do by myself. And that's why I'm leaving you.

HELMER (*jumps up*).   What did you say!

NORA.   I have to be by myself if I am to find out about myself and about all the other things too. So I can't stay here with you any longer.

HELMER.   Nora, Nora!

NORA.   I'm leaving now. I'm sure Kristine will put me up for tonight.

HELMER.   You're out of your mind! I won't let you! I forbid you!

NORA.   You can't forbid me anything any more; it won't do any good. I'm taking my own things with me. I won't accept anything from you, either now or later.

HELMER.   But this is madness!

NORA.   Tomorrow I'm going home— I mean back to my old home town. It will be easier for me to find some kind of job there.

HELMER.   Oh, you blind, inexperienced creature—!

NORA.   I must see to it that I get experience, Torvald.

HELMER.   Leaving your home, your husband, your children! Not a thought of what people will say!

NORA.   I can't worry about that. All I know is that I have to leave.

HELMER.   Oh, this is shocking! Betraying your most sacred duties like this!

NORA.   And what do you consider my most sacred duties?

HELMER.   Do I need to tell you that? They are your duties to your husband and your children.

NORA.   I have other duties equally sacred.

HELMER.   You do not. What duties would they be?

NORA.   My duties to myself.

HELMER.   You are a wife and a mother before you are anything else.

NORA.   I don't believe that any more. I believe I am first of all a human being, just as much as you—or at any rate that I must try to become one. Oh, I know very well that most people agree with you, Torvald, and that it says something like that in all the books. But what people say and what the books say is no longer enough for me. I have to think about these things myself and see if I can't find the answers.

HELMER.   You mean to tell me you don't know what your proper place in your own home is? Don't you have a reliable guide in such matters? Don't you have religion?

NORA.   Oh but Torvald—I don't really know what religion is.

HELMER.   What are you saying!

NORA.   All I know is what the Reverend Hansen told me when he prepared me for confirmation. He said that religion was *this* and it was *that*. When I get by myself, away from here, I'll have to look into that, too. I have to decide if what the Reverend Hansen said was right, or anyway if it is right for *me*.

HELMER.   Oh, this is unheard of in a young woman! If religion can't guide you, let me appeal to your conscience. For surely you have moral feelings? Or—answer me—maybe you don't?

NORA.   Well, you see, Torvald, I don't really know what to say. I just don't know. I am confused about these things. All I know is that my ideas are quite different from yours. I have just found out that the laws are different from what I thought they were, but in no way can I get it into my head that those laws are right. A woman shouldn't have the right to spare her dying old father or save her husband's life! I just can't believe that.

HELMER.   You speak like a child. You don't understand the society you live in.

NORA.   No, I don't. But I want to find out about it. I have to make up my mind who is right, society or I.

HELMER.   You are sick, Nora; you have a fever. I really don't think you are in your right mind.

NORA.   I have never felt so clearheaded and sure of myself as I do tonight.

HELMER.   And clearheaded and sure of yourself you're leaving your husband and children?

NORA. Yes.

HELMER.   Then there is only one possible explanation.

NORA.   What?

HELMER.   You don't love me any more.

NORA.   No, that's just it.

HELMER.   Nora! Can you say that?

NORA.   I am sorry, Torvald, for you have always been so good to me. But I can't help it. I don't love you any more.

HELMER (*with forced composure*).   And this too is a clear and sure conviction?

NORA.   Completely clear and sure. That's why I don't want to stay here any more.

HELMER.   And are you ready to explain to me how I came to forfeit your love?

NORA.   Certainly I am. It was tonight, when the wonderful didn't happen. That was when I realized you were not the man I thought you were.

HELMER.   You have to explain. I don't understand.

NORA.   I have waited patiently for eight years, for I wasn't such a fool that I thought the wonderful is something that happens any old day. Then this—thing—came crashing in on me, and then there wasn't a doubt in my mind that now—now comes the wonderful. When Krogstad's letter was in that mailbox, never for a moment did it even occur to me that you would submit to his conditions. I was so absolutely certain that you would say to him: make the whole thing public—tell everybody. And when that had happened—

HELMER.   Yes, then what? When I surrendered my wife to shame and disgrace—!

NORA.   When that had happened, I was absolutely certain that you would stand up and take the blame and say, "I'm the guilty one."

HELMER.   Nora!

NORA.   You mean I never would have accepted such a sacrifice from you? Of course not. But what would my protests have counted against yours? *That* was the wonderful I was hoping for in terror. And to prevent that I was going to kill myself.

HELMER.   I'd gladly work nights and days for you, Nora—endure sorrow and want for your sake. But nobody sacrifices his *honor* for his love.

NORA.   A hundred thousand women have done so.

HELMER.   Oh, you think and talk like a silly child.

NORA.   All right. But you don't think and talk like the man I can live with. When you had gotten over your fright—not because of what threatened *me* but because of the risk to *you*—and the whole danger was past, then you acted as if nothing at all had happened. Once again I was your little songbird, your doll, just as before, only now you had to handle her even more carefully, because she was so frail and weak. (*Rises.*) Torvald—that moment I realized that I had been living here for eight years with a stranger and had borne him three children— Oh, I can't stand thinking about it! I feel like tearing myself to pieces!

HELMER (*heavily*).   I see it, I see it. An abyss has opened up between us. —Oh but Nora—surely it can be filled?

NORA.   The way I am now I am no wife for you.

HELMER.   I have it in me to change.

NORA.   Perhaps—if your doll is taken from you.

HELMER.   To part—to part from you! No, no, Nora! I can't grasp that thought!

NORA (*goes out, right*).   All the more reason why it has to be. (*She returns with her outdoor clothes and a small bag, which she sets down on the chair by the table.*)

HELMER.   Nora, Nora! Not now! Wait till tomorrow.

NORA (*putting on her coat*).   I can't spend the night in a stranger's rooms.

HELMER.   But couldn't we live here together like brother and sister—?

NORA (*tying on her hat*).   You know very well that wouldn't last long—. (*Wraps her shawl around her.*) Goodbye, Torvald. I don't want to see the children. I know I leave them in better hands than mine. The way I am now I can't be anything to them.

HELMER.   But some day, Nora—some day—?

NORA.   How can I tell? I have no idea what's going to become of me.

HELMER.   But you're still my wife, both as you are now and as you will be.

NORA.   Listen, Torvald—when a wife leaves her husband's house, the way I am doing now, I have heard he has no more legal responsibilities for her. At any rate, I now release you from all responsibility. You are not to feel yourself obligated to me for anything, and I have no obligations to you. There has to be full freedom on both sides. Here is your ring back. Now give me mine.

HELMER.   Even this?

NORA.   Even this.

HELMER.   Here it is.

NORA.   There. So now it's over. I'm putting the keys here. The maids know everything about the house—better than I. Tomorrow, after I'm gone, Kristine will come over and pack my things from home. I want them sent after me.

HELMER.   Over! It's all over! Nora, will you never think of me?

NORA.   I'm sure I'll often think of you and the children and this house.

HELMER.   May I write to you, Nora?

NORA.   No—never. I won't have that.

HELMER.   But send you things—? You must let me—

NORA.   Nothing, nothing.

HELMER.   —help you, when you need help—

NORA.   I told you, no; I won't have it. I'll accept nothing from strangers.

HELMER.   Nora—can I never again be more to you than a stranger?

NORA (*picks up her bag*).   Oh Torvald—then the most wonderful of all would have to happen—

HELMER.   Tell me what that would be—!

NORA.   For that to happen, both you and I would have to change so that— Oh Torvald, I no longer believe in the wonderful.

HELMER.   But I *will* believe. Tell me! Change, so that—?

NORA.   So that our living together would become a true marriage. Goodbye. (*She goes out through the hall.*)

HELMER (*sinks down on a chair near the door and covers his face with his hands*).   Nora! Nora! (*Looks around him and gets up.*) All empty. She's gone. (*With sudden hope.*) The most wonderful—?!

(*From downstairs comes the sound of a heavy door slamming shut.*)

QUESTIONS

1. How do the following contribute to the characterizations of Nora at the beginning of the play: (a) her husband's nicknames for her, (b) her fondness for sweets, (c) her games with her children, (d) her prodigality with money, and (e) her deceptions? What evidence is there that these characteristics may reflect both her own nature and conformity to her husband's expectations of her? What definition of marriage does she imply in her remarks to Mrs. Linde about how she may continue to act as long as she remains "young and pretty" (page 1089)? It was socially proper at the time of the play for Norwegian wives to address their husbands by their last names; what does Nora's use of Helmer's first name suggest about their relationship?

2. What are the various functions of Nora's conversation with Mrs. Linde in Act 1? Consider it from these perspectives: (a) the exposition of prior events and the definition of Nora's dilemma; (b) further revelations of Nora's character, both in the past and during the conversation; (c) the insight into herself that Nora gains from Mrs. Linde's history; (d) definitions of legal and moral standards of the time indicated by the prior actions of both women.

3. What are the symbolic meanings of the title? Why is it more appropriate than A *Doll's House?* Is Nora the only "doll" in the play?

4. How much time passes during the present action of the play, from the opening of Act 1 to the final curtain? What events that occurred before the first act may be considered causes for the present action? What events that take place during the present are reported rather than dramatized on the stage?

5. What is the significance of Mrs. Linde's former and present relationship to Krogstad? To what extent can Krogstad be labeled "villain"? Compare his motives and actions (in the past and in the present) with those of Helmer; with those of Dr. Rank.

6. Characterize Dr. Rank. What are his strengths? his weaknesses? Structurally and morally he may be contrasted to Krogstad—but is he a model of virtue?

7. The major characters can be described thus: Nora and Helmer are protagonist and antagonist; Mrs. Linde is a foil to Nora; and both Krogstad and Dr. Rank are foils to Helmer. By evaluating the actions and motives of the foil characters, locate Nora and Helmer on a scale of human value. To what extent do the foil characters offer models for the central characters? To what extent do they offer them examples of actions to be avoided?

8. What positive gains does Nora make in the course of the action? What must she learn in order to perform her final act? Is that act a triumph, or a failure, or some of both? (For the play's first performance in Berlin, Ibsen was pressured into creating a conventionally "happy ending"— Nora is persuaded by Helmer not to leave him for the sake of their children, and so sacrifices herself to their need for a mother. Why is the present ending truer to the themes Ibsen presents?)

9. Compare Nora and Helmer as developing characters. What opportunities for change does Helmer have? How does he respond to them? Consider the extent to which Nora and Helmer share the responsibility for having created "a doll house" of their marriage. Evaluate Nora's leaving him as an opportunity for Helmer.

10. From the first moments of the play, money is a recurring topic. Consider the importance it has in the motivations and actions of the five major characters. Can you establish a rank-order of more or less admirable attitudes toward it? Can you separate examples of genuine need from examples of desire for gain? Is the influence of money on the lives of these characters limited to the time and society in which they lived, or are there parallels to our time?

11. Consider the ways in which the marriage of Nora and Helmer is typical rather than uniquely theirs.

12. Assess the thematic importance of deception and honesty, of self-deception and self-discovery.

13. Explore the implications of this interpretation: "A Doll House represents a woman imbued with the idea of becoming a person, but it proposes nothing categorical about women becoming people; in fact, its real theme has nothing to do with the sexes. It is the irrepressible conflict of two different personalities which have founded themselves on two radically different estimates of reality" (Robert M. Adams, "Ibsen on the Contrary," in Modern Drama, ed. Anthony Caputi [New York: Norton, 1966], 345).

Tennessee Williams
The Glass Menagerie

Characters

AMANDA WINGFIELD, *the mother, a little woman of great but confused vitality clinging frantically to another time and place. Her characterization must be carefully created, not copied from type. She is not paranoiac, but her life is paranoia. There is much to admire in* AMANDA, *and as much to love and pity as there is to laugh at. Certainly she has endurance and a kind of heroism, and though her foolishness makes her unwittingly cruel at times, there is tenderness in her slight person.*

LAURA WINGFIELD, *her daughter.* AMANDA, *having failed to establish contact with reality, continues to live vitally in her illusions, but* LAURA's *situation is even graver. A childhood illness has left her crippled, one leg slightly shorter than the other, and held in a brace. This defect need not be more than suggested on the stage. Stemming from this,* LAURA's *separation increases till she is like a piece of her own glass collection, too exquisitely fragile to move from the shelf.*

TOM WINGFIELD, *her son and the narrator of the play. A poet with a job in a warehouse. His nature is not remorseless, but to escape from a trap he has to act without pity.*

JIM O'CONNOR, *the gentleman caller, a nice, ordinary, young man.*

THE GLASS MENAGERIE   First performed in 1944; developed from a short story, "Portrait of a Girl in Glass" (published later in *One Arm and Other Stories*). Tennessee Williams (1911–1983) was born Thomas Lanier Williams in Mississippi, the son of a traveling salesman. In 1918 the family moved to St. Louis when the father was made a sales manager of International Shoe Company. Here, while the family lived in a succession of rented apartments, Tom published his first story at sixteen, graduated from high school, attended the University of Missouri for three years, worked at a menial job in the shoe company (1932–1935), had a nervous breakdown, and finished his education at Washington University and the University of Iowa. Adopting "Tennessee" as his writing name, he then embarked on a life that took him to Chicago, New Orleans, Los Angeles, Mexico City, New York, Key West, and other cities while he wrote steadily, supporting himself with odd jobs. *The Glass Menagerie*, his first commercial success, rescued him from penury. The play reflects his St. Louis years, although his real father (given to alcoholic excess) never disappeared from home; his sister (two years his elder) did have dates, was not handicapped, and did not have a glass collection; a younger brother (eight years Tom's junior) does not appear; and "Miss Edwina" (Williams's mother and his guest at the first performance) has written, "The only resemblance I have to Amanda is that we both like jonquils."

Scene.   *An alley in St. Louis.*

Part 1. Preparation for a gentleman caller.
Part 2. The gentleman calls.

Time: Now and the Past.

SCENE 1

The Wingfield apartment is in the rear of the building, one of those vast hive-like conglomerations of cellular living-units that flower as warty growths in overcrowded urban centers of lower middle-class population and are symptomatic of the impulse of this largest and fundamentally enslaved section of American society to avoid fluidity and differentiation and to exist and function as one interfused mass of automatism.

The apartment faces an alley and is entered by a fire-escape, a structure whose name is a touch of accidental poetic truth, for all of these huge buildings are always burning with the slow and implacable fires of human desperation. The fire-escape is part of what we see—that is, the landing of it and steps descending from it.

The scene is memory and is therefore nonrealistic. Memory takes a lot of poetic license. It omits some details; others are exaggerated, according to the emotional value of the articles it touches, for memory is seated predominantly in the heart. The interior is therefore rather dim and poetic.

At the rise of the curtain, the audience is faced with the dark, grim rear wall of the Wingfield tenement. This building is flanked on both sides by dark, narrow alleys which run into murky canyons of tangled clotheslines, garbage cans and the sinister latticework of neighboring fire-escapes. It is up and down these side alleys that exterior entrances and exits are made, during the play. At the end of Tom's *opening commentary, the dark tenement wall slowly becomes transparent and reveals the interior of the ground floor Wingfield apartment.*

Nearest the audience is the living room, which also serves as a sleeping room for Laura, *the sofa unfolding to make her bed. Just beyond, separated from the living room by a wide arch or second proscenium with transparent faded portieres (or second curtain), is the dining room. In an old-fashioned what-not in the living room are seen scores of transparent glass animals. A blown-up photograph of the father hangs on the wall of the living room to the left of the archway. It is the face of a very handsome young man in a dough-boy's First World War cap. He is gallantly smiling, ineluctably smiling, as if to say, "I will be smiling forever."*

Also hanging on the wall, near the photograph, are a typewriter keyboard chart and a Gregg shorthand diagram. An upright typewriter on a small table stands beneath the charts.

The audience hears and sees the opening scene in the dining room through both the transparent fourth wall of the building and the transparent gauze portieres of the dining-room arch. It is during this revealing scene that the fourth wall slowly ascends, out of sight. This transparent exterior wall is not brought down again until the very end of the play, during TOM's *final speech.*

The narrator is an undisguised convention of the play. He takes whatever license with dramatic convention as is convenient to his purposes.

TOM *enters, dressed as a merchant sailor, and strolls across the front of the stage to the fire-escape. There he stops and lights a cigarette. He addresses the audience.*

TOM.   Yes, I have tricks in my pocket, I have things up my sleeve. But I am the opposite of a stage magician. He gives you illusion that has the appearance of truth. I give you truth in the pleasant disguise of illusion.

To begin with, I turn back time. I reverse it to that quaint period, the thirties, when the huge middle class of America was matriculating in a school for the blind. Their eyes had failed them, or they had failed their eyes, and so they were having their fingers pressed forcibly down on the fiery Braille alphabet of a dissolving economy.

In Spain there was revolution. Here there was only shouting and confusion. In Spain there was Guernica.° Here there were disturbances of labor, sometimes pretty violent, in otherwise peaceful cities such as Chicago, Cleveland, Saint Louis . . . This is the social background of the play. (*Music.*)

The play is memory. Being a memory play, it is dimly lighted, it is sentimental, it is not realistic. In memory everything seems to happen to music. That explains the fiddle in the wings.

I am the narrator of the play, and also a character in it. The other characters are my mother, Amanda, my sister, Laura, and a gentleman caller who appears in the final scenes. He is the most realistic character in the play, being an emissary from a world of reality that we were somehow set apart from. But since I have a poet's weakness for symbols, I am using this character also as a symbol; he is the long delayed but always expected something that we live for.

There is a fifth character in the play who doesn't appear except in this larger-than-life-size photograph over the mantel. This is our father who left us a long time ago. He was a telephone man who fell in

---

Guernica: A town in northern Spain destroyed in 1937 during the Spanish Civil War by German bombers, in the first mass air attack on an urban community.

love with long distances; he gave up his job with the telephone company and skipped the light fantastic out of town . . .

The last we heard of him was a picture post-card from Mazatlán, on the Pacific coast of Mexico, containing a message of two words— "Hello—Good-bye!" and no address.

I think the rest of the play will explain itself . . . (AMANDA's *voice becomes audible through the portieres.* TOM *divides the portieres and enters the upstage area.* AMANDA *and* LAURA *are seated at a drop-leaf table. Eating is indicated by gestures without food or utensils.* AMANDA *faces the audience.* TOM *and* LAURA *are seated in profile. The interior has lit up softly and through the scrim we see* AMANDA *and* LAURA *seated at the table in the upstage area.*)

AMANDA (*calling*).   Tom?

TOM.   Yes, Mother.

AMANDA.   We can't say grace until you come to the table!

TOM.   Coming, Mother. (*He bows slightly and withdraws, reappearing a few moments later in his place at the table.*)

AMANDA (*to her son*).   Honey, don't *push* with your *fingers.* If you have to push with something, the thing to push with is a crust of bread. And chew—chew! Animals have sections in their stomachs which enable them to digest food without mastication, but human beings are supposed to chew their food before they swallow it down. Eat food leisurely, son, and really enjoy it. A well-cooked meal has lots of delicate flavors that have to be held in the mouth for appreciation. So chew your food and give your salivary glands a chance to function!

TOM (*deliberately lays his imaginary fork down and pushes his chair back from the table*).   I haven't enjoyed one bite of this dinner because of your constant directions on how to eat it. It's you that makes me rush through meals with your hawk-like attention to every bite I take. Sickening— spoils my appetite—all this discussion of—animals' secretion—salivary glands—mastication!

AMANDA (*lightly*).   Temperament like a Metropolitan star! (*He rises and crosses downstage.*) You're not excused from the table.

TOM.   I'm getting a cigarette.

AMANDA.   You smoke too much.

LAURA (*rises*).   I'll bring in the blancmange. (TOM *remains standing with his cigarette by the portieres during the following.*)

AMANDA (*rising*).   No, sister, no, sister—you be the lady this time and I'll be the darky.

LAURA.   I'm already up.

AMANDA.   Resume your seat, little sister—I want you fresh and pretty—for gentlemen callers!

LAURA.   I'm not expecting any gentlemen callers.

AMANDA (*crossing out to kitchenette. Airily*).   Sometimes they come when they are least expected! Why, I remember one Sunday afternoon in Blue Mountain—(*enters kitchenette*).

TOM.   I know what's coming!

LAURA.   Yes. But let her tell it.

TOM.   Again?

LAURA.   She loves to tell it.

AMANDA (*returning with a bowl of dessert*).   One Sunday afternoon in Blue Mountain—your mother received—*seventeen!*—gentlemen callers! Why, sometimes there weren't chairs enough to accommodate them all. We had to send the nigger over to bring in folding chairs from the parish house.

TOM (*remaining at portieres*).   How did you entertain those gentlemen callers?

AMANDA.   I understood the art of conversation!

TOM.   I bet you could talk.

AMANDA.   Girls in those days *knew* how to talk, I can tell you.

TOM.   Yes?

AMANDA.   They knew how to entertain their gentlemen callers. It wasn't enough for a girl to be possessed of a pretty face and a graceful figure—although I wasn't slighted in either respect. She also needed to have a nimble wit and a tongue to meet all occasions.

TOM.   What did you talk about?

AMANDA.   Things of importance going on in the world! Never anything coarse or common or vulgar. (*She addresses* TOM *as though he were seated in the vacant chair at the table though he remains by the portieres. He plays this scene as though he held the book.*) My callers were gentlemen—all! Among my callers were some of the most prominent young planters of the Mississippi Delta—planters and sons of planters! (*TOM motions for music and a spot of light on* AMANDA. *Her eyes lift, her face glows, her voice becomes rich and elegiac.*)

There was young Champ Laughlin who later became vice-president of the Delta Planters Bank. Hadley Stevenson who was drowned in Moon Lake and left his widow one hundred and fifty thousand in Government bonds. There were the Cutrere brothers, Wesley and Bates. Bates was one of my bright particular beaux! He got in a quarrel with that wild Wainwright boy. They shot it out on the floor of Moon Lake Casino. Bates was shot through the stomach. Died in the ambulance on his way to Memphis. His widow was so well-provided for, came into eight or ten thousand acres, that's all. She married him on the rebound—never loved her—carried my picture on him the night he died! And there was that boy that every girl in the Delta had set her cap for! That beautiful, brilliant young Fitzhugh boy from Greene County!

TOM.   What did he leave his widow?

AMANDA.   He never married! Gracious, you talk as though all of my old admirers had turned up their toes to the daisies!

TOM.   Isn't this the first you've mentioned that still survives?

AMANDA.   That Fitzhugh boy went North and made a fortune— came to be known as the Wolf of Wall Street! He had the Midas touch, whatever he touched turned to gold! And I could have been Mrs. Duncan J. Fitzhugh, mind you! But—I picked your *father!*

LAURA (*rising*).   Mother, let me clear the table.

AMANDA.   No, dear, you go in front and study your typewriter chart. Or practice your shorthand a little. Stay fresh and pretty!—It's almost time for our gentlemen callers to start arriving. (*She flounces girl-ishly toward the kitchenette.*) How many do you suppose we're going to entertain this afternoon? (TOM *throws down the paper and jumps up with a groan.*)

LAURA (*alone in the dining room*).   I don't believe we're going to receive any, Mother.

AMANDA (*reappearing, airily*).   What? No one—not one? You must be joking! (LAURA *nervously echoes her laugh. She slips in a fugitive man-ner through the half-open portieres and draws them gently behind her. A shaft of very clear light is thrown on her face against the faded tapestry of the cur-tains. Music: "The Glass Menagerie"° under faintly. Lightly*) Not one gen-tleman caller? It can't be true! There must be a flood, there must have been a tornado!

LAURA.   It isn't a flood, it's not a tornado, Mother. I'm just not popular like you were in Blue Mountain . . . (TOM *utters another groan. LAURA glances at him with a faint, apologetic smile. Her voice catching a little.*) Mother's afraid I'm going to be an old maid. (*The scene dims out with "Glass Menagerie" music.*)

SCENE 2

LAURA *is seated in the delicate ivory chair at the small claw-foot table. She wears a dress of soft violet material for a kimono—her hair tied back from her forehead with a ribbon. She is washing and polishing her collection of glass. AMANDA appears on the fire-escape steps. At the sound of her ascent, LAURA*

Music . . . Menagerie": Music for the play, including "The Glass Menagerie" theme, was composed by Paul Bowles (1910–1999), American composer, novelist, and short story writer.

catches her breath, thrusts the bowl of ornaments away and seats herself stiffly before the diagram of the typewriter keyboard as though it held her spellbound. Something has happened to AMANDA. *It is written in her face as she climbs to the landing: a look that is grim and hopel~~ and a little absurd. She has on one of those cheap or imitation velvety-looking cloth coats with imitation fur collar. Her hat is five or six years old, one of those dreadful cloche hats that were worn in the late twenties, and she is clasping an enormous black patent-leather pocketbook with nickel clasps and initials. This is her full-dress outfit, the one she usually wears to the D.A.R. Before entering she looks through the door. She purses her lips, opens her eyes very wide, rolls them upward and shakes her head. Then she slowly lets herself in the door. Seeing her mother's expression* LAURA *touches her lips with a nervous gesture.*

LAURA.   Hello, Mother, I was— (*She makes a nervous gesture toward the chart on the wall.* AMANDA *leans against the shut door and stares at* LAURA *with a martyred look.*)

AMANDA.   Deception? Deception? (*She slowly removes her hat and gloves, continuing the sweet suffering stare. She lets the hat and gloves fall on the floor—a bit of acting.*)

LAURA (*shakily*).   How was the D.A.R. meeting? (AMANDA *slowly opens her purse and removes a dainty white handkerchief which she shakes out delicately and delicately touches to her lips and nostrils.*) Didn't you go to the D.A.R. meeting, Mother?

AMANDA (*faintly, almost inaudibly*).   —No.—No. (*Then more forcibly*) I did not have the strength—to go to the D.A.R. In fact, I did not have the courage! I wanted to find a hole in the ground and hide myself in it forever! (*She crosses slowly to the wall and removes the diagram of the typewriter keyboard. She holds it in front of her for a second, staring at it sweetly and sorrowfully—then bites her lips and tears it in two pieces.*)

LAURA (*faintly*).   Why did you do that, Mother? (AMANDA *repeats the same procedure with the chart of the Gregg Alphabet.*) Why are you—

AMANDA.   Why? Why? How old are you, Laura?

LAURA.   Mother, you know my age.

AMANDA.   I thought you were an adult; it seems that I was mistaken. (*She crosses slowly to the sofa and sinks down and stares at* LAURA.)

LAURA.   Please don't stare at me, Mother. (AMANDA *closes her eyes and lowers her head. There is a ten-second pause.*)

AMANDA.   What are we going to do, what is going to become of us, what is the future? (*There is another pause.*)

LAURA.   Has something happened, Mother? (AMANDA *draws a long breath and takes out the handkerchief again. Dabbing process.*) Mother, has—something happened?

AMANDA.   I'll be all right in a minute, I'm just bewildered—(*she hesitates*)—by life.

LAURA.   Mother, I wish that you would tell me what's happened!

AMANDA.   As you know, I was supposed to be inducted into my office at the D.A.R. this afternoon. But I stopped off at Rubicam's Business College to speak to your teachers about your having a cold and ask them what progress they thought were you making down there.

LAURA.   Oh . . .

AMANDA.   I went to the typing instructor and introduced myself as your mother. She didn't know who you were. "Wingfield," she said. "We don't have any such student enrolled at the school!"

I assured her she did, that you had been going to classes since early in January.

"I wonder," she said, "if you could be talking about that terribly shy little girl who dropped out of school after only a few days' attendance?"

"No," I said, "Laura, my daughter, has been going to school every day for the past six weeks!"

"Excuse me," she said. She took the attendance book out and there was your name, unmistakably printed, and all the dates you were absent until they decided that you had dropped out of school.

I still said, "No, there must have been some mistake! There must have been some mix-up in the records!"

And she said, "No—I remember her perfectly now. Her hands shook so that she couldn't hit the right keys! The first time we gave a speed-test, she broke down completely—was sick at the stomach and almost had to be carried into the wash-room! After that morning she never showed up any more. We phoned the house but never got any answer"—While I was working at Famous and Barr, I suppose, demonstrating those—

Oh! (*She indicates a brassiere with her hands.*) I felt so weak I could barely keep on my feet! I had to sit down while they got me a glass of water! Fifty dollars' tuition, all of our plans—my hopes and ambitions for you—just gone up the spout, just gone up the spout like that. (LAURA *draws a long breath and gets awkwardly to her feet. She crosses to the victrola and winds it up.*) What are you doing?

LAURA.   Oh! (*She releases the handle and returns to her seat.*)

AMANDA.   Laura, where have you been going when you've gone out pretending that you were going to business college?

LAURA.   I've just been going out walking.

AMANDA.   That's not true.

LAURA.   It is. I just went walking.

AMANDA.   Walking? Walking? In winter? Deliberately courting pneumonia in that light coat? Where did you walk to, Laura?

LAURA. All sorts of places—mostly in the park.

AMANDA. Even after you'd started catching that cold?

LAURA. It was the lesser of two evils, Mother. I couldn't go back up. I—threw up—on the floor!

AMANDA. From half past seven till after five every day you mean to tell me you walked around in the park, because you wanted me to think that you were still going to Rubicam's Business College?

LAURA. It wasn't as bad as it sounds. I went inside places to get warmed up.

AMANDA. Inside where?

LAURA. I went in the art museum and the bird-houses at the Zoo. I visited the penguins every day! Sometimes I did without lunch and went to the movies. Lately I've been spending most of my afternoons in the Jewel-box, that big glass house where they raise the tropical flowers.

AMANDA. You did all this to deceive me, just for deception? (LAURA *looks down.*) Why?

LAURA. Mother, when you're disappointed, you get that awful suffering look on your face, like the picture of Jesus's mother in the museum!

AMANDA. Hush!

LAURA. I couldn't face it. (*Pause. A whisper of strings.*)

AMANDA (*hopelessly fingering the huge pocketbook*). So what are we going to do the rest of our lives? Stay home and watch the parades go by? Amuse ourselves with the glass menagerie, darling? Eternally play those worn-out phonograph records your father left as a painful reminder of him? We won't have a business career—we've given that up because it gave us nervous indigestion! (*Laughs wearily.*) What is there left but dependency all our lives? I know so well what becomes of unmarried women who aren't prepared to occupy a position. I've seen such pitiful cases in the South—barely tolerated spinsters living upon the grudging patronage of sister's husband or brother's wife!—stuck away in some little mouse-trap of a room—encouraged by one in-law to visit another—little birdlike women without any nest—eating the crust of humility all their life!

Is that the future that we've mapped out for ourselves? I swear it's the only alternative I can think of! (*She pauses.*) It isn't a very pleasant alternative, is it? (*She pauses again.*) Of course—some girls *do* marry. (LAURA *twists her hands nervously.*) Haven't you ever liked some boy?

LAURA. Yes. I liked one once. (*Rises.*) I came across his picture a while ago.

AMANDA (*with some interest*). He gave you his picture?

LAURA. No, it's in the year-book.

AMANDA (*disappointed*).   Oh—a high-school boy.

LAURA.   Yes. His name was Jim. (LAURA *lifts the heavy annual from the claw-foot table.*) Here he is in *The Pirates of Penzance.*°

AMANDA (*absently*).   The what?

LAURA.   The operetta the senior class put on. He had a wonderful voice and we sat across the aisle from each other Mondays, Wednesdays and Fridays in the Aud. Here he is with the silver cup for debating! See his grin?

AMANDA (*absently*).   He must have had a jolly disposition.

LAURA.   He used to call me—Blue Roses.

AMANDA.   Why did he call you such a name as that?

LAURA.   When I had that attack of pleurosis—he asked me what was the matter when I came back. I said pleurosis—he thought that I said Blue Roses! So that's what he always called me after that. Whenever he saw me, he'd holler, "Hello, Blue Roses!" I didn't care for the girl he went out with. Emily Meisenbach. Emily was the best-dressed girl at Soldan. She never struck me, though, as being sincere . . . It says in the Personal Section—they're engaged. That's—six years ago! They must be married by now.

AMANDA.   Girls that aren't cut out for business careers usually wind up married to some nice man. (*Gets up with a spark of revival.*) Sister, that's what you'll do! (LAURA *utters a startled, doubtful laugh. She reaches quickly for a piece of glass.*)

LAURA.   But, Mother—

AMANDA.   Yes? (*Crossing to photograph.*)

LAURA (*in a tone of frightened apology*).   I'm—crippled!

AMANDA.   Nonsense! Laura, I've told you never, never to use that word. Why, you're not crippled, you just have a little defect—hardly noticeable, even! When people have some slight disadvantage like that, they cultivate other things to make up for it—develop charm—and vivacity—and—*charm!* That's all you have to do! (*She turns again to the photograph.*) One thing your father had *plenty of*—was *charm!* (TOM *motions to the fiddle in the wings. The scene fades out with music.*)

SCENE 3

Tom speaks from the fire-escape landing.

TOM.   After the fiasco at Rubicam's Business College, the idea of getting a gentleman caller for Laura began to play a more and more im-

The . . . Penzance: comic operetta (1880) by Gilbert and Sullivan

portant part in Mother's calculations. It became an obsession. Like some archetype of the universal unconscious, the image of the gentleman caller haunted our small apartment . . .

An evening at home rarely passed without some allusion to this image, this specter, this hope . . . Even when he wasn't mentioned, his presence hung in Mother's preoccupied look and in my sister's frightened, apologetic manner—hung like a sentence passed upon the Wingfields!

Mother was a woman of action as well as words. She began to take logical steps in the planned direction. Late that winter and in the early spring—realizing that extra money would be needed to properly feather the nest and plume the bird—she conducted a vigorous campaign on the telephone, roping in subscribers to one of those magazines for matrons called *The Home-maker's Companion*, the type of journal that features the serialized sublimations of ladies of letters who think in terms of delicate cup-like breasts, slim, tapering waists, rich, creamy thighs, eyes like woodsmoke in autumn, fingers that soothe and caress like strains of music, bodies as powerful as Etruscan sculpture. (AMANDA *enters with phone on long extension cord. She is spotted in the dim stage.*)

AMANDA.   Ida Scott? This is Amanda Wingfield! We *missed* you at the D.A.R. last Monday! I said to myself: She's probably suffering with that sinus condition! How is the sinus condition?

Horrors! Heaven have mercy!—You're a Christian martyr, yes, that's what you are, a Christian martyr!

Well, I just now happened to notice that your subscription to the *Companion's* about to expire! Yes, it expires with the next issue, honey!—just when that wonderful new serial by Bessie Mae Hopper is getting off to such an exciting start. Oh, honey, it's something that you can't miss! You remember how *Gone with the Wind* took everybody by storm? You simply couldn't go out if you hadn't read it. All everybody *talked* was Scarlett O'Hara. Well, this is a book that critics already compare to *Gone with the Wind*. It's the *Gone with the Wind* of the post–World War generation—What?—Burning?—Oh, honey, don't let them burn, go take a look in the oven and I'll hold the wire! Heavens—I think she's hung up!

(*Before the stage is lighted, the violent voices of* TOM *and* AMANDA *are heard. They are quarreling behind the portieres. In front of them stands* LAURA *with clenched hands and panicky expression. A clear pool of light on her figure throughout this scene.*)

TOM.   What in Christ's name am I—
AMANDA (*shrilly*).   Don't you use that—
TOM.   Supposed to do!

AMANDA.   Expression! Not in my—

TOM.   Ohhh!

AMANDA.   Presence! Have you gone out of your senses?

TOM.   I have, that's true, *driven* out!

AMANDA.   What is the matter with you, you—big—big—IDIOT!

TOM.   Look!—I've got *no thing*, no single thing—

AMANDA.   Lower your voice!

TOM.   In my life here that I can call my OWN! Everything is—

AMANDA.   Stop that shouting!

TOM.   Yesterday you confiscated my books! You have the nerve to—

AMANDA.   I took that horrible novel back to the library—yes! That hideous book by that insane Mr. Lawrence.° (TOM *laughs wildly*.) I cannot control the output of diseased minds or people who cater to them—(TOM *laughs still more wildly*.) BUT I WON'T ALLOW SUCH FILTH BROUGHT INTO MY HOUSE! No, no, no, no, no!

TOM.   House, house! Who pays rent on it, who makes a slave of himself to—

AMANDA (*fairly screeching*).   Don't you DARE to—

TOM.   No, no, *I* mustn't say things. *I've* got to just—

AMANDA.   Let me tell you—

TOM.   I don't want to hear any more! (*He tears the portieres open. The upstage area is lit with a turgid smoky red glow. AMANDA's hair is in metal curlers and she wears a very old bathrobe, much too large for her slight figure, a relic of the faithless Mr. Wingfield. An upright typewriter and a wild disarray of manuscripts is on the drop-leaf table. The quarrel was probably precipitated by AMANDA's interruption of his creative labor. A chair lies overthrown on the floor. Their gesticulating shadows are cast on the ceiling by the fiery glow.*)

AMANDA.   You *will* hear more, you—

TOM.   No, I won't hear more, I'm going out!

AMANDA.   You come right back in—

TOM.   Out, out, out! Because I'm—

AMANDA.   Come back here, Tom Wingfield! I'm not through talking to you!

TOM.   Oh, go—

LAURA (*desperately*).   —Tom!

AMANDA.   You're going to listen, and no more insolence from you! I'm at the end of my patience!

Mr. Lawrence: D. H. Lawrence, author of "The Rocking-Horse Winner" (page 285), emphasized in his novels the force and importance of sexuality in human life.

Tom (*comes back toward her*).   What do you think I'm at? Aren't I supposed to have any patience to reach the end of, Mother? I know, I know. It seems unimportant to you, what I'm *doing*—what I *want* to do—having a little *difference* between them! You don't think that—

Amanda.   I think you've been doing things that you're ashamed of. That's why you act like this. I don't believe that you go every night to the movies. Nobody goes to the movies night after night. Nobody in their right minds goes to the movies as often as you pretend to. People don't go to the movies at nearly midnight, and movies don't let out at two a.m. Come in stumbling. Muttering to yourself like a maniac! You get three hours' sleep and then go to work. Oh, I can picture the way you're doing down there. Moping, doping, because you're in no condition.

Tom (*wildly*).   No, I'm in no condition!

Amanda.   What right have you got to jeopardize your job? Jeopardize the security of all of us? How do you think we'd manage if you were—

Tom.   Listen! You think I'm crazy *about* the *warehouse*? (*He bends fiercely toward her slight figure.*) You think I'm in love with the Continental Shoemakers? You think I want to spend fifty-five *years* down there in that—*celotex interior!* with—*fluorescent*—*tubes!* Look! I'd rather somebody picked up a crowbar and battered out my brains—than go back mornings! I *go!* Every time you come in yelling that God damn "*Rise and Shine!*" "*Rise and Shine!*" I say to myself, "How *lucky dead* people are!" But I get up. I *go!* For sixty-five dollars a month I give up all that I dream of doing and being *ever!* And you say self—*self's* all I ever think of. Why, listen, if self is what I thought of, Mother, I'd be where he is—GONE! (*Pointing to father's picture.*) As far as the system of transportation reaches! (*He starts past her. She grabs his arm.*) Don't grab at me, Mother!

Amanda.   Where are you going?

Tom.   I'm going to the *movies!*

Amanda.   I don't believe that lie!

Tom (*crouching toward her, overtowering her tiny figure. She backs away, gasping*).   I'm going to opium dens! Yes, opium dens, dens of vice and criminals' hang-outs, Mother. I've joined the Hogan gang, I'm a hired assassin, I carry a tommy-gun in a violin case! I run a string of cat-houses in the Valley! They call me Killer, Killer Wingfield, I'm leading a double-life, a simple, honest warehouse worker by day, by night a dynamic *czar* of the *underworld, Mother.* I go to gambling casinos, I spin away fortunes on the roulette table! I wear a patch over one eye and a false mustache, sometimes I put on green whiskers. On those occasions they call me—*El Diablo!* Oh, I could tell you things to make you sleepless! My enemies plan to dynamite this place. They're going to blow us all sky-high some night! I'll be glad, very happy, and so will you! You'll go up, up on a broomstick, over Blue Mountain with seventeen gentlemen callers! You ugly—babbling old—*witch* . . . (*He goes through a series of violent, clumsy movements, seizing his overcoat, lunging to the door, pulling it fiercely open. The women watch him, aghast. His arm catches in the sleeve of the coat as he struggles to pull it on. For a moment he is pinioned by the bulky garment. With an outraged groan he tears the coat off again, splitting the shoulder of it, and hurls it across the room. It strikes against the shelf of* LAURA's *glass collection, there is a tinkle of shattering glass.* LAURA *cries out as if wounded. Music: "The Glass Menagerie."*)

LAURA (*shrilly*).   My glass!—menagerie . . . (*She covers her face and turns away. But* AMANDA *is still stunned and stupefied by the "ugly witch" so that she barely notices this occurrence. Now she recovers her speech.*)

AMANDA (*in an awful voice*).   I won't speak to you—until you apologize!

(*She crosses through the portieres and draws them together behind her.* TOM *is left with* LAURA. LAURA *clings weakly to the mantel with her face averted.* TOM *stares at her stupidly for a moment. Then he crosses to shelf. Drops awkwardly on knees to collect the fallen glass, glancing at* LAURA *as if he would speak but couldn't. "The Glass Menagerie" steals in as the scene dims out.*)

SCENE 4

The interior of the apartment is dark. There is a faint light in the alley. A deep-voiced bell in a church is tolling the hour of five as the scene commences.

TOM *appears at the top of the alley. After each solemn boom of the bell in the tower, he shakes a little noise-maker or rattle as if to express the tiny spasm of man in contrast to the sustained power and dignity of the Almighty. This and the unsteadiness of his advance make it evident that he has been drinking. As he climbs the few steps to the fire-escape landing, light steals up inside.* LAURA *appears in night-dress, observing* TOM's *empty bed in the front room.* TOM *fishes in his pockets for his door-key, removing a motley assortment of articles in the search, including a perfect shower of movie-ticket stubs and an empty bottle. At last he finds the key, but just as he is about to insert it, it slips from his fingers. He strikes a match and crouches below the door.*

TOM (*bitterly*).   One crack—and it falls through!
LAURA (*opens the door*).   Tom! Tom, what are you doing?
TOM.   Looking for a door-key.
LAURA.   Where have you been all this time?

TOM.   I have been to the movies.

LAURA.   All this time at the movies?

TOM.   There was a very long program. There was a Garbo picture and a Mickey Mouse and a travelogue and a newsreel and a preview of coming attractions. And there was an organ solo and a collection for the milk-fund—simultaneously—which ended up in a terrible fight between a fat lady and an usher!

LAURA (*innocently*).   Did you have to stay through everything?

TOM.   Of course! And, oh, I forgot! There was a big stage show! The headliner on this stage show was Malvolio the Magician. He performed wonderful tricks, many of them, such as pouring water back and forth between pitchers. First it turned to wine and then it turned to beer and then it turned to whiskey. I know it was whiskey it finally turned into because he needed somebody to come up out of the audience to help him, and I came up—both shows! It was Kentucky Straight Bourbon. A very generous fellow, he gave souvenirs. (*He pulls from his back pocket a shimmering rainbow-colored scarf.*) He gave me this. This is his magic scarf. You can have it, Laura. You wave it over a canary cage and you get a bowl of goldfish. You wave it over the goldfish bowl and they fly away canaries . . . But the wonderfullest trick of all was the coffin trick. We nailed him into a coffin and he got out of the coffin without removing one nail. (*He has come inside.*) There is a trick that would come in handy for me—get me out of this 2 by 4 situation! (*Flops onto bed and starts removing shoes.*)

LAURA.   Tom—Shhh!

TOM.   What're you shushing me for?

LAURA.   You'll wake up Mother.

TOM.   Goody, goody! Pay 'er back for all those "Rise an' Shines." (*Lies down, groaning.*) You know it don't take much intelligence to get yourself into a nailed-up coffin, Laura. But who in hell ever got himself out of one without removing one nail? (*As if in answer, the father's grinning photograph lights up. Scene dims out. Immediately following the church bell is heard striking six. At the sixth stroke the alarm clock goes off in* AMANDA's *room, and after a few moments we hear her calling: "Rise and Shine! Rise and Shine! Laura, go tell your brother to rise and shine!"*)

TOM (*sitting up slowly*).   I'll rise—but I won't shine. (*The light increases.*)

AMANDA.   Laura, tell your brother his coffee is ready.

LAURA (*slips into front room*).   Tom!—It's nearly seven. Don't make Mother nervous. (*He stares at her stupidly. Beseechingly*) Tom, speak to Mother this morning. Make up with her, apologize, speak to her!

Tom.   She won't to me. It's her that started not speaking.

Laura.   If you just say you're sorry she'll start speaking.

Tom.   Her not speaking—is that such a tragedy?

Laura.   Please—please!

Amanda (*calling from kitchenette*).   Laura, are you going to do what I asked you to do, or do I have to get dressed and go out myself?

Laura.   Going, going—soon as I get on my coat! (*She pulls on a shapeless felt hat with nervous, jerky movement, pleadingly glancing at* Tom. *Rushes awkwardly for coat. The coat is one of* Amanda's, *inaccurately made-over, the sleeves too short for* Laura.) Butter and what else?

Amanda (*entering upstage*).   Just butter. Tell them to charge it.

Laura.   Mother, they make such faces when I do that.

Amanda.   Sticks and stones can break our bones, but the expression on Mr. Garfinkel's face won't harm us! Tell your brother his coffee is getting cold.

Laura (*at door*).   Do what I asked you, will you, will you, Tom? (*He looks sullenly away.*)

Amanda.   Laura, go now or just don't go at all!

Laura (*rushing out*).   Going—going! (*A second later she cries out.* Tom *springs up and crosses to door.* Amanda *rushes anxiously in.* Tom *opens the door.*)

Tom.   Laura?

Laura.   I'm all right. I slipped, but I'm all right.

Amanda (*peering anxiously after her*).   If anyone breaks a leg on those fire-escape steps, the landlord ought to be sued for every cent he possesses! (*She shuts door. Remembers she isn't speaking and returns to the other room.*)

(*As* Tom *enters listlessly for his coffee, she turns her back to him and stands rigidly facing the window on the gloomy gray vault of the areaway. Its light on her face with its aged but childish features is cruelly sharp, satirical as a Daumier print.*

(*Music under:* "Ave Maria."

(Tom *glances sheepishly but sullenly at her averted figure and slumps at the table. The coffee is scalding hot; he sips it and gasps and spits it back in the cup. At his gasp,* Amanda *catches her breath and half turns. Then catches herself and turns back to window.* Tom *blows on his coffee, glancing sidewise at his mother. She clears her throat.* Tom *clears his. He starts to rise. Sinks back down again, scratches his head, clears his throat again.* Amanda *coughs.* Tom *raises his cup in both hands to blow on it, his eyes staring over the rim of it at his mother for several moments. Then he slowly sets the cup down and awkwardly and hesitantly rises from the chair.*)

Tom (*hoarsely*).   Mother. I—I apologize, Mother. (Amanda *draws a quick, shuddering breath. Her face works grotesquely. She breaks into childlike tears.*) I'm sorry for what I said, for everything that I said, I didn't mean it.

AMANDA (*sobbingly*).   My devotion has made me a witch and so I make myself hateful to my children!

TOM.   *No,* you *don't.*

AMANDA.   I worry so much, don't sleep, it makes me nervous!

TOM (*gently*).   I understand that.

AMANDA.   I've had to put up a solitary battle all these years. But you're my right-hand bower! Don't fall down, don't fail!

TOM (*gently*).   I try, Mother.

AMANDA (*with great enthusiasm*).   Try and you will SUCCEED! (*The notion makes her breathless.*) Why, you—you're just *full* of natural endowments! Both of my children—they're *unusual* children! Don't you think I know it? I'm so—*proud!* Happy and—feel I've—so much to be thankful for but— Promise me one thing, son!

TOM.   What, Mother?

AMANDA.   Promise, son, you'll—never be a drunkard!

TOM (*turns to her grinning*).   I will never be a drunkard, Mother.

AMANDA.   That's what frightened me so, that you'd been drinking. Eat a bowl of Purina!

TOM.   Just coffee, Mother.

AMANDA.   Shredded wheat biscuit?

TOM.   No. No, Mother, just coffee.

AMANDA.   You can't put in a day's work on an empty stomach. You've got ten minutes—don't gulp! Drinking too-hot liquids makes cancer of the stomach . . . Put cream in.

TOM.   No, thank you.

AMANDA.   To cool it.

TOM.   No! No, thank you, I want it black.

AMANDA.   I know, but it's not good for you. We have to do all that we can to build ourselves up. In these trying times we live in, all that we have to cling to is—each other . . . That's why it's so important to—Tom, I—I sent out your sister so I could discuss something with you. If you hadn't spoken I would have spoken to you. (*Sits down.*)

TOM (*gently*).   What is it, Mother, that you want to discuss?

AMANDA.   *Laura!*

TOM (*puts his cup down slowly. Music: "The Glass Menagerie"*). Oh.—Laura . . .

AMANDA (*touching his sleeve*).   You know how Laura is. So quiet but—still water runs deep! She notices things and I think she—broods about them. (TOM *looks up.*) A few days ago I came in and she was crying.

TOM.   What about?

AMANDA.   You.

TOM.   Me?

AMANDA.   She has an idea that you're not happy here.

TOM.   What gave her that idea?

AMANDA.   What gives her any idea? However, you do act strangely. I—I'm not criticizing, understand *that!* I know your ambitions do not lie in the warehouse, that like everybody in the whole wide world—you've had to—make sacrifices, but—Tom—Tom—life's not easy, it calls for—Spartan endurance! There's so many things in my heart that I cannot describe to you! I've never told you but I—*loved* your father . . .

TOM (*gently*).   I know that, Mother.

AMANDA.   And you—when I see you taking after his ways! Staying out late—and—well, you *had* been drinking the night you were in that—terrifying condition! Laura says that you hate the apartment and that you go out nights to get away from it! Is that true, Tom?

TOM.   No. You say there's so much in your heart that you can't describe to me. That's true of me, too. There's so much in my heart that I can't describe to *you!* So let's respect each other's—

AMANDA.   But, why—*why*, Tom—are you always so *restless?* Where do you *go* to, nights?

TOM.   I—go to the movies.

AMANDA.   Why do you go to the movies so much, Tom?

TOM.   I go to the movies because—I like adventure. Adventure is something I don't have much of at work, so I go to the movies.

AMANDA.   But, Tom, you go to the movies *entirely* too *much!*

TOM.   I like a lot of adventure. (AMANDA *looks baffled, then hurt. As the familiar inquisition resumes he becomes hard and impatient again.* AMANDA *slips back to her querulous attitude toward him.*)

AMANDA.   Most young men find adventure in their careers.

TOM.   Then most young men are not employed in a warehouse.

AMANDA.   The world is full of young men employed in warehouses and offices and factories.

TOM.   Do all of them find adventure in their careers?

AMANDA.   They do or they do without it! Not everybody has a craze for adventure.

TOM.   Man is by instinct a lover, a hunter, a fighter, and none of those instincts are given much play at the warehouse!

AMANDA.   Man is by instinct! Don't quote instincts to me! Instinct is something that people have got away from! It belongs to animals! Christian adults don't want it!

TOM.   What do Christian adults want, then, Mother?

AMANDA.   Superior things! Things of the mind and the spirit! Only animals have to satisfy instincts! Surely your aims are somewhat higher than theirs! Than monkeys—pigs—

TOM.   I reckon they're not.

AMANDA.   You're joking. However, that isn't what I wanted to discuss.

TOM (*rising*).   I haven't much time.

AMANDA (*pushing his shoulders*).   Sit down.

TOM.   You want me to punch in red at the warehouse, Mother?

AMANDA.   You have five minutes. I want to talk about Laura.

TOM.   All right! What about Laura?

AMANDA.   We have to be making some plans and provisions for her. She's older than you, two years, and nothing has happened. She just drifts along doing nothing. It frightens me terribly how she just drifts along.

TOM.   I guess she's the type that people call home girls.

AMANDA.   There's no such type, and if there is, it's a pity! That is unless the home is hers, with a husband!

TOM.   What?

AMANDA.   Oh, I can see the handwriting on the wall as plain as I see the nose in front of my face! It's terrifying! More and more you remind me of your father! He was out all hours without explanation!— Then *left! Goodbye!* And me with the bag to hold. I saw that letter you got from the Merchant Marine. I know what you're dreaming of. I'm not standing here blindfolded. (*She pauses.*) Very well, then. Then *do* it! But not till there's somebody to take your place.

TOM.   What do you mean?

AMANDA.   I mean that as soon as Laura has got somebody to take care of her, married, a home of her own, independent—why, then you'll be free to go wherever you please, on land, on sea, whichever way the wind blows you! But until that time you've got to look out for your sister. I don't say me because I'm old and don't matter! I say your sister because she's young and dependent.

I put her in business college—a dismal failure! Frightened her so it made her sick at the stomach. I took her over to the Young People's League at the church. Another fiasco. She spoke to nobody, nobody spoke to her. Now all she does is fool with those pieces of glass and play those worn-out records. What kind of a life is that for a girl to lead?

TOM.   What can I do about it?

AMANDA.   Overcome selfishness! Self, self, self is all that you ever think of! (TOM *springs up and crosses to get his coat. It is ugly and bulky. He pulls on a cap with earmuffs.*) Where is your muffler? Put your wool muffler on! (*He snatches it angrily from the closet and tosses it about his neck and pulls both ends tight.*) Tom! I haven't said what I had in mind to ask you.

Tom.   I'm too late to—

Amanda (*catching his arm—very importunately. Then shyly*). Down at the warehouse, aren't there some—nice young men?

Tom.   No!

Amanda.   There *must* be—*some* . . .

Tom.   Mother—(*Gesture.*)

Amanda.   Find out one that's clean-living—doesn't drink and— ask him out for sister!

Tom.   What?

Amanda.   For *sister!* To *meet!* Get *acquainted!*

Tom (*stamping to door*).   Oh, my *go-osh!*

Amanda.   Will you? (*He opens door. Imploringly*) Will you? (*He starts down.*) Will you? Will you, dear?

Tom (*calling back*).   YES! (Amanda *closes the door hesitantly and with a troubled but faintly hopeful expression.*)

Amanda (*moves into spotlight at the phone*).   Ella Cartwright? This is Amanda Wingfield!

How are you, honey?

How is that kidney condition? (*There is a five-second pause.*)

Horrors! (*There is another pause.*)

You're a Christian martyr, yes, honey, that's what you are, a Christian martyr! Well, I just now happened to notice in my little red book that your subscription to the *Companion* has just run out! I knew that you wouldn't want to miss out on the wonderful serial starting in this new issue. It's by Bessie Mae Hopper, the first thing she's written since *Honeymoon for Three.* Wasn't that a strange and interesting story? Well, this one is even lovelier, I believe. It has a sophisticated, society background. It's all about the horsey set on Long Island!

SCENE 5

It is early dusk of a spring evening. Supper has just been finished in the Wingfield apartment. Amanda *and* Laura *in light-colored dresses are removing dishes from the table, in the upstage area, which is shadowy, their movements formalized almost as a dance or ritual, their moving forms as pale and silent as moths.* Tom, *in white shirt and trousers, rises from the table and crosses toward the fire-escape.*

Amanda (*as he passes her*).   Son, will you do me a favor?

TOM.   What?

AMANDA.   Comb your hair! You look so pretty when your hair is combed! (TOM *slouches on sofa with evening paper. Enormous caption "Franco Triumphs."*) There is only one respect in which I would like you to emulate your father.

TOM.   What respect is that?

AMANDA.   The care he always took of his appearance. He never allowed himself to look untidy. (*He throws down the paper and crosses to fire-escape.*) Where are you going?

TOM.   I'm going out to smoke.

AMANDA.   You smoke too much. A pack a day at fifteen cents a pack. How much would that amount to in a month? Thirty times fifteen is how much, Tom? Figure it out and you will be astounded at what you could save. Enough to give you a night-school course in accounting at Washington U! Just think what a wonderful thing that would be for you, Son!

TOM.   I'd rather smoke. (*He steps out on landing, letting the screen door slam.*)

AMANDA (*sharply*).   I know! That's the tragedy of it . . . (*Alone, she turns to look at her husband's picture. Dance music: "All the World Is Waiting for the Sunrise!"*)

TOM (*to the audience*).   Across the alley from us was the Paradise Dance Hall. On evenings in spring the windows and doors were open and the music came outdoors. Sometimes the lights were turned out except for a large glass sphere that hung from the ceiling. It would turn slowly about and filter the dusk with delicate rainbow colors. Then the orchestra played a waltz or a tango, something that had a slow and sensuous rhythm. Couples would come outside, to the relative privacy of the alley. You could see them kissing behind ash-pits and telephone poles. This was the compensation for lives that passed like mine, without any change or adventure. Adventure and change were imminent in this year. They were waiting around the corner for all these kids. Suspended in the mist over Berchtesgaden,° caught in the folds of Chamberlain's umbrella—.° In Spain there was Guernica! But here there was only hot swing music and liquor, dance halls, bars, and movies, and sex that hung in the gloom like a chandelier and flooded the world with

---

Berchtesgaden: Hitler's Bavarian summer retreat   **Chamberlain's umbrella:** Neville Chamberlain, British prime minister (1937–1940), who always carried a furled umbrella, and whose name has become a symbol for appeasement, returned from a conference with Hitler in Munich in 1938 with a signed agreement that he proclaimed meant "Peace in our time." One year later, German troops invaded Poland, beginning World War II.

brief, deceptive rainbows . . . All the world was waiting for bombardments! (AMANDA *turns from the picture and comes outside.*)

AMANDA (*sighing*).   A fire-escape landing's a poor excuse for a porch. (*She spreads a newspaper on a step and sits down, gracefully and demurely as if she were settling into a swing on a Mississippi veranda.*) What are you looking at?

TOM.   The moon.

AMANDA.   Is there a moon this evening?

TOM.   It's rising over Garfinkel's Delicatessen.

AMANDA.   So it is! A little silver slipper of a moon. Have you made a wish on it yet?

TOM.   Um-hum.

AMANDA.   What did you wish for?

TOM.   That's a secret.

AMANDA.   A secret, huh? Well, I won't tell mine either. I will be just as mysterious as you.

TOM.   I bet I can guess what yours is.

AMANDA.   Is my head so transparent?

TOM.   You're not a sphinx.

AMANDA.   No, I don't have secrets. I'll tell you what I wished for on the moon. Success and happiness for my precious children! I wish for that whenever there's a moon, and when there isn't a moon, I wish for it, too.

TOM.   I thought perhaps you wished for a gentleman caller.

AMANDA.   Why do you say that?

TOM.   Don't you remember asking me to fetch one?

AMANDA.   I remember suggesting that it would be nice for your sister if you brought home some nice young man from the warehouse. I think that I've made that suggestion more than once.

TOM.   Yes, you have made it repeatedly.

AMANDA.   Well?

TOM.   We are going to have one.

AMANDA.   *What?*

TOM.   A gentleman caller! (*The annunciation is celebrated with music.* AMANDA *rises.*)

AMANDA.   You mean you have asked some nice young man to come over?

TOM.   Yep. I've asked him to dinner.

AMANDA.   You really did?

TOM.   I did!

AMANDA.   You did, and did he—*accept?*

TOM.   He did!

AMANDA.   Well, well—well, well! That's—lovely!

TOM.   I thought that you would be pleased.

AMANDA.   It's definite, then?

TOM.   Very definite.

AMANDA.   Soon?

TOM.   Very soon.

AMANDA.   For heaven's sake, stop putting on and tell me some things, will you?

TOM.   What things do you want me to tell you?

AMANDA.   *Naturally* I would like to know when he's *coming!*

TOM.   He's coming tomorrow.

AMANDA.   *Tomorrow?*

TOM.   Yep. Tomorrow.

AMANDA.   But, Tom!

TOM.   Yes, Mother?

AMANDA.   Tomorrow gives me no time!

TOM.   Time for what?

AMANDA.   Preparations! Why didn't you phone me at once, as soon as you asked him, the minute that he accepted? Then, don't you see, I could have been getting ready!

TOM.   You don't have to make any fuss.

AMANDA.   Oh, Tom, Tom, Tom, of course I have to make a fuss! I want things nice, not sloppy! Not thrown together. I'll certainly have to do some fast thinking, won't I?

TOM.   I don't see why you have to think at all.

AMANDA.   You just don't know. We can't have a gentleman caller in a pig-sty! All my wedding silver has to be polished, the monogrammed table linen ought to be laundered! The windows have to be washed and fresh curtains put up. And how about clothes? We have to *wear* something, don't we?

TOM.   Mother, this boy is no one to make a fuss over!

AMANDA.   Do you realize he's the first young man we've introduced to your sister? It's terrible, dreadful, disgraceful that poor little sister has never received a single gentleman caller! Tom, come inside! (*She opens the screen door.*)

TOM.   What for?

AMANDA.   I want to ask you some things.

TOM.   If you're going to make such a fuss, I'll call it off, I'll tell him not to come!

AMANDA.   You certainly won't do anything of the kind. Nothing offends people worse than broken engagements. It simply means I'll have to work like a Turk! We won't be brilliant, but we'll pass inspection. Come on inside. (TOM *follows, groaning.*) Sit down.

TOM.   Any particular place you would like me to sit?

AMANDA.   Thank heavens I've got the new sofa! I'm also making payments on a floor lamp I'll have sent out! And put the chintz covers on, they'll brighten things up! Of course I'd hoped to have these walls repapered . . . What is the young man's name?

TOM.   His name is O'Connor.

AMANDA.   That, of course, means fish—tomorrow is Friday! I'll have that salmon loaf—with Durkee's dressing! What does he do? He works at the warehouse?

TOM.   Of course! How else would I—

AMANDA.   Tom, he—doesn't drink?

TOM.   Why do you ask me that?

AMANDA.   Your father *did!*

TOM.   Don't get started on that!

AMANDA.   He *does* drink, then?

TOM.   Not that I know of!

AMANDA.   Make sure, be certain! The last thing I want for my daughter's a boy who drinks!

TOM.   Aren't you being a little bit premature? Mr. O'Connor has not yet appeared on the scene!

AMANDA.   But will tomorrow. To meet your sister, and what do I know about his character? Nothing! Old maids are better off than wives of drunkards!

TOM.   Oh, my God!

AMANDA.   Be still!

TOM (*leaning forward to whisper*).   Lots of fellows meet girls whom they don't marry!

AMANDA.   Oh, talk sensibly, Tom—and don't be sarcastic! (*She has gotten a hairbrush.*)

TOM.   What are you doing?

AMANDA.   I'm brushing that cow-lick down! What is this young man's position at the warehouse?

TOM (*submitting grimly to the brush and the interrogation*).   This young man's position is that of a shipping clerk, Mother.

AMANDA.   Sounds to me like a fairly responsible job, the sort of a job *you* would be in if you just had more *get-up*. What is his salary? Have you any idea?

TOM.   I would judge it to be approximately eighty-five dollars a month.

AMANDA.   Well—not princely, but—

TOM.   Twenty more than I make.

AMANDA.   Yes, how well I know! But for a family man, eighty-five dollars a month is not much more than you can just get by on . . .

TOM.   Yes, but Mr. O'Connor is not a family man.

AMANDA.   He might be, mightn't he? Some time in the future?

TOM.   I see. Plans and provisions.

AMANDA.   You are the only young man that I know of who ignores the fact that the future becomes the present, the present the past, and the past turns into everlasting regret if you don't plan for it!

TOM.   I will think that over and see what I can make of it.

AMANDA.   Don't be supercilious with your mother! Tell me some more about this—what do you call him?

TOM.   James D. O'Connor. The D. is for Delaney.

AMANDA.   Irish on *both* sides! *Gracious!* And doesn't drink?

TOM.   Shall I call him up and ask him right this minute?

AMANDA.   The only way to find out about these things is to make discreet inquiries at the proper moment. When I was a girl in Blue Mountain and it was suspected that a young man drank, the girl whose attentions he had been receiving, if any girl *was*, would sometimes speak to the minister of his church, or rather her father would if her father was living, and sort of feel him out on the young man's character. That is the way such things are discreetly handled to keep a young woman from making a tragic mistake!

TOM.   Then how did you happen to make a tragic mistake?

AMANDA.   That innocent look of your father's had everyone fooled! He *smiled*—the world was *enchanted*! No girl can do worse than put herself at the mercy of a handsome appearance! I hope that Mr. O'Connor is not too good-looking.

TOM.   No, he's not too good-looking. He's covered with freckles and hasn't too much of a nose.

AMANDA.   He's not right-down homely, though?

TOM.   Not right-down homely. Just medium homely, I'd say.

AMANDA.   Character's what to look for in a man.

TOM.   That's what I've always said, Mother.

AMANDA.   You've never said anything of the kind and I suspect you would never give it a thought.

TOM.   Don't be so suspicious of me.

AMANDA.   At least I hope he's the type that's up and coming.

TOM.   I think he really goes in for self-improvement.

AMANDA.   What reason have you to think so?

TOM.   He goes to night school.

AMANDA (*beaming*).   Splendid! What does he do, I mean study?

TOM.   Radio engineering and public speaking!

AMANDA.   Then he has visions of being advanced in the world! Any young man who studies public speaking is aiming to have an executive job some day! And radio engineering? A thing for the future! Both of these facts are very illuminating. Those are the sort of things that a mother should know concerning any young man who comes to call on her daughter. Seriously or—not.

TOM.   One little warning. He doesn't know about Laura. I didn't let on that we had dark ulterior motives. I just said, why don't you come and have dinner with us? He said okay and that was the whole conversation.

AMANDA.   I bet it was! You're eloquent as an oyster. However, he'll know about Laura when he gets here. When he sees how lovely and sweet and pretty she is, he'll thank his lucky stars he was asked to dinner.

TOM.   Mother, you mustn't expect too much of Laura.

AMANDA.   What do you mean?

TOM.   Laura seems all those things to you and me because she's ours and we love her. We don't even notice she's crippled any more.

AMANDA.   Don't say crippled! You know that I never allow that word to be used!

TOM.   But face facts, Mother. She is and—that's not all—

AMANDA.   What do you mean "not all"?

TOM.   Laura is very different from other girls.

AMANDA.   I think the difference is all to her advantage.

TOM.   Not quite all—in the eyes of others—strangers—she's terribly shy and lives in a world of her own and those things make her seem a little peculiar to people outside the house.

AMANDA.   Don't say peculiar.

TOM.   Face the facts. She is. (*The dance-hall music changes to a tango that has a minor and somewhat ominous tone.*)

AMANDA.   In what way is she peculiar—may I ask?

TOM (*gently*).   She lives in a world of her own—a world of—little glass ornaments, Mother . . . (*Gets up.* AMANDA *remains holding the brush, looking at him, troubled.*) She plays old phonograph records and—that's about all—(*He glances at himself in the mirror and crosses to door.*)

AMANDA (*sharply*).   Where are you going?

TOM.   I'm going to the movies. (*Out screen door.*)

AMANDA.   Not to the movies, every night to the movies! (*Follows quickly to screen door.*) I don't believe you always go to the movies! (*He is gone.* AMANDA *looks worriedly after him for a moment. Then vitality and optimism return and she turns from the door, crossing to portieres.*) Laura! Laura!

LAURA (*answers from kitchenette*).   Yes, Mother.

AMANDA.   Let those dishes go and come in front! (LAURA *appears with dish towel.* AMANDA *speaks to her gaily.*) Laura, come here and make a wish on the moon!

LAURA (*entering*).   Moon—moon?

AMANDA.   A little silver slipper of a moon. Look over your left shoulder, Laura, and make a wish! (LAURA *looks faintly puzzled as if called out of sleep.* AMANDA *seizes her shoulders and turns her at an angle by the door.*)

LAURA.   What shall I wish for, Mother?

AMANDA (*her voice trembling and her eyes suddenly filled with tears*). Happiness! Good fortune! (*The sound of the violin rises and the stage dims out.*)

SCENE 6

TOM.   And so the following evening I brought Jim home to dinner. I had known Jim slightly in high school. In high school Jim was a hero. He had tremendous Irish good nature and vitality with the scrubbed and polished look of white chinaware. He seemed to move in a continual spotlight. He was a star in basketball, captain of the debating club, president of the senior class and the glee club and he sang the male lead in the annual light operas. He was always running or bounding, never just walking. He seemed always at the point of defeating the law of gravity. He was shooting with such velocity through his adolescence that you would logically expect him to arrive at nothing short of the White House by the time he was thirty. But Jim apparently ran into more interference after his graduation from Soldan. His speed had definitely slowed. Six years after he left high school he was holding a job that wasn't much better than mine.

He was the only one at the warehouse with whom I was on friendly terms. I was valuable to him as someone who could remember his former glory, who had seen him win basketball games and the silver cup in debating. He knew of my secret practice of retiring to a cabinet of the washroom to work on poems when business was slack in the warehouse. He called me Shakespeare. And while the other boys in the warehouse regarded me with suspicious hostility, Jim took a humorous attitude toward me. Gradually his attitude affected the others, their hostility wore off and they also began to smile at me as people smile at an oddly fashioned dog who trots across their paths at some distance.

I knew that Jim and Laura had known each other at Soldan, and I had heard Laura speak admiringly of his voice. I didn't know if Jim remembered her or not. In high school Laura had been as unobtrusive as

Jim had been astonishing. If he did remember Laura, it was not as my sister, for when I asked him to dinner, he grinned and said, "You know, Shakespeare, I never thought of you as having folks!"

He was about to discover that I did . . .

(*The light dims out on* TOM *and comes up in the* Wingfield *living room —a delicate lemony light. It is about five on a Friday evening of late spring which comes "scattering poems in the sky."*

(AMANDA *has worked like a Turk in preparation for the gentleman caller. The results are astonishing. The new floor lamp with its rose-silk shade is in place, a colored paper lantern conceals the broken light fixture in the ceiling, new billowing white curtains are at the windows, chintz covers are on chairs and sofa, a pair of new sofa pillows make their initial appearance. Open boxes and tissue paper are scattered on the floor.*

(LAURA *stands in the middle with lifted arms while* AMANDA *crouches before her, adjusting the hem of a new dress, devout and ritualistic. The dress is colored and designed by memory. The arrangement of* LAURA's *hair is changed; it is softer and more becoming. A fragile, unearthly prettiness has come out in* LAURA: *she is like a piece of translucent glass touched by light, given a momentary radiance, not actual, not lasting.*)

AMANDA (*impatiently*).   Why are you trembling?

LAURA.   Mother, you've made me nervous!

AMANDA.   How have I made you nervous?

LAURA.   By all this fuss! You make it seem so important!

AMANDA.   I don't understand you, Laura. You couldn't be satisfied with just sitting home, and yet whenever I try to arrange something for you, you seem to resist it. (*She gets up.*) Now take a look at yourself. No, wait! Wait just a moment—I have an idea!

LAURA.   What is it now? (AMANDA *produces two powder puffs which she wraps in handkerchiefs and stuffs in* LAURA's *bosom.*)

LAURA.   Mother, what are you doing?

AMANDA.   They call them "Gay Deceivers"!

LAURA.   I won't wear them.

AMANDA.   You will!

LAURA.   Why should I?

AMANDA.   Because, to be painfully honest, your chest is flat.

LAURA.   You make it seem like we were setting a trap.

AMANDA.   All pretty girls are a trap, a pretty trap, and men expect them to be. Now look at yourself, young lady. This is the prettiest you will ever be! (*She stands back to admire* LAURA.) I've got to fix myself now! You're going to be surprised by your mother's appearance! (*She crosses through portieres, humming gaily.* LAURA *moves slowly to the long mirror and stares solemnly at herself. A wind blows the white curtain inward in a slow, graceful motion and with a faint, sorrowful sighing.* AMANDA *speaks from somewhere behind the portieres.*) It isn't dark enough yet. (LAURA *turns slowly before the mirror with a troubled look.*)

AMANDA (*laughing, still not visible*).   I'm going to show you something. I'm going to make a spectacular appearance!

LAURA.   What is it, Mother?

AMANDA.   Possess your soul in patience—you will see! Something I've resurrected from that old trunk! Styles haven't changed so terribly much after all . . . (*She parts the portieres.*) Now just look at your mother! (*She wears a girlish frock of yellow voile with a blue silk sash. She carries a bunch of jonquils—the legend of her youth is nearly revived. Now she speaks feverishly.*) This is the dress in which I led the cotillion. Won the cakewalk twice at Sunset Hill, wore one spring to the Governor's ball in Jackson! See how I sashayed around the ballroom, Laura? (*She raises her skirt and does a mincing step around the room.*) I wore it on Sundays for my gentlemen callers! I had it on the day I met your father—I had malaria fever all that spring. The change of climate from East Tennessee to the Delta—weakened resistance—I had a little temperature all the time—not enough to be serious—just enough to make me restless and giddy!—Invitations poured in—parties all over the Delta!— "Stay in bed," said Mother, "you have fever!"—but I just wouldn't.—I took quinine but kept on going, going!—Evenings, dances!—Afternoons, long, long rides! Picnics—lovely!—So lovely, that country in May.—All lacy with dogwood, literally flooded with jonquils!—That was the spring I had the craze for jonquils. Jonquils became an absolute obsession. Mother said, "Honey, there's no more room for jonquils." And still I kept on bringing in more jonquils. Whenever, wherever I saw them, I'd say, "Stop! Stop! I see jonquils!" I made the young men help me gather the jonquils! It was a joke, Amanda and her jonquils! Finally there were no more vases to hold them, every available space was filled with jonquils. No vases to hold them? All right, I'll hold them myself! And then I—(*She stops in front of the picture. Music.*) met your father! Malaria and jonquils and then—this—boy . . . (*She switches on the rose-colored lamp.*) I hope they get here before it starts to rain. (*She crosses upstage and places the jonquils in bowl on table.*) I gave your brother a little extra change so he and Mr. O'Connor could take the service car home.

LAURA (*with altered look*).   What did you say his name was?

AMANDA.   O'Connor.

LAURA.   What is his first name?

AMANDA.   I don't remember. Oh, yes, I do. It was—Jim! (LAURA *sways slightly and catches hold of a chair.*)

LAURA (*faintly*).   Not—Jim!

AMANDA.   Yes, that was it, it was Jim! I've never known a Jim that wasn't nice! (*The music becomes ominous.*)

LAURA.   Are you sure his name is Jim O'Connor?

AMANDA.   Yes. Why?

LAURA.   Is he the one that Tom used to know in high school?

AMANDA.   He didn't say so. I think he just got to know him at the warehouse.

LAURA.   There was a Jim O'Connor we both knew in high school —(*Then, with effort*) If that is the one that Tom is bringing to dinner— you'll have to excuse me, I won't come to the table.

AMANDA.   What sort of nonsense is this?

LAURA.   You asked me once if I'd ever liked a boy. Don't you re- member I showed you this boy's picture?

AMANDA.   You mean the boy you showed me in the year-book?

LAURA.   Yes, that boy.

AMANDA.   Laura, Laura, were you in love with that boy?

LAURA.   I don't know, Mother. All I know is I couldn't sit at the table if it was him!

AMANDA.   It won't be him! It isn't the least bit likely. But whether it is or not, you will come to the table. You will not be ex- cused.

LAURA.   I'll have to be, Mother.

AMANDA.   I don't intend to humor your silliness, Laura. I've had too much from you and your brother, both! So just sit down and com- pose yourself till they come. Tom has forgotten his key so you'll have to let them in, when they arrive.

LAURA (*panicky*).   Oh, Mother—*you* answer the door!

AMANDA (*lightly*).   I'll be in the kitchen—busy!

LAURA.   Oh, Mother, please answer the door, don't make me do it!

AMANDA (*crossing into kitchenette*).   I've got to fix the dressing for the salmon. Fuss, fuss—silliness!—over a gentleman caller! (*Door swings shut. LAURA is left alone. She utters a low moan and turns off the lamp— sits stiffly on the edge of the sofa, knotting her fingers together. TOM and JIM appear on the fire-escape steps and climb to landing. Hearing their approach, LAURA rises with a panicky gesture. She retreats to the portieres. The door- bell rings. LAURA catches her breath and touches her throat. Low drums sound. AMANDA calls.*) Laura, sweetheart! The door! (*LAURA stares at it without moving.*)

JIM.   I think we just beat the rain.

TOM. Uh-huh. (*He rings again, nervously.* JIM *whistles and fishes for a cigarette.*)

AMANDA (*very, very gaily*). Laura, that is your brother and Mr. O'Connor! Will you let them in, darling? (LAURA *crosses toward kitchenette door.*)

LAURA (*breathlessly*). Mother—you go to the door! (AMANDA *steps out of the kitchenette and stares furiously at* LAURA. *She points imperiously at the door.*) Please, please!

AMANDA (*in a fierce whisper*). What is the matter with you, you silly thing?

LAURA (*desperately*). Please, you answer it, *please!*

AMANDA. I told you I wasn't going to humor you, Laura. Why have you chosen this moment to lose your mind?

LAURA. Please, please, please, you go!

AMANDA. You'll have to go to the door because I can't!

LAURA (*despairingly*). I can't either!

AMANDA. *Why?*

LAURA. I'm *sick!*

AMANDA. I'm sick too—of your nonsense! Why can't you and your brother be normal people? Fantastic whims and behavior. (TOM *gives a long ring.*) Preposterous goings on! Can you give me one reason—(*She calls out lyrically.*) Coming! Just one second!—why you should be afraid to open a door? Now you answer it, Laura!

LAURA. Oh, oh, oh . . . (*She returns through the portieres, darts to the victrola, winds it frantically and turns it on.*)

AMANDA. Laura Wingfield, you march right to that door!

LAURA. Yes—yes, Mother! (*A faraway, scratchy rendition of "Dardanella" softens the air and gives her strength to move through it. She slips to the door and draws it cautiously open.* TOM *enters with the caller,* JIM O'CONNOR.)

TOM. Laura, this is Jim. Jim, this is my sister, Laura.

JIM (*stepping inside*). I didn't know that Shakespeare had a sister!

LAURA (*retreating stiff and trembling from the door*). How—how do you do?

JIM (*heartily extending his hand*). Okay! (LAURA *touches it hesitantly with hers.*) Your hand's *cold*, Laura!

LAURA. Yes, well—I've been playing the victrola . . .

JIM. Must have been playing classical music on it! You ought to play a little hot swing music to warm you up!

LAURA. Excuse me—I haven't finished playing the victrola . . . (*She turns awkwardly and hurries into the front room. She pauses a second by the victrola. Then she catches her breath and darts through the portieres like a frightened deer.)*

JIM (*grinning*).   What was the matter?

TOM.   Oh—with Laura? Laura is—terribly shy.

JIM.   Shy, huh? It's unusual to meet a shy girl nowadays. I don't believe you ever mentioned you had a sister.

TOM.   Well, now you know. I have one. Here is the *Post Dispatch*. You want a piece of it?

JIM.   Uh-huh.

TOM.   What piece? The comics?

JIM.   Sports! (*Glances at it.*) Ole Dizzy Dean is on his bad behavior.

TOM (*uninterested*).   Yeah? (*Lights a cigarette and crosses back to fire-escape door.*)

JIM.   Where are *you* going?

TOM.   I'm going out on the terrace.

JIM (*goes after him*).   You know, Shakespeare—I'm going to sell you a bill of goods!

TOM.   What goods?

JIM.   A course I'm taking.

TOM.   Huh.

JIM.   In public speaking! You and me, we're not the warehouse type.

TOM.   Thanks—that's good news. But what has public speaking got to do with it?

JIM.   It fits you for—executive positions!

TOM.   Awww.

JIM.   I tell you it's done a helluva lot for me.

TOM.   In what respect?

JIM.   In every! Ask yourself what is the difference between you an' me and men in the office down front? Brains?—No!—Ability?—No! Then what? Just one little thing—

TOM.   What is that one little thing?

JIM.   Primarily it amounts to—social poise! Being able to square up to people and hold your own on any social level!

AMANDA (*from the kitchenette*).   Tom?

TOM.   Yes, Mother?

AMANDA.   Is that you and Mr. O'Connor?

TOM.   Yes, Mother.

AMANDA.   Well, you just make yourselves comfortable in there.

TOM.   Yes, Mother.

AMANDA.   Ask Mr. O'Connor if he would like to wash his hands.

JIM.   Aw, no—no—thank you—I took care of that at the warehouse. Tom—

TOM.   Yes?

JIM.   Mr. Mendoza was speaking to me about you.

TOM.   Favorably?

JIM.   What do you think?

TOM.   Well—

JIM.   You're going to be out of a job if you don't wake up.

TOM.   I am waking up—

JIM.   You show no signs.

TOM.   The signs are interior. I'm planning to change. (*He leans over the rail speaking with quiet exhilaration. The incandescent marquees and signs of the first-run movie houses light his face from across the alley. He looks like a voyager.*) I'm right at the point of committing myself to a future that doesn't include the warehouse and Mr. Mendoza or even a night-school course in public speaking.

JIM.   What are you gassing about?

TOM.   I'm tired of the movies.

JIM.   Movies!

TOM.   Yes, movies! Look at them—(*a wave toward the marvels of Grand Avenue*) all of those glamorous people—having adventures—hogging it all, gobbling the whole thing up! You know what happens? People go to the *movies* instead of *moving*! Hollywood characters are supposed to have all the adventures for everybody in America, while everybody in America sits in a dark room and watches them have them! Yes, until there's a war. That's when adventure becomes available to the masses! *Everyone's* dish, not only Gable's! Then the people in the dark room come out of the dark room to have some adventures themselves—Goody, goody!—It's our turn now, to go to the South Sea Island—to make a safari—to be exotic, far-off!—But I'm not patient. I don't want to wait till then. I'm tired of the *movies* and I am *about* to move!

JIM (*incredulously*).   Move?

TOM.   Yes.

JIM.   When?

TOM.   Soon!

JIM.   Where? Where? (*The music seems to answer the question, while* TOM *thinks it over. He searches in his pockets.*)

TOM.   I'm starting to boil inside. I know I seem dreamy, but inside—well, I'm boiling!—Whenever I pick up a shoe, I shudder a little thinking how short life is and what I am doing!—Whatever that means, I know it doesn't mean shoes—except as something to wear on a traveler's feet! (*Finds paper.*) Look—

JIM.   What?

TOM.   I'm a member.

JIM (*reading*).   The Union of Merchant Seamen.

TOM.   I paid my dues this month, instead of the light bill.

JIM.   You will regret it when they turn the lights off.

TOM.   I won't be here.

JIM.   How about your mother?

TOM.   I'm like my father. The bastard son of a bastard! See how he grins? And he's been absent going on sixteen years!

JIM.   You're just talking, you drip. How does your mother feel about it?

TOM.   Shh!—Here comes Mother! Mother is not acquainted with my plans!

AMANDA (*coming through the portieres*).   Where are you all?

TOM.   On the terrace, Mother. (*They start inside. She advances to them. TOM is distinctly shocked at her appearance. Even JIM blinks a little. He is making his first contact with girlish Southern vivacity and in spite of the night-school course in public speaking is somewhat thrown off the beam by the unexpected outlay of social charm. Certain responses are attempted by JIM but are swept aside by AMANDA's gay laughter and chatter. TOM is embarrassed but after the first shock JIM reacts very warmly. He grins and chuckles, is altogether won over.*)

AMANDA (*coyly smiling, shaking her girlish ringlets*).   Well, well, well, so this is Mr. O'Connor. Introductions entirely unnecessary. I've heard so much about you from my boy. I finally said to him, Tom—good gracious!—why don't you bring this paragon to supper? I'd like to meet this nice young man at the warehouse!—Instead of just hearing him sing your praises so much! I don't know why my son is so stand-offish— that's not Southern behavior! Let's sit down and—I think we could stand a little more air in here! Tom, leave the door open. I felt a nice fresh breeze a moment ago. Where has it gone? Mmm, so warm already! And not quite summer, even. We're going to burn up when summer really gets started. However, we're having—we're having a very light supper. I think light things are better fo' this time of year. The same as light clothes are. Light clothes an' light food are what warm weather calls fo'. You know our blood gets so thick during th' winter—it takes a while fo' us to *adjust* ou'selves!—when the season changes . . . It's come so quick this year. I wasn't prepared. All of a sudden—heavens! Already summer!—I ran to the trunk an' pulled out this light dress— Terribly old! Historical almost! But feels so good—so good an' co-ol, y' know . . .

TOM.   Mother—

AMANDA.   Yes, honey?

TOM.   How about—supper?

AMANDA.   Honey, you go ask Sister if supper is ready! You know that Sister is in full charge of supper! Tell her you hungry boys are waiting for it. (*To* JIM) Have you met Laura?

JIM.   She—

AMANDA.   Let you in? Oh, good, you've met already! It's rare for a girl as sweet an' pretty as Laura to be domestic! But Laura, is, thank heavens, not only pretty but very domestic. I'm not at all. I never was a bit. I never could make a thing but angel-food cake. Well, in the south we had so many servants. Gone, gone, gone. All vestige of gracious living! Gone completely! I wasn't prepared for what the future brought me. All of my gentlemen callers were sons of planters and so of course I assumed that I would be married to one and raise my family on a large piece of land with plenty of servants. But man proposes—and woman accepts the proposal!—to vary that old, old saying° a little bit—I married no planter! I married a man who worked for the telephone company!—That gallantly smiling gentleman over there! (*Points to the picture.*) A telephone man who—fell in love with long-distance!—Now he travels and I don't even know where!—But what am I going on for about my—tribulations? Tell me yours—I hope you don't have any! Tom?

TOM (*returning*).   Yes, Mother.

AMANDA.   Is supper nearly ready?

TOM.   It looks to me like supper is on the table.

AMANDA.   Let me look—(*She rises prettily and looks through portieres.*) Oh, lovely!—But where is Sister?

TOM.   Laura is not feeling well and she says that she thinks she'd better not come to the table.

AMANDA.   What?—Nonsense!—Laura? Oh, Laura!

LAURA (*off stage, faintly*).   Yes, Mother.

AMANDA.   You really must come to the table. We won't be seated until you come to the table! Come in, Mr. O'Connor. You sit over there, and I'll—Laura? Laura Wingfield! You're keeping us waiting, honey! We can't say grace until you come to the table! (*The kitchenette door is pushed weakly open and* LAURA *comes in. She is obviously quite faint, her lips trembling, her eyes wide and staring. She moves unsteadily toward the table. Outside a summer storm is coming abruptly. The white curtains billow inward at the windows and there is a sorrowful murmur and deep*

---

old . . . saying: "Man proposes, but God disposes" (Thomas à Kempis [1380–1471], *Imitation of Christ*)

blue dusk. LAURA *suddenly stumbles—she catches at a chair with a faint moan.*)

TOM.   Laura!

AMANDA.   Laura! (*There is a clap of thunder. Despairingly*) Why, Laura, you *are* sick, darling! Tom, help your sister into the living room, dear! Sit in the living room, Laura—rest on the sofa. Well! (*To* JIM *as* TOM *helps his sister to the sofa in the living room*) Standing over the hot stove made her ill!—I told her that it was just too warm this evening, but—(TOM *comes back to the table.*) Is Laura all right now?

TOM.   Yes.

AMANDA.   What *is* that? Rain? A nice cool rain has come up! (*She gives the gentleman caller a frightened look.*) I think we may—have grace—now . . . (TOM *looks at her stupidly.*) Tom, honey—you say grace!

TOM.   Oh . . . "For these and all thy mercies—" (*They bow their heads,* AMANDA *stealing a nervous glance at* JIM. *In the living room,* LAURA, *stretched on the sofa, clenches her hand to her lips, to hold back a shuddering sob.*) God's Holy Name be praised—(*The scene dims out.*)

SCENE 7

Half an hour later. Dinner is just being finished in the dining room. LAURA *is still huddled upon the sofa, her feet drawn under her, her head resting on a pale blue pillow, her eyes wide and mysteriously watchful. The new floor lamp with its shade of rose-colored silk gives a soft, becoming light to her face, bringing out the fragile, unearthly prettiness which usually escapes attention. There is a steady murmur of rain, but it is slackening and soon stops; the air outside becomes pale and luminous as the moon breaks out. A moment after the curtain rises, the lights in both rooms flicker and go out.*

JIM.   Hey, there, Mr. Light Bulb!

AMANDA (*laughs nervously*).   Where was Moses when the lights went out? Ha-ha. Do you know the answer to that one, Mr. O'Connor?

JIM.   No, Ma'am, what's the answer?

AMANDA.   In the dark! (JIM *laughs appreciatively.*) Everybody sit still. I'll light the candles. Isn't it lucky we have them on the table? Where's a match? Which of you gentlemen can provide a match?

JIM.   Here.

AMANDA.   Thank you, sir.

JIM.   Not at all, Ma'am!

AMANDA.   I guess the fuse has burnt out. Mr. O'Connor, can you tell a burnt-out fuse? I know I can't and Tom is a total loss when it comes to mechanics. (*They rise from the table and go into the kitchenette, from where their voices are heard.*) Oh, be careful you don't bump into something. We don't want our gentleman caller to break his neck. Now wouldn't that be a fine howdy-do?

JIM.   Ha-ha! Where is the fuse box?

AMANDA.   Right here next to the stove. Can you see anything?

JIM.   Just a minute.

AMANDA.   Isn't electricity a mysterious thing? Wasn't it Benjamin Franklin who tied a key to a kite? We live in such a mysterious universe, don't we? Some people say that science clears up all the mysteries for us. In my opinion it only creates more! Have you found it yet?

JIM.   No, Ma'am. All these fuses look okay to me.

AMANDA.   Tom!

TOM.   Yes, Mother?

AMANDA.   That light bill I gave you several days ago. The one I told you we got the notices about?

TOM.   Oh—Yeah.

AMANDA.   You didn't neglect to pay it by chance?

TOM.   Why, I—

AMANDA.   Didn't! I might have known it!

JIM.   Shakespeare probably wrote a poem on that light bill, Mrs. Wingfield.

AMANDA.   I might have known better than to trust him with it! There's such a high price for negligence in this world!

JIM.   Maybe the poem will win a ten-dollar prize.

AMANDA.   We'll just have to spend the remainder of the evening in the nineteenth century, before Mr. Edison made the Mazda lamp!

JIM.   Candlelight is my favorite kind of light.

AMANDA.   That shows you're romantic! But that's no excuse for Tom. Well, we got through dinner. Very considerate of them to let us get through dinner before they plunged us into everlasting darkness, wasn't it, Mr. O'Connor?

JIM.   Ha-ha!

AMANDA.   Tom, as a penalty for your carelessness you can help me with the dishes.

JIM.   Let me give you a hand.

AMANDA.   Indeed you will not!

JIM.   I ought to be good for something.

AMANDA.   Good for something? (*Her tone is rhapsodic.*) You? Why, Mr. O'Connor nobody, *nobody's* given me this much entertainment in years—as you have!

JIM.   Aw, now, Mrs. Wingfield!

AMANDA.   I'm not exaggerating, not one bit! But Sister is all by her lonesome. You go keep her company in the parlor! I'll give you this lovely old candelabrum that used to be on the altar at the church of the Heavenly Rest. It was melted a little out of shape when the church burnt down. Lightning struck it one spring. Gypsy Jones was holding a revival at the time and he intimated that the church was destroyed because the Episcopalians gave card parties.

JIM.   Ha-ha.

AMANDA.   And how about you coaxing Sister to drink a little wine? I think it would be good for her! Can you carry both at once?

JIM.   Sure. I'm Superman!

AMANDA.   Now, Thomas, get into this apron! (JIM *comes into the dining room, carrying the candelabrum, its candles lighted, in one hand and a glass of wine in the other. The door of the kitchenette swings closed on* AMANDA's *gay laughter; the flickering light approaches the portieres.* LAURA *sits up nervously as he enters. Her speech at first is low and breathless from the almost intolerable strain of being alone with a stranger. At first, before* JIM's *warmth overcomes her paralyzing shyness,* LAURA's *voice is thin and breathless, as though she had just run up a steep flight of stairs.* JIM's *attitude is gently humorous. While the incident is apparently unimportant, it is to* LAURA *the climax of her secret life.*)

JIM.   Hello, there, Laura.

LAURA (*faintly*).   Hello. (*She clears her throat.*)

JIM.   How are you feeling now? Better?

LAURA.   Yes. Yes, thank you.

JIM.   This is for you. A little dandelion wine. (*He extends it toward her with extravagant gallantry.*)

LAURA.   Thank you.

JIM.   Drink it—but don't get drunk! (*He laughs heartily.* LAURA *takes the glass uncertainly, laughs shyly.*) Where shall I set the candles?

LAURA.   Oh—oh, anywhere . . .

JIM.   How about here on the floor? Any objections?

LAURA.   No.

JIM.   I'll spread a newspaper to catch the drippings. I like to sit on the floor. Mind if I do?

LAURA.   Oh, no.

JIM.   Give me a pillow?

LAURA.   What?

JIM.   A pillow!

LAURA.   Oh . . . (*Hands him one quickly.*)

JIM.   How about you? Don't you like to sit on the floor?

LAURA.   Oh—yes.

JIM.   Why don't you, then?

LAURA.   I—will.

JIM.   Take a pillow! (LAURA *does. Sits on the other side of the cande-labrum.* JIM *crosses his legs and smiles engagingly at her.*) I can't hardly see you sitting way over there.

LAURA.   I can—see you.

JIM.   I know, but that's not fair. I'm in the limelight. (LAURA *moves her pillow closer.*) Good! Now I can see you! Comfortable?

LAURA.   Yes.

JIM.   So am I. Comfortable as a cow! Will you have some gum?

LAURA.   No, thank you.

JIM.   I think I will indulge, with your permission. (*He musingly unwraps it and holds it up.*) Think of the fortune made by the guy that invented the first piece of chewing gum. Amazing, huh? The Wrigley Building is one of the sights of Chicago.—I saw it summer before last when I went up to the Century of Progress.° Did you take in the Century of Progress?

LAURA.   No, I didn't.

JIM.   Well, it was quite a wonderful exposition. What impressed me most was the Hall of Science. Gives you an idea of what the future will be in America, even more wonderful than the present time is! (*There is a pause.* JIM *smiles at her.*) Your brother tells me you're shy. Is that right, Laura?

LAURA.   I—don't know.

JIM.   I judge you to be an old-fashioned type of girl. Well, I think that's a pretty good type to be. Hope you don't think I'm being too personal—do you?

LAURA (*hastily, out of embarrassment*).   I believe I *will* take a piece of gum, if you—don't mind. (*Clearing her throat.*) Mr. O'Connor, have you—kept up with your singing?

JIM.   Singing? Me?

LAURA.   Yes. I remember what a beautiful voice you had.

JIM.   When did you hear me sing?

(*Voice off stage in the pause:*

O blow, ye winds, heigh-ho,
A-roving I will go!
I'm off to my love
With a boxing glove—
Ten thousand miles away!*)

JIM.   You say you've heard me sing?

Century of Progress: World's Fair in Chicago, 1933–1934

LAURA.   Oh, yes! Yes, very often . . . I—don't suppose—you re-member me—at all?

JIM (*smiling doubtfully*).   You know I have an idea I've seen you be-fore. I had that idea soon as you opened the door. It seems almost like I was about to remember your name. But the name that I started to call you—wasn't a name! And so I stopped myself before I said it.

LAURA.   Wasn't it—Blue Roses?

JIM (*springs up. Grinning*).   Blue Roses!—My gosh, yes—Blue Roses! That's what I had on my tongue when you opened the door! Isn't it funny what tricks your memory plays? I didn't connect you with high school somehow or other. But that's where it was; it was high school. I didn't even know you were Shakespeare's sister! Gosh, I'm sorry.

LAURA.   I didn't expect you to. You—barely knew me!

JIM.   But we did have a speaking acquaintance, huh?

LAURA.   Yes, we—spoke to each other.

JIM.   When did you recognize me?

LAURA.   Oh, right away!

JIM.   Soon as I came in the door?

LAURA.   When I heard your name I thought it was probably you. I knew that Tom used to know you a little in high school. So when you came in the door—well, then I was—sure.

JIM.   Why didn't you *say* something, then?

LAURA (*breathlessly*).   I didn't know what to say, I was—too surprised!

JIM.   For goodness sakes! You know, this sure is funny!

LAURA.   Yes! Yes, isn't it, though . . .

JIM.   Didn't we have a class in something together?

LAURA.   Yes, we did.

JIM.   What class was that?

LAURA.   It was—singing—chorus!

JIM.   Aw!

LAURA.   I sat across the aisle from you in the Aud.

JIM.   Aw.

LAURA.   Mondays, Wednesdays and Fridays.

JIM.   Now I remember—you always came in late.

LAURA.   Yes, it was so hard for me getting upstairs. I had that brace on my leg—it clumped so loud!

JIM.   I never heard any clumping.

LAURA (*wincing at the recollection*).   To me it sounded like—thunder!

JIM.   Well, well, well, I never even noticed.

LAURA.   And everybody was seated before I came in. I had to walk in front of all those people. My seat was in the back row. I had to go clumping all the way up the aisle with everyone watching!

JIM.   You shouldn't have been self-conscious.

LAURA.   I know, but I was. It was always such a relief when the singing started.

JIM.   Aw, yes, I've placed you now! I used to call you Blue Roses. How was it that I got started calling you that?

LAURA.   I was out of school a little while with pleurosis. When I came back you asked me what was the matter. I said I had pleurosis—you thought I said Blue Roses. That's what you always called me after that!

JIM.   I hope you didn't mind.

LAURA.   Oh, no—I liked it. You see, I wasn't acquainted with many—people . . .

JIM.   As I remember you sort of stuck by yourself.

LAURA.   I—I—never have had much luck at—making friends.

JIM.   I don't see why you wouldn't.

LAURA.   Well, I—started out badly.

JIM.   You mean being—

LAURA.   Yes, it sort of—stood between me—

JIM.   You shouldn't have let it!

LAURA.   I know, but it did, and—

JIM.   You were shy with people!

LAURA.   I tried not to be but never could—

JIM.   Overcome it?

LAURA.   No, I—I never could!

JIM.   I guess being shy is something you have to work out of kind of gradually.

LAURA (*sorrowfully*).   Yes—I guess it—

JIM.   Takes time!

LAURA.   Yes—

JIM.   People are not so dreadful when you know them. That's what you have to remember! And everybody has problems, not just you, but practically everybody has got some problems. You think of yourself as having the only problems, as being the only one who is disappointed. But just look around you and you will see lots of people as disappointed as you are. For instance, I hoped when I was going to high school that I would be further along at this time, six years later, than I am now—You remember that wonderful write-up I had in *The Torch*?

LAURA.   Yes! (*She rises and crosses to table.*)

JIM.   It said I was bound to succeed in anything I went into! (LAURA *returns with the annual.*) Holy Jeez! *The Torch!* (*He accepts it reverently. They smile across it with mutual wonder.* LAURA *crouches beside him and they begin to turn through it.* LAURA's *shyness is dissolving in his warmth.*)

LAURA.   Here you are in *The Pirates of Penzance!*

JIM (*wistfully*).   I sang the baritone lead in that operetta.

LAURA (*raptly*).   So—*beautifully!*

JIM (*protesting*).   Aw—

LAURA.   Yes, yes—beautifully—beautifully!

JIM.   You heard me?

LAURA.   All three times!

JIM.   No!

LAURA.   Yes!

JIM.   All three performances?

LAURA (*looking down*).   Yes.

JIM.   Why?

LAURA.   I—wanted to ask you to—autograph my program.

JIM.   Why didn't you ask me to?

LAURA.   You were always surrounded by your own friends so much that I never had a chance to.

JIM.   You should have just—

LAURA.   Well, I—thought you might think I was—

JIM.   Thought I might think you was—what?

LAURA.   Oh—

JIM (*with reflective relish*).   I was beleaguered by females in those days.

LAURA.   You were terribly popular!

JIM.   Yeah—

LAURA.   You had such a—friendly way—

JIM.   I was spoiled in high school.

LAURA.   Everybody—liked you!

JIM.   Including you?

LAURA.   I—yes, I—I did, too—(*She gently closes the book in her lap.*)

JIM.   Well, well, well!—Give me that program, Laura. (*She hands it to him. He signs it with a flourish.*) There you are—better late than never!

LAURA.   Oh, I—what a—surprise!

JIM.   My signature isn't worth very much right now. But some day—maybe—it will increase in value! Being disappointed is one thing and being discouraged is something else. I am disappointed but I am not discouraged. I'm twenty-three years old. How old are you?

LAURA.   I'll be twenty-four in June.

JIM.   That's not old age!

LAURA.   No, but—

JIM.   You finished high school?

LAURA (*with difficulty*).   I didn't go back.

JIM.   You mean you dropped out?

LAURA.   I made bad grades in my final examinations. (*She rises and replaces the book and the program. Her voice is strained.*) How is—Emily Meisenbach getting along?

JIM.   Oh, that kraut-head!

LAURA.   Why do you call her that?

JIM.   That's what she was.

LAURA.   You're not still—going with her?

JIM.   I never see her.

LAURA.   It said in the Personal Section that you were—engaged!

JIM.   I know, but I wasn't impressed by that—propaganda!

LAURA.   It wasn't—the truth?

JIM.   Only in Emily's optimistic opinion!

LAURA.   Oh—(JIM *lights a cigarette and leans indolently back on his elbows smiling at* LAURA *with a warmth and charm which lights her inwardly with altar candles. She remains by the table and turns in her hands a piece of glass to cover her tumult.*)

JIM (*after several reflective puffs on a cigarette*).   What have you done since high school? (*She seems not to hear him.*) Huh? (LAURA *looks up.*) I said what have you done since high school, Laura?

LAURA.   Nothing much.

JIM.   You must have been doing something these six long years.

LAURA.   Yes.

JIM.   Well, then, such as what?

LAURA.   I took a business course at business college—

JIM.   How did that work out?

LAURA.   Well, not very—well—I had to drop out, it gave me—indigestion—

JIM (*laughs gently*).   What are you doing now?

LAURA.   I don't do anything—much. Oh, please don't think I sit around doing nothing! My glass collection takes up a good deal of time. Glass is something you have to take good care of.

JIM.   What did you say—about glass?

LAURA.   Collection I said—I have one—(*She clears her throat and turns away again, acutely shy.*)

JIM (*abruptly*).   You know what I judge to be the trouble with you? Inferiority complex! Know what that is? That's what they call it when someone low-rates himself! I understand it because I had it, too. Although my case was not so aggravated as yours seems to be. I had it until I took up public speaking, developed my voice, and learned that I had an aptitude for science. Before that time I never thought of myself as being outstanding in any way whatsoever! Now I've never made a regular study of it, but I have a friend who says I can analyze people better than doctors that make a profession of it. I don't claim that to be necessarily true, but I can sure guess a person's psychology, Laura! (*Takes out his gum.*) Excuse me, Laura. I always take it out when the flavor is gone. I'll use this scrap of paper to wrap it in. I know how it is to get it stuck on a shoe. Yep—that's what I judge to be your principal trouble. A lack of confidence in yourself as a person. You don't have the proper amount of faith in yourself. I'm basing that fact on a number of your remarks and also on certain observations I've made. For instance that clumping you thought was so awful in high school. You say that you even dreaded to walk into class. You see what you did? You dropped out of school, you gave up an education because of a clump, which as far as I know was practically non-existent! A little physical defect is what you have. Hardly noticeable even! Magnified thousands of times by imagination! You know what my strong advice to you is? Think of yourself as *superior* in some way!

LAURA.   In what way would I think?

JIM.   Why, man alive, Laura! Just look about you a little. What do you see? A world full of common people! All of 'em born and all of 'em going to die! Which of them has one-tenth of your good points! Or mine! Or anyone else's, as far as that goes—Gosh! Everybody excels in some one thing. Some in many! (*Unconsciously glances at himself in the mirror.*) All you've got to do is discover in *what!* Take me, for instance. (*He adjusts his tie at the mirror.*) My interest happens to lie in electrodynamics. I'm taking a course in radio engineering at night school, Laura, on top of a fairly responsible job at the warehouse. I'm taking that course and studying public speaking.

LAURA.   Ohhhh.

JIM.   Because I believe in the future of television! (*Turning back to her.*) I wish to be ready to go up right along with it. Therefore I'm planning to get in on the ground floor. In fact I've already made the right connections and all that remains is for the industry itself to get under way! Full steam—(*His eyes are starry.*) Knowledge—Zzzzzp! Money— Zzzzzzp!—*Power!* That's the cycle democracy is built on! (*His attitude is convincingly dynamic.* LAURA *stares at him, even her shyness eclipsed in her absolute wonder. He suddenly grins.*) I guess you think I think a lot of myself?

LAURA.   No—o-o-o, I—

JIM.   Now how about you? Isn't there something you take more interest in than anything else?

LAURA.   Well, I do—as I said—have my—glass collection—(*A peal of girlish laughter from the kitchenette.*)

JIM.   I'm not right sure I know what you're talking about. What kind of glass is it?

LAURA.   Little articles of it, they're ornaments mostly! Most of them are little animals made out of glass, the tiniest little animals in the world. Mother calls them a glass menagerie! Here's an example of one, if you'd like to see it! This one is one of the oldest. It's nearly thirteen. (*Music: "The Glass Menagerie." JIM stretches out his hand.*) Oh, be careful—if you breathe, it breaks!

JIM.   I'd better not take it. I'm pretty clumsy with things.

LAURA.   Go on, I trust you with him! (*Places it in his palm.*) There now—you're holding him gently! Hold him over the light, he loves the light! You see how the light shines through him?

JIM.   It sure does shine!

LAURA.   I shouldn't be partial, but he is my favorite one.

JIM.   What kind of thing is this one supposed to be?

LAURA.   Haven't you noticed the single horn on his forehead?

JIM.   A unicorn, huh?

LAURA.   Mmm-hmmm!

JIM.   Unicorns, aren't they extinct in the modern world?

LAURA.   I know!

JIM.   Poor little fellow, he must feel sort of lonesome.

LAURA (*smiling*).   Well, if he does he doesn't complain about it. He stays on a shelf with some horses that don't have horns and all of them seem to get along nicely together.

JIM.   How do you know?

LAURA (*lightly*).   I haven't heard any arguments among them!

JIM (*grinning*).   No arguments, huh? Well, that's a pretty good sign! Where shall I set him?

LAURA.   Put him on the table. They all like a change of scenery once in a while!

JIM (*stretching*).   Well, well, well, well—Look how big my shadow is when I stretch!

LAURA.   Oh, oh, yes—it stretches across the ceiling!

JIM (*crossing to door*).   I think it's stopped raining. (*Opens fire-escape door.*) Where does the music come from?

LAURA.   From the Paradise Dance Hall across the alley.

JIM.   How about cutting the rug a little, Miss Wingfield?

LAURA.   Oh, I—

JIM.   Or is your program filled up? Let me have a look at it. (*Grasps imaginary card.*) Why, every dance is taken! I'll just have to scratch some out. (*Waltz music: "La Golondrina."*) Ahhh, a waltz! (*He executes some sweeping turns by himself then holds his arms toward* LAURA.)

LAURA (*breathlessly*).   I—can't dance!

JIM.   There you go, that inferiority stuff!

LAURA.   I've never danced in my life!

JIM.   Come on, try!

LAURA.   Oh, but I'd step on you!

JIM.   I'm not made out of glass.

LAURA.   How—how—how do we start?

JIM.   Just leave it to me. You hold your arms out a little.

LAURA.   Like this?

JIM.   A bit higher. Right. Now don't tighten up, that's the main thing about it—relax.

LAURA (*laughing breathlessly*).   It's hard not to.

JIM.   Okay.

LAURA.   I'm afraid you can't budge me.

JIM.   What do you bet I can't? (*He swings her into motion.*)

LAURA.   Goodness, yes, you can!

JIM.   Let yourself go, now, Laura, just let yourself go.

LAURA.   I'm—

JIM.   Come on!

LAURA.   Trying!

JIM.   Not so stiff—Easy does it!

LAURA.   I know but I'm—

JIM.   Loosen th' backbone! There now, that's a lot better.

LAURA.   Am I?

JIM.   Lots, lots better! (*He moves her about the room in a clumsy waltz.*)

LAURA.   Oh, my!

JIM.   Ha-ha!

LAURA.   Oh, my goodness!

JIM.   Ha-ha-ha! (*They suddenly bump into the table.* JIM *stops.*) What did we hit on?

LAURA.   Table.

JIM.   Did something fall off it? I think—

LAURA.   Yes.

JIM.   I hope it wasn't the little glass horse with the horn!

LAURA.   Yes.

JIM.   Aw, aw, aw. Is it broken?

LAURA.   Now it is just like all the other horses.

JIM.   It's lost its—

LAURA.   Horn! It doesn't matter. Maybe it's a blessing in disguise.

JIM.   You'll never forgive me. I bet that was your favorite piece of glass.

LAURA.   I don't have favorites much. It's no tragedy, Freckles. Glass breaks so easily. No matter how careful you are. The traffic jars the shelves and things fall off them.

JIM.   Still I'm awfully sorry that I was the cause.

LAURA (*smiling*).   I'll just imagine he had an operation. The horn was removed to make him feel less—freakish! (*They both laugh.*) Now he will feel more at home with the other horses, the ones that don't have horns . . .

JIM.   Ha-ha, that's very funny! (*Suddenly serious.*) I'm glad to see that you have a sense of humor. You know—you're—well—very different! Surprisingly different from anyone else I know! (*His voice becomes soft and hesitant with a genuine feeling.*) Do you mind me telling you that? (LAURA *is abashed beyond speech.*) I mean it in a nice way . . . (LAURA *nods shyly, looking away.*) You make me feel sort of—I don't know how to put it! I'm usually pretty good at expressing things, but— this is something that I don't know how to say! (LAURA *touches her throat and clears it—turns the broken unicorn in her hands. His voice becomes softer.*) Has anyone ever told you that you were pretty? (*Pause: music.* LAURA *looks up slowly, with wonder, and shakes her head.*)

Well, you are! In a very different way from anyone else. And all the nicer because of the difference, too. (*His voice becomes low and husky.* LAURA *turns away, nearly faint with the novelty of her emotions.*) I wish that you were my sister. I'd teach you to have some confidence in yourself. The different people are not like other people, but being different is nothing to be ashamed of. Because other people are not such wonderful people. They're one hundred times one thousand. You're one times one! They walk all over the earth. You just stay here. They're common as—weeds, but—you—well, you're—*Blue Roses!* (*Music changes.*)

LAURA.   But blue is wrong for—roses . . .

JIM.   It's right for you!—You're—pretty!

LAURA.   In what respect am I pretty?

JIM.   In all respects—believe me! Your eyes—your hair—are pretty! Your hands are pretty! (*He catches hold of her hand.*) You think I'm making this up because I'm invited to dinner and have to be nice. Oh, I could do that! I could put on an act for you, Laura, and say lots of things without being very sincere. But this time I am. I'm talking to you sincerely. I happened to notice you had this inferiority complex that keeps you from feeling comfortable with people. Somebody needs to build your confidence up and make you proud instead of shy and turning away and—blushing—Somebody—ought to—Ought to—*kiss* you, Laura! (*His hand slips slowly up her arm to her shoulder. Music swells tumultuously. He suddenly turns her about and kisses her on the lips. When he releases her,* LAURA *sinks on the sofa with a bright, dazed look.* JIM *backs away and fishes in his pocket for a cigarette.*) Stumble-john! (*He lights a cigarette, avoiding her look. There is a peal of girlish laughter from* AMANDA *in the kitchenette.* LAURA *slowly raises and opens her hand. It still contains the little broken glass animal. She looks at it with a tender, bewildered expression.*)

Stumble-john! I shouldn't have done that—That was way off beam. You don't smoke, do you? (*She looks up, smiling, not hearing the question. He sits beside her a little gingerly. She looks at him speechlessly—waiting. He coughs decorously and moves a little farther aside as he considers the situation and senses her feelings, dimly, with perturbation. He speaks gently.*) Would you—care for a—mint? (*She doesn't seem to hear him but her look grows brighter even.*) Peppermint—Life-Saver? My pocket's a regular drug store—wherever I go . . . (*He pops a mint in his mouth. Then gulps and decides to make a clean breast of it. He speaks slowly and gingerly.*) Laura, you know, if I had a sister like you, I'd do the same thing as Tom. I'd bring out fellows and—introduce her to them. The right type of boys of a type to—appreciate her. Only—well—he made a mistake with me. Maybe I've got no call to be saying this. That may not have been the idea in having me over. But what if it was? There's nothing wrong about that. The only trouble is that in my case—I'm not in a situation to—do the right thing. I can't take down your number and say I'll phone. I can't call up next week and—ask for a date. I thought I had better explain the situation in case you—misunderstood it and—hurt your feelings . . . (*Pause. Slowly, very slowly,* LAURA's *look changes, her eyes returning slowly from his to the ornament in her palm.* AMANDA *utters another gay laugh in the kitchenette.*)

LAURA (*faintly*). You—won't—call again?

JIM. No, Laura, I can't. (*He rises from the sofa.*) As I was just explaining. I've—got strings on me. Laura, I've—been going steady! I go out all of the time with a girl named Betty. She's a home-girl like you, and Catholic, and Irish, and in a great many ways we—get along fine. I met her last summer on a moonlight boat trip up the river to Alton, on the *Majestic.* Well—right away from the start it was—love! (LAURA *sways slightly forward and grips the arm of the sofa. He fails to notice, now enrapt in his own comfortable being.*) Being in love has made a new man of me! (*Leaning stiffly forward, clutching the arm of the sofa,* LAURA *struggles visibly with her storm. But* JIM *is oblivious; she is a long way off.*) The power of love is really pretty tremendous! Love is something that—changes the whole world, Laura! (*The storm abates a little and* LAURA *leans back. He notices her again.*) It happened that Betty's aunt took sick, she got a wire and had to go to Centralia. So Tom—when he asked me to dinner—I naturally just accepted the invitation, not knowing that you—that he—that I—(*He stops awkwardly.*) Huh —I'm a stumble-john! (*He flops back on the sofa. The holy candles in the altar of* LAURA's *face have been snuffed out. There is a look of almost infinite desolation.* JIM *glances at her uneasily.*) I wish that you would—say something. (*She bites her lip which was trembling and then bravely smiles. She opens her hand again on the broken glass ornament. Then she gently takes his hand and raises it level with her own. She carefully places the unicorn in the palm of his hand, then pushes his fingers closed upon it.*) What are you—doing that for? You want me to have him—Laura? (*She nods.*) What for?

LAURA.   A—souvenir . . . (*She rises unsteadily and crouches beside the victrola to wind it up. At this moment* AMANDA *rushes brightly back into the living room. She bears a pitcher of fruit punch in an old-fashioned cut-glass pitcher and a plate of macaroons. The plate has a gold border and poppies painted on it.*)

AMANDA.   Well, well, well! Isn't the air delightful after the shower? I've made you children a little liquid refreshment. (*She turns gaily to* JIM.) Jim, do you know that song about lemonade?

   "Lemonade, lemonade,
      Made in the shade and stirred with a spade—
      Good enough for any old maid!"

JIM (*uneasily*).   Ha-ha! No—I never heard it.

AMANDA.   Why, Laura! You look so serious!

JIM.   We were having a serious conversation.

AMANDA.   Good! Now you're better acquainted!

JIM (*uncertainly*).   Ha-ha! Yes.

AMANDA.   You modern young people are much more serious-minded than my generation. I was so gay as a girl!

JIM.   You haven't changed, Mrs. Wingfield.

AMANDA.   Tonight I'm rejuvenated! The gaiety of the occasion, Mr. O'Connor! (*She tosses her head with a peal of laughter. Spills lemonade.*) Oooo! I'm baptizing myself!

JIM.   Here—let me—

AMANDA (*setting the pitcher down*).   There now. I discovered we had some maraschino cherries. I dumped them in, juice and all!

JIM.   You shouldn't have gone to that trouble, Mrs. Wingfield.

AMANDA.   Trouble, trouble? Why, it was loads of fun! Didn't you hear me cutting up in the kitchen? I bet your ears were burning! I told Tom how outdone with him I was for keeping you to himself so long a time! He should have brought you over much, much sooner! Well, now that you've found your way, I want you to be a frequent caller! Not just occasional but all the time. Oh, we're going to have a lot of gay times together! I see them coming! Mmm, just breathe that air! So fresh, and the moon's so pretty! I'll skip back out—I know where my place is when young folks are having a—serious conversation!

JIM.   Oh, don't go out, Mrs. Wingfield. The fact of the matter is I've got to be going.

AMANDA.   Going, now? You're joking! Why, it's only the shank of the evening, Mr. O'Connor!

JIM.   Well, you know how it is.

AMANDA.   You mean you're a young workingman and have to keep workingmen's hours. We'll let you off early tonight. But only on the condition that next time you stay later.

What's the best night for you? Isn't Saturday night the best night for you workingmen?

JIM.   I have a couple of time-clocks to punch, Mrs. Wingfield. One at morning, another at night!

AMANDA.   My, but you *are* ambitious! You work at night, too?

JIM.   No, Ma'am, not work but—Betty! (*He crosses deliberately to pick up his hat. The band at the Paradise Dance Hall goes into a tender waltz.*)

AMANDA.   Betty? Betty? Who's—Betty! (*There is an ominous cracking sound in the sky.*)

JIM.   Oh, just a girl. The girl I go steady with! (*He smiles charmingly. The sky falls.*)

AMANDA (*a long-drawn exhalation*).   Ohhhh. . . . Is it a serious romance, Mr. O'Connor?

JIM.   We're going to be married the second Sunday in June.

AMANDA.   Ohhhh—how nice! Tom didn't mention that you were engaged to be married.

JIM.   The cat's not out of the bag at the warehouse yet. You know how they are. They call you Romeo and stuff like that. (*He stops at the oval mirror to put on his hat. He carefully shapes the brim and the crown to give a discreetly dashing effect.*) It's been a wonderful evening, Mrs. Wingfield. I guess this is what they mean by Southern hospitality.

AMANDA.   It really wasn't anything at all.

JIM.   I hope it don't seem like I'm rushing off. But I promised Betty I'd pick her up at the Wabash depot, an' by the time I get my jalopy down there her train'll be in. Some women are pretty upset if you keep 'em waiting.

AMANDA.   Yes, I know—The tyranny of women! (*Extends her hand.*) Good-bye, Mr. O'Connor. I wish you luck—and happiness— and success! All three of them, and so does Laura—Don't you Laura?

LAURA.   Yes!

JIM (*taking her hand*).   Good-bye Laura. I'm certainly going to trea- sure that souvenir. And don't you forget the good advice I gave you. (*Raises his voice to a cheery shout.*) So long, Shakespeare! Thanks again, ladies—Good night! (*He grins and ducks jauntily out. Still bravely gri- macing,* AMANDA *closes the door on the gentleman caller. Then she turns back to the room with a puzzled expression. She and* LAURA *don't dare to face each other.* LAURA *crouches beside the victrola to wind it.*)

AMANDA (*faintly*).   Things have a way of turning out so badly. I don't believe that I would play the victrola. Well, well—well—Our gentleman caller was engaged to be married! (*She raises her voice.*) Tom!

TOM (*from the kitchenette*).   Yes, Mother?

AMANDA.   Come in here a minute. I want to tell you something awfully funny.

TOM (*enters with a macaroon and a glass of lemonade*).   Has the gentleman caller gotten away already?

AMANDA.   The gentleman caller has made an early departure. What a wonderful joke you played on us!

TOM.   How do you mean?

AMANDA.   You didn't mention that he was engaged to be married.

TOM.   Jim? Engaged?

AMANDA.   That's what he just informed us.

TOM.   I'll be jiggered! I didn't know about that.

AMANDA.   That seems very peculiar.

TOM.   What's peculiar about it?

AMANDA.   Didn't you call him your best friend down at the warehouse?

TOM.   He is, but how did I know?

AMANDA.   It seems extremely peculiar that you wouldn't know your best friend was going to be married!

TOM.   The warehouse is where I work, not where I know things about people!

AMANDA.   You don't know things anywhere! You live in a dream; you manufacture illusions! (*He crosses to the door.*) Where are you going?

TOM.   I'm going to the movies.

AMANDA.   That's right, now that you've had us make such fools of ourselves. The effort, the preparations, all the expense! The new floor lamp, the rug, the clothes for Laura! All for what? To entertain some other girl's fiancé! Go to the movies, go! Don't think about us, a mother deserted, an unmarried sister who's crippled and has no job! Don't let anything interfere with your selfish pleasure! Just go, go, go— to the movies!

TOM.   All right, I will! The more you shout about my selfishness to me the quicker I'll go, and I won't go to the movies!

AMANDA.   Go, then! Then go to the moon—you selfish dreamer!

(TOM *smashes his glass on the floor. He plunges out of the fire-escape, slamming the door.* LAURA *screams in fright. The dance-hall music becomes louder.* TOM *goes to the rail and grips it desperately, lifting his face in the chill white moonlight penetrating the narrow abyss of the alley.*

(TOM's *closing speech is timed with what is happening inside the house. The interior scene is played as though viewed through soundproof glass.* AMANDA *appears to be making a comforting speech to* LAURA *who is huddled upon the sofa. Now that we cannot hear the mother's speech, her silliness is gone and she has dignity and tragic beauty.* LAURA's *dark hair hides her face until at the end of the speech she lifts it to smile at her mother.* AMANDA's *gestures are slow and graceful, almost dance-like, as she comforts her daughter. At the end of her speech she glances a moment at the father's picture—then withdraws through the portieres. At the close of* TOM's *speech,* LAURA *blows out the candles, ending the play.*)

TOM.   I didn't go to the moon, I went much further—for time is the longest distance between two places—Not long after that I was fired for writing a poem on the lid of a shoe-box. I left Saint Louis. I descended the steps of this fire-escape for a last time and followed, from then on, in my father's footsteps, attempting to find in motion what was lost in space—I traveled around a great deal. The cities swept about me like dead leaves, leaves that were brightly colored but torn away from the branches. I would have stopped, but I was pursued by something. It always came upon me unawares, taking me altogether by surprise. Perhaps it was a familiar bit of music. Perhaps it was only a piece of transparent glass—Perhaps I am walking along a street at night, in some strange city, before I have found companions. I pass the lighted window of a shop where perfume is sold. The window is filled with pieces of colored glass, tiny transparent bottles in delicate colors, like bits of a shattered rainbow. Then all at once my sister touches my shoulder. I turn around and look into her eyes . . . Oh, Laura, Laura, I tried to leave you behind me, but I am more faithful than I intended to be! I reach for a cigarette, I cross the street, I run into the movies or a bar, I buy a drink, I speak to the nearest stranger—anything that can blow your candles out! (LAURA *bends over the candles.*) For nowadays

the world is lit by lightning! Blow out your candles, Laura—and so
goodbye . . .
(*She blows the candles out.*)

QUESTIONS

1. In presenting Scene 1, the author says: "The scene is memory and is therefore nonrealistic." To whose memory does he refer? Why should memory
be nonrealistic? List the different ways in which the play is nonrealistic.
What, according to Tom in his opening speech, is the ultimate aim of this
nonrealistic method of presentation?

2. How does the kind of language Tom uses as a narrator differ from that he
uses as a character? What would happen to the play if Tom used the first
kind of language throughout?

3. What is Tom's dilemma? Why is he always quarreling with his mother?
What is his attitude toward Laura? Why does he finally leave? Does he
ever resolve his dilemma?

4. What qualities possessed by Tom, and by him alone, make him the proper
narrator of the play?

5. Laura is the pivotal character in the play, as evidenced by its title and by
the fact that the main actions of the play revolve around her. What are
the symptoms and causes of her mental condition? Can they all be traced
to her physical defect? What qualities make her a sympathetic character?
How does her relationship with her mother differ from Tom's?

6. What symbolic meanings has Laura's glass menagerie? What, especially,
is symbolized by the unicorn? How and why does her reaction to Jim's
breaking the unicorn differ from her reaction to Tom's breaking several
pieces at the end of Scene 3? Why does she give the broken unicorn to Jim
as a souvenir? What future do you predict for her? What symbolism has her
blowing out the candles at the end of the play?

7. The author tells us (page 1143) that "Amanda, having failed to establish
contact with reality, continues to live vitally in her illusions." What part
of this statement could be applied to Laura as well? What part could not?
What are the chief instances in the play of Amanda's having lost "contact
with reality"? What are her chief illusions? What are her strengths? How
is she both cruel and tender with her children? What qualities has she in
common with Jim, the gentleman caller? Why do you suppose her husband left her?

8. The author describes Jim O'Connor as "a nice, ordinary, young man"
(page 1143). Tom (in Scene 1) describes him as "the most realistic character, being an emissary from that world of reality that we were set apart
from." In what ways is Jim "nice"? In what ways is he "ordinary"? In what
ways and in what sense is he more "realistic" than the Wingfields? Does
this mean that he is without delusions? What would you predict for his
future? Of what is he symbolic?

9. Account for Jim's treatment of Laura in Scene 7.

10. What trait do Laura, Amanda, and Tom all share, which makes Jim more realistic than they? Explain the dramatic irony in Amanda's remark to Tom, in their final dialogue, "You don't know things anywhere! You live in a dream; you manufacture illusions!"

11. What respective claims have Tom, Laura, and Amanda for being considered the protagonist of the play? For which character would it be most crucial to the success or failure of a production to obtain a highly accomplished actor or actress? Why?

12. The play is set in the 1930s. Of what significance are the many references throughout the play to its social and historical background? How are these larger events and the Wingfields' domestic lives related?

13. The play is divided into seven scenes. If you were to produce it with one intermission, where would you put the intermission? For what reasons?

Luis Valdez
Los Vendidos

Characters

HONEST SANCHO
SECRETARY
FARMWORKER

JOHNNY PACHUCO
REVOLUCIONARIO
MEXICAN-AMERICAN

SCENE: HONEST SANCHO's *Used Mexican Lot and Mexican Curio Shop. Three models are on display in* HONEST SANCHO's *shop. To the right, there is a* REVOLUCIONARIO, *complete with sombrero, carrilleras and carabina 30-30.° At center, on the floor, there is the* FARMWORKER, *under a broad straw sombrero. At stage left is the* PACHUCO, *filero° in hand.* HONEST SANCHO *is moving among his models, dusting them off and preparing for another day of business.*

SANCHO.   Bueno, bueno, mis monos, vamos a ver a quién vendemos ahora, ¿no? (*To audience*) ¡Quihubo!° I'm Honest Sancho and this is my shop. Antes fui contratista, pero ahora logré mi negocito.° All I need now is a customer. (*A bell rings offstage.*) Ay, a customer!

SECRETARY (*entering*).   Good morning, I'm Miss Jimenez from . . .

SANCHO.   Ah, una chicana! Welcome, welcome Señorita Jiménez.

SECRETARY (*Anglo pronunciation*).   JIM-enez.

SANCHO.   ¿Qué?

LOS VENDIDOS   First performed in 1967. The title may be translated both "men who are sold" and "the sellouts," i.e., traitors to the cause. Luis Valdez was born in 1940 in Delano, California, the son of migrant farmworkers (*campesinos*). Although his early education was interrupted by the need to work in the fields, he earned a B.A. in English from San Jose State College in 1964 and then joined the San Francisco Mime Troupe performing political and satirical plays in public parks. In 1965 he founded El Teatro Campesino in Delano to present satirical skits (called "Actos") in support of the farmworkers' cause and as a means of political protest. Like others of the Actos, *Los Vendidos* was presented free to an audience in a park. Subsequently, in 1972, it won an Emmy in a television production for the Corporation for Public Broadcasting. At the time of its writing, Ronald Reagan was governor of California and another film actor, George Murphy, was a U.S. senator.

carrilleras . . . 30-30: cartridge belts and 30-30 rifle   filero: switchblade
Bueno . . . Quihubo!: Good, good, my cuties, let's see who we can sell now. What's going on?   Antes fui . . . negocito: I used to be a contractor, but now I run my little business.

SECRETARY.   My name is Miss JIM-enez. Don't you speak English? What's wrong with you?

SANCHO.   Oh, nothing, Señorita JIM-enez. I'm here to help you.

SECRETARY.   That's better. As I was starting to say, I'm a secretary from Governor Reagan's office, and we're looking for a Mexican type for the administration.

SANCHO.   Well, you come to the right place, lady. This is Honest Sancho's Used Mexican Lot, and we got all types here. Any particular type you want?

SECRETARY.   Yes, we were looking for somebody suave . . .

SANCHO.   Suave.

SECRETARY.   Debonaire.

SANCHO.   De buen aire.

SECRETARY.   Dark.

SANCHO.   Prieto.

SECRETARY.   But of course, not too dark.

SANCHO.   No muy prieto.

SECRETARY.   Perhaps, beige.

SANCHO.   Beige, just the tone. Asi como cafecito con leche,° ¿no?

SECRETARY.   One more thing. He must be hard-working.

SANCHO.   That could only be one model. Step right over here to the center of the shop, lady. (*They cross to the* FARMWORKER.) This is our standard farmworker model. As you can see, in the words of our beloved Senator George Murphy, he is "built close to the ground." Also, take special notice of his 4-ply Goodyear huaraches,° made from the rain tire. This wide-brimmed sombrero is an extra added feature; keeps off the sun, rain and dust.

SECRETARY.   Yes, it does look durable.

SANCHO.   And our farmworker model is friendly. Muy amable.° Watch. (*Snaps his fingers.*)

FARMWORKER (*lifts up head*). Buenos días, señorita. (*His head drops.*)

SECRETARY.   My, he is friendly.

SANCHO.   Didn't I tell you? Loves his patrones!° But his most attractive feature is that he's hard-working. Let me show you. (*Snaps fingers.* FARMWORKER *stands.*)

FARMWORKER.   ¡El jale!° (*He begins to work.*)

SANCHO.   As you can see he is cutting grapes.

SECRETARY.   Oh, I wouldn't know.

Asi . . . leche: Like coffee with milk   **huaraches:** sandals   **Muy amable:** Very friendly   **patrones:** bosses   **El jale:** The job

SANCHO.   He also picks cotton. (*Snaps.* FARMWORKER *begins to pick cotton.*)

SECRETARY.   Versatile, isn't he?

SANCHO.   He also picks melons. (*Snaps.* FARMWORKER *picks melons.*) That's his slow speed for late in the season. Here's his fast speed. (*Snap.* FARMWORKER *picks faster.*)

SECRETARY.   Chihuahua.° . . . I mean, goodness, he sure is a hardworker.

SANCHO (*pulls the* FARMWORKER *to his feet*).   And that isn't the half of it. Do you see these little holes on his arms that appear to be pores? During those hot sluggish days in the field when the vines or the branches get so entangled, it's almost impossible to move, these holes emit a certain grease that allows our model to slip and slide right through the crop with no trouble at all.

SECRETARY.   Wonderful. But is he economical?

SANCHO.   Economical? Señorita, you are looking at the Volkswagen of Mexicans. Pennies a day is all it takes. One plate of beans and tortillas will keep him going all day. That, and chile. Plenty of chile. Chile jalapeños, chile verde, chile colorado. But, of course, if you do give him chile (*Snap.* FARMWORKER *turns left face. Snap.* FARMWORKER *bends over.*), then you have to change his oil filter once a week.

SECRETARY.   What about storage?

SANCHO.   No problem. You know these new farm labor camps our Honorable Governor Reagan has built out by Parlier or Raisin City? They were designed with our model in mind. Five, six, seven, even ten in one of those shacks will give you no trouble at all. You can also put him in old barns, old cars, riverbanks. You can even leave him out in the field overnight with no worry!

SECRETARY.   Remarkable.

SANCHO.   And here's an added feature: every year at the end of the season, this model goes back to Mexico and doesn't return, automatically, until next spring.

SECRETARY.   How about that. But tell me, does he speak English?

SANCHO.   Another outstanding feature is that last year this model was programmed to go out on STRIKE! (*Snap.*)

FARMWORKER.   ¡Huelga! ¡Huelga! Hermanos, sálganse de esos files.° (*Snap. He stops.*)

SECRETARY.   No! Oh no, we can't strike in the State Capitol.

SANCHO.   Well, he also scabs. (*Snap.*)

Chihuahua: Hot damn!   **¡Huelga! . . . files:** Strike! Strike! Brothers, leave those rows.

FARMWORKER.   Me vendo barato, ¿y qué?° (*Snap.*)

SECRETARY.   That's much better, but you didn't answer my question. Does he speak English?

SANCHO.   Bueno . . . no, pero° he has other . . .

SECRETARY.   No.

SANCHO.   Other features.

SECRETARY.   No! He just won't do!

SANCHO.   Okay, okay, pues.° We have other models.

SECRETARY.   I hope so. What we need is something a little more sophisticated.

SANCHO.   Sophisti-qué?

SECRETARY.   An urban model.

SANCHO.   Ah, from the city! Step right back. Over here in this corner of the shop is exactly what you're looking for. Introducing our new 1969 JOHNNY PACHUCO° model! This is our fast-back model. Streamlined. Built for speed, low-riding, city life. Take a look at some of these features. Mag shoes, dual exhausts, green chartreuse paint-job, dark-tint windshield, a little poof on top. Let me just turn him on. (*Snap.* JOHNNY *walks to stage center with a* PACHUCO *bounce.*)

SECRETARY.   What was that?

SANCHO.   That, señorita, was the Chicano shuffle.

SECRETARY.   Okay, what does he do?

SANCHO.   Anything and everything necessary for city life. For instance, survival: he knife fights. (*Snaps.* JOHNNY *pulls out a switchblade and swings at* SECRETARY. SECRETARY *screams.*) He dances. (*Snap.*)

JOHNNY (*singing*).   "Angel Baby, my Angel Baby . . ." (*Snap.*)

SANCHO.   And here's a feature no city model can be without. He gets arrested, but not without resisting, of course. (*Snap.*)

JOHNNY.   En la madre, la placa.° I didn't do it! I didn't do it!

(JOHNNY *turns and stands up against an imaginary wall, legs spread out, arms behind his back.*)

SECRETARY.   Oh no, we can't have arrests! We must maintain law and order.

SANCHO.   But he's bilingual.

SECRETARY.   Bilingual?

SANCHO.   Simón que yes. He speaks English! Johnny, give us some English. (*Snap.*)

JOHNNY (*comes downstage*).   Fuck-you!

Me vendo . . . qué?: My price is cheap, so what?   **Bueno . . . pero:** Well, no, but
pues: then   **Pachuco:** a slang term for an urban tough   **En la . . . placa:** Oh, oh,
the cops

SECRETARY (*gasps*). Oh! I've never been so insulted in my whole life!

SANCHO. Well, he learned it in your school.

SECRETARY. I don't care where he learned it.

SANCHO. But he's economical.

SECRETARY. Economical?

SANCHO. Nickels and dimes. You can keep Johnny running on hamburgers, Taco Bell tacos, Lucky Lager beer, Thunderbird wine, yesca . . .

SECRETARY. Yesca?

SANCHO. Mota.

SECRETARY. Mota?

SANCHO. Leños° . . . marijuana. (*Snap.* JOHNNY *inhales on an imaginary joint.*)

SECRETARY. That's against the law!

JOHNNY (*big smile, holding his breath*). Yeah.

SANCHO. He also sniffs glue. (*Snap.* JOHNNY *inhales glue, big smile.*)

JOHNNY. Tha's too much, man, ése.°

SECRETARY. No, Mr. Sancho, I don't think this . . .

SANCHO. Wait a minute, he has other qualities I know you'll love. For example, an inferiority complex. (*Snap.*)

JOHNNY (*to* SANCHO). You think you're better than me, huh, ése? (*Swings switchblade.*)

SANCHO. He can also be beaten and he bruises. Cut him and he bleeds, kick him and he . . . (*He beats, bruises and kicks* PACHUCO.) Would you like to try it?

SECRETARY. Oh, I couldn't.

SANCHO. Be my guest. He's a great scapegoat.

SECRETARY. No really.

SANCHO. Please.

SECRETARY. Well, all right. Just once. (*She kicks* PACHUCO.) Oh, he's so soft.

SANCHO. Wasn't that good? Try again.

SECRETARY (*kicks* PACHUCO). Oh, he's wonderful! (*She kicks him again.*)

SANCHO. Okay, that's enough, lady. You'll ruin the merchandise. Yes, our Johnny Pachuco model can give you many hours of pleasure. Why, the LAPD just bought twenty of these to train their rookie cops on. And talk about maintenance. Señorita, you are looking at an entirely self-supporting machine. You're never going to find our Johnny

Leños: Joints   **ése:** man

Pachuco model on the relief rolls. No, sir, this model knows how to liberate.

SECRETARY.   Liberate?

SANCHO.   He steals. (*Snap.* JOHNNY *rushes to* SECRETARY *and steals her purse.*)

JOHNNY.   ¡Dame esa bolsa, vieja!° (*He grabs the purse and runs. Snap by* SANCHO, *he stops.* SECRETARY *runs after* JOHNNY *and grabs purse away from him, kicking him as she goes.*)

SECRETARY.   No, no, no! We can't have any more thieves in the State Administration. Put him back.

SANCHO.   Okay, we still got other models. Come on, Johnny, we'll sell you to some old lady. (SANCHO *takes* JOHNNY *back to his place.*)

SECRETARY.   Mr. Sancho, I don't think you quite understand what we need. What we need is something that will attract the women voters. Something more traditional, more romantic.

SANCHO.   Ah, a lover. (*He smiles meaningfully.*) Step right over here, señorita. Introducing our standard Revolucionario and/or Early California Bandit type. As you can see, he is well-built, sturdy, durable. This is the International Harvester of Mexicans.

SECRETARY.   What does he do?

SANCHO.   You name it, he does it. He rides horses, stays in the mountains, crosses deserts, plains, rivers, leads revolutions, follows revolutions, kills, can be killed, serves as a martyr, hero, movie star. Did I say movie star? Did you ever see *Viva Zapata? Viva Villa, Villa Rides, Pancho Villa Returns, Pancho Villa Goes Back, Pancho Villa Meets Abbott and Costello?*

SECRETARY.   I've never seen any of those.

SANCHO.   Well, he was in all of them. Listen to this. (*Snap.*)

REVOLUCIONARIO (*scream*).   ¡Viva Villaaaaa!

SECRETARY.   That's awfully loud.

SANCHO.   He has a volume control. (*He adjusts volume. Snap.*)

REVOLUCIONARIO (*mousey voice*).   Viva Villa.

SECRETARY.   That's better.

SANCHO.   And even if you didn't see him in the movies, perhaps you saw him on TV. He makes commercials. (*Snap.*)

REVOLUCIONARIO.   Is there a Frito Bandito in your house?

SECRETARY.   Oh, yes, I've seen that one!

SANCHO.   Another feature about this one is that he is economical. He runs on raw horsemeat and tequila!

SECRETARY.   Isn't that rather savage?

¡Dame . . . vieja!: Give me that purse, old lady!

SANCHO.   Al contrario,° it makes him a lover. (*Snap.*)

REVOLUCIONARIO (*to* SECRETARY).   Ay, mamasota, cochota, ven pa 'ca!° (*He grabs* SECRETARY *and folds her back, Latin-lover style.*)

SANCHO (*Snap.* REVOLUCIONARIO *goes back upright*).   Now wasn't that nice?

SECRETARY.   Well, it was rather nice.

SANCHO.   And finally, there is one outstanding feature about this model I know the ladies are going to love: he's a genuine antique! He was made in Mexico in 1910!

SECRETARY.   Made in Mexico?

SANCHO.   That's right. Once in Tijuana, twice in Guadalajara, three times in Cuernavaca.

SECRETARY.   Mr. Sancho, I thought he was an American product.

SANCHO.   No, but . . .

SECRETARY.   No, I'm sorry. We can't buy anything but American made products. He just won't do.

SANCHO.   But he's an antique!

SECRETARY.   I don't care. You still don't understand what we need. It's true we need Mexican models, such as these, but it's more important that he be American.

SANCHO.   American?

SECRETARY.   That's right, and judging from what you've shown me, I don't think you have what we want. Well, my lunch hour's almost over, I better . . .

SANCHO.   Wait a minute! Mexican but American?

SECRETARY.   That's correct.

SANCHO.   Mexican but . . . (*A sudden flash.*) American! Yeah, I think we've got exactly what you want. He just came in today! Give me a minute. (*He exits. Talks from backstage.*) Here he is in the shop. Let me just get some papers off. There. Introducing our new 1970 Mexican-American! Ta-ra-ra-raaaa! (SANCHO *brings out the* MEXICAN-AMERICAN *model, a clean-shaven middle-class type in a business suit, with glasses.*)

SECRETARY (*impressed*).   Where have you been hiding this one?

SANCHO.   He just came in this morning. Ain't he a beauty? Feast your eyes on him! Sturdy U.S. Steel frame, streamlined, modern. As a matter of fact, he is built exactly like our Anglo models, except that he comes in a variety of darker shades: naugahyde, leather or leatherette.

SECRETARY.   Naugahyde.

SANCHO.   Well, we'll just write that down. Yes, señorita, this model represents the apex of American engineering! He is bilingual, college

Al contrario: On the contrary   **Ay . . . pa 'ca:** Hey, c'mere, big mama!

educated, ambitious! Say the word "acculturate" and he accelerates. He is intelligent, well-mannered, clean. Did I say clean? (*Snap.* MEXICAN-AMERICAN *raises his arm.*) Smell.

SECRETARY (*smells*).   Old Sobaco, my favorite.

SANCHO (*Snap.* MEXICAN-AMERICAN *turns toward* SANCHO). Eric? (*To* SECRETARY) We call him Eric García. (*To* ERIC) I want you to meet Miss JIM-enez, Eric.

MEXICAN-AMERICAN.   Miss JIM-enez, I am delighted to make your acquaintance. (*He kisses her hand.*)

SECRETARY.   Oh, my, how charming!

SANCHO.   Did you feel the suction? He has seven especially engineered suction cups right behind his lips. He's a charmer all right!

SECRETARY.   How about boards, does he function on boards?

SANCHO.   You name them, he is on them. Parole boards, draft boards, school boards, taco quality control boards, surf boards, two by fours.

SECRETARY.   Does he function in politics?

SANCHO.   Señorita, you are looking at a political machine. Have you ever heard of the OEO, EOC, COD, WAR ON POVERTY? That's our model! Not only that, he makes political speeches.

SECRETARY.   May I hear one?

SANCHO.   With pleasure. (*Snap.*) Eric, give us a speech.

MEXICAN-AMERICAN.   Mr. Congressman, Mr. Chairman, members of the board, honored guests, ladies and gentlemen. (SANCHO *and* SECRETARY *applaud.*) Please, please. I come before you as a Mexican-American to tell you about the problems of the Mexican. The problems of the Mexican stem from one thing and one thing only: he's stupid. He's uneducated. He needs to stay in school. He needs to be ambitious, forward-looking, harder-working. He needs to think American, American, American, American, American! God bless America! God bless America! God bless America! (*He goes out of control.* SANCHO *snaps frantically and the* MEXICAN-AMERICAN *finally slumps forward, bending at the waist.*)

SECRETARY.   Oh my, he's patriotic too!

SANCHO.   Sí, señorita, he loves his country. Let me just make a little adjustment here. (*Stands* MEXICAN-AMERICAN *up.*)

SECRETARY.   What about upkeep? Is he economical?

SANCHO.   Well, no, I won't lie to you. The Mexican-American costs a little bit more, but you get what you pay for. He's worth every extra cent. You can keep him running on dry Martinis, Langendorf bread . . .

SECRETARY.   Apple pie?

Sancho. Only Mom's. Of course, he's also programmed to eat Mexican food at ceremonial functions, but I must warn you, an overdose of beans will plug up his exhaust.

Secretary. Fine! There's just one more question. How much do you want for him?

Sancho. Well, I tell you what I'm gonna do. Today and today only, because you've been so sweet, I'm gonna let you steal this model from me! I'm gonna let you drive him off the lot for the simple price of, let's see, taxes and license included, $15,000.

Secretary. Fifteen thousand dollars? For a Mexican!!!!

Sancho. Mexican? What are you talking about? This is a Mexican-American! We had to melt down two pachucos, a farmworker and three gabachos° to make this model! You want quality, but you gotta pay for it! This is no cheap run-about. He's got class!

Secretary. Okay, I'll take him.

Sancho. You will?

Secretary. Here's your money.

Sancho. You mind if I count it?

Secretary. Go right ahead.

Sancho. Well, you'll get your pink slip in the mail. Oh, do you want me to wrap him up for you? We have a box in the back.

Secretary. No, thank you. The Governor is having a luncheon this afternoon, and we need a brown face in the crowd. How do I drive him?

Sancho. Just snap your fingers. He'll do anything you want. (Secretary snaps. Mexican-American steps forward.)

Mexican-American. ¡Raza querida, vamos levantando armas para liberarnos de estos desgraciados gabachos que nos explotan! Vamos . . .°

Secretary. What did he say?

Sancho. Something about taking up arms, killing white people, etc.

Secretary. But he's not supposed to say that!

Sancho. Look, lady, don't blame me for bugs from the factory. He's your Mexican-American, you bought him, now drive him off the lot!

Secretary. But he's broken!

Sancho. Try snapping another finger. (Secretary snaps. Mexican-American comes to life again.)

---

gabachos: whites   ¡Raza querida . . . Vamos: Beloved members of our Mexican race, let's take up arms to free ourselves from those damned whites who exploit us! Let's go . . .

MEXICAN-AMERICAN.   Esta gran humanidad ha dicho basta! ¡Y se ha puesto en marcha! ¡Basta! ¡Basta! ¡Viva la raza! ¡Viva la causa! ¡Viva la huelga! ¡Vivan los brown berets! ¡Vivan los estudiantes!° ¡Chicano power! (*The* MEXICAN-AMERICAN *turns toward the* SECRETARY, *who gasps and backs up. He keeps turning toward the* PACHUCO, FARMWORKER *and* REVOLUCIONARIO, *snapping his fingers and turning each of them on, one by one.*)

PACHUCO (*Snap. To* SECRETARY). I'm going to get you, baby! ¡Viva la raza!

FARMWORKER (*Snap. To* SECRETARY). ¡Viva la huelga! ¡Viva la huelga! ¡Viva la huelga!

REVOLUCIONARIO (*Snap. To* SECRETARY). ¡Viva la revolución! (*The three models join together and advance toward the* SECRETARY, *who backs up and runs out of the shop screaming.* SANCHO *is at the other end of the shop holding his money in his hand. All freeze. After a few seconds of silence, the* PACHUCO *moves and stretches, shaking his arms and loosening up. The* FARMWORKER *and* REVOLUCIONARIO *do the same.* SANCHO *stays where he is, frozen to his spot.*)

JOHNNY.   Man, that was a long one, ése. (*Others agree with him.*)

FARMWORKER.   How did we do?

JOHNNY.   Pretty good, look at all that lana,° man! (*He goes over to* SANCHO *and removes the money from his hand.* SANCHO *stays where he is.*)

REVOLUCIONARIO.   En la madre, look at all the money.

JOHNNY.   We keep this up, we're going to be rich.

FARMWORKER.   They think we're machines.

REVOLUCIONARIO.   Burros.

JOHNNY.   Puppets.

MEXICAN-AMERICAN.   The only thing I don't like is how come I always get to play the goddamn Mexican-American?

JOHNNY.   That's what you get for finishing high school.

FARMWORKER.   How about our wages, ése?

JOHNNY.   Here it comes right now, $3,000 for you, $3,000 for you, $3,000 for you and $3,000 for me. The rest we put back into the business.

MEXICAN-AMERICAN.   Too much, man. Hey, where you vatos° going tonight?

FARMWORKER.   I'm going over to Concha's. There's a party.

JOHNNY.   Wait a minute, vatos. What about our salesman? I think he needs an oil job.

Esta . . . estudiantes!: This great mass of humanity has done enough talking! It has begun to march! Enough! Enough! Long live our race! Long live our cause! Long live the strike! Long live the brown berets! Long live the students!   **lana:** money   **vatos:** guys

REVOLUCIONARIO. Leave him to me. (*The* PACHUCO, FARM-WORKER *and* MEXICAN-AMERICAN *exit, talking loudly about their plans for the night. The* REVOLUCIONARIO *goes over to* SANCHO, *removes his derby hat and cigar, lifts him up and throws him over his shoulder.* SANCHO *hangs loose, lifeless. To audience*) He's the best model we got! ¡Ajúa!° (*Exit.*)

QUESTIONS

1. "Honest Sancho" runs his "Used Mexican Lot" like a used car lot. How is this metaphorical context developed in the play? How is the satire directed at both used car salesmen and a Mexican who has sold out his race?
2. Explore the stereotyping that characterizes the "models" that Honest Sancho offers for sale. At whom is the satire directed—the four "models," or people who stereotype others? What is the implication of these men being presented as if they were machines?
3. Of the characters in the play, only Miss Jimenez escapes being portrayed as a machine. Is she therefore treated sympathetically by the play?
4. How effective is the surprise ending?
5. How do you think an audience composed entirely of Mexican Americans would respond to this play? an audience of Anglos? a mixed audience? Would there be differences among these audiences as to how comic the play is?

SUGGESTIONS FOR WRITING

1. Review the chapter on "Characterization" in the Fiction section of this book, paying particular attention to the qualities that contribute to a convincing character. Write an essay demonstrating that one or more characters in one of the plays in the preceding chapter displays those qualities. If you are permitted the space to write a longer essay, extend the essay to include two of these plays, one more realistic than the other.
2. After reviewing the chapter on "Plot" in the Fiction section of this book, write an analysis of the plot of one of the plays in chapter 1. To what extent does plot help to determine whether a play is realistic or nonrealistic?
3. The three plays in this chapter represent a range from realistic to nonrealistic conventions. Using the materials in the opening discussion of those conventions, write an essay on realistic elements in *A Doll House* or *The Glass Menagerie*; or an essay on nonrealistic elements in *The Glass Menagerie* or "Los Vendidos." In each case, consider the way in which the conventions are used to represent human realities and themes.
4. In any classification of the plays in chapter 1, Glaspell's "Trifles" would undoubtedly be called realistic, Albee's "The Sandbox" nonrealistic. Write an essay in which you classify either of the other plays in chapter 1 based on the criterion of faithfulness "to the outer appearances of life."

¡Ajúa!: Wow!

5. Write an essay ranking the plays in chapter 1 in terms of their presentation of "life's inner meanings"—their revelation of "human truth."

6. You have had the opportunity to read seven plays thus far. Write an essay in which you use some or all of them to create a hypothesis about the correlation between realistic conventions and significant insights into human behavior.

7. Through the centuries, theatrical producers and writers have sometimes sought to modernize older plays, chiefly by recasting them in the conventions of contemporary theater. Considering the plays you have read so far, and considering the remainder of the plays as you read on in this book, write an essay in which you explore what would be necessary to modernize one of them. Would you find it always appropriate to remove the nonrealistic elements in the play so as to appeal to today's audience—or might you want to adapt the play for that part of the audience that prefers musical dramas?

Chapter Three

Tragedy and Comedy

The two masks of drama—one with the corners of its mouth turned down expressing agony or suffering, the other with the corners of its mouth turned up expressing joy or laughter—are familiar everywhere. Derived from masks actually worn by the actors in ancient Greek plays, they symbolize two principal modes of drama. Indeed, just as life gravitates between tears and laughter, they seem to imply that all drama is divided between **tragedy** and **comedy**.

But drama is an ancient literary form; in its development from the beginnings to the present it has produced a rich variety of plays. Can all these plays be classified under two terms? If our answer to this question is Yes, we must define the terms very broadly. If our answer is No, then how many terms do we need, and where do we stop? Polonius, in *Hamlet*, says of a visiting troupe of players that they can act "tragedy, comedy, history, pastoral, pastoral-comical, historical-pastoral, tragical-historical, tragical-comical-historical-pastoral, scene individable, or poem unlimited." Like Polonius himself, his list seems ridiculous. Moreover, even if we adopted these terms, and more, could we be sure that they would accurately classify all plays or that a new play, written tomorrow, would not demand a totally new category?

The discussion that follows proceeds on four assumptions. First, perfect definitions and an airtight system of classification are impossible. There exist no views of tragedy and comedy that have not been challenged and no classification system that unequivocally provides for all examples. Second, it is quite unnecessary that we classify each play we read or see. The most important questions to ask about a play are not "Is this a tragedy?" or "Is this a comedy?" but "Does this play furnish an enjoyable, valid, and significant experience?" Third, the quality of experience furnished by a play may be partially dependent on our perception of its relationship to earlier literary forms, and therefore familiarity with traditional notions of tragedy and comedy is important for our understanding and appreciation of plays. Many of the conventions used in specific plays have been determined by the kind of play the author intended to write. Other plays have been written in deliberate defiance of these conventions. Fourth, whether or not tragedy and comedy be taken as the two all-inclusive dramatic modes, they are certainly, as symbolized by the masks, the two principal ones, and useful points, therefore, from which to begin discussion.

The popular distinctions between comedy and tragedy are fairly simple: comedy is funny; tragedy is sad. Comedy has a happy ending, tragedy an unhappy one. The typical ending for comedy is a marriage; the typical ending for tragedy is a death. There is some truth in these notions, but only some. Some plays called comedies make no attempt to be funny. Successful tragedies, though they involve suffering and sadness, do not leave the spectator depressed. Some funny plays have sad endings: they send the viewer away with a lump in the throat. A few plays usually classified as tragedies do not have unhappy endings but conclude with the protagonist's triumph. In short, the popular distinctions are unreliable. Though we need not abandon them entirely, we must take a more complex view. Let us begin with tragedy.

The first great theorist of dramatic art was Aristotle (384–322 B.C.), whose discussion of tragedy in *Poetics* has dominated critical thought ever since. A very brief summary of Aristotle's view will be helpful.

A tragedy, so Aristotle wrote, is the imitation in dramatic form of an action that is serious and complete, with incidents arousing pity and fear wherewith it effects a **catharsis** of such emotions. The language used is pleasurable and appropriate throughout to the situation. The chief characters are noble personages ("better than ourselves," says Aristotle), and the actions they perform are noble actions. The plot involves a change in the protagonist's fortune, in which he usually, but not always, falls from happiness to misery. The protagonist, though not perfect, is hardly a bad person; his misfortunes result not from character deficiencies but rather from what Aristotle calls **hamartia,** a criminal act committed in ignorance of some material fact or even for the sake of a greater good. A tragic plot has organic unity: the events follow not just *after* one another but *because* of one another. The best tragic plots involve a reversal (a change from one state of things within the play to its opposite) or a discovery (a change from ignorance to knowledge) or both.

In the more extensive account that follows, we will not attempt to delineate the boundaries of tragedy or necessarily describe it at its greatest. Instead, we will describe a common understanding of tragedy as a point of departure for further discussion. Nor shall we enter into the endless controversies over what Aristotle meant by "catharsis" or over which of his statements are meant to apply to all tragedies and which only to the best ones. The important thing is that Aristotle had important insights into the nature of some of the greatest tragedies and that, rightly or wrongly interpreted, his conceptions are the basis for a kind of archetypal notion of tragedy that has dominated critical thought. What are the central features of that archetype? (The following summary retains Aristotle's reference to the tragic protagonist in masculine terms; however, the definitions apply equally to female protagonists such as Sophocles's Antigone and Shakespeare's Cleopatra.)

1.   The tragic hero is a man of noble stature. He has a greatness about him. He is not an ordinary man but one of outstanding quality. In Greek and in Shakespearean tragedy, he is usually a prince or a king. We may, if we wish, set down this predilection of former times for kings as tragic heroes as an undemocratic prejudice that regarded some men to be of nobler "blood" than others—preeminent by virtue of their aristocratic birth. But it is only partially that. We may with equal validity regard the hero's kingship as the symbol rather than as the cause of his greatness. He is great not primarily by virtue of his kingship but by his possession of extraordinary powers, by qualities of passion or aspiration or nobility of mind. The tragic hero's kingship is also a symbol of his initial good fortune, the mark of his high position. If the hero's fall is to arouse in us the emotions of pity and fear, it must be a fall from a height. A clumsy man tripping over his shoelace is comic, not tragic— even if it could cause him serious physical pain.

2.   The tragic hero is good, though not perfect, and his fall results from his committing what Aristotle calls "an act of injustice" (*hamartia*) either through ignorance or from a conviction that some greater good will be served. This act is, nevertheless, a criminal one, and the good hero is still responsible for it, even if he is totally unaware of its criminality and is acting out of the best intentions. Some later critics ignore Aristotle's insistence on the hero's commission of a guilty act and choose instead to blame the hero's fall on a flaw in his character or personality. Such a notion misrepresents Aristotle's view both of tragedy and of a basically just natural order. It implies a world in which personality alone, not one's actions, can bring on catastrophe.

Aristotle notwithstanding, there is a critical tradition that attributes the fall of the hero to a so-called "tragic flaw"—some fault of character such as inordinate ambition, quickness to anger, a tendency to jealousy, or overweening pride. Conversely, the protagonist's vulnerability has been attributed to some excess of virtue—a nobility of character that unfits him for life among ordinary mortals. But whatever it be—a criminal act, a fault of character, or excessive virtue—the protagonist is personally responsible for his downfall.

3. The hero's downfall, therefore, is his own fault, the result of his own free choice—not the result of pure accident or someone else's villainy or some overriding malignant fate. Accident, villainy, or fate may contribute to the downfall but only as cooperating agents: they are not alone responsible. The combination of the hero's greatness and his responsibility for his own downfall is what entitles us to describe his downfall as tragic rather than as merely pathetic. In common speech these two adjectives are often confused. If a father of ten children is accidentally killed at a street corner, the event, strictly speaking, is pathetic, not tragic. When a weak man succumbs to his weakness and comes to a bad end, the event should be called pathetic, not tragic. The tragic event involves a fall from greatness, brought about, at least partially, by the agent's free action.

4. Nevertheless, the hero's misfortune is not wholly deserved. The punishment exceeds the crime. We do not come away from tragedy with the feeling that "he got what he had coming to him" but rather with the sad sense of a waste of human potential. For what most impresses us about the tragic hero is not his weakness but his greatness. He is, in a sense, "larger than life," or, as Aristotle said, "better than ourselves." He reveals to us the dimensions of human possibility. He is a person mainly admirable, and his fall therefore fills us with pity and fear.

5. Yet the tragic fall is not pure loss. Though it may result in the protagonist's death, it involves, before his death, some increase in awareness, some gain in self-knowledge—as Aristotle puts it, some "discovery"—a change from ignorance to knowledge. On the level of plot, the discovery may be merely learning the truth about some fact or situation of which the protagonist was ignorant, but on the level of character it is accompanied or followed by a significant insight, a fuller self-knowledge, an increase not only in knowledge but in wisdom. Often this increase in wisdom involves some sort of reconciliation with the universe or with the protagonist's situation. He exits not cursing his fate but accepting it and acknowledging that it is to some degree just.

6. Though it arouses solemn emotions—pity and fear, says Aristotle, but compassion and awe might be better terms—tragedy, when well performed, does not leave its audience in a state of depression. Though we cannot be sure what Aristotle meant by his term "catharsis," some sort of emotional release at the end is a common experience of those who witness great tragedies on the stage. They have

been greatly moved by pity, fear, and associated emotions, but they are not left emotionally beaten down or dejected. Instead, there may be a feeling almost of exhilaration. This feeling is a response to the tragic action. With the fall of the hero and his gain in wisdom or self-knowledge, there is, besides the appalling sense of human waste, a fresh recognition of human greatness, a sense that human life has unrealized potentialities. Though the hero may be defeated, he at least has dared greatly, and he gains understanding from his defeat.

Is the comic mask laughing or smiling? The question is more important than it may at first appear, for usually we laugh *at* something but smile *with* someone. The laugh expresses recognition of some absurdity in human behavior; the smile expresses pleasure in someone's company or good fortune.

The comic mask may be interpreted both ways. Comedy, Northrop Frye has said, lies between satire and romance. Historically, there have been two chief kinds of comedy—**scornful comedy** and **romantic comedy,** laughing comedy and smiling comedy. Of the two, scornful or satiric comedy is the older and probably still the more dominant.

The most essential difference between tragedy and comedy, particularly scornful comedy, is in their depiction of human nature. Where tragedy emphasizes human greatness, comedy delineates human weakness. Where tragedy celebrates human freedom, comedy points up human limitations. Wherever human beings fail to measure up to their own resolutions or to their own self-conceptions, wherever they are guilty of hypocrisy, vanity, or folly, wherever they fly in the face of good sense and rational behavior, comedy exhibits their absurdity and invites us to laugh at them. Where tragedy tends to say, with Shakespeare's Hamlet, "What a piece of work is a man! how noble in reason! how infinite in faculty! in form and moving how express and admirable! in action how like an angel! in apprehension how like a god!" comedy says, with Shakespeare's Puck, "Lord, what fools these mortals be!"

Because comedy exposes human folly, its function is partly critical and corrective. Where tragedy challenges us with a vision of human possibility, comedy reveals to us a spectacle of human ridiculousness that it makes us want to avoid. No doubt, we should not exaggerate this function of comedy. We go to the theater primarily for enjoyment, not to receive lessons in personality or character development. Nevertheless, laughter may be educative at the same time that it is enjoyable. The comedies of Aristophanes and Molière, of Ben Jonson and Congreve, are, first of all, good fun, but, secondly, they are antidotes for human folly.

Romantic or smiling comedy, as opposed to scornful comedy, and as exemplified by many plays of Shakespeare—*A Midsummer Night's Dream, As You Like It, Twelfth Night, Much Ado About Nothing, The Tempest*, for instance—puts its emphasis upon sympathetic rather than ridiculous characters. These characters—likable, not given up to folly or vanity—are placed in various kinds of difficulties from which, at the end of the play, they are rescued, attaining their ends or having their good fortunes restored. Though different from the protagonists of scornful comedy, however, these characters are not the commanding or lofty figures that tragic protagonists are. They are sensible and good rather than noble, aspiring, and grand. They do not strike us with awe as the tragic protagonist does. They do not so challengingly test the limits of human possibility. In short, they move in a smaller world. Romantic comedies, therefore, do not occupy a different universe from satiric comedies; they simply lie at opposite sides of the same territory. The romantic comedy, moreover, though its protagonists are sympathetic, has usually a number of lesser characters whose folly is held up to ridicule. The satiric comedy, on the other hand, frequently has minor characters—often a pair of young lovers—who are sympathetic and likable. The difference between the two kinds of comedy may be only a matter of whether we laugh at the primary or at the secondary characters.

There are other differences between comedy and tragedy. The norms of comedy are primarily social. Where tragedies tend to isolate their protagonists to emphasize their uniqueness, comedies put their protagonists in the midst of a group to emphasize their commonness. Where tragic protagonists possess overpowering individuality, so that plays are often named after them (for example, *Oedipus Rex, Othello*), comic protagonists tend to be types of individuals, and the plays in which they appear are often named for the type (for example, Molière's *Tartuffe, or The Impostor*, Congreve's *The Double Dealer*). We judge tragic protagonists by absolute moral standards, by how far they soar above society. We judge comic protagonists by social standards, by how well they adjust to society and conform to the expectations of the group.

Finally, comic plots are less likely than tragic plots to exhibit the high degree of organic unity—of logical cause-and-effect progression—that Aristotle required of tragedy. Plausibility, in fact, is not usually the central characteristic of a comic plot. Unlikely coincidences, improbable disguises, mistaken identities—these are the stuff of which comedy is made; and, as long as they make us laugh and, at the same time, help to illuminate human nature and human folly, we need not greatly care. Not that plausibility is no longer important—only that other things are more important, and these other things are often achieved by the most outrageous violations of probability.

This is particularly true regarding the comic ending. *Conventionally*, comedies have a happy ending. The happy ending is, indeed, a *convention* of comedy, which is to say that a comedy ends happily because comedies end happily—that is the nature of the form—not necessarily because a happy ending is a plausible outcome of the events that have preceded it. The greatest masters of comedy—Aristophanes, Shakespeare, Molière—have often been extremely arbitrary in the manner in which they achieved their endings. The accidental discovery of a lost will, rescue by an act of divine intervention (*deus ex machina*), the sudden reform of a mean-spirited person into a friendly person—such devices have been used by the greatest comic writers. And, even where the ending is achieved more plausibly, comedy asks us to forget for the time being that in actuality life has no endings except for death. Marriage, which provides the ending for so many comedies, is really a beginning.

And now, though we do not wish to imitate the folly of Polonius, it is well that we define two additional terms: melodrama and farce. In the two-part classification suggested by the two symbolic masks, melodrama belongs with tragedy, and farce with comedy; but the differences are sufficient to make the two new terms useful.

Melodrama, like tragedy, attempts to arouse feelings of fear and pity, but it does so ordinarily through cruder means. The conflict is an oversimplified one between good and evil depicted in absolute terms. Plot is emphasized at the expense of characterization. Sensational incidents provide the staple of the plot. The young mother and her baby are evicted into a howling storm by the villain holding the mortgage; the heroine is tied to the railroad tracks as the express train approaches. Most important, good finally triumphs over evil, and the ending is happy. Typically, at the end, the hero marries the heroine; villainy is foiled or crushed. Melodrama may, of course, have different degrees of power and subtlety; it is not always as crude as its crudest examples. But in it, moral issues are typically oversimplified, and good is finally triumphant. Melodrama does not provide the complex insights of tragedy. It is usually commercial rather than literary. Much of what television and films present as science fiction, police or medical dramas, and thrillers are examples of melodrama.

Farce, more consistently than comedy, is aimed at rousing explosive laughter. But again the means are cruder. The conflicts are violent and usually at the physical level. Plot is emphasized at the expense of characterization, improbable situations and coincidence at the expense of articulated plot. Comic implausibility is raised to heights of absurd impossibility. Coarse wit, practical jokes, and physical action are staples. Characters trip over benches, insult each other, run into walls, knock each other down, get into brawls. Performed with gusto, farce may be hilariously funny. Psychologically, it may boost our spirits and purge us of hostility and aggression. In content, however, like melodrama, it is usually commercial rather than literary. Contemporary farces are a staple of the movies.

Now we have four classifications—tragedy, comedy, melodrama, farce—the latter two as appendages of the former. But none of these classifications is rigid. They blend into each other and defy exact definition. If we take them too seriously, the tragic mask may laugh, and the comic mask weep.

REVIEWING CHAPTER THREE

1. Summarize the main points of Aristotle's definition of tragedy, indicating where possible how these characteristics arouse responses from the audience.
2. Define the two major types of comedy, satiric and romantic, in terms of their materials and their effects on audiences.
3. Explain how melodrama and farce are related to the major genres of tragedy and comedy.
4. As you read the plays in this chapter, identify any melodramatic events in the tragedies and any farcical elements in the comedies.

Sophocles

Oedipus Rex

The plots of Greek tragedies were based on legends with which Greek audiences were more or less familiar (as American audiences, for example, would be familiar with the major events in a historical play based on the life of Lincoln). These plays often owed much of their impact to the audience's previous knowledge of the characters and their fate, for it enabled the playwright to make powerful use of dramatic irony and allusion. Much of the audience's delight, in addition, came from seeing how the playwright worked out the details of the story. The

purpose of this introductory note is therefore to supply such information as the play's first audiences might be presumed to have had.

Because of a prophecy that their new son would kill his father,
Laius and Jocasta, King and Queen of Thebes, gave their infant to a
shepherd with orders that he be left on a mountainside to die. The
shepherd, however, after having pinned the babe's ankles together,
took pity on him and gave him instead to a Corinthian shepherd. This
shepherd in turn presented him to Polybus and Merope, King and
Queen of Corinth, who, childless, adopted him as their own. The child
was given the name Oedipus ("Swollen-foot") because of the injury to
his ankles.

When grown to manhood at Polybus's court, Oedipus was accused
by a drunken guest of not being his father's son. Though reassured by
Polybus and Merope, he was still disturbed and traveled to consult the
Delphic oracle. The oracle, without answering the question about his
parentage, prophesied that Oedipus would kill his father and beget
children by his mother. Horrified, resolved to avert this fate, Oedipus
determined never to return to Corinth. Traveling from Delphi, he came
to a place where three roads met and was ordered off the road by a man
in a chariot. Blows were exchanged, and Oedipus killed the man and
four of his attendants. Later, on the outskirts of Thebes, he encountered the Sphinx, a monster with the head of a woman, wings of an eagle, and body of a lion, which was terrorizing Thebes by slaying all who
failed to answer her riddle ("What goes on four legs in the morning,
two legs at noon, and three legs in the evening?"). When Oedipus correctly answered the riddle ("man, for he crawls as an infant, walks erect
as a man, and uses a staff in old age"), the Sphinx destroyed herself. As
a reward, Oedipus was named King of Thebes to replace the recently
slain Laius and was given the hand of Jocasta in marriage. With her, he
ruled Thebes successfully for some years and had four children—two
sons and two daughters. Then the city was afflicted by a plague. It is at
this point that the action of Sophocles's play begins.

The play was first performed in Athens about 430 B.C. In the
present version, prepared by Dudley Fitts and Robert Fitzgerald, the
translators use spellings for the proper names that are closer to the
original Greek than the more familiar Anglicized spellings used in
this note. Sophocles (496?–406 B.C.), an active and devoted citizen
of Athens during its democratic period, served as an elected general
in an Athenian military expedition and held other posts of civic responsibility, but was most importantly its leading and most prolific
tragic playwright.

Characters

OEDIPUS, *King of Thebes, supposed son of Polybus and Meropê, King and*
    Queen of Corinth
IOKASTÊ, *wife of Oedipus and widow of the late King Laïos*
KREON, *brother of Iokastê, a prince of Thebes*
TEIRESIAS, *a blind seer who serves Apollo*
PRIEST
MESSENGER, *from Corinth*
SHEPHERD, *former servant of Laïos*
SECOND MESSENGER, *from the palace*
CHORUS OF THEBAN ELDERS
CHORAGOS, *leader of the Chorus*
ANTIGONE and ISMENE, *young daughters of Oedipus and Iokastê. They*
    appear in the Exodus but do not speak.
SUPPLIANTS, GUARDS, SERVANTS

THE SCENE. *Before the palace of* OEDIPUS, *King of Thebes. A central
door and two lateral doors open onto a platform which runs the length of the
façade. On the platform, right and left, are altars; and three steps lead down
into the orchêstra, or chorus-ground. At the beginning of the action these
steps are crowded by suppliants who have brought branches and chaplets of
olive leaves and who sit in various attitudes of despair.* OEDIPUS *enters.*

PROLOGUE

OEDIPUS.   My children, generations of the living
    In the line of Kadmos,° nursed at his ancient hearth:
    Why have you strewn yourselves before these altars
    In supplication, with your boughs and garlands?
    The breath of incense rises from the city   5
    With a sound of prayer and lamentation.
                      Children,
    I would not have you speak through messengers,
    And therefore I have come myself to hear you—
    I, Oedipus, who bear the famous name.
    (*To a* PRIEST) You, there, since you are eldest in the company, 10
    Speak for them all, tell me what preys upon you,
    Whether you come in dread, or crave some blessing:
    Tell me, and never doubt that I will help you
    In every way I can; I should be heartless
    Were I not moved to find you suppliant here.   15

2. **Kadmos:** Founder of Thebes

PRIEST.   Great Oedipus, O powerful king of Thebes!
        You see how all the ages of our people
        Cling to your altar steps: here are boys
        Who can barely stand alone, and here are priests
        By weight of age, as I am a priest of God,   20
        And young men chosen from those yet unmarried;
        As for the others, all that multitude,
        They wait with olive chaplets in the squares,
        At the two shrines of Pallas, and where Apollo
        Speaks in the glowing embers.
                                    Your own eyes   25
        Must tell you: Thebes is tossed on a murdering sea
        And can not lift her head from the death surge.
        A rust consumes the buds and fruits of the earth;
        The herds are sick; children die unborn,
        And labor is vain. The god of plague and pyre   30
        Raids like detestable lightning through the city,
        And all the house of Kadmos is laid waste,
        All emptied, and all darkened: Death alone
        Battens upon the misery of Thebes.
        You are not one of the immortal gods, we know;   35
        Yet we have come to you to make our prayer
        As to the man surest in mortal ways
        And wisest in the ways of God. You saved us
        From the Sphinx, that flinty singer, and the tribute
        We paid to her so long; yet you were never   40
        Better informed than we, nor could we teach you:
        A god's touch, it seems, enabled you to help us.

        Therefore, O mighty power, we turn to you:
        Find us our safety, find us a remedy,
        Whether by counsel of the gods or of men.   45
        A king of wisdom tested in the past
        Can act in a time of troubles, and act well.
        Noblest of men, restore
        Life to your city! Think how all men call you
        Liberator for your boldness long ago;   50
        Ah, when your years of kingship are remembered,
        Let them not say *We rose, but later fell*—
        Keep the State from going down in the storm!
        Once, years ago, with happy augury,
        You brought us fortune; be the same again!   55
        No man questions your power to rule the land:

But rule over men, not over a dead city!
Ships are only hulls, high walls are nothing,
When no life moves in the empty passageways.
OEDIPUS.   Poor children! You may be sure I know   60
All that you longed for in your coming here.
I know that you are deathly sick; and yet,
Sick as you are, not one is as sick as I.
Each of you suffers in himself alone
His anguish, not another's; but my spirit   65
Groans for the city, for myself, for you.

I was not sleeping, you are not waking me.
No, I have been in tears for a long while
And in my restless thought walked many ways.
In all my search I found one remedy,   70
And I have adopted it: I have sent Kreon,
Son of Menoikeus, brother of the queen,
To Delphi, Apollo's place of revelation,
To learn there, if he can,
What act or pledge of mine may save the city.   75
I have counted the days, and now, this very day,
I am troubled, for he has overstayed his time.
What is he doing? He has been gone too long.
Yet whenever he comes back, I should do ill
Not to take any action the god orders.   80
PRIEST.   It is a timely promise. At this instant
They tell me Kreon is here.
OEDIPUS.   O Lord Apollo!
May his news be fair as his face is radiant!
PRIEST.   Good news, I gather! he is crowned with bay,
The chaplet is thick with berries.
OEDIPUS.   We shall soon know;   85
He is near enough to hear us now. (*Enter* KREON.) O prince:
Brother: son of Menoikeus:
What answer do you bring us from the god?
KREON.   A strong one. I can tell you, great afflictions
Will turn out well, if they are taken well.   90
OEDIPUS.   What was the oracle? These vague words
Leave me still hanging between hope and fear.
KREON.   Is it your pleasure to hear me with all these
Gathered around us? I am prepared to speak,
But should we not go in?
OEDIPUS.   Speak to them all,   95
It is for them I suffer, more than for myself.

KREON.   Then I will tell you what I heard at Delphi.
    In plain words
    The god commands us to expel from the land of Thebes
    An old defilement we are sheltering.   100
    It is a deathly thing, beyond cure;
    We must not let it feed upon us longer.
OEDIPUS.   What defilement? How shall we rid ourselves of it?
KREON.   By exile or death, blood for blood. It was
    Murder that brought the plague-wind on the city.   105
OEDIPUS.   Murder of whom? Surely the god has named him?
KREON.   My lord: Laïos once ruled this land,
    Before you came to govern us.
OEDIPUS.   I know;
    I learned of him from others; I never saw him.
KREON.   He was murdered; and Apollo commands us now   110
    To take revenge upon whoever killed him.
OEDIPUS.   Upon whom? Where are they? Where shall we find a clue
    To solve that crime after so many years?
KREON.   Here in this land, he said. Search reveals
    Things that escape an inattentive man.   115
OEDIPUS.   Tell me: Was Laïos murdered in his house,
    Or in the fields, or in some foreign country?
KREON.   He said he planned to make a pilgrimage.
    He did not come home again.
OEDIPUS.   And was there no one,
    No witness, no companion, to tell what happened?   120
KREON.   They were all killed but one, and he got away,
    So frightened that he could remember one thing only.
OEDIPUS.   What was that one thing? One may be the key
    To everything, if we resolve to use it.
KREON.   He said that a band of highwaymen attacked them,   125
    Outnumbered them, and overwhelmed the king.
OEDIPUS.   Strange, that a highwayman should be so daring—
    Unless some faction here bribed him to do it.
KREON.   We thought of that. But after Laïos's death
    New troubles arose and we had no avenger.   130
OEDIPUS.   What troubles could prevent your hunting down the killers?
KREON.   The riddling Sphinx's song
    Made us deaf to all mysteries but her own.
OEDIPUS.   Then once more I must bring what is dark to light.
    It is most fitting that Apollo shows,   135
    As you do, this compunction for the dead.
    You shall see how I stand by you, as I should,

Avenging this country and the god as well,
And not as though it were for some distant friend,
But for my own sake, to be rid of evil.   140
Whoever killed King Laïos might—who knows?—
Lay violent hands even on me—and soon.
I act for the murdered king in my own interest.

Come, then, my children: leave the altar steps,
Lift up your olive boughs!
                              One of you go   145
And summon the people of Kadmos to gather here.
I will do all that I can; you may tell them that. (*Exit a* PAGE.)
So, with the help of God,
We shall be saved—or else indeed we are lost.
PRIEST.   Let us rise, children. It was for this we came,   150
And now the king has promised it.
Phoibus° has sent us an oracle; may he descend
Himself to save us and drive out the plague. (*Exeunt* OEDIPUS *and*
KREON *into the palace by the central door. The* PRIEST *and the* SUPPLIANTS
disperse right and left. After a short pause the CHORUS *enters the orchêstra.*)

PÁRODOS°

STROPHE 1

CHORUS.   What is God singing in his profound
          Delphi of gold and shadow?   155
          What oracle for Thebes, the sunwhipped city?
          Fear unjoints me, the roots of my heart tremble.
          Now I remember, O Healer, your power, and wonder:
          Will you send doom like a sudden cloud, or weave it
          Like nightfall of the past?   160
          Speak to me, tell me, O
          Child of golden Hope, immortal Voice.

---

152. **Phoibus:** Apollo, god of light and truth
Párodos: The song or ode chanted by the chorus on their entry. It is accompanied by
dancing and music played on a flute. The chorus, in this play, represents elders of the city of
Thebes. They remain on stage (on a level lower than the principal actors) for the remainder of the play. The choral odes and dances serve to separate one scene from another (there
was no curtain in Greek theater) as well as to comment on the action, reinforce the emotion, and interpret the situation. The chorus also performs dance movements during certain portions of the scenes themselves. *Strophe* and *antistrophe* are terms denoting the movement and countermovement of the chorus from one side of their playing area to the other.
When the chorus participates in dialogue with the other characters, their lines are spoken
by the Choragos, their leader.

ANTISTROPHE 1

Let me pray to Athenê, the immortal daughter of Zeus,
And to Artemis her sister
Who keeps her famous throne in the market ring,   165
And to Apollo, archer from distant heaven—
O gods, descend! Like three streams leap against
The fires of our grief, the fires of darkness;
Be swift to bring us rest!
As in the old time from the brilliant house   170
Of air you stepped to save us, come again!

STROPHE 2

Now our afflictions have no end,
Now all our stricken host lies down
And no man fights off death with his mind;
The noble plowland bears no grain,   175
And groaning mothers can not bear—
See, how our lives like birds take wing,
Like sparks that fly when a fire soars,
To the shore of the god of evening.

ANTISTROPHE 2

The plague burns on, it is pitiless,   180
Though pallid children laden with death
Lie unwept in the stony ways,
And old gray women by every path
Flock to the strand about the altars
There to strike their breasts and cry   185
Worship of Phoibus in wailing prayers:
Be kind, God's golden child!

STROPHE 3

There are no swords in this attack by fire,
No shields, but we are ringed with cries.
Send the besieger plunging from our homes   190
Into the vast sea-room of the Atlantic
Or into the waves that foam eastward of Thrace—
For the day ravages what the night spares—
Destroy our enemy, lord of the thunder!
Let him be riven by lightning from heaven!   195

ANTISTROPHE 3

Phoibus Apollo, stretch the sun's bowstring,
That golden cord, until it sing for us,
Flashing arrows in heaven!
                                 Artemis, Huntress,
Race with flaring lights upon our mountains!
O scarlet god,° O golden-banded brow,   200
O Theban Bacchos in a storm of Maenads, (*Enter* OEDIPUS, *center.*)
Whirl upon Death, that all the Undying hate!
Come with blinding torches, come in joy!

SCENE 1

OEDIPUS.   Is this your prayer? It may be answered. Come,
    Listen to me, act as the crisis demands,   205
    And you shall have relief from all these evils.

    Until now I was a stranger to this tale,
    As I had been a stranger to the crime.
    Could I track down the murderer without a clue?
    But now, friends,   210
    As one who became a citizen after the murder,
    I make this proclamation to all Thebans:
    If any man knows by whose hand Laïos, son of Labdakos,
    Met his death, I direct that man to tell me everything,
    No matter what he fears for having so long withheld it.   215
    Let it stand as promised that no further trouble
    Will come to him, but he may leave the land in safety.
    Moreover: If anyone knows the murderer to be foreign,
    Let him not keep silent: he shall have his reward from me.
    However, if he does conceal it; if any man   220
    Fearing for his friend or for himself disobeys this edict,
    Hear what I propose to do:

    I solemnly forbid the people of this country,
    Where power and throne are mine, ever to receive that man
    Or speak to him, no matter who he is, or let him   225
    Join in sacrifice, lustration, or in prayer.
    I decree that he be driven from every house,
    Being, as he is, corruption itself to us: the Delphic

---

200. scarlet god: Bacchos, god of wine and revelry; the Maenads were his female attendants.

Voice of Apollo has pronounced this revelation.
Thus I associate myself with the oracle   230
And take the side of the murdered king.
As for the criminal, I pray to God—
Whether it be a lurking thief, or one of a number—
I pray that that man's life be consumed in evil and wretchedness.
And as for me, this curse applies no less   235
If it should turn out that the culprit is my guest here,
Sharing my hearth.
                          You have heard the penalty.
I lay it on you now to attend to this
For my sake, for Apollo's, for the sick
Sterile city that heaven has abandoned.   240
Suppose the oracle had given you no command:
Should this defilement go uncleansed for ever?
You should have found the murderer: your king,
A noble king, had been destroyed!
                                Now I,
Having the power that he held before me,   245
Having his bed, begetting children there
Upon his wife, as he would have, had he lived—
Their son would have been my children's brother,
If Laïos had had luck in fatherhood!
(And now his bad fortune has struck him down)—   250
I say I take the son's part, just as though
I were his son, to press the fight for him
And see it won! I'll find the hand that brought
Death to Labdakos's and Polydoros's child,
Heir of Kadmos's and Agenor's line.°   255
And as for those who fail me,
May the gods deny them the fruit of the earth,
Fruit of the womb, and may they rot utterly!
Let them be wretched as we are wretched, and worse!

For you, for loyal Thebans, and for all   260
Who find my actions right, I pray the favor
Of justice, and of all the immortal gods.
CHORAGOS.   Since I am under oath, my lord, I swear
    I did not do the murder, I can not name
    The murderer. Phoibus ordained the search;   265
    Why did he not say who the culprit was?

255. Labdakos, Polydoros, Kadmos, and Agenor: father, grandfather, great-grandfather,
and great-great-grandfather of Laïos

OEDIPUS.   An honest question. But no man in the world
  Can make the gods do more than the gods will.
CHORAGOS.   There is an alternative, I think—
OEDIPUS.   Tell me.
  Any or all, you must not fail to tell me.   270
CHORAGOS.   A lord clairvoyant to the lord Apollo,
  As we all know, is the skilled Teiresias.
  One might learn much about this from him, Oedipus.
OEDIPUS.   I am not wasting time:
  Kreon spoke of this, and I have sent for him—   275
  Twice, in fact; it is strange that he is not here.
CHORAGOS.   The other matter—that old report—seems useless.
OEDIPUS.   What was that? I am interested in all reports.
CHORAGOS.   The king was said to have been killed by highwaymen.
OEDIPUS.   I know. But we have no witness to that.   280
CHORAGOS.   If the killer can feel a particle of dread,
  Your curse will bring him out of hiding!
OEDIPUS.   No.
  The man who dared that act will fear no curse.
  (*Enter the blind seer* TEIRESIAS, *led by a* PAGE.)
CHORAGOS.   But there is one man who may detect the criminal.
  This is Teiresias, this is the holy prophet   285
  In whom, alone of all men, truth was born.
OEDIPUS.   Teiresias: seer: student of mysteries,
  Of all that's taught and all that no man tells,
  Secrets of Heaven and secrets of the earth:
  Blind though you are, you know the city lies   290
  Sick with plague; and from this plague, my lord,
  We find that you alone can guard or save us.

  Possibly you did not hear the messengers?
  Apollo, when we sent to him,
  Sent us back word that this great pestilence   295
  Would lift, but only if we established clearly
  The identity of those who murdered Laïos.
  They must be killed or exiled.
                                          Can you use
  Birdflight° or any art of divination
  To purify yourself, and Thebes, and me   300

---

299. Birdflight: Prophets predicted the future or divined the unknown by observing the
flight of birds.

From this contagion? We are in your hands.
There is no fairer duty
Than that of helping others in distress.

TEIRESIAS.   How dreadful knowledge of the truth can be
When there's no help in truth! I knew this well,   305
But did not act on it: else I should not have come.

OEDIPUS.   What is troubling you? Why are your eyes so cold?

TEIRESIAS.   Let me go home. Bear your own fate, and I'll
Bear mine. It is better so: trust what I say.

OEDIPUS.   What you say is ungracious and unhelpful   310
To your native country. Do not refuse to speak.

TEIRESIAS.   When it comes to speech, your own is neither temperate
Nor opportune. I wish to be more prudent.

OEDIPUS.   In God's name, we all beg you—

TEIRESIAS.   You are all ignorant.
No; I will never tell you what I know.   315
Now it is my misery; then, it would be yours.

OEDIPUS.   What! You do know something, and will not tell us?
You would betray us all and wreck the State?

TEIRESIAS.   I do not intend to torture myself, or you.
Why persist in asking? You will not persuade me.   320

OEDIPUS.   What a wicked old man you are! You'd try a stone's
Patience! Out with it! Have you no feeling at all?

TEIRESIAS.   You call me unfeeling. If you could only see
The nature of your own feelings . . .

OEDIPUS.   Why,
Who would not feel as I do? Who could endure   325
Your arrogance toward the city?

TEIRESIAS.   What does it matter?
Whether I speak or not, it is bound to come.

OEDIPUS.   Then, if "it" is bound to come, you are bound to tell me.

TEIRESIAS.   No, I will not go on. Rage as you please.

OEDIPUS.   Rage? Why not!
                                And I'll tell you what I think: 330
You planned it, you had it done, you all but
Killed him with your own hands: if you had eyes,
I'd say the crime was yours, and yours alone.

TEIRESIAS.   So? I charge you, then,
Abide by the proclamation you have made: 335
From this day forth
Never speak again to these men or me;
You yourself are the pollution of this country.

OEDIPUS.   You dare say that! Can you possibly think you have
 Some way of going free, after such insolence?   340
TEIRESIAS.   I have gone free. It is the truth sustains me.
OEDIPUS.   Who taught you shamelessness? It was not your craft.
TEIRESIAS.   You did. You made me speak. I did not want to.
OEDIPUS.   Speak what? Let me hear it again more clearly.
TEIRESIAS.   Was it not clear before? Are you tempting me? 345
OEDIPUS.   I did not understand it. Say it again.
TEIRESIAS.   I say that you are the murderer whom you seek.
OEDIPUS.   Now twice you have spat out infamy. You'll pay for it!
TEIRESIAS.   Would you care for more? Do you wish to be really angry?
OEDIPUS.   Say what you will. Whatever you say is worthless. 350
TEIRESIAS.   I say you live in hideous shame with those
 Most dear to you. You can not see the evil.
OEDIPUS.   Can you go on babbling like this for ever?
TEIRESIAS.   I can, if there is power in truth.
OEDIPUS.   There is:
 But not for you, not for you,   355
 You sightless, witless, senseless, mad old man!
TEIRESIAS.   You are the madman. There is no one here
 Who will not curse you soon, as you curse me.
OEDIPUS.   You child of total night! I would not touch you;
 Neither would any man who sees the sun.   360
TEIRESIAS.   True: it is not from you my fate will come.
 That lies within Apollo's competence,
 As it is his concern.
OEDIPUS.   Tell me, who made
 These fine discoveries? Kreon? or someone else?
TEIRESIAS.   Kreon is no threat. You weave your own doom. 365
OEDIPUS.   Wealth, power, craft of statesmanship!
 Kingly position, everywhere admired!
 What savage envy is stored up against these,
 If Kreon, whom I trusted, Kreon my friend,
 For this great office which the city once   370
 Put in my hands unsought—if for this power
 Kreon desires in secret to destroy me!

 He has bought this decrepit fortune-teller, this
 Collector of dirty pennies, this prophet fraud—
 Why, he is no more clairvoyant than I am!
OEDIPUS.   Tell us: 375
 Has your mystic mummery ever approached the truth?
 When that hellcat the Sphinx was performing here,

What help were you to these people?
Her magic was not for the first man who came along:
It demanded a real exorcist. Your birds—   380
What good were they? or the gods, for the matter of that?
But I came by,
Oedipus, the simple man, who knows nothing—
I thought it out for myself, no birds helped me!
And this is the man you think you can destroy,   385
That you may be close to Kreon when he's king!
Well, you and your friend Kreon, it seems to me,
Will suffer most. If you were not an old man,
You would have paid already for your plot.
CHORAGOS.   We can not see that his words or yours   390
Have been spoken except in anger, Oedipus,
And of anger we have no need. How to accomplish
The god's will best: that is what most concerns us.
TEIRESIAS.   You are a king. But where argument's concerned
I am your man, as much a king as you.   395
I am not your servant, but Apollo's.
I have no need of Kreon or Kreon's name.

Listen to me. You mock my blindness, do you?
But I say that you, with both your eyes, are blind:
You can not see the wretchedness of your life,   400
Nor in whose house you live, no, nor with whom.
Who are your father and mother? Can you tell me?
You do not even know the blind wrongs
That you have done them, on earth and in the world below.
But the double lash of your parents' curse will whip you   405
Out of this land some day, with only night
Upon your precious eyes.
Your cries then—where will they not be heard?
What fastness of Kithairon° will not echo them?
And that bridal-descant of yours—you'll know it then,   410
The song they sang when you came here to Thebes
And found your misguided berthing.
All this, and more, that you can not guess at now,
Will bring you to yourself among your children.

Be angry, then. Curse Kreon. Curse my words.   415
I tell you, no man that walks upon the earth
Shall be rooted out more horribly than you.

409. **Kithairon:** the mountain where Oedipus was taken to be exposed as an infant

OEDIPUS.   Am I to bear this from him?—Damnation
    Take you! Out of this place! Out of my sight!
TEIRESIAS.   I would not have come at all if you had not asked me. 420
OEDIPUS.   Could I have told that you'd talk nonsense, that
    You'd come here to make a fool of yourself, and of me?
TEIRESIAS.   A fool? Your parents thought me sane enough.
OEDIPUS.   My parents again!— Wait: who were my parents?
TEIRESIAS.   This day will give you a father, and break your heart. 425
OEDIPUS.   Your infantile riddles! Your damned abracadabra!
TEIRESIAS.   You were a great man once at solving riddles.
OEDIPUS.   Mock me with that if you like; you will find it true.
TEIRESIAS.   It was true enough. It brought about your ruin.
OEDIPUS.   But if it saved the town?
TEIRESIAS (*to the* PAGE).   Boy, give me your hand.   430
OEDIPUS.   Yes, boy; lead him away.
                          —While you are here
    We can do nothing. Go; leave us in peace.
TEIRESIAS.   I will go when I have said what I have to say.
    How can you hurt me? And I tell you again:
    The man you have been looking for all this time,   435
    The damned man, the murderer of Laïos,
    That man is in Thebes. To your mind he is foreign-born,
    But it will soon be shown that he is a Theban,
    A revelation that will fail to please.
                           A blind man,
    Who has his eyes now; a penniless man, who is rich now;   440
    And he will go tapping the strange earth with his staff.
    To the children with whom he lives now he will be
    Brother and father—the very same; to her
    Who bore him, son and husband—the very same
    Who came to his father's bed, wet with his father's blood.   445
    Enough. Go think that over.
    If later you find error in what I have said,
    You may say that I have no skill in prophecy.
    (*Exit* TEIRESIAS, *led by his* PAGE. OEDIPUS *goes into the palace.*)

ODE 1

STROPHE 1

CHORUS.   The Delphic stone of prophecies
    Remembers ancient regicide   450
    And a still bloody hand.
    That killer's hour of flight has come.

He must be stronger than riderless
Coursers of untiring wind,
For the son° of Zeus armed with his father's thunder   455
Leaps in lightning after him;
And the Furies hold his track, the sad Furies.

ANTISTROPHE 1

Holy Parnassos'° peak of snow
Flashes and blinds that secret man,
That all shall hunt him down: 460
Though he may roam the forest shade
Like a bull gone wild from pasture
To rage through glooms of stone,
Doom comes down on him; flight will not avail him;
For the world's heart calls him desolate,   465
And the immortal voices follow, for ever follow.

STROPHE 2

But now a wilder thing is heard
From the old man skilled at hearing Fate in the wing-beat of a bird.
Bewildered as a blown bird, my soul hovers and can not find
Foothold in this debate, or any reason or rest of mind.   470
But no man ever brought—none can bring
Proof of strife between Thebes' royal house,
Labdakos's line, and the son of Polybos;
And never until now has any man brought word
Of Laïos's dark death staining Oedipus the King.   475

ANTISTROPHE 2

Divine Zeus and Apollo hold
Perfect intelligence alone of all tales ever told;
And well though this diviner works, he works in his own night;
No man can judge that rough unknown or trust in second sight,
For wisdom changes hands among the wise.   480
Shall I believe my great lord criminal
At a raging word that a blind old man let fall?
I saw him, when the carrion woman° faced him of old,
Prove his heroic mind. These evil words are lies.

---

455. son: Apollo   **458. Parnassos:** mountain sacred to Apollo   **483. woman:** the Sphinx

SCENE 2

KREON.   Men of Thebes: 485
  I am told that heavy accusations
  Have been brought against me by King Oedipus.

  I am not the kind of man to bear this tamely.

  If in these present difficulties
  He holds me accountable for any harm to him   490
  Through anything I have said or done—why, then,
  I do not value life in this dishonor.
  It is not as though this rumor touched upon
  Some private indiscretion. The matter is grave.
  The fact is that I am being called disloyal   495
  To the State, to my fellow citizens, to my friends.
CHORAGOS.   He may have spoken in anger, not from his mind.
KREON.   But did you not hear him say I was the one
  Who seduced the old prophet into lying?
CHORAGOS.   The thing was said; I do not know how seriously.   500
KREON.   But you were watching him! Were his eyes steady?
  Did he look like a man in his right mind?
CHORAGOS.   I do not know.
  I can not judge the behavior of great men.
  But here is the king himself. (*Enter* OEDIPUS.)
OEDIPUS.   So you dared come back.
  Why? How brazen of you to come to my house,   505
  You murderer!
                Do you think I do not know
  That you plotted to kill me, plotted to steal my throne?
  Tell me, in God's name: am I coward, a fool,
  That you should dream you could accomplish this?
  A fool who could not see your slippery game?   510
  A coward, not to fight back when I saw it?
  You are the fool, Kreon, are you not? hoping
  Without support or friends to get a throne?
  Thrones may be won or bought: you could do neither.
KREON.   Now listen to me. You have talked; let me talk, too.   515
  You can not judge unless you know the facts.
OEDIPUS.   You speak well: there is one fact; but I find it hard
  To learn from the deadliest enemy I have.
KREON.   That above all I must dispute with you.

OEDIPUS.   That above all I will not hear you deny.   520
KREON.   If you think there is anything good in being stubborn
    Against all reason, then I say you are wrong.
OEDIPUS.   If you think a man can sin against his own kind
    And not be punished for it, I say you are mad.
KREON.   I agree. But tell me: what have I done to you?   525
OEDIPUS.   You advised me to send for that wizard, did you not?
KREON.   I did. I should do it again.
OEDIPUS.   Very well. Now tell me:
    How long has it been since Laïos—
KREON.   What of Laïos?
OEDIPUS.   Since he vanished in that onset by the road?
KREON.   It was long ago, a long time.
OEDIPUS.   And this prophet,   530
    Was he practicing here then?
KREON.   He was; and with honor, as now.
OEDIPUS.   Did he speak of me at that time?
KREON.   He never did,
    At least, not when I was present.
OEDIPUS.   But . . . the enquiry?
    I suppose you held one?
KREON.   We did, but we learned nothing.
OEDIPUS.   Why did the prophet not speak against me then?   535
KREON.   I do not know; and I am the kind of man
    Who holds his tongue when he has no facts to go on.
OEDIPUS.   There's one fact that you know, and you could tell it.
KREON.   What fact is that? If I know it, you shall have it.
OEDIPUS.   If he were not involved with you, he could not say   540
    That it was I who murdered Laïos.
KREON.   If he says that, you are the one that knows it!—
    But now it is my turn to question you.
OEDIPUS.   Put your questions. I am no murderer.
KREON.   First, then: You married my sister?
OEDIPUS.   I married your sister. 545
KREON.   And you rule the kingdom equally with her?
OEDIPUS.   Everything that she wants she has from me.
KREON.   And I am the third, equal to both of you?
OEDIPUS.   That is why I call you a bad friend.
KREON.   No. Reason it out, as I have done.   550
    Think of this first: Would any sane man prefer
    Power, with all a king's anxieties,

To that same power and the grace of sleep?
Certainly not I.
I have never longed for the king's power—only his rights.   555
Would any wise man differ from me in this?
As the matters stand, I have my way in everything
With your consent, and no responsibilities.
If I were king, I should be a slave to policy.
How could I desire a scepter more   560
Than what is now mine—untroubled influence?
No, I have not gone mad; I need no honors,
Except those with the perquisites I have now.
I am welcome everywhere; every man salutes me,
And those who want your favor seek my ear,   565
Since I know how to manage what they ask.
Should I exchange this ease for that anxiety?
Besides, no sober mind is treasonable.
I hate anarchy
And never would deal with any man who likes it.   570

Test what I have said. Go to the priestess
At Delphi, ask if I quoted her correctly.
And as for this other thing: if I am found
Guilty of treason with Teiresias,
Then sentence me to death. You have my word   575
It is a sentence I should cast my vote for—
But not without evidence!
                You do wrong
When you take good men for bad, bad men for good.
A true friend thrown aside—why, life itself
Is not more precious!
                In time you will know this well: 580
For time, and time alone, will show the just man,
Though scoundrels are discovered in a day.
CHORAGOS.   This is well said, and a prudent man would ponder it.
    Judgments too quickly formed are dangerous.
OEDIPUS.   But is he not quick in his duplicity?   585
    And shall I not be quick to parry him?
    Would you have me stand still, hold my peace, and let
    This man win everything, through my inaction?
KREON.   And you want—what is it, then? To banish me?
OEDIPUS.   No, not exile. It is your death I want,   590
    So that all the world may see what treason means.

KREON.   You will persist, then? You will not believe me?
OEDIPUS.   How can I believe you?
KREON.   Then you are a fool.
OEDIPUS.   To save myself?
KREON.   In justice, think of me.
OEDIPUS.   You are evil incarnate.
KREON.   But suppose that you are wrong? 595
OEDIPUS.   Still I must rule.
KREON.   But not if you rule badly.
OEDIPUS.   O city, city!
KREON.   It is my city, too!
CHORAGOS.   Now, my lords, be still. I see the queen,
        Iokastê, coming from her palace chambers;
        And it is time she came, for the sake of you both.   600
        This dreadful quarrel can be resolved through her. (*Enter* IOKASTÊ.)
IOKASTÊ.   Poor foolish men, what wicked din is this?
        With Thebes sick to death, is it not shameful
        That you should rake some private quarrel up?
        (*To* OEDIPUS) Come into the house.
                            —And you, Kreon, go now: 605
        Let us have no more of this tumult over nothing.
KREON.   Nothing? No, sister: what your husband plans for me
        Is one of two great evils: exile or death.
OEDIPUS.   He is right.
                    Why, woman I have caught him squarely
        Plotting against my life.
KREON.   No! Let me die   610
        Accurst if ever I have wished you harm!
IOKASTÊ.   Ah, believe it, Oedipus!
        In the name of the gods, respect this oath of his
        For my sake, for the sake of these people here!

STROPHE 1

CHORAGOS.   Open your mind to her, my lord. Be ruled by her, I beg you!
OEDIPUS.   What would you have me do?   616
CHORAGOS.   Respect Kreon's word. He has never spoken like a fool,
        And now he has sworn an oath.
OEDIPUS.   You know what you ask?
CHORAGOS.   I do.
OEDIPUS.   Speak on, then.

CHORAGOS.   A friend so sworn should not be baited so,
    In blind malice, and without final proof.   620
OEDIPUS.   You are aware, I hope, that what you say
    Means death for me, or exile at the least.

STROPHE 2

CHORAGOS.   No, I swear by Helios, first in heaven!
                May I die friendless and accurst,
          The worst of deaths, if ever I meant that!   625
          It is the withering fields
               That hurt my sick heart:
        Must we bear all these ills,
              And now your blood as well?
OEDIPUS.   Then let him go. And let me die, if I must,   630
    Or be driven by him in shame from the land of Thebes.
    It is your unhappiness, and not his talk,
    That touches me.
              As for him—
    Wherever he goes, hatred will follow him.
KREON.   Ugly in yielding, as you were ugly in rage!   635
    Natures like yours chiefly torment themselves.
OEDIPUS.   Can you not go? Can you not leave me?
KREON.   I can.
    You do not know me; but the city knows me,
    And in its eyes I am just, if not in yours. (*Exit* KREON.)

ANTISTROPHE 1

CHORAGOS.   Lady Iokastê, did you not ask the King to go to his
    chambers?   640
IOKASTÊ.   First tell me what has happened.
CHORAGOS.   There was suspicion without evidence; yet it rankled
    As even false charges will.
IOKASTÊ.   On both sides?
CHORAGOS.   On both.
IOKASTÊ.   But what was said?
CHORAGOS.   Oh let it rest, let it be done with!
    Have we not suffered enough?   645
OEDIPUS.   You see to what your decency has brought you:
    You have made difficulties where my heart saw none.

ANTISTROPHE 2

CHORAGOS.   Oedipus, it is not once only I have told you—
                    You must know I should count myself unwise
                To the point of madness, should I now forsake you—   650
                    You, under whose hand,
                        In the storm of another time,
                    Our dear land sailed out free.
                        But now stand fast at the helm!
IOKASTÊ.   In God's name, Oedipus, inform your wife as well: 655
        Why are you so set in this hard anger?
OEDIPUS.   I will tell you, for none of these men deserves
        My confidence as you do. It is Kreon's work,
        His treachery, his plotting against me.
IOKASTÊ.   Go on, if you can make this clear to me.   660
OEDIPUS.   He charges me with the murder of Laïos.
IOKASTÊ.   Has he some knowledge? Or does he speak from hearsay?
OEDIPUS.   He would not commit himself to such a charge,
        But he has brought in that damnable soothsayer
        To tell his story.
IOKASTÊ.   Set your mind at rest.   665
        If it is a question of soothsayers, I tell you
        That you will find no man whose craft gives knowledge
        Of the unknowable.
                        Here is my proof:
        An oracle was reported to Laïos once
        (I will not say from Phoibus himself, but from   670
        His appointed ministers, at any rate)
        That his doom would be death at the hands of his own son—
        His son, born of his flesh and of mine!

        Now, you remember the story: Laïos was killed
        By marauding strangers where three highways meet;   675
        But his child had not been three days in this world
        Before the king had pierced the baby's ankles
        And left him to die on a lonely mountainside.

        Thus, Apollo never caused that child
        To kill his father, and it was not Laïos's fate   680
        To die at the hands of his son, as he had feared.
        This is what prophets and prophecies are worth!

Have no dread of them.
                              It is God himself
Who can show us what he wills, in his own way.

OEDIPUS.   How strange a shadowy memory crossed my mind,   685
  Just now while you were speaking; it chilled my heart.

IOKASTÊ.   What do you mean? What memory do you speak of?

OEDIPUS.   If I understand you, Laïos was killed
  At a place where three roads meet.

IOKASTÊ.   So it was said;
  We have no later story.

OEDIPUS.   Where did it happen?   690

IOKASTÊ.   Phokis, it is called: at a place where the Theban Way
  Divides into the roads toward Delphi and Daulia.

OEDIPUS.   When?

IOKASTÊ.   We had the news not long before you came
  And proved the right to your succession here.

OEDIPUS.   Ah, what net has God been weaving for me?   695

IOKASTÊ.   Oedipus! Why does this trouble you?

OEDIPUS.   Do not ask me yet.
  First, tell me how Laïos looked, and tell me
  How old he was.

IOKASTÊ.   He was tall, his hair just touched
  With white; his form was not unlike your own.

OEDIPUS.   I think that I myself may be accurst   700
  By my own ignorant edict.

IOKASTÊ.   You speak strangely.
  It makes me tremble to look at you, my king.

OEDIPUS.   I am not sure that the blind man can not see.
  But I should know better if you were to tell me—

IOKASTÊ.   Anything—though I dread to hear you ask it.   705

OEDIPUS.   Was the king lightly escorted, or did he ride
  With a large company, as a ruler should?

IOKASTÊ.   There were five men with him in all: one was a herald;
  And a single chariot, which he was driving.

OEDIPUS.   Alas, that makes it plain enough!
                                        But who—   710
  Who told you how it happened?

IOKASTÊ.   A household servant,
  The only one to escape.

OEDIPUS.   And is he still
  A servant of ours?

IOKASTÊ.   No; for when he came back at last
    And found you enthroned in the place of the dead king,
    He came to me, touched my hand with his, and begged   715
    That I would send him away to the frontier district
    Where only the shepherds go—
    As far away from the city as I could send him.
    I granted his prayer; for although the man was a slave,
    He had earned more than this favor at my hands.   720
OEDIPUS.   Can he be called back quickly?
IOKASTÊ.   Easily.
    But why?
OEDIPUS.   I have taken too much upon myself
    Without enquiry; therefore I wish to consult him.
IOKASTÊ.   Then he shall come.
                                But am I not one also
    To whom you might confide these fears of yours?   725
OEDIPUS.   That is your right; it will not be denied you,
    Now least of all; for I have reached a pitch
    Of wild foreboding. Is there anyone
    To whom I should sooner speak?

    Polybos of Corinth is my father.   730
    My mother is a Dorian: Meropê.
    I grew up chief among the men of Corinth
    Until a strange thing happened—
    Not worth my passion, it may be, but strange.
    At a feast, a drunken man maundering in his cups   735
    Cries out that I am not my father's son!

    I contained myself that night, though I felt anger
    And a sinking heart. The next day I visited
    My father and mother, and questioned them. They stormed,
    Calling it all the slanderous rant of a fool;   740
    And this relieved me. Yet the suspicion
    Remained always aching in my mind;
    I knew there was talk; I could not rest;
    And finally, saying nothing to my parents,
    I went to the shrine at Delphi.   745

    The god dismissed my question without reply;
    He spoke of other things.
                       Some were clear,

Full of wretchedness, dreadful, unbearable:
As, that I should lie with my own mother, breed
Children from whom all men would turn their eyes;   750
And that I should be my father's murderer.

I heard all this, and fled. And from that day
Corinth to me was only in the stars
Descending in that quarter of the sky,
As I wandered farther and farther on my way   755
To a land where I should never see the evil
Sung by the oracle. And I came to this country
Where, so you say, King Laïos was killed.

I will tell you all that happened there, my lady.

There were three highways   760
Coming together at a place I passed;
And there a herald came towards me, and a chariot
Drawn by horses, with a man such as you describe
Seated in it. The groom leading the horses
Forced me off the road at his lord's command;   765
But as this charioteer lurched over towards me
I struck him in my rage. The old man saw me
And brought his double goad down upon my head
As I came abreast.
                        He was paid back, and more!
Swinging my club in this right hand I knocked him   770
Out of his car, and he rolled on the ground.
                                            I killed him.

I killed them all.
Now if that stranger and Laïos were—kin,
Where is a man more miserable than I?
More hated by the gods? Citizen and alien alike   775
Must never shelter me or speak to me—
I must be shunned by all.
                        And I myself
Pronounced this malediction upon myself!

Think of it: I have touched you with these hands,
These hands that killed your husband. What defilement!   780

Am I all evil, then? It must be so,
Since I must flee from Thebes, yet never again
See my own countrymen, my own country,
For fear of joining my mother in marriage
And killing Polybos, my father.
Ah,   785
If I was created so, born to this fate,
Who could deny the savagery of God?

O holy majesty of heavenly powers!
May I never see that day! Never!
Rather let me vanish from the race of men   790
Than know the abomination destined me!
CHORAGOS.   We too, my lord, have felt dismay at this.
    But there is hope: you have yet to hear the shepherd.
OEDIPUS.   Indeed, I fear no other hope is left me.
IOKASTÊ.   What do you hope from him when he comes?
OEDIPUS.   This much: 795
    If his account of the murder tallies with yours,
    Then I am cleared.
IOKASTÊ.   What was it that I said
    Of such importance?
OEDIPUS.   Why, "marauders," you said,
    Killed the king, according to this man's story.
    If he maintains that still, if there were several,   800
    Clearly the guilt is not mine: I was alone.
    But if he says one man, singlehanded, did it,
    Then the evidence all points to me.
IOKASTÊ.   You may be sure that he said there were several;
    And can he call back that story now? He can not.   805
    The whole city heard it as plainly as I.
    But suppose he alters some detail of it:
    He can not ever show that Laïos's death
    Fulfilled the oracle: for Apollo said
    My child was doomed to kill him; and my child—   810
    Poor baby!—it was my child that died first.

No. From now on, where oracles are concerned,
    I would not waste a second thought on any.
OEDIPUS.   You may be right.
But come: let someone go
For the shepherd at once. This matter must be settled.   815

Iokastê.   I will send for him.
  I would not wish to cross you in anything.
  And surely not in this.—Let us go in. (*Exeunt into the palace.*)

ODE 2

STROPHE 1

Chorus.   Let me be reverent in the ways of right,
  Lowly the paths I journey on;   820
  Let all my words and actions keep
  The laws of the pure universe
  From highest Heaven handed down
  For Heaven is their bright nurse,
  Those generations of the realms of light;   825
  Ah, never of mortal kind were they begot,
  Nor are they slaves of memory, lost in sleep:
  Their Father is greater than Time, and ages not.

ANTISTROPHE 1

  The tyrant is a child of Pride
  Who drinks from his great sickening cup   830
  Recklessness and vanity,
  Until from his high crest headlong
  He plummets to the dust of hope.
  That strong man is not strong.
  But let no fair ambition be denied;   835
  May God protect the wrestler for the State
  In government, in comely policy,
  Who will fear God, and on His ordinance wait.

STROPHE 2

  Haughtiness and the high hand of disdain
  Tempt and outrage God's holy law;   840
  And any mortal who dares hold
  No immortal Power in awe
  Will be caught up in a net of pain:
  The price for which his levity is sold.
  Let each man take due earnings, then,   845
  And keep his hands from holy things,
  And from blasphemy stand apart—

Else the crackling blast of heaven
Blows on his head, and on his desperate heart.
Though fools will honor impious men,   850
In their cities no tragic poet sings.

ANTISTROPHE 2

Shall we lose faith in Delphi's obscurities,
We who have heard the world's core
Discredited, and the sacred wood
Of Zeus at Elis praised no more?   855
The deeds and the strange prophecies
Must make a pattern yet to be understood.
Zeus, if indeed you are lord of all,
Throned in light over night and day,
Mirror this in your endless mind: 860
Our masters call the oracle
Words on the wind, and the Delphic vision blind!
Their hearts no longer know Apollo,
And reverence for the gods has died away.

SCENE 3

Enter IOKASTÊ.

IOKASTÊ.   Princes of Thebes, it has occurred to me   865
    To visit the altars of the gods, bearing
    These branches as a suppliant, and this incense.
    Our king is not himself: his noble soul
    Is overwrought with fantasies of dread,
    Else he would consider   870
    The new prophecies in the light of the old.
    He will listen to any voice that speaks disaster,
    And my advice goes for nothing. (*She approaches the altar, right.*)
                        To you, then, Apollo,
    Lycéan lord, since you are nearest, I turn in prayer.
    Receive these offerings, and grant us deliverance   875
    From defilement. Our hearts are heavy with fear
    When we see our leader distracted, as helpless sailors
    Are terrified by the confusion of their helmsman. (*Enter* MESSENGER.)
MESSENGER.   Friends, no doubt you can direct me:
    Where shall I find the house of Oedipus,   880
    Or, better still, where is the king himself?

CHORAGOS.   It is this very place, stranger; he is inside.
    This is his wife and mother of his children.
MESSENGER.   I wish her happiness in a happy house,
    Blest in all the fulfillment of her marriage.   885
IOKASTÊ.   I wish as much for you: your courtesy
    Deserves a like good fortune. But now, tell me:
    Why have you come? What have you to say to us?
MESSENGER.   Good news, my lady, for your house and your husband.
IOKASTÊ.   What news? Who sent you here?
MESSENGER.   I am from Corinth.   890
    The news I bring ought to mean joy for you,
    Though it may be you will find some grief in it.
IOKASTÊ.   What is it? How can it touch us in both ways?
MESSENGER.   The word is that the people of the Isthmus
    Intend to call Oedipus to be their king.   895
IOKASTÊ.   But old King Polybos—is he not reigning still?
MESSENGER.   No. Death holds him in his sepulcher.
IOKASTÊ.   What are you saying? Polybos is dead?
MESSENGER.   If I am not telling the truth, may I die myself.
IOKASTÊ (*to a* MAIDSERVANT).   Go in, go quickly; tell this to your master. 900
    O riddlers of God's will, where are you now!
    This was the man whom Oedipus, long ago,
    Feared so, fled so, in dread of destroying him—
    But it was another fate by which he died. (*Enter* OEDIPUS, *center.*)
OEDIPUS.   Dearest Iokastê, why have you sent for me?   905
IOKASTÊ.   Listen to what this man says, and then tell me
    What has become of the solemn prophecies.
OEDIPUS.   Who is this man? What is his news for me?
IOKASTÊ.   He has come from Corinth to announce your father's
    death!
OEDIPUS.   Is it true, stranger? Tell me in your own words.   910
MESSENGER.   I can not say it more clearly: the king is dead.
OEDIPUS.   Was it by treason? Or by an attack of illness?
MESSENGER.   A little thing brings old men to their rest.
OEDIPUS.   It was sickness, then?
MESSENGER.   Yes, and his many years.
OEDIPUS.   Ah!   915
    Why should a man respect the Pythian hearth,° or
    Give heed to the birds that jangle above his head?
    They prophesied that I should kill Polybos,

916. **Pythian hearth:** Delphi

Kill my own father; but he is dead and buried,
And I am here—I never touched him, never,   920
Unless he died of grief for my departure,
And thus, in a sense, through me. No. Polybos
Has packed the oracles off with him underground.
They are empty words.

IOKASTÊ.   Had I not told you so?
OEDIPUS.   You had; it was my faint heart that betrayed me.   925
IOKASTÊ.   From now on never think of those things again.
OEDIPUS.   And yet—must I not fear my mother's bed?
IOKASTÊ.   Why should anyone in this world be afraid,
   Since Fate rules us and nothing can be foreseen?
   A man should live only for the present day.   930

   Have no more fear of sleeping with your mother:
   How many men, in dreams, have lain with their mothers!
   No reasonable man is troubled by such things.
OEDIPUS.   That is true; only—
   If only my mother were not still alive!   935
   But she is alive. I can not help my dread.
IOKASTÊ.   Yet this news of your father's death is wonderful.
OEDIPUS.   Wonderful. But I fear the living woman.
MESSENGER.   Tell me who is this woman that you fear?
OEDIPUS.   It is Meropê, man; the wife of King Polybos.   940
MESSENGER.   Meropê? Why should you be afraid of her?
OEDIPUS.   An oracle of the gods, a dreadful saying.
MESSENGER.   Can you tell me about it or are you sworn to silence?
OEDIPUS.   I can tell you, and I will.
   Apollo said through his prophet that I was the man   945
   Who should marry his own mother, shed his father's blood
   With his own hands. And so, for all these years
   I have kept clear of Corinth, and no harm has come—
   Though it would have been sweet to see my parents again.
MESSENGER.   And is this the fear that drove you out of Corinth? 950
OEDIPUS.   Would you have me kill my father?
MESSENGER.   As for that
   You must be reassured by the news I gave you.
OEDIPUS.   If you could reassure me, I would reward you.
MESSENGER.   I had that in mind, I will confess; I thought
   I could count on you when you returned to Corinth.   955
OEDIPUS.   No: I will never go near my parents again.
MESSENGER.   Ah, son, you still do not know what you are doing—

OEDIPUS.   What do you mean? In the name of God tell me!

MESSENGER.   —If these are your reasons for not going home.

OEDIPUS.   I tell you, I fear the oracle may come true.   960

MESSENGER.   And guilt may come upon you through your parents?

OEDIPUS.   That is the dread that is always in my heart.

MESSENGER.   Can you not see that all your fears are groundless?

OEDIPUS.   Groundless? Am I not my parents' son?

MESSENGER.   Polybos was not your father.

OEDIPUS.   Not my father?   965

MESSENGER.   No more your father than the man speaking to you.

OEDIPUS.   But you are nothing to me!

MESSENGER.   Neither was he.

OEDIPUS.   Then why did he call me son?

MESSENGER.   I will tell you:
    Long ago he had you from my hands, as a gift.

OEDIPUS.   Then how could he love me so, if I was not his?   970

MESSENGER.   He had no children, and his heart turned to you.

OEDIPUS.   What of you? Did you buy me? Did you find me by chance?

MESSENGER.   I came upon you in the woody vales of Kithairon.

OEDIPUS.   And what were you doing there?

MESSENGER.   Tending my flocks.

OEDIPUS.   A wandering shepherd?

MESSENGER.   But your savior, son, that day. 975

OEDIPUS.   From what did you save me?

MESSENGER.   Your ankles should tell you that.

OEDIPUS.   Ah, stranger, why do you speak of that childhood pain?

MESSENGER.   I pulled the skewer that pinned your feet together.

OEDIPUS.   I have had the mark as long as I can remember.

MESSENGER.   That was why you were given the name you bear.   980

OEDIPUS.   God! Was it my father or my mother who did it?
    Tell me!

MESSENGER.   I do not know. The man who gave you to me
    Can tell you better than I.

OEDIPUS.   It was not you that found me, but another?

MESSENGER.   It was another shepherd gave you to me.   985

OEDIPUS.   Who was he? Can you tell me who he was?

MESSENGER.   I think he was said to be one of Laïos's people.

OEDIPUS.   You mean the Laïos who was king here years ago?

MESSENGER.   Yes; King Laïos; and the man was one of his herdsmen.

OEDIPUS.   Is he still alive? Can I see him?

MESSENGER.   These men here   990
    Know best about such things.

OEDIPUS.   Does anyone here
   Know this shepherd that he is talking about?
   Have you seen him in the fields, or in the town?
   If you have, tell me. It is time things were made plain.
CHORAGOS.   I think the man he means is that same shepherd   995
   You have already asked to see. Iokastê perhaps
   Could tell you something.
OEDIPUS.   Do you know anything
   About him, Lady? Is he the man we have summoned?
   Is that the man this shepherd means?
IOKASTÊ.   Why think of him?
   Forget this herdsman. Forget it all.
   This talk is a waste of time.   1000
OEDIPUS.   How can you say that,
   When the clues to my true birth are in my hands?
IOKASTÊ.   For God's love, let us have no more questioning!
   Is your life nothing to you?
   My own is pain enough for me to bear.   1005
OEDIPUS.   You need not worry. Suppose my mother a slave,
   And born of slaves: no baseness can touch you.
IOKASTÊ.   Listen to me, I beg you: do not do this thing!
OEDIPUS.   I will not listen; the truth must be made known.
IOKASTÊ.   Everything that I say is for your own good!
OEDIPUS.   My own good 1010
   Snaps my patience, then; I want none of it.
IOKASTÊ.   You are fatally wrong! May you never learn who you are!
OEDIPUS.   Go, one of you, and bring the shepherd here.
   Let us leave this woman to brag of her royal name.
IOKASTÊ.   Ah, miserable!   1015
   That is the only word I have for you now.
   That is the only word I can ever have. (*Exit into the palace.*)
CHORAGOS.   Why has she left us, Oedipus? Why has she gone
   In such a passion of sorrow? I fear this silence:
   Something dreadful may come of it.
OEDIPUS.   Let it come!   1020
   However base my birth, I must know about it.
   The Queen, like a woman, is perhaps ashamed
   To think of my low origin. But I
   Am a child of Luck; I can not be dishonored.
   Luck is my mother; the passing months, my brothers,   1025
   Have seen me rich and poor.
                     If this is so,

How could I wish that I were someone else?
How could I not be glad to know my birth?

ODE 3

STROPHE

CHORUS.   If ever the coming time were known
    To my heart's pondering,   1030
    Kithairon, now by Heaven I see the torches
    At the festival of the next full moon,
    And see the dance, and hear the choir sing
    A grace to your gentle shade:
    Mountain where Oedipus was found,   1035
    O mountain guard of a noble race!
    May the god° who heals us lend his aid,
    And let that glory come to pass
    For our king's cradling-ground.

ANTISTROPHE

    Of the nymphs that flower beyond the years,   1040
    Who bore you,° royal child,
    To Pan of the hills or the timberline Apollo,
    Cold in delight where the upland clears,
    Or Hermês for whom Kyllenê's heights° are piled?
    Or flushed as evening cloud,   1045
    Great Dionysis, roamer of mountains,
    He—was it he who found you there,
    And caught you up in his own proud
    Arms from the sweet god-ravisher
    Who laughed by the Muses' fountains?   1050

SCENE 4

OEDIPUS.   Sirs: though I do not know the man,
    I think I see him coming, this shepherd we want:
    He is old, like our friend here, and the men
    Bringing him seem to be servants of my house.

1037. god: Apollo   1041. Who bore you: The chorus is suggesting that perhaps
Oedipus is the son of one of the immortal nymphs and of a god—Pan, Apollo, Hermes, or
Dionysis. The "sweet god-ravisher" (line 1049) is the presumed mother.
1044. Kyllenê's heights: the mountain where Hermes was born

But you can tell, if you have ever seen him.   1055
    (*Enter* SHEPHERD *escorted by* SERVANTS.)
CHORAGOS.   I know him, he was Laïos's man. You can trust him.
OEDIPUS.   Tell me first, you from Corinth: is this the shepherd
    We were discussing?
MESSENGER.   This is the very man.
OEDIPUS (*to* SHEPHERD).   Come here. No, look at me. You must answer
    Everything I ask.— You belonged to Laïos?   1060
SHEPHERD.   Yes: born his slave, brought up in his house.
OEDIPUS.   Tell me: what kind of work did you do for him?
SHEPHERD.   I was a shepherd of his, most of my life.
OEDIPUS.   Where mainly did you go for pasturage?
SHEPHERD.   Sometimes Kithairon, sometimes the hills near-by. 1065
OEDIPUS.   Do you remember ever seeing this man out there?
SHEPHERD.   What would he be doing there? This man?
OEDIPUS.   This man standing here. Have you ever seen him before?
SHEPHERD.   No. At least, not to my recollection.
MESSENGER.   And that is not strange, my lord. But I'll refresh 1070
    His memory: he must remember when we two
    Spent three whole seasons together, March to September,
    On Kithairon or thereabouts. He had two flocks;
    I had one. Each autumn I'd drive mine home
    And he would go back with his to Laïos's sheepfold.—   1075
    Is this not true, just as I have described it?
SHEPHERD.   True, yes; but it was all so long ago.
MESSENGER.   Well, then: do you remember, back in those days,
    That you gave me a baby boy to bring up as my own?
SHEPHERD.   What if I did? What are you trying to say?   1080
MESSENGER.   King Oedipus was once that little child.
SHEPHERD.   Damn you, hold your tongue!
OEDIPUS.   No more of that!
    It is your tongue needs watching, not this man's.
SHEPHERD.   My king, my master, what is it I have done wrong?
OEDIPUS.   You have not answered his question about the boy.   1085
SHEPHERD.   He does not know . . . He is only making trouble . . .
OEDIPUS.   Come, speak plainly, or it will go hard with you.
SHEPHERD.   In God's name, do not torture an old man!
OEDIPUS.   Come here, one of you; bind his arms behind him.
SHEPHERD.   Unhappy king! What more do you wish to learn?   1090
OEDIPUS.   Did you give this man the child he speaks of?
SHEPHERD.   I did.
    And I would to God I had died that very day.

OEDIPUS.   You will die now unless you speak the truth.
SHEPHERD.   Yet if I speak the truth, I am worse than dead.
OEDIPUS (*to* ATTENDANT).   He intends to draw it out, apparently— 1095
SHEPHERD.   No! I have told you already that I gave him the boy.
OEDIPUS.   Where did you get him? From your house? From somewhere else?
SHEPHERD.   Not from mine, no. A man gave him to me.
OEDIPUS.   Is that man here? Whose house did he belong to?
SHEPHERD.   For God's love, my king, do not ask me any more!   1100
OEDIPUS.   You are a dead man if I have to ask you again.
SHEPHERD.   Then . . . Then the child was from the palace of Laïos.
OEDIPUS.   A slave child? or a child of his own line?
SHEPHERD.   Ah, I am on the brink of dreadful speech!
OEDIPUS.   And I of dreadful hearing. Yet I must hear.   1105
SHEPHERD.   If you must be told, then . . .
                             They said it was Laïos's child;

But it is your wife who can tell you about that.
OEDIPUS.   My wife—Did she give it to you?
SHEPHERD.
                                 My lord, she did.
OEDIPUS.   Do you know why?
SHEPHERD.
                      I was told to get rid of it.
OEDIPUS.   Oh heartless mother!
SHEPHERD.
                      But in dread of prophecies . . .   1110
OEDIPUS.   Tell me.
SHEPHERD.   It was said that the boy would kill his own father.
OEDIPUS.   Then why did you give him over to this old man?
SHEPHERD.   I pitied the baby, my king,
And I thought that this man would take him far away
To his own country.
                He saved him—but for what a fate!   1115
For if you are what this man says you are,
No man living is more wretched than Oedipus.
OEDIPUS.   Ah God!
It was true!
        All the prophecies!
                —Now,
O Light, may I look on you for the last time!   1120
I, Oedipus,
Oedipus, damned in his birth, in his marriage damned,
Damned in the blood he shed with his own hand!
(*He rushes into the palace.*)

ODE 4

STROPHE 1

CHORUS.   Alas for the seed of men.
    What measure shall I give these generations   1125
    That breathe on the void and are void
    And exist and do not exist?
    Who bears more weight of joy
    Than mass of sunlight shifting in images,
    Or who shall make his thought stay on   1130
    That down time drifts away?
    Your splendor is all fallen.
    O naked brow of wrath and tears,
    O change of Oedipus!
    I who saw your days call no man blest—   1135
    Your great days like ghósts góne.

ANTISTROPHE 1

    That mind was a strong bow.
    Deep, how deep you drew it then, hard archer,
    At a dim fearful range,
    And brought dear glory down!   1140
    You overcame the stranger°—
    The virgin with her hooking lion claws—
    And though death sang, stood like a tower
    To make pale Thebes take heart.
    Fortress against our sorrow!   1145
    True king, giver of laws,
    Majestic Oedipus!
    No prince in Thebes had ever such renown,
    No prince won such grace of power.

STROPHE 2

    And now of all men ever known   1150
    Most pitiful is this man's story:
    His fortunes are most changed; his state
    Fallen to a low slave's
    Ground under bitter fate.
    O Oedipus, most royal one!   1155
    The great door° that expelled you to the light

1141. stranger: the Sphinx   1156. door: Iokastê's womb

Gave at night—ah, gave night to your glory:
As to the father, to the fathering son.
All understood too late.
How could that queen whom Laïos won,   1160
The garden that he harrowed at his height,
Be silent when that act was done?

ANTISTROPHE 2

But all eyes fail before time's eye,
All actions come to justice there.
Though never willed, though far down the deep past,   1165
Your bed, your dread sirings,
Are brought to book at last.
Child by Laïos doomed to die,
Then doomed to lose that fortunate little death,
Would God you never took breath in this air   1170
That with my wailing lips I take to cry:
For I weep the world's outcast.
I was blind, and now I can tell why:
Asleep, for you had given ease of breath
To Thebes, while the false years went by.   1175

EXODOS°

Enter, from the palace, SECOND MESSENGER.

SECOND MESSENGER.   Elders of Thebes, most honored in this land,
     What horrors are yours to see and hear, what weight
     Of sorrow to be endured, if, true to your birth,
     You venerate the line of Labdakos!
     I think neither Istros nor Phasis, those great rivers,   1180
     Could purify this place of all the evil
     It shelters now, or soon must bring to light—
     Evil not done unconsciously, but willed.

     The greatest griefs are those we cause ourselves.
CHORAGOS.   Surely, friend, we have grief enough already;   1185
     What new sorrow do you mean?
SECOND MESSENGER.   The queen is dead.
CHORAGOS.   O miserable queen! But at whose hand?

Exodos: final scene

SECOND MESSENGER.   Her own.
   The full horror of what happened you can not know,
For you did not see it; but I, who did, will tell you
As clearly as I can how she met her death.   1190

When she had left us,
In passionate silence, passing through the court,
She ran to her apartment in the house,
Her hair clutched by the fingers of both hands.
She closed the doors behind her; then, by that bed   1195
Where long ago the fatal son was conceived—
That son who should bring about his father's death—
We heard her call upon Laïos, dead so many years,
And heard her wail for the double fruit of her marriage,
A husband by her husband, children by her child.   1200

Exactly how she died I do not know:
For Oedipus burst in moaning and would not let us
Keep vigil to the end: it was by him
As he stormed about the room that our eyes were caught.
From one to another of us he went, begging a sword,   1205
Hunting the wife who was not his wife, the mother
Whose womb had carried his own children and himself.
I do not know: it was none of us aided him,
But surely one of the gods was in control!
For with a dreadful cry   1210
He hurled his weight, as though wrenched out of himself,
At the twin doors: the bolts gave, and he rushed in.
And there we saw her hanging, her body swaying
From the cruel cord she had noosed about her neck.
A great sob broke from him, heartbreaking to hear,   1215
As he loosened the rope and lowered her to the ground.

I would blot out from my mind what happened next!
For the king ripped from her gown the golden brooches
That were her ornament, and raised them, and plunged them down
Straight into his own eyeballs, crying, "No more,   1220
No more shall you look on the misery about me,
The horrors of my own doing! Too long you have known
The faces of those whom I should never have seen,
Too long been blind to those for whom I was searching!
From this hour, go in darkness!" And as he spoke,   1225

He struck his eyes—not once, but many times;
And the blood spattered his beard,
Bursting from his ruined sockets like red hail.
So from the unhappiness of two this evil has sprung,
A curse on the man and woman alike. The old   1230
Happiness of the house of Labdakos
Was happiness enough: where is it today?
It is all wailing and ruin, disgrace, death—all
The misery of mankind that has a name—
And it is wholly and for ever theirs.   1235

CHORAGOS.   Is he in agony still? Is there no rest for him?

SECOND MESSENGER.   He is calling for someone to open the doors wide
So that all the children of Kadmos may look upon
His father's murderer, his mother's—no,
I can not say it!
                 And then he will leave Thebes,   1240
Self-exiled, in order that the curse
Which he himself pronounced may depart from the house.
He is weak, and there is none to lead him,
So terrible is his suffering.
                 But you will see:
Look, the doors are opening; in a moment   1245
You will see a thing that would crush a heart of stone.

(*The central door is opened;* OEDIPUS, *blinded, is led in.*)

CHORAGOS.   Dreadful indeed for me to see.
Never have my own eyes
Looked on a sight so full of fear.

Oedipus!   1250
What madness came upon you, what daemon
Leaped on your life with heavier
Punishment than a mortal man can bear?
No: I can not even
Look at you, poor ruined one.   1255
And I would speak, question, ponder,
If I were able. No.
You make me shudder.

OEDIPUS.   God. God.
Is there a sorrow greater?   1260
Where shall I find harbor in this world?
My voice is hurled far on a dark wind.
What has God done to me?

CHORAGOS.   Too terrible to think of, or to see.

STROPHE 1

OEDIPUS.   O cloud of night,   1265
    Never to be turned away: night coming on,
    I can not tell how: night like a shroud!
    My fair winds brought me here.
                    O God. Again
    The pain of the spikes where I had sight,
    The flooding pain   1270
    Of memory, never to be gouged out.
CHORAGOS.   This is not strange.
    You suffer it all twice over, remorse in pain,
    Pain in remorse.

ANTISTROPHE 1

OEDIPUS.   Ah dear friend   1275
    Are you faithful even yet, you alone?
    Are you still standing near me, will you stay here,
    Patient, to care for the blind?
                   The blind man!
    Yet even blind I know who it is attends me,
    By the voice's tone—   1280
    Though my new darkness hide the comforter.
CHORAGOS.   Oh fearful act!
    What god was it drove you to rake black
    Night across your eyes?

STROPHE 2

OEDIPUS.   Apollo. Apollo. Dear   1285
    Children, the god was Apollo.
    He brought my sick, sick fate upon me.
    But the blinding hand was my own!
    How could I bear to see
    When all my sight was horror everywhere?   1290
CHORAGOS.   Everywhere; that is true.
OEDIPUS.   And now what is left?
    Images? Love? A greeting even,
    Sweet to the senses? Is there anything?
    Ah, no, friends: lead me away.   1295
    Lead me away from Thebes.
                 Lead the great wreck
    And hell of Oedipus, whom the gods hate.

CHORAGOS.   Your misery, you are not blind to that.
    Would God you had never found it out!

ANTISTROPHE 2

OEDIPUS.   Death take the man who unbound   1300
    My feet on that hillside
    And delivered me from death to life! What life?
    If only I had died,
    This weight of monstrous doom
    Could not have dragged me and my darlings down.   1305
CHORAGOS.   I would have wished the same.
OEDIPUS.   Oh never to have come here
    With my father's blood upon me! Never
    To have been the man they call his mother's husband!
    Oh accurst! Oh child of evil,   1310
    To have entered that wretched bed—
                        the selfsame one!
    More primal than sin itself, this fell to me.
CHORAGOS.   I do not know what words to offer you.
    You were better dead than alive and blind.
OEDIPUS.   Do not counsel me any more. This punishment   1315
    That I have laid upon myself is just.
    If I had eyes,
    I do not know how I could bear the sight
    Of my father, when I came to the house of Death,
    Or my mother: for I have sinned against them both   1320
    So vilely that I could not make my peace
    By strangling my own life.
                        Or do you think my children,
    Born as they were born, would be sweet to my eyes?
    Ah never, never! Nor this town with its high walls,
    Nor the holy images of the gods.
                        For I,   1325
    Thrice miserable!—Oedipus, noblest of all the line
    Of Kadmos, have condemned myself to enjoy
    These things no more, by my own malediction
    Expelling that man whom the gods declared
    To be a defilement in the house of Laïos.   1330
    After exposing the rankness of my own guilt,
    How could I look men frankly in the eyes?
    No, I swear it.
    If I could have stifled my hearing at its source,

I would have done it and made all this body   1335
A tight cell of misery, blank to light and sound:
So I should have been safe in my dark mind
Beyond external evil.
                        Ah Kithairon!
Why did you shelter me? When I was cast upon you,
Why did I not die? Then I should never   1340
Have shown the world my execrable birth.

Ah Polybos! Corinth, city that I believed
The ancient sea of my ancestors: how fair
I seemed, your child! And all the while this evil
Was cancerous within me!
                        For I am sick,   1345
In my own being, sick in my origin.

O three roads, dark ravine, woodland and way
Where three roads met: you, drinking my father's blood,
My own blood, spilled by my own hand: can you remember
The unspeakable things I did there, and the things   1350
I went on from there to do?
                        O marriage, marriage!
The act that engendered me, and again the act
Performed by the son in the same bed—
                        Ah, the net
Of incest, mingling fathers, brothers, sons,
With brides, wives, mothers: the last evil   1355
That can be known by men: no tongue can say
How evil!
          No. For the love of God, conceal me
Somewhere far from Thebes; or kill me; or hurl me
Into the sea, away from men's eyes for ever.

Come, lead me. You need not fear to touch me.   1360
   Of all men, I alone can bear this guilt. (*Enter* Kreon.)
Choragos.   Kreon is here now. As to what you ask,
   He may decide the course to take. He only
   Is left to protect the city in your place.
Oedipus.   Alas, how can I speak to him? What right have I   1365
   To beg his courtesy whom I have deeply wronged?
Kreon.   I have not come to mock you, Oedipus,
   Or to reproach you, either.
      (*To* Attendants)   —You, standing there:

If you have lost all respect for man's dignity,
At least respect the flame of Lord Helios: 1370
Do not allow this pollution to show itself
Openly here, an affront to the earth
And Heaven's rain and the light of day. No, take him
Into the house as quickly as you can.
For it is proper   1375
That only the close kindred see his grief.

OEDIPUS.   I pray you in God's name, since your courtesy
Ignores my dark expectation, visiting
With mercy this man of all men most execrable:
Give me what I ask for—for your good, not for mine.   1380

KREON.   And what is it that you turn to me begging for?

OEDIPUS.   Drive me out of this country as quickly as may be
To a place where no human voice can ever greet me.

KREON.   I should have done that before now—only,
God's will had not been wholly revealed to me.   1385

OEDIPUS.   But his command is plain: the parricide
Must be destroyed. I am that evil man.

KREON.   That is the sense of it, yes; but as things are,
We had best discover clearly what is to be done.

OEDIPUS.   You would learn more about a man like me?   1390

KREON.   You are ready now to listen to the god.

OEDIPUS.   I will listen. But it is to you
That I must turn for help. I beg you, hear me.

The woman in there—
Give her whatever funeral you think proper: 1395
She is your sister.
                        —But let me go, Kreon!
Let me purge my father's Thebes of the pollution
Of my living here, and go out to the wild hills,
To Kithairon, that has won such fame with me,
The tomb my mother and father appointed for me,   1400
And let me die there, as they willed I should.
And yet I know
Death will not ever come to me through sickness
Or in any natural way: I have been preserved
For some unthinkable fate. But let that be.   1405

As for my sons, you need not care for them.
They are men, they will find some way to live.

But my poor daughters, who have shared my table,
Who never before have been parted from their father—
Take care of them, Kreon; do this for me.   1410

And will you let me touch them with my hands
A last time, and let us weep together?
Be kind, my lord,
Great prince, be kind!
                   Could I but touch them,
They would be mine again, as when I had my eyes.   1415
(*Enter* ANTIGONE *and* ISMENE, *attended.*)
Ah, God!
Is it my dearest children I hear weeping?
Has Kreon pitied me and sent my daughters?
KREON.   Yes, Oedipus: I knew that they were dear to you
In the old days, and know you must love them still.   1420
OEDIPUS.   May God bless you for this—and be a friendlier
Guardian to you than he has been to me!

Children, where are you?
Come quickly to my hands: they are your brother's—
Hands that have brought your father's once clear eyes   1425
To this way of seeing—
                Ah dearest ones,
I had neither sight nor knowledge then, your father
By the woman who was the source of his own life!
And I weep for you—having no strength to see you—
I weep for you when I think of the bitterness   1430
That men will visit upon you all your lives.
What homes, what festivals can you attend
Without being forced to depart again in tears?
And when you come to marriageable age,
Where is the man, my daughters, who would dare   1435
Risk the bane that lies on all my children?
Is there any evil wanting? Your father killed
His father; sowed the womb of her who bore him;
Engendered you at the fount of his own existence!
That is what they will say of you.

                    Then, whom   1440
Can you ever marry? There are no bridegrooms for you,
And your lives must wither away in sterile dreaming.

O Kreon, son of Menoikeus!
You are the only father my daughters have,
Since we, their parents, are both of us gone for ever.   1445
They are your own blood: you will not let them
Fall into beggary and loneliness;
You will keep them from the miseries that are mine!
Take pity on them; see, they are only children,
Friendless except for you. Promise me this,   1450
Great prince, and give me your hand in token of it.
(KREON *clasps his right hand.*)
Children:
I could say much, if you could understand me,
But as it is, I have only this prayer for you:
Live where you can, be as happy as you can—   1455
Happier, please God, than God has made your father.

KREON.   Enough. You have wept enough. Now go within.

OEDIPUS.   I must; but it is hard.

KREON.   Time eases all things.

OEDIPUS.   You know my mind, then?

KREON.   Say what you desire.

OEDIPUS.   Send me from Thebes!

KREON.   God grant that I may!   1460

OEDIPUS.   But since God hates me . . .

KREON.   No, he will grant your wish.

OEDIPUS.   You promise?

KREON.   I can not speak beyond my knowledge.

OEDIPUS.   Then lead me in.

KREON.   Come now, and leave your children.

OEDIPUS.   No! Do not take them from me!

KREON.   Think no longer
That you are in command here, but rather think   1465
How, when you were, you served your own destruction. (*Exeunt
into the house all but the* CHORUS; *the* CHORAGOS *chants directly to
the audience.*)

CHORAGOS.   Men of Thebes: look upon Oedipus.

This is the king who solved the famous riddle
And towered up, most powerful of men.
No mortal eyes but looked on him with envy,   1470
Yet in the end ruin swept over him.

Let every man in mankind's frailty
Consider his last day; and let none

Presume on his good fortune until he find
Life, at his death, a memory without pain.   1475

QUESTIONS

1. The oracles had prophesied that Oedipus would kill his father and beget children by his mother. Is Oedipus therefore *made* to do these things? Is the play premised on the notion that Oedipus is bound or free—the puppet of fate or the creator of his own fate? Or some of each?

2. Outline the actions presented on the stage: begin where the play begins, with the people turning to their king for relief from the plague, and disregard for the moment the revelation of incidents that preceded the play. Then summarize the antecedent actions as they are gradually revealed. In what ways are Oedipus's stage actions consistent with his prior actions? In what ways are they different? How do these two sets of actions reveal him to be a person of extraordinary stature?

3. What is Oedipus's primary motivation throughout the action of the play? What were his motives in actions prior to the play? What characters try to dissuade him from pursuing his purpose, and why do they do so? How do his subjects regard him?

4. Is any common pattern of behavior exhibited in Oedipus's encounters with Laïos, with Teiresias, and with Kreon? Is there any justification for his anger with Teiresias? For his suspicion of Kreon? Why?

5. Oedipus's original question, "Who killed Laïos?" soon turns into the question "Who am I?" On the level of plot, the answer is "Son of Laïos and Iokastê, father's murderer, mother's husband." What is the answer at the level of character—that is, in a psychological or philosophical sense?

6. What philosophical issues are raised by Iokastê's judgment on the oracles (Scene 2)? How does the chorus respond to her judgment? How does the play resolve these issues?

7. Why does Oedipus blind himself? Is this an act of weakness or of strength? Why does he ask Kreon to drive him from Thebes? Does he feel that his fate has been just or unjust? Is his suffering, in fact, deserved? Partially deserved? Undeserved?

8. There is a good deal in the play about seeing and blindness. What purpose does this serve? How is Oedipus contrasted with Teiresias? How does Oedipus at the beginning of the play contrast with Oedipus at the end? Why is his blinding himself dramatically appropriate?

9. In what sense may Oedipus be regarded as a better man, though a less fortunate one, at the end of the play than at the beginning? What has he gained from his experience?

10. Some critics have suggested that Oedipus's answer to the Sphinx's riddle was incomplete—that the answer should have been not just man but Oedipus himself—and that Oedipus was as ignorant of the whole truth here as he is when he lays his curse in Scene 1 on the murderer of Laïos. Does this suggestion make sense? On how many legs does Oedipus walk at the end of the play?

11. If the answer to the Sphinx's riddle is not just man but Oedipus himself, may the answer to Oedipus's question "Who am I?" pertain not only to Oedipus but also to man, or at least to civilized Western man? What characteristics of Oedipus as an individual are also characteristics of man in the Western world? Is Sophocles writing only about Oedipus the king, or is he saying something about man's presumed place and his real place in the universe?

12. What purposes are served by the appearance of Antigone and Ismene in the Exodos?

13. What purposes does the chorus serve in the play? Whom does it speak for? Comment on the function of each of the four Odes.

14. What does the final speech of the Choragos tell us about human life?

15. A central formal feature of the play is its use of dramatic irony. Point out speeches by Oedipus, especially in the Prologue and Scene 1, that have a different or a larger meaning for the audience than for Oedipus himself. Sophocles's title literally translates "Oedipus the Tyrant," but the word *tyrant* denoted a ruler who had earned his position through his own intelligence and strength rather than by inheritance—it was not a negative term. Given that, what ironies are suggested by Sophocles's title?

16. The plot of *Oedipus Rex* has been called one of the most perfect dramatic plots ever devised. Why is it admired? What are its outstanding characteristics?

William Shakespeare
Othello, the Moor of Venice

Characters

DUKE OF VENICE
BRABANTIO, *a Senator*
OTHER SENATORS
GRATIANO, *Brabantio's brother*
LODOVICO, *Brabantio's kinsman*
OTHELLO, *a noble Moor in the service of the Venetian state*
CASSIO, *his lieutenant*
IAGO, *his ensign*
MONTANO, *Othello's predecessor in the government of Cyprus*
RODERIGO, *a Venetian gentleman*
CLOWN, *Othello's servant*
DESDEMONA, *Brabantio's daughter and Othello's wife*
EMILIA, *Iago's wife*
BIANCA, *Cassio's mistress*
SAILOR, MESSENGER, HERALD, OFFICERS, GENTLEMEN, MUSICIANS,
    and ATTENDANTS

SCENE. *Venice, and a seaport in Cyprus.*

OTHELLO, THE MOOR OF VENICE   First performed in 1604. The general historical background of the action is probably sometime between 1470 and 1522, a period when Venice, an independent city-state headed by a duke (or doge) elected by the heads of the noble families, was the strongest sea power of the Christian world and included Cyprus and Rhodes among its dominions. Its chief rival for power in the Mediterranean was the Turkish or Ottomite empire. Venetian law required that the commander-in-chief of its forces be an alien, not a Venetian citizen, to prevent political ambition from interfering with his duties. Othello, a black African of royal blood and a soldier of great experience, fulfills the qualifications. The events and characters of the play are fictional, and in any case Shakespeare was not overly concerned with historical accuracy.

William Shakespeare (1564–1616) was born in Stratford-upon-Avon but went to London as a young man and made his fortune as an actor, playwright, and part-owner of the Globe Theatre. He did not supervise the publication of his plays, and the two earliest printings of *Othello*—the quarto of 1622 and the folio of 1623—differ in various ways. Modern editors must rely on judgment and scholarship in reconciling the two to arrive at their texts. The version presented here is that of G. B. Harrison, from *Shakespeare: The Complete Works* (New York: Harcourt, 1952). The editors of this book have selected some notes from Harrison's text and supplemented them with newly created notes.

ACT 1

SCENE 1. Venice. A street.

Enter RODERIGO *and* IAGO.

RODERIGO.   Tush, never tell me! I take it much unkindly
    That thou, Iago, who hast had my purse
    As if the strings were thine, shouldst know of this.
IAGO.   'Sblood, but you will not hear me.
    If ever I did dream of such a matter,   5
    Abhor me.
RODERIGO.   Thou told'st me thou didst hold him in thy hate.
IAGO.   Despise me if I do not. Three great ones of the city,
    In personal suit to make me his Lieutenant,
    Off-capped to him. And, by the faith of man,   10
    I know my price, I am worth no worse a place.
    But he, as loving his own pride and purposes,
    Evades them, with a bombast circumstance
    Horribly stuffed with epithets of war.
    And, in conclusion,   15
    Nonsuits° my mediators, for, "Certes," says he,
    "I have already chose my officer."
    And what was he?
    Forsooth, a great arithmetician,°
    One Michael Cassio, a Florentine,   20
    A fellow almost damned in a fair wife,°
    That never set a squadron in the field,
    Nor the division of a battle knows
    More than a spinster, unless the bookish theoric,
    Wherein the toged Consuls° can propose   25
    As masterly as he—mere prattle without practice
    Is all his soldiership. But he, sir, had the election.
    And I, of whom his° eyes had seen the proof
    At Rhodes, at Cyprus, and on other grounds
    Christian and heathen, must be beeled° and calmed   30
    By debitor and creditor. This countercaster,°

---

16. Nonsuits: Rejects the petition of   **19. arithmetician:** Contemporary books on military tactics are full of elaborate diagrams and numerals to explain military formations. Cassio is a student of such books.   **21. almost . . . wife:** A much-disputed phrase. There is an Italian proverb, "You have married a fair wife? You are damned." If Iago has this in mind, he means by *almost* that Cassio is about to marry.   **25. toged Consuls:** senators in togas [Eds.]   **28. his:** Othello's [Eds.]   **30. beeled:** placed on the lee (or unfavorable) side   **31. countercaster:** calculator (repeating the idea of arithmetician). Counters were used in making calculations.

He, in good time,° must his Lieutenant be,
And I—God bless the mark!—his Moorship's Ancient.°
RODERIGO.   By Heaven, I rather would have been his hangman.
IAGO.   Why, there's no remedy. 'Tis the curse of service,   35
    Preferment goes by letter and affection,
    And not by old gradation,° where each second
    Stood heir to the first. Now, sir, be judge yourself
    Whether I in any just term am affined°
    To love the Moor.
RODERIGO.   I would not follow him, then.   40
IAGO.   Oh, sir, content you,
    I follow him to serve my turn upon him.
    We cannot all be masters, nor all masters
    Cannot be truly followed. You shall mark
    Many a duteous and knee-crooking knave   45
    That doting on his own obsequious bondage
    Wears out his time, much like his master's ass,
    For naught but provender, and when he's old, cashiered.
    Whip me such honest knaves. Others there are
    Who, trimmed in forms and visages of duty,   50
    Keep yet their hearts attending on themselves,
    And throwing but shows of service on their lords
    Do well thrive by them, and when they have lined their coats
    Do themselves homage. These fellows have some soul,
    And such a one do I profess myself. For, sir,   55
    It is as sure as you are Roderigo,
    Were I the Moor, I would not be Iago.
    In following him, I follow but myself.
    Heaven is my judge, not I for love and duty,
    But seeming so, for my peculiar° end.   60
    For when my outward action doth demonstrate
    The native act and figure of my heart
    In compliment extern, 'tis not long after
    But I will wear my heart upon my sleeve
    For daws to peck at. I am not what I am.   65
RODERIGO.   What a full fortune does the thick-lips owe°
    If he can carry 't thus!°

---

32. in good time: a phrase expressing indignation   **33. Ancient:** Ensign, the third officer in the company of which Othello is Captain and Cassio Lieutenant
36–37. Preferment . . . gradation: Promotion comes through private recommendation and favoritism and not by order of seniority.   **39. affined:** tied by affection   **60. peculiar:** personal [Eds.]   **66. owe:** own   **67. carry 't thus:** i.e., bring off this marriage

IAGO.   Call up her father,
  Rouse him. Make after him, poison his delight,
  Proclaim him in the streets. Incense her kinsmen,
  And though he in a fertile climate dwell,   70
  Plague him with flies. Though that his joy be joy,
  Yet throw such changes of vexation on 't
  As it may lose some color.
RODERIGO.   Here is her father's house, I'll call aloud.
IAGO.   Do, with like timorous° accent and dire yell   75
  As when, by night and negligence, the fire
  Is spied in populous cities.
RODERIGO.   What ho, Brabantio! Signior Brabantio, ho!
IAGO.   Awake! What ho, Brabantio! Thieves! Thieves! Thieves!
  Look to your house, your daughter and your bags!°   80
  Thieves! Thieves! (BRABANTIO *appears above, at a window.*)
BRABANTIO.   What is the reason of this terrible summons?
  What is the matter there?
RODERIGO.   Signior, is all your family within?
IAGO.   Are your doors locked?
BRABANTIO.   Why, wherefore ask you this?   85
IAGO.   'Zounds, sir, you're robbed. For shame, put on your gown,
  Your heart is burst, you have lost half your soul.
  Even now, now, very now, an old black ram
  Is tupping your white ewe. Arise, arise,
  Awake the snorting° citizens with the bell,   90
  Or else the Devil° will make a grandsire of you.
  Arise, I say.
BRABANTIO.   What, have you lost your wits?
RODERIGO.   Most reverend signior, do you know my voice?
BRABANTIO.   Not I. What are you?
RODERIGO.   My name is Roderigo.
BRABANTIO.   The worser welcome.   95
  I have charged thee not to haunt about my doors.
  In honest plainness thou hast heard me say
  My daughter is not for thee, and now, in madness,
  Being full of supper and distempering draughts,
  Upon malicious bravery° dost thou come   100
  To start° my quiet.

---

75. timorous: terrifying   **80. bags:** moneybags   **90. snorting:** snoring
91. Devil: The Devil in old pictures and woodcuts was represented as black.
100. bravery: defiance   **101. start:** startle

RODERIGO.   Sir, sir, sir—
BRABANTIO.   But thou must needs be sure
My spirit and my place have in them power
To make this bitter to thee.
RODERIGO.   Patience, good sir.
BRABANTIO.   What tell'st thou me of robbing? This is Venice,   105
My house is not a grange.°
RODERIGO.   Most grave Brabantio,
In simple and pure soul I come to you.
IAGO.   'Zounds, sir, you are one of those that will not serve God if the
Devil bid you. Because we come to do you service and you think
we are ruffians, you'll have your daughter covered with a Barbary°
horse, you'll have your nephews° neigh to you, you'll have coursers
for cousins,° and jennets° for germans.°   112
BRABANTIO.   What profane wretch art thou?
IAGO.   I am one, sir, that comes to tell you your daughter and the Moor
are now making the beast with two backs.
BRABANTIO.   Thou art a villain.
IAGO.   You are—a Senator.
BRABANTIO.   This thou shalt answer. I know thee, Roderigo.
RODERIGO.   Sir, I will answer anything. But I beseech you
If 't be your pleasure and most wise consent,
As partly I find it is, that your fair daughter,   120
At this odd-even° and dull watch o' the night,
Transported with no worse nor better guard
But with a knave of common hire, a gondolier,
To the gross clasps of a lascivious Moor—
If this be known to you, and your allowance,°   125
We then have done you bold and saucy wrongs.
But if you know not this, my manners tell me
We have your wrong rebuke. Do not believe
That, from the sense of all civility,°
I thus would play and trifle with your reverence.   130
Your daughter, if you have not given her leave,
I say again, hath made a gross revolt,
Tying her duty, beauty, wit, and fortunes
In an extravagant° and wheeling° stranger

---

106. **grange:** lonely farm   110. **Barbary:** Moorish   111. **nephews:** grandsons
112. **cousins:** near relations   **jennets:** Moorish ponies   **germans:** kinsmen
121. **odd-even:** about midnight   125. **your allowance:** by your permission
129. **from . . . civility:** contrary to all decency [Eds.]   134. **extravagant:** vagabond
wheeling: wandering

    Of here and everywhere. Straight satisfy yourself.   135
    If she be in her chamber or your house,
    Let loose on me the justice of the state
    For thus deluding you.
BRABANTIO.   Strike on the tinder,° ho!
    Give me a taper!° Call up all my people!
    This accident is not unlike my dream.   140
    Belief of it oppresses me already.
    Light, I say! Light! (*Exit above.*)
IAGO.   Farewell, for I must leave you.
    It seems not meet, nor wholesome to my place,°
    To be produced—as if I stay I shall—
    Against the Moor. For I do know the state,   145
    However this may gall him with some check,
    Cannot with safety cast° him. For he's embarked
    With such loud reason to the Cyprus wars,
    Which even now stand in act,° that, for their souls,
    Another of his fathom they have none   150
    To lead their business. In which regard,
    Though I do hate him as I do Hell pains,
    Yet for necessity of present life
    I must show out a flag and sign of love,
    Which is indeed but sign. That you shall surely find him,   155
    Lead to the Sagittary° the raisèd search,
    And there will I be with him. So farewell.
    (*Exit* IAGO. *Enter, below,* BRABANTIO, *in his nightgown,*° *and* SER-
    VANTS *with torches.*)
BRABANTIO.   It is too true an evil. Gone she is,
    And what's to come of my despisèd time
    Is naught but bitterness. Now, Roderigo,   160
    Where didst thou see her? Oh, unhappy girl!
    With the Moor, say'st thou? Who would be a father!
    How didst thou know 'twas she? Oh, she deceives me
    Past thought! What said she to you? Get more tapers.
    Raise all my kindred. Are they married, think you?   165
RODERIGO.   Truly, I think they are.
BRABANTIO.   Oh Heaven! How got she out? Oh, treason of the blood!
    Fathers, from hence trust not your daughters' minds

---

138. tinder: the primitive method of making fire, used before the invention of matches
139. taper: candle   **143. place:** i.e., as Othello's officer   **147. cast:** dismiss from
service   **149. stand in act:** are under way [Eds.]   **156. Sagittary:** presumably some
inn in Venice [Eds.]   **157. s.d. nightgown:** dressing-gown [Eds.]

By what you see them act. Are there not charms°
By which the property° of youth and maidhood   170
May be abused?° Have you not read, Roderigo,
Of some such thing?
RODERIGO.   Yes, sir, I have indeed.
BRABANTIO.   Call up my brother.—Oh, would you had had her!—
Some one way, some another.—Do you know
Where we may apprehend her and the Moor?   175
RODERIGO.   I think I can discover him, if you please
To get good guard and go along with me.
BRABANTIO.   Pray you, lead on. At every house I'll call,
I may command° at most. Get weapons, ho!
And raise some special officers of night.   180
On, good Roderigo, I'll deserve your pains.° (*Exeunt*.)

SCENE 2. *Another street.*

Enter OTHELLO, IAGO, *and* ATTENDANTS *with torches.*

IAGO.   Though in the trade of war I have slain men,
Yet do I hold it very stuff o' the conscience
To do no contrivèd murder. I lack iniquity
Sometimes to do me service. Nine or ten times
I had thought to have yerked him° here under the ribs.   5
OTHELLO.   'Tis better as it is.
IAGO.   Nay, but he prated
And spoke such scurvy and provoking terms
Against your honor
That, with the little godliness I have,
I did full hard forbear him. But I pray you, sir,   10
Are you fast married? Be assured of this,
That the Magnifico is much beloved,
And hath in his effect a voice potential
As double as° the Duke's. He will divorce you,
Or put upon you what restraint and grievance   15
The law, with all his might to enforce it on,
Will give him cable.
OTHELLO.   Let him do his spite.
My services which I have done the signiory°

---

169. **charms:** magic spells   170. **property:** nature   171. **abused:** deceived
179. **command:** find supporters   181. **deserve your pains:** reward your labor
5. **yerked him:** stabbed Brabantio [Eds.]   13–14. **potential . . . as:** twice as powerful as
18. **signiory:** state of Venice

Shall out-tongue his complaints. 'Tis yet to know°—
Which, when I know that boasting is an honor,   20
I shall promulgate—I fetch my life and being
From men of royal siege,° and my demerits°
May speak unbonneted to as proud a fortune
As this that I have reached. For know, Iago,
But that I love the gentle Desdemona,   25
I would not my unhousèd° free condition
Put into circumscription and confine
For the sea's worth. But look! What lights come yond?

IAGO.   Those are the raisèd father and his friends.
    You were best go in.

OTHELLO.   Not I, I must be found.   30
    My parts, my title, and my perfect soul°
    Shall manifest me rightly. Is it they?

IAGO.   By Janus, I think no.
    (*Enter* CASSIO, *and certain* OFFICERS *with torches.*)

OTHELLO.   The servants of the Duke, and my Lieutenant.
    The goodness of the night upon you, friends!   35
    What is the news?

CASSIO.   The Duke does greet you, General,
    And he requires your haste-posthaste appearance,
    Even on the instant.

OTHELLO.   What is the matter, think you?

CASSIO.   Something from Cyprus, as I may divine.
    It is a business of some heat. The galleys   40
    Have sent a dozen sequent messengers
    This very night at one another's heels,
    And many of the consuls, raised and met,
    Are at the Duke's already. You have been hotly called for
    When, being not at your lodging to be found,   45
    The Senate hath sent about three several° quests
    To search you out.

OTHELLO.   'Tis well I am found by you.
    I will but spend a word here in the house
    And go with you. (*Exit.*)

CASSIO.   Ancient, what makes he here?

IAGO.   Faith, he tonight hath boarded a land carrack.°   50
    If it prove lawful prize, he's made forever.

19. yet to know: not widely known [Eds.]   **22. siege:** rank [Eds.]   **demerits:**
deserts   **26. unhousèd:** unmarried   **31. perfect soul:** clear conscience [Eds.]
46. several: separate   **50. carrack:** large merchant ship

CASSIO. I do not understand.

IAGO.   He's married.

CASSIO.   To who? (*Re-enter* OTHELLO.)

IAGO. Marry,° to—Come, Captain, will you go?

OTHELLO.   Have with you.

CASSIO. Here comes another troop to seek for you.

IAGO. It is Brabantio. General, be advised,   55
 He comes to bad intent.
 (*Enter* BRABANTIO, RODERIGO, *and* OFFICERS *with torches and weapons.*)

OTHELLO.   Holloa! Stand there!

RODERIGO. Signior, it is the Moor.

BRABANTIO.   Down with him, thief!
 (*They draw on both sides.*)

IAGO. You, Roderigo! Come, sir, I am for you.

OTHELLO. Keep up° your bright swords, for the dew will rust them.
 Good signior, you shall more command with years   60
 Than with your weapons.

BRABANTIO. O thou foul thief, where hast thou stowed my daughter?
 Damned as thou art, thou hast enchanted her.
 For I'll refer me to all things of sense
 If she in chains of magic were not bound,   65
 Whether a maid so tender, fair, and happy,
 So opposite to marriage that she shunned
 The wealthy curlèd darlings of our nation,
 Would ever have, to incur a general mock,
 Run from her guardage° to the sooty bosom   70
 Of such a thing as thou, to fear, not to delight.
 Judge me the world if 'tis not gross in sense°
 That thou hast practiced on her with foul charms,
 Abused her delicate youth with drugs or minerals
 That weaken motion.° I'll have 't disputed on,°   75
 'Tis probable, and palpable to thinking.
 I therefore apprehend and do attach° thee
 For an abuser of the world, a practicer
 Of arts inhibited and out of warrant.°
 Lay hold upon him. If he do resist,   80
 Subdue him at his peril.

---

53. Marry: a mild oath [Eds.] **59. Keep up:** Sheathe **70. guardage:** guardianship
72. gross in sense: obvious [Eds.] **75. motion:** sense **disputed on:** argued in the
law courts [Eds.] **77. attach:** arrest **79. inhibited . . . warrant:** forbidden and illegal [Eds.]

OTHELLO.   Hold your hands,
   Both you of my inclining and the rest.
   Were it my cue to fight, I should have known it
   Without a prompter. Where will you that I go
   To answer this your charge?
BRABANTIO.   To prison, till fit time   85
   Of law and course of direct session
   Call thee to answer.
OTHELLO.   What if I do obey?
   How may the Duke be therewith satisfied,
   Whose messengers are here about my side
   Upon some present business of the state   90
   To bring me to him?
FIRST OFFICER.   'Tis true, most worthy signior.
   The Duke's in council, and your noble self
   I am sure is sent for.
BRABANTIO.   How? The Duke in council?
   In this time of the night? Bring him away.
   Mine's not an idle cause. The Duke himself,   95
   Or any of my brothers of the state,
   Cannot but feel this wrong as 'twere their own.
   For if such actions may have passage free,
   Bondslaves and pagans shall our statesmen be. (*Exeunt.*)

SCENE 3. *A council chamber.*

The DUKE *and* SENATORS *sitting at a table*, OFFICERS *attending.*

DUKE.   There is no composition° in these news°
   That gives them credit.
FIRST SENATOR.   Indeed they are disproportioned.
   My letters say a hundred and seven galleys.
DUKE.   And mine, a hundred and forty.
SECOND SENATOR.   And mine, two hundred.
   But though they jump not on a just account°—   5
   As in these cases, where the aim reports,°
   'Tis oft with difference—yet do they all confirm
   A Turkish fleet, and bearing up to Cyprus.
DUKE.   Nay, it is possible enough to judgment.
   I do not so secure me in the error,°   10

---

1. composition: agreement   news: reports   5. jump . . . account: do not agree
with an exact estimate   6. aim reports: i.e., intelligence reports of an enemy's intention often differ in the details   10. I . . . error: I do not consider myself free from danger, because the reports may not all be accurate.

But the main article° I do approve
In fearful° sense.
SAILOR (*within*).   What ho! What ho! What ho!
FIRST OFFICER.   A messenger from the galleys. (*Enter* SAILOR.)
DUKE.   Now, what's the business?
SAILOR.   The Turkish preparation makes for Rhodes.
   So was I bid report here to the state   15
   By Signior Angelo.
DUKE.   How say you by this charge?
FIRST SENATOR.   This cannot be,
   By no assay of reason. 'Tis a pageant
   To keep us in false gaze. When we consider
   The importancy of Cyprus to the Turk,   20
   And let ourselves again but understand
   That as it more concerns the Turk than Rhodes,
   So may he with more facile question bear it,°
   For that it stands not in such warlike brace
   But altogether lacks the abilities   25
   That Rhodes is dressed in—if we make thought of this,
   We must not think the Turk is so unskillful
   To leave that latest which concerns him first,
   Neglecting an attempt of ease and gain
   To wake and wage a danger profitless.   30
DUKE.   Nay, in all confidence, he's not for Rhodes.
FIRST OFFICER.   Here is more news. (*Enter a* MESSENGER.)
MESSENGER.   The Ottomites,° Reverend and Gracious,
   Steering with due course toward the isle of Rhodes,
   Have there injointed° them with an after-fleet.°   35
FIRST SENATOR.   Aye, so I thought. How many, as you guess?
MESSENGER.   Of thirty sail. And now they do restem°
   Their backward course, bearing with frank appearance
   Their purposes toward Cyprus. Signior Montano,
   Your trusty and most valiant servitor,
   With his free duty recommends° you thus,   40
   And prays you to believe him.
DUKE.   'Tis certain then for Cyprus.
   Marcus Luccicos, is not he in town?
FIRST SENATOR.   He's now in Florence.   45
DUKE.   Write from us to him, post-posthaste dispatch.

---

11. main article: general report   **12. fearful:** to be feared   **23. with . . . it:** take it more easily   **33. Ottomites:** Turks   **35. injointed:** joined   **after-fleet:** second fleet   **37. restem:** steer again   **41. recommends:** advises [Eds.]

FIRST SENATOR.   Here comes Brabantio and the valiant Moor.
    (*Enter* BRABANTIO, OTHELLO, IAGO, RODERIGO, *and* OFFICERS.)
DUKE.   Valiant Othello, we must straight employ you
    Against the general enemy Ottoman.
    (*To* BRABANTIO) I did not see you. Welcome, gentle signior,   50
    We lacked your counsel and your help tonight.
BRABANTIO.   So did I yours. Good your Grace, pardon me,
    Neither my place nor aught I heard of business
    Hath raised me from my bed, nor doth the general care
    Take hold on me. For my particular° grief   55
    Is of so floodgate and o'erbearing nature
    That it engluts and swallows other sorrows,
    And it is still itself.
DUKE.   Why, what's the matter?
BRABANTIO.   My daughter! Oh, my daughter!
ALL.   Dead?
BRABANTIO.   Aye, to me.
    She is abused, stol'n from me and corrupted   60
    By spells and medicines bought of mountebanks.
    For nature so preposterously to err,
    Being not deficient, blind, or lame of sense,
    Sans° witchcraft could not.
DUKE.   Whoe'er he be that in this foul proceeding   65
    Hath thus beguiled your daughter of herself
    And you of her, the bloody book of law
    You shall yourself read in the bitter letter
    After your own sense—yea, though our proper° son
    Stood in your action.
BRABANTIO.   Humbly I thank your Grace.   70
    Here is the man, this Moor, whom now, it seems,
    Your special mandate for the state affairs
    Hath hither brought.
ALL.   We are very sorry for 't.
DUKE (*to* OTHELLO).   What in your own part can you say to this?
BRABANTIO.   Nothing but this is so.   75
OTHELLO.   Most potent, grave, and reverend signiors,
    My very noble and approved good masters,
    That I have ta'en away this old man's daughter,
    It is most true—true, I have married her.

---

55. particular: personal   **64. Sans:** Without   **69. proper:** own

The very head and front of my offending   80
Hath this extent, no more. Rude am I in my speech,
And little blest with the soft phrase of peace,
For since these arms of mine had seven years' pith
Till now some nine moons wasted, they have used
Their dearest action in the tented field;   85
And little of this great world can I speak,
More than pertains to feats of broil and battle,
And therefore little shall I grace my cause
In speaking for myself. Yet, by your gracious patience,
I will a round unvarnished tale° deliver   90
Of my whole course of love—what drugs, what charms,
What conjuration and what mighty magic—
For such proceeding I am charged withal—
I won his daughter.
BRABANTIO.   A maiden never bold,
Of spirit so still and quiet that her motion   95
Blushed at herself, and she—in spite of nature,
Of years, of country, credit,° everything—
To fall in love with what she feared to look on!
It is a judgment maimed and most imperfect
That will confess perfection so could err   100
Against all rules of nature, and must be driven
To find out practices of cunning Hell
Why this should be. I therefore vouch again
That with some mixtures powerful o'er the blood,
Or with some dram conjured to this effect,   105
He wrought upon her.
DUKE.   To vouch this is no proof
Without more certain and more overt test
Than these thin habits and poor likelihoods
Of modern seeming° do prefer against him.
FIRST SENATOR.   But, Othello, speak.   110
Did you by indirect and forcèd courses
Subdue and poison this young maid's affections?
Or came it by request, and such fair question
As soul to soul affordeth?
OTHELLO.   I do beseech you
Send for the lady to the Sagittary,   115

90. round . . . tale: direct, unadorned account   97. credit: reputation
108–9. thin . . . seeming: superficial, unlikely, and trivial suppositions [Eds.]

And let her speak of me before her father.
If you do find me foul in her report,
The trust, the office I do hold of you,
Not only take away, but let your sentence
Even fall upon my life.
DUKE.   Fetch Desdemona hither.   120
OTHELLO.   Ancient, conduct them, you best know the place.
     (*Exeunt* IAGO *and* ATTENDANTS.)
     And till she come, as truly as to Heaven
     I do confess the vices of my blood,
     So justly to your grave ears I'll present
     How I did thrive in this fair lady's love   125
     And she in mine.
DUKE.   Say it, Othello.
OTHELLO.   Her father loved me, oft invited me,
     Still° questioned me the story of my life
     From year to year, the battles, sieges, fortunes,
     That I have passed.   130
     I ran it through, even from my boyish days
     To the very moment that he bade me tell it.
     Wherein I spake of most disastrous chances,
     Of moving accidents by flood and field,
     Of hairbreadth 'scapes i' the imminent deadly breach,   135
     Of being taken by the insolent foe
     And sold to slavery, of my redemption thence,
     And portance in my travels' history.
     Wherein of antres° vast and deserts idle,
     Rough quarries, rocks, and hills whose heads touch heaven, 140
     It was my hint to speak—such was the process.
     And of the cannibals that each other eat,
     The anthropophagi,° and men whose heads
     Do grow beneath their shoulders. This to hear
     Would Desdemona seriously incline.   145
     But still the house affairs would draw her thence,
     Which ever as she could with haste dispatch,
     She'd come again, and with a greedy ear
     Devour up my discourse. Which I observing,
     Took once a pliant hour and found good means   150
     To draw from her a prayer of earnest heart
     That I would all my pilgrimage dilate,

---

128. Still: Always   139. antres: caves   143. anthropophagi: cannibals

Whereof by parcels she had something heard,
But not intentively. I did consent,
And often did beguile her of her tears   155
When I did speak of some distressful stroke
That my youth suffered. My story being done,
She gave me for my pains a world of sighs.
She swore, in faith, 'twas strange, 'twas passing strange,
'Twas pitiful, 'twas wondrous pitiful.   160
She wished she had not heard it, yet she wished
That Heaven had made her such a man. She thanked me,
And bade me, if I had a friend that loved her,
I should but teach him how to tell my story
And that would woo her. Upon this hint° I spake.   165
She loved me for the dangers I had passed,
And I loved her that she did pity them.
This only is the witchcraft I have used.
Here comes the lady, let her witness it.
(*Enter* DESDEMONA, IAGO, *and* ATTENDANTS.)
DUKE.   I think this tale would win my daughter too.   170
Good Brabantio,
Take up this mangled matter at the best.°
Men do their broken weapons rather use
Than their bare hands.
BRABANTIO.   I pray you hear her speak.
If she confess that she was half the wooer,   175
Destruction on my head if my bad blame
Light on the man! Come hither, gentle mistress.
Do you perceive in all this noble company
Where most you owe obedience?
DESDEMONA.   My noble father,
I do perceive here a divided duty.   180
To you I am bound for life and education,
My life and education both do learn me
How to respect you; you are the lord of duty,
I am hitherto your daughter. But here's my husband,
And so much duty as my mother showed   185
To you, preferring you before her father,
So much I challenge that I may profess
Due to the Moor my lord.

---

165. hint: opportunity [Eds.]   **172. Take . . . best:** Make the best settlement you can of this confused business.

BRABANTIO.   God be with you! I have done.
    Please it your Grace, on to the state affairs.
    I had rather to adopt a child than get° it.   190
    Come hither, Moor.
    I here do give thee that with all my heart
    Which, but thou hast already, with all my heart
    I would keep from thee. For your sake, jewel,
    I am glad at soul I have no other child,   195
    For thy escape would teach me tyranny,
    To hang clogs on them. I have done, my lord.
DUKE.   Let me speak like yourself, and lay a sentence°
    Which, as a grise° or step, may help these lovers
    Into your favor.   200
    When remedies are past, the griefs are ended
    By seeing the worst, which late on hopes depended.
    To mourn a mischief that is past and gone
    Is the next way to draw new mischief on.
    What cannot be preserved when fortune takes,   205
    Patience her injury a mockery makes.
    The robbed that smiles steals something from the thief.
    He robs himself that spends a bootless grief.
BRABANTIO.   So let the Turk of Cyprus us beguile,
    We lose it not so long as we can smile.   210
    He bears the sentence well that nothing bears
    But the free comfort which from thence he hears.
    But he bears both the sentence and the sorrow
    That, to pay grief, must of poor patience borrow.
    These sentences, to sugar or to gall,   215
    Being strong on both sides, are equivocal.
    But words are words. I never yet did hear
    That the bruisèd heart was piercèd through the ear.
    I humbly beseech you, proceed to the affairs of state.
DUKE.   The Turk with a most mightly preparation makes for Cyprus.
    Othello, the fortitude of the place is best known to you, and though
    we have there a substitute° of most allowed sufficiency, yet opinion, a
    sovereign mistress of effects, throws a more safer voice on you. You
    must therefore be content to slubber° the gloss of your new fortunes
    with this more stubborn and boisterous expedition.   225
OTHELLO.   The tyrant custom, most grave Senators,
    Hath made the flinty and steel couch of war

---

190 **get:** beget   198. **sentence:** proverbial saying   199. **grise:** degree
222. **substitute:** deputy commander   224. **slubber:** tarnish

My thrice-driven bed of down. I do agnize°
A natural and prompt alacrity
I find in hardness,° and do undertake   230
These present wars against the Ottomites.
Most humbly therefore bending to your state,
I crave fit disposition for my wife,
Due reference of place and exhibition,°
With such accommodation and besort°   235
As levels with her breeding.
DUKE.   If you please,
    Be 't at her father's.
BRABANTIO.   I'll not have it so.
OTHELLO.   Nor I.
DESDEMONA.   Nor I. I would not there reside,
    To put my father in impatient thoughts
    By being in his eye. Most gracious Duke,   240
    To my unfolding lend your prosperous° ear,
    And let me find a charter in your voice
    To assist my simpleness.
DUKE.   What would you, Desdemona?
DESDEMONA.   That I did love the Moor to live with him,   245
    My downright violence and storm of fortunes
    May trumpet to the world. My heart's subdued
    Even to the very quality° of my lord.
    I saw Othello's visage in his mind,
    And to his honors and his valiant parts°   250
    Did I my soul and fortunes consecrate.
    So that, dear lords, if I be left behind,
    A moth of peace, and he go to the war,
    The rites for which I love him are bereft me,
    And I a heavy interim shall support   255
    By his dear absence. Let me go with him.
OTHELLO.   Let her have your voices.
    Vouch with me, Heaven, I therefore beg it not
    To please the palate of my appetite,
    Nor to comply with heat—the young affects   260
    In me defunct°—and proper satisfaction,
    But to be free and bounteous to her mind.°

---

228. **agnize:** confess   230. **hardness:** hardship   234. **exhibition:** allowance
235. **besort:** attendants   241. **prosperous:** favorable   248. **quality:** profession
250. **parts:** qualities   260–61. **young . . . defunct:** In me the passion of youth is
dead.   262. **to . . . mind:** Othello repeats Desdemona's claim that this is a marriage of
minds.

And Heaven defend your good souls, that you think
I will your serious and great business scant
For she is with me. No, when light-winged toys   265
Of feathered Cupid seel° with wanton dullness
My speculative and officed instruments,°
That my disports° corrupt and taint my business,
Let housewives make a skillet of my helm,
And all indign° and base adversities   270
Make head against my estimation!°
DUKE.   Be it as you shall privately determine,
     Either for her stay or going. The affair cries haste,
     And speed must answer 't. You must hence tonight.
DESDEMONA.   Tonight, my lord?
DUKE.   This night.
OTHELLO.   With all my heart.   275
DUKE.   At nine i' the morning here we'll meet again.
     Othello, leave some officer behind,
     And he shall our commission bring to you,
     With such things else of quality and respect
     As doth import you.
OTHELLO.   So please your Grace, my Ancient,   280
     A man he is of honesty and trust.
     To his conveyance I assign my wife,
     With what else needful your good Grace shall think
     To be sent after me.
DUKE.   Let it be so.
     Good night to everyone. (*To* BRABANTIO) And, noble signior,   285
     If virtue no delighted beauty lack,
     Your son-in-law is far more fair than black.°
FIRST SENATOR.   Adieu, brave Moor. Use Desdemona well.
BRABANTIO.   Look to her, Moor, if thou hast eyes to see.
     She has deceived her father, and may thee.   290
     (*Exeunt* DUKE, SENATORS, OFFICERS, *etc.*)
OTHELLO.   My life upon her faith! Honest Iago,
     My Desdemona must I leave to thee.
     I prithee, let thy wife attend on her,
     And bring them after in the best advantage.

---

266. seel: close up   **267. speculative . . . instruments:** powers of sight and action; i.e., my efficiency as your general   **268. disports:** amusements   **270. indign:** unworthy   **271. estimation:** reputation   **286–87. If . . . black:** If worthiness is a beautiful thing in itself, your son-in-law, though black, has beauty.

Come, Desdemona, I have but an hour   295
Of love, of worldly matters and direction,
To spend with thee. We must obey the time.
(*Exeunt* OTHELLO *and* DESDEMONA.)

RODERIGO.   Iago!

IAGO.   What sayest thou, noble heart?

RODERIGO.   What will I do, thinkest thou?   300

IAGO.   Why, go to bed and sleep.

RODERIGO.   I will incontinently° drown myself.

IAGO.   If thou dost, I shall never love thee after. Why, thou silly
gentleman!

RODERIGO.   It is silliness to live when to live is torment, and then
have we a prescription to die when death is our physician.   306

IAGO.   Oh, villainous! I have looked upon the world for four times seven
years, and since I could distinguish betwixt a benefit and an injury I
never found man that knew how to love himself. Ere I would say I
would drown myself for the love of a guinea hen, I would change my
humanity with a baboon.   311

RODERIGO.   What should I do? I confess it is my shame to be so fond,
but it is not in my virtue° to amend it.

IAGO.   Virtue! A fig! 'Tis in ourselves that we are thus or thus. Our bodies are gardens, to the which our wills are gardeners. So that if we
will plant nettles or sow lettuce, set hyssop and weed up thyme,
supply it with one gender of herbs or distract it with many, either
to have it sterile with idleness or manured with industry—why, the
power and corrigible° authority of this lies in our wills. If the balance of our lives had not one scale of reason to poise another of
sensuality, the blood and baseness of our natures would conduct us
to most preposterous conclusions. But we have reason to cool our
raging motions, our carnal stings, our unbitted lusts, whereof I take
this that you call love to be a sect or scion.°

RODERIGO.   It cannot be.   325

IAGO.   It is merely a lust of the blood and a permission of the will. Come,
be a man! Drown thyself? Drown cats and blind puppies! I have pro-
fessed me thy friend, and I confess me knit to thy deserving with
cables of perdurable toughness. I could never better stead thee
than now. Put money in thy purse, follow thou the wars, defeat
thy favor with an usurped beard°—I say put money in thy purse.

---

302. incontinently: immediately   **313. virtue:** strength [Eds.]
319. corrigible: correcting, directing   **324. sect or scion:** Both words mean a slip
taken from a tree and planted to produce a new growth.   **330–31. defeat . . . beard:**
disguise your face by growing a beard

It cannot be that Desdemona should long continue her love to the Moor—put money in thy purse—nor he his to her. It was a violent commencement, and thou shalt see an answerable sequestration°—put but money in thy purse. These Moors are changeable in their wills.°—Fill thy purse with money. The food that to him now is as luscious as locusts shall be to him shortly as bitter as coloquintida.° She must change for youth. When she is sated with his body, she will find the error of her choice. She must have change, she must—therefore put money in thy purse. If thou wilt needs damn thyself, do it a more delicate way than drowning. Make all the money thou canst.° If sanctimony and a frail vow betwixt an erring° barbarian and a supersubtle Venetian be not too hard for my wits and all the tribe of Hell, thou shalt enjoy her—therefore make money. A pox of drowning thyself! It is clean out of the way. Seek thou rather to be hanged in compassing thy joy than to be drowned and go without her.   347

RODERIGO.   Wilt thou be fast to my hopes if I depend on the issue?

IAGO.   Thou art sure of me. Go, make money. I have told thee often, and I retell thee again and again, I hate the Moor. My cause is hearted,° thine hath no less reason. Let us be conjunctive in our revenge against him. If thou canst cuckold him thou dost thyself a pleasure, me a sport. There are many events in the womb of time which will be delivered. Traverse, go, provide thy money. We will have more of this tomorrow. Adieu.   355

RODERIGO.   Where shall we meet i' the morning?

IAGO.   At my lodging.

RODERIGO.   I'll be with thee betimes.

IAGO.   Go to, farewell. Do you hear, Roderigo?

RODERIGO.   What say you?   360

IAGO.   No more of drowning, do you hear?

RODERIGO.   I am changed. I'll go sell all my land. (*Exit.*)

IAGO.   Thus do I ever make my fool my purse,
    For I mine own gained knowledge should profane
    If I would time expend with such a snipe   365
    But for my sport and profit. I hate the Moor,
    And it is thought abroad that 'twixt my sheets
    He's done my office. I know not if 't be true,
    But I for mere suspicion in that kind
    Will do as if for surety. He holds me well,   370

334–35. **answerable sequestration:** corresponding separation; i.e., reaction
336. **wills:** desires [Eds.]   338. **coloquintida:** a bitter purgative [Eds.]
342. **Make . . . canst:** Turn all you can into ready cash.   343. **erring:** vagabond
351. **hearted:** heartfelt

The better shall my purpose work on him.
Cassio's a proper° man. Let me see now,
To get his place, and to plume up° my will
In double knavery—How, how?—Let's see.—
After some time, to abuse Othello's ear   375
That he is too familiar with his wife.
He hath a person and a smooth dispose
To be suspected,° framed to make women false.
The Moor is of a free and open nature
That thinks men honest that but seem to be so,   380
And will as tenderly be led by the nose
As asses are.
I have't. It is engendered. Hell and night
Must bring this monstrous birth to the world's light. (*Exit.*)

ACT 2

SCENE 1.   A seaport in Cyprus. An open place near the wharf.

Enter MONTANO *and two* GENTLEMEN.

MONTANO.   What from the cape can you discern at sea?
FIRST GENTLEMAN.   Nothing at all. It is a high-wrought flood.
I cannot 'twixt the heaven and the main
Descry a sail.
MONTANO.   Methinks the wind hath spoke aloud at land,   5
A fuller blast ne'er shook our battlements.
If it hath ruffianed so upon the sea,
What ribs of oak, when mountains melt on them,
Can hold the mortise? What shall we hear of this?
SECOND GENTLEMAN.   A segregation° of the Turkish fleet.   10
For do but stand upon the foaming shore,
The chidden billow seems to pelt the clouds,
The wind-shaked surge, with high and monstrous mane,
Seems to cast water on the burning Bear,
And quench the guards of the ever-fixèd Pole.°   15
I never did like molestation view
On the enchafèd flood.
MONTANO.   If that the Turkish fleet
Be not ensheltered and embayed, they are drowned.
It is impossible to bear it out. (*Enter a* THIRD GENTLEMAN.)

---

372. **proper:** handsome   373. **plume up:** glorify   377-78. **He . . . suspected:** He
has an easy way about him that is naturally suspected.   10. **segregation:** separation
14-15. **cast . . . Pole:** drown the constellations [Eds.]

THIRD GENTLEMAN.   News, lads! Our wars are done.   20
 The desperate tempest hath so banged the Turks
 That their designment halts. A noble ship of Venice
 Hath seen a grievous wreck and sufferance°
 On most part of their fleet.
MONTANO.   How! Is this true?
THIRD GENTLEMAN.   The ship is here put in,   25
 A Veronesa. Michael Cassio,
 Lieutenant to the warlike Moor Othello,
 Is come on shore, the Moor himself at sea,
 And is in full commission here for Cyprus.
MONTANO.   I am glad on 't. 'Tis a worthy governor.   30
THIRD GENTLEMAN.   But this same Cassio, though he speak of comfort
 Touching the Turkish loss, yet he looks sadly
 And prays the Moor be safe, for they were parted
 With foul and violent tempest.
MONTANO.   Pray Heavens he be,
 For I have served him, and the man commands   35
 Like a full soldier. Let's to the seaside, ho!
 As well to see the vessel that's come in
 As to throw out our eyes for brave Othello,
 Even till we make the main and the aerial blue
 An indistinct regard.
THIRD GENTLEMAN.   Come, let's do so.   40
 For every minute is expectancy
 Of more arrivance. (*Enter* CASSIO.)
CASSIO.   Thanks, you the valiant of this warlike isle
 That so approve the Moor! Oh, let the heavens
 Give him defense against the elements,   45
 For I have lost him on a dangerous sea.
MONTANO.   Is he well shipped?
CASSIO.   His bark is stoutly timbered, and his pilot
 Of very expert and approved allowance.
 Therefore my hopes, not surfeited to death,   50
 Stand in bold cure.
 (*A cry within:* "A sail, a sail, a sail!" *Enter a* FOURTH GENTLEMAN.)
 What noise?
FOURTH GENTLEMAN.   The town is empty. On the brow o' the sea
 Stand ranks of people and they cry "A sail!"
CASSIO.   My hopes do shape him for the governor. (*Guns heard.*)   55

---

23. sufferance: damage

SECOND GENTLEMAN.   They do discharge their shot of courtesy.
  Our friends, at least.
CASSIO.   I pray you, sir, go forth,
  And give us truth who 'tis that is arrived.
SECOND GENTLEMAN.   I shall. (*Exit.*)
MONTANO.   But, good Lieutenant, is your General wived?   60
CASSIO.   Most fortunately. He hath achieved a maid
  That paragons description and wild fame,
  One that excels the quirks of blazoning pens
  And in the essential vesture of creation
  Does tire the ingener.° (*Re-enter* SECOND GENTLEMAN.)
                          How now! Who has put in?   65
SECOND GENTLEMAN.   'Tis one Iago, Ancient to the General.
CASSIO.   He has had most favorable and happy speed.
  Tempests themselves, high seas, and howling winds,
  The guttered rocks, and congregated sands,
  Traitors ensteeped to clog the guiltless keel,   70
  As having sense of beauty, do omit
  Their mortal° natures, letting go safely by
  The divine Desdemona.
MONTANO.   What is she?
CASSIO.   She that I spake of, our great Captain's captain,
  Left in the conduct of the bold Iago,   75
  Whose footing here anticipates our thoughts
  A sennight's° speed. Great Jove, Othello guard,
  And swell his sail with thine own powerful breath,
  That he may bless this bay with his tall ship,
  Make love's quick pants in Desdemona's arms,   80
  Give renewed fire to our extinct spirits,
  And bring all Cyprus comfort.
  (*Enter* DESDEMONA, EMILIA, IAGO, RODERIGO, *and* ATTENDANTS.)
                          Oh, behold,
  The riches of the ship is come on shore!
  Ye men of Cyprus, let her have your knees.
  Hail to thee, lady! And the grace of Heaven,   85
  Before, behind thee, and on every hand,
  Enwheel thee round!

63–65. One . . . ingener: One that is too good for the fancy phrases (*quirks*) of painting
pens (i.e., poets) and in her absolute perfection wearies the artist (i.e., the painter)
ingener: inventor   **72. mortal:** deadly   **77. sennight's:** week's

DESDEMONA.   I thank you, valiant Cassio.
    What tidings can you tell me of my lord?
CASSIO.   He is not yet arrived, nor know I aught
    But that he's well and will be shortly here.   90
DESDEMONA.   Oh, but I fear—How lost you company?
CASSIO.   The great contention of the sea and skies
    Parted our fellowship.—But hark! A sail.
    (*A cry within:* "A sail, a sail!" *Guns heard.*)
SECOND GENTLEMAN.   They give their greeting to the citadel.
    This likewise is a friend.
CASSIO.   See for the news. (*Exit* GENTLEMAN.)   95
    Good Ancient, you are welcome. (*To* EMILIA) Welcome, mistress.
    Let it not gall your patience, good Iago,
    That I extend my manners. 'Tis my breeding
    That gives me this bold show of courtesy. (*Kissing her.*)
IAGO.   Sir, would she give you so much of her lips   100
    As of her tongue she oft bestows on me,
    You'd have enough.
DESDEMONA.   Alas, she has no speech.
IAGO.   In faith, too much,
    I find it still when I have list° to sleep.
    Marry, before your ladyship, I grant,   105
    She puts her tongue a little in her heart
    And chides with thinking.
EMILIA.   You have little cause to say so.
IAGO.   Come on, come on. You are pictures° out of doors,
    Bells° in your parlors, wildcats in your kitchens,   110
    Saints in your injuries,° devils being offended,
    Players in your housewifery, and housewives in your beds.
DESDEMONA.   Oh, fie upon thee, slanderer!
IAGO.   Nay, it is true, or else I am a Turk.
    You rise to play, and go to bed to work.   115
EMILIA.   You shall not write my praise.
IAGO.   No, let me not.
DESDEMONA.   What wouldst thou write of me if thou shouldst praise
    me?
IAGO.   O gentle lady, do not put me to 't,
    For I am nothing if not critical.
DESDEMONA.   Come on, assay.°—There's one gone to the harbor?   120

---

104. list: desire   **109. pictures:** i.e., painted and dumb   **110. Bells:** i.e., ever clacking   **111. Saints . . . injuries:** Saints when you hurt anyone else   **120. assay:** try

IAGO.   Aye, madam.

DESDEMONA (*aside*).   I am not merry, but I do beguile
    The thing I am by seeming otherwise.—
    Come, how wouldst thou praise me?

IAGO.   I am about it, but indeed my invention   125
    Comes from my pate as birdlime does from frieze°—
    It plucks out brains and all. But my Muse labors,
    And thus she is delivered:
    If she be fair and wise, fairness and wit,
    The one's for use, the other useth it.   130

DESDEMONA.   Well praised! How if she be black° and witty?

IAGO.   If she be black, and thereto have a wit,
    She'll find a white° that shall her blackness fit.

DESDEMONA.   Worse and worse.

EMILIA.   How if fair and foolish?   135

IAGO.   She never yet was foolish that was fair,
    For even her folly helped her to an heir.

DESDEMONA.   These are old fond paradoxes to make fools laugh i' the
    alehouse. What miserable praise hast thou for her that's foul and
    foolish?   140

IAGO.   There's none so foul, and foolish thereunto,
    But does foul pranks which fair and wise ones do.

DESDEMONA.   Oh, heavy ignorance! Thou praisest the worst best. But
    what praise couldst thou bestow on a deserving woman indeed, one
    that in the authority of her merit did justly put on the vouch of
    very malice itself?°   146

IAGO.   She that was ever fair and never proud,
    Had tongue at will° and yet was never loud,
    Never lacked gold and yet went never gay,
    Fled from her wish and yet said "Now I may";   150
    She that, being angered, her revenge being nigh,
    Bade her wrong stay and her displeasure fly;
    She that in wisdom never was so frail
    To change the cod's head for the salmon's tail;°
    She that could think and ne'er disclose her mind,   155
    See suitors following and not look behind;
    She was a wight, if ever such wight were—

125–26. my . . . frieze: my literary effort (*invention*) is as hard to pull out of my head as frieze
(cloth with a nap)   **131. black:** brunette, dark-complexioned [Eds.]   **133. white:**
with a pun on *wight* (line 156), man, person   **144–46. one . . . itself:** one so deserving
that even malice would declare her good   **148. tongue . . . will:** a ready flow of words
154. To . . . tail: To prefer the tail end of a good thing to the head of a poor thing

DESDEMONA.   To do what?

IAGO.   To suckle fools and chronicle small beer.°

DESDEMONA.   Oh, most lame and impotent conclusion! Do not learn of
him, Emilia, though he be thy husband. How say you, Cassio? Is he
not a most profane and liberal° counselor?   162

CASSIO.   He speaks home,° madam. You may relish him more in the
soldier than in the scholar.

IAGO (*aside*).   He takes her by the palm. Aye, well said, whisper. With as
little a web as this will I ensnare as great a fly as Cassio. Aye, smile
upon her, do, I will gyve thee in thine own courtship.° You say true,
'tis so indeed. If such tricks as these strip you out of your Lieuten-
antry, it had been better you had not kissed your three fingers° so
oft, which now again you are most apt to play the sir° in. Very good,
well kissed! An excellent courtesy! 'Tis so indeed. Yet again your
fingers to your lips? Would they were clyster pipes° for your sake!
(*Trumpet within.*) The Moor! I know his trumpet.   173

CASSIO.   'Tis truly so.

DESDEMONA.   Let's meet him and receive him.   175

CASSIO.   Lo where he comes! (*Enter* OTHELLO *and* ATTENDANTS.)

OTHELLO.   O my fair warrior!°

DESDEMONA.   My dear Othello!

OTHELLO.   It gives me wonder great as my content
To see you here before me. O my soul's joy!
If after every tempest come such calms,   180
May the winds blow till they have wakened death!
And let the laboring bark climb hills of seas
Olympus-high, and duck again as low
As Hell's from Heaven! If it were now to die,
'Twere now to be most happy, for I fear   185
My soul hath her content so absolute
That not another comfort like to this
Succeeds in unknown fate.

DESDEMONA.   The Heavens forbid
But that our loves and comforts should increase,
Even as our days do grow!

---

159. **suckle . . . beer:** nurse babies and keep petty household accounts (i.e., even the best
woman belongs in the nursery and kitchen) [Eds.]   162. **liberal:** gross   163. **home:**
bluntly [Eds.]   167. **gyve . . . courtship:** trap you with your own show of courtesy
[Eds.]   169. **kissed . . . fingers:** a gesture of gallantry   170. **play the sir:** act the
fine gentleman   172. **clyster pipes:** an enema syringe   177. **warrior:** because she
is a soldier's wife

OTHELLO.   Amen to that, sweet powers!   190
  I cannot speak enough of this content.
  It stops me here,° it is too much of joy.
  And this, and this, the greatest discords be (*Kissing her.*)
  That e'er our hearts shall make!
IAGO (*aside*).   Oh, you are well tuned now,
  But I'll set down the pegs° that make this music,   195
  As honest as I am.
OTHELLO.   Come, let us to the castle.
  News, friends! Our wars are done, the Turks are drowned.
  How does my old acquaintance of this isle?
  Honey, you shall be well desired in Cyprus,
  I have found great love amongst them. O my sweet,   200
  I prattle out of fashion, and I dote
  In mine own comforts. I prithee, good Iago,
  Go to the bay and disembark my coffers.°
  Bring thou the master° to the citadel.
  He is a good one, and his worthiness   205
  Does challenge much respect. Come, Desdemona,
  Once more well met at Cyprus. (*Exeunt all but* IAGO *and* RODERIGO.)
IAGO.   Do thou meet me presently at the harbor. Come hither. If thou
  beest valiant—as they say base men being in love have then a no-
  bility in their natures more than is native to them—list me. The
  Lieutenant tonight watches on the court of guard. First, I must tell
  thee this. Desdemona is directly in love with him.   212
RODERIGO.   With him! Why, 'tis not possible.
IAGO.   Lay thy finger thus,° and let thy soul be instructed. Mark me with
  what violence she first loved the Moor, but for bragging and telling
  her fantastical lies. And will she love him still for prating? Let not
  thy discreet heart think it. Her eye must be fed, and what delight
  shall she have to look on the Devil? When the blood is made dull
  with the act of sport, there should be, again to inflame it and to give
  satiety a fresh appetite, loveliness in favor,° sympathy in years, manners, and beauties, all which the Moor is defective in. Now, for want
  of these required conveniences, her delicate tenderness will find itself abused, begin to heave the gorge, disrelish and abhor the Moor.
  Very nature will instruct her in it and compel her to some second

---

192. **here:** i.e., in the heart   195. **set . . . pegs:** i.e., make you sing out of tune.
A stringed instrument was tuned by the pegs.   203. **coffers:** trunks
204. **master:** captain of the ship   214. **thus:** i.e., on the lips   220. **favor:** face

choice. Now, sir, this granted—as it is a most pregnant and unforced position°—who stands so eminently in the degree of this fortune as Cassio does? A knave very voluble, no further conscionable° than in putting on the mere form of civil and humane seeming° for the better compassing of his salt° and most hidden loose affection? Why, none, why, none. A slipper° and subtle knave, a finder-out of occasions, that has an eye can stamp and counterfeit advantages,° though true advantage never present itself. A devilish knave! Besides, the knave is handsome, young, and hath all those requisites in him that folly and green minds look after. A pestilent complete knave, and the woman hath found him already.   235

RODERIGO.   I cannot believe that in her. She's full of most blest condition.°

IAGO.   Blest fig's-end!° The wine she drinks is made of grapes. If she had been blest, she would never have loved the Moor. Blest pudding! Didst thou not see her paddle with the palm of his hand? Didst not mark that?   241

RODERIGO.   Yes, that I did, but that was but courtesy.

IAGO.   Lechery, by his hand, an index and obscure prologue to the history of lust and foul thoughts. They met so near with their lips that their breaths embraced together. Villainous thoughts, Roderigo! When these mutualities so marshal the way, hard at hand comes the master and main exercise, the incorporate° conclusion. Pish! But, sir, be you ruled by me. I have brought you from Venice. Watch you tonight. For the command, I'll lay 't upon you. Cassio knows you not. I'll not be far from you. Do you find some occasion to anger Cassio, either by speaking too loud, or tainting° his discipline, or from what other course you please which the time shall more favorably minister.

RODERIGO.   Well.   253

IAGO.   Sir, he is rash and very sudden in choler,° and haply may strike at you. Provoke him, that he may, for even out of that will I cause these of Cyprus to mutiny, whose qualification shall come into no true taste again but by the displanting of Cassio. So shall you have a shorter journey to your desires by the means I shall then have to prefer° them, and the impediment most profitably removed without the which there were no expectation of our prosperity.   260

RODERIGO.   I will do this, if I can bring it to any opportunity.

225–26. pregnant . . . position: very significant and probable argument   227. no . . . conscionable: who has no more conscience   228. humane seeming: courteous appearance   229. salt: lecherous   230. slipper: slippery   231. stamp . . . advantages: forge false opportunities   237. condition: disposition   238. fig's-end: nonsense [Eds.]   247. incorporate: bodily   251. tainting: disparaging   254. choler: anger   259. prefer: promote

IAGO.   I warrant thee. Meet me by and by at the citadel. I must fetch his
    necessaries ashore. Farewell.
RODERIGO.   Adieu. (*Exit.*)
IAGO.   That Cassio loves her, I do well believe it.   265
    That she loves him, 'tis apt and of great credit.°
    The Moor, howbeit that I endure him not,
    Is of a constant, loving, noble nature,
    And I dare think he'll prove to Desdemona
    A most dear husband. Now, I do love her too,   270
    Not out of absolute lust, though peradventure
    I stand accountant for as great a sin,
    But partly led to diet° my revenge
    For that I do suspect the lusty Moor
    Hath leaped into my seat. The thought whereof   275
    Doth like a poisonous mineral gnaw my inwards,
    And nothing can or shall content my soul
    Till I am evened with him, wife for wife.
    Or failing so, yet that I put the Moor
    At least into a jealousy so strong   280
    That judgment cannot cure. Which thing to do,
    If this poor trash of Venice, whom I trash
    For his quick hunting,° stand the putting-on,
    I'll have our Michael Cassio on the hip,
    Abuse him to the Moor in the rank garb°—   285
    For I fear Cassio with my nightcap too—
    Make the Moor thank me, love me, and reward me
    For making him egregiously an ass
    And practicing upon his peace and quiet
    Even to madness. 'Tis here, but yet confused.   290
    Knavery's plain face is never seen till used. (*Exit.*)

SCENE 2. *A street.*

Enter a HERALD *with a proclamation,* PEOPLE *following.*

HERALD.   It is Othello's pleasure, our noble and valiant General, that
    upon certain tidings now arrived, importing the mere perdition° of
    the Turkish fleet, every man put himself into triumph°—some to
    dance, some to make bonfires, each man to what sport and revels
    his addiction leads him. For, besides these beneficial news, it is the

266. apt . . . credit: likely and very creditable   273. diet: feed
282–83. trash . . . hunting: hold back from outrunning the pack [Eds.]   285. rank
garb: gross manner; i.e., by accusing him of being Desdemona's lover   2. mere
perdition: absolute destruction   3. put . . . triumph: celebrate

celebration of his nuptial. So much was his pleasure should be proclaimed. All offices° are open, and there is full liberty of feasting from this present hour of five till the bell have told eleven. Heaven bless the isle of Cyprus and our noble General Othello! (*Exeunt.*)

SCENE 3.   *A hall in the castle.*

Enter OTHELLO, DESDEMONA, CASSIO, *and* ATTENDANTS.

OTHELLO.   Good Michael, look you to the guard tonight.
    Let's teach ourselves that honorable stop,
    Not to outsport discretion.°
CASSIO.   Iago hath directions what to do,
    But notwithstanding with my personal eye   5
    Will I look to 't.
OTHELLO.   Iago is most honest.
    Michael, good night. Tomorrow with your earliest
    Let me have speech with you. (*To* DESDEMONA) Come, my dear love,
    The purchase made, the fruits are to ensue—
    That profit's yet to come 'tween me and you.   10
    Good night. (*Exeunt all but* CASSIO. *Enter* IAGO.)
CASSIO.   Welcome, Iago. We must to the watch.
IAGO.   Not this hour, Lieutenant, 'tis not yet ten o'clock. Our General cast° us thus early for the love of his Desdemona, who let us not therefore blame. He hath not yet made wanton the night with her, and she is sport for Jove.   16
CASSIO.   She's a most exquisite lady.
IAGO.   And, I'll warrant her, full of game.
CASSIO.   Indeed she's a most fresh and delicate creature.
IAGO.   What an eye she has! Methinks it sounds a parley to   20
    provocation.
CASSIO.   An inviting eye, and yet methinks right modest.
IAGO.   And when she speaks, is it not an alarum to love?
CASSIO.   She is indeed perfection.
IAGO.   Well, happiness to their sheets! Come, Lieutenant, I have a stoup of wine, and there without are a brace of Cyprus gallants that would fain have a measure to the health of black Othello.   27
CASSIO.   Not tonight, good Iago. I have very poor and unhappy brains for drinking. I could well wish courtesy would invent some other custom of entertainment.   30

---

7. **offices:** the kitchen and buttery—i.e., free food and drink for all   3. **outsport discretion:** let the fun go too far.   14. **cast:** dismissed

IAGO.   Oh, they are our friends. But one cup—I'll drink for you.

CASSIO.   I have drunk but one cup tonight, and that was craftily quali-
fied° too, and behold what innovation it makes here. I am unfortunate in the infirmity, and dare not task my weakness with any more.

IAGO.   What, man! 'Tis a night of revels. The gallants desire it.   35

CASSIO.   Where are they?

IAGO.   Here at the door. I pray you call them in.

CASSIO.   I'll do 't, but it dislikes me. (*Exit.*)

IAGO.   If I can fasten but one cup upon him,
  With that which he hath drunk tonight already,   40
  He'll be as full of quarrel and offense
  As my young mistress' dog. Now my sick fool Roderigo,
  Whom love hath turned almost the wrong side out,
  To Desdemona hath tonight caroused
  Potations pottle-deep, and he's to watch.   45
  Three lads of Cyprus, noble swelling spirits
  That hold their honors in a wary distance,°
  The very elements° of this warlike isle,
  Have I tonight flustered with flowing cups,
  And they watch too. Now, 'mongst this flock of drunkards, 50
  Am I to put our Cassio in some action
  That may offend the isle. But here they come.
  If consequence do but approve my dream,
  My boat sails freely, both with wind and stream.
  (*Re-enter* CASSIO, *with him* MONTANO *and* GENTLEMEN, SERVANTS
  following with wine.)

CASSIO.   'Fore God, they have given me a rouse already.   55

MONTANO.   Good faith, a little one—not past a pint, as I am a soldier.

IAGO.   Some wine, ho! (*Sings*)
     "And let me the cannikin clink, clink
     And let me the cannikin clink.
      A soldier's a man,   60
      A life's but a span.°
     Why, then let a soldier drink."

  Some wine, boys!

CASSIO.   'Fore God, an excellent song.

32–33. qualified: diluted [Eds.] 47. hold . . . distance: are very sensitive about their
honor [Eds.] 48. very elements: typical specimens 61. span: lit., the measure between the thumb and little finger of the outstretched hand; about 9 inches

IAGO.   I learned it in England, where indeed they are most potent in pot-
ting.° Your Dane, your German, and your swag-bellied Hollander—
Drink, ho!—are nothing to your English.   67
CASSIO.   Is your Englishman so expert in his drinking?
IAGO.   Why, he drinks you with facility your Dane dead drunk, he
sweats not to overthrow your Almain,° he gives your Hollander a
vomit° ere the next pottle can be filled.   71
CASSIO.   To the health of our General!
MONTANO.   I am for it, Lieutenant, and I'll do you justice.
IAGO.   O sweet England! (*Sings*)
                    "King Stephen was a worthy peer,   75
                        His breeches cost him but a crown.
                    He held them sixpence all too dear,
                        With that he called the tailor lown.°

                    "He was a wight of high renown,
                        And thou art but of low degree.   80
                    'Tis pride that pulls the country down.
                        Then take thine auld cloak about thee."
        Some wine, ho!
CASSIO.   Why, this is a more exquisite song than the other.
IAGO.   Will you hear 't again?   85
CASSIO.   No, for I hold him to be unworthy of his place that does those
things. Well, God's above all, and there be souls must be saved and
there be souls must not be saved.
IAGO.   It's true, good Lieutenant.
CASSIO.   For mine own part—no offense to the General, nor any man
of quality—I hope to be saved.   91
IAGO.   And so do I too, Lieutenant.
CASSIO.   Aye, but, by your leave, not before me. The Lieutenant is to
be saved before the Ancient. Let's have no more of this, let's to our
affairs. God forgive us our sins! Gentlemen, let's look to our busi-
ness. Do not think, gentlemen, I am drunk. This is my Ancient,
this is my right hand and this is my left. I am not drunk now, I can
stand well enough and speak well enough.   98
ALL.   Excellent well.
CASSIO.   Why, very well, then, you must not think then that I am drunk.
(*Exit.*)
MONTANO.   To the platform, masters. Come, let's set the watch. 101

65–66. potting: drinking   **70. Almain:** German   **gives . . . vomit:** drinks as
much as will make a Dutchman throw up   **78. lown:** lout

IAGO.   You see this fellow that is gone before.
    He is a soldier fit to stand by Caesar
    And give direction. And do but see his vice.
    'Tis to his virtue a just equinox,   105
    The one as long as the other. 'Tis pity of him.
    I fear the trust Othello puts him in
    On some odd time of his infirmity
    Will shake this island.
MONTANO.   But is he often thus?
IAGO.   'Tis evermore the prologue to his sleep.   110
    He'll watch the horologe a double set,°
    If drink rock not his cradle.
MONTANO.   It were well
    The General were put in mind of it.
    Perhaps he sees it not, or his good nature
    Prizes the virtue that appears in Cassio   115
    And looks not on his evils. Is not this true? (*Enter* RODERIGO.)
IAGO (*aside to him*).   How now, Roderigo! I pray you, after the Lieu-
    tenant. Go. (*Exit* RODERIGO.)
MONTANO.   And 'tis great pity that the noble Moor
    Should hazard such a place as his own second   120
    With one of an ingraft infirmity.
    It were an honest action to say
    So to the Moor.
IAGO.   Not I, for this fair island.
    I do love Cassio well, and would do much
    To cure him of this evil—But hark! What noise?   125
    (*A cry within:* "Help! Help!" *Re-enter* CASSIO, *driving in*
    RODERIGO.)
CASSIO.   'Zounds! You rogue! You rascal!
MONTANO.   What's the matter, Lieutenant?
CASSIO.   A knave teach me my duty! But I'll beat the knave into a
    wicker bottle.
RODERIGO.   Beat me!   130
CASSIO.   Does thou prate, rogue? (*Striking* RODERIGO.)
MONTANO.   Nay, good Lieutenant (*staying him*),
                            I pray you sir, hold your hand.
CASSIO.   Let me go, sir, or I'll knock you o'er the mazzard.°
MONTANO.   Come, come, you're drunk.
CASSIO.   Drunk! (*They fight.*)   135

111. watch . . . set: stay awake the clock twice round   **133. mazzard:** head

IAGO (*aside to* RODERIGO).   Away, I say. Go out and cry a mutiny.
   (*Exit* RODERIGO.)
   Nay, good Lieutenant! God's will, gentlemen!
   Help, ho!—Lieutenant—sir—Montano—sir—
   Help, masters!—Here's a goodly watch indeed! (*A bell rings.*)
   Who's that that rings the bell?—Diablo, ho!   140
   The town will rise. God's will, Lieutenant, hold—
   You will be ashamed forever. (*Re-enter* OTHELLO *and*
   ATTENDANTS.)
OTHELLO.   What is the matter here?
MONTANO.   'Zounds, I bleed still, I am hurt to death. (*Faints.*)
OTHELLO.   Hold, for your lives!
IAGO.   Hold, ho! Lieutenant—sir—Montano—gentlemen—   145
   Have you forgot all sense of place and duty?
   Hold! The General speaks to you. Hold, hold, for shame!
OTHELLO.   Why, how now, ho! From whence ariseth this?
   Are we turned Turks, and to ourselves do that
   Which Heaven hath forbid the Ottomites?   150
   For Christian shame, put by this barbarous brawl.
   He that stirs next to carve for his own rage
   Holds his soul light, he dies upon his motion.
   Silence that dreadful bell. It frights the isle
   From her propriety. What is the matter, masters?   155
   Honest Iago, that look'st dead with grieving,
   Speak, who began this? On thy love, I charge thee.
IAGO.   I do not know. Friends all but now, even now,
   In quarter and in terms like bride and groom
   Devesting them for bed. And then, but now,   160
   As if some planet had unwitted men,
   Swords out, and tilting one at other's breast
   In opposition bloody. I cannot speak
   Any beginning to this peevish odds,
   And would in action glorious I had lost   165
   Those legs that brought me to a part of it!
OTHELLO.   How comes it, Michael, you are thus forgot?°
CASSIO.   I pray you, pardon me, I cannot speak.
OTHELLO.   Worthy Montano, you were wont be civil.
   The gravity and stillness of your youth   170
   The world hath noted, and your name is great
   In mouths of wisest censure.° What's the matter

167. are thus forgot: have so forgotten yourself   **172. censure:** judgment

That you unlace your reputation thus
And spend your rich opinion° for the name
Of a night brawler? Give me answer to it.   175
MONTANO.   Worthy Othello, I am hurt to danger.
   Your officer, Iago, can inform you—
While I spare speech, which something now offends me—
Of all that I do know. Nor know I aught
By me that's said or done amiss this night,   180
Unless self-charity° be sometimes a vice,
And to defend ourselves it be a sin
When violence assails us.
OTHELLO.   Now, by Heaven,
   My blood begins my safer guides to rule,
And passion, having my best judgment collied,°   185
Assays to lead the way. If I once stir,
Or do but lift this arm, the best of you
Shall sink in my rebuke. Give me to know
How this foul rout began, who set it on,
And he that is approved° in this offense,   190
Though he had twinned with me, both at a birth,
Shall lose me. What! In a town of war,
Yet wild, the people's hearts brimful of fear,
To manage private and domestic quarrel,
In night, and on the court and guard of safety!   195
'Tis monstrous. Iago, who began 't?
MONTANO.   If partially affined or leagued in office,
   Thou dost deliver more or less than truth,
Thou art no soldier.
IAGO.   Touch me not so near.
   I had rather have this tongue cut from my mouth   200
Than it should do offense to Michael Cassio.
Yet I persuade myself to speak the truth
Shall nothing wrong him. Thus it is, General.
Montano and myself being in speech,
There comes a fellow crying out for help,   205
And Cassio following him with determined sword
To execute upon him. Sir, this gentleman
Steps in to Cassio and entreats his pause.
Myself the crying fellow did pursue

---

174. **opinion:** reputation [Eds.]   181. **self-charity:** love for oneself
185. **collied:** darkened   190. **approved:** proved guilty

Lest by his clamor—as it so fell out—   210
The town might fall in fright. He, swift of foot,
Outran my purpose, and I returned the rather
For that I heard the clink and fall of swords,
And Cassio high in oath, which till tonight
I ne'er might say before. When I came back—   215
For this was brief—I found them close together,
At blow and thrust, even as again they were
When you yourself did part them.
More of this matter cannot I report.
But men are men, the best sometimes forget.   220
Though Cassio did some little wrong to him,
As men in rage strike those that wish them best,
Yet surely Cassio, I believe, received
From him that fled some strange indignity,
Which patience could not pass.

OTHELLO.   I know, Iago,   225
Thy honesty and love doth mince this matter,
Making it light to Cassio. Cassio, I love thee,
But never more be officer of mine. (*Re-enter* DESDEMONA,
attended.)
Look, if my gentle love be not raised up!
I'll make thee an example.

DESDEMONA.   What's the matter?   230

OTHELLO.   All's well now, sweeting. Come away to bed.
(*To* MONTANO, *who is led off*)
Sir, for your hurts, myself will be your surgeon.
Lead him off.
Iago, look with care about the town,
And silence those whom this vile brawl distracted.   235
Come, Desdemona. 'Tis the soldier's life
To have their balmy slumbers waked with strife.
(*Exeunt all but* IAGO *and* CASSIO.)

IAGO.   What, are you hurt, Lieutenant?

CASSIO.   Aye, past all surgery.

IAGO.   Marry, Heaven forbid!   240

CASSIO.   Reputation, reputation, reputation! Oh, I have lost my
reputation! I have lost the immortal part of myself, and what remains is bestial. My reputation, Iago, my reputation!

IAGO.   As I am an honest man, I thought you had received some bodily
wound. There is more sense in that than in reputation. Reputation
is an idle and most false imposition, oft got without merit and lost

without deserving. You have lost no reputation at all unless you repute yourself such a loser. What, man! There are ways to recover the General again. You are but now cast in his mood,° a punishment more in policy° than in malice—even so as one would beat his offenseless dog to affright an imperious lion.° Sue to him again and he's yours.   252

CASSIO.   I will rather sue to be despised than to deceive so good a commander with so slight, so drunken, and so indiscreet an officer. Drunk? And speak parrot°? And squabble? Swagger? Swear? And discourse fustian° with one's own shadow? O thou invisible spirit of wine, if thou hast no name to be known by, let us call thee devil!   258

IAGO.   What was he that you followed with your sword? What had he done to you?   260

CASSIO.   I know not.

IAGO.   Is 't possible?

CASSIO.   I remember a mass of things, but nothing distinctly—a quarrel, but nothing wherefore. Oh God, that men should put an enemy in their mouths to steal away their brains! That we should, with joy, pleasance, revel, and applause, transform ourselves into beasts!   266

IAGO.   Why, but you are now well enough. How came you thus recovered?

CASSIO.   It hath pleased the devil drunkenness to give place to the devil wrath. One unperfectness shows me another, to make me frankly despise myself.   271

IAGO.   Come, you are too severe a moraler. As the time, the place, and the condition of this country stands, I could heartily wish this had not befallen. But since it is as it is, mend it for your own good.   274

CASSIO.   I will ask him for my place again, he shall tell me I am a drunkard! Had I as many mouths as Hydra, such an answer would stop them all. To be now a sensible man, by and by a fool, and presently a beast! Oh, strange! Every inordinate cup is unblest, and the ingredient is a devil.

IAGO.   Come, come, good wine is a good familiar creature, if it be well used. Exclaim no more against it. And, good Lieutenant, I think you think I love you.   282

CASSIO.   I have well approved it, sir. I drunk!

---

249. cast . . . mood: dismissed because he is in a bad mood   250. in policy: i.e., because he must appear to be angry before the Cypriots   250–51. even . . . lion: a proverb meaning that when the lion sees the dog beaten, he will know what is coming to him   255. speak parrot: babble   256. fustian: nonsense

IAGO.   You or any man living may be drunk at some time, man. I'll tell you what you shall do. Our General's wife is now the General. I may say so in this respect, for that he hath devoted and given up himself to the contemplation, mark, and denotement of her parts and graces. Confess yourself freely to her, importune her help to put you in your place again. She is of so free, so kind, so apt, so blessed a disposition, she holds it a vice in her goodness not to do more than she is requested. This broken joint between you and her husband entreat her to splinter° and, my fortunes against any lay° worth naming, this crack of your love shall grow stronger than it was before.   293

CASSIO.   You advise me well.

IAGO.   I protest, in the sincerity of love and honest kindness.

CASSIO.   I think it freely, and betimes in the morning I will beseech the virtuous Desdemona to undertake for me. I am desperate of my fortunes if they check me here.

IAGO.   You are in the right. Good night, Lieutenant, I must to the watch.

CASSIO.   Good night, honest Iago. (*Exit.*)   300

IAGO.   And what's he then that says I play the villain?
    When this advice is free I give and honest,
    Probal° to thinking, and indeed the course
    To win the Moor again? For 'tis most easy
    The inclining Desdemona to subdue   305
    In any honest suit. She's framed as fruitful
    As the free elements. And then for her
    To win the Moor, were 't to renounce his baptism,
    All seals and symbols of redeemèd sin,
    His soul is so enfettered to her love   310
    That she may make, unmake, do what she list,
    Even as her appetite shall play the god
    With his weak function.° How am I then a villain
    To counsel Cassio to this parallel course,
    Directly to his good? Divinity of Hell!   315
    When devils will the blackest sins put on,
    They do suggest at first with heavenly shows,
    As I do now. For whiles this honest fool
    Plies Desdemona to repair his fortunes,
    And she for him pleads strongly to the Moor,   320
    I'll pour this pestilence into his ear,
    That she repeals° him for her body's lust,

---

292. **splinter:** put in splints   **lay:** bet   303. **Probal:** Probable
313. **function:** mental faculties [Eds.]   322. **repeals:** calls back

And by how much she strives to do him good,
She shall undo her credit with the Moor.
So will I turn her virtue into pitch,   325
And out of her own goodness make the net
That shall enmesh them all. (*Enter* RODERIGO.)
                       How now, Roderigo!

RODERIGO.   I do follow here in the chase, not like a hound that hunts
    but one that fills up the cry. My money is almost spent, I have been
    tonight exceedingly well cudgeled, and I think the issue will be I
    shall have so much experience from my pains and so, with no
    money at all and a little more wit, return again to Venice.   332

IAGO.   How poor are they that have not patience!
    What wound did ever heal but by degrees?
    Thou know'st we work by wit and not by witchcraft,   335
    And wit depends on dilatory Time.
    Does 't not go well? Cassio hath beaten thee,
    And thou by that small hurt hast cashiered Cassio.
    Though other things grow fair against the sun,
    Yet fruits that blossom first will first be ripe.   340
    Content thyself awhile. By the mass, 'tis morning.
    Pleasure and action make the hours seem short.
    Retire thee, go where thou art billeted.
    Away, I say. Thou shalt know more hereafter.
    Nay, get thee gone. (*Exit* RODERIGO.)
                       Two things are to be done: 345
    My wife must move for Cassio to her mistress,
    I'll set her on,
    Myself the while to draw the Moor apart
    And bring him jump° when he may Cassio find
    Soliciting his wife. Aye, that's the way.   350
    Dull not device by coldness and delay. (*Exit.*)

ACT 3

SCENE 1. *Before the castle.*

Enter CASSIO *and some* MUSICIANS.

CASSIO.   Masters, play here, I will content your pains°—
    Something that's brief, and bid "Good morrow, General."°
    (*Music. Enter* CLOWN.)

---

349. jump: at the moment   **1. content your pains:** reward your labor   **2. bid . . .**
General.": It was a common custom to play or sing a song beneath the bedroom window of
a distinguished guest or of a newly wedded couple on the morning after their wedding night.

CLOWN.   Why, masters, have your instruments been in Naples, that they speak i' the nose thus?

FIRST MUSICIAN.   How, sir, how?   5

CLOWN.   Are these, I pray you, wind instruments?

FIRST MUSICIAN.   Aye, marry are they, sir.

CLOWN.   Oh, thereby hangs a tail.

FIRST MUSICIAN.   Whereby hangs a tale, sir?

CLOWN.   Marry, sir, by many a wind instrument that I know. But, masters, here's money for you. And the General so likes your music that he desires you, for love's sake, to make no more noise with it.   12

FIRST MUSICIAN.   Well, sir, we will not.

CLOWN.   If you have any music that may not be heard, to 't again. But, as they say, to hear music the General does not greatly care.   15

FIRST MUSICIAN.   We have none such, sir.

CLOWN.   Then put up your pipes in your bag, for I'll away. Go, vanish into air, away! (*Exeunt* MUSICIANS.)

CASSIO.   Dost thou hear, my honest friend?

CLOWN.   No, I hear not your honest friend, I hear you.   20

CASSIO.   Prithee keep up thy quillets.° There's a poor piece of gold for thee. If the gentlewoman that attends the General's wife be stirring, tell her there's one Cassio entreats her a little favor of speech. Wilt thou do this?

CLOWN.   She is stirring, sir. If she will stir hither, I shall seem to notify unto her.   26

CASSIO.   Do, good my friend. (*Exit* CLOWN. *Enter* IAGO.)
                         In happy time, Iago.

IAGO.   You have not been abed, then?

CASSIO.   Why, no, the day had broke
     Before we parted. I have made bold, Iago,   30
     To send in to your wife. My suit to her
     Is that she will to virtuous Desdemona
     Procure me some access.

IAGO.   I'll send her to you presently,
     And I'll devise a mean to draw the Moor
     Out of the way, that your convérse and business   35
     May be more free.

CASSIO.   I humbly thank you for 't. (*Exit* IAGO.)
                         I never knew
     A Florentine more kind and honest. (*Enter* EMILIA.)

---

21. keep . . . quillets: put away your wisecracks

EMILIA.   Good morrow, good Lieutenant. I am sorry
  For your displeasure, but all will sure be well.   40
  The General and his wife are talking of it,
  And she speaks for you stoutly. The Moor replies
  That he you hurt is of great fame in Cyprus
  And great affinity,° and that in wholesome wisdom
  He might not but refuse you. But he protests he loves you,   45
  And needs no other suitor but his likings
  To take the safest occasion by the front
  To bring you in again.
CASSIO.   Yet I beseech you
  If you think fit, or that it may be done,
  Give me advantage of some brief discourse   50
  With Desdemona alone.
EMILIA.   Pray you, come in.
  I will bestow you where you shall have time
  To speak your bosom freely.
CASSIO.   I am much bound to you. (*Exeunt.*)

SCENE 2.   *A room in the castle.*

Enter OTHELLO, IAGO, *and* GENTLEMEN.

OTHELLO.   These letters give, Iago, to the pilot,
  And by him do my duties to the Senate.
  That done, I will be walking on the works.°
  Repair there to me.
IAGO.   Well, my good lord, I'll do 't.
OTHELLO.   This fortification, gentlemen, shall we see 't?   5
GENTLEMEN.   We'll wait upon your lordship. (*Exeunt.*)

SCENE 3.   *The garden of the castle.*

Enter DESDEMONA, CASSIO, *and* EMILIA.

DESDEMONA.   Be thou assured, good Cassio, I will do
  All my abilities in thy behalf.
EMILIA.   Good madam, do. I warrant it grieves my husband
  As if the case were his.

---

44. affinity: kindred   **3. works:** fortifications

DESDEMONA.   Oh, that's an honest fellow. Do not doubt, Cassio,   5
    But I will have my lord and you again
    As friendly as you were.
CASSIO.   Bounteous madam,
    Whatever shall become of Michael Cassio,
    He's never anything but your true servant.
DESDEMONA.   I know 't. I thank you. You do love my lord.   10
    You have known him long, and be you well assured
    He shall in strangeness stand no farther off
    Than in a politic distance.°
CASSIO.   Aye, but lady,
    That policy may either last so long,
    Or feed upon such nice and waterish diet,   15
    Or breed itself so out of circumstance,
    That, I being absent and my place supplied,
    My General will forget my love and service.
DESDEMONA.   Do not doubt° that. Before Emilia here
    I give thee warrant of thy place. Assure thee,   20
    If I do vow a friendship, I'll perform it
    To the last article. My lord shall never rest.
    I'll watch him tame and talk him out of patience,
    His bed shall seem a school, his board a shrift.°
    I'll intermingle every thing he does   25
    With Cassio's suit. Therefore be merry, Cassio,
    For thy solicitor shall rather die
    Than give thy cause away. (*Enter* OTHELLO *and* IAGO, *at a distance.*)
EMILIA.   Madam, here comes my lord.
CASSIO.   Madam, I'll take my leave.   30
DESDEMONA.   Nay, stay and hear me speak.
CASSIO.   Madam, not now. I am very ill at ease,
    Unfit for mine own purposes.
DESDEMONA.   Well, do your discretion. (*Exit* CASSIO.)
IAGO.   Ha! I like not that.   35
OTHELLO.   What dost thou say?
IAGO.   Nothing, my lord. Or if—I know not what.
OTHELLO.   Was not that Cassio parted from my wife?
IAGO.   Cassio, my lord! No, sure, I cannot think it,
    That he would steal away so guilty-like,   40
    Seeing you coming.

12–13: **He . . . distance:** i.e., his apparent coldness to you shall only be so much as his
official position demands for reasons of policy.   **19. doubt:** fear   **24. shrift:** place
of confession [Eds.]

OTHELLO.   I do believe 'twas he.
DESDEMONA.   How now, my lord!
    I have been talking with a suitor here,
    A man that languishes in your displeasure.
OTHELLO.   Who is 't you mean?   45
DESDEMONA.   Why, your Lieutenant, Cassio. Good my lord,
    If I have any grace or power to move you,
    His present reconciliation take.°
    For if he be not one that truly loves you,
    That errs in ignorance and not in cunning,   50
    I have no judgment in an honest face.
    I prithee call him back.
OTHELLO.   Went he hence now?
DESDEMONA.   Aye, sooth, so humbled
    That he hath left part of his grief with me,
    To suffer with him. Good love, call him back.   55
OTHELLO.   Not now, sweet Desdemona, some other time.
DESDEMONA.   But shall 't be shortly?
OTHELLO.   The sooner, sweet, for you.
DESDEMONA.   Shall 't be tonight at supper?
OTHELLO.   No, not tonight.
DESDEMONA.   Tomorrow dinner then?
OTHELLO.   I shall not dine at home.
    I meet the captains at the citadel.   60
DESDEMONA.   Why, then tomorrow night or Tuesday morn,
    On Tuesday noon, or night, on Wednesday morn.
    I prithee name the time, but let it not
    Exceed three days. In faith, he's penitent,
    And yet his trespass, in our common reason—   65
    Save that, they say, the wars must make examples
    Out of their best—is not almost° a fault
    To incur a private check.° When shall he come?
    Tell me, Othello. I wonder in my soul
    What you would ask me that I should deny,   70
    Or stand so mammering° on. What! Michael Cassio,
    That came a-wooing with you, and so many a time
    When I have spoke of you dispraisingly
    Hath ta'en your part—to have so much to do
    To bring him in! Trust me, I could do much—   75

48. His . . . take: Accept his immediate apology and forgive him.
67. not almost: hardly   **68. check:** rebuke   **71. mammering:** hesitating

OTHELLO.   Prithee, no more. Let him come when he will.
    I will deny thee nothing.
DESDEMONA.   Why, this is not a boon.
    'Tis as I should entreat you wear your gloves,
    Or feed on nourishing dishes, or keep you warm,
    Or sue to you to do a peculiar profit   80
    To your own person. Nay, when I have a suit
    Wherein I mean to touch your love indeed,
    It shall be full of poise and difficult weight,
    And fearful to be granted.
OTHELLO.   I will deny thee nothing.
    Whereon I do beseech thee grant me this,   85
    To leave me but a little to myself.
DESDEMONA.   Shall I deny you? No. Farewell, my lord.
OTHELLO.   Farewell, my Desdemona. I'll come to thee straight.
DESDEMONA.   Emilia, come. Be as your fancies teach you.
    Whate'er you be, I am obedient.   90
    (*Exeunt* DESDEMONA *and* EMILIA.)
OTHELLO.   Excellent wretch! Perdition catch my soul
    But I do love thee! And when I love thee not,
    Chaos is come again.
IAGO.   My noble lord—
OTHELLO.   What dost thou say, Iago?
IAGO.   Did Michael Cassio, when you wooed my lady,   95
    Know of your love?
OTHELLO.   He did, from first to last. Why dost thou ask?
IAGO.   But for a satisfaction of my thought,
    No further harm.
OTHELLO.   Why of thy thought, Iago?
IAGO.   I did not think he had been acquainted with her.   100
OTHELLO.   Oh yes, and went between us very oft.
IAGO.   Indeed!
OTHELLO.   Indeed! Aye, indeed. Discern'st thou aught in that?
    Is he not honest?
IAGO.   Honest, my lord!
OTHELLO.   Honest! Aye, honest.
IAGO.   My lord, for aught I know.
OTHELLO.   What dost thou think?   105
IAGO.   Think, my lord!
OTHELLO.   Think, my lord! By Heaven, he echoes me
    As if there were some monster in his thought
    Too hideous to be shown. Thou dost mean something.

I heard thee say even now that thou likedst not that 110
When Cassio left my wife. What didst not like?
And when I told thee he was of my counsel
In my whole course of wooing, thou criedst "Indeed!"
And didst contract and purse thy brow together
As if thou then hadst shut up in thy brain 115
Some horrible conceit. If thou dost love me,
Show me thy thought.
IAGO.   My lord, you know I love you.
OTHELLO.   I think thou dost,
And for I know thou'rt full of love and honesty
And weigh'st thy words before thou givest them breath, 120
Therefore these stops of thine fright me the more.
For such things in a false disloyal knave
Are tricks of custom, but in a man that's just
They're close delations,° working from the heart,
That passion cannot rule.
IAGO.   For Michael Cassio, 125
I dare be sworn I think that he is honest.
OTHELLO.   I think so too.
IAGO.   Men should be what they seem,
Or those that be not, would they might seem none!°
OTHELLO.   Certain, men should be what they seem.
IAGO.   Why, then I think Cassio's an honest man. 130
OTHELLO.   Nay, yet there's more in this.
I prithee speak to me as to thy thinkings,
As thou dost ruminate, and give thy worst of thoughts
The worst of words.
IAGO.   Good my lord, pardon me.
Though I am bound to every act of duty, 135
I am not bound to that all slaves are free to.
Utter my thoughts? Why, say they are vile and false,
As where's that palace whereinto foul things
Sometimes intrude not? Who has a breast so pure
But some uncleanly apprehensions 140
Keep leets° and law days, and in session sit
With meditations lawful?
OTHELLO.   Thou dost conspire against thy friend, Iago,
If thou but think'st him wronged and makest his ear
A stranger to thy thoughts.

124. **close delations:** concealed accusations   128. **seem none:** i.e., not seem to be
honest men   141. **leets:** courts

IAGO.   I do beseech you—   145
    Though I perchance am vicious in my guess,
    As, I confess, it is my nature's plague
    To spy into abuses, and oft my jealousy°
    Shapes faults that are not—that your wisdom yet,
    From one that so imperfectly conceits,°   150
    Would take no notice, nor build yourself a trouble
    Out of his scattering and unsure observance.°
    It were not for your quiet nor your good,
    Nor for my manhood, honesty, or wisdom,
    To let you know my thoughts.
OTHELLO.   What dost thou mean?   155
IAGO.   Good name in man and woman, dear my lord,
    Is the immediate jewel of their souls.
    Who steals my purse steals trash—'tis something, nothing,
    'Twas mine, 'tis his, and has been slave to thousands—
    But he that filches from me my good name   160
    Robs me of that which not enriches him
    And makes me poor indeed.
OTHELLO.   By Heaven, I'll know thy thoughts.
IAGO.   You cannot, if my heart were in your hand,
    Nor shall not, whilst 'tis in my custody.   165
OTHELLO.   Ha!
IAGO.   Oh, beware, my lord, of jealousy.
    It is the green-eyed monster which doth mock
    The meat it feeds on. That cuckold lives in bliss
    Who, certain of his fate, loves not his wronger.°
    But, oh, what damnèd minutes tells he o'er   170
    Who dotes, yet doubts, suspects, yet strongly loves!
OTHELLO.   Oh misery!
IAGO.   Poor and content is rich, and rich enough,
    But riches fineless° is as poor as winter
    To him that ever fears he shall be poor.   175
    Good God, the souls of all my tribe defend
    From jealousy!
OTHELLO.   Why, why is this?
    Think'st thou I'd make a life of jealousy,
    To follow still the changes of the moon
    With fresh suspicions? No, to be once in doubt   180

---

148. jealousy: suspicion   **150. conceits:** conceives   **152. observance:** observation
168–69. That . . . wronger: i.e., the cuckold who hates his wife and knows her falseness is
not tormented by suspicious jealousy.   **174. fineless:** limitless

Is once to be resolved.° Exchange me for a goat
When I shall turn the business of my soul
To such exsufflicate° and blown surmises,
Matching thy inference.° 'Tis not to make me jealous
To say my wife is fair, feeds well, loves company,   185
Is free of speech, sings, plays, and dances well.
Where virtue is, these are more virtuous.
Nor from mine own weak merits will I draw
The smallest fear or doubt of her revolt,
For she had eyes, and chose me. No, Iago,   190
I'll see before I doubt, when I doubt, prove,
And on the proof, there is no more but this—
Away at once with love or jealousy!

IAGO.   I am glad of it, for now I shall have reason
To show the love and duty that I bear you   195
With franker spirit. Therefore, as I am bound,
Receive it from me. I speak not yet of proof.
Look to your wife. Observe her well with Cassio.
Wear your eye thus, not jealous nor secure.°
I would not have your free and noble nature   200
Out of self-bounty° be abused. Look to 't.
I know our country disposition well.
In Venice° they do let Heaven see the pranks
They dare not show their husbands. Their best conscience
Is not to leave 't undone, but keep 't unknown.   205

OTHELLO.   Dost thou say so?

IAGO.   She did deceive her father, marrying you,
And when she seemed to shake and fear your looks,
She loved them most.

OTHELLO.   And so she did.

IAGO.   Why, go to, then.
She that so young could give out such a seeming   210
To seel° her father's eyes up close as oak—
He thought 'twas witchcraft—but I am much to blame.
I humbly do beseech you of your pardon
For too much loving you.

180–81. to . . . resolved: whenever I find myself in doubt I at once seek out the truth.
182–84. When . . . inference: When I shall allow that which concerns me most dearly to
be influenced by such trifling suggestions as yours   exsufflicate: blown up like a bubble
199. secure: overconfident   201. self-bounty: natural goodness
203. In Venice: Venice was notorious for its loose women; the Venetian courtesans were
among the sights of Europe and were much commented upon by travelers.
211. seel: blind

OTHELLO.   I am bound to thee forever.
IAGO.   I see this hath a little dashed your spirits.   215
OTHELLO.   Not a jot, not a jot.
IAGO.   I' faith, I fear it has.
    I hope you will consider what is spoke
    Comes from my love. But I do see you're moved.
    I am to pray you not to strain my speech
    To grosser issues nor to larger reach   220
    Than to suspicion.
OTHELLO.   I will not.
IAGO.   Should you do so, my lord,
    My speech should fall into such vile success
    As my thoughts aim not at. Cassio's my worthy friend.—
    My lord, I see you're moved.
OTHELLO.   No, not so much moved.   225
    I do not think but Desdemona's honest.°
IAGO.   Long live she so! And long live you to think so!
OTHELLO.   And yet, how nature erring from itself—
IAGO.   Aye, there's the point. As—to be bold with you—
    Not to affect° many proposèd matches   230
    Of her own clime, complexion, and degree,
    Whereto we see in all things nature tends°—
    Foh! One may smell in such a will most rank,°
    Foul disproportion, thoughts unnatural.
    But pardon me. I do not in position   235
    Distinctly speak of her, though I may fear
    Her will, recoiling to her better judgment,
    May fall to match° you with her country forms,°
    And happily° repent.
OTHELLO.   Farewell, farewell.
    If more thou dost perceive, let me know more.   240
    Set on thy wife to observe. Leave me, Iago.
IAGO (*going*).   My lord, I take my leave.
OTHELLO.   Why did I marry? This honest creature doubtless
    Sees and knows more, much more, than he unfolds.

---

226. honest: When applied to Desdemona, "honest" means "chaste," but applied to Iago it has the modern meaning of "open and sincere."   **230. affect:** be inclined to
232. in . . . tends: i.e., a woman naturally marries a man of her own country, color, and rank.   **233. will . . . rank:** desire most lustful   **238. match:** compare   **country forms:** the appearance of her countrymen, i.e., white men   **239. happily:** haply, by chance

IAGO (*returning*).   My lord, I would I might entreat your honor   245
    To scan this thing no further. Leave it to time.
    Though it be fit that Cassio have his place,
    For sure he fills it up with great ability,
    Yet if you please to hold him off awhile,
    You shall by that perceive him and his means.   250
    Note if your lady strain his entertainment°
    With any strong or vehement importunity—
    Much will be seen in that. In the meantime,
    Let me be thought too busy in my fears—
    As worthy cause I have to fear I am—   255
    And hold her free, I do beseech your Honor.
OTHELLO.   Fear not my government.°
IAGO.   I once more take my leave. (*Exit.*)
OTHELLO.   This fellow's of exceeding honesty,
    And knows all qualities, with a learned spirit,   260
    Of human dealings. If I do prove her haggard,°
    Though that her jesses° were my dear heartstrings,
    I'd whistle her off and let her down the wind
    To prey at fortune.° Haply, for° I am black
    And have not those soft parts of conversation   265
    That chamberers° have, or for I am declined
    Into the vale of years—yet that's not much—
    She's gone, I am abused, and my relief
    Must be to loathe her. Oh, curse of marriage,
    That we can call these delicate creatures ours,   270
    And not their appetites! I had rather be a toad
    And live upon the vapor of a dungeon
    Than keep a corner in the thing I love
    For others' uses. Yet, 'tis the plague of great ones,
    Prerogatived are they less than the base.   275
    'Tis destiny unshunnable, like death.
    Even then this forkèd plague° is fated to us
    When we do quicken.° Desdemona comes.
    (*Re-enter* DESDEMONA *and* EMILIA.)

---

251. strain his entertainment: urge you to receive him   **257. government:** self-control   **261. haggard:** a wild hawk   **261–64. If . . . fortune:** Othello keeps up the imagery of falconry throughout. He means: If I find that she is wild, I'll whistle her off the game and let her go where she will, for she's not worth keeping.   **262. jesses:** the straps attached to a hawk's legs   **264. Haply, for:** Perhaps, because [Eds.]   **266. chamberers:** playboys   **277. forkèd plague:** i.e., to be a cuckold   **278. quicken:** stir in our mother's womb

If she be false, oh, then Heaven mocks itself!
I'll not believe 't.
DESDEMONA.   How now, my dear Othello!   280
  Your dinner, and the generous° islanders
  By you invited, do attend your presence.
OTHELLO.   I am to blame.
DESDEMONA.   Why do you speak so faintly?
  Are you not well?
OTHELLO.   I have a pain upon my forehead here.   285
DESDEMONA.   Faith, that's with watching,° 'twill away again.
  Let me but bind it hard, within this hour
  It will be well.
OTHELLO.   Your napkin° is too little,
  (*He puts the handkerchief from him, and it drops.*)
  Let it alone. Come, I'll go in with you.
DESDEMONA.   I am very sorry that you are not well.   290
  (*Exeunt* OTHELLO *and* DESDEMONA.)
EMILIA.   I am glad I have found this napkin.
  This was her first remembrance from the Moor.
  My wayward° husband hath a hundred times
  Wooed me to steal it, but she so loves the token,
  For he conjured° her she should ever keep it,   295
  That she reserves it evermore about her
  To kiss and talk to. I'll have the work ta'en out,°
  And give 't to Iago. What he will do with it
  Heaven knows, not I.
  I nothing know, but for his fantasy.° (*Re-enter* IAGO.)   300
IAGO.   How now! What do you here alone?
EMILIA.   Do not you chide, I have a thing for you.
IAGO.   A thing for me? It is a common thing—
EMILIA.   Ha!
IAGO.   To have a foolish wife.   305
EMILIA.   Oh, is that all? What will you give me now
  For that same handkerchief?
IAGO.   What handkerchief?
EMILIA.   What handkerchief!
  Why, that the Moor first gave to Desdemona,
  That which so often you did bid me steal.   310

---

281. **generous:** noble   286. **watching:** lack of sleep   288. **napkin:** handkerchief
293. **wayward:** unaccountable   295. **conjured:** begged with an oath
297. **work . . . out:** pattern copied   300. **fantasy:** whim

IAGO.   Hast stol'n it from her?

EMILIA.   No, faith, she let it drop by negligence,
And, to the advantage, I being here took 't up.
Look, here it is.

IAGO.   A good wench. Give it me.

EMILIA.   What will you do with 't, that you have been so earnest   315
To have me filch it?

IAGO (*snatching it*).   Why, what's that to you?

EMILIA.   If 't be not for some purpose of import,
Give 't me again. Poor lady, she'll run mad
When she shall lack it.

IAGO.   Be not acknown on 't,° I have use for it.   320
Go, leave me. (*Exit* EMILIA.)
I will in Cassio's lodging lose this napkin,
And let him find it. Trifles light as air
Are to the jealous confirmations strong
As proofs of Holy Writ. This may do something.   325
The Moor already changes with my poison.
Dangerous conceits° are in their natures poisons,
Which at the first are scarce found to distaste,
But, with a little, act upon the blood,
Burn like the mines of sulphur. I did say so.°   330
Look where he comes! (*Re-enter* OTHELLO.)
                     Not poppy,° nor mandragora,°
Nor all the drowsy syrups of the world,
Shall ever medicine thee to that sweet sleep
Which thou owedst° yesterday,

OTHELLO.   Ha! Ha! False to me?

IAGO.   Why, how now, General! No more of that.   335

OTHELLO.   Avaunt! Be gone! Thou hast set me on the rack.
I swear 'tis better to be much abused
Than but to know 't a little.

IAGO.   How now, my lord!

OTHELLO.   What sense had I of her stol'n hours of lust?
I saw 't not, thought it not, it harmed not me.   340
I slept the next night well, was free and merry.
I found not Cassio's kisses on her lips.

---

320. Be . . . 't: Know nothing about it   327. conceits: ideas [Eds.]   330. I . . .
so: As Iago says this, Othello is seen approaching, with all the signs of his agitation out-
wardly visible.   331. poppy: opium   mandragora: called also mandrake—a root
used as a drug to bring sleep   334. owedst: owned

He that is robbed, not wanting° what is stol'n,
Let him not know 't and he's not robbed at all.
IAGO.   I am sorry to hear this.   345
OTHELLO.   I had been happy if the general camp,
   Pioners° and all, had tasted her sweet body,
   So I had nothing known. Oh, now forever
   Farewell the tranquil mind! Farewell content!
   Farewell the plumèd troop and the big wars   350
   That make ambition virtue! Oh farewell,
   Farewell the neighing steed and the shrill trump,
   The spirit-stirring drum, the ear-piercing fife,
   The royal banner, and all quality,
   Pride, pomp, and circumstance of glorious war!   355
   And, O you mortal engines,° whose rude throats
   The immortal Jove's dread clamors counterfeit,
   Farewell! Othello's occupation's gone!
IAGO.   Is 't possible, my lord?
OTHELLO.   Villain, be sure thou prove my love a whore,   360
   Be sure of it, give me the ocular proof.
   Or by the worth of man's eternal soul,
   Thou hadst been better have been born a dog
   Than answer my waked wrath!
IAGO.   Is 't come to this?
OTHELLO.   Make me to see 't, or at the least so prove it   365
   That the probation° bear no hinge nor loop
   To hang a doubt on, or woe upon thy life!
IAGO.   My noble lord—
OTHELLO.   If thou dost slander her and torture me,
   Never pray more, abandon all remorse.°   370
   On horror's head horrors accumulate,
   Do deeds to make Heaven weep, all earth amazed,
   For nothing canst thou to damnation add
   Greater than that.
IAGO.   Oh, grace! Oh, Heaven defend me!
   Are you a man? Have you a soul or sense?   375
   God be wi' you, take mine office. O wretched fool,
   That livest to make thine honesty a vice!
   O monstrous world! Take note, take note, O world,
   To be direct and honest is not safe.

---

343. wanting: missing   **347. Pioners:** Pioneers, the lowest type of soldier
356. mortal engines: deadly cannon   **366. probation:** proof   **370. remorse:** pity

I thank you for this profit, and from hence   380
I'll love no friend, sith° love breeds such offense.
OTHELLO.   Nay, stay. Thou shouldst be honest.
IAGO.   I should be wise, for honesty's a fool,
    And loses that it works for.
OTHELLO.   By the world,
    I think my wife be honest, and think she is not.   385
    I think that thou are just, and think thou art not.
    I'll have some proof. Her name, that was as fresh
    As Dian's° visage, is now begrimed and black
    As mine own face. If there be cords, or knives,
    Poison, or fire, or suffocating streams,   390
    I'll not endure it. Would I were satisfied!
IAGO.   I see, sir, you are eaten up with passion.
    I do repent me that I put it to you.
    You would be satisfied?
OTHELLO.   Would! Nay, I will.
IAGO.   And may, but how? How satisfied, my lord?   395
    Would you, the supervisor,° grossly gape on?
    Behold her topped?
OTHELLO.   Death and damnation! Oh!
IAGO.   It were a tedious difficulty, I think,
    To bring them to that prospect. Damn them then,
    If ever mortal eyes do see them bolster°   400
    More than their own! What then? How then?
    What shall I say? Where's satisfaction?
    It is impossible you should see this,
    Were they as prime° as goats, as hot as monkeys,
    As salt° as wolves in pride,° and fools as gross   405
    As ignorance made drunk. But yet I say
    If imputation° and strong circumstances,
    Which lead directly to the door of truth,
    Will give you satisfaction, you may have 't.
OTHELLO.   Give me a living reason she's disloyal.   410
IAGO.   I do not like the office.
    But sith I am entered in this cause so far,
    Pricked to 't by foolish honesty and love,
    I will go on. I lay with Cassio lately,
    And being troubled with a raging tooth,   415

381. sith: since   388. Dian: Diana, goddess of chastity
396. supervisor: looker-on   400. bolster: sleep together   404. prime: lustful
405. salt: eager   pride: in heat   407. imputation: probability

I could not sleep.
There are a kind of men so loose of soul
That in their sleeps will mutter their affairs.
One of this kind is Cassio.
In sleep I heard him say "Sweet Desdemona,   420
Let us be wary, let us hide our loves."
And then, sir, would he gripe° and wring my hand,
Cry "O sweet creature!" and then kiss me hard,
As if he plucked up kisses by the roots
That grew upon my lips. Then laid his leg   425
Over my thigh, and sighed and kissed, and then
Cried "Cursed fate that gave thee to the Moor!"

OTHELLO.   Oh, monstrous! Monstrous!

IAGO.   Nay, this was but his dream.

OTHELLO.   But this denoted a foregone conclusion.
    'Tis a shrewd doubt,° though it be but a dream.   430

IAGO.   And this may help to thicken other proofs
    That do demonstrate thinly.

OTHELLO.   I'll tear her all to pieces.

IAGO.   Nay, but be wise. Yet we see nothing done.
    She may be honest yet. Tell me this:
    Have you not sometimes seen a handkerchief   435
    Spotted with strawberries in your wife's hand?

OTHELLO.   I gave her such a one, 'twas my first gift.

IAGO.   I know not that. But such a handkerchief—
    I am sure it was your wife's—did I today
    See Cassio wipe his beard with.

OTHELLO.   If it be that—   440

IAGO.   If it be that, or any that was hers,
    It speaks against her with the other proofs.

OTHELLO.   Oh, that the slave had forty thousand lives!
    One is too poor, too weak, for my revenge.
    Now do I see 'tis true. Look here, Iago,   445
    All my fond love thus do I blow to Heaven—
    'Tis gone.
    Arise, black Vengeance, from thy hollow cell!
    Yield up, O Love, thy crown and hearted throne
    To tyrannous hate! Swell, bosom, with thy fraught,°   450
    For 'tis of aspics'° tongues!

---

422. **gripe:** grip   430. **shrewd doubt:** bitter suspicion   450. **fraught:** freight
451. **aspics':** asps'

IAGO.   Yet be content.
OTHELLO.   Oh, blood, blood, blood!
IAGO.   Patience, I say. Your mind perhaps may change.
OTHELLO.   Never, Iago. Like to the Pontic Sea,
    Whose icy current and compulsive course   455
    Ne'er feels retiring ebb but keeps due on
    To the Propontic and the Hellespont;
    Even so my bloody thoughts, with violent pace,
    Shall ne'er look back, ne'er ebb to humble love,
    Till that a capable° and wide revenge   460
    Swallow them up. Now, by yond marble Heaven,
    In the due reverence of a sacred vow (*kneels*)
    I here engage my words.
IAGO.   Do not rise yet. (*Kneels.*)
    Witness, you ever burning lights above,
    You elements that clip° us round about,   465
    Witness that here Iago doth give up
    The execution of his wit,° hands, heart,
    To wronged Othello's service! Let him command,
    And to obey shall be in me remorse,°
    What bloody business ever. (*They rise.*)
OTHELLO.   I greet thy love,   470
    Not with vain thanks, but with acceptance bounteous,
    And will upon the instant put thee to 't.
    Within these three days let me hear thee say
    That Cassio's not alive.
IAGO.   My friend is dead. 'Tis done at your request.   475
    But let her live.
OTHELLO.   Damn her, lewd minx! Oh, damn her!
    Come, go with me apart. I will withdraw,
    To furnish me with some swift means of death
    For the fair devil. Now art thou my Lieutenant.   480
IAGO.   I am your own forever. (*Exeunt.*)

SCENE 4. BEFORE THE CASTLE.

Enter DESDEMONA, EMILIA, *and* CLOWN.

DESDEMONA.   Do you know, sirrah, where Lieutenant Cassio lies?
CLOWN.   I dare not say he lies anywhere.

---

460. capable: comprehensive   **465. clip:** embrace   **467. wit:** mind [Eds.]
469. remorse: solemn obligation

DESDEMONA. Why, man?

CLOWN. He's a soldier, and for one to say a soldier lies is stabbing.

DESDEMONA. Go to. Where lodges he?   5

CLOWN. To tell you where he lodges is to tell you where I lie.

DESDEMONA. Can anything be made of this?

CLOWN. I know not where he lodges, and for me to devise a lodging,
      and say he lies here or he lies there, were to lie in mine own throat.

DESDEMONA. Can you inquire him out and be edified by report?° 10

CLOWN. I will catechize the world for him; that is, make questions
      and by them answer.

DESDEMONA. Seek him, bid him come hither. Tell him I have moved
      my lord on his behalf and hope all will be well.

CLOWN. To do this is within the compass of man's wit, and therefore
      I will attempt the doing it. (*Exit.*)   16

DESDEMONA. Where should I lose that handkerchief, Emilia?

EMILIA. I know not, madam.

DESDEMONA. Believe me, I had rather have lost my purse
      Full of crusados. And, but my noble Moor   20
      Is true of mind and made of no such baseness
      As jealous creatures are, it were enough
      To put him to ill thinking.

EMILIA.   Is he not jealous?

DESDEMONA. Who, he? I think the sun where he was born
      Drew all such humors from him.

EMILIA.   Look where he comes.   25

DESDEMONA. I will not leave him now till Cassio
      Be called to him. (*Enter* OTHELLO.)
                          How is 't with you, my lord?

OTHELLO. Well, my good lady. (*Aside*) Oh, hardness to dissemble!
      How do you, Desdemona?

DESDEMONA.   Well, my good lord.

OTHELLO. Give me your hand. This hand is moist,° my lady.   30

DESDEMONA. It yet has felt no age nor known no sorrow.

OTHELLO. This argues fruitfulness and liberal heart.
      Hot, hot, and moist—this hand of yours requires
      A sequester from liberty, fasting and prayer,
      Much castigation, exercise devout.   35
      For here's a young and sweating devil here,
      That commonly rebels. 'Tis a good hand,
      A frank one.

_____

10. edified by report: enlightened by the information. Desdemona speaks with mock
pomposity.   **30. moist:** A hot moist palm was believed to show desire.

DESDEMONA.   You may indeed say so,
    For 'twas that hand that gave away my heart.
OTHELLO.   A liberal° hand. The hearts of old gave hands,   40
    But our new heraldry is hands, not hearts.°
DESDEMONA.   I cannot speak of this. Come now, your promise.
OTHELLO.   What promise, chuck?°
DESDEMONA.   I have sent to bid Cassio come speak with you.
OTHELLO.   I have a salt and sorry rheum offends me.   45
    Lend me thy handkerchief.
DESDEMONA.   Here, my lord.
OTHELLO.   That which I gave you.
DESDEMONA.   I have it not about me.
OTHELLO.   Not?
DESDEMONA.   No indeed, my lord.
OTHELLO.   That's a fault. That handkerchief
    Did an Egyptian to my mother give.   50
    She was a charmer, and could almost read
    The thoughts of people. She told her while she kept it
    'Twould make her amiable and subdue my father
    Entirely to her love, but if she lost it
    Or made a gift of it, my father's eye   55
    Should hold her loathèd and his spirits should hunt
    After new fancies. She dying gave it me,
    And bid me, when my fate would have me wive,
    To give it her. I did so. And take heed on 't,
    Make it a darling like your precious eye.   60
    To lose 't or give 't away were such perdition
    As nothing else could match.
DESDEMONA.   Is 't possible?
OTHELLO.   'Tis true. There's magic in the web of it.
    A sibyl that had numbered in the world
    The sun to course two hundred compasses   65
    In her prophetic fury sewed the work.
    The worms were hallowed that did breed the silk,
    And it was dyed in mummy which the skillful
    Conserved° of maiden's hearts.
DESDEMONA.   Indeed! Is 't true?

---

40. liberal: overgenerous   **40–41. The . . . hearts:** Once love and deeds went
together, but now it is all deeds (i.e., faithlessness) and no love.   **43. chuck:** A term of
affection, but not the kind of word with which a person of Othello's dignity would normally
address his wife. He is beginning to treat her with contemptuous familiarity.
69. Conserved: Prepared

OTHELLO.   Most veritable, therefore look to 't well.   70
DESDEMONA.   Then would God that I had never seen 't.
OTHELLO.   Ha! Wherefore?
DESDEMONA.   Why do you speak so startingly and rash?
OTHELLO.   Is 't lost? Is 't gone? Speak, is it out o' the way?
DESDEMONA.   Heaven bless us!   75
OTHELLO.   Say you?
DESDEMONA.   It is not lost, but what an if it were?
OTHELLO.   How!
DESDEMONA.   I say it is not lost.
OTHELLO.   Fetch 't, let me see it.
DESDEMONA.   Why, so I can, sir, but I will not now.   80
    This is a trick to put me from my suit.
    Pray you let Cassio be received again.
OTHELLO.   Fetch me the handkerchief. My mind misgives.
DESDEMONA.   Come, come,
    You'll never meet a more sufficient man.   85
OTHELLO.   The handkerchief!
DESDEMONA.   I pray talk me of Cassio.
OTHELLO.   The handkerchief!
DESDEMONA.   A man that all this time
    Hath founded his good fortunes on your love,
    Shared dangers with you—
OTHELLO.   The handkerchief!   90
DESDEMONA.   In sooth, you are to blame.
OTHELLO.   Away! (*Exit.*)
EMILIA.   Is not this man jealous?
DESDEMONA.   I ne'er saw this before.
    Sure there's some wonder in this handkerchief.   95
    I am most unhappy in the loss of it.
EMILIA.   'Tis not a year or two shows us a man.°
    They are all but stomachs and we all but food.
    They eat us hungerly, and when they are full
    They belch us. Look you, Cassio and my husband.   100
    (*Enter* CASSIO *and* IAGO.)
IAGO.   There is no other way, 'tis she must do 't.
    And, lo, the happiness!° Go and impórtune her.
DESDEMONA.   How now, good Cassio! What's the news with you?
CASSIO.   Madam, my former suit. I do beseech you
    That by your virtuous means I may again   105

97. 'Tis . . . man: It does not take a couple of years to discover the nature of a man; i.e., he soon shows his real nature.   102. And . . . happiness!: What good luck, here she is!

Exist, and be a member of his love
Whom I with all the office of my heart
Entirely honor. I would not be delayed.
If my offense be of such mortal kind
That nor my service past nor present sorrows   110
Nor purposed merit in futurity
Can ransom me into his love again,
But to know so must be my benefit.
So shall I clothe me in a forced content
And shut myself up in some other course   115
To Fortune's alms.
DESDEMONA.   Alas, thrice-gentle Cassio!
My advocation° is not now in tune.
My lord is not my lord, nor should I know him
Were he in favor° as in humor altered.
So help me every spirit sanctified,   120
As I have spoken for you all my best
And stood within the blank° of his displeasure
For my free speech! You must awhile be patient.
What I can do I will, and more I will
Than for myself I dare. Let that suffice you.   125
IAGO.   Is my lord angry?
EMILIA.   He went hence but now,
And certainly in strange unquietness.
IAGO.   Can he be angry? I have seen the cannon
When it hath blown his ranks into the air,
And, like the Devil, from his very arm   130
Puffed his own brother, and can he be angry?
Something of moment then. I will go meet him.
There's matter in 't indeed if he be angry.
DESDEMONA.   I prithee do so. (*Exit* IAGO.)
                         Something sure of state,
Either from Venice, or some unhatched practice   135
Made demonstrable° here in Cyprus to him,
Hath puddled his clear spirit. And in such cases
Men's natures wrangle with inferior things,
Though great ones are their object. 'Tis even so,
For let our finger ache and it indues   140
Our other healthful members even to that sense

---

117. **advocation:** advocacy   119. **favor:** face [Eds.]   122. **blank:** aim
135–36. **unhatched . . . demonstrable:** some plot, not yet matured, which has been revealed

Of pain. Nay, we must think men are not gods,
Nor of them look for such observancy
As fits the bridal.° Beshrew me much, Emilia,
I was, unhandsome warrior° as I am,   145
Arraigning his unkindness with my soul,
But now I find I had suborned the witness,°
And he's indicted falsely.

EMILIA.   Pray Heaven it be state matters, as you think,
And no conception nor no jealous toy°   150
Concerning you.

DESDEMONA.   Alas the day, I never gave him cause!

EMILIA.   But jealous souls will not be answered so.
They are not ever jealous for the cause,
But jealous for they are jealous. 'Tis a monster   155
Begot upon itself, born on itself.

DESDEMONA.   Heaven keep that monster from Othello's mind!

EMILIA.   Lady, amen.

DESDEMONA.   I will go seek him. Cassio, walk hereabout.
If I do find him fit, I'll move your suit,   160
And seek to effect it to my uttermost.

CASSIO.   I humbly thank your ladyship.
    (*Exeunt* DESDEMONA *and* EMILIA. *Enter* BIANCA.)

BIANCA.   Save you, friend Cassio!

CASSIO.   What make you from home?
How is it with you, my most fair Bianca?
I' faith, sweet love, I was coming to your house.   165

BIANCA.   And I was going to your lodging, Cassio.
What, keep a week away? Seven days and nights?
Eightscore eight hours? And lovers' absent hours,
More tedious than the dial eightscore times?
Oh, weary reckoning!

CASSIO.   Pardon me, Bianca.   170
I have this while with leaden thoughts been pressed,
But I shall in a more continuate time
Strike off this score of absence. Sweet Bianca,
    (*Giving her* DESDEMONA's *handkerchief*)
Take me this work out.

---

144. bridal: honeymoon   **145. unhandsome warrior:** clumsy soldier. Desdemona continually thinks of herself as Othello's companion in arms. Cf. 1.3.248 ff.
147. suborned the witness: corrupted the evidence; i.e., misunderstood his behavior [Eds.]
150. jealous toy: silly suspicion

BIANCA.   O Cassio, whence came this?
    This is some token from a newer friend.   175
    To the felt absence now I feel a cause.
    Is 't come to this? Well, well.
CASSIO.   Go to, woman!
    Throw your vile guesses in the Devil's teeth,
    From whence you have them. You are jealous now
    That this is from some mistress, some remembrance.   180
    No, by my faith, Bianca.
BIANCA.   Why, whose is it?
CASSIO.   I know not, sweet. I found it in my chamber.
    I like the work well. Ere it be demanded—
    As like enough it will—I'd have it copied.
    Take it, and do 't, and leave me for this time.   185
BIANCA.   Leave you! Wherefore?
CASSIO.   I do attend here on the General,
    And think it no addition,° nor my wish
    To have him see me womaned.°
BIANCA.   Why, I pray you?
CASSIO.   Not that I love you not.
BIANCA.   But that you do not love me.   190
    I pray you bring me on the way a little,
    And say if I shall see you soon at night.
CASSIO.   'Tis but a little way that I can bring you,
    For I attend here. But I'll see you soon.
BIANCA.   'Tis very good, I must be circumstanced.° (*Exeunt.*)   195

ACT 4

SCENE 1. Cyprus. Before the castle.

Enter OTHELLO and IAGO.

IAGO.   Will you think so?
OTHELLO.   Think so, Iago!
IAGO.   What,
    To kiss in private?
OTHELLO.   An unauthorized kiss.

---

188. addition: honor   **189. womaned:** with a woman   **195. circumstanced:** put
off

IAGO.   Or to be naked with her friend in bed
    An hour or more, not meaning any harm?
OTHELLO.   Naked in bed, Iago, and not mean harm!   5
    It is hypocrisy against the Devil.
    They that mean virtuously and yet do so,
    The Devil their virtue tempts and they tempt Heaven.
IAGO.   So they do nothing, 'tis a venial° slip.
    But if I give my wife a handkerchief—   10
OTHELLO.   What then?
IAGO.   Why, then, 'tis hers, my lord, and being hers,
    She may, I think, bestow 't on any man.
OTHELLO.   She is protectress of her honor too.
    May she give that?   15
IAGO.   Her honor is an essence that's not seen.
    They have it very oft that have it not.
    But for the handkerchief—
OTHELLO.   By Heaven, I would most gladly have forgot it.
    Thou said'st—oh, it comes o'er my memory,   20
    As doth the raven o'er the infected house
    Boding to all°—he had my handkerchief.
IAGO.   Aye, what of that?
OTHELLO.   That's not so good now.
IAGO.   What
    If I had said I had seen him do you wrong?
    Or heard him say—as knaves be such abroad,   25
    Who having, by their own importunate suit,
    Or voluntary dotage of some mistress,
    Convincèd or supplied° them, cannot choose
    But they must blab—
OTHELLO.   Hath he said anything?
IAGO.   He hath, my lord, but be you well assured,   30
    No more than he'll unswear.
OTHELLO.   What hath he said?
IAGO.   Faith, that he did—I know not what he did.
OTHELLO.   What? What?
IAGO.   Lie—
OTHELLO.   With her?
IAGO.   With her, on her, what you will.   34

---

9. venial: pardonable   **21–22. As doth the raven . . . all:** As an evil omen (such as a raven overhead) brings evil tidings to all who live in a plague-infested house [Eds.]
28. Convincèd or supplied: Overcome or satisfied their desires

OTHELLO.   Lie° with her! Lie on her!—We say lie on her when they
   belie her.—Lie with her. 'Zounds, that's fulsome!° Handkerchief—
   confessions—handkerchief!—To confess, and be hanged for his
   labor. First to be hanged, and then to confess. I tremble at it. Nature
   would not invest herself in such shadowing passion without some
   instruction.° It is not words that shake me thus. Pish! Noses, ears,
   and lips. Is 't possible?—Confess?—Handkerchief?—Oh, devil!
   (*Falls in a trance.*)   41
IAGO.   Work on,
   My medicine, work! Thus credulous fools are caught,
   And many worthy and chaste dames even thus,
   All guiltless, meet reproach. What ho! My lord!   45
   My lord, I say! Othello! (*Enter* CASSIO.)
                                        How now, Cassio!
CASSIO.   What's the matter?
IAGO.   My lord is fall'n into an epilepsy.
   This is his second fit, he had one yesterday.
CASSIO.   Rub him about the temples.
IAGO.   No, forbear,   50
   The lethargy° must have his quiet course.
   If not, he foams at mouth and by and by
   Breaks out to savage madness. Look, he stirs.
   Do you withdraw yourself a little while,
   He will recover straight. When he is gone,   55
   I would on great occasion speak with you. (*Exit* CASSIO.)
   How is it, General? Have you not hurt your head?°
OTHELLO.   Dost thou mock me?
IAGO.   I mock you! No, by Heaven.
   Would you would bear your fortune like a man!
OTHELLO.   A hornèd man's a monster and a beast.   60
IAGO.   There's many a beast, then, in a populous city,
   And many a civil monster.
OTHELLO.   Did he confess it?
IAGO.   Good sir, be a man.
   Think every bearded fellow that's but yoked°
   May draw with you.° There's millions now alive   65

35–41. Lie . . . devil: Othello breaks into incoherent muttering before he falls down in
a fit.   **36. fulsome:** disgusting   **38–40. Nature . . . instruction:** Nature would not
fill me with such overwhelming emotion unless there was some cause.
51. lethargy: epileptic fit   **57. Have . . . head?:** With brutal cynicism Iago asks
whether Othello is suffering from cuckold's headache.   **64. yoked:** married
65. draw with you: be your yoke fellow

That nightly lie in those unproper beds
Which they dare swear peculiar.° Your case is better.
Oh, 'tis the spite of Hell, the Fiend's arch-mock,
To lip° a wanton in a secure couch°
And to suppose her chaste! No, let me know,   70
And knowing what I am, I know what she shall be.

OTHELLO.   Oh, thou art wise, 'tis certain.

IAGO.   Stand you awhile apart,
Confine yourself but in a patient list.°
Whilst you were here o'erwhelmèd with your grief—
A passion most unsuiting such a man—   75
Cassio came hither. I shifted him away,
And laid good 'scuse upon your ecstasy,°
Bade him anon return and here speak with me,
The which he promised. Do but encave yourself,
And mark the fleers, the gibes, and notable scorns,   80
That dwell in every region of his face.
For I will make him tell the tale anew,
Where, how, how oft, how long ago, and when
He hath and is again to cope° your wife.
I say but mark his gesture. Marry, patience,   85
Or I shall say you are all in all in spleen,
And nothing of a man.

OTHELLO.   Dost thou hear, Iago?
I will be found most cunning in my patience,
But—dost thou hear?—most bloody.

IAGO.   That's not amiss.
But yet keep time in all. Will you withdraw? (OTHELLO *retires*.) 90
Now will I question Cassio of Bianca,
A housewife° that by selling her desires
Buys herself bread and clothes. It is a creature
That dotes on Cassio, as 'tis the strumpet's plague
To beguile many and be beguiled by one.   95
He, when he hears of her, cannot refrain
From the excess of laughter. Here he comes. (*Re-enter* CASSIO.)
As he shall smile, Othello shall go mad,
And his unbookish° jealousy must construe

66–67. **That . . . peculiar:** That lie nightly in beds which they believe are their own but
which others have shared   69. **lip:** kiss   **secure couch:** lit., a carefree bed; i.e., a
bed which has been used by the wife's lover, but secretly   73. **patient list:** confines of
patience   77. **ecstasy:** fit   84. **cope:** encounter   92. **housewife:** hussy
99. **unbookish:** unlearned

Poor Cassio's smiles, gestures, and light behavior   100
   Quite in the wrong. How do you now, Lieutenant?
Cassio.   The worser that you give me the addition°
   Whose want even kills me.
Iago.   Ply Desdemona well, and you are sure on 't.
   Now, if this suit lay in Bianca's power,   105
   How quickly should you speed!
Cassio.   Alas, poor caitiff!°
Othello.   Look how he laughs already!
Iago.   I never knew a woman love man so.
Cassio.   Alas, poor rogue! I think i' faith, she loves me.
Othello.   Now he denies it faintly and laughs it out.   110
Iago.   Do you hear, Cassio?
Othello.   Now he impórtunes him
   To tell it o'er. Go to. Well said, well said.
Iago.   She gives it out that you shall marry her.
   Do you intend to?
Cassio.   Ha, ha, ha!   115
Othello.   Do you triumph, Roman?° Do you triumph?
Cassio.   I marry her! What, a customer!° I prithee bear some charity
   to my wit. Do not think it so unwholesome. Ha, ha, ha!
Othello.   So, so, so, so. They laugh that win.
Iago.   Faith, the cry goes that you shall marry her.   120
Cassio.   Prithee say true.
Iago.   I am a very villain else.
Othello.   Have you scored° me? Well.
Cassio.   This is the monkey's own giving out. She is persuaded I
   will marry her out of her own love and flattery, not out of my
   promise.   126
Othello.   Iago beckons me, now he begins the story.
Cassio.   She was here even now. She haunts me in every place. I was
   the other day talking on the sea bank with certain Venetians, and
   thither comes the bauble, and, by this hand, she falls me thus about
   my neck—   131
Othello.   Crying "O dear Cassio!" as it were. His gesture imports it.
Cassio.   So hangs and lolls and weeps upon me, so hales and pulls me.
   Ha, ha, ha!

---

102. **addition:** title (Lieutenant) which he has lost   106. **caitiff:** wretch
116. **triumph, Roman:** The word "triumph" suggests "Roman" because the Romans celebrated their victories with triumphs, elaborate shows, and processions.   117. **customer:**
harlot   123. **scored:** marked, as with a blow from a whip

OTHELLO.   Now he tells how she plucked him to my chamber. Oh, I
see that nose of yours, but not that dog I shall throw it to.   136
CASSIO.   Well, I must leave her company.
IAGO.   Before me!° Look where she comes.
CASSIO.   'Tis such another fitchew!° Marry, a perfumed one.
(*Enter* BIANCA.)
What do you mean by this haunting of me?   140
BIANCA.   Let the Devil and his dam haunt you! What did you mean by
that same handkerchief you gave me even now? I was a fine fool to
take it. I must take out the work? A likely piece of work, that you should
find it in your chamber and not know who left it there! This is some
minx's token, and I must take out the work? There, give it your hobby-
horse. Wheresoever you had it, I'll take out no work on 't.   146
CASSIO.   How now, my sweet Bianca! How now! How now!
OTHELLO.   By Heaven, that should be my handkerchief!
BIANCA.   An° you'll come to supper tonight, you may. An you will
not, come when you are next prepared for. (*Exit.*)   150
IAGO.   After her, after her.
CASSIO.   Faith, I must, she'll rail i' the street else.
IAGO.   Will you sup there?
CASSIO.   Faith, I intend so.
IAGO.   Well, I may chance to see you, for I would very fain speak with
you.   156
CASSIO.   Prithee, come, will you?
IAGO.   Go to. Say no more. (*Exit* CASSIO.)
OTHELLO (*advancing*).   How shall I murder him, Iago?
IAGO.   Did you perceive how he laughed at his vice?   160
OTHELLO.   Oh, Iago!
IAGO.   And did you see the handkerchief?
OTHELLO.   Was that mine?
IAGO.   Yours, by this hand. And to see how he prizes the foolish woman
your wife? She gave it him, and he hath given it his whore.   165
OTHELLO.   I would have him nine years a-killing. A fine woman! A
fair woman! A sweet woman!
IAGO.   Nay, you must forget that.
OTHELLO.   Aye, let her rot, and perish, and be damned tonight, for she
shall not live. No, my heart is turned to stone, I strike it and it
hurts my hand. Oh, the world hath not a sweeter creature. She
might lie by an emperor's side, and command him tasks.   172
IAGO.   Nay, that's not your way.°

---

138. Before me!: By my soul!   **139. fitchew:** polecat   **149. An:** If
173. Nay . . . way: i.e., don't get soft thoughts about her

OTHELLO.   Hang her! I do but say what she is, so delicate with her
   needle, an admirable musician—oh, she will sing the savageness
   out of a bear—of so high and plenteous wit and invention—   176
IAGO.   She's the worse for all this.
OTHELLO.   Oh, a thousand times. And then, of so gentle a condition!
IAGO.   Aye, too gentle.
OTHELLO.   Nay, that's certain. But yet the pity of it, Iago! O Iago, the
   pity of it, Iago!   181
IAGO.   If you are so fond over her iniquity, give her patent to offend,
   for if it touch not you, it comes near nobody.
OTHELLO.   I will chop her into messes.° Cuckold me!
IAGO.   Oh, 'tis foul in her.   185
OTHELLO.   With mine officer!
IAGO.   That's fouler.
OTHELLO.   Get me some poison, Iago, this night. I'll not expostulate
   with her, lest her body and beauty unprovide my mind again. This
   night, Iago.   190
IAGO.   Do it not with poison, strangle her in her bed, even the bed she
   hath contaminated.
OTHELLO.   Good, good. The justice of it pleases. Very good.
IAGO.   And for Cassio, let me be his undertaker.°
   You shall hear more by midnight.   195
OTHELLO.   Excellent good. (*A trumpet within.*) What trumpet is that
   same?
IAGO.   Something from Venice, sure. 'Tis Lodovico
   Come from the Duke. And see, your wife is with him.
   (*Enter* LODOVICO, DESDEMONA, *and* ATTENDANTS.)
LODOVICO.   God save the worthy General!   200
OTHELLO.   With all my heart, sir.
LODOVICO.   The Duke and Senators of Venice greet you. (*Gives him a
   letter.*)
OTHELLO.   I kiss the instrument of their pleasures.
   (*Opens the letter, and reads.*)
DESDEMONA.   And what's the news, good Cousin Lodovico?
IAGO.   I am very glad to see you, signior.   205
   Welcome to Cyprus.
LODOVICO.   I thank you. How does Lieutenant Cassio?
IAGO.   Lives, sir.
DESDEMONA.   Cousin, there's fall'n between him and my lord
   An unkind breach, but you shall make all well.   210

---

184. messes: mincemeat [Eds.]   **194. be his undertaker:** undertake to manage his
business. In Shakespeare's plays the word does *not* mean "mortician."

OTHELLO.   Are you sure of that?
DESDEMONA.   My lord?
OTHELLO (*reads*).   "This fail you not to do, as you will—"
LODOVICO.   He did not call, he's busy in the paper.
   Is there division 'twixt my lord and Cassio?   215
DESDEMONA.   A most unhappy one. I would do much
   To atone° them, for the love I bear to Cassio.
OTHELLO.   Fire and brimstone!
DESDEMONA.   My lord?
OTHELLO.   Are you wise?°
DESDEMONA.   What, is he angry?
LODOVICO.   Maybe the letter moved him,
   For, as I think, they do command him home,   220
   Deputing Cassio in his government.
DESDEMONA.   By my troth, I am glad on 't.
OTHELLO.   Indeed!
DESDEMONA.   My lord?
OTHELLO.   I am glad to see you mad.
DESDEMONA.   Why, sweet Othello?
OTHELLO.   Devil! (*Striking her.*)
DESDEMONA.   I have not deserved this.   225
LODOVICO.   My lord, this would not be believed in Venice
   Though I should swear I saw 't. 'Tis very much.
   Make her amends, she weeps.
OTHELLO.   O devil, devil!
   If that the earth could teem with a woman's tears,
   Each drop she falls would prove a crocodile.°   230
   Out of my sight!
DESDEMONA.   I will not stay to offend you. (*Going.*)
LODOVICO.   Truly, an obedient lady.
   I do beseech your lordship, call her back.
OTHELLO.   Mistress!
DESDEMONA.   My lord?   235
OTHELLO.   What would you with her, sir?
LODOVICO.   Who, I, my lord?
OTHELLO.   Aye, you did wish that I would make her turn.
   Sir, she can turn and turn, and yet go on
   And turn again. And she can weep, sir, weep.

---

217. **atone:** reconcile   218. **Are you wise?:** i.e., in saying you bear love to Cassio
229–30. **If . . . crocodile:** If the earth could breed from woman's tears, each tear that she
lets fall would become a crocodile. It was believed that the crocodile would cry and sob to
attract the sympathetic passer-by, who was then snapped up.

And she's obedient, as you say, obedient,   240
Very obedient.—Proceed you in your tears—
Concerning this, sir—oh, well-painted passion!°—
I am commanded home.—Get you away.
I'll send for you anon.—Sir, I obey the mandate,
And will return to Venice.—Hence, avaunt! (*Exit* Desdemona.)
Cassio shall have my place. And, sir, tonight,   246
I do entreat that we may sup together.
You are welcome, sir, to Cyprus.—Goats and monkeys! (*Exit.*)
Lodovico.   Is this the noble Moor whom our full Senate
Call all-in-all sufficient? This the nature   250
Whom passion could not shake? Whose solid virtue
The shot of accident nor dart of chance
Could neither graze nor pierce?
Iago.   He is much changed.
Lodovico.   Are his wits safe? Is he not light of brain?
Iago.   He's that he is. I may not breathe my censure°   255
What he might be. If what he might he is not,
I would to Heaven he were!
Lodovico.   What, strike his wife!
Iago.   Faith, that was not so well, yet would I knew
That stroke would prove the worst!
Lodovico.   Is it his use?
Or did the letters work upon his blood,   260
And new-create this fault?
Iago.   Alas, alas!
It is not honesty in me to speak
What I have seen and known. You shall observe him,
And his own courses will denote him so
That I may save my speech. Do but go after,   265
And mark how he continues.
Lodovico.   I am sorry that I am deceived in him. (*Exeunt.*)

SCENE 2. A room in the castle.

Enter Othello *and* Emilia.

Othello.   You have seen nothing, then?
Emilia.   Nor ever heard, nor ever did suspect.
Othello.   Yes, you have seen Cassio and she together.

242. **passion:** emotion [Eds.]   255. **censure:** opinion [Eds.]

EMILIA.   But then I saw no harm, and then I heard
    Each syllable that breath made up between them.   5
OTHELLO.   What, did they never whisper?
EMILIA.   Never, my lord.
OTHELLO.   Nor send you out o' the way?
EMILIA.   Never.
OTHELLO.   To fetch her fan, her gloves, her mask, nor nothing?
EMILIA.   Never, my lord.   10
OTHELLO.   That's strange.
EMILIA.   I durst, my lord, to wager she is honest,
    Lay down my soul at stake. If you think other,
    Remove your thought, it doth abuse your bosom.
    If any wretch have put this in your head,   15
    Let Heaven requite it with the serpent's curse!
    For if she be not honest, chaste, and true,
    There's no man happy, the purest of their wives
    Is foul as slander.
OTHELLO.   Bid her come hither. Go. (*Exit* EMILIA.)
    She says enough. Yet she's a simple bawd   20
    That cannot say as much. This is a subtle whore,
    A closet lock and key of villainous secrets.
    And yet she'll kneel and pray, I have seen her do 't.
    (*Enter* DESDEMONA *with* EMILIA.)
DESDEMONA.   My lord, what is your will?
OTHELLO.   Pray, chuck, come hither.
DESDEMONA.   What is your pleasure?
OTHELLO.   Let me see your eyes.   25
    Look in my face.
DESDEMONA.   What horrible fancy's this?
OTHELLO (*to* EMILIA).   Some of your function,° mistress.
    Leave procreants alone and shut the door,
    Cough, or cry hem, if anybody come.
    Your mystery,° your mystery. Nay, dispatch. (*Exit* EMILIA.)   30
DESDEMONA.   Upon my knees, what doth your speech import?
    I understand a fury in your words,
    But not the words.
OTHELLO.   Why, what art thou?
DESDEMONA.   Your wife, my lord, your true and loyal wife.

---

27. **Some . . . function:** Get about your business, i.e., prostitution. Othello pretends that
Emilia is keeper of a brothel and Desdemona one of the women.
30. **mystery:** profession

OTHELLO.   Come, swear it, damn thyself,   35
    Lest, being like one of Heaven,° the devils themselves
    Should fear to seize thee. Therefore be double-damned.
    Swear thou art honest.
DESDEMONA.   Heaven doth truly know it.
OTHELLO.   Heaven truly knows that thou art false as Hell.
DESDEMONA.   To whom, my lord? With whom? How am I false?   40
OTHELLO.   O Desdemona! Away! Away! Away!
DESDEMONA.   Alas the heavy day! Why do you weep!
    Am I the motive of these tears, my lord?
    If haply you my father do suspect
    An instrument of this your calling-back,   45
    Lay not your blame on me. If you have lost him,
    Why, I have lost him too.
OTHELLO.   Had it pleased Heaven
    To try me with affliction, had they rained
    All kinds of sores and shames on my bare head,
    Steeped me in poverty to the very lips,   50
    Given to captivity me and my utmost hopes,
    I should have found in some place of my soul
    A drop of patience. But, alas, to make me
    A fixèd figure for the time of scorn
    To point his slow unmoving finger at!   55
    Yet could I bear that too, well, very well.
    But there where I have garnered up my heart,
    Where either I must live or bear no life,
    The fountain from the which my current runs
    Or else dries up—to be discarded thence!   60
    Or keep it as a cistern for foul toads
    To knot and gender in! Turn thy complexion there,
    Patience, thou young and rose-lipped cherubin—
    Aye, there, look grim as Hell!
DESDEMONA.   I hope my noble lord esteems me honest.   65
OTHELLO.   Oh, aye, as summer flies are in the shambles,°
    That quicken even with blowing.° O thou weed,
    Who art so lovely fair and smell'st so sweet
    That the sense aches at thee, would thou hadst ne'er been born!
DESDEMONA.   Alas, what ignorant sin have I committed?   70

---

36. being . . . Heaven: because you look like an angel   66. shambles: slaughterhouse
67. quicken . . . blowing: come to life as soon as the eggs are laid

OTHELLO.   Was this fair paper,° this most goodly book,
  Made to write "whore" upon? What committed!
  Committed! O thou public commoner!°
  I should make very forges of my cheeks
  That would to cinders burn up modesty   75
  Did I but speak thy deeds. What committed!
  Heaven stops the nose at it, and the moon winks.
  The bawdy wind, that kisses all it meets,
  Is hushed within the hollow mine of earth
  And will not hear it. What committed!   80
  Impudent strumpet!
DESDEMONA.   By Heaven, you do me wrong.
OTHELLO.   Are not you a strumpet?
DESDEMONA.   No, as I am a Christian.
  If to preserve this vessel for my lord
  From any other foul unlawful touch
  Be not to be a strumpet, I am none.   85
OTHELLO.   What, not a whore?
DESDEMONA.   No, as I shall be saved.
OTHELLO.   Is 't possible?
DESDEMONA.   Oh, Heaven forgive us!
OTHELLO.   I cry you mercy, then.
  I took you for that cunning whore of Venice
  That married with Othello. (*Raising his voice*) You mistress,   90
  That have the office opposite to Saint Peter,
  And keep the gate of Hell! (*Re-enter* EMILIA.)
                    You, you, aye, you!
  We have done our course, there's money for your pains.
  I pray you turn the key, and keep our counsel. (*Exit.*)
EMILIA.   Alas, what does this gentleman conceive?   95
  How do you, madam? How do you, my good lady?
DESDEMONA.   Faith, half-asleep.
EMILIA.   Good madam, what's the matter with my lord?
DESDEMONA.   With who?
EMILIA.   Why, with my lord, madam.   100
DESDEMONA.   Who is thy lord?
EMILIA.   He that is yours, sweet lady.
DESDEMONA.   I have none. Do not talk to me, Emilia.
  I cannot weep, nor answer have I none

---

71. fair paper: i.e., her white body   **73. public commoner:** one who offers herself to
all comers

But what should go by water.° Prithee tonight
Lay on my bed my wedding sheets. Remember,   105
And call thy husband hither.
EMILIA.   Here's a change indeed! (*Exit*.)
DESDEMONA.   'Tis meet I should be used so, very meet.
    How have I been behaved that he might stick
    The small'st opinion on my least misuse?°
    (*Re-enter* EMILIA *with* IAGO.)
IAGO.   What is your pleasure, madam? How is 't with you?   110
DESDEMONA.   I cannot tell. Those that do teach young babes
    Do it with gentle means and easy tasks.
    He might have chid me so, for, in good faith,
    I am a child to chiding.
IAGO.   What's the matter, lady?
EMILIA.   Alas, Iago, my lord hath so bewhored her,   115
    Thrown such despite and heavy terms upon her,
    As true hearts cannot bear.
DESDEMONA.   Am I that name, Iago?
IAGO.   What name, fair lady?
DESDEMONA.   Such as she says my lord did say I was.
EMILIA.   He called her whore. A beggar in his drink   120
    Could not have laid such terms upon his callet.°
IAGO.   Why did he so?
DESDEMONA.   I do not know. I am sure I am none such.
IAGO.   Do not weep, do not weep. Alas the day!
EMILIA.   Hath she forsook so many noble matches,   125
    Her father and her country and her friends,
    To be called whore? Would it not make one weep?
DESDEMONA.   It is my wretched fortune.
IAGO.   Beshrew him for 't!
    How comes this trick upon him?
DESDEMONA.   Nay, Heaven doth know.
EMILIA.   I will be hanged if some eternal villain,   130
    Some busy and insinuating rogue,
    Some cogging, cozening slave, to get some office,
    Have not devised this slander. I'll be hanged else.
IAGO.   Fie, there is no such man, it is impossible.
DESDEMONA.   If any such there be, heaven pardon him!   135

104. go by water: be expressed in tears   **109. misuse:** mistake   **121. callet:** slut
[Eds.]

EMILIA.   A halter pardon him! And Hell gnaw his bones!
    Why should he call her whore? Who keeps her company?
    What place? What time? What form? What likelihood?
    The Moor's abused by some most villainous knave,
    Some base notorious knave, some scurvy fellow.   140
    O Heaven, that such companions° Thou'dst unfold,°
    And put in every honest hand a whip
    To lash the rascals naked through the world
    Even from the east to the west!
IAGO.   Speak withindoor.°
EMILIA.   Oh, fie upon them! Some such squire he was   145
    That turned your wit the seamy side without,
    And made you to suspect me with the Moor.
IAGO.   You are a fool. Go to.°
DESDEMONA.   O good Iago,
    What shall I do to win my lord again?
    Good friend, go to him, for, by this light of Heaven,   150
    I know not how I lost him. Here I kneel.
    If e'er my will did trespass 'gainst his love
    Either in discourse of thought or actual deed,
    Or that mine eyes, mine ears, or any sense
    Delighted them in any other form,   155
    Or that I do not yet,° and ever did,
    And ever will, though he do shake me off
    To beggarly divorcement, love him dearly,
    Comfort forswear me! Unkindness may do much,
    And his unkindness may defeat my life,   160
    But never taint my love. I cannot say "whore,"
    It doth abhor me now I speak the word.
    To do the act that might the addition° earn
    Not the world's mass of vanity° could make me.
IAGO.   I pray you be content, 'tis but his humor.   165
    The business of the state does him offense,
    And he does chide with you.
DESDEMONA.   If 'twere no other—
IAGO.   'Tis but so, I warrant. (*Trumpets within.*)
    Hark how these instruments summon to supper!
    The messengers of Venice stay the meat.°   170

141. **companions:** low creatures   **unfold:** bring to light
144. **Speak withindoor:** Don't shout so loud that all the street will hear you.
148. **Go to:** an expression of derision   156. **yet:** still [Eds.]   163. **addition:** title
164. **vanity:** i.e., riches   170. **meat:** serving of supper

Go in, and weep not, all things shall be well.
(*Exeunt* DESDEMONA *and* EMILIA. *Enter* RODERIGO.)
How now, Roderigo!
RODERIGO.   I do not find that thou dealest justly with me.
IAGO.   What in the contrary?
RODERIGO.   Every day thou daffest me with some device, Iago, and
    rather, as it seems to me now, keepest from me all conveniency
    than suppliest me with the least advantage of hope. I will indeed no
    longer endure it, nor am I yet persuaded to put up in peace what al-
    ready I have foolishly suffered.   179
IAGO.   Will you hear me, Roderigo?
RODERIGO.   Faith, I have heard too much, for your words and perfor-
    mances are no kin together.
IAGO.   You charge me most unjustly.
RODERIGO.   With naught but truth. I have wasted myself out of my
    means. The jewels you have had from me to deliver to Desdemona
    would half have corrupted a votarist.° You have told me she hath
    received them, and returned me expectations and comforts of sud-
    den respect and acquaintance, but I find none.   188
IAGO.   Well, go to, very well.
RODERIGO.   Very well! Go to! I cannot go to, man, nor 'tis not very well.
    By this hand, I say 'tis very scurvy, and begin to find myself fopped
    in it.   192
IAGO.   Very well.
RODERIGO.   I tell you 'tis not very well. I will make myself known to
    Desdemona. If she will return me my jewels, I will give over my suit
    and repent my unlawful solicitation. If not, assure yourself I will seek
    satisfaction of you.   197
IAGO.   You have said now.°
RODERIGO.   Aye, and said nothing but what I protest intendment of
    doing.
IAGO.   Why, now I see there's mettle in thee, and even from this instant
    do build on thee a better opinion than ever before. Give me thy hand,
    Roderigo. Thou hast taken against me a most just exception, but yet
    I protest I have dealt most directly in thy affair.   204
RODERIGO.   It hath not appeared.
IAGO.   I grant indeed it hath not appeared, and your suspicion is not
    without wit and judgment. But, Roderigo, if thou hast that in thee
    indeed which I have greater reason to believe now than ever—I
    mean purpose, courage, and valor—this night show it. If thou the

186. votarist: nun   **198. You . . . now:** or in modern slang, "Oh yeah."

next night following enjoy not Desdemona, take me from this world
with treachery and devise engines° for my life.   211
RODERIGO.   Well, what is it? Is it within reason and compass?
IAGO.   Sir, there is especial commission come from Venice to depute
Cassio in Othello's place.
RODERIGO.   Is that true? Why, then Othello and Desdemona return
again to Venice.   216
IAGO.   Oh, no. He goes into Mauritania, and takes away with him the
fair Desdemona, unless his abode be lingered here by some accident,
wherein none can be so determinate as the removing of Cassio.
RODERIGO.   How do you mean, "removing of" him?   220
IAGO.   Why, by making him uncapable of Othello's place, knocking
out his brains.
RODERIGO.   And that you would have me to do?
IAGO.   Aye, if you dare do yourself a profit and a right. He sups tonight
with a harlotry,° and thither will I go to him. He knows not yet of
his honorable fortune. If you will watch his going thence, which I
will fashion to fall out between twelve and one, you may take him
at your pleasure. I will be near to second your attempt, and he shall
fall between us. Come, stand not amazed at it, but go along with
me. I will show you such a necessity in his death that you shall
think yourself bound to put it on him. It is now high suppertime
and the night grows to waste. About it.   232
RODERIGO.   I will hear further reason for this.
IAGO.   And you shall be satisfied. (*Exeunt.*)

SCENE 3.   *Another room in the castle.*

Enter OTHELLO, LODOVICO, DESDEMONA, EMILIA, *and* ATTENDANTS.

LODOVICO.   I do beseech you, sir, trouble yourself no further.
OTHELLO.   Oh, pardon me, 'twill do me good to walk.
LODOVICO.   Madam, good night. I humbly thank your ladyship.
DESDEMONA.   Your Honor is most welcome.
OTHELLO.   Will you walk, sir?
   Oh—Desdemona—   5
DESDEMONA.   My lord?
OTHELLO.   Get you to bed on the instant, I will be returned forthwith.
Dismiss your attendant there. Look it be done.
DESDEMONA.   I will, my lord.
   (*Exeunt* OTHELLO, LODOVICO, *and* ATTENDANTS.)

---

211. engines: instruments of torture   **225. harlotry:** harlot

EMILIA.   How goes it now? He looks gentler than he did.   10
DESDEMONA.   He says he will return incontinent.°
   He hath commanded me to go to bed,
   And bade me to dismiss you.
EMILIA.   Dismiss me!
DESDEMONA.   It was his bidding, therefore, good Emilia,
   Give me my nightly wearing, and adieu.   15
   We must not now displease him.
EMILIA.   I would you had never seen him!
DESDEMONA.   So would not I. My love doth so approve him
   That even his stubbornness, his checks, his frowns—
   Prithee, unpin me—have grace and favor in them.   20
EMILIA.   I have laid those sheets you bade me on the bed.
DESDEMONA.   All's one. Good faith, how foolish are our minds!
   If I do die before thee, prithee shroud me
   In one of those same sheets.
EMILIA.   Come, come, you talk.
DESDEMONA.   My mother had a maid called Barbary.   25
   She was in love, and he she loved proved mad
   And did forsake her. She had a song of "willow"°—
   An old thing 'twas, but it expressed her fortune,
   And she died singing it. That song tonight
   Will not go from my mind. I have much to do   30
   But to go hang my head all at one side
   And sing it like poor Barbary. Prithee, dispatch.
EMILIA.   Shall I go fetch your nightgown?
DESDEMONA.   No, unpin me here.
   This Lodovico is a proper man.
EMILIA.   A very handsome man.   35
DESDEMONA.   He speaks well.
EMILIA.   I know a lady in Venice would have walked barefoot to Pales-
   tine for a touch of his nether lip.
DESDEMONA (singing).
   "The poor soul sat sighing by a sycamore tree,
      Sing all a green willow.   40
   Her hand on her bosom, her head on her knee,
      Sing willow, willow, willow.
   The fresh streams ran by her, and murmured her moans,
      Sing willow, willow, willow.
   Her salt tears fell from her, and softened the stones—"   45

11. incontinent: immediately   **27. willow:** the emblem of the forlorn lover

Lay by these—(*singing*)
    "Sing willow, willow, willow,"
Prithee, hie thee, he'll come anon.—(*singing*)
    "Sing all a green willow must be my garland.
    Let nobody blame him, his scorn I approve—"   50
Nay, that's not next. Hark! Who is 't that knocks?
EMILIA.   It's the wind.
DESDEMONA (*singing*).
    "I called my love false love, but what said he then?
    Sing willow, willow, willow.
    If I court moe° women, you'll couch with moe men."   55
So get thee gone, good night. Mine eyes do itch.
Doth that bode weeping?
EMILIA.   'Tis neither here nor there.
DESDEMONA.   I have heard it said so. Oh, these men, these men!
Dost thou in conscience think—tell me, Emilia—
That there be women do abuse their husbands   60
In such gross kind?
EMILIA.   There be some such, no question.
DESDEMONA.   Wouldst thou do such a deed for all the world?
EMILIA.   Why, would not you?
DESDEMONA.   No, by this heavenly light!
EMILIA.   Nor I neither by this heavenly light.
I might do 't as well i' the dark.   65
DESDEMONA.   Would thou do such a deed for all the world?
EMILIA.   The world's a huge thing. It is a great price
For a small vice.
DESDEMONA.   In troth, I think thou wouldst not.
EMILIA.   In troth, I think I should, and undo 't when I had done. Marry, I
would not do such a thing for a joint ring,° nor for measures of lawn,°
nor for gowns, petticoats, nor caps, nor any petty exhibition;° but for
the whole world—why, who would not make her husband a cuckold
to make him a monarch? I should venture Purgatory for 't.   73
DESDEMONA.   Beshrew me if I would do such a wrong for the whole
world.
EMILIA.   Why, the wrong is but a wrong i' the world, and having the
world for your labor, 'tis a wrong in your own world and you might
quickly make it right.   78
DESDEMONA.   I do not think there is any such woman.

---

55. moe: more   70. joint ring: ring made in two pieces, a lover's gift   measures of
lawn: lengths of finest linen [Eds.]   71. petty exhibition: small allowance of money

EMILIA.   Yes, a dozen, and as many to the vantage as would store the
  world they played for.
  But I do think it is their husbands' faults
  If wives do fall. Say that they slack their duties
  And pour our treasures into foreign laps,
  Or else break out in peevish jealousies,   85
  Throwing restraint upon us, or say they strike us,
  Or scant our former having in despite,°
  Why, we have galls,° and though we have some grace,
  Yet have we some revenge. Let husbands know
  Their wives have sense like them. They see and smell   90
  And have their palates both for sweet and sour,
  As husbands have. What is it that they do
  When they change us for others? Is it sport?
  I think it is. And doth affection breed it?
  I think it doth. Is 't frailty that thus errs?   95
  It is so too. And have not we affections,
  Desires for sport, and frailty, as men have?
  Then let them use us well. Else let them know
  The ills we do, their ills instruct us so.
DESDEMONA.   Good night, good night. Heaven me such uses send, 100
  Not to pick bad from bad, but by bad mend! (*Exeunt.*)

ACT 5

SCENE 1. *Cyprus. A street.*

Enter IAGO *and* RODERIGO.

IAGO.   Here, stand behind this bulk, straight will he come.
  Wear thy good rapier bare, and put it home.
  Quick, quick, fear nothing. I'll be at thy elbow.
  It makes us, or it mars us. Think on that,
  And fix most firm thy resolution.   5
RODERIGO.   Be near at hand. I may miscarry in 't.
IAGO.   Here, at thy hand. Be bold, and take thy stand. (*Retires.*)
RODERIGO.   I have no great devotion to the deed,
  And yet he hath given me satisfying reasons.
  'Tis but a man gone. Forth, my sword. He dies.   10

---

87. scant . . . despite: for spite cut down our allowance   **88. galls:** bile, the cause of
bitterness

IAGO.   I have rubbed this young quat° almost to the sense,°
    And he grows angry. Now, whether he kill Cassio,
    Or Cassio him, or each do kill the other,
    Every way makes my gain. Live Roderigo,°
    He calls me to a restitution large   15
    Of gold and jewels that I bobbed from him
    As gifts to Desdemona.
    It must not be. If Cassio do remain,
    He hath a daily beauty in his life
    That makes me ugly,° and besides, the Moor   20
    May unfold me to him. There stand I in much peril.
    No, he must die. Be 't so. I hear him coming. (*Enter* CASSIO.)
RODERIGO.   I know his gait, 'tis he. Villain, thou diest!
    (*Makes a pass at* CASSIO.)
CASSIO.   That thrust had been mine enemy indeed
    But that my coat is better than thou know'st.   25
    I will make proof of thine. (*Draws, and wounds* RODERIGO.)
RODERIGO.   Oh, I am slain!
    (IAGO *from behind wounds* CASSIO *in the leg, and exits.*)
CASSIO.   I am maimed for ever. Help, ho! Murder! Murder!
    (*Falls. Enter* OTHELLO.)
OTHELLO.   The voice of Cassio. Iago keeps his word.
RODERIGO.   Oh, villain that I am!
OTHELLO.   It is even so.
CASSIO.   Oh, help, ho! Light! A surgeon!   30
OTHELLO.   'Tis he. O brave Iago, honest and just,
    That hast such noble sense of thy friend's wrong!
    Thou teachest me. Minion,° your dear friend lies dead,
    And your unblest fate hies. Strumpet, I come!
    Forth of my heart those charms, thine eyes, are blotted.   35
    Thy bed lust-stained shall with lust's blood be spotted.
    (*Exit. Enter* LODOVICO *and* GRATIANO.)
CASSIO.   What ho! No watch?° No passage?° Murder! Murder!
GRATIANO.   'Tis some mischance, the cry is very direful.
CASSIO.   Oh, help!
LODOVICO.   Hark!   40
RODERIGO.   Oh, wretched villain!

---

11. **quat:** pimple   **sense:** quick   14. **Live Roderigo:** If Roderigo lives [Eds.]
19–20. **He . . . ugly:** By comparison with him I am a poor thing. Iago is conscious of his
lack of social graces.   33. **Minion:** Darling, in a bad sense   37. **watch:** police
No passage?: Nobody passing?

LODOVICO.   Two or three groan. It is a heavy° night.
    These may be counterfeits. Let's think 't unsafe
    To come in to the cry without more help.
RODERIGO.   Nobody come? Then I shall bleed to death.   45
LODOVICO.   Hark! (*Re-enter* IAGO, *with a light.*)
GRATIANO.   Here's one comes in his shirt, with light and weapons.
IAGO.   Who's there? Whose noise is this that cries on murder?
LODOVICO.   We do not know.
IAGO.   Did not you hear a cry?
CASSIO.   Here, here! For Heaven's sake, help me!
IAGO.   What's the matter?   50
GRATIANO.   This is Othello's Ancient, as I take it.
LODOVICO.   The same indeed, a very valiant fellow.
IAGO.   What are you here that cry so grievously?
CASSIO.   Iago? Oh, I am spoiled, undone by villains! Give me some
    help.   55
IAGO.   Oh me, Lieutenant! What villains have done this?
CASSIO.   I think that one of them is hereabout,
    And cannot make away.
IAGO.   Oh, treacherous villains!
    (*To* LODOVICO *and* GRATIANO) What are you there?
    Come in and give some help.
RODERIGO.   Oh, help me here!   60
CASSIO.   That's one of them.
IAGO.   Oh, murderous slave! Oh, villain!
    (*Stabs* RODERIGO.)
RODERIGO.   Oh, damned Iago! Oh, inhuman dog!
IAGO.   Kill men i' the dark! Where be these bloody thieves?
    How silent is this town! Ho! Murder! Murder!
    What may you be? Are you of good or evil?   65
LODOVICO.   As you shall prove us, praise us.
IAGO.   Signior Lodovico?
LODOVICO.   He, sir.
IAGO.   I cry your mercy. Here's Cassio hurt by villains.
GRATIANO.   Cassio!   70
IAGO.   How is 't, brother?
CASSIO.   My leg is cut in two.
IAGO.   Marry, Heaven forbid!
    Light, gentlemen. I'll bind it with my shirt. (*Enter* BIANCA.)
BIANCA.   What is the matter, ho? Who is 't that cried?

42. **heavy:** thick

IAGO.   Who is 't that cried!   75
BIANCA.   Oh, my dear Cassio! My sweet Cassio!
    Oh, Cassio, Cassio, Cassio!
IAGO.   Oh, notable strumpet! Cassio, may you suspect
    Who they should be that have thus mangled you?
CASSIO.   No.   80
GRATIANO.   I am sorry to find you thus. I have been to seek you.
IAGO.   Lend me a garter. Oh, for a chair,
    To bear him easily hence!
BIANCA.   Alas, he faints! Oh, Cassio, Cassio, Cassio!
IAGO.   Gentlemen all, I do suspect this trash   85
    To be a party in this injury.
    Patience awhile, good Cassio. Come, come
    Lend me a light. Know we this face or no?
    Alas, my friend and my dear countryman
    Roderigo? No—yes, sure. Oh Heaven! Roderigo.   90
GRATIANO.   What, of Venice?
IAGO.   Even he, sir. Did you know him?
GRATIANO.   Know him! Aye.
IAGO.   Signior Gratiano? I cry you gentle pardon.
    These bloody accidents must excuse my manners,
    That so neglected you.
GRATIANO.   I am glad to see you.   95
IAGO.   How do you, Cassio? Oh, a chair, a chair!
GRATIANO.   Roderigo!
IAGO.   He, he, 'tis he. (*A chair brought in.*) Oh, that's well said, the chair.
    Some good man bear him carefully from hence.
    I'll fetch the General's surgeon. (*To* BIANCA) For you, mistress,   100
    Save you your labor. He that lies slain here, Cassio,
    Was my dear friend. What malice between you?
CASSIO.   None in the world, nor do I know the man.
IAGO (*to* BIANCA).   What, look you pale? Oh, bear him out o' the air.
    (CASSIO *and* RODERIGO *are borne off.*)
    Stay you, good gentlemen. Look you pale, mistress?   105
    Do you perceive the gastness of her eye?
    Nay, if you stare, we shall hear more anon.
    Behold her well, I pray you look upon her.
    Do you see, gentlemen? Nay, guiltiness will speak,
    Though tongues were out of use. (*Enter* EMILIA.)   110
EMILIA.   'Las, what's the matter? What's the matter, husband?
IAGO.   Cassio hath here been set on in the dark
    By Roderigo and fellows that are 'scaped.
    He's almost slain, and Roderigo dead.

EMILIA.   Alas, good gentleman! Alas, good Cassio!   115
IAGO.   This is the fruit of whoring. Prithee, Emilia,
   Go know of Cassio where he supped tonight.
   What, do you shake at that?
BIANCA.   He supped at my house, but I therefore shake not.
IAGO.   Oh, did he so? I charge you, go with me.   120
EMILIA.   Fie, fie upon thee, strumpet!
BIANCA.   I am no strumpet, but of life as honest
   As you that thus abuse me.
EMILIA.   As I! Foh! Fie upon thee!
IAGO.   Kind gentlemen, let's go see poor Cassio dressed.°
   Come, mistress, you must tell's another tale.   125
   Emilia, run you to the citadel,
   And tell my lord and lady what hath happened!
   Will you go on afore? I pray. (*Aside*) This is the night
   That either makes me or fordoes me quite. (*Exeunt.*)

SCENE 2. *A bedchamber in the castle.* DESDEMONA *in bed asleep, a light burning.*

   Enter OTHELLO.

OTHELLO.   It is the cause,° it is the cause, my soul.
   Let me not name it to you, you chaste stars!
   It is the cause. Yet I'll not shed her blood,
   Nor scar that whiter skin of hers than snow
   And smooth as monumental alabaster.   5
   Yet she must die, else she'll betray more men.
   Put out the light, and then put out the light.
   If I quench thee, thou flaming minister,°
   I can again thy former light restore,
   Should I repent me. But once put out thy light,   10
   Thou cunning'st° pattern of excelling nature,
   I know not where is that Promethean heat
   That can thy light relume. When I have plucked the rose,
   I cannot give it vital growth again,
   It needs must wither. I'll smell it on the tree. (*Kissing her*) 15
   Ah, balmy breath, that dost almost persuade
   Justice to break her sword! One more, one more.
   Be thus when thou art dead, and I will kill thee,

---

124. dressed: i.e., his wound dressed   **1. It . . . cause:** The meaning of the opening lines of this speech has been much discussed. The *cause* is Desdemona's supposed faithlessness; Othello, at this moment, sees himself as embodied justice, the avenger of man betrayed by woman.   **8. minister:** servant   **11. cunning'st:** most skillfully made

And love thee after. One more, and this the last.
So sweet was ne'er so fatal. I must weep,   20
But they are cruel tears. This sorrow's heavenly,
It strikes where it doth love. She wakes.
DESDEMONA.   Who's there? Othello?
OTHELLO.   Aye, Desdemona.
DESDEMONA.   Will you come to bed, my lord?
OTHELLO.   Have you prayed tonight, Desdemona?
DESDEMONA.   Aye, my lord.   25
OTHELLO.   If you bethink yourself of any crime
    Unreconciled as yet to Heaven and grace,
    Solicit for it straight.
DESDEMONA.   Alas, my lord, what may you mean by that?
OTHELLO.   Well, do it, and be brief. I will walk by.   30
    I would not kill thy unprepar**è**d spirit.
    No, Heaven forfend! I would not kill thy soul.
DESDEMONA.   Talk you of killing?
OTHELLO.   Aye, I do.
DESDEMONA.   Then Heaven
    Have mercy on me!
OTHELLO.   Amen, with all my heart!
DESDEMONA.   If you say so, I hope you will not kill me.   35
OTHELLO. Hum!
DESDEMONA.   And yet I fear you, for you are fatal then
    When your eyes roll so. Why I should fear I know not,
    Since guiltiness I know not, but yet I feel I fear.
OTHELLO.   Think on thy sins.
DESDEMONA.   They are loves I bear to you.   40
OTHELLO.   Aye, and for that thou diest.
DESDEMONA.   That death's unnatural that kills for loving.
    Alas, why gnaw you so your nether lip?
    Some bloody passion shakes your very frame.
    These are portents, but yet I hope, I hope,   45
    They do not point on me.
OTHELLO.   Peace, and be still!
DESDEMONA.   I will so. What's the matter?
OTHELLO.   That handkerchief which I so loved and gave thee
    Thou gavest to Cassio.
DESDEMONA.   No, by my life and soul!
    Send for the man, and ask him.
OTHELLO.   Sweet soul, take heed,   50
    Take heed of perjury, thou art on thy deathbed.

DESDEMONA.   Aye, but not yet to die.
OTHELLO.   Yes, presently.°
   Therefore confess thee freely of thy sin,
   For to deny each article with oath
   Cannot remove nor choke the strong conception   55
   That I do groan withal. Thou art to die.
DESDEMONA.   Then Lord have mercy on me!
OTHELLO.   I say amen.
DESDEMONA.   And have you mercy too! I never did
   Offend you in my life, never loved Cassio
   But with such general warranty of Heaven   60
   As I might love. I never gave him token.
OTHELLO.   By Heaven, I saw my handkerchief in 's hand.
   O perjured woman! Thou dost stone° my heart,
   And makest me call what I intend to do
   A murder, which I thought a sacrifice.   65
   I saw the handkerchief.
DESDEMONA.   He found it, then,
   I never gave it him. Send for him hither.
   Let him confess a truth.
OTHELLO.   He hath confessed.
DESDEMONA.   What, my lord?
OTHELLO.   That he hath used thee.
DESDEMONA.   How? Unlawfully?
OTHELLO.   Aye.   70
DESDEMONA.   He will not say so.
OTHELLO.   No, his mouth is stopped.
   Honest Iago hath ta'en order for 't.
DESDEMONA.   Oh, my fear interprets! What, is he dead?
OTHELLO.   Had all his hairs been lives, my great revenge
   Had stomach for them all.   75
DESDEMONA.   Alas, he is betrayed, and I undone!
OTHELLO.   Out, strumpet! Weep'st thou for him to my face?
DESDEMONA.   Oh, banish me, my lord, but kill me not!
OTHELLO.   Down, strumpet!
DESDEMONA.   Kill me tomorrow, let me live tonight!   80
OTHELLO.   Nay, if you strive—
DESDEMONA.   But half an hour!
OTHELLO.   Being done, there is no pause.
DESDEMONA.   But while I say one prayer!

---

52. presently: at once   **63. stone:** turn to stone

OTHELLO.   It is too late. (*He stifles her.*)
EMILIA (*within*).   My lord, my lord! What ho! My lord, my lord!
OTHELLO.   What noise is this? Not dead? Not yet quite dead?   85
    I that am cruel am yet merciful,
    I would not have thee linger in thy pain.
    So, so.
EMILIA (*within*).   What ho! My lord, my lord!
OTHELLO.   Who's there?
EMILIA (*within*).   Oh, good my lord, I would speak a word with you!
OTHELLO.   Yes, 'tis Emilia. By and by. She's dead.   90
    'Tis like she comes to speak of Cassio's death.
    The noise was here. Ha! No more moving?
    Still as the grave. Shall she come in? Were 't good?
    I think she stirs again. No. What's best to do?
    If she come in, she'll sure speak to my wife.   95
    My wife! My wife! What wife? I have no wife.
    Oh, insupportable! Oh, heavy hour!
    Methinks it should be now a huge eclipse
    Of sun and moon, and that the affrighted globe
    Should yawn° at alteration.
EMILIA (*within*).   I do beseech you   100
    That I may speak with you, O good my lord!
OTHELLO.   I had forgot thee. Oh, come in, Emilia.
    Soft, by and by. Let me the curtains° draw.
    What art thou? (*Unlocks the door. Enter* EMILIA.)
            What's the matter with thee now?
EMILIA.   Oh, my good lord, yonder's foul murders done!   105
OTHELLO.   What, now?
EMILIA.   But now, my lord.
OTHELLO.   It is the very error of the moon.
    She comes more nearer earth than she was wont
    And makes men mad.   110
EMILIA.   Cassio, my lord, hath killed a young Venetian
    Called Roderigo.
OTHELLO.   Roderigo killed!
    And Cassio killed!
EMILIA.   No, Cassio is not killed.
OTHELLO.   Not Cassio killed! Then murder's out of tune,
    And sweet revenge grows harsh.   115

---

100. yawn: split open in an earthquake [Eds.]   **103. curtains:** i.e., of the bed

DESDEMONA.   Oh, falsely, falsely murdered!
EMILIA.   Alas, what cry is that?
OTHELLO.   That! What?
EMILIA.   Out and alas! That was my lady's voice.
    Help! Help, ho! Help! O lady, speak again!
    Sweet Desdemona! O sweet mistress, speak!   120
DESDEMONA.   A guiltless death I die.
EMILIA.   Oh, who hath done this deed?
DESDEMONA.   Nobody, I myself. Farewell.
    Commend me to my kind lord. Oh, farewell! (*Dies.*)
OTHELLO.   Why, how should she be murdered?
EMILIA.   Alas, who knows? 125
OTHELLO.   You heard her say herself it was not I.
EMILIA.   She said so. I must needs report the truth.
OTHELLO.   She's like a liar gone to burning Hell.
    'Twas I that killed her.
EMILIA.   Oh, the more angel she,
    And you the blacker devil!   130
OTHELLO.   She turned to folly, and she was a whore.
EMILIA.   Thou dost belie her, and thou art a devil.
OTHELLO.   She was false as water.
EMILIA.   Thou art rash as fire to say
    That she was false. Oh, she was heavenly true!
OTHELLO.   Cassio did top her, ask thy husband else.   135
    Oh, I were damned beneath all depth in Hell
    But that I did proceed upon just grounds
    To this extremity. Thy husband knew it all.
EMILIA.   My husband!
OTHELLO.   Thy husband.   140
EMILIA.   That she was false to wedlock?
OTHELLO.   Aye, with Cassio. Nay, had she been true,
    If Heaven would make me such another world
    Of one entire and perfect chrysolite,
    I'd not have sold her for it.
EMILIA.   My husband!   145
OTHELLO.   Aye, 'twas he that told me first.
    An honest man he is, and hates the slime
    That sticks on filthy deeds.
EMILIA.   My husband!
OTHELLO.   What needs this iteration, woman? I say thy husband.
EMILIA.   Oh, mistress, villainy hath made mocks with love!   150
    My husband say that she was false!

OTHELLO.   He, woman.
    I say thy husband. Dost understand the word?
    My friend, thy husband, honest, honest Iago.
EMILIA.   If he say so, may his pernicious soul
    Rot half a grain a day! He lies to the heart.   155
    She was too fond of her most filthy bargain.
OTHELLO.   Ha!
EMILIA.   Do thy worst.
    This deed of thine is no more worthy Heaven
    Than thou wast worthy her.
OTHELLO.   Peace, you were best.   160
EMILIA.   Thou hast not half that power to do me harm
    As I have to be hurt. O gull! O dolt!
    As ignorant as dirt! Thou hast done a deed—
    I care not for thy sword, I'll make thee known,
    Though I lost twenty lives. Help! Help! ho! Help!   165
    The Moor hath killed my mistress! Murder! Murder!
    (*Enter* MONTANO, GRATIANO, IAGO, *and others.*)
MONTANO.   What is the matter? How now, General!
EMILIA.   Oh, are you come, Iago? You have done well,
    That men must lay their murders on your neck.
GRATIANO.   What is the matter?   170
EMILIA.   Disprove this villain, if thou be'st a man.
    He says thou told'st him that his wife was false.
    I know thou didst not, thou'rt not such a villain.
    Speak, for my heart is full.
IAGO.   I told him what I thought, and told no more   175
    Than what he found himself was apt and true.
EMILIA.   But did you ever tell him she was false?
IAGO.   I did.
EMILIA.   You told a lie, an odious, damnèd lie,
    Upon my soul, a lie, a wicked lie!   180
    She false with Cassio! Did you say with Cassio?
IAGO.   With Cassio, mistress. Go to, charm your tongue.°
EMILIA.   I will not charm my tongue, I am bound to speak.
    My mistress here lies murdered in her bed.
ALL.   Oh, Heavens forfend!   185
EMILIA.   And your reports have set the murder on.
OTHELLO.   Nay, stare not, masters. It is true indeed.
GRATIANO.   'Tis a strange truth.

182. **charm your tongue:** be silent

MONTANO.　Oh, monstrous act!

EMILIA.　　　　　　　Villainy, villainy, villainy!
　I think upon 't. I think I smell 't. Oh, villainy!　　　　190
　I thought so then. I'll kill myself for grief.
　Oh, villainy, villainy!

IAGO.　What, are you mad? I charge you, get you home.

EMILIA.　Good gentlemen, let me have leave to speak.
　'Tis proper I obey him, but not now.　　　　　　　195
　Perchance, Iago, I will ne'er go home.

OTHELLO.　Oh! Oh! Oh! (*Falling on the bed.*)

EMILIA.　　　　　Nay, lay thee down and roar,
　For thou has killed the sweetest innocent
　That e'er did lift up eye.

OTHELLO (*rising*).　　　Oh, she was foul!
　I scarce did know you, Uncle. There lies your niece,　200
　Whose breath indeed these hands have newly stopped.
　I know this act shows horrible and grim.

GRATIANO.　Poor Desdemona! I am glad thy father's dead.
　Thy match was mortal to him, and pure grief
　Shore his old thread in twain. Did he live now,　　205
　This sight would make him do a desperate turn—
　Yea, curse his better angel from his side,
　And fall to reprobation.°

OTHELLO.　'Tis pitiful, but yet Iago knows
　That she with Cassio hath the act of shame　　　210
　A thousand times committed. Cassio confessed it.
　And she did gratify his amorous works
　With that recognizance and pledge of love
　Which I first gave her, I saw it in his hand.
　It was a handkerchief, an antique token　　　215
　My father gave my mother.

EMILIA.　Oh, Heaven! Oh, heavenly powers!

IAGO.　'Zounds! Hold your peace.

EMILIA.　　　　　　'Twill out, 'twill out. I peace!
　No, I will speak as liberal as the north.°
　Let Heaven and men and devils, let them all,　　220
　All, all, cry shame against me, yet I'll speak.

IAGO.　Be wise, and get you home.

EMILIA.　　　　　　　I will not.
　(IAGO *offers to stab* EMILIA.)

---

208. reprobation: damnation; i.e., by self-murder　　**219. liberal . . . north:** as freely as
the north wind, which is loud and bitter

GRATIANO.   Fie!
   Your sword upon a woman!
EMILIA.   O thou dull Moor! That handkerchief thou speak'st of
   I found by fortune and did give my husband,   225
   For often with a solemn earnestness,
   More than indeed belonged to such a trifle,
   He begged of me to steal it.
IAGO.   Villainous whore!
EMILIA.   She give it Cassio! No, alas, I found it,
   And I did give 't my husband.
IAGO.   Filth, thou liest!   230
EMILIA.   By Heaven, I do not, I do not, gentlemen.
   Oh, murderous coxcomb! What should such a fool
   Do with so good a wife!
OTHELLO.   Are there no stones° in Heaven
   But what serve for the thunder? Precious villain!
   (*He runs at* IAGO. IAGO, *from behind, stabs* EMILIA, *and exits.*)
GRATIANO.   The woman falls. Sure, he hath killed his wife.   235
EMILIA.   Aye. Aye. Oh, lay me by my mistress' side.
GRATIANO.   He's gone, but his wife's killed.
MONTANO.   'Tis a notorious villain. Take you this weapon,
   Which I have here recovered from the Moor.
   Come, guard the door without, let him not pass,   240
   But kill him rather. I'll after that same villain,
   For 'tis a damnèd slave. (*Exeunt all but* OTHELLO *and* EMILIA.)
OTHELLO.   I am not valiant neither,
   But every puny whipster gets my sword.
   But why should honor outlive honesty?
   Let it go all.
EMILIA.   What did thy song bode, lady?   245
   Hark, canst thou hear me? I will play the swan,
   And die in music. (*Singing*)
        "Willow, willow, willow."
   Moor, she was chaste. She loved thee, cruel Moor,
   So come my soul to bliss as I speak true.
   So speaking as I think, I die, I die. (*Dies.*)   250
OTHELLO.   I have another weapon in this chamber.
   It is a sword of Spain, the ice brook's temper.—
   Oh, here it is. Uncle, I must come forth.
GRATIANO (*within*).   If thou attempt it, it will cost thee dear.
   Thou hast no weapon, and perforce must suffer.   255

233. stones: thunderbolts

OTHELLO.   Look in upon me then, and speak with me,
  Or, naked° as I am, I will assault thee. (*Re-enter* GRATIANO.)
GRATIANO.   What is the matter?
OTHELLO.   Behold, I have a weapon,
  A better never did itself sustain
  Upon a soldier's thigh. I have seen the day   260
  That with this little arm and this good sword
  I have made my way through more impediments
  Than twenty times your stop. But, oh, vain boast!
  Who can control his fate? 'Tis not so now.
  Be not afraid, though you do see me weaponed.   265
  Here is my journey's end, here is my butt°
  And very sea mark of my utmost sail.
  Do you go back dismayed? 'Tis a lost fear.
  Man but a rush° against Othello's breast,
  And he retires. Where should Othello go?   270
  Now, how dost thou look now? O ill-starred wench!
  Pale as thy smock! When we shall meet at compt,°
  This look of thine will hurl my soul from Heaven
  And fiends will snatch at it. Cold, cold, my girl!
  Even like thy chastity. Oh, cursèd slave!   275
  Whip me, ye devils,
  From the possession of this heavenly sight!
  Blow me about in winds! Roast me in sulphur!
  Wash me in steep-down gulfs of liquid fire!
  O Desdemona! Desdemona! Dead!   280
  Oh! Oh! Oh!
  (*Enter* LODOVICO, MONTANO, CASSIO *carried in a chair, and*
  OFFICERS *with* IAGO, *prisoner*.)
LODOVICO.   Where is this rash and most unfortunate man?
OTHELLO.   That's he that was Othello. Here I am.
LODOVICO.   Where is the viper? Bring the villain forth.
OTHELLO.   I look down toward his feet,° but that's a fable.   285
  If that thou be'st a devil, I cannot kill thee. (*Wounds* IAGO.)
LODOVICO.   Wrench his sword from him.
IAGO.   I bleed, sir, but not killed.
OTHELLO.   I am not sorry neither. I'd have thee live,
  For, in my sense, 'tis happiness to die.

---

257. **naked:** unarmed   266. **butt:** aim   269. **Man . . . rush:** Attack with only a
reed   272. **compt:** account; i.e., the Day of Judgment   285. **toward his feet:** i.e.,
to see if he has the cloven hoof of a devil

LODOVICO.   O thou Othello, that wert once so good,   290
    Fall'n in the practice° of a damnèd slave,
    What shall be said to thee?
OTHELLO.   Why, anything.
    An honorable murderer, if you will,
    For naught did I in hate, but all in honor.
LODOVICO.   This wretch hath part confessed his villainy.   295
    Did you and he consent in Cassio's death?
OTHELLO.   Aye.
CASSIO.   Dear General, I never gave you cause.
OTHELLO.   I do believe it, and I ask your pardon.
    Will you, I pray, demand that demi-devil   300
    Why he hath thus ensnared my soul and body?
IAGO.   Demand me nothing. What you know, you know.
    From this time forth I never will speak word.
LODOVICO.   What, not to pray?
GRATIANO.   Torments will ope your lips.
OTHELLO.   Well, thou dost best.   305
LODOVICO.   Sir, you shall understand what hath befall'n,
    Which, as I think, you know not. Here is a letter
    Found in the pocket of the slain Roderigo,
    And here another. The one of them imports
    The death of Cassio to be undertook   310
    By Roderigo.
OTHELLO.   Oh, villain!
CASSIO.   Most heathenish and most gross!
LODOVICO.   Now here's another discontented paper,
    Found in his pocket too. And this, it seems,
    Roderigo meant to have sent this damnèd villain   315
    But that, belike, Iago in the interim
    Came in and satisfied him.
OTHELLO.   Oh, the pernicious caitiff!
    How come you, Cassio, by that handkerchief
    That was my wife's?
CASSIO.   I found it in my chamber.
    And he himself confessed but even now   320
    That there he dropped it for a special purpose
    Which wrought to his desire.
OTHELLO.   O fool! Fool! Fool!

---

291. Fall'n . . . practice: Destroyed by the plotting

CASSIO.   There is besides in Roderigo's letter
    How he upbraids Iago, that he made him
    Brave° me upon the watch, whereon it came   325
    That I was cast.° And even but now he spake
    After long seeming dead, Iago hurt him,
    Iago set him on.
LODOVICO.   You must forsake this room, and go with us.
    Your power and your command is taken off,   330
    And Cassio rules in Cyprus. For this slave,
    If there be any cunning cruelty
    That can torment him much and hold him long,°
    It shall be his. You shall close prisoner rest
    Till that the nature of your fault be known   335
    To the Venetian state. Come, bring away.
OTHELLO.   Soft you, a word or two before you go.
    I have done the state some service, and they know 't.
    No more of that. I pray you, in your letters,
    When you shall these unlucky deeds relate,   340
    Speak of me as I am, nothing extenuate,
    Nor set down aught in malice. Then must you speak
    Of one that loved not wisely but too well;
    Of one not easily jealous, but, being wrought,
    Perplexed in the extreme; of one whose hand,   345
    Like the base Indian, threw a pearl away
    Richer than all his tribe; of one whose subdued eyes,
    Albeit unusèd to the melting mood,
    Drop tears as fast as the Arabian trees
    Their medicinable gum. Set you down this,   350
    And say besides that in Aleppo once,
    Where a malignant and a turbaned Turk
    Beat a Venetian and traduced the state,
    I took by the throat the circumcisèd dog
    And smote him, thus. (*Stabs himself.*)   355
LODOVICO.   Oh, bloody period!
GRATIANO.   All that's spoke is marred.
OTHELLO.   I kissed thee ere I killed thee. No way but this,
    Killing myself, to die upon a kiss. (*Falls on the bed, and dies.*)
CASSIO.   This did I fear, but thought he had no weapon,
    For he was great of heart.

---

325. Brave: Insult   **326. cast:** dismissed   **333. long:** i.e., in dying

LODOVICO (*to* IAGO).   O Spartan° dog,   360
    More fell° than anguish, hunger, or the sea!
    Look on the tragic loading of this bed:
    This is thy work. The object poisons sight,
    Let it be hid.° Gratiano, keep the house,
    And seize upon the fortunes of the Moor,   365
    For they succeed on you. To you, Lord Governor,
    Remains the censure of this hellish villain,
    The time, the place, the torture.
    Oh, enforce it!
    Myself will straight aboard, and to the state   370
    This heavy act with heavy heart relate. (*Exeunt.*)

QUESTIONS

1. In what ways is Othello, in the first two acts, shown to be a person of extraordinary quality?
2. Is Othello a person jealous "by nature"? Does he show any disposition to jealousy in the first two acts? What does he say about himself in his final soliloquy? (There has been much critical controversy over the psychological probability of Othello's being roused so quickly to such a high pitch of jealousy in Act 3. Some have explained it by attributing a predisposition to jealousy in Othello; others have attributed it to the almost superhuman Machiavellian cleverness of Iago, which would have taken in any husband. In general, however, Shakespeare was less interested in psychological consistency and the subtle tracing of motivation—which are modern interests—than he was in theatrical effectiveness and the orchestration of emotions. Perhaps the question we should properly ask is not "How probable is Othello's jealousy?" but "How vital and effective has Shakespeare rendered it?")
3. Who is more naturally suspicious of human nature—Othello or Iago?
4. Is something of Othello's nobility manifested even in the scale of his jealousy? How does he respond to his conviction that Desdemona has been unfaithful to him? Would a lesser man have responded in the same way? Why or why not?
5. How does Othello's final speech reestablish his greatness?
6. What are Iago's motivations in his actions toward Othello, Cassio, and Roderigo? What is his philosophy? How does his technique in handling Roderigo differ from his technique in handling Othello and Cassio? Why?
7. In rousing Othello's suspicions against Desdemona (3.3), Iago uses the same technique, in part, that he had used with Othello in inculpating

---

360. Spartan: i.e., hardhearted   **361. fell:** cruel   **364. Let . . . hid:** At these words the curtains are closed across the inner stage (or chamber, if this scene was acted aloft), concealing all three bodies.

Cassio (2.3) and that he later uses with Lodovico in inculpating Othello (4.2). What is this technique? Why is it effective? How does he change his tactics in the opening of 4.1?

8. What opinions of Iago, before his exposure, are expressed by Othello, Desdemona, Cassio, and Lodovico? Is Othello the only one taken in by him? Does his own wife think him capable of villainy?

9. Though Othello is the protagonist, the majority of soliloquies and asides are given to Iago. Why?

10. The difference between Othello and Desdemona that Iago plays on most is that of color, and, reading the play today, we may be tempted to see the play as being centrally about race relations. However, only one other character, besides Othello, makes much of this difference in color. Which one? Is this character sympathetically portrayed? What attitude toward Othello himself, and his marriage, is taken by the Duke, Cassio, Lodovico, Emilia, Desdemona herself? What differences between Othello and Desdemona, besides color, are used by Iago to undermine Othello's confidence in Desdemona's fidelity? What differences between them does Othello himself take into account?

11. What are Desdemona's principal character traits? In what ways are she and Emilia character foils? Is she entirely discreet in pleading Cassio's case to Othello? Why or why not? Why does she lie about the handkerchief (3.4)?

12. Like Sophocles in *Oedipus Rex*, Shakespeare makes extensive use of dramatic irony in this play. Point out effective examples.

13. Unlike *Oedipus Rex*, *Othello* contains comedy. For what purposes is it used? What larger difference in effect between *Othello* and *Oedipus Rex* does this use of comedy contribute to?

14. Find several occasions when chance and coincidence are involved in the plot (for example, Bianca's entry in 4.1). How important are these to the development of the plot? To what extent do they *cause* subsequent events to happen?

15. As much responsible as any other quality for the original popularity and continued vitality of *Othello* is its poetry. What are some of the prominent characteristics of that poetry (language, imagery, rhythm)? What speeches are particularly memorable or effective? Though most of the play is written in blank verse, some passages are written in rhymed iambic pentameter couplets and others in prose. Can you suggest any reasons for Shakespeare's use of these other mediums?

16. How would the effect of the play have been different if Othello had died *before* discovering Desdemona's innocence?

Molière

Tartuffe

or The Impostor

Characters

MADAME PERNELLE, *Orgon's mother*
ORGON, *Elmire's husband*
ELMIRE, *Orgon's second wife*
DAMIS, *Orgon's son, Elmire's stepson*
MARIANE, *Orgon's daughter, Elmire's stepdaughter, in love with Valère*
VALÈRE, *in love with Mariane*
CLÉANTE, *Orgon's brother-in-law, Elmire's brother*
TARTUFFE, *a hypocrite*
DORINE, *Mariane's lady's-maid*
MONSIEUR LOYAL, *a bailiff*
A POLICE OFFICER
FLIPOTE, *Mme. Pernelle's maid*

The scene throughout is a room in Orgon's house in Paris.

ACT 1

SCENE 1

Enter MADAME PERNELLE, FLIPOTE, ELMIRE, DORINE, CLÉANTE, MARIANE, *and* DAMIS.

MADAME PERNELLE.   Come, come, Flipote; it's time I left this place.

TARTUFFE, OR THE IMPOSTOR   First performed in Paris in 1669 (two earlier versions of the play, in 1664 and 1667, were banned by authorities on religious grounds), during the reign of "the Sun King," Louis XIV, a time in social and aristocratic circles when great emphasis was placed on elegance in dress, manners, and taste. Translated by Richard Wilbur. Molière (1622–73) was born Jean-Baptiste Poquelin in Paris and was given excellent schooling by his father, a successful furniture maker with a position at court. He took "Molière" as his stage-name when, at the age of twenty-one, he joined a traveling theater company. The rest of his life was spent in the theater as actor, manager, and author. Though twice sent to prison for debts, and often in trouble with the civil authorities for his satiric writing, he enjoyed a certain amount of royal favor after his establishment in Paris in 1658, when the king provided him with a theater where he worked for the rest of his life. In his productions of *Tartuffe* Molière took the role of Orgon.

ELMIRE.   I can't keep up, you walk at such a pace.
MADAME PERNELLE.   Don't trouble, child; no need to show me out.
   It's not your manners I'm concerned about.
ELMIRE.   We merely pay you the respect we owe.   5
   But, Mother, why this hurry? Must you go?
MADAME PERNELLE.   I must. This house appalls me. No one in it
   Will pay attention for a single minute.
   Children, I take my leave much vexed in spirit.
   I offer good advice, but you won't hear it.   10
   You all break in and chatter on and on.
   It's like a madhouse with the keeper gone.
DORINE.   If . . .
MADAME PERNELLE.   Girl, you talk too much, and I'm afraid
   You're far too saucy for a lady's-maid.
   You push in everywhere and have your say.   15
DAMIS.   But . . .
MADAME PERNELLE.   You, boy, grow more foolish every day.
   To think my grandson should be such a dunce!
   I've said a hundred times, if I've said it once,
   That if you keep the course on which you've started,
   You'll leave your worthy father broken-hearted.   20
MARIANE.   I think . . .
MADAME PERNELLE.   And you, his sister, seems so pure,
   So shy, so innocent, and so demure.
   But you know what they say about still waters.
   I pity parents with secretive daughters.
ELMIRE.   Now, Mother . . .
MADAME PERNELLE.   And as for you, child, let me add   25
   That your behavior is extremely bad,
   And a poor example for these children, too.
   Their dear, dead mother did far better than you.
   You're much too free with money, and I'm distressed
   To see you so elaborately dressed.   30
   When it's one's husband that one aims to please,
   One has no need of costly fripperies.
CLÉANTE.   Oh, Madam, really . . .
MADAME PERNELLE.   You are her brother, Sir,
   And I respect and love you; yet if I were
   My son, this lady's good and pious spouse,   35
   I wouldn't make you welcome in my house.
   You're full of worldly counsels which, I fear,
   Aren't suitable for decent folk to hear.

    I've spoken bluntly, Sir; but it behooves us
    Not to mince words when righteous fervor moves us.   40
DAMIS.   Your man Tartuffe is full of holy speeches . . .
MADAME PERNELLE.   And practices precisely what he preaches.
    He's a fine man, and should be listened to.
    I will not hear him mocked by fools like you.
DAMIS.   Good God! Do you expect me to submit   45
    To the tyranny of that carping hypocrite?
    Must we forgo all joys and satisfactions
    Because that bigot censures all our actions?
DORINE.   To hear him talk—and he talks all the time—
    There's nothing one can do that's not a crime.   50
    He rails at everything, your dear Tartuffe.
MADAME PERNELLE.   Whatever he reproves deserves reproof.
    He's out to save your souls, and all of you
    Must love him, as my son would have you do.
DAMIS.   Ah no, Grandmother, I could never take   55
    To such a rascal, even for my father's sake.
    That's how I feel, and I shall not dissemble.
    His every action makes me seethe and tremble
    With helpless anger, and I have no doubt
    That he and I will shortly have it out.   60
DORINE.   Surely it is a shame and a disgrace
    To see this man usurp the master's place—
    To see this beggar who, when first he came,
    Had not a shoe or shoestring to his name
    So far forget himself that he behaves   65
    As if the house were his, and we his slaves.
MADAME PERNELLE.   Well, mark my words, your souls would fare far
      better
    If you obeyed his precepts to the letter.
DORINE.   You see him as a saint. I'm far less awed;
    In fact, I see right through him. He's a fraud.   70
MADAME PERNELLE.   Nonsense!
DORINE.   His man Laurent's the same, or worse;
    I'd not trust either with a penny purse.
MADAME PERNELLE.   I can't say what his servant's morals may be;
    His own great goodness I can guarantee.
    You all regard him with distaste and fear   75
    Because he tells you what you're loath to hear,
    Condemns your sins, points out your moral flaws,
    And humbly strives to further Heaven's cause.

DORINE.   If sin is all that bothers him, why is it
    He's so upset when folk drop in to visit?   80
    Is Heaven so outraged by a social call
    That he must prophesy against us all?
    I'll tell you what I think: if you ask me,
    He's jealous of my mistress' company.
MADAME PERNELLE.   Rubbish! (*To* ELMIRE) He's not alone, child, in
    complaining   85
    Of all your promiscuous entertaining.
    Why, the whole neighborhood's upset, I know,
    By all these carriages that come and go,
    With crowds of guests parading in and out
    And noisy servants loitering about.   90
    In all of this, I'm sure there's nothing vicious;
    But why give people cause to be suspicious?
CLÉANTE.   They need no cause; they'll talk in any case.
    Madam, this world would be a joyless place
    If, fearing what malicious tongues might say,   95
    We locked our doors and turned our friends away.
    And even if one did so dreary a thing,
    D'you think those tongues would cease their chattering?
    One can't fight slander; it's a losing battle;
    Let us instead ignore their tittle-tattle.   100
    Let's strive to live by conscience' clear decrees,
    And let the gossips gossip as they please.
DORINE.   If there is talk against us, I know the source:
    It's Daphne and her little husband, of course.
    Those who have greatest cause for guilt and shame   105
    Are quickest to besmirch a neighbor's name.
    When there's a chance for libel, they never miss it;
    When something can be made to seem illicit
    They're off at once to spread the joyous news,
    Adding to fact what fantasies they choose.   110
    By talking up their neighbor's indiscretions
    They seek to camouflage their own transgressions,
    Hoping that others' innocent affairs
    Will lend a hue of innocence to theirs,
    Or that their own black guilt will come to seem   115
    Part of a general shady color-scheme.
MADAME PERNELLE.   All that is quite irrelevant. I doubt
    That anyone's more virtuous and devout
    Than dear Orante; and I'm informed that she

Condemns your mode of life most vehemently.   120
DORINE.   Oh, yes, she's strict, devout, and has no taint
     Of worldliness; in short, she seems a saint.
     But it was time which taught her that disguise;
     She's thus because she can't be otherwise.
     So long as her attractions could enthrall,   125
     She flounced and flirted and enjoyed it all,
     But now that they're no longer what they were
     She quits a world which fast is quitting her,
     And wears a veil of virtue to conceal
     Her bankrupt beauty and her lost appeal.   130
     That's what becomes of old coquettes today:
     Distressed when all their lovers fall away,
     They see no recourse but to play the prude,
     And so confer a style on solitude.
     Thereafter, they're severe with everyone,   135
     Condemning all our actions, pardoning none,
     And claiming to be pure, austere, and zealous
     When, if the truth were known, they're merely jealous,
     And cannot bear to see another know
     The pleasures time has forced them to forgo.   140
MADAME PERNELLE (*initially to* ELMIRE).   That sort of talk is what you
     like to hear;
     Therefore you'd have us all keep still, my dear,
     While Madam rattles on the livelong day.
     Nevertheless, I mean to have my say.
     I tell you that you're blest to have Tartuffe   145
     Dwelling, as my son's guest, beneath this roof;
     That Heaven has sent him to forestall its wrath
     By leading you, once more, to the true path;
     That all he reprehends is reprehensible,
     And that you'd better heed him, and be sensible.   150
     These visits, balls, and parties in which you revel
     Are nothing but inventions of the Devil.
     One never hears a word that's edifying:
     Nothing but chaff and foolishness and lying,
     As well as vicious gossip in which one's neighbor   155
     Is cut to bits with epee, foil, and saber.
     People of sense are driven half-insane
     At such affairs, where noise and folly reign
     And reputations perish thick and fast.
     As a wise preacher said on Sunday last,   160
     Parties are Towers of Babylon, because

The guests all babble on with never a pause;
And then he told a story which, I think . . .
(*To* CLÉANTE) I heard that laugh, Sir, and I saw that wink!
Go find your silly friends and laugh some more!   165
Enough; I'm going; don't show me to the door.
I leave this household much dismayed and vexed;
I cannot say when I shall see you next.
(*Slapping* FLIPOTE) Wake up, don't stand there gaping into space!
I'll slap some sense into that stupid face.   170
Move, move, you slut. (*Exeunt* MADAME PERNELLE, FLIPOTE,
   ELMIRE, MARIANE, *and* DAMIS.)

SCENE 2*

CLÉANTE.   I think I'll stay behind;
   I want no further pieces of her mind.
   How that old lady . . .
DORINE.   Oh, what wouldn't she say
   If she could hear you speak of her that way!
   She'd thank you for the *lady*, but I'm sure   5
   She'd find the *old* a little premature.
CLÉANTE.   My, what a scene she made, and what a din!
   And how this man Tartuffe has taken her in!
DORINE.   Yes, but her son is even worse deceived;
   His folly must be seen to be believed.   10
   In the late troubles, he played an able part
   And served his king with wise and loyal heart,
   But he's quite lost his senses since he fell
   Beneath Tartuffe's infatuating spell.
   He calls him brother, and loves him as his life,   15
   Preferring him to mother, child, or wife.
   In him and him alone will he confide;
   He's made him his confessor and his guide;
   He pets and pampers him with love more tender
   Than any pretty mistress could engender,   20
   Gives him the place of honor when they dine,
   Delights to see him gorging like a swine,
   Stuffs him with dainties till his guts distend,

---

*In English and in most modern plays, a "scene" is a continuous section of the action in one setting, and acts are not usually divided into scenes unless there is a shift in setting or a shift in time. In older French drama, however, a scene is any portion of the play involving one group of characters, and a new scene begins, without interruption of the action, whenever any important character enters or exits.

And when he belches, cries "God bless you, friend!"
In short, he's mad; he worships him; he dotes;   25
His deeds he marvels at, his words he quotes,
Thinking each act a miracle, each word
Oracular as those that Moses heard.
Tartuffe, much pleased to find so easy a victim,
Has in a hundred ways beguiled and tricked him,   30
Milked him of money, and with his permission
Established here a sort of Inquisition.
Even Laurent, his lackey, dares to give
Us arrogant advice on how to live;
He sermonizes us in thundering tones   35
And confiscates our ribbons and colognes.
Last week he tore a kerchief into pieces
Because he found it pressed in a *Life of Jesus:*
He said it was a sin to juxtapose
Unholy vanities and holy prose.   40

SCENE 3

Enter ELMIRE, MARIANE, *and* DAMIS.

ELMIRE (*to* CLÉANTE).   You did well not to follow; she stood in the door
And said *verbatim* all she'd said before.
I saw my husband coming. I think I'd best
Go upstairs now, and take a little rest.
CLÉANTE.   I'll wait and greet him here; then I must go.   5
I've really only time to say hello.
DAMIS.   Sound him about my sister's wedding, please.
I think Tartuffe's against it, and that he's
Been urging Father to withdraw his blessing.
As you well know, I'd find that most distressing.   10
Unless my sister and Valère can marry,
My hopes to wed *his* sister will miscarry,
And I'm determined . . .
DORINE.   He's coming. (*Exeunt* ELMIRE, MARIANE,
    and DAMIS.)

SCENE 4

Enter ORGON.

ORGON.   Ah, Brother, good-day.
CLÉANTE.   Well, welcome back. I'm sorry I can't stay.
How was the country? Blooming, I trust, and green?

ORGON.   Excuse me, Brother; just one moment.
   (*To* DORINE)   Dorine . . .
   (*To* CLÉANTE) To put my mind at rest, I always learn   5
   The household news the moment I return.
   (*To* DORINE) Has all been well, these two days I've been gone?
   How are the family? What's been going on?
DORINE.   Your wife, two days ago, had a bad fever,
   And a fierce headache which refused to leave her.   10
ORGON.   Ah. And Tartuffe?
DORINE.   Tartuffe? Why, he's round and red,
   Bursting with health, and excellently fed.
ORGON.   Poor fellow!
DORINE.   That night, the mistress was unable
   To take a single bite at the dinner-table.
   Her headache-pains, she said, were simply hellish.   15
ORGON.   Ah. And Tartuffe?
DORINE.   He ate his meal with relish,
   And zealously devoured in her presence
   A leg of mutton and a brace of pheasants.
ORGON.   Poor fellow!
DORINE.   Well, the pains continued strong,
   And so she tossed and tossed the whole night long,   20
   Now icy-cold, now burning like a flame.
   We sat beside her bed till morning came.
ORGON.   Ah. And Tartuffe?
DORINE.   Why, having eaten, he rose
   And sought his room, already in a doze,
   Got into his warm bed, and snored away   25
   In perfect peace until the break of day.
ORGON.   Poor fellow!
DORINE.   After much ado, we talked her
   Into dispatching someone for the doctor.
   He bled her, and the fever quickly fell.
ORGON.   Ah. And Tartuffe?
DORINE.   He bore it very well.   30
   To keep his cheerfulness at any cost,
   And make up for the blood *Madame* had lost,
   He drank, at lunch, four beakers full of port.
ORGON.   Poor fellow!
DORINE.   Both are doing well, in short.
   I'll go and tell *Madame* that you've expressed   35
   Keen sympathy and anxious interest. (*Exit.*)

SCENE 5

CLÉANTE.   That girl was laughing in your face, and though
    I've no wish to offend you, even so
    I'm bound to say that she had some excuse.
    How can you possibly be such a goose?
    Are you so dazed by this man's hocus-pocus   5
    That all the world, save him, is out of focus?
    You've given him clothing, shelter, food, and care;
    Why must you also . . .
ORGON.   Brother, stop right there.
    You do not know the man of whom you speak.
CLÉANTE.   I grant you that. But my judgment's not so weak   10
    That I can't tell, by his effect on others . . .
ORGON.   Ah, when you meet him, you two will be like brothers!
    There's been no loftier soul since time began.
    He is a man who . . . a man who . . . an excellent man.
    To keep his precepts is to be reborn,   15
    And view this dunghill of a world with scorn.
    Yes, thanks to him I'm a changed man indeed.
    Under his tutelage my soul's been freed
    From earthly loves, and every human tie:
    My mother, children, brother, and wife could die,   20
    And I'd not feel a single moment's pain.
CLÉANTE.   That's a fine sentiment, Brother; most humane.
ORGON.   Oh, had you seen Tartuffe as I first knew him,
    Your heart, like mine, would have surrendered to him.
    He used to come into our church each day   25
    And humbly kneel nearby, and start to pray.
    He'd draw the eyes of everybody there
    By the deep fervor of his heartfelt prayer;
    He'd sigh and weep, and sometimes with a sound
    Of rapture he would bend and kiss the ground;   30
    And when I rose to go, he'd run before
    To offer me holy-water at the door.
    His serving-man, no less devout than he,
    Informed me of his master's poverty;
    I gave him gifts, but in his humbleness   35
    He'd beg me every time to give him less.
    "Oh, that's too much," he'd cry, "too much by twice!
    I don't deserve it. The half, Sir, would suffice."
    And when I wouldn't take it back, he'd share

Half of it with the poor, right then and there.   40
At length, Heaven prompted me to take him in
To dwell with us, and free our souls from sin.
He guides our lives, and to protect my honor
Stays by my wife, and keeps an eye upon her;
He tells me whom she sees, and all she does,   45
And seems more jealous than I ever was!
And how austere he is! Why, he can detect
A mortal sin where you would least suspect;
In smallest trifles, he's extremely strict.
Last week, his conscience was severely pricked   50
Because, while praying, he had caught a flea
And killed it, so he felt, too wrathfully.
CLÉANTE.   Good God, man! Have you lost your common sense—
Or is this all some joke at my expense?
How can you stand there and in all sobriety . . .   55
ORGON.   Brother, your language savors of impiety.
Too much free-thinking's made your faith unsteady,
And as I've warned you many times already,
'Twill get you into trouble before you're through.
CLÉANTE.   So I've been told before by dupes like you: 60
Being blind, you'd have all others blind as well;
The clear-eyed man you call an infidel,
And he who sees through humbug and pretense
Is charged, by you, with want of reverence.
Spare me your warnings, Brother; I have no fear   65
Of speaking out, for you and Heaven to hear,
Against affected zeal and pious knavery.
There's true and false in piety, as in bravery,
And just as those whose courage shines the most
In battle, are the least inclined to boast,   70
So those whose hearts are truly pure and lowly
Don't make a flashy show of being holy.
There's a vast difference, so it seems to me,
Between true piety and hypocrisy:
How do you fail to see it, may I ask?   75
Is not a face quite different from a mask?
Cannot sincerity and cunning art,
Reality and semblance, be told apart?
Are scarecrows just like men, and do you hold
That a false coin is just as good as gold?   80
Ah, Brother, man's a strangely fashioned creature

Who seldom is content to follow Nature,
But recklessly pursues his inclination
Beyond the narrow bounds of moderation,
And often, by transgressing Reason's laws,   85
Perverts a lofty aim or noble cause.
A passing observation, but it applies.
ORGON.   I see, dear Brother, that you're profoundly wise;
You harbor all the insight of the age.
You are our one clear mind, our only sage,   90
The era's oracle, its Cato too,
And all mankind are fools compared to you.
CLÉANTE.   Brother, I don't pretend to be a sage,
Nor have I all the wisdom of the age.
There's just one insight I would dare to claim: 95
I know that true and false are not the same;
And just as there is nothing I more revere
Than a soul whose faith is steadfast and sincere,
Nothing that I more cherish and admire
Than honest zeal and true religious fire,   100
So there is nothing that I find more base
Than specious piety's dishonest face—
Than these bold mountebanks, these histrios
Whose impious mummeries and hollow shows
Exploit our love of Heaven, and make a jest   105
Of all that men think holiest and best;
These calculating souls who offer prayers
Not to their Maker, but as public wares,
And seek to buy respect and reputation
With lifted eyes and sighs of exaltation;   110
These charlatans, I say, whose pilgrim souls
Proceed, by way of Heaven, toward earthly goals,
Who weep and pray and swindle and extort,
Who preach the monkist life, but haunt the court,
Who make their zeal the partner of their vice—   115
Such men are vengeful, sly, and cold as ice,
And when there is an enemy to defame
They cloak their spite in fair religion's name,
Their private spleen and malice being made
To seem a high and virtuous crusade,   120
Until, to mankind's reverent applause,
They crucify their foe in Heaven's cause.
Such knaves are all too common; yet, for the wise,
True piety isn't hard to recognize,

And, happily, these present times provide us   125
With bright examples to instruct and guide us.
Consider Ariston and Périandre;
Look at Oronte, Alcidamas, Clitandre;
Their virtue is acknowledged; who could doubt it?
But you won't hear them beat the drum about it.   130
They're never ostentatious, never vain,
And their religion's moderate and humane;
It's not their way to criticize and chide:
They think censoriousness a mark of pride,
And therefore, letting others preach and rave,   135
They show, by deeds, how Christians should behave.
They think no evil of their fellow man,
But judge of him as kindly as they can.
They don't intrigue and wangle and conspire;
To lead a good life is their one desire;   140
The sinner wakes no rancorous hate in them;
It is the sin alone which they condemn;
Nor do they try to show a fiercer zeal
For Heaven's cause than Heaven itself could feel.
These men I honor, these men I advocate   145
As models for us all to emulate.
Your man is not their sort at all, I fear:
And, while your praise of him is quite sincere,
I think that you've been dreadfully deluded.

ORGON.   Now then, dear Brother, is your speech concluded?   150
CLÉANTE.   Why yes.
ORGON.   Your servant, Sir. (*He turns to go.*)
CLÉANTE.   No, Brother; wait.
There's one more matter. You agreed of late
That young Valère might have your daughter's hand.
ORGON.   I did.
CLÉANTE.   And set the date, I understand.
ORGON.   Quite so.
CLÉANTE.   You've now postponed it; is that true?   155
ORGON.   No doubt.
CLÉANTE.   The match no longer pleases you?
ORGON.   Who knows?
CLÉANTE.   D'you mean to go back on your word?
ORGON.   I won't say that.
CLÉANTE.   Has anything occurred
Which might entitle you to break your pledge?
ORGON.   Perhaps.

CLÉANTE.   Why must you hem, and haw, and hedge?   160
    The boy asked me to sound you in this affair . . .
ORGON.   It's been a pleasure.
CLÉANTE.   But what shall I tell Valère?
ORGON.   Whatever you like.
CLÉANTE.   But what have you decided?
    What are your plans?
ORGON.   I plan, Sir, to be guided
    By Heaven's will.
CLÉANTE.   Come, Brother, don't talk rot.   165
    You've given Valère your word; will you keep it, or not?
ORGON.   Good day.
CLÉANTE.   This looks like poor Valère's undoing;
    I'll go and warn him that there's trouble brewing. (*Exit.*)

ACT 2

SCENE 1

Enter MARIANE.

ORGON.   Mariane.
MARIANE.   Yes, Father?
ORGON.   A word with you; come here.
MARIANE.   What are you looking for?
ORGON (*peering into a small closet*).   Eavesdroppers, dear.
    I'm making sure we shan't be overheard.
    Someone in there could catch our every word.
    Ah, good, we're safe. Now, Mariane, my child,   5
    You're a sweet girl who's tractable and mild,
    Whom I hold dear, and think most highly of.
MARIANE.   I'm deeply grateful, Father, for your love.
ORGON.   That's well said, Daughter; and you can repay me
    If, in all things, you'll cheerfully obey me.   10
MARIANE.   To please you, Sir, is what delights me best.
ORGON.   Good, good. Now, what d'you think of Tartuffe, our guest?
MARIANE.   I, Sir?
ORGON.   Yes, Weigh your answer; think it through.
MARIANE.   Oh, dear. I'll say whatever you wish me to.
ORGON.   That's wisely said, my Daughter. Say of him, then,   15
    That he's the very worthiest of men,
    And that you're fond of him, and would rejoice

In being his wife, if that should be my choice.
Well?
MARIANE.   What?
ORGON.   What's that?
MARIANE.   I . . .
ORGON.   Well?
MARIANE.   Forgive me, pray.
ORGON.   Did you not hear me?
MARIANE.   Of *whom*, Sir, must I say   20
    That I am fond of him, and would rejoice
    In being his wife, if that should be your choice?
ORGON.   Why, of Tartuffe.
MARIANE.   But, Father, that's false, you know.
    Why would you have me say what isn't so?
ORGON.   Because I am resolved it shall be true.   25
    That it's my wish should be enough for you.
MARIANE.   You can't mean, father . . .
ORGON.   Yes, Tartuffe shall be
    Allied by marriage to this family,
    And he's to be your husband, is that clear?
    It's a father's privilege . . .   30

SCENE 2

Enter DORINE.
ORGON (*to* DORINE).   What are you doing in here?
    Is curiosity so fierce a passion
    With you, that you must eavesdrop in this fashion?
DORINE.   There's lately been a rumor going about—
    Based on some hunch or chance remark, no doubt—   5
    That you mean Mariane to wed Tartuffe.
    I've laughed it off, of course, as just a spoof.
ORGON.   You find it so incredible?
DORINE.   Yes, I do.
    I won't accept that story, even from you.
ORGON.   Well, you'll believe it when the thing is done.   10
DORINE.   Yes, yes, of course. Go on and have your fun.
ORGON.   I've never been more serious in my life.
DORINE.   Ha!
ORGON.   Daughter, I mean it; you're to be his wife.
DORINE.   No, don't believe your father; it's all a hoax.
ORGON.   See here, young woman . . .

DORINE.   Come, Sir, no more jokes;   15
  You can't fool us.
ORGON.   How dare you talk this way?
DORINE.   All right, then: we believe you, sad to say.
  But how a man like you, who looks so wise
  And wears a moustache of such splendid size,
  Can be so foolish as to . . .
ORGON.   Silence, please!   20
  My girl, you take too many liberties,
  I'm master here, as you must not forget.
DORINE.   Do let's discuss this calmly; don't be upset.
  You can't be serious, Sir, about this plan.
  What should that bigot want with Mariane?   25
  Praying and fasting ought to keep him busy.
  And then, in terms of wealth and rank, what is he?
  Why should a man of property like you
  Pick out a beggar son-in-law?
ORGON.   That will do.
  Speak of his poverty with reverence.   30
  His is a pure and saintly indigence
  Which far transcends all worldly pride and pelf.
  He lost his fortune, as he says himself,
  Because he cared for Heaven alone, and so
  Was careless of his interests here below.   35
  I mean to get him out of his present straits
  And help him to recover his estates—
  Which, in his part of the world, have no small fame.
  Poor though he is, he's a gentleman just the same.
DORINE.   Yes, so he tells us; and, Sir, it seems to me   40
  Such pride goes very ill with piety.
  A man whose spirit spurns this dungy earth
  Ought not to brag of lands and noble birth;
  Such worldly arrogance will hardly square
  With meek devotion and the life of prayer.   45
  . . . But this approach, I see, has drawn a blank;
  Let's speak, then, of his person, not his rank.
  Doesn't it seem to you a trifle grim
  To give a girl like her to a man like him?
  When two are so ill-suited, can't you see   50
  What the sad consequence is bound to be?
  A young girl's virtue is imperilled, Sir,
  When such a marriage is imposed on her;
  For if one's bridegroom isn't to one's taste,

It's hardly an inducement to be chaste,   55
And many a man with horns upon his brow
Has made his wife·the thing that she is now.
It's hard to be a faithful wife, in short,
To certain husbands of a certain sort,
And he who gives his daughter to a man she hates   60
Must answer for her sins at Heaven's gates.
Think, Sir, before you play so risky a role.

ORGON.   This servant-girl presumes to save my soul!

DORINE.   You would do well to ponder what I've said.

ORGON.   Daughter, we'll disregard this dunderhead.   65
Just trust your father's judgment. Oh, I'm aware
That I once promised you to young Valère;
But now I hear he gambles, which greatly shocks me;
What's more, I've doubts about his orthodoxy.
His visits to church, I note, are very few.   70

DORINE.   Would you have him go at the same hours as you,
And kneel nearby, to be sure of being seen?

ORGON.   I can dispense with such remarks, Dorine.
(To MARIANE) Tartuffe, however, is sure of Heaven's blessing,
And that's the only treasure worth possessing.   75
This match will bring you joys beyond all measure;
Your cup will overflow with every pleasure;
You two will interchange your faithful loves
Like two sweet cherubs, or two turtle-doves.
No harsh word shall be heard, no frown be seen,   80
And he shall make you happy as a queen.

DORINE.   And she'll make him a cuckold, just wait and see.

ORGON.   What language!

DORINE.   Oh, he's a man of destiny;
He's *made* for horns, and what the stars demand
Your daughter's virtue surely can't withstand.   85

ORGON.   Don't interrupt me further. Why can't you learn
That certain things are none of your concern?

DORINE.   It's for your own sake that I interfere. (*She repeatedly
interrupts* ORGON *just as he is turning to speak to his daughter.*)

ORGON.   Most kind of you. Now, hold your tongue, d'you hear?

DORINE.   If I didn't love you . . .

ORGON.   Spare me your affection.   90

DORINE.   I love you, Sir, in spite of your objection.

ORGON.   Blast!

DORINE.   I can't bear, Sir, for your honor's sake,
To let you make this ludicrous mistake.

ORGON.   You mean to go on talking?

DORINE.   If I didn't protest
   This sinful marriage, my conscience couldn't rest.   95

ORGON.   If you don't hold your tongue, you little shrew . . .

DORINE.   What, lost your temper? A pious man like you?

ORGON.   Yes! Yes! You talk and talk. I'm maddened by it.
   Once and for all, I tell you to be quiet.

DORINE.   Well, I'll be quiet. But I'll be thinking hard.   100

ORGON.   Think all you like, but you had better guard
   That saucy tongue of yours, or I'll . . .
   (*Turning back to* MARIANE)
                                        Now, child,
   I've weighed this matter fully.

DORINE (*aside*).   It drives me wild
   That I can't speak. (ORGON *turns his head, and she is silent.*)

ORGON.   Tartuffe is no young dandy,
   But, still, his person . . .

DORINE (*aside*).   Is as sweet as candy.   105

ORGON.   Is such that, even if you shouldn't care
   For his other merits . . .
   (*He turns and stands facing* DORINE, *arms crossed.*)

DORINE (*aside*).   They'll make a lovely pair.
   If I were she, no man would marry me
   Against my inclination, and go scot-free.
   He'd learn, before the wedding-day was over,   110
   How readily a wife can find a lover.

ORGON (*to* DORINE).   It seems you treat my orders as a joke.

DORINE.   Why, what's the matter? 'Twas not to you I spoke.

ORGON.   What *were* you doing?

DORINE.   Talking to myself, that's all.

ORGON.   Ah! (*Aside*) One more bit of impudence and gall,   115
   And I shall give her a good slap in the face. (*He puts himself in
   position to slap her;* DORINE, *whenever he glances at her, stands
   immobile and silent.*)
   Daughter, you shall accept, and with good grace,
   The husband I've selected . . . Your wedding-day . . .
   (*To* DORINE) Why don't you talk to yourself?

DORINE.   I've nothing to say.

ORGON.   Come, just one word.

DORINE.   No thank you, Sir. I pass.   120

ORGON.   Come, speak; I'm waiting.

DORINE.   I'd not be such an ass.

ORGON (*turning to* MARIANE).   In short, dear Daughter, I mean to be
    obeyed,
    And you must bow to the sound choice I've made.
DORINE (*moving away*).   I'd not wed such a monster, even in jest.
    (ORGON *attempts to slap her, but misses.*)
ORGON.   Daughter, that maid of yours is a thorough pest;   125
    She makes me sinfully annoyed and nettled.
    I can't speak further; my nerves are too unsettled.
    She's so upset me by her insolent talk,
    I'll calm myself by going for a walk. (*Exit.*)

SCENE 3

DORINE (*returning*).   Well, have you lost your tongue, girl? Must I play
    Your part, and say the lines you ought to say?
    Faced with a fate so hideous and absurd,
    Can you not utter one dissenting word?
MARIANE.   What good would it do? A father's power is great.   5
DORINE.   Resist him now, or it will be too late.
MARIANE.   But . . .
DORINE.   Tell him one cannot love at a father's whim;
    That you shall marry for yourself, not him;
    That since it's you who are to be the bride,
    It's you, not he, who must be satisfied;   10
    And that if his Tartuffe is so sublime,
    He's free to marry him at any time.
MARIANE.   I've bowed so long to Father's strict control,
    I couldn't oppose him now, to save my soul.
DORINE.   Come, come, Mariane. Do listen to reason, won't you?   15
    Valère has asked your hand. Do you love him, or don't you?
MARIANE.   Oh, how unjust of you! What can you mean
    By asking such a question, dear Dorine?
    You know the depth of my affection for him;
    I've told you a hundred times how I adore him.   20
DORINE.   I don't believe in everything I hear;
    Who knows if your professions were sincere?
MARIANE.   They were, Dorine, and you do me wrong to doubt it;
    Heaven knows that I've been all too frank about it.
DORINE.   You love him, then?
MARIANE.   Oh, more than I can express.   25
DORINE.   And he, I take it, care for you no less?
MARIANE.   I think so.

DORINE.   And you both, with equal fire,
  Burn to be married?
MARIANE.   That is our one desire.
DORINE.   What of Tartuffe, then? What of your father's plan?
MARIANE.   I'll kill myself, if I'm forced to wed that man.   30
DORINE.   I hadn't thought of that recourse. How splendid!
  Just die, and all your troubles will be ended!
  A fine solution. Oh, it maddens me
  To hear you talk in that self-pitying key.
MARIANE.   Dorine, how harsh you are! It's most unfair   35
  You have no sympathy for my despair.
DORINE.   I've none at all for people who talk drivel
  And, faced with difficulties, whine and snivel.
MARIANE.   No doubt I'm timid, but it would be wrong . . .
DORINE.   True love requires a heart that's firm and strong.   40
MARIANE.   I'm strong in my affection for Valère,
  But coping with my father is his affair.
DORINE.   But if your father's brain has grown so cracked
  Over his dear Tartuffe that he can retract
  His blessing, though your wedding-day was named,   45
  It's surely not Valère who's to be blamed.
MARIANE.   If I defied my father, as you suggest,
  Would it not seem unmaidenly, at best?
  Shall I defend my love at the expense
  Of brazenness and disobedience?   50
  Shall I parade my heart's desires, and flaunt . . .
DORINE.   No, I ask nothing of you. Clearly you want
  To be Madame Tartuffe, and I feel bound
  Not to oppose a wish so very sound.
  What right have I to criticize the match?   55
  Indeed, my dear, the man's a brilliant catch.
  Monsieur Tartuffe! Now, there's a man of weight!
  Yes, yes, Monsieur Tartuffe, I'm bound to state,
  Is quite a person; that's not to be denied;
  'Twill be no little thing to be his bride.   60
  The world already rings with his renown;
  He's a great noble—in his native town;
  His ears are red, he has a pink complexion,
  And all in all, he'll suit you to perfection.
MARIANE.   Dear God!

DORINE.   Oh, how triumphant you will feel   65
   At having caught a husband so ideal!
MARIANE.   Oh, do stop teasing, and use your cleverness
   To get me out of this appalling mess.
   Advise me, and I'll do whatever you say.
DORINE.   Ah no, a dutiful daughter must obey   70
   Her father, even if he weds her to an ape.
   You've a bright future; why struggle to escape?
   Tartuffe will take you back where his family lives,
   To a small town aswarm with relatives—
   Uncles and cousins whom you'll be charmed to meet.   75
   You'll be received at once by the elite,
   Calling upon the bailiff's wife, no less—
   Even, perhaps, upon the mayoress,
   Who'll sit you down in the *best* kitchen chair.
   Then, once a year, you'll dance at the village fair   80
   To the drone of bagpipes—two of them, in fact—
   And see a puppet-show, or an animal act.
   Your husband . . .
MARIANE.   Oh, you turn my blood to ice!
   Stop torturing me, and give me your advice.
DORINE (*threatening to go*).   Your servant, Madam.
MARIANE.   Dorine, I beg of you . . .   85
DORINE.   No, you deserve it; this marriage must go through.
MARIANE.   Dorine!
DORINE.   No.
MARIANE.   Not Tartuffe! You know I think him . . .
DORINE.   Tartuffe's your cup of tea, and you shall drink him.
MARIANE.   I've always told you everything, and relied . . .
DORINE.   No. You deserve to be tartuffified.   90
MARIANE.   Well, since you mock me and refuse to care,
   I'll henceforth seek my solace in despair:
   Despair shall be my counselor and friend,
   And help me bring my sorrows to an end. (*She starts to leave.*)
DORINE.   There now, come back; my anger has subsided.   95
   You do deserve some pity, I've decided.
MARIANE.   Dorine, if Father makes me undergo
   This dreadful martyrdom, I'll die, I know.
DORINE.   Don't fret; it won't be difficult to discover
   Some plan of action . . . But here's Valère, your lover.   100

SCENE 4

Enter VALÈRE.

VALÈRE. Madam, I've just received some wondrous news
Regarding which I'd like to hear your views.
MARIANE. What news?
VALÈRE.   You're marrying Tartuffe.
MARIANE.   I find
That Father does have such a match in mind.
VALÈRE. Your father, Madam . . .
MARIANE.   . . . has just this minute said   5
That it's Tartuffe he wishes me to wed.
VALÈRE. Can he be serious?
MARIANE.   Oh, indeed, he can;
He's clearly set his heart upon the plan.
VALÈRE. And what position do you propose to take,
Madam?
MARIANE. Why—I don't know.
VALÈRE.   For heaven's sake—   10
You don't know?
MARIANE.   No.
VALÈRE.   Well, well!
MARIANE.   Advise me, do.
VALÈRE. Marry the man. That's my advice to you.
MARIANE. That's your advice?
VALÈRE.   Yes.
MARIANE.   Truly?
VALÈRE.   Oh, absolutely.
You couldn't choose more wisely, more astutely.
MARIANE. Thanks for this counsel; I'll follow it, of course.   15
VALÈRE. Do, do; I'm sure 'twill cost you no remorse.
MARIANE. To give it didn't cause your heart to break.
VALÈRE. I gave it, Madam, only for your sake.
MARIANE. And it's for your sake that I take it, Sir.
DORINE (*withdrawing to the rear of the stage*). Let's see which
fool will prove the stubborner.   20
VALÈRE. So! I am nothing to you, and it was flat
Deception when you . . .
MARIANE.   Please, enough of that.
You've told me plainly that I should agree
To wed the man my father's chosen for me,
And since you've deigned to counsel me so wisely,   25
I promise, Sir, to do as you advise me.

VALÈRE.   Ah, no, 'twas not by me that you were swayed.
No, your decision was already made;
Though now, to save appearances, you protest
That you're betraying me at my behest.   30
MARIANE.   Just as you say.
VALÈRE.   Quite so, And I now see
That you were never truly in love with me.
MARIANE.   Alas, you're free to think so if you choose.
VALÈRE.   I choose to think so, and here's a bit of news:
You've spurned my hand, but I know where to turn   35
For kinder treatment, as you shall quickly learn.
MARIANE.   I'm sure you do. Your noble qualities
Inspire affection . . .
VALÈRE.   Forget my qualities, please.
They don't inspire you overmuch, I find.
But there's another lady I have in mind   40
Whose sweet and generous nature will not scorn
To compensate me for the loss I've borne.
MARIANE.   I'm no great loss, and I'm sure that you'll transfer
Your heart quite painlessly from me to her.
VALÈRE.   I'll do my best to take it in my stride.   45
The pain I feel at being cast aside
Time and forgetfulness may put an end to.
Or if I can't forget, I shall pretend to.
No self-respecting person is expected
To go on loving once he's been rejected.   50
MARIANE.   Now, that's a fine, high-minded sentiment.
VALÈRE.   One to which any sane man would assent.
Would you prefer it if I pined away
In hopeless passion till my dying day?
Am I to yield you to a rival's arms   55
And not console myself with other charms?
MARIANE.   Go then: console yourself; don't hesitate.
I wish you to; indeed, I cannot wait.
VALÈRE.   You wish me to?
MARIANE.   Yes.
VALÈRE.   That's the final straw.
Madam, farewell. Your wish shall be my law. (He starts to   60
leave, and then returns repeatedly.)
MARIANE.   Splendid.
VALÈRE (coming back again).
                This breach, remember, is of your making;
It's you who've driven me to the step I'm taking.

MARIANE.   Of course.
VALÈRE (*coming back again*).
                    Remember, too, that I am merely
    Following your example.
MARIANE.   I see that clearly.
VALÈRE.   Enough. I'll go and do your bidding, then.   65
MARIANE.   Good.
VALÈRE (*coming back again*).
                    You shall never see my face again.
MARIANE.   Excellent.
VALÈRE (*walking to the door, then turning about*).
                    Yes?
MARIANE.   What?
VALÈRE.   What's that? What did you say?
MARIANE.   Nothing. You're dreaming.
VALÈRE.   Ah. Well, I'm on my way.
    Farewell, *Madame*. (*He moves slowly away*.)
MARIANE.   Farewell.
DORINE (*to* MARIANE).   If you ask me,
    Both of you are as mad as mad can be.   70
    Do stop this nonsense, now. I've only let you
    Squabble so long to see where it would get you.
    Whoa there, Monsieur Valère! (*She goes and seizes* VALÈRE *by the
    arm; he makes a great show of resistance*.)
VALÈRE.   What's this, Dorine?
DORINE.   Come here.
VALÈRE.   No, no, my heart's too full of spleen.
    Don't hold me back; her wish must be obeyed.   75
DORINE.   Stop!
VALÈRE.   It's too late now; my decision's made.
DORINE.   Oh, pooh!
MARIANE (*aside*).   He hates the sight of me, it's plain.
    I'll go, and so deliver him from pain.
DORINE (*leaving* VALÈRE, *running after* MARIANE.)
    And now *you* run away! Come back.
MARIANE.   No, No.
    Nothing you say will keep me here. Let go!   80
VALÈRE (*aside*).   She cannot bear my presence, I perceive.
    To spare her further torment, I shall leave.
DORINE (*leaving* MARIANE, *running after* VALÈRE).   Again! You'll not
        escape, Sir; don't you try it.
    Come here, you two. Stop fussing, and be quiet. (*She takes
    VALÈRE by the hand, then MARIANE, and draws them together*.)

VALÈRE (*to* DORINE).   What do you want of me?
MARIANE (*to* DORINE).   What is the point of this? 85
DORINE.   We're going to have a little armistice.
    (*To* VALÈRE) Now weren't you silly to get so overheated?
VALÈRE.   Didn't you see how badly I was treated?
DORINE (*to* MARIANE).   Aren't you a simpleton, to have lost your head?
MARIANE.   Didn't you hear the hateful things he said?   90
DORINE (*to* VALÈRE).   You're both great fools. Her sole desire, Valère,
    Is to be yours in marriage. To that I'll swear.
    (*To* MARIANE) He loves you only, and he wants no wife
    But you, Mariane. On that I'll stake my life.
MARIANE (*to* VALÈRE).   Then why you advised me so, I cannot see. 95
VALÈRE (*to* MARIANE).   On such a question, why ask advice of *me*?
DORINE.   Oh, you're impossible. Give me your hands, you two.
    (*To* VALÈRE) Yours first.
VALÈRE (*giving* DORINE *his hand*).   But why?
DORINE (*to* MARIANE).   And now a hand from you.
MARIANE (*also giving* DORINE *her hand*).
    What are you doing?
DORINE.   There: a perfect fit.
    You suit each other better than you'll admit. (VALÈRE *and*   100
MARIANE *hold hands for some time without looking at each other.*)
VALÈRE (*turning toward* MARIANE).   Ah, come, don't be so haughty.
    Give a man
    A look of kindness, won't you, Mariane? (MARIANE *turns toward*
    VALÈRE *and smiles.*)
DORINE.   I tell you, lovers are completely mad!
VALÈRE (*to* MARIANE).   Now come, confess that you were very bad
    To hurt my feelings as you did just now.   105
    I have a just complaint, you must allow.
MARIANE.   *You* must allow that you were most unpleasant . . .
DORINE.   Let's table that discussion for the present;
    Your father has a plan which must be stopped.
MARIANE.   Advise us, then; what means must we adopt?   110
DORINE.   We'll use all manner of means, and all at once.
    (*To* MARIANE) Your father's addled; he's acting like a dunce.
    Therefore you'd better humor the old fossil.
    Pretend to yield to him, be sweet and docile,
    And then postpone, as often as necessary,   115
    The day on which you have agreed to marry.
    You'll thus gain time, and time will turn the trick.
    Sometimes, for instance, you'll be taken sick,
    And that will seem good reason for delay;

Or some bad omen will make you change the day—   120
You'll dream of muddy water, or you'll pass
A dead man's hearse, or break a looking-glass.
If all else fails, no man can marry you
Unless you take his ring and say "I do."
But now, let's separate. If they should find   125
Us talking here, our plot might be divined.
(*To* VALÈRE) Go to your friends, and tell them what's occurred,
And have them urge her father to keep his word.
Meanwhile, we'll stir her brother into action,
And get Elmire, as well, to join our faction.   130
Good-bye.

VALÈRE (*to* MARIANE).
         Though each of us will do his best,
  It's your true heart on which my hopes shall rest.

MARIANE (*to* VALÈRE).   Regardless of what Father may decide,
  None but Valère shall claim me as his bride.

VALÈRE.   Oh, how those words content me! Come what will . . .   135

DORINE.   Oh, lovers, lovers! Their tongues are never still.
  Be off, now.

VALÈRE (*turning to go, then turning back*).
         One last word . . .

DORINE.   No time to chat:
  You leave by this door; and *you* leave by that. (DORINE *pushes them,*
  by the shoulders, toward opposing doors. Exeunt MARIANE *and* VALÈRE.)

ACT 3

SCENE 1

Enter DAMIS.

DAMIS.   May lightning strike me even as I speak,
  May all men call me cowardly and weak,
  If any fear or scruple holds me back
  From settling things, at once, with that great quack!

DORINE.   Now, don't give way to violent emotion.   5
  Your father's merely talked about this notion,
  And words and deeds are far from being one.
  Much that is talked about is left undone.

DAMIS.   No, I must stop that scoundrel's machinations;
  I'll go and tell him off; I'm out of patience.   10

DORINE.   Do calm down and be practical. I had rather
    My mistress dealt with him—and with your father.
    She has some influence with Tartuffe, I've noted.
    He hangs upon her words, seems most devoted,
    And may, indeed, be smitten by her charm.   15
    Pray Heaven it's true! 'Twould do our cause no harm.
    She sent for him, just now, to sound him out
    On this affair you're so incensed about;
    She'll find out where he stands, and tell him, too,
    What dreadful strife and trouble will ensue   20
    If he lends countenance to your father's plan.
    I couldn't get in to see him, but his man
    Says that he's almost finished with his prayers.
    Go, now. I'll catch him when he comes downstairs.
DAMIS.   I want to hear this conference, and I will.   25
DORINE.   No, they must be alone.
DAMIS.   Oh, I'll keep still.
DORINE.   Not you. I know your temper. You'd start a brawl,
    And shout and stamp your foot and spoil it all.
    Go on.
DAMIS.   I won't; I have a perfect right . . .
DORINE.   Lord, you're a nuisance! He's coming; get out of sight.   30
    (DAMIS *conceals himself in a closet at the rear of the stage*.)

SCENE 2

    Enter TARTUFFE.

TARTUFFE (*observing* DORINE, *and calling to his manservant offstage*).
    Hang up my hair-shirt, put my scourge in place,
    And pray, Laurent, for Heaven's perpetual grace.
    I'm going to the prison now, to share
    My last few coins with the poor wretches there.
DORINE (*aside*).   Dear God, what affectation! What a fake!   5
TARTUFFE.   You wished to see me?
DORINE.   Yes . . .
TARTUFFE (*taking a handkerchief from his pocket*).
                           For mercy's sake,
    Please take this handkerchief, before you speak.
DORINE.   What?
TARTUFFE.   Cover that bosom, girl. The flesh is weak,
    And unclean thoughts are difficult to control.
    Such sights as that can undermine the soul.   10

DORINE.   Your soul, it seems, has very poor defenses,
  And flesh makes quite an impact on your senses.
  It's strange that you're so easily excited;
  My own desires are not so soon ignited;
  And if I saw you naked as a beast,   15
  Not all your hide would tempt me in the least.
TARTUFFE.   Girl, speak more modestly; unless you do,
  I shall be forced to take my leave of you.
DORINE.   Oh, no, it's I who must be on my way;
  I've just one little message to convey.   20
  Madame is coming down, and begs you, Sir,
  To wait and have a word or two with her.
TARTUFFE.   Gladly.
DORINE (*aside*).   *That* had a softening effect!
  I think my guess about him was correct.   25
TARTUFFE.   Will she be long?
DORINE.   No: that's her step I hear.
  Ah, here she is, and I shall disappear. (*Exit.*)

SCENE 3

  Enter ELMIRE.

TARTUFFE.   May Heaven, whose infinite goodness we adore,
  Preserve your body and soul forevermore,
  And bless your days, and answer thus the plea
  Of one who is its humblest votary.
ELMIRE.   I thank you for that pious wish. But please,   5
  Do take a chair and let's be more at ease. (*They sit down.*)
TARTUFFE.   I trust that you are once more well and strong?
ELMIRE.   Oh, yes: the fever didn't last for long.
TARTUFFE.   My prayers are too unworthy, I am sure,
  To have gained from heaven this most gracious cure;   10
  But lately, Madam, my every supplication
  Has had for object your recuperation.
ELMIRE.   You shouldn't have troubled so. I don't deserve it.
TARTUFFE.   Your health is priceless, Madam, and to preserve it
  I'd gladly give my own, in all sincerity.   15
ELMIRE.   Sir, you outdo us all in Christian charity.
  You've been most kind. I count myself your debtor.
TARTUFFE.   'Twas nothing, Madam. I long to serve you better.
ELMIRE.   There's a private matter I'm anxious to discuss.
  I'm glad there's no one here to hinder us.   20

TARTUFFE.   I too am glad; it floods my heart with bliss
    To find myself alone with you like this.
    For just this chance I've prayed with all my power—
    But prayed in vain, until this happy hour.
ELMIRE.   This won't take long, Sir, and I hope you'll be   25
    Entirely frank and unconstrained with me.
TARTUFFE.   Indeed, there's nothing I had rather do
    Than bare my inmost heart and soul to you.
    First, let me say that what remarks I've made
    About the constant visits you are paid   30
    Were prompted not by any mean emotion,
    But rather by a pure and deep devotion,
    A fervent zeal . . .
ELMIRE.   No need for explanation.
    Your sole concern, I'm sure, was my salvation.
TARTUFFE (*taking* ELMIRE's *hand and pressing her fingertips*).   Quite so;
    and such great fervor do I feel . . .
ELMIRE.   Ooh! Please! You're pinching!
TARTUFFE.   'Twas from excess of zeal.
    I never meant to cause you pain, I swear.
    I'd rather . . . (*He places his hand on* ELMIRE's *knee.*)
ELMIRE.   What can your hand be doing there?
TARTUFFE.   Feeling your gown; what soft, fine-woven stuff!
ELMIRE.   Please, I'm extremely ticklish. That's enough. (*She draws her*   40
chair away; TARTUFFE *pulls his after her.*)
TARTUFFE (*fondling the lace collar of her gown*).   My, my, what lovely
    lacework on your dress!
    The workmanship's miraculous, no less.
    I've not seen anything to equal it.
ELMIRE.   Yes, quite. But let's talk business for a bit.
    They say my husband means to break his word   45
    And give his daughter to you, Sir. Had you heard?
TARTUFFE.   He did once mention it. But I confess
    I dream of quite a different happiness.
    It's elsewhere, Madam, that my eyes discern
    The promise of that bliss for which I yearn.   50
ELMIRE.   I see: you care for nothing here below.
TARTUFFE.   Ah, well—my heart's not made of stone, you know.
ELMIRE.   All your desires mount heavenward, I'm sure,
    In scorn of all that's earthly and impure.
TARTUFFE.   A love of heavenly beauty does not preclude   55
    A proper love for earthly pulchritude;
    Our senses are quite rightly captivated

By perfect works our Maker has created.
Some glory clings to all that Heaven has made;
In you, all Heaven's marvels are displayed.   60
On that fair face, such beauties have been lavished,
The eyes are dazzled and the heart is ravished;
How could I look on you, O flawless creature,
And not adore the Author of all Nature,
Feeling a love both passionate and pure   65
For you, his triumph of self-portraiture?
At first, I trembled lest that love should be
A subtle snare that Hell had laid for me;
I vowed to flee the sight of you, eschewing
A rapture that might prove my soul's undoing;   70
But soon, fair being, I became aware
That my deep passion could be made to square
With rectitude, and with my bounden duty.
I thereupon surrendered to your beauty.
It is, I know, presumptuous on my part   75
To bring you this poor offering of my heart,
And it is not my merit, Heaven knows,
But your compassion on which my hopes repose.
You are my peace, my solace, my salvation;
On you depends my bliss—or desolation;   80
I bide your judgment and, as you think best,
I shall be either miserable or blest.

ELMIRE.   Your declaration is most gallant, Sir,
But don't you think it's out of character?
You'd have done better to restrain your passion   85
And think before you spoke in such a fashion.
It ill becomes a pious man like you . . .

TARTUFFE.   I may be pious, but I'm human too:
With your celestial charms before his eyes,
A man has not the power to be wise.   90
I know such words sound strangely, coming from me,
But I'm no angel, nor was meant to be,
And if you blame my passion, you must needs
Reproach as well the charms on which it feeds.
Your loveliness I had no sooner seen   95
Than you became my soul's unrivalled queen;
Before your seraph glance, divinely sweet,
My heart's defenses crumbled in defeat,
And nothing fasting, prayer, or tears might do
Could stay my spirit from adoring you.   100

My eyes, my sighs have told you in the past
What now my lips make bold to say at last,
And if, in your great goodness, you will deign
To look upon your slave, and ease his pain,—
If, in compassion for my soul's distress,   105
You'll stoop to comfort my unworthiness,
I'll raise to you, in thanks for that sweet manna,
An endless hymn, an infinite hosanna.
With me, of course, there need be no anxiety,
No fear of scandal or of notoriety.   110
These young court gallants, whom all the ladies fancy,
Are vain in speech, in action rash and chancy;
When they succeed in love, the world soon knows it;
No favor's granted them but they disclose it
And by the looseness of their tongues profane   115
The very altar where their hearts have lain.
Men of my sort, however, love discreetly,
And one may trust our reticence completely.
My keen concern for my good name insures
The absolute security of yours;
In short, I offer you, my dear Elmire,   120
Love without scandal, pleasure without fear.
ELMIRE.   I've heard your well-turned speeches to the end,
And what you urge I clearly apprehend.
Aren't you afraid that I may take a notion   125
To tell my husband of your warm devotion,
And that, supposing he were duly told,
His feelings toward you might grow rather cold?
TARTUFFE.   I know, dear lady, that your exceeding charity
Will lead your heart to pardon my temerity;   130
That you'll excuse my violent affection
As human weakness, human imperfection;
And that—O fairest!—you will bear in mind
That I'm but flesh and blood, and am not blind.
ELMIRE.   Some women might do otherwise, perhaps   135
But I shall be discreet about your lapse;
I'll tell my husband nothing of what's occurred
If, in return you'll give your solemn word
To advocate as forcefully as you can
The marriage of Valère and Mariane,   140
Renouncing all desire to dispossess
Another of his rightful happiness,
And . . .

SCENE 4

DAMIS (*emerging from the closet where he has been hiding*).
        No! we'll not hush up this vile affair;
  I heard it all inside that closet there,
  Where Heaven, in order to confound the pride
  Of this great rascal, prompted me to hide.
  Ah, now I have my long-awaited chance   5
  To punish his deceit and arrogance,
  And give my father clear and shocking proof
  Of the black character of his dear Tartuffe.
ELMIRE.   Ah no, Damis; I'll be content if he
  Will study to deserve my leniency.   10
  I've promised silence—don't make me break my word;
  To make a scandal would be too absurd.
  Good wives laugh off such trifles, and forget them;
  Why should they tell their husbands, and upset them?
DAMIS.   You have your reasons for taking such a course,   15
  And I have reasons, too, of equal force.
  To spare him now would be insanely wrong.
  I've swallowed my just wrath for far too long
  And watched this insolent bigot bringing strife
  And bitterness into our family life.   20
  Too long he's meddled in my father's affairs,
  Thwarting my marriage-hopes, and poor Valère's.
  It's high time that my father was undeceived,
  And now I've proof that can't be disbelieved—
  Proof that was furnished me by Heaven above.   25
  It's too good not to take advantage of.
  This is my chance, and I deserve to lose it
  If, for one moment, I hesitate to use it.
ELMIRE.   Damis . . .
DAMIS.   No, I must do what I think right.
  Madam, my heart is bursting with delight,   30
  And, say whatever you will, I'll not consent
  To lose the sweet revenge on which I'm bent.
  I'll settle matters without more ado;
  And here, most opportunely, is my cue.

SCENE 5

   Enter ORGON.

DAMIS.   Father, I'm glad you've joined us. Let us advise you
  Of some fresh news which doubtless will surprise you.

You've just now been repaid with interest
For all your loving-kindness to our guest.
He's proved his warm and grateful feelings toward you;   5
It's with a pair of horns he would reward you.
Yes, I surprised him with your wife, and heard
His whole adulterous offer, every word.
She, with her all too gentle disposition,
Would not have told you of his proposition;   10
But I shall not make terms with brazen lechery,
And feel that not to tell you would be treachery.
ELMIRE.   And I hold that one's husband's peace of mind
Should not be spoilt by tattle of this kind.
One's honor doesn't require it: to be proficient   15
In keeping men at bay is quite sufficient.
These are my sentiments, and I wish, Damis,
That you had heeded me and held your peace. (*Exit* ELMIRE.)

SCENE 6

ORGON.   Can it be true, this dreadful thing I hear?
TARTUFFE.   Yes, Brother, I'm a wicked man, I fear:
A wretched sinner, all depraved and twisted,
The greatest villain that has ever existed.
My life's one heap of crimes, which grows each minute;   5
There's naught but foulness and corruption in it;
And I perceive that Heaven, outraged by me,
Has chosen this occasion to mortify me.
Charge me with any deed you wish to name;
I'll not defend myself, but take the blame,   10
Believe what you are told, and drive Tartuffe
Like some base criminal from beneath your roof;
Yes, drive me hence, and with a parting curse:
I shan't protest, for I deserve far worse.
ORGON (*to* DAMIS).   Ah, you deceitful boy, how dare you try   15
To stain his purity with so foul a lie?
DAMIS.   What! Are you taken in by such a bluff?
Did you not hear . . . ?
ORGON.   Enough, you rogue, enough!
TARTUFFE.   Ah, Brother, let him speak; you're being unjust.
Believe his story; the boy deserves your trust.   20
Why, after all, should you have faith in me?
How can you know what I might do, or be?

Is it on my good actions that you base
Your favor? Do you trust my pious face?
Ah, no, don't be deceived by hollow shows;   25
I'm far, alas, from being what men suppose;
Though the world takes me for a man of worth,
I'm truly the most worthless man on earth.
(*To* DAMIS) Yes, my dear son, speak out now: call me the chief
Of sinners, a wretch, a murderer, a thief;   30
Load me with all the names men most abhor;
I'll not complain; I've earned them all, and more;
I'll kneel here while you pour them on my head
As a just punishment for the life I've led.
ORGON (*to* TARTUFFE).   This is too much, dear Brother.
    (*To* DAMIS)   Have you no heart? 35
DAMIS.   Are you so hoodwinked by this rascal's art . . .?
ORGON.   Be still, you monster.
    (*To* TARTUFFE)   Brother, I pray you, rise.
    (*To* DAMIS) Villain!
DAMIS.   But . . .
ORGON.   Silence!
DAMIS.   Can't you realize . . .?
ORGON.   Just one word more, and I'll tear you limb from limb.
TARTUFFE.   In God's name, Brother, don't be harsh with him.   40
    I'd rather far be tortured at the stake
    Than see him bear one scratch for my poor sake.
ORGON (*to* DAMIS).   Ingrate!
TARTUFFE.   If I must beg you, on bended knee,
    To pardon him . . .
ORGON (*falling to his knees, addressing* TARTUFFE).
                        Such goodness cannot be!
    (*To* DAMIS) Now, *there's* true charity!
DAMIS.   What, you . . . ?
ORGON.   Villain, be still! 45
    I know your motives; I know you wish him ill:
    Yes, all of you—wife, children, servants, all—
    Conspire against him and desire his fall,
    Employing every shameful trick you can
    To alienate me from this saintly man.   50
    Ah, but the more you seek to drive him away,
    The more I'll do to keep him. Without delay,
    I'll spite this household and confound its pride
    By giving him my daughter as his bride.
DAMIS.   You're going to force her to accept his hand?   55

ORGON.   Yes, and this very night, d'you understand?
 I shall defy you all, and make it clear
 That I'm the one who gives the orders here.
 Come, wretch, kneel down and clasp his blessed feet,
 And ask his pardon for your black deceit.   60
DAMIS.   I ask that swindler's pardon? Why, I'd rather . . .
ORGON.   So! You insult him, and defy your father!
 A stick! A stick! (*To* TARTUFFE) No, no—release me, do.
 (*To* DAMIS) Out of my house this minute! Be off with you,
 And never dare set foot in it again.   65
DAMIS.   Well, I shall go, but . . .
ORGON.   Well, go quickly, then.
 I disinherit you; an empty purse
 Is all you'll get from me—except my curse! (*Exit* DAMIS.)

SCENE 7

ORGON.   How he blasphemed your goodness! What a son!
TARTUFFE.   Forgive him, Lord, as I've already done.
 (*To* ORGON) You can't know how it hurts when someone tries
 To blacken me in my dear Brother's eyes.
ORGON.   Ahh!
TARTUFFE.   The mere thought of such ingratitude   5
 Plunges my soul into so dark a mood . . .
 Such horror grips my heart . . . I gasp for breath,
 And cannot speak, and feel myself near death.
ORGON (*running, in tears, to the door through which he has just driven his*
 son).   You blackguard! Why did I spare you? Why did I not
 Break you in little pieces on the spot?   10
 Compose yourself, and don't be hurt, dear friend.
TARTUFFE.   These scenes, these dreadful quarrels, have got to end.
 I've much upset your household, and I perceive
 That the best thing will be for me to leave.
ORGON.   What are you saying!
TARTUFFE.   They're all against me here;   15
 They'd have you think me false and insincere.
ORGON.   Ah, what of that? Have I ceased believing in you?
TARTUFFE.   Their adverse talk will certainly continue,
 And charges which you now repudiate
 You may find credible at a later date.   20
ORGON.   No, Brother, never.
TARTUFFE.   Brother, a wife can sway
 Her husband's mind in many a subtle way.

ORGON.   No, no.

TARTUFFE.   To leave at once is the solution;
  Thus only can I end their persecution.

ORGON.   No, no, I'll not allow it; you shall remain.   25

TARTUFFE.   Ah, well; 'twill mean much martyrdom and pain,
  But if you wish it . . .

ORGON.   Ah!

TARTUFFE.   Enough; so be it.
  But one thing must be settled, as I see it.
  For your dear honor, and for our friendship's sake,
  There's one precaution I feel bound to take.   30
  I shall avoid your wife, and keep away . . .

ORGON.   No, you shall not, whatever they may say.
  It pleases me to vex them, and for spite
  I'd have them see you with her day and night.
  What's more, I'm going to drive them to despair   35
  By making you my only son and heir;
  This very day, I'll give to you alone
  Clear deed and title to everything I own.
  A dear, good friend and son-in-law-to-be
  Is more than wife, or child, or kin to me.   40
  Will you accept my offer, dearest son?

TARTUFFE.   In all things, let the will of Heaven be done.

ORGON.   Poor fellow! Come, we'll go draw up the deed.
  Then let them burst with disappointed greed! (*Exeunt.*)

ACT 4

SCENE 1

  Enter CLÉANTE *and* TARTUFFE.

CLÉANTE.   Yes, all the town's discussing it, and truly,
  Their comments do not flatter you unduly.
  I'm glad we've met, Sir, and I'll give my view
  Of this sad matter in a word or two.
  As for who's guilty, that I shan't discuss;   5
  Let's say it was Damis who caused the fuss;
  Assuming, then, that you have been ill-used
  By young Damis, and groundlessly accused,
  Ought not a Christian to forgive, and ought
  He not to stifle every vengeful thought?   10

Should you stand by and watch a father make
His only son an exile for your sake?
Again I tell you frankly, be advised:
The whole town, high and low, is scandalized;
This quarrel must be mended, and my advice is   15
Not to push matters to a further crisis.
No, sacrifice your wrath to God above,
And help Damis regain his father's love.
TARTUFFE.   Alas, for my part I should take great joy
In doing so. I've nothing against the boy.   20
I pardon all, I harbor no resentment;
To serve him would afford me much contentment.
But Heaven's interest will not have it so:
If he comes back, then I shall have to go.
After his conduct—so extreme, so vicious—   25
Our further intercourse would look suspicious.
God knows what people would think! Why, they'd describe
My goodness to him as a sort of bribe;
They'd say that out of guilt I made pretense
Of loving-kindness and benevolence—   30
That, fearing my accuser's tongue, I strove
To buy his silence with a show of love.
CLÉANTE.   Your reasoning is badly warped and stretched,
And these excuses, Sir, are most far-fetched.
Why put yourself in charge of Heaven's cause?   35
Does Heaven need our help to enforce its laws?
Leave vengeance to the Lord, Sir; while we live,
Our duty's not to punish, but forgive;
And what the Lord commands, we should obey
Without regard to what the world may say.   40
What! Shall the fear of being misunderstood
Prevent our doing what is right and good?
No, no; let's simply do what Heaven ordains,
And let no other thoughts perplex our brains.
TARTUFFE.   Again, Sir, let me say that I've forgiven   45
Damis, and thus obeyed the laws of Heaven;
But I am not commanded by the Bible
To live with one who smears my name with libel.
CLÉANTE.   Were you commanded, Sir, to indulge the whim
Of poor Orgon, and to encourage him   50
In suddenly transferring to your name
A large estate to which you have no claim?

TARTUFFE.   'Twould never occur to those who know me best
   To think I acted from self-interest.
   The treasures of this world I quite despise;   55
   Their specious glitter does not charm my eyes;
   And if I have resigned myself to taking
   The gift which my dear Brother insists on making,
   I do so only, as he well understands,
   Lest so much wealth fall into wicked hands,   60
   Lest those to whom it might descend in time
   Turn it to purposes of sin and crime,
   And not, as I shall do, make use of it
   For Heaven's glory and mankind's benefit.
CLÉANTE.   Forget these trumped-up fears. Your argument   65
   Is one the rightful heir might well resent;
   It is a moral burden to inherit
   Such wealth, but give Damis a chance to bear it.
   And would it not be worse to be accused
   Of swindling, than to see that wealth misused?   70
   I'm shocked that you allowed Orgon to broach
   This matter, and that you feel no self-reproach;
   Does true religion teach that lawful heirs
   May freely be deprived of what is theirs?
   And if the Lord has told you in your heart   75
   That you and young Damis must dwell apart,
   Would it not be the decent thing to beat
   A generous and honorable retreat,
   Rather than let the son of the house be sent,
   For your convenience, into banishment?   80
   Sir, if you wish to prove the honesty
   Of your intentions . . .
TARTUFFE.   Sir, it is half-past three.
   I've certain pious duties to attend to,
   And hope my prompt departure won't offend you. (*Exit.*)
CLÉANTE.   Damn. (*Starts to leave.*)

SCENE 2

   Enter ELMIRE, MARIANE, *and* DORINE.

DORINE.   Stay, Sir, and help Mariane, for Heaven's sake!
   She's suffering so, I fear her heart will break.
   Her father's plan to marry her off tonight
   Has put the poor child in a desperate plight.
   I hear him coming. Let's stand together, now,

And see if we can't change his mind, somehow,
About this match we all deplore and fear.

SCENE 3

Enter ORGON.

ORGON.   Hah! Glad to find you all assembled here.
   (*To* MARIANE) This contract, child, contains your happiness,
   And what it says I think your heart can guess.
MARIANE (*falling to her knees*).   Sir, by that Heaven which sees me here
     distressed,
   And by whatever else can move your breast,   5
   Do not employ a father's power, I pray you,
   To crush my heart and force it to obey you,
   Nor by your harsh commands oppress me so
   That I'll begrudge the duty which I owe—
   And do not so embitter and enslave me   10
   That I shall hate the very life you gave me.
   If my sweet hopes must perish, if you refuse
   To give me to the one I've dared to choose,
   Spare me at least—I beg you, I implore—
   The pain of wedding one whom I abhor;   15
   And do not, by a heartless use of force,
   Drive me to contemplate some desperate course.
ORGON (*feeling himself touched by her*).   Be firm, my soul. No human
     weakness, now.
MARIANE.   I don't resent your love for him. Allow
   Your heart free rein, Sir; give him your property,   20
   And if that's not enough, take mine from me;
   He's welcome to my money; take it, do,
   But don't, I pray, include my person too.
   Spare me, I beg you; and let me end the tale
   Of my sad days behind a convent veil.   25
ORGON.   A convent! Hah! When crossed in their amours,
   All lovesick girls have the same thought as yours.
   Get up! The more you loathe the man, and dread him,
   The more ennobling it will be to wed him.
   Marry Tartuffe, and mortify your flesh!   30
   Enough; don't start that whimpering afresh.
DORINE.   But why . . . ?
ORGON.   Be still, there. Speak when you're spoken to.
   Not one more bit of impudence out of you.
CLÉANTE.   If I may offer a word of counsel here . . .

ORGON.   Brother, in counseling you have no peer;   35
    All your advice is forceful, sound, and clever;
    I don't propose to follow it, however.
ELMIRE (*to* ORGON).   I am amazed, and don't know what to say;
    Your blindness simply takes my breath away.
    You are indeed bewitched, to take no warning   40
    From our account of what occurred this morning.
ORGON.   Madam, I know a few plain facts, and one
    Is that you're partial to my rascal son;
    Hence, when he sought to make Tartuffe the victim
    Of a base lie, you dared not contradict him.   45
    Ah, but you underplayed your part, my pet;
    You should have looked more angry, more upset.
ELMIRE.   When men make overtures, must we reply
    With righteous anger and a battle-cry?
    Must we turn back their amorous advances   50
    With sharp reproaches and with fiery glances?
    Myself, I find such offers merely amusing,
    And make no scenes and fusses in refusing;
    My taste is for good-natured rectitude,
    And I dislike the savage sort of prude   55
    Who guards her virtue with her teeth and claws,
    And tears men's eyes out for the slightest cause;
    The Lord preserve me from such honor as that,
    Which bites and scratches like an alley-cat!
    I've found that a polite and cool rebuff   60
    Discourages a lover quite enough.
ORGON.   I know the facts, and I shall not be shaken.
ELMIRE.   I marvel at your power to be mistaken.
    Would it, I wonder, carry weight with you
    If I could *show* you that our tale was true?   65
ORGON.   Show me?
ELMIRE.   Yes.
ORGON.   Rot.
ELMIRE.   Come, what if I found a way
    To make you see the facts as plain as day?
ORGON.   Nonsense.
ELMIRE.   Do answer me; don't be absurd.
    I'm not now asking you to trust our word.
    Suppose that from some hiding-place in here   70
    You learned the whole sad truth by eye and ear—
    What would you say of your good friend, after that?

ORGON.   Why, I'd say . . . nothing, by Jehosophat!
    It can't be true.
ELMIRE.   You've been too long deceived,
    And I'm quite tired of being disbelieved.   75
    Come now: let's put my statement to the test,
    And you shall see the truth made manifest.
ORGON.   I'll take that challenge. Now do your uttermost.
    We'll see how you make good your empty boast.
ELMIRE (*to* DORINE).   Send him to me.
DORINE.   He's crafty; it may be hard   80
    To catch the cunning scoundrel off his guard.
ELMIRE.   No, amorous men are gullible. Their conceit
    So blinds them that they're never hard to cheat.
    Have him come down. (*Exit* DORINE. *To* CLÉANTE *and* MARIANE)
        Please leave us, for a bit. (*They leave.*)

SCENE 4

ELMIRE.   Pull up this table, and get under it.
ORGON.   What?
ELMIRE.   It's essential that you be well-hidden.
ORGON.   Why there?
ELMIRE.   Oh, Heavens! Just do as you are bidden.
    I have my plans; we'll soon see how they fare.
    Under the table, now; and once you're there,   5
    Take care that you are neither seen nor heard.
ORGON.   Well, I'll indulge you, since I gave my word
    To see you through this infantile charade.
ELMIRE.   Once it is over, you'll be glad we played.
    (*To her husband, who is now under the table*) I'm going to act
        quite strangely, now, and you   10
    Must not be shocked at anything I do.
    Whatever I may say, you must excuse
    As part of that deceit I'm forced to use.
    I shall employ sweet speeches in the task
    Of making that impostor drop his mask;   15
    I'll give encouragement to his bold desires,
    And furnish fuel to his amorous fires.
    Since it's for your sake, and for his destruction,
    That I shall seem to yield to his seduction,
    I'll gladly stop whenever you decide   20
    That all your doubts are fully satisfied.

I'll count on you, as soon as you have seen
What sort of man he is, to intervene,
And not expose me to his odious lust
One moment longer than you feel you must.   25
Remember: you're to save me from my plight
Whenever . . . He's coming! Hush! Keep out of sight!

SCENE 5

Enter TARTUFFE.

TARTUFFE.   You wish to have a word with me, I'm told.
ELMIRE.   Yes. I've a little secret to unfold.
    Before I speak, however, it would be wise
    To close that door, and look about for spies.
    (TARTUFFE *goes to the door, closes it, and returns.*)   5
    The very last thing that must happen now
    Is a repetition of this morning's row.
    I've never been so badly caught off guard.
    Oh, how I feared for you! You saw how hard
    I tried to make that troublesome Damis
    Control his dreadful temper, and hold his peace.   10
    In my confusion, I didn't have the sense
    Simply to contradict his evidence;
    But as it happened, that was for the best,
    And all has worked out in our interest.
    This storm has only bettered your position;   15
    My husband doesn't have the least suspicion,
    And now, in mockery of those who do,
    He bids me be continually with you.
    And that is why, quite fearless of reproof,
    I now can be alone with my Tartuffe,   20
    And why my heart—perhaps too quick to yield—
    Feels free to let its passion be revealed.
TARTUFFE.   Madam, your words confuse me. Not long ago,
    You spoke in quite a different style, you know.
ELMIRE.   Ah, Sir, if that refusal made you smart,   25
    It's little that you know of woman's heart,
    Or what that heart is trying to convey
    When it resists in such a feeble way!
    Always, at first, our modesty prevents
    The frank avowal of tender sentiments;   30
    However high the passion which inflames us,

Still, to confess its power somehow shames us.
Thus we reluct, at first, yet in a tone
Which tells you that our heart is overthrown,
That what our lips deny, our pulse confesses,   35
And that, in time, all noes will turn to yesses.
I fear my words are all too frank and free,
And a poor proof of woman's modesty;
But since I'm started, tell me, if you will—
Would I have tried to make Damis be still,   40
Would I have listened, calm and unoffended,
Until your lengthy offer of love was ended,
And been so very mild in my reaction,
Had your sweet words not given me satisfaction?
And when I tried to force you to undo   45
The marriage plans my husband has in view,
What did my urgent pleading signify
If not that I admired you, and that I
Deplored the thought that someone else might own
Part of a heart I wished for mine alone?   50
TARTUFFE.   Madam, no happiness is so complete
As when, from lips we love, come words so sweet;
Their nectar floods my every sense, and drains
In honeyed rivulets through all my veins.
To please you is my joy, my only goal;   55
Your love is the restorer of my soul;
And yet I must beg leave, now, to confess
Some lingering doubts as to my happiness.
Might this not be a trick? Might not the catch
Be that you wish me to break off the match   60
With Mariane, and so have feigned to love me?
I shan't quite trust your fond opinion of me
Until the feelings you've expressed so sweetly
Are demonstrated somewhat more concretely,
And you have shown, by certain kind concessions,   65
That I may put my faith in your professions.
ELMIRE (*coughs, to warn her husband*).   Why be in such a hurry?
     Must my heart
Exhaust its bounty at the very start?
To make that sweet admission cost me dear,
But you'll not be content, it would appear,   70
Unless my store of favors is disbursed
To the last farthing, and at the very first.

TARTUFFE. The less we merit, the less we dare to hope,
  And with our doubts, mere words can never cope.
  We trust no promised bliss till we receive it;   75
  Not till a joy is ours can we believe it.
  I, who so little merit your esteem,
  Can't credit this fulfillment of my dream,
  And shan't believe it, Madam, until I savor
  Some palpable assurance of your favor.   80
ELMIRE. My, how tyrannical your love can be,
  And how it flusters and perplexes me!
  How furiously you take one's heart in hand,
  And make your every wish a fierce command!
  Come, must you hound and harry me to death?   85
  Will you not give me time to catch my breath?
  Can it be right to press me with such force,
  Give me no quarter, show me no remorse,
  And take advantage, by your stern insistence,
  Of the fond feelings which weaken my resistance?   90
TARTUFFE. Well, if you look with favor upon my love,
  Why, then, begrudge me some clear proof thereof?
ELMIRE. But how can I consent without offense
  To Heaven, toward which you feel such reverence?
TARTUFFE. If Heaven is all that holds you back, don't worry.   95
  I can remove that hindrance in a hurry.
  Nothing of that sort need obstruct our path.
ELMIRE. Must one not be afraid of Heaven's wrath?
TARTUFFE. Madam, forget such fears, and be my pupil,
  And I shall teach you how to conquer scruple.   100
  Some joys, it's true, are wrong in Heaven's eyes;
  Yet Heaven is not averse to compromise;
  There is a science, lately formulated,
  Whereby one's conscience may be liberated,
  And any wrongful act you care to mention   105
  May be redeemed by purity of intention.
  I'll teach you, Madam, the secrets of that science;
  Meanwhile, just place on me your full reliance.
  Assuage my keen desires, and feel no dread:
  The sin, if any, shall be on my head. (ELMIRE *coughs, this time*
    more loudly.)   110
  You've a bad cough.
ELMIRE.   Yes, yes. It's bad indeed.
TARTUFFE (*producing a little paper bag*). A bit of licorice may be what
  you need.

ELMIRE.   No, I've a stubborn cold, it seems. I'm sure it
    Will take much more than licorice to cure it.
TARTUFFE.   How aggravating.
ELMIRE.   Oh, more than I can say.   115
TARTUFFE.   If you're still troubled, think of things this way:
    No one shall know our joys, save us alone,
    And there's no evil till the act is known;
    It's scandal, Madam, which makes it an offense,
    And it's no sin to sin in confidence.   120
ELMIRE (*having coughed once more*).   Well, clearly I must do as you
    require,
    And yield to your importunate desire.
    It is apparent, now, that nothing less
    Will satisfy you, and so I acquiesce.
    To go so far is much against my will;   125
    I'm vexed that it should come to this; but still,
    Since you are so determined on it, since you
    Will not allow mere language to convince you,
    And since you ask for concrete evidence, I
    See nothing for it, now, but to comply.   130
    If this is sinful, if I'm wrong to do it,
    So much the worse for him who drove me to it.
    The fault can surely not be charged to me.
TARTUFFE.   Madam, the fault is mine, if fault there be,
    And . . .
ELMIRE.   Open the door a little, and peek out;   135
    I wouldn't want my husband poking about.
TARTUFFE.   Why worry about the man? Each day he grows
    More gullible; one can lead him by the nose.
    To find us here would fill him with delight,
    And if he saw the worst, he'd doubt his sight.   140
ELMIRE.   Nevertheless, do step out for a minute
    Into the hall, and see that no one's in it. (*Exit* TARTUFFE.)

SCENE 6

ORGON (*coming out from under the table*).   That man's a perfect
    monster, I must admit!
    I'm simply stunned. I can't get over it.
ELMIRE.   What, coming out so soon? how premature!
    Get back in hiding, and wait until you're sure.
    Stay till the end, and be convinced completely;   5
    We mustn't stop till things are proved concretely.

ORGON.   Hell never harbored anything so vicious!

ELMIRE.   Tut, don't be hasty. Try to be judicious.

Wait, and be certain that there's no mistake.

No jumping to conclusions, for Heaven's sake! (*She places*   10
ORGON *behind her, as* TARTUFFE *re-enters.*)

SCENE 7

TARTUFFE (*not seeing* ORGON).   Madam, all things have worked out
to perfection;

I've given the neighboring rooms a full inspection;

No one's about; and now I may at last . . .

ORGON (*intercepting him*).   Hold on, my passionate fellow, not so fast!

I should advise a little more restraint.   5

Well, so you thought you'd fool me, my dear saint!

How soon you wearied of the saintly life—

Wedding my daughter, and coveting my wife!

I've long suspected you, and had a feeling

That soon I'd catch you at your double-dealing.   10

Just now, you've given me evidence galore;

It's quite enough; I have no wish for more.

ELMIRE (*to* TARTUFFE).   I'm sorry to have treated you so slyly,

But circumstances forced me to be wily.

TARTUFFE.   Brother, you can't think . . .

ORGON.   No more talk from you;   15

Just leave this household, without more ado.

TARTUFFE.   What I had intended . . .

ORGON.   That seems fairly clear.

Spare me your falsehoods and get out of here.

TARTUFFE.   No, I'm the master, and you're the one to go!

This house belongs to me, I'll have you know,   20

And I shall show you that you can't hurt *me*

By this contemptible conspiracy,

That those who cross me know not what they do,

And that I've means to expose and punish you,

Avenge offended Heaven, and make you grieve   25

That ever you dared order me to leave. (*Exit.*)

SCENE 8

ELMIRE.   What was the point of all that angry chatter?

ORGON.   Dear God, I'm worried. This is no laughing matter.

ELMIRE.   How so?

ORGON.   I fear I understood his drift.
   I'm much disturbed about that deed of gift.
ELMIRE.   You gave him . . . ?
ORGON.   Yes, it's all been drawn and signed.   5
   But one thing more is weighing on my mind.
ELMIRE.   What's that?
ORGON.   I'll tell you; but first let's see if there's
   A certain strong-box in his room upstairs. (*Exeunt.*)

ACT 5

SCENE 1

   Enter ORGON *and* CLÉANTE.

CLÉANTE.   Where are you going so fast?
ORGON.   God knows!
CLÉANTE.   Then wait;
   Let's have a conference, and deliberate
   On how this situation's to be met.
ORGON.   That strong-box has me utterly upset;
   This is the worst of many, many shocks.   5
CLÉANTE.   Is there some fearful mystery in that box?
ORGON.   My poor friend Argas brought that box to me
   With his own hands, in utmost secrecy;
   'Twas on the very morning of his flight.
   It's full of papers which, if they came to light,   10
   Would ruin him—or such is my impression.
CLÉANTE.   Then why did you let it out of your possession?
ORGON.   Those papers vexed my conscience, and it seemed best
   To ask the counsel of my pious guest.
   The cunning scoundrel got me to agree   15
   To leave the strong-box in his custody,
   So that, in case of an investigation,
   I could employ a slight equivocation
   And swear I didn't have it, and thereby,
   At no expense to conscience, tell a lie.   20
CLÉANTE.   It looks to me as if you're out on a limb.
   Trusting him with that box, and offering him
   That deed of gift, were actions of a kind
   Which scarcely indicate a prudent mind.
   With two such weapons, he has the upper hand,   25

And since you're vulnerable, as matters stand,
You erred once more in bringing him to bay.
You should have acted in some subtler way.
ORGON.   Just think of it: behind that fervent face,
A heart so wicked, and a soul so base!   30
I took him in, a hungry beggar, and then . . .
Enough, by God! I'm through with pious men:
Henceforth I'll hate the whole false brotherhood,
And persecute them worse than Satan could.
CLÉANTE.   Ah, there you go—extravagant as ever!   35
Why can you not be rational? You never
Manage to take the middle course, it seems,
But jump, instead, between absurd extremes.
You've recognized your recent grave mistake
In falling victim to a pious fake;   40
Now, to correct that error, must you embrace
An even greater error in its place,
And judge our worthy neighbors as a whole
By what you've learned of one corrupted soul?
Come, just because one rascal made you swallow   45
A show of zeal which turned out to be hollow,
Shall you conclude that all men are deceivers,
And that, today, there are no true believers?
Let atheists make that foolish inference;
Learn to distinguish virtue from pretense,   50
Be cautious in bestowing admiration,
And cultivate a sober moderation.
Don't humor fraud, but also don't asperse
True piety; the latter fault is worse,
And it is best to err, if err one must,   55
As you have done, upon the side of trust.

SCENE 2

Enter DAMIS.

DAMIS.   Father, I hear that scoundrel's uttered threats
Against you; that he pridefully forgets
How, in his need, he was befriended by you,
And means to use your gifts to crucify you.
ORGON.   It's true, my boy. I'm too distressed for tears.   5
DAMIS.   Leave it to me, Sir; let me trim his ears.

Faced with such insolence, we must not waver.
I shall rejoice in doing you the favor
Of cutting short his life, and your distress.
CLÉANTE.   What a display of young hotheadedness!   10
Do learn to moderate your fits of rage.
In this just kingdom, this enlightened age,
One does not settle things by violence.

SCENE 3

Enter MADAME PERNELLE, DORINE, MARIANE, *and* ELMIRE.

MADAME PERNELLE.   I hear strange tales of very strange events.
ORGON.   Yes, strange events which these two eyes beheld.
The man's ingratitude is unparalleled.
I save a wretched pauper from starvation,
House him, and treat him like a blood relation,   5
Shower him every day with my largesse,
Give him my daughter, and all that I possess;
And meanwhile the unconscionable knave
Tries to induce my wife to misbehave;
And not content with such extreme rascality,   10
Now threatens me with my own liberality,
And aims, by taking base advantage of
The gifts I gave him out of Christian love,
To drive me from my house, a ruined man,
And make me end a pauper, as he began.   15
DORINE.   Poor fellow!
MADAME PERNELLE.   No, my son, I'll never bring
Myself to think him guilty of such a thing.
ORGON.   How's that?
MADAME PERNELLE.   The righteous always were maligned.
ORGON.   Speak clearly, Mother. Say what's on your mind.
MADAME PERNELLE.   I mean that I can smell a rat, my dear.   20
You know how everybody hates him, here.
ORGON.   That has no bearing on the case at all.
MADAME PERNELLE.   I told you a hundred times, when you were small,
That virtue in this world is hated ever;
Malicious men may die, but malice never.   25
ORGON.   No doubt that's true, but how does it apply?
MADAME PERNELLE.   They've turned you against him by a clever lie.
ORGON.   I've told you, I was there and saw it done.

MADAME PERNELLE.   Ah, slanderers will stop at nothing, Son.
ORGON.   Mother, I'll lose my temper . . . For the last time,   30
  I tell you I was witness to the crime.
MADAME PERNELLE.   The tongues of spite are busy night and noon,
  And to their venom no man is immune.
ORGON.   You're talking nonsense. Can't you realize
  I saw it; saw it; saw it with my eyes?   35
  Saw, do you understand me? Must I shout it
  Into your ears before you'll cease to doubt it?
MADAME PERNELLE.   Appearances can deceive, my son. Dear me,
  We cannot always judge by what we see.
ORGON.   Drat! Drat!
MADAME PERNELLE.   One often interprets things awry;   40
  Good can seem evil to a suspicious eye.
ORGON.   Was I to see his pawing at Elmire
  As an act of charity?
MADAME PERNELLE.   Till his guilt is clear,
  A man deserves the benefit of the doubt.
  You should have waited, to see how things turned out.   45
ORGON.   Great God in Heaven, what more proof did I need?
  Was I to sit there, watching, until he'd . . .
  You drive me to the brink of impropriety.
MADAME PERNELLE.   No, no, a man of such surpassing piety
  Could not do such a thing. You cannot shake me.   50
  I don't believe it, and you shall not make me.
ORGON.   You vex me so that, if you weren't my mother,
  I'd say to you . . . some dreadful thing or other.
DORINE.   It's your turn now, Sir, not to be listened to;
  You'd not trust us, and now she won't trust you.   55
CLÉANTE.   My friends, we're wasting time which should be spent
  In facing up to our predicament.
  I fear that scoundrel's threats weren't made in sport.
DAMIS.   Do you think he'd have the nerve to go to court?
ELMIRE.   I'm sure he won't: they'd find it all too crude   60
  A case of swindling and ingratitude.
CLÉANTE.   Don't be too sure. He won't be at a loss
  To give his claims a high and righteous gloss;
  And clever rogues with far less valid cause
  Have trapped their victims in a web of laws.   65
  I say again that to antagonize
  A man so strongly armed was most unwise.
ORGON.   I know it; but the man's appalling cheek
  Outraged me so, I couldn't control my pique.

CLÉANTE.   I wish to Heaven that we could devise   70
    Some truce between you, or some compromise.
ELMIRE.   If I had known what cards he held, I'd not
    Have roused his anger by my little plot.
ORGON (*to* DORINE, *as* M. LOYAL *enters*).   What is that fellow looking
    for? Who is he?
    Go talk to him—and tell him that I'm busy.   75

SCENE 4

MONSIEUR LOYAL.   Good day, dear sister. Kindly let me see
    Your master.
DORINE.   He's involved with company,
    And cannot be disturbed just now, I fear.
MONSIEUR LOYAL.   I hate to intrude; but what has brought me here
    Will not disturb your master, in any event.   5
    Indeed, my news will make him most content.
DORINE.   Your name?
MONSIEUR LOYAL.   Just say that I bring greetings from
    Monsieur Tartuffe, on whose behalf I've come.
DORINE (*to* ORGON).   Sir, he's a very gracious man, and bears
    A message from Tartuffe, which, he declares,   10
    Will make you most content.
CLÉANTE.   Upon my word,
    I think this man had best be seen, and heard.
ORGON.   Perhaps he has some settlement to suggest.
    How shall I treat him? What manner would be best?
CLÉANTE.   Control your anger, and if he should mention   15
    Some fair adjustment, give him your full attention.
MONSIEUR LOYAL.   Good health to you, good Sir. May Heaven confound
    Your enemies, and may your joys abound.
ORGON (*aside, to* CLÉANTE).   A gentle salutation: it confirms
    My guess that he is here to offer terms   20
MONSIEUR LOYAL.   I've always held your family most dear;
    I served your father, Sir, for many a year.
ORGON.   Sir, I must ask your pardon; to my shame,
    I cannot now recall your face or name.
MONSIEUR LOYAL.   Loyal's my name; I come from Normandy,   25
    And I'm a bailiff, in all modesty.
    For forty years, praise God, it's been my boast
    To serve with honor in that vital post,
    And I am here, Sir, if you will permit
    The liberty, to serve you with this writ . . .   30

ORGON.   To—*what?*

MONSIEUR LOYAL.   Now, please, Sir, let us have no friction:
It's nothing but an order of eviction.
You are to move your goods and family out
And make way for new occupants, without
Deferment or delay, and give the keys . . .   35

ORGON.   I? Leave this house?

MONSIEUR LOYAL.   Why yes, Sir, if you please.
This house, Sir, from the cellar to the roof,
Belongs now to the good Monsieur Tartuffe,
And he is lord and master of your estate
By virtue of a deed of present date,   40
Drawn in due form, with clearest legal phrasing . . .

DAMIS.   Your insolence is utterly amazing!

MONSIEUR LOYAL.   Young man, my business here is not with you,
But with your wise and temperate father, who,
Like every worthy citizen, stands in awe   45
Of justice, and would never obstruct the law.

ORGON.   But . . .

MONSIEUR LOYAL.   Not for a million, Sir, would you rebel
Against authority; I know that well.
You'll not make trouble, Sir, or interfere
With the execution of my duties here.   50

DAMIS.   Someone may execute a smart tattoo
On that black jacket of yours, before you're through.

MONSIEUR LOYAL.   Sir, bid your son be silent. I'd much regret
Having to mention such a nasty threat
Of violence, in writing my report.   55

DORINE (*aside*).   This man Loyal's a most disloyal sort!

MONSIEUR LOYAL.   I love all men of upright character,
And when I agreed to serve these papers, Sir,
It was your feelings that I had in mind.
I couldn't bear to see the case assigned   60
To someone else, who might esteem you less
And so subject you to unpleasantness.

ORGON.   What's more unpleasant than telling a man to leave
His house and home?

MONSIEUR LOYAL.   You'd like a short reprieve?
If you desire it, Sir, I shall not press you,   65
But wait until tomorrow to dispossess you.
Splendid. I'll come and spend the night here, then,
Most quietly, with half a score of men.

For form's sake, you might bring me, just before
You go to bed, the keys to the front door.   70
My men, I promise, will be on their best
Behavior, and will not disturb your rest.
But bright and early, Sir, you must be quick
And move out all your furniture, every stick:
The men I've chosen are both young and strong,   75
And with their help it shouldn't take you long.
In short, I'll make things pleasant and convenient,
And since I'm being so extremely lenient,
Please show me, Sir, a like consideration,
And give me your entire cooperation.   80

ORGON (aside).   I may be all but bankrupt, but I vow
    I'd give a hundred louis, here and now,
    Just for the pleasure of landing one good clout
    Right on the end of that complacent snout.

CLÉANTE.   Careful; don't make things worse.

DAMIS.   My bootsole itches   85
    To give that beggar a good kick in the breeches.

DORINE.   Monsieur Loyal, I'd love to hear the whack
    Of a stout stick across your fine broad back.

MONSIEUR LOYAL.   Take care: a woman too may go to jail if
    She uses threatening language to a bailiff.   90

CLÉANTE.   Enough, enough, Sir. This must not go on.
    Give me that paper, please, and then begone.

MONSIEUR LOYAL.   Well, au revoir. God give you all good cheer!
    (Leaving.)

ORGON.   May God confound you, and him who sent you here!

SCENE 5

ORGON.   Now, Mother, was I right or not? This writ
    Should change your notion of Tartuffe a bit.
    Do you perceive his villainy at last?

MADAME PERNELLE.   I'm thunderstruck. I'm utterly aghast.

DORINE.   Oh, come, be fair. You mustn't take offense   5
    At this new proof of his benevolence.
    He's acting out of selfless love, I know.
    Material things enslave the soul, and so
    He kindly arranged your liberation
    From all that might endanger your salvation.   10

ORGON.   Will you not ever hold your tongue, you dunce?

CLÉANTE.   Come, you must take some action, and at once.

ELMIRE.   Go tell the world of the low trick he's tried.
  The deed of gift is surely nullified
  By such behavior, and public rage will not   15
  Permit the wretch to carry out his plot.

SCENE 6

  Enter VALÈRE.

VALÈRE.   Sir, though I hate to bring you more bad news,
  Such is the danger that I cannot choose.
  A friend who is extremely close to me
  And knows my interest in your family
  Has, for my sake, presumed to violate   5
  The secrecy that's due to things of state,
  And sends me word that you are in a plight
  From which your one salvation lies in flight.
  That scoundrel who's imposed upon you so
  Denounced you to the King an hour ago   10
  And, as supporting evidence, displayed
  The strong-box of a certain renegade
  Whose secret papers, so he testified,
  You had disloyally agreed to hide.
  I don't know just what charges may be pressed,   15
  But there's a warrant out for your arrest;
  Tartuffe has been instructed, furthermore,
  To guide the arresting officer to your door.
CLÉANTE.   He's clearly done this to facilitate
  His seizure of your house and your estate.   20
ORGON.   That man, I must say, is a vicious beast!
VALÈRE.   Quick, Sir; you mustn't tarry in the least.
  My carriage is outside, to take you hence;
  This thousand louis should cover all expense.
  Let's lose no time, or you shall be undone;   25
  The sole defense, in this case, is to run.
  I shall go with you all the way, and place you
  In a safe refuge to which they'll never trace you.
ORGON.   Alas, dear boy, I wish that I could show you
  My gratitude for everything I owe you.   30
  But now is not the time; I pray the Lord
  That I may live to give you your reward.
  Farewell, my dears; be careful . . .
CLÉANTE.   Brother, hurry.
  We shall take care of things; you needn't worry.

SCENE 7

Enter TARTUFFE *conducting a* POLICE OFFICER.

TARTUFFE.   Gently, Sir, gently; stay right where you are.
No need for haste; your lodging isn't far.
You're off to prison, by order of the Prince.
ORGON.   This is the crowning blow, you wretch; and since
It means my total ruin and defeat,   5
Your villainy is now at last complete.
TARTUFFE.   You needn't try to provoke me; it's no use.
Those who serve heaven must expect abuse.
CLÉANTE.   You are indeed most patient, sweet, and blameless.
DORINE.   How he exploits the name of Heaven! It's shameless.   10
TARTUFFE.   Your taunts and mockeries are all for naught;
To do my duty is my only thought.
MARIANE.   Your love of duty is most meritorious,
And what you've done is little short of glorious.
TARTUFFE.   All deeds are glorious, Madam, which obey   15
The sovereign Prince who sent me here today.
ORGON.   I rescued you when you were destitute;
Have you forgotten that, you thankless brute?
TARTUFFE.   No, no, I well remember everything;
But my first duty is to serve my King.   20
That obligation is so paramount
That other claims, beside it, do not count;
And for it I would sacrifice my wife,
My family, my friend, or my own life.
ELMIRE.   Hypocrite!
DORINE.   All that we most revere, he uses   25
To cloak his plots and camouflage his ruses.
CLÉANTE.   If it is true that you are animated
Be pure and loyal zeal, as you have stated,
Why was this zeal not roused until you'd sought
To make Orgon a cuckold, and been caught?   30
Why weren't you moved to give your evidence
Until your outraged host had driven you hence?
I shan't say that the gift of all his treasure
Ought to have damped your zeal in any measure;
But if he is a traitor, as you declare,   35
How could you condescend to be his heir?
TARTUFFE (*to the* OFFICER).   Sir, spare me all this clamor; it's growing
    shrill.
Please carry out your orders, if you will.

OFFICER.   Yes, I've delayed too long, Sir. Thank you kindly.
    You're just the proper person to remind me.   40
    Come, you are off to join the other boarders
    In the King's prison, according to his orders.
TARTUFFE.   Who? I, Sir?
OFFICER.   Yes.
TARTUFFE.   To prison? This can't be true!
OFFICER.   I owe an explanation, but not to you.
    (*To* ORGON) Sir, all is well; rest easy, and be grateful.   45
    We serve a Prince to whom all sham is hateful,
    A Prince who sees into our inmost hearts,
    And can't be fooled by any trickster's arts.
    His royal soul, though generous and human,
    Views all things with discernment and acumen;   50
    His sovereign reason is not lightly swayed,
    And all his judgments are discreetly weighed.
    He honors righteous men of every kind,
    And yet his zeal for virtue is not blind,
    Nor does his love of piety numb his wits   55
    And make him tolerant of hypocrites.
    'Twas hardly likely that this man could cozen
    A King who's foiled such liars by the dozen.
    With one keen glance the King perceived the whole
    Perverseness and corruption of his soul,   60
    And thus high Heaven's justice was displayed:
    Betraying you, the rogue stood self-betrayed.
    The King soon recognized Tartuffe as one
    Notorious by another name, who'd done
    So many vicious crimes that one could fill   65
    Ten volumes with them, and be writing still.
    But to be brief: our sovereign was appalled
    By this man's treachery toward you, which he called
    The last, worst villainy of a vile career,
    And bade me follow the impostor here   70
    To see how gross his impudence could be,
    And force him to restore your property.
    Your private papers, by the King's command,
    I hereby seize and give into your hand.
    The King, by royal order, invalidates   75
    The deed which gave this rascal your estates,
    And pardons, furthermore, your grave offense
    In harboring an exile's documents.

By these decrees, our Prince rewards you for
Your loyal deeds in the late civil war,   80
And shows how heartfelt is his satisfaction
In recompensing any worthy action,
How much he prizes merit, and how he makes
More of men's virtues than of their mistakes.
DORINE.   Heaven be praised!
MADAME PERNELLE.   I breathe again, at last.   85
ELMIRE.   We're safe.
MARIANE.   I can't believe the danger's past.
ORGON (*to* TARTUFFE).   Well, traitor, now you see . . .
CLÉANTE.   Ah, Brother, please,
Let's not descend to such indignities.
Leave the poor wretch to his unhappy fate,
And don't say anything to aggravate   90
His present woes; but rather hope that he
Will soon embrace an honest piety,
And mend his ways, and by a true repentance
Move our just King to moderate his sentence.
Meanwhile, go kneel before your sovereign's throne   95
And thank him for the mercies he has shown.
ORGON.   Well said: let's go at once and, gladly kneeling,
Express the gratitude which all are feeling.
Then, when that first great duty has been done,
We'll turn with pleasure to a second one,   100
And give Valère, whose love has proven so true,
The wedded happiness which is his due.

QUESTIONS

1. The title character does not appear on the stage until Act 3, though he is the topic of all conversation preceding his entrance. How has he gained entrance to Orgon's household, and what is his function there? What expectations do you have about him before he appears? Do his actions hold any surprises for you?

2. Orgon as protagonist is preyed upon by his antagonist Tartuffe, but also displays characteristics that make him easily victimized. What are these, and how are they revealed not only in his dealings with Tartuffe but in other actions? What kinds of internal conflicts does he have?

3. The romantic subplot of Mariane and Valère suffers the traditional difficulties of a "blocking" father and a lovers' quarrel. Trace how these difficulties are overcome, and discuss the ways in which the subplot is integrated into the major plot. How is it more than an amusing contrast to the plot of Tartuffe's rise and fall?

4. What are Mme. Pernelle's complaints about her son's family? What set of values does she uphold? How does the first act define the moral and social values of the society in which the play is set?

5. A *raisonneur* is a character in a play who speaks for the author, providing commentary and correcting the mistaken ideas of others. How do Cléante and Dorine represent normative values? How are they more than mere mouthpieces for Molière?

6. This play employs some of the devices of farce. Identify these, and indicate how they support characterization, plot, and meaning in the play. In particular, how does the scene in which Orgon is hidden under the table (4.5) provide physical action that parallels meaning?

7. How does the scene with M. Loyal provide a miniature version of Tartuffe's relations with Orgon?

8. One early version of the play was called *Tartuffe, or The Hypocrite*. What implications does that title have, and how do they differ from those of the present title? Which more accurately captures the themes of the play?

9. Is the king's intervention in the final scene plausible? It resolves the conflicts between the antagonist and the protagonist, but to what extent does it provide a conclusion to the themes the play has raised?

10. Acts 1–3 flow continuously without any breaks in time. How much time is presumed to have elapsed between Acts 3 and 4, and between Acts 4 and 5? What is the effect of a play's action taking no more time than its stage performance? How closely do other plays in this book match this use of time?

11. Early versions of the play were suppressed because they were thought to satirize religion. Is that an accurate estimation of this play? Why, or why not? Aside from Tartuffe's actions and speeches, what information does the play provide about religious belief and behavior?

12. Aside from the use of poetry for dialogue, would you judge this play to be more realistic or nonrealistic?

Anton Chekhov
The Boor
A Jest in One Act

Characters

YELENA IVANOVNA POPOVA, *a little widow with dimpled cheeks, a landowner*
GRIGORY STEPANOVICH SMIRNOV, *a middle-aged gentleman farmer*
LUKA, Mme. *Popova's footman, an old man*

The drawing room in Mme. Popova's manor house. Mme. Popova, in deep mourning, her eyes fixed on a photograph, and Luka.

LUKA.   It isn't right, madam. You're just killing yourself. The maid and the cook have gone berrying, every living thing rejoices, even the cat knows how to enjoy life and wanders through the courtyard catching birds, but you stay in the house as if it were a convent and take no pleasure at all. Yes, really! It's a whole year now, I figure, that you haven't left the house!

MME. POPOVA.   And I never will leave it . . . What for? My life is over. He lies in his grave, and I have buried myself within these four walls. We are both dead.

LUKA.   There you go again! I oughtn't to listen to you, really. Nikolay Mihailovich is dead, well, there is nothing to do about it, it's the will of God; may the kingdom of Heaven be his. You have grieved over it, and that's enough; there's a limit to everything. One can't cry and wear mourning forever. The time came when my old woman, too, died. Well? I grieved over it, I cried for a month, and that was enough for her, but to go on wailing all my life, why, the old woman isn't worth it. (*Sighs.*) You've forgotten all your neighbors. You don't go out and

THE BOOR   First performed in 1888. Translated by Avrahm Yarmolinsky. This, one of the one-act plays Chekhov referred to as "vaudevilles," was his first genuine stage success, and was so popular in production that he called it his "milch-cow" (his "cash-cow," a rich source of income for him). Anton Chekhov (1860–1904)—also the author of "Gooseberries" in the fiction section of this book (page 202)—was educated as a physician but gave up his profession when he was financially successful as a writer. The title is transliterated "Medved," a Russian word that means "bear," and metaphorically has been interpreted to imply "boor" and "brute"; all three words have been used as names for this play. For a note on Russian names, see page 202.

you won't receive anyone. We live, excuse me, like spiders—we never see the light of day. The mice have eaten the livery. And it isn't as if there were no nice people around—the county is full of gentlemen. A regiment is quartered at Ryblov and every officer is a good-looker, you can't take your eyes off them. And every Friday there's a ball at the camp, and 'most every day the military band is playing. Eh, my dear lady, you're young and pretty, just peaches and cream, and you could lead a life of pleasure. Beauty doesn't last forever, you know. In ten years' time you'll find yourself wanting to strut like a pea-hen and dazzle the officers, but it will be too late.

MME. POPOVA (*resolutely*).   I beg you never to mention this to me again! You know that since Nikolay Mihailovich died, life has been worth nothing to me. You think that I am alive, but it only seems so to you! I vowed to myself that never to the day of my death would I take off my mourning or see the light. Do you hear me? Let his shade see how I love him! Yes, I know, it is no secret to you that he was often unjust to me, cruel, and . . . even unfaithful, but I shall be true to the end, and prove to him how I can love. There, in the other world, he will find me just the same as I was before he died . . .

LUKA.   Instead of talking like that, you ought to go and take a walk in the garden, or have Toby or Giant put in the shafts° and drive out to pay calls on the neighbors.

MME. POPOVA.   Oh! (*Weeps.*)

LUKA.   Madam! Dear madam! What's wrong? Bless you!

MME. POPOVA.   He was so fond of Toby! When he drove out to the Korchagins and the Vlasovs it was always with Toby. What a wonderful driver he was! How graceful he was, when he pulled at the reins with all his might! Do you remember? Toby, Toby! Tell them to give him an extra measure of oats today.

LUKA.   Very well, madam. (*The doorbell rings sharply.*)

MME. POPOVA (*startled*).   Who is it? Say that I am at home to no one.

LUKA.   Very good, madam. (*Exits.*)

MME. POPOVA (*looking at the photograph*).   You shall see, *Nicolas*, how I can love and forgive. My love will die only with me, when my poor heart stops beating. (*Laughs through her tears.*) And aren't you ashamed? I am a good, faithful little wife, I've locked myself in and shall remain true to you to the grave, and you . . . aren't you ashamed, you naughty boy? You were unfaithful to me, you made scenes, you left me alone for weeks . . . (LUKA *enters.*)

---

put . . . shafts: harnessed to the carriage

LUKA (*disturbed*).   Madam, someone is asking for you, wants to see you . . .

MME. POPOVA.   But you told him, didn't you, that since my husband's death I receive no one?

LUKA.   Yes, I did, but he wouldn't listen to me, he says it's a very urgent matter.

MME. POPOVA.   I do not re-ceive anyone!

LUKA.   I told him, but . . . he's a perfect devil . . . he curses and barges right in . . . he's in the dining-room now.

MME. POPOVA (*annoyed*).   Very well, ask him in . . . What rude people! (*Exit* LUKA.) How irritating! What do they want of me? Why do they have to intrude on my solitude? (*Sighs.*) No, I see I shall really have to enter a convent. (*Pensively.*) Yes, a convent . . . (*Enter* SMIRNOV *and* LUKA.)

SMIRNOV (*to* LUKA).   Blockhead, you talk too much. You jackass! (*Seeing* MME. POPOVA, *with dignity*) Madam, I have the honor to introduce myself: Landowner Grigory Stepanovich Smirnov, lieutenant of the artillery, retired. I am compelled to disturb you in connection with a very weighty matter.

MME. POPOVA (*without offering her hand*).   What do you wish?

SMIRNOV.   At his death your late husband, with whom I had the honor of being acquainted, was in my debt to the amount of 1200 rubles, for which I hold two notes. As I have to pay interest on a loan to the Land Bank tomorrow, I must request you, madam, to pay me the money today.

MME. POPOVA.   Twelve hundred. . . . And for what did my husband owe you the money?

SMIRNOV.   He used to buy oats from me.

MME. POPOVA (*sighing, to* LUKA).   So don't forget, Luka, to tell them to give Toby an extra measure of oats. (*Exit* LUKA. *To* SMIRNOV) If Nikolay Mihailovich owed you money, I shall pay you, of course; but you must excuse me, I haven't any ready cash today. The day after tomorrow my steward will be back from town and I will see that he pays you what is owing to you, but just now I cannot comply with your request. Besides, today is exactly seven months since my husband's death and I am in no mood to occupy myself with money matters.

SMIRNOV.   And I am in the mood to be carried out feet foremost if I don't pay the interest tomorrow. They'll seize my estate!

MME. POPOVA.   The day after tomorrow you will receive your money.

SMIRNOV.   I need the money today, not the day after tomorrow.

MME. POPOVA.   I am sorry, but I cannot pay you today.

SMIRNOV.   And I can't wait till the day after tomorrow.

MME. POPOVA.   But what can I do if I don't have the money now!

SMIRNOV.   So you can't pay me?

MME. POPOVA.   No, I can't.

SMIRNOV.   H'm . . . So that's your last word?

MME. POPOVA.   My last word.

SMIRNOV.   Your last word? Positively?

MME. POPOVA.   Positively.

SMIRNOV.   Many thanks. I'll make a note of it. (*Shrugs his shoulders.*) And they want me to keep cool! I meet the tax commissioner on the road, and he asks me: "Why are you always in a bad humor, Grigory Stepanovich?" But in heaven's name, how can I help being in a bad humor? I'm in desperate need of money. I left home yesterday morning at dawn and called on all my debtors and not one of them paid up! I wore myself out, slept the devil knows where, in some Jewish inn next to a barrel of vodka . . . Finally I come here, fifty miles from home, hoping to get something, and I'm confronted with a "mood." How can I help getting in a temper?

MME. POPOVA.   I thought I made it clear to you that you will get your money as soon as my steward returns from town.

SMIRNOV.   I didn't come to your steward, but to you! What the devil—pardon the expression—do I care for your steward!

MME. POPOVA.   Excuse me, sir, I am not accustomed to such language or to such a tone. I won't listen to you any more. (*Exits rapidly.*)

SMIRNOV.   That's a nice thing! Not in the mood . . . husband died seven months ago! What about me? Do I have to pay the interest or don't I? I'm asking you: do I have to pay the interest or don't I? Well, your husband died, you're not in the mood, and all that . . . and your steward, devil take him, has gone off somewhere, but what do you want me to do? Am I to escape my creditors in a balloon, eh? Or take a running start and dash my head against a wall? I call on Gruzdev, he's not at home, Yaroshevich is hiding, I had an awful row with Kuritzyn and nearly threw him out of the window; Mazutov has an upset stomach, and this one isn't in the mood! Not one scoundrel will pay up! And it's all because I've spoiled them, because I'm a milksop, a softy, a weak sister. I'm too gentle with them altogether! But wait! You'll find out what I'm like! I won't let you make a fool of me, devil take it! I'll stay right here till she pays up! Ugh! I'm in a perfect rage today, in a rage! Every one of my nerves is trembling with fury, I can hardly breathe. Ouf! Good Lord, I even feel sick! (*Shouts.*) You there! (*Enter* LUKA.)

LUKA.   What do you wish?

SMIRNOV. Give me some *kvass*° or a drink of water! (*Exit* LUKA.) No, but the logic of it! A fellow is in desperate need of cash, is on the point of hanging himself, but she won't pay up, because, you see, she isn't in the mood to occupy herself with money matters! Real petticoat logic! That's why I've never liked to talk to women, and I don't now. I'd rather sit on a powder-keg than talk to a woman. Brr! I'm getting gooseflesh—that skirt made me so furious! I just have to see one of these poetic creatures from a distance and my very calves begin to twitch with rage. It's enough to make me yell for help. (*Enter* LUKA.)

LUKA (*handing* SMIRNOV *a glass of water*).   Madam is ill and will see no one.

SMIRNOV.   Get out! (*Exit* LUKA.) Ill and will see no one! All right, don't see me. I'll sit here until you pay up. If you're sick for a week, I'll stay a week; if you're sick a year, I'll stay a year. I'll get my own back, my good woman. You won't get round me with your widow's weeds and your dimples . . . We know those dimples! (*Shouts through the window.*) Semyon, take out the horses! We're not leaving so soon! I'm staying on! Tell them at the stables to give the horses oats. You blockhead, you've let the left outrider's leg get caught in the reins again! (*Mimicking the coachman.*) "It don't matter" . . . I'll show you "don't matter." (*Walks away from the window.*) It's horrible . . . the heat is terrific, nobody has paid up, I slept badly, and here's this skirt in mourning, with her moods! I have a headache. Shall I have some vodka? Yes, I think I will. (*Shouts.*) You there! (*Enter* LUKA.)

LUKA.   What do you wish?

SMIRNOV.   Give me a glass of vodka. (*Exit* LUKA.) Ouf! (*Sits down and looks himself over.*) I cut a fine figure, I must say! All dusty, boots dirty, unwashed, uncombed, straw on my vest. The little lady must have taken me for a highwayman. (*Yawns.*) It's a bit uncivil to barge into a drawing-room in such shape, but never mind . . . I'm no caller, just a creditor, and there are no rules as to what the creditor should wear. (*Enter* LUKA.)

LUKA (*handing* SMIRNOV *the vodka*).   You allow yourself too many liberties, sir . . .

SMIRNOV (*crossly*).   What?

LUKA.   I . . . nothing . . . I just meant . . .

SMIRNOV.   To whom do you think you're talking? Shut up!

LUKA (*aside*).   There's a demon in the house . . . The Evil Spirit must have brought him . . . (*Exit* LUKA.)

___

kvass: homemade fermented drink

SMIRNOV.   Oh, what a rage I'm in! I'm mad enough to grind the whole world to powder. I feel sick. (*Shouts.*) You there! (*Enter* MME. POPOVA.)

MME. POPOVA (*with downcast eyes*).   Sir, in my solitude I've long since grown unaccustomed to the human voice, and I cannot bear shouting. I beg you not to disturb my peace!

SMIRNOV.   Pay me my money and I'll drive off.

MME. POPOVA.   I told you in plain language, I have no ready cash now. Wait till the day after tomorrow.

SMIRNOV.   And I had the honor of telling you in plain language that I need the money today, not the day after tomorrow. If you don't pay me today, I'll have to hang myself tomorrow.

MME. POPOVA.   But what shall I do if I have no money? How odd!

SMIRNOV.   So you won't pay me now, eh?

MME. POPOVA.   I can't.

SMIRNOV.   In that case I stay and I'll sit here till I get the money. (*Sits down.*) You'll pay me the day after tomorrow? Excellent. I'll sit here till the day after tomorrow. (*Jumps up.*) I ask you: Do I have to pay the interest tomorrow or don't I? Or do you think I'm joking?

MME. POPOVA.   Sir, I beg you not to shout. This is no stable.

SMIRNOV.   Never mind the stable, I'm asking you: Do I have to pay the interest tomorrow or not?

MME. POPOVA.   You don't know how to behave in the presence of ladies!

SMIRNOV.   No, madam, I do know how to behave in the presence of ladies!

MME. POPOVA.   No, you do not! You are a rude, ill-bred man! Decent people don't talk to women that way!

SMIRNOV.   Admirable! How would you like me to talk to you? In French, eh? (*Rages, and lisps.*) Madame, je vous prie,° I am delighted that you do not pay me my money . . . Ah, pardonnez-moi if I have discommoded you! It's such delightful weather today! And how your mourning becomes you! (*Scrapes his foot.*)

MME. POPOVA.   That's rude and silly.

SMIRNOV (*mimicking her*).   Rude and silly! I don't know how to behave in the presence of ladies! Madam, I've seen more ladies than you've seen sparrows! I've fought three duels on account of women, I've jilted twelve women and been jilted by nine! Yes, madam! Time was when I played the fool, sentimentalized, used honeyed words, went out of my way to please, bowed and scraped . . . I used to love, pine, sigh at

---

Madame . . . prie: Madam, I beg of you

the moon, feel blue, melt, freeze . . . I loved passionately, madly, all sorts of ways, devil take me; I chattered like a magpie about the emancipation of women, I wasted half my fortune on affairs of the heart, but now, please excuse me! Now you won't bamboozle me! Enough! Dark eyes, burning eyes, ruby lips, dimpled cheeks, the moon, whispers, timid breathing . . . I wouldn't give a brass farthing for all this now, madam. Present company excepted, all women, young or old, put on airs, pose, gossip, are liars to the marrow of their bones, are malicious, vain, petty, cruel, revoltingly unreasonable, and as for this (*taps his forehead*), pardon my frankness, a sparrow can give ten points to any philosopher in skirts! You look at one of these poetic creatures: she's all muslin and fluff, an airy demi-goddess, a million transports, but look into her soul and what do you see but a common crocodile! (*Grips the back of his chair so that it cracks and breaks.*) But what is most revolting, this crocodile for some reason imagines that the tender feelings are her special province, her privilege, her monopoly! Why, devil take it, hang me by my feet on that nail, but can a woman love anything except a lap-dog? When she's in love all she can do is whimper and turn on the waterworks! While a man suffers and makes sacrifices, her love finds expression only in swishing her train and trying to get a firmer grip on your nose. You, madam, have the misfortune of being a woman, so you know the nature of women down to the ground. Tell me honestly, then, did you ever see a woman who was sincere, faithful, and constant? You never did! Only old women and frights are faithful and constant. You'll sooner come across a horned cat or a white woodcock than a constant woman!

MME. POPOVA.   Allow me to ask, then, who, in your opinion, is faithful and constant in love? Not man?

SMIRNOV.   Yes, madam, man!

MME. POPOVA.   Man! (*With bitter laughter.*) Man is faithful and constant in love! That's news! (*Hotly.*) What earthly right do you have to say that? Men faithful and constant! If such is the case, let me tell you that of all the men I have ever known my late husband was the best. I loved him passionately, with my whole soul, as only a young, deep-natured woman can love. I gave him my youth, my happiness, my life, my fortune; I lived and breathed by him; I worshiped him like a heathen, and . . . and what happened? This best of men deceived me shamelessly at every step! After his death I found a whole drawerful of love letters in his desk, and while he was alive—I can't bear to recall it!—he would leave me alone for weeks on end; he made love to other women before my very eyes, and he was unfaithful to me; he squandered my money and mocked my feelings. And in spite of it all, I loved him and was faithful to him. More than that, he died, and I am still faithful to him, still constant. I have buried myself forever within these four walls, and I will not take off my mourning till I go to my grave.

SMIRNOV (*laughing scornfully*).   Mourning! I wonder who you take me for! As if I didn't know why you are masquerading in black like this and why you've buried yourself within four walls! Of course I do! It's so mysterious, so poetic! Some cadet or some puny versifier will ride past the house, glance at the windows, and say to himself: "Here lives the mysterious Tamara who, for love of her husband, has buried herself within four walls." We know those tricks!

MME. POPOVA (*flaring up*).   What! How dare you say this to me!

SMIRNOV.   You've buried yourself alive, but you haven't forgotten to powder your nose.

MME. POPOVA.   How dare you talk to me like that!

SMIRNOV.   Please don't scream, I'm not your steward! Allow me to call a spade a spade. I'm no woman and I'm used to talking straight from the shoulder! So please don't shout!

MME. POPOVA.   I'm not shouting, you are shouting! Please leave me alone!

SMIRNOV.   Pay me my money, and I'll go.

MME. POPOVA.   I won't give you any money.

SMIRNOV.   No, madam, you will!

MME. POPOVA.   Just to spite you, I won't give you a penny. Only leave me alone!

SMIRNOV.   I haven't the pleasure of being either your husband or your fiancé, so kindly, no scenes. (*Sits down.*) I don't like them.

MME. POPOVA (*choking with rage*).   You've sat down?

SMIRNOV.   I've sat down.

MME. POPOVA.   I ask you to leave.

SMIRNOV.   Give me my money . . . (*Aside*) Oh, what a rage I'm in, what a rage!

MME. POPOVA.   Such impudence! I don't want to talk to you. Please get out. (*Pause.*) Are you going? No?

SMIRNOV.   No.

MME. POPOVA.   No?

SMIRNOV.   No!

MME. POPOVA.   Very well, then. (*Enter* LUKA.)

MME. POPOVA.   Luka, show this gentleman out!

LUKA (*approaching* SMIRNOV).   Sir, be good enough to leave when you are asked to. Don't be—

SMIRNOV (*jumping to his feet*).   Shut up! Who do you think you're talking to! I'll make hash of you!

LUKA (*clutching at his heart*).   Mercy on us! Holy saints! (*Drops into an armchair.*) Oh, I'm sick, I'm sick! I can't get my breath!

MME. POPOVA.   But where is Dasha? Dasha? (*Shouts.*) Dasha! Pelageya! Dasha! (*Rings.*)

LUKA.   Oh, they've all gone berrying . . . There's no one here . . . I'm sick, water!

MME. POPOVA (*to* SMIRNOV).   Please, get out!

SMIRNOV.   Can't you be a little more civil?

MME. POPOVA (*clenching her fists and stamping her feet*).   You're a boor! A brute, a bully, a monster!

SMIRNOV.   What! What did you say?

MME. POPOVA.   I said that you were a brute, a monster.

SMIRNOV (*advancing upon her*).   Excuse me, but what right have you to insult me?

MME. POPOVA.   Yes, I insulted you. What of it? Do you think I'm afraid of you?

SMIRNOV.   And you think, just because you're a poetic creature, you can insult people with impunity, eh? I challenge you!

LUKA.   Mercy on us! Holy saints! Water!

SMIRNOV.   We'll shoot it out!

MME. POPOVA.   Just because you have big fists and bellow like a bull, you think I'm afraid of you, eh? Bully!

SMIRNOV.   I challenge you! I won't allow anybody to insult me, and it makes no difference to me that you're a woman, a member of the weaker sex.

MME. POPOVA (*trying to outshout him*).   Brute, brute, brute!

SMIRNOV.   It's high time to abandon the prejudice that men alone must pay for insults. Equal rights are equal rights, devil take it! I challenge you!

MME. POPOVA.   You want to shoot it out? Well and good.

SMIRNOV.   This very minute.

MME. POPOVA.   This very minute. I have my husband's pistols. I'll bring them directly. (*Walks rapidly away and turns back.*) What pleasure it will give me to put a bullet into your brazen head! Devil take you! (*Exits.*)

SMIRNOV.   I'll bring her down like a duck. I'm no boy, no sentimental puppy. There's no weaker sex as far as I'm concerned.

LUKA.   Master, kind sir! (*Going down on his knees.*) Have pity on an old man, do me a favor—go away from here! You've frightened me to death, and now you want to fight a duel!

SMIRNOV (*not listening to him*).   A duel! That's equal rights, that's emancipation! That's equality of the sexes for you! I'll bring her down as a matter of principle. But what a woman! (*Mimics her.*) "Devil take you . . . I'll put a bullet into your brazen head." What a woman! She flushed and her eyes shone! She accepted the challenge!

Word of honor, it's the first time in my life that I've seen one of that stripe.

LUKA.   Kind master, please go away, and I will pray for you always.

SMIRNOV.   That's a woman! That's the kind I understand! A real woman! Not a sour-faced, spineless crybaby, but a creature all fire and gunpowder, a cannonball! It's a pity I have to kill her!

LUKA (crying).   Sir, kind sir, please go away!

SMIRNOV.   I positively like her! Positively! Even though she has dimples in her cheeks, I like her! I am even ready to forgive her the debt . . . And I'm not angry any more. A remarkable woman! (Enter MME. POPOVA with the pistols.)

MME. POPOVA.   Here are the pistols. But before we fight, please show me how to shoot. I never held a pistol in my hands before.

LUKA.   Lord, have mercy on us! I'll go and look for the gardener and the coachman. Why has this calamity befallen us? (Exit.)

SMIRNOV (examining the pistols).   You see, there are several makes of pistols. There are Mortimers, specially made for duelling, they are fired with the percussion cap. What you have here are Smith and Wesson triple-action, central-fire revolvers with extractors. Excellent pistols! Worth ninety rubles a pair at least. You hold the revolver like this . . . (Aside.) The eyes, the eyes! A woman to set you on fire!

MME. POPOVA.   Like this?

SMIRNOV.   Yes, like this. Then you cock the trigger . . . and you take aim like this . . . throw your head back a little! Stretch your arm out properly . . . Like this . . . Then you press this gadget with this finger, and that's all there is to it. . . . The main thing is: keep cool and take aim slowly. . . . And try not to jerk your arm.

MME. POPOVA.   Very well. It's inconvenient to shoot indoors, let's go into the garden.

SMIRNOV.   All right. Only I warn you, I'll fire into the air.

MME. POPOVA.   That's all that was wanting. Why?

SMIRNOV.   Because . . . because . . . It's my business why.

MME. POPOVA.   You're scared, eh? Ah, ah, ah! No, sir, don't try to get out of it! Be so good as to follow me. I shan't rest until I've drilled a hole in your forehead . . . this forehead that I hate so! Scared?

SMIRNOV.   Yes, I am scared.

MME. POPOVA.   You're lying! Why do you refuse to fight?

SMIRNOV.   Because . . . because I . . . like you.

MME. POPOVA (laughing bitterly).   He likes me! He dares to say that he likes me! (Shows him the door.) You may go.

SMIRNOV (silently puts down the revolver, takes his cap and walks to the door; there he stops and for half a minute the pair look at each other without *a word; then he says, hesitatingly approaching* MME. POPOVA).   Listen . . . Are you still angry? I'm in a devil of a temper myself, but you see . . . how shall I put it? . . . the thing is . . . you see . . . it's this way . . . in fact . . . (*Shouts.*) Well, am I to blame if I like you? (*Clutches the back of his chair; it cracks and breaks.*) The devil! What fragile furniture you have! I like you. You understand. I've almost fallen in love.

MME. POPOVA.   Go away from me. I hate you.

SMIRNOV.   God, what a woman! Never in my life have I seen anything like her! I'm lost. I'm done for. I'm trapped like a mouse.

MME. POPOVA.   Go away, or I'll shoot.

SMIRNOV.   Shoot! You can't understand what happiness it would be to die before those enchanting eyes . . . to die of a revolver shot fired by this little velvet hand! I've lost my mind. Think a moment and decide right now, because if I leave this house, we'll never see each other again. Decide. I'm a landed gentleman, a decent fellow, with an income of ten thousand a year; I can put a bullet through a penny thrown into the air; I have a good stable. Will you be my wife?

MME. POPOVA (*indignant, brandishing the revolver*).   We'll shoot it out! Come along! Get your pistol.

SMIRNOV.   I've lost my mind. I don't understand anything. (*Shouts.*) You there! Some water!

MME. POPOVA (*shouts*).   Come! Let's shoot it out!

SMIRNOV.   I've lost my mind. I've fallen in love like a boy, like a fool. (*Seizes her by the hand; she cries out with pain.*) I love you. (*Goes down on his knees.*) I love you as I've never loved before. I jilted twelve women and was jilted by nine. But I didn't love one of them as I do you. I've gotten sentimental. I'm melting. I'm weak as water. Here I am on my knees like a fool, and I offer you my hand. It's a shame, a disgrace! For five years I've not been in love. I took a vow. And suddenly I'm bowled over, swept off my feet. I offer you my hand—yes or no? You won't? Then don't! (*Rises and walks rapidly to the door.*)

MME. POPOVA.   Wait a minute.

SMIRNOV (*stops*).   Well?

MME. POPOVA.   Never mind. Go . . . But no, wait a minute . . . No, go, go! I detest you! Or no . . . don't go! Oh, if you knew how furious I am, how furious! (*Throws the revolver on the table.*) My fingers are cramped from holding this vile thing. (*Tears her handkerchief in a fit of temper.*) What are you standing there for? Get out!

SMIRNOV.   Good-by.

MME. POPOVA.   Yes, yes, go! (*Shouts.*) Where are you going? Wait a minute . . . But no, go away . . . Oh, how furious I am! Don't come near me, don't come near me!

SMIRNOV (*approaching her*).   I'm disgusted with myself! Falling in love like a moon-calf, going down on my knees. It gives me gooseflesh. (*Rudely.*) I love you. What on earth made me fall in love with you? Tomorrow I have to pay the interest. And we've started mowing. And here are you! . . . (*Puts his arm around her waist.*) I shall never forgive myself for this.

MME. POPOVA.   Get away from me! Hands off! I hate you! Let's shoot it out!

(*A prolonged kiss. Enter* LUKA *with an ax, the gardener with a rake, the coachman with a pitchfork, and hired men with sticks.*)

LUKA (*catching sight of the pair kissing*).   Mercy on us! Holy saints! (*Pauses.*)

MME. POPOVA (*dropping her eyes*).   Luka, tell them at the stables that Toby isn't to have any oats at all today.

QUESTIONS

1. Both Mme. Popova and Smirnov have settled preconceptions about themselves and their relations with other people. Define these as precisely as possible. Can you infer the origins of these preconceptions? What have been their life experiences leading up to their confrontation?
2. Ostensibly, the plot of the play is based on the resolution of the conflict between the two characters, and ends with the typical conclusion of a romantic comedy. But both of the characters also discover in themselves an inner conflict. Define both kinds of conflicts (external and internal), and demonstrate that the apparently simple plot is in fact complex.
3. How do the attitudes and reactions of the servant Luka contrast to those of Mme. Popova and Smirnov? Does he provide a standard by which their extreme behavior is judged?
4. One critic has claimed that the kiss that ends the play is both inevitable and predictable, given the personalities of the two characters and their exaggerated behavior. What support can you find for that assertion?
5. What is the effect of Mme. Popova's ordering extra oats for Toby the horse, and of her final command that he should have no oats at all? What motivates her in each case? What is the symbolic meaning of this reversal?
6. Unlike most realistic drama, this play makes extensive use of soliloquies and asides. Would you say, then, that this is a nonrealistic play? What elements of farce can you discover in it?

SUGGESTIONS FOR WRITING

1. One of the structural devices regularly used by Shakespeare is contrast in tone, content, or effect. In tragedies, he follows a scene of high seriousness with a comic scene (commonly called **comic relief,** because like a "relief map," it delineates for us by contrast the heights of emotion that we have just experienced). Conversely, in comedies, we often encounter actions that

threaten dire consequences or remind the audience of the less pleasant side of life (no one has labeled this "tragic relief," though that might be an appropriate term). Using "Los Vendidos," *Tartuffe*, "The Boor," or *A Midsummer Night's Dream*, write an essay that explores the emotional effects of these contrasts.

2. Using one of the plays in this chapter, write an essay demonstrating the idea that the conclusion of a tragedy or of a comedy has a mixed effect on the audience—that tragedy does not produce unmitigated woe and depression, that comedy leaves its audience not only laughing but with a renewed sense of its own limitations.

3. Explore the emotional effects of the conclusions of one or more of the following: Glaspell's "Trifles," Albee's "The Sandbox," Ibsen's *A Doll House*, Williams's *The Glass Menagerie*.

4. Write an essay about one of the seven plays in chapters 1 and 2 showing it to be an example of one of the four dramatic categories defined in this chapter—tragedy, comedy, melodrama, or farce. If your choice does not wholly fit into one of the categories, explore the ways in which it has characteristics of more than one of them.

Plays for Further Reading

Christopher Durang
For Whom the Southern Belle Tolls
(or "The Further Adventures of Amanda and Her Children")

Characters

AMANDA, *the mother*
LAWRENCE, *the son*
TOM, *the other son*
GINNY

Lights up on a fussy living room setting. Enter AMANDA, *the Southern belle mother.*

AMANDA.   Rise and shine! Rise and shine! (*Calls off*) Lawrence, honey, come on out here and let me have a look at you! (*Enter* LAWRENCE, *who limps across the room. He is very sensitive, and is wearing what are clearly his dress clothes.* AMANDA *fiddles with his bow tie and stands back to admire him.*)

AMANDA.   Lawrence, honey, you look lovely.

LAWRENCE.   No, I don't mama. I have a pimple on the back of my neck.

AMANDA.   Don't say the word "pimple," honey, it's common. Now your brother Tom is bringing home a girl from the warehouse for you to meet, and I want you to make a good impression, honey.

LAWRENCE.   It upsets my stomach to meet people, mama.

AMANDA.   Oh, Lawrence honey, you're so sensitive it makes me want to hit you.

LAWRENCE.   I don't need to meet people, mama. I'm happy just by myself, playing with my collection of glass cocktail stirrers. (LAWRENCE *limps over to a table on top of which sits a glass jar filled with glass swizzle sticks.*)

AMANDA.   Lawrence, you are a caution. Only retarded people and alcoholics are interested in glass cocktail stirrers.

FOR WHOM THE SOUTHERN BELLE TOLLS   First performed in 1994 and published in *The Best American Short Plays 1993–1994.* Christopher Durang, prize-winning actor and playwright, was born in 1949 in Montclair, New Jersey, and graduated from Harvard and the Yale School of Drama. His first big success was the Off-Broadway production in 1981 of *Sister Mary Ignatius Explains It All for You.* The characters in this play are derived from Tennessee Williams's *The Glass Menagerie* (page 1143).

LAWRENCE (*picking up some of them*).   Each one of them has a special name, mama. This one is called Stringbean because it's long and thin; and this one is called Stringbean because it's long and thin; and this one is called Blue because it's blue.

AMANDA.   All my children have such imagination, why was I so blessed? Oh, Lawrence honey, how are you going to get on in the world if you just stay home all day, year after year, playing with your collection of glass cocktail stirrers?

LAWRENCE.   I don't like the world, mama, I like it here in this room.

AMANDA.   I know you do, Lawrence honey, that's part of your charm. Some days. But, honey, what about making a living?

LAWRENCE.   I can't work, mama. I'm crippled. (*He limps over to the couch and sits.*)

AMANDA.   There is nothing wrong with your leg, Lawrence honey, all the doctors have told you that. This limping thing is an affectation.

LAWRENCE.   I only know how I feel, mama.

AMANDA.   Oh if only I had connections in the Mafia, I'd have someone come and break both your legs.

LAWRENCE.   Don't try to make me laugh, mama. You know I have asthma.

AMANDA.   Your asthma, your leg, your eczema. You're just a mess, Lawrence.

LAWRENCE.   I have scabs from the itching, mama.

AMANDA.   That's lovely, Lawrence. You must tell us more over dinner.

LAWRENCE.   Alright.

AMANDA.   That was a joke, Lawrence.

LAWRENCE.   Don't try to make me laugh, mama. My asthma.

AMANDA.   Now, Lawrence, I don't want you talking about your ailments to the feminine caller your brother Tom is bringing home from the warehouse, honey. No nice-bred young lady likes to hear a young man discussing his eczema, Lawrence.

LAWRENCE.   What else can I talk about, mama?

AMANDA.   Talk about the weather. Or Red China.

LAWRENCE.   Or my collection of glass cocktail stirrers?

AMANDA.   I suppose so, honey, if the conversation comes to some godawful standstill. Otherwise, I'd shut up about it. Conversation is an art, Lawrence. Back at Blue Mountain, when I had seventeen gentlemen callers, I was able to converse with charm and vivacity for six hours without stop and never once mention eczema or bone cancer or vivisection. Try to emulate me, Lawrence, honey. Charm and vivacity. And charm. And vivacity. And charm.

LAWRENCE. Well, I'll try, but I doubt it.

AMANDA. Me too, honey. But we'll go through the motions anyway, won't we?

LAWRENCE. I don't know if I want to meet some girl who works in a warehouse, mama.

AMANDA. Your brother Tom says she's a lovely girl with a nice personality. And where else does he meet girls except the few who work at the warehouse? He only seems to meet men at the movies. Your brother goes to the movies entirely too much. I must speak to him about it.

LAWRENCE. It's unfeminine for a girl to work at a warehouse.

AMANDA. Lawrence, honey, if you can't go out the door without getting an upset stomach or an attack of vertigo, then we got to find some nice girl who's willing to support you. Otherwise, how am I ever going to get you out of this house and off my hands?

LAWRENCE. Why do you want to be rid of me, mama?

AMANDA. I suppose it's unmotherly of me, dear, but you really get on my nerves. Limping around the apartment, pretending to have asthma. If only some nice girl would marry you and I knew you were taken care of, then I'd feel free to start to live again. I'd join Parents Without Partners, I'd go to dinner dances, I'd have a life again. Rather than just watch you mope about this stupid apartment. I'm not bitter, dear, it's just that I hate my life.

LAWRENCE. I understand, mama.

AMANDA. Do you, dear? Oh, you're cute. Oh listen, I think I hear them.

TOM (*from off-stage*). Mother, I forgot my key.

LAWRENCE. I'll be in the other room. (*Starts to limp away.*)

AMANDA. I want you to let them in, Lawrence.

LAWRENCE. Oh, I couldn't, mama. She'd see I limp.

AMANDA. Then don't limp, damn it.

TOM (*from off-stage*). Mother, are you there?

AMANDA. Just a minute, Tom, honey. Now, Lawrence, you march over to that door or I'm going to break all your swizzle sticks.

LAWRENCE. Mama, I can't.

AMANDA. Lawrence, you're a grown boy. Now you answer that door like any normal person.

LAWRENCE. I can't.

TOM. Mother, I'm going to break the door down in a minute.

AMANDA. Just be patient, Tom. Now you're causing a scene, Lawrence. I want you to answer that door.

LAWRENCE. My eczema itches.

AMANDA. I'll itch it for you in a second, Lawrence.

TOM. Alright, I'm breaking it down. (*Sound of door breaking down. Enter* TOM *and* GINNY BENNETT, *a vivacious girl dressed in factory clothes.*)

AMANDA. Oh, Tom, you got in.

TOM. Why must we go through this every night? You know the stupid fuck won't open the door, so why don't you let him alone about it? (*To* GINNY) My kid brother has a thing about answering doors. He thinks people will notice his limp and his asthma and his eczema.

LAWRENCE. Excuse me. I think I hear someone calling me in the other room. (*Limps off, calls to imaginary person*) Coming!

AMANDA. Now see what you've done. He's probably going to refuse to come to the table due to your insensitivity. Oh, was any woman as cursed as I? With one son who's too sensitive and another one who's this big ox. I'm sorry, how rude of me. I'm Amanda Wingvalley. You must be Virginia Bennett from the warehouse. Tom has spoken so much about you I feel you're almost one of the family, preferably a daughter-in-law. Welcome, Virginia.

GINNY (*speaking very loudly*). Call me Ginny or Gin. But just don't call me late for dinner! (*Roars with laughter.*)

AMANDA. Oh, how amusing. (*Whispers to* TOM) Why is she shouting? Is she deaf?

GINNY. You're asking why I am speaking loudly. It's so that I can be heard! I am taking a course in public speaking, and so far we've covered organizing your thoughts and speaking good and loud so the people in the back of the room can hear you.

AMANDA. Public speaking. How impressive. You must be interested in improving yourself.

GINNY (*truly not having heard*). What?

AMANDA (*loudly*). YOU MUST BE INTERESTED IN IMPROVING YOURSELF.

GINNY (*loudly and happily*). YES I AM!

TOM. When's dinner? I want to get this over with fast if everyone's going to shout all evening.

GINNY. What?

AMANDA (*to* GINNY). Dinner is almost ready, Ginny.

GINNY. Who's Freddy?

AMANDA. Oh, Lord. No, dear. DINNER IS READY.

GINNY. Oh good. I'm as hungry as a bear! (*Growls enthusiastically.*)

AMANDA. You must be very popular at the warehouse, Ginny.

GINNY.   No popsicle for me, ma'am, although I will take you up on some gin.

AMANDA (*confused*).   What?

GINNY (*loudly*).   I WOULD LIKE SOME GIN.

AMANDA.   Well, fine. I think I'd like to get drunk too. Tom, why don't you go and make two Southern ladies some nice summer gin and tonics? And see if your sister would like a lemonade.

TOM.   Sister?

AMANDA.   I'm sorry, did I say sister? I meant brother.

TOM (*calling as he exits*).   Hey, four eyes, you wanna lemonade?

AMANDA.   Tom's so amusing. He calls Lawrence four eyes even though he doesn't wear glasses.

GINNY.   And does Lawrence wear glasses?

AMANDA (*confused*).   What?

GINNY.   You said Tom called Lawrence four eyes even though he doesn't wear glasses, and I wondered if Lawrence wore glasses. Because that would, you see, explain it.

AMANDA (*looks at her with despair*).   Ah. I don't know. I'll have to ask Lawrence someday. Speaking of Lawrence, let me go check on the supper and see if I can convince him to come out here and make conversation with you.

GINNY.   No, thank you, ma'am, I'll just have the gin.

AMANDA.   What?

GINNY.   What?

AMANDA.   Never mind. I'll be back. Or with luck I won't. (AMANDA *exits.* GINNY *looks around uncomfortably, and crosses to the table with the collection of glass cocktail stirrers.*)

GINNY.   They must drink a lot here. (*Enter* TOM *with a glass of gin for* GINNY.)

TOM.   Here's some gin for Ginny.

GINNY.   What?

TOM.   Here's your poison.

GINNY.   No, thanks, I'll just wait here.

TOM.   Have you ever thought all that loud machinery at the warehouse may be affecting your hearing?

GINNY.   Scenery? You mean, like trees? Yeah, I like trees.

TOM.   I like trees, too.

AMANDA (*from off-stage*).   Now you get out of that bed this minute, Lawrence Wingvalley, or I'm going to give that overbearing girl your entire collection of glass gobbledygook—is that clear? (AMANDA *pushes in* LAWRENCE, *who is wearing a nightshirt.*)

AMANDA.   I believe Lawrence would like to visit with you, Ginny.

GINNY (*shows her drink*).   Tom brought me my drink already, thank you, Mrs. Wingvalley.

AMANDA.   You know a hearing aid isn't really all that expensive, dear, you might look into that.

GINNY.   No, if I have the gin, I don't really want any gator aid. Never liked the stuff anyway. But you feel free.

AMANDA.   Thank you, dear. I will. Come, Tom, come to the kitchen and help me prepare the dinner. And we'll let the two young people converse. Remember, Lawrence. Charm and vivacity.

TOM.   I hope this dinner won't take long, mother. I don't want to get to the movies too late.

AMANDA.   Oh shut up about the movies. (AMANDA *and* TOM *exit.* LAWRENCE *stands still, uncomfortable.* GINNY *looks at him pleasantly. Silence for a while.*)

GINNY.   Hi.

LAWRENCE.   Hi. (*Pause.*) I'd gone to bed.

GINNY.   I never eat bread. It's too fattening. I have to watch my figure if I want to get ahead in the world. Why are you wearing that nightshirt?

LAWRENCE.   I'd gone to bed. I wasn't feeling well. My leg hurts and I have a headache, and I have palpitations of the heart.

GINNY.   I don't know. Hum a few bars, and I'll see.

LAWRENCE.   We've met before, you know.

GINNY.   I've never seen snow. Is it exciting?

LAWRENCE.   We were in high school together. You were voted Girl Most Likely To Succeed. We sat next to one another in glee club.

GINNY.   I'm sorry, I really can't hear you. You're talking too softly.

LAWRENCE (*louder*).   You used to call me BLUE ROSES.

GINNY.   Blue Roses? Oh yes, I remember, sort of. Why did I do that?

LAWRENCE.   I had been absent from school for several months, and when I came back, you asked me where I'd been, and I said I'd been sick with viral pneumonia, but you thought I said "blue roses."

GINNY.   I didn't get much of that, but I remember you now. You used to make a spectacle of yourself every day in glee class, clumping up the aisle with this great big noisy leg brace on your leg. God, you made a racket.

LAWRENCE.   I was always so afraid people were looking at me, and pointing. But then eventually mama wouldn't let me wear the leg brace anymore. She gave it to the Salvation Army.

GINNY.   I've never been in the army. How long were you in for?

LAWRENCE.   I've never been in the army. I have asthma.

GINNY.   You do? May I see it?

LAWRENCE (*confused*).   See it?

GINNY.   Well, sure unless you don't want to.

LAWRENCE.   Maybe you want to see my collection of glass cocktail stirrers. (*He limps to the table, and limps back to her, holding his collection. Holds up a stick.*) I call this one Stringbean, because it's long and thin.

GINNY.   Thank you. (*Puts it in her glass and stirs it.*)

LAWRENCE (*fairly appalled*).   They're not for use. (*Takes it back from her.*) They're a collection.

GINNY.   Well, I guess I stirred it enough.

LAWRENCE.   They're my favorite thing in the world. (*Holds up another one.*) I call this one Q-tip, because I realized it looks like a Q-tip, except it's made out of glass and doesn't have little cotton swabs at the end of it. (*She looks blank.*) Q-TIPS.

GINNY.   Really? (*She takes it and puts it in her ear.*)

LAWRENCE.   No! Don't put it in your ear. (*Takes it back.*) Now it's disgusting.

GINNY.   Well, I didn't think it was a Q-tip, but that's what you said it was.

LAWRENCE.   I call it that. I think I'm going to throw it out now. (*Holds up another one.*) I call this one Pinocchio because if you hold it perpendicular to your nose it makes your nose look long. (*He holds it to his nose.*)

GINNY.   Uh huh.

LAWRENCE.   And I call this one Henry Kissinger, because he wears glasses and it's made of glass.

GINNY.   Uh huh. (*Takes it and stirs her drink.*)

LAWRENCE.   No! They're just for looking, not for stirring. Mama, she's making a mess with my collection.

AMANDA (*from off-stage*).   Oh shut up about your collection, honey, you're probably driving the poor girl bananas.

GINNY.   No bananas, thank you! My nutritionist says I should avoid potassium. You know what I take your trouble to be, Lawrence?

LAWRENCE.   Mama says I'm retarded.

GINNY.   I know you're tired, I figured that's why you put on the nightshirt, but this won't take long. I judge you to be lacking in self-confidence. Am I right?

LAWRENCE.   Well, I am afraid of people and things, and I have a lot of ailments.

GINNY.   But that makes you special, Lawrence.

LAWRENCE.   What does?

GINNY.   I don't know. Whatever you said. And that's why you should present yourself with more confidence. Throw back your shoulders, and say, "HI! HOW YA DOIN'?" Now you try it.

LAWRENCE (*unenthusiastically, softly*).   Hello. How are you?

GINNY (*looking at watch, in response to his supposed question*).   I
don't know, it's about 8:30, but this won't take long and then you can
go to bed. Alright, now try it. (*Booming*) "HI! HOW YA DOIN'?"

LAWRENCE.   Hi. How ya doin'?

GINNY.   Now swagger a bit. (*Kinda butch*) HI. HOW YA DOIN'?

LAWRENCE (*imitates her fairly successfully*).   HI. HOW YA DOIN'?

GINNY.   Good, Lawrence. That's much better. Again. (AMANDA
and TOM *enter from behind them and watch this.*) HI! HOW YA DOIN'?

LAWRENCE.   HI! HOW YA DOIN'?

GINNY.   THE BRAVES PLAYED A HELLUVA GAME,
DON'TCHA THINK?

LAWRENCE.   THE BRAVES PLAYED A HELLUVA GAME,
DON'TCHA THINK?

AMANDA.   Oh God I feel sorry for their children. Is this the only
girl who works at the warehouse, Tom?

GINNY.   HI, MRS. WINGVALLEY. YOUR SON LAWRENCE
AND I ARE GETTING ON JUST FINE. AREN'T WE,
LAWRENCE?

AMANDA.   Please, no need to shout, I'm not deaf, even if you are.

GINNY.   What?

AMANDA.   I'm glad you like Lawrence.

GINNY.   What?

AMANDA.   I'M GLAD YOU LIKE LAWRENCE.

GINNY.   What?

AMANDA.   WHY DON'T YOU MARRY LAWRENCE?

GINNY (*looks shocked; has heard this*).   Oh.

LAWRENCE.   Oh, mama.

GINNY.   Oh dear, I see. So that's why Shakespeare asked me here.

AMANDA (*To* TOM).   Shakespeare?

TOM.   The first day of work she asked me my name, and I said
Tom Wingvalley, and she thought I said Shakespeare.

GINNY.   Oh dear. Mrs. Wingvalley, if I had a young brother as
nice and as special as Lawrence is, I'd invite girls from the warehouse
home to meet him too.

AMANDA.   I'm sure I don't know what you mean.

GINNY.   And you're probably hoping I'll say that I'll call again.

AMANDA.   Really, we haven't even had dinner yet. Tom,
shouldn't you be checkin' on the roast pigs' feet?

TOM.   I guess so. If anything interesting happens, call me. (*Exits.*)

GINNY.   But I'm afraid I won't be calling on Lawrence again.

LAWRENCE.   This is so embarrassing. I told you I wanted to stay in
my room.

AMANDA.   Hush up, Lawrence.

GINNY.   But, Lawrence, I don't want you to think that I won't be calling because I don't like you. I do like you.

LAWRENCE.   You do?

GINNY.   Sure. I like everybody. But I got two time clocks to punch, Mrs. Wingvalley. One at the warehouse, and one at night.

AMANDA.   At night? You have a second job? That is ambitious.

GINNY.   Not a second job, ma'am. Betty.

AMANDA.   Pardon?

GINNY.   Now who's deaf, eh what? Betty. I'm involved with a girl named Betty. We've been going together for about a year. We're saving money so that we can buy a farmhouse and a tractor together. So you (*to* LAWRENCE) can see why I can't visit your son, though I wish I could. No hard feelings, Lawrence. You're a good kid.

LAWRENCE (*offers her another swizzle stick*).   I want you to keep this. It's my very favorite one. I call it Thermometer because it looks like a thermometer.

GINNY.   You want me to have this?

LAWRENCE.   Yes, as a souvenir.

GINNY (*offended*).   Well, there's no need to call me a queer. Fuck you and your stupid swizzle sticks. (*Throws the offered gift upstage.*)

LAWRENCE (*very upset*).   You've broken it!

GINNY.   What?

LAWRENCE.   You've broken it. YOU'VE BROKEN IT.

GINNY.   So I've broken it. Big fuckin' deal. You have twenty more of them here.

AMANDA.   Well, I'm so sorry you have to be going.

GINNY.   What?

AMANDA.   Hadn't you better be going?

GINNY.   What?

AMANDA.   Go away!

GINNY.   Well I guess I can tell when I'm not wanted. I guess I'll go now.

AMANDA.   You and Betty must come over some evening. Preferably when we're out.

GINNY.   I wasn't shouting. (*Calls off*) So long, Shakespeare. See you at the warehouse. (*To* LAWRENCE) So long, Lawrence. I hope your rash gets better.

LAWRENCE (*saddened, holding the broken swizzle stick*).   You broke Thermometer.

GINNY.   What?

LAWRENCE.   YOU BROKE THERMOMETER!

GINNY.   Well, what was a thermometer doing in with the swizzle sticks anyway?

LAWRENCE.   Its name was Thermometer, you nitwit!

AMANDA.   Let it go, Lawrence. There'll be other swizzle sticks. Goodbye, Virginia.

GINNY.   I sure am hungry. Any chance I might be able to take a sandwich with me?

AMANDA.   Certainly you can shake hands with me, if that will make you happy.

GINNY.   I said I'm hungry.

AMANDA.   Really, dear? What part of Hungary are you from?

GINNY.   Oh never mind. I guess I'll go.

AMANDA.   That's right. You have two time clocks. It must be getting near to when you punch in Betty.

GINNY.   Well, so long, everybody. I had a nice time. (*Exits.*)

AMANDA.   Tom, come in here please. Lawrence, I don't believe I would play the victrola right now.

LAWRENCE.   What victrola?

AMANDA.   Any victrola. (*Enter* TOM.)

TOM.   Yes, mother? Where's Ginny?

AMANDA.   The feminine caller made a hasty departure.

TOM.   Old four eyes bored her to death, huh?

LAWRENCE.   Oh, drop dead.

TOM.   We should have you institutionalized.

AMANDA.   That's the first helpful thing you've said all evening, but first things first. You played a little joke on us, Tom.

TOM.   What are you talking about?

AMANDA.   You didn't mention that your friend is already spoken for.

TOM.   Really? I didn't even think she liked men.

AMANDA.   Yes, well. It seems odd that you know so little about a person you see every day at the warehouse.

TOM.   The warehouse is where I work, not where I know things about people.

AMANDA.   The disgrace. The expense of the pigs' feet, a new tie for Lawrence. And you—bringing a lesbian into this house. We haven't had a lesbian in this house since your grandmother died, and now you have the audacity to bring in that . . . that . . .

LAWRENCE.   Dyke.

AMANDA.   Thank you, Lawrence. That overbearing, booming-voiced bull dyke. Into a Christian home.

TOM.   Oh look, who cares? No one in their right mind would marry four eyes here.

AMANDA.   You have no Christian charity, or filial devotion, or fraternal affection.

TOM.   I don't want to listen to this. I'm going to the movies.

AMANDA.   You go to the movies to excess, Tom. It isn't healthy.

LAWRENCE.   While you're out, could you stop at the liquor store and get me some more cocktail stirrers? She broke Thermometer, and she put Q-tip in her ear.

AMANDA.   Listen to your brother, Tom. He's pathetic. How are we going to support ourselves once you go? And I know you want to leave. I've seen the brochure for the merchant marines in your underwear drawer. And the application to the Air Force. And your letter of inquiry to the Ballet Trockadero. So I'm not unaware of what you're thinking. But don't leave us until you fulfill your duties here, Tom. Help brother find a wife, or a job, or a doctor. Or consider euthanasia. But don't leave me here all alone, saddled with him.

LAWRENCE.   Mama, don't you like me?

AMANDA.   Of course, dear. I'm just making jokes.

LAWRENCE.   Be careful of my asthma.

AMANDA.   I'll try, dear. Now why don't you hold your breath in case you get a case of terminal hiccups?

LAWRENCE.   Alright. (*Holds his breath.*)

TOM.   I'm leaving.

AMANDA.   Where are you going?

TOM.   I'm going to the movies.

AMANDA.   I don't believe you go to the movies. What did you see last night?

TOM.   Hyapatia Lee in "Beaver City."

AMANDA.   And the night before that?

TOM.   I don't remember. "Humpy Busboys" or something.

AMANDA.   Humpy what?

TOM.   Nothing. Leave me alone.

AMANDA.   These are not mainstream movies, Tom. Why can't you see a normal movie like "The Philadelphia Story." Or "The Bitter Tea of General Yen"?

TOM.   Those movies were made in the 1930s.

AMANDA.   They're still good today.

TOM.   I don't want to have this conversation. I'm going to the movies.

AMANDA.   That's right, go to the movies! Don't think about us, a mother alone, an unmarried brother who thinks he's crippled and has no job. Stop holding your breath, Lawrence, mama was kidding. (*Back to* TOM) Don't let anything interfere with your selfish pleasure. Go see your pornographic trash that's worse than anything Mr. D.H. Lawrence ever envisioned. Just go, go, go—to the movies!

TOM.   Alright, I will! And the more you shout about my selfishness and my taste in movies the quicker I'll go, and I won't just go to the movies!

AMANDA.   Go then! Go to the moon—you selfish dreamer! (TOM *exits.*) Oh Lawrence, honey, what's to become of us?

LAWRENCE.   Tom forgot his newspaper, mama.

AMANDA.   He forgot a lot more than that, Lawrence honey. He forgot his mama and brother. (AMANDA *and* LAWRENCE *stay in place.* TOM *enters down right and stands apart from them in a spot. He speaks to the audience.*)

TOM.   I didn't go to the moon, I went to the movies. In Amsterdam. A long, lonely trip working my way on a freighter. They had good movies in Amsterdam. They weren't in English, but I didn't really care. And as for my mother and brother—well, I was adopted anyway. So I didn't miss them.

Or at least so I thought. For something pursued me. It always came upon me unawares, it always caught me by surprise. Sometimes it would be a swizzle stick in someone's vodka glass, or sometimes it would just be a jar of pigs' feet. But then all of a sudden my brother touches my shoulder, and my mother puts her hands around my neck, and everywhere I look I am reminded of them. And in all the bars I go to there are those damn swizzle sticks everywhere. I find myself thinking of my brother Lawrence. And of his collection of glass. And of my mother. I begin to think that their story would maybe make a good novel, or even a play. A mother's hopes, a brother's dreams. Pathos, humor, even tragedy. But then I lose interest, I really haven't the energy. So I'll leave them both, dimly lit, in my memory. For nowadays the world is lit by lightning, and when we get those colored lights going, it feels like I'm on LSD. Or some other drug. Or maybe it's the trick of memory, and the fact that life is very, very sad. Play with your cocktail stirrers, Lawrence. And so, good-bye.

AMANDA (*calling over in* TOM's *direction*).   Tom, I hear you out on the porch talking. Who are you talking to?

TOM.   No one, mother. I'm just on my way to the movies.

AMANDA   Well, try not to be too late, you have to work early at the warehouse tomorrow. And please don't bring home any visitors from the movies, I'm not up to it after that awful girl. Besides, if some sailor misses his boat, that's no reason you have to put him up in your room. You're too big-hearted, son.

TOM.   Yes, mother. See you later. (*Exits.*)

LAWRENCE.   Look at the light through the glass, mama. (*Looks through a swizzle stick.*) Isn't it amazin'?

AMANDA.   Yes, I guess it is, Lawrence. Oh, but both my children are weird. What have I done, O Lord, to deserve them?

LAWRENCE.   Just lucky, mama.

AMANDA.   Don't make jokes, Lawrence. Your asthma. Your eczema. My life.

LAWRENCE.   Don't be sad, mama. We have each other for company and amusement.

AMANDA.   That's right. It's always darkest before the dawn. Or right before a typhoon sweeps up and kills everybody.

LAWRENCE.   Oh, poor mama, let me try to cheer you up with my collection. Is that a good idea?

AMANDA.   It's just great, Lawrence. Thank you.

LAWRENCE.   I call this one Daffodil, because its yellow, and daffodils are yellow.

AMANDA.   Uh huh.

LAWRENCE (*holds up another one*).   And I call this one Curtain Rod because it reminds me of a curtain rod.

AMANDA.   Uh huh.

LAWRENCE.   And I call this one Ocean, because it's blue, and the ocean is . . .

AMANDA.   I THOUGHT YOU CALLED THE BLUE ONE BLUE, YOU IDIOT CHILD! DO I HAVE TO LISTEN TO THIS PATHETIC PRATTLING THE REST OF MY LIFE??? CAN'T YOU AT LEAST BE CONSISTENT???

LAWRENCE (*pause; hurt*).   No, I guess I can't.

AMANDA.   Well, try, can't you? (*Silence.*) I'm sorry, Lawrence. I'm a little short-tempered today.

LAWRENCE.   That's alright. (*Silence.*)

AMANDA (*trying to make up*).   Do you have any other swizzle sticks with names, Lawrence?

LAWRENCE.   Yes, I do. (*Holds one up.*) I call this one "Mama." (*He throws it over his shoulder onto the floor.*)

AMANDA.   Well, that's lovely, Lawrence, thank you.

LAWRENCE.   I guess I can be a little short-tempered too.

AMANDA.   Yes, well, whatever. I think we won't kill each other this evening, alright?

LAWRENCE.   Alright.

AMANDA.   I'll just distract myself from my rage and despair, and read about other people's rage and despair in the newspaper, shall I? (*Picks up Tom's newspaper.*) Your brother has the worst reading and viewing taste of any living creature. This is just a piece of filth. (*Reads*) Man Has Sex With Chicken, Then Makes Casserole. (*Closes the paper.*) Disgusting. Oh, Lawrence honey, look—it's the Evening Star. (*She holds the paper out in front of them.*) Let's make a wish on it, honey, shall we?

LAWRENCE. Alright, mama. (AMANDA *holds up the newspaper, and she and* LAWRENCE *close their eyes and make a wish.*)

AMANDA. What did you wish for, darlin'?

LAWRENCE. More swizzle sticks.

AMANDA. You're so predictable, Lawrence. It's part of your charm, I guess.

LAWRENCE. What did you wish for, mama?

AMANDA. The same thing, honey. Maybe just a little happiness, too, but mostly just some more swizzle sticks.

(*Sad music.* AMANDA *and* LAWRENCE *look up at the Evening Star. Fade to black.*)

QUESTIONS

1. To appreciate this play, you'll need to be familiar with Tennessee Williams's *The Glass Menagerie* (page 1143). What attitude toward that play is suggested by the change of the family name from "Wingfield" to "Wingvalley"?

2. This play changes the sex of Laura (Lawrence, here) and Jim (Ginny), and replaces Laura's collection of glass animal figurines with Lawrence's collection of glass swizzle sticks. How are Amanda and Tom different from their originals? Note other shifts and replacements, and consider their effect on audience responses. (For example, Williams has Amanda preparing salmon loaf for dinner, while Durang's Amanda cooks roasted pigs' feet.)

3. Although she doesn't recognize it, Amanda identifies her son Tom as homosexual, and Ginny is a lesbian. How do these sexual orientations contribute to the play?

4. *The Glass Menagerie* evokes sympathy for its characters. What does this parody play evoke in the way of audience response?

5. A parody such as this may have a serious purpose—to provide a critique of the work it is spoofing, or to make use of the original work in order to develop a different theme, or some of each. Or it may have no purpose beyond poking fun. What would you say is the purpose of Durang's play?

Arthur Miller
Death of a Salesman
Certain Private Conversations in Two Acts and a Requiem

Characters

WILLY LOMAN
LINDA, *his wife*
BIFF ⎱ *his sons*
HAPPY ⎰
UNCLE BEN, *his older brother*
HOWARD WAGNER, *his employer*
THE WOMAN

CHARLEY, *a neighbor*
BERNARD, *Charley's son*
JENNY, *Charley's secretary*
STANLEY, *a waiter*
MISS FORSYTHE ⎱ *young women*
LETTA   ⎰

The action takes place in Willy Loman's house and yard and in various places he visits in the New York and Boston of today.

ACT 1

A melody is heard, played upon a flute. It is small and fine, telling of grass and trees and the horizon. The curtain rises.

Before us is the Salesman's house. We are aware of towering, angular shapes behind it, surrounding it on all sides. Only the blue light of the sky falls upon the house and forestage; the surrounding area shows an angry glow of orange. As more light appears, we see a solid vault of apartment houses around the small, fragile-seeming home. An air of the dream clings to the place, a dream rising out of reality. The kitchen at center seems actual enough, for there is a kitchen table with three chairs, and a refrigerator. But no other fixtures are seen. At the back of the kitchen there is a draped entrance, which leads to the living-room. To the right of the kitchen, on a level raised two feet, is a bedroom furnished only with a brass bedstead and a straight chair. On a shelf over the bed a silver athletic trophy stands. A window opens onto the apartment house at the side.

DEATH OF A SALESMAN   First performed in 1949. Arthur Miller (1915–2005) was born in New York City, the son of a well-to-do manufacturer whose financial losses in the Depression forced a move to Brooklyn in 1929. Here Miller graduated from high school and worked in an automobile parts warehouse for two years before entering the University of Michigan, where he won three drama prizes. After graduation in 1938, he returned to Brooklyn, married, and fathered a son and daughter. *Death of a Salesman* was his third Broadway play.

Behind the kitchen, on a level raised six and a half feet, is the boys' bed-
room, at present barely visible. Two beds are dimly seen, and at the back of
the room a dormer window. (This bedroom is above the unseen living-room.)
At the left a stairway curves up to it from the kitchen.

The entire setting is wholly, or, in some places, partially transparent.
The roofline of the house is one-dimensional; under and over it we see the
apartment buildings. Before the house lies an apron, curving beyond the
forestage into the orchestra. This forward area serves as the back yard as well
as the locale of all Willy's *imaginings and of his city scenes. Whenever the*
action is in the present the actors observe the imaginary wall-lines, entering
the house only through its door at the left. But in the scenes of the past these
boundaries are broken, and characters enter or leave a room by stepping
"through" a wall onto the forestage.

From the right, Willy Loman, *the Salesman, enters, carrying two large*
sample cases. The flute plays on. He hears but is not aware of it. He is past
sixty years of age, dressed quietly. Even as he crosses the stage to the door-
way of the house, his exhaustion is apparent. He unlocks the door, comes into
the kitchen, and thankfully lets his burden down, feeling the soreness of his
palms. A word-sigh escapes his lips—it might be "Oh, boy, oh, boy." He
closes the door, then carries his cases out into the living-room, through the
draped kitchen doorway.

Linda, *his wife, has stirred in her bed at the right. She gets out and puts*
on a robe, listening. Most often jovial, she has developed an iron repression
of her exceptions to Willy's *behavior—she more than loves him, she admires*
him, as though his mercurial nature, his temper, his massive dreams and lit-
tle cruelties, served her only as sharp reminders of the turbulent longings
within him, longings which she shares but lacks the temperament to utter and
follow to their end.

Linda *(hearing* Willy *outside the bedroom, calls with some trepida-*
tion).   Willy!

Willy.   It's all right. I came back.

Linda.   Why? What happened? (*Slight pause.*) Did something
happen, Willy?

Willy.   No, nothing happened.

Linda.   You didn't smash the car, did you?

Willy (*with casual irritation*).   I said nothing happened. Didn't you
hear me?

Linda.   Don't you feel well?

Willy.   I'm tired to the death. (*The flute has faded away. He sits on*
the bed beside her, a little numb.) I couldn't make it. I just couldn't make
it, Linda.

LINDA (*very carefully, delicately*).   Where were you all day? You look terrible.

WILLY.   I got as far as a little above Yonkers. I stopped for a cup of coffee. Maybe it was the coffee.

LINDA.   What?

WILLY (*after a pause*).   I suddenly couldn't drive any more. The car kept going off onto the shoulder, y'know?

LINDA (*helpfully*).   Oh. Maybe it was the steering again. I don't think Angelo knows the Studebaker.

WILLY.   No, it's me, it's me. Suddenly I realize I'm goin' sixty miles an hour and I don't remember the last five minutes. I'm—I can't seem to—keep my mind to it.

LINDA.   Maybe it's your glasses. You never went for your new glasses.

WILLY.   No, I see everything. I came back ten miles an hour. It took me nearly four hours from Yonkers.

LINDA (*resigned*).   Well, you'll just have to take a rest, Willy, you can't continue this way.

WILLY.   I just got back from Florida.

LINDA.   But you didn't rest your mind. Your mind is overactive, and the mind is what counts, dear.

WILLY.   I'll start out in the morning. Maybe I'll feel better in the morning. (*She is taking off his shoes.*) These goddam arch supports are killing me.

LINDA.   Take an aspirin. Should I get you an aspirin? It'll soothe you.

WILLY (*with wonder*).   I was driving along, you understand? And I was fine. I was even observing the scenery. You can imagine, me looking at scenery, on the road every week of my life. But it's so beautiful up there, Linda, the trees are so thick, and the sun is warm. I opened the windshield and just let the warm air bathe over me. And then all of a sudden I'm goin' off the road! I'm tellin' ya, I absolutely forgot I was driving. If I'd've gone the other way over the white line I might've killed somebody. So I went on again—and five minutes later I'm dreamin' again, and I nearly—(*He presses two fingers against his eyes.*) I have such thoughts, I have such strange thoughts.

LINDA.   Willy, dear. Talk to them again. There's no reason why you can't work in New York.

WILLY.   They don't need me in New York. I'm the New England man. I'm vital in New England.

LINDA.   But you're sixty years old. They can't expect you to keep traveling every week.

WILLY.   I'll have to send a wire to Portland. I'm supposed to see Brown and Morrison tomorrow morning at ten o'clock to show the line. Goddammit, I could sell them! (*He starts putting on his jacket.*)

LINDA (*taking the jacket from him*).   Why don't you go down to the place tomorrow and tell Howard you've simply got to work in New York? You're too accommodating, dear.

WILLY.   If old man Wagner was alive I'd a been in charge of New York now! That man was a prince, he was a masterful man. But that boy of his, that Howard, he don't appreciate. When I went north the first time, the Wagner Company didn't know where New England was!

LINDA.   Why don't you tell those things to Howard, dear?

WILLY (*encouraged*).   I will, I definitely will. Is there any cheese?

LINDA.   I'll make you a sandwich.

WILLY.   No, go to sleep. I'll take some milk. I'll be up right away. The boys in?

LINDA.   They're sleeping. Happy took Biff on a date tonight.

WILLY (*interested*).   That so?

LINDA.   It was so nice to see them shaving together, one behind the other, in the bathroom. And going out together. You notice? The whole house smells of shaving lotion.

WILLY.   Figure it out. Work a lifetime to pay off a house. You finally own it, and there's nobody to live in it.

LINDA.   Well, dear, life is a casting off. It's always that way.

WILLY.   No, no, some people—some people accomplish something. Did Biff say anything after I went this morning?

LINDA.   You shouldn't have criticized him, Willy, especially after he just got off the train. You mustn't lose your temper with him.

WILLY.   When the hell did I lose my temper? I simply asked him if he was making any money. Is that a criticism?

LINDA.   But, dear, how could he make any money?

WILLY (*worried and angered*).   There's such an undercurrent in him. He became a moody man. Did he apologize when I left this morning?

LINDA.   He was crestfallen, Willy. You know how he admires you. I think if he finds himself, then you'll both be happier and not fight any more.

WILLY.   How can he find himself on a farm? Is that a life? A farmhand? In the beginning, when he was young, I thought, well, a young man, it's good for him to tramp around, take a lot of different jobs. But it's more than ten years now and he has yet to make thirty-five dollars a week!

LINDA.   He's finding himself, Willy.

WILLY.   Not finding yourself at the age of thirty-four is a disgrace!

LINDA.   Shh!

WILLY.   The trouble is he's lazy, goddammit!

LINDA.   Willy, please!

WILLY.   Biff is a lazy bum!

LINDA.   They're sleeping. Get something to eat. Go on down.

WILLY.   Why did he come home? I would like to know what brought him home.

LINDA.   I don't know. I think he's still lost, Willy. I think he's very lost.

WILLY.   Biff Loman is lost. In the greatest country in the world a young man with such—personal attractiveness, gets lost. And such a hard worker. There's one thing about Biff—he's not lazy.

LINDA.   Never.

WILLY (*with pity and resolve*).   I'll see him in the morning; I'll have a nice talk with him. I'll get him a job selling. He could be big in no time. My God! Remember how they used to follow him around in high school? When he smiled at one of them their faces lit up. When he walked down the street . . . (*He loses himself in reminiscences.*)

LINDA (*trying to bring him out of it*).   Willy, dear, I got a new kind of American-type cheese today. It's whipped.

WILLY.   Why do you get American when I like Swiss?

LINDA.   I just thought you'd like a change—

WILLY.   I don't want change! I want Swiss cheese. Why am I always being contradicted?

LINDA (*with a covering laugh*).   I thought it would be a surprise.

WILLY.   Why don't you open a window in here, for God's sake?

LINDA (*with infinite patience*).   They're all open, dear.

WILLY.   The way they boxed us in here. Bricks and windows, windows and bricks.

LINDA.   We should've bought the land next door.

WILLY.   The street is lined with cars. There's not a breath of fresh air in the neighborhood. The grass don't grow any more, you can't raise a carrot in the back yard. They should've had a law against apartment houses. Remember those two beautiful elm trees out there? When I and Biff hung the swing between them?

LINDA.   Yeah, like being a million miles from the city.

WILLY.   They should've arrested the builder for cutting those down. They massacred the neighborhood. (*Lost*) More and more I think of those days, Linda. This time of year it was lilac and wisteria. And then the peonies would come out, and the daffodils. What fragrance in this room!

LINDA.   Well, after all, people had to move somewhere.

WILLY.   No, there's more people now.

LINDA.   I don't think there's more people. I think—

WILLY.   There's more people! That's what's ruining this country! Population is getting out of control. The competition is maddening! Smell the stink from that apartment house! And another one on the other side . . . How can they whip cheese?

(On WILLY's *last line*, BIFF *and* HAPPY *raise themselves up in their beds, listening.*)

LINDA.   Go down, try it. And be quiet.

WILLY (*turning to* LINDA, *guiltily*).   You're not worried about me, are you, sweetheart?

BIFF.   What's the matter?

HAPPY.   Listen!

LINDA.   You've got too much on the ball to worry about.

WILLY.   You're my foundation and my support, Linda.

LINDA.   Just try to relax, dear. You make mountains out of molehills.

WILLY.   I won't fight with him any more. If he wants to go back to Texas, let him go.

LINDA.   He'll find his way.

WILLY.   Sure. Certain men just don't get started till later in life. Like Thomas Edison, I think. Or B. F. Goodrich. One of them was deaf. (*He starts for the bedroom doorway.*) I'll put my money on Biff.

LINDA.   And Willy—if it's warm Sunday we'll drive in the country. And we'll open the windshield, and take lunch.

WILLY.   No, the windshields don't open on the new cars.

LINDA.   But you opened it today.

WILLY.   Me? I didn't. (*He stops.*) Now isn't that peculiar! Isn't that a remarkable—(*He breaks off in amazement and fright as the flute is heard distantly.*)

LINDA.   What, darling?

WILLY.   That is the most remarkable thing.

LINDA.   What, dear?

WILLY.   I was thinking of the Chevvy. (*Slight pause.*) Nineteen twenty-eight . . . when I had that red Chevvy—(*Breaks off.*) That's funny! I coulda sworn I was driving that Chevvy today.

LINDA.   Well, that's nothing. Something must've reminded you.

WILLY.   Remarkable. Ts. Remember those days? The way Biff used to simonize that car? The dealer refused to believe there was eighty thousand miles on it. (*He shakes his head.*) Heh! (*To* LINDA) Close your eyes, I'll be right up. (*He walks out of the bedroom.*)

HAPPY (*to* BIFF).   Jesus, maybe he smashed up the car again!

LINDA (*calling after* WILLY).   Be careful on the stairs, dear! The cheese is on the middle shelf! (*She turns, goes over to the bed, takes his jacket, and goes out of the bedroom.*)

(*Light has risen on the boys' room. Unseen,* WILLY *is heard talking to himself,* "Eighty thousand miles," *and a little laugh.* BIFF *gets out of bed, comes downstage a bit, and stands attentively.* BIFF *is two years older than his brother* HAPPY, *well built, but in these days bears a worn air and seems less self-assured. He has succeeded less, and his dreams are stronger and less acceptable than* HAPPY'S. HAPPY *is tall, powerfully made. Sexuality is like a visible color on him, or a scent that many women have discovered. He, like his brother, is lost, but in a different way, for he has never allowed himself to turn his face toward defeat and is thus more confused and hard-skinned, although seemingly more content.*)

HAPPY (*getting out of bed*).   He's going to get his license taken away if he keeps that up. I'm getting nervous about him, y'know, Biff?

BIFF.   His eyes are going.

HAPPY.   No, I've driven with him. He sees all right. He just doesn't keep his mind on it. I drove into the city with him last week. He stops at a green light and then it turns red and he goes. (*He laughs.*)

BIFF.   Maybe he's color-blind.

HAPPY.   Pop? Why he's got the finest eye for color in the business. You know that.

BIFF (*sitting down on his bed*).   I'm going to sleep.

HAPPY.   You're not still sour on Dad, are you, Biff?

BIFF.   He's all right, I guess.

WILLY (*underneath them, in the living-room*).   Yes, sir, eighty thousand miles—eighty-two thousand!

BIFF.   You smoking?

HAPPY (*holding out a pack of cigarettes*).   Want one?

BIFF (*taking a cigarette*).   I can never sleep when I smell it.

WILLY.   What a simonizing job, heh!

HAPPY (*with deep sentiment*).   Funny, Biff, y'know? Us sleeping in here again? The old beds. (*He pats his bed affectionately.*) All the talk that went across those two beds, huh? Our whole lives.

BIFF.   Yeah. Lotta dreams and plans.

HAPPY (*with a deep and masculine laugh*).   About five hundred women would like to know what was said in this room. (*They share a soft laugh.*)

BIFF.   Remember that big Betsy something—what the hell was her name—over on Bushwick Avenue?

HAPPY (*combing his hair*).   With the collie dog!

BIFF.   That's the one. I got you in there, remember?

HAPPY.   Yeah, that was my first time—I think. Boy, there was a pig! (*They laugh, almost crudely.*) You taught me everything I know about women. Don't forget that.

BIFF.   I bet you forgot how bashful you used to be. Especially with girls.

HAPPY.   Oh, I still am, Biff.

BIFF.   Oh, go on.

HAPPY.   I just control it, that's all. I think I got less bashful and you got more so. What happened, Biff? Where's the old humor, the old confidence? (*He shakes* BIFF's *knee.* BIFF *gets up and moves restlessly about the room.*) What's the matter?

BIFF.   Why does Dad mock me all the time?

HAPPY.   He's not mocking you, he—

BIFF.   Everything I say there's a twist of mockery on his face. I can't get near him.

HAPPY.   He just wants you to make good, that's all. I wanted to talk to you about Dad for a long time, Biff. Something's—happening to him. He—talks to himself.

BIFF.   I noticed that this morning. But he always mumbled.

HAPPY.   But not so noticeable. It got so embarrassing I sent him to Florida. And you know something? Most of the time he's talking to you.

BIFF.   What's he say about me?

HAPPY.   I can't make it out.

BIFF.   What's he say about me?

HAPPY.   I think the fact that you're not settled, that you're still kind of up in the air . . .

BIFF.   There's one or two other things depressing him, Happy.

HAPPY.   What do you mean?

BIFF.   Never mind. Just don't lay it all to me.

HAPPY.   But I think if you just got started—I mean—is there any future for you out there?

BIFF.   I'll tell ya, Hap, I don't know what the future is. I don't know—what I'm supposed to want.

HAPPY.   What do you mean?

BIFF.   Well, I spent six or seven years after high school trying to work myself up. Shipping clerk, salesman, business of one kind or another. And it's a measly manner of existence. To get on that subway on the hot mornings in summer. To devote your whole life to keeping stock, or making phone calls, or selling or buying. To suffer fifty weeks of the year for the sake of a two-week vacation, when all you really desire is to be outdoors, with your shirt off. And always to have to get ahead of the next fella. And still—that's how you build a future.

HAPPY.   Well, you really enjoy it on a farm? Are you content out there?

BIFF (*with rising agitation*).   Hap, I've had twenty or thirty different kinds of jobs since I left home before the war, and it always turns out the same. I just realized it lately. In Nebraska when I herded cattle, and the Dakotas, and Arizona, and now in Texas. It's why I came home now, I guess, because I realized it. This farm I work on, it's spring there now, see? And they've got about fifteen new colts. There's nothing more inspiring or—beautiful than the sight of a mare and a new colt. And it's cool there now, see? Texas is cool now, and it's spring. And whenever spring comes to where I am, I suddenly get the feeling, my God, I'm not gettin' anywhere! What the hell am I doing, playing around with horses, twenty-eight dollars a week! I'm thirty-four years old, I oughta be makin' my future. That's when I come running home. And now, I get here, and I don't know what to do with myself. (*After a pause.*) I've always made a point of not wasting my life, and everytime I come back here I know that all I've done is to waste my life.

HAPPY.   You're a poet, you know that, Biff? You're a—you're an idealist!

BIFF.   No, I'm mixed up very bad. Maybe I oughta get married. Maybe I oughta get stuck into something. Maybe that's my trouble. I'm like a boy. I'm not married, I'm not in business, I just—I'm like a boy. Are you content, Hap? You're a success, aren't you? Are you content?

HAPPY.   Hell, no!

BIFF.   Why? You're making money, aren't you?

HAPPY (*moving about with energy, expressiveness*).   All I can do now is wait for the merchandise manager to die. And suppose I get to be merchandise manager? He's a good friend of mine, and he just built a terrific estate on Long Island. And he lived there about two months and sold it, and now he's building another one. He can't enjoy it once it's finished. And I know that's just what I would do. I don't know what the hell I'm workin' for. Sometimes I sit in my apartment—all alone. And I think of the rent I'm paying. And it's crazy. But then, it's what I always wanted. My own apartment, a car, and plenty of women. And still, goddammit, I'm lonely.

BIFF (*with enthusiasm*).   Listen, why don't you come out West with me?

HAPPY.   You and I, heh?

BIFF.   Sure, maybe we could buy a ranch. Raise cattle, use our muscles. Men built like we are should be working out in the open.

HAPPY (*avidly*).   The Loman Brothers, heh?

BIFF (*with vast affection*).   Sure, we'd be known all over the counties!

HAPPY (*enthralled*).   That's what I dream about, Biff. Sometimes I want to just rip my clothes off in the middle of the store and outbox that goddam merchandise manager. I mean I can outbox him, outrun, and outlift anybody in that store, and I have to take orders from those common, petty sons-of-bitches till I can't stand it any more.

BIFF.   I'm tellin' you, kid, if you were with me I'd be happy out there.

HAPPY (*enthused*).   See, Biff, everybody around me is so false that I'm constantly lowering my ideals . . .

BIFF.   Baby, together we'd stand up for one another, we'd have someone to trust.

HAPPY.   If I were around you—

BIFF.   Hap, the trouble is we weren't brought up to grub for money. I don't know how to do it.

HAPPY.   Neither can I!

BIFF.   Then let's go!

HAPPY.   The only thing is—what can you make out there?

BIFF.   But look at your friend. Builds an estate and then hasn't the peace of mind to live in it.

HAPPY.   Yeah, but when he walks into the store the waves part in front of him. That's fifty-two thousand dollars a year coming through the revolving door, and I got more in my pinky finger than he's got in his head.

BIFF.   Yeah, but you just said—

HAPPY.   I gotta show some of those pompous, self-important executives over there that Hap Loman can make the grade. I want to walk into the store the way he walks in. Then I'll go with you, Biff. We'll be together yet, I swear. But take those two we had tonight. Now weren't they gorgeous creatures?

BIFF.   Yeah, yeah, most gorgeous I've had in years.

HAPPY.   I get that any time I want, Biff. Whenever I feel disgusted. The only trouble is, it gets like bowling or something. I just keep knockin' them over and it doesn't mean anything. You still run around a lot?

BIFF.   Naa. I'd like to find a girl—steady, somebody with substance.

HAPPY.   That's what I long for.

BIFF.   Go on! You'd never come home.

HAPPY.   I would! Somebody with character, with resistance! Like Mom, y'know? You're gonna call me a bastard when I tell you this. That girl Charlotte I was with tonight is engaged to be married in five weeks. (*He tries on his new hat.*)

BIFF.   No kiddin'!

HAPPY.   Sure, the guy's in line for the vice-presidency of the store. I don't know what gets into me, maybe I just have an overdeveloped sense of competition or something, but I went and ruined her, and furthermore I can't get rid of her. And he's the third executive I've done that to. Isn't that a crummy characteristic? And to top it all, I go to their weddings! (*Indignantly, but laughing*) Like I'm not supposed to take bribes. Manufacturers offer me a hundred-dollar bill now and then to throw an order their way. You know how honest I am, but it's like this girl, see. I hate myself for it. Because I don't want the girl, and, still, I take it and—I love it!

BIFF.   Let's go to sleep.

HAPPY.   I guess we didn't settle anything, heh?

BIFF.   I just got one idea that I think I'm going to try.

HAPPY.   What's that?

BIFF.   Remember Bill Oliver?

HAPPY.   Sure, Oliver is very big now. You want to work for him again?

BIFF.   No, but when I quit he said something to me. He put his arm on my shoulder, and he said, "Biff, if you ever need anything, come to me."

HAPPY.   I remember that. That sounds good.

BIFF.   I think I'll go to see him. If I could get ten thousand or even seven or eight thousand dollars I could buy a beautiful ranch.

HAPPY.   I bet he'd back you. 'Cause he thought highly of you, Biff. I mean, they all do. You're well liked, Biff. That's why I say to come back here, and we both have the apartment. And I'm tellin' you, Biff, any babe you want . . .

BIFF.   No, with a ranch I could do the work I like and still be something. I just wonder though. I wonder if Oliver still thinks I stole that carton of basketballs.

HAPPY.   Oh, he probably forgot that long ago. It's almost ten years. You're too sensitive. Anyway, he didn't really fire you.

BIFF.   Well, I think he was going to. I think that's why I quit. I was never sure whether he knew or not. I know he thought the world of me, though. I was the only one he'd let lock up the place.

WILLY (*below*).   You gonna wash the engine, Biff?

HAPPY.   Shh! (BIFF *looks at* HAPPY, *who is gazing down, listening.* WILLY *is mumbling in the parlor.*) You hear that? (*They listen.* WILLY *laughs warmly.*)

BIFF (*growing angry*).   Doesn't he know Mom can hear that?

WILLY.   Don't get your sweater dirty, Biff! (*A look of pain crosses* BIFF's *face.*)

HAPPY.   Isn't that terrible? Don't leave again, will you? You'll find a job here. You gotta stick around. I don't know what to do about him, it's getting embarrassing.

WILLY.   What a simonizing job!

BIFF.   Mom's hearing that!

WILLY.   No kiddin', Biff, you got a date? Wonderful!

HAPPY.   Go on to sleep. But talk to him in the morning, will you?

BIFF (*reluctantly getting into bed*).   With her in the house. Brother!

HAPPY (*getting into bed*).   I wish you'd have a good talk with him. (*The light on their room begins to fade.*)

BIFF (*to himself in bed*).   That selfish, stupid . . .

HAPPY.   Sh . . . Sleep, Biff.

(*Their light is out. Well before they have finished speaking,* WILLY's *form is dimly seen below in the darkened kitchen. He opens the refrigerator, searches in there, and takes out a bottle of milk. The apartment houses are fading out, and the entire house and surroundings become covered with leaves. Music insinuates itself as the leaves appear.*)

WILLY.   Just wanna be careful with those girls, Biff, that's all. Don't make any promises. No promises of any kind. Because a girl, y'know, they always believe what you tell 'em, and you're very young, Biff, you're too young to be talking seriously to girls. (*Light rises on the kitchen.* WILLY, *talking, shuts the refrigerator door and comes downstage to the kitchen table. He pours milk into a glass. He is totally immersed in himself, smiling faintly.*) Too young entirely, Biff. You want to watch your schooling first. Then when you're all set, there'll be plenty of girls for a boy like you. (*He smiles broadly at a kitchen chair.*) That so? The girls pay for you? (*He laughs.*) Boy, you must really be makin' a hit. (WILLY *is gradually addressing—physically—a point offstage, speaking through the wall of the kitchen, and his voice has been rising in volume to that of a normal conversation.*) I been wondering why you polish the car so careful. Ha! Don't leave the hubcaps, boys. Get the chamois to the hubcaps. Happy, use newspaper on the windows, it's the easiest thing. Show him how to do it, Biff! You see, Happy? Pad it up, use it like a pad. That's it, that's it, good work. You're doin' all right, Hap. (*He pauses, then nods in approbation for a few seconds, then looks upward.*) Biff, first thing we gotta do when we get time is clip that big branch over the house. Afraid it's gonna fall in a storm and hit the roof. Tell you what. We get a rope and sling her around, and then we climb up there with a couple of saws and take her down. Soon as you finish the car, boys, I wanna see ya. I got a surprise for you, boys.

BIFF (*offstage*).   Whatta ya got, Dad?

WILLY.   No, you finish first. Never leave a job till you're finished—remember that. (*Looking toward the "big trees"*) Biff, up in Albany I saw a beautiful hammock. I think I'll buy it next trip, and we'll hang it right between those two elms. Wouldn't that be something? Just swingin' there under those branches. Boy, that would be . . . (YOUNG BIFF *and* YOUNG HAPPY *appear from the direction* WILLY *was addressing.* HAPPY *carries rags and a pail of water.* BIFF, *wearing a sweater with a block* "S," *carries a football.*)

BIFF (*pointing in the direction of the car offstage*).   How's that, Pop, professional?

WILLY.   Terrific. Terrific job, boys. Good work, Biff.

HAPPY.   Where's the surprise, Pop?

WILLY.   In the back seat of the car.

HAPPY.   Boy! (*He runs off.*)

BIFF.   What is it, Dad? Tell me, what'd you buy?

WILLY (*laughing, cuffs him*).   Never mind, something I want you to have.

BIFF (*turns and starts off*).   What is it, Hap?

HAPPY (*offstage*).   It's a punching bag!

BIFF.   Oh, Pop!

WILLY.   It's got Gene Tunney's signature on it! (HAPPY *runs onstage with a punching bag.*)

BIFF.   Gee, how'd you know we wanted a punching bag?

WILLY.   Well, it's the finest thing for the timing.

HAPPY (*lies down on his back and pedals with his feet*).   I'm losing weight, you notice, Pop?

WILLY (*to* HAPPY).   Jumping rope is good too.

BIFF.   Did you see the new football I got?

WILLY (*examining the ball*).   Where'd you get a new ball?

BIFF.   The coach told me to practice my passing.

WILLY.   That so? And he gave you the ball, heh?

BIFF.   Well, I borrowed it from the locker room. (*He laughs confidentially.*)

WILLY (*laughing with him at the theft*).   I want you to return that.

HAPPY.   I told you he wouldn't like it!

BIFF (*angrily*).   Well, I'm bringing it back!

WILLY (*stopping the incipient argument, to* HAPPY).   Sure, he's gotta practice with a regulation ball, doesn't he? (*To* BIFF) Coach'll probably congratulate you on your initiative!

BIFF.   Oh, he keeps congratulating my initiative all the time, Pop.

WILLY.   That's because he likes you. If somebody else took that ball there'd be an uproar. So what's the report, boys, what's the report?

BIFF.   Where'd you go this time, Dad? Gee, we were lonesome for you.

WILLY (*pleased, puts an arm around each boy and they come down to the apron*).   Lonesome, heh?

BIFF.   Missed you every minute.

WILLY.   Don't say? Tell you a secret, boys. Don't breathe it to a soul. Someday I'll have my own business, and I'll never have to leave home any more.

HAPPY.   Like Uncle Charley, heh?

WILLY.   Bigger than Uncle Charley! Because Charley is not— liked. He's liked, but he's not—well liked.

BIFF.   Where'd you go this time, Dad?

WILLY.   Well, I got on the road, and I went north to Providence. Met the Mayor.

BIFF.   The Mayor of Providence!

WILLY.   He was sitting in the hotel lobby.

BIFF.   What'd he say?

WILLY.   He said, "Morning!" And I said, "You got a fine city here, Mayor." And then he had coffee with me. And then I went to Waterbury. Waterbury is a fine city. Big clock city, the famous Waterbury clock. Sold a nice bill there. And then Boston—Boston is the cradle of the Revolution. A fine city. And a couple of other towns in Mass., and on to Portland and Bangor and straight home!

BIFF.   Gee, I'd love to go with you sometime, Dad.

WILLY.   Soon as summer comes.

HAPPY.   Promise?

WILLY.   You and Hap and I, and I'll show you all the towns. America is full of beautiful towns and fine, upstanding people. And they know me, boys, they know me up and down New England. The finest people. And when I bring you fellas up, there'll be open sesame for all of us, 'cause one thing, boys: I have friends. I can park my car in any street in New England, and the cops protect it like their own. This summer, heh?

BIFF *and* HAPPY (*together*).   Yeah! You bet!

WILLY.   We'll take our bathing suits.

HAPPY.   We'll carry your bags, Pop!

WILLY.   Oh, won't that be something! Me comin' into the Boston stores with you boys carryin' my bags. What a sensation! (BIFF *is prancing around, practicing passing the ball.*) You nervous, Biff, about the game?

BIFF.   Not if you're gonna be there.

WILLY.   What do they say about you in school, now that they made you captain?

HAPPY.   There's a crowd of girls behind him everytime the classes change.

BIFF (*taking* WILLY'*s hand*).   This Saturday, Pop, this Saturday—just for you, I'm going to break through for a touchdown.

HAPPY.   You're supposed to pass.

BIFF.   I'm takin' one play for Pop. You watch me, Pop, and when I take off my helmet, that means I'm breakin' out. Then you watch me crash through that line!

WILLY (*kisses* BIFF).   Oh, wait'll I tell this in Boston! (BERNARD *enters in knickers. He is younger than* BIFF, *earnest and loyal, a worried boy.*)

BERNARD.   Biff, where are you? You're supposed to study with me today.

WILLY.   Hey, looka Bernard. What're you lookin' so anemic about, Bernard?

BERNARD.   He's gotta study, Uncle Willy. He's got Regents° next week.

HAPPY (*tauntingly, spinning* BERNARD *around*).   Let's box, Bernard!

BERNARD.   Biff! (*He gets away from* HAPPY.) Listen, Biff, I heard Mr. Birnbaum say that if you don't start studyin' math he's gonna flunk you, and you won't graduate. I heard him!

WILLY.   You better study with him, Biff. Go ahead now.

BERNARD.   I heard him!

BIFF.   Oh, Pop, you didn't see my sneakers! (*He holds up a foot for* WILLY *to look at.*)

WILLY.   Hey, that's a beautiful job of printing!

BERNARD (*wiping his glasses*).   Just because he printed University of Virginia on his sneakers doesn't mean they've got to graduate him, Uncle Willy!

WILLY (*angrily*).   What're you talking about? With scholarships to three universities they're gonna flunk him?

BERNARD.   But I heard Mr. Birnbaum say—

WILLY.   Don't be a pest, Bernard! (*To his* BOYS) What an anemic!

BERNARD.   Okay, I'm waiting for you in my house, Biff. (BERNARD *goes off. The* LOMANS *laugh.*)

WILLY.   Bernard is not well liked, is he?

BIFF.   He's liked, but he's not well liked.

HAPPY.   That's right, Pop.

WILLY.   That's just what I mean. Bernard can get the best marks in school, y'understand, but when he gets out in the business world, y'understand, you are going to be five times ahead of him. That's why I thank Almighty God you're both built like Adonises. Because the man

---

Regents: a statewide proficiency examination administered in New York high schools

who makes an appearance in the business world, the man who creates personal interest, is the man who gets ahead. Be liked and you will never want. You take me, for instance. I never have to wait in line to see a buyer. "Willy Loman is here!" That's all they have to know, and I go right through.

BIFF.   Did you knock them dead, Pop?

WILLY.   Knocked 'em cold in Providence, slaughtered 'em in Boston.

HAPPY (*on his back, pedaling again*).   I'm losing weight, you notice, Pop? (LINDA *enters, as of old, a ribbon in her hair, carrying a basket of washing.*)

LINDA (*with youthful energy*).   Hello, dear!

WILLY.   Sweetheart!

LINDA.   How'd the Chevvy run?

WILLY.   Chevrolet, Linda, is the greatest car ever built. (*To the* BOYS) Since when do you let your mother carry wash up the stairs?

BIFF.   Grab hold there, boy!

HAPPY.   Where to, Mom?

LINDA.   Hang them up on the line. And you better go down to your friends, Biff. The cellar is full of boys. They don't know what to do with themselves.

BIFF.   Ah, when Pop comes home they can wait!

WILLY (*laughs appreciatively*).   You better go down and tell them what to do, Biff.

BIFF.   I think I'll have them sweep out the furnace room.

WILLY.   Good work, Biff.

BIFF (*goes through wall-line of kitchen to doorway at back and calls down*). Fellas! Everybody sweep out the furnace room! I'll be right down!

VOICES.   All right! Okay, Biff.

BIFF.   George and Sam and Frank, come out back! We're hangin' up the wash! Come on, Hap, on the double! (*He and* HAPPY *carry out the basket.*)

LINDA.   The way they obey him!

WILLY.   Well, that's training, the training. I'm tellin' you, I was sellin' thousands and thousands, but I had to come home.

LINDA.   Oh, the whole block'll be at that game. Did you sell anything?

WILLY.   I did five hundred gross in Providence and seven hundred gross in Boston.

LINDA.   No! Wait a minute, I've got a pencil. (*She pulls pencil and paper out of her apron pocket.*) That makes your commission . . . Two hundred—my God! Two hundred and twelve dollars!

WILLY.   Well, I didn't figure it yet, but . . .

LINDA.   How much did you do?

WILLY.   Well, I—I did—about a hundred and eighty gross in Providence. Well no—it came to—roughly two hundred gross on the whole trip.

LINDA (*without hesitation*).   Two hundred gross. That's . . . (*She figures.*)

WILLY.   The trouble was that three of the stores were half closed for inventory in Boston. Otherwise I woulda broke records.

LINDA.   Well, it makes seventy dollars and some pennies. That's very good.

WILLY.   What do we owe?

LINDA.   Well, on the first there's sixteen dollars on the refrigerator—

WILLY.   Why sixteen?

LINDA.   Well, the fan belt broke, so it was a dollar eighty.

WILLY.   But it's brand new.

LINDA.   Well, the man said that's the way it is. Till they work themselves in, y'know. (*They move through the wall-line into the kitchen.*)

WILLY.   I hope we didn't get stuck on that machine.

LINDA.   They got the biggest ads of any of them!

WILLY.   I know, it's a fine machine. What else?

LINDA.   Well, there's nine-sixty for the washing machine. And for the vacuum cleaner there's three and a half due on the fifteenth. Then the roof, you got twenty-one dollars remaining.

WILLY.   It doesn't leak, does it?

LINDA.   No, they did a wonderful job. Then you owe Frank for the carburetor.

WILLY.   I'm not going to pay that man! That goddam Chevrolet, they ought to prohibit the manufacture of that car!

LINDA.   Well, you owe him three and a half. And odds and ends, comes to around a hundred and twenty dollars by the fifteenth.

WILLY.   A hundred and twenty dollars! My God, if business don't pick up I don't know what I'm gonna do!

LINDA.   Well, next week you'll do better.

WILLY.   Oh, I'll knock 'em dead next week. I'll go to Hartford. I'm very well liked in Hartford. You know, the trouble is, Linda, people don't seem to take to me. (*They move onto the forestage.*)

LINDA.   Oh, don't be foolish.

WILLY.   I know it when I walk in. They seem to laugh at me.

LINDA.   Why? Why would they laugh at you? Don't talk that way, Willy. (WILLY *moves to the edge of the stage.* LINDA *goes into the kitchen and starts to darn stockings.*)

WILLY.   I don't know the reason for it, but they just pass me by. I'm not noticed.

LINDA.   But you're doing wonderful, dear. You're making seventy to a hundred dollars a week.

WILLY.   But I gotta be at it ten, twelve hours a day. Other men— I don't know—they do it easier. I don't know why—I can't stop myself —I talk too much. A man oughta come in with a few words. One thing about Charley. He's a man of few words, and they respect him.

LINDA.   You don't talk too much, you're just lively.

WILLY (*smiling*).   Well, I figure, what the hell, life is short, a couple of jokes. (*To himself*) I joke too much! (*The smile goes.*)

LINDA.   Why? You're—

WILLY.   I'm fat. I'm very—foolish to look at, Linda. I didn't tell you, but Christmas time I happened to be calling on F. H. Stewarts, and a salesman I know, as I was going in to see the buyer I heard him say something about—walrus. And I—I cracked him right across the face. I won't take that. I simply will not take that. But they do laugh at me. I know that.

LINDA.   Darling . . .

WILLY.   I gotta overcome it. I know I gotta overcome it. I'm not dressing to advantage, maybe.

LINDA.   Willy, darling, you're the handsomest man in the world—

WILLY.   Oh, no, Linda.

LINDA.   To me you are. (*Slight pause.*) The handsomest. (*From the darkness is heard the laughter of a woman.* WILLY *doesn't turn to it, but it continues through* LINDA's *lines.*) And the boys, Willy. Few men are idolized by their children the way you are. (*Music is heard as, behind a scrim to the left of the house,* THE WOMAN, *dimly seen, is dressing.*)

WILLY (*with great feeling*).   You're the best there is, Linda, you're a pal, you know that? On the road—on the road I want to grab you sometimes and just kiss the life outa you.

(*The laughter is loud now, and he moves into a brightening area at the left, where* THE WOMAN *has come from behind the scrim and is standing, putting on her hat, looking into a "mirror" and laughing.*)

WILLY.   'Cause I get so lonely—especially when business is bad and there's nobody to talk to. I get the feeling that I'll never sell anything again, that I won't make a living for you, or a business, a business for the boys. (*He talks through* THE WOMAN's *subsiding laughter;* THE WOMAN *primps at the "mirror."*) There's so much I want to make for—

THE WOMAN.   Me? You didn't make me, Willy. I picked you.

WILLY (*pleased*).   You picked me?

THE WOMAN (*who is quite proper-looking,* WILLY's *age*).   I did. I've been sitting at that desk watching all the salesmen go by, day in, day out. But you've got such a sense of humor, and we do have such a good time together, don't we?

WILLY.   Sure, sure. (*He takes her in his arms.*) Why do you have to go now?

THE WOMAN.   It's two o'clock . . .

WILLY.   No, come on in! (*He pulls her.*)

THE WOMAN.   . . . my sisters'll be scandalized. When'll you be back?

WILLY.   Oh, two weeks about. Will you come up again?

THE WOMAN.   Sure thing. You do make me laugh. It's good for me. (*She squeezes his arm, kisses him.*) And I think you're a wonderful man.

WILLY.   You picked me, heh?

THE WOMAN.   Sure. Because you're so sweet. And such a kidder.

WILLY.   Well, I'll see you next time I'm in Boston.

THE WOMAN.   I'll put you right through to the buyers.

WILLY (*slapping her bottom*).   Right. Well, bottoms up!

THE WOMAN (*slaps him gently and laughs*).   You just kill me, Willy. (*He suddenly grabs her and kisses her roughly.*) You kill me. And thanks for the stockings. I love a lot of stockings. Well, good night.

WILLY.   Good night. And keep your pores open!

THE WOMAN.   Oh, Willy!

(THE WOMAN *bursts out laughing, and* LINDA's *laughter blends in.* THE WOMAN *disappears into the dark. Now the area at the kitchen table brightens.* LINDA *is sitting where she was at the kitchen table, but now is mending a pair of her silk stockings.*)

LINDA.   You are, Willy. The handsomest man. You've got no reason to feel that—

WILLY (*coming out of* THE WOMAN's *dimming area and going over to* LINDA).   I'll make it all up to you, Linda. I'll—

LINDA.   There's nothing to make up, dear. You're doing fine, better than—

WILLY (*noticing her mending*).   What's that?

LINDA.   Just mending my stockings. They're so expensive—

WILLY (*angrily, taking them from her*).   I won't have you mending stockings in this house! Now throw them out! (LINDA *puts the stockings in her pocket.*)

BERNARD (*entering on the run*).   Where is he? If he doesn't study!

WILLY (*moving to the forestage, with great agitation*).   You'll give him the answers!

BERNARD.   I do, but I can't on a Regents! That's a state exam! They're liable to arrest me!

WILLY.   Where is he? I'll whip him, I'll whip him!

LINDA.   And he'd better give back that football, Willy, it's not nice.

WILLY.   Biff! Where is he? Why is he taking everything?

LINDA.   He's too rough with the girls, Willy. All the mothers are afraid of him!

WILLY.   I'll whip him!

BERNARD.   He's driving the car without a license! (THE WOMAN's *laugh is heard.*)

WILLY.   Shut up!

LINDA.   All the mothers—

WILLY.   Shut up!

BERNARD (*backing quietly away and out*).   Mr. Birnbaum says he's stuck up.

WILLY.   Get outa here!

BERNARD.   If he doesn't buckle down he'll flunk math! (*He goes off.*)

LINDA.   He's right, Willy, you've gotta—

WILLY (*exploding at her*).   There's nothing the matter with him! You want him to be a worm like Bernard? He's got spirit, personality . . . (*As he speaks,* LINDA, *almost in tears, exits into the living-room.* WILLY *is alone in the kitchen, wilting and staring. The leaves are gone, it is night again, and the apartment houses look down from behind.*) Loaded with it. Loaded! What is he stealing? He's giving it back, isn't he? Why is he stealing? What did I tell him? I never in my life told him anything but decent things. (HAPPY *in pajamas has come down the stairs;* WILLY *suddenly becomes aware of* HAPPY's *presence.*)

HAPPY.   Let's go now, come on.

WILLY (*sitting down at the kitchen table*).   Huh! Why did she have to wax the floors herself? Everytime she waxes the floors she keels over. She knows that!

HAPPY.   Shh! Take it easy. What brought you back tonight?

WILLY.   I got an awful scare. Nearly hit a kid in Yonkers. God! Why didn't I go to Alaska with my brother Ben that time! Ben! That man was a genius, that man was success incarnate! What a mistake! He begged me to go.

HAPPY.   Well, there's no use in—

WILLY.   You guys! There was a man started with the clothes on his back and ended up with diamond mines!

HAPPY.   Boy, someday I'd like to know how he did it.

WILLY.   What's the mystery? The man knew what he wanted and went out and got it! Walked into a jungle, and comes out, the age of twenty-one, and he's rich! The world is an oyster, but you don't crack it open on a mattress.

HAPPY.   Pop, I told you I'm gonna retire you for life.

WILLY.   You'll retire me for life on seventy goddam dollars a week? And your women and your car and your apartment, and you'll retire me for life! Christ's sake, I couldn't get past Yonkers today! Where are you guys, where are you? The woods are burning! I can't drive a car! (CHARLEY *has appeared in the doorway. He is a large man, slow of speech, laconic, immovable. In all he says, despite what he says, there is pity, and, now, trepidation. He has a robe over pajamas, slippers on his feet. He enters the kitchen.*)

CHARLEY.   Everything all right?

HAPPY.   Yeah, Charley, everything's . . .

WILLY.   What's the matter?

CHARLEY.   I heard some noise. I thought something happened. Can't we do something about the walls? You sneeze in here, and in my house hats blow off.

HAPPY.   Let's go to bed, Dad. Come on. (CHARLEY *signals to* HAPPY *to go.*)

WILLY.   You go ahead, I'm not tired at the moment.

HAPPY (*to* WILLY).   Take it easy, huh? (*He exits.*)

WILLY.   What're you doin' up?

CHARLEY (*sitting down at the kitchen table opposite* WILLY). Couldn't sleep good. I had a heartburn.

WILLY.   Well, you don't know how to eat.

CHARLEY.   I eat with my mouth.

WILLY.   No, you're ignorant. You gotta know about vitamins and things like that.

CHARLEY.   Come on, let's shoot. Tire you out a little.

WILLY (*hesitantly*).   All right. You got cards?

CHARLEY (*taking a deck from his pocket*).   Yeah, I got them. Some-place. What is it with those vitamins?

WILLY (*dealing*).   They build up your bones. Chemistry.

CHARLEY.   Yeah, but there's no bones in a heartburn.

WILLY.   What are you talkin' about? Do you know the first thing about it?

CHARLEY.   Don't get insulted.

WILLY.   Don't talk about something you don't know anything about. (*They are playing. Pause.*)

CHARLEY.   What're you doin' home?

WILLY.   A little trouble with the car.

CHARLEY.   Oh. (*Pause.*) I'd like to take a trip to California.

WILLY.   Don't say.

CHARLEY.   You want a job?

WILLY.   I got a job, I told you that. (*After a slight pause*) What the hell are you offering me a job for?

CHARLEY.   Don't get insulted.

WILLY.   Don't insult me.

CHARLEY.   I don't see no sense in it. You don't have to go on this way.

WILLY.   I got a good job. (*Slight pause.*) What do you keep coming in here for?

CHARLEY.   You want me to go?

WILLY (*after a pause, withering*).   I can't understand it. He's going back to Texas again. What the hell is that?

CHARLEY.   Let him go.

WILLY.   I got nothin' to give him, Charley, I'm clean, I'm clean.

CHARLEY.   He won't starve. None a them starve. Forget about him.

WILLY.   Then what have I got to remember?

CHARLEY.   You take it too hard. To hell with it. When a deposit bottle is broken you don't get your nickel back.

WILLY.   That's easy enough for you to say.

CHARLEY.   That ain't easy for me to say.

WILLY.   Did you see the ceiling I put up in the living-room?

CHARLEY.   Yeah, that's a piece of work. To put up a ceiling is a mystery to me. How do you do it?

WILLY.   What's the difference?

CHARLEY.   Well, talk about it.

WILLY.   You gonna put up a ceiling?

CHARLEY.   How could I put up a ceiling?

WILLY.   Then what the hell are you bothering me for?

CHARLEY.   You're insulted again.

WILLY.   A man who can't handle tools is not a man. You're disgusting.

CHARLEY.   Don't call me disgusting, Willy. (UNCLE BEN, *carrying a valise and an umbrella, enters the forestage from around the right corner of the house. He is a stolid man, in his sixties, with a mustache and an authoritative air. He is utterly certain of his destiny, and there is an aura of far places about him. He enters exactly as* WILLY *speaks.*)

WILLY.   I'm getting awfully tired, Ben. (BEN's *music is heard.* BEN *looks around at everything.*)

CHARLEY.   Good, keep playing; you'll sleep better. Did you call me Ben? (BEN *looks at his watch.*)

WILLY.   That's funny. For a second there you reminded me of my brother Ben.

BEN.   I only have a few minutes. (*He strolls, inspecting the place.* WILLY *and* CHARLEY *continue playing.*)

CHARLEY.   You never heard from him again, heh? Since that time?

WILLY.   Didn't Linda tell you? Couple of weeks ago we got a letter from his wife in Africa. He died.

CHARLEY.   That so.

BEN (*chuckling*).   So this is Brooklyn, eh?

CHARLEY.   Maybe you're in for some of his money.

WILLY.   Naa, he had seven sons. There's just one opportunity I had with that man . . .

BEN.   I must make a train, William. There are several properties I'm looking at in Alaska.

WILLY.   Sure, sure! If I'd gone with him to Alaska that time, everything would've been totally different.

CHARLEY.   Go on, you'd froze to death up there.

WILLY.   What're you talking about?

BEN.   Opportunity is tremendous in Alaska, William. Surprised you're not up there.

WILLY.   Sure, tremendous.

CHARLEY.   Heh?

WILLY.   There was the only man I ever met who knew the answers.

CHARLEY.   Who?

BEN.   How are you all?

WILLY (*taking a pot, smiling*).   Fine, fine.

CHARLEY.   Pretty sharp tonight.

BEN.   Is Mother living with you?

WILLY.   No, she died a long time ago.

CHARLEY.   Who?

BEN.   That's too bad. Fine specimen of a lady, Mother.

WILLY (*to* CHARLEY).   Heh?

BEN.   I'd hoped to see the old girl.

CHARLEY.   Who died?

BEN.   Heard anything from Father, have you?

WILLY (*unnerved*).   What do you mean, who died?

CHARLEY (*taking a pot*).   What're you talkin' about?

BEN (*looking at his watch*).   William, it's half-past eight!

WILLY (*as though to dispel his confusion he angrily stops* CHARLEY's *hand*).   That's my build!

CHARLEY.   I put the ace—

WILLY.   If you don't know how to play the game I'm not gonna throw my money away on you!

CHARLEY (*rising*).   It was my ace, for God's sake!

WILLY.   I'm through, I'm through!

BEN.   When did Mother die?

WILLY.   Long ago. Since the beginning you never knew how to play cards.

CHARLEY (*picks up the cards and goes to the door*).   All right! Next time I'll bring a deck with five aces.

WILLY.   I don't play that kind of game!

CHARLEY (*turning to him*).   You ought to be ashamed of yourself!

WILLY.   Yeah?

CHARLEY.   Yeah! (*He goes out.*)

WILLY (*slamming the door after him*).   Ignoramus!

BEN (*as WILLY comes toward him through the wall-line of the kitchen*). So you're William.

WILLY (*shaking BEN's hand*).   Ben! I've been waiting for you so long! What's the answer? How did you do it?

BEN.   Oh, there's a story in that. (*LINDA enters the forestage, as of old, carrying the wash basket.*)

LINDA.   Is this Ben?

BEN (*gallantly*).   How do you do, my dear.

LINDA.   Where've you been all these years? Willy's always wondered why you—

WILLY (*pulling BEN away from her impatiently*).   Where is Dad? Didn't you follow him? How did you get started?

BEN.   Well, I don't know how much you remember.

WILLY.   Well, I was just a baby, of course, only three or four years old—

BEN.   Three years and eleven months.

WILLY.   What a memory, Ben!

BEN.   I have many enterprises, William, and I have never kept books.

WILLY.   I remember I was sitting under the wagon in—was it Nebraska?

BEN.   It was South Dakota, and I gave you a bunch of wild flowers.

WILLY.   I remember you walking away down some open road.

BEN (*laughing*).   I was going to find Father in Alaska.

WILLY.   Where is he?

BEN.   At that age I had a very faulty view of geography, William. I discovered after a few days that I was heading due south, so instead of Alaska, I ended up in Africa.

LINDA.   Africa!

WILLY.   The Gold Coast!

BEN.   Principally diamond mines.

LINDA.   Diamond mines!

BEN.   Yes, my dear. But I've only a few minutes—

WILLY.   No! Boys! Boys! (YOUNG BIFF *and* HAPPY *appear.*) Listen to this. This is your Uncle Ben, a great man! Tell my boys, Ben!

BEN.   Why, boys, when I was seventeen I walked into the jungle, and when I was twenty-one I walked out. (*He laughs.*) And by God I was rich.

WILLY (*to the* BOYS).   You see what I been talking about? The greatest things can happen!

BEN (*glancing at his watch*).   I have an appointment in Ketchikan Tuesday week.

WILLY.   No, Ben! Please tell about Dad. I want my boys to hear. I want them to know the kind of stock they spring from. All I remember is a man with a big beard, and I was in Mamma's lap, sitting around a fire, and some kind of high music.

BEN.   His flute. He played the flute.

WILLY.   Sure, the flute, that's right! (*New music is heard, a high, rollicking tune.*)

BEN.   Father was a very great and a very wild-hearted man. We would start in Boston, and he'd toss the whole family into the wagon, and then he'd drive the team right across the country; through Ohio and Indiana, Michigan, Illinois, and all the Western states. And we'd stop in the towns and sell the flutes that he'd made on the way. Great inventor, Father. With one gadget he made more in a week than a man like you could make in a lifetime.

WILLY.   That's just the way I'm bringing them up, Ben—rugged, well liked, all-around.

BEN.   Yeah? (*To* BIFF) Hit that, boy—hard as you can. (*He pounds his stomach.*)

BIFF.   Oh, no, sir!

BEN (*taking boxing stance*).   Come on, get to me! (*He laughs.*)

WILLY.   Go to it, Biff! Go ahead, show him!

BIFF.   Okay! (*He cocks his fists and starts in.*)

LINDA (*to* WILLY).   Why must he fight, dear?

BEN (*sparring with* BIFF).   Good boy! Good boy!

WILLY.   How's that, Ben, heh?

HAPPY.   Give him the left, Biff!

LINDA.   Why are you fighting?

BEN.   Good boy! (*Suddenly comes in, trips* BIFF, *and stands over him, the point of his umbrella poised over* BIFF's *eye.*)

LINDA.   Look out, Biff!

BIFF.   Gee!

BEN (*patting* BIFF's *knee*).   Never fight fair with a stranger, boy. You'll never get out of the jungle that way. (*Taking* LINDA's *hand and bowing*) It was an honor and a pleasure to meet you, Linda.

LINDA (*withdrawing her hand coldly, frightened*).   Have a nice —trip.

BEN (*to* WILLY).   And good luck with your—what do you do?

WILLY.   Selling.

BEN.   Yes. Well . . . (*He raises his hand in farewell to all.*)

WILLY.   No, Ben, I don't want you to think . . . (*He takes* BEN's *arm to show him.*) It's Brooklyn, I know, but we hunt too.

BEN.   Really, now.

WILLY.   Oh, sure, there's snakes and rabbits and—that's why I moved out here. Why, Biff can fell any one of these trees in no time! Boys! Go right over to where they're building the apartment house and get some sand. We're gonna rebuild the entire front stoop right now! Watch this, Ben!

BIFF.   Yes, sir! On the double, Hap!

HAPPY (*as he and* BIFF *run off*).   I lost weight, Pop, you notice? (CHARLEY *enters in knickers, even before the* BOYS *are gone.*)

CHARLEY.   Listen, if they steal any more from that building the watchman'll put the cops on them!

LINDA (*to* WILLY).   Don't let Biff . . . (BEN *laughs lustily.*)

WILLY.   You shoulda seen the lumber they brought home last week. At least a dozen six-by-tens worth all kinds a money.

CHARLEY.   Listen, if that watchman—

WILLY.   I gave them hell, understand. But I got a couple of fearless characters there.

CHARLEY.   Willy, the jails are full of fearless characters.

BEN (*clapping* WILLY *on the back, with a laugh at* CHARLEY).   And the stock exchange, friend!

WILLY (*joining in* BEN's *laughter*).   Where are the rest of your pants?

CHARLEY.   My wife bought them.

WILLY.   Now all you need is a golf club and you can go upstairs and go to sleep. (*To* BEN) Great athlete! Between him and his son Bernard they can't hammer a nail!

BERNARD (*rushing in*).   The watchman's chasing Biff!

WILLY (*angrily*).   Shut up! He's not stealing anything!

LINDA (*alarmed, hurrying off left*).   Where is he? Biff, dear! (*She exits.*)

WILLY (*moving toward the left, away from* BEN).   There's nothing wrong. What's the matter with you?

BEN.   Nervy boy. Good!

WILLY (*laughing*).   Oh, nerves of iron, that Biff!

CHARLEY.   Don't know what it is. My New England man comes back and he's bleedin', they murdered him up there.

WILLY.   It's contacts, Charley, I got important contacts!

CHARLEY (*sarcastically*).   Glad to hear it, Willy. Come in later, we'll shoot a little casino. I'll take some of your Portland money. (*He laughs at* WILLY *and exits.*)

WILLY (*turning to* BEN).   Business is bad, it's murderous. But not for me, of course.

BEN.   I'll stop by on my way back to Africa.

WILLY (*longingly*).   Can't you stay a few days? You're just what I need, Ben, because I—I have a fine position here, but I—well, Dad left when I was such a baby and I never had a chance to talk to him and I still feel—kind of temporary about myself.

BEN.   I'll be late for my train. (*They are at opposite ends of the stage.*)

WILLY.   Ben, my boys—can't we talk? They'd go into the jaws of hell for me, but I—

BEN.   William, you're being first-rate with your boys. Outstanding, manly chaps!

WILLY (*hanging on to his words*).   Oh, Ben, that's good to hear! Because sometimes I'm afraid that I'm not teaching them the right kind of—Ben, how should I teach them?

BEN (*giving great weight to each word, and with a certain vicious audacity*).   William, when I walked into the jungle, I was seventeen. When I walked out I was twenty-one. And, by God, I was rich! (*He goes off into the darkness around the right corner of the house.*)

WILLY.   . . . was rich! That's just the spirit I want to imbue them with! To walk into a jungle! I was right! (BEN *is gone, but* WILLY *is still speaking to him as* LINDA, *in nightgown and robe, enters the kitchen, glances around for* WILLY, *then goes to the door of the house, looks out and sees him. Comes down to his left. He looks at her.*)

LINDA.   Willy, dear? Willy?

WILLY.   I was right!

LINDA.   Did you have some cheese? (*He can't answer.*) It's very late, darling. Come to bed, heh?

WILLY (*looking straight up*).   Gotta break your neck to see a star in this yard.

LINDA.   You coming in?

WILLY.   Whatever happened to that diamond watch fob? Remember? When Ben came from Africa that time? Didn't he give me a watch fob with a diamond in it?

LINDA.   You pawned it, dear. Twelve, thirteen years ago. For Biff's radio correspondence course.

WILLY.   Gee, that was a beautiful thing. I'll take a walk.

LINDA.   But you're in your slippers.

WILLY (*starting to go around the house at the left*).   I was right! I was! (*Half to* LINDA, *as he goes, shaking his head*) What a man! There was a man worth talking to. I was right!

LINDA (*calling after* WILLY).   But in your slippers, Willy! (WILLY *is almost gone when* BIFF, *in his pajamas, comes down the stairs and enters the kitchen.*)

BIFF.   What is he doing out there?

LINDA.   Sh!

BIFF.   God Almighty, Mom, how long has he been doing this?

LINDA.   Don't, he'll hear you.

BIFF.   What the hell is the matter with him?

LINDA.   It'll pass by morning.

BIFF.   Shouldn't we do anything?

LINDA.   Oh, my dear, you should do a lot of things, but there's nothing to do, so go to sleep. (HAPPY *comes down the stairs and sits on the steps.*)

HAPPY.   I never heard him so loud, Mom.

LINDA.   Well, come around more often; you'll hear him. (*She sits down at the table and mends the lining of* WILLY's *jacket.*)

BIFF.   Why didn't you ever write me about this, Mom?

LINDA.   How would I write to you? For over three months you had no address.

BIFF.   I was on the move. But you know I thought of you all the time. You know that, don't you, pal?

LINDA.   I know, dear, I know. But he likes to have a letter. Just to know that there's still a possibility for better things.

BIFF.   He's not like this all the time, is he?

LINDA.   It's when you come home he's always the worst.

BIFF.   When I come home?

LINDA.   When you write you're coming, he's all smiles, and talks about the future, and—he's just wonderful. And then the closer you seem to come, the more shaky he gets, and then, by the time you get here, he's arguing, and he seems angry at you. I think it's just that maybe he can't bring himself to—to open up to you. Why are you so hateful to each other? Why is that?

BIFF (*evasively*).   I'm not hateful, Mom.

LINDA.   But you no sooner come in the door than you're fighting!

BIFF.   I don't know why. I mean to change. I'm tryin', Mom, you understand?

LINDA. Are you home to stay now?

BIFF. I don't know. I want to look around, see what's doin'.

LINDA. Biff, you can't look around all your life, can you?

BIFF. I just can't take hold, Mom. I can't take hold of some kind of a life.

LINDA. Biff, a man is not a bird to come and go with the springtime.

BIFF. Your hair . . . (*He touches her hair.*) Your hair got so gray.

LINDA. Oh, it's been gray since you were in high school. I just stopped dyeing it, that's all.

BIFF. Dye it again, will ya? I don't want my pal looking old. (*He smiles.*)

LINDA. You're such a boy! You think you can go away for a year and . . . You've got to get it into your head now that one day you'll knock on this door and there'll be strange people here—

BIFF. What are you talking about? You're not even sixty, Mom.

LINDA. But what about your father?

BIFF (*lamely*). Well, I meant him, too.

HAPPY. He admires Pop.

LINDA. Biff, dear, if you don't have any feeling for him, then you can't have any feeling for me.

BIFF. Sure I can, Mom.

LINDA. No. You can't just come to see me, because I love him. (*With a threat, but only a threat, of tears*) He's the dearest man in the world to me, and I won't have anyone making him feel unwanted and low and blue. You've got to make up your mind now, darling, there's no leeway any more. Either he's your father and you pay him that respect, or else you're not to come here. I know he's not easy to get along with—nobody knows that better than me—but . . .

WILLY (*from the left, with a laugh*). Hey, hey, Biffo!

BIFF (*starting to go out after* WILLY). What the hell is the matter with him? (HAPPY *stops him.*)

LINDA. Don't—don't go near him!

BIFF. Stop making excuses for him! He always, always wiped the floor with you. Never had an ounce of respect for you.

HAPPY. He's always had respect for—

BIFF. What the hell do you know about it?

HAPPY (*surlily*). Just don't call him crazy!

BIFF. He's got no character—Charley wouldn't do this. Not in his own house—spewing out that vomit from his mind.

HAPPY. Charley never had to cope with what he's got to.

BIFF. People are worse off than Willy Loman. Believe me, I've seen them.

LINDA.   Then make Charley your father, Biff. You can't do that, can you? I don't say he's a great man. Willy Loman never made a lot of money. His name was never in the paper. He's not the finest character that ever lived. But he's a human being, and a terrible thing is happening to him. So attention must be paid. He's not to be allowed to fall into his grave like an old dog. Attention, attention must be finally paid to such a person. You called him crazy—

BIFF.   I didn't mean—

LINDA.   No, a lot of people think he's lost his—balance. But you don't have to be very smart to know what his trouble is. The man is exhausted.

HAPPY.   Sure!

LINDA.   A small man can be just as exhausted as a great man. He works for a company thirty-six years this March, opens up unheard-of territories to their trademark, and now in his old age they take his salary away.

HAPPY (*indignantly*).   I didn't know that, Mom.

LINDA.   You never asked, my dear! Now that you get your spending money someplace else you don't trouble your mind with him.

HAPPY.   But I gave you money last—

LINDA.   Christmas time, fifty dollars! To fix the hot water it cost ninety-seven fifty! For five weeks he's been on straight commission, like a beginner, an unknown!

BIFF.   Those ungrateful bastards!

LINDA.   Are they any worse than his sons? When he brought them business, when he was young, they were glad to see him. But now his old friends, the old buyers that loved him so and always found some order to hand him in a pinch—they're all dead, retired. He used to be able to make six, seven calls a day in Boston. Now he takes his valises out of the car and puts them back and takes them out again and he's exhausted. Instead of walking he talks now. He drives seven hundred miles, and when he gets there no one knows him any more, no one welcomes him. And what goes through a man's mind, driving seven hundred miles home without having earned a cent? Why shouldn't he talk to himself? Why? When he has to go to Charley and borrow fifty dollars a week and pretend to me that it's his pay? How long can that go on? How long? You see what I'm sitting here and waiting for? And you tell me he has no character? The man who never worked a day but for your benefit? When does he get the medal for that? Is this his reward—to turn around at the age of sixty-three and find his sons, who he loved better than his life, one a philandering bum—

HAPPY.   Mom!

LINDA. That's all you are, my baby! (*To* BIFF) And you! What happened to the love you had for him? You were such pals! How you used to talk to him on the phone every night! How lonely he was till he could come home to you!

BIFF. All right, Mom, I'll live here in my room, and I'll get a job. I'll keep away from him, that's all.

LINDA. No, Biff. You can't stay here and fight all the time.

BIFF. He threw me out of this house, remember that.

LINDA. Why did he do that? I never knew why.

BIFF. Because I know he's a fake and he doesn't like anybody around who knows!

LINDA. Why a fake? In what way? What do you mean?

BIFF. Just don't lay it all at my feet. It's between me and him— that's all I have to say. I'll chip in from now on. He'll settle for half my pay check. He'll be all right. I'm going to bed. (*He starts for the stairs.*)

LINDA. He won't be all right.

BIFF (*turning on the stairs, furiously*). I hate this city and I'll stay here. Now what do you want?

LINDA. He's dying, Biff. (HAPPY *turns quickly to her, shocked.*)

BIFF (*after a pause*). Why is he dying?

LINDA. He's been trying to kill himself.

BIFF (*with great horror*). How?

LINDA. I live from day to day.

BIFF. What're you talking about?

LINDA. Remember I wrote you that he smashed up the car again? In February?

BIFF. Well?

LINDA. The insurance inspector came. He said that they have evidence. That all these accidents in the last year—weren't— weren't—accidents.

HAPPY. How can they tell that? That's a lie.

LINDA. It seems there's a woman . . . (*She takes a breath as—*)

BIFF (*sharply but contained*). What woman?

LINDA (*simultaneously*).   . . . and this woman . . .

LINDA. What?

BIFF. Nothing. Go ahead.

LINDA. What did you say?

BIFF. Nothing. I just said what woman?

HAPPY. What about her?

LINDA. Well, it seems she was walking down the road and saw his car. She says that he wasn't driving fast at all, and that he didn't skid. She says he came to that little bridge, and then deliberately smashed into the railing, and it was only the shallowness of the water that saved him.

BIFF.   Oh, no, he probably just fell asleep again.

LINDA.   I don't think he fell asleep.

BIFF.   Why not?

LINDA.   Last month . . . (*With great difficulty*) Oh, boys, it's so hard to say a thing like this! He's just a big stupid man to you, but I tell you there's more good in him than in many other people. (*She chokes, wipes her eyes.*) I was looking for a fuse. The lights blew out, and I went down to the cellar. And behind the fuse box—it happened to fall out—was a length of rubber pipe—just short.

HAPPY.   No kidding?

LINDA.   There's a little attachment on the end of it. I knew it right away. And sure enough, on the bottom of the water heater there's a new little nipple on the gas pipe.

HAPPY (*angrily*).   That—jerk.

BIFF.   Did you have it taken off?

LINDA.   I'm—I'm ashamed to. How can I mention it to him? Every day I go down and take away that little rubber pipe. But, when he comes home, I put it back where it was. How can I insult him that way? I don't know what to do. I live from day to day, boys. I tell you, I know every thought in his mind. It sounds so old-fashioned and silly, but I tell you he put his whole life into you and you've turned your backs on him. (*She is bent over in the chair, weeping, her face in her hands.*) Biff, I swear to God! Biff, his life is in your hands!

HAPPY (*to* BIFF).   How do you like that damned fool!

BIFF (*kissing her*).   All right, pal, all right. It's all settled now. I've been remiss. I know that, Mom. But now I'll stay, and I swear to you, I'll apply myself. (*Kneeling in front of her, in a fever of self-reproach*) It's just—you see, Mom, I don't fit in business. Not that I won't try. I'll try, and I'll make good.

HAPPY.   Sure you will. The trouble with you in business was you never tried to please people.

BIFF.   I know, I—

HAPPY.   Like when you worked for Harrison's. Bob Harrison said you were tops, and then you go and do some damn fool thing like whistling whole songs in the elevator like a comedian.

BIFF (*against* HAPPY).   So what? I like to whistle sometimes.

HAPPY.   You don't raise a guy to a responsible job who whistles in the elevator!

LINDA.   Well, don't argue about it now.

HAPPY.   Like when you'd go off and swim in the middle of the day instead of taking the line around.

BIFF (*his resentment rising*).   Well, don't you run off? You take off sometimes, don't you? On a nice summer day?

HAPPY.   Yeah, but I cover myself!

LINDA.   Boys!

HAPPY.   If I'm going to take a fade the boss can call any number where I'm supposed to be and they'll swear to him that I just left. I'll tell you something that I hate to say, Biff, but in the business world some of them think you're crazy.

BIFF (*angered*).   Screw the business world!

HAPPY.   All right, screw it! Great, but cover yourself!

LINDA.   Hap, Hap!

BIFF.   I don't care what they think! They've laughed at Dad for years, and you know why? Because we don't belong in this nuthouse of a city! We should be mixing cement on some open plain, or—or carpenters. A carpenter is allowed to whistle! (WILLY *walks in from the entrance of the house, at left.*)

WILLY.   Even your grandfather was better than a carpenter. (*Pause. They watch him.*) You never grew up. Bernard does not whistle in the elevator, I assure you.

BIFF (*as though to laugh* WILLY *out of it*).   Yeah, but you do, Pop.

WILLY.   I never in my life whistled in an elevator! And who in the business world thinks I'm crazy?

BIFF.   I didn't mean it like that, Pop. Now don't make a whole thing out of it, will ya?

WILLY.   Go back to the West! Be a carpenter, a cowboy, enjoy yourself!

LINDA.   Willy, he was just saying—

WILLY.   I heard what he said!

HAPPY (*trying to quiet* WILLY).   Hey, Pop, come on now . . .

WILLY (*continuing over* HAPPY's *line*).   They laugh at me, heh? Go to Filene's, go to the Hub, go to Slattery's, Boston. Call out the name Willy Loman and see what happens! Big shot!

BIFF.   All right, Pop.

WILLY.   Big!

BIFF.   All right!

WILLY.   Why do you always insult me?

BIFF.   I didn't say a word. (*To* LINDA) Did I say a word?

LINDA.   He didn't say anything, Willy.

WILLY (*going to the doorway of the living-room*).   All right, good night, good night.

LINDA.   Willy, dear, he just decided . . .

WILLY (*to* BIFF).   If you get tired hanging around tomorrow, paint the ceiling I put up in the living-room.

BIFF.   I'm leaving early tomorrow.

HAPPY.   He's going to see Bill Oliver, Pop.

WILLY (*interestedly*).   Oliver? For what?

BIFF (*with reserve, but trying, trying*).   He always said he'd stake me. I'd like to go into business, so maybe I can take him up on it.

LINDA.   Isn't that wonderful?

WILLY.   Don't interrupt. What's wonderful about it? There's fifty men in the City of New York who'd stake him. (*To* BIFF) Sporting goods?

BIFF.   I guess so. I know something about it and—

WILLY.   He knows something about it! You know sporting goods better than Spalding, for God's sake! How much is he giving you?

BIFF.   I don't know, I didn't even see him yet, but—

WILLY.   Then what're you talkin' about?

BIFF (*getting angry*).   Well, all I said was I'm gonna see him, that's all!

WILLY (*turning away*).   Ah, you're counting your chickens again.

BIFF (*starting left for the stairs*).   Oh, Jesus, I'm going to sleep!

WILLY (*calling after him*).   Don't curse in this house!

BIFF (*turning*).   Since when did you get so clean?

HAPPY (*trying to stop them*).   Wait a . . .

WILLY.   Don't use that language to me! I won't have it!

HAPPY (*grabbing* BIFF, *shouts*).   Wait a minute! I got an idea. I got a feasible idea. Come here, Biff, let's talk this over now, let's talk some sense here. When I was down in Florida last time, I thought of a great idea to sell sporting goods. It just came back to me. You and I, Biff—we have a line, the Loman Line. We train a couple of weeks, and put on a couple of exhibitions, see?

WILLY.   That's an idea!

HAPPY.   Wait! We form two basketball teams, see? Two water-polo teams. We play each other. It's a million dollars' worth of publicity. Two brothers, see? The Loman Brothers. Displays in the Royal Palms —all the hotels. And banners over the ring and the basketball court: "Loman Brothers." Baby, we could sell sporting goods!

WILLY.   That is a one-million-dollar idea!

LINDA.   Marvelous!

BIFF.   I'm in great shape as far as that's concerned.

HAPPY.   And the beauty of it is, Biff, it wouldn't be like a business. We'd be out playin' ball again . . .

BIFF (*enthused*).   Yeah, that's . . .

WILLY.   Million-dollar . . .

HAPPY.   And you wouldn't get fed up with it, Biff. It'd be the family again. There'd be the old honor, and comradeship, and if you wanted to go off for a swim or somethin'—well, you'd do it! Without some smart cooky gettin' up ahead of you!

WILLY.   Lick the world! You guys together could absolutely lick the civilized world.

BIFF.   I'll see Oliver tomorrow. Hap, if we could work that out . . .

LINDA.   Maybe things are beginning to—

WILLY (*wildly enthused, to* LINDA).   Stop interrupting! (*To* BIFF) But don't wear sport jacket and slacks when you see Oliver.

BIFF.   No, I'll—

WILLY.   A business suit, and talk as little as possible, and don't crack any jokes.

BIFF.   He did like me. Always liked me.

LINDA.   He loved you!

WILLY (*to* LINDA).   Will you stop! (*To* BIFF) Walk in very serious. You are not applying for a boy's job. Money is to pass. Be quiet, fine, and serious. Everybody likes a kidder, but nobody lends him money.

HAPPY.   I'll try to get some myself, Biff. I'm sure I can.

WILLY.   I see great things for you kids, I think your troubles are over. But remember, start big and you'll end big. Ask for fifteen. How much you gonna ask for?

BIFF.   Gee, I don't know—

WILLY.   And don't say, "Gee," "Gee" is a boy's word. A man walking in for fifteen thousand dollars does not say "Gee!"

BIFF.   Ten, I think, would be top though.

WILLY.   Don't be so modest. You always started too low. Walk in with a big laugh. Don't look worried. Start off with a couple of your good stories to lighten things up. It's not what you say, it's how you say it—because personality always wins the day.

LINDA.   Oliver always thought the highest of him—

WILLY.   Will you let me talk?

BIFF.   Don't yell at her, Pop, will ya?

WILLY (*angrily*).   I was talking, wasn't I?

BIFF.   I don't like you yelling at her all the time, and I'm tellin' you, that's all.

WILLY.   What're you, takin' over this house?

LINDA.   Willy—

WILLY (*turning on her*).   Don't take his side all the time, goddammit!

BIFF (*furiously*).   Stop yelling at her!

WILLY (*suddenly pulling on his cheek, beaten down, guilt ridden*). Give my best to Bill Oliver—he may remember me. (*He exits through the living-room doorway.*)

LINDA (*her voice subdued*).   What'd you have to start that for? (BIFF *turns away.*) You see how sweet he was as soon as you talked hopefully? (*She goes over to* BIFF.) Come up and say good night to him. Don't let him go to bed that way.

HAPPY.   Come on, Biff, let's buck him up.

LINDA.   Please, dear. Just say good night. It takes so little to make him happy. Come. (*She goes through the living-room doorway, calling upstairs from within the living-room.*) Your pajamas are hanging in the bathroom, Willy!

HAPPY (*looking toward where* LINDA *went out*).   What a woman! They broke the mold when they made her. You know that, Biff?

BIFF.   He's off salary. My God, working on commission!

HAPPY.   Well, let's face it: he's no hot-shot selling man. Except that sometimes, you have to admit, he's a sweet personality.

BIFF (*decidedly*).   Lend me ten bucks, will ya? I want to buy some new ties.

HAPPY.   I'll take you to a place I know. Beautiful stuff. Wear one of my striped shirts tomorrow.

BIFF.   She got gray. Mom got awful old. Gee, I'm gonna go in to Oliver tomorrow and knock him for a—

HAPPY.   Come on up. Tell that to Dad. Let's give him a whirl. Come on.

BIFF (*steamed up*).   You know, with ten thousand bucks, boy!

HAPPY (*as they go into the living-room*).   That's the talk, Biff, that's the first time I've heard the old confidence out of you! (*From within the living-room, fading off*) You're gonna live with me, kid, and any babe you want just say the word . . . (*The last lines are hardly heard. They are mounting the stairs to their parents' bedroom.*)

LINDA (*entering her bedroom and addressing* WILLY, *who is in the bathroom. She is straightening the bed for him*).   Can you do anything about the shower? It drips.

WILLY (*from the bathroom*).   All of a sudden everything falls to pieces! Goddam plumbing, oughta be sued, those people. I hardly finished putting it in and the thing . . . (*His words rumble off.*)

LINDA.   I'm just wondering if Oliver will remember him. You think he might?

WILLY (*coming out of the bathroom in his pajamas*).   Remember him? What's the matter with you, you crazy? If he'd've stayed with Oliver he'd be on top by now! Wait'll Oliver gets a look at him. You don't know the average caliber any more. The average young man to-day—(*he is getting into bed*)—is got a caliber of zero. Greatest thing in the world for him was to bum around. (BIFF *and* HAPPY *enter the bedroom. Slight pause.* WILLY *stops short, looking at* BIFF.) Glad to hear it, boy.

HAPPY.   He wanted to say good night to you, sport.

WILLY (*to* BIFF).   Yeah. Knock him dead, boy. What'd you want to tell me?

BIFF.   Just take it easy, Pop. Good night. (*He turns to go.*)

WILLY (*unable to resist*).   And if anything falls off the desk while you're talking to him—like a package or something—don't you pick it up. They have office boys for that.

LINDA.   I'll make a big breakfast—

WILLY.   Will you let me finish? (*To* BIFF) Tell him you were in the business in the West. Not farm work.

BIFF.   All right, Dad.

LINDA.   I think everything—

WILLY (*going right through her speech*).   And don't undersell yourself. No less than fifteen thousand dollars.

BIFF (*unable to bear him*).   Okay. Good night, Mom. (*He starts moving.*)

WILLY.   Because you got a greatness in you, Biff, remember that. You got all kinds of greatness . . . (*He lies back, exhausted.* BIFF *walks out.*)

LINDA (*calling after* BIFF).   Sleep well, darling!

HAPPY.   I'm going to get married, Mom. I wanted to tell you.

LINDA.   Go to sleep, dear.

HAPPY (*going*).   I just wanted to tell you.

WILLY.   Keep up the good work. (HAPPY *exits.*) God . . . remember that Ebbets Field° game? The championship of the city?

LINDA.   Just rest. Should I sing to you?

WILLY.   Yeah. Sing to me. (LINDA *hums a soft lullaby.*) When that team came out—he was the tallest, remember?

LINDA.   Oh, yes. And in gold. (BIFF *enters the darkened kitchen, takes a cigarette, and leaves the house. He comes downstage into a golden pool of light. He smokes, staring at the night.*)

WILLY.   Like a young god. Hercules—something like that. And the sun, the sun all around him. Remember how he waved to me? Right up from the field, with the representatives of three colleges standing by?

Ebbets Field: A baseball stadium, the home of the Brooklyn Dodgers, torn down in 1960. Because it was used primarily for baseball, its locker rooms were called clubhouses.

And the buyers I brought, and the cheers when he came out—Loman, Loman, Loman! God Almighty, he'll be great yet. A star like that, magnificent, can never really fade away! (*The light on* WILLY *is fading. The gas heater begins to glow through the kitchen wall, near the stairs, a blue flame beneath the red coils.*)

LINDA (*timidly*).   Willy dear, what has he got against you?

WILLY.   I'm so tired. Don't talk any more. (BIFF *slowly returns to the kitchen. He stops, stares toward the heater.*)

LINDA.   Will you ask Howard to let you work in New York?

WILLY.   First thing in the morning. Everything'll be all right. (BIFF *reaches behind the heater and draws out a length of rubber tubing. He is horrified and turns his head toward* WILLY'S *room, still dimly lit, from which the strains of* LINDA'S *desperate but monotonous humming rise.* WILLY *stares through the window into the moonlight.*) Gee, look at the moon moving between the buildings! (BIFF *wraps the tubing around his hand and quickly goes up the stairs.*)

ACT 2

Music is heard, gay and bright. The curtain rises as the music fades away. WILLY, *in shirt sleeves, is sitting at the kitchen table, sipping coffee, his hat in his lap.* LINDA *is filling his cup when she can.*

WILLY.   Wonderful coffee. Meal in itself.

LINDA.   Can I make you some eggs?

WILLY.   No. Take a breath.

LINDA.   You look so rested, dear.

WILLY.   I slept like a dead one. First time in months. Imagine, sleeping till ten on a Tuesday morning. Boys left nice and early, heh?

LINDA.   They were out of here by eight o'clock.

WILLY.   Good work!

LINDA.   It was so thrilling to see them leaving together. I can't get over the shaving lotion in this house!

WILLY (*smiling*).   Mmm—

LINDA.   Biff was very changed this morning. His whole attitude seemed to be hopeful. He couldn't wait to get downtown to see Oliver.

WILLY.   He's heading for a change. There's no question, there simply are certain men that take longer to get—solidified. How did he dress?

LINDA.   His blue suit. He's so handsome in that suit. He could be a—anything in that suit! (WILLY *gets up from the table.* LINDA *holds his jacket for him.*)

WILLY.   There's no question, no question at all. Gee, on the way home tonight I'd like to buy some seeds.

LINDA (*laughing*).   That'd be wonderful. But not enough sun gets back there. Nothing'll grow any more.

WILLY.   You wait, kid, before it's all over we're gonna get a little place out in the country, and I'll raise some vegetables, a couple of chickens . . .

LINDA.   You'll do it yet, dear. (WILLY *walks out of his jacket.* LINDA *follows him.*)

WILLY.   And they'll get married, and come for a weekend. I'd build a little guest house. 'Cause I got so many fine tools, all I'd need would be a little lumber and some peace of mind.

LINDA (*joyfully*).   I sewed the lining . . .

WILLY.   I would build two guest houses, so they'd both come. Did he decide how much he's going to ask Oliver for?

LINDA (*getting him into his jacket*).   He didn't mention it, but I imagine ten or fifteen thousand. You going to talk to Howard today?

WILLY.   Yeah. I'll put it to him straight and simple. He'll just have to take me off the road.

LINDA.   And, Willy, don't forget to ask for a little advance, because we've got the insurance premium. It's the grace period now.

WILLY.   That's a hundred . . . ?

LINDA.   A hundred and eight, sixty-eight. Because we're a little short again.

WILLY.   Why are we short?

LINDA.   Well, you had the motor job on the car . . .

WILLY.   That goddam Studebaker!

LINDA.   And you got one more payment on the refrigerator . . .

WILLY.   But it just broke again!

LINDA.   Well, it's old, dear.

WILLY.   I told you we should've bought a well-advertised machine. Charley bought a General Electric and it's twenty years old and it's still good, that son-of-a-bitch.

LINDA.   But, Willy—

WILLY.   Whoever heard of a Hastings refrigerator? Once in my life I would like to own something outright before it's broken! I'm always in a race with the junkyard! I just finished paying for the car and it's on its last legs. The refrigerator consumes belts like a goddam maniac. They time those things. They time them so when you finally paid for them, they're used up.

LINDA (*buttoning up his jacket as he unbuttons it*).   All told, about two hundred dollars would carry us, dear. But that includes the last payment on the mortgage. After this payment, Willy, the house belongs to us.

WILLY.   It's twenty-five years!

LINDA.   Biff was nine years old when we bought it.

WILLY.   Well, that's a great thing. To weather a twenty-five year mortgage is—

LINDA.   It's an accomplishment.

WILLY.   All the cement, lumber, the reconstruction I put in this house! There ain't a crack to be found in it any more.

LINDA.   Well, it served its purpose.

WILLY.   What purpose? Some stranger'll come along, move in, and that's that. If only Biff would take this house, and raise a family . . . (*He starts to go.*) Good-by, I'm late.

LINDA (*suddenly remembering*).   Oh, I forgot! You're supposed to meet them for dinner.

WILLY.   Me?

LINDA.   At Frank's Chop House on Forty-eighth near Sixth Avenue.

WILLY.   Is that so! How about you?

LINDA.   No, just the three of you. They're gonna blow you to a big meal!

WILLY.   Don't say! Who thought of that?

LINDA.   Biff came to me this morning, Willy, and he said, "Tell Dad, we want to blow him to a big meal." Be there six o'clock. You and your two boys are going to have dinner.

WILLY.   Gee whiz! That's really somethin'. I'm gonna knock Howard for a loop, kid. I'll get an advance, and I'll come home with a New York job. Goddammit, now I'm gonna do it!

LINDA.   Oh, that's the spirit, Willy!

WILLY.   I will never get behind a wheel the rest of my life!

LINDA.   It's changing, Willy, I can feel it changing!

WILLY.   Beyond a question. G'by, I'm late. (*He starts to go again.*)

LINDA (*calling after him as she runs to the kitchen table for a handkerchief*).   You got your glasses?

WILLY (*feels for them, then comes back in*).   Yeah, yeah, got my glasses.

LINDA (*giving him the handkerchief*).   And a handkerchief.

WILLY.   Yeah, handkerchief.

LINDA.   And your saccharine?

WILLY.   Yeah, my saccharine.

LINDA.   Be careful on the subway stairs. (*She kisses him, and a silk stocking is seen hanging from her hand. WILLY notices it.*)

WILLY. Will you stop mending stockings? At least while I'm in the house. It gets me nervous. I can't tell you. Please. (LINDA *hides the stocking in her hand as she follows* WILLY *across the forestage in front of the house.*)

LINDA. Remember, Frank's Chop House.

WILLY (*passing the apron*). Maybe beets would grow out there.

LINDA (*laughing*). But you tried so many times.

WILLY. Yeah. Well, don't work hard today. (*He disappears around the right corner of the house.*)

LINDA. Be careful! (*As* WILLY *vanishes,* LINDA *waves to him. Suddenly the phone rings. She runs across the stage and into the kitchen and lifts it.*) Hello? Oh, Biff! I'm so glad you called, I just . . . Yes, sure, I just told him. Yes, he'll be there for dinner at six o'clock, I didn't forget. Listen, I was just dying to tell you. You know that little rubber pipe I told you about? That he connected to the gas heater? I finally decided to go down the cellar this morning and take it away and destroy it. But it's gone! Imagine? He took it away himself, it isn't there! (*She listens.*) When? Oh, then you took it. Oh—nothing, it's just that I'd hoped he'd taken it away himself. Oh, I'm not worried, darling, because this morning he left in such high spirits, it was like the old days! I'm not afraid any more. Did Mr. Oliver see you? . . . Well, you wait there then. And make a nice impression on him, darling. Just don't perspire too much before you see him. And have a nice time with Dad. He may have big news too! . . . That's right, a New York job. And be sweet to him tonight, dear. Be loving to him. Because he's only a little boat looking for a harbor. (*She is trembling with sorrow and joy.*) Oh, that's wonderful, Biff, you'll save his life. Thanks, darling. Just put your arm around him when he comes into the restaurant. Give him a smile. That's the boy . . . Good-by, dear . . . You got your comb? . . . That's fine. Good-by, Biff dear.

(*In the middle of her speech,* HOWARD WAGNER, *thirty-six, wheels on a small typewriter table on which is a wire-recording machine and proceeds to plug it in. This is on the left forestage. Light slowly fades on* LINDA *as it rises on* HOWARD. HOWARD *is intent on threading the machine and only glances over his shoulder as* WILLY *appears.*)

WILLY. Pst! Pst!

HOWARD. Hello, Willy, come in.

WILLY. Like to have a little talk with you, Howard.

HOWARD. Sorry to keep you waiting. I'll be with you in a minute.

WILLY. What's that, Howard?

HOWARD. Didn't you ever see one of these? Wire recorder.

WILLY. Oh. Can we talk a minute?

HOWARD.   Records things. Just got delivery yesterday. Been driving me crazy, the most terrific machine I ever saw in my life. I was up all night with it.

WILLY.   What do you do with it?

HOWARD.   I bought it for dictation, but you can do anything with it. Listen to this. I had it home last night. Listen to what I picked up. The first one is my daughter. Get this. (*He flicks the switch and "Roll Out the Barrel" is heard being whistled.*) Listen to that kid whistle.

WILLY.   That is lifelike, isn't it?

HOWARD.   Seven years old. Get that tone.

WILLY.   Ts, ts. Like to ask a little favor of you . . . (*The whistling breaks off, and the voice of* HOWARD's *daughter is heard.*)

HIS DAUGHTER.   "Now you, Daddy."

HOWARD.   She's crazy for me! (*Again the same song is whistled.*) That's me! Ha! (*He winks.*)

WILLY.   You're very good! (*The whistling breaks off again. The machine runs silent for a moment.*)

HOWARD.   Sh! Get this now, this is my son.

HIS SON.   "The capital of Alabama is Montgomery; the capital of Arizona is Phoenix; the capital of Arkansas is Little Rock; the capital of California is Sacramento . . ." (*and on, and on*).

HOWARD (*holding up five fingers*).   Five years old, Willy!

WILLY.   He'll make an announcer some day!

HIS SON (*continuing*).   "The capital . . ."

HOWARD.   Get that—alphabetical order! (*The machine breaks off suddenly.*) Wait a minute. The maid kicked the plug out.

WILLY.   It certainly is a—

HOWARD.   Sh, for God's sake!

HIS SON.   "It's nine o'clock, Bulova watch time. So I have to go to sleep."

WILLY.   That really is—

HOWARD.   Wait a minute! The next is my wife. (*They wait.*)

HOWARD'S VOICE.   "Go on, say something." (*Pause.*) "Well, you gonna talk?"

HIS WIFE.   "I can't think of anything."

HOWARD'S VOICE.   "Well, talk—it's turning."

HIS WIFE (*shyly, beaten*).   "Hello." (*Silence.*) "Oh, Howard, I can't talk into this . . ."

HOWARD (*snapping the machine off*).   That was my wife.

WILLY.   That is a wonderful machine. Can we—

HOWARD.   I tell you, Willy, I'm gonna take my camera, and my bandsaw, and all my hobbies, and out they go. This is the most fascinating relaxation I ever found.

WILLY.   I think I'll get one myself.

HOWARD.   Sure, they're only a hundred and a half. You can't do without it. Supposing you wanna hear Jack Benny, see? But you can't be at home at that hour. So you tell the maid to turn the radio on when Jack Benny comes on, and this automatically goes on with the radio . . .

WILLY.   And when you come home you . . .

HOWARD.   You can come home twelve o'clock, one o'clock, any time you like, and you get yourself a Coke and sit yourself down, throw the switch, and there's Jack Benny's program in the middle of the night!

WILLY.   I'm definitely going to get one. Because lots of time I'm on the road, and I think to myself, what I must be missing on the radio!

HOWARD.   Don't you have a radio in the car?

WILLY.   Well, yeah, but who ever thinks of turning it on?

HOWARD.   Say, aren't you supposed to be in Boston?

WILLY.   That's what I want to talk to you about, Howard. You got a minute? (*He draws a chair in from the wing.*)

HOWARD.   What happened? What're you doing here?

WILLY.   Well . . .

HOWARD.   You didn't crack up again, did you?

WILLY.   Oh, no. No . . .

HOWARD.   Geez, you had me worried there for a minute. What's the trouble?

WILLY.   Well, tell you the truth, Howard, I've come to the decision that I'd rather not travel any more.

HOWARD.   Not travel! Well, what'll you do?

WILLY.   Remember, Christmas time, when you had the party here? You said you'd try to think of some spot for me here in town.

HOWARD.   With us?

WILLY.   Well, sure.

HOWARD.   Oh, yeah, yeah. I remember. Well, I couldn't think of anything for you, Willy.

WILLY.   I tell ya, Howard. The kids are all grown up, y'know. I don't need much any more. If I could take home—well, sixty-five dollars a week, I could swing it.

HOWARD.   Yeah, but Willy, see I—

WILLY.   I tell ya why, Howard. Speaking frankly and between the two of us, y'know—I'm just a little tired.

HOWARD.   Oh, I could understand that, Willy. But you're a road man, Willy, and we do a road business. We've only got a half-dozen salesmen on the floor here.

WILLY.   God knows, Howard, I never asked a favor of any man. But I was with the firm when your father used to carry you in here in his arms.

HOWARD.   I know that, Willy, but—

WILLY.   Your father came to me the day you were born and asked me what I thought of the name of Howard, may he rest in peace.

HOWARD.   I appreciate that, Willy, but there just is no spot here for you. If I had a spot I'd slam you right in, but I just don't have a single solitary spot. (*He looks for his lighter.* WILLY *has picked it up and gives it to him. Pause.*)

WILLY (*with increasing anger*).   Howard, all I need to set my table is fifty dollars a week.

HOWARD.   But where am I going to put you, kid?

WILLY.   Look, it isn't a question of whether I can sell merchandise, is it?

HOWARD.   No, but it's a business, kid, and everybody's gotta pull his own weight.

WILLY (*desperately*).   Just let me tell you a story, Howard—

HOWARD.   'Cause you gotta admit, business is business.

WILLY (*angrily*).   Business is definitely business, but just listen for a minute. You don't understand this. When I was a boy—eighteen, nineteen—I was already on the road. And there was a question in my mind as to whether selling had a future for me. Because in those days I had a yearning to go to Alaska. See, there were three gold strikes in one month in Alaska, and I felt like going out. Just for the ride, you might say.

HOWARD (*barely interested*).   Don't say.

WILLY.   Oh, yeah, my father lived many years in Alaska. He was an adventurous man. We've got quite a little streak of self-reliance in our family. I thought I'd go out with my older brother and try to locate him, and maybe settle in the North with the old man. And I was almost decided to go, when I met a salesman in the Parker House. His name was Dave Singleman. And he was eighty-four years old, and he'd drummed merchandise in thirty-one states. And old Dave, he'd go up to his room, y'understand, put on his green velvet slippers—I'll never forget—and pick up his phone and call the buyers, and without ever leaving his room, at the age of eighty-four, he made his living. And when I saw that, I realized that selling was the greatest career a man could want. 'Cause what could be more satisfying than to be able to go, at the age of eighty-four, into twenty or thirty different cities, and pick up a phone, and be remembered and loved and helped by so many different people? Do you know? when he died—and by the way he died the death of a salesman, in his green velvet slippers in the smoker of the New York, New Haven and Hartford, going into Boston—when he died, hundreds of salesmen and buyers were at his funeral. Things were sad on a lotta trains for months after that. (*He stands up.* HOWARD *has not looked at him.*) In those days there was personality in it, Howard. There was respect, and comradeship, and gratitude in it. Today, it's all cut and dried, and there's no chance for bringing friendship to bear—or personality. You see what I mean? They don't know me any more.

HOWARD (*moving away, to the right*).   That's just the thing, Willy.

WILLY.   If I had forty dollars a week—that's all I'd need. Forty dollars, Howard.

HOWARD.   Kid, I can't take blood from a stone, I—

WILLY (*desperation is on him now*).   Howard, the year Al Smith° was nominated, your father came to me and—

HOWARD (*starting to go off*).   I've got to see some people, kid.

WILLY (*stopping him*).   I'm talking about your father! There were promises made across this desk! You mustn't tell me you've got people to see—I put thirty-four years into this firm, Howard, and now I can't pay my insurance! You can't eat the orange and throw the peel away—a man is not a piece of fruit! (*After a pause.*) Now pay attention. Your father—in 1928 I had a big year. I averaged a hundred and seventy dollars a week in commissions.

HOWARD (*impatiently*).   Now, Willy, you never averaged—

WILLY (*banging his hand on the desk*).   I averaged a hundred and seventy dollars a week in the year of 1928! And your father came to me —or rather, I was in the office here—it was right over this desk—and he put his hand on my shoulder—

HOWARD (*getting up*).   You'll have to excuse me, Willy, I gotta see some people. Pull yourself together. (*Going out*) I'll be back in a little while. (*On* HOWARD's *exit, the light on his chair grows very bright and strange.*)

WILLY.   Pull myself together! What the hell did I say to him? My God, I was yelling at him! How could I! (WILLY *breaks off, staring at the light, which occupies the chair, animating it. He approaches this chair, standing across the desk from it.*) Frank, Frank, don't you remember what you told me that time? How you put your hand on my shoulder, and

---

Al Smith: Four-term governor of New York and the 1928 Democratic nominee for president, who lost to Herbert Hoover.

Frank . . . (*He leans on the desk and as he speaks the dead man's name he accidentally switches on the recorder, and instantly*)

HOWARD'S SON.   ". . . of New York is Albany. The capital of Ohio is Cincinnati, the capital of Rhode Island is . . ." (*The recitation continues.*)

WILLY (*leaping away with fright, shouting*).   Ha! Howard! Howard! Howard!

HOWARD (*rushing in*).   What happened?

WILLY (*pointing at the machine, which continues nasally, childishly, with the capital cities*).   Shut it off! Shut it off!

HOWARD (*pulling the plug out*).   Look, Willy . . .

WILLY (*pressing his hands to his eyes*).   I gotta get myself some coffee. I'll get some coffee . . . (WILLY *starts to walk out.* HOWARD *stops him.*)

HOWARD (*rolling up the cord*).   Willy, look . . .

WILLY.   I'll go to Boston.

HOWARD.   Willy, you can't go to Boston for us.

WILLY.   Why can't I go?

HOWARD.   I don't want you to represent us. I've been meaning to tell you for a long time now.

WILLY.   Howard, are you firing me?

HOWARD.   I think you need a good long rest, Willy.

WILLY.   Howard—

HOWARD.   And when you feel better, come back, and we'll see if we can work something out.

WILLY.   But I gotta earn money, Howard. I'm in no position to—

HOWARD.   Where are your sons? Why don't your sons give you a hand?

WILLY.   They're working on a very big deal.

HOWARD.   This is no time for false pride, Willy. You go to your sons and tell them that you're tired. You've got two great boys, haven't you?

WILLY.   Oh, no question, no question, but in the meantime . . .

HOWARD.   Then that's that, heh?

WILLY.   All right, I'll go to Boston tomorrow.

HOWARD.   No, no.

WILLY.   I can't throw myself on my sons. I'm not a cripple!

HOWARD.   Look, kid, I'm busy this morning.

WILLY (*grasping* HOWARD'S *arm*).   Howard, you've got to let me go to Boston!

HOWARD (*hard, keeping himself under control*).   I've got a line of people to see this morning. Sit down, take five minutes, and pull yourself together, and then go home, will ya? I need the office, Willy. (*He starts to go, turns, remembering the recorder, starts to push off the table holding the recorder.*) Oh, yeah. Whenever you can this week, stop by and drop off the samples. You'll feel better, Willy, and then come back and we'll talk. Pull yourself together, kid, there's people outside. (HOWARD *exits, pushing the table off left.* WILLY *stares into space, exhausted. Now the music is heard*—BEN's *music—first distantly, then closer, closer. As* WILLY *speaks,* BEN *enters from the right. He carries valise and umbrella.*)

WILLY.   Oh, Ben, how did you do it? What is the answer? Did you wind up the Alaska deal already?

BEN.   Doesn't take much time if you know what you're doing. Just a short business trip. Boarding ship in an hour. Wanted to say good-by.

WILLY.   Ben, I've got to talk to you.

BEN (*glancing at his watch*).   Haven't the time, William.

WILLY (*crossing the apron to* BEN).   Ben, nothing's working out. I don't know what to do.

BEN.   Now look here, William. I've bought timberland in Alaska and I need a man to look after things for me.

WILLY.   God, timberland! Me and my boys in those grand outdoors!

BEN.   You've a new continent at your doorstep, William. Get out of these cities, they're full of talk and time payments and courts of law. Screw on your fists and you can fight for a fortune up there.

WILLY.   Yes, yes! Linda, Linda! (LINDA *enters as of old, with the wash.*)

LINDA.   Oh, you're back?

BEN.   I haven't much time.

WILLY.   No, wait! Linda, he's got a proposition for me in Alaska.

LINDA.   But you've got—(*To* BEN) He's got a beautiful job here.

WILLY.   But in Alaska, kid, I could—

LINDA.   You're doing well enough, Willy!

BEN (*to* LINDA).   Enough for what, my dear?

LINDA (*frightened of* BEN *and angry at him*).   Don't say those things to him! Enough to be happy right here, right now. (*To* WILLY, *while* BEN *laughs*) Why must everybody conquer the world? You're well liked, and the boys love you, and someday—(*to* BEN)—why, old man Wagner told him just the other day that if he keeps it up he'll be a member of the firm, didn't he, Willy?

WILLY.   Sure, sure. I am building something with this firm, Ben, and if a man is building something he must be on the right track, mustn't he?

BEN.   What are you building? Lay your hand on it. Where is it?

WILLY (*hesitantly*).   That's true, Linda, there's nothing.

LINDA.   Why? (*To* BEN) There's a man eighty-four years old—

WILLY.   That's right, Ben, that's right. When I look at that man I say, what is there to worry about?

BEN.   Bah!

WILLY.   It's true, Ben. All he has to do is go into any city, pick up the phone, and he's making his living and you know why?

BEN (*picking up his valise*).   I've got to go.

WILLY (*holding BEN back*).   Look at this boy! (BIFF, *in his high-school sweater, enters carrying suitcase.* HAPPY *carries* BIFF's *shoulder guards, gold helmet, and football pants.*) Without a penny to his name, three great universities are begging for him, and from there the sky's the limit, because it's not what you do, Ben. It's who you know and the smile on your face! It's contacts, Ben, contacts! The whole wealth of Alaska passes over the lunch table at the Commodore Hotel, and that's the wonder, the wonder of this country, that a man can end with diamonds here on the basis of being liked! (*He turns to* BIFF.) And that's why when you get out on that field today, it's important. Because thousands of people will be rooting for you and loving you. (*To* BEN, *who has again begun to leave*) And Ben! when he walks into a business office his name will sound out like a bell and all the doors will open to him! I've seen it, Ben, I've seen it a thousand times! You can't feel it with your hand like timber, but it's there!

BEN.   Good-by, William.

WILLY.   Ben, am I right? Don't you think I'm right? I value your advice.

BEN.   There's a new continent at your doorstep, William. You could walk out rich. Rich! (*He is gone.*)

WILLY.   We'll do it here, Ben! You hear me? We're gonna do it here! (YOUNG BERNARD *rushes in. The gay music of the* BOYS *is heard.*)

BERNARD.   Oh, gee, I was afraid you left already!

WILLY.   Why? What time is it?

BERNARD.   It's half-past one!

WILLY.   Well, come on, everybody! Ebbets Field next stop! Where's the pennants? (*He rushes through the wall-line of the kitchen and out into the living-room.*)

LINDA (*to* BIFF).   Did you pack fresh underwear?

BIFF (*who has been limbering up*).   I want to go!

BERNARD.   Biff, I'm carrying your helmet, ain't I?

HAPPY.   No, I'm carrying the helmet.

BERNARD.   Oh, Biff, you promised me.

HAPPY.   I'm carrying the helmet.

BERNARD.   How am I going to get in the locker room?

LINDA.   Let him carry the shoulder guards. (*She puts her coat and hat on in the kitchen.*)

BERNARD. Can I, Biff? 'Cause I told everybody I'm going to be in the locker room.

HAPPY. In Ebbets Field it's the clubhouse.

BERNARD. I meant the clubhouse, Biff!

HAPPY. Biff!

BIFF (*grandly, after a slight pause*). Let him carry the shoulder guards.

HAPPY (*as he gives* BERNARD *the shoulder guards*). Stay close to us now. (WILLY *rushes in with the pennants.*)

WILLY (*handing them out*). Everybody wave when Biff comes out on the field. (HAPPY *and* BERNARD *run off.*) You set now, boy? (*The music has died away.*)

BIFF. Ready to go, Pop. Every muscle is ready.

WILLY (*at the edge of the apron*). You realize what this means?

BIFF. That's right, Pop.

WILLY (*feeling* BIFF's *muscles*). You're comin' home this afternoon captain of the All-Scholastic Championship Team of the City of New York.

BIFF. I got it, Pop. And remember, pal, when I take off my helmet, that touchdown is for you.

WILLY. Let's go! (*He is starting out, with his arms around* BIFF, *when* CHARLEY *enters, as of old, in knickers.*) I got no room for you, Charley.

CHARLEY. Room? For what?

WILLY. In the car.

CHARLEY. You goin' for a ride? I wanted to shoot some casino.

WILLY (*furiously*). Casino! (*Incredulously*) Don't you realize what today is?

LINDA. Oh, he knows, Willy. He's just kidding you.

WILLY. That's nothing to kid about!

CHARLEY. No, Linda, what's goin' on?

LINDA. He's playing in Ebbets Field.

CHARLEY. Baseball in this weather?

WILLY. Don't talk to him. Come on, come on! (*He is pushing them out.*)

CHARLEY. Wait a minute, didn't you hear the news?

WILLY. What?

CHARLEY. Don't you listen to the radio? Ebbets Field just blew up.

WILLY. You go to hell! (CHARLEY *laughs. Pushing them out*) Come on, come on! We're late.

CHARLEY (*as they go*). Knock a homer, Biff, knock a homer!

WILLY (*the last to leave, turning to* CHARLEY). This is the greatest day of his life.

CHARLEY. Willy, when are you going to grow up?

WILLY.   Yeah, heh? When this game is over, Charley, you'll be
laughing out the other side of your face. They'll be calling him another
Red Grange.° Twenty-five thousand a year.
    CHARLEY (*kidding*).   Is that so?
    WILLY.   Yeah, that's so.
    CHARLEY.   Well, then, I'm sorry, Willy. But tell me something.
    WILLY.   What?
    CHARLEY.   Who is Red Grange?
    WILLY.   Put up your hands. Goddam you, put up your hands!
(CHARLEY, *chuckling, shakes his head and walks away, around the left corner of the stage.* WILLY *follows him. The music rises to a mocking frenzy.*)
Who the hell do you think you are, better than anybody else? You don't
know everything, you big, ignorant, stupid . . . Put up your hands!
    (*Light rises, on the right side of the forestage, on a small table in the re-
ception room of* CHARLEY's *office. Traffic sounds are heard.* BERNARD, *now
mature, sits whistling to himself. A pair of tennis rackets and an overnight
bag are on the floor beside him.*)
    WILLY (*offstage*).   What are you walking away for? Don't walk
away! If you're going to say something say it to my face! I know you
laugh at me behind my back. You'll laugh out of the other side of your
goddam face after this game. Touchdown! Touchdown! Eighty thousand people! Touchdown! Right between the goal posts.
    (BERNARD *is a quiet, earnest, but self-assured young man.* WILLY's
voice is coming from right upstage now. BERNARD *lowers his feet off the table
and listens.* JENNY, *his father's secretary, enters.*)
    JENNY (*distressed*).   Say, Bernard, will you go out in the hall?
    BERNARD.   What is that noise? Who is it?
    JENNY.   Mr. Loman. He just got off the elevator.
    BERNARD (*getting up*).   Who's he arguing with?
    JENNY.   Nobody. There's nobody with him. I can't deal with him
any more, and your father gets all upset everytime he comes. I've got a
lot of typing to do, and your father's waiting to sign it. Will you see
him?
    WILLY (*entering*).   Touchdown! Touch—(*He sees* JENNY.) Jenny,
Jenny, good to see you. How're ya? Workin'? Or still honest?
    JENNY.   Fine. How've you been feeling?
    WILLY.   Not much any more, Jenny. Ha, Ha! (*He is surprised to see
the rackets.*)
    BERNARD.   Hello, Uncle Willy.

Red Grange: famous All-American running back at the University of Illinois (1923–1925)

WILLY (*almost shocked*).   Bernard! Well, look who's here! (*He comes quickly, guiltily, to* BERNARD *and warmly shakes his hand.*)

BERNARD.   How are you? Good to see you.

WILLY.   What are you doing here?

BERNARD.   Oh, just stopped by to see Pop. Get off my feet till my train leaves. I'm going to Washington in a few minutes.

WILLY.   Is he in?

BERNARD.   Yes, he's in his office with the accountant. Sit down.

WILLY (*sitting down*).   What're you going to do in Washington?

BERNARD.   Oh, just a case I've got there, Willy.

WILLY.   That so? (*Indicating the rackets*) You going to play tennis there?

BERNARD.   I'm staying with a friend who's got a court.

WILLY.   Don't say. His own tennis court. Must be fine people, I bet.

BERNARD.   They are, very nice. Dad tells me Biff's in town.

WILLY (*with a big smile*).   Yeah, Biff's in. Working on a very big deal, Bernard.

BERNARD.   What's Biff doing?

WILLY.   Well, he's been doing very big things in the West. But he decided to establish himself here. Very big. We're having dinner. Did I hear your wife had a boy?

BERNARD.   That's right. Our second.

WILLY.   Two boys! What do you know!

BERNARD.   What kind of deal has Biff got?

WILLY.   Well, Bill Oliver—very big sporting goods man—he wants Biff very badly. Called him in from the West. Long distance, carte blanche, special deliveries. Your friends have their own private tennis court?

BERNARD.   You still with the old firm, Willy?

WILLY (*after a pause*).   I'm—I'm overjoyed to see how you made the grade, Bernard, overjoyed. It's an encouraging thing to see a young man really—really—Looks very good for Biff—very—(*He breaks off, then*) Bernard—(*He is so full of emotion, he breaks off again.*)

BERNARD.   What is it, Willy?

WILLY (*small and alone*).   What—what's the secret?

BERNARD.   What secret?

WILLY.   How—how did you? Why didn't he ever catch on?

BERNARD.   I wouldn't know that, Willy.

WILLY (*confidentially, desperately*).   You were his friend, his boy-hood friend. There's something I don't understand about it. His life ended after that Ebbets Field game. From the age of seventeen nothing good ever happened to him.

BERNARD.   He never trained himself for anything.

WILLY.   But he did, he did. After high school he took so many correspondence courses. Radio mechanics; television; God knows what, and never made the slightest mark.

BERNARD (*taking off his glasses*).   Willy, do you want to talk candidly?

WILLY (*rising, faces* BERNARD).   I regard you as a very brilliant man, Bernard. I value your advice.

BERNARD.   Oh, the hell with the advice, Willy. I couldn't advise you. There's just one thing I've always wanted to ask you. When he was supposed to graduate, and the math teacher flunked him—

WILLY.   Oh, that son-of-a-bitch ruined his life.

BERNARD.   Yeah, but, Willy, all he had to do was go to summer school and make up that subject.

WILLY.   That's right, that's right.

BERNARD.   Did you tell him not to go to summer school?

WILLY.   Me? I begged him to go. I ordered him to go!

BERNARD.   Then why wouldn't he go?

WILLY.   Why? Why! Bernard, that question has been trailing me like a ghost for the last fifteen years. He flunked the subject, and laid down and died like a hammer hit him!

BERNARD.   Take it easy, kid.

WILLY.   Let me talk to you—I got nobody to talk to. Bernard, Bernard, was it my fault? Y'see? It keeps going around in my mind, maybe I did something to him. I got nothing to give him.

BERNARD.   Don't take it so hard.

WILLY.   Why did he lay down? What is the story there? You were his friend!

BERNARD.   Willy, I remember, it was June, and our grades came out. And he'd flunked math.

WILLY.   That son-of-a-bitch!

BERNARD.   No, it wasn't right then. Biff just got very angry, I remember, and he was ready to enroll in summer school.

WILLY (*surprised*).   He was?

BERNARD.   He wasn't beaten by it at all. But then, Willy, he disappeared from the block for almost a month. And I got the idea that he'd gone up to New England to see you. Did he have a talk with you then? (WILLY *stares in silence.*) Willy?

WILLY (*with a strong edge of resentment in his voice*).   Yeah, he came to Boston. What about it?

BERNARD.   Well, just that when he came back—I'll never forget this, it always mystifies me. Because I thought so well of Biff, even though he'd always taken advantage of me. I loved him. Willy, y'know? And he came back after that month and took his sneakers—remember those sneakers with "University of Virginia" printed on them? He was so proud of those, wore them every day. And he took them down in the cellar, and burned them up in the furnace. We had a fist fight. It lasted at least half an hour. Just the two of us, punching each other down the cellar, and crying right through it. I've often thought of how strange it was that I knew he'd given up his life. What happened in Boston, Willy? (WILLY *looks at him as at an intruder.*) I just bring it up because you asked me.

WILLY (*angrily*).   Nothing. What do you mean, "What happened?" What's that got to do with anything?

BERNARD.   Well, don't get sore.

WILLY.   What are you trying to do, blame it on me? If a boy lays down is that my fault?

BERNARD.   Now, Willy, don't get—

WILLY.   Well, don't—don't talk to me that way! What does that mean, "What happened?" (CHARLEY *enters. He is in his vest, and he carries a bottle of bourbon.*)

CHARLEY.   Hey, you're going to miss that train. (*He waves the bottle.*)

BERNARD.   Yeah, I'm going. (*He takes the bottle.*) Thanks, Pop. (*He picks up his rackets and bag.*) Good-by, Willy, and don't worry about it. You know, "If at first you don't succeed . . ."

WILLY.   Yes, I believe in that.

BERNARD.   But sometimes, Willy, it's better for a man just to walk away.

WILLY.   Walk away?

BERNARD.   That's right.

WILLY.   But if you can't walk away?

BERNARD (*after a slight pause*).   I guess that's when it's tough. (*Extending his hand*) Good-by, Willy.

WILLY (*shaking* BERNARD's *hand*).   Good-by, boy.

CHARLEY (*an arm on* BERNARD's *shoulder*).   How do you like this kid? Gonna argue a case in front of the Supreme Court.

BERNARD (*protesting*).   Pop!

WILLY (*genuinely shocked, pained, and happy*).   No! The Supreme Court!

BERNARD.   I gotta run. 'By Dad!

CHARLEY.   Knock 'em dead, Bernard! (BERNARD *goes off.*)

WILLY (*as* CHARLEY *takes out his wallet*).   The Supreme Court! And he didn't even mention it!

CHARLEY (*counting out money on the desk*).   He don't have to—he's gonna do it.

WILLY.   And you never told him what to do, did you? You never took any interest in him.

CHARLEY.   My salvation is that I never took any interest in anything. There's some money—fifty dollars. I got an accountant inside.

WILLY.   Charley, look . . . (*With difficulty*) I got my insurance to pay. If you can manage it—I need a hundred and ten dollars. (CHARLEY *doesn't reply for a moment; merely stops moving.*) I'd draw it from my bank but Linda would know, and I . . .

CHARLEY.   Sit down, Willy.

WILLY (*moving toward the chair*).   I'm keeping an account of everything, remember. I'll pay every penny back. (*He sits.*)

CHARLEY.   Now listen to me, Willy.

WILLY.   I want you to know I appreciate . . .

CHARLEY (*sitting down on the table*).   Willy, what're you doin'? What the hell is goin' on in your head?

WILLY.   Why? I'm simply . . .

CHARLEY.   I offered you a job. You can make fifty dollars a week. And I won't send you on the road.

WILLY.   I've got a job.

CHARLEY.   Without pay? What kind of a job is a job without pay? (*He rises.*) Now, look, kid, enough is enough. I'm no genius but I know when I'm being insulted.

WILLY.   Insulted!

CHARLEY.   Why don't you want to work for me?

WILLY.   What's the matter with you? I've got a job.

CHARLEY.   Then what're you walkin' in here every week for?

WILLY (*getting up*).   Well, if you don't want me to walk in here—

CHARLEY.   I am offering you a job.

WILLY.   I don't want your goddam job!

CHARLEY.   When the hell are you going to grow up?

WILLY (*furiously*).   You big ignoramus, if you say that to me again I'll rap you one! I don't care how big you are! (*He's ready to fight. Pause.*)

CHARLEY (*kindly, going to him*).   How much do you need, Willy?

WILLY.   Charley, I'm strapped. I'm strapped. I don't know what to do. I was just fired.

CHARLEY.   Howard fired you?

WILLY.   That snotnose. Imagine that? I named him. I named him Howard.

CHARLEY.   Willy, when're you gonna realize that them things don't mean anything? You named him Howard, but you can't sell that.

The only thing you got in this world is what you can sell. And the funny thing is that you're a salesman, and you don't know that.

WILLY. I've always tried to think otherwise, I guess. I always felt that if a man was impressive, and well liked, that nothing—

CHARLEY. Why must everybody like you? Who liked J. P. Morgan? Was he impressive? In a Turkish bath he'd look like a butcher. But with his pockets on he was very well liked. Now listen, Willy, I know you don't like me, and nobody can say I'm in love with you, but I'll give you a job because—just for the hell of it, put it that way. Now what do you say?

WILLY. I—I just can't work for you, Charley.

CHARLEY. What're you, jealous of me?

WILLY. I can't work for you, that's all, don't ask me why.

CHARLEY (*angered, takes out more bills*). You been jealous of me all your life, you damned fool! Here, pay your insurance. (*He puts the money in* WILLY's *hand.*)

WILLY. I'm keeping strict accounts.

CHARLEY. I've got some work to do. Take care of yourself. And pay your insurance.

WILLY (*moving to the right*). Funny, y'know? After all the high-ways, and the trains, and the appointments, and the years, you end up worth more dead than alive.

CHARLEY. Willy, nobody's worth nothin' dead. (*After a slight pause.*) Did you hear what I said? (WILLY *stands still, dreaming.*) Willy!

WILLY. Apologize to Bernard for me when you see him. I didn't mean to argue with him. He's a fine boy. They're all fine boys, and they'll end up big—all of them. Someday they'll all play tennis to-gether. Wish me luck, Charley. He saw Bill Oliver today.

CHARLEY. Good luck.

WILLY (*on the verge of tears*). Charley, you're the only friend I got. Isn't that a remarkable thing? (*He goes out.*)

CHARLEY. Jesus!

(CHARLEY *stares after him a moment and follows. All light blacks out. Suddenly raucous music is heard, and a red glow rises behind the screen at right.* STANLEY, *a young waiter, appears, carrying a table, followed by* HAPPY, *who is carrying two chairs.*)

STANLEY (*putting the table down*). That's all right, Mr. Loman, I can handle it myself. (*He turns and takes the chairs from* HAPPY *and places them at the table.*)

HAPPY (*glancing around*). Oh, this is better.

STANLEY. Sure, in the front there you're in the middle of all kinds a noise. Whenever you got a party, Mr. Loman, you just tell me and I'll put you back here. Y'know, there's a lotta people they don't like it private, because when they go out they like to see a lotta action around them because they're sick and tired to stay in the house by theirself. But I know you, you ain't from Hackensack. You know what I mean?

HAPPY (*sitting down*).   So how's it coming, Stanley?

STANLEY.   Ah, it's a dog's life. I only wish during the war they'd a took me in the Army. I coulda been dead by now.

HAPPY.   My brother's back, Stanley.

STANLEY.   Oh, he come back, heh? From the Far West.

HAPPY.   Yeah, big cattle man, my brother, so treat him right. And my father's coming too.

STANLEY.   Oh, your father too!

HAPPY.   You got a couple of nice lobsters?

STANLEY.   Hundred per cent, big.

HAPPY.   I want them with the claws.

STANLEY.   Don't worry, I don't give you no mice. (HAPPY *laughs.*) How about some wine? It'll put a head on the meal.

HAPPY.   No. You remember, Stanley, that recipe I brought you from overseas? With the champagne in it?

STANLEY.   Oh, yeah, sure. I still got it tacked up yet in the kitchen. But that'll have to cost a buck apiece anyways.

HAPPY.   That's all right.

STANLEY.   What'd you, hit a number or somethin'?

HAPPY.   No, it's a little celebration. My brother is—I think he pulled off a big deal today. I think we're going into business together.

STANLEY.   Great! That's the best for you. Because a family business, you know what I mean?—that's the best.

HAPPY.   That's what I think.

STANLEY.   'Cause what's the difference? Somebody steals? It's in the family. Know what I mean? (*Sotto voce*) Like this bartender here. The boss is goin' crazy what kinda leak he's got in the cash register. You put it in but it don't come out.

HAPPY (*raising his head*).   Sh!

STANLEY.   What?

HAPPY.   You notice I wasn't lookin' right or left, was I?

STANLEY.   No.

HAPPY.   And my eyes are closed.

STANLEY.   So what's the—?

HAPPY.   Strudel's comin'.

STANLEY (*catching on, looks around*).   Ah, no, there's no—(*He breaks off as a furred, lavishly dressed girl enters and sits at the next table. Both follow her with their eyes.*) Geez, how'd ya know?

HAPPY. I got radar or something. (*Staring directly at her profile*) Oooooooo . . . Stanley.

STANLEY. I think that's for you, Mr. Loman.

HAPPY. Look at that mouth. Oh, God. And the binoculars.

STANLEY. Geez, you got a life, Mr. Loman.

HAPPY. Wait on her.

STANLEY (*going to the* GIRL'*s table*). Would you like a menu, ma'am?

GIRL. I'm expecting someone, but I'd like a—

HAPPY. Why don't you bring her—excuse me, miss, do you mind? I sell champagne, and I'd like you to try my brand. Bring her a champagne, Stanley.

GIRL. That's awfully nice of you.

HAPPY. Don't mention it. It's all company money. (*He laughs.*)

GIRL. That's a charming product to be selling, isn't it?

HAPPY. Oh, gets to be like everything else. Selling is selling, y'know.

GIRL. I suppose.

HAPPY. You don't happen to sell, do you?

GIRL. No, I don't sell.

HAPPY. Would you object to a compliment from a stranger? You ought to be on a magazine cover.

GIRL (*looking at him a little archly*). I have been. (STANLEY *comes in with a glass of champagne.*)

HAPPY. What'd I say before, Stanley? You see? She's a cover girl.

STANLEY. Oh, I could see, I could see.

HAPPY (*to the* GIRL). What magazine?

GIRL. Oh, a lot of them. (*She takes the drink.*) Thank you.

HAPPY. You know what they say in France, don't you? "Champagne is the drink of the complexion"—Hya, Biff! (BIFF *has entered and sits with* HAPPY.)

BIFF. Hello, kid. Sorry I'm late.

HAPPY. I just got here. Uh, Miss—?

GIRL. Forsythe.

HAPPY. Miss Forsythe, this is my brother.

BIFF. Is Dad here?

HAPPY. His name is Biff. You might've heard of him. Great football player!

GIRL. Really? What team?

HAPPY. Are you familiar with football?

GIRL. No, I'm afraid I'm not.

HAPPY. Biff is quarterback with the New York Giants.

GIRL.   Well, that is nice, isn't it? (*She drinks.*)

HAPPY.   Good health.

GIRL.   I'm happy to meet you.

HAPPY.   That's my name. Hap. It's really Harold, but at West Point they called me Happy.

GIRL (*now really impressed*).   Oh, I see. How do you do? (*She turns her profile.*)

BIFF.   Isn't Dad coming?

HAPPY.   You want her?

BIFF.   Oh, I could never make that.

HAPPY.   I remember the time that idea would never come into your head. Where's the old confidence, Biff?

BIFF.   I just saw Oliver—

HAPPY.   Wait a minute. I've got to see that old confidence again. Do you want her? She's on call.

BIFF.   Oh, no. (*He turns to look at the* GIRL.)

HAPPY.   I'm telling you. Watch this. (*Turning to the* GIRL) Honey? (*She turns to him.*) Are you busy?

GIRL.   Well, I am . . . but I could make a phone call.

HAPPY.   Do that, will you, honey? And see if you can get a friend. We'll be here for a while. Biff is one of the greatest football players in the country.

GIRL (*standing up*).   Well, I'm certainly happy to meet you.

HAPPY.   Come back soon.

GIRL.   I'll try.

HAPPY.   Don't try, honey, try hard. (*The* GIRL *exits.* STANLEY *follows, shaking his head in bewildered admiration.*) Isn't that a shame now? A beautiful girl like that? That's why I can't get married. There's not a good woman in a thousand. New York is loaded with them, kid!

BIFF.   Hap, look—

HAPPY.   I told you she was on call!

BIFF (*strangely unnerved*).   Cut it out, will ya? I want to say something to you.

HAPPY.   Did you see Oliver?

BIFF.   I saw him all right. Now look, I want to tell Dad a couple of things and I want you to help me.

HAPPY.   What? Is he going to back you?

BIFF.   Are you crazy? You're out of your goddam head, you know that?

HAPPY.   Why? What happened?

BIFF (*breathlessly*).   I did a terrible thing today, Hap. It's been the strangest day I ever went through. I'm all numb, I swear.

HAPPY.   You mean he wouldn't see you?

BIFF.   Well, I waited for six hours for him, see? All day. Kept sending my name in. Even tried to date his secretary so she'd get me to him, but no soap.

HAPPY.   Because you're not showin' the old confidence, Biff. He remembered you, didn't he?

BIFF (*stopping* HAPPY *with a gesture*).   Finally, about five o'clock, he comes out. Didn't remember who I was or anything. I felt like such an idiot, Hap.

HAPPY.   Did you tell him my Florida idea?

BIFF.   He walked away. I saw him for one minute. I got so mad I could've torn the walls down! How the hell did I ever get the idea I was a salesman there? I even believed myself that I'd been a salesman for him! And then he gave me one look and—I realized what a ridiculous lie my whole life has been! We've been talking in a dream for fifteen years. I was a shipping clerk.

HAPPY.   What'd you do?

BIFF (*with great tension and wonder*).   Well, he left, see. And the secretary went out. I was all alone in the waiting-room. I don't know what came over me, Hap. The next thing I know I'm in his office—paneled walls, everything. I can't explain it. I—Hap, I took his fountain pen.

HAPPY.   Geez, did he catch you?

BIFF.   I ran out. I ran down all eleven flights. I ran and ran and ran.

HAPPY.   That was an awful dumb—what'd you do that for?

BIFF (*agonized*).   I don't know, I just—wanted to take something, I don't know. You gotta help me, Hap, I'm gonna tell Pop.

HAPPY.   You crazy? What for?

BIFF.   Hap, he's got to understand that I'm not the man somebody lends that kind of money to. He thinks I've been spiting him all these years and it's eating him up.

HAPPY.   That's just it. You tell him something nice.

BIFF.   I can't.

HAPPY.   Say you got a lunch date with Oliver tomorrow.

BIFF.   So what do I do tomorrow?

HAPPY.   You leave the house tomorrow and come back at night and say Oliver is thinking it over. And he thinks it over for a couple of weeks, and gradually it fades away and nobody's the worse.

BIFF.   But it'll go on forever!

HAPPY.   Dad is never so happy as when he's looking forward to something! (WILLY *enters.*) Hello, scout!

WILLY.   Gee, I haven't been here in years! (STANLEY *has followed* WILLY *in and sets a chair for him.* STANLEY *starts off but* HAPPY *stops him.*)

HAPPY.   Stanley! (STANLEY *stands by, waiting for an order.*)

BIFF (*going to* WILLY *with guilt, as to an invalid*).   Sit down, Pop. You want a drink?

WILLY.   Sure, I don't mind.

BIFF.   Let's get a load on.

WILLY.   You look worried.

BIFF.   N-no. (*To* STANLEY) Scotch all around. Make it doubles.

STANLEY.   Doubles, right. (*He goes.*)

WILLY.   You had a couple already, didn't you?

BIFF.   Just a couple, yeah.

WILLY.   Well, what happened, boy? (*Nodding affirmatively, with a smile*) Everything go all right?

BIFF (*takes a breath, then reaches out and grasps* WILLY'S *hand*). Pal . . . (*He is smiling bravely, and* WILLY *is smiling too.*) I had an experience today.

HAPPY.   Terrific, Pop.

WILLY.   That so? What happened?

BIFF (*high, slightly alcoholic, above the earth*).   I'm going to tell you everything from first to last. It's been a strange day. (*Silence. He looks around, composes himself as best he can, but his breath keeps breaking the rhythm of his voice.*) I had to wait quite a while for him, and—

WILLY.   Oliver?

BIFF.   Yeah, Oliver. All day, as a matter of cold fact. And a lot of—instances—facts, Pop, facts about my life came back to me. Who was it, Pop? Who ever said I was a salesman with Oliver?

WILLY.   Well, you were.

BIFF.   No, Dad, I was a shipping clerk.

WILLY.   But you were practically—

BIFF (*with determination*).   Dad, I don't know who said it first, but I was never a salesman for Bill Oliver.

WILLY.   What're you talking about?

BIFF.   Let's hold on to the facts tonight, Pop. We're not going to get anywhere bullin' around. I was a shipping clerk.

WILLY (*angrily*).   All right, now listen to me—

BIFF.   Why don't you let me finish?

WILLY.   I'm not interested in stories about the past or any crap of that kind because the woods are burning, boys, you understand? There's a big blaze going on all around. I was fired today.

BIFF (*shocked*).   How could you be?

WILLY.   I was fired, and I'm looking for a little good news to tell your mother, because the woman has waited and the woman has suffered. The gist of it is that I haven't got a story left in my head, Biff. So don't give me a lecture about facts and aspects. I am not interested. Now what've you got to say to me? (STANLEY *enters with three drinks. They wait until he leaves.*) Did you see Oliver?

BIFF.   Jesus, Dad!

WILLY.   You mean you didn't go up there?

HAPPY.   Sure he went up there.

BIFF.   I did. I—saw him. How could they fire you?

WILLY (*on the edge of his chair*).   What kind of a welcome did he give you?

BIFF.   He won't even let you work on commission?

WILLY.   I'm out! (*Driving*) So tell me, he gave you a warm welcome?

HAPPY.   Sure, Pop, sure!

BIFF (*driven*).   Well, it was kind of—

WILLY.   I was wondering if he'd remember you. (*To* HAPPY) Imagine, man doesn't see him for ten, twelve years and gives him that kind of a welcome!

HAPPY.   Damn right!

BIFF (*trying to return to the offensive*).   Pop look—

WILLY.   You know why he remembered you, don't you? Because you impressed him in those days.

BIFF.   Let's talk quietly and get this down to the facts, huh?

WILLY (*as though* BIFF *had been interrupting*).   Well, what happened? It's great news, Biff. Did he take you into his office or'd you talk in the waiting-room?

BIFF.   Well, he came in, see, and—

WILLY (*with a big smile*).   What'd he say? Betcha he threw his arm around you.

BIFF.   Well, he kinda—

WILLY.   He's a fine man. (*To* HAPPY) Very hard man to see, y'know.

HAPPY (*agreeing*).   Oh, I know.

WILLY (*to* BIFF).   Is that where you had the drinks?

BIFF.   Yeah, he gave me a couple of—no, no!

HAPPY (*cutting in*).   He told him my Florida idea.

WILLY.   Don't interrupt. (*To* BIFF) How'd he react to the Florida idea?

BIFF.   Dad, will you give me a minute to explain?

WILLY.   I've been waiting for you to explain since I sat down here! What happened? He took you into his office and what?

BIFF.   Well—I talked. And—and he listened, see.

WILLY.   Famous for the way he listens, y'know. What was his answer?

BIFF.   His answer was—(*He breaks off, suddenly angry.*) Dad, you're not letting me tell you what I want to tell you!

WILLY (*accusing, angered*).   You didn't see him, did you?

BIFF.   I did see him!

WILLY.   What'd you insult him or something? You insulted him, didn't you?

BIFF.   Listen, will you let me out of it, will you just let me out of it!

HAPPY.   What the hell!

WILLY.   Tell me what happened!

BIFF (*to* HAPPY).   I can't talk to him!

(*A single trumpet note jars the ear. The light of green leaves stains the house, which holds the air of night and a dream.* YOUNG BERNARD *enters and knocks on the door of the house.*)

YOUNG BERNARD (*frantically*).   Mrs. Loman, Mrs. Loman!

HAPPY.   Tell him what happened!

BIFF (*to* HAPPY).   Shut up and leave me alone!

WILLY.   No, no! You had to go and flunk math!

BIFF.   What math? What're you talking about?

YOUNG BERNARD.   Mrs. Loman, Mrs. Loman! (LINDA *appears in the house, as of old.*)

WILLY (*wildly*).   Math, math, math!

BIFF.   Take it easy, Pop!

YOUNG BERNARD.   Mrs. Loman!

WILLY (*furiously*).   If you hadn't flunked you'd've been set by now!

BIFF.   Now, look, I'm gonna tell you what happened, and you're going to listen to me.

YOUNG BERNARD.   Mrs. Loman!

BIFF.   I waited six hours—

HAPPY.   What the hell are you saying?

BIFF.   I kept sending in my name but he wouldn't see me. So finally he . . . (*He continues unheard as light fades low on the restaurant.*)

YOUNG BERNARD.   Biff flunked math!

LINDA.   No!

YOUNG BERNARD.   Birnbaum flunked him! They won't graduate him!

LINDA.   But they have to. He's gotta go to the university. Where is he? Biff! Biff!

YOUNG BERNARD.   No, he left. He went to Grand Central.

LINDA.   Grand—You mean he went to Boston!

YOUNG BERNARD.   Is Uncle Willy in Boston?

LINDA.   Oh, maybe Willy can talk to the teacher. Oh, the poor, poor boy! (*Light on house area snaps out.*)

BIFF (*at the table, now audible, holding up a gold fountain pen*).   . . . so I'm washed up with Oliver, you understand? Are you listening to me?

WILLY (*at a loss*).   Yeah, sure. If you hadn't flunked—

BIFF.   Flunked what? What're you talking about?

WILLY.   Don't blame everything on me! I didn't flunk math—you did! What pen?

HAPPY.   That was awful dumb, Biff, a pen like that is worth—

WILLY (*seeing the pen for the first time*).   You took Oliver's pen?

BIFF (*weakening*).   Dad, I just explained it to you.

WILLY.   You stole Bill Oliver's fountain pen!

BIFF.   I didn't exactly steal it! That's just what I've been explaining to you!

HAPPY.   He had it in his hand and just then Oliver walked in, so he got nervous and stuck it in his pocket!

WILLY.   My God, Biff!

BIFF.   I never intended to do it, Dad!

OPERATOR'S VOICE.   Standish Arms, good evening!

WILLY (*shouting*).   I'm not in my room!

BIFF (*frightened*).   Dad, what's the matter? (*He and* HAPPY *stand up.*)

OPERATOR.   Ringing Mr. Loman for you!

WILLY.   I'm not there, stop it!

BIFF (*horrified, gets down on one knee before* WILLY).   Dad, I'll make good, I'll make good. (WILLY *tries to get to his feet.* BIFF *holds him down.*) Sit down now.

WILLY.   No, you're no good, you're no good for anything.

BIFF.   I am, Dad, I'll find something else, you understand? Now don't worry about anything. (*He holds up* WILLY's *face.*) Talk to me, Dad.

OPERATOR.   Mr. Loman does not answer. Shall I page him?

WILLY (*attempting to stand, as though to rush and silence the* OPERATOR).   No, no, no!

HAPPY.   He'll strike something, Pop.

WILLY.   No, no . . .

BIFF (*desperately, standing over* WILLY).   Pop, listen! Listen to me! I'm telling you something good. Oliver talked to his partner about the Florida idea. You listening? He—he talked to his partner, and he came to me . . . I'm going to be all right, you hear? Dad, listen to me, he said it was just a question of the amount!

WILLY.   Then you . . . got it?

HAPPY.   He's gonna be terrific, Pop!

WILLY (*trying to stand*).   Then you got it, haven't you? You got it! You got it!

BIFF (*agonized, holds* WILLY *down*).   No, no. Look, Pop. I'm supposed to have lunch with them tomorrow. I'm just telling you this so you'll know that I can still make an impression, Pop. And I'll make good somewhere, but I can't go tomorrow, see?

WILLY.   Why not? You simply—

BIFF.   But the pen, Pop!

WILLY.   You give it to him and tell him it was an oversight!

HAPPY.   Sure, have lunch tomorrow!

BIFF.   I can't say that—

WILLY.   You were doing a crossword puzzle and accidentally used his pen!

BIFF.   Listen, kid, I took those balls years ago, now I walk in with his fountain pen? That clinches it, don't you see? I can't face him like that! I'll try elsewhere.

PAGE'S VOICE.   Paging Mr. Loman!

WILLY.   Don't you want to be anything?

BIFF.   Pop, how can I go back?

WILLY.   You don't want to be anything, is that what's behind it?

BIFF (*now angry at* WILLY *for not crediting his sympathy*).   Don't take it that way! You think it was easy walking into that office after what I'd done to him? A team of horses couldn't have dragged me back to Bill Oliver!

WILLY.   Then why'd you go?

BIFF.   Why did I go? Why did I go! Look at you! Look at what's become of you! (*Off left,* THE WOMAN *laughs.*)

WILLY.   Biff, you're going to go to that lunch tomorrow, or—

BIFF.   I can't go. I've got no appointment!

HAPPY.   Biff, for . . . !

WILLY.   Are you spiting me?

BIFF.   Don't take it that way! Goddammit!

WILLY (*strikes* BIFF *and falters away from the table*).   You rotten little louse! Are you spiting me?

THE WOMAN.   Someone's at the door, Willy!

BIFF.   I'm no good, can't you see what I am?

HAPPY (*separating them*).   Hey, you're in a restaurant! Now cut it out, both of you! (*The* GIRLS *enter.*) Hello, girls, sit down. (THE WOMAN *laughs, off left.*)

MISS FORSYTHE.   I guess we might as well. This is Letta.

THE WOMAN.   Willy, are you going to wake up?

BIFF (*ignoring* WILLY).   How're ya, miss, sit down. What do you drink?

MISS FORSYTHE.   Letta might not be able to stay long.

LETTA.   I gotta get up very early tomorrow. I got jury duty. I'm so excited! Were you fellows ever on a jury?

BIFF.   No, but I been in front of them! (*The* GIRLS *laugh.*) This is my father.

LETTA.   Isn't he cute? Sit down with us, Pop.

HAPPY.   Sit him down, Biff!

BIFF (*going to him*).   Come on, slugger, drink us under the table. To hell with it! Come on, sit down, pal. (*On* BIFF'S *last insistence,* WILLY *is about to sit.*)

THE WOMAN (*now urgently*).   Willy, are you going to answer the door! (*THE* WOMAN'S *call puts* WILLY *back. He starts right, befuddled.*)

BIFF.   Hey, where are you going?

WILLY.   Open the door.

BIFF.   The door?

WILLY.   The washroom . . . the door . . . where's the door?

BIFF (*leading* WILLY *to the left*).   Just go straight down. (*WILLY moves left.*)

THE WOMAN.   Willy, Willy, are you going to get up, get up, get up, get up? (*WILLY exits left.*)

LETTA.   I think it's sweet you bring your daddy along.

MISS FORSYTHE.   Oh, he isn't really your father!

BIFF (*at left, turning to her resentfully*).   Miss Forsythe, you've just seen a prince walk by. A fine, troubled prince. A hard-working, unappreciated prince. A pal, you understand? A good companion. Always for his boys.

LETTA.   That's so sweet.

HAPPY.   Well, girls, what's the program? We're wasting time. Come on, Biff. Gather round. Where would you like to go?

BIFF.   Why don't you do something for him?

HAPPY.   Me!

BIFF.   Don't you give a damn for him, Hap?

HAPPY.   What're you talking about? I'm the one who—

BIFF.   I sense it, you don't give a good goddam about him. (*He takes the rolled-up hose from his pocket and puts it on the table in front of* HAPPY.) Look what I found in the cellar, for Christ's sake. How can you bear to let it go on?

HAPPY.   Me? Who goes away? Who runs off and—

BIFF.   Yeah, but he doesn't mean anything to you. You could help him—I can't! Don't you understand what I'm talking about? He's going to kill himself, don't you know that?

HAPPY.   Don't I know it! Me!

BIFF.   Hap, help him! Jesus . . . help him . . . Help me, help me, I can't bear to look at his face! (*Ready to weep, he hurries out, up right.*)

HAPPY (*starting after him*).   Where are you going?

MISS FORSYTHE.   What's he so mad about?

HAPPY.   Come on, girls, we'll catch up with him.

MISS FORSYTHE (*as* HAPPY *pushes her out*).   Say, I don't like that temper of his!

HAPPY.   He's just a little overstrung, he'll be all right!

WILLY (*off left, as* THE WOMAN *laughs*).   Don't answer! Don't answer!

LETTA.   Don't you want to tell your father—

HAPPY.   No, that's not my father. He's just a guy. Come on, we'll catch Biff, and, honey, we're going to paint this town! Stanley, where's the check! Hey, Stanley! (*They exit,* STANLEY *looks toward left.*)

STANLEY (*calling to* HAPPY *indignantly*).   Mr. Loman! Mr. Loman! (STANLEY *picks up a chair and follows them off. Knocking is heard off left.* THE WOMAN *enters, laughing.* WILLY *follows her. She is in a black slip; he is buttoning his shirt. Raw, sensuous music accompanies their speech.*)

WILLY.   Will you stop laughing? Will you stop?

THE WOMAN.   Aren't you going to answer the door? He'll wake the whole hotel.

WILLY.   I'm not expecting anybody.

THE WOMAN.   Whyn't you have another drink, honey, and stop being so damn self-centered.

WILLY.   I'm so lonely.

THE WOMAN.   You know you ruined me, Willy? From now on, whenever you come to the office, I'll see that you go right through to the buyers. No waiting at my desk any more, Willy. You ruined me.

WILLY.   That's nice of you to say that.

THE WOMAN.   Gee, you are self-centered! Why so sad? You are the saddest, self-centeredest soul I ever did see-saw. (*She laughs. He kisses her.*) Come on inside, drummer boy. It's silly to be dressing in the middle of the night. (*As knocking is heard*) Aren't you going to answer the door?

WILLY.   They're knocking on the wrong door.

THE WOMAN.   But I felt the knocking. And he heard us talking in here. Maybe the hotel's on fire!

WILLY (*his terror rising*).   It's a mistake.

THE WOMAN.   Then tell him to go away!

WILLY.   There's nobody there.

THE WOMAN.   It's getting on my nerves, Willy. There's somebody standing out there and it's getting on my nerves!

WILLY (*pushing her away from him*).   All right, stay in the bathroom here, and don't come out. I think there's a law in Massachusetts about it, so don't come out. It may be the new room clerk. He looked very mean. So don't come out. It's a mistake, there's no fire. (*The knocking is heard again. He takes a few steps away from her, and she vanishes into the wing. The light follows him, and now he is facing* YOUNG BIFF, *who carries a suitcase.* BIFF *steps toward him. The music is gone.*)

BIFF.   Why didn't you answer?

WILLY.   Biff! What are you doing in Boston?

BIFF.   Why didn't you answer? I've been knocking for five minutes, I called you on the phone—

WILLY.   I just heard you. I was in the bathroom and had the door shut. Did anything happen home?

BIFF.   Dad—I let you down.

WILLY.   What do you mean?

BIFF.   Dad . . .

WILLY.   Biffo, what's this about? (*Putting his arm around* BIFF) Come on, let's go downstairs and get you a malted.

BIFF.   Dad, I flunked math.

WILLY.   Not for the term?

BIFF.   The term. I haven't got enough credits to graduate.

WILLY.   You mean to say Bernard wouldn't give you the answers?

BIFF.   He did, he tried, but I only got sixty-one.

WILLY.   And they wouldn't give you four points.

BIFF.   Birnbaum refused absolutely. I begged him, Pop, but he won't give me those points. You gotta talk to him before they close the school. Because if he saw the kind of man you are, and you just talked to him in your way, I'm sure he'd come through for me. The class came right before practice, see, and I didn't go enough. Would you talk to him? He'd like you, Pop. You know the way you could talk.

WILLY.   You're on. We'll drive right back.

BIFF.   Oh, Dad, good work! I'm sure he'll change it for you!

WILLY.   Go downstairs and tell the clerk I'm checkin' out. Go right down.

BIFF.   Yes, sir! See, the reason he hates me, Pop—one day he was late for class so I got up at the blackboard and imitated him. I crossed my eyes and talked with a lithp.

WILLY (*laughing*).   You did? The kids like it?

BIFF.   They nearly died laughing!

WILLY.   Yeah? What'd you do?

BIFF. The thquare root of thixty twee is . . . (WILLY *bursts out laughing;* BIFF *joins him*). And in the middle of it he walked in! (WILLY *laughs and* THE WOMAN *joins in off-stage.*)

WILLY (*without hesitation*).   Hurry downstairs and—

BIFF.   Somebody in there?

WILLY.   No, that was next door. (THE WOMAN *laughs off-stage.*)

BIFF.   Somebody got in your bathroom!

WILLY.   No, it's the next room, there's a party.

THE WOMAN (*enters, laughing. She lisps this*).   Can I come in? There's something in the bathtub, Willy, and it's moving! (WILLY *looks at* BIFF, *who is staring open-mouthed and horrified at* THE WOMAN.)

WILLY.   Ah—you better go back to your room. They must be finished painting by now. They're painting her room so I let her take a shower here. Go back, go back . . . (*He pushes her.*)

THE WOMAN (*resisting*).   But I've got to get dressed, Willy, I can't—

WILLY.   Get out of here! Go back, go back . . . (*Suddenly striving for the ordinary*) This is Miss Francis, Biff, she's a buyer. They're painting her room. Go back, Miss Francis, go back . . .

THE WOMAN.   But my clothes, I can't go out naked in the hall!

WILLY (*pushing her off-stage*).   Get outa here! Go back, go back! (BIFF *slowly sits down on his suitcase as the argument continues off-stage.*)

THE WOMAN.   Where's my stockings? You promised me stockings, Willy!

WILLY.   I have no stockings here!

THE WOMAN.   You had two boxes of size nine sheers for me, and I want them!

WILLY.   Here, for God's sake, will you get outa here!

THE WOMAN (*enters holding a box of stockings*).   I just hope there's nobody in the hall. That's all I hope. (*To* BIFF) Are you football or baseball?

BIFF.   Football.

THE WOMAN (*angry, humiliated*).   That's me too. G'night. (*She snatches her clothes from* WILLY *and walks out.*)

WILLY (*after a pause*).   Well, better get going. I want to get to the school first thing in the morning. Get my suits out of the closet. I'll get my valise. (BIFF *doesn't move.*) What's the matter? (BIFF *remains motionless, tears falling.*) She's a buyer. Buys for J. H. Simmons. She lives down the hall—they're painting. You don't imagine—(*He breaks off. After a pause*) Now listen, pal, she's just a buyer. She sees merchandise in her room and they have to keep it looking just so . . . (*Pause. Assuming command*) All right, get my suits. (BIFF *doesn't move.*) Now stop crying and do as I say. I gave you an order. Biff, I gave you an order! Is that what you do when I give you an order? How dare you cry! (*Putting his arm around* BIFF) Now look, Biff, when you grow up you'll under-stand about these things. You mustn't—you mustn't overemphasize a thing like this. I'll see Birnbaum first thing in the morning.

BIFF.   Never mind.

WILLY (*getting down beside* BIFF).   Never mind! He's going to give you those points. I'll see to it.

BIFF.   He wouldn't listen to you.

WILLY.   He certainly will listen to me. You need those points for the U. of Virginia.

BIFF.   I'm not going there.

WILLY.   Heh? If I can't get him to change that mark you'll make it up in summer school. You've got all summer to—

BIFF (*his weeping breaking from him*).   Dad . . .

WILLY (*infected by it*).   Oh, my boy . . .

BIFF.   Dad . . .

WILLY.   She's nothing to me, Biff. I was lonely, I was terribly lonely.

BIFF.   You—you gave her Mama's stockings! (*His tears break through and he rises to go.*)

WILLY (*grabbing for* BIFF).   I gave you an order!

BIFF.   Don't touch me, you—liar!

WILLY.   Apologize for that!

BIFF.   You fake! You phony little fake! You fake! (*Overcome, he turns quickly and weeping fully goes out with his suitcase.* WILLY *is left on the floor on his knees.*)

WILLY.   I gave you an order! Biff, come back here or I'll beat you! Come back here! I'll whip you! (STANLEY *comes quickly in from the right and stands in front of* WILLY, *who shouts at him.*) I gave you an order . . .

STANLEY.   Hey, let's pick it up, pick it up, Mr. Loman. (*He helps* WILLY *to his feet.*) Your boys left with the chippies. They said they'll see you home. (*A second waiter watches some distance away.*)

WILLY.   But we were supposed to have dinner together. (*Music is heard,* WILLY's *theme.*)

STANLEY.   Can you make it?

WILLY.   I'll—sure. I can make it. (*Suddenly concerned about his clothes*) Do I—I look all right?

STANLEY.   Sure, you look all right. (*He flicks a speck off* WILLY's *lapel.*)

WILLY.   Here—here's a dollar.

STANLEY.   Oh, your son paid me. It's all right.

WILLY (*putting it in* STANLEY's *hand*).   No, take it. You're a good boy.

STANLEY.   Oh, no, you don't have to . . .

WILLY. Here's some more, I don't need it any more. (*After a slight pause.*) Tell me—is there a seed store in the neighborhood?

STANLEY. Seeds? You mean like to plant? (*As* WILLY *turns,* STANLEY *slips the money back into his jacket pocket.*)

WILLY. Yes. Carrots, peas . . .

STANLEY. Well, there's hardware stores on Sixth Avenue, but it may be too late now.

WILLY (*anxiously*). Oh, I'd better hurry. I've got to get some seeds. (*He starts off to the right.*) I've got to get some seeds, right away. Nothing's planted. I don't have a thing in the ground. (WILLY *hurries out as the light goes down.* STANLEY *moves over to the right after him, watches him off. The other waiter has been staring at* WILLY.)

STANLEY (*to the waiter*). Well, whatta you looking at?

(*The waiter picks up the chairs and moves off right.* STANLEY *takes the table and follows him. The light fades on this area. There is a long pause, the sound of the flute coming over. The light gradually rises on the kitchen, which is empty.* HAPPY *appears at the door of the house, followed by* BIFF. HAPPY *is carrying a large bunch of long-stemmed roses. He enters the kitchen, looks around for* LINDA. *Not seeing her, he turns to* BIFF, *who is just outside the house door, and makes a gesture with his hands, indicating "Not here, I guess." He looks into the living-room and freezes. Inside,* LINDA, *unseen, is seated,* WILLY'S *coat on her lap. She rises ominously and quietly and moves toward* HAPPY, *who backs up into the kitchen, afraid.*)

HAPPY. Hey, what're you doing? (LINDA *says nothing but moves toward him implacably.*) Where's Pop? (*He keeps backing to the right, and now* LINDA *is in full view of the doorway to the living-room.*) Is he sleeping?

LINDA. Where were you?

HAPPY (*trying to laugh it off*). We met two girls, Mom, very fine types. Here, we brought you some flowers. (*Offering them to her*) Put them in your room, Ma. (*She knocks them to the floor at* BIFF'S *feet. He has now come inside and closed the door behind him. She stares at* BIFF, *silent.*) Now what'd you do that for? Mom, I want you to have some flowers—

LINDA (*cutting* HAPPY *off, violently to* BIFF). Don't you care whether he lives or dies?

HAPPY (*going to the stairs*). Come upstairs, Biff.

BIFF (*with a flare of disgust, to* HAPPY). Go away from me! (*To* LINDA) What do you mean, lives or dies? Nobody's dying around here, pal.

LINDA. Get out of my sight! Get out of here!

BIFF. I wanna see the boss.

LINDA. You're not to go near him!

BIFF. Where is he? (*He moves into the living-room and* LINDA *follows.*)

LINDA (*shouting after* BIFF). You invite him to dinner. He looks forward to it all day—(BIFF *appears in his parents' bedroom, looks around, and exits*)—and then you desert him there. There's no stranger you'd do that to!

HAPPY. Why? He had a swell time with us. Listen, when I— (LINDA *comes back into the kitchen*)—desert him I hope I don't outlive the day!

LINDA. Get out of here!

HAPPY. Now look, Mom . . .

LINDA. Did you have to go to women tonight? You and your lousy rotten whores! (BIFF *re-enters the kitchen.*)

HAPPY. Mom, all we did was follow Biff around trying to cheer him up! (*To* BIFF) Boy, what a night you gave me!

LINDA. Get out of here, both of you, and don't come back! I don't want you tormenting him any more. Go on now, get your things together! (*To* BIFF) You can sleep in his apartment. (*She starts to pick up the flowers and stops herself.*) Pick up this stuff, I'm not your maid any more. Pick it up, you bum, you! (HAPPY *turns his back to her in refusal.* BIFF *slowly moves over and gets down on his knees, picking up the flowers.*)

LINDA. You're a pair of animals! Not one, not another living soul would have had the cruelty to walk out on that man in a restaurant!

BIFF (*not looking at her*). Is that what he said?

LINDA. He didn't have to say anything. He was so humiliated he nearly limped when he came in.

HAPPY. But, Mom, he had a great time with us—

BIFF (*cutting him off violently*). Shut up! (*Without another word,* HAPPY *goes upstairs.*)

LINDA. You! You didn't even go in to see if he was all right!

BIFF (*still on the floor in front of* LINDA, *the flowers in his hand; with self-loathing*). No. Didn't. Didn't do a damned thing. How do you like that, heh? Left him babbling in a toilet.

LINDA. You louse. You . . .

BIFF. Now you hit it on the nose! (*He gets up, throws the flowers in the wastebasket.*) The scum of the earth, and you're looking at him!

LINDA. Get out of here!

BIFF. I gotta talk to the boss, Mom. Where is he?

LINDA. You're not going near him. Get out of this house!

BIFF (*with absolute assurance, determination*). No. We're gonna have an abrupt conversation, him and me.

LINDA.   You're not talking to him! (*Hammering is heard from outside the house, off right.* BIFF *turns toward the noise.* LINDA *is suddenly pleading.*) Will you please leave him alone?

BIFF.   What's he doing out there?

LINDA.   He's planting a garden!

BIFF (*quietly*).   Now? Oh, my God! (BIFF *moves outside,* LINDA *following. The light dies down on them and comes up on the center of the apron as* WILLY *walks into it. He is carrying a flashlight, a hoe, and a handful of seed packets. He raps the top of the hoe sharply to fix it firmly, and then moves to the left, measuring off the distance with his foot. He holds the flashlight to look at the seed packets, reading off the instructions. He is in the blue of night.*)

WILLY.   Carrots . . . quarter-inch apart. Rows . . . one-foot rows. (*He measures it off.*) One foot. (*He puts down a package and measures off.*) Beets. (*He puts down another package and measures again.*) Lettuce. (*He reads the package, puts it down.*) One foot—(*He breaks off as* BEN *appears at the right and moves slowly down to him.*) What a proposition, ts, ts. Terrific, terrific. 'Cause she suffered, Ben, the woman has suffered. You understand me? A man can't go out the way he came in. Ben, a man has got to add up to something. You can't, you can't—(BEN *moves toward him as though to interrupt.*) You gotta consider, now. Don't answer so quick. Remember, it's a guaranteed twenty-thousand-dollar proposition. Now look, Ben, I want you to go through the ins and outs of this thing with me. I've got nobody to talk to, Ben, and the woman has suffered, you hear me?

BEN (*standing still, considering*).   What's the proposition?

WILLY.   It's twenty-thousand dollars on the barrelhead. Guaranteed, gilt-edged, you understand?

BEN.   You don't want to make a fool of yourself. They might not honor the policy.

WILLY.   How can they dare refuse? Didn't I work like a coolie to meet every premium on the nose? And now they don't pay off? Impossible!

BEN.   It's called a cowardly thing, William.

WILLY.   Why? Does it take more guts to stand here the rest of my life ringing up a zero?

BEN (*yielding*).   That's a point, William. (*He moves, thinking, turns.*) And twenty-thousand—that *is* something one can feel with the hand, it is there.

WILLY (*now assured, with rising power*).   Oh, Ben, that's the whole beauty of it! I can see it like a diamond shining in the dark, hard and rough, that I can pick up and touch in my hand. Not like—like an appointment! This would not be another damned-fool appointment, Ben, and it changes all the aspects. Because he thinks I'm nothing, see, and so he spites me. But the funeral—(*Straightening up*) Ben, that funeral will be massive! They'll come from Maine, Massachusetts, Vermont, New Hampshire! All the old-timers with the strange license plates— that boy will be thunderstruck, Ben, because he never realized—I am known! Rhode Island, New York, New Jersey—I am known, Ben, and he'll see it with his eyes once and for all. He'll see what I am. He's in for a shock, that boy!

BEN (*coming down to the edge of the garden*).   He'll call you a coward.

WILLY (*suddenly fearful*).   No, that would be terrible.

BEN.   Yes. And a damned fool.

WILLY.   No, no, he mustn't, I won't have it! (*He is broken and desperate.*)

BEN.   He'll hate you, William. (*The gay music of the* BOYS *is heard.*)

WILLY.   Oh, Ben, how do we get back to all the great times? Used to be so full of light, and comradeship, the sleigh-riding in winter and the ruddiness of his cheeks. And always some kind of good news coming up, always something nice coming up ahead. And never let me carry the valises in the house, and simonizing, simonizing that little red car! Why, why can't I give him something and not have him hate me?

BEN.   Let me think about it. (*He glances at his watch.*) I still have a little time. Remarkable proposition, but you've got to be sure you're not making a fool of yourself. (BEN *drifts off upstage and goes out of sight.* BIFF *comes down from the left.*)

WILLY (*suddenly conscious of* BIFF, *turns and looks up at him, then begins picking up the packages of seeds in confusion*).   Where the hell is that seed? (*Indignantly*) You can't see nothing out here! They boxed in the whole goddam neighborhood!

BIFF.   There are people all around here. Don't you realize that?

WILLY.   I'm busy. Don't bother me.

BIFF (*taking the hoe from* WILLY).   I'm saying good-by to you, Pop. (WILLY *looks at him, silent, unable to move.*) I'm not coming back any more.

WILLY.   You're not going to see Oliver tomorrow?

BIFF.   I've got no appointment, Dad.

WILLY.   He put his arms around you, and you've got no appointment?

BIFF.   Pop, get this now, will you? Every time I've left it's been a fight that sent me out of here. Today I realized something about myself and I tried to explain it to you and I—I think I'm just not smart enough to make any sense out of it for you. To hell with whose fault it is or anything like that. (*He takes* WILLY's *arm.*) Let's just wrap it up, heh? Come on in, we'll tell Mom. (*He gently tries to pull* WILLY *to left.*)

WILLY (*frozen, immobile, with guilt in his voice*).   No, I don't want to see her.

BIFF.   Come on! (*He pulls again, and* WILLY *tries to pull away.*)

WILLY (*highly nervous*).   No, no, I don't want to see her.

BIFF (*tries to look into* WILLY's *face, as if to find the answer there*). Why don't you want to see her?

WILLY (*more harshly now*).   Don't bother me, will you?

BIFF.   What do you mean, you don't want to see her? You don't want them calling you yellow do you? This isn't your fault; it's me, I'm a bum. Now come inside! (WILLY *strains to get away.*) Did you hear what I said to you? (WILLY *pulls away and quickly goes by himself into the house.* BIFF *follows.*)

LINDA (*to* WILLY).   Did you plant, dear?

BIFF (*at the door, to* LINDA).   All right, we had it out. I'm going and I'm not writing any more.

LINDA (*going to* WILLY *in the kitchen*).   I think that's the best way, dear. 'Cause there's no use drawing it out, you'll just never get along. (WILLY *does not respond.*)

BIFF.   People ask where I am and what I'm doing, you don't know, and you don't care. That way it'll be off your mind and you can start brightening up again. All right? That clears it, doesn't it? (WILLY *is silent, and* BIFF *goes to him.*) You gonna wish me luck, scout? (*He extends his hand.*) What do you say?

LINDA.   Shake his hand, Willy.

WILLY (*turning to her, seething with hurt*).   There's no necessity to mention the pen at all, y'know.

BIFF (*gently*).   I've got no appointment, Dad.

WILLY (*erupting fiercely*).   He put his arm around . . . ?

BIFF.   Dad, you're never going to see what I am, so what's the use of arguing? If I strike oil I'll send you a check. Meantime forget I'm alive.

WILLY (*to* LINDA).   Spite, see?

BIFF.   Shake hands, Dad.

WILLY.   Not my hand.

BIFF.   I was hoping not to go this way.

WILLY.   Well, this is the way you're going. Good-by. (BIFF *looks at him a moment, then turns sharply and goes to the stairs.* WILLY *stops him with*) May you rot in hell if you leave this house!

BIFF (*turning*).   Exactly what is it that you want from me?

WILLY.   I want you to know, on the train, in the mountains, in the valleys, wherever you go, that you cut down your life for spite!

BIFF.   No, no.

WILLY.   Spite, spite, is the word of your undoing! And when you're down and out, remember what did it. When you're rotting somewhere beside the railroad tracks, remember, and don't you dare blame it on me!

BIFF.   I'm not blaming it on you!

WILLY.   I won't take the rap for this, you hear? (HAPPY *comes down the stairs and stands on the bottom step, watching.*)

BIFF.   That's just what I'm telling you!

WILLY (*sinking into a chair at the table, with full accusation*).   You're trying to put a knife in me—don't think I don't know what you're doing!

BIFF.   All right, phony! Then let's lay it on the line. (*He whips the rubber tube out of his pocket and puts it on the table.*)

HAPPY.   You crazy—

LINDA.   Biff! (*She moves to grab the hose, but* BIFF *holds it down with his hand.*)

BIFF.   Leave it there! Don't move it!

WILLY (*not looking at it*).   What is that?

BIFF.   You know goddam well what that is.

WILLY (*caged, wanting to escape*).   I never saw that.

BIFF.   You saw it. The mice didn't bring it into the cellar! What is this supposed to do, make a hero out of you? This supposed to make me sorry for you?

WILLY.   Never heard of it.

BIFF.   There'll be no pity for you, you hear it? No pity!

WILLY (*to* LINDA).   You hear the spite!

BIFF.   No, you're going to hear the truth—what you are and what I am!

LINDA.   Stop it!

WILLY.   Spite!

HAPPY (*coming down toward* BIFF).   You cut it out now!

BIFF (*to* HAPPY).   The man don't know who we are! The man is gonna know! (*To* WILLY) We never told the truth for ten minutes in this house!

HAPPY.   We always told the truth!

BIFF (*turning on him*).   You big blow, are you the assistant buyer? You're one of two assistants to the assistant, aren't you?

HAPPY.   Well, I'm practically—

BIFF.   You're practically full of it! We all are! And I'm through with it. (*To* WILLY) Now hear this, Willy, this is me.

WILLY.   I know you!

BIFF.   You know why I had no address for three months? I stole a suit in Kansas City and I was in jail. (*To* LINDA, *who is sobbing*) Stop crying. I'm through with it. (LINDA *turns away from them, her hands covering her face.*)

WILLY.   I suppose that's my fault!

BIFF.   I stole myself out of every job since high school!

WILLY.   And whose fault is that?

BIFF.   And I never got anywhere because you blew me so full of hot air I could never stand taking orders from anybody! That's whose fault it is!

WILLY.   I hear that!

LINDA.   Don't, Biff!

BIFF.   It's goddam time you heard that! I had to be boss big shot in two weeks, and I'm through with it!

WILLY.   Then hang yourself! For spite, hang yourself!

BIFF.   No! Nobody's hanging himself, Willy! I ran down eleven flights with a pen in my hand today. And suddenly I stopped, you hear me? And in the middle of that office building, do you hear this? I stopped in the middle of that building and I saw—the sky. I saw the things that I love in this world. The work and the food and time to sit and smoke. And I looked at the pen and said to myself, what the hell am I grabbing this for? Why am I trying to become what I don't want to be? What am I doing in an office, making a contemptuous, begging fool of myself, when all I want is out there, waiting for me the minute I say I know who I am! Why can't I say that, Willy? (*He tries to make* WILLY *face him, but* WILLY *pulls away and moves to the left.*)

WILLY (*with hatred, threateningly*).   The door of your life is wide open!

BIFF.   Pop! I'm a dime a dozen, and so are you!

WILLY (*turning on him now in an uncontrolled outburst*).   I am not a dime a dozen! I am Willy Loman, and you are Biff Loman! (BIFF *starts for* WILLY, *but is blocked by* HAPPY. *In his fury,* BIFF *seems on the verge of attacking his father.*)

BIFF.   I am not a leader of men, Willy, and neither are you. You were never anything but a hard-working drummer who landed in the ash can like all the rest of them! I'm one dollar an hour, Willy! I tried seven states and couldn't raise it. A buck an hour! Do you gather my meaning? I'm not bringing home any prizes any more, and you're going to stop waiting for me to bring them home!

WILLY (*directly to* BIFF).   You vengeful, spiteful mutt! (BIFF *breaks from* HAPPY. WILLY, *in fright, starts up the stairs.* BIFF *grabs him.*)

BIFF (*at the peak of his fury*).   Pop, I'm nothing! I'm nothing, Pop. Can't you understand that? There's no spite in it any more. I'm just what I am, that's all. (BIFF'*s fury has spent itself, and he breaks down, sobbing, holding on to* WILLY, *who dumbly fumbles for* BIFF'*s face.*)

WILLY (*astonished*).   What're you doing? What're you doing? (*To* LINDA) Why is he crying?

BIFF (*crying, broken*).   Will you let me go, for Christ's sake? Will you take that phony dream and burn it before something happens? (*Struggling to contain himself, he pulls away and moves to the stairs.*) I'll go in the morning. Put him—put him to bed. (*Exhausted,* BIFF *moves up the stairs to his room.*)

WILLY (*after a long pause, astonished, elevated*).   Isn't that—isn't that remarkable? Biff—he likes me!

LINDA.   He loves you, Willy!

HAPPY (*deeply moved*).   Always did, Pop.

WILLY.   Oh, Biff! (*Staring wildly*) He cried! Cried to me. (*He is choking with his love, and now cries out his promise.*) That boy—that boy is going to be magnificent! (BEN *appears in the light just outside the kitchen.*)

BEN.   Yes, outstanding, with twenty thousand behind him.

LINDA (*sensing the racing of his mind, fearfully, carefully*).   Now come to bed, Willy. It's all settled now.

WILLY (*finding it difficult not to rush out of the house*).   Yes, we'll sleep. Come on. Go to sleep, Hap.

BEN.   And it does take a great kind of man to crack the jungle. (*In accents of dread,* BEN'*s idyllic music starts up.*)

HAPPY (*his arm around* LINDA).   I'm getting married, Pop, don't forget it. I'm changing everything. I'm gonna run that department before the year is up. You'll see, Mom. (*He kisses her.*)

BEN.   The jungle is dark but full of diamonds, Willy. (WILLY *turns, moves, listening to* BEN.)

LINDA.   Be good. You're both good boys, just act that way, that's all.

HAPPY.   'Night, Pop. (*He goes upstairs.*)

LINDA (*to* WILLY).   Come, dear.

BEN (*with greater force*).   One must go in to fetch a diamond out.

WILLY (*to* LINDA, *as he moves slowly along the edge of the kitchen, toward the door*).   I just want to get settled down, Linda. Let me sit alone for a little.

LINDA (*almost uttering her fear*).   I want you upstairs.

WILLY (*taking her in his arms*).   In a few minutes, Linda. I couldn't sleep right now. Go on, you look awful tired. (*He kisses her.*)

BEN.   Not like an appointment at all. A diamond is rough and hard to the touch.

WILLY.   Go on now. I'll be right up.

LINDA.   I think this is the only way, Willy.

WILLY.   Sure, it's the best thing.

BEN.   Best thing!

WILLY.   The only way. Everything is gonna be—go on, kid, get to bed. You look so tired.

LINDA.   Come right up.

WILLY.   Two minutes. (LINDA *goes into the living-room, then reappears in her bedroom.* WILLY *moves just outside the kitchen door.*) Loves me. (*Wonderingly*) Always loved me. Isn't that a remarkable thing? Ben, he'll worship me for it!

BEN (*with promise*).   It's dark there, but full of diamonds.

WILLY.   Can you imagine that magnificence with twenty thousand dollars in his pocket?

LINDA (*calling from her room*).   Willy! Come up!

WILLY (*calling into the kitchen*).   Yes, yes. Coming! It's very smart, you realize that, don't you, sweetheart? Even Ben sees it. I gotta go, baby. 'By! 'By! (*Going over to* BEN, *almost dancing*) Imagine? When the mail comes he'll be ahead of Bernard again!

BEN.   A perfect proposition all around.

WILLY.   Did you see how he cried to me? Oh, if I could kiss him, Ben!

BEN.   Time, William, time!

WILLY.   Oh, Ben, I always knew one way or another we were gonna make it, Biff and I!

BEN (*looking at his watch*).   The boat. We'll be late. (*He moves slowly off into the darkness.*)

WILLY (*elegiacally, turning to the house*).   Now when you kick off, boy, I want a seventy-yard boot, and get right down the field under the ball, and when you hit, hit low and hit hard, because it's important, boy. (*He swings around and faces the audience.*) There's all kinds of important people in the stands, and the first thing you know . . . (*Suddenly realizing he is alone*) Ben! Ben, where do I . . . ? (*He makes a sudden movement of search.*) Ben, how do I . . . ?

LINDA (*calling*).   Willy, you coming up?

WILLY (*uttering a gasp of fear, whirling about as if to quiet her*).   Sh! (*He turns as if to find his way; sounds, faces, voices, seem to be swarming in upon him and he flicks at them, crying*) Sh! Sh! (*Suddenly music, faint and high, stops him. It rises in intensity, almost to an unbearable scream. He goes up and down on his toes, and rushes off around the house.*) Shhh!

LINDA.   Willy? (*There is no answer.* LINDA *waits.* BIFF *gets up off his bed. He is still in his clothes.* HAPPY *sits up.* BIFF *stands there listening.* LINDA, *with real fear*) Willy, answer me! Willy! (*There is the sound of a car starting and moving away at full speed.*) No!

BIFF (*rushing down the stairs*).   Pop!

(*As the car speeds off, the music crashes down in a frenzy of sound, which becomes the soft pulsation of a single cello string.* BIFF *slowly returns to his bedroom. He and* HAPPY *gravely don their jackets.* LINDA *slowly walks out of her room. The music has developed into a dead march. The leaves of day are appearing over everything.* CHARLEY *and* BERNARD, *somberly dressed, appear and knock on the kitchen door.* BIFF *and* HAPPY *slowly descend the stairs to the kitchen as* CHARLEY *and* BERNARD *enter. All stop a moment when* LINDA, *in clothes of mourning, bearing a little bunch of roses, comes through the draped doorway into the kitchen. She goes to* CHARLEY *and takes his arm. Now all move toward the audience, through the wall-line of the kitchen. At the limit of the apron,* LINDA *lays down the flowers, kneels, and sits back on her heels. All stare down at the grave.*)

REQUIEM

CHARLEY.   It's getting dark, Linda. (LINDA *doesn't react. She stares at the grave.*)

BIFF.   How about it, Mom? Better get some rest, heh? They'll be closing the gate soon. (LINDA *makes no move. Pause.*)

HAPPY (*deeply angered*).   He had no right to do that. There was no necessity for it. We would've helped him.

CHARLEY (*grunting*).   Hmmm.

BIFF.   Come along, Mom.

LINDA.   Why didn't anybody come?

CHARLEY.   It was a nice funeral.

LINDA.   But where are all the people he knew? Maybe they blame him.

CHARLEY.   Naa. It's a rough world, Linda. They wouldn't blame him.

LINDA.   I can't understand it. At this time especially. First time in thirty-five years we were just about free and clear. He only needed a little salary. He was even finished with the dentist.

CHARLEY.   No man only needs a little salary.

LINDA.   I can't understand it.

BIFF.   There were a lot of nice days. When he'd come home from a trip; or on Sundays, making the stoop; finishing the cellar; putting on the new porch; when he built the extra bathroom; and put up the garage. You know something, Charley, there's more of him in that front stoop than in all the sales he ever made.

CHARLEY.   Yeah. He was a happy man with a batch of cement.

LINDA.   He was so wonderful with his hands.

BIFF.   He had the wrong dreams. All, all, wrong.

HAPPY (*almost ready to fight* BIFF).   Don't say that!

BIFF.   He never knew who he was.

CHARLEY (*stopping* HAPPY'S *movement and reply. To* BIFF).   Nobody dast blame this man. You don't understand: Willy was a salesman. And for a salesman, there is no rock bottom to the life. He don't put a bolt to a nut, he don't tell you the law or give you medicine. He's a man way out there in the blue, riding on a smile and a shoeshine. And when they start not smiling back—that's an earthquake. And then you get yourself a couple of spots on your hat, and you're finished. Nobody dast blame this man. A salesman is got to dream, boy. It comes with the territory.

BIFF.   Charley, the man didn't know who he was.

HAPPY (*infuriated*).   Don't say that!

BIFF.   Why don't you come with me, Happy?

HAPPY.   I'm not licked that easily. I'm staying right in this city, and I'm gonna beat this racket! (*He looks at* BIFF, *his chin is set.*) The Loman Brothers!

BIFF.   I know who I am, kid.

HAPPY.   All right, boy. I'm gonna show you and everybody else that Willy Loman did not die in vain. He had a good dream. It's the only dream you can have—to come out number-one man. He fought it out here and this is where I'm gonna win it for him.

BIFF (*with a hopeless glance at* HAPPY, *bends toward his mother*). Let's go, Mom.

LINDA.   I'll be with you in a minute. Go on, Charley. (*He hesitates.*) I want to, just for a minute. I never had a chance to say good-by. (CHARLEY *moves away, followed by* HAPPY. BIFF *remains a slight distance up and left of* LINDA. *She sits there, summoning herself. The flute begins, not far away, playing behind her speech.*) Forgive me, dear. I can't cry. I don't know what it is, but I can't cry. I don't understand it. Why did you ever do that? Help me, Willy, I can't cry. It seems to me that you're just on another trip. I keep expecting you. Willy, dear, I can't cry. Why did you do it? I search and search and I search, and I can't understand it, Willy. I made the last payment on the house today. Today, dear. And there'll be nobody home. (*A sob rises in her throat.*) We're free and clear. (*Sobbing more fully, released*) We're free. (BIFF *comes slowly toward her.*) We're free . . . We're free . . .

(BIFF *lifts her to her feet and moves out up right with her in his arms.* LINDA *sobs quietly.* BERNARD *and* CHARLEY *come together and follow them, followed by* HAPPY. *Only the music of the flute is left on the darkening stage as over the house the hard towers of the apartment buildings rise into sharp focus, and the curtain falls.*)

QUESTIONS

1. Critics have disagreed as to whether *Death of a Salesman* can be called a tragedy. Most of the debate centers on whether or not Willy Loman has the stature of a tragic hero. How would you answer this question? What admirable characteristics does Willy have? Could any of his desires or motivations be called noble? Consider particularly Willy's motivations in committing suicide. In what respect are they to be admired? In what respect are they mistaken? Does Willy make any "discovery" before his death? If so, does it involve an increased self-knowledge?

   Miller himself has said that he did not set out to "write a tragedy" in this play, but "to show the truth" as he saw it. It is nevertheless clear from his various comments about the play that he regards it as a tragedy, with Willy as its hero. In his article "Tragedy and the Common Man" he has written that "the tragic feeling is evoked in us when we are in the presence of a character who is ready to lay down his life, if need be, to secure one thing—his sense of personal dignity." Is this remark applicable to Willy Loman?

2. Regardless of your answers to question 1, there can be little doubt that Willy Loman is the victim of a "tragic flaw." Can you isolate that flaw? Is it Willy's own tragic flaw that causes his downfall? Is it society's? Is it a combination of both?

3. Willy is generally assumed to be the protagonist of *Death of a Salesman*, but a case can also be made for its being Biff's play. Consider the play in terms of both interpretations. If Willy is the protagonist, who or what constitutes the antagonistic force? Is the antagonist the same if one considers Biff as protagonist? Explain.

4. Which characters change during the course of the play? In what respects?

5. Some critics have viewed *Death of a Salesman* entirely as a social commentary. To what extent do you consider this evaluation valid or invalid?

6. Discuss the interaction of the characters in *Death of a Salesman*. What effect has Willy had upon his sons' lives? They on his? Linda has been described as "the perfect wife." Do you find her so? What has been her effect on the lives of her husband and children? Willy's brother Ben is in many ways a character foil to Willy. To what extent, if any, has Ben's "success" contributed to Willy's failure? What is Ben's role in the play? What function do Charley and Bernard serve in the play?

7. What purposes are served by the Requiem? What ironies does it contain? What would be lost by its omission from the play?

8. To what extent is *Death of a Salesman* a realistic play? To what extent is it nonrealistic? Describe as precisely as you can the nonrealistic devices used by Miller in the play, and comment on their purpose.

Rich Orloff
Oedi

Characters

OEDIPUS, *King of Thebes, early thirties*
TIRESIAS, *a blind, old seer*
CREON, *Oedipus's advisor and brother-in-law*
JOCASTA, *Oedipus's wife, among other things*
THE TOWN CRIER, *heard off-stage*

Ancient Greece. Around 4 p.m.

A room in the palace of OEDIPUS *the king, simply furnished. A chair and perhaps a column or two. The chair should be in the style of ancient Greece, without backs. In the distance, we hear the call of the* TOWN CRIER.

TOWN CRIER *(off-stage).*   Hear ye, hear ye! Four o'clock and all is well. Details at eleven. For the best in dining delicacies, treat yourself to Hecuba's House of Hummus! Try their babagonoosh! . . . Plato says, "It's ideal!" (TIRESIAS *and* CREON *enter.* TIRESIAS *is blind and uses a cane.)*

CREON.   Oedipus!

OEDIPUS.   Creon, my trusted aide; Tiresias, noble seer. At last you have returned! My mind has been able to dwell on nothing save what news you may have found on your journey.

TIRESIAS.   If it is good news for which you wait, you wait in vain. I see nothing but gloom and doom!

OEDIPUS.   Creon, is that true?

CREON.   Oedipus, my dear brother-in-law, perhaps we should hold off telling you anything until we have gathered all of our information.

OEDIPUS.   I cannot wait. Ever since the plague has hit our beloved Thebes, the people insist that we find the killer of their former king, as they are convinced that until we punish the murderer, the plague shall

OEDI (pronounced "Eddie")   First performed in 1998 by the Carousel Theatre Company in New York City, and published in *The Best American Short Plays 1997–1998*. A native of Chicago, Rich Orloff graduated from Oberlin College and now lives in New York. Orloff writes: "For years I had wanted to create a new adaptation of one of the world's greatest tragedies, turning it into a comedy while maintaining most of the key story elements. When I found a way to look at the events in *Oedipus Rex* from a different angle, I knew I had a fun play."

continue. As their new king, I owe them the truth as quickly as possible. Besides, the latest polls show my popularity's plummeting.

CREON. Yes, but—

OEDIPUS. There is no time for "but"s. I created the Creon Commission to ferret out the facts of this fearsome felony, and I demand to know what you have learned.

CREON. Well, first we visited the oracles of Delphi to see what they could tell us.

OEDIPUS. Were the oracles helpful?

TIRESIAS. Well, you know oracles. It's hard to get a straight answer out of them.

CREON. They did tell us that old king Laios was murdered by his own son.

OEDIPUS. But that's crazy. Laios had no son.

CREON. Acually, we discovered he did, many years ago, but the child was banished as an infant. People assumed the child died in the wilderness.

OEDIPUS. Poor child. I feel his pain, as if it were my own.

TIRESIAS. Funny you should say that.

CREON. We did some checking, and learned the child had been rescued by a shepherd.

OEDIPUS. Oh, good.

CREON. And the child grew up to be about your height, your weight, and according to descriptions, he looked a lot like you.

OEDIPUS. What a coincidence.

CREON. Oedipus, how to put this . . . You know how much I admire you. When you first came to town, it was I who encouraged the people to make you king. And as you know, well, before we made you king, well, we never did a lot of checking into your background.

OEDIPUS. I have led a completely pious life.

CREON. I'm sure it's been very pious, but, well, in between those many, many years of piety, you never murdered anyone, did you?

OEDIPUS. I want to state unequivocally that I have never murdered anyone, depending on a very strict legal definition of murder.

CREON. Did you, say, kill anyone on your journey here?

OEDIPUS. Let me recall my journey. I decided it was time to leave Corinth and seek my fortune in the world. So I decided to journey to Thebes. I stopped off for a visit with the poet Sappho, who I used to think had a crush on me but now I have my doubts, and then I continued on the Thebes Highway. When I got to town of Phokis, I met a hostile band of travelers. One of them said something obnoxious to me, so I clubbed them all to death. Other than that, I didn't kill anyone.

TIRESIAS.   What'd the man say that was so obnoxious?

OEDIPUS.   He called me a mama's boy.

TIRESIAS.   For that you clubbed him to death?

OEDIPUS.   What can I say? He got my goat, and I liked my goat very much.

CREON.   Well, Oedipus, I don't know how to tell you this, but we learned that Laios was clubbed to death in the town of Phokis. And everyone in his party was killed before they got out of Phokis.

OEDIPUS.   You're not suggesting I— I'd never kill a king. It's—It's inappropriate.

CREON.   But he was on a religious pilgrimage.

OEDIPUS.   You mean—

TIRESIAS.   He always dressed down for those things.

OEDIPUS.   Then it's possible . . . I . . .

TIRESIAS.   If the sandal fits.

OEDIPUS.   But Tiresias, you prophesized that Laios would be killed by his own son. I never even met the man before. (CREON *and* TIRESIAS *say nothing.*) This is going to be a real bad news day, isn't it?

CREON.   Oedipus, we discovered Polybus and Merope weren't your real parents. You're an orphan.

OEDIPUS.   Wow, this is a lot to deal with.

TIRESIAS.   We also know that the son of Laios had a birthmark in the shape of an olive on the bottom of his left foot. (CREON *stares at* OEDIPUS's *left foot.*)

OEDIPUS.   Well, we'll just have to search all of Greece until we find out where that child is. Let's start at the end of the kingdom and work our way back.

CREON.   I think we must start here.

OEDIPUS.   But I hate taking off my sandals. It always takes so long to lace them back up.

CREON.   The people will be furious unless you can prove your innocence.

OEDIPUS.   You really think they'll be angry?

TIRESIAS.   Is the earth flat? (OEDIPUS *unlaces his left sandal and lifts his left foot. On the bottom of his foot is a birthmark in the shape of a huge green olive with a red pimento.*)

OEDIPUS.   As you can see, my foot has no such mark.

CREON.   It looks like an olive to me.

OEDIPUS.   Tiresias?

TIRESIAS.   I see nothing.

OEDIPUS.   I'll go with Tiresias.

CREON.   Oedi, admit it. That's an olive.

OEDIPUS.   I prefer to think of it as an unripe eggplant with ketchup on it.

CREON.   It's an olive.

OEDIPUS.   Okay, okay. Technically speaking, it's an olive. I must be the son of Laios, and I've killed my own father in a rage! I did a very bad thing. Now can we drop it?

CREON.   I'm sorry, my lord, but given your public statements on the matter, I'm afraid I can't.

OEDIPUS.   Oh, woe to me and those who dwell in my house! I've slain a king, and I promised the people I'd put the killer to death. I even said "Read my lips." But wait! One thing isn't clear.

TIRESIAS.   Here comes the messy part.

OEDIPUS.   If I'm Laios's son, and if Laios was married to Jocasta, who is now my wife, that means, that means, that means—Laios must've had a previous wife, right?

CREON.   I'm afraid not.

OEDIPUS.   Did he ever fool around on the side?

CREON.   Never.

OEDIPUS.   Sperm donor?

CREON.   Nope.

OEDIPUS.   Are you saying my wife is also, my, my . . .

TIRESIAS.   Bullseye!

OEDIPUS.   Oh my gods! Oh my gods! I've married my mother!! No wonder she always knows what I want for breakfast. Oh my gods! I've murdered my father and married my mother!

TIRESIAS.   It could be worse. You could've murdered your mother and married your father. Then you'd be in real trouble.

OEDIPUS.   Who else knows?

CREON.   Don't worry. Only the staff of the Creon Commission, all of whom are completely trustworthy.

TOWN CRIER (off-stage).   Hear ye, hear ye! The King is shtupping his mother, details at 11!

OEDIPUS.   Oh, wretched day! Oh, cursed life! How can I expunge the evil deed from my soul? There is only one way! I must pluck out my eyes immediately! (OEDIPUS tries to pluck out his eyes, but CREON holds his arms back.)

CREON.   Don't do it!

OEDIPUS.   Let go of me!

TIRESIAS.   Don't do it! You'll have a moment's satisfaction, and a lifetime of wondering if your toga's on straight.

OEDIPUS.   Okay, okay. Let go . . . Does my beloved wife know about this?

CREON.   Not yet.

OEDIPUS.   Oh, how can I break this news to her? How can I tell her without breaking her heart? Her face is too lovely for tears. Her soul is too pure for grief.

JOCASTA (off-stage).   Yoo-hoo, oh, Oedi!

CREON.   The queen approaches.

OEDIPUS (calling out).   In here, snookums! (JOCASTA enters. She's easily thirty or more years older than OEDIPUS. If she happens to be short and speaks with a slight old world inflection, so much the better.)

JOCASTA.   Oedileh, I was wondering if—Oh, am I disturbing something?

(Simultaneously)

OEDIPUS.	CREON.
Yes!	No. We were just leaving.
	Right, Tiresias?

TIRESIAS.   Oh right. It's time for me to practice my musical instrument.

JOCASTA.   Lyre?

TIRESIAS.   No, honestly. (CREON and TIRESIAS exit.)

JOCASTA.   I didn't know you were in a meeting.

OEDIPUS.   It was the most important meeting of my life.

JOCASTA.   More important than when we met and you became my blintz of bliss?

OEDIPUS.   Jocasta, I must tell you something most horrible, worse than the most terrible news you could imagine.

JOCASTA.   You didn't like my brisket last night?

OEDIPUS.   That's not it.

JOCASTA.   What a relief. I was afraid I used too many bay leaves.

OEDIPUS.   Oh, I cannot bear to tell you.

JOCASTA.   My toga's too short, isn't it? You think a woman my age—

OEDIPUS.   Your toga's fine.

JOCASTA.   Are we having problems I'm unaware of in the horizontal department?

OEDIPUS.   No, everything's fine in the— Jocasta, I just received the preliminary report of the Creon Commission.

JOCASTA.   Oh, good. As soon as we name the murderer of Laios and make him drink some seltzer with a shpritz of hemlock, I know your approval rating will bounce right back.

OEDIPUS.   I don't think so.

JOCASTA.   Why not?

OEDIPUS.   Jocasta, my beloved . . .

JOCASTA.   Oedipus, my Corinthian column of love . . .

OEDIPUS.   Jocasta . . . The murderer of your late husband stands before you.

JOCASTA.   You killed Laios?

OEDIPUS.   Yes.

JOCASTA.   Oh, no! Horror of horrors! I suddenly feel like plucking—

OEDIPUS.   Don't pluck your eyes out!

JOCASTA.   No, I feel like plucking a chicken. I'm so stressed. How are we going to put a spin on this so the public doesn't hate you?

OEDIPUS.   Don't you hate me?

JOCASTA.   Nah.

OEDIPUS.   But I murdered your first husband!

JOCASTA.   How can I hate you for something I thought of doing every single day of our marriage?

OEDIPUS.   I thought you loved him.

JOCASTA.   Feh.

OEDIPUS.   You didn't love him?

JOCASTA.   What's to love? The man snored, he had bad breath, and when I think of the things that man made me do . . .

OEDIPUS.   You mean, in the bedroom?

JOCASTA.   Worse, in the kitchen. I'd make him a nice roast chicken, and he'd make me melt some feta cheese on it. The man had no class.

OEDIPUS.   But when I first met you, you were in deep mourning.

JOCASTA.   My press people insisted. I wanted to go sunbathing on Crete.

OEDIPUS.   I didn't know.

JOCASTA.   So you see, my darling, the news is not that bad at all.

OEDIPUS.   But I have not told you all of it, and the news that remains is so horrendous my lips can barely form the shapes to say the misbegotten words.

JOCASTA.   Can it wait? In fifteen minutes, I have my belly dancercize class.

OEDIPUS.   Jocasta, do you remember the prophecy of Tiresias that your husband would be murdered by your son?

JOCASTA.   Yes, also remember he prophesied . . . *The Iliad* would never make it as a novel.

OEDIPUS.   Jocasta, I . . . I cannot tell you. The shame is too deep.

JOCASTA.   Don't feel ashamed, my beloved.

OEDIPUS.   Please say no more. Your words of affection only make it more difficult.

JOCASTA.   Why?

OEDIPUS.   Because . . . Because there's reason to believe that, by some ferocious folly of the fates, you married your own son.

JOCASTA.   So?

OEDIPUS.   Did you hear me? I'm your son!

JOCASTA.   So tell me something I don't know.

OEDIPUS.   You know I'm your son?

JOCASTA.   From the first moment you came into town. I took one look at those eyes, that smile, that—oh, wait a second, you have a little shmutz on your forehead. (JOCASTA *licks her fingers and begins to wipe* OEDI's *forehead.*)

OEDIPUS.   Stop that!

JOCASTA.   I just want you should look presentable.

OEDIPUS.   How could you know I was your son and not tell me?

JOCASTA.   I didn't think it was significant.

OEDIPUS.   You married me!

JOCASTA.   You asked.

OEDIPUS.   I know, but—

JOCASTA.   I would've been happy just dating; you were the one in a hurry. "Marry me, Jocasta, and I'll be the happiest man on earth." What mother could refuse such an offer?

OEDIPUS.   But I killed Dad!

JOCASTA.   So? He never liked you anyway.

OEDIPUS.   He didn't?

JOCASTA.   Once he heard Tiresias's prediction that you were destined to murder him, he insisted you be sent away. I said, "Can't we wait and see? Maybe he'll just wound you a little."

OEDIPUS.   This is the most devastating day of my life.

JOCASTA.   Look, you're here and all is well, so unless there's some more news, I want to get to my belly dancercize class. Next week we start navel exercises, so I need to be in ship shape.

OEDIPUS.   Don't you think we have some issues to discuss?

JOCASTA.   Like what?

OEDIPUS.   Like the fact that we can no longer live as husband and wife.

JOCASTA.   Why not?

OEDIPUS.   Because you're my mother!

JOCASTA.   You say that like it's negative.

OEDIPUS.   Men cannot marry their mothers!

JOCASTA.   None of my friends feel that way.

OEDIPUS.   But—

JOCASTA.   From what I've heard, most men marry women who remind them of their mothers. So I figure why settle for second best when you can have the real thing?

OEDIPUS.   But I can't have sex with you knowing you're my mother.

JOCASTA.   Not even on weekends?

OEDIPUS.   No!

JOCASTA.   I bet you want to do it with Helen, that Trojan slut, don't you?

OEDIPUS.   No.

JOCASTA.   Then who do you want to do it with?

OEDIPUS.   I want to be with a woman to whom I'm not already related.

JOCASTA.   I see. So now the whole family's not good enough to have sex with.

OEDIPUS.   Will you be reasonable?! I'm a public official. I'm a role model.

JOCASTA.   So? Look at the Gods. The immortal Zeus has slept with his half-sister, his quarter-sister, his sixteenth-sister. If our own immortal gods get to boff their relatives, why can't you?

OEDIPUS.   Because you're not just a relative, you're my mother!

JOCASTA.   Must you make everything so complex, Oedipus? . . .(*If the audience moans, . . . she addresses them.*) Hey, it's better than the navel joke, so be grateful.

OEDIPUS.   Jocasta, this abomination against nature cannot continue.

JOCASTA.   Look, Oedileh, I understand this is traumatic for you. But in a healthy marriage, you work through these things.

OEDIPUS.   We don't have a healthy marriage!

JOCASTA.   You want we should see a counselor?

OEDIPUS.   No!

JOCASTA.   Then what are you saying?

OEDIPUS.   Mom . . . I want a divorce. (JOCASTA *breaks into hysterical crying.*)

JOCASTA.   I never thought I'd hear such a thing from my own son.

OEDIPUS.   Oh, wretched day, oh monstrous doom. And I'm sure when Sophocles hears about this, he'll try to turn it into another one of his lurid docudramas.

JOCASTA.   Listen, sweetheart, don't split up something wonderful.

OEDIPUS.   But I must do something so the people . . . will forgive my unfortunate foray into forbidden familial fornication.

JOCASTA.   Call in your advisors. See what they say.

OEDIPUS. (*calling out*).   Get me Creon and Tiresias! (CREON *and* TIRESIAS *enter.*)

CREON.   Yes, my lord?

OEDIPUS.   That was fast.

TIRESIAS.   Well, um, uh, we remembered I left something in your outer office, and—

OEDIPUS.   Have you two been spying on me?

CREON.   We have dedicated our hearts and souls to you. How could you accuse us of such a monstrosity?

TOWN CRIER *(off-stage)*.   Hear ye! Hear ye! Jocasta refuses to grant Oedipus a divorce! Details at 11, followed by a special report and a half-hour of wisecracks by the village idiot.

TIRESIAS.   First thing in the morning, I promise to find the source of these leaks.

OEDIPUS *(temper rising)*.   If I find out either of you—

CREON.   I have been busy, my lord, making some initial inquiries into public response to the crisis.

OEDIPUS.   And what have you learned?

CREON.   The people are confused. 85% of those polled strongly agreed with the statement, "If two people love each other, nothing else in a marriage is important."

JOCASTA.   Aha!

CREON.   But 54% also believe that those who commit incest should be boiled alive in non-virgin olive oil.

OEDIPUS.   Of course, if I didn't know she was my mother, does it still fit the technical legal definition of incest?

CREON.   Oedipus, get real.

OEDIPUS.   And give up a life in politics? Never.

TIRESIAS.   Why don't you start a war? That's always a good distraction.

OEDIPUS.   I'm not going to start a war just to boost my approval rating.

TIRESIAS.   How about a major rescue mission?

OEDIPUS.   No! Oh, what can I do?

CREON.   Well, from my polling, I definitely think that divorce would be unwise. To separate at a time of personal crisis would lose the family vote.

JOCASTA.   Oh, what a happy day this is! Let the ouzo° pour!

CREON.   But we still don't have a solution to the crisis.

OEDIPUS.   As far as I'm concerned, there's only one answer which will prove to the people I show my remorse for my sins.

TIRESIAS.   You don't mean—

OEDIPUS.   I must pluck out my eyes!

JOCASTA.   You do that; don't expect me to lead you to the bathroom in the middle of the night.

OEDIPUS.   I must do it! It's my only chance to earn the forgiveness of my people.

JOCASTA.   Wouldn't a sincere "I'm sorry" suffice?

---

ouzo: aniseed-flavoured Greek liqueur

OEDIPUS.   No! Give me your golden pins. (OEDI *grabs two large pins from* JOCASTA's *toga or hair.*)

CREON.   Oedipus, don't!

OEDIPUS.   Don't try to stop me, I warn you!

TIRESIAS.   You fool!

OEDIPUS.   Get away, or I'll punish you for trying to stop me!

TIRESIAS.   What are you going to do, make me deaf?

OEDIPUS.   Silence! Stand back! *(Raising the pins.)* I declare myself guilty of wretchedness and sin! From this hour forth, I go in darkness! (OEDIPUS *is about to plunge the pins into his eyes, but he stops at the last moment.)* Or: Maybe I'll just cut off the offending organ which caused the sinful deed. That's it! I'll save my sight, but lose my jewels.

JOCASTA.   Oedipus, no!

OEDIPUS.   I declare myself guilty of wretchedness and sin! From this hour forth, I go in eunuchness! (OEDIPUS *is about to plunge the pins into his pelvic region, but stops at the last moment.)* Or: Maybe I'll just cut off my arm. It's a more visible symbol anyway. People will never know if I've really castrated myself, but if I cut off my arm, my left arm, or maybe just one of my fingers, since we're talking symbolic action, anyway!

JOCASTA.   Maybe you could just give some money to charity.

TIRESIAS.   Maybe if you bit your lip and cried in public.

OEDIPUS.   I give up.

CREON.   You know, Oedipus, the more I think about it, the more I wonder, why are we driving ourselves into such a tizzy? You know how fickle the people are. Today they'll want to burn you at the stake; in a week, they'll be obsessed with the latest gossip about the gods.

OEDIPUS.   But—

CREON.   All we need is one good speech and a heartfelt explanation.

OEDIPUS.   But how can we explain such a monstrous deed?

CREON.   Well, it's not like you married your mother on purpose.

JOCASTA.   Oh, no, he'd be too embarrassed to do that.

OEDIPUS.   Jocasta!

TIRESIAS.   I see the future!

OEDIPUS.   What do you see?

TIRESIAS.   The Olympics will never catch on.

OEDIPUS.   Oh, what am I to do? If only the gods would give me a sign.

CREON.   Maybe they have.

OEDIPUS.   They have?

CREON.   Run with me a little. Tiresias saw your fate when you were born; you tried your best not to live it out, but there are powers beyond those of we poor mortals.

OEDIPUS.   I get it! Any efforts to forswear malfeasance were futile; it was the fault of the fates!

CREON.   Exactly.

OEDIPUS.   I'll make a speech where I'll take complete responsibility for my actions, but none of the blame.

TIRESIAS.   Now that's good political thinking.

CREON.   We'll say you wanted to smite out your eyes, but you placed your sense of public duty ahead of your own desires.

OEDIPUS.   That's good.

TIRESIAS (*imagining a headline*).   "Oedipus Rex, Tragic Hero."

OEDIPUS.   I like the sound of that!

CREON.   We'll start working on a speech for you immediately, my lord.

OEDIPUS. It must be brilliant, Creon.

CREON.   It *will* be brilliant.

JOCASTA.   And what will this speech say about us, about me?

OEDIPUS.   Oh . . . right. (JOCASTA *looks at* OEDIPUS. *He's uncomfortable looking back.*)

JOCASTA.   If you really want me to go, I don't want to be a burden. I'll just go. (JOCASTA *begins to leave.*)

OEDIPUS.   Let the speech say . . . I cannot, and will not, apologize for marrying the greatest woman I've ever known!

JOCASTA.   You mean it?

OEDIPUS.   I love you Jocasta, and true love is as Greek as mom, the flag and spinach pie.

JOCASTA.   Oh, Oedi, darling!

OEDIPUS.   Jocasta, my love!

JOCASTA.   My hero!

OEDIPUS.   My dearest!

JOCASTA.   Sweetie! (OEDIPUS *and* JOCASTA *embrace warmly.*)

TOWN CRIER (*off-stage*).   Hear ye, hear ye! Love conquers all! And when I say all, believe me, I mean all! (*The lights fade.*)

QUESTIONS

1. To appreciate this short play you will need to have read Sophocles's *Oedipus Rex* (page 1216). Begin by taking note of the differences in the actions of this version of the Oedipus story.
2. Orloff calls this "a fun play." Identify the sources of "fun" in this parody of a great tragedy. What examples of wordplay do you find (such as the question "Is the earth flat?" or the puns on "lyre/liar" and on "navel exercises . . . ship shape"). How many examples of alliteration of words beginning with "f" do you find?

3. Jocasta is characterized as a stereotypical "Jewish mother," in her vocabulary, her speech patterns, her motherly concerns, and in her observation of kosher food laws that prohibit mixing meat and dairy products in a meal. Besides adding another source of humor, what does this characterization add to the plot?

4. The play has many examples of contemporary American political jargon and thinking (concern for polls and approval ratings, for example). Find as many of them as you can.

5. This play satirizes two distinct things, the seriousness of the great tragedy and modern politics. Which, would you say, is thematically more important here?

William Shakespeare

A Midsummer Night's Dream

Characters

THESEUS, *Duke of Athens*

HIPPOLYTA, *Queen of the Amazons, conquered by Theseus and betrothed to him*

PHILOSTRATE, *Theseus's Master of the Revels*

EGEUS, *an Athenian nobleman, Hermia's father*

HERMIA, *Egeus's daughter in love with Lysander*

HELENA, *a young Athenian in love with Demetrius*

LYSANDER, *a young Athenian in love with Hermia*

DEMETRIUS, *a young Athenian in love with Hermia and Egeus's choice for her*

OBERON, *King of the Fairies*

TITANIA, *Queen of the Fairies*

PUCK (or ROBIN GOODFELLOW), *Oberon's jester and henchman*

PEASEBLOSSOM, COBWEB, MOTH, MUSTARDSEED, *Titania's attendant fairies*

PETER QUINCE, *a carpenter who acts the role of* PROLOGUE

NICK BOTTOM, *a weaver who acts the role of* PYRAMUS

FRANCIS FLUTE, *a bellows mender who acts the role of* THISBE

TOM SNOUT, *a tinker who acts the role of* WALL

A MIDSUMMER NIGHT'S DREAM   There is no recorded first performance, but the play is customarily dated 1594–95. It combines story material from Greek mythology (the marriage of Theseus and Hippolyta), typical confusions, frustrations, and fulfillments of young love (Hermia and Lysander, Helena and Demetrius), folklore about fairies and elves (Titania, Oberon, and Puck), a drama of star-crossed lovers drawn from Latin literature (the Pyramus and Thisbe play-within-a-play), and down-to-earth, uneducated working men familiar to Shakespeare's audiences. While its multiple plots amply illustrate that "the course of true love never did run smooth," it completes the promise of its title by making dreams come true. Mixing references to midsummer festivals and May Day rituals, the play evokes an atmosphere of superstition and celebration, while at the same time displaying the sophistication of courtly behavior. Appropriate to the presence of the mythical Theseus and Hippolyta, the location of the action is "Athens," but there is no attempt to represent an actual time or geographical place.

This play was first printed in a quarto in 1600, and a subsequent quarto in 1619 and the folio of 1623 are based on that first printing. The present text has been edited from the first quarto and adopts some suggestions from several of Shakespeare's earliest editors. For a brief summary of Shakespeare's life, see the note introducing *Othello, the Moor of Venice* (page 1263).

SNUG, *a joiner who acts the role of* LION
ROBIN STARVELING, *a tailor who acts the role of* MOONSHINE
Other FAIRIES *and* ATTENDANTS

SCENE. *Athens and the woods near it.*

ACT 1

SCENE 1. *The court of Theseus.*

Enter THESEUS, HIPPOLYTA, PHILOSTRATE, *and* ATTENDANTS.

THESEUS.   Now, fair Hippolyta, our nuptial hour
  Draws on apace. Four happy days bring in
  Another moon; but, O, methinks, how slow
  This old moon wanes! She lingers° my desires,
  Like to a stepdame or a dowager   5
  Long withering out a young man's revenue.°
HIPPOLYTA.   Four days will quickly steep° themselves in night;
  Four nights will quickly dream away the time;
  And then the moon, like to a silver bow
  New bent in heaven, shall behold the night   10
  Of our solemnities.
THESEUS.   Go, Philostrate,
  Stir up the Athenian youth to merriments.
  Awake the pert and nimble spirit of mirth.
  Turn melancholy forth to funerals:
  The pale companion is not for our pomp.°   15
  (*Exit* PHILOSTRATE.)
  Hippolyta, I wooed thee with my sword
  And won thy love doing thee injuries;
  But I will wed thee in another key,
  With pomp, with triumph, and with reveling.
  (*Enter* EGEUS, *his daughter* HERMIA, LYSANDER, *and* DEMETRIUS.)

EGEUS.   Happy be Theseus, our renownèd Duke!   20
THESEUS.   Thanks, good Egeus. What's the news with thee?
EGEUS.   Full of vexation come I, with complaint
  Against my child, my daughter Hermia.—

---

4. lingers: delays   **5–6. Like . . . revenue:** i.e., like a stepmother or widowed mother
who controls her son's inheritance   **7. steep:** absorb   **15. pomp:** celebration

Stand forth, Demetrius.—My noble lord,
This man hath my consent to marry her.—   25
Stand forth, Lysander.—And, my gracious Duke,
This man hath bewitched the bosom of my child.
Thou, thou Lysander, thou hast given her rhymes
And interchanged love tokens with my child.
Thou hast by moonlight at her window sung   30
With feigning voice verses of feigning° love,
And stol'n the impression of her fantasy°
With bracelets of thy hair, rings, gauds, conceits,
Knacks,° trifles, nosegays, sweetmeats—messengers
Of strong prevailment in° unhardened youth.   35
With cunning hast thou filched my daughter's heart,
Turned her obedience, which is due to me,
To stubborn harshness. And, my gracious Duke,
Be it so° she will not here before Your Grace
Consent to marry with Demetrius,   40
I beg the ancient privilege of Athens:
As she is mine, I may dispose of her,
Which shall be either to this gentleman
Or to her death, according to our law
Immediately° provided in that case.   45

THESEUS.   What say you, Hermia? Be advised, fair maid.
To you your father should be as a god,
One that composed your beauties, yea; and one
To whom you are but as a form in wax
By him imprinted, and within his power   50
To leave the figure or disfigure it.°
Demetrius is a worthy gentleman.

HERMIA.   So is Lysander.

THESEUS.   In himself he is;
But in this kind,° wanting° your father's voice,
The other must be held the worthier.   55

HERMIA.   I would my father looked but with my eyes.

THESEUS.   Rather your eyes must with his judgment look.

HERMIA.   I do entreat Your Grace to pardon me.
I know not by what power I am made bold,

---

31. feigning . . . feigning: The words imply both pretending and yearning.
32. And . . . fantasy: And made a deceitful impression on her imagination
33–34. gauds . . . Knacks: insignificant presents and compliments   35. prevailment
in: influence on   39. Be it so: If   45. Immediately: Expressly   51. leave . . .
or disfigure it: let it be or destroy it   54. kind: case   wanting: without

Nor how it may concern my modesty°   60
In such a presence here to plead my thoughts;
But I beseech Your Grace that I may know
The worst that may befall me in this case
If I refuse to wed Demetrius.
THESEUS.   Either to die the death or to abjure   65
Forever the society of men.
Therefore, fair Hermia, question your desires,
Know of your youth, examine well your blood,
Whether, if you yield not to your father's choice,
You can endure the livery of a nun,   70
For aye° to be in shady cloister mewed,°
To live a barren sister all your life,
Chanting faint hymns to the cold fruitless moon.
Thrice blessèd they that master so their blood
To undergo such maiden pilgrimage;   75
But earthlier° happy is the rose distilled°
Than that which, withering on the virgin thorn,
Grows, lives, and dies in single blessedness.
HERMIA.   So will I grow, so live, so die, my lord,
Ere I will yield my virgin patent° up   80
Unto his lordship, whose unwishèd yoke
My soul consents not to give sovereignty.
THESEUS.   Take time to pause, and by the next new moon—
The sealing day betwixt my love and me
For everlasting bond of fellowship—   85
Upon that day either prepare to die
For disobedience to your father's will,
Or else to wed Demetrius, as he would,
Or on Diana's altar to protest°
For aye austerity and single life.   90
DEMETRIUS.   Relent, sweet Hermia, and, Lysander, yield
Thy crazèd° title to my certain right.
LYSANDER.   You have her father's love, Demetrius;
Let me have Hermia's. Do you marry him.
EGEUS.   Scornful Lysander! True, he hath my love,   95
And what is mine my love shall render him.

---

60. **concern my modesty:** seem to be inappropriate for an unmarried young woman
71. **for aye:** forever   **mewed:** caged up   76. **earthlier:** in worldly terms
distilled: plucked and made into perfume   80. **virgin patent:** the privilege of my
virginity   89. **protest:** swear an oath   92. **crazèd:** flawed

And she is mine, and all my right of her
I do estate° unto Demetrius.
LYSANDER.   I am, my lord, as well derived° as he,
    As well possessed;° my love is more than his;   100
    My fortunes every way as fairly ranked,
    If not with vantage,° as Demetrius';
    And, which is more than all these boasts can be,
    I am beloved of beauteous Hermia.
    Why should not I then prosecute my right?   105
    Demetrius, I'll avouch it to his head,°
    Made love to° Nedar's daughter, Helena,
    And won her soul; and she, sweet lady, dotes,
    Devoutly dotes, dotes in idolatry
    Upon this spotted and inconstant° man.   110
THESEUS.   I must confess that I have heard so much,
    And with Demetrius thought to have spoke thereof;
    But, being overfull of self-affairs,
    My mind did lose it. But, Demetrius, come,
    And come, Egeus, you shall go with me;   115
    I have some private schooling for you both.
    For you, fair Hermia, look you° arm yourself
    To fit your fancies to your father's will,
    Or else the law of Athens yields you up—
    Which by no means we may extenuate—   120
    To death or to a vow of single life.
    Come, my Hippolyta. What cheer, my love?
    Demetrius and Egeus, go along.
    I must employ you in some business
    Against° our nuptial, and confer with you   125
    Of something nearly that° concerns yourselves.
EGEUS.   With duty and desire we follow you.
    (*Exeunt all but* HERMIA *and* LYSANDER.)
LYSANDER.   How now, my love, why is your cheek so pale?
    How chance the roses there do fade so fast?
HERMIA.   Belike° for want of rain, which I could well   130
    Beteem° them from the tempest of my eyes.

---

98. estate: bestow   **99. as well derived:** equal in rank
100. well possessed: equally wealthy   **102. vantage:** superiority   **106. avouch . . .
head:** declare it to his face   **107. Made love to:** Courted, pursued   **110. spotted
and inconstant:** immoral and unfaithful   **117. look you:** take care to
125. Against: In preparation for   **126. nearly that:** that privately
130. Belike: Probably   **131. Beteem:** Send forth

LYSANDER.   Ay me! For aught that I could ever read,
    Could ever hear by tale or history,
    The course of true love never did run smooth;
    But either it was different in blood—°   135
HERMIA.   O cross! Too high to be enthralled to low.
LYSANDER.   Or else misgraffèd in respect of years—°
HERMIA.   O spite! Too old to be engaged to young.
LYSANDER.   Or else it stood upon the choice of friends—°
HERMIA.   O hell, to choose love by another's eyes!   140
LYSANDER.   Or if there were a sympathy in choice,
    War, death, or sickness did lay siege to it,
    Making it momentany° as a sound,
    Swift as a shadow, short as any dream,
    Brief as the lightning in the collied° night   145
    That in a spleen unfolds° both heaven and earth,
    And ere a man hath power to say "Behold!"
    The jaws of darkness do devour it up.
    So quick° bright things come to confusion.°
HERMIA.   If then true lovers have been ever crossed,°   150
    It stands as an edict in destiny.
    Then let us teach our trial patience,
    Because it is a customary cross,
    As due to love as thoughts, and dreams, and sighs,
    Wishes, and tears, poor fancy's followers.°   155
LYSANDER.   A good persuasion. Therefore, hear me, Hermia:
    I have a widow aunt, a dowager
    Of great revenue, and she hath no child.
    From Athens is her house remote seven leagues;
    And she respects me as her only son.   160
    There, gentle Hermia, may I marry thee,
    And to that place the sharp Athenian law
    Cannot pursue us. If thou lovest me, then,
    Steal forth thy father's house tomorrow night;
    And in the wood, a league without° the town,   165
    Where I did meet thee once with Helena
    To do observance to a morn of May,°
    There will I stay for thee.

135. **blood:** hereditary rank   137. **misgraffèd . . . years:** badly matched in age
139. **friends:** kinsmen   143. **momentany:** momentary   145. **collied:** black as
coal   146. **in a spleen unfolds:** reveals in a sudden flash   149. **quick:** living (as
well as quickly)   **confusion:** destruction   150. **ever crossed:** always thwarted
155. **fancy's followers:** love's accompaniments   165. **without:** outside
167. **do . . . May:** observe May Day rituals

HERMIA.   My good Lysander!
    I swear to thee, by Cupid's strongest bow,
    By his best arrow° with the golden head,   170
    By the simplicity of Venus' doves,°
    By that which knitteth souls and prospers loves,
    And by that fire which burned the Carthage queen
    When the false Trojan under sail was seen,°
    By all the vows that ever men have broke,   175
    In number more than ever women spoke,
    In that same place thou hast appointed me
    Tomorrow truly will I meet with thee.
LYSANDER.   Keep promise, love. Look, here comes Helena.
    (*Enter* HELENA.)
HERMIA.   God speed, fair Helena! Whither away?   180
HELENA.   Call you me fair? That "fair" again unsay.
    Demetrius loves your fair.° O happy fair!°
    Your eyes are lodestars,° and your tongue's sweet air°
    More tunable than lark to shepherd's ear
    When wheat is green, when hawthorn buds appear.   185
    Sickness is catching. O, were favor° so,
    Yours would I catch, fair Hermia, ere I go;
    My ear should catch your voice, my eye your eye,
    My tongue should catch your tongue's sweet melody.
    Were the world mine, Demetrius being bated,°   190
    The rest I'd give to be to you translated.
    O, teach me how you look and with what art
    You sway the motion° of Demetrius' heart.
HERMIA.   I frown upon him, yet he loves me still.
HELENA.   O, that your frowns would teach my smiles such skill!   195
HERMIA.   I give him curses, yet he gives me love.
HELENA.   O, that my prayers could such affection move!
HERMIA.   The more I hate, the more he follows me.
HELENA.   The more I love, the more he hateth me.
HERMIA.   His folly, Helena, is no fault of mine.   200
HELENA.   None, but your beauty. Would that fault were mine!

---

170. best arrow: Cupid shot two kinds of arrows, golden-headed to cause love and
leaden-headed to cause hatred.   **171. simplicity . . . doves:** Innocent doves pulled the
chariot of Venus.   **173–74. Carthage . . . seen:** Dido, Queen of Carthage, burned herself to death when she was deserted by her Trojan lover Aeneas.   **182. your fair:** your
beauty   **happy fair:** you fortunate beauty   **183. lodestars:** guiding stars, attracting
Demetrius's look   **air:** music   **186. favor:** appearance, good looks
190. bated: excepted   **193. sway the motion:** control the inclination

HERMIA.   Take comfort. He no more shall see my face.
Lysander and myself will fly this place.
Before the time I did Lysander see
Seemed Athens as a paradise to me.°   205
O, then, what graces in my love do dwell,
That he hath turned a heaven unto a hell?
LYSANDER.   Helen, to you our minds we will unfold.
Tomorrow night, when Phoebe° doth behold
Her silver visage in the watery glass,°   210
Decking with liquid pearl the bladed grass,
A time that lovers' flights doth still° conceal,
Through Athens' gates have we devised to steal.
HERMIA.   And in the wood, where often you and I
Upon faint primrose beds were wont to lie,   215
Emptying our bosoms of their counsel sweet,
There my Lysander and myself shall meet,
And thence from Athens turn away our eyes
To seek new friends and stranger companies.
Farewell, sweet playfellow. Pray thou for us,   220
And good luck grant thee thy Demetrius!
Keep word, Lysander. We must starve our sight
From lovers' food till morrow deep midnight.
LYSANDER.   I will, my Hermia. (*Exit* HERMIA.) Helena, adieu.
As you on him, Demetrius dote on you! (*Exit.*)   225
HELENA.   How happy some o'er other some° can be!
Through Athens I am thought as fair as she.
But what of that? Demetrius thinks not so;
He will not know what all but he do know.
And as he errs, doting on Hermia's eyes,   230
So I, admiring of his qualities.
Things base and vile, holding no quantity,°
Love can transpose to form and dignity.
Love looks not with the eyes, but with the mind,
And therefore is winged Cupid painted blind.   235
Nor hath Love's mind of any judgment taste;°
Wings and no eyes figure° unheedy haste.

204–5. Before . . . me: Before I fell in love with Lysander (and thus ran into all the
problems with my father and Demetrius), Athens was a heavenly place to me.
209. Phoebe: Diana, goddess of chastity, identified with the moon
210. watery glass: reflective surface of lakes, etc.   212. still: always
226. o'er . . . some: in contrast to others   232. holding no quantity: having no shape
or proportion   236. Nor . . . taste: i.e., love has no ability to judge
237. figure: represent

And therefore is Love said to be a child,
Because in choice he is so oft beguiled.
As waggish boys in game themselves forswear,   240
So the boy Love is perjured everywhere.
For ere Demetrius looked on Hermia's eyne,°
He hailed down oaths that he was only mine;
And when this hail some heat from Hermia felt,
So he dissolved, and showers of oaths did melt.   245
I will go tell him of fair Hermia's flight.
Then to the wood will he tomorrow night
Pursue her; and for this intelligence
If I have thanks, it is a dear expense.°
But herein mean I to enrich my pain,   250
To have his sight thither and back again. (*Exit.*)

SCENE 2. *Peter Quince's house in Athens.*

Enter PETER QUINCE *the carpenter,* NICK BOTTOM *the weaver,* SNUG
the joiner, FLUTE *the bellows mender,* SNOUT *the tinker, and* STARVE-
LING *the tailor.*

QUINCE.   Is all our company here?
BOTTOM.   You were best to call them generally,° man by man, according to the scrip.°
QUINCE.   Here is the scroll of every man's name which is thought fit,
through all Athens, to play in our interlude° before the Duke and
the Duchess on his wedding day at night.   6
BOTTOM.   First, good Peter Quince, say what the play treats on, then
read the names of the actors, and so grow to a point.
QUINCE.   Marry,° our play is "The most lamentable comedy and most
cruel death of Pyramus and Thisbe."   10
BOTTOM.   A very good piece of work, I assure you, and a merry. Now,
good Peter Quince, call forth your actors by the scroll. Masters,
spread yourselves.
QUINCE.   Answer as I call you. Nick Bottom, the weaver.
BOTTOM.   Ready. Name what part I am for, and proceed.   15
QUINCE.   You, Nick Bottom, are set down for Pyramus.

---

242. eyne: eyes   **249. dear expense:** something that costs a lot (Either Demetrius
will find it difficult to repay her by thanking her, or she will be paying a lot for the little
thanks she gets.)
2. generally: Bottom means "individually," but uses a word that means the opposite.
3. scrip: scrap of paper (Bottom means "script.")   **5. interlude:** play
9. Marry: Indeed (originally a mild oath, "by the Virgin Mary")

BOTTOM.   What is Pyramus? A lover or a tyrant?

QUINCE.   A lover, that kills himself most gallant for love.

BOTTOM.   That will ask some tears in the true performing of it. If I do
    it, let the audience look to their eyes. I will move storms; I will
    condole° in some measure. To the rest—yet my chief humor° is for
    a tyrant. I could play Ercles° rarely, or a part to tear a cat in, to
    make all split.°   23

> "The raging rocks
> And shivering shocks   25
> Shall break the locks
>   Of prison gates;
> And Phibbus' car°
> Shall shine from far
> And make and mar   30
>   The foolish Fates."

This was lofty! Now name the rest of the players. This is Ercles' vein, a
    tyrant's vein. A lover is more condoling.

QUINCE.   Francis Flute, the bellows mender.

FLUTE.   Here, Peter Quince.   35

QUINCE.   Flute, you must take Thisbe on you.

FLUTE.   What is Thisbe? A wandering knight?

QUINCE.   It is the lady that Pyramus must love.

FLUTE.   Nay, faith, let not me play a woman. I have a beard coming.

QUINCE.   That's all one. You shall play it in a mask, and you may
    speak as small° as you will.   41

BOTTOM.   An° I may hide my face, let me play Thisbe too. I'll speak
    in a monstrous little voice: "Thisne, Thisne!" "Ah, Pyramus, my
    lover dear! Thy Thisbe dear, and lady dear!"

QUINCE.   No, no, you must play Pyramus, and Flute, you Thisbe.   45

BOTTOM.   Well, proceed.

QUINCE.   Robin Starveling, the tailor.

STARVELING.   Here, Peter Quince.

QUINCE.   Robin Starveling, you must play Thisbe's mother. Tom
    Snout, the tinker.   50

SNOUT.   Here, Peter Quince.

---

21. **condole:** express grief   **humor:** temperament, inclination
22. **Ercles:** Hercules, portrayed in old plays as a ranting character   **to tear . . . split:**
to rant and bluster, and cause great commotion in the audience
28. **Phibbus' car:** the chariot of Phoebus the sun god   41. **small:** in a shrill voice
42. **An:** If

QUINCE. You, Pyramus' father; myself, Thisbe's father; Snug, the joiner, you, the lion's part; and I hope here is a play fitted.

SNUG. Have you the lion's part written? Pray you, if it be, give it me, for I am slow of study.   55

QUINCE. You may do it extempore, for it is nothing but roaring.

BOTTOM. Let me play the lion too. I will roar that I will do any man's heart good to hear me. I will roar that I will make the Duke say, "Let him roar again, let him roar again."   59

QUINCE. An you should do it too terribly, you would fright the Duchess and the ladies, that they would shriek; and that were enough to hang us all.   63

ALL. That would hang us, every mother's son.

BOTTOM. I grant you, friends, if you should fright the ladies out of their wits, they would have no more discretion but to hang us; but I will aggravate° my voice so that I will roar you as gently as any sucking dove;° I will roar you an 'twere any nightingale.   67

QUINCE. You can play no part but Pyramus; for Pyramus is a sweet-faced man, a proper° man as one shall see in a summer's day, a most lovely gentlemanlike man. Therefore you must needs play Pyramus.   71

BOTTOM. Well, I will undertake it. What beard were I best to play it in?

QUINCE. Why, what you will.

BOTTOM. I will discharge it in either your straw-color beard, your orange-tawny beard, your purple-in-grain° beard, or your French-crown-color° beard, your perfect yellow.   76

QUINCE. Some of your French crowns° have no hair at all, and then you will play barefaced. But, masters, here are your parts. And I am to entreat you, request you, and desire you to con° them by tomorrow night, and meet me in the palace wood, a mile without the town, by moonlight. There will we rehearse; for if we meet in the city, we shall be dogged with company, and our devices known. In the meantime I will draw a bill of properties, such as our play wants. I pray you, fail me not.   84

BOTTOM. We will meet, and there we may rehearse most obscenely° and courageously. Take pains, be perfect. Adieu.

---

66. aggravate: He intends to mean "moderate."   67. sucking dove: a combination of two symbols of innocence and mildness, "sitting dove" and "sucking lamb"
69. proper: handsome   75. purple-in-grain: dyed a deep red color
75–76. French-crown-color: gold-colored (after the French coin)   77. crowns: heads (gone bald from syphilis, the "French disease")   79. con: learn, memorize
85. obscenely: Bottom probably means "seemly," properly.

QUINCE.   At the Duke's oak we meet.
BOTTOM.   Enough. Hold, or cut bowstrings.° (*Exeunt.*)

ACT 2

SCENE 1. *A wood near Athens.*

Enter from opposite sides of the stage a FAIRY *and* PUCK.

PUCK.   How now, spirit, whither wander you?
FAIRY.   Over hill, over dale,
    Thorough bush, thorough brier,
  Over park, over pale,°
    Thorough flood, thorough fire,   5
  I do wander everywhere,
  Swifter than the moon's sphere;
  And I serve the Fairy Queen,
  To dew her orbs° upon the green.
  The cowslips tall her pensioners° be.   10
  In their gold coats spots you see;
  Those be rubies, fairy favors;
  In those freckles live their savors.
I must go seek some dewdrops here
And hang a pearl in every cowslip's ear.   15
Farewell, thou lob° of spirits; I'll be gone.
Our Queen and all her elves come here anon.
PUCK.   The King doth keep his revels here tonight.
Take heed the Queen come not within his sight.
For Oberon is passing fell and wrath,°   20
Because that she as her attendant hath
A lovely boy, stolen from an Indian king;
She never had so sweet a changeling.°
And jealous Oberon would have the child
Knight of his train, to trace° the forests wild.   25
But she perforce° withholds the lovèd boy,
Crowns him with flowers, and makes him all her joy.
And now they never meet in grove or green,

---

88. **Hold . . . bowstrings:** An unexplained phrase, possibly from archery; Bottom's meaning is apparently "Either we do this well, or we give up on it." (Characteristically, Bottom insists on having the last word.)   **4. pale:** fence   **9. orbs:** "fairy rings," circles of darker grass in a meadow   **10. pensioners:** the Queen's bodyguards   **16. lob:** lout, bumpkin   **20. passing . . . wrath:** extremely fierce in his anger   **23. changeling:** a child stolen by fairies   **25. trace:** roam through   **26. perforce:** by force

> By fountain clear, or spangled starlight sheen,
> But they do square,° that all their elves for fear   30
> Creep into acorn cups and hide them there.

FAIRY.   Either I mistake your shape and making quite,
> Or else you are that shrewd and knavish sprite
> Called Robin Goodfellow. Are not you he
> That frights the maidens of the villagery,   35
> Skim milk,° and sometimes labor in the quern,°
> And bootless° make the breathless huswife churn,
> And sometimes make the drink to bear no barm,°
> Mislead night wanderers, laughing at their harm?
> Those that "Hobgoblin" call you, and "Sweet Puck,"   40
> You do their work, and they shall have good luck.
> Are you not he?

PUCK.   Thou speakest aright;
> I am that merry wanderer of the night.
> I jest to Oberon and make him smile
> When I a fat and bean-fed horse beguile,   45
> Neighing in likeness of a filly foal;
> And sometimes lurk I in a gossip's° bowl
> In very likeness of a roasted crab,°
> And when she drinks, against her lips I bob
> And on her withered dewlap° pour the ale.   50
> The wisest aunt, telling the saddest° tale,
> Sometimes for three-foot stool mistaketh me;
> Then slip I from her bum, down topples she,
> And "Tailor" cries, and falls into a cough;
> And then the whole quire° hold their hips and laugh,   55
> And waxen in their mirth, and neeze,° and swear
> A merrier hour was never wasted there.
> But, room,° fairy! Here comes Oberon.

FAIRY.   And here my mistress. Would that he were gone!
> (*Enter from one side* OBERON, *the King of the Fairies with his train, and
> from the other side* TITANIA, *the Queen of the Fairies with her train.*)

OBERON.   Ill met by moonlight, proud Titania.   60

---

30. **square:** quarrel, argue   36. **Skim milk:** Steal the cream   **quern:** handmill for
grinding grain   37. **bootless:** in vain (because the cream won't turn to butter)
38. **barm:** yeast (preventing the ale from fermenting)   47. **gossip's:** old woman's
48. **crab:** crab apple, added to a drink for flavor   50. **dewlap:** loose skin under the
chin   51. **saddest:** most serious   55. **quire:** company   56. **waxen . . . neeze:**
laugh loudly and sneeze   58. **room:** make room, stand aside

TITANIA.   What, jealous Oberon? Fairies, skip hence.
      I have forsworn his bed and company.
OBERON.   Tarry, rash wanton.° Am not I thy lord?
TITANIA.   Then I must be thy lady; but I know
      When thou hast stolen away from Fairyland   65
      And in the shape of Corin° sat all day,
      Playing on pipes of corn and versing love
      To amorous Phillida.° Why art thou here
      Come from the farthest step of India,
      But that, forsooth, the bouncing Amazon,   70
      Your buskined° mistress and your warrior love,
      To Theseus must be wedded, and you come
      To give their bed joy and prosperity.
OBERON.   How canst thou thus for shame, Titania,
      Glance at my credit° with Hippolyta,   75
      Knowing I know thy love to Theseus?
      Didst not thou lead him through the glimmering night
      From Perigenia,° whom he ravishèd?
      And make him with fair Aegles° break his faith,
      With Ariadne° and Antiopa?°   80
TITANIA.   These are the forgeries of jealousy;
      And never, since the middle summer's spring,
      Met we on hill, in dale, forest, or mead,
      By pavèd fountain or by rushy brook,
      Or in the beachèd margent° of the sea,   85
      To dance our ringlets° to the whistling wind,
      But with thy brawls thou hast disturbed our sport.
      Therefore the winds, piping to us in vain,
      As in revenge, have sucked up from the sea
      Contagious fogs which, falling in the land,   90
      Hath every pelting° river made so proud
      That they have overborne their continents.°
      The ox hath therefore stretched his yoke° in vain,
      The plowman lost his sweat, and the green corn°
      Hath rotted ere his youth attained a beard;   95
      The fold° stands empty in the drownèd field,

63. **wanton:** willful creature   66, 68. **Corin, Phillida:** typical names in pastoral poetry
71. **buskined:** wearing hunting boots   75. **Glance . . . credit:** Insult my good name
78–80. **Perigenia, Aegles, Ariadne, Antiopa:** various amorous conquests of Theseus
85. **margent:** margin   86. **ringlets:** round dances   91. **pelting:** paltry,
insignificant   92. **overborne . . . continents:** flooded over their banks
93. **stretched his yoke:** dragged heavily on its yoke in plowing   94. **corn:** wheat or
other grain   96. **fold:** sheep pen

And crows are fatted with the murrain° flock;
The nine-men's morris° is filled up with mud,
And the quaint mazes° in the wanton° green
For lack of tread are undistinguishable.   100
The human mortals want their winter° here;
No night is now with hymn or carol blessed.
Therefore° the moon, the governess of floods,
Pale in her anger, washes all the air,
That rheumatic diseases do abound.   105
And thorough this distemperature° we see
The seasons alter: hoary-headed frosts
Fall in the fresh lap of the crimson rose,
And on old Hiems'° thin and icy crown
An odorous chaplet of sweet summer buds   110
Is, as in mockery, set. The spring, the summer,
The childing° autumn, angry winter, change
Their wonted liveries,° and the mazèd° world
By their increase now knows not which is which.
And this same progeny of evils comes   115
From our debate, from our dissension.
We are their parents and original.
OBERON.   Do you amend it, then. It lies in you.
Why should Titania cross her Oberon?
I do but beg a little changeling boy   120
To be my henchman.
TITANIA.   Set your heart at rest.
The fairy land buys not the child of me.
His mother was a vot'ress of my order,°
And in the spicèd Indian air by night
Full often hath she gossiped by my side   125
And sat with me on Neptune's yellow sands,
Marking th' embarkèd traders on the flood,°
When we have laughed to see the sails conceive

---

97. **murrain:** killed by the plague   98. **nine-men's morris:** a lawn marked out for playing a game of this name   99. **quaint mazes:** a series of paths laid out for another kind of
game   **wanton:** growing luxuriantly   101. **want their winter:** miss the sports and
festivities of wintertime   103. **Therefore:** As a result (of our quarreling)
106. **distemperature:** natural disturbance   109. **Hiems':** Winter's
112. **childing:** pregnant (ready for harvesting)   113. **wonted liveries:** normal appearances   **mazèd:** confused, amazed   123. **vot'ress . . . order:** devoted follower, as if
a nun worshipping me   127. **embarkèd . . . flood:** merchant ships beginning their
voyage

And grow big-bellied with the wanton wind;
Which she, with pretty and with swimming gait,   130
Following—her womb then rich with my young squire—
Would imitate, and sail upon the land
To fetch me trifles, and return again
As from a voyage, rich with merchandise.
But she, being mortal, of that boy did die;   135
And for her sake do I rear up her boy,
And for her sake I will not part with him.

OBERON.   How long within this wood intend you stay?

TITANIA.   Perchance till after Theseus' wedding day.
If you will patiently dance in our round°   140
And see our moonlight revels, go with us;
If not, shun me, and I will spare° your haunts.

OBERON.   Give me that boy, and I will go with thee.

TITANIA.   Not for thy fairy kingdom. Fairies, away!
We shall chide° downright, if I longer stay.   145
(*Exeunt* TITANIA *with her train.*)

OBERON.   Well, go thy way. Thou shalt not from this grove
Till I torment thee for this injury.
My gentle Puck, come hither. Thou rememb'rest
Since once I sat upon a promontory,
And heard a mermaid on a dolphin's back   150
Uttering such dulcet and harmonious breath°
That the rude sea grew civil at her song,
And certain stars shot madly from their spheres
To hear the sea-maid's music?

PUCK.   I remember.

OBERON.   That very time I saw, but thou couldst not,   155
Flying between the cold moon and the earth
Cupid, all armed. A certain aim he took
At a fair vestal° thronèd by the west,
And loosed his love shaft smartly from his bow
As it should pierce a hundred thousand hearts;   160
But I might see young Cupid's fiery shaft
Quenched in the chaste beams of the watery moon,
And the imperial vot'ress passèd on,
In maiden meditation, fancy-free.°

---

140. round: circle dance   **142. spare:** avoid   **145. chide:** quarrel
151. dulcet . . . breath: sweet and melodious song   **158. fair vestal:** beautiful vestal
virgin (presumably a compliment to Elizabeth, "the Virgin Queen")
164. fancy-free: not touched by sexual desire

Yet marked I where the bolt° of Cupid fell: 165
It fell upon a little western flower,
Before milk-white, now purple with love's wound,
And maidens call it love-in-idleness.°
Fetch me that flower; the herb I showed thee once.
The juice of it on sleeping eyelids laid   170
Will make or man or° woman madly dote
Upon the next live creature that it sees.
Fetch me this herb, and be thou here again
Ere the leviathan° can swim a league.
PUCK.   I'll put a girdle round about the earth°   175
In forty minutes. (*Exit.*)
OBERON.   Having once this juice,
I'll watch Titania when she is asleep
And drop the liquor of it in her eyes.
The next thing then she waking looks upon,
Be it on lion, bear, or wolf, or bull,   180
On meddling monkey, or on busy ape,
She shall pursue it with the soul of love.
And ere I take this charm from off her sight,
As I can take it with another herb,
I'll make her render up her page to me.   185
But who comes here? I am invisible,
And I will overhear their conference.
(*Enter* DEMETRIUS *followed by* HELENA.)
DEMETRIUS.   I love thee not; therefore pursue me not.
Where is Lysander and fair Hermia?
The one I'll slay; the other slayeth me.   190
Thou toldst me they were stol'n unto this wood;
And here am I, and wode° within this wood;
Because I cannot meet my Hermia.
Hence, get thee gone, and follow me no more.
HELENA.   You draw me, you hardhearted adamant!°   195
But yet you draw not iron, for my heart
Is true as steel. Leave you° your power to draw,
And I shall have no power to follow you.

---

165. bolt: arrow   **168. love-in-idleness:** popular name for the pansy   **171. or . . .
or:** either . . . or   **174. leviathan:** whale   **175. put . . . earth:** fly around the
world   **192. wode:** frantic, insane   **195. adamant:** a very hard magnetic stone
197. Leave you: If you will give up

DEMETRIUS.   Do I entice you? Do I speak you fair?°
    Or rather do I not in plainest truth   200
    Tell you I do not nor I cannot love you?
HELENA.   And even for that do I love you the more.
    I am your spaniel; and, Demetrius,
    The more you beat me I will fawn on you.
    Use me but as your spaniel, spurn me, strike me,   205
    Neglect me, lose me, only give me leave,
    Unworthy as I am, to follow you.
    What worser place can I beg in your love—
    And yet a place of high respect with me—
    Than to be usèd as you use your dog?   210
DEMETRIUS.   Tempt not too much the hatred of my spirit,
    For I am sick when I do look on thee.
HELENA.   And I am sick when I look not on you.
DEMETRIUS.   You do impeach° your modesty too much
    To leave the city and commit yourself   215
    Into the hands of one that loves you not,
    To trust the opportunity of night
    And the ill counsel of a desert° place
    With the rich worth of your virginity.
HELENA.   Your virtue is my privilege.° For that   220
    It is not night when I do see your face,
    Therefore I think I am not in the night;
    Nor doth this wood lack worlds of company,
    For you, in my respect,° are all the world.
    Then how can it be said I am alone   225
    When all the world is here to look on me?
DEMETRIUS.   I'll run from thee and hide me in the brakes,°
    And leave thee to the mercy of wild beasts.
HELENA.   The wildest hath not such a heart as you.
    Run when you will. The story shall be changed: 230
    Apollo flies and Daphne holds the chase,°
    The dove pursues the griffin,° the mild hind°
    Makes speed to catch the tiger—bootless° speed,
    When cowardice pursues and valor flies!

---

199. **speak you fair:** speak kindly to you   214. **impeach:** discredit, call into question
218. **desert:** wild and uninhabited   220. **Your . . . privilege:** Your goodness will defend me.   224. **in my respect:** to me   227. **brakes:** bushes, thickets
231. **Apollo . . . chase:** Reversing the mythical story, the pursuer and pursued change
roles.   232. **griffin:** a mythical monster, half-eagle and half-lion   **hind:** female
deer   233. **bootless:** fruitless

DEMETRIUS.   I will not stay thy questions.° Let me go!   235
    Or if thou follow me, do not believe
    But I shall do thee mischief in the wood.
HELENA.   Ay, in the temple, in the town, the field,
    You do me mischief. Fie, Demetrius!
    Your wrongs do set a scandal on my sex.   240
    We cannot fight for love, as men may do;
    We should be wooed and were not made to woo.
    (*Exit* DEMETRIUS.)
    I'll follow thee and make a heaven of hell,
    To die upon the hand I love so well. (*Exit.*)
OBERON.   Fare thee well, nymph. Ere he do leave this grove   245
    Thou shalt fly him, and he shall seek thy love.
    (*Enter* PUCK.)
    Hast thou the flower there? Welcome, wanderer.
PUCK.   Ay, there it is.
OBERON.   I pray thee, give it me.
    I know a bank where the wild thyme blows,°
    Where oxlips and the nodding violet grows,   250
    Quite overcanopied with luscious woodbine,
    With sweet muskroses and with eglantine.
    There sleeps Titania sometime of the night,
    Lulled in these flowers with dances and delight;
    And there the snake throws her enameled skin,°   255
    Weed° wide enough to wrap a fairy in.
    And with the juice of this I'll streak her eyes
    And make her full of hateful fantasies.
    Take thou some of it, and seek through this grove.
    A sweet Athenian lady is in love   260
    With a disdainful youth. Anoint his eyes,
    But do it when the next thing he espies
    May be the lady. Thou shalt know the man
    By the Athenian garments he hath on.
    Effect it with some care, that he may prove   265
    More fond° on her than she upon her love;
    And look thou meet me ere the first cock crow.
PUCK.   Fear not, my lord, your servant shall do so. (*Exeunt.*)

---

235. stay thy questions: listen to your arguments   **249. blows:** blooms
255. throws . . . skin: sheds its shiny skin   **256. Weed:** Garment
266. fond: foolishly doting

SCENE 2. *Another part of the wood.*

Enter TITANIA *with her train.*

TITANIA.   Come, now a roundel° and a fairy song;
　　　Then, for the third part of a minute, hence,
　　　Some to kill cankers° in the muskrose buds,
　　　Some war with reremice° for their leathern wings
　　　To make my small elves coats, and some keep back　　　　　　5
　　　The clamorous owl, that nightly hoots and wonders
　　　At our quaint spirits. Sing me now asleep,
　　　Then to your offices, and let me rest.
　　　(FAIRIES *sing and dance.*)
FIRST FAIRY.   You spotted snakes with double tongue,
　　　　Thorny hedgehogs, be not seen;　　　　　　　　　　　10
　　　Newts and blindworms,° do no wrong;
　　　　Come not near our Fairy Queen!
CHORUS (*dancing*).   Philomel,° with melody
　　　　Sing in our sweet lullaby;
　　　Lulla, lulla, lullaby, lulla, lulla, lullaby.　　　　　　　　15
　　　　Never harm
　　　　Nor spell nor charm
　　　Come our lovely lady nigh.
　　　So good night, with lullaby.
FIRST FAIRY.   Weaving spiders, come not here;　　　　　　　20
　　　　Hence, you long-legged spinners, hence!
　　　Beetles black, approach not near;
　　　　Worm nor snail, do no offense.
CHORUS (*dancing*).   Philomel, with melody
　　　　Sing in our sweet lullaby;　　　　　　　　　　　　　25
　　　Lulla, lulla, lullaby, lulla, lulla, lullaby.
　　　　Never harm
　　　　Nor spell nor charm
　　　Come our lovely lady nigh.
　　　So good night, with lullaby.　　　　　　　　　　　　　30
　　　(TITANIA *sleeps.*)
SECOND FAIRY.   Hence, away! Now all is well.
　　　One aloof stand sentinel.

---

1. roundel: round dance   **3. cankers:** cankerworms or other parasites
4. reremice: bats   **11. Newts . . . blindworms:** varieties of lizard erroneously considered venomous   **13. Philomel:** the nightingale, so called from a tale in Ovid's
Metamorphoses

(*Exeunt* FAIRIES, *leaving one as sentinel. Enter* OBERON, *who squeezes the flower on* TITANIA's *eyelids.*)

OBERON.   What thou seest when thou dost wake,
    Do it for thy true love take;
    Love and languish for his sake.   35
    Be it ounce,° or cat, or bear,
    Pard,° or boar with bristled hair,
    In thy eye that shall appear
    When thou wak'st, it is thy dear.
    Wake when some vile thing is near. (*Exit.*)   40
    (*Enter* LYSANDER *and* HERMIA.)

LYSANDER.   Fair love, you faint with wandering in the wood;
    And to speak truth, I have forgot our way.
    We'll rest us, Hermia, if you think it good,
    And tarry for the comfort of the day.

HERMIA.   Be it so, Lysander. Find you out a bed,   45
    For I upon this bank will rest my head.

LYSANDER.   One turf shall serve as pillow for us both;
    One heart, one bed, two bosoms, and one troth.°

HERMIA.   Nay, good Lysander, for my sake, my dear,
    Lie further off yet. Do not lie so near.   50

LYSANDER.   O, take the sense,° sweet, of my innocence!
    Love takes the meaning in love's conference.°
    I mean that my heart unto yours is knit,
    So that but one heart we can make of it;
    Two bosoms interchainèd with an oath—   55
    So then two bosoms and a single troth.
    Then by your side no bed-room me deny,
    For lying so, Hermia, I do not lie.

HERMIA   Lysander riddles very prettily.
    Now much beshrew° my manners and my pride   60
    If Hermia meant to say Lysander lied.
    But, gentle friend, for love and courtesy
    Lie further off, in human modesty.
    Such separation as may well be said
    Becomes a virtuous bachelor and a maid,   65
    So far be distant, and good night, sweet friend.
    Thy love ne'er alter till thy sweet life end!

---

36. ounce: lynx   **37. Pard:** Leopard   **48. troth:** pledged faithfulness
51. take the sense: understand the meaning   **52. Love . . . conference:** Lovers can
understand each other.   **60. beshrew:** condemn

LYSANDER.   Amen, amen, to that fair prayer, say I,
    And then end life when I end loyalty!
    Here is my bed. Sleep give thee all his rest!   70
HERMIA.   With half that wish the wisher's eyes be pressed!
    (*They sleep apart. Enter* PUCK.)
PUCK.   Through the forest have I gone,
    But Athenian found I none
    On whose eyes I might approve°
    This flower's force in stirring love.   75
    Night and silence.—Who is here?
    Weeds of Athens he doth wear.
    This is he, my master said,
    Despisèd the Athenian maid;
    And here the maiden, sleeping sound,   80
    On the dank and dirty ground.
    Pretty soul, she durst not lie
    Near this lack-love, this kill-courtesy.
    Churl, upon thy eyes I throw
    All the power this charm doth owe.°   85
    When thou wak'st, let love forbid
    Sleep his seat on thy eyelid.
    So awake when I am gone,
    For I must now to Oberon. (*Exit.*)
    (*Enter* DEMETRIUS *running, pursued by* HELENA.)
HELENA.   Stay, though thou kill me, sweet Demetrius!   90
DEMETRIUS.   I charge thee, hence, and do not haunt me thus.
HELENA.   O, wilt thou darkling° leave me? Do not so.
DEMETRIUS.   Stay, on thy peril! I alone will go. (*Exit.*)
HELENA.   O, I am out of breath in this fond chase!
    The more my prayer, the lesser is my grace.°   95
    Happy is Hermia, wheresoe'er she lies,
    For she hath blessèd and attractive eyes.
    How came her eyes so bright? Not with salt tears;
    If so, my eyes are oftener washed than hers.
    No, no, I am as ugly as a bear,   100
    For beasts that meet me run away for fear.
    Therefore no marvel though Demetrius
    Do, as a monster,° fly my presence thus.
    What wicked and dissembling glass of mine

74. **approve:** test   85. **owe:** own   92. **darkling:** in the dark
95. **my grace:** the favor he gives me   103. **as a monster:** as if I were a monster

Made me compare with Hermia's sphery eyne?°   105
But who is here? Lysander, on the ground?
Dead, or asleep? I see no blood, no wound.
Lysander, if you live, good sir, awake!
LYSANDER (*awaking*).   And run through fire I will for thy sweet sake.
Transparent° Helena! Nature shows art,   110
That through thy bosom makes me see thy heart.
Where is Demetrius? O, how fit a word
Is that vile name to perish on my sword!
HELENA.   Do not say so, Lysander; say not so.
What though he love your Hermia? Lord, what though?   115
Yet Hermia still loves you. Then be content.
LYSANDER.   Content with Hermia? No! I do repent
The tedious minutes I with her have spent.
Not Hermia but Helena I love.
Who will not change a raven for a dove?   120
The will° of man is by his reason swayed,
And reason says you are the worthier maid.
Things growing are not ripe until their season;
So I, being young, till now ripe not to reason.
And, touching now the point of human skill,°   125
Reason becomes the marshal to my will
And leads me to your eyes, where I o'erlook°
Love's stories written in love's richest book.
HELENA.   Wherefore° was I to this keen mockery born?
When at your hands did I deserve this scorn?   130
Is 't not enough, is 't not enough, young man,
That I did never—no, nor never can—
Deserve a sweet look from Demetrius' eye,
But you must flout my insufficiency?
Good troth, you do me wrong, good sooth, you do,   135
In such disdainful manner me to woo.
But fare you well. Perforce I must confess
I thought you lord of more true gentleness.°
O, that a lady, of one man refused,
Should of° another therefore be abused! (*Exit.*)   140
LYSANDER.   She sees not Hermia. Hermia, sleep thou there,
And never mayst thou come Lysander near!
For as a surfeit of the sweetest things

---

105. **sphery eyne:** starlike eyes   110. **Transparent:** Radiant, honest, and clear
121. **will:** passion   125. **touching . . . skill:** now having reached full judgment
127. **o'erlook:** read   129. **Wherefore:** Why   138. **lord . . . gentleness:** a more
courteous man   139–40. **of . . . of:** by . . . by (also in line 148)

The deepest loathing to the stomach brings,
Or as the heresies that men do leave   145
Are hated most of those they did deceive,°
So thou, my surfeit and my heresy,
Of all be hated, but the most of me!
And, all my powers, address your love and might
To honor Helen and to be her knight! (*Exit.*)   150
HERMIA (*awaking*).   Help me, Lysander, help me! Do thy best
To pluck this crawling serpent from my breast!
Ay me, for pity! What a dream was here!
Lysander, look how I do quake with fear.
Methought a serpent ate my heart away,   155
And you sat smiling at his cruel prey.
Lysander! What, removed? Lysander! Lord!
What, out of hearing? Gone? No sound, no word?
Alack, where are you? Speak, an if you hear;
Speak, of all loves!° I swoon almost with fear.   160
No? Then I well perceive you are not nigh.
Either death, or you, I'll find immediately.
(*Exit.* TITANIA *remains, asleep.*)

ACT 3

SCENE 1. *The scene continues, with* TITANIA *still sleeping.*

Enter BOTTOM, QUINCE, SNOUT, STARVELING, FLUTE, *and* SNUG.

BOTTOM.   Are we all met?
QUINCE.   Pat, pat; and here's a marvelous convenient place for our
    rehearsal. This green plot shall be our stage, this hawthorn brake
    our tiring-house,° and we will do it in action as we will do it before
    the Duke.   5
BOTTOM.   Peter Quince?
QUINCE.   What sayest thou, bully° Bottom?
BOTTOM.   There are things in this comedy of Pyramus and Thisbe that
    will never please. First, Pyramus must draw a sword to kill himself,
    which the ladies cannot abide. How answer you that?   10
SNOUT.   By 'r lakin, a parlous fear.°
STARVELING.   I believe we must leave the killing out, when all is done.

145–46. as . . . deceive: as men who give up heretical beliefs are most extreme in
denouncing their former heresies   160. of all loves: for the sake of love
3–4. brake . . . tiring-house: thicket our dressing room   7. bully: admirable fellow
11. By . . . fear: By the Virgin, a fearful danger

BOTTOM.   Not a whit. I have a device to make all well. Write me° a prologue, and let the prologue seem to say, we will do no harm with
our swords, and that Pyramus is not killed indeed; and for the more
better assurance, tell them that I, Pyramus, am not Pyramus but Bottom the weaver. This will put them out of fear.   17
QUINCE.   Well, we will have such a prologue, and it shall be written
in eight and six.°
BOTTOM.   No, make it two more: let it be written in eight and eight.°
SNOUT.   Will not the ladies be afeard of the lion?   21
STARVELING.   I fear it, I promise you.
BOTTOM.   Masters, you ought to consider with yourself, to bring in—
God shield us!—a lion among ladies is a most dreadful thing. For
there is not a more fearful wildfowl than your lion living, and we
ought to look to 't.   26
SNOUT.   Therefore another prologue must tell he is not a lion.
BOTTOM.   Nay, you must name his name, and half his face must be
seen through the lion's neck, and he himself must speak through,
saying thus or to the same defect:° "Ladies," or "Fair ladies, I would
wish you," or "I would request you," or "I would entreat you, not to
fear, not to tremble; my life for yours.° If you think I come hither
as a lion, it were pity of my life. No, I am no such thing; I am a man
as other men are." And there indeed let him name his name, and
tell them plainly he is Snug the joiner.   35
QUINCE.   Well, it shall be so. But there is two hard things: that is, to
bring the moonlight into a chamber; for, you know, Pyramus and
Thisbe meet by moonlight.
SNOUT.   Doth the moon shine that night we play our play?
BOTTOM.   A calendar, a calendar! Look in the almanac. Find out
moonshine, find out moonshine.   41
QUINCE.   Yes, it doth shine that night.
BOTTOM.   Why then may you leave a casement of the great chamber
window where we play open, and the moon may shine in at the
casement.   45
QUINCE.   Ay, or else one must come in with a bush of thorns and a
lantern° and say he comes to disfigure° or to present the person of
Moonshine. Then there is another thing: we must have a wall in

---

13. Write me: I suggest you write ("me" does not imply "for me to speak")
19–20. eight and six, eight and eight: refers to numbers of syllables per line in poetry
30. defect: he means "effect"   **32. my . . . yours:** I'd give my life rather than see you
harmed.   **46–47. bush . . . lantern:** In popular lore, the "man in the moon" was not
the round face we see there but a man carrying a lantern and a bundle of thorn branches,
accompanied by his dog.   **47. disfigure:** he means "figure," represent

the great chamber; for Pyramus and Thisbe, says the story, did talk
through the chink of a wall.   50

SNOUT.   You can never bring in a wall. What say you, Bottom?

BOTTOM.   Some man or other must present Wall. And let him have
some plaster, or some loam,° or some roughcast° about him, to signify wall; or let him hold his fingers thus, and through that cranny
shall Pyramus and Thisbe whisper.   55

QUINCE.   If that may be, then all is well. Come, sit down, every
mother's son, and rehearse your parts. Pyramus, you begin. When
you have spoken your speech, enter into that brake, and so everyone according to his cue. (*Enter* PUCK.)

PUCK (*aside*).   What hempen homespuns° have we swaggering here
So near the cradle of the Fairy Queen?   61
What, a play toward?° I'll be an auditor;
An actor, too, perhaps, if I see cause.

QUINCE.   Speak, Pyramus. Thisbe, stand forth.

BOTTOM (*as Pyramus*).   "Thisbe, the flowers of odious savors sweet—"

QUINCE.   Odors, odors.   66

BOTTOM.   "—Odors savors sweet;
    So hath thy breath, my dearest Thisbe dear.
    But hark, a voice! Stay thou but here awhile,
    And by and by I will to thee appear." (*Exit.*)   70

PUCK.   A stranger Pyramus than e'er played here. (*Exit.*)

FLUTE.   Must I speak now?

QUINCE.   Ay, marry, must you; for you must understand he goes but to
see a noise that he heard, and is to come again.

FLUTE (*as Thisbe*).   "Most radiant Pyramus, most lily-white of hue,
    Of color like the red rose on triumphant brier,   76
Most brisky juvenal° and eke° most lovely Jew,°
    As true as truest horse that yet would never tire.
I'll meet thee, Pyramus, at Ninny's tomb."

QUINCE.   "Ninus'° tomb," man. Why, you must not speak that yet.
That you answer to Pyramus. You speak all your part at once, cues
and all. Pyramus, enter. Your cue is past; it is "never tire."   82

FLUTE.   O—"As true as truest horse, that yet would never tire."

(*Enter* PUCK, *and* BOTTOM *wearing an ass's head.*)

BOTTOM.   "If I were fair, Thisbe, I were only thine."

---

53. loam, roughcast: materials used to plaster walls   **60. hempen homespuns:** men
who dress in coarse, homemade fabrics—poor louts   **62. toward:** being prepared
77. brisky juvenal: lively young man   **eke:** also   **Jew:** a meaningless echo of the
first syllable of "juvenal"   **80. Ninus:** mythical founder of Ninevah

QUINCE.   O, monstrous! O, strange! We are haunted!   85
    Pray, masters! Fly, masters! Help!
    (*Exeunt* QUINCE, SNOUT, STARVELING, FLUTE, *and* SNUG.)
PUCK.   I'll follow you, I'll lead you about a round,
        Thorough bog, thorough bush, thorough brake,
            thorough brier.
    Sometimes a horse I'll be, sometimes a hound,
        A hog, a headless bear, sometimes a fire;   90
    And neigh, and bark, and grunt, and roar, and burn,
    Like horse, hound, hog, bear, fire, at every turn. (*Exit.*)
BOTTOM.   Why do they run away? This is a knavery of them to make
    me afeard.
    (*Enter* SNOUT.)
SNOUT.   O Bottom, thou art changed! What do I see on thee?   95
BOTTOM.   What do you see? You see an ass head of your own, do you?
    (*Exit* SNOUT. *Enter* QUINCE.)
QUINCE.   Bless thee, Bottom, bless thee! Thou art translated.° (*Exit.*)
BOTTOM.   I see their knavery. This is to make an ass of me, to fright
    me, if they could. But I will not stir from this place, do what they
    can. I will walk up and down here, and will sing, that they shall
    hear I am not afraid (*he sings*):   101
            The ouzel° cock so black of hue,
                With orange-tawny bill,
            The throstle° with his note so true,
                The wren with little quill—°   105
TITANIA (*awaking*).   What angel wakes me from my flowery bed?
BOTTOM (*sings*).
            The finch, the sparrow, and the lark,
                The plainsong° cuckoo gray,
            Whose note full many a man doth mark,
                And dares not answer nay—°   110
    For indeed, who would set his wit to° so foolish a bird? Who would
    give a bird the lie,° though he cry "cuckoo" never so?
TITANIA.   I pray thee, gentle mortal, sing again.
    Mine ear is much enamored of thy note;
    So is mine eye enthrallèd to thy shape;   115

---

97. **translated:** transformed   102. **ousel:** blackbird (in England, a songbird)
104. **throstle:** thrush   105. **little quill:** piping song   108. **plainsong:** a simple,
repetitive melody   110. **dares . . . nay:** cannot deny that he is a cuckold (which the
song of the cuckoo seems to reveal)   111. **set his wit to:** attempt to answer
112. **give . . . lie:** call the bird a liar

And thy fair virtue's force° perforce doth move me
On the first view to say, to swear, I love thee.

BOTTOM.   Methinks, mistress, you should have little reason for that.
And yet to say the truth, reason and love keep little company together nowadays—the more the pity that some honest neighbors
will not make them friends. Nay, I can gleek° upon occasion.   121

TITANIA.   Thou art as wise as thou art beautiful.

BOTTOM.   Not so, neither. But if I had wit enough to get out of this
wood, I have enough to serve mine own turn.°

TITANIA.   Out of this wood do not desire to go.   125
Thou shalt remain here, whether thou wilt or no.
I am a spirit of no common rate.°
The summer still doth tend upon my state,°
And I do love thee. Therefore, go with me.
I'll give thee fairies to attend on thee,   130
And they shall fetch thee jewels from the deep,
And sing while thou on pressèd flowers dost sleep.
And I will purge thy mortal grossness so
That thou shalt like an airy spirit go.
Peaseblossom, Cobweb, Moth, and Mustardseed!   135
(Enter PEASEBLOSSOM, COBWEB, MOTH,° and MUSTARDSEED.)

PEASEBLOSSOM.   Ready.

COBWEB.   And I.

MOTH.   And I.

MUSTARDSEED.   And I.

ALL.   Where shall we go?

TITANIA.   Be kind and courteous to this gentleman.
Hop in his walks and gambol in his eyes;
Feed him with apricots and dewberries,   140
With purple grapes, green figs, and mulberries;
The honey bags steal from the humble-bees,
And for night tapers crop their waxen thighs
And light them at the fiery glowworms' eyes,
To have my love to bed and to arise;   145
And pluck the wings from painted butterflies
To fan the moonbeams from his sleeping eyes.
Nod to him, elves, and do him courtesies.

---

116. fair . . . force: the power of your beauty   121. gleek: make a witty joke
124. serve . . . turn: take care of myself   127. rate: rank
128. still . . . state: always attends upon me   136 s.d. MOTH: Pronounced like
"mote," the word may refer to a speck or to the insect.

PEASEBLOSSOM. Hail, mortal!

COBWEB. Hail!   150

MOTH. Hail!

MUSTARDSEED. Hail!

BOTTOM. I cry your worships mercy,° heartily. I beseech your worship's name.

COBWEB. Cobweb.   155

BOTTOM. I shall desire you of more acquaintance, good Master Cobweb. If I cut my finger,° I shall make bold with you.—Your name, honest gentleman?

PEASEBLOSSOM. Peaseblossom.

BOTTOM. I pray you, commend me to Mistress Squash,° your mother, and to Master Peascod,° your father. Good Master Peaseblossom, I shall desire you of more acquaintance too.—Your name, I beseech you, sir?   163

MUSTARDSEED. Mustardseed.

BOTTOM. Good Master Mustardseed, I know your patience well. That same cowardly, giantlike ox-beef° hath devoured many a gentleman of your house. I promise you, your kindred hath made my eyes water ere now. I desire you of more acquaintance, good Master Mustardseed.

TITANIA. Come wait upon him; lead him to my bower.   170
    The moon methinks looks with a watery eye;
And when she weeps, weeps° every little flower,
    Lamenting some enforcèd° chastity.
    Tie up my lover's tongue; bring him silently.
(*Exeunt.*)

SCENE 2. *The scene continues.*

Enter OBERON.

OBERON. I wonder if Titania be awaked,
    Then, what it was that next came in her eye,
    Which she must dote on in extremity. (*Enter* PUCK.)
    Here comes my messenger. How now, mad spirit?
    What night-rule° now about this haunted° grove?   5

---

153. cry . . . mercy: I beg pardon of your worships (assuming the Fairies to be important dignitaries) for asking presumptuous questions.   **157. cut my finger:** cobwebs were used to stop bleeding from a cut   **160, 161. Squash, Peascod:** names for an unripe and a ripe pea pod   **166. ox-beef:** mustard is a common condiment for beef
172. weeps: causes dew   **173. enforcèd:** violated   **5. night-rule:** mischief, night's sport   **haunted:** much visited

PUCK.   My mistress with a monster is in love.
     Near to her close and consecrated bower,
     While she was in her dull and sleeping hour,
     A crew of patches,° rude mechanicals,°
     That work for bread upon Athenian stalls,°   10
     Were met together to rehearse a play
     Intended for great Theseus' nuptial day.
     The shallowest thickskin of that barren° sort,
     Who Pyramus presented, in their sport
     Forsook his scene and entered in a brake.   15
     When I did him at this advantage take,
     An ass's noll° I fixèd on his head.
     Anon his Thisbe must be answerèd,
     And forth my mimic° comes. When they him spy,
     As wild geese that the creeping fowler° eye,   20
     Or russet-pated choughs,° many in sort,
     Rising and cawing at the gun's report,
     Sever themselves and madly sweep the sky,
     So, at his sight, away his fellows fly;
     And, at our stamp, here o'er and o'er one falls;   25
     He "Murder!" cries and help from Athens calls.
     Their sense thus weak, lost with their fears thus strong,
     Made senseless things begin to do them wrong,
     For briers and thorns at their apparel snatch;
     Some, sleeves—some, hats; from yielders all things catch.   30
     I led them on in this distracted fear
     And left sweet Pyramus translated there,
     When in that moment, so it came to pass,
     Titania waked and straightway loved an ass.
OBERON.   This falls out better than I could devise.   35
     But hast thou yet latched° the Athenian's eyes
     With the love juice, as I did bid thee do?
PUCK.   I took him sleeping—that is finished too—
     And the Athenian woman by his side,
     That, when he waked, of force° she must be eyed.   40
     (Enter HERMIA followed by DEMETRIUS.)
OBERON.   Stand close. This is the same Athenian.
PUCK.   This is the woman, but not this the man.

9. **patches:** clowns   **mechanicals:** workingmen   10. **stalls:** market shops
13. **barren:** empty-headed   17. **noll:** head   19. **mimic:** actor
20. **fowler:** bird hunter   21. **russet-pated choughs:** gray-headed crow-like birds
36. **latched:** caught, snared   40. **of force:** necessarily

DEMETRIUS.   O, why rebuke you him that loves you so?
Lay breath so bitter on your bitter foe.
HERMIA.   Now I but chide, but I should use thee worse,   45
For thou, I fear, hast given me cause to curse.
If thou hast slain Lysander in his sleep,
Being o'er shoes in blood, plunge in the deep
And kill me too.
The sun was not so true unto the day   50
As he to me. Would he have stolen away
From sleeping Hermia? I'll believe as soon
This whole earth may be bored, and that the moon
May through the center creep, and so displease
Her brother's noontide with th' Antipodes.°   55
It cannot be but thou hast murdered him,
So should a murderer look, so dead,° so grim.
DEMETRIUS.   So should the murdered look, and so should I,
Pierced through the heart with your stern cruelty.
Yet you, the murderer, look as bright, as clear   60
As yonder Venus in her glimmering sphere.
HERMIA.   What's this to my Lysander? Where is he?
Ah, good Demetrius, wilt thou give him me?
DEMETRIUS.   I had rather give his carcass to my hounds.
HERMIA.   Out, dog! Out, cur! Thou driv'st me past the bounds   65
Of maiden's patience. Hast thou slain him, then?
Henceforth be never numbered among men.
O, once tell true, tell true, even for my sake!
Durst thou have looked upon him being awake?
And hast thou killed him sleeping? O brave touch!   70
Could not a worm, an adder, do so much?
An adder did it; for with doubler° tongue
Than thine, thou serpent, never adder stung.
DEMETRIUS.   You spend your passion on a misprised° mood.
I am not guilty of Lysander's blood,   75
Nor is he dead, for aught that I can tell.
HERMIA.   I pray thee, tell me then that he is well.
DEMETRIUS.   And if I could, what should I get therefor?
HERMIA.   A privilege never to see me more.
And from thy hated presence part I so.   80
See me no more, whether he be dead or no. (*Exit.*)

---

55. Her . . . Antipodes: The sun shining on the opposite side of the earth
57. dead: deadly   **72. doubler:** twice as deceitful   **74. misprised:** mistaken

DEMETRIUS.   There is no following her in this fierce vein,
        Here therefore for a while I will remain.
        So sorrow's heaviness doth heavier grow
        For debt that bankrupt sleep doth sorrow owe,   85
        Which now in some slight measure it will pay,
        If for his tender here I make some stay.°
        (*He lies down and sleeps.*)
OBERON.   What hast thou done? Thou hast mistaken quite
        And laid the love juice on some true love's sight!
        Of thy misprision must perforce ensue   90
        Some true love turned, and not a false turned true.
PUCK.   Then fate o'errules, that, one man holding troth,
        A million fail, confounding oath on oath.°
OBERON.   About the wood go swifter than the wind,
        And Helena of Athens look thou find.   95
        All fancy-sick° she is and pale of cheer°
        With sighs of love that cost the fresh blood dear.
        By some illusion see thou bring her here.
        I'll charm his eyes against she do appear.°
PUCK.   I go, I go, look how I go,   100
        Swifter than arrow from the Tartar's bow. (*Exit.*)
OBERON (*applying the flower juice to* DEMETRIUS' *eyes*).
            Flower of this purple dye,
            Hit with Cupid's archery,
            Sink in apple of his eye.
            When his love he doth espy,   105
            Let her shine as gloriously
            As the Venus of the sky.
            When thou wak'st, if she be by,
            Beg of her for remedy. (*Enter* PUCK.)
PUCK.   Captain of our fairy band,   110
            Helena is here at hand,
            And the youth, mistook by me,
            Pleading for a lover's fee.°
            Shall we their fond pageant° see?
            Lord, what fools these mortals be!   115

84–87. So . . . stay: A man in sorrow cannot sleep, even when the sorrow increases his
need for sleep, but I will try to let sleep give me ease by lying here.   **92–93. one . . .
oath:** for one man true in love there are a million who fail, breaking oath after oath
96. fancy-sick: lovesick   **cheer:** face   **99. against . . . appear:** to prepare for her
arrival   **113. fee:** reward   **114. fond pageant:** display of foolishness

OBERON.   Stand aside. The noise they make
         Will cause Demetrius to awake.
PUCK.   Then will two at once woo one;
         That must needs be sport alone.
         And those things do best please me   120
         That befall preposterously.
(OBERON *and* PUCK *stand aside. Enter* HELENA *followed by*
LYSANDER.)
LYSANDER.   Why should you think that I should woo in scorn?
    Scorn and derision never come in tears.
    Look when I vow, I weep, and vows so born,
      In their nativity all truth appears.°   125
    How can these things in me seem scorn to you,
    Bearing the badge of faith to prove them true?
HELENA.   You do advance your cunning more and more.
    When truth kills truth,° O, devilish-holy fray!
    These vows are Hermia's. Will you give her o'er?   130
      Weigh oath with oath, and you will nothing weigh.
    Your vows to her and me, put in two scales,
    Will even weigh, and both as light as tales.
LYSANDER.   I had no judgment when to her I swore.
HELENA.   Nor none, in my mind, now you give her o'er.   135
LYSANDER.   Demetrius loves her, and he loves not you.
DEMETRIUS (*awaking*).   O Helen, goddess, nymph, perfect, divine!
    To what, my love, shall I compare thine eyne?
    Crystal is muddy.° O, how ripe in show
    Thy lips, those kissing cherries, tempting grow!   140
    That pure congealèd white, high Taurus° snow,
    Fanned with the eastern wind, turns to a crow
    When thou hold'st up thy hand.° O, let me kiss
    This princess of pure white, this seal° of bliss!
HELENA.   O spite! O hell! I see you all are bent   145
    To set against me for your merriment.
    If you were civil and knew courtesy,
    You would not do me thus much injury,
    Can you not hate me, as I know you do,
    But you must join in souls to mock me too?   150

124–25. vows . . . appears: vows made by a weeping person are always sincere
129. truth kills truth: one vow cancels the other—he has sworn love to both Helena and
Hermia   **139. Crystal is muddy:** Compared to her eyes, crystal would look opaque.
141. Taurus: a mountain range in Asia Minor   **142–43. turns . . . hand:** seems black
compared to her white hand   **144. seal:** guarantee

If you were men, as men you are in show,
You would not use a gentle lady so,
To vow, and swear, and superpraise my parts,
When I am sure you hate me with your hearts.
You both are rivals and love Hermia,   155
And now both rivals to mock Helena.
A trim° exploit, a manly enterprise,
To conjure tears up in a poor maid's eyes
With your derision! None of noble sort
Would so offend a virgin and extort°   160
A poor soul's patience, all to make you sport.
LYSANDER.   You are unkind, Demetrius. Be not so.
For you love Hermia, this you know I know.
And here, with all good will, with all my heart,
In Hermia's love I yield you up my part;   165
And yours of Helena to me bequeath,
Whom I do love, and will do till my death.
HELENA.   Never did mockers waste more idle breath.
DEMETRIUS.   Lysander, keep thy Hermia, I will none.
If e'er I loved her, all that love is gone.   170
My heart to her but as guestwise sojourned,°
And now to Helen is it home returned,
There to remain.
LYSANDER.   Helen, it is not so.
DEMETRIUS.   Disparage not the faith thou dost not know,
Lest, to thy peril, thou aby° it dear.   175
Look where thy love comes; yonder is thy dear.
(*Enter* HERMIA.)
HERMIA.   Dark night, that from the eye his function takes,
The ear more quick of apprehension makes;
Wherein it doth impair the seeing sense,
It pays the hearing double recompense.   180
Thou art not by mine eye, Lysander, found;
Mine ear, I thank it, brought me to thy sound.
But why unkindly didst thou leave me so?
LYSANDER.   Why should he stay, whom love doth press to go?
HERMIA.   What love could press Lysander from my side?   185
LYSANDER.   Lysander's love, that would not let him bide—
Fair Helena, who more engilds the night

---

157. trim: fine   160. extort: torture   171. My . . . sojourned: My heart only
made a short visit to her   175. aby: pay for

Than all yon fiery oes and eyes of light.°
Why seek'st thou me? Could not this make thee know
The hate I bear thee made me leave thee so?   190
HERMIA.   You speak not as you think. It cannot be.
HELENA.   Lo, she is one of this confederacy!
Now I perceive they have conjoined all three
To fashion this false sport, in spite of me.°
Injurious Hermia, most ungrateful maid!   195
Have you conspired, have you with these contrived
To bait° me with this foul derision?
Is all the counsel that we two have shared—
The sisters' vows, the hours that we have spent
When we have chid the hasty-footed time   200
For parting us—O, is all forgot?
All schooldays' friendship, childhood innocence?
We, Hermia, like two artificial° gods
Have with our needles created both one flower,
Both on one sampler, sitting on one cushion,   205
Both warbling of one song, both in one key,
As if our hands, our sides, voices, and minds
Had been incorporate.° So we grew together,
Like to a double cherry, seeming parted,
But yet an union in partition,   210
Two lovely berries molded on one stem;
So, with two seeming bodies but one heart,
Two of the first, like coats in heraldry,
Due but to one and crownèd with one crest.°
And will you rend our ancient love asunder   215
To join with men in scorning your poor friend?
It is not friendly, 'tis not maidenly.
Our sex, as well as I, may chide you for it,
Though I alone do feel the injury.
HERMIA.   I am amazèd at your passionate words.   220
I scorn you not. It seems that you scorn me.
HELENA.   Have you not set Lysander, as in scorn,
To follow me and praise my eyes and face?
And made your other love, Demetrius,

---

188. oes . . . light: stars   194. in spite of me: to spite me   197. bait: tease or
torment   203. artificial: artistically creative   208. incorporate: one single body
213–14. Two . . . crest: As if we were a married couple whose separate coats of arms were
merged into a single one.

Who even but now did spurn me with his foot,   225
To call me goddess, nymph, divine, and rare,
Precious, celestial? Wherefore speaks he this
To her he hates? And wherefore doth Lysander
Deny your love, so rich within his soul,
And tender me, forsooth, affection,   230
But by your setting on, by your consent?
What though I be not so in grace as you,
So hung upon with love, so fortunate,
But miserable most, to love unloved?
This you should pity rather than despise.   235

HERMIA.   I understand not what you mean by this.

HELENA.   Ay, do! Persever,° counterfeit sad° looks,
Make mouths upon me when I turn my back,
Wink each at other, hold the sweet jest up,
This sport, well carried, shall be chronicled.°   240
If you have any pity, grace, or manners,
You would not make me such an argument.°
But fare ye well. 'Tis partly my own fault,
Which death, or absence, soon shall remedy.

LYSANDER.   Stay, gentle Helena; hear my excuse,   245
My love, my life, my soul, fair Helena!

HELENA.   O excellent!

HERMIA (to LYSANDER).   Sweet, do not scorn her so.

DEMETRIUS (to LYSANDER).   If she cannot entreat, I can compel.

LYSANDER.   Thou canst compel no more than she entreat.
Thy threats have no more strength than her weak prayers.   250
Helen, I love thee, by my life, I do!
I swear by that which I will lose for thee,
To prove him false that says I love thee not.

DEMETRIUS (to HELENA).   I say I love thee more than he can do.

LYSANDER.   If thou say so, withdraw, and prove it° too.   255

DEMETRIUS.   Quick, come!

HERMIA.   Lysander, whereto tends all this?

LYSANDER.   Away, you Ethiope!°

DEMETRIUS.   No, no; he'll
Seem to break loose; take on as you° would follow,
But yet come not. You are a tame man. Go!

237. **Persever:** Keep the game going   **sad:** serious   240. **chronicled:** written in
history books   242. **argument:** subject for a story   255. **prove it:** i.e., by fighting a
duel   257. **Ethiope:** exaggerating the comparative darkness of Hermia's complexion and
hair   258. **take on as you:** pretend you are trying to

LYSANDER (*to* HERMIA).   Hang off, thou cat, thou burr! Vile thing, let
   loose,   260
   Or I will shake thee from me like a serpent!
HERMIA.   Why are you grown so rude? What change is this,
   Sweet love?
LYSANDER.   Thy love? Out, tawny Tartar, out!
   Out, loathèd med'cine!° O hated potion, hence!
HERMIA.   Do you not jest?
HELENA.   Yes, sooth, and so do you.   265
LYSANDER.   Demetrius, I will keep my word with thee.
DEMETRIUS.   I would I had your bond,° for I perceive
   A weak bond° holds you. I'll not trust your word.
LYSANDER.   What, should I hurt her, strike her, kill her dead?
   Although I hate her, I'll not harm her so.   270
HERMIA.   What, can you do me greater harm than hate?
   Hate me? Wherefore? O me, what news, my love?
   Am not I Hermia? Are not you Lysander?
   I am as fair now as I was erewhile.°
   Since night you loved me; yet since night you left me.   275
   Why, then you left me—O, the gods forbid!—
   In earnest, shall I say?
LYSANDER.   Ay, by my life!
   And never did desire to see thee more.
   Therefore be out of hope, of question, of doubt;
   Be certain, nothing truer. 'Tis no jest   280
   That I do hate thee and love Helena.
HERMIA (*to* HELENA).   O me! You juggler! You cankerblossom!°
   You thief of love! What, have you come by night
   And stol'n my love's heart from him?
HELENA.   Fine, i' faith!
   Have you no modesty, no maiden shame,   285
   No touch of bashfulness? What, will you tear
   Impatient answers from my gentle tongue?
   Fie, fie! You counterfeit, you puppet,° you!
HERMIA.   "Puppet"? Why, so! Ay, that way goes the game.
   Now I perceive that she hath made compare   290
   Between our statures; she hath urged her height,
   And with her personage, her tall personage,

---

264. med'cine: poison   **267–68. bond; bond:** written agreement; Hermia's grasp
274. erewhile: a short while ago   **282. cankerblossom:** worm that destroys the bud of
a flower   **288. puppet:** little doll (referring to Hermia's shortness)

Her height, forsooth, she hath prevailed with him.
And are you grown so high in his esteem
Because I am so dwarfish and so low?   295
How low am I, thou painted maypole? Speak!
How low am I? I am not yet so low
But that my nails can reach unto thine eyes.

HELENA.   I pray you, though you mock me, gentlemen,
Let her not hurt me. I was never curst;°   300
I have no gift at all in shrewishness;
I am a right maid° for my cowardice.
Let her not strike me. You perhaps may think,
Because she is something lower than myself,
That I can match her.

HERMIA.   Lower? Hark, again!   305

HELENA.   Good Hermia, do not be so bitter with me.
I evermore did love you, Hermia,
Did ever keep your counsels, never wronged you,
Save that, in love unto Demetrius,
I told him of your stealth unto this wood.   310
He followed you; for love I followed him.
But he hath chid me hence and threatened me
To strike me, spurn me, nay, to kill me too.
And now, so° you will let me quiet go,
To Athens will I bear my folly back   315
And follow you no further. Let me go.
You see how simple and how fond I am.

HERMIA.   Why, get you gone. Who is 't that hinders you?

HELENA.   A foolish heart, that I leave here behind.

HERMIA.   What, with Lysander?

HELENA.   With Demetrius.   320

LYSANDER.   Be not afraid; she shall not harm thee, Helena.

DEMETRIUS.   No, sir, she shall not, though you take her part.

HELENA.   O, when she is angry, she is keen and shrewd.°
She was a vixen when she went to school,
And though she be but little, she is fierce.   325

HERMIA.   "Little" again? Nothing but "low" and "little"?
Why will you suffer her to flout me thus?
Let me come to her.

---

300. **curst:** fierce, sharp-tongued   302. **right maid:** truly feminine   314. **so:** if
323. **keen and shrewd:** fierce and sharp-tongued

LYSANDER.   Get you gone, you dwarf!
   You minimus,° of hindering knotgrass° made!
   You bead, you acorn!
DEMETRIUS.   You are too officious   330
   In her behalf that scorns your services.
   Let her alone. Speak not of Helena;
   Take not her part. For, if thou dost intend
   Never so little show of love to her,
   Thou shalt aby it.
LYSANDER.   Now she holds me not.   335
   Now follow, if thou dar'st, to try whose right,
   Of thine or mine, is most in Helena. (*Exit.*)
DEMETRIUS.   Follow? Nay, I'll go with thee, cheek by jowl.
   (*Exeunt* LYSANDER *and* DEMETRIUS.)
HERMIA.   You, mistress, all this coil° is 'long of you.°
   Nay, go not back.
HELENA.   I will not trust you, I,   340
   Nor longer stay in your curst company.
   Your hands than mine are quicker for a fray;
   My legs are longer, though, to run away. (*Exit.*)
HERMIA.   I am amazed and know not what to say. (*Exit.*)
OBERON.   This is thy negligence. Still thou mistak'st,   345
   Or else committ'st thy knaveries willfully.
PUCK.   Believe me, king of shadows, I mistook.
   Did not you tell me I should know the man
   By the Athenian garments he had on?
   And so far blameless proves my enterprise   350
   That I have 'nointed an Athenian's eyes;
   And so far am I glad it so did sort,
   As this their jangling I esteem a sport.
OBERON.   Thou seest these lovers seek a place to fight.
   Hie therefore, Robin, overcast the night;   355
   The starry welkin° cover thou anon°
   With drooping fog as black as Acheron,°
   And lead these testy rivals so astray
   As one come not within another's way.
   Like to Lysander sometimes frame thy tongue,   360
   Then stir Demetrius up with bitter wrong,
   And sometimes rail thou like Demetrius.
   And from each other look thou lead them thus,

---

329. **minimus:** tiniest creature   **knotgrass:** a weed supposed to be able to stunt one's
growth   339. **coil:** fighting   **'long of you:** your fault   356. **welkin:** sky
anon: immediately   357. **Acheron:** river of Hades

Till o'er their brows death-counterfeiting sleep
With leaden legs and batty wings doth creep.   365
Then crush this herb into Lysander's eye,
Whose liquor hath this virtuous property,
To take from thence all error with his might
And make his eyeballs roll with wonted sight.°
When they next wake, all this derision   370
Shall seem a dream and fruitless vision,
And back to Athens shall the lovers wend
With league whose date till death shall never end.°
Whiles I in this affair do thee employ,
I'll to my queen and beg her Indian boy;   375
And then I will her charmèd eye release
From monster's view, and all things shall be peace.
PUCK.   My fairy lord, this must be done with haste,
For night's swift dragons cut the clouds full fast,
And yonder shines Aurora's harbinger,°   380
At whose approach ghosts, wand'ring here and there,
Troop home to churchyards. Damnèd spirits all,
That in crossways and floods have burial,
Already to their wormy beds are gone.°
For fear lest day should look their shames upon,   385
They willfully themselves exile from light
And must for aye° consort with black-browed night.
OBERON.   But we are spirits of another sort.°
I with the Morning's love have oft made sport,
And, like a forester, the groves may tread   390
Even till the eastern gate, all fiery red,
Opening on Neptune with fair blessèd beams,
Turns into yellow gold his salt green streams.
But notwithstanding, haste, make no delay.
We may effect this business yet ere day. (*Exit.*)   395
PUCK.   Up and down, up and down,
        I will lead them up and down.
        I am feared in field and town.
        Goblin,° lead them up and down.
Here comes one. (*Enter* LYSANDER.)   400

367–69. hath . . . sight: has the power to remove his mistaken vision and make him see as
he used to   373. With . . . end: Everlastingly united   379–80. night's . . .
harbinger: The dragons that draw night's chariot are speeding away, and the precursor of
dawn, the morning star Venus, has risen.   382–84. Damnèd . . . gone: The ghosts of
those who were damned for their suicide have ceased their night wandering.   387. for
aye: forever   388. of another sort: not damned, and so able to function in daylight as
well as night   399. Goblin: Puck refers to himself, using one of his names, "Hobgoblin."

LYSANDER.   Where art thou, proud Demetrius? Speak thou now.
PUCK (*imitates* DEMETRIUS' *voice*).   Here, villain, drawn° and ready.
　　　Where art thou?
LYSANDER.   I will be with thee straight.
PUCK.   Follow me, then,
　　　To plainer ground. (LYSANDER *follows the voice. Enter* DEMETRIUS.)
DEMETRIUS.   Lysander! Speak again!
　　　Thou runaway, thou coward, art thou fled?   405
　　　Speak! In some bush? Where dost thou hide thy head?
PUCK (*imitates* LYSANDER's *voice*).   Thou coward, art thou bragging to
　　　the stars,
　　　Telling the bushes that thou look'st for wars,
　　　And wilt not come? Come, recreant,° come, thou child,
　　　I'll whip thee with a rod. He is defiled   410
　　　That draws a sword on thee.
DEMETRIUS.   Yea, art thou there?
PUCK.   Follow my voice. We'll try° no manhood here.
　　　(*Exeunt all three.* LYSANDER *returns.*)
LYSANDER.   He goes before me and still dares me on.
　　　When I come where he calls, then he is gone.
　　　The villain is much lighter-heeled than I.   415
　　　I followed fast but faster he did fly,
　　　That fallen am I in dark uneven way,
　　　And here will rest me. Come, thou gentle day!
　　　For if but once thou show me thy gray light,
　　　I'll find Demetrius and revenge this spite.   420
　　　(*He lies down and sleeps. Enter* PUCK *leading* DEMETRIUS.)
PUCK.   Ho, ho, ho! Coward, why com'st thou not?
DEMETRIUS.   Abide° me, if thou dar'st, for well I wot°
　　　Thou runn'st before me, shifting every place,
　　　And dar'st not stand nor look me in the face.
　　　Where art thou now?
PUCK.   Come hither. I am here.   425
DEMETRIUS.   Nay, then, thou mock'st me. Thou shalt buy this dear,°
　　　If ever I thy face by daylight see.
　　　Now go thy way. Faintness constraineth me
　　　To measure out my length on this cold bed.

---

402. drawn: with my sword in my hand   **409. recreant:** traitor, coward
412. try: test   **422. Abide:** Wait for   **wot:** know   **426. buy this dear:** pay
plenty for this

By day's approach look to be visited.   430
(*He lies down and sleeps. Enter* HELENA.)
HELENA.   O weary night, O long and tedious night,
 Abate° thy hours! Shine comforts from the east,
That I may back to Athens by daylight
 From these that my poor company detest;
And sleep, that sometimes shuts up sorrow's eye,   435
Steal me awhile from mine own company.
(*She lies down and sleeps.*)
PUCK.   Yet but three? Come one more;
   Two of both kinds makes up four.
   Here she comes, curst° and sad.
   Cupid is a knavish lad,   440
   Thus to make poor females mad. (*Enter* HERMIA.)
HERMIA.   Never so weary, never so in woe,
 Bedabbled with the dew and torn with briers,
I can no further crawl, no further go;
 My legs can keep no pace with my desires.   445
Here will I rest me till the break of day.
Heavens shield Lysander, if they mean a fray!
(*She lies down and sleeps.*)
PUCK.   On the ground
 Sleep sound.
 I'll apply   450
 To your eye,
Gentle lover, remedy. (*He squeezes the juice on* LYSANDER's *eyes.*)
 When thou wak'st,
 Thou tak'st
 True delight   455
 In the sight
Of thy former lady's eye;
And the country proverb known,
That every man should take his own,
In your waking shall be shown: 460
 Jack shall have Jill;
 Naught shall go ill;
The man shall have his mare again, and all shall be well. (*Exit.
The four lovers remain, asleep.*)

432. Abate: Shorten   **439. curst:** ill-tempered

ACT 4

SCENE 1. *The action continues, with the four lovers still asleep on the ground.*

Enter Titania, Bottom, *and* Fairies, *and behind them* Oberon.

Titania.   Come, sit thee down upon this flowery bed,
　　While I thy amiable° cheeks do coy,°
　　And stick muskroses in thy sleek smooth head,
　　And kiss thy fair large ears, my gentle joy.
Bottom.   Where's Peaseblossom?   5
Peaseblossom.   Ready.
Bottom.   Scratch my head, Peaseblossom. Where's Monsieur°
　　Cobweb?
Cobweb.   Ready.
Bottom.   Monsieur Cobweb, good monsieur, get you your weapons in
　　your hand, and kill me a red-hipped humble-bee on the top of a
　　thistle; and, good monsieur, bring me the honey bag. Do not fret
　　yourself too much in the action, monsieur; and, good monsieur, have
　　a care the honey bag break not. I would be loath to have you over-
　　flown with a honey bag, signor. (*Exit* Cobweb.) Where's Monsieur
　　Mustardseed?   16
Mustardseed.   Ready.
Bottom.   Give me your neaf,° Monsieur Mustardseed. Pray you, leave
　　your courtesy,° good monsieur.
Mustardseed.   What's your will?   20
Bottom.   Nothing, good monsieur, but to help Cavalery° Cobweb to
　　scratch. I must to the barber's, monsieur, for methinks I am mar-
　　velous hairy about the face; and I am such a tender ass, if my hair
　　do but tickle me I must scratch.
Titania.   What, wilt thou hear some music, my sweet love?   25
Bottom.   I have a reasonable good ear in music. Let's have the tongs
　　and the bones.° (Fairies *play rustic music.*)
Titania.   Or say, sweet love, what thou desirest to eat.
Bottom.   Truly, a peck of provender. I could munch your good dry oats.
　　Methinks I have a great desire to a bottle° of hay. Good hay, sweet
　　hay, hath no fellow.°   31

---

2. amiable: lovely   **coy:** caress   **7, 21. Monsieur, Cavalery:** terms appropriate for
addressing French and Italian gentlemen ("Cavalery" for "Cavaliere")   **18. neaf:** fist
18–19. leave . . . courtesy: there's no need to keep bowing   **26–27. tongs . . . bones:**
crude rustic musical instruments, both creating monotone percussion effects   **30. bottle:**
bundle   **31. fellow:** equal

TITANIA.   I have a venturous fairy that shall seek
    The squirrel's hoard, and fetch thee new nuts.
BOTTOM.   I had rather have a handful or two of dried peas. But, I pray
    you, let none of your people stir me. I have an exposition° of sleep
    come upon me.   36
TITANIA.   Sleep thou, and I will wind thee in my arms.
    Fairies, begone, and be all ways away. (*Exeunt* FAIRIES.)
    So doth the woodbine the sweet honeysuckle
    Gently entwist; the female ivy so   40
    Enrings the barky fingers of the elm.
    O, how I love thee! How I dote on thee!
    (*They sleep. Enter* PUCK.)
OBERON (*coming forward*).   Welcome, good Robin. Seest thou this
        sweet sight?
    Her dotage now I do begin to pity.
    For, meeting her of late behind the wood   45
    Seeking sweet favors for this hateful fool,
    I did upbraid her and fall out with her.
    For she his hairy temples then had rounded
    With coronet of fresh and fragrant flowers;
    And that same dew, which sometime on the buds   50
    Was wont to swell like round and orient pearls,
    Stood now within the pretty flowerets' eyes
    Like tears that did their own disgrace bewail.
    When I had at my pleasure taunted her,
    And she in mild terms begged my patience,   55
    I then did ask of her her changeling child,
    Which straight she gave me, and her fairy sent
    To bear him to my bower in Fairyland.
    And, now I have the boy, I will undo
    This hateful imperfection of her eyes.   60
    And, gentle Puck, take this transformèd scalp
    From off the head of this Athenian swain,
    That he, awaking when the other do,
    May all to Athens back again repair,°
    And think no more of this night's accidents   65
    But as the fierce vexation of a dream.
    But first I will release the Fairy Queen.

---

35. exposition: Bottom means "disposition" or "inclination."   **64. repair:** return

(*He applies the antidote to* TITANIA's *eyes.*)
    Be as thou wast wont to be;
    See as thou wast wont to see.
    Dian's bud o'er Cupid's flower°   70
    Hath such force and blessèd power.
Now, my Titania, wake you, my sweet queen.
TITANIA (*awaking*).   My Oberon! What visions have I seen!
Methought I was enamored of an ass.
OBERON.   There lies your love.
TITANIA.   How came these things to pass?   75
    O, how mine eyes do loathe his visage now!
OBERON.   Silence awhile. Robin, take off this head.
    Titania, music call, and strike more dead
    Than common sleep of all these five the sense.°
TITANIA.   Music, ho! Music, such as charmeth sleep! (*Music.*)   80
PUCK (*to* BOTTOM, *removing the ass's head from him*).
    Now, when thou wak'st, with thine own fool's eyes peep.
OBERON.   Sound, music! Come, my queen, take hands with me,
    And rock the ground whereon these sleepers be.
    (*They dance.*)
    Now thou and I are new in amity,
    And will tomorrow midnight solemnly   85
    Dance in Duke Theseus' house triumphantly,
    And bless it to all fair prosperity.
    There shall the pairs of faithful lovers be
    Wedded, with Theseus, all in jollity.
PUCK.   Fairy King, attend, and mark: 90
    I do hear the morning lark.
OBERON.   Then, my queen, in silence sad,°
    Trip we after night's shade.
    We the globe can compass soon,
    Swifter than the wandering moon.   95
TITANIA.   Come, my lord, and in our flight
    Tell me how it came this night
    That I sleeping here was found
    With these mortals on the ground.
    (*Exeunt* TITANIA, OBERON, *and* PUCK. *Hunting horns sound, and en-*
    ter THESEUS *with his train,* HIPPOLYTA, *and* EGEUS.)

---

70. Dian's . . . flower: a flower sacred to the goddess of chastity Diana, over the flower
transformed by the arrow of Cupid (the pansy)   **78–79. strike . . . sense:** put all five of
them (Bottom and the four lovers) into a deeper sleep than normal   **92. sad:** serious

THESEUS.   Go, one of you, find out the forester,   100
    For now our observation° is performed;
    And since we have the vaward° of the day,
    My love shall hear the music of my hounds.
    Uncouple° in the western valley; let them go.
    Dispatch, I say, and find the forester.   105
    (*Exit an* ATTENDANT.)
    We will, fair queen, up to the mountain's top
    And mark the musical confusion
    Of hounds and echo in conjunction.
HIPPOLYTA.   I was with Hercules and Cadmus once
    When in a wood of Crete they bayed° the bear   110
    With hounds of Sparta. Never did I hear
    Such gallant chiding,° for, besides the groves,
    The skies, the fountains, every region near
    Seemed all one mutual cry. I never heard
    So musical a discord, such sweet thunder.   115
THESEUS.   My hounds are bred out of the Spartan kind,
    So flewed, so sanded;° and their heads are hung
    With ears that sweep away the morning dew;
    Crook-kneed, and dewlapped° like Thessalian bulls;
    Slow in pursuit, but matched in mouth like bells,   120
    Each under each.° A cry more tunable
    Was never holloed to nor cheered with horn
    In Crete, in Sparta, nor in Thessaly.
    Judge when you hear. But soft! What nymphs are these?
EGEUS.   My lord, this is my daughter here asleep,   125
    And this Lysander; this Demetrius is;
    This Helena, old Nedar's Helena.
    I wonder of their being here together.
THESEUS.   No doubt they rose up early to observe
    The rite of May, and hearing our intent,   130
    Came here in grace of our solemnity.°
    But speak, Egeus. Is not this the day
    That Hermia should give answer of her choice?
EGEUS.   It is, my lord.

---

101. **observation:** May morning ritual   102. **vaward:** earliest part
104. **Uncouple:** Unleash   110. **bayed:** brought to bay   112. **chiding:** barking
117. **flewed, sanded:** with hanging cheeks, sand-colored   119. **dewlapped:** with folds
of skin hanging under their chins   120–21. **matched . . . each:** barking in harmony,
like bells, from high to low   131. **in . . . solemnity:** to honor our marriage ceremony

THESEUS.   Go bid the huntsmen wake them with their horns.   135
(*Exit an* ATTENDANT. *Shouting and horns sounding off-stage. The four lovers start up.*)
Good morrow, friends. Saint Valentine° is past.
Begin these woodbirds but to couple now?
LYSANDER.   Pardon, my lord. (*They kneel.*)
THESEUS.   I pray you all, stand up. (*They stand.*)
I know you two are rival enemies;
How comes this gentle concord in the world,   140
That hatred is so far from jealousy°
To sleep by hate and fear no enmity?
LYSANDER.   My lord, I shall reply amazedly,
Half sleep, half waking; but as yet, I swear,
I cannot truly say how I came here.   145
But, as I think—for truly would I speak,
And now I do bethink me, so it is—
I came with Hermia hither. Our intent
Was to be gone from Athens, where we might,
Without the peril° of the Athenian law—   150
EGEUS.   Enough, enough, my lord; you have enough.
I beg the law, the law, upon his head.
They would have stol'n away; they would, Demetrius,
Thereby to have defeated you and me,
You of your wife and me of my consent,   155
Of my consent that she should be your wife.
DEMETRIUS.   My lord, fair Helen told me of their stealth,
Of this their purpose hither to this wood,
And I in fury hither followed them,
Fair Helena in fancy following me.   160
But, my good lord, I wot not by what power—
But by some power it is—my love to Hermia,
Melted as the snow, seems to me now
As the remembrance of an idle gaud°
Which in my childhood I did dote upon;   165
And all the faith, the virtue of my heart,
The object and the pleasure of mine eye,
Is only Helena. To her, my lord,
Was I betrothed ere I saw Hermia,

---

136. Saint Valentine: the day on which birds were thought to choose a mate
141. jealousy: suspicion or fear of danger   **150. Without the peril:** Beyond the
danger   **164. idle gaud:** worthless toy

But like a sickness did I loathe this food;   170
But, as in health, come to my natural taste,
Now I do wish it, love it, long for it,
And will forevermore be true to it.

THESEUS.   Fair lovers, you are fortunately met.
Of this discourse we more will hear anon.   175
Egeus, I will overbear your will;
For in the temple, by and by, with us
These couples shall eternally be knit.
And, for the morning now is something worn,
Our purposed hunting shall be set aside.   180
Away with us to Athens. Three and three,
We'll hold a feast in great solemnity.
Come, Hippolyta.
(*Exeunt* THESEUS, HIPPOLYTA, EGEUS, *and train.*)

DEMETRIUS.   These things seem small and undistinguishable,
Like far-off mountains turnèd into clouds.   185

HERMIA.   Methinks I see these things with parted° eye,
When everything seems double.

HELENA.   So methinks;
And I have found Demetrius like a jewel,
Mine own, and not mine own.

DEMETRIUS.   Are you sure
That we are awake? It seems to me   190
That yet we sleep, we dream. Do not you think
The Duke was here, and bid us follow him?

HERMIA.   Yea, and my father.

HELENA.   And Hippolyta.

LYSANDER.   And he did bid us follow to the temple.

DEMETRIUS.   Why, then, we are awake. Let's follow him,   195
And by the way let us recount our dreams.
(*Exeunt the four lovers.*)

BOTTOM (*awaking*).   When my cue comes, call me, and I will answer.
My next is "Most fair Pyramus." Heigh-ho! Peter Quince! Flute,
the bellows mender! Snout, the tinker! Starveling! God's my life,°
stolen hence and left me asleep! I have had a most rare vision. I
have had a dream, past the wit of man to say what dream it was.
Man is but an ass if he go about to expound this dream. Methought
I was—there is no man can tell what. Methought I was—and

---

186. parted: out of focus   **199. God's my life:** God save me.

methought I had—but man is but a patched fool° if he will offer to
say what methought I had. The eye of man hath not heard, the ear
of man hath not seen, man's hand is not able to taste, his tongue to
conceive, nor his heart to report,° what my dream was. I will get
Peter Quince to write a ballad° of this dream. It shall be called
"Bottom's Dream," because it hath no bottom,° and I will sing it in
the latter end of a play, before the Duke. Peradventure, to make it
the more gracious, I shall sing it at her° death. (*Exit.*)   211

SCENE 2. *Athens.* QUINCE's *house.*

Enter QUINCE, FLUTE, SNOUT, *and* STARVELING.

QUINCE.   Have you sent to Bottom's house? Is he come home yet?
STARVELING.   He cannot be heard of. Out of doubt he is transported.°
FLUTE.   If he come not, then the play is marred. It goes not forward.
   Doth it?
QUINCE.   It is not possible. You have not a man in all Athens able to
   discharge Pyramus but he.   6
FLUTE.   No, he hath simply the best wit° of any handicraft man in
   Athens.
QUINCE.   Yea, and the best person° too, and he is a very paramour for
   a sweet voice.   10
FLUTE.   You must say "paragon." A paramour is, God bless us, a thing
   of naught.° (*Enter* SNUG.)
SNUG.   Masters, the Duke is coming from the temple, and there is two
   or three lords and ladies more married. If our sport had gone forward,
   we had all been made men.°   15
FLUTE.   O sweet bully Bottom! Thus hath he lost sixpence a day during
   his life;° he could not have scaped sixpence a day. An the Duke had
   not given him sixpence a day for playing Pyramus, I'll be hanged.
   He would have deserved it. Sixpence a day in Pyramus, or nothing.
   (*Enter* BOTTOM.)
BOTTOM.   Where are these lads? Where are these hearts?   20
QUINCE.   Bottom! O most courageous day! O most happy hour!

---

204. patched fool: a court jester in motley   **205–7. The eye . . . report:** Bottom typically mixes up senses and what they report.   **208. ballad:** Printed poems related the
latest sensational (and sometimes fictitious) news, a sixteenth-century version of supermar-
ket tabloids.   **209. hath no bottom:** is profound beyond measuring (also, has no basis
in reality)   **211. her:** presumably, Thisbe's   **2. transported:** stolen away by the
fairies   **7. wit:** intelligence   **9. best person:** handsomest   **12. of naught:** immoral   **15. made men:** men who have made it in life   **16–17. sixpence . . . life:** a
generous royal pension, equivalent to a craftsman's daily wage

BOTTOM.   Masters, I am to discourse wonders.° But ask me not what; for if I tell you, I am no true Athenian. I will tell you everything, right as it fell out.

QUINCE.   Let us hear, sweet Bottom.   25

BOTTOM.   Not a word of me. All that I will tell you is that the Duke hath dined. Get your apparel together, good strings° to your beards, new ribbons to your pumps;° meet presently at the palace; every man look o'er his part; for the short and the long is, our play is pre-ferred.° In any case, let Thisbe have clean linen; and let not him that plays the lion pare his nails, for they shall hang out for the lion's claws. And, most dear actors, eat no onions nor garlic, for we are to utter sweet breath; and I do not doubt but to hear them say it is a sweet comedy. No more words. Away! Go, away! (*Exeunt.*)   34

ACT 5

SCENE 1. Athens. The palace of Theseus.

Enter THESEUS, HIPPOLYTA, PHILOSTRATE, LORDS, *and* ATTEN-DANTS.

HIPPOLYTA.   'Tis strange, my Theseus, that these lovers speak of.

THESEUS.   More strange than true. I never may believe
These antique fables nor these fairy toys.°
Lovers and madmen have such seething brains,
Such shaping fantasies,° that apprehend°   5
More than cool reason ever comprehends.°
The lunatic, the lover, and the poet
Are of imagination all compact.°
One sees more devils than vast hell can hold;
That is the madman. The lover, all as frantic,   10
Sees Helen's beauty in a brow of Egypt.°
The poet's eye, in a fine frenzy rolling,
Doth glance from heaven to earth, from earth to heaven;
And as imagination bodies forth
The forms of things unknown, the poet's pen   15

---

22. am . . . wonders: have wonderful things to tell you   **27. good strings:** for tying on their beards   **28. pumps:** shoes   **29. preferred:** accepted for consideration, "on the short list"   **3. fairy toys:** trivial fairy stories   **5. fantasies:** imaginations **apprehend:** perceive, imagine   **6. comprehends:** understands   **8. Are . . . com-pact:** Are composed entirely of imagination   **11. Helen's . . . Egypt:** the beauty of Helen of Troy in the (ugly) face of a gypsy

Turns them to shapes and gives to airy nothing
A local habitation and a name.
Such tricks hath strong imagination
That if it would but apprehend some joy,
It comprehends some bringer° of that joy;   20
Or in the night, imagining some fear,
How easy is a bush supposed a bear!

HIPPOLYTA.   But all the story of the night told over,
And all their minds transfigured so together,
More witnesseth than fancy's images°   25
And grows to something of great constancy;°
But, howsoever, strange and admirable.°

(*Enter* LYSANDER, DEMETRIUS, HERMIA, *and* HELENA.)

THESEUS.   Here come the lovers, full of joy and mirth.
Joy, gentle friends! Joy and fresh days of love
Accompany your hearts!

LYSANDER.   More than to us   30
Wait in your royal walks, your board, your bed!

THESEUS.   Come now, what masques,° what dances shall we have
To wear away this long age of three hours
Between our after-supper and bedtime?
Where is our usual manager of mirth?   35
What revels are in hand? Is there no play
To ease the anguish of a torturing hour?
Call Philostrate.

PHILOSTRATE.   Here, mighty Theseus.

THESEUS.   Say, what abridgment° have you for this evening?
What masque? What music? How shall we beguile   40
The lazy time, if not with some delight?

PHILOSTRATE (*giving him a paper*).   There is a brief° how many sports
    are ripe.
Make choice of which Your Highness will see first.

THESEUS (*reads*).   "The battle with the Centaurs,° to be sung
By an Athenian eunuch to the harp"?   45
We'll none of that. That have I told my love,
In glory of my kinsman Hercules.

---

20. comprehends . . . bringer: invents some cause   **25. More . . . images:** Seems evidence of more than just imaginary things   **26. constancy:** consistency, certainty
27. admirable: wonderful   **32. masques:** courtly entertainments
39. abridgment: pastime, entertainment   **42. brief:** summary list   **44. battle . . .
Centaurs:** probably refers to a mythical story in which the centaurs (half human, half
horse) attempted to steal a bride from her husband, but were defeated with the help of
Hercules

(*He reads.*) "The riot of the tipsy Bacchanals,
Tearing the Thracian singer in their rage"?°
That is an old device; and it was played   50
When I from Thebes came last a conqueror.
(*He reads.*) "The thrice three Muses mourning for the death
Of Learning, late deceased in beggary"?
That is some satire, keen and critical,
Not sorting with° a nuptial ceremony.   55
(*He reads.*) "A tedious brief scene of young Pyramus
And his love Thisbe; very tragical mirth"?
Merry and tragical? Tedious and brief?
That is, hot ice and wondrous strange snow.
How shall we find the concord of this discord?   60

PHILOSTRATE.   A play there is, my lord, some ten words long,
Which is as brief as I have known a play.
But by ten words, my lord, it is too long,
Which makes it tedious. For in all the play
There is not one word apt, one player fitted.   65
And tragical, my noble lord, it is,
For Pyramus therein doth kill himself,
Which, when I saw rehearsed, I must confess,
Made mine eyes water; but more merry tears
The passion of loud laughter never shed.   70

THESEUS.   What are they that do play it?

PHILOSTRATE.   Hardhanded men that work in Athens here,
Which never labored in their minds till now,
And now have toiled their unbreathed° memories
With this same play, against° your nuptial.   75

THESEUS.   And we will hear it.

PHILOSTRATE.   No, my noble lord,
It is not for you. I have heard it over,
And it is nothing, nothing in the world—
Unless you can find sport in their intents,
Extremely stretched° and conned° with cruel pain,   80
To do you service.

THESEUS.   I will hear that play;
For never anything can be amiss
When simpleness and duty tender it.

48–49. The riot . . . rage: The poet Orpheus was torn to pieces by a mob of drunken
women (worshippers of the god of wine Bacchus).   **55. sorting with:** appropriate to
74. unbreathed: inexperienced, undeveloped   **75. against:** in preparation for
80. stretched: strained   **conned:** memorized

Go, bring them in, and take your places, ladies.
(*Exit* PHILOSTRATE.)
HIPPOLYTA.   I love not to see wretchedness o'ercharged,°   85
  And duty in his service° perishing.
THESEUS.   Why, gentle sweet, you shall see no such thing.
HIPPOLYTA.   He says they can do nothing in this kind.
THESEUS.   The kinder we, to give them thanks for nothing.
  Our sport shall be to take what they mistake;   90
  And what poor duty cannot do, noble respect
  Takes it in might, not merit.°
  Where I have come, great clerks° have purposèd
  To greet me with premeditated welcomes,
  Where I have seen them shiver and look pale,   95
  Make periods in the midst of sentences,
  Throttle their practiced accent in their fears,
  And in conclusion dumbly have broke off,
  Not paying me a welcome. Trust me, sweet,
  Out of this silence yet I picked a welcome,   100
  And in the modesty of fearful duty
  I read as much as from the rattling tongue
  Of saucy and audacious eloquence.
  Love, therefore, and tongue-tied simplicity
  In least speak most, to my capacity.°   105
  (*Enter* PHILOSTRATE.)
PHILOSTRATE.   So please Your Grace, the Prologue is addressed.°
THESEUS.   Let him approach.
  (*Flourish of trumpets. Enter* QUINCE *for the Prologue.*)
PROLOGUE.   If we offend, it is with our good will.
    That you should think, we come not to offend,
  But with good will. To show our simple skill,   110
    That is the true beginning of our end.
  Consider, then, we come but in despite.
    We do not come, as minding° to content you,
  Our true intent is. All for your delight
    We are not here. That you should here repent you,   115
  The actors are at hand, and, by their show,
  You shall know all that you are like to know.
THESEUS.   This fellow doth not stand upon points.°

<hr>

85. wretchedness o'ercharged: poor men trying to do too much
86. in his service: in attempting to serve   **91–92. noble . . . merit:** i.e., a noble mind
is more concerned with the good intention than with the poor performance   **93. great
clerks:** learned scholars   **105. In . . . capacity:** Are most eloquent when they say less,
in my judgment   **106. addressed:** ready   **113. minding:** intending
118. stand upon points: pay attention to punctuation marks (and thus, doesn't make his
points clearly)

LYSANDER.　He hath rid his prologue like a rough colt; he knows not the stop.° A good moral, my lord: it is not enough to speak, but to speak true.

HIPPOLYTA.　Indeed, he hath played on his prologue like a child on a recorder:° a sound, but not in government.°

THESEUS.　His speech was like a tangled chain: nothing impaired, but all disordered. Who is next?　　　　　　　　　　　　　　125

(*Enter* BOTTOM *as* PYRAMUS, FLUTE *as* THISBE, SNOUT *as* WALL, STARVELING *as* MOONSHINE, *and* SNUG *as* LION.)

PROLOGUE.　Gentles, perchance you wonder at this show,
　　But wonder on, till truth make all things plain.
This man is Pyramus, if you would know.
　　This beauteous lady Thisbe is, certain.
This man with lime and roughcast doth present　　　　　　130
　　Wall, that vile wall which did these lovers sunder,
And through Wall's chink, poor souls, they are content
　　To whisper. At the which let no man wonder.
This man, with lantern, dog, and bush of thorn,
　　Presenteth Moonshine; for, if you will know,　　　　　135
By moonshine did these lovers think no scorn°
　　To meet at Ninus' tomb, there, there to woo.
This grisly beast, which Lion hight° by name,
　　The trusty Thisbe coming first by night
Did scare away, or rather did affright;　　　　　　　　　140
　　And as she fled, her mantle she did fall,°
　　Which Lion vile with bloody mouth did stain.
Anon comes Pyramus, sweet youth and tall,°
　　And finds his trusty Thisbe's mantle slain;
Whereat, with blade, with bloody, blameful blade,　　　145
　　He bravely broached his boiling bloody breast.
And Thisbe, tarrying in mulberry shade,
　　His dagger drew, and died. For all the rest,
Let Lion, Moonshine, Wall, and lovers twain
At large discourse, while here they do remain.　　　　　150

(*Exeunt* PROLOGUE, PYRAMUS, THISBE, MOONSHINE, *and* LION.)

THESEUS.　I wonder if the lion be to speak.

DEMETRIUS.　No wonder, my lord. One lion may, when many asses do.

WALL.　In this same interlude° it doth befall
　　That I, one Snout by name, present a wall,

---

120. stop: reining in an untrained colt, and punctuation mark　　**123. recorder:** a wind instrument like a flute　　**government:** control　　**136. think no scorn:** not regard it as disgraceful　　**138. hight:** is named　　**141. did fall:** dropped　　**143. tall:** brave　　**153. interlude:** play

And such a wall as I would have you think   155
That had in it a crannied hole or chink,
Through which the lovers, Pyramus and Thisbe,
Did whisper often, very secretly.
This loam, this roughcast, and this stone doth show
That I am that same wall; the truth is so.   160
And this the cranny is, right and sinister,°
Through which the fearful lovers are to whisper.

THESEUS.   Would you desire lime and hair to speak better?

DEMETRIUS.   It is the wittiest partition that ever I heard discourse,
my lord. (*Enter* PYRAMUS.)   165

THESEUS.   Pyramus draws near the wall. Silence!

PYRAMUS.   O grim-looked night! O night with hue so black!
    O night, which ever art when day is not!
O night, O night! Alack, alack, alack,
    I fear my Thisbe's promise is forgot!   170
And thou, O wall, O sweet, O lovely wall,
    That stand'st between her father's ground and mine,
Thou wall, O wall, O sweet and lovely wall,
    Show me thy chink, to blink through with mine eyne. (WALL
        holds up his fingers.)
Thanks, courteous wall. Jove shield thee well for this.   175
    But what see I? No Thisbe do I see.
O wicked wall, through whom I see no bliss!
    Cursed be thy stones for thus deceiving me!

THESEUS.   The wall, methinks, being sensible,° should curse again.°

PYRAMUS.   No, in truth, sir, he should not. "Deceiving me" is Thisbe's
cue: she is to enter now, and I am to spy her through the wall. You
shall see, it will fall pat° as I told you. Yonder she comes. (*Enter*
THISBE.)

THISBE.   O wall, full often hast thou heard my moans   183
    For parting my fair Pyramus and me.
My cherry lips have often kissed thy stones,
    Thy stones with lime and hair knit up in thee.

PYRAMUS.   I see a voice. Now will I to the chink,
    To spy an I can hear my Thisbe's face.
    Thisbe!

THISBE.   My love! Thou art my love, I think.

---

161. right and sinister: running from right to left, horizontal   **179. sensible:** capable
of feeling   **curse again:** curse back at him   **182. fall pat:** happen precisely

PYRAMUS.   Think what thou wilt, I am thy lover's grace,   190
    And like Limander° am I trusty still.
THISBE.   And I like Helen,° till the Fates me kill.
PYRAMUS.   Not Shafalus° to Procrus° was so true.
THISBE.   As Shafalus to Procrus, I to you.
PYRAMUS.   O, kiss me through the hole of this vile wall!   195
THISBE.   I kiss the wall's hole, not your lips at all.
PYRAMUS.   Wilt thou at Ninny's tomb meet me straightway?
THISBE.   'Tide° life, 'tide death, I come without delay.
    (*Exeunt* PYRAMUS *and* THISBE.)
WALL.   Thus have I, Wall, my part dischargèd so,
    And, being done, thus Wall away doth go. (*Exit.*)   200
THESEUS.   Now is the mural down between the two neighbors.
DEMETRIUS.   No remedy, my lord, when walls are so willful to hear
    without warning.°
HIPPOLYTA.   This is the silliest stuff that ever I heard.
THESEUS.   The best in this kind are but shadows,° and the worst are no
    worse, if imagination amend them.   206
HIPPOLYTA.   It must be your imagination then, and not theirs.
THESEUS.   If we imagine no worse of them than they of themselves,
    they may pass for excellent men. Here come two noble beasts in, a
    man and a lion.   210
    (*Enter* LION *and* MOONSHINE.)
LION.   You, ladies, you, whose gentle hearts do fear
    The smallest monstrous mouse that creeps on floor,
May now perchance both quake and tremble here,
    When lion rough in wildest rage doth roar.
Then know that I, as Snug the joiner, am   215
A lion fell,° nor else no lion's dam;
For, if I should as lion come in strife
Into this place, 'twere pity on my life.°
THESEUS.   A very gentle beast, and of a good conscience.
DEMETRIUS.   The very best at a beast, my lord, that e'er I saw.   220
LYSANDER.   This lion is a very fox for his valor.°
THESEUS.   True, and a goose for his discretion.°

191–93. Limander, Helen, Shafalus, Procrus: mangled references to famous pairs of
lovers—Leander and Hero (not Helen), Cephalus and Procris   **198. 'Tide:** Betide,
come   **203. without warning:** i.e., without telling the parents of the elopement
205. shadows: mere representations, not true-to-life   **216. fell:** fierce
218. 'twere . . . life: it would cost me my life   **221. is . . . valor:** his valor is chiefly
just craftiness   **222. goose . . . discretion:** more foolish than he is discreet

DEMETRIUS.   Not so, my lord, for his valor cannot carry his discretion,
and the fox carries the goose.

THESEUS.   His discretion, I am sure, cannot carry his valor, for the goose
carries not the fox. It is well. Leave it to his discretion, and let us
listen to the moon.   227

MOON.   This lanthorn doth the hornèd moon present—

DEMETRIUS.   He should have worn the horns on his head.°

THESEUS.   He is no crescent, and his horns are invisible within the cir-
cumference.°   231

MOON.   This lanthorn doth the hornèd moon present;
Myself the man i' the moon do seem to be.

THESEUS.   This is the greatest error of all the rest. The man should be
put into the lanthorn. How is it else the man i' the moon?   235

DEMETRIUS.   He dares not come there for the candle, for you see it is
already in snuff.°

HIPPOLYTA.   I am aweary of this moon. Would he would change!

THESEUS.   It appears, by his small light of discretion, that he is in the
wane; but yet, in courtesy, in all reason, we must stay the time.   240

LYSANDER.   Proceed, Moon.

MOON.   All that I have to say is to tell you that the lanthorn is the
moon, I, the man i' the moon, this thornbush my thornbush, and
this dog my dog.

DEMETRIUS.   Why, all these should be in the lanthorn, for all these are
in the moon. But silence! Here comes Thisbe. (*Enter* THISBE.) 246

THISBE.   This is old Ninny's tomb. Where is my love?

LION (*roaring*).   O!

DEMETRIUS.   Well roared, Lion.

(THISBE *runs off, dropping her mantle.*)

THESEUS.   Well run, Thisbe.   250

HIPPOLYTA.   Well shone, Moon. Truly, the moon shines with a good
grace.

(LION *shakes* THISBE's *mantle, drops it, and exits.*)

THESEUS.   Well moused,° Lion. (*Enter* PYRAMUS.)

DEMETRIUS.   And then came Pyramus.

LYSANDER.   And so the lion vanished.   255

PYRAMUS.   Sweet Moon, I thank thee for thy sunny beams;
I thank thee, Moon, for shining now so bright;

---

229. on his head: a cuckold was said to sprout horns   **230–31. He . . . circumfer-
ence:** The horns of a crescent moon are not visible when the moon is full.   **237. in
snuff:** smoking, in need of having its wick trimmed   **253. moused:** shaken, as a cat
shakes a mouse

For, by thy gracious, golden, glittering gleams,
    I trust to take of truest Thisbe sight.
      But stay, O spite!   260
      But mark, poor knight,
    What dreadful dole° is here?
      Eyes, do you see?
      How can it be?
    O dainty duck! O dear!   265
      Thy mantle good,
    What, stained with blood?
    Approach, ye Furies fell!°
      O Fates,° come, come,
    Cut thread and thrum;°   270
    Quail,° crush, conclude, and quell!°
THESEUS.   This passion, and the death of a dear friend, would go near
    to make a man look sad.°
HIPPOLYTA.   Beshrew my heart, but I pity the man.
PYRAMUS.   O, wherefore, Nature, didst thou lions frame?   275
    Since lion vile hath here deflowered my dear,
    Which is—no, no, which was—the fairest dame
    That lived, that loved, that liked, that looked with cheer.
      Come, tears, confound,
      Out, sword, and wound   280
    The pap° of Pyramus;
      Ay, that left pap,
      Where heart doth hop. (*Stabs himself.*)
    Thus die I, thus, thus, thus.
      Now am I dead,   285
      Now am I fled;
    My soul is in the sky.
      Tongue, lose thy light;
      Moon, take thy flight. (*Exit* MOONSHINE.)
    Now die, die, die, die, die. (*Dies.*)   290
DEMETRIUS.   No die, but an ace, for him; for he is but one.°
LYSANDER.   Less than an ace, man; for he is dead, he is nothing.

---

262. dole: grievous sight   **268. Furies fell:** fierce avenging goddesses of Greek mythology   **269. Fates:** the three Greek goddesses who spun, drew out, and cut the thread of life   **270. Cut thread and thrum:** i.e., destroy everything   **271. Quail:** Overpower **quell:** slay   **272–73. This . . . sad:** i.e., this acting of violent sorrow is so absurd that you could only be sad if you had some genuine cause (such as the death of a friend) to add to it   **281. pap:** breast   **291. No . . . one:** Bottom is not even a whole die (singular of dice), only the side of the cube with one spot on it.

THESEUS.   With the help of a surgeon he might yet recover, and yet
  prove an ass.°
HIPPOLYTA.   How chance Moonshine is gone before Thisbe comes
  back and finds her lover?   296
THESEUS.   She will find him by starlight. (*Enter* THISBE.)
  Here she comes; and her passion ends the play.
HIPPOLYTA.   Methinks she should not use a long one for such a Pyra-
  mus. I hope she will be brief.   300
DEMETRIUS.   A mote° will turn the balance, which Pyramus, which
  Thisbe, is the better: he for a man, God warrant us; she for a
  woman, God bless us.
LYSANDER.   She hath spied him already with those sweet eyes.
DEMETRIUS.   And thus she means,° videlicet:°   305
THISBE.   Asleep, my love?
    What, dead, my dove?
  O Pyramus, arise!
    Speak, speak. Quite dumb?
    Dead, dead? A tomb   310
  Must cover thy sweet eyes.
    These lily lips,
    This cherry nose,
  These yellow cowslip cheeks,
    Are gone, are gone!   315
    Lovers, make moan.
  His eyes were green as leeks.
    O Sisters Three,°
    Come, come to me,
  With hands as pale as milk;   320
    Lay them in gore,
    Since you have shore°
  With shears his thread of silk.
    Tongue, not a word.
    Come, trusty sword,   325
  Come, blade, my brest imbrue.° (*Stabs herself.*)
    And farewell, friends.
    Thus Thisbe ends.
  Adieu, adieu, adieu. (*Dies.*)
THESEUS.   Moonshine and Lion are left to bury the dead.   330
DEMETRIUS.   Ay, and Wall too.

---

294. ass: similar in pronunciation to "ace" in Shakespeare's time   **301. mote:** speck
305. means: moans   **videlicet:** (Latin) as follows   **318. Sisters Three:** the Fates
322. shore: cut   **326. imbrue:** make bloody

BOTTOM (*starting up, as* FLUTE *does also*).   No, I assure you, the wall is down that parted their fathers. Will it please you to see the epilogue, or to hear a Bergomask° dance between two of our company?   334
(*The other players enter.*)

THESEUS.   No epilogue, I pray you; for your play needs no excuse. Never excuse; for when the players are all dead, there need none to be blamed. Marry, if he that writ it had played Pyramus and hanged himself in Thisbe's garter, it would have been a fine tragedy; and so it is, truly, and very notably discharged. But, come, your Bergomask. Let your epilogue alone. (*A dance.*) The iron tongue° of midnight hath told twelve.   341
Lovers, to bed, 'tis almost fairy time.
I fear we shall outsleep the coming morn
As much as we this night have overwatched.°
This palpable-gross° play hath well beguiled   345
The heavy° gait of night. Sweet friends, to bed.
A fortnight hold we this solemnity,
In nightly revels and new jollity. (*Exeunt.*)
(*Enter* PUCK *carrying a broom.*)

PUCK.   Now the hungry lion roars,
        And the wolf behowls the moon,   350
    Whilst the heavy° plowman snores,
        All with weary task fordone.°
    Now the wasted brands do glow,°
        Whilst the screech owl, screeching loud,
    Puts the wretch that lies in woe   355
        In remembrance of a shroud.
    Now it is the time of night
        That the graves, all gaping wide,
    Every one lets forth his sprite,°
        In the church-way paths to glide.   360
    And we fairies, that do run
        By the triple Hecate's team°
    From the presence of the sun,
        Following darkness like a dream,
    Now are frolic.° Not a mouse   365
        Shall disturb this hallowed house.

---

334. Bergomask: a rough country dance   **340–341. iron tongue:** bell   **344. over-watched:** stayed awake too long   **345. palpable-gross:** obviously crude
346. heavy: dull   **351. heavy:** exhausted   **352. fordone:** overcome
353. wasted . . . glow: burned out logs are now only embers   **359. sprite:** ghost
362. triple Hecate's team: the dragons that pull the chariot of the moon (The goddess Hecate had three forms: Luna or Cynthia in the heavens, Diana on the earth, and Proserpina in the underworld.)   **365. frolic:** merry

I am sent with broom before,
To sweep the dust behind° the door.
(*Enter* OBERON *and* TITANIA *with all their train of* FAIRIES.)
OBERON.   Through the house give glimmering light,
  By the dead and drowsy fire;   370
Every elf and fairy sprite
  Hop as light as bird from brier;
And this ditty, after me,
Sing, and dance it trippingly.
TITANIA.   First, rehearse° your song by rote,   375
To each word a warbling note.
Hand in hand, with fairy grace,
Will we sing, and bless this place.
(*Song and dance.*)
OBERON.   Now, until the break of day,
Through this house each fairy stray.   380
To the best bride-bed will we,
Which by us shall blessèd be;
And the issue there create°
Ever shall be fortunate.
So shall all the couples three   385
Ever true in loving be;
And the blots of Nature's hand
Shall not in their issue stand;
Never mole, harelip, nor scar,
Nor mark prodigious,° such as are   390
Despisèd in nativity,
Shall upon their children be.
With this field dew consecrate,°
Every fairy take his gait,°
And each several° chamber bless,   395
Through this palace, with sweet peace;
And the owner of it blest
Ever shall in safety rest.
Trip away; make no stay;
Meet me all by break of day.   400
(*Exeunt* OBERON, TITANIA, *and* FAIRIES.)

---

368. behind: from behind (where presumably a sloppy housekeeper has missed it)
375. rehearse: perform   **383. issue there create:** children conceived there
390. mark prodigious: monstrous birthmark   **393. consecrate:** blessed
394. take his gait: go his way   **395. several:** separate

PUCK (*to the audience*).   If we shadows have offended,
  Think but this, and all is mended,
  That you have but slumbered here
  While these visions did appear.
  And this weak and idle theme,   405
  No more yielding but° a dream,
  Gentles, do not reprehend.
  If you pardon, we will mend.°
  And, as I am an honest Puck,
  If we have unearnèd luck   410
  Now to scape the serpent's tongue,°
  We will make amends ere long;
  Else the Puck a liar call.
  So, good night unto you all.
  Give me your hands,° if we be friends,   415
  And Robin shall restore amends.° (*Exit.*)

QUESTIONS

1. The play contains six love plots, all resolved by the conclusion of the drama. Trace each of these plots from their origins to their resolutions: (1) Hippolyta and Theseus; (2) Hermia and Lysander; (3) Helena and Demetrius; (4) Titania and Oberon; (5) Titania and Bottom; and (6) "Pyramus and Thisbe." Be sure to include any expository material that precedes the action of the play.

2. In addition to the love plots, the play includes the plot of Quince, Bottom, and the other craftsmen preparing their play. How are the goals of these men like and unlike the goals displayed in the lovers' plots?

3. In what ways does the play make the two young men and the two young women similar in characterization? What is the thematic importance of this similarity?

4. There are two pairs of mature lovers—Hippolyta and Theseus, and Titania and Oberon. Sometimes in staging the play, the same actress takes the role of Hippolyta and Titania, the same actor Theseus and Oberon. What thematic ideas might be reinforced by this double casting?

5. Explore the nonrealistic elements of the play. Consider the following: (1) the mythological characters; (2) the supernatural characters; (3) the magical potions; (4) the elapsed time of the play, and its identification with "midsummer" (June 20–21). What truths are being expressed by these nonrealistic means? In particular, what unpleasant or grim realities are alluded to in the dialogue of the fairies?

---

406. No . . . but: Yielding no more than   **408. mend:** improve   **411. serpent's tongue:** hissing of the audience   **415. Give . . . hands:** Applaud   **416. restore amends:** give future satisfaction in return

6. Of the seven plots identified in questions 1 and 2 above, which is most realistic in terms of motivation and character, and which is least realistic?
When considering this question, disregard the supernatural or mythological identifications and explore the characters as human beings.

7. The word "dream" has two relevant meanings in the play: (1) an imaginary event that occurs while sleeping, and (2) the hope, ambition, or aspiration that motivates a person's actions. Explore the occurrences of both
kinds of "dream" (and include in your investigation the synonymous word
"vision"). What universal dream about love and marriage lies at the center of the play? (See Oberon's blessing at the end of 5.1 and Puck's jingle
about Jack and Jill at 3.3.458–63).

8. Until the triple marriage preceding Act 5, there is only one married couple in the play—Titania and Oberon. How does their relationship cast
doubt on the universal dream you identified in the preceding question?

9. "The course of true love never did run smooth," says Lysander (1.1.134).
Is this a sufficient statement of the themes of the play? Of the various obstacles that interfere with the smooth course of love, which are imposed
upon the lovers by outside forces, and which arise from within the lovers'
own feelings? Do the external or the internal obstacles play a larger role?

10. This play contains elements of both "smiling" and "laughing" comedy (see
page 1213). Identify these as fully as you can, and determine which type
predominates.

11. We often leave the performance of a comedy with mixed feelings—
pleasure arising from seeing the success of sympathetic characters overcoming obstacles to their happiness, and a renewed sense that such success does not often occur in real life but depends upon the conventions of
comic drama. How does this play explicitly remind the audience of these
limitations in real life?

August Wilson
Fences

Characters

TROY MAXSON
JIM BONO, *Troy's friend*
ROSE, *Troy's wife*
LYONS, *Troy's oldest son by previous marriage*
GABRIEL, *Troy's brother*
CORY, *Troy and Rose's son*
RAYNELL, *Troy's daughter*

The setting is the yard which fronts the only entrance to the Maxson household, an ancient two-story brick house set back off a small alley in a big-city neighborhood. The entrance to the house is gained by two or three steps leading to a wooden porch badly in need of paint.

A relatively recent addition to the house and running its full width, the porch lacks congruence. It is a sturdy porch with a flat roof. One or two chairs of dubious value sit at one end where the kitchen window opens onto the porch. An old-fashioned icebox stands silent guard at the opposite end.

The yard is a small dirt yard, partially fenced, except for the last scene, with a wooden sawhorse, a pile of lumber, and other fence-building equipment set off to the side. Opposite is a tree from which hangs a ball made of rags. A baseball bat leans against the tree. Two oil drums serve as garbage receptacles and sit near the house at right to complete the setting.

FENCES   First produced in 1985. The setting is a black neighborhood in Pittsburgh, reminiscent of the author's childhood home where he was one of six children raised by their mother in the absence of their white father. August Wilson (born in 1945) quit the football team and dropped out of high school when he was sixteen but continued his education by reading in the public library, where he developed the goal of being a writer. After a series of jobs, he moved to St. Paul, Minnesota, and became involved with the Playwrights Center in Minneapolis. *Fences* is one of ten projected plays dealing with African American experience in the twentieth century (one play for each decade). The action of the play begins ten years after Jackie Robinson (1919–1972) became the first black to play major league baseball. Prior to that time blacks were limited to playing in the Negro Leagues; two of the legendary players in the Leagues were Josh Gibson (1911–1947), called "the Babe Ruth" of the Negro Leagues, and the venerable Satchel Paige (1906–1982). Probably the most celebrated black athlete of the first half of the century was the heavyweight boxing champion Joe Louis (1914–1981).

Near the turn of the century, the destitute of Europe sprang on the city with tenacious claws and an honest and solid dream. The city devoured them. They swelled its belly until it burst into a thousand furnaces and sewing machines, a thousand butcher shops and bakers' ovens, a thousand churches and hospitals and funeral parlors and money-lenders. The city grew. It nourished itself and offered each man a partnership limited only by his talent, his guile, and his willingness and capacity for hard work. For the immigrants of Europe, a dream dared and won true.

The descendants of African slaves were offered no such welcome or participation. They came from places called the Carolinas and the Virginias, Georgia, Alabama, Mississippi, and Tennessee. They came strong, eager, searching. The city rejected them and they fled and settled along the riverbanks and under bridges in shallow, ramshackle houses made of sticks and tarpaper. They collected rags and wood. They sold the use of their muscles and their bodies. They cleaned houses and washed clothes, they shined shoes, and in quiet desperation and vengeful pride, they stole, and lived in pursuit of their own dream: that they could breathe free, finally, and stand to meet life with the force of dignity and whatever eloquence the heart could call upon.

By 1957, the hard-won victories of the European immigrants had solidified the industrial might of America. War had been confronted and won with new energies that used loyalty and patriotism as its fuel. Life was rich, full, and flourishing. The Milwaukee Braves won the World Series, and the hot winds of change that would make the sixties a turbulent, racing, dangerous, and provocative decade had not yet begun to blow full.

ACT 1

SCENE 1

It is 1957. TROY and BONO enter the yard, engaged in conversation. TROY is fifty-three years old, a large man with thick, heavy hands; it is this largeness that he strives to fill out and make an accommodation with. Together with his blackness, his largeness informs his sensibilities and the choices he has made in his life.

Of the two men, BONO is obviously the follower. His commitment to their friendship of thirty-odd years is rooted in his admiration of TROY's honesty, capacity for hard work, and his strength, which BONO seeks to emulate.

It is Friday night, payday, and the one night of the week the two men engage in a ritual of talk and drink. TROY is usually the most talkative and at times he can be crude and almost vulgar, though he is capable of rising to profound heights of expression. The men carry lunch buckets and wear or carry burlap aprons and are dressed in clothes suitable to their jobs as garbage collectors.

BONO.   Troy, you ought to stop that lying!

TROY.   I ain't lying! The nigger had a watermelon this big. (*He indicates with his hands.*) Talking about . . . "What watermelon, Mr. Rand?" I liked to fell out! "What watermelon, Mr. Rand?" . . . And it sitting there big as life.

BONO.   What did Mr. Rand say?

TROY.   Ain't said nothing. Figure if the nigger too dumb to know he carrying a watermelon, he wasn't gonna get much sense out of him. Trying to hide that great big watermelon under his coat. Afraid to let the white man see him carry it home.

BONO.   I'm like you . . . I ain't got no time for them kind of people.

TROY.   Now what he look like getting mad cause he see the man from the union talking to Mr. Rand?

BONO.   He come to me talking about . . . "Maxson gonna get us fired." I told him to get away from me with that. He walked away from me calling you a troublemaker. What Mr. Rand say?

TROY.   Ain't said nothing. He told me to go down the Commissioner's office next Friday. They called me down there to see them.

BONO.   Well, as long as you got your complaint filed, they can't fire you. That's what one of them white fellows tell me.

TROY.   I ain't worried about them firing me. They gonna fire me 'cause I asked a question? That's all I did. I went to Mr. Rand and asked him, "Why? Why you got the white mens driving and the colored lifting?" Told him, "what's the matter, don't I count? You think only white fellows got sense enough to drive a truck. That ain't no paper job! Hell, anybody can drive a truck. How come you got all whites driving and the colored lifting?" He told me "take it to the union." Well, hell, that's what I done! Now they wanna come up with this pack of lies.

BONO.   I told Brownie if the man come and ask him any questions . . . just tell the truth! It ain't nothing but something they done trumped up on you cause you filed a complaint on them.

TROY.   Brownie don't understand nothing. All I want them to do is change the job description. Give everybody a chance to drive the truck. Brownie can't see that. He ain't got that much sense.

BONO.   How you figure he be making out with that gal be up at Taylors' all the time . . . that Alberta gal?

TROY.   Same as you and me. Getting just as much as we is. Which is to say nothing.

BONO.   It is, huh? I figure you doing a little better than me . . . and I ain't saying what I'm doing.

TROY.   Aw, nigger, look here . . . I know you. If you had got anywhere near that gal, twenty minutes later you be looking to tell somebody. And the first one you gonna tell . . . that you gonna want to brag to . . . is me.

BONO.   I ain't saying that. I see where you be eyeing her.

TROY.   I eye all the women. I don't miss nothing. Don't never let nobody tell you Troy Maxson don't eye the women.

BONO.   You been doing more than eyeing her. You done bought her a drink or two.

TROY.   Hell yeah, I bought her a drink! What that mean? I bought you one, too. What that mean cause I buy her a drink? I'm just being polite.

BONO.   It's all right to buy her one drink. That's what you call being polite. But when you wanna be buying two or three . . . that's what you call eyeing her.

TROY.   Look here, as long as you known me . . . you ever known me to chase after women?

BONO.   Hell yeah! Long as I done known you. You forgetting I knew you when.

TROY.   Naw, I'm talking about since I been married to Rose?

BONO.   Oh, not since you been married to Rose. Now, that's the truth, there. I can say that.

TROY.   All right then! Case closed.

BONO.   I see you be walking up around Alberta's house. You supposed to be at Taylors' and you be walking up around there.

TROY.   What you watching where I'm walking for? I ain't watching after you.

BONO.   I seen you walking around there more than once.

TROY.   Hell, you liable to see me walking anywhere! That don't mean nothing cause you see me walking around there.

BONO.   Where she come from anyway? She just kinda showed up one day.

TROY.   Tallahassee. You can look at her and tell she one of them Florida gals. They got some big healthy women down there. Grow them right up out the ground. Got a little bit of Indian in her. Most of them niggers down in Florida got some Indian in them.

BONO.   I don't know about that Indian part. But she damn sure big and healthy. Woman wear some big stockings. Got them great big old legs and hips as wide as the Mississippi River.

TROY.   Legs don't mean nothing. You don't do nothing but push them out of the way. But them hips cushion the ride!

BONO.   Troy, you ain't got no sense.

TROY.   It's the truth! Like you riding on Goodyears!

(ROSE *enters from the house. She is ten years younger than* TROY; *her devotion to him stems from her recognition of the possibilities of her life without him: a succession of abusive men and their babies, a life of partying and running the streets, the Church, or aloneness with its attendant pain and frustration. She recognizes* TROY's *spirit as a fine and illuminating one and she either ignores or forgives his faults, only some of which she recognizes. Though she doesn't drink, her presence is an integral part of the Friday night rituals. She alternates between the porch and the kitchen, where supper preparations are under way.*)

ROSE.   What you all out here getting into?

TROY.   What you worried about what we getting into for? This is men talk, woman.

ROSE.   What I care what you all talking about? Bono, you gonna stay for supper?

BONO.   No, I thank you, Rose. But Lucille says she cooking up a pot of pigfeet.

TROY.   Pigfeet! Hell, I'm going home with you! Might even stay the night if you got some pigfeet. You got something in there to top them pigfeet, Rose?

ROSE.   I'm cooking up some chicken. I got some chicken and collard greens.

TROY.   Well, go on back in the house and let me and Bono finish what we was talking about. This is men talk. I got some talk for you later. You know what kind of talk I mean. You go on and powder it up.

ROSE.   Troy Maxson, don't you start that now!

TROY (*puts his arms around her*).   Aw, woman . . . come here. Look here, Bono . . . when I met this woman . . . I got out that place, say, "Hitch up my pony, saddle up my mare . . . there's a woman out there for me somewhere. I looked here. Looked there. Saw Rose and latched on to her." I latched on to her and told her—I'm gonna tell you the truth—I told her, "Baby, I don't wanna marry, I just wanna be your man." Rose told me . . . tell him what you told me, Rose.

ROSE.   I told him if he wasn't the marrying kind, then move out the way so the marrying kind could find me.

TROY.   That's what she told me. "Nigger, you in my way. You blocking the view! Move out the way so I can find me a husband." I thought it over two or three days. Come back—

ROSE.   Ain't no two or three days nothing. You was back the same night.

TROY.   Come back, told her . . . "Okay, baby . . . but I'm gonna buy me a banty rooster and put him out there in the backyard . . . and when he see a stranger come, he'll flap his wings and crow . . ." Look here, Bono, I could watch the front door by myself . . . it was that back door I was worried about.

ROSE.   Troy, you ought not talk like that. Troy ain't doing nothing but telling a lie.

TROY.   Only thing is . . . when we first got married . . . forget the rooster . . . we ain't had no yard!

BONO.   I hear you tell it. Me and Lucille was staying down there on Logan Street. Had two rooms with the outhouse in the back. I ain't mind the outhouse none. But when that goddamn wind blow through there in the winter . . . that's what I'm talking about! To this day I wonder why in the hell I ever stayed down there for six long years. But see, I didn't know I could do no better. I thought only white folks had inside toilets and things.

ROSE.   There's a lot of people don't know they can do no better than they doing now. That's just something you got to learn. A lot of folks still shop at Bella's.

TROY.   Ain't nothing wrong with shopping at Bella's. She got fresh food.

ROSE.   I ain't said nothing about if she got fresh food. I'm talking about what she charge. She charge ten cents more than the A&P.

TROY.   The A&P ain't never done nothing for me. I spends my money where I'm treated right. I go down to Bella, say, "I need a loaf of bread, I'll pay you Friday." She give it to me. What sense that make when I got money to go and spend it somewhere else and ignore the person who done right by me? That ain't in the Bible.

ROSE.   We ain't talking about what's in the Bible. What sense it make to shop there when she overcharge?

TROY.   You shop where you want to. I'll do my shopping where the people been good to me.

ROSE.   Well, I don't think it's right for her to overcharge. That's all I was saying.

BONO.   Look here . . . I got to get on. Lucille going be raising all kind of hell.

TROY.   Where you going, nigger? We ain't finished this pint. Come here, finish this pint.

BONO.   Well, hell, I am . . . if you ever turn the bottle loose.

TROY (*hands him the bottle*).   The only thing I say about the A&P is I'm glad Cory got that job down there. Help him take care of his school clothes and things. Gabe done moved out and things getting tight around here. He got that job. . . . He can start to look out for himself.

ROSE.   Cory done went and got recruited by a college football team.

TROY.   I told that boy about that football stuff. The white man ain't gonna let him get nowhere with that football. I told him when he first come to me with it. Now you come telling me he done went and got more tied up in it. He ought to go and get recruited in how to fix cars or something where he can make a living.

ROSE.   He ain't talking about making no living playing football. It's just something the boys in school do. They gonna send a recruiter by to talk to you. He'll tell you he ain't talking about making no living playing football. It's a honor to be recruited.

TROY.   It ain't gonna get him nowhere. Bono'll tell you that.

BONO.   If he be like you in the sports . . . he's gonna be all right. Ain't but two men ever played baseball as good as you. That's Babe Ruth and Josh Gibson. Them's the only two men ever hit more home runs than you.

TROY.   What it ever get me? Ain't got a pot to piss in or a window to throw it out of.

ROSE.   Times have changed since you was playing baseball, Troy. That was before the war. Times have changed a lot since then.

TROY.   How in hell they done changed?

ROSE.   They got lots of colored boys playing ball now. Baseball and football.

BONO.   You right about that, Rose. Times have changed, Troy. You just come along too early.

TROY.   There ought not never have been no time called too early! Now you take that fellow . . . what's that fellow they had playing right field for the Yankees back then? You know who I'm talking about, Bono. Used to play right field for the Yankees.

ROSE.   Selkirk?

TROY.   Selkirk! That's it! Man batting .269, understand? .269. What kind of sense that make? I was hitting .432 with thirty-seven home runs! Man batting .269 and playing right field for the Yankees! I saw Josh Gibson's daughter yesterday. She walking around with raggedy shoes on her feet. Now I bet you Selkirk's daughter ain't walking around with raggedy shoes on her feet! I bet you that!

ROSE.   They got a lot of colored baseball players now. Jackie Robinson was the first. Folks had to wait for Jackie Robinson.

TROY.   I done seen a hundred niggers play baseball better than Jackie Robinson. Hell, I know some teams Jackie Robinson couldn't even make! What you talking about Jackie Robinson. Jackie Robinson wasn't nobody. I'm talking about if you could play ball then they ought to have let you play. Don't care what color you were. Come telling me I come along too early. If you could play . . . then they ought to have let you play. (TROY *takes a long drink from the bottle.*)

ROSE.   You gonna drink yourself to death. You don't need to be drinking like that.

TROY.   Death ain't nothing. I done seen him. Done wrassled with him. You can't tell me nothing about death. Death ain't nothing but a fastball on the outside corner. And you know what I'll do to that! Lookee here, Bono . . . am I lying? You get one of them fastballs, about waist high, over the outside corner of the plate where you can get the meat of the bat on it . . . and good god! You can kiss it goodbye. Now, am I lying?

BONO.   Naw, you telling the truth there. I seen you do it.

TROY.   If I'm lying . . . that 450 feet worth of lying! (*Pause.*) That's all death is to me. A fastball on the outside corner.

ROSE.   I don't know why you want to get on talking about death.

TROY.   Ain't nothing wrong with talking about death. That's part of life. Everybody gonna die. You gonna die, I'm gonna die. Bono's gonna die. Hell, we all gonna die.

ROSE.   But you ain't got to talk about it. I don't like to talk about it.

TROY.   You the one brought it up. Me and Bono was talking about baseball . . . you tell me I'm gonna drink myself to death. Ain't that right, Bono? You know I don't drink this but one night out of the week. That's Friday night. I'm gonna drink just enough to where I can handle it. Then I cuts it loose. I leave it alone. So don't you worry about me drinking myself to death. 'Cause I ain't worried about Death. I done seen him. I done wrestled with him.

Look here, Bono . . . I looked up one day and Death was marching straight at me. Like Soldiers on Parade! The Army of Death was marching straight at me. The middle of July, 1941. It got real cold just like it be winter. It seem like Death himself reached out and touched me on the shoulder. He touch me just like I touch you. I got cold as ice and Death standing there grinning at me.

ROSE.   Troy, why don't you hush that talk.

TROY.   I say . . . what you want, Mr. Death? You be wanting me? You done brought your army to be getting me? I looked him dead in the eye. I wasn't fearing nothing. I was ready to tangle. Just like I'm ready to tangle now. The Bible say be ever vigilant. That's why I don't get but so drunk. I got to keep watch.

ROSE.   Troy was right down there in Mercy Hospital. You remember he had pneumonia? Laying there with a fever talking plumb out of his head.

TROY.   Death standing there staring at me . . . carrying that sickle in his hand. Finally he say, "You want bound over for another year?" See, just like that . . . "You want bound over for another year?" I told him, "Bound over hell! Let's settle this now!"

It seem like he kinda fell back when I said that, and all the cold went out of me. I reached down and grabbed that sickle and threw it just as far as I could throw it . . . and me and him commenced to wrestling.

We wrestled for three days and three nights. I can't say where I found the strength from. Every time it seemed like he was gonna get the best of me, I'd reach way down deep inside myself and find the strength to do him one better.

ROSE.   Every time Troy tell that story he find different ways to tell it. Different things to make up about it.

TROY.   I ain't making up nothing. I'm telling you the facts of what happened. I wrestled with Death for three days and three nights and I'm standing here to tell you about it. (*Pause.*) All right. At the end of the third night we done weakened each other to where we can't hardly move. Death stood up, throwed on his robe . . . had him a white robe with a hood on it. He throwed on that robe and went off to look for his sickle. Say, "I'll be back." Just like that. "I'll be back." I told him, say, "Yeah, but . . . you gonna have to find me!" I wasn't no fool. I wasn't going looking for him. Death ain't nothing to play with. And I know he's gonna get me. I know I got to join his army . . . his camp followers. But as long as I keep my strength and see him coming . . . as long as I keep up my vigilance . . . he's gonna have to fight to get me. I ain't going easy.

BONO.   Well, look here, since you got to keep up your vigilance . . . let me have the bottle.

TROY.   Aw hell, I shouldn't have told you that part. I should have left out that part.

ROSE.   Troy be talking that stuff and half the time don't even know what he be talking about.

TROY.   Bono know me better than that.

BONO.   That's right. I know you. I know you got some Uncle Remus° in your blood. You got more stories than the devil got sinners.

TROY.   Aw hell, I done seen him too! Done talked with the devil.

ROSE.   Troy, don't nobody wanna be hearing all that stuff. (LYONS *enters the yard from the street. Thirty-four years old,* TROY'*s son by a previous marriage, he sports a neatly trimmed goatee, sport coat, white shirt, tieless and buttoned at the collar. Though he fancies himself a musician, he is more caught up in the rituals and "idea" of being a musician than in the actual practice of the music. He has come to borrow money from* TROY, *and while he knows he will be successful, he is uncertain as to what extent his lifestyle will be held up to scrutiny and ridicule.*)

LYONS.   Hey, Pop.

TROY.   What you come "Hey, Popping" me for?

LYONS.   How you doing, Rose? (*He kisses her.*) Mr. Bono. How you doing?

Uncle Remus: black narrator of folk tales in a series of books by Joel Chandler Harris (1848–1908)

BONO.   Hey, Lyons . . . how you been?

TROY.   He must have been doing all right. I ain't seen him around here last week.

ROSE.   Troy, leave your boy alone. He come by to see you and you wanna start all that nonsense.

TROY.   I ain't bothering Lyons. (*Offers him the bottle.*) Here . . . get you a drink. We got an understanding. I know why he come by to see me and he know I know.

LYONS.   Come on, Pop . . . I just stopped by to say hi . . . see how you was doing.

TROY.   You ain't stopped by yesterday.

ROSE.   You gonna stay for supper, Lyons? I got some chicken cooking in the oven.

LYONS.   No, Rose . . . thanks. I was just in the neighborhood and thought I'd stop by for a minute.

TROY.   You was in the neighborhood all right, nigger. You telling the truth there. You was in the neighborhood cause it's my payday.

LYONS.   Well, hell, since you mentioned it . . . let me have ten dollars.

TROY.   I'll be damned! I'll die and go to hell and play blackjack with the devil before I give you ten dollars.

BONO.   That's what I wanna know about . . . that devil you done seen.

LYONS.   What . . . Pop done seen the devil? You too much, Pops.

TROY.   Yeah, I done seen him. Talked to him too!

ROSE.   You ain't seen no devil. I done told you that man ain't had nothing to do with the devil. Anything you can't understand, you want to call it the devil.

TROY.   Look here, Bono . . . I went down to see Hertzberger about some furniture. Got three rooms for two-ninety-eight. That what it say on the radio. "Three rooms . . . two-ninety-eight." Even made up a little song about it. Go down there . . . man tell me I can't get no credit. I'm working every day and can't get no credit. What to do? I got an empty house with some raggedy furniture in it. Cory ain't got no bed. He's sleeping on a pile of rags on the floor. Working every day and can't get no credit. Come back here—Rose'll tell you—madder than hell. Sit down . . . try to figure what I'm gonna do. Come a knock on the door. Ain't been living here but three days. Who know I'm here? Open the door . . . devil standing there bigger than life. White fellow . . . white fellow . . . got on good clothes and everything. Standing there with a clipboard in his hand. I ain't had to say nothing. First words come out of his mouth was . . . "I understand you need some furniture and can't get no credit." I liked to fell over. He say, "I'll give you all the credit you want, but you got to pay the interest on it." I told him, "Give me three rooms worth and charge whatever you want." Next day a truck pulled up here and two men unloaded them three rooms. Man what drove the truck give me a book. Say send ten dollars, first of every month to the address in the book and everything will be all right. Say if I miss a payment the devil was coming back and it'll be hell to pay. That was fifteen years ago. To this day . . . the first of the month I send my ten dollars, Rose'll tell you.

Rose.   Troy lying.

Troy.   I ain't never seen that man since. Now you tell me who else that could have been but the devil? I ain't sold my soul or nothing like that, you understand. Naw, I wouldn't have truck with the devil about nothing like that. I got my furniture and pays my ten dollars the first of the month just like clockwork.

Bono.   How long you say you been paying this ten dollars a month?

Troy.   Fifteen years!

Bono.   Hell, ain't you finished paying for it yet? How much the man done charged you?

Troy.   Ah hell, I done paid for it. I done paid for it ten times over! The fact is I'm scared to stop paying it.

Rose.   Troy lying. We got that furniture from Mr. Glickman. He ain't paying no ten dollars a month to nobody.

Troy.   Aw hell, woman. Bono know I ain't that big a fool.

Lyons.   I was just getting ready to say . . . I know where there's a bridge for sale.

Troy.   Look here, I'll tell you this . . . it don't matter to me if he was the devil. It don't matter if the devil give credit. Somebody has got to give it.

Rose.   It ought to matter. You going around talking about having truck with the devil . . . God's the one you gonna have to answer to. He's the one gonna be at the Judgment.

Lyons.   Yeah, well, look here, Pop . . . let me have that ten dollars. I'll give it back to you. Bonnie got a job working at the hospital.

Troy.   What I tell you, Bono? The only time I see this nigger is when he wants something. That's the only time I see him.

Lyons.   Come on, Pop, Mr. Bono don't want to hear all that. Let me have the ten dollars. I told you Bonnie working.

Troy.   What that mean to me? "Bonnie working." I don't care if she working. Go ask her for the ten dollars if she working. Talking about "Bonnie working." Why ain't you working?

Lyons.   Aw, Pop, you know I can't find no decent job. Where am I gonna get a job at? You know I can't get no job.

TROY.   I told you I know some people down there. I can get you on
the rubbish if you want to work. I told you that the last time you came
by here asking me for something.

LYONS.   Naw, Pop . . . thanks. That ain't for me. I don't wanna
be carrying nobody's rubbish. I don't wanna be punching nobody's
time clock.

TROY.   What's the matter, you too good to carry people's rubbish?
Where you think that ten dollars you talking about come from? I'm just
supposed to haul people's rubbish and give my money to you cause you
too lazy to work. You too lazy to work and wanna know why you ain't
got what I got.

ROSE.   What hospital Bonnie working at? Mercy?

LYONS.   She's down at Passavant working in the laundry.

TROY.   I ain't got nothing as it is. I give you that ten dollars and I
got to eat beans the rest of the week. Naw . . . you ain't getting no ten
dollars here.

LYONS.   You ain't got to be eating no beans. I don't know why you
wanna say that.

TROY.   I ain't got no extra money. Gabe done moved over to
Miss Pearl's paying her the rent and things done got tight around here.
I can't afford to be giving you every payday.

LYONS.   I ain't asked you to give me nothing. I asked you to loan
me ten dollars. I know you got ten dollars.

TROY.   Yeah, I got it. You know why I got it? 'Cause I don't
throw my money away out there in the streets. You living the fast
life . . . wanna be a musician . . . running around in them clubs and
things . . . then, you learn to take care of yourself. You ain't gonna
find me going and asking nobody for nothing. I done spent too many
years without.

LYONS.   You and me is two different people, Pop.

TROY.   I done learned my mistake and learned to do what's right
by it. You still trying to get something for nothing. Life don't owe you
nothing. You owe it to yourself. Ask Bono. He'll tell you I'm right.

LYONS.   You got your way of dealing with the world . . . I got mine.
The only thing that matters to me is the music.

TROY.   Yeah, I can see that! It don't matter how you gonna
eat . . . where your next dollar is coming from. You telling the truth
there.

LYONS.   I know I got to eat. But I got to live too. I need something
that gonna help me to get out of the bed in the morning. Make me feel
like I belong in the world. I don't bother nobody. I just stay with the
music 'cause that's the only way I can find to live in the world. Other-

wise there ain't no telling what I might do. Now I don't come criticizing you and how you live. I just come by to ask you for ten dollars. I don't wanna hear all that about how I live.

TROY.   Boy, your mamma did a hell of a job raising you.

LYONS.   You can't change me, Pop. I'm thirty-four years old. If you wanted to change me, you should have been there when I was growing up. I come by to see you . . . ask for ten dollars and you want to talk about how I was raised. You don't know nothing about how I was raised.

ROSE.   Let the boy have ten dollars, Troy.

TROY (*to* LYONS).   What the hell you looking at me for? I ain't got no ten dollars. You know what I do with my money. (*To* ROSE) Give him ten dollars if you want him to have it.

ROSE.   I will. Just as soon as you turn it loose.

TROY (*handing* ROSE *the money*).   There it is. Seventy-six dollars and forty-two cents. You see this, Bono? Now, I ain't gonna get but six of that back.

ROSE.   You ought to stop telling that lie. Here, Lyons. (*She hands him the money.*)

LYONS.   Thanks, Rose. Look . . . I got to run . . . I'll see you later.

TROY.   Wait a minute. You gonna say, "thanks, Rose" and ain't gonna look to see where she got that ten dollars from? See how they do me, Bono?

LYONS.   I know she got it from you, Pop. Thanks. I'll give it back to you.

TROY.   There he go telling another lie. Time I see that ten dollars . . . he'll be owing me thirty more.

LYONS.   See you, Mr. Bono.

BONO.   Take care, Lyons!

LYONS.   Thanks, Pop. I'll see you again. (LYONS *exits the yard.*)

TROY.   I don't know why he don't go and get him a decent job and take care of that woman he got.

BONO.   He'll be all right, Troy. The boy is still young.

TROY.   The *boy* is thirty-four years old.

ROSE.   Let's not get off into all that.

BONO.   Look here . . . I got to be going. I got to be getting on. Lucille gonna be waiting.

TROY (*puts his arm around* ROSE).   See this woman, Bono? I love this woman. I love this woman so much it hurts. I love her so much . . . I done run out of ways of loving. So I got to go back to basics. Don't you come by my house Monday morning talking about time to go to work . . . 'cause I'm still gonna be stroking!

ROSE.   Troy! Stop it now!

BONO.   I ain't paying him no mind, Rose. That ain't nothing but gin-talk. Go on, Troy. I'll see you Monday.

TROY.   Don't you come by my house, nigger! I done told you what I'm gonna be doing. (*The lights go down to black.*)

SCENE 2

The lights come up on ROSE *hanging up clothes. She hums and sings softly to herself. It is the following morning.*

ROSE (*sings*).   Jesus, be a fence all around me every day
        Jesus, I want you to protect me as I travel on my way.
        Jesus, be a fence all around me every day.
(TROY *enters from the house.*)
        Jesus, I want you to protect me
        As I travel on my way.
(*To* TROY) 'Morning. You ready for breakfast? I can fix it soon as I finish hanging up these clothes.

TROY.   I got the coffee on. That'll be all right. I'll just drink some of that this morning.

ROSE.   That 651 hit yesterday. That's the second time this month. Miss Pearl hit for a dollar . . . seem like those that need the least always get lucky. Poor folks can't get nothing.

TROY.   Them numbers don't know nobody. I don't know why you fool with them. You and Lyons both.

ROSE.   It's something to do.

TROY.   You ain't doing nothing but throwing your money away.

ROSE.   Troy, you know I don't play foolishly. I just play a nickel here and nickel there.

TROY.   That's two nickels you done thrown away.

ROSE.   Now I hit sometimes . . . that makes up for it. It always comes in handy when I do hit. I don't hear you complaining then.

TROY.   I ain't complaining now. I just say it's foolish. Trying to guess out of six hundred ways which way the number gonna come. If I had all the money niggers, these Negroes, throw away on numbers for one week—just one week—I'd be a rich man.

ROSE.   Well, you wishing and calling it foolish ain't gonna stop folks from playing numbers. That's one thing for sure. Besides . . . some good things come from playing numbers. Look where Pope done bought him that restaurant off of numbers.

TROY.   I can't stand niggers like that. Man ain't had two dimes to rub together. He walking around with his shoes all run over bumming money for cigarettes. All right. Got lucky there and hit the numbers . . .

ROSE.   Troy, I know all about it.

TROY.   Had good sense, I'll say that for him. He ain't throwed his money away. I seen niggers hit the numbers and go through two thousand dollars in four days. Man bought him that restaurant down there . . . fixed it up real nice . . . and then didn't want nobody to come in it! A Negro go in there and can't get no kind of service. I seen a white fellow come in there and order a bowl of stew. Pope picked all the meat out the pot for him. Man ain't had nothing but a bowl of meat! Negro come behind him and ain't got nothing but the potatoes and carrots. Talking about what numbers do for people, you picked a wrong example. Ain't done nothing but make a worser fool out of him than he was before.

ROSE.   Troy, you ought to stop worrying about what happened at work yesterday.

TROY.   I ain't worried. Just told me to be down there at the Commissioner's office on Friday. Everybody think they gonna fire me. I ain't worried about them firing me. You ain't got to worry about that. (*Pause.*) Where's Cory? Cory in the house? (*Calls*) Cory?

ROSE.   He gone out.

TROY.   Out, huh? He gone out 'cause he know I want him to help me with this fence. I know how he is. That boy scared of work. (GABRIEL *enters. He comes halfway down the alley and, hearing* TROY'S *voice, stops.*) He ain't done a lick of work in his life.

ROSE.   He had to go to football practice. Coach wanted them to get in a little extra practice before the season start.

TROY.   I got his practice . . . running out of here before he get his chores done.

ROSE.   Troy, what is wrong with you this morning? Don't nothing set right with you. Go on back in there and go to bed . . . get up on the other side.

TROY.   Why something got to be wrong with me? I ain't said nothing wrong with me.

ROSE.   You got something to say about everything. First it's the numbers . . . then it's the way the man runs his restaurant . . . then you done got on Cory. What's it gonna be next? Take a look up there and see if the weather suits you . . . or is it gonna be how you gonna put up the fence with the clothes hanging in the yard.

TROY.   You hit the nail on the head then.

ROSE.   I know you like I know the back of my hand. Go on in there and get you some coffee . . . see if that straighten you up. 'Cause you ain't right this morning. (TROY *starts into the house and sees* GABRIEL. GABRIEL *starts singing.* TROY'S *brother, he is seven years younger than* TROY. *Injured in World War II, he has a metal plate in his head. He*

carries an old trumpet tied around his waist and believes with every fiber of
his being that he is the Archangel Gabriel. He carries a chipped basket with
an assortment of discarded fruits and vegetables he has picked up in the strip
district and which he attempts to sell.)

GABRIEL (*singing*).   Yes, ma'am, I got plums
              You ask me how I sell them
              Oh ten cents apiece
              Three for a quarter
              Come and buy now
              'Cause I'm here today
              And tomorrow I'll be gone

(GABRIEL *enters the yard.*) Hey, Rose!

ROSE.   How you doing, Gabe?

GABRIEL.   There's Troy . . . Hey, Troy!

TROY.   Hey, Gabe. (*Exit into kitchen.*)

ROSE (*to* GABRIEL).   What you got there?

GABRIEL.   You know what I got, Rose. I got fruits and vegetables.

ROSE (*looking in basket*).   Where's all these plums you talking
about?

GABRIEL.   I ain't got no plums today, Rose. I was just singing that.
Have some tomorrow. Put me in a big order for plums. Have enough
plums tomorrow for St. Peter and everybody. (TROY *reenters from*
kitchen, crosses to steps.) Troy's mad at me.

TROY.   I ain't mad at you. What I got to be mad at you about? You
ain't done nothing to me.

GABRIEL.   I just moved over to Miss Pearl's to keep out from in
your way. I ain't mean no harm by it.

TROY.   Who said anything about that? I ain't said anything about
that.

GABRIEL.   You ain't mad at me, is you?

TROY.   Naw . . . I ain't mad at you, Gabe. If I was mad at you I'd
tell you about it.

GABRIEL.   Got me two rooms. In the basement. Got my own
door too. Wanna see my key? (*He holds up a key.*) That's my own
key! Ain't nobody else got a key like that. That's my key! My two
rooms!

TROY.   Well, that's good, Gabe. You got your own key . . . that's
good.

ROSE.   You hungry, Gabe? I was just fixing to cook Troy his
breakfast.

GABRIEL.   I'll take some biscuits. You got some biscuits? Did you
know when I was in heaven . . . every morning me and St. Peter would
sit down by the gate and eat some big fat biscuits? Oh, yeah! We had

us a good time. We'd sit there and eat us them biscuits and then St. Peter would go off to sleep and tell me to wake him up when it's time to open the gates for the judgment.

ROSE. Well, come on . . . I'll make up a batch of biscuits. (*Exits into the house.*)

GABRIEL. Troy . . . St. Peter got your name in the book. I seen it. It say . . . Troy Maxson. I say . . . I know him! He got the same name like what I got. That's my brother!

TROY. How many times you gonna tell me that, Gabe?

GABRIEL. Ain't got my name in the book. Don't have to have my name. I done died and went to heaven. He got your name though. One morning St. Peter was looking at his book . . . marking it up for the judgment . . . and he let me see your name. Got it in there under M. Got Rose's name . . . I ain't seen it like I seen yours . . . but I know it's in there. He got a great big book. Got everybody's name what was ever been born. That's what he told me. But I seen your name. Seen it with my own eyes.

TROY. Go on in the house there. Rose going to fix you something to eat.

GABRIEL. Oh, I ain't hungry. I done had breakfast with Aunt Jemimah. She come by and cooked me up a whole mess of flapjacks. Remember how we used to eat them flapjacks?

TROY. Go on in the house and get you something to eat now.

GABRIEL. I got to sell my plums. I done sold some tomatoes. Got me two quarters. Wanna see? (*He shows* TROY *his quarters.*) I'm gonna save them and buy me a new horn so St. Peter can hear me when it's time to open the gates. (GABRIEL *stops suddenly. Listens.*) Hear that? That's the hellhounds. I got to chase them out of here. Go on get out of here! Get out! (GABRIEL *exits singing.*)

> Better get ready for the judgment
> Better get ready for the judgment
> My Lord is coming down

(ROSE *enters from the house.*)

TROY. He's gone off somewhere.

GABRIEL (*offstage*). Better get ready for the judgment

> Better get ready for the judgment morning
> Better get ready for the judgment
> My God is coming down.

ROSE. He ain't eating right. Miss Pearl say she can't get him to eat nothing.

TROY. What you want me to do about it, Rose? I done did everything I can for the man. I can't make him get well. Man got half his head blown away . . . what you expect?

ROSE.   Seem like something ought to be done to help him.

TROY.   Man don't bother nobody. He just mixed up from that metal plate he got in his head. Ain't no sense for him to go back into the hospital.

ROSE.   Least he be eating right. They can help him take care of himself.

TROY.   Don't nobody wanna be locked up, Rose. What you wanna lock him up for? Man go over there and fight the war . . . messin' around with them Japs, get half his head blown off . . . and they give him a lousy three thousand dollars. And I had to swoop down on that.

ROSE.   Is you fixing to go into that again?

TROY.   That's the only way I got a roof over my head . . . 'cause of that metal plate.

ROSE.   Ain't no sense you blaming yourself for nothing. Gabe wasn't in no condition to manage that money. You done what was right by him. Can't nobody say you ain't done what was right by him. Look how long you took care of him . . . till he wanted to have his own place and moved over there with Miss Pearl.

TROY.   That ain't what I'm saying, woman! I'm just stating the facts. If my brother didn't have that metal plate in his head . . . I wouldn't have a pot to piss in or a window to throw it out of. And I'm fifty-three years old. Now see if you can understand that! (TROY *gets up from the porch and starts to exit the yard.*)

ROSE.   Where you going off to? You been running out of here every Saturday for weeks. I thought you was gonna work on this fence?

TROY.   I'm gonna walk down to Taylors'. Listen to the ball game. I'll be back in a bit. I'll work on it when I get back. (*He exits the yard. The lights go to black.*)

SCENE 3

The lights come up on the yard. It is four hours later. ROSE *is taking down the clothes from the line.* CORY *enters carrying his football equipment.*

ROSE.   Your daddy like to had a fit with you running out of here this morning without doing your chores.

CORY.   I told you I had to go to practice.

ROSE.   He say you were supposed to help him with this fence.

CORY.   He been saying that the last four or five Saturdays, and then he don't never do nothing, but go down to Taylors'. Did you tell him about the recruiter?

ROSE.   Yeah, I told him.

CORY.   What he say?

ROSE.   He ain't said nothing too much. You get in there and get started on your chores before he gets back. Go on and scrub down them steps before he gets back here hollering and carrying on.

CORY.   I'm hungry. What you got to eat, Mama?

ROSE.   Go on and get started on your chores. I got some meat loaf in there. Go on and make you a sandwich . . . and don't leave no mess in there. (CORY *exits into the house.* ROSE *continues to take down the clothes.* TROY *enters the yard and sneaks up and grabs her from behind.*) Troy! Go on, now. You liked to scared me to death. What was the score of the game? Lucille had me on the phone and I couldn't keep up with it.

TROY.   What I care about the game? Come here, woman. (*He tries to kiss her.*)

ROSE.   I thought you went down Taylors' to listen to the game. Go on, Troy! You supposed to be putting up this fence.

TROY (*attempting to kiss her again*).   I'll put it up when I finish with what is at hand.

ROSE.   Go on, Troy. I ain't studying you.

TROY (*chasing after her*).   I'm studying you . . . fixing to do my homework!

ROSE.   Troy, you better leave me alone.

TROY.   Where's Cory? That boy brought his butt home yet?

ROSE.   He's in the house doing his chores.

TROY (*calling*).   Cory! Get your butt out here, boy! (ROSE *exits into the house with the laundry.* TROY *goes over to the pile of wood, picks up a board, and starts sawing.* CORY *enters from the house.*) You just now coming in here from leaving this morning?

CORY.   Yeah, I had to go to football practice.

TROY.   Yeah, what?

CORY.   Yessir.

TROY.   I ain't but two seconds off you noway. The garbage sitting in there overflowing . . . you ain't done none of your chores . . . and you come in here talking about "Yeah."

CORY.   I was just getting ready to do my chores now, Pop . . .

TROY.   Your first chore is to help me with this fence on Saturday. Everything else come after that. Now get that saw and cut them boards. (CORY *takes the saw and begins cutting the boards.* TROY *continues working. There is a long pause.*)

CORY.   Hey, Pop . . . why don't you buy a TV?

TROY.   What I want with a TV? What I want one of them for?

CORY.   Everybody got one. Earl, Ba Bra . . . Jesse!

TROY.   I ain't asked you who had one. I say what I want with one?

CORY.   So you can watch it. They got lots of things on TV. Baseball games and everything. We could watch the World Series.

TROY.   Yeah . . . and how much this TV cost?

CORY.   I don't know. They got them on sale for around two hundred dollars.

TROY.   Two hundred dollars, huh?

CORY.   That ain't that much, Pop.

TROY.   Naw, it's just two hundred dollars. See that roof you got over your head at night? Let me tell you something about that roof. It's been over ten years since that roof was last tarred. See now . . . the snow come this winter and sit up there on that roof like it is . . . and it's gonna seep inside. It's just gonna be a little bit . . . ain't gonna hardly notice it. Then the next thing you know, it's gonna be leaking all over the house. Then the wood rot from all that water and you gonna need a whole new roof. Now, how much you think it cost to get that roof tarred?

CORY.   I don't know.

TROY.   Two hundred and sixty-four dollars . . . cash money. While you thinking about a TV, I got to be thinking about the roof . . . and whatever else go wrong here. Now if you had two hundred dollars, what would you do . . . fix the roof or buy a TV?

CORY.   I'd buy a TV. Then when the roof started to leak . . . when it needed fixing . . . I'd fix it.

TROY.   Where you gonna get the money from? You done spent it for a TV. You gonna sit up and watch the water run all over your brand new TV.

CORY.   Aw, Pop. You got money. I know you do.

TROY.   Where I got it at, huh?

CORY.   You got it in the bank.

TROY.   You wanna see my bankbook? You wanna see that seventy-three dollars and twenty-two cents I got sitting up in there?

CORY.   You ain't got to pay for it all at one time. You can put a down payment on it and carry it on home with you.

TROY.   Not me. I ain't gonna owe nobody nothing if I can help it. Miss a payment and they come and snatch it right out your house. Then what you got? Now, soon as I get two hundred dollars clear, then I'll buy a TV. Right now, as soon as I get two hundred and sixty-four dollars, I'm gonna have this roof tarred.

CORY.   Aw . . . Pop!

TROY.   You go on and get you two hundred dollars and buy one if ya want it. I got better things to do with my money.

CORY.   I can't get no two hundred dollars. I ain't never seen two hundred dollars.

TROY.   I'll tell you what . . . you get you a hundred dollars and I'll put the other hundred with it.

CORY.   All right, I'm gonna show you.

TROY.   You gonna show me how you can cut them boards right now. (CORY *begins to cut the boards. There is a long pause.*)

CORY.   The Pirates won today. That makes five in a row.

TROY.   I ain't thinking about the Pirates. Got an all-white team. Got that boy . . . that Puerto Rican boy . . . Clemente. Don't even half-play him. That boy could be something if they give him a chance. Play him one day and sit him on the bench the next.

CORY.   He gets a lot of chances to play.

TROY.   I'm talking about playing regular. Playing every day so you can get your timing. That's what I'm talking about.

CORY.   They got some white guys on the team that don't play every day. You can't play everybody at the same time.

TROY.   If they got a white fellow sitting on the bench . . . you can bet your last dollar he can't play! The colored guy got to be twice as good before he get on the team. That's why I don't want you to get all tied up in them sports. Man on the team and what it get him? They got colored on the team and don't use them. Same as not having them. All them teams the same.

CORY.   The Braves got Hank Aaron and Wes Covington. Hank Aaron hit two home runs today. That makes forty-three.

TROY.   Hank Aaron ain't nobody. That what you supposed to do. That's how you supposed to play the game. Ain't nothing to it. It's just a matter of timing . . . getting the right follow-through. Hell, I can hit forty-three home runs right now!

CORY.   Not off no major-league pitching, you couldn't.

TROY.   We had better pitching in the Negro leagues. I hit seven home runs off of Satchel Paige. You can't get no better than that!

CORY.   Sandy Koufax. He's leading the league in strikeouts.

TROY.   I ain't thinking of no Sandy Koufax.

CORY.   You got Warren Spahn and Lew Burdette. I bet you couldn't hit no home runs off of Warren Spahn.

TROY.   I'm through with it now. You go on and cut them boards. (*Pause.*) Your mama tell me you done got recruited by a college football team? Is that right?

CORY.   Yeah. Coach Zellman say the recruiter gonna be coming by to talk to you. Get you to sign the permission papers.

TROY.   I thought you supposed to be working down there at the A&P. Ain't you suppose to be working down there after school?

CORY.   Mr. Stawicki say he gonna hold my job for me until after the football season. Say starting next week I can work weekends.

TROY.   I thought we had an understanding about this football stuff? You suppose to keep up with your chores and hold that job down at the A&P. Ain't been around here all day on a Saturday. Ain't none of your chores done . . . and now you telling me you done quit your job.

CORY.   I'm going to be working weekends.

TROY.   You damn right you are! And ain't no need for nobody coming around here to talk to me about signing nothing.

CORY.   Hey, Pop . . . you can't do that. He's coming all the way from North Carolina.

TROY.   I don't care where he coming from. The white man ain't gonna let you get nowhere with that football noway. You go on and get your book-learning so you can work yourself up in that A&P or learn how to fix cars or build houses or something, get you a trade. That way you have something can't nobody take away from you. You go on and learn how to put your hands to some good use. Besides hauling people's garbage.

CORY.   I get good grades, Pop. That's why the recruiter wants to talk with you. You got to keep up your grades to get recruited. This way I'll be going to college. I'll get a chance . . .

TROY.   First you gonna get your butt down there to the A&P and get your job back.

CORY.   Mr. Stawicki done already hired somebody else 'cause I told him I was playing football.

TROY.   You a bigger fool than I thought . . . to let somebody take away your job so you can play some football. Where you gonna get your money to take out your girlfriend and whatnot? What kind of foolishness is that to let somebody take away your job?

CORY.   I'm still gonna be working weekends.

TROY.   Naw . . . naw. You getting your butt out of here and finding you another job.

CORY.   Come on, Pop! I got to practice. I can't work after school and play football too. The team needs me. That's what Coach Zellman say . . .

TROY.   I don't care what nobody else say. I'm the boss . . . you understand? I'm the boss around here. I do the only saying what counts.

CORY.   Come on, Pop!

TROY.   I asked you . . . did you understand?

CORY.   Yeah . . .

TROY.   What?!

CORY.   Yessir.

TROY.   You go on down there to that A&P and see if you can get your job back. If you can't do both . . . then you quit the football team. You've got to take the crookeds with the straights.

CORY.   Yessir. (*Pause.*) Can I ask you a question?

TROY.   What the hell you wanna ask me? Mr. Stawicki the one you got the questions for.

CORY.   How come you ain't never liked me?

TROY.   Liked you? Who the hell say I got to like you? What law is there say I got to like you? Wanna stand up in my face and ask a damn fool-ass question like that. Talking about liking somebody. Come here, boy, when I talk to you. (CORY *comes over to where* TROY *is working. He stands slouched over and* TROY *shoves him on his shoulder.*) Straighten up, goddammit! I asked you a question . . . what law is there say I got to like you?

CORY.   None.

TROY.   Well, all right then! Don't you eat every day? (*Pause.*) Answer me when I talk to you! Don't you eat every day?

CORY.   Yeah.

TROY.   Nigger, as long as you in my house, you put that sir on the end of it when you talk to me!

CORY.   Yes . . . sir.

TROY.   You eat every day.

CORY.   Yessir!

TROY.   Got a roof over your head.

CORY.   Yessir!

TROY.   Got clothes on your back.

CORY.   Yessir.

TROY.   Why you think that is?

CORY.   'Cause of you.

TROY.   Ah, hell I know it's 'cause of me . . . but why do you think that is?

CORY (*hesitant*).   'Cause you like me.

TROY.   Like you? I go out of here every morning . . . bust my butt . . . putting up with them crackers every day . . . 'cause I like you? You are the biggest fool I ever saw. (*Pause.*) It's my job. It's my responsibility! You understand that? A man got to take care of his family. You live in my house . . . sleep you behind on my bedclothes . . . fill you belly up with my food . . . 'cause you my son. You my flesh and blood. Not 'cause I like you! 'Cause it's my duty to take care of you. I owe a responsibility to you! Let's get this straight right here . . . before it go along any further . . . I ain't got to like you. Mr. Rand don't give me my money come payday 'cause he likes me. He give me 'cause he owe me. I done give you everything I had to give you. I gave you your life! Me and your mama worked that out between us. And liking your black ass wasn't part of the bargain.

Don't you try and go through life worrying about if somebody like you or not. You best be making sure they doing right by you. You understand what I'm saying, boy?

CORY.   Yessir.

TROY.   Then get the hell out of my face, and get on down to that A&P. (ROSE *has been standing behind the screen door for much of the scene. She enters as* CORY *exits.*)

ROSE.   Why don't you let the boy go ahead and play football, Troy? Ain't no harm in that. He's just trying to be like you with the sports.

TROY.   I don't want him to be like me! I want him to move as far away from my life as he can get. You the only decent thing that ever happened to me. I wish him that. But I don't wish him a thing else from my life. I decided seventeen years ago that boy wasn't getting involved in no sports. Not after what they did to me in the sports.

ROSE.   Troy, why don't you admit you was too old to play in the major leagues? For once . . . why don't you admit that?

TROY.   What do you mean too old? Don't come telling me I was too old. I just wasn't the right color. Hell, I'm fifty-three years old and can do better than Selkirk's .269 right now!

ROSE.   How's was you gonna play ball when you were over forty? Sometimes I can't get no sense out of you.

TROY.   I got good sense, woman. I got sense enough not to let my boy get hurt over playing no sports. You been mothering that boy too much. Worried about if people like him.

ROSE.   Everything that boy do . . . he do for you. He wants you to say "Good job, son." That's all.

TROY.   Rose, I ain't got time for that. He's alive. He's healthy. He's got to make his own way. I made mine. Ain't nobody gonna hold his hand when he get out there in that world.

ROSE.   Times have changed from when you was young, Troy. People change. The world's changing around you and you can't even see it.

TROY (*slow, methodical*).   Woman . . . I do the best I can do. I come in here every Friday. I carry a sack of potatoes and a bucket of lard. You all line up at the door with your hands out. I give you the lint from my pockets. I give you my sweat and my blood. I ain't got no tears. I done spent them. We go upstairs in that room at night . . . and I fall down on you and try to blast a hole into forever. I get up Monday morning . . . find my lunch on the table. I go out. Make my way. Find my strength to carry me through to the next Friday. (*Pause.*) That's all I got, Rose. That's all I got to give. I can't give nothing else. (TROY *exits into the house. The lights go down to black.*)

SCENE 4

It is Friday. Two weeks later. Cory *starts out of the house with his football equipment. The phone rings.*

Cory (*calling*).   I got it! (*He answers the phone and stands in the screen door talking.*) Hello? Hey, Jesse. Naw . . . I was just getting ready to leave now.

Rose (*calling*).   Cory!

Cory.   I told you, man, them spikes is all tore up. You can use them if you want, but they ain't no good. Earl got some spikes.

Rose (*calling*).   Cory!

Cory (*calling to* Rose).   Mam? I'm talking to Jesse. (*Into phone*) When she say that? (*Pause.*) Aw, you lying, man. I'm gonna tell her you said that.

Rose (*calling*).   Cory, don't you go nowhere!

Cory.   I got to go to the game, Ma! (*Into the phone*) Yeah, hey, look, I'll talk to you later. Yeah, I'll meet you over Earl's house. Later. Bye, Ma. (Cory *exits the house and starts out the yard.*)

Rose.   Cory, where you going off to? You got that stuff all pulled out and thrown all over your room.

Cory (*in the yard*).   I was looking for my spikes. Jesse wanted to borrow my spikes.

Rose.   Get up there and get that cleaned up before your daddy get back in here.

Cory.   I got to go to the game! I'll clean it up when I get back. (Cory *exits.*)

Rose.   That's all he need to do is see that room all messed up. (Rose *exits into the house.* Troy *and* Bono *enter the yard.* Troy *is dressed in clothes other than his work clothes.*)

Bono.   He told him the same thing he told you. Take it to the union.

Troy.   Brownie ain't got that much sense. Man wasn't thinking about nothing. He wait until I confront them on it . . . then he wanna come crying seniority. (*Calls*) Hey, Rose!

Bono.   I wish I could have seen Mr. Rand's face when he told you.

Troy.   He couldn't get it out of his mouth! Liked to bit his tongue! When they called me down there to the Commissioner's office . . . he thought they was gonna fire me. Like everybody else.

Bono.   I didn't think they was gonna fire you. I thought they was gonna put you on the warning paper.

Troy.   Hey, Rose! (*To* Bono) Yeah, Mr. Rand like to bit his tongue. (Troy *breaks the seal on the bottle, takes a drink, and hands it to* Bono.)

BONO. I see you run right down to Taylors' and told that Alberta gal.

TROY (*calling*). Hey Rose! (*To* BONO) I told everybody. Hey, Rose! I went down there to cash my check.

ROSE (*entering from the house*). Hush all that hollering, man! I know you out here. What they say down there at the Commissioner's office?

TROY. You supposed to come when I call you, woman. Bono'll tell you that. (*To* BONO) Don't Lucille come when you call her?

ROSE. Man, hush your mouth. I ain't no dog . . . talk about "come when you call me."

TROY (*puts his arm around* ROSE). You hear this, Bono? I had me an old dog used to get uppity like that. You say, "C'mere, Blue!" . . . and he just lay there and look at you. End up getting a stick and chasing him away trying to make him come.

ROSE. I ain't studying you and your dog. I remember you used to sing that old song.

TROY (*he sings*). Hear it ring! Hear it ring! I had a dog his name was Blue.

ROSE. Don't nobody wanna hear you sing that old song.

TROY (*sings*). You know Blue was mighty true.

ROSE. Used to have Cory running around here singing that song.

BONO. Hell, I remember that song myself.

TROY (*sings*). You know Blue was a good old dog.
    Blue treed a possum in a hollow log.
That was my daddy's song. My daddy made up that song.

ROSE. I don't care who made it up. Don't nobody wanna hear you sing it.

TROY (*makes a song like calling a dog*). Come here, woman.

ROSE. You come in here carrying on, I reckon they ain't fired you. What they say down there at the Commissioner's office?

TROY. Look here, Rose . . . Mr. Rand called me into his office today when I got back from talking to them people down there . . . it come from up top . . . he called me in and told me they was making me a driver.

ROSE. Troy, you kidding!

TROY. No I ain't. Ask Bono.

ROSE. Well, that's great, Troy. Now you don't have to hassle them people no more. (LYONS *enters from the street.*)

TROY. Aw hell, I wasn't looking to see you today. I thought you was in jail. Got it all over the front page of the *Courier* about them raiding Sefus's place . . . where you be hanging out with all them thugs.

LYONS.   Hey, Pop . . . that ain't got nothing to do with me. I don't go down there gambling. I go down there to sit in with the band. I ain't got nothing to do with the gambling part. They got some good music down there.

TROY.   They got some rogues . . . is what they got.

LYONS.   How you been, Mr. Bono? Hi, Rose.

BONO.   I see where you playing down at the Crawford Grill tonight.

ROSE.   How come you ain't brought Bonnie like I told you? You should have brought Bonnie with you, she ain't been over in a month of Sundays.

LYONS.   I was just in the neighborhood . . . thought I'd stop by.

TROY.   Here he come . . .

BONO.   Your daddy got a promotion on the rubbish. He's gonna be the first colored driver. Ain't got to do nothing but sit up there and read the paper like them white fellows.

LYONS.   Hey, Pop . . . if you knew how to read you'd be all right.

BONO.   Naw . . . naw . . . you mean if the nigger knew how to *drive* he'd be all right. Been fighting with them people about driving and ain't even got a license. Mr. Rand know you ain't got no driver's license?

TROY.   Driving ain't nothing. All you do is point the truck where you want it to go. Driving ain't nothing.

BONO.   Do Mr. Rand know you ain't got no driver's license? That's what I'm talking about. I ain't asked if driving was easy. I asked if Mr. Rand know you ain't got no driver's license.

TROY.   He ain't got to know. The man ain't got to know my business. Time he find out, I have two or three driver's licenses.

LYONS (*going into his pocket*).   Say, look here, Pop . . .

TROY.   I knew it was coming. Didn't I tell you, Bono? I know what kind of "Look here, Pop" that was. The nigger fixing to ask me for some money. It's Friday night. It's my payday. All them rogues down there on the avenue . . . the ones that ain't in jail . . . and Lyons is hopping in his shoes to get down there with them.

LYONS.   See, Pop . . . if you give somebody else a chance to talk sometimes, you'd see that I was fixing to pay you back your ten dollars like I told you. Here . . . I told you I'd pay you when Bonnie got paid.

TROY.   Naw . . . you go ahead and keep that ten dollars. Put it in the bank. The next time you feel like you wanna come by here and ask me for something . . . you go on down there and get that.

LYONS.   Here's your ten dollars, Pop. I told you I don't want you to give me nothing. I just wanted to borrow ten dollars.

TROY.   Naw . . . you go on and keep that for the next time you want to ask me.

LYONS.   Come on, Pop . . . here go your ten dollars.

ROSE.   Why don't you go on and let the boy pay you back, Troy?

LYONS.   Here you go, Rose. If you don't take it I'm gonna have to hear about it for the next six months. (*He hands her the money.*)

ROSE.   You can hand yours over here too, Troy.

TROY.   You see this, Bono. You see how they do me.

BONO.   Yeah, Lucille do me the same way. (GABRIEL *is heard singing offstage. He enters.*)

GABRIEL.   Better get ready for the Judgment! Better get ready for . . . Hey! . . . Hey! There's Troy's boy!

LYONS.   How are you doing, Uncle Gabe!

GABRIEL.   Lyons . . . The King of the Jungle! Rose . . . hey, Rose. Got a flower for you. (*He takes a rose from his pocket.*) Picked it myself. That's the same rose like you is!

ROSE.   That's right nice of you, Gabe.

LYONS.   What you been doing, Uncle Gabe?

GABRIEL.   Oh, I been chasing hellhounds and waiting on the time to tell St. Peter to open the gates.

LYONS.   You been chasing hellhounds, huh? Well . . . you doing the right thing, Uncle Gabe. Somebody got to chase them.

GABRIEL.   Oh, yeah . . . I know it. The devil's strong. The devil ain't no pushover. Hellhounds snipping at everybody's heels. But I got my trumpet waiting on the judgment time.

LYONS.   Waiting on the Battle of Armageddon, huh?

GABRIEL.   Ain't gonna be too much of a battle when God get to waving that Judgment sword. But the people's gonna have a hell of a time trying to get into heaven if them gates ain't open.

LYONS (*putting his arm around* GABRIEL).   You hear this, Pop. Uncle Gabe, you all right!

GABRIEL (*laughing with* LYONS).   Lyons! King of the Jungle.

ROSE.   You gonna stay for supper, Gabe? Want me to fix you a plate?

GABRIEL.   I'll take a sandwich, Rose. Don't want no plate. Just wanna eat with my hands. I'll take a sandwich.

ROSE.   How about you, Lyons? You staying? Got some short ribs cooking.

LYONS.   Naw, I won't eat nothing till after we finished playing. (*Pause.*) You ought to come down and listen to me play, Pop.

TROY.   I don't like that Chinese music. All that noise.

ROSE.   Go on in the house and wash up, Gabe . . . I'll fix you a sandwich.

GABRIEL (*to* LYONS, *as he exits*).   Troy's mad at me.

LYONS.   What you mad at Uncle Gabe for, Pop?

ROSE.   He thinks Troy's mad at him 'cause he moved over to Miss Pearl's.

TROY.   I ain't mad at the man. He can live where he want to live at.

LYONS.   What he move over there for? Miss Pearl don't like nobody.

ROSE.   She don't mind him none. She treats him real nice. She just don't allow all that singing.

TROY.   She don't mind that rent he be paying . . . that's what she don't mind.

ROSE.   Troy, I ain't going through that with you no more. He's over there 'cause he want to have his own place. He can come and go as he please.

TROY.   Hell, he could come and go as he please here. I wasn't stopping him. I ain't put no rules on him.

ROSE.   It ain't the same thing, Troy. And you know it. (GABRIEL *comes to the door.*) Now, that's the last I wanna hear about that. I don't wanna hear nothing else about Gabe and Miss Pearl. And next week . . .

GABRIEL.   I'm ready for my sandwich, Rose.

ROSE.   And next week . . . when that recruiter come from that school . . . I want you to sign that paper and go on and let Cory play football. Then that'll be the last I have to hear about that.

TROY (*to* ROSE *as she exits into the house*).   I ain't thinking about Cory nothing.

LYONS.   What . . . Cory got recruited? What school he going to?

TROY.   That boy walking around here smelling his piss . . . thinking he's grown. Thinking he's gonna do what he want, irrespective of what I say. Look here, Bono . . . I left the Commissioner's office and went down to the A&P . . . that boy ain't working down there. He lying to me. Telling me he got his job back . . . telling me he working weekends . . . telling me he working after school . . . Mr. Stawicki tell me he ain't working down there at all!

LYONS.   Cory just growing up. He's just busting at the seams trying to fill out your shoes.

TROY.   I don't care what he's doing. When he get to the point where he wanna disobey me . . . then it's time for him to move on. Bono'll tell you that. I bet he ain't never disobeyed his daddy without paying the consequences.

BONO.   I ain't never had a chance. My daddy came on through . . . but I ain't never knew him to see him . . . or what he had on his mind or where he went. Just moving on through. Searching out the New Land. That's what the old folks used to call it. See a fellow moving around from place to place . . . woman to woman . . . called it searching out the New Land. I can't say if he ever found it. I come along, didn't want no kids. Didn't know if I was gonna be in one place long enough to fix on them right as their daddy. I figured I was going searching too. As it turned out I been hooked up with Lucille near about as long as your daddy been with Rose. Going on sixteen years.

TROY.   Sometimes I wish I hadn't known my daddy. He ain't cared nothing about no kids. A kid to him wasn't nothing. All he wanted was for you to learn how to walk so he could start you to working. When it come time for eating . . . he ate first. If there was anything left over, that's what you got. Man would sit down and eat two chickens and give you the wing.

LYONS.   You ought to stop that, Pop. Everybody feed their kids. No matter how hard times is . . . everybody care about their kids. Make sure they have something to eat.

TROY.   The only thing my daddy cared about was getting them bales of cotton in to Mr. Lubin. That's the only thing that mattered to him. Sometimes I used to wonder why he was living. Wonder why the devil hadn't come and got him. "Get them bales of cotton in to Mr. Lubin" and find out he owe him money . . .

LYONS.   He should have just went on and left when he saw he couldn't get nowhere. That's what I would have done.

TROY.   How he gonna leave with eleven kids? And where he gonna go? He ain't knew how to do nothing but farm. No, he was trapped and I think he knew it. But I'll say this for him . . . he felt a responsibility toward us. Maybe he ain't treated us the way I felt he should have . . . but without that responsibility he could have walked off and left us . . . made his own way.

BONO.   A lot of them did. Back in those days what you talking about . . . they walk out their front door and just take on down one road or another and keep on walking.

LYONS.   There you go! That's what I'm talking about.

BONO.   Just keep on walking till you come to something else. Ain't you never heard of nobody having the walking blues? Well, that's what you call it when you just take off like that.

TROY.   My daddy ain't had them walking blues! What you talking about? He stayed right there with his family. But he was just as evil as he could be. My mama couldn't stand him. Couldn't stand that evilness. She run off when I was about eight. She sneaked off one night after he had gone to sleep. Told me she was coming back for me. I ain't never seen her no more. All his women run off and left him. He wasn't good for nobody.

When my turn come to head out, I was fourteen and got to sniffing around Joe Canewell's daughter. Had us an old mule we called Greyboy. My daddy sent me out to do some plowing and I tied up Greyboy and went to fooling around with Joe Canewell's daughter. We done found us a nice little spot, got real cozy with each other. She about thirteen and we done figured we was grown anyway . . . so we down there enjoying ourselves . . . ain't thinking about nothing. We didn't know Greyboy had got loose and wandered back to the house and my daddy was looking for me. We down there by the creek enjoying ourselves when my daddy come up on us. Surprised us. He had them leather straps off the mule and commenced to whupping me like there was no tomorrow. I jumped up, mad and embarrassed. I was scared of my daddy. When he commenced to whupping on me . . . quite naturally I run to get out of the way. (*Pause.*) Now I thought he was mad 'cause I ain't done my work. But I see where he was chasing me off so he could have the gal for himself. When I see what the matter of it was, I lost all fear of my daddy. Right there is where I become a man . . . at fourteen years of age. (*Pause.*) Now it was my turn to run him off. I picked up them same reins that he had used on me. I picked up them reins and commenced to whupping on him. The gal jumped up and run off . . . and when my daddy turned to face me, I could see why the devil had never come to get him . . . 'cause he was the devil himself. I don't know what happened. When I woke up, I was laying right there by the creek, and Blue . . . this old dog we had . . . was licking my face. I thought I was blind. I couldn't see nothing. Both my eyes were swollen shut. I laid there and cried. I didn't know what I was gonna do. The only thing I knew was the time had come for me to leave my daddy's house. And right there the world suddenly got big. And it was a long time before I could cut it down to where I could handle it.

Part of that cutting down was when I got to the place where I could feel him kicking in my blood and knew that the only thing that separated us was the matter of a few years. (GABRIEL *enters from the house with a sandwich.*)

LYONS. What you got there, Uncle Gabe?

GABRIEL. Got me a ham sandwich. Rose gave me a ham sandwich.

TROY. I don't know what happened to him. I done lost touch with everybody except Gabriel. But I hope he's dead. I hope he found some peace.

LYONS. That's a heavy story, Pop. I didn't know you left home when you was fourteen.

TROY. I didn't know nothing. The only part of the world I knew was the forty-two acres of Mr. Lubin's land. That's all I knew about life.

LYONS.   Fourteen's kinda young to be out on your own. (*Phone rings.*) I don't even think I was ready to be out on my own at fourteen. I don't know what I would have done.

TROY.   I got up from the creek and walked on down to Mobile. I was through with farming. Figured I could do better in the city. So I walked the two hundred miles to Mobile.

LYONS.   Wait a minute . . . you ain't walked no two hundred miles, Pop. Ain't nobody gonna walk no two hundred miles. You talking about some walking there.

BONO.   That's the only way you got anywhere back in them days.

LYONS.   Shhh. Damn if I wouldn't have hitched a ride with somebody!

TROY.   Who you gonna hitch it with? They ain't had no cars and things like they got now. We talking about 1918.

ROSE (*entering*).   What you all out here getting into?

TROY (*to* ROSE).   I'm telling Lyons how good he got it. He don't know nothing about this I'm talking.

ROSE.   Lyons, that was Bonnie on the phone. She say you supposed to pick her up.

LYONS.   Yeah, okay, Rose.

TROY.   I walked on down to Mobile and hitched up with some of them fellows that was heading this way. Got up here and found out . . . not only couldn't you get a job . . . you couldn't find no place to live. I thought I was in freedom. Shhh. Colored folks living down there on the riverbanks in whatever kind of shelter they could find for themselves. Right down there under the Brady Street Bridge. Living in shacks made of sticks and tarpaper. Messed around there and went from bad to worse. Start stealing. First it was food. Then I figured, hell, if I steal money I can buy me some food. Buy me some shoes too! One thing led to another. Met your mama. I was young and anxious to be a man. Met your mama and had you. What I do that for? Now I got to worry about feeding you and her. Got to steal three times as much. Went out one day looking for somebody to rob . . . that's what I was, a robber. I'll tell you the truth. I'm ashamed of it today. But it's the truth. Went to rob this fellow . . . pulled out my knife . . . and he pulled out a gun. Shot me in the chest. I felt just like somebody had taken a hot branding iron and laid it on me. When he shot me I jumped at him with my knife. They told me I killed him and they put me in the penitentiary and locked me up for fifteen years. That's where I met Bono. That's where I learned how to play baseball. Got out that place and your mama had taken you and went on to make life without me. Fifteen years was a long time for her to wait. But that fifteen years cured me of that robbing stuff. Rose'll tell you. She asked me when I met her if I had gotten all that foolishness out of my system. And I told her, "Baby, it's you and baseball all what count with me." You hear me, Bono? I mean it too. She say, "Which one comes first?" I told her, "Baby, ain't no doubt it's baseball . . . but you stick and get old with me and we'll both outlive this baseball." Am I right, Rose? And it's true.

ROSE.   Man, hush your mouth. You ain't said no such thing. Talking about, "Baby, you know you'll always be number one with me." That's what you was talking.

TROY.   You hear that, Bono. That's why I love her.

BONO.   Rose'll keep you straight. You get off the track, she'll straighten you up.

ROSE.   Lyons, you better get on up and get Bonnie. She waiting on you.

LYONS (*gets up to go*).   Hey, Pop, why don't you come on down to the Grill and hear me play?

TROY.   I ain't going down there. I'm too old to be sitting around in them clubs.

BONO.   You got to be good to play down at the Grill.

LYONS.   Come on, Pop . . .

TROY.   I got to get up in the morning.

LYONS.   You ain't got to stay long.

TROY.   Naw, I'm gonna get my supper and go on to bed.

LYONS.   Well, I got to go. I'll see you again.

TROY.   Don't you come around my house on my payday.

ROSE.   Pick up the phone and let somebody know you coming. And bring Bonnie with you. You know I'm always glad to see her.

LYONS.   Yeah, I'll do that, Rose. You take care now. See you, Pop. See you, Mr. Bono. See you, Uncle Gabe.

GABRIEL.   Lyons! King of the Jungle! (LYONS *exits*.)

TROY.   Is supper ready, woman? Me and you got some business to take care of. I'm gonna tear it up too.

ROSE.   Troy, I done told you now!

TROY (*puts his arm around* BONO).   Aw hell, woman . . . this is Bono. Bono like family. I done known this nigger since . . . how long I done know you?

BONO.   It's been a long time.

TROY.   I done know this nigger since Skippy was a pup. Me and him done been through some times.

BONO.   You sure right about that.

TROY.   Hell, I done know him longer than I known you. And we still standing shoulder to shoulder. Hey, look here, Bono . . . a man can't ask for no more than that. (*Drinks to him.*) I love you, nigger.

BONO.   Hell, I love you too . . . I got to get home see my woman. You got yours in hand. I got to go get mine. (BONO *starts to exit as* CORY *enters the yard, dressed in his football uniform. He gives* TROY *a hard, uncompromising look.*)

CORY.   What you do that for, Pop? (*He throws his helmet down in the direction of* TROY.)

ROSE.   What's the matter? Cory . . . what's the matter?

CORY.   Papa done went up to the school and told Coach Zellman I can't play football no more. Wouldn't even let me play the game. Told him to tell the recruiter not to come.

ROSE.   Troy . . .

TROY.   What you Troying me for. Yeah, I did it. And the boy know why I did it.

CORY.   Why you wanna do that to me? That was the one chance I had.

ROSE.   Ain't nothing wrong with Cory playing football, Troy.

TROY.   The boy lied to me. I told the nigger if he wanna play football . . . to keep up his chores and hold down that job at the A&P. That was the conditions. Stopped down there to see Mr. Stawicki . . .

CORY.   I can't work after school during the football season, Pop! I tried to tell you that Mr. Stawicki's holding my job for me. You don't never want to listen to nobody. And then you wanna go and do this to me!

TROY.   I ain't done nothing to you. You done it to yourself.

CORY.   Just 'cause you didn't have a chance! You just scared I'm gonna be better than you, that's all.

TROY.   Come here.

ROSE.   Troy . . . (CORY *reluctantly crosses over to* TROY.)

TROY.   All right! See. You done made a mistake.

CORY.   I didn't even do nothing!

TROY.   I'm gonna tell you what your mistake was. See . . . you swung at the ball and didn't hit it. That's strike one. See, you in the batter's box now. You swung and you missed. That's strike one. Don't you strike out! (*Lights fade to black.*)

ACT 2

SCENE 1

The following morning. CORY *is at the tree hitting the ball with the bat. He tries to mimic* TROY, *but his swing is awkward, less sure.* ROSE *enters from the house.*

ROSE. Cory, I want you to help me with this cupboard.

CORY. I ain't quitting the team. I don't care what Poppa say.

ROSE. I'll talk to him when he gets back. He had to go see about your Uncle Gabe. The police done arrested him. Say he was disturbing the peace. He'll be back directly. Come on in here and help me clean out the top of this cupboard. (CORY *exits into the house.* ROSE *sees* TROY *and* BONO *coming down the alley.*) Troy . . . what they say down there?

TROY. Ain't said nothing. I give them fifty dollars and they let him go. I'll talk to you about it. Where's Cory?

ROSE. He's in there helping me clean out these cupboards.

TROY. Tell him to get his butt out here. (TROY *and* BONO *go over to the pile of wood.* BONO *picks up the saw and begins sawing. To* BONO) All they want is the money. That makes six or seven times I done went down there and got him. See me coming they stick out their *hands.*

BONO. Yeah. I know what you mean. That's all they care about . . . that money. They don't care about what's right. (*Pause.*) Nigger, why you got to go and get some hard wood? You ain't doing nothing but building a little old fence. Get you some soft pine wood. That's all you need.

TROY. I know what I'm doing. This is outside wood. You put pine wood inside the house. Pine wood is inside wood. This here is outside wood. Now you tell me where the fence is gonna be?

BONO. You don't need this wood. You can put it up with pine wood and it'll stand as long as you gonna be here looking at it.

TROY. How you know how long I'm gonna be here, nigger? Hell, I might just live forever. Live longer than old man Horsely.

BONO. That's what Magee used to say.

TROY. Magee's a damn fool. Now you tell me who you ever heard of gonna pull their own teeth with a pair of rusty pliers.

BONO. The old folks . . . my granddaddy used to pull his teeth with pliers. They ain't had no dentists for the colored folks back then.

TROY. Get clean pliers! You understand? Clean pliers! Sterilize them! Besides we ain't living back then. All Magee had to do was walk over to Doc Goldblum's.

BONO. I see where you and that Tallahassee gal . . . that Alberta . . . I see where you all done got tight.

TROY. What you mean "got tight"?

BONO. I see where you be laughing and joking with her all the time.

TROY. I laughs and jokes with all of them, Bono. You know me.

BONO. That ain't the kind of laughing and joking I'm talking about. (CORY *enters from the house.*)

CORY.   How you doing, Mr. Bono?

TROY.   Cory? Get that saw from Bono and cut some wood. He talking about the wood's too hard to cut. Stand back there, Jim, and let that young boy show you how it's done.

BONO.   He's sure welcome to it. (CORY *takes the saw and begins to cut the wood*.) Whew-e-e! Look at that. Big old strong boy. Look like Joe Louis. Hell, must be getting old the way I'm watching that boy whip through that wood.

CORY.   I don't see why Mama want a fence around the yard noways.

TROY.   Damn if I know either. What the hell she keeping out with it? She ain't got nothing nobody want.

BONO.   Some people build fences to keep people out . . . and other people build fences to keep people in. Rose wants to hold on to you all. She loves you.

TROY.   Hell, nigger, I don't need nobody to tell me my wife loves me. Cory . . . go on in the house and see if you can find that other saw.

CORY.   Where's it at?

TROY.   I said find it! Look for it till you find it! (CORY *exits into the house*.) What's that supposed to mean? Wanna keep us in?

BONO.   Troy . . . I done known you seem like damn near my whole life. You and Rose both. I done know both of you all for a long time. I remember when you met Rose. When you was hitting them baseball out the park. A lot of them old gals was after you then. You had the pick of the litter. When you picked Rose, I was happy for you. That was the first time I knew you had any sense. I said . . . My man Troy knows what he's doing . . . I'm gonna follow this nigger . . . he might take me somewhere. I been following you too. I done learned a whole heap of things about life watching you. I done learned how to tell where the shit lies. How to tell it from the alfalfa. You done learned me a lot of things. You showed me how to not make the same mistakes . . . to take life as it comes along and keep putting one foot in front of the other. (*Pause*.) Rose a good woman, Troy.

TROY.   Hell, nigger, I know she a good woman. I been married to her for eighteen years. What you got on your mind, Bono?

BONO.   I just say she a good woman. Just like I say anything. I ain't got to have nothing on my mind.

TROY.   You just gonna say she a good woman and leave it hanging out there like that? Why you telling me she a good woman?

BONO.   She loves you, Troy. Rose loves you.

TROY.   You saying I don't measure up. That's what you trying to say. I don't measure up 'cause I'm seeing this other gal. I know what you trying to say.

BONO.   I know what Rose means to you, Troy. I'm just trying to say I don't want to see you mess up.

TROY.   Yeah, I appreciate that, Bono. If you was messing around on Lucille I'd be telling you the same thing.

BONO.   Well, that's all I got to say. I just say that because I love you both.

TROY.   Hell, you know me . . . I wasn't out there looking for nothing. You can't find a better woman than Rose. I know that. But seems like this woman just stuck onto me where I can't shake her loose. I done wrestled with it, tried to throw her off me . . . but she just stuck on tighter. Now she's stuck on for good.

BONO.   You's in control . . . that's what you tell me all the time. You responsible for what you do.

TROY.   I ain't ducking the responsibility of it. As long as it sets right in my heart . . . then I'm okay. 'Cause that's all I listen to. It'll tell me right from wrong every time. And I ain't talking about doing Rose no bad turn. I love Rose. She done carried me a long ways and I love and respect her for that.

BONO.   I know you do. That's why I don't want to see you hurt her. But what you gonna do when she find out? What you got then? If you try and juggle both of them . . . sooner or later you gonna drop one of them. That's common sense.

TROY.   Yeah, I hear what you saying, Bono. I been trying to figure a way to work it out.

BONO.   Work it out right, Troy. I don't want to be getting all up between you and Rose's business . . . but work it so it come out right.

TROY.   Ah hell, I get all up between you and Lucille's business. When you gonna get that woman that refrigerator she been wanting? Don't tell me you ain't got no money now. I know who your banker is. Mellon don't need that money bad as Lucille want that refrigerator. I'll tell you that.

BONO.   Tell you what I'll do . . . when you finish building this fence for Rose . . . I'll buy Lucille that refrigerator.

TROY.   You done stuck your foot in your mouth now! (*Grabs up a board and begins to saw.* BONO *starts to walk out of the yard.*) Hey, nigger . . . where you going?

BONO.   I'm going home. I know you don't expect me to help you now. I'm protecting my money. I wanna see you put that fence up by yourself. That's what I want to see. You'll be here another six months without me.

TROY.   Nigger, you ain't right.

BONO.   When it comes to my money . . . I'm right as fireworks on the Fourth of July.

TROY.   All right, we gonna see now. You better get out your bank-book. (BONO *exits, and* TROY *continues to work.* ROSE *enters from the house.*)

ROSE.   What they say down there? What's happening with Gabe?

TROY.   I went down there and got him out. Cost me fifty dollars. Say he was disturbing the peace. Judge set up a hearing for him in three weeks. Say to show cause why he shouldn't be recommitted.

ROSE.   What was he doing that cause them to arrest him?

TROY.   Some kids was teasing him and he run them off home. Say he was howling and carrying on. Some folks seen him and called the police. That's all it was.

ROSE.   Well, what's you say? What'd you tell the judge?

TROY.   Told him I'd look after him. It didn't make no sense to recommit the man. He stuck out his big greasy palm and told me to give him fifty dollars and take him on home.

ROSE.   Where's he at now? Where'd he go off to?

TROY.   He's gone about his business. He don't need nobody to hold his hand.

ROSE.   Well, I don't know. Seem like that would be the best place for him if they did put him into the hospital. I know what you're gonna say. But that's what I think would be best.

TROY.   The man done had his life ruined fighting for what? And they wanna take and lock him up. Let him be free. He don't bother nobody.

ROSE.   Well, everybody got their own way of looking at it I guess. Come on and get your lunch. I got a bowl of lima beans and some corn-bread in the oven. Come and get something to eat. Ain't no sense you fretting over Gabe. (*Turns to go into the house.*)

TROY.   Rose . . . got something to tell you.

ROSE.   Well, come on . . . wait till I get this food on the table.

TROY.   Rose! (*She stops and turns around.*) I don't know how to say this. (*Pause.*) I can't explain it none. It just sort of grows on you till it gets out of hand. It starts out like a little bush . . . and the next thing you know it's a whole forest.

ROSE.   Troy . . . what is you talking about?

TROY.   I'm talking, woman, let me talk. I'm trying to find a way to tell you . . . I'm gonna be a daddy. I'm gonna be somebody's daddy.

ROSE. Troy . . . you're not telling me this? You're gonna be . . . what?

TROY. Rose . . . now . . . see . . .

ROSE. You telling me you gonna be somebody's daddy? You telling your *wife* this? (GABRIEL *enters from the street. He carries a rose in his hand.*)

GABRIEL. Hey, Troy! Hey, Rose!

ROSE. I have to wait eighteen years to hear something like this.

GABRIEL. Hey, Rose . . . I got a flower for you. (*He hands it to her.*) That's a rose. Same rose like you is.

ROSE. Thanks, Gabe.

GABRIEL. Troy, you ain't mad at me is you? Them bad mens come and put me away. You ain't mad at me is you?

TROY. Naw, Gabe, I ain't mad at you.

ROSE. Eighteen years and you wanna come with this.

GABRIEL (*takes a quarter out of his pocket*).   See what I got? Got a brand new quarter.

TROY. Rose . . . it's just . . .

ROSE. Ain't nothing you can say, Troy. Ain't no way of explaining that.

GABRIEL. Fellow that give me this quarter had a whole mess of them. I'm gonna keep this quarter till it stop shining.

ROSE. Gabe, go on in the house there. I got some watermelon in the Frigidaire. Go on and get you a piece.

GABRIEL. Say, Rose . . . you know I was chasing hellhounds and them bad mens come and get me and take me away. Troy helped me. He come down there and told them they better let me go before he beat them up. Yeah, he did!

ROSE. You go on and get you a piece of watermelon, Gabe. Them bad mens is gone now.

GABRIEL. Okay, Rose . . . gonna get me some watermelon. The kind with the stripes on it. (GABRIEL *exits into the house.*)

ROSE. Why, Troy? Why? After all these years to come dragging this in to me now. It don't make no sense at your age. I could have expected this ten or fifteen years ago, but not now.

TROY. Age ain't got nothing to do with it, Rose.

ROSE. I done tried to be everything a wife should be. Everything a wife could be. Been married eighteen years and I got to live to see the day you tell me you been seeing another woman and done fathered a child by her. And you know I ain't never wanted no half nothing in my family. My whole family is half. Everybody got different fathers and mothers . . . my two sisters and my brother. Can't hardly tell who's who.

Can't never sit down and talk about Papa and Mama. It's your papa and your mama and my papa and my mama . . .

TROY.   Rose . . . stop it now.

ROSE.   I ain't never wanted that for none of my children. And now you wanna drag your behind in here and tell me something like this.

TROY.   You ought to know. It's time for you to know.

ROSE.   Well, I don't want to know, goddamn it!

TROY.   I can't just make it go away. It's done now. I can't wish the circumstance of the thing away.

ROSE.   And you don't want to either. Maybe you want to wish me and my boy away. Maybe that's what you want? Well, you can't wish us away. I've got eighteen years of my life invested in you. You ought to have stayed upstairs in my bed where you belong.

TROY.   Rose . . . now listen to me . . . we can get a handle on this thing. We can talk this out . . . come to an understanding.

ROSE.   All of a sudden it's "we." Where was "we" at when you was down there rolling around with some godforsaken woman? "We" should have come to an understanding before you started making a damn fool of yourself. You're a day late and a dollar short when it comes to an understanding with me.

TROY.   It's just . . . She gives me a different idea . . . a different understanding about myself. I can step out of this house and get away from the pressures and problems . . . be a different man. I ain't got to wonder how I'm gonna pay the bills or get the roof fixed. I can just be a part of myself that I ain't never been.

ROSE.   What I want to know . . . is do you plan to continue seeing her. That's all you can say to me.

TROY.   I can sit up in her house and laugh. Do you understand what I'm saying? I can laugh out loud . . . and it feels good. It reaches all the way down to the bottom of my shoes. (*Pause.*) Rose, I can't give that up.

ROSE.   Maybe you ought to go on and stay down there with her . . . if she's a better woman than me.

TROY.   It ain't about nobody being a better woman or nothing. Rose, you ain't the blame. A man couldn't ask for no woman to be a better wife than you've been. I'm responsible for it. I done locked myself into a pattern trying to take care of you all that I forgot about myself.

ROSE.   What the hell was I there for? That was my job, not somebody else's.

TROY.   Rose, I done tried all my life to live decent . . . to live a clean . . . hard . . . useful life. I tried to be a good husband to you. In every way I knew how. Maybe I come into the world backwards, I don't know. But . . . you born with two strikes on you before you come to the plate. You got to guard it closely . . . always looking for the curve ball on the inside corner. You can't afford to let none get past you. You can't afford a call strike. If you going down . . . you going down swinging. Everything lined up against you. What you gonna do? I fooled them, Rose. I bunted. When I found you and Cory and a halfway decent job . . . I was safe. Couldn't nothing touch me. I wasn't gonna strike out no more. I wasn't going back to the penitentiary. I wasn't gonna lay in the streets with a bottle of wine. I was safe. I had me a family. A job. I wasn't gonna get that last strike. I was on first looking for one of them boys to knock me in. To get me home.

ROSE.   You should have stayed in my bed, Troy.

TROY.   Then when I saw that gal . . . she firmed up my backbone. And I got to thinking that if I tried . . . I just might be able to steal second. Do you understand after eighteen years I wanted to steal second.

ROSE.   You should have held me tight. You should have grabbed me and held on.

TROY.   I stood on first base for eighteen years and I thought . . . well, goddamn it . . . go on for it!

ROSE.   We're not talking about baseball! We're talking about you going off to lay in bed with another woman . . . and then bring it home to me. That's what we're talking about. We ain't talking about no baseball.

TROY.   Rose, you're not listening to me. I'm trying the best I can to explain it to you. It's not easy for me to admit that I been standing in the same place for eighteen years.

ROSE.   I been standing with you! I been right here with you, Troy. I got a life too. I gave eighteen years of my life to stand in the same spot with you. Don't you think I ever wanted other things? Don't you think I had dreams and hopes? What about my life? What about me. Don't you think it ever crossed my mind to want to know other men? That I wanted to lay up somewhere and forget about my responsibilities? That I wanted someone to make me laugh so I could feel good? You not the only one who's got wants and needs. But I held on to you, Troy. I took all my feelings, my wants and needs, my dreams . . . and buried them inside you. I planted a seed and watched and prayed over it. I planted myself inside you and waited to bloom. And it didn't take me no eighteen years to find out the soil was hard and rocky and it wasn't never gonna bloom.

But I held on to you, Troy. I held you tighter. You was my husband. I owed you everything I had. Every part of me I could find to give you.

And upstairs in that room . . . with the darkness falling in on me . . . I gave everything I had to try and erase the doubt that you wasn't the finest man in the world. And wherever you was going . . . I wanted to be there with you. 'Cause you was my husband. 'Cause that's the only way I was gonna survive as your wife. You always talking about what you give . . . and what you don't have to give. But you take too. You take . . . and don't even know nobody's giving! (*Turns to exit into the house;* TROY *grabs her arm.*)

TROY.   You say I take and don't give!

ROSE.   Troy! You're hurting me!

TROY.   You say I take and don't give!

ROSE.   Troy . . . you're hurting my arm! Let go!

TROY.   I done give you everything I got. Don't you tell that lie on me.

ROSE.   Troy!

TROY.   Don't you tell that lie on me! (CORY *enters from the house.*)

CORY.   Mama!

ROSE.   Troy. You're hurting me.

TROY.   Don't you tell me about my taking and giving. (CORY *comes up behind* TROY *and grabs him.* TROY, *surprised, is thrown off balance just as* CORY *throws a glancing blow that catches him on the chest and knocks him down.* TROY *is stunned, as is* CORY.)

ROSE.   Troy. Troy. No! (TROY *gets to his feet and starts at* CORY.) Troy . . . no. Please! Troy! (ROSE *pulls on* TROY *to hold him back.* TROY *stops himself.*)

TROY (*to* CORY).   All right. That's strike two. You stay away from around me, boy. Don't you strike out. You living with a full count. Don't you strike out. (TROY *exits out the yard as the lights go down.*)

SCENE 2

It is six months later, early afternoon. TROY *enters from the house and starts to exit the yard.* ROSE *enters from the house.*

ROSE.   Troy, I want to talk to you.

TROY.   All of a sudden, after all this time, you want to talk to me, huh? You ain't wanted to talk to me for months. You ain't wanted to talk to me last night. You ain't wanted no part of me then. What you wanna talk to me about now?

ROSE.   Tomorrow's Friday.

TROY.   I know what day tomorrow is. You think I don't know tomorrow's Friday? My whole life I ain't done nothing but look to see Friday coming and you got to tell me it's Friday.

ROSE.   I want to know if you're coming home.

TROY.   I always come home, Rose. You know that. There ain't never been a night I ain't come home.

ROSE.   That ain't what I mean . . . and you know it. I want to know if you're coming straight home after work.

TROY.   I figure I'd cash my check . . . hang out at Taylors' with the boys . . . maybe play a game of checkers . . .

ROSE.   Troy, I can't live like this. I won't live like this. You livin' on borrowed time with me. It's been going on six months now you ain't been coming home.

TROY.   I be here every night. Every night of the year. That's 365 days.

ROSE.   I want you to come home tomorrow after work.

TROY.   Rose . . . I don't mess up my pay. You know that now. I take my pay and I give it to you. I don't have no money but what you give me back. I just want to have a little time to myself . . . a little time to enjoy life.

ROSE.   What about me? When's my time to enjoy life?

TROY.   I don't know what to tell you, Rose. I'm doing the best I can.

ROSE.   You ain't been home from work but time enough to change your clothes and run out . . . and you wanna call that the best you can do?

TROY.   I'm going over to the hospital to see Alberta. She went into the hospital this afternoon. Look like she might have the baby early. I won't be gone long.

ROSE.   Well, you ought to know. They went over to Miss Pearl's and got Gabe today. She said you told them to go ahead and lock him up.

TROY.   I ain't said no such thing. Whoever told you that is telling a lie. Pearl ain't doing nothing but telling a big fat lie.

ROSE.   She ain't had to tell me. I read it on the papers.

TROY.   I ain't told them nothing of the kind.

ROSE.   I saw it right there on the papers.

TROY.   What it say, huh?

ROSE.   It said you told them to take him.

TROY.   Then they screwed that up, just the way they screw up everything. I ain't worried about what they got on the paper.

ROSE.   Say the government send part of his check to the hospital and the other part to you.

TROY.   I ain't got nothing to do with that if that's the way it works. I ain't made up the rules about how it work.

ROSE.   You did Gabe just like you did Cory. You wouldn't sign the paper for Cory . . . but you signed for Gabe. You signed that paper. (*The telephone is heard ringing inside the house.*)

TROY.   I told you I ain't signed nothing, woman! The only thing I signed was the release form. Hell, I can't read, I don't know what they had on that paper! I ain't signed nothing about sending Gabe away.

ROSE.   I said send him to the hospital . . . you said let him be free . . . now you done went down there and signed him to the hospital for half his money. You went back on yourself, Troy. You gonna have to answer for that.

TROY.   See now . . . you been over there talking to Miss Pearl. She done got mad 'cause she ain't getting Gabe's rent money. That's all it is. She's liable to say anything.

ROSE.   Troy, I seen where you signed the paper.

TROY.   You ain't seen nothing I signed. What she doing got papers on my brother anyway? Miss Pearl telling a big fat lie. And I'm gonna tell her about it too! You ain't seen nothing I signed. Say . . . you ain't seen nothing I signed. (ROSE *exits into the house to answer the telephone. Presently she returns.*)

ROSE.   Troy . . . that was the hospital. Alberta had the baby.

TROY.   What she have? What is it?

ROSE.   It's a girl.

TROY.   I better get on down to the hospital to see her.

ROSE.   Troy . . .

TROY.   Rose . . . I got to go see her now. That's only right . . . what's the matter . . . the baby's all right, ain't it?

ROSE.   Alberta died having the baby.

TROY.   Died . . . you say she's dead? Alberta's dead?

ROSE.   They said they done all they could. They couldn't do nothing for her.

TROY.   The baby? How's the baby?

ROSE.   They say it's healthy. I wonder who's gonna bury her.

TROY.   She had family, Rose. She wasn't living in the world by herself.

ROSE.   I know she wasn't living in the world by herself.

TROY.   Next thing you gonna want to know if she had any insurance.

ROSE.   Troy, you ain't got to talk like that.

TROY.   That's the first thing that jumped out your mouth. "Who's gonna bury her?" Like I'm fixing to take on that task for myself.

ROSE.   I am your wife. Don't push me away.

TROY.   I ain't pushing nobody away. Just give me some space. That's all. Just give me some room to breathe. (ROSE *exits into the house.* TROY *walks about the yard. With a quiet rage that threatens to consume him.*) All right . . . Mr. Death. See now . . . I'm gonna tell you what I'm gonna do. I'm gonna take and build me a fence around this yard. See? I'm gonna build me a fence around what belongs to me. And then I want you to stay on the other side. See? You stay over there until you're ready for me. Then you come on. Bring your army. Bring your sickle. Bring your wrestling clothes. I ain't gonna fall down on my vigilance this time. You ain't gonna sneak up on me no more. When you ready for me . . . when the top of your list say Troy Maxson . . . that's when you come around here. You come up and knock on the front door. Ain't nobody else got nothing to do with this. This is between you and me. Man to man. You stay on the other side of that fence until you ready for me. Then you come up and knock on the front door. Anytime you want. I'll be ready for you. (*The lights go down to black.*)

SCENE 3

The lights come up on the porch. It is late evening three days later. ROSE *sits listening to the ball game waiting for* TROY. *The final out of the game is made and* ROSE *switches off the radio.* TROY *enters the yard carrying an infant wrapped in blankets. He stands back from the house and calls.*

ROSE *enters and stands on the porch. There is a long, awkward silence, the weight of which grows heavier with each passing second.*

TROY.   Rose . . . I'm standing here with my daughter in my arms. She ain't but a wee bittie little old thing. She don't know nothing about grownups' business. She innocent . . . and she ain't got no mama.

ROSE.   What you telling me for, Troy? (*She turns and exits into the house.*)

TROY.   Well . . . I guess we'll just sit out here on the porch. (*He sits down on the porch. There is an awkward indelicateness about the way he handles the baby. His largeness engulfs and seems to swallow it. He speaks loud enough for* ROSE *to hear*) A man's got to do what's right for him. I ain't sorry for nothing I done. It felt right in my heart. (*To the baby*) What you smiling at? Your daddy's a big man. Got these great big old hands. But sometimes he's scared. And right now your daddy's scared 'cause we sitting out here and ain't got no home. Oh, I been homeless before. I ain't had no little baby with me. But I been homeless. You just be out on the road by your lonesome and you see one of them trains coming and you just kinda go like this . . . (*He sings as a lullaby.*)

       Please, Mr. Engineer let a man ride the line
       Please, Mr. Engineer let a man ride the line
       I ain't got no ticket please let me ride the blinds

(ROSE *enters from the house.* TROY, *hearing her steps behind him, stands and faces her.*) She's my daughter, Rose. My own flesh and blood. I can't deny her no more than I can deny them boys. (*Pause.*) You and them boys is my family. You and them and this child is all I got in the world. So I guess what I'm saying is . . . I'd appreciate it if you'd help me take care of her.

ROSE.   Okay, Troy . . . you're right. I'll take care of your baby for you . . . 'cause . . . like you say . . . she's innocent . . . and you can't visit the sins of the father upon the child. A motherless child has got a hard time. (*She takes the baby from him.*) From right now . . . this child got a mother. But you a womanless man. (ROSE *turns and exits into the house with the baby. Lights go down to black.*)

SCENE 4

It is two months later. LYONS *enters from the street. He knocks on the door and calls.*

LYONS.   Hey, Rose! (*Pause.*) Rose!

ROSE (*from inside the house*).   Stop that yelling. You gonna wake up Raynell. I just got her to sleep.

LYONS.   I just stopped by to pay Papa this twenty dollars I owe him. Where's Papa at?

ROSE.   He should be here in a minute. I'm getting ready to go down to the church. Sit down and wait on him.

LYONS.   I got to go pick up Bonnie over her mother's house.

ROSE.   Well, sit it down there on the table. He'll get it.

LYONS (*enters the house and sets the money on the table*).   Tell Papa I said thanks. I'll see you again.

ROSE.   All right, Lyons. We'll see you. (LYONS *starts to exit as* CORY *enters.*)

CORY.   Hey, Lyons.

LYONS.   What's happening, Cory? Say man, I'm sorry I missed your graduation. You know I had a gig and couldn't get away. Otherwise, I would have been there, man. So what you doing?

CORY.   I'm trying to find a job.

LYONS.   Yeah I know how that go, man. It's rough out here. Jobs are scarce.

CORY.   Yeah, I know.

LYONS.   Look here, I got to run. Talk to Papa . . . he know some people. He'll be able to help you get a job. Talk to him . . . see what he say.

CORY.   Yeah . . . all right, Lyons.

LYONS.   You take care. I'll talk to you soon. We'll find some time to talk. (LYONS *exits the yard.* CORY *wanders over to the tree, picks up the bat, and assumes a batting stance. He studies an imaginary pitcher and swings. Dissatisfied with the result, he tries again.* TROY *enters. They eye each other for a beat.* CORY *puts the bat down and exits the yard.* TROY *starts into the house as* ROSE *exits with* RAYNELL. *She is carrying a cake.*)

TROY.   I'm coming in and everybody's going out.

ROSE.   I'm taking this cake down to the church for the bake sale. Lyons was by to see you. He stopped by to pay you your twenty dollars. It's laying in there on the table.

TROY (*going into his pocket*).   Well . . . here go this money.

ROSE.   Put it in there on the table, Troy. I'll get it.

TROY.   What time you coming back?

ROSE.   Ain't no use in you studying me. It don't matter what time I come back.

TROY.   I just asked you a question, woman. What's the matter . . . can't I ask you a question?

ROSE.   Troy, I don't want to go into it. Your dinner's in there on the stove. All you got to do is heat it up. And don't you be eating the rest of them cakes in there. I'm coming back for them. We having a bake sale at the church tomorrow. (ROSE *exits the yard.* TROY *sits down on the step, takes a pint bottle from his pocket, opens it, and drinks. He begins to sing.*)

TROY.   Hear it ring! Hear it ring!

Had an old dog his name was Blue
You know Blue was mighty true
You know Blue was a good old dog
Blue trees a possum in a hollow log
You know from that he was a good old dog. (BONO *enters the yard.*)

BONO.   Hey, Troy.

TROY.   Hey, what's happening, Bono?

BONO.   I just thought I'd stop by to see you.

TROY.   What you stop by and see me for? You ain't stopped by in a month of Sundays. Hell, I must owe you money or something.

BONO.   Since you got your promotion I can't keep up with you. Used to see you every day. Now I don't even know what route you working.

TROY.   They keep switching me around. Got me out in Greentree now . . . hauling white folks' garbage.

BONO.   Greentree, huh? You lucky, at least you ain't got to be lifting them barrels. Damn if they ain't getting heavier. I'm gonna put in my two years and call it quits.

TROY.   I'm thinking about retiring myself.

BONO.   You got it easy. You can *drive* for another five years.

TROY.   It ain't the same, Bono. It ain't like working the back of the truck. Ain't got nobody to talk to . . . feel like you working by yourself. Naw, I'm thinking about retiring. How's Lucille?

BONO.   She all right. Her arthritis get to acting up on her sometime. Saw Rose on my way in. She going down to the church, huh?

TROY.   Yeah, she took up going down there. All them preachers looking for somebody to fatten their pockets. (*Pause.*) Got some gin here.

BONO.   Naw, thanks. I just stopped by to say hello.

TROY.   Hell, nigger . . . you can take a drink. I ain't never known you to say no to a drink. You ain't got to work tomorrow.

BONO.   I just stopped by. I'm fixing to go over to Skinner's. We got us a domino game going over his house every Friday.

TROY.   Nigger, you can't play no dominoes. I used to whup you four games out of five.

BONO.   Well, that learned me. I'm getting better.

TROY.   Yeah? Well, that's all right.

BONO.   Look here . . . I got to be getting on. Stop by sometime, huh?

TROY.   Yeah, I'll do that, Bono. Lucille told Rose you bought her a new refrigerator.

BONO.   Yeah, Rose told Lucille you had finally built your fence . . . so I figured we'd call it even.

TROY.   I knew you would.

BONO.   Yeah . . . okay. I'll be talking to you.

TROY.   Yeah, take care, Bono. Good to see you. I'm gonna stop over.

BONO.   Yeah. Okay, Troy. (BONO *exits.* TROY *drinks from the bottle.*)

TROY.   Old Blue died and I dig his grave
    Let him down with a golden chain
    Every night when I hear old Blue bark
    I know Blue treed a possum in Noah's Ark.
    Hear it ring! Hear it ring!

(CORY *enters the yard. They eye each other for a beat.* TROY *is sitting in the middle of the steps.* CORY *walks over.*)

CORY.   I got to get by.

TROY.   Say what? What's you say?

CORY.   You in my way. I got to get by.

TROY.   You got to get by where? This is my house. Bought and paid for. In full. Took me fifteen years. And if you wanna go in my house and I'm sitting on the steps . . . you say excuse me. Like your mama taught you.

CORY.   Come on, Pop . . . I got to get by. (CORY *starts to maneuver his way past* TROY. TROY *grabs his leg and shoves him back.*)

TROY.   You just gonna walk over top of me?

CORY.   I live here too!

TROY (*advancing toward him*).   You just gonna walk over top of me in my own house?

CORY.   I ain't scared of you.

TROY.   I ain't asked if you was scared of me. I asked you if you was fixing to walk over top of me in my own house? That's the question. You ain't gonna say excuse me? You just gonna walk over top of me?

CORY.   If you wanna put it like that.

TROY.   How else am I gonna put it?

CORY.   I was walking by you to go into the house 'cause you sitting on the steps drunk, singing to yourself. You can put it like that.

TROY.   Without saying excuse me??? (CORY *doesn't respond.*) I asked you a question. Without saying excuse me???

CORY.   I ain't got to say excuse me to you. You don't count around here no more.

TROY.   Oh, I see . . . I don't count around here no more. You ain't got to say excuse me to your daddy. All of a sudden you done got so grown that your daddy don't count around here no more . . . Around here in his own house and yard that he done paid for with the sweat of his brow. You done got so grown to where you gonna take over. You gonna take over my house. Is that right? You gonna wear my pants. You gonna go in there and stretch out on my bed. You ain't got to say excuse me 'cause I don't count around here no more. Is that right?

CORY.   That's right. You always talking this dumb stuff. Now, why don't you just get out my way?

TROY.   I guess you got someplace to sleep and something to put in your belly. You got that, huh? You got that? That's what you need. You got that, huh?

CORY.   You don't know what I got. You ain't got to worry about what I got.

TROY.   You right! You one hundred percent right! I done spent the last seventeen years worrying about what you got. Now it's your turn, see? I'll tell you what to do. You grown . . . we done established that. You a man. Now, let's see you act like one. Turn your behind around and walk out this yard. And when you get out there in the alley . . . you can forget about this house. See? 'Cause this is my house. You go on and be a man and get your own house. You can forget about this. 'Cause this is mine. You go on and get yours 'cause I'm through with doing for you.

CORY.   You talking about what you did for me . . . what'd you ever give me?

TROY.   Them feet and bones! That pumping heart, nigger! I give you more than anybody else is ever gonna give you.

CORY.   You ain't never gave me nothing! You ain't never done nothing but hold me back. Afraid I was gonna be better than you. All you ever did was try and make me scared of you. I used to tremble every time you called my name. Every time I heard your footsteps in the house. Wondering all the time . . . what's Papa gonna say if I do this? . . . What's he gonna say if I do that? . . . What's Papa gonna say if I turn on the radio? And Mama, too . . . she tries . . . but she's scared of you.

TROY.   You leave your mama out of this. She ain't got nothing to do with this.

CORY.   I don't know how she stand you . . . after what you did to her.

TROY.   I told you to leave your mama out of this! (*He advances toward* CORY.)

CORY.   What you gonna do . . . give me a whupping? You can't whup me no more. You're too old. You just an old man.

TROY (*shoves him on his shoulder*).   Nigger! That's what you are. You just another nigger on the street to me!

CORY.   You crazy! You know that?

TROY.   Go on now! You got the devil in you. Get on away from me!

CORY.   You just a crazy old man . . . talking about I got the devil in me.

TROY.   Yeah, I'm crazy! If you don't get on the other side of that yard . . . I'm gonna show you how crazy I am! Go on . . . get the hell out of my yard.

CORY.   It ain't your yard. You took Uncle Gabe's money he got from the army to buy this house and then you put him out.

TROY (*advances on* CORY).   Get your black ass out of my yard! (TROY's *advance backs* CORY *up against the tree.* CORY *grabs up the bat.*)

CORY.   I ain't going nowhere! Come on . . . put me out! I ain't scared of you.

TROY.   That's my bat!

CORY.   Come on!

TROY.   Put my bat down!

CORY.   Come on, put me out. (*Swings at* TROY, *who backs across the yard.*) What's the matter? you so bad . . . put me out! (TROY *advances toward* CORY. *Backing up*) Come on! Come on!

TROY.   You're gonna have to use it! You wanna draw that bat back on me . . . you're gonna have to use it.

CORY.   Come on! . . . Come on! (CORY *swings the bat at* TROY *a second time. He misses.* TROY *continues to advance toward him.*)

TROY.   You're gonna have to kill me! You wanna draw that bat back on me. You're gonna have to kill me. (CORY, *backed up against the tree, can go no farther.* TROY *taunts him. He sticks out his head and offers him a target.*) Come on! Come on! (CORY *is unable to swing the bat.* TROY *grabs it.*) Then I'll show you. (CORY *and* TROY *struggle over the bat. The struggle is fierce and fully engaged.* TROY *ultimately is the stronger and takes the bat from* CORY *and stands over him ready to swing. He stops himself.*) Go on and get away from around my house. (CORY, *stung by his defeat, picks himself up, walks slowly out of the yard and up the alley.*)

CORY.   Tell Mama I'll be back for my things.

TROY.   They'll be on the other side of that fence. (CORY *exits.*) I can't taste nothing. Hallelujah! I can't taste nothing no more. (TROY *assumes a batting posture and begins to taunt Death, the fastball on the outside corner.*) Come on! It's between you and me now! Come on! Anytime you want! Come on! I be ready for you . . . but I ain't gonna be easy. (*The lights go down on the scene.*)

SCENE 5

The time is 1965. The lights come up in the yard. It is the morning of TROY's *funeral. A funeral plaque with a light hangs beside the door. There is a small garden plot off to the side. There is noise and activity in the house as* ROSE *and* BONO *have gathered. The door opens and* RAYNELL, *seven years old, enters dressed in a flannel nightgown. She crosses to the garden and pokes around with a stick.* ROSE *calls from the house.*

ROSE.   Raynell!

RAYNELL.   Mam?

ROSE.   What you doing out there?

RAYNELL.   Nothing. (ROSE *comes to the door.*)

ROSE.   Girl, get in here and get dressed. What you doing?

RAYNELL.   Seeing if my garden growed.

ROSE.   I told you it ain't gonna grow overnight. You got to wait.

RAYNELL.   It don't look like it never gonna grow. Dag!

Rose. I told you a watched pot never boils. Get in here and get dressed.

Raynell. This ain't even no pot, Mama.

Rose. You just have to give it a chance. It'll grow. Now you come on and do what I told you. We got to be getting ready. This ain't no morning to be playing around. You hear me?

Raynell. Yes, mam. (Rose *exits into the house.* Raynell *continues to poke at her garden with a stick.* Cory *enters. He is dressed in a Marine corporal's uniform, and carries a duffel bag. His posture is that of a military man, and his speech has a clipped sternness.*)

Cory (*to* Raynell). Hi. (*Pause.*) I bet your name is Raynell.

Raynell. Uh huh.

Cory. Is your mama home? (Raynell *runs up on the porch and calls through the screen door.*)

Raynell. Mama . . . there's some man out here. Mama? (Rose *comes to the door.*)

Rose. Cory? Lord have mercy! Look here, you all! (Rose *and* Cory *embrace in a tearful reunion as* Bono *and* Lyons *enter from the house dressed in funeral clothes.*)

Bono. Aw, looka here . . .

Rose. Done got all grown up!

Cory. Don't cry, Mama. What you crying about?

Rose. I'm just so glad you made it.

Cory. Hey Lyons. How you doing, Mr. Bono. (Lyons *goes to embrace* Cory.)

Lyons. Look at you, man. Look at you. Don't he look good, Rose. Got them Corporal stripes.

Rose. What took you so long?

Cory. You know how the Marines are, Mama. They got to get all their paperwork straight before they let you do anything.

Rose. Well, I'm sure glad you made it. They let Lyons come. Your Uncle Gabe's still in the hospital. They don't know if they gonna let him out or not. I just talked to them a little while ago.

Lyons. A Corporal in the United States Marines.

Bono. Your daddy knew you had it in you. He used to tell me all the time.

Lyons. Don't he look good, Mr. Bono?

Bono. Yeah, he remind me of Troy when I first met him. (*Pause.*) Say, Rose, Lucille's down at the church with the choir. I'm gonna go down and get the pallbearers lined up. I'll be back to get you all.

Rose. Thanks, Jim.

Cory. See you, Mr. Bono.

LYONS (*with his arm around* RAYNELL).   Cory . . . look at Raynell. Ain't she precious? She gonna break a whole lot of hearts.

ROSE.   Raynell, come and say hello to your brother. This is your brother, Cory. You remember Cory?

RAYNELL.   No, Mam.

CORY.   She don't remember me, Mama.

ROSE.   Well, we talk about you. She heard us talk about you. (*To* RAYNELL) This is your brother, Cory. Come on and say hello.

RAYNELL.   Hi.

CORY.   Hi. So you're Raynell. Mama told me a lot about you.

ROSE.   You all come on into the house and let me fix you some breakfast. Keep up your strength.

CORY.   I ain't hungry, Mama.

LYONS.   You can fix me something, Rose. I'll be in there in a minute.

ROSE.   Cory, you sure you don't want nothing? I know they ain't feeding you right.

CORY.   No, Mama . . . thanks. I don't feel like eating. I'll get something later.

ROSE.   Raynell . . . get on upstairs and get that dress on like I told you. (ROSE *and* RAYNELL *exit into the house*.)

LYONS.   So . . . I hear you thinking about getting married.

CORY.   Yeah, I done found the right one, Lyons. It's about time.

LYONS.   Me and Bonnie been split up about four years now. About the time Papa retired. I guess she just got tired of all them changes I was putting her through. (*Pause*.) I always knew you was gonna make something out yourself. Your head was always in the right direction. So . . . you gonna stay in . . . make it a career . . . put in your twenty years?

CORY.   I don't know. I got six already, I think that's enough.

LYONS.   Stick with Uncle Sam and retire early. Ain't nothing out here. I guess Rose told you what happened with me. They got me down the workhouse. I thought I was being slick cashing other people's checks.

CORY.   How much time you doing?

LYONS.   They give me three years. I got that beat now. I ain't got but nine more months. It ain't so bad. You learn to deal with it like anything else. You got to take the crookeds with the straights. That's what Papa used to say. He used to say that when he struck out. I seen him strike out three times in a row . . . and the next time up he hit the ball over the grandstand. Right out there in Homestead Field. He wasn't satisfied hitting in the seats . . . he want to hit it over everything! After the game he had two hundred people standing around waiting to shake his hand. You got to take the crookeds with the straights. Yeah, Papa was something else.

CORY.   You still playing?

LYONS.   Cory . . . you know I'm gonna do that. There's some fellows down there we got us a band . . . we gonna try and stay together when we get out . . . but yeah, I'm still playing. It still helps me to get out of bed in the morning. As long as it do that I'm gonna be right there playing and trying to make some sense out of it.

ROSE (*calling*).   Lyons, I got these eggs in the pan.

LYONS.   Let me go on and get these eggs, man. Get ready to go bury Papa. (*Pause.*) How you doing? You doing all right? (CORY *nods.* LYONS *touches him on the shoulder and they share a moment of silent grief.* LYONS *exits into the house.* CORY *wanders about the yard.* RAYNELL *enters.*)

RAYNELL.   Hi.

CORY.   Hi.

RAYNELL.   Did you used to sleep in my room?

CORY.   Yeah . . . that used to be my room.

RAYNELL.   That's what Papa call it. "Cory's room." It got your football in the closet. (ROSE *comes to the door.*)

ROSE.   Raynell, get in there and get them good shoes on.

RAYNELL.   Mama, can't I wear these? Them other ones hurt my feet.

ROSE.   Well, they just gonna have to hurt your feet for a while. You ain't said they hurt your feet when you went down to the store and got them.

RAYNELL.   They didn't hurt then. My feet done got bigger.

ROSE.   Don't you give me no backtalk now. You get in there and get them shoes on. (RAYNELL *exits into the house.*) Ain't too much changed. He still got that piece of rag tied to that tree. He was out here swinging that bat. I was just ready to go back in the house. He swung that bat and then he just fell over. Seem like he swung it and stood there with this grin on his face . . . and then he just fell over. They carried him on down to the hospital, but I knew there wasn't no need . . . why don't you come on in the house?

CORY.   Mama . . . I got something to tell you. I don't know how to tell you this . . . but I've got to tell you . . . I'm not going to Papa's funeral.

ROSE.   Boy, hush your mouth. That's your daddy you talking about. I don't want to hear that kind of talk this morning. I done raised you to come to this? You standing there all healthy and grown talking about you ain't going to your daddy's funeral?

CORY.   Mama . . . listen . . .

ROSE.   I don't want to hear it, Cory. You just get that thought out of your head.

CORY.   I can't drag Papa with me everywhere I go. I've got to say no to him. One time in my life I've got to say no.

ROSE.   Don't nobody have to listen to nothing like that. I know you and your daddy ain't seen eye to eye, but I ain't got to listen to that kind of talk this morning. Whatever was between you and your daddy . . . the time has come to put it aside. Just take it and set it over there on the shelf and forget about it. Disrespecting your daddy ain't gonna make you a man, Cory. You got to find a way to come to that on your own. Not going to your daddy's funeral ain't gonna make you a man.

CORY.   The whole time I was growing up . . . living in his house . . . Papa was like a shadow that followed you everywhere. It weighed on you and sunk into your flesh. It would wrap around you and lay there until you couldn't tell which one was you anymore. That shadow digging in your flesh. Trying to crawl in. Trying to live through you. Everywhere I looked, Troy Maxson was staring back at me . . . hiding under the bed . . . in the closet. I'm just saying I've got to find a way to get rid of that shadow, Mama.

ROSE.   You just like him. You got him in you good.

CORY.   Don't tell me that, Mama.

ROSE.   You Troy Maxson all over again.

CORY.   I don't want to be Troy Maxson. I want to be me.

ROSE.   You can't be nobody but who you are, Cory. That shadow wasn't nothing but you growing into yourself. You either got to grow into it or cut it down to fit you. But that's all you got to make life with. That's all you got to measure yourself against that world out there. Your daddy wanted you to be everything he wasn't . . . and at the same time he tried to make you into everything he was. I don't know if he was right or wrong . . . but I do know he meant to do more good than he meant to do harm. He wasn't always right. Sometimes when he touched he bruised. And sometimes when he took me in his arms he cut.

When I first met your daddy I thought . . . Here is a man I can lay down with and make a baby. That's the first thing I thought when I seen him. I was thirty years old and had done seen my share of men. But when he walked up to me and said, "I can dance a waltz that'll make you dizzy," I thought, Rose Lee, here is a man that you can open yourself up to and be filled to bursting. Here is a man that can fill all them empty spaces you been tipping around the edges of. One of them empty spaces was being somebody's mother.

I married your daddy and settled down to cooking his supper and keeping clean sheets on the bed. When your daddy walked through the house he was so big he filled it up. That was my first mistake. Not to make him leave some room for me. For my part in the matter. But at that time I wanted that. I wanted a house that I could sing in. And that's what your daddy gave me. I didn't know to keep up his strength I had to give up little pieces of mine. I did that. I took on his life as mine and mixed up the pieces so that you couldn't hardly tell which was which anymore. It was my choice. It was my life and I didn't have to live it like that. But that's what life offered me in the way of being a woman and I took it. I grabbed hold of it with both hands.

By the time Raynell came into the house, me and your daddy had done lost touch with one another. I didn't want to make my blessing off of nobody's misfortune . . . but I took on to Raynell like she was all them babies I had wanted and never had. (*The phone rings.*) Like I'd been blessed to relive a part of my life. And if the Lord see fit to keep up my strength . . . I'm gonna do her just like your daddy did you . . . I'm gonna give her the best of what's in me.

RAYNELL (*entering, still with her old shoes*).   Mama . . . Reverend Tollivier on the phone. (ROSE *exits into the house.*)

RAYNELL.   Hi.

CORY.   Hi.

RAYNELL.   You in the Army or the Marines?

CORY.   Marines.

RAYNELL.   Papa said it was the Army. Did you know Blue?

CORY.   Blue? Who's Blue?

RAYNELL.   Papa's dog what he sing about all the time.

CORY (*singing*).   Hear it ring! Hear it ring!
>   I had a dog his name was Blue
>   You know Blue was mighty true
>   You know Blue was a good old dog
>   Blue treed a possum in a hollow log
>   You know from that he was a good old dog.
>   Hear it ring! Hear it ring! (RAYNELL *joins in singing.*)

CORY *and* RAYNELL.   Blue treed a possum out on a limb
>   Blue looked at me and I looked at him
>   Grabbed that possum and put him in a sack
>   Blue stayed there till I came back
>   Old Blue's feets was big and round
>   Never allowed a possum to touch the ground.

Old Blue died and I dug his grave
I dug his grave with a silver spade
Let him down with a golden chain
And every night I call his name
Go on Blue, you good dog you
Go on Blue, you good dog you

RAYNELL.   Blue laid down and died like a man
Blue laid down and died . . .

BOTH.   Blue laid down and died like a man
Now he's treeing possums in the Promised Land
I'm gonna tell you this to let you know
Blue's gone where the good dogs go
When I hear old Blue bark
When I hear old Blue bark
Blue treed a possum in Noah's Ark
Blue treed a possum in Noah's Ark.

(ROSE *comes to the screen door.*)

ROSE.   Cory, we gonna be ready to go in a minute.

CORY (*to* RAYNELL).   You go on in the house and change them shoes like Mama told you so we can go to Papa's funeral.

RAYNELL.   Okay, I'll be back. (RAYNELL *exits into the house.* CORY *gets up and crosses over to the tree.* ROSE *stands in the screen door watching him.* GABRIEL *enters from the alley.*)

GABRIEL (*calling*).   Hey, Rose!

ROSE.   Gabe?

GABRIEL.   I'm here, Rose. Hey Rose, I'm here! (ROSE *enters from the house.*)

ROSE.   Lord . . . Look here, Lyons!

LYONS.   See, I told you, Rose . . . I told you they'd let him come.

CORY.   How you doing, Uncle Gabe?

LYONS.   How you doing, Uncle Gabe?

GABRIEL.   Hey, Rose. It's time. It's time to tell St. Peter to open the gates. Troy, you ready? You ready, Troy. I'm gonna tell St. Peter to open the gates. You get ready now. (GABRIEL, *with great fanfare, braces himself to blow. The trumpet is without a mouthpiece. He puts the end of it into his mouth and blows with great force, like a man who has been waiting some twenty-odd years for this single moment. No sound comes out of the trumpet. He braces himself and blows again with the same result. A third time he blows. There is a weight of impossible description that falls away and leaves him bare and exposed to a frightful realization. It is a trauma that a sane and normal mind would be unable to withstand. He be-*

gins to dance. A slow, strange dance, eerie and life-giving. A dance of atavistic signature and ritual. LYONS *attempts to embrace him.* GABRIEL *pushes* LYONS *away. He begins to howl in what is an attempt at song, or perhaps a song turning back into itself in an attempt at speech. He finishes his dance and the gates of heaven stand open as wide as God's closet.*) That's the way that go!

QUESTIONS

1. Construct a chronological biography of Troy Maxson. How naturally do the expository materials figure into the conversations where they are revealed (that is, what reasons does Troy have for summarizing his past at various points in the play)?

2. Describe the condition of the marriage of Rose and Troy at the opening of the play. What are their habits? How well-meshed are they? What about their marriage has made Troy discontented?

3. What are Troy's relationships to the other characters—Bono, Lyons, Gabriel? Show how these are compounded of both conflict and congruence of feelings.

4. Define the conflicts between Cory and Troy, showing how they develop. In what ways do they resemble those between Troy and his father? What does Troy want to protect Cory from, and what direction does he want him to take? What unspoken dangers does Cory face as a Marine in 1965?

5. Explore the various meanings of the title, from the literal fence Troy is building (why is he? what purpose will it serve?) to the more figurative fences, the obstacles that Troy has faced and overcome. What does the title have to do with Troy's career as a baseball player? How are Troy's victories ironic? (For example, he achieves his wish to become a driver, but what effect does that have on his relationship with Bono? Does it bring him happiness?)

6. What similarities and contrasts exist between this play and *Death of a Salesman*? How is Troy like and unlike Willy Loman in his situations and in his temperament? What is his attitude toward the importance of being "liked"? Does Troy lie to himself or to others?

7. What aspects of this play make it convincingly realistic in its conventions? What qualities of African American urban life in the late fifties does it capture? What universal themes are conveyed within this restricted, specific milieu?

Glossary of Terms

These definitions sometimes repeat and sometimes differ in language from those in the text. Where they differ, the intention is to give a fuller sense of the term's meaning by allowing the reader a double perspective on it. Page numbers refer to the discussions in the text, which in most but not all cases are fuller than those in the glossary. Multiple page references may indicate separate discussions in the various sections of this book—Fiction, Poetry, Drama.

Absurd, Drama of the   A type of drama, allied to *comedy*, radically nonrealistic in both content and presentation, that emphasizes the absurdity, emptiness, or meaninglessness of life. 1061–1062

Accent   In this book, the same as *stress*. A syllable given more prominence in pronunciation than its neighbors is said to be accented. 838

Allegory   A narrative or description that has a second meaning beneath the surface, often relating each literal term to a fixed, corresponding abstract idea or moral principle; usually, the ulterior meanings belong to a pre-existing system of ideas or principles. 281–82, 743

Alliteration   The repetition at close intervals of the initial consonant sounds of accented syllables or important words (for example, *map*–*moon*, *kill*–*code*, *preach*–*approve*). Important words and accented syllables beginning with vowels may also be said to alliterate with each other inasmuch as they all have the same lack of an initial consonant sound (for example, "*Inebriate* of *Air*—am *I* "). 824

Allusion   A reference, explicit or implicit, to something in previous literature or history. (The term is reserved by some writers for implicit references only, such as those in "in Just—," 782; and "On His Blindness," 783, but the distinction between the two kinds of reference is not always clear-cut.) 778–81

Anapest   A metrical foot consisting of two unaccented syllables followed by one accented syllable (for example, ŭn-dĕr-stánd). 842

Anapestic meter   A *meter* in which a majority of the feet are anapests. (But see *Triple meter*.) 842

Anaphora   Repetition of an opening word or phrase in a series of lines. 833

Antagonist   Any force in a story or play that is in conflict with the *protagonist*. An antagonist may be another person, an aspect of the physical or social environment, or a destructive element in the protagonist's own nature. See *Conflict*. 104

Apostrophe   A figure of speech in which someone absent or dead or something nonhuman is addressed as if it were alive and present and could reply. 720

Approximate rhyme   (also known as *imperfect rhyme, near rhyme, slant rhyme*, or *oblique rhyme*) A term used for words in a rhyming pattern that have some kind of sound correspondence but are not perfect rhymes. See *Rhyme*. Approximate rhymes occur occasionally in patterns where most of the rhymes are perfect (for example, *push-rush* in "Leda and the Swan," 788), and sometimes are used systematically in place of perfect rhyme (for example, "Mr. Z," 774). 825

Artistic unity   That condition of a successful literary work whereby all its elements work together for the achievement of its central purpose. In an artistically unified work nothing is included that is irrelevant to the central purpose, nothing is omitted that is essential to it, and the parts are arranged in the most effective order for the achievement of that purpose. 109

Aside   A brief speech in which a character turns from the person being addressed to speak directly to the audience; a dramatic device for letting the audience know what a character is really thinking or feeling as opposed to what the character pretends to think or feel. 1028

Assonance   The repetition at close intervals of the vowel sounds of accented syllables or important words (for example, hat–ran–amber, vein–made). 824

Aubade   A poem about dawn; a morning love song; or a poem about the parting of lovers at dawn. 980

Ballad   A fairly short narrative poem written in a songlike *stanza* form. Examples: "Ballad of Birmingham," 658; "La Belle Dame sans Merci," 975. Also see *Folk ballad*.

Blank verse   Unrhymed iambic pentameter. 852

Cacophony   A harsh, discordant, unpleasant-sounding choice and arrangement of sounds. 867

Caesura   A speech pause occurring within a line. See *Grammatical pause* and *Rhetorical pause*. 839

Catharsis   A term used by Aristotle to describe some sort of emotional release experienced by the audience at the end of a successful tragedy. 1210–1213

Chance   The occurrence of an event that has no apparent cause in antecedent events or in predisposition of character. 109–110

Character   Any of the persons presented in a story or play. 163

Developing (or *dynamic*) *character*   A *character* who during the course of a work undergoes a permanent change in some distinguishing moral qualities or personal traits or outlook. 164–65

Flat character   A *character* whose distinguishing moral qualities or personal traits are summed up in one or two traits. 163–64

Foil character   A minor character whose situation or actions parallel those of a major character, and thus by contrast sets off or illuminates the major character; most often the contrast is complimentary to the major character.

Round character   A *character* whose distinguishing moral qualities or personal traits are complex and many-sided. 163–64

Static character   A *character* who is the same sort of person at the end of a work as at the beginning. 164

Stock character   A stereotyped character: one whose nature is familiar to us from prototypes in previous literature. 164

Characterization   The various literary means by which characters are presented. 161–65

Chorus   A group of actors speaking or chanting in unison, often while going through the steps of an elaborate formalized dance; a characteristic device of Greek drama for conveying communal or group emotion. 1077, 1222

Climax   The turning point or high point in a *plot*. 110

Coincidence   The chance concurrence of two events having a peculiar correspondence between them. 109–110

Comedy   A type of drama, opposed to *tragedy*, having usually a happy ending, and emphasizing human limitation rather than human greatness. 1209–10, 1213–15

Scornful comedy   A type of *comedy* whose main purpose is to expose and ridicule human folly, vanity, or hypocrisy. 1213

Romantic comedy   A type of *comedy* whose likable and sensible main characters are placed in difficulties from which they are rescued at the end of the play, either attaining their ends or having their good fortunes restored. 1213–14

Comic relief   In a *tragedy*, a comic scene that follows a scene of seriousness and by contrast intensifies the emotions aroused by the serious scene. 1426–27

Commercial fiction   Fiction written to meet the taste of a wide popular audience and relying usually on tested formulas for satisfying such taste. 62–67

Conflict   A clash of actions, desires, ideas, or goals in the *plot* of a story or drama. Conflict may exist between the main *character* and some other person or persons; between the main character and some external force—physical nature, society, or "fate"; or between the main character and some destructive element in his or her own nature. 104–105

Connotation   What a word suggests beyond its basic dictionary definition; a word's overtones of meaning. 686–91

Consonance   The repetition at close intervals of the final consonant sounds of accented syllables or important words (for example, book–plaque–thicker). 824

Continuous form   That *form* of a poem in which the lines follow each other without formal grouping, the only breaks being dictated by units of meaning. 883

Couplet   Two successive lines, usually in the same *meter*, linked by *rhyme*. 887

Dactyl   A metrical foot consisting of one accented syllable followed by two unaccented syllables (for example, mér-ří-lў). 842

Dactylic meter   A *meter* in which a majority of the feet are dactyls. (But see *Triple meter*.) 842

Denotation   The basic definition or dictionary meaning of a word. 686–91

Denouement   That portion of a *plot* that reveals the final outcome of its conflicts or the solution of its mysteries.

Deus ex machina ("god from the machine")   The resolution of a *plot* by use of a highly improbable chance or coincidence (so named from the practice of some Greek dramatists of having a god descend from heaven at the last possible minute—in the theater by means of a stage machine—to rescue the *protagonist* from an impossible situation). 109

Developing character   See *Character*.

Didactic writing   Poetry, fiction, or drama having as a primary purpose to teach or preach. 905

Dilemma   A situation in which a *character* must choose between two courses of action, both undesirable. 106

Dimeter   A metrical line containing two feet. 843

Direct presentation of character   That method of *characterization* in which the author, by exposition or analysis, tells us directly what a *character* is like, or has someone else in the story do so. 162–63

Double rhyme   A rhyme in which the repeated vowel is in the second last syllable of the words involved (for example, *politely–rightly–sprightly*); one form of *feminine rhyme*. 825, 829

Dramatic convention   Any dramatic device which, though it departs from reality, is implicitly accepted by author and audience as a means of representing reality. 1076–78

Dramatic exposition   The presentation through dialogue of information about events that occurred before the action of a play, or that occur offstage or between the staged actions; this may also refer to the presentation of information about individual characters' backgrounds or the general situation (political, historical, etc.) in which the action takes place.

Dramatic framework   The situation, whether actual or fictional, realistic or fanciful, in which an author places his or her characters in order to express the *theme*. 676

Dramatic irony   See *Irony*.

Dramatic point of view   See *Point of view*.

Dramatization   The presentation of character or of emotion through the speech or action of characters rather than through exposition, analyses, or description by the author. See *Indirect presentation of character*. 163–64

Duple meter   A *meter* in which a majority of the feet contain two syllables. *Iambic* and *trochaic* are both duple meters. 842

Dynamic character   See *Character*.

Editorializing   Writing that departs from the narrative or dramatic mode and instructs the reader how to think or feel about the events of a story or the behavior of a *character*. 337

End rhyme   Rhymes that occur at the ends of lines. 825

End-stopped line   A line that ends with a natural speech pause, usually marked by punctuation. 839

English (or *Shakespearean*) *sonnet*   A *sonnet* rhyming *ababcdcdefefgg*. Its content or structure ideally parallels the rhyme scheme, falling into three coordinate *quatrains* and a concluding *couplet;* but it is sometimes structured, like the *Italian sonnet*, into *octave* and *sestet*, the principal break in thought coming at the end of the eighth line. 887

Epiphany   A moment or event in which a *character* achieves a spiritual insight into life or into her or his own circumstances. 165

Euphony   A smooth, pleasant-sounding choice and arrangement of sounds. 867

Expected rhythm   The rhythmic expectation set up by the basic *meter* of a poem. 850

Extended figure (also known as *sustained figure*)   A *figure of speech* (usually *metaphor, simile, personification,* or *apostrophe*) sustained or developed through a considerable number of lines or through a whole poem. 725–26

Extrametrical syllables   In metrical verse, extra unaccented syllables added at the beginnings or endings of lines; these may be either a feature of the metrical *form* of a poem (example, "Is my team plowing," odd-numbered lines, 674) or occur as exceptions to the *form* (example, "Virtue," lines 9 and 11, 843). In *iambic* lines, they occur at the end of the line; in *trochaic*, at the beginning. 843

Falling action   That segment of the *plot* that comes between the *climax* and the conclusion. 110

Fantasy   A kind of fiction that pictures creatures or events beyond the boundaries of known reality. 283–84

Farce   A type of drama related to *comedy* but emphasizing improbable situations, violent conflicts, physical action, and coarse wit over *characterization* or articulated *plot*. 1215–1216

Feminine rhyme   A rhyme in which the repeated accented vowel is in either the second or third last syllable of the words involved (for example, *cei*ling–*appeal*–ing; *hur*rying–*scur*rying). 825

Figurative language   Language employing *figures of speech*; language that cannot be taken literally or only literally. 714

Figure of speech   Broadly, any way of saying something other than the ordinary way; more narrowly (and for the purposes of this book) a way of saying one thing and meaning another. 715–24

First-person point of view   See *Point of view*.

Fixed form   A *form* of poem in which the length and pattern are prescribed by previous usage or tradition, such as *sonnet*, *villanelle*, and so on. 886

Flat character   See *Character*.

Foil character   See *Character*.

Folk ballad   A narrative poem designed to be sung, composed by an anonymous author, and transmitted orally for years or generations before being written down. It has usually undergone modification through the process of oral transmission. 660

Foot   The basic unit used in the *scansion* or measurement of verse. A foot usually contains one accented syllable and one or two unaccented syllables (the *spondaic foot* is a modification of this principle). 841

Form   The external pattern or shape of a poem, describable without reference to its content, as *continuous form*, *stanzaic form*, *fixed form* (and their varieties), *free verse*, and *syllabic verse*. 883. See *Structure*.

Free verse   Nonmetrical poetry in which the basic rhythmic unit is the line, and in which pauses, line breaks, and formal patterns develop organically from the requirements of the individual poem rather than from established poetic forms. 839

Grammatical pause (also known as *caesura*)   A pause introduced into the reading of a line by a mark of punctuation. 851

Hamartia   In Greek tragedy, a criminal act committed in ignorance of some material fact or even for the sake of a greater good. 1210

Happy ending   An ending in which events turn out well for a sympathetic *protagonist*. 107–108

Heard rhythm   The actual *rhythm* of a metrical poem as we hear it when it is read naturally. The heard rhythm mostly conforms to but sometimes departs from or modifies the *expected rhythm*. 850

Hexameter   A metrical line containing six feet. 843

Hyperbole   See *Overstatement*.

Iamb   A metrical *foot* consisting of one unaccented syllable followed by one accented syllable (for example, rě-heárse). 842

Iambic meter   A *meter* in which the majority of feet are *iambs*. The most common English meter. 842

Imagery   The representation through language of sense experience. 700–703

Indeterminate ending   An ending in which the central problem or *conflict* is left unresolved. 108–109

Indirect presentation of character   That method of *characterization* in which the author shows us a *character* in action, compelling us to infer what the character is like from what is said or done by the character. 162–63

Internal rhyme   A rhyme in which one or both of the rhyme-words occurs *within* the line. 825

Irony   A situation or a use of language involving some kind of incongruity or discrepancy. 334–37, 760–65. Three kinds of irony are distinguished in this book:

    Verbal irony   A *figure of speech* in which what is said is the opposite of what is meant. 334–35, 760–61

    Dramatic irony   An incongruity or discrepancy between what a *character* says or thinks and what the reader knows to be true (or between what a character perceives and what the author intends the reader to perceive). 335, 762–63

    Irony of situation   A situation in which there is an incongruity between appearance and reality, or between expectation and fulfillment, or between the actual situation and what would seem appropriate. 336, 764

Italian (or *Petrarchan*) *sonnet*   A *sonnet* consisting of an *octave* rhyming *abbaabba* and of a *sestet* using any arrangement of two or three additional rhymes, such as *cdcdcd* or *cdecde*. 886

Literary fiction   Fiction written with serious artistic intentions, providing an imagined experience yielding authentic insights into some significant aspect of life. 62–67

Masculine rhyme (also known as *single rhyme*)   A rhyme in which the repeated accented vowel sound is in the final syllable of the words involved (for example, *dance-pants, scald-recalled*). 824

Melodrama   A type of drama related to *tragedy* but featuring sensational incidents, emphasizing *plot* at the expense of *characterization*, relying on cruder conflicts (virtuous *protagonist* versus villainous *antagonist*), and having a *happy ending* in which good triumphs over evil. 1215

Metaphor   A *figure of speech* in which an implicit comparison is made between two things essentially unlike. It may take one of four forms: (1) that in which the literal term and the figurative term are *both* named; (2) that in which the literal term is *named* and the figurative term *implied*; (3) that in which the literal term is *implied* and the figurative term *named*; (4) that in which *both* the literal and the figurative terms are *implied*. 715–18

Meter   The regular patterns of accent that underlie metrical verse; the measurable repetition of accented and unaccented syllables in poetry. 840

Metonymy   A *figure of speech* in which some significant aspect or detail of an experience is used to represent the whole experience. In this book the single term *metonymy* is used for what are sometimes distinguished as two separate figures: *synecdoche* (the use of the part for the whole) and *metonymy* (the use of something closely related for the thing actually meant). 721–22

Metrical variations   Departures from the basic metrical pattern (see *substitution, extrametrical syllables*). 843

Monometer   A metrical line containing one *foot*. 843

Moral   A rule of conduct or maxim for living expressed or implied as the "point" of a literary work. Compare *Theme*. 649

Motivation   The incentives or goals that, in combination with the inherent natures of characters, cause them to behave as they do. In *commercial fiction* actions may be unmotivated, insufficiently motivated, or implausibly motivated. 163

Mystery   An unusual set of circumstances for which the reader craves an explanation; used to create *Suspense*. 105–106

Narrator   In drama a *character*, found in some plays, who, speaking directly to the audience, introduces the action and provides a string of commentary between the dramatic scenes. The narrator may or may not be a major character in the action itself. 1077

Nonrealistic drama   Drama that, in content, presentation, or both, departs markedly from fidelity to the outward appearances of life. 1074–78

Objective point of view   See *Point of view.*

Octave   (1) an eight-line *stanza.* (2) the first eight lines of a *sonnet,* especially one structured in the manner of an *Italian sonnet.* 886

Omniscient point of view   See *Point of view.*

Onomatopoeia   The use of words that supposedly mimic their meaning in their sound (for example, *boom, click, plop*). 865

Onomatopoetic language   Language employing *onomatopoeia.*

Overstatement (or *hyperbole*)   A *figure of speech* in which exaggeration is used in the service of truth. 757–58

Oxymoron   A compact verbal paradox in which two successive words seemingly contradict one another. 900

Paradox   A statement or situation containing apparently contradictory or incompatible elements. 756

Paradoxical situation   A situation containing apparently but not actually incompatible elements. The celebration of a fifth birthday anniversary by a twenty-year-old man is paradoxical but explainable if the man was born on February 29. The Christian doctrines that Christ was born of a virgin and is both God and man are, for a Christian believer, paradoxes (that is, apparently impossible but true). 756

Paradoxical statement (or *verbal paradox*)   A *figure of speech* in which an apparently self-contradictory statement is nevertheless found to be true. 756

Paraphrase   A restatement of the content of a poem designed to make its *prose meaning* as clear as possible. 670–71

Pentameter   A metrical line containing five feet. 843

Personification   A *figure of speech* in which human attributes are given to an animal, an object, or a concept. 718–719

Petrarchan sonnet   See *Italian sonnet.*

Phonetic intensive   A word whose sound, by an obscure process, to some degree suggests its meaning. As differentiated from *onomatopoetic* words, the meanings of phonetic intensives do not refer explicitly to sounds. 865

Playwright   A maker of plays. 1027

Plot   The sequence of incidents or events of which a story or play is composed. 103

Plot manipulation   A situation in which an author gives the *plot* a twist or turn unjustified by preceding action or by the characters involved. 109

Poeticizing   Writing that uses immoderately heightened or distended language to sway the reader's feelings. 337

Point of view   The angle of vision from which a story is told. 227. The four basic points of view are as follows:

Omniscient point of view   The author tells the story using the third person, knowing all and free to tell us anything, including what the characters are thinking or feeling and why they act as they do. 228–29

Third-person limited point of view   The author tells the story using the third person, but is limited to a complete knowledge of one *character* in the story and tells us only what that one character thinks, feels, sees, or hears. 229–30

First-person point of view   The story is told by one of its characters, using the first person. 230–31

Objective (or *Dramatic*) *point of view*   The author tells the story using the third person, but is limited to reporting what the characters say or do; the author does not interpret their behavior or tell us their private thoughts or feelings. 231–33

Prose meaning   That part of a poem's *total meaning* that can be separated out and expressed through *paraphrase*. 791

Prose poem   Usually a short composition having the intentions of poetry but written in prose rather than *verse*. 840

Protagonist   The central *character* in a story or play. 104

Quatrain   (1) A four-line *stanza*. (2) A four-line division of a *sonnet* marked off by its rhyme scheme. 887

Realistic drama   Drama that attempts, in content and in presentation, to preserve the illusion of actual, everyday life. 1074–78

Refrain   A repeated word, phrase, line, or group of lines, normally at some fixed position in a poem written in *stanzaic form*. 826

Rhetorical pause (also known as *caesura*)   A natural pause, unmarked by punctuation, introduced into the reading of a line by its phrasing or syntax. 851

Rhetorical poetry   Poetry using artificially eloquent language, that is, language too high-flown for its occasion and unfaithful to the full complexity of human experience. 904

Rhetorical stress   In natural speech, as in prose and poetic writing, the stressing of words or syllables so as to emphasize meaning and sentence structure. 839

Rhythm   Any wavelike recurrence of motion or sound. 838

Rhyme   The repetition of the accented vowel sound and all succeeding sounds in important or importantly positioned words (for example, *old–cold, vane–reign, court–report, order–recorder*). The above definition applies to *perfect rhyme* and assumes that the accented vowel sounds involved are preceded by differing consonant sounds.

If the preceding consonant sound is the same (for example, *manse–romance*, *style–stile*), or if there is no preceding consonant sound in either word (for example, *aisle–isle*, *alter–altar*), or if the same word is repeated in the rhyming position (for example, *hill–hill*), the words are called *identical rhymes*. Both perfect rhymes and identical rhymes are to be distinguished from *approximate rhymes*. 824–25

Rhyme scheme   Any fixed pattern of rhymes characterizing a whole poem or its stanzas. 885–86

Rising action   That development of *plot* in a story or play that precedes and leads up to the climax. 110

Romantic comedy   See *Comedy*.

Round character   See *Character*.

Run-on line   A line which has no natural speech pause at its end, allowing the sense to flow uninterruptedly into the succeeding line. 839

Sarcasm   Bitter or cutting speech; speech intended by its speaker to give pain to the person addressed. 760

Satire   A kind of literature that ridicules human folly or vice with the purpose of bringing about reform or of keeping others from falling into similar folly or vice. 760

Scansion   The process of measuring verse, that is, of marking accented and unaccented syllables, dividing the lines into feet, identifying the metrical pattern, and noting significant variations from that pattern. 843

Scornful comedy   See *Comedy*.

Sentimentality   Unmerited or contrived tender feeling; that quality in a work that elicits or seeks to elicit tears through an oversimplification or falsification of reality. 337–38, 904

Sentimental poetry   Poetry that attempts to manipulate the reader's emotions in order to achieve a greater emotional response than the poem itself really warrants. (A sentimental novel or film is sometimes called, pejoratively, a "tear-jerker.") 904

Sestet   (1) A six-line *stanza*. (2) The last six lines of a *sonnet* structured on the Italian model. 886

Setting   The context in time and place in which the action of a story occurs.

Shakespearean sonnet   See *English sonnet*.

Simile   A *figure of speech* in which an explicit comparison is made between two things essentially unlike. The comparison is made explicit by the use of some such word or phrase as *like*, *as*, *than*, *similar to*, *resembles*, or *seems*. 715

Single rhyme   See *Masculine rhyme*.

Situational irony   See *Irony.*

Soliloquy   A speech in which a *character,* alone on the stage, addresses himself or herself; a soliloquy is a "thinking out loud," a dramatic means of letting an audience know a character's thoughts and feelings. 1028

Sonnet   A *fixed form* of fourteen lines, normally iambic pentameter, with a rhyme scheme conforming to or approximating one of two main types—the *Italian* or the *English.* 886

Spondee   A metrical *foot* consisting of two syllables equally or almost equally accented (for example, *true–blue*). 842

Stanza   A group of lines whose metrical pattern (and usually its rhyme scheme as well) is repeated throughout a poem. 884

Stanzaic form   The *form* taken by a poem when it is written in a series of units having the same number of lines and usually other characteristics in common, such as metrical pattern or rhyme scheme. 884

Static character   See *Character.*

Stock character   See *Character.*

Stream of consciousness   Narrative that presents the private thoughts of a *character* without commentary or interpretation by the author. 230

Stress   In this book, the same as *Accent.* But see 838 (footnote).

Structure   The sequential arrangement of plot elements in fiction or drama. 103; in poetry, the internal organization of content (see *Form*). 883

Substitution   In metrical verse, the replacement of the expected metrical *foot* by a different one (for example, a *trochee* occurring in an *iambic* line). 843

Surprise   An unexpected turn in the development of a *plot.* 107

Surprise ending   A completely unexpected revelation or turn of *plot* at the conclusion of a story or play. 107

Suspense   That quality in a story or play that makes the reader eager to discover what happens next and how it will end. 105–107

Sustained figure   See *Extended figure.*

Syllabic verse   *Verse* measured by the number of syllables rather than the number of feet per line. 857

Symbol   Something that means *more* than what it is; an object, person, situation, or action that in addition to its literal meaning suggests other meanings as well. 274–81, 735–42

Synecdoche   A *figure of speech* in which a part is used for the whole. In this book it is subsumed under the term *Metonymy.* 721–22

Synesthesia   Presentation of one sense experience in terms usually associated with another sensation. 873

Tercet   A three-line *stanza* exhibited in *terza rima* and *villanelle* as well as in other poetic forms. 698, 888

Terza rima   An interlocking rhyme scheme with the pattern *aba bcb cdc*, etc. 897–98

Tetrameter   A metrical line containing four feet. 843

Theme   The central idea or unifying generalization implied or stated by a literary work. 188–94, 670

Third-person limited point of view   See *Point of view*.

Tone   The writer's or speaker's attitude toward the subject, the audience, or herself or himself; the emotional coloring, or emotional meaning, of a work. 804–808

Total meaning   The total experience communicated by a poem. It includes all those dimensions of experience by which a poem communicates—sensuous, emotional, imaginative, and intellectual—and it can be communicated in no other words than those of the poem itself. 791

Tragedy   A type of drama, opposed to *comedy*, which depicts the causally related events that lead to the downfall and suffering of the *protagonist*, a person of unusual moral or intellectual stature or outstanding abilities. 1209–1213

Trimeter   A metrical line containing three feet. 843

Triple meter   A *meter* in which a majority of the feet contain three syllables. (Actually, if more than 25 percent of the feet in a poem are triple, its effect is more triple than duple, and it ought perhaps to be referred to as triple meter.) *Anapestic* and *dactylic* are both triple meters. 842

Trochaic meter   A *meter* in which the majority of feet are trochees. 842

Trochee   A metrical foot consisting of one accented syllable followed by one unaccented syllable (for example, bár-tĕr). 842

Truncation   In metric verse, the omission of an unaccented syllable at either end of a line (for example, "Introduction to *Songs of Innocence*," 853). 843

Understatement   A *figure of speech* that consists of saying less than one means, or of saying what one means with less force than the occasion warrants. 758

Unhappy ending   An ending that turns out unhappily for a sympathetic *protagonist*. 108

Verbal irony   See *Irony*.

Verse   Metrical language; the opposite of *prose*.

Villanelle   A nineteen-line *fixed form* consisting of five tercets rhymed *aba* and a concluding quatrain rhymed *abaa*, with lines 1 and 3 of the first *tercet* serving as refrains in an alternating pattern through line 15 and then repeated as lines 18 and 19. 888

Copyrights and Acknowledgments

SOPHOCLES "Oedipus Rex" from *Sophocles, The Oedipus Cycle: An English Version* by Robert Fitzgerald and Dudley Fitts. Copyright 1949 by Harcourt Brace & Company and renewed 1977 by Cornelia Fitts and Robert Fitzgerald. Reprinted by permission of Harcourt, Inc.

GARY SOTO "Small Town with One Road" by Gary Soto. From *New and Selected Poems*, copyright © 1995 by Gary Soto. Used with permission of Chronicle Books, LLC, San Francisco. Visit ChronicleBooks.com.

WOLE SOYINKA "Telephone Conversation," copyright © 1965 by Wole Soyinka.

WILLIAM STAFFORD "Traveling through the dark" from *Stories That Could Be True* (Harper & Row: 1960). Copyright © 1960 by William Stafford. Reprinted by permission of the author.

WALLACE STEVENS "Death of Soldier," "Disillusionment of Ten O'Clock," "The Snow Man," and "Sunday Morning" from *The Collected Poems of Wallace Stevens* by Wallace Stevens, copyright © 1954 by Wallace Stevens and renewed 1982 by Holly Stevens. Used by permission of Alfred A. Knopf, a division of Random House, Inc.

LEON STOKESBURY "Listening to My Mothers Comic Banter with Sackboys and Servers" by Leon Stokesbury, from *The Kenyan Review, 2002*.

ELIZABETH TALLENT "No One's a Mystery" from *Time with Children*. Copyright 1987 by Alfred A. Knopf, a division of Random House, Inc.

DYLAN THOMAS "Do Not Go Gentle into That Good Night" by Dylan Thomas, from *The Poems of Dylan Thomas*, copyright © 1952 by Dylan Thomas. Reprinted by permission of New Directions Publishing Group. "Fern Hill" by Dylan Thomas, from *The Poems of Dylan Thomas*, copyright © 1945 by The Trustees for the Copyrights of Dylan Thomas. Reprinted by permission of New Directions Publishing Group.

JEAN TOOMER "Reapers" from *Cane* by Jean Toomer. Copyright © 1923 by Boni & Liveright, renewed 1951 by Jean Toomer. Reprinted by permission of Liveright Publishing Corporation.

CHASE TWICHELL "Blurry Cow" from *The Odds*, by Chase Twichell, © 1986. Reprinted by permission of the University of Pittsburgh Press.

JOHN UPDIKE "A & P" from *Pigeon Feathers and Other Stories*, copyright 1962 by John Updike. Published by Alfred A. Knopf, a division of Random House, Inc. "Telephone Poles" and "Recital" from *Collected Poems 1953-1993* by John Updike, copyright © 1993 by John Updike. Used by permission of Alfred A. Knopf, A division of Random House, Inc.

LUIS VALDEZ "Los Vendidos" from *Luis Valdez—Early Works: Actos, Bernabe, Pensamiento Serpentino*. Copyright © 1971 by Luis Valdez. Reprinted by permission of Arte Público Press, University of Houston.

MONA VAN DUYN "What the Motorcycle Said" from *If It Be Not I* by Mona Van Duyn, copyright © 1959 by Mona Van Duyn. Used by permission of Alfred A. Knopf, a division of Random House, Inc.

DEREK WALCOTT "The Virgins" from *Sea Grapes* by Derek Walcott. Copyright © 1976 by Derek Walcott. Reprinted by permission of Farrar, Straus and Giroux, LLC.,

Index of Authors, Titles, and First Lines

Authors' names appear in capitals, titles of selections in italics. A number in bold face indicates the page of the selection, and numbers in roman type indicate the pages where the selection is discussed.